PENGUIN BOOKS

The Penguin Companion to European Union

'As eloquent as it is comprehensive, th
anyone who wants to understand the
always been plenty of heat in the Europ ... -
vides the light.' Philip Stephens, author ... *Pound*

'I recommend this book to anyone wanting a comprehensive, well-balanced and well-informed account of today's Europe.' Chris Patten, Chancellor of Oxford University

'The EU has not been very successful in explaining itself to outsiders, and opinions on the Union, especially in the English-speaking word, are too often based on prejudice or hearsay. In this *Companion*, two experienced insiders provide the kind of precise information and analysis which is the prerequisite for sound judgement.' Norman Davies, author of *Europe: A History* and *Vanished Kingdoms*

'The *Penguin Companion* stands out as a lucid and well-written introduction to the EU . . . comprehensive, accurate and readable – technical enough for the expert, yet accessible for the intelligent lay reader.' *The European*

'This is a highly useful and affordable multi-disciplinary supplement to undergraduate reading lists. Entries are excellent in terms of scope and clarity of treatment.' *Journal of Common Market Studies*

'The *Penguin Companion* provides American students of politics with a unique insight into the dynamics of Europe's emerging federal system.' Fred Kempe, President, Atlantic Council and author of *Berlin 1961*

'A friendly guide through Europe . . . a very useful reference book which will help interested readers and students alike.' *Times Higher Education*

ABOUT THE AUTHORS

Anthony Teasdale was educated at Balliol and Nuffield Colleges, Oxford, where he took a first in PPE and an MPhil in Politics. A former research fellow of Nuffield College, he has worked in the European Parliament and EU Council of Ministers in Brussels, and as Special Adviser at the Foreign and Commonwealth Office and HM Treasury in London. A visiting fellow at the European Institute of the London School of Economics, he has most recently served as deputy chief of staff to the President of the European Parliament and as a director in its administration.

Timothy Bainbridge was educated at Gonville and Caius College, Cambridge, where he took a BA in Classics and a PhD in the History of Art. After working in the Conservative Research Department in London, he served as a senior political adviser in the European Parliament from 1974 to 1999, based in Brussels, Luxembourg and London. Married with one son, his principal interests were classical music and the history of art. Dr Bainbridge died in 2004, at the age of 57, after a long struggle with leukaemia.

ANTHONY TEASDALE and
TIMOTHY BAINBRIDGE

The Penguin Companion to European Union

Fourth Edition

PENGUIN BOOKS

PENGUIN BOOKS

Published by the Penguin Group
Penguin Books Ltd, 80 Strand, London WC2R 0RL, England
Penguin Group (USA) Inc., 375 Hudson Street, New York, New York 10014, USA
Penguin Group (Canada), 90 Eglinton Avenue East, Suite 700, Toronto, Ontario, Canada M4P 2Y3
(a division of Pearson Penguin Canada Inc.)
Penguin Ireland, 25 St Stephen's Green, Dublin 2, Ireland (a division of Penguin Books Ltd)
Penguin Group (Australia), 707 Collins Street, Melbourne, Victoria 3008, Australia
(a division of Pearson Australia Group Pty Ltd)
Penguin Books India Pvt Ltd, 11 Community Centre, Panchsheel Park, New Delhi – 110 017, India
Penguin Group (NZ), 67 Apollo Drive, Rosedale, Auckland 0632, New Zealand
(a division of Pearson New Zealand Ltd)
Penguin Books (South Africa) (Pty) Ltd, Block D, Rosebank Office Park,
181 Jan Smuts Avenue, Parktown North, Gauteng 2193, South Africa

Penguin Books Ltd, Registered Offices: 80 Strand, London WC2R 0RL, England

www.penguin.com

First published 1995
Reprinted with corrections 1996
Reprinted with revisions 1997
Second edition 1998
Reprinted with revisions 2000
Third edition 2002
Reprinted with revisions 2003
Fourth edition 2012
001

Typeset in 11/13pt Minion
Typeset by Jouve (UK), Milton Keynes
Printed in England by Clays Ltd, St Ives plc

ISBN: 978–0–141–02118–8

www.greenpenguin.co.uk

We hope to reach again a Europe united but purged of the slavery of ancient, classical times – a Europe in which men will be proud to say, 'I am a European'. We hope to see a Europe where men of every country will think as much of being a European as of belonging to their native land, and that without losing any part of their love and loyalty to their birthplace. We hope wherever they go in this wide domain, to which we set no limits in the European continent, they will truly feel 'Here I am at home. I am a citizen of this country too'.

Winston Churchill,
Amsterdam, 9 May 1948

Contents

Preface **ix**
Note to the Reader **xii**

The Penguin Companion to European Union **1**

Bibliography **855**
Synoptic Index **863**

Preface

This is the fourth edition of *The Penguin Companion to European Union*, originally co-authored by Timothy Bainbridge and myself in 1995. It is designed to offer the intelligent generalist a single-volume introduction to the complexities of one of the least understood but most powerful political systems in the modern world. It is written for people who are interested in politics but are not experts in the ways and byways of the European Union.

The philosophy behind the book is perhaps best expressed in the words of Jonathan Swift: 'Providence never intended to make the management of public affairs a mystery to be comprehended by a few persons of sublime genius.' Rather like Gulliver on his travels, even politically alert readers who venture into European Union territory can quickly find themselves tied down by a thousand opaque or mystical concepts and categories that make it difficult to move forward. Timothy and I decided to try to show that the EU can be as penetrable and comprehensible as any other power structure – and indeed in many ways more interesting, because of its unique, international character. We deliberately chose an 'A to Z' format because we believed that thinking and learning about Europe in a modular way – moving from one subject to another as a person's interest takes them – not only replicated the way that we ourselves had discovered the subject, but was also more satisfying for the reader.

Nobody can or will wish to explore every aspect of what has been the expanding universe of EU politics over the last half century, but many people do genuinely want to know more about its history, institutions, policies and personalities. In over 350 interlocking entries, this book attempts to promote such an understanding, in an easy and convenient format. It is not just a dictionary, but a 'companion', in the sense that it aims to present not only facts, but arguments and analysis too.

Readers will quickly find that the *Penguin Companion* displays a strong historical bias, founded upon the belief that an essential part of any understanding of the new European political system is a proper knowledge of the course of post-war integration and an appreciation of how it differs from what came before or might otherwise have been. The multiple and messy compromises that have shaped the contours of its institutions and policies at every stage only make sense in the context of the assumptions, pressures and interests of their time. Those advocates or detractors of European integration who attribute some linear inevitability to the course of its development do a disservice to this remarkable historical phenomenon.

The Penguin Companion is not focused exclusively on the European Union, a feature reflected in the absence of the word 'the' before 'European Union' in its title. It seeks to take proper account of the large number of other political institutions and bodies operating at European level, some of which pre-date the Union or overlap with it. Nor is the book's aim to give an absolutely up-to-the-minute account of every specific aspect of European institutions and policies, but rather to explain their key features, political dynamics and (where appropriate) underpinnings in law. In any case, European developments often move on at high speed, so it is inevitable that, by the time this fourth edition is published, it will already be out-of-date in some important aspects. The book's treatment of the fast-moving eurozone debt crisis, which came to head just as the text was being finalized, displays a natural caution in this regard.

The reader also may detect something of a British emphasis in the issues, events and personalities chosen for inclusion in the *Penguin Companion*. This is not simply a reflection of the background and interests of the book's authors, but is also the product of a conscious choice. In recent decades, the European issue has, in different forms, repeatedly proved central to British political debate, yet the level of understanding of how the EU system actually operates is still surprisingly low, even within political and media circles. This book is a modest attempt to improve the quality and accuracy of discussion about European issues in Britain – a polity which, by temperament, history and institutional ethos, is unlikely ever to embrace the process of European integration with much enthusiasm.

The last edition of this book was published nearly a decade ago. Attempting to do justice to the many changes that have taken place since 2003 has compounded the inherent challenge of compressing so many dimensions of European politics into a single volume. Inevitably, some entries that featured in earlier editions have had to be sacrificed for reasons of space, whilst not all the new material prepared for this edition has found a home in the final text. Unpublished entries, as well as a detailed chronology of post-war European integration, are accessible at www.penguincompaniontoeu.com, where readers may also leave comments on the text.

In preparing the successive editions of the *Penguin Companion*, the authors have benefited greatly from the generous advice and support of many people over many years. Among those who assisted Timothy Bainbridge in the preparation of the first three editions of the book were Alexander and Bettina Bainbridge, Paul Beaumont, Janet Berry, Antonella Collaro, Avis Furness, Alastair Graham, Casilda Grigg, Patricia Halligan, Alison Harries, Barbara

Horn, Lindsay Kirkby, Julianne Mulholland, Alan Reekie, Elspeth Senior, Pat Walsh, Deborah Warren and Helen Williams. Having co-authored the first edition with Tim, I was delighted to resume this role for the latest edition and undertake a 'stem to stern' refit and updating of the text.

I am immensely grateful for the help and encouragement I have received from my editors at Penguin – Adam Freudenheim, Rose Goddard, Ronnie Hanna, Kristen Harrison, Jodie Greenwood, Georgina Laycock, Rachel Love, Stefan McGrath and Ruth Stimson – as well as my literary agent, Andrew Lownie. John Flatman and Claire Meyer have provided indispensable practical assistance of various kinds, whilst Federico Cucchi undertook outstanding research assistance on a number of entries and tables, as well as the bibliography. I would like to thank my employer, the European Parliament, for encouraging me in this project – whilst stressing that it is in no way implicated in the book's arguments or conclusions – as well as the staff of the libraries of the three main EU institutions for their assistance in retrieving various materials unavailable on the world wide web.

I have also been privileged to draw on insights offered in conversation on European issues by many friends, colleagues and experts over many years. They include Eschel Alpermann, Paul Arthur, Timothy Beyer Helm, John Biesmans, Graham Bishop, Vernon Bogdanor, Jim Cloos, Nicholas Crosby, Brendan Donnelly, James Elles, Roland Freudenstein, Charles Grant, John Hunt, David Levy, Roger Liddle, Guy Milton, Praveen Moman, Robert Moreland, Maciej Popowski, Jamie Shea, Larry Siedentop, Thomas Subelack, Dick Taverne, Andrew Tyrie, Klaus Welle, Michael Welsh, Martin Westlake and Graham Ziegner. Several kindly took the time to comment on specific entries, for which I am very grateful.

I would like to express my special appreciation to four individuals. Maurice Fraser was 'present at the creation' when Timothy and I first had the idea of putting together an 'A to Z of Europe': his contribution and encouragement have been invaluable at every stage. Richard Corbett generously read much of the manuscript of this latest edition: his thoughtful and penetrating suggestions have greatly improved the text. Quentin Huxham kindly put at my disposal his formidable understanding of European politics, helped me revise and update a number of entries on the policies of the Union in particular, and commented incisively on many other parts of the book. Finally, my wife, Jacqui, has been hugely supportive throughout the project: without her enthusiasm, patience, kindness and understanding, the publication of this new edition would simply not have been possible.

Notwithstanding the great help which so many people have given to the writing of the successive editions of this book, any errors of fact or judgement remain the responsibility of the authors alone.

Anthony Teasdale

15 March 2012

Note to the Reader

Reference to the Treaties

Reference is made throughout this book to the various **Treaties** on which the European Union is founded. This is done for two reasons. First, the most distinctive feature of the European Union is the principle of **sovereignty-sharing** through supranational law. As the Treaties are the supreme embodiment of such law, an appreciation of what they say and mean is crucial to any serious understanding of the Union's institutions and policies. Second, the citing of the relevant treaty references allows interested readers to research issues in greater depth by consulting either the treaty texts themselves or other specialist sources.

The majority of treaty references in this book are to the Treaty on the Functioning of the European Union (TFEU) and the Treaty on European Union (TEU). These two texts are updated versions of the 1957 **Treaty of Rome** and the 1992 **Maastricht Treaty** respectively. The first established the **European Economic Community** (EEC); the second amended the EEC Treaty, renamed the EEC as the European Community, and most importantly created the European Union. The two treaties exist in parallel to one another and provide the central legal architecture of today's Union. Other recent treaties can only be understood in that context: the 1986 **Single European Act** (SEA) amended the first document, whilst the 1997 **Amsterdam Treaty**, 2001 **Nice Treaty** and the 1997 **Lisbon Treaty** (which entered into force in December 2009) amended both texts. Efforts in the early 2000s to amalgamate the Rome and Maastricht Treaties into a single document, in the form of a **European Constitution**, failed. The subsequent Lisbon Treaty accepted the duality of the existing legal situation, but imported into one or other of the two treaties many of the changes originally foreseen in the draft Constitution.

The situation is further complicated by the fact that the 1957 EEC Treaty had been preceded five years earlier by a **Treaty of Paris** founding a **European Coal and Steel Community** (ECSC) and that the EEC Treaty was itself paralleled by a second treaty, also signed in Rome at the same time, establishing a **European Atomic Energy Community** (EAEC or Euratom). There were thus, strictly speaking, two Treaties of Rome, and three **European Communities** – the ECSC, EEC and Euratom. The 1965 **Merger Treaty** amalgamated most of their institutional structures. The ECSC Treaty lapsed after 50 years, in 2002. As a result, today the European Union (defined by the TEU and TFEU) and Euratom exist side by side. Even if technically Euratom is separate to the Union, it is normally considered to be part of it, not least because it uses the same institutions.

In the absence of any indication to the contrary, the year cited for any treaty in this book is the one in which the treaty in question was signed, not that of its entry into force. In conformity with normal academic usage, the various treaties are often referred to by their initials. References to the Treaty of Rome before the Maastricht Treaty came into force (in 1993) use the initials EEC; after that date, it is denoted by EC; and since the Lisbon Treaty, by TFEU. Successive changes to the Treaties have also involved adding to, and so renumbering some of, their articles. The old article numbers are referred to only when it seems useful or necessary for readers to know them. As a result of these changes, for example, the original Article 113 EEC, dealing with external trade policy, was renumbered Article 133 EC and is now Article 207 TFEU.

The Penguin Companion to European Union

A

Abatement

Under the **Fontainebleau Agreement** of June 1984, aimed at resolving the long-running **British Budget dispute**, the United Kingdom is refunded part of its contribution to the annual **Budget** of the European Union. The sum, which is calculated annually, is technically known as the abatement, but more commonly as the 'British Budget rebate'. It is called an abatement because the deduction is made at source and so is never passed from London to Brussels, whereas the ad hoc series of rebates which Britain received in the early 1980s, before the Fontainebleau deal, were cash refunds passing in the opposite direction, designed to boost spending on European projects in Britain. As a result, the UK government enjoys complete freedom over how the abatement is spent.

Most member states face a mismatch between their contributions and receipts under the Union's Budget. However, the divergence in Britain's case has long been unusually wide and negative: on the basis of figures compiled by HM Treasury, the UK made gross payments to the EU Budget in 2010 of € 18.5 billion and received € 6.6 billion in return, resulting in a gross contribution of € 12 billion. After the application of the abatement – calculated at 66 per cent of the difference between 'unabated' payments and receipts, subject to certain qualifications – the gross contribution was reduced by € 3.6 billion, resulting in a UK net contribution of € 8.4 billion. In that year, Britain was the second largest net contributor to the EU Budget, after Germany (€ 13.7 billion), followed by France (€ 7.6 billion) and Italy (€ 6.7 billion). Over the period 1985–2010, the UK abatement averaged € 3.6 billion per year and totalled € 92.5 billion (in nominal terms).

Accession

The formal act of joining the European Union is known as 'accession' and the legal text that marks the successful conclusion of the negotiations between an applicant state and the existing **member states** is known as a *Treaty of Accession*. Annexed to the latter and forming an integral part of it is an *Act of Accession*, in which the precise conditions of membership and the detailed adjustments to the Union's founding **Treaties** are specified. The procedures governing accession are set out in Article 49 TEU.

Acts of Accession set out the institutional changes necessary for **enlargement**, affecting notably the composition of the various EU institutions and bodies, as well as the number of official and working **languages** of the Union. Although new member states will undertake in their Act of Accession to respect the ***acquis communautaire*** in its entirety, they may be given specific periods of adjustment, known as **transitional periods**, if too rapid an adoption of certain policies might cause serious difficulty in either the new or existing member states. In addition, a country will automatically be given a **derogation** from stage three of **Economic and Monetary Union** (EMU), namely the adoption of the single currency and common monetary policy, if it is unable to meet the necessary **convergence criteria.**

If several countries are set to join the Union at the same time, one accession treaty will be concluded with all of them collectively, rather than a series of separate treaties with each individually. Accession treaties require **ratification** not only in each acceding state – where **referenda** are sometimes held – but also in all existing member states, 'in accordance with their respective constitutional requirements'. The latter process will always include approval by each **national parliament** and it can logically extend to use of the referendum too. So far there has only been one example of an existing member state holding a referendum on a planned enlargement: in April 1972, President Georges Pompidou invited the French public to endorse the accession of Denmark, Ireland, Norway and the United Kingdom to the Community. Although this proposal was approved by a wide margin, ironically the Norwegian people rejected the membership of their own country five months later.

ACP states

Nearly all the countries of sub-Saharan Africa, the Caribbean and the Pacific enjoy a special status in their relations with the European Union. As members of the African, Caribbean and Pacific Group of States – established by an agreement signed in Georgetown, Guyana, in June 1975 – they have been formally associated with the Union and its member states under successive Lomé Conventions (1975–2000) and Cotonou Agreements (since 2000). These agreements have offered the ACP states preferential export access to EU markets, as well as development aid from the intergovernmental **European Development Fund** (EDF) and finance from the **European Investment Bank** (EIB). As such, the ACP states are the principal beneficiaries of EU **development policy**.

When the ACP system was established in 1975, there were 46 participating countries, nearly all former French or British colonies; the number has since increased to 79, with the most recent admissions being Cuba in 2000 and Timor-Leste (East Timor) in 2003. Of the present total, about half are members of the Commonwealth, and 40 feature among the world's 49 least developed countries (LDCs), as defined by the United Nations. The 79 ACP states are now organized, for administrative and negotiating purposes, into seven geographical areas – namely five African regions, as well as the Caribbean and the Pacific. The total population of the ACP states is almost 700 million people.

The EU's relations with the ACP states are structured through an ACP–EU Council of Ministers, comprised of representatives of all the member governments on both sides, as well as the **European Commission**, which meets formally at least once a year. Ministers are supported at official level by a Committee of Ambassadors, which meets regularly in Brussels. The presidency of the ACP–EU Council rotates annually, alternating between states on each side. Since the **Lisbon Treaty** came into force in December 2009, the **High Representative** for **Common Foreign and Security Policy** (CFSP) has the right to serve as the president on the EU side, but has chosen to delegate that role to the six-month, rotating **presidency** of the (EU) **Council of Ministers** (which exercised it before). A parliamentary dimension to relations is provided by the ACP–EU Joint Parliamentary Assembly (JPA): it brings together 79 ACP representatives and 79 Members of the **European Parliament** (MEPs), with co-presidents from each side. The JPA has three standing committees, meets in plenary session twice a year for one week, rotating between ACP and EU countries, and adopts resolutions of a non-binding nature.

The internal structure of the ACP Group of States mirrors the broader ACP–EU arrangements in that it is also based on a Council of Ministers, supported by a Committee of Ambassadors. In addition, summit meetings of ACP heads of state and government were launched in 1997 and held every two or three years until 2008. An ACP secretariat, headed by a secretary general, is based in Brussels.

In recent years, the preferential trade access extended by the EU to the 39 'richer' ACP states that do not feature on the UN's list of LDCs has come under increasing criticism, on the grounds that it is non-reciprocal and contradicts the principle of non-discrimination within the World Trade Organization (WTO). In order to make its ACP trade arrangements WTO-compatible, the Union is currently negotiating a series of Economic Partnership Agreements (EPAs) with the ACP states, based on reciprocity, whilst attempting to group the countries on a regional basis.

Acquis communautaire

The phrase *acquis communautaire* – sometimes translated into English as 'the Community patrimony' – denotes the whole range of principles, policies, laws, formal practices, obligations and objectives that have been agreed within the European Union to date. It necessarily includes the **Treaties** in their entirety, all legislation (see **legal acts**) adopted under them, and all **international agreements** entered into by the Union. It also includes judgements of the **European Court of Justice** (ECJ) and agreements within and between the EU institutions about their operation. Recognition of ECJ rulings is something of cardinal importance, since this ensures acceptance by the member states of the **primacy** of EU law and the principle of **direct effect**. The *acquis communautaire* is also normally deemed to encompass 'softer' commitments, notably long-term political objectives agreed by heads of government in meetings of the **European Council**, even though these usually have no legal force.

The significance of the *acquis communautaire* is most obvious when a new member state joins the Union (see **enlargement**). **Accession** countries are deemed to be 'in the same situation as the present member states in respect of declarations or resolutions of, or other positions taken up by, the European Council or Council . . . [or] adopted by common agreement of the member states'. Accordingly, they are required to 'observe the principles and guidelines deriving from those declarations, resolutions or other positions' and to 'take such measures as may be necessary to ensure their implementation' (Article 3.2 of the Act of Accession for Bulgaria and Romania).

Sometimes enlargement is used to impose a stricter version of the *acquis communautaire* than that actually applying to existing member states. All 12 member states acceding to the EU in 2004 and 2007 had to accept an obligation for their currencies to join the single currency, once the **convergence criteria** had been met, even though two existing member states (United Kingdom and Denmark) had earlier negotiated de jure **opt-outs**, and one (Sweden) had secured a seemingly permanent de facto opt-out without foundation in law.

Action Committee for the United States of Europe (ACUSE)

The Action Committee for the United States of Europe was founded by **Jean Monnet** in October 1955, following his resignation as President of the **High Authority** of the **European Coal and Steel Community** (ECSC) the previous year. Its purpose was to act as an international pressure group for closer European integration, bringing together leading political figures from the founding member states, plus, in later years, the United Kingdom. The committee was in effect Monnet's personal response to the rejection of the proposed **European Defence Community** (EDC) by the French National

Assembly in August 1954 and the need it revealed to convince a wider swathe of Europe's political élite of the merits of **supranationalism**. With a staff of only five, Monnet ran the committee from his brother-in-law's apartment at 83 Avenue Foch, in central Paris, to which he commuted every day for many years from his home near Versailles.

The creation of the Action Committee helped give impetus to the negotiations that were already taking place among **the Six** in 1955–6, launched at the **Messina Conference**, that led to the **Treaty of Rome** establishing the **European Economic Community** (EEC) in March 1957. The marked scepticism (and often opposition) of many on the mainstream left in continental Europe to successive European treaties during the 1950s meant that Monnet placed a special emphasis on involving Socialist, Social Democratic and trade-union leaders in the committee, to complement the stronger support already witnessed among Christian Democrats and Liberals. His notion of the committee as an open network, rather than a classic confederation, freed it from many of the doctrinal or organizational disputes that often infect such bodies. Describing its working method, Monnet said: 'We come to agreement on resolutions – the word is not used by chance – that parties and organizations in power or in opposition pledge themselves to propose or defend in their own country.' Although Monnet eventually succeeded in bringing together almost a hundred political parties as members, the committee never lost its informal and visionary character. In a famous phrase, ACUSE was described by French journalist Jean-Jacques Servan-Schreiber as a 'kind of federal authority of the mind'.

During the 1960s, the Action Committee served as a focus for opposition to the determined **intergovernmentalism** of French President **Charles de Gaulle** in his approach to Europe. Monnet used it as a vehicle to issue declarations opposing several of the General's key foreign policy positions, including notably his exclusion of the United Kingdom from the Community. He actively fostered closer links with the political world in London: in 1968, at a rare moment of convergence on Europe in British politics, the Conservative, Labour and Liberal parties all joined the committee, together with the Trades Union Congress (TUC). However, with the relaunch of the Community after de Gaulle's departure from power in 1969 and its **enlargement** in 1973, both the need for, and role of, the Action Committee became less clear-cut. Monnet suddenly dissolved the committee in May 1975, on the twenty-fifth anniversary of the declaration by **Robert Schuman** proposing the ECSC.

Additionality

'Additionality' is the principle whereby sums received from the **Budget** of the European Union in support of particular programmes or projects within member states – most commonly from the **structural funds** – should be additional to those received from national government sources, rather than a substitute for them. The great temptation, which few member states have been able to resist, is to allow some receipts from the EU Budget to take the place of national spending. The **European Commission** has put in place a variety of procedures in an attempt to prevent such substitution, but inevitably the additionality principle has proved easier to police in respect of specific projects that are co-financed at national and European levels – for example, the construction of airports or motorways – than it has for broader categories of expenditure, such as the overall level of regional development aid.

Adenauer, Konrad (1876–1967)

Chancellor of the Federal Republic of Germany from 1949 to 1963, Konrad Adenauer was the central figure in the reconstruction of West Germany after the Second World War and its reintegration into western Europe and the Atlantic Alliance.

A lawyer by training, Adenauer entered politics at the age of 30, serving as a local councillor in Cologne; by 1917, he had been elected the city's mayor. He was sceptical towards the concentration of power in Berlin and became chairman of the national consultative body for local government in 1922. A leading member of the Catholic-based Centre Party before and during the Weimar Republic, he was forced from office by the Nazis in 1933. After a long period of internal exile, during which he was briefly imprisoned twice, Adenauer returned to the political stage in 1945. He was reappointed as mayor of Cologne and became a co-founder of the new Christian Democratic Union (CDU), which aimed to unite both Catholics and Protestants in a single centre-right party. In 1948–9, he served as president of the transitional Parliamentary Council of the three western occupation zones and played a key role in negotiations with the Allies on the constitution (Basic Law) of the new Federal Republic. In August 1949, at the age of 73, he was elected to the Bundestag – in a contest where the new Christian Democrats did unexpectedly well against their Social Democrat rivals – and was chosen the following month, by a one-vote margin, to become the first Federal Chancellor. His advocacy of Bonn as the capital of the new republic reflected his strong determination to shape the latter in the moderate, internationalist mould of Rhineland politics, rather than the classic pattern of Prussian militarism and centralism.

In foreign policy, Adenauer's chancellorship was driven by a desire to ensure that the Federal Republic acted on the lessons of the Nazi disaster. He wanted his country to play a full part in the post-war democratic community of nations, anchored in the new international structures created under American leadership. In his vision, West Germany would be a reliable ally in the Atlantic Alliance, would reconcile itself fully with its old adversary, France, and would help build a pan-European political system in which a significant measure of the country's resurgent sovereignty could be dissolved. By such means, as Wolfram Hanrieder has put it, the Bonn government would make a claim to 'political and legal equality in the name of European integration and the Western alliance', rather than that of 'discredited German nationalism' (*West German Foreign Policy, 1949–1963*, 1980).

Adenauer's simultaneous Atlanticism and pro-Europeanism found particular favour in Washington, which supported both the reindustrialization and the rearmament of West Germany in an international framework. In return, the Chancellor took a hard line in relations with the Soviet Union, refusing to maintain diplomatic contact with any other country that recognized East Germany (the **Hallstein** Doctrine). He secured the admission of the Federal Republic to the **Council of Europe** in 1950 and to the **North Atlantic Treaty Organization** (NATO) in 1955. Acting as his own foreign minister from 1951 to 1955, Adenauer ensured the country's position as a founder member of the **European Coal and Steel Community** (ECSC) and resolved the long-running dispute with France over the **Saarland**. In 1952, in defiance of domestic public opinion, he reached agreement with Israel on reparations for the Holocaust, and in 1955, travelling to Moscow, he extracted Soviet agreement to the return of German prisoners of war still held in the USSR. Given negative attitudes towards Germany in many countries at the time, as well as the striking lack of support he received from the opposition SPD, these were no minor achievements. SPD leader Kurt Schumacher, for example, condemned the new ECSC as 'conservative, capitalist, clerical and dominated by cartels'.

When the process of European integration stalled in the mid-1950s – with the refusal of the French National Assembly to ratify the **European Defence Community** (EDC) in August 1954 – Adenauer lent his support to the **Beyen Plan** to create a **common market** and **customs union**, leading to the launch of the **European Economic Community** (EEC) in January 1958. He then overcame his initial scepticism towards **Charles de Gaulle**, who returned to power in France in June that year, and sought to work with him on European issues, although often with difficulty. Relations were strained by the General's hostility to the United States, his openness to the Soviet Union, his effort to 'intergovernmentalize' the European Communities through the **Fouchet Plan**, and his dramatic and divisive **veto** of British membership in January 1963. However, Adenauer avoided confronting de Gaulle and tried to respond positively to any approach from Paris that could deepen bilateral Franco-German cooperation, even at the cost of discomforting other member states. The symbolically important **Elysée Treaty**, signed in January 1963, only a few days after de Gaulle's veto, was a powerful case in point: many within Adenauer's party felt that the Chancellor had been manipulated by the General.

Despite his strong commitment of principle to closer European integration, Adenauer was pragmatic in the methods that might achieve it. He saw Franco-German reconciliation and European unity as largely synonymous, but rarely took the lead himself in advancing specific initiatives, preferring to leave it to others to float proposals to which he usually responded sympathetically, even if their directions might diverge. In the spring of 1950, he first supported 'a customs union and customs parliament' uniting France and Germany, 'like those which unified Germany after the Napoleonic wars', then advocated the complete fusion of the two countries, and finally accepted the French proposal, set out in the **Schuman Plan**, for a pooling of their coal and steel industries, under supranational control, an initiative which he welcomed as 'the beginning of a federal structure of Europe'. Conversely, however, when describing a conversation with the French President a decade later, in July 1960, Adenauer could hardly be accused of displaying an excess of supranational zeal: 'de Gaulle and I were agreed that we should not allow [the European Communities] to develop into super-states, given that they had no formal responsibilities. They had to be confined to their role of giving technical advice.'

At home, the distinctive 'social market economy' pioneered by Adenauer's economics minister (and successor as Chancellor), Ludwig Erhard, helped to generate the Federal Republic's post-war *Wirtschaftswunder* or 'economic miracle'. Its careful mix of free-market economics and social regulation appealed to the national mood. Growing prosperity also helped facilitate the reintegration of 10 million refugees into the new republic. Carried forward by speedy reconstruction and rising living standards, the Christian Democrats increased their share of the vote in the 1953 and 1957 general elections, winning an absolute majority of votes cast in the latter contest on the slogan of 'Safety First: No Experiments'.

In 1959, however, Adenauer's usually acute political skills failed badly, when he initially nominated Erhard, without his prior agreement, to the vacant post of Federal President, and then decided to enter the contest himself, only to quickly withdraw. The high watermark of the Chancellor's fortunes had passed. An increasingly flexible and resourceful SPD benefited politically from the construction of the Berlin Wall in August 1961, and in the following month's general election, the CDU-CSU lost its overall majority in the Bundestag. The price of forming a coalition with the (Liberal) Free Democrats was a commitment by Adenauer himself to leave office within two years: in October 1963, at the age of 87, he duly retired as Chancellor. With the near simultaneous resignation of Harold Macmillan as British prime minister and the assassination of US President John F. Kennedy five weeks later, Adenauer's departure marked a turning-point in European politics, increasing the predominance of de Gaulle. The former Chancellor continued as a member of the Bundestag and chairman of the CDU for another three years. In retirement, he published four volumes of memoirs, covering the years 1945 to 1963.

By virtue of his dignity, experience and authority, Adenauer was the ideal embodiment of the 'new Germany' that emerged from the ruins of 1945. In the words of Wolfram Hanrieder, the 'rapid transformation from hated and destroyed foe to respected and valued ally in such a short time after a major war is almost unprecedented in history'. Adenauer played an absolutely crucial role in engineering this process. His courteous, dutiful and hard-working manner belied a politician of great agility, clarity and tenacity. Stephen Spender met him in 1945, at the age of 69, and described him thus: 'He has an energetic, though somewhat insignificant appearance: a long lean oval face, almost no hair, small blue active eyes, a little button nose and a reddish complexion. He looks remarkably young and he has the quietly confident manner of a successful and attentive young man' (*European Witness*, 1946). Adenauer was an extremely astute and determined politician who built a European and international reputation which none of his successors as Chancellor has yet been able to match.

Advocate-general

The **European Court of Justice** (ECJ) is composed of 27 judges and eight advocates-general. The role of advocate-general – which is known in several jurisdictions among the founding **Six** member states of the European Union but has no equivalent in English law – is to present, on the basis of the facts and arguments submitted by all parties, a 'reasoned submission' in open court. This submission, known as the Opinion, seeks to identify the points of law at issue, to remind the Court of precedents with a bearing on the case, and, most importantly, to recommend what judgement the Court should reach. The judges then retire to deliberate in camera without the advocate-general being present. The Court very often, but not always, follows the advocate-general's recommendation, which is therefore widely taken as an early indication of the Court's likely ruling. Although the Opinion has no legal force in its own right, it is printed, together with the final judgement, in *European Court Reports*. Traditionally, advocates-general prepared Opinions on all cases before the Court. However, in recent years, they have concentrated on cases that are particularly complex or involve new points of law.

Under Articles 252–3 TFEU, the eight advocates-general, like judges, are appointed by common accord of the member states of the Union, for a renewable term of six years, on a rotating basis, with half the appointees (four) retiring every three years. (The **Council of Ministers** has the right, acting unanimously, in response to a request from the Court, to increase the number of advocates-general.) By convention among the member states, five of the eight positions as advocate-general are occupied by individuals from the five largest member states (France, Germany, Italy, Spain and the United Kingdom), with the other three posts rotating in alphabetical order among the remaining (currently 22) member states. Since Poland entered the Union in 2004, it has campaigned for the right to nominate an advocate-general.

Agencies

An agency of the European Union is a specialist public authority set up under European law, separate from the Union's **institutions** and with its own **legal personality**. There are currently 33 such agencies, the earliest dating from 1975. Recent years have witnessed a significant expansion in the number of agencies: before 1990, there were only two agencies; during the 1990s, 11 agencies were created; since then, the total has more than doubled. Whilst initially agencies tended to conduct research for and offer advice to the **European Commission**, their role has widened with time. They have been increasingly assigned the tasks of administering certain policies, conducting risk assessment and contributing to the compliance and enforcement of **EU law**. From 2000 to 2010, the cost of agencies increased from approximately € 100 million to over € 1.5 billion per year and their staff complement rose from 1,000 to over 5,000 people.

An incentive for the Commission to spin off agencies lies in the fact that their operating costs are attributed not to the administrative chapter of the institution's budget (so-called Heading 5), but to the relevant policy chapters (Headings 1–4). The financial displacement this causes can free up resources to cover other Commission personnel and operating costs at the centre. The converse effect is to squeeze expenditure available for the pursuit of policy objectives. Agencies are also freer than the Commission to hire staff on temporary contracts (see **Eurocrats**) and some are permitted to raise income from outside sources. About two-thirds of agency staff are 'temporary agents'. The Community Plant Variety Office (CPVO), which has the unique right to assign industrial property rights for plant varieties, is entirely self-financing, whilst the European Medicines Agency (EMA), which offers a Union-wide registration procedure for new medicinal products, raises three-quarters of its income from fees paid by the pharmaceutical industry. The three new EU agencies established in 2011 to regulate the financial markets – the European Banking Authority (EBA), the European Insurance and Occupational Pensions Authority (EIOPA) and the European Securities and Markets Authority (ESMA) – are partially co-financed by the relevant national public authorities.

Increasing recourse to the agency model has met with criticism from the **European Parliament** in particular, which fears that the entities created are less amenable to political oversight and control than conventional Commission directorates-general. The Parliament has also insisted on granting '**discharge**' to the accounts of each of the agencies separately, rather than collectively or in conjunction with the Commission's accounts. The nomination of the members of the boards of many, but not all, agencies is now subject to de facto, and in some cases de jure, approval by the Parliament, which usually holds 'hearings' of directors-designate. In order to increase support within the **Council of Ministers** for the use of agencies, a deliberate policy of decentralization has been pursued, with most such bodies now being located away from the three **seats of the EU institutions** – **Brussels**, Luxembourg and Strasbourg – in over two dozen other cities across the Union.

Most EU agencies operate in what was, before the **Lisbon Treaty**, the first or European Community '**pillar**' of the European Union. Twenty-seven agencies of this kind either provide services, information or advice to the European Commission (and sometimes national authorities) or engage in risk assessment, inspection and/or the promotion of compliance with and enforcement of EU law. A small number of agencies in the second category – notably the CVPO, European Aviation Safety Agency (EASA), European Chemicals Agency (ECA) and Office for Harmonization in the Internal Market (OHIM) – have been entrusted with the power to adopt technical decisions that are legally binding on third parties. The three new supervisory agencies established in 2011 to oversee the financial services sector – the EBA, EIOPA and ESMA – may propose delegated and implementing measures for formal adoption by the Commission (see **comitology**).

With the abolition of the 'pillared' structure of the Union, three agencies created under the old 'third pillar' for **Justice and Home Affairs** (JHA), and relating to police and judicial cooperation in criminal matters – Europol, Eurojust and the European Police College (CEPOL) – will become conventional Community-style agencies in due course, and are already partly financed by the Union. There are also three separate agencies in the field of **Common Foreign and Security Policy** (CFSP), previously the 'second pillar' of the Union, which report to the Council of Ministers and are currently funded by subscriptions from the member states, with the Union's **High Representative** chairing their governing boards: the European Union Institute for Security Studies (EUISS), European Union Satellite Centre (EUSC) and European Defence Agency (EDA).

In addition to the 33 EU agencies listed above, the European Commission itself has established six internal 'executive agencies' in Brussels to administer specific, technical aspects of policies within that institution, together with seven 'European Joint Undertakings' (EJUs), which are essentially public–private partnerships in the field of **research and development policy**.

Details of the names, roles, and locations of all EU agencies can be found on the European Commission website. Agencies are not to be confused with EU 'bodies', which are often organizations whose existence is specifically provided for in the **Treaties**, but which are not themselves institutions. Examples of 'bodies' are the two main advisory fora to the EU institutions – the **European Economic and Social Committee** (EESC) and the **Committee of the Regions** – as well as the new **European External Action Service** (EEAS), the **European Investment Bank** (EIB), the European **Ombudsman** and the European Data Protection Supervisor (EDPS).

Albert–Ball Report

Commissioned by the **European Parliament**, the Albert–Ball Report was published in August 1983 under the title *Towards European Economic Recovery in the 1980s*. The authors were two leading European economists, Michel Albert, former head of French *Commissariat général du Plan*, and Professor James Ball, principal of London Business School. Their 110-page report – which reads more as a series of interlinking personal essays than a single set of policy recommendations – was one of the first analyses to draw attention, in a systematic and quantified way, to the 'opportunity cost' of the Community's failure to establish a true **single market** and to the difficulty confronted by business in taking advantage of the potential economies of scale that flowed from the logic of **free movement** in the founding **Treaties**.

The authors claimed specifically that restrictions placed by national regulations on the free movement of goods, services and capital were costing the European economy around two per cent of GDP: 'like the peasants of the Middle Ages who had to pay a tithe to the lord', everyone in employment in Europe 'works on average one week per year' simply to pay for the retention of these barriers. To capture this phenomenon, the Albert–Ball Report coined the phrase 'the cost of **non-Europe**', subsequently popularized by the **Cecchini Report** in 1988. It declared that 'the main obstacle to the economic growth of the European countries is what we must call *non-Europe*' and that 'the low level of cooperation and the weakness of common policies' meant that the Community was 'declining on a slippery slope of non-growth' and failing to realise the 'multiplier effect' of joint action.

The Franco-British provenance of the Albert–Ball Report gave it additional credibility in opinion-forming circles, whilst its emphasis on supply-side reform promoted its appeal in finance ministries. The report played an important part in generating wider support for the idea of completing the single market, which was already being canvassed by the **Kangaroo Group** and others in the European Parliament – including the latter's special committee on European economic recovery which invited Albert and Ball to undertake their study – and by the European Round Table (ERT) of leading industrialists. The single-market objective was taken up by **Jacques Delors** – whom Michel Albert knew well from his time as French finance minister – when he became President of the **European Commission** in January 1985, was endorsed by EC heads of government in March that year, and was converted into a legislative programme by the **Cockfield White Paper** three months later, with the specific aim of removing all remaining barriers to the free movement of goods, services, capital and persons by the end of 1992.

Allied Command Europe (ACE)

Until 2008, the military command structure of the **North Atlantic Treaty Organization** (NATO) was organized on a geographic, rather than functional, basis, with Allied Command Europe being the name given to its European sphere of operations. ACE was one of two geographic commands within an overarching framework, known as Allied Command Operations (ACO), created in 2002. The other was the US-based Allied Command Transformation (ACT), previously known as Allied Command Atlantic. ACE and ACT have now been subsumed by ACO, which is based at **Supreme Headquarters Allied Powers Europe** (SHAPE), near Mons, Belgium. SHAPE, the original home of ACE, retains its European designation for purely historic reasons.

ACE had two 'regional commands': Allied Forces North Europe, based in Brunssum, Netherlands, and headed by a British or German general; and Allied Forces South Europe, based in Naples, Italy, and headed by a US general. Each of these two regional commands had separate air and naval forces, as well as a series of sub-regional commands, located in various centres. Under the new system, the Brunssum and Naples facilities have become 'joint force commands' (JFCs), with the first coordinating NATO operations in Afghanistan, and the second, NATO operations in the Balkans. Each JFC now has access to the old sub-regional commands, although for practical reasons the latter remain formally assigned to one or other of the two JFCs.

Allied Rapid Reaction Corps (ARRC)

The creation of the Allied Rapid Reaction Corps was a product of the overall review of the role and structure of the **North Atlantic Treaty Organization** (NATO) undertaken in the early 1990s. With the receding threat of a massive armed attack against any of the NATO states, the Alliance's 'New Strategic Concept' (agreed at the NATO summit in Rome in November 1991) laid emphasis on the need for smaller forces with 'enhanced flexibility and mobility', including 'immediate and rapid reaction elements able to respond to a wide range of eventualities'. The ARRC was headquartered in Rheindahlen, Germany, after it became operational in May 1995, and moved to Innsworth, United Kingdom, in 2010. The corps has a peacetime establishment of 400 personnel and includes forces from 15 countries. It must be ready for deployment worldwide within five to 30 days, with a complement of up to 25,000 troops. It has so far seen service in Bosnia and Herzegovina (IFOR, 1995–6), Kosovo (KFOR, 1999) and Afghanistan (ISAF, 2006). The success of the ARRC has prompted the creation of four more 'high readiness forces' within the NATO system: such forces are available for both NATO and European Union missions and work closely with the (non-NATO) **Eurocorps**, which has been given such high-readiness status by NATO.

Amsterdam Treaty

The Amsterdam Treaty represented the third large-scale revision of the **Treaties** upon which the European Union is founded, following the 1986 **Single European Act** (SEA) and the 1992 **Maastricht Treaty**. The text was agreed at the Amsterdam meeting of the **European Council** on 16–17 June 1997, after more than a year of negotiation, and was formally signed on 2 October 1997. Following **ratification** by the then 15 member states, it came into force on 1 May 1999.

The negotiations which led to the Amsterdam Treaty were set in train by a commitment in the Maastricht Treaty that a new **Intergovernmental Conference** (IGC) would be convened in 1996. This undertaking was designed to reconcile some of the more integrationist member states to what they saw as the ambiguous outcome in Maastricht. The declared purpose of the second IGC was to review (and if appropriate, extend) the new decision-making procedures introduced under the Maastricht Treaty, notably the **co-decision procedure** between the **Council of Ministers** and **European Parliament**; to examine (and again by implication, extend) the system of **qualified majority voting** (QMV) in the Council, in the context of the likely **enlargement** of the Union; to consider extending Community **competence** in certain fields (civil protection, energy and tourism); and to attempt to agree a so-called '**hierarchy of acts**', whereby the various categories of **legal act** and legislative procedures within the EU would be brought together in a single coherent listing.

In preparation for the 1996 IGC, the Corfu European Council in June 1994 set up a Reflection Group, composed mainly of representatives of the foreign ministers and tasked with identifying the issues at stake and areas of potential agreement. The creation of such a group was a modest attempt to make the process of treaty revision more open and intelligible to the public, following the bruising **Maastricht ratification crisis** of 1992–3. However, the group's final report, presented to the Madrid European Council in December 1995, was non-committal, avoiding concrete proposals for new treaty language. Heads of government simply welcomed the report as a 'sound basis' for the IGC's work.

The IGC was formally convened in Turin on 26 March 1996. Its role was 'to examine the improvements which will have to be made to the Treaties to bring the Union into line with today's realities and tomorrow's requirements'. The European Parliament was to be 'closely associated' with the IGC, and the applicant countries and those of the **European Economic Area** (EEA) were briefed on its proceedings and given an opportunity to contribute their views. Negotiations in the 1996–7 IGC took somewhat longer than expected, as the British Conservative government of John Major, badly damaged by party divisions over Europe and facing a general election in May 1997 at the latest, had little political interest in an early outcome. A number of outstanding issues were held over until a new UK government, with a more constructive attitude, was in a position to make compromises.

The Amsterdam Treaty as eventually agreed in June 1997 falls into two distinct parts. The first, by far the longest, part contains 'substantive amendments' to the existing Treaties. The second part 'simplified' those Treaties by pruning them of provisions which were no longer considered relevant, rewriting the articles as necessary, and repealing the 1965 **Merger Treaty**. Annexed to the treaty were 13 **protocols** and 50 declarations.

The Amsterdam Treaty simplified and speeded up the co-decision procedure, by allowing legislation to be adopted at first reading, without a Council common position, either if the Council agrees to the Parliament's amendments or if neither the Parliament nor Council wish to make any changes to the Commission proposal. It also extended the number of policy areas to which co-decision applied (from 15 to 32 **legal bases**), to include **transport policy**, **development policy**, **non-discrimination**, fraud, some aspects of **social and employment policy**, and further aspects of **environment policy**. The assent procedure (now **consent procedure**) was extended to the Parliament in decisions on its own **uniform electoral procedure**.

The field of QMV in the Council was similarly extended in 24 (existing or new) legal bases, including **enhanced cooperation**, **equal treatment** between men and women, social and employment policy, **research and development policy**, public health, visa policy, **transparency**, customs cooperation and fraud. Limited use of QMV was allowed for the first time in the intergovernmental '**pillar**' for **Justice and Home Affairs** (JHA), created by the Maastricht Treaty, subject to an 'emergency break'. The extension of QMV would probably have gone wider, but for a hardening of position by the German government towards the end of the IGC negotiations, as Chancellor **Helmut Kohl** concluded that he could not afford to dilute the veto power of the *Länder* governments in policy areas where they had domestic competence. On the vexed question of the system of voting under QMV – and especially the relative voting weights of large and small member states – the IGC made no progress. This problem and the linked issue of the number of Commissioners were referred to a future IGC (by Protocol 11), so setting in train a process that led to the negotiation of the **Nice Treaty** three years later. The IGC equally failed to secure agreement on whether the Union should enjoy competence in the fields of civil protection, energy and tourism, or in defining a hierarchy of acts.

The Amsterdam Treaty did, however, introduce a variety of other reforms which could be presented as helping adapt the Union's institutions to further enlargement or as generally updating their operation. The number of Members of the European Parliament (MEPs) was capped at 700 (although it was subsequently increased to 732 by the Nice Treaty and to 751 by the **Lisbon Treaty**). The position of the President of the **European Commission** was strengthened: henceforth his or her agreement was required for the nomination of other Commissioners, whilst the Commission as a whole would 'work under the political guidance of its President'. The Treaty established (restrictive) ground-rules for the use of enhanced cooperation – to allow sub-groups of member states to integrate further and faster – in a wider, more heterogeneous Union. A new provision on the possible **suspension** of a member state's rights was introduced to provide a sanction against 'serious and persistent breaches' of fundamental rights. The United Kingdom's **opt-out** on the **Social Chapter** was ended and a new chapter added on employment. A protocol was added to the Treaties on the application of the principles of **subsidiarity** and **proportionality** in EU decision-making.

In the intergovernmental pillars for **Common Foreign and Security Policy** (CFSP) and JHA, a number of important changes resulted from the Amsterdam deal. In CFSP, the post of **High Representative** for CFSP was established and the institutional link between the **Western European Union** (WEU) and the EU was formalized. The WEU's '**Petersberg tasks**' – encompassing humanitarian and rescue tasks, peacekeeping, and crisis management, including peacemaking – were defined as EU functions. Policy relating to visas, asylum, immigration and judicial cooperation in civil matters was 'communautized', moving from the JHA pillar into the Community pillar over a five-year period. Within the remaining area of intergovernmental cooperation, the provisions on police and judicial cooperation in criminal matters were strengthened, and the **European Court of Justice** (ECJ) was given a limited jurisdiction in this field for the first time. The **Schengen** *acquis* on **free movement** across frontiers was also incorporated into the Treaties.

Antici and Mertens Groups

The Antici and Mertens Groups, composed of trusted mid-rank officials from the **permanent representations** of the member states of the European Union, prepare the weekly meetings of **COREPER** within the **Council of Ministers**. The Antici Group services COREPER II, which meets at the level of permanent representatives (ambassadors) and covers the major political issues being discussed in the Council; the Mertens Group performs a similar role for COREPER I, which brings together deputy permanent representatives and handles most sectoral issues.

The two groups meet weekly, the afternoon before their respective COREPER meetings: they prepare the agendas of those meetings, clarify the negotiating positions of the member states (and sometimes broker deals between them), and generally attempt to ensure that the Council system works as smoothly as possible. The groups act in effect as the interface between the multitude of Council working groups (in specific policy areas or on individual pieces of draft legislation) and the final process of dispute-settlement at ambassadorial and ministerial levels. The Commission and Council secretariat take part in their meetings, which are chaired by the country holding the rotating **presidency** of the Council. The Antici and Mertens Groups greatly facilitate the work of the presidency, by offering a forum in which to judge how ripe issues are for discussion at higher level and float compromise proposals to resolve them.

The Antici and Mertens Groups were established respectively in 1975 and 1993, in response to the growing volume and complexity of business before the Council. They are named after Paolo Massimo Antici, an Italian civil servant who proposed his group initially as a means of clearing certain technical items more quickly (such as agreeing Council minutes), and Vincent Mertens de Wilmars, the then Belgian permanent representative, who used his country's presidency of the Council to extend the improved preparation and coordination already achieved in the Antici Group to the wide-ranging and more sporadic business of COREPER I.

'Anticis' perform a special task at the quarterly meetings of the **European Council**. They meet in a room next to the heads of government and receive a continuous, near-verbatim account of proceedings in the summit room, which they then pass on to other officials from their national representations in distilled form. They are also given other politically-sensitive assignments from time to time: for example, the Antici Group met (for a second time) each week in the autumn of 2009 to discuss Council preparations for the introduction of the **Lisbon Treaty**.

In spring 2003, the Union's **Political and Security Committee** (PSC) developed a 'Nicolaidis Group', which is a looser arrangement than the Antici and Mertens Groups, but modelled on the same principles. It is named after Milton Nicolaidis, the then Greek representative on the PSC, who subsequently became a senior official in the Council secretariat.

Arctic Council

Established by the Ottawa Declaration of 1996, the Arctic Council is an intergovernmental forum for the discussion of marine, environmental and human development issues common to the Arctic region. The eight countries with territorial claims within the Arctic Circle – Denmark, Finland, Sweden, Norway, Iceland, Canada, the United States and Russia – comprise the members of the Council. Nine other countries in the northern hemisphere – including Germany, France, the United Kingdom, Italy and China – have observer status. (As a result, all the **Group of Eight** (G8) states sit in the Council either as members or observers.) Six indigenous communities are also recognized as 'permanent participants'. The presidency of the Council rotates every two years among the eight members, with the country in the chair providing the secretariat. The Council holds at least one ministerial meeting every second year, with a committee of 'senior Arctic officials' convening every six months, backed by five working groups.

A Conference of Parliamentarians of the Arctic Region (CPAR) brings together representatives of the national parliaments of the eight Arctic states, as well as the **European Parliament**. The observers and 'permanent participants' also take part. The Conference meets every second year, hosted in turn by participating parliaments. Its most recent meeting was held in September 2010 on the premises of the European Parliament in Brussels. A standing committee convenes between meetings of the Conference and enjoys observer status within the Arctic Council. See also **Barents Euro-Arctic Council** (BEAC).

Article 352

It is usually asserted that the EU institutions act exclusively on the basis of limited or 'conferred' powers, namely only in areas and under conditions assigned to the Union by the signatory states in the **Treaties**, and that they may not go beyond such powers. Article 5 TEU states that the European Union 'shall act only within the limits of the competences conferred upon it by the Member States in the Treaties to attain the objectives set out therein. Competences not conferred upon the Union in the Treaties remain with the Member States.' However, the emergence of a wide interpretation of EU **competence** by the **European Court of Justice** (ECJ), drawing on the principle of 'implied' powers, has rendered this less of a constraint than it might at first seem. Equally, from the outset, the **Treaty of Rome** provided a legal basis for the adoption of measures not explicitly sanctioned by the powers contained in specific treaty articles, but which might nonetheless be deemed desirable by the Union's institutions in pursuit of its broader objectives.

The basis for this potentially open-ended capacity to act by the **Council of Ministers**, on the basis of a proposal from the **European Commission**, is to be found in Article 352 TFEU. As originally drafted in 1957, Article 235 EEC, subsequently renumbered Article 308 EC, read as follows:

> *If action by the Community should prove necessary to attain, in the course of the operation of the* ***common market****, one of the objectives of the Community and this Treaty*

has not provided the necessary powers, the Council shall, acting unanimously on a proposal from the Commission and after consulting the European Parliament, take the appropriate measures.

The **Lisbon Treaty**, which came into effect in December 2009, amended that provision, now Article 352 TFEU, so that it reads:

If action by the Union should prove necessary, within the framework of the policies defined in the Treaties, to attain one of the objectives set out in the Treaties, and the Treaties have not provided the necessary powers, the Council, acting unanimously on a proposal from the Commission and after obtaining the **consent** *of the European Parliament, shall adopt the appropriate measures.*

(The original wording still remains for Article 203 in the parallel **Euratom** Treaty.)

Over the years, this treaty article – which has increasingly become known as the 'flexibility clause' – has provided the legal foundation for the development of new common policies or instruments not previously foreseen. For example, the initial elaboration of the Community's regional, environmental and consumer policies relied on use of the then Article 235, before successive treaty changes introduced more explicit **legal bases** for those policies. The evolution of **cooperation agreements** between the EU and third countries also depended for many years, at least in part, on this article. Today, it is only invoked by the Council about ten times a year: during the six years 2004–9, for example, 66 legal acts were adopted that relied solely or jointly on Article 308 as a legal base. It was used, for example, to impose personal sanctions against specific individuals who were suspected of involvement in the assassination of former Lebanese prime minister Rafiq Hariri, of violating the arms embargo against the Democratic Republic of Congo, and of breaking international law in Darfur, as well as those being sought by the International Criminal Tribunal for the former Yugoslavia (ICTY). In February 2007, it was used as the basis for establishing the new European Union Agency for Fundamental Rights, and in December 2008, as the basis for a directive to identify and designate critical European infrastructures, with a view to protecting them from potential terrorist attack.

In some cases, the use of Article 352 and its predecessors by the Council has proved controversial, with accusations that the EU institutions have exploited it to engage in deliberate 'competence stretching', despite the need for unanimous agreement within the Council to use it. If the article had not existed, the member states would have had to have found other legal means of cooperating outside the EU framework, for example by separate treaty or convention, subject to national parliamentary **ratification**. Criticism has been compounded by the fairly generous interpretation that the European Court has given to the scope of the article. In a landmark judgement in 1971, the ECJ took a broad view of the meaning of the critical words 'in the course of the operation of the common market' – now superseded in any case by the more wide-ranging phrase 'within the framework of the policies defined in the Treaties' – in this instance allowing the Commission to negotiate the European Road Transport Agreement and so develop a stronger role in external relations (**ERTA case**; Case 22/70).

The Court does not, of course, always rule in favour of the use of Article 352. In 1994, it rejected the suggestion that the Union might accede to the **European Convention on Human Rights** (ECHR) on the basis of this article, on the grounds that this would be a 'constitutional' decision, taken without going through the normal process of treaty amendment. The article, the ECJ said, 'cannot be used as the basis for the adoption of provisions whose effect would, in substance, be to amend the Treaty without following the procedure which [the latter] provides for that purpose' (Opinion 2/94).

As early as 1972, the **Vedel Report** had recommended that use of Article 235 should be subject to the approval of the **European Parliament**. The member states resisted this idea in successive rounds of treaty reform, until in the Lisbon Treaty, they finally conceded that the Parliament should acquire a right of veto, through the **consent procedure**. Lisbon also specifies that this article cannot be used in respect of actions under the **Common Foreign and Security Policy** (CFSP), now that the '**pillared' structure** of the Union, established by the 1992 **Maastricht Treaty**, has been abolished.

Over the years, another suggestion has been that approval by **national parliaments** should, in some form, also be a precondition for using Article 352. The Lisbon Treaty makes a nod in this direction, by obliging the Commission to draw any proposals it makes under the article to the attention of national parliaments. However, following the ruling of the German Federal Constitutional Court on the Lisbon Treaty in June 2009, the Bundestag and Bundesrat enacted, as a condition for ratification of the treaty, a specific safeguard to ensure that the German government could not agree to any use of Article 352 in the future without obtaining explicit national parliamentary authorization for this in law (see **Karlsruhe judgements**). A similar requirement was instituted in Britain in July 2011 by the European Union Act, giving the House of Commons a de facto power of veto over use of Article 352, and other national parliaments may insist on following suit. The development of such a 'safety-catch' is likely to reduce the willingness of the Commission to make proposals under this article in the future.

Articles 114 and 115

Articles 114 and 115 TFEU provide the legal basis for what is commonly known as **harmonization**, namely the elimination – either by the creation of new common standards or by mutual recognition of existing national standards – of the barriers to trade that spring from member states' different requirements in respect of health, safety, technical specifications, consumer protection and product standards generally. As such, Articles 114 and 115 are of fundamental importance to the realization of the **single market** – itself defined in Article 26 TFEU as 'an area without internal frontiers in which the **free movement** of goods, persons, services and capital is ensured in accordance with the provisions of the Treaties'.

Until the 1986 **Single European Act** (SEA), progress towards the single market had been slow, partly because the original Article 100 EEC required the **Council of Ministers** to act by **unanimity** in this field. Although Article 100 remained in force, its place as the **legal base** for the majority of single market measures was taken by a new provision, Article 100a, introduced by the Single Act, which provided for **qualified majority voting** (QMV) to be used in the Council. The **cooperation procedure** between the Council and **European Parliament**, now replaced by the **co-decision procedure**, was also introduced. (With subsequent treaty revisions, Articles 100 and 100a EEC became Articles 94 and 95 EC respectively, and since the **Lisbon Treaty**, Articles 115 and 114 TFEU, with their order reversed.)

Key exceptions from Article 114 are 'fiscal provisions . . . the free movement of persons . . . [and] the rights and interests of employed persons', which continue to be dealt with under Article 115. Member states are also allowed to 'maintain national provisions' in respect of the 'protection of the environment or the working environment' (Article 114(4) TFEU), as well as in certain sensitive fields listed in Article 36 TFEU, notably public morality, public security, health, heritage and industrial property. However, these latter restrictions must be approved by the **European Commission** and may not constitute 'a means of arbitrary discrimination or a disguised restriction on trade' between member states.

Association agreement

Association agreements are one of several types of **international agreement** concluded by the European Union: 'The Union may conclude with one or more third countries or international organizations agreements establishing an association involving reciprocal rights and obligations, common action and special procedure' (Article 217 TFEU, previously Article 310 EC). Such agreements are more comprehensive than either trade or **cooperation agreements**. They create a framework for dialogue and joint action across a wide range of political, economic and trade relations, and they normally include a free trade agreement of some kind.

Currently, six types of association agreement can be identified, although the distinction between them is something that has developed pragmatically and is not defined in any single legally-binding text:

i) 'Pre-**accession** partnership agreements' negotiated with countries aspiring to become members of the European Union. These agreements make explicit provision for eventual full membership of the Union, without guaranteeing it. The **Europe Agreements** concluded with the central and eastern European countries in the 1990s and the earlier association agreements with Greece in 1961 and **Turkey** in 1963 (the latter now superseded by a **customs union**) fall into this category;
ii) the **European Economic Area** (EEA) Agreement with three of the four (non-member) states within the **European Free Trade Association** (EFTA) – **Iceland,** Liechtenstein (see **micro-states**) and **Norway**. Like pre-accession partnership agreements, the EEA Agreement foresees accession to the Union for those states that wish to join;
iii) Stabilization and Association Agreements (SAAs) so far concluded with six of the seven countries of the western Balkans, under the Stabilization and Association Process (SAP), starting in 2001. All of the countries of the western Balkans aspire to EU membership and five have so far applied;
iv) Euro-Mediterranean Agreements concluded with seven countries in the Mediterranean Basin, including Israel, between 1995 and 2002;
v) the Cotonou 'Partnership Agreement' concluded collectively with the 79 **ACP states** in 2000 (and updated in 2005). The word 'association' was dropped from the title of this agreement because some developing countries considered it to have a neo-colonial connotation;
vi) individual association agreements – each one with a slightly different title – concluded with Mexico, Chile and South Africa between 1997 and 2002.

Where an agreement is concluded with a single country, relations between the parties are usually institutionalized through an 'association council', meeting annually or biannually, which brings together national government ministers (from the associated countries), on the one side, and Commissioners and representatives of both the Council of Ministers and the member states, on the other. The presidency of an association council rotates, on a six-monthly basis, between the two sides. Since the **Lisbon Treaty** came into force in December 2009, the **High Representative** for **Common Foreign and Security Policy** (CFSP) has the right to chair association councils on the EU side (other than with candidate countries for **enlargement**), but has chosen to delegate that role to the six-month, rotating **presidency** of the (EU) **Council of Ministers** (which exercised it before). Meetings of each association council are prepared at official level by an association committee. There are special arrangements for relations with groupings of states, notably within the ACP and EEA. Between six and 12 association councils are usually held in any given year.

Like most other international agreements, association agreements are negotiated by the **European Commission**, on the basis of a mandate from the **Council of Ministers**, with the latter adopting the text that results. Until the **Lisbon Treaty**, the Council acted by unanimity; now it proceeds by **qualified majority voting** (QMV), unless a policy area covered by the agreement still requires unanimity in the Council. Since the 1987 **Single European Act** (SEA), the text of any association agreement has required the assent, now termed **consent**, of the **European Parliament** before it may finally be adopted in the Council.

B

Balkans crisis

See **Yugoslavia**.

Baltic states

In 1918, in the immediate aftermath of the Russian revolution and the First World War, the three Baltic states of Estonia, Latvia and Lithuania secured independence from Russia, having been subsumed within the latter's imperial territories since the eighteenth century. (Finland also became independent from Russia and was referred to, at that time, as a 'Baltic state'.) During the Second World War, the Baltic states were successively occupied by Soviet and German troops, and then by Soviet troops once again. In 1944, they were incorporated as 'Soviet socialist republics' within the USSR. However, under the influence of *glasnost* and *perestroika* in the late 1980s, freedom movements sprung up in all three countries, with Lithuania declaring independence in March 1990, in the face of resistance from Moscow. Estonia and Latvia followed suit in August 1991, four months before the final collapse of the Soviet Union.

The newly independent Baltic states moved rapidly to assert a Western vocation, mainly through fear of potential Russian aggression. (Even after the independence of Belarus, Estonia and Latvia still share a border with Russia, and Lithuania abuts the Russian enclave of **Kaliningrad**.) In addition to joining the **Council of Europe** and the **Organization for Security and Cooperation in Europe** (OSCE), they quickly sought membership of the **North Atlantic Treaty Organization** (NATO), acceding to the new **Partnership for Peace** in 1994 and signing Membership Action Plans (MAPs) in 1999. In parallel, the Baltic states concluded **Europe Agreements** with the European Union in July 1994 and applied for membership in autumn 1995. They also secured associate membership of the **Western European Union** (WEU) in 1994. The Russian military withdrawal from the Baltic states was completed the same year, earlier than from East Germany. The Baltic states joined NATO in March 2004 and the European Union two months later.

In November 1991, the three Baltic states created a joint parliamentary forum, known as the Baltic Assembly, loosely modelled on the **Nordic Council**. In June 1994, they carried the logic one step further, by establishing a parallel structure for executive dialogue, called the Baltic Council of Ministers (like the Nordic Council of Ministers). An annual meeting between the two bodies is known as the Baltic Council – a title previously used by the representatives of independence movements in 1989. The 60-strong Baltic Assembly meets for one session per year and works by consensus, with each national delegation exercising an equal, block vote. The Assembly has six committees and three political groups: the Social Democratic party, Centrist party, and the Conservative/Right party. The three Baltic states also established a Baltic Free Trade Area (BAFTA) in 1994, followed by a common visa régime. BAFTA ceased to exist when they joined the EU a decade later.

Bank for International Settlements (BIS)

The world's oldest international financial institution, the BIS was founded in 1930, in conjunction with the Young plan to reorder post-First World War reparations and indebtedness. Its role is to encourage cooperation between central banks and to promote international monetary and financial stability. Most European countries' central banks, including the **European Central Bank** (ECB), participate in the activities of the BIS, together with the central banks of most of the emerging market economies. The Bank's headquarters are in Basle, Switzerland, where it employs a staff of over 500, with representative offices in Hong Kong and Mexico City. Some 85 per cent of the BIS' total share capital is in the hands of the participating central banks.

About 120 central banks and international institutions place deposits with the BIS. In 2010, such deposits (whether in currency or gold) amounted to around € 250 billion or approximately five per cent of total foreign exchange reserves worldwide. Sometimes known as the 'central banks' central bank', the BIS organizes bi-monthly meetings of governors and other senior officials, and cooperates closely with the International Monetary Fund (IMF). The BIS acts as a framework for the development of international regulatory standards in the banking sector – for example, the Basle I, II and III solvency requirements – through its 'Basle Committee' on banking supervision. Such standards are transposed into EU law by legislative proposals tabled by the **European Commission**. The BIS hosts the Financial Stability Board (FSB) established by the **Group of Twenty** (G20) to promote and oversee the global regulation of financial markets. It also collates and publishes a variety of statistics on central and commercial banking. In the period of the European Payments Union (1950–58), instituted by the then **Organization for European Economic Cooperation** (OEEC), the BIS acted as the clearing-house for the settlement of payments.

Barents Euro-Arctic Council (BEAC)

Founded in January 1993 on the basis of the Kirkenes Declaration, signed in the town of that name in northern Norway, BEAC is an intergovernmental forum to promote closer cooperation and economic development within the Barents Sea region. This is an area in the northernmost part of Europe – comprised of parts of Finland, Norway, Sweden and north-west Russia – which has five million inhabitants and covers a land mass twice the size of France, together with territorial waters bordering the resource-rich Arctic Ocean. In addition to the four countries directly affected, BEAC's membership also comprises Denmark and **Iceland**, as well as the **European Commission**, on behalf of the European Union. Six individual EU member states have observer status, together with the United States, Canada and Japan.

Alongside the **Black Sea Economic Cooperation** (BSEC) and the **Council of the Baltic Sea States** (CBSS), BEAC is an example of the emergence of new forms of regional cooperation in the post-Soviet era. It is also one of four 'northern regional councils' now operating in the most northerly parts of Europe, the others being the **Nordic Council**, the **Arctic Council** and the CBSS. The four bodies participate collectively in the Northern Dimension policy, adopted jointly by the EU, Norway, Iceland and Russia at a special **summit** meeting in Helsinki in November 2006.

BEAC's work is organized through meetings of foreign ministers, chaired by a presidency that rotates between the four core countries every second year, and is supported by a series of working groups and an International Barents Secretariat, based in Kirkenes. In January 2003, on the tenth anniversary of the Kirkenes Declaration, heads of government of BEAC countries held their first, and so far only, Barents summit. A Barents Regional Council brings together BEAC member states, regional authorities and representatives of indigenous peoples. It is assisted by a Barents Regional Committee, composed of civil servants and divided into working groups. Since 1999, five BEAC parliamentary conferences of national and regional parliamentarians have also been held, the most recent being in Luleå, Sweden, in May 2011.

Barroso, José Manuel

See **European Commission**.

Belgo-Luxembourg Economic Union (BLEU)

BLEU was set up under a convention signed between Belgium and Luxembourg in 1921, initially for a period of 50 years, Luxembourg having failed to establish a similar arrangement with France. Customs controls between the two countries were effectively removed in May 1922. The Union was dissolved in 1940 and reactivated in 1945. Since 1972, it has been renewed by tacit agreement for ten-year periods, most recently in December 2002. The key economic commitments of the union were that the two countries held their gold and foreign exchange reserves in common, and that their currencies – the Belgian and Luxembourg francs – were maintained at parity and were legal tender in each other's country. The advent of **Economic and Monetary Union** (EMU) in Europe – with a single currency, the **euro**, and a common monetary policy for **eurozone** countries – has rendered these provisions redundant. Equally the BLEU practice of compiling common customs statistics was superseded by an EU obligation to present national statistics from 1999 onwards.

Benelux

The word Benelux is an acronym formed from the first syllables of Belgium, the Netherlands and Luxembourg. It came into general use in the post-war years to signify a **customs union** founded between the three states in 1948 and elaborated ten years later into a broader economic union. The Benelux arrangement – providing for the **free movement** of goods, services, capital and labour between the participating countries – was very much seen as a model for the wider economic integration of western Europe. However, as the **European Economic Community** (EEC) developed from 1958 onwards, the rationale for Benelux receded, even if for many years it was still some way in advance of the rest of the Community in its chosen fields of activity. The vanguard role once played by Benelux has more recently been performed by the **Schengen** Agreement and Convention – to which the three Benelux states were founding parties – for complete free movement across the frontiers of participating states.

The Benelux Customs Union was established on 1 January 1948 and grew out of the existing **Belgo-Luxembourg Economic Union** (BLEU), founded in 1921 (including the common denomination of their two countries' currencies), and an agreement in September 1944 between the three governments-in-exile in London to include the Netherlands in certain provisions of the BLEU after the war. A decade later, in February 1958, the three countries signed a successor Treaty of Economic Union in The Hague, which was concluded for a period of 50 years and came into force in November 1960. Article 233 of the **Treaty of Rome**, now Article 350 TFEU, acknowledged BLEU and Benelux, explicitly allowing such 'regional unions' to exist and flourish within the new Community framework. In advance of the expiry of the 1960 treaty in 2010, a successor treaty, establishing a 'Benelux Union', was signed in The Hague in June 2008 and concluded for an unlimited period.

The 1948 Benelux arrangement was significantly more ambitious than BLEU, with a broader range of goals: common employment and social security policies, close coordination of macro-economic and budgetary policies, and the eventual adoption of a full monetary and fiscal union, with a single currency and harmonized taxes. Although the latter objectives were not realized, the Benelux countries did succeed in abolishing internal restrictions on trade and adopting a common external tariff some years ahead of the Community as a whole, and in pioneering a passport-free area with common treatment of third-country nationals, something that remains to be achieved throughout the Union several decades later. The 2010 treaty extends the areas of cooperation to intellectual property, sustainable development, and justice and home affairs.

The Benelux institutional structure bears a distinct resemblance to that adopted by **the Six** in designing the European Communities in the 1950s. It reflects the common perceptions of the architects of both systems about the political importance of supranational structures, representational bodies and legal adjudication in economic integration. Crucially, however, the system lacks an independent executive body of the kind represented by the **European Commission**. Benelux is governed by a Committee of Ministers, assisted by a consultative Inter-Parliamentary Council, a consultative economic and social council, and a court of justice.

The Benelux Committee of Ministers, which acts by unanimity, meets at both ministerial and official level. The Committee comprises foreign and finance ministers, as well as other ministers as appropriate; its presidency rotates every six months. Ministerial meetings are prepared by senior civil servants in a 'Benelux Council' – with roughly the equivalent role to **COREPER** in the EU system – and there are about a dozen official committees or working groups. Regulations adopted by the Committee are binding on the three states in question but are not directly applicable in their national legal systems. In parallel, conventions may be adopted. The Benelux Court of Justice, whose work only began in 1975, is comprised of judges from the three countries' supreme courts and is responsible for the uniform interpretation of common legal undertakings. The Benelux Inter-Parliamentary Council – known as the 'Benelux Parliament' – is composed of 21 Dutch, 21 Belgian and seven Luxembourg parliamentarians: in the Belgian case, the representatives come from both national and regional parliaments. It has seven committees and members sit by political group. Its presidency and physical location rotate on a biennial basis, although administrative support is provided by the Belgian parliament. The Benelux Economic and Social Council is comprised of 27 members drawn equally from comparable bodies in the three countries. The Benelux secretariat in based in Brussels and comprises about 60 staff. By convention, the secretary general is always of Dutch nationality, with two deputy secretaries general drawn from the other states. The administrative costs of Benelux are met by direct contributions from the three countries: Belgium and the Netherlands pay 48.5 per cent each and Luxembourg the remainder.

The word 'Benelux' was invented in 1947 by F. M. Aspelagh, the Brussels correspondent of *The Economist*, to describe the proposed customs union between the three countries. In search of an original and amusing way of popularizing the concept, the author initially lighted on the word 'Nebelux'. 'After some hesitation I changed it to "Benelux". That sounded much better, but I was still not completely satisfied. It sounded more like a brand of vacuum cleaner than a concept of economic geography. Nonetheless I decided to give it a chance, and used it for the first time in *The Economist* on 6 August 1947. The rest is history.'

Benelux is the only survivor of a number of comparable customs unions proposed in the late 1940s and 1950s. France and Italy discussed such a union in 1949, and later considered joining the Benelux arrangement. This was opposed by the Netherlands, on the grounds that it might disrupt the progress then beginning to be made on a broader front in the **Council of Europe** and the **Organization for European Economic Cooperation** (OEEC). With exotic names like Fritalux and Finebel – to which must be added the land of Bizonia, an amalgamation of the British and American sectors of occupied Germany – these projects now survive only as fossils in the bedrock of European integration.

Berlaymont

The Berlaymont building, located at the junction of rue de la Loi and Rond-Point Schuman in Brussels, is the headquarters of the **European Commission**, the executive of the European Union and by far the largest of its institutions. Built between 1963 and 1969, the 13-storey office complex was originally financed by the Belgian government – from the pension fund of former colonial civil servants in the Belgian Congo – as a means of strengthening the claim of Brussels to serve as the administrative capital of the then **European Communities**. The project succeeded in this aim: in 1965, the governments of the member states designated the city as the provisional location of the Commission, a decision that was made definitive in 1992 when the various **seats of the EU institutions** were finally settled. The building occupies the site of the former convent and school of a Catholic order, the *Dames du Berlaymont*. Designed by Belgian architect Lucien de Vestel, its distinctive star shape – with four wings radiating from a central hub – was loosely modelled on the then voguish UNESCO building in Paris (of 1958).

Before the Berlaymont opened in 1969, the Commission services were dispersed across eight buildings in what gradually became known as the *quartier européen* of Brussels. It was headquartered first at 51–55 rue Belliard and then in a series of interlocking offices on the other side of the Rond-Point Schuman: the 'JECL' complex occupying the whole triangle bordered by rue de la Joyeuse Entrée, Avenue Cortenbergh and the Parc du Cinquantenaire. The

Commission continued to use the JECL until its demolition in 2006; its replacement now plays host to the **European External Action Service** (EEAS); The Berlaymont was originally able to house the bulk of the Commission's directorates-general and other services, but as the administration grew in numbers, it became increasingly the preserve of the institution's more senior staff.

In 1990, the walls of the Berlaymont were discovered to have a high content of asbestos, which was potentially injurious to health. From 1991 to 2004, the building was closed for complete reconstruction. The Commissioners and central services were moved to the smaller Breydel building nearby, with other staff relocated in a large number of (often) rented office buildings across the city. When the Berlaymont reopened, this pattern of dispersion was largely maintained: the Commission currently occupies offices at nearly 70 different addresses in Brussels, about half of which are in the European quarter.

On its completion in July 2004, five years late, the revamped Berlaymont was purchased by the Commission from the Belgian government for some € 550 million. It is a lighter, more environmentally-friendly and more technically sophisticated building than its predecessor. The installation of an additional glass façade around the building also means that its external appearance differs markedly from the earlier version. Comprised of thousands of adjustable louvre windows, this façade both regulates the temperature within the building and reduces external noise. Today the Berlaymont houses around one tenth of the Commission's 25,000 staff. European Commissioners and their ***cabinets*** have offices on the 12th and 13th floors. The college of Commissioners meets in the '**Jean Monnet** room' on the 13th floor, which also houses a private dining room for the use of Commissioners and a small restaurant for senior staff, known as *La Convivialité*. The Commission's secretariat general, legal service and other central services are housed on the lower floors.

Better Law-Making

'Better law-making' is a generic term used to denote efforts to improve the coherence and quality of the legislative process within the European Union – from the inception of draft law through to its application in practice. The stress is characteristically on those stages of the law-making process that are 'upstream' or 'downstream' of the formal adoption of measures by the EU institutions, although it does not exclude the process of enactment.

The issues encompassed by better law-making thus include the advance consultation of outside bodies by the **European Commission** before it tables legislative proposals; the use of impact assessments to identify the likely effects of such proposals as they are being drafted or enacted; the simplification of the existing body of **EU law** to make it more comprehensible to the citizen; the possible resort to 'soft law' as an alternative to formal legislation; the development of an improved system of legislative planning within and between the institutions; arrangements for the adoption of administrative law (**comitology**); and the successful implementation and enforcement of **legal acts** once adopted. Greater openness in law-making and the closer involvement of **national parliaments** in the EU legislative process are sometimes also cited as components of the same agenda.

The Commission, **Council of Ministers** and **European Parliament** concluded an **Inter-Institutional Agreement** (IIA) on Better Law-Making in December 2003, after two years of negotiation. This sets out certain general principles to be followed in drafting, enacting and implementing law, and contains a number of commitments by the Commission in particular. The Commission and the Parliament have tended to be more interested than the Council in seeking action in this area, mainly because they see it as a way of safeguarding or increasing their power (respectively). For the Commission, the use of advance consultation, soft law and impact assessments, for example, has the potential at least to reduce its exposure to the vagaries of the Council and Parliament. For the Parliament, by contrast, the very notion of better law-making legitimizes its interest in being involved at every stage in the legislative process, rather than simply at the moment it is invited to propose amendments to draft proposals.

Initially, the phrase 'better law-making' was used interchangeably with 'better regulation', when both terms entered into circulation in the early 2000s. Better regulation now more usually refers to attempts to simplify the existing or prospective body of EU law. Simplification is undertaken in three main ways: by withdrawing outdated proposals (known as 'screening'); consolidating existing laws on the same subject into a single text, either informally ('consolidation') or legally ('codification'); or by using the opportunity of passing a new piece of legislation to incorporate (without modification) the existing law in the same field ('recasting'), so that there is one, more coherent text.

When recasting is used – and the Parliament has argued for it to become routine – disputes sometimes arise between the Commission and Parliament (and occasionally the Council too) about whether the amendments proposed to the Commission's proposal may deliberately or inadvertently touch on existing law. Since the Commission enjoys an exclusive **right of initiative** in proposing changes to EU law, it is extremely keen to avoid a situation where recasting may allow changes to be made, by the back door, to aspects of the existing law in a way that it had not envisaged or intended.

The genesis of 'better regulation' lies with the Molitor Group, a committee of national experts set up by the European Commission in 1994 and named after its German chairman, Bernhard Molitor. An initiative of the German government, the group was concerned with legislative and administrative simplification at European and national levels, with a view to improving the functioning of the **single market** and competitiveness of the European economy. The Molitor Group's report was presented at the Cannes meeting of the **European Council** in June 1995.

Recently, the distinction between 'better law-making' and 'better regulation' has been confused once again, as the Commission has chosen to replace both terms with the single concept of 'smart regulation' and widened the latter to include **subsidiarity** and other logically seperate notions.

Beyen Plan

After the failure to establish the **European Defence Community** (EDC) in 1954, **the Six** decided to look for new areas into which they could extend the kind of supranational collaboration they had begun with the **European Coal and Steel Community** (ECSC) in 1951. On 4 April 1955, Johan Willem Beyen (1897–1976), foreign minister of the Netherlands, submitted a memorandum proposing the creation of a **common market** and **customs union** among the ECSC partners. Instead of advancing cautiously, sector by sector, he suggested that the member states should aim to address all sectors at once, creating a single, integrated economy. This notion led directly – via the **Messina Conference** in June 1955 and the work of the **Spaak Committee** over the following year – to the **Treaty of Rome** establishing the **European Economic Community** (EEC) in March 1957. As such, the Beyen Plan has a strong claim to be a key text in the history of European integration, and Beyen himself to be one of the forgotten **founding fathers** of the European Union.

Beyen had first developed his thinking publicly in 1952, when he entered the Dutch government, after working at the International Monetary Fund (IMF) and **Bank for International Settlements** (BIS). He was dissatisfied with the very slow progress being made in dismantling restrictions on trade in post-war Europe. He argued that efforts to integrate the western European economy – notably through the **Organization for European Economic Cooperation** (OEEC) and the European Payments Union which it had spawned – were insufficiently ambitious. His experience of intergovernmental discussions at the IMF and BIS had convinced him that progress would depend on pursuing the same supranational logic that informed the new (but sectoral) ECSC. More immediately, he also wanted to forestall any possibility of the smaller, open economies, such as his own, being excluded from bilateral deals on trade and investment between the larger countries – of the kind that France and West Germany were considering – by shifting the debate to a multilateral level.

Beyen scored an early success in 1953, by making the establishment of 'a common market among the member states, based on the **free movement** of goods, capital and persons' one of the goals of the proposed **European Political Community** (EPC), although the means to achieve this objective were not spelt out in any detail. When plans for the EPC collapsed in the wake of the failure of the EDC, he was anxious to salvage the concept and gave it greater substance in his April 1955 memorandum. He convinced his Belgian and Luxembourg opposite numbers, **Paul-Henri Spaak** and Joseph Bech, as well as **Jean Monnet**, of the 'creative force of [this] positive idea' (as he later put it) for revitalizing the process of European unity. The establishment of a horizontal common market, underpinned by a custom union, quickly became the central focus of the negotiations among the Six in 1955–6.

Before and during the deliberations of the Spaak Committee, Beyen played an important, but unsuccessful, role in trying to secure British involvement in the emerging plans. He visited London in June and November 1955, only to be rebuffed in meetings with the then Chancellor of the Exchequer, R. A. Butler. The latter had described the ECSC in the early 1950s as 'Schumania' and now dismissed the Messina Conference as the political equivalent of 'archaeological excavations' in Sicily of little concern to Britain.

Black Sea Economic Cooperation (BSEC)

The BSEC Organization was set up in June 1992, under an agreement signed by Bulgaria, Romania, **Turkey** and the then Soviet Union, as an intergovernmental forum for economic cooperation and consultation on regional issues in the Black Sea area. As well as Russia, the membership now also extends to Albania, Armenia, Azerbaijan, Georgia, Greece, Moldova, Montenegro, Serbia and Ukraine, 'encompassing territories of the Black Sea littoral states, the Balkans and Caucasus'. Observer status is open to outside parties and currently includes the **European Commission**, on behalf of the European Union, seven individual EU member states and the United States. BSEC itself acquired observer status at the UN General Assembly in 1999 and undertakes a variety of cooperative projects with various UN bodies in the region.

BSEC has a Council of Ministers, chaired by a rotating six-month presidency, supported by 16 working groups on different economic sectors. Its work is prepared by a Committee of Senior Officials and supported by an international secretariat based in Istanbul. A Parliamentary Assembly, comprised of delegates from national parliaments, meets twice yearly in a city of the presidency country. An International Centre for Black Sea Studies was set up in Athens in 1998 and a Black Sea Trade and Development Bank became operational in Thessaloniki in 1999.

Black Wednesday

On Wednesday 16 September 1992, the government of the United Kingdom was forced to suspend the pound sterling's membership of the **Exchange-Rate Mechanism** (ERM) of the **European Monetary System** (EMS). This proved to be a seminal moment not only in British economic policy – involving a devaluation of some 25 per cent – but also in British domestic politics: the authority of the Conservative government of John Major was hugely damaged, his party became increasingly divided over Europe, and Britain's relations with EU partners suffered a period of turbulence until he left office in May 1997. Major himself subsequently described Black Wednesday as 'an embarrassment for the United Kingdom' and 'a political disaster'.

Britain had only joined the ERM in October 1990, after a long battle in government between a reluctant prime minister, **Margaret Thatcher** – who was to lose office only a month later – and her successive Chancellors of the Exchequer (Nigel Lawson and John Major) and Foreign Secretaries (Geoffrey Howe and Douglas Hurd). Lawson resigned from the government in October 1989 because of disputes with Thatcher over his closet 'shadowing' of the Deutschmark. In the event, delayed too long, both the timing and rate of entry proved inappropriate. **German reunification** was soon to generate economic stresses and strains that spilled across the whole system: a Deutschmark–Ostmark parity of one-to-one, imposed unilaterally by German Chancellor **Helmut Kohl**, led to a big increase in the money supply in his country, forcing the Bundesbank to raise interest rates. The Deutschmark rose in value, whilst sterling and other weak currencies were forced towards the bottom of their fluctuation bands, without any clear plan for maintaining their parities. In joining the ERM at an unexpectedly high bilateral rate of 2.95 Deutschmarks to the pound – set equally unilaterally by Thatcher without Bundesbank agreement – the British Treasury had inadvertently exacerbated the problem, creating circumstances in which the German central bank would feel less commitment than it should to supporting the British currency through intervention in the markets. With both inflation and interest rates also high in Britain, which was approaching the peak of an economic cycle, the UK's economic situation was not sufficiently robust to sustain entry at the time and at the rate chosen.

The Germans, for their part, were trapped in the classic position of an anchor currency facing difficulties: if they allowed the money supply to expand, they would export inflation to other countries; if they kept raising interest rates, they would export deflation. The British response was unsatisfactory: instead of maintaining high interest rates, and indeed perhaps raising them further, whilst seeking a downward realignment of weak currencies, the Treasury pursued the opposite policy. The new Major government tried to take advantage of the credibility offered by the 'new monetary framework' of the ERM to lower interest rates (from 14 to 10 per cent) and engaged in 'open-mouth operations' in support of sterling's ERM parity. In early August 1992, the prime minister was even quoted as saying that his long-term ambition was for sterling to become the 'strongest currency in Europe'. At an informal meeting of the **Ecofin Council** in Bath on 5–6 September 1992, the British Chancellor, Norman Lamont, conscious of the increasing incoherence of the situation, pleaded with Germany to revalue the Deutschmark. The German finance minister and Bundesbank president, Theo Waigel and Helmut Schlesinger, responded by suggesting that weaker currencies should rather adjust downwards, a solution which Lamont refused. In effect, as Moniek Wolters has put it, neither of the key assumptions on which the ERM had come to depend any longer applied – namely that Germany would have low inflation and interest rates, and that 'the Bundesbank would defend exchange rates, provided that members of the system made the necessary interest-rate adjustments to protect their currencies' ('The 1992–93 ERM Crisis', unpublished paper).

Pressures intensified in the run-up to the **French referendum on the Maastricht Treaty**, due on Sunday 20 September. The Danes had already rejected the Treaty on 2 June, the ratification process had been put on hold in Britain since that date, and the issue of the linkage between ratification and prospects for **Economic and Monetary Union** (EMU) had become widely understood over the summer. As a 'no' vote looked increasingly possible in France, traders sold currencies whose value would be certain to fall if the EMU project was seriously dented, if not abandoned, by any French rejection. By selling the pound short, at a rate which many believed too high but which the government said it would defend in all circumstances, the scene was set for a spectacular 'one-way bet' in the currency markets.

The British government entered the week before the French referendum absolutely determined to resist the speculative onslaught. Major declared that 'the soft option, the devaluer's option, the inflationary option, would be a betrayal of our future'. Pressures came to a head on the Wednesday, four days before the French vote. The Bank of England deployed around a third of the UK's foreign currency reserves in an effort to hold the pound within its ERM band. Following a series of crisis meetings of senior ministers, the Chancellor raised interest rates from 10 to 12 per cent, and then again to 15 per cent, to try to prevent the currency from haemorrhaging. At 7.00 p.m., Lamont announced that, after an 'extremely difficult day', sterling would temporarily leave the ERM. The currency's value immediately fell from 2.80 Deutschmarks to 2.20 – and from 2.00 to 1.50 US dollars – and drifted down further thereafter. The cost to the Treasury, in terms of foreign currency reserves lost, was estimated at some £3.3 billion. One hedge-fund trader alone, George Soros, famously made over $1 billion from speculation against sterling on that day.

The Italian lire followed sterling in departing the ERM, although unlike the pound, it re-entered four years later. The Spanish peseta was devalued by five per cent. The UK economy appeared to benefit from devaluation and the authorities put in place a new system of monetary policy-making that proved increasingly effective from 1992 to 1997. The inflationary side effects of sterling's fall were unexpectedly muted: it proved a rare example of a large-scale devaluation whose competitive benefits were not offset by rising prices. Reflecting an emerging consensus among economists about the merits of an independent monetary policy, the first major act of the new Labour government of **Tony Blair** in May 1997 was to transfer responsibility for the setting of interest rates from the Treasury to the Bank of England.

Although sterling's enforced exit from the ERM probably hastened UK economic recovery in the 1990s, the events of Black Wednesday were widely considered to be the most serious economic policy failure in Britain since the IMF crisis of 1976, and possibly the biggest political setback suffered by any government since the **Suez crisis** in 1956. It shattered the reputation of the Conservative government for economic competence, perhaps the most electorally valuable legacy of the 'Thatcher revolution'. The party's opinion poll rating fell from 43 to 29 per cent in a matter of days, and remained at that low level for the remainder of Major's term in office (and indeed much of the decade after). Black Wednesday also greatly weakened the self-confidence of pro-European forces in British politics and cemented a pervasive scepticism of EMU – and indeed a wider **Euroscepticism** – that persists to this day. Although departure from the ERM was originally meant to be temporary, successive British governments have refused to consider rejoining the mechanism.

In the aftermath of Black Wednesday, it became extremely difficult to secure approval of the **Maastricht Treaty** in Britain. Major's government was only able to relaunch the ratification process by a majority of three votes in the House of Commons in November 1992, where a growing Conservative revolt, exploited by an expedient opposition, imperilled his position. The UK component of a Europe-wide **Maastricht ratification crisis** culminated in a dramatic series of Commons votes in July 1993, in which endorsement of the treaty was only made possible by the prime minister threatening to call an early general election. Many of those who most strongly resented the failure of ERM membership had also displayed, as Hugo Young put it, 'an intense, sometimes tearful, loyalty to Margaret Thatcher in the hour of her deposing' (see below): Maastricht became their opportunity for revenge. Together, Thatcher's fall over Europe, Black Wednesday and Maastricht fuelled what Kenneth Clarke has called a 'Tory civil war on Europe', leaving the Conservative Party broken-backed in government and deeply sceptical about European integration in opposition. Although Black Wednesday helped to catapult Blair, in 1997, to the largest Commons majority of any incoming government since the Second World War, its deeper legacy was to make it impossible for the new prime minister decisively to shift public opinion in favour of Europe, as he wished, during his own decade in power.

Further reading: Philip Stephens, *Politics and the Pound: The Tories, the Economy and Europe*, 1997; Hugo Young, *This Blessed Plot: Britain and Europe from Churchill to Blair*, 1999.

Blair, Tony (born 1953)

Tony Blair was British prime minister from May 1997 to June 2007. Despite a classically Tory background – of public school, Oxford and the Bar – Blair became a Labour MP before the age of 30, at the height of his party's anti-Europeanism. In the early 1990s, he emerged as a leading front-bench 'modernizer', committed to abandoning left-wing policies on the economy, defence and Europe, and to distancing the party from the trade unions. He succeeded John Smith as Labour Party leader on the latter's sudden death in the run-up to the 1994 **European elections**. In opposition, he successfully rebranded the party as 'New Labour', dropped its symbolic commitment to public ownership (by repealing Clause Four of its constitution), and adroitly exploited Conservative divisions on a number of issues, notably Europe.

The only Labour leader ever to win three successive general elections (in 1997, 2001 and 2005), Blair pursued a distinctive foreign policy as prime minister. His approach combined simultaneous pro-Europeanism and pro-Americanism, to a degree not witnessed since Harold Macmillan in the early 1960s. He became a close political ally of the two US Presidents with whom he dealt, the Democrat Bill Clinton and Republican George W. Bush. At the same time, unlike his Conservative predecessors since 1979, **Margaret Thatcher** and John Major, Blair neither wished to, nor was forced to, define Britain against the European mainstream. Instead, during his decade-long tenure at Number 10, he attempted to reposition Britain as a more positive force in the European Union.

From the start, Blair sought to handle relations with European partners in as non-confrontational a way as possible, attempting to draw a line under the isolation and non-cooperation of the late 1980s and mid-1990s. More actively, he sought to ensure that any major new European initiative would not exclude Britain, and might be shaped positively by Britain to reflect its interests. In practice, this approach meant that he had to accept the need for ongoing institutional reform, whilst attempting to avoid unnecessary or controversial extensions of Union **competence** or **qualified majority voting** (QMV) in the **Council of Ministers**. It also involved conceding that the '**pillared structure**' of the **Maastricht Treaty** could be dismantled, provided that Britain retained its existing **opt-out** in **Justice and Home Affairs** (JHA) and that **unanimity** was maintained on most decisions in **Common Foreign and Security Policy** (CFSP). He committed Britain in principle to joining the single currency, the **euro**, whilst seeking to retain maximum discretion over whether and when this might happen in practice.

In other areas of European policy, Blair was happy to continue the approach of previous British governments, in attempting to reorient Europe's internal policy priorities towards liberalization and economic reform; to ensure that legislation on the **single market**, the environment and employment enhanced, rather than inhibited, competitiveness; to promote the continued **enlargement** of the European Union and reform of the **Common Agricultural Policy** (CAP); and to ally with other net contributors in preventing any significant growth of the EU **Budget**, whilst in parallel seeking to minimize the UK's own net contribution to it.

The Blair years in Europe may be divided into three phases: the first running from the British general election of May 1997 to the terrorist attacks of 11 September 2001; the second from '9/11' until the French referendum of June 2005; and the third from June 2005 until his retirement two years later. If the first period was characterized by broad success in advancing Britain's goals in Europe, the second phase was one in which Britain increasingly lost control of the European agenda, with the 2003 Iraq war dividing Europe into Atlanticists and 'Europeanists', in a way which Blair deeply wished to avoid. It also so weakened his position at home that he was increasingly unable to pursue a coherent policy abroad. During this period, British diplomacy in Europe confronted the limits of his policy of 'positive engagement'. The third phase was a period of recovery, during which – working in parallel with José Manuel Barroso as President of the **European Commission** – Blair gradually regained the initiative and was able briefly to impact positively on European priorities once again.

Elected to office, Blair quickly concluded negotiations on the **Amsterdam Treaty** in June 1997 – agreeing certain extensions of EU competence and QMV in the Council that Major would by then have found politically impossible, as well as opting Britain into the controversial **Social Chapter**. The UK **presidency** of the Council in the first half of 1998 offered the new prime minister the chance to showcase his more cooperative diplomatic style across a range of issues. He then pushed further and faster than his Foreign Office wanted in the development of a **Common Security and Defence Policy** (CSDP). He agreed a Franco-British plan for defence cooperation with French President Jacques Chirac – the **Saint-Malo Declaration** of December

1998 – which allowed the possibility that a future European defence force might operate independently of the **North Atlantic Treaty Organization** (NATO).

Blair's successful early dealings with Chirac reflected a broader tendency of seeking to build pragmatic, ad hoc alliances with other governmental leaders, regardless of party, to carry forward specific policy objectives. His early allies included not only the German Chancellor, Gerhard Schröder, but the Spanish conservative prime minister, José María Aznar, the Belgian Liberal leader, Guy Verhofstadt, and the Dutch and Italian centre-left premiers, Wim Kok and Romano Prodi – the last of whom he supported to become Commission President in 1999. All were seen as modernizers in their own countries and as potential supporters of economic reform in Europe. Progress was registered in acceptance in March 1999 of the Agenda 2000 proposals to prepare for enlargement, modernize the structural funds and reform the CAP, as well as in agreement a year later to the **Lisbon Strategy** to make Europe 'the most dynamic, knowledge-based economy in the world by 2010'.

Blair was also able to exploit such links, at least initially, to minimize the threat from the re-emergence of the institutional reform agenda: the modest **Nice Treaty** which resulted from an **Intergovernmental Conference** (IGC) in 2000 was seen as another British negotiating success, with **ratification** problems arising in France and Ireland (the latter voting 'no' in a referendum in spring 2001), rather than the United Kingdom.

At home, however, the political situation was more constrained. Blair was forced (in October 1997) to bow to pressure from his Chancellor of the Exchequer, Gordon Brown, to signal that Britain would not enter EMU stage three in the lifetime of his first term of government, as well as to make membership contingent on 'five economic tests' of a largely domestic character. These tests were imposed in addition to the formal **convergence criteria** in the Maastricht Treaty, which apart from membership of the **Exchange-Rate Mechanism** (ERM), Britain already met. Blair seems to have thought that he was simply deferring a decision on the timing of future entry (and convinced European leaders accordingly), but when he tried to return to the question during his second term in office, he found he had lost control over the issue to his Chancellor. An increasingly sceptical Brown was able to postpone membership indefinitely.

The terrorist attacks of 11 September 2001 marked an important turning point in the politics of Blair's relationship with his European partners and opened a second phase in his European policy. Although the crisis initially generated huge goodwill towards the United States, its consequences cast Blair in the role of George W. Bush's alter ego on the world stage, and forced him to take sides in 2002–3 between two very different alignments of European states, in an increasingly bitter battle about the merits of invading Iraq.

The division of Europe into '**old and new Europe**' identified by US Defense Secretary Donald Rumsfeld required Blair to make perhaps the most painful decision of his premiership: to choose whether or not to support the United States at the price of making enemies within the European Union and diminishing Britain's ability to 'lead in Europe'. It posed a challenge to his whole philosophy of seeking to influence both Washington and Brussels simultaneously by serving as a privileged mediator and bridge between the two.

Blair's strategy of bilateral diplomacy in Europe became increasingly difficult to sustain. His relations with both the French President and German Chancellor cooled rapidly, a process compounded by a secret Chirac–Schröder deal in October 2002, which bounced the **European Council** into agreeing in effect to freeze CAP spending over the 2007–13 future financing period. Aznar was voted out of office in March 2004, and three months later, Blair chose to join most centre-right leaders (other than Chirac) in preventing Verhofstadt from becoming Commission President (having previously agreed to support him). Instead, he backed Chris Patten and José Manuel Barroso in quick succession.

Institutional problems also began to cast a shadow over the middle Blair years, as the scope of the 'Future of Europe' debate continuously widened, and help explain the prime minister's scepticism towards Verhofstadt. The latter's Belgian presidency of the Council, starting in July 2001 quickly asserted a maximalist agenda, seeking to move beyond what it saw as the disappointing outcomes of Amsterdam and Nice towards a **European Constitution**. By contrast, in a keynote speech in Warsaw in October 2000, Blair opposed the idea of a constitution, arguing for a non-binding charter of competences instead, and proposed an upper chamber for the **European Parliament**, to be chosen from national parliamentarians. He found that there were surprisingly few governments resisting the first concept and even fewer takers for the second. The Laeken Declaration, to which he hesitantly agreed, in December 2001, spoke for the first time of a constitution being a serious possibility. The **Convention on the Future of Europe,** which met from April 2002 – an institutional innovation about which the Foreign Office had misgivings – took this concept as its starting point. The convention's chairman, **Valéry Giscard d'Estaing**, quickly guided the body towards a constitutional treaty, proposing a single text, rather than a series of options, as Britain would have preferred.

The outcome of the Convention (and the IGC that followed) was ambiguous. It broadly respected the UK's bottom line about where extensions of QMV should apply and endorsed the creation of a new post of full-time **President of the European Council**, a change strongly advocated by Blair. The prime minister was forced, however, to accept that the **Charter of**

Fundamental Rights should become legally binding and that the Maastricht 'pillars' be demolished. He was keen to avoid a difficult debate about the treaty on ratification and wanted to use his large majority in the Commons to push it through. He was receptive when President Chirac proposed to him that, if possible, all member states should refuse to hold **referenda**. However, as his domestic political problems deepened – partly as a result of accusations that the government had lied over intelligence reports before the Iraq War – his resistance to populist clamour for a referendum crumbled. In April 2004, he announced, to incredulity among pro-Europeans in Britain and abroad, that if a constitutional treaty were finally to be agreed – as it was two months later – the UK would only ratify the treaty after the electorate had endorsed it in a referendum. This decision sent shock waves through the European political establishment, making it inevitable that several other countries would have to follow suit.

Although Blair had extracted himself from an immediate difficulty, with the Eurosceptic press hailing him as a hero, he had built up a much bigger, looming problem. Britain would not want to hold its referendum until after as many other countries as possible had already voted in favour, so building pressure for a 'yes' vote there too. However, a UK vote in such circumstances would inevitably pose the de facto question of whether Britain stayed in the European Union, so considerably raising the stakes. In Paris, certain senior civil servants started to draw up plans for a 'rearguard' membership of the Union for countries that might vote 'no' (with potential candidates being Britain, Poland and the Czech Republic).

Ironically, it was Chirac's significant miscalculation in calling a referendum of his own that was unexpectedly to let Blair off the hook of any future 'no' vote in the UK. The rejection of the constitutional text in the **French and Dutch referenda** of May–June 2005 immobilized the document in its existing form and made the issue of a vote in Britain redundant. In one bound, Blair was free of the growing contradiction which had enveloped his position on Europe. It seemed that a constitution which he had not really wanted would never take effect – or if it did, it would almost certainly be scaled down sufficiently so as not to require popular endorsement. Blair could attempt to pick up the pieces and resume the pattern of relations he was forging before September 11 and the Iraq War. In doing so, he also hoped to take advantage of the confusion in France about what kind of Europe they as a nation wanted, and whether or not it might be possible.

The final phase of Blair's policy on Europe began in effect with a speech to the European Parliament on 23 June 2005, three weeks after the French referendum. Preparing the ground for his second UK presidency of the Council, in the latter half of the year, he argued that Europe should come to terms with the rejection of the constitution and focus instead on delivering policy results for the people. In a powerful intervention that made a big impact on an initially sceptical audience, he said: 'It is time to give ourselves a reality check. To receive the wake-up call. The people are blowing the trumpets round the city walls. Are we listening? Have we the political will to go out and meet them, so that they regard our leadership as part of the solution, not the problem?'

Blair's solution – pursued during the UK presidency – was to try to identify areas of common action that could offer tangible evidence of Europe adding value for the citizen. Working in tandem with Barroso, he prioritized the relaunch of the floundering Lisbon Strategy for economic reform and action to address the policy implications of Europe's ageing and shrinking population, to boost the size and quality of the workforce, and develop a more coherent common energy policy within the Union. In effect, Blair was arguing that, rather than see Europe as a bulwark against globalization, it should be a vehicle for embracing and promoting change. Barroso encapsulated this agenda in the phrase 'a Europe of results'. The new Blair–Barroso tandem was helped by the accession to the EU of eight former Communist countries of central and eastern Europe in May 2004, many of which had a positive attitude to reform. Blair exploited these circumstances in December 2005 to fend off pressure radically to reduce or even abandon the UK **abatement**, in the context of the new deal on EU spending being negotiated for 2007–13, eventually conceding about a fifth of its value over seven years.

Blair's post-2005 policy successes were mitigated in part by the sudden resurgence of the European Constitution, which had been widely declared dead. The determination of the new German Chancellor, Angela Merkel, to salvage at least part of the constitutional treaty during her presidency of the Council in the first half of 2007 proved remarkably effective. A detailed agreement was reached by the European Council in June 2007, shortly before Blair relinquished the premiership to Brown, with an IGC called to finalize the text thereafter. The new 'Reform Treaty', subsequently renamed the **Lisbon Treaty**, reiterated many features of the Constitution, whilst offering the UK additional safeguards on JHA and the Charter of Fundamental Rights: Britain would enjoy a complete opt-out on the former, wherever it wished (including in some cases retrospectively), and the latter would not create new rights that were justiciable in the British courts. The changes to the treaty were sufficient to enable Brown to claim that no referendum would now be necessary, even though most of the rest of the text looked suspiciously like its predecessor.

The overall verdict on Blair's premiership in Europe is inevitably mixed. Formally speaking, he succeeded in fulfilling his promise that, during his years in office, Britain would 'never be isolated in Europe'. He avoided having to threaten to veto a European treaty, associated Britain with deeper cooperation in defence and security, and opted the UK into the Social Chapter. He managed to provide 'leadership in Europe' on some important British priorities, notably in promoting enlargement and economic reform. However, he proved unwilling to risk serious unpopularity over the single currency and was unable to halt the drive to deeper institutional integration, even if he blunted its sharper edges. The Iraq War forced him to make enemies in Europe as the price for supporting the United States, critically weakening his position on several fronts. Although he recovered some of his momentum, by the time he left office, the UK was engaged in negotiating further exemptions from policies that would apply to other member states. Ironically, the 'opt-out mentality of an opt-out government' of which Labour had once accused John Major, seemed to have become the default position of both main parties in power.

On leaving office, Blair was immediately appointed the Middle East peace envoy of the 'Quartet' group (of the **United Nations**, United States, European Union and Russia). He subsequently established 'personal faith' and sports foundations and published his memoirs, *A Journey*, in 2010. Strongly promoted by Sarkozy, Blair emerged in autumn 2007 as a potential candidate for the new post of President of the European Council, to be established under the Lisbon Treaty. However, when the treaty was finally ratified in October 2009, his hopes were dashed as Merkel declined to endorse him, Sarkozy withdrew his support and several heads of government indicated that they preferred a candidate from a smaller member state within the **eurozone**. In June 2010, Blair became the first major international figure to argue for an elected 'President of Europe' – presumably combining the roles of President of the Commission and President of the European Council – as a means of providing 'strong, collective leadership and direction' to defend and project European power on the world stage.

Brezhnev Doctrine

In 1968, the year of the 'Prague Spring' uprising in Czechoslovakia, Leonid Brezhnev, General Secretary of the Communist Party of the Soviet Union, announced that the USSR had the right to interfere in the internal affairs of its satellite states in central and eastern Europe if it appeared that Communism or the hegemony of Moscow were under threat. The 'socialist commonwealth as a whole', represented by the Soviet Union, he said, could intervene if hostile ideological forces were at work in member countries. This became known as the Brezhnev Doctrine, although it was merely the formal expression of what had been the case de facto since Stalin's time. Under the terms of the **Warsaw Pact**, the Soviet Union was entitled to keep military forces in the satellite states. The Brezhnev Doctrine – which gave precedence to the unity of the Soviet bloc over the rights and equality of states – was challenged by the principles laid down in Basket I of the **Helsinki Final Act**, negotiated within the **Conference on Security and Cooperation in Europe** (CSCE), among which were respect for **sovereignty**, non-interference in internal affairs, and the inviolability of frontiers. Although all Warsaw Pact states were signatories to the Final Act, the Brezhnev Doctrine remained a feature of Soviet foreign policy until it was abrogated by Mikhail Gorbachev in 1988.

Briand, Aristide (1862–1932)

Aristide Briand was a leading Socialist politician of the French Third Republic, several times prime minister and foreign minister from 1925 until his death seven years later. He was one of the first advocates of what he called 'a system of European Federal Union', which he proposed to the **League of Nations** in September 1929. He drew his inspiration from the Pan-American Union. The 27 European members of the League agreed to discuss the proposal, and in May 1930 the French government circulated a memorandum setting out the proposal in more detail. Briand's memorandum was largely the work of Alexis Léger, a senior official in the Quai d'Orsay, better known as the poet Saint-John Perse, who was awarded the Nobel Prize for Literature in 1960.

The Briand memorandum spoke of the need for 'a permanent régime of solidarity based on international agreements for the rational organization of Europe'. Interestingly, it cited 'the possibilities of enlarging the economic market' as one of the reasons why such an organization was imperative, and drew attention to the 20,000 kilometres of new national frontiers which had been created within Europe by the Treaty of Versailles. Throughout the memorandum, Briand stressed that any Federal Union was not intended to supplant the League, but instead to work within it as one of the regional organizations specifically sanctioned by the League Covenant. The proposal fell well short of a 'federal' arrangement in the conventional sense: 'It is on the plane of absolute **sovereignty** and of entire political independence that the understanding between European nations must be brought about . . . under a system of federal union fully compatible with respect for traditions and for the characteristics peculiar to each people.' The Briand memorandum was considered in detail by a special study group chaired by Eric Drummond, Secretary General of the League. There the proposal 'died a lingering death, killed by increasing international friction and mistrust' (A. C. Temperley, *The Whispering Gallery of Europe*, 1938).

Briand is frequently cited, especially by French writers, as one of the **founding fathers** of European integration, if not the European Community.

At the time he made his proposal for a European Federal Union, he was honorary president of the Pan-European Union (see **Pan-Europa**). Jointly with Gustav Stresemann and Austen Chamberlain, he was awarded the Nobel Peace Prize in 1926, in recognition of his achievement in negotiating the Locarno Pacts. In *Makers of Modern Europe* (1930), **Carlo Sforza** described Briand's patriotism as 'intense, so deep and so serene that its aggressive side disappears'. A remark by Briand – quoted by Sforza – about Joan of Arc is revealing: 'Why did she waste so much energy in expelling the English? In a few generations we should have assimilated all of them; and what a splendid race we might have made.'

British Budget dispute

Reduced to its essentials, the British Budget dispute – which overshadowed the United Kingdom's relations with the rest of the European Community from 1979 until 1984 – was generated by a significant mismatch between the country's contributions and receipts under the Community **Budget**. Both the pre-1979 Labour government and the subsequent Conservative administration of **Margaret Thatcher** believed this situation to be inequitable and sought changes to alleviate the problem. Various temporary solutions were agreed in the early 1980s, mainly in the form of one-off rebates (or cash refunds) designed to boost Community spending in the UK. A longer-term settlement was only reached in the form of the **Fontainebleau Agreement** in June 1984, guaranteeing Britain a permanent **abatement** at source.

At the time of entry negotiations, it became apparent that, because of the way the Community's system of **own resources** operated, the United Kingdom, with its relatively high imports from outside the Community and therefore high revenue from external tariffs and levies, would be a substantial contributor to the Budget. On the receipts side, by contrast, the relative efficiency of British agriculture meant that payments to the UK under the **Common Agricultural Policy** (CAP), which represented by far the largest share of EC spending (75 per cent in 1975), were relatively modest. As a result, although (at the time) among the poorer member states in terms of per capita gross national product (GNP), Britain found itself both to have the lowest receipts from Community funds per head and to be the second largest net contributor to the Budget, after Germany. This problem was initially sidestepped in several ways: the British were given a seven-year **transitional period**, they were told that new spending policies from which they could expect to benefit would soon be established, and they were assured that if an 'unacceptable situation' were to arise, the Community would find an equitable solution.

Although the **European Regional Development Fund** (ERDF) was established with strong British support between 1972 and 1975, it was clearly too small in scale to make a real difference to the overall pattern of the UK's contributions and receipts. Accordingly, the budgetary question featured in the Labour government's **renegotiation** of the terms of entry in 1974–5. At the Dublin meeting of the **European Council** in March 1975 a 'corrective mechanism', with which London expressed itself satisfied, was developed. However, the mechanism had one fatal flaw: it was triggered only if the member state concerned had an overall deficit on its balance of trade. Thanks to the rapid exploitation of North Sea oil, this would no longer to be the case for Britain, and nothing was ever paid to the UK under the Dublin arrangement.

When the Conservatives took office in May 1979, the transitional period was over, and the forecasts of British net contributions to the Budget showed all too clearly that the problem was getting worse: from 1980 onwards, Community membership seemed likely to cost the UK almost £1 billion a year. This was the moment at which, in the view of Christopher Tugendhat, the European Commissioner (from Britain) then responsible for the Budget, 'an act of statesmanship' on the part of the French and German leaders, **Valéry Giscard d'Estaing** and Helmut Schmidt, 'could have solved the British budget problem before it got out of hand'. Instead, they chose to turn the issue into 'a trial of strength' between the major member states (*Making Sense of Europe*, 1986). At the Dublin European Council meeting in November 1979, Margaret Thatcher was provoked into demanding 'our money back', a phrase that called into question the idea of own resources belonging to the Community as of right. It also suggested that the British stance was prompted by the idea of a ***juste retour*** – rather than by broader notions of equity or mutual solidarity.

Temporary solutions to the problem were found for the years 1980, 1981 and 1982. By 1983, however, circumstances had changed in the UK's favour. The Community was running out of money, and the volume of revenue from own resources, notably from **value-added tax** (VAT) receipts, could be increased only with the unanimous agreement of all member states (including **ratification** by **national parliaments**). At the Stuttgart European Council in June 1983, Thatcher made it very clear that her consent to any additional own resources was conditional upon a permanent solution to the British Budget problem and upon new measures to enforce greater **budgetary discipline** in the Community. A change in French attitudes was perhaps prompted by the realization in Paris that, in the wake of any **enlargement** to include Spain and Portugal, France was also likely to become a net contributor to the Community Budget. A further ad hoc arrangement was made for the British net contribution for 1983.

Twelve months of intense negotiations followed, including difficult European Council meetings, ending in failure, in December 1983 and March 1984. At the European Council meeting in Fontainebleau, near Paris, in June 1984, agreement was finally reached to calculate the disparity in the British Budget contribution on the basis of the difference between the British share of Community expenditure and the proportion of the Community's VAT-based revenue contributed by the UK. The abatement, as it was known, was to be paid for each year in the form of a reduced VAT-based contribution in the following year, a method that had the advantage (as most member states saw it) of keeping the **European Parliament** out of the picture, the Parliament's budgetary powers being limited to the expenditure side. The revision of the own resources system, under which the VAT ceiling was raised from 1.0 to 1.4 per cent (of overall national revenue from this source, adjusted in accordance with a uniform 'base'), would allow the UK a further ad hoc abatement of one billion ECU for 1984 and thereafter a two-thirds reduction in the difference between the British contribution to VAT-based revenue and the amount of Community expenditure in the UK. As had been the case since 1982, a special arrangement was made that allowed Germany – by far the biggest net contributor to the Budget – to pay a reduced share of what would otherwise have been a substantial proportion of the British rebate. In its first full year of operation (1985), the new abatement amounted to about £1 billion, and since then it has totalled € 92.5 billion (1985–2010) and averaged € 3.6 billion per year (in nominal terms).

Since the Fontainebleau Agreement, the abatement has regularly been called into question, but so far it has survived on each occasion that the own resources decision, adopted in the **Council of Ministers** by **unanimity**, has been revised. Although the fundamental mismatch between contributions and receipts at the heart of the British budget problem has remained, the relative situation has eased somewhat, as the number of net contributor member states has steadily grown. In some years, the post-abatement outcome for the UK is now more satisfactory than the positions of France and Italy (both of which were larger net contributors in 2009, for example), but in other years it remains less so (as in 2010). However, in the absence of a reappraisal of the structure of EU revenue and expenditure from first principles, it is difficult to see how an alternative solution for Britain could work.

Although Thatcher's pugnacious negotiating style irritated and alienated the leaders of some other member states – notably the Greek socialist prime minister, Andreas Papandreou, whose inaugural 1983 **presidency** of the Council was marred by the dispute and who famously remarked that 'it would be a great relief if Britain left the Community' – it is doubtful if anything less than her tenacity, allied to a mastery of complex detail, could have yielded, in the end, so satisfactory a result to the UK. Nor was it perhaps realistic to expect that a new British government so firmly committed to the restraint of domestic public expenditure, in a country where membership of the Community remained controversial, could easily have let the issue lie. In retrospect, it reflects little credit on many of the participants at the time that the problem should have absorbed so much of the time and energy of officials and politicians across Europe, which could have been directed at more pressing issues, and taken so long to resolve.

British referendum on EC membership (June 1975)

Until it became part of the Labour party's policy for the **renegotiation** of the terms of membership in 1972, no political party in the United Kingdom had been in favour of holding a **referendum** on whether the country should be a member state of the European Community. In December 1969, a backbench motion calling for a referendum had been defeated in the House of Commons, opposed not only by Harold Wilson's Labour government, but leading members of all opposition parties, whether or not they were in favour of membership. The subsequent Conservative government of **Edward Heath**, elected in June 1970, secured entry on the basis of a series of hard-fought votes in the Commons.

Wilson returned to power in March 1974, committed (for reasons of internal party management) to renegotiate the 'Tory terms' of membership and submit the outcome to the people, either through a general election or a referendum. The government completed its largely notional renegotiation in March 1975 and introduced a Referendum Bill, which was passed by the House of Commons the following month. Divisions within the Labour party led to ministers being allowed to express divergent views publicly under an unprecedented 'agreement to differ'. As the European issue cut across the normal dividing lines between the political parties, the referendum campaign was fought by two all-party organizations: 'Britain in Europe', in favour of continued Community membership, and the 'National Referendum Campaign', against it. In addition to advertising and other campaign activity, each organization prepared a booklet circulated to all households at public expense. In parallel, the government circulated its own document, *Britain's New Deal in Europe*, in which it summarized the results of the renegotiation and committed itself to abide by the decision of the electorate. An information unit in the Cabinet Office provided factual briefing for the public.

A lively campaign pitted many of the leading personalities in British politics both together and against one another in unusual combinations. The 'yes' campaign, under the effective slogan 'Keep Britain in Europe', brought together decade-long rivals Wilson and Heath, as well as the Home Secretary, **Roy Jenkins**, who had earlier resigned as Wilson's deputy leader in protest at his handling of Europe, and **Margaret Thatcher**, who had recently displaced Heath as Conservative leader in a bitter struggle. Only Heath and Jenkins were prepared to appear together on the same platform. The 'no' campaign combined some of the most rhetorically capable figures in Labour politics – notably Tony Benn, Michael Foot and Peter Shore – but they failed to reach beyond the left of their party, other than to an increasingly discredited Enoch Powell, the ex-Conservative whose populism had helped prepare the ground for Thatcher's takeover of the Conservative party.

The referendum was held on Thursday 5 June 1975, with 64.5 per cent of the electorate taking part. The question posed was: 'Do you think that the United Kingdom should stay in the European Community (the Common Market)?' In the event, 67.2 per cent of votes were cast in favour (17,378,581) and 32.8 per cent against (8,470,073). Results were counted on a county basis, other than in Northern Ireland. All counties of the United Kingdom, except the Shetlands and the Western Isles, voted for continued membership.

The decisive outcome was not entirely a surprise. The advocates of a 'yes' vote fought a much more attractive and credible campaign, drawing on modern public relations techniques. Each side was given £125,000 from public funds. Published accounts revealed that Britain in Europe spent £1.48 million and their opponents less than one-tenth of that sum (£131,000). More fundamentally, although British public opinion had long been sceptical about entry to the Community – with a two-thirds majority against joining at the time the Conservatives were elected in June 1970 – the actual experience of membership, together with the Labour government shifting towards acceptance of its continuation, had been reassuring. This was compounded by the fact that most national newspapers, as well as trade unions and business groups, came out increasingly strongly in favour of Britain remaining in the Community. In January 1975, there was already an eight per cent lead for the 'yes' camp in the opinion polls, and this advantage continued to increase as the spring proceeded.

The first national plebiscite in British political history – and the only one to be held for another 36 years – the referendum of June 1975 failed definitively to settle the question of Community membership. It did not even resolve differences within the Labour Party, which by 1983 had moved in favour of withdrawal. At best, it rendered Labour's hostility during the 1980s an electoral liability, creating a brief pro-European consensus in mainstream British politics before Margaret Thatcher as Conservative prime minister voiced increasingly strong Eurosceptic tendencies from 1988 onwards.

Further reading: David Butler and Uwe Kitzinger, *The 1975 Referendum*, 1976.

Bruges speech

On 20 September 1988, **Margaret Thatcher**, then British prime minister, delivered a speech at the College of Europe in Bruges, Belgium, which turned out to be her most important public pronouncement on Europe during more than a decade in power. The 'Bruges speech', as it instantly became known, set out Thatcher's philosophy of European integration, based on a combination of 'willing and active cooperation between independent sovereign states', opposition to efforts to 'suppress nationhood and concentrate power at the centre of a European conglomerate', and resistance to 'attempts to introduce collectivism and corporatism at European level'. She argued that, instead of wasting energy on 'arcane institutional debates' and attempting to establish an **Economic and Monetary Union** (EMU), the European Community should work within its existing treaty arrangements – defined most recently by the 1986 **Single European Act** (SEA) – and use them to pursue an active free-market, free-trade agenda, based on greater economic liberalization, completion of the **single market** and reform of the **Common Agricultual Policy** (CAP). 'The basic framework is there: the **Treaty of Rome** was intended as a charter for economic liberty. But that is not how it has always been read, still less applied.'

The central thrust of the Bruges speech – expressing a preference for **intergovernmentalism** over **supranationalism** in Europe and a fear that the Community's policies were increasingly interventionist – was encapsulated in its most memorable phrase: 'We have not successfully rolled back the frontiers of the state in Britain, only to see them reimposed at a European level, with a European super-state exercising a new dominance from Brussels.' In effect, these words marked the moment at which Thatcher clearly distanced herself from the emerging priorities of **Jacques Delors**, whose reappointment as President of the **European Commission** she had endorsed only three months earlier. She saw the Bruges speech as an important counterblast against Delors' plans – supported by **François Mitterrand**, who had been re-elected as President of France in the spring of that year – to move beyond the single market programme of the mid-1980s towards both a single currency and a Social Europe.

The Bruges speech did not call into question the United Kingdom's membership of the Community: 'Britain does not dream of some cosy, isolated existence on the fringes of the Community. Britain's destiny is in Europe, as part of the Community.' Nor was Thatcher opposed to the member states working 'more closely together on the things we can do better together than alone . . . whether it be in trade, in defence, or in our relations with the rest of the world'. However, she emphasized that closer cooperation should respect the pre-eminence and diversity of nations: 'Europe will be stronger precisely because it has France as France, Spain as Spain, Britain as Britain – each with its own customs, traditions and identity. It would be folly to try to fit them into some sort of identikit European personality.' She also linked Europe's diversity with the plight of the countries of central and eastern Europe, trapped under Communism. In words that jarred with the prevailing orthodoxy in 1988, she declared:

Europe is not the creation of the Treaty of Rome ... The European Community is one manifestation of ... European identity, but it is not the only one. We must never forget that east of the Iron Curtain, people who once enjoyed a full share of European culture, freedom and identity have been cut off from their roots. We shall always look on Warsaw, Prague and Budapest as great European cities.

The Bruges speech was to prove both controversial and significant. In effect, Thatcher was using her political capital to draw a new dividing line on Europe, forcing people to take sides on the increasingly 'federalist' agenda of Delors – although interestingly she did not use the word 'federal' in her speech – in a way reminiscent of opposition by **Charles de Gaulle** to the plans of Commission President **Walter Hallstein** in the 1960s. In the immediate term, she was to discover that few European leaders shared her concerns to anything like the same degree. Instead, the institutional and policy deepening of the Community found increasing favour, particularly following the collapse of the Berlin Wall the following year. Governments of the left tended to welcome Delors' emphasis on Social Europe, and Thatcher was left isolated in opposing the adoption of the Community **Social Charter** at the Strasbourg European Council in December 1989. Governments of the centre-right were generally reassured when the **Delors Report** of April 1989 envisaged the creation of EMU along lines acceptable to the highly cautious German Bundesbank. On the same day as Thatcher spoke in Bruges, the Conservative prime minister of Denmark, Poul Schlüter, gave a little-reported speech at the Reform Club in London, in which he argued that the era of the nation state in Europe was over.

Brussels

The national capital of Belgium, Brussels is the de facto 'capital of Europe'. With a population of approximately one million, half of whom are non-Belgian in origin, Brussels is one of the most ethnically diverse major cities in Europe. It also has one of the highest proportions of people involved in government and politics. Around 30,000 (of the 46,000) employees of the European Union **institutions**, otherwise known as **Eurocrats**, are based in Brussels, with the figure rising towards 100,000 once family members are included. A further 30,000 people are estimated to be working directly or indirectly in international governmental activity, or dependent on it, in the city. Brussels has been home to the **North Atlantic Treaty Organization** (NATO) since it was expelled from Paris in 1966, with around 4,000 staff and diplomats based there. The presence of the EU alone is thought to contribute over 15 per cent of the total economy of the Brussels region, with international organizations overall generating around a fifth.

The diplomatic community in Brussels is one of the largest in the world –

with 169 countries represented in the city and over 25,000 individuals posted there, working in missions to Belgium, the EU and NATO. Many Europe-wide interest groups and lobbying bodies, notably trade associations and non-governmental organizations (NGOs), now base themselves in Brussels, and an increasing number of multinational corporations and specialist consultancies locate public-affairs staff in the city. Well over a hundred regions within Europe have separate representational offices in Brussels. The city also hosts the second largest international press corps in the world, after Washington – with nearly a thousand journalists accredited to the **European Commission** – and has an even bigger concentration of translators and interpreters than either Geneva or New York.

Strictly speaking, three EU institutions and three other major bodies are based in Brussels: the European Commission, **Council of Ministers** and **European Council** (of EU heads of government), together with the **European External Action Service** (EEAS) and the advisory **European Economic and Social Committee** (EESC) and **Committee of the Regions**. Over three-quarters of the staff in the Commission's directorates-general are located in Brussels, with the remainder either in Luxembourg (around 3,500) or in third countries. Meetings of the Council of Ministers and its various bodies take place in Brussels throughout the year – except in April, June and October, when ministerial meetings at least are held in Luxembourg. All meetings of the European Council are now held in Brussels too. Like the 3,200-strong Council secretariat, the 27 **permanent representations** of the EU member states are located in Brussels, together with the diplomatic missions of third countries accredited to the Union. In addition, although not formally based in Brussels, the **European Parliament** now has over half of its nearly 7,000 staff in the city, including nearly all policy-related personnel, with the remainder located at its traditional administrative centre in Luxembourg. Whilst the 12 monthly plenary sessions of the Parliament still take place in Strasbourg, France, most meetings of the parliamentary committees and **political groups** are held in Brussels, as well as, since 1993, between four and six two-day 'mini-plenary' sessions at various times in the year.

The principal buildings of the EU institutions in Brussels are located in what has become known as the *quartier européen*, which stretches a distance of about 1.5 kilometres, between the Rond-Point Schuman and Place du Luxembourg, in the eastern part of the city. This workaday area – dubbed the 'valley of the Eurocrats' by Belgian urban historian Thierry Demey – features two main clusters of buildings, linked only by a railway line and a complex web of streets. In the first cluster, the European Commission has its headquarters in the 13-storey **Berlaymont** building (at 200 rue de la Loi), with the Council of Ministers located in the Justus Lipsius or 'Consilium' building directly opposite (at 175 rue de la Loi). The second, more recent, cluster is to be found on the south side of rue Belliard, and revolves around the huge *Espace Léopold* complex occupied by European Parliament (at 60 rue Wiertz), one of the largest office installations in Europe. The headquarters of the EESC and Committee of the Regions are near by, in the **Jacques Delors** building (at 99–101 rue Belliard).

The 'European quarter' has grown up largely piecemeal, through a series of ad hoc decisions over half a century, rather than as a result of any coherent masterplan. The original choice of the Schuman area as the location for the Commission and Council was haphazard and the subsequent commitment by the Brussels' authorities to contain the European institutions within that area proved unsustainable. Many architects cite the development of this part of Brussels as an object lesson of how *not* to engage in urban planning. Unfavourable comparisons are drawn with the conscious design and interplay between government buildings to be found in the centres of other federal capitals, notably Washington DC, where positive narratives are often told about the history and cultures of political communities. With the possible exception of the barrel-vaulted glass roof of the European Parliament, redolent of the Crystal Palace, the EU buildings in Brussels conspicuously fail to communicate any political signal, except perhaps about the anonymity of officialdom. The elaborate system of government even in the Brussels region, let alone the country as a whole, complicates this situation. No single jurisdiction is responsible for the area occupied by the principal EU buildings. See also **seats of EU institutions**.

Further reading: Thierry Demey, *Bruxelles, capitale de l'Europe*, 2007.

Brussels Treaty

Meeting at the Palais des Académies in Brussels on 17 March 1948, the United Kingdom, France and the **Benelux** countries signed a 'Treaty for collaboration in economic, social and cultural matters and for collective self-defence'. Initially proposed by George Marshall, the US Secretary of State who authored the **Marshall Plan** for the economic reconstruction of post-war western Europe, the 'Western Union' initiative, as it became known, provided the potential for the development of a **European army** and was strongly supported by the Labour government in Britain at the time.

Concluded for 50 years, the Brussels Treaty built upon the Franco-British **Dunkirk Treaty** signed the previous year and was intended ostensibly to protect the signatory states from any 'renewal by Germany of a policy of aggression', as the preamble put it. The real purpose of the treaty, however, was to respond to American pressure that western European states unite in the face of the escalating threat from the Soviet Union and the growing division of Europe into two competing blocs. As such it was, in the words of

Richard Mayne, 'the first post-war treaty to recognize the potential danger from Soviet military power' (*The Community of Europe*, 1962). At the heart of the treaty was an automatic military assistance clause, which stated: 'If any of the High Contracting Parties should be the object of an armed attack in Europe, the other High Contracting Parties will, in accordance with the provisions of Article 51 of the Charter of the **United Nations**, afford the Party so attacked all the military and other aid and assistance in their power' (Article 4, subsequently Article 5). In addition, at the suggestion of the Benelux states, the treaty envisaged that its signatories would work for 'the elimination of conflict in their economic policies, the coordination of production and the development of commercial exchanges', as well as conclude conventions in the fields of social security and cultural exchange. Policies would be elaborated through intergovernmental consultations in a ministerial Council.

Introducing the proposed text in the House of Commons in January 1948, the British Foreign Secretary, Ernest Bevin, declared: 'The time for consolidation of Western Europe is ripe . . . The old-fashioned concept of the balance of power should be discontinued.' Britain, he said, was now 'thinking of Western Europe as a unity'. Taken with the pronouncements of **Winston Churchill**, now leader of the opposition, the Brussels Treaty gave rise to great hopes that the United Kingdom was prepared to take the lead in post-war European unification. The British government hosted the secretariat of the Western Union in London and was happy to see the rapid development of its 'military command', based in Fontainebleau, outside Paris, initially with 12 divisions at its disposal.

Despite this promising start, the Brussels Treaty was quickly overtaken by events. As the **Cold War** intensified, most strikingly with the blockade of Berlin from June 1948, there was a compelling need for the United States formally to guarantee western Europe's collective defence. In Washington, the US Senate lifted its opposition to endorsing military treaties with countries outside the Americas. Discussions with the United States and Canada, as well as a number of other European countries, about their potential signature of the Brussels Treaty led to a different outcome – the decision to create a new, parallel body, the **North Atlantic Treaty Organization** (NATO), established by the North Atlantic Treaty of April 1949. Formally speaking, unlike the Brussels Treaty, the North Atlantic Treaty did not commit its signatories to automatic mutual defence – as the approval of the Senate still remained necessary before the United States could go to war – but in practice, the advent of NATO rendered the Western Union redundant, denying it any possibility of developing a meaningful military role. The latter's Council agreed in December 1950 to dissolve its military structure in Fontainebleau, transferring it to NATO. With this decision, as Pierre Gerbet has written, 'genuinely European military structures disappeared, replaced by Atlantic ones. The opportunity to create a

"European pillar" of the Atlantic Alliance – as certain French leaders wanted, but which both the military and [the other] allies rejected on the grounds of efficiency – was not grasped' (*Dictionnaire historique de l'Europe unie*, 2009). The economic provisions of the Brussels Treaty were not pursued either, whilst the social and cultural ones were devolved to the **Council of Europe**, created in May 1949.

The Western Union was converted into the **Western European Union** (WEU) in October 1954, when ministers agreed amendments to the Brussels Treaty (which became known inelegantly as the 'Modified Brussels Treaty') and admitted Germany and Italy as members. In parallel, Germany was allowed to rearm and to join NATO. The reference to potential German aggression in the original treaty was diplomatically replaced by a commitment 'to promote the unity and to encourage the progressive integration of Europe'. The WEU would work in close cooperation with NATO and rely on it 'for information and advice on military matters'. A new WEU Assembly was created, composed of those national parliamentarians from Brussels Treaty states who already sat in the Consultative Assembly of the Council of Europe. A provision in the treaty allowed it to continue, after it expired in 1998, unless or until its signatory states chose individually to denounce it. The treaty thus remained in force, even though the WEU had in effect been absorbed as part of the **Common Security and Defence Policy** (CSDP) of the European Union. However, in March 2010, the contracting parties finally announced that they had 'collectively decided to terminate' the Modified Brussels Treaty as from the end of June 2011.

The **Lisbon Treaty**, which came into force in December 2009, in effect replicates Article 5 of the Modified Brussels Treaty, by instituting a mutual defence clause within the EU. Article 42 (7) TEU states: 'If a Member State is the victim of armed aggression on its territory, the other Member States shall have towards it an obligation of aid and assistance by all the means in their power, in accordance with Article 51 of the United Nations Charter.' This obligation is subject to the proviso that it 'shall not prejudice the specific character of the security and defence policy of certain Member States', so might be interpreted as exempting, if they wish, those countries that claim **neutrality**.

Budget

The annual Budget of the European Union amounted to € 126.5 billion in 2011, equivalent to almost exactly one per cent (1.01) of the gross national income (GNI) – the reference indicator used for budgetary calculations since 2007 – of the 27 member states of the Union. In volume terms, the sum was slightly larger than the whole of the Romanian economy, about the same as total public expenditure in Denmark, and broadly equivalent to spending on public healthcare in the United Kingdom. (By contrast, total public expenditure in the 27 member states at national, regional and local levels amounted to € 6.3 trillion in 2011, or just over half of their combined GNI.)

To finance such expenditure, the Union has at its disposal potential revenue, in the form of **own resources**, of up to 1.23 per cent of GNI. However, in recent years, the annual Budget has been consistently set below that ceiling (which has never been reached). Very often, the Budget itself has also been underspent, with surplus funds being returned to the member states (as at the end of 2010). Article 310(1) TFEU prohibits the Union from running a budget deficit.

The level of Community, subsequently Union, expenditure rose rapidly in the 1960s to 1980s, with the broadening and deepening of common policies that required significant financial resources, first for the **Common Agricultural Policy** (CAP) and subsequently for the **structural funds**. Whereas spending represented only 0.03 per cent of Community gross domestic product (GDP) in 1960, it had risen to 0.73 per cent by 1970, and 0.80 per cent in 1980. A series of budgetary crises in the 1980s resulted in a new and increasingly effective system of 'budgetary discipline' being put in place. Since 1988, the annual Budget has been located in a set of 'financial perspectives' – now known as the Multiannual Financial Framework (MFF) – which is agreed between the EU institutions and establishes detailed expenditure ceilings for (currently) a seven-year period. The annual **budgetary process** – based on a proposal from the **European Commission** and then agreement on final numbers by the **Council of Ministers** and the **European Parliament** (the twin arms of the 'budgetary authority') – operates within this framework, thus significantly constraining the possibility of sudden surges in spending.

Over the last two decades, the share of EU spending in the total European economy has been held broadly constant, usually at a little under one per cent. Planned expenditure during the decade 2000–9 varied between 1.02 and 1.11 per cent of GNI, with the out-turn coming in at between 0.88 and 0.97 per cent of GNI. The planned 2011 Budget, at 1.01 per cent of GNI, was thus at the lower end of recent experience. The current MFF, covering the years 2007–13, envisages expenditure of 0.94 per cent of GNI in 2013. Although spending on this scale falls well short of a level that would have a perceptible macro-economic effect in the Union as a whole – as the **MacDougall Report** foresaw in the 1970s – its impact can still be very important in specific countries at specific times. For Ireland, Greece, Spain and Portugal, EU spending represented a significant boost to GDP during the 1980s and 1990s, with resulting infrastructure playing an important part in the modernization of their economies. In 1991, net receipts in Ireland represented fully 6.3 per cent of its GNP. In 2009, Hungary and Poland benefited to the tune of 2.6 and 1.9 per cent, and the **Baltic states** by an average of 4.0 per cent.

The composition (as opposed to level) of the EU Budget has changed significantly over time: whereas the CAP represented less than 10 per cent of Community spending in 1965, it rose dramatically to 88 per cent five years later, and since then has been in steady and continuous decline, at an average rate of about one per cent per year, to 71 per cent in 1980, 51 per cent in 2000, and 41.3 per cent in 2011. Conversely, the various structural funds have increased significantly: taken together, the **European Social Fund** (ESF), the **European Regional Development Fund** (ERDF) and the **Cohesion Fund** have risen from around five per cent of the Budget in 1975 (the Cohesion Fund only came on stream in 1993) to a quarter in 2005 and over a third in 2011 (36.0 per cent). These two trends have left just under a quarter of the Budget consistently available for other policy priorities (together with administration).

Since the 1990s, the Commission has pushed for higher priority to be given to spending on 'modernizing' policies – such as research and development, transport, energy, education and culture – as well as on external relations, including the **Common Foreign and Security Policy** (CFSP), and on **Justice and Home Affairs** (JHA). However, progress in shifting spending priorities in these directions has been slow and laborious, hindered recently by the fact that many of the new **accession** states from central and eastern Europe are substantial recipients from both the CAP and structural funds. Less than a tenth of the 2011 Budget was devoted to headings relating to 'competitiveness for growth and employment' (9.5 per cent) and still less to external relations (6.2 per cent) and JHA (1.3 per cent).

More precisely, of the € 126.5 billion in payment appropriations provided in the 2011 Budget, € 56.4 billion were devoted to the CAP, CFP and **environment policy**; € 41.7 billion to the ESF, ERDF and Cohesion Fund; € 11.6 billion to **research and development policy**, **education policy**, **cultural policy**, **energy policy**, enterprise and the **single market**, **transport policy** and the information society; € 8.1 billion to the administration of the EU institutions, bodies and **agencies**; € 7.2 billion to **development policy**, **enlargement**, humanitarian aid, pre-accession support, **European Neighbourhood Policy** (ENP) and CFSP; and € 1.5 billion to JHA and citizenship.

European Union expenditure, 1960–2010

	1960	1965	1970	1975	1980	1985	1990	1995	2000	2005	2010
Total EU expenditure (billion euro, nominal)	0.06	0.34	3.58	6.1	16.46	28.83	45.61	66.57	80.45	104.8	120.49
Per capita expenditure (euro, nominal)	0.3	1.9	19	24	63	131	139	183	213	227	241
Union expenditure as percentage of public-sector expenditure in member states	0.1	0.3	2.0	1.2	1.7	1.8	2.0	2.1	2.0	2.2	2.0
Union expenditure as percentage of EU GDP (GNI since 2007)	0.03	0.11	0.74	0.54	0.8	0.93	0.94	1.04	1.07	1.08	1.02
Own resources ceiling as percentage of EU GDP (GNI since 2007)	–	–	–	–	–	–	1.2	1.2	1.27	1.24	1.23

Source: European Commission

Budgetary process

The annual **Budget** of the European Union embraces the revenue derived from '**own resources**', on the one hand, and expenditure undertaken on both the policies of the Union and the running costs of its institutions, on the other. In practice, however, the annual procedure for the adoption of the EU Budget centres upon the proposals for spending, as the revenue side is in effect already predetermined by a combination of an overall ceiling on own resources set by member-state governments and the specific amount assigned for any particular year in the Multiannual Financial Framework (MFF) – previously known as the 'financial perspectives' – currently agreed between the institutions every seven years. The EU's annual Budget thus differs from the budgets of most member states, which adjust both revenue and expenditure each year. It differs particularly from the annual Budget Statement in the United Kingdom, which is concerned primarily with the raising of revenue. Another important feature is that the EU, unlike its member states, is not permitted to run a budget deficit. Although the Union may engage in borrowing and lending activities separately, expenditure must be matched by revenue in each budgetary year (Article 310(1) TFEU).

Responsibility for drawing up and implementing the EU Budget rests with the **European Commission**. The **Council of Ministers** and the **European Parliament** together constitute the Union's joint 'budgetary authority', which is entitled to (and invariably chooses to) amend the Commission's proposal before agreeing and enacting the final document. An annual audit of the Budget is carried out retrospectively by the **Court of Auditors**, backed by a parliamentary '**discharge' procedure**.

A single Budget for the various **European Communities** was introduced by the 1965 **Merger Treaty**. Initially, the institutional dialogue concerning the adoption of the Budget, like the legislative process, involved only the Commission and Council (with the pro forma association of the Parliament, which could suggest changes that were almost invariably rejected by the Council). In 1970 and 1975, however, two Budgetary **Treaties** significantly strengthened the position of the Parliament. The move from direct financial contributions by member states to a system of own resources argued for the establishment, in parallel, of a greater degree of parliamentary accountability at European level. (Indeed, the Dutch parliament insisted on this as a condition for **ratification**.) The 1970 Budgetary Treaty made the Parliament part of the budgetary authority and gave it the power to reject the Budget in its entirety. It also introduced a distinction between **compulsory expenditure** – which was mostly on the **Common Agricultural Policy** (CAP), and where the Council had the last say – and non-compulsory expenditure (most other spending), where the Parliament could determine the final outcome within a 'margin' settled in advance. This distinction – which created separate political cultures around the two fields of spending – was abolished by the **Lisbon Treaty**, which took effect in December 2009.

The budgetary process is set out in Article 314 TFEU, and each of the main stages has to be completed by a specific deadline in the course of the year preceding that to which the Budget relates. The initial stage involves the drawing up of estimates by each institution (by 1 July) and the consolidation of these by the Commission into a single Draft Budget (DB). The estimates of the Council and Parliament relate essentially to administrative expenditure, whereas those of the Commission cover both policy and administration, and are therefore much greater in size. (For example, the 2011 Budget provided for total Commission expenditure of some € 122 billion – of which only € 3.3 billion was administrative – whereas the spending of all other institutions and bodies together was less than € 5.0 billion.)

The Draft Budget must be sent by the Commission to the Council and Parliament by 1 September. It is often sent earlier: the Draft Budget for 2012, for example, was communicated by the Commission on 20 April 2011. The Council considers the proposal and adopts its position thereon – in the form of amendments to specific spending lines, passed by **qualified majority voting** (QMV) – by 1 October. It then communicates its position to the Parliament, which has 42 days within which to propose further amendments of its own. The Parliament's amendments are submitted to the plenary by its budgets committee; to pass they need to secure the support of an absolute majority of the members (currently 378 out of 754 MEPs). If the Parliament approves the Draft Budget as amended by the Council or simply takes no action within the 42-day period – either of which outcome is very unlikely – the Budget is deemed to be adopted. More usually, as a result of diverging amendments tabled by the Council and Parliament, a Conciliation Committee will be convened (by the President of the European Parliament) with a view to reconciling the positions of the two institutions.

The Conciliation Committee brings together an equal number of representatives of the Council and Parliament (27 each), with the Commission invited to 'take all necessary initiatives' to find agreement between them. The committee has a maximum of 21 days in which to meet – including at the level of smaller, preparatory 'trialogues' – and its meetings are chaired alternately by each side. If the committee can agree, both the Council and Parliament then have two weeks in which to endorse the joint text. If the committee cannot agree (or the Parliament rejects the outcome of the committee), the Commission has to come forward with a new Budget proposal (as happened in late November 2010). In the unlikely event of the Council rejecting the result of the committee (in which all its members are represented), the Parliament may reconfirm its original amendments, by a three-fifths majority, and the Budget will stand adopted on that basis.

The budgetary procedure outlined above was introduced by the Lisbon Treaty and used for the first time in autumn 2010 for the 2011 EU Budget. It replaced a rather more complex process that had operated since the 1970 Budgetary Treaty. This involved two readings, rather than a single reading, before the Council and Parliament moved to the decisive, conciliation phase. There was a Preliminary Draft Budget (PDB) before the Draft Budget, and the treatment of amendments to compulsory and non-compulsory expenditure diverged significantly, with the Parliament concentrating on the latter. In addition to proposing changes to certain budget lines, the Parliament could also unilaterally threaten to place (or actually place) items of non-compulsory spending 'in reserve' (Chapter 100) until the substance or management of a particular Commission policy was altered in some way. All of these features of the budgetary process have now disappeared (although details of them can be found in previous editions of this *Companion*).

There were two occasions under the old procedure – in December 1979 and December 1984 – when the Parliament rejected the Draft Budget because of the inability of the two institutions to agree over spending priorities. (At that time, rejection required not only that an absolute majority of Members of the European Parliament (MEPs) vote against, but that they represent two-thirds of the votes cast.) On a third occasion, in December 1985, the President of the Parliament declared the following year's Budget adopted, even though the Council claimed that the Parliament's amendments had exceeded the 'maximum rate' of increase for non-compulsory expenditure which was allowed (under the system then prevailing). The Council successfully challenged the decision in the **European Court of Justice** (ECJ), although the latter also found that the maximum rate had not been properly determined in the first place. The Budget eventually agreed (in July 1986) took account of the Parliament's amendments.

The consequences of any rejection of the Draft Budget by the Parliament (or indeed the Council) are limited by the fact that spending continues but at the previous level. A system known as 'provisional twelfths' comes into effect, which requires expenditure in each month (by budget chapter) to be no more than one-twelfth of the nominal total in the previous year. This system continues until a new Budget is adopted, with the possibility of the Council authorizing additional expenditure (by qualified majority) if necessary in the interim. The provisional-twelfths situation is more complicated than it may immediately appear, because the profile of payments made by the Commission varies considerably over the year, with a substantial proportion of CAP payments, in particular, being made in the first quarter.

The Treaties allow the Commission to submit draft 'amending' budgets to take account of unforeseen circumstances during the year in question. Transfers of appropriations may also be made between budget lines, to take account of shifting policy priorities or practical needs, although the degree of flexibility is limited. In the course of 2010, for example, there were ten amending budgets of various sizes.

All EU spending entered into the Budget must have a **legal base**, established separately through the routine legislative process, for it to take effect. The distinction between authorization and appropriation is thus maintained. However, within agreed limits, the Parliament and Council are allowed to propose a number of 'pilot projects and preparatory actions' each year for specific new policies not yet sanctioned in law. Some of these projects – if subsequently endorsed by the Commission, given a legal base and assigned resources in future Budgets – may develop into significant EU spending programmes in their own right.

Although the budgetary procedure and the Budget itself operate on an annual basis, from early on the EU developed an increasing number of multi-annual spending programmes which involved obligations spread over longer periods than twelve months. To facilitate this, the Budget allows for 'differentiated appropriations', with a distinction drawn between commitments and payments at least for the Commission, which has to deliver spending on substantive policy, not just administration. In any given year, the level of commitments tends to be higher than that of payments (by about 15 per cent). Adding current commitments to those carried over from previous years, the result is that outstanding commitments often amount to around 125 per cent of the EU Budget for any particular calendar year.

Overall there is now a structural bias in the EU system towards a high degree of budgetary discipline. As a result of the regular budget crises that occurred between 1979 and 1986 – which coincided with the Commission's simultaneous difficulty in controlling CAP expenditure and its ambition to significantly increase non-agricultural spending – certain net-contributor member states, notably Germany, the Netherlands and the United Kingdom, pushed successfully for de facto multi-annual budgeting to be adopted within the Community. A lively debate on the need for greater budgetary discipline led in 1988 to the adoption by heads of government for the first time of multi-annual 'financial perspectives', providing agreed figures for broad headings of expenditure over a five-year period (and since then on a seven-year cycle: 1993–9, 2000–6 and 2007–13).

The development of the financial perspectives – formalized by an **Inter-Institutional Agreement** (IIA) between the Council, Commission and Parliament – tied the hands of all three institutions in the annual budgetary process, especially the latter two. The Commission was forced to decide some years in advance on the spending totals and breakdown it wished to see and then justify them to heads of government. The effect was greatly to reduce the rate of increase in spending over time. Equally, the Parliament was no longer able to exploit the maximum rate of increase or its capacity to reorder non-compulsory spending priorities each year. As the Parliament was not a party to multi-annual deals struck every five, then seven, years in the European Council, it was faced with an essentially 'take-it-or-leave-it' situation when it came to negotiate with the Council and Commission over the resulting IIA. Although the Parliament was able to extract some concessions – for example, in April 2006 it obtained an additional € 4.0 billion (on top of a planned € 921 billion total) for the current 2007–13 MFF, plus € 2.5 billion in additional **European Investment Bank** (EIB) lending and some greater oversight over the Commission's administration of spending programmes – the reality was that budgetary politics became much more 'routinized' in the Union, to the advantage of national finance ministers.

Since the late 1980s, the EU's annual budget has consistently been set at below the ceiling of own resources available, and in most years the institutions have then spent less than the budget ceiling provided, with some of the unused payments being returned to national finance ministries. (The Budget was underspent by an average of € 4.9 billion during the years 2008–10.) The distribution of spending within annual budgets has corresponded closely, with occasional adjustments, to the profile agreed in advance for the the multiannual financing periods. This outcome has been achieved notwithstanding successive enlargements and a gradual reordering of spending priorities over time, with CAP spending falling from over 60 per cent of the total budget in 1988 to 43 per cent in 2011. The detailed operation of the annual budgetary process has been greatly facilitated by the arrangements for budgetary discipline. Not once between 1984 and 1988 was it possible for the budget to be agreed and adopted by the end of the preceding financial year. Since 1989, however, this has always been achieved.

The Lisbon Treaty finally gave treaty status to the Union's multi-annual budgetary framework. Henceforth the MFF takes the form of a legally-binding Council **regulation**, rather than an IIA, which can only be adopted with the **consent** of the Parliament. It is an open question how far this change will reverse the de facto loss of power over both the level and composition of EU spending which the Parliament suffered with the development of the financial perspectives. The need for the Parliament's formal endorsement of any MFF gives it a potentially very powerful weapon against the 'pre-cooking' of a deal by the Council and Commission, but equally the use of that weapon could have significant negative political consequences for all the institutions. Likewise the Parliament is, on balance, strengthened by the abolition of the distinction between compulsory and non-compulsory expenditure, which has the potential to make the Council and Parliament genuinely co-equal for the first time in the annual budgetary process. However, when the new budgetary process was first used in the autumns of 2010 and 2011, the Parliament was frustrated on both occasions by the Council in its attempt to support the real-terms increase in spending proposed by the Commission. As one official put it, the Parliment seemed 'disoriented by the move it had long advocated, from having the last word over two-thirds of the Budget to having an equal say with the Council over 100 per cent'.

C

Cabinet

In a European Union context, the French word *cabinet* denotes the private office of a senior office-holder in one of the European institutions. The concept derives from the French administrative tradition, where ministerial *cabinets* – composed of a small group of personally-chosen civil servants, together with some advisers drawn from outside government – act as the key interface between the minister and his or her department. *Cabinets* are also to be found in Belgium, Italy, Spain and Portugal. (In Italy, they have a largely legalistic, rather than policy-oriented, function.)

Unlike in Britain, where the principle of 'ministerial responsibility' within government usually assures a seamless relationship between a minister and policy advice from officials, the *cabinet* system often witnesses a more detached relationship between the two. Members of *cabinets* often become active advocates of their master's wishes, both internally against established interests within the bureaucracy, and externally vis-à-vis outside audiences. Relations between senior *cabinet* staff and their opposite numbers in departments can sometimes be problematic. Ezra Suleiman, in his classic account of the French civil service (*Politics, Power and Bureaucracy in France*, 1975), notes that the distinction between *chef de cabinet* and the director general of a ministry can institutionalize a 'particularly acute conflict at the apex of the French administrative system'. In Paris, as in Brussels, *cabinets* often attract what Edward Page has called 'a distinctive form of bureaucratic politician who, as a political appointee of one form or another, can advance his or her career' by serving close to those entrusted with executive power (*People who run Europe*, 1997).

The President and members of the **European Commission** – currently 27 individuals in total – each have *cabinets*, as do the Presidents of the other EU institutions. (The immediate support staff of the Secretaries General of the various institutions are also known as *cabinets*, although the latter are usually administrative offices with a less obviously political character.) Appointments to *cabinets* are much sought after among **Eurocrats** in Brussels, both because of the influence that members can wield on behalf of their bosses, and because their proximity to power gives them wide access and exposure at senior levels within the organization. The combination of visibility and experience of dealing with a wide range of business, both within and between directorates-general, often results in faster-track career advancement for *cabinet* members, who are often 'parachuted' into head of unit or director level posts towards the end of their service with Commissioners. A high percentage of the Commission's most senior officials have worked, at some point, in *cabinet* positions.

The growing size and influence of *cabinets* within the Commission became a source of some controversy during the 1980s and 1990s. As Commission President, **Jacques Delors** relied particularly heavily on key *cabinet* figures, some of whom became as powerful as, if not more powerful than, most other Commissioners – and certainly more influential than the Secretary General of the institution. (The long-serving **Émile Noël** retired very soon after Delors and his team took over.) The *chef de cabinet*, Pascal Lamy, known less than affectionately as the 'Beast of the **Berlaymont**', and his deputy, François Lamoureux, proved to be very significant players in their own right. Criticism of their (largely effective) style was accentuated by the limitations of the tradition, at that time, that nearly all *cabinet* staff came from the same member state as the Commissioner who appointed them: eight of the 11 policy advisers in Delors' cabinet were French. His successor but one, Romano Prodi, decided in 1999 to limit the size of his own team to nine advisers, with each of his Commissioner colleagues allowed only six, plus a press spokesman. The *chef* and deputy *chef de cabinet* had henceforth to be of different nationalities, and in total only three of any Commissioner's seven top staffers could be of the same nationality, and at least two of them had to be women. The limit on numbers proved unsustainable and has now in effect been reversed. The *cabinet* of the current Commission President, José Manuel Barroso, comprises 12 policy advisers of seven nationalities, plus two press spokesmen and 23 assistants. The other Commissioners usually have eight policy advisers, plus a spokesman, and up to 11 assistants. The increase in the number of Commissioners from 20 to 27 in recent years, as a result of **enlargement**, has further doomed the attempt to contain the '*cabinet* culture'. In all, some 250 policy advisers and spokesmen, as well as over 300 assistants, now serve in Commissioners' *cabinets* at any given moment.

In addition to the support they give to Commissioners individually, the *cabinets* play an important part in the Commission's collective decision-making process. *Chefs de cabinets* convene weekly before each full Commission meeting to try to reach agreement on all points on the agenda. (These meetings usually occur on Mondays and Wednesdays respectively.) In advance of the discussion among *chefs*, the individual members of the various *cabinets* covering specific subject areas come together in (somewhat incongruously named) 'special *chefs*' meetings, to prepare the ground and thrash out detailed compromises in their fields. These preparatory meetings, which act as 'gatekeeper' to any full Commission discussion, can often be arduous: the meetings of *chefs de cabinet* in January 2007 and June 2008 to finalize complex Commission 'packages' of measures on climate change and social policy were each over six hours' long. The climate-change discussion, aimed at agreeing carbon reduction targets for each member state, forced the *chefs de cabinet* to defend the national interests of their Commissioners: the meeting was referred to ironically by one participant as the equivalent of '**COREPER** III'.

Cassis de Dijon case

The 1979 judgement of the **European Court of Justice** (ECJ) in the case known as 'Cassis de Dijon' *(Rewe-Zentrale AG* v *Bundesmonopolverwaltung für Branntwein,* Case 120/78) established that a product lawfully manufactured and on sale in one EU member state may be imported into another without restriction. This principle, sometimes known as **mutual recognition** of product standards, is of the greatest importance in facilitating the **free movement of goods** within the **single market** and can obviate the need for detailed **harmonization** of product standards to guarantee such circulation.

Cassis de Dijon is a blackcurrant-based liqueur, often drunk with white wine or champagne, manufactured in France. The West German spirits monopoly sought to ban its import into the German market on the grounds that its alcoholic content (15 to 20 per cent by volume) was below the minimum laid down by German law for liqueurs (32 per cent). The ECJ did not accept this argument, finding that although the German restriction might not be discriminatory in intent, it was discriminatory in effect, especially as the stated justification for the rule – ironically to discourage alcoholism by banning the consumption of low-alcohol liqueurs – could be more easily achieved by other means.

The Court's ruling gave a new dynamic to then Article 30 EEC, now Article 34 TFEU, which states that 'Quantitative restrictions on imports and all measures having equivalent effect shall be prohibited between Member States.' Restrictive technical standards of this kind could be deemed to have 'equivalent effect' and could thus be struck down by the courts, even when they applied equally to domestic and foreign producers. As Stephen Weatherill and Paul Beaumont have written, this was an area where, until the ruling, it was 'widely assumed that legislative harmonization of divergent national rules was required to eliminate obstacles to interstate trade. *Cassis de Dijon* is crucial to the integration of the market through the application of Article 30 by the courts' (*EU Law*, 1999).

Subsequently, the ECJ struck down a number of other national restrictions on similar grounds. These included Italian bans on non wine-based vinegars and on pasta made from soft wheat, an overly prescriptive German rule on the composition of beer, and a French attempt to limit the sale of coffee whiteners. In the Keck judgement of 1993 (Case 267/91), the Court chose to limit the scope of the Cassis de Dijon ruling, by clarifying that it should only apply to restrictions affecting the 'designation, form, size, weight, composition, presentation, labelling [and] packaging' of a good, as opposed to arrangements for its sale (unless the latter discriminated against imports in fact or law). The Court's 1989 ruling against the (then) restriction on Sunday trading in the United Kingdom – the Torfaen Borough Council case (Case 145/88) – would not therefore have been possible after 1993.

Cecchini Report

In the **Cockfield White Paper** of June 1985, the **European Commission** identified the legislative measures that would be needed if the **single market** were to be completed within the European Community by the target date set by heads of government of December 1992. In April 1988, a committee of experts, chaired by a senior Commission official, Paolo Cecchini, assessed the likely economic effect of successful completion of the single-market programme. Published by the Commission under the title *1992: The European Challenge*, the Cecchini Report surveyed the range of barriers that still stood in the way of the free flow of goods, services, capital and people within the Community. The report calculated that the continuing fragmentation of markets along national lines by 'technical, physical and fiscal frontiers' was costing the Community some five per cent of its gross domestic product (GDP) annually. It suggested that removal of remaining barriers would deliver a one-off increase of up to seven per cent of GDP over a seven-year period, and could then generate additional, ongoing non-inflationary growth of about one per cent a year after that. The identification of this 'cost of **non-Europe**' – a phrase derived from the **Albert–Ball Report** of five years before – helped provide political impetus for the ongoing single market programme. The report's findings, which encompassed 13 volumes by economic sector, were based in part on a survey among 11,000 businessmen, who cited frontier formalities and the failure to agree on Europe-wide product standards as the key elements in the problem. The academic foundations of the report were set out in Michael Emerson et al., *The Economics of 1992*, 1988.

Central bank governors

There was no reference to the governors of the central banks of the EC member states in the original text of the **Treaty of Rome**. They were first given institutional standing in May 1964, when the **Ecofin Council** (Council of Economics and Finance Ministers) decided to complement the existing **Monetary Committee** by establishing a parallel body to coordinate the activities of the various national central banks at Community level. The resulting forum, known as the Committee of Central Bank Governors, brought together the governors and their senior staff, with a limited remit to 'hold consultations concerning the general principles and the broad lines of policy of the central banks' and to 'exchange information at regular intervals about the most important measures that fall within [their] competence'.

In practice, the committee's work was given real substance only once the promotion of exchange-rate stability became a major Community objective during the 1970s. The first attempt to develop **Economic and Monetary Union** (EMU) in Europe, following the 1970 **Werner Report**, led to a major enhancement of the committee's role. In March 1971, it was entrusted with coordinating intervention on the currency markets to sustain the so-called 'Snake'. A decision of the Ecofin Council of the same month strengthened cooperation between central banks in respect of interest rates and money supply. Two years later, in April 1973, the committee was appointed in its entirety to serve as the board of governors of the new **European Monetary Cooperation Fund** (EMCF).

Although the Werner-inspired EMU project failed, the development of the **European Monetary System** (EMS) from January 1979 onwards once again strengthened the position of the central bank governors, with increasing importance attached to monetary policy as a key component of macro-economic management and a growing trend to make central banks legally independent of governments. When it was decided to relaunch the EMU process at the European Council meeting in Hanover in June 1988, by commissioning the **Delors Report**, the membership of the committee for the new study was composed almost exclusively of the central bank governors.

The Delors Committee designed several of the key features of the three-stage move to EMU that followed, including the requirements that both the national central banks and the new central monetary authority, eventually established as the **European Central Bank** (ECB), should be legally independent. The remit and organization of the Committee of Central Bank Governors were strengthened, in preparation for the beginning of stage one of EMU in July 1990, as the Delors Report suggested. A Council decision (of March 1990) explicitly tasked the committee with holding consultations on, and promoting the coordination of, the monetary policies of the member states, with the aim of achieving price stability. Its chairman, elected annually, was given the formal right to attend meetings of the Ecofin Council when it was dealing with matters 'involving the tasks of the Committee'. In parallel, the committee's existing secretariat – composed of national officials on secondment and based at the **Bank for International Settlements** (BIS) in Basle – was significantly strengthened.

Under the provisions of the 1992 **Maastricht Treaty**, the Committee of

Central Bank Governors and the EMCF were merged in January 1994, at the start of stage two of EMU, to form the **European Monetary Institute** (EMI). In June 1998, seven months before the start of stage three, the EMI was transformed into the European Central Bank. The central bank governors of those EU member states within stage three sit on the ECB's Governing Council, which meets monthly and sets interest rates for the **eurozone**. They are joined by the governors from member states outside the eurozone on the ECB's General Council, which has an advisory and technical role and meets less regularly than the Governing Council.

Central Commission for Navigation on the Rhine (CCNR)

With its headquarters in Strasbourg, the Central Commission for Navigation on the Rhine is the world's longest surviving international organization – and thus the oldest pan-European body – having been established by the Congress of Vienna in 1815. Governed by the Convention of Mannheim (1868) and its five subsequent protocols, the CCNR is responsible for all aspects of navigation and shipping on the Rhine, including regulation of traffic, registration of vessels, maintenance of the waterway, safety and pollution. The four riparian states (France, Germany, the Netherlands and Switzerland), together with Belgium, take part in its work. Each of the countries nominates four Commissioners and two deputy commissioners, who meet together in plenary session twice a year, passing resolutions which represent in effect the collective position of their respective governments. Ten committees and eight working groups carry forward the Commission's business in the interim. The president of the Commission serves a two-year term, with the post rotating among the five member states. Ministers meet periodically to provide political orientation to the Commission's work. An international court, the Chamber of Appeal, was established in 1963 by the Strasbourg Convention to promote the settlement of legal disputes arising over navigation of the Rhine. The 1,320 kilometre-long river is Europe's busiest waterway, along which some 300 million tonnes of freight are transported each year, three times the volume carried on the Danube (where navigation is regulated by the **Danube Commission**, modelled on the CCNR).

Central European Free Trade Agreement (CEFTA)

The Central European Free Trade Agreement was signed by the **Visegrád** countries – Poland, Hungary and Czechoslovakia – in December 1992 in Kraków, Poland. Its purpose was to create a **free trade area** and **single market** among the participating states by 2001. Except for certain 'sensitive' products, duties on all industrial goods in CEFTA were removed in 1997. The three founding countries already had bilateral free trade agreements with each other and **Europe Agreements** with the European Union, in preparation for membership of the latter in due course. They were soon joined by Slovenia (1996), Romania (1997) and Bulgaria (1999). **Accession** by all of the foregoing countries to the Union in 2004 and 2007 required them to leave CEFTA, which would have otherwise ceased to exist but for its expansion to include the remainder of the Balkan states. **Croatia** joined in 2003, FYR Macedonia in 2006, and Albania, Bosnia and Herzegovina, Montenegro and Serbia in 2007, along with Moldova later the same year. As a result, CEFTA has become in effect a free trade area for south-east Europe. The criteria for membership were loosened in 2005 to require that participants have only an **association agreement** with the EU, rather than arrangements that explicitly envisage eventual membership.

Central European Initiative (CEI)

Founded in November 1989, as the collapse of **Communism** gathered pace, the CEI was the first new forum to be established for regional cooperation in central, eastern and south-east Europe. Since then, it has provided a framework for promoting economic recovery and democratization, as well as cooperation in the fields of the environment, transport and energy. Today the organization acts as a bridge between those countries within the region that are member states of the European Union and those that aspire to membership in the future.

The CEI began life as the Alps–Adriatic working group or 'Quadrilateral Initiative' of the Italian government, encompassing Austria, Hungary and **Yugoslavia**, as well as Italy. In 1990, it was joined by Czechoslovakia (becoming the Pentagonal Initiative) and a year later by Poland (Hexagonal Initiative). The current name was adopted in 1992, on the accession of **Croatia**, Slovenia and Bosnia and Herzegovina. By 1996, the CEI had been extended south and eastwards to include Albania, Belarus, Bulgaria, Macedonia, Moldova, Romania and Ukraine. Today, the CEI encompasses 18 countries, half of which are now EU member states.

The CEI holds an annual summit meeting of heads of government, hosted by the country occupying its rotating presidency. Foreign ministers meet twice a year and finance ministers annually. Day-to-day decisions are taken by an official-level committee of national coordinators. Parliamentary and business 'dimensions' bring together national legislators and chambers of commerce. Financial contributions from member states, notably Italy, have enabled the CEI to establish a series of funds to co-finance joint projects. The most important of these is the CEI Trust Fund, administered in conjunction with the **European Bank for Reconstruction and Development** (EBRD). The CEI has a small secretariat based in Trieste, including a staff devoted specifically to securing EU funding for its projects and encouraging CEI involvement in EU programmes. The CEI's working language is English.

Charlemagne Prize

The International Charlemagne Prize (*Karlspreis*), awarded annually by an independent foundation drawing on citizens of Aachen (Aix la Chapelle) – the German town close to the borders of Belgium and the Netherlands – is intended to honour those who have made an outstanding contribution to the process of European unification. First awarded in 1950 to **Richard Coudenhove-Kalergi**, the prize has since been given to a wide variety of European and American personalities. They include the various **founding fathers** – **Alcide de Gasperi** (1952), **Jean Monnet** (1953), **Konrad Adenauer** (1954), **Paul-Henri Spaak** (1957) and **Robert Schuman** (1958) – as well as to **Winston Churchill** (1956), General George Marshall (1959; see **Marshall Plan**), **Walter Hallstein** (1961), **Edward Heath** (1963), **Roy Jenkins** (1972), Konstantinos Karamanlis (1978), King Juan Carlos of Spain (1982), Henry Kissinger (1987), **François Mitterrand** and **Helmut Kohl** (jointly in 1988), Václav Havel (1991), **Jacques Delors** (1992), **Tony Blair** (1999), Bill Clinton (2000), **Valéry Giscard d'Estaing** (2003), Pope John Paul II (2004) and Angela Merkel (2008). On three occasions, the prize has been awarded to a collective entity: the **European Commission** (1969), the people of **Luxembourg** (1986) and the **euro** (2002). The prize-winner's medal shows Charlemagne, who was crowned as Holy Roman Emperor in Aachen in 800, seated on his throne.

Charter of Fundamental Rights

At the meeting of the **European Council** (of EU heads of governments) in Cologne in June 1999 it was decided that 'at the present stage of development of the European Union, the fundamental rights applicable at Union level should be consolidated in a Charter and thereby made more evident'. The proposed Charter should inter alia 'contain the fundamental rights and freedoms, as well as basic procedural rights' guaranteed by the **European Convention on Human Rights** (ECHR) and take account of economic and social rights contained in the **Social Charters** of both the **Council of Europe** and European Union. The exact legal status of the new Charter was left undecided, the European Council adding only that consideration would be given at some future date as to 'whether, and, if so, how the Charter should be integrated into the **Treaties**'.

The background to the proposal was the strong feeling, especially on the political left, that if the European Union was to progress beyond being an essentially economic construct with political aspirations, it was in need of a stronger statement of values and rights. As the possibility of the Union becoming a signatory to the ECHR under existing treaty arrangements had been ruled out by the **European Court of Justice** (ECJ) in 1994 (Opinion 2/94), many believed that the best solution would be for the Union to draw up a document of its own. This sentiment was compounded by awareness that the German Federal Constitutional Court had signalled that it would not necessarily accept the **primacy** of **EU law** over national law unless there were treaty-based guarantees that the law respected fundamental rights (see **Karlsruhe judgements**). The new German social democrat government of Gerhard Schröder, elected in September 1998, decided to make the issue a high priority of its European policy. Schröder secured the support of French President Jacques Chirac for such an initiative, a move which was accepted without enthusiasm by British prime minister **Tony Blair**.

At its meeting in Tampere in October 1999, the European Council entrusted the drafting of the Charter to an innovative forum, a Convention, composed of 15 representatives of the members of the European Council, 16 Members of the **European Parliament** (MEPs), 30 members of **national parliaments**, and a member of the **European Commission** representing the Commission President. (This 'Convention method', rather than the immediate convening of an **Intergovernmental Conference** (IGC), was subsequently employed in 2002–3 for the purpose of drafting the **European Constitution** that eventually became, in diluted form, the **Lisbon Treaty**.)

The Convention met for the first time in December 1999. The chairman was Roman Herzog, the recently-retired President of Germany. A small drafting committee, composed of representatives of the Convention's constituent elements, prepared texts for submission to the whole meeting. The Charter was agreed by the Convention in September 2000, adopted at the meeting of the European Council in Nice in December that year, and thereafter 'solemnly proclaimed' jointly by the European Parliament, the Commission and the **Council of Ministers**. In a declaration annexed to the **Nice Treaty**, the member states committed themselves to considering the status of the Charter at the next IGC.

The Charter contains 54 articles divided into seven chapters: Dignity, Freedoms, Equality, Solidarity, Citizens' Rights, Justice, and General Provisions. The rights contained in the Charter fall into three broad categories. First are the basic universal rights – such as the right to life, freedom from arbitrary detention, presumption of innocence and the right to a fair trial – as set out in the ECHR and in the constitutions of most member states. Second are the civil and political rights associated with **European citizenship**. Third, and most controversial as far as differences between member states are concerned, are the economic and social rights pertaining to employment, health care, living standards, working conditions and other areas covered by the **Social Charters** of the Council of Europe and European Union. On the one hand, there are member states – such as the United Kingdom – in which there is relatively little formal recognition of such rights and, on the other, member states in which such rights are legally guaranteed.

The most controversial point, especially in a UK context, is the 'right of collective bargaining and action', including strike action, set out in Article 28. The British government fought hard in the Convention to secure the least constraining form of wording on this point.

Apart from disagreements, major or minor, within the Convention on the substance or formulation of particular rights, certain differences of approach became evident in the Convention's proceedings. First, there were those who interpreted the Convention's mandate as exclusively one of consolidation, namely the Charter was not to break new ground but assemble and codify existing rights, whether contained in the ECHR, the EU Treaties or law made under the latter. Others regarded the drawing up of the Charter as an opportunity to move the Union forward in an area not systematically touched on in EU law and envisaged the Charter as an essential component of a future European Constitution. Second, there was the question of whether the Charter should be declaratory only or whether it should possess the force of law. If the latter, what should be the relation between the Charter and the Treaties? Should it eventually be incorporated into the Treaties, or should it remain separate, even though this would mean that certain rights were in the Treaties (such as the right of **free movement**) and others – perhaps more fundamental – were not? Third, given that all the Union's member states and all applicant states were signatories to the ECHR, there was thought by some to be a risk of confusion, duplication of effort, and conflicting jurisdiction arising from the existence of a separate EU Charter.

The Convention took a relatively expansive view of what constituted 'rights' at European level, whilst seeking to limit them to freedoms and protections already recognized in law, in some form – through the provisions of the ECHR and EU Treaties, EU legislation adopted under the Treaties, and rulings of either the European Court of Human Rights in Strasbourg or the ECJ in Luxembourg. (An annex to the Charter explained the precise origin of each right contained therein in such terms.) The Charter included rights in relation to issues that had arisen only relatively recently – for example, human cloning (Article 3.2) and data protection (Article 8). However, in some areas, the absoluteness of the right in question was qualified by the addition of phrases such as 'in accordance with the national laws governing the exercise of this right' (for example, in Article 10.2 on conscientious objection) or 'in accordance with Union law and national laws and practices' (for example, in Articles 30 and 34 on protection from unfair dismissal and entitlement to social security). In other cases, certain rights were not proclaimed but merely 'recognized' (for example, Article 25 on the rights of the elderly). It may be questioned whether some of the rights listed were really fundamental, such as 'the right of access to a free placement service' (Article 29), and there were other inclusions of questionable relevance, such as the observation that 'political parties at Union level contribute to expressing the political will of the citizens of the Union' (Article 12).

The Charter, as proclaimed by the institutions in 2000, did not possess the force of law, and, unlike the ECHR, there was no machinery for its enforcement. However, Article 6 TEU, introduced by the 1992 **Maastricht Treaty**, already obliged the Union to respect fundamental rights – as guaranteed by the ECHR and 'as they result from the constitutional traditions common to the Member States' – as 'general principles' of Union law. On one reading, the Charter could be seen as a statement of what these common traditions were, on which the Court could draw. Article 52 of the Charter attempted to minimize any inconsistency with the ECHR, by stating that where rights in the former corresponded to those already guaranteed by the latter, the two should be regarded as identical in 'meaning and scope'. The Charter was addressed specifically to the institutions and bodies of the Union and 'to the Member States only when they are implementing Union law' and did 'not establish any new power of task' for the Union or 'modify powers and tasks defined by the Treaties' (Article 51).

The **Convention on the Future of Europe** in 2002–3 agreed that the text of the Charter of Fundamental Rights should be made legally binding and feature (as Part Two) in the proposed European Constitution. Both the Convention and the subsequent IGC (in 2003–4) made minor adjustments to the wording of the text, notably in respect of its scope of application. At the insistence of the British and other governments hesitant about making the Charter legally binding, Article 51 was strengthened to assert that the EU institutions and bodies would need to respect 'the limits of the powers of the Union' in applying the Charter, which itself did 'not extend the field of application of Union law'. Article 52 was modified to state that where the Charter 'recognizes fundamental rights as they result from the constitutional traditions common to the Member States, those rights shall be interpreted in harmony with those traditions'. Equally, 'full account shall be taken of national laws and practices as specified in this Charter'.

The European Constitution was abandoned following its rejection in the **French and Dutch referenda** of May and June 2005. When it was revived as the Reform Treaty, subsequently the Lisbon Treaty, no further changes were made to the text of the Charter of Fundamental Rights. However, instead of the Charter featuring in the body of the treaty, there was simply a cross-reference to the text, stating: 'The Union recognizes the rights, freedoms and principles set out in the Charter of Fundamental Rights of the European Union . . . which shall have the same legal value as the Treaties. The provisions of the Charter shall not extend in any way the **competences** of the Union as defined in the Treaties' (Article 6 TEU).

In parallel, as a condition for agreeing to the new treaty, the United

Kingdom took the lead in negotiating a **protocol**, by which – 'in order to clarify' the application of the Charter, but 'without prejudice' to its impact on other member states – it secured what it presented as a de facto **opt-out** from some, at least, of its legal effects. The Polish government chose to follow suit, adding its name to the protocol at the last minute. Protocol 30 to the Treaties, introduced by the Lisbon Treaty, makes clear that the Charter does not 'extend the ability' of the ECJ or of either the British or Polish courts to find the laws or administrative acts of those countries to be inconsistent with rights asserted in the Charter. It states, in particular, that nothing in the section on workers' rights creates any 'justiciable rights' applicable to the UK or Poland, except in so far as either country itself chooses to provide for such rights in national law. Moreover, where the Charter refers to national laws and practices, 'it shall only apply in Poland or the United Kingdom to the extent that the rights or principles that it contains are recognized in the law or practices' of those two member states. The legal effectiveness of the assurances given in the protocol is still far from clear, as much will depend on the specific interpretation given by the ECJ in any dispute between the provisions of the Charter and those of domestic UK or Polish law.

The Charter of Fundamental Rights was 'reproclaimed' by the Commission, Council and Parliament in a ceremony – disrupted by Eurosceptic MEPs – in the chamber of the European Parliament in Strasbourg on 12 December 2007, a day before the Lisbon Treaty itself was signed. Subsequently, Czech President Václav Klaus sought and obtained a similar 'opt-out' to that provided for the UK and Poland, as the quid pro quo for agreeing to sign his country's act of ratification in November 2009, so ending the Lisbon ratification crisis of 2008–9. The EU heads of government agreed that the text of Protocol 30 would be amended, by widening it to include the Czech Republic, on the occasion of the next substantive treaty change.

Charter of Paris

The signing of the Charter of Paris for a New Europe on 21 November 1990 by the states participating in the **Conference on Security and Cooperation in Europe** (CSCE) was widely regarded as marking the formal end of the **Cold War**. Made possible by the collapse of Soviet hegemony in central and eastern Europe, the Charter reiterated the ideas and principles set out in the **Helsinki Final Act** and marked the transition of the CSCE from a negotiating process to a permanent institution, with a formal structure. The signatory states declared that 'henceforth our relations will be founded on respect and cooperation' and asserted the need for 'a new quality of political dialogue'. The CSCE was renamed the **Organization for Security and Cooperation in Europe** (OSCE) in 1995.

The CSCE summit in Paris in November 1990 is politically significant in a second respect. The decision of British prime minister **Margaret Thatcher** to attend the meeting, rather than stay in London to shore up support in an increasingly competitive Conservative party leadership contest, is thought to have played a part in her unexpected failure to win outright victory on the first ballot of that election. She received news of the result at the British Embassy on 20 November and resigned as prime minister two days later, as her position became untenable.

Christian Democracy

The largest and most successful family of centre and centre-right political parties in post-war continental Europe, Christian Democracy played a central part in European integration during the 1950s. Tracing their intellectual antecedents back to the nineteenth century, Christian Democrat parties were mainly descended from those political forces which sided with the Church in the disputes between Church and state, and which took the lead in opposing the essentially secular Socialist parties based upon universal suffrage. Between the First and Second World Wars, such parties were often strongly associated with Catholicism. After 1945, modern Christian Democracy reflected a desire to bring together both Catholic and Protestant forces in a broader movement, whilst its rapid rise lay partly in the discrediting of most other elements on the right of the political spectrum through association with Fascism. Christian Democrat parties usually saw themselves as forces of 'national unity', located in the centre of the political spectrum – even if objectively they largely occupied space on the centre-right – and several attached importance to their links with the Christian trade unions that often existed in countries where the Catholic Church had been powerful.

After the Second World War, many of the characteristic tenets of Christian Democracy – a belief in a balance between personal freedom and individual responsibility, the desire to mix market economics and social justice, strong opposition to nationalism and equal support for international cooperation – chimed well with the domestic political moods in Germany, Italy and the **Benelux** countries, in particular. Christian Democrat parties became the leading political forces in these five countries during the 1950s – a phenomenon which helps explain both their central role in European integration and the influence on the new Community institutions of their thinking at that time. Christian Democrats also started strongly in France, but dwindled with the rise of Gaullism. Three of Europe's leading Christian Democrats of that era – **Konrad Adenauer**, **Alcide de Gasperi** and **Robert Schuman** – are usually cited as among the '**founding fathers**' of the European Union. Unlike certain Socialist parties, the Christian Democrats voted solidly in favour of the **Treaty of Paris** and the

Treaties of Rome, establishing the various **European Communities**, when they were submitted for **ratification** in **national parliaments**. The first President of the **European Commission** was a German Christian Democrat, **Walter Hallstein**.

Further reading: David Hanley, *Christian Democracy in Europe: a Comparative Perspective*, 1994; R. E. M. Irving, *The Christian Democratic Parties of Western Europe*, 1979.

Churchill, Winston (1874–1965)

After taking a decisive stand against the appeasement of Nazi Germany during the 1930s, Winston Churchill became prime minister of the United Kingdom in May 1940 at a critical moment in the history of his country and that of Europe. As Britain's war leader, he played a decisive role in securing Allied victory. After unexpectedly losing power in the 1945 general election, he served as Leader of the Opposition during the post-war Labour government of Clement Attlee, returning to office in 1951. He then served a second term as prime minister, retiring in 1955, to be replaced by his long-time heir apparent and Foreign Secretary, Anthony Eden. In the years after the war, Churchill enjoyed immense moral authority, not only in Britain but across Europe as a whole. His advocacy of European unification was thus a position of great political significance.

Writing before the war – in the New York *Saturday Evening Post* on 15 February 1930 – Churchill had been one of the first political figures to express support for what he called a '**United States of Europe**'. His advocacy of greater European unity reflected his view that the League of Nations needed to be underpinned by large regional groupings. During the war, his belief that the future of Europe might be bound up with closer integration was expressed in his so-called 'morning thoughts' in January 1943, in which he envisaged 'an instrument of European government' as part of an international post-war settlement. Such a structure might help contain not only any revival of German power, after that country's defeat, but also address the potential problem of Soviet influence in central and eastern Europe, which he already foresaw.

Allied victory in the Second World War left Churchill in an exceptionally strong position to shape the contours of post-war Europe. Ironically, at this moment, the British public ejected him from power by a crushing margin, electing a Labour government with its sights set firmly on domestic reconstruction. In opposition after July 1945, Churchill devoted several major speeches to the theme of a united Europe. His reputation as a pioneer of post-war integration rests more than anything else on his **Zurich speech** of 19 September 1946, in which he reiterated his call for a United States of Europe, based now on Franco-German reconciliation, and proposed the creation of a **Council of Europe** as a stepping stone towards that goal. As in his Fulton speech in March 1946, warning of the rise of Soviet power and the descent of an 'iron curtain' across the continent, he was, as Paul Addison has written, 'attempting to detach his audience from wartime emotions and prepare them for a new post-war reality' (*Churchill: The Unexpected Hero*, 2006). Twenty months after Zurich, in May 1948, at the **Congress of Europe** in The Hague, over which he presided, Churchill called for a European Assembly as 'the voice of United Europe' and explained that European unity required 'some sacrifice or merger of national **sovereignty**', adding that 'it is also possible and not less agreeable to regard it as the gradual assumption by all the nations concerned of that larger sovereignty which can alone protect their diverse and distinctive customs and characteristics and their national traditions'. In August 1950, as a member of the Consultative Assembly of the very Council of Europe he had proposed, Churchill moved a resolution calling for the immediate establishment of a 'unified **European army**', in which he implied that Britain would 'play an honourable and active part'. In parallel, following the announcement of the **Schuman Plan**, he criticized the Attlee government for not participating in the negotiations for the creation of a supranational **European Coal and Steel Community** (ECSC), whether or not Britain were to join.

In the event, on returning to power in October 1951, at the age of 77, Churchill did not materially alter the European policies of the previous Labour government. The new administration declined to participate in the new ECSC, even though the United States would have welcomed it, and took no part in the discussions about either the **European Defence Community** (EDC) or **European Political Community** (EPC), even though these latter initiatives had flowed indirectly from his own proposal of a European army in 1950. As a result, there has been a lively debate among historians about the true nature of Churchill's views on Europe. In part, his failure to push for closer British involvement in 1951–5 may simply have reflected a dwindling ability to resist the deep and growing hostility of Eden towards supranational European institutions. More fundamentally, the choices of government appear to have brought into relief a duality of view that Churchill had long harboured, in which Britain's involvement in Europe needed to be reconciled with an equal and opposite priority: the continued strength and survival of the British Empire and Commonwealth.

As early as his *Saturday Evening Post* article in 1930, Churchill had written: 'The attitude of Great Britain toward unification or "federal links" would, in the first instance, be determined by her dominant conception of a United British Empire. Every step that tends to make Europe more prosperous and more peaceful is conducive to British interests . . . We have our own dream and our own task. We are with Europe, but not of it. We are linked, but not comprised. We are interested and associated, but not absorbed.' In similar vein, in his Zurich speech 16 years later, he referred to Britain as 'the friend and sponsor of the new Europe', rather than necessarily as the country defining it as the new leader from within.

However, in most of his subsequent pronouncements in opposition, Churchill took a more ambitious view. In the House of Commons in January 1948, he said that a 'European policy of unity can perfectly well be reconciled with and adjusted to our obligations to the Commonwealth and Empire, of which we are the heart and centre'. At The Hague in May that year, he talked of the 'Council of Europe, including Great Britain linked with her Empire and Commonwealth' being one of the 'great groups' of what he hoped would be a new international order. A week later, addressing a rally organized by the Committee for a United Europe at the Royal Albert Hall, Churchill said that 'if Europe united is to be a living force, Britain will have to play her full part as a member of the European family' and spoke of 'the idea of a united Europe in which our country will play a decisive part'. He said that the self-governing Dominions 'feel with us that Britain is geographically and historically a part of Europe, and that they also have their inheritance in Europe'.

Churchill's view was that the United Kingdom's world role should be located at the point of overlap between 'three great circles': the Commonwealth, the Atlantic Alliance and Europe. Britain would be the 'vital link' at the centre of a global system defined in effect by the winners of the Second World War. However, in its reduced condition after the war, Britain was to find it increasingly difficult to juggle between the imperatives of these competing arenas. During 'Churchill's Indian summer', his second government largely avoided the hard choices that were crowding in. Subsequently, his successors proceeded to liquidate the Empire, tested the limits of its 'special relationship' with the United States to breaking-point during the **Suez crisis**, and stepped aside as moves towards closer European integration gathered pace.

Winston Churchill's political career was exceptionally long and eventful. He served in the House of Commons for over six decades, 30 of those years as a minister. His views certainly evolved over time and may ultimately have been inconsistent on both the European question and some others. One thing is certain: that Churchill lent his enormous prestige to the cause of European unity in the years immediately after the Second World War was a matter of cardinal importance for the subsequent development of the continent.

Citizens' initiative and petitions

Article 10(1) TEU, introduced by the **Lisbon Treaty**, states that the European Union 'shall be founded on representative democracy'. The direct election of Members of the **European Parliament** (MEPs) and the accountability of member-state representatives in the **European Council** and **Council of Ministers** to **national parliaments** and electorates are cited as evidence of this principle in EU decision-making. However, in a spirit of direct participatory democracy, the Lisbon Treaty also institutes a new mechanism, known as the 'citizens' initiative', by which individual members of the general public, acting collectively, may seek to influence the political agenda of the institutions.

Since the foundation of the Communities, citizens have always enjoyed the right to petition the European Parliament over individual grievances, the application of existing policies and the possible development of new ones. This right was provided for in the Parliament's rules of procedure, starting in 1953, and was given treaty status by the 1992 **Maastricht Treaty** (Article 24 TFEU). The Parliament established a separate petitions committee in 1987 to investigate issues raised by petitions and recommend appropriate action. The number of petitions has grown over time, from 57 to more than a thousand a year, with some attracting a very large number of signatures. The petitions flowing from organized campaigns to ban the testing of cosmetics on animals, step up action against the illegal trade in bushmeat and concentrate all of the Parliament's own meetings in Brussels have each received more than a million signatures. After a petition has been found admissible and considered in the petitions committee, it may be referred to the appropriate policy committee in the Parliament or drawn to the attention of the **European Commission**, the **Ombudsman** or the authorities in a member state. The petitions committee submits an annual report to the Parliament.

The absence of any obvious process of follow-up to petitions in the Parliament led to the suggestion that the act of petitioning the Union might be better (or at least, additionally) directed at the Commission, which enjoys the **right of initiative** for EU legislation. The **Convention on the Future of Europe** (2002–3) took up this question and – drawing on the fact that some form of citizens' initiative exists at national level in 11 member states – proposed that the possibility of tabling a mass petition to the Commission be guaranteed at European level, although this right would be limited to suggestions for new **legal acts** by the Union. This proposal survived the transition from the **European Constitution** to the Lisbon Treaty and now Article 11(4) TEU provides that:

> *Not less than one million citizens who are nationals of a significant number of Member States may take the initiative of inviting the European Commission, within the framework of its powers, to submit any appropriate proposal on matters where citizens consider that a legal act of the Union is required for the purpose of implementing the Treaties.*

The 'procedures and conditions' for the exercise of the citizens' initiative are to be decided in law, 'including the minimum number of Member States from which such citizens must come' (Article 24 TFEU). Accordingly, in November 2009, the Commission published a Green Paper to consult with the public on the practical arrangements for the citizens' initiative, and in March 2010, it came forward with a draft **regulation**, to be adopted jointly by the Council and Parliament under the **co-decision procedure**. The Commission proposed that the one million signatures should come from at least one third of member states (currently nine) and that the threshold for support in each state should be set at the relatively low figure of 750 times the number of its MEPs (the number would thus vary between 4,500 signatories in Luxembourg or Malta and 74,000 in Germany). The signatures could be collected either in paper form or electronically and would be submitted on a standard-format 'statement of support', which would require each citizen to show their passport, identity card or social security number, in order to verify who they were.

The Commission itself would establish a mandatory, central online register for proposed citizens' initiatives. The subject of any initiative would need to meet the two conditions set down in the treaty, namely that the issue 'falls within the framework of the powers of the Commission to make a proposal' and 'concerns a matter where a legal act of the Union can be adopted for the purpose of implementing the Treaties'. Proposals that were 'manifestly against the values of the Union' would be rejected. (The implication is that a petition on the death penalty, abortion, defence or the **seats of EU institutions**, for example, would be ruled inadmissible.) In submitting a proposed initiative, the organizers would need to specify the treaty base under which the proposal would fall. However, only after accumulating 300,000 signatures, would they have formally to verify the admissibility of the proposal with the Commission, which would have two months in which to object. From the moment of registration, there would be a one-year period during which the million signatures could be collected. If successful, the initiative would then be considered by the Commission, which promises to signal within four months 'the action it intends to take, if any, and its reasons for doing so'.

The European Parliament insisted on a number of changes in the Commission proposal to make the arrangements more user-friendly. The number of member states from which signatures would be required was reduced from a third to a quarter (currently seven). The organizers of a petition will now need to form a 'citizens' committee', comprising residents of at least seven different member states. The admissibility check will be conducted at the beginning of the process, rather than after 300,000 signatures have been collected. Instead of a blanket obligation on those signing to provide proof of identity, the member states are left free to decide whether to impose this requirement: 18 countries will do so (including France, Italy, Poland and Spain), whilst nine (including Germany, the Netherlands and the United Kingdom) will not. If an initiative secures one million signatures, the organizers will be given the opportunity to present it at a public hearing to be held in the Parliament's premises.

After months of negotiation, these revisions to the Commission's proposal were agreed at first reading between the Council and Parliament in December 2010. Within a week of the deal, the measure was endorsed both by the plenary of the Parliament and the **General Affairs Council** (GAC), with the new system entering into force in April 2012.

Cockfield White Paper

When the former French finance minister, **Jacques Delors**, became President of the **European Commission** in January 1985, he sought to identify one or more major political projects on which he could work in his new role. Drawing on the analysis of the **Albert–Ball Report** of July 1983, which lamented the economic cost of '**non-Europe**', the British and some other governments, as well as the **European Parliament**, had been striving for some time to raise the priority attached to completing the **single market** within the European Community. Delors concluded that significant momentum could be established behind this goal: among the major states, the UK and Germany would be supportive and France persuadable on the basis of his own advocacy. In March 1985, the **European Council** endorsed this approach. It committed the member states to the completion of 'a single large market by 1992' – the lifespan of two four-year terms of the Commission – and called upon the latter body to draw up 'a detailed programme with a specific timetable before its next meeting'.

It fell to (Lord) Arthur Cockfield (1916–2007), a little-known former British Treasury minister and newly-appointed Commissioner for the internal market and taxation, to come forward with a detailed plan to convert the general commitment to the single market into concrete action. The White Paper which he produced for the June 1985 European Council in Milan was to prove a landmark document. Breathtaking in its ambition, it identified 282 legislative initiatives that would be needed to establish a 'frontier-free' market in goods, services and capital, and proposed a fast-track timetable for their adoption (with deadlines both for the Commission to draft proposals and for the **Council of Ministers** to decide on them. These measures focused on three kinds of barrier to trade: physical barriers (remaining frontier controls), technical barriers (notably different product standards) and fiscal barriers (different rates of excise duty and **value-added tax** (VAT)).

The White Paper was innovative in breaking with the Commission's tradition of dealing with proposals piecemeal and sometimes avoiding necessary but unpopular measures. As Cockfield subsequently noted: 'It was essential that we had a properly structured programme covering all the vital elements of the internal market. It was no good proceeding as previous Commissions had done by picking out subjects that happened to catch the eye of particular member states. It had to be the lot' (*The European Union: Creating the Single Market*, 1994).

Cockfield convinced Delors of this high-risk approach, arguing that it would decisively shape the way the single market was seen. By publishing the White Paper only two weeks before the Milan summit, the Commission was able, as he put it, 'to give heads of government sufficient time to read the document and appreciate the immense importance of the opportunity being opened up', but not 'to give their officials enough time to pick it to pieces'. The strategy worked brilliantly: the European Council endorsed the White Paper, and the single-market legislative programme that followed was to dominate Community decision-making for the rest of the decade.

As Geoffrey Howe, the British Foreign Secretary who was instrumental in Cockfield's appointment, notes wryly in his memoirs: 'For a moment Arthur succeeded, because of their common enthusiasm for the single market, in winning the simultaneous admiration of both **Margaret Thatcher** and Jacques Delors. It was a short-lived achievement: for very soon it was Delors, and not [Thatcher], who was able to rely on Arthur's tenacious commitment to his cause' (*Conflict of Loyalty*, 1994). For the political impact of the Cockfield White Paper went far beyond the immediate policy agenda of completing the single market. It fed directly into the ongoing debate about European institutional reform, strengthening the hand of both Delors and integrationist member states in arguing for an **Intergovernmental Conference** (IGC) to update the **Treaty of Rome**. The Milan European Council accordingly agreed – against the objections of the British, Danish and Greek governments – to convene the IGC which quickly drafted the **Single European Act** (SEA), widening the remit of **qualified majority voting** (QMV) in the Council of Ministers to include most single-market measures. Cockfield in turn used this extension of QMV to drive through a large part of his programme, applying the same determination, tenacity and attention to detail that had characterized the drafting of his original White Paper.

Although (or perhaps because) Cockfield was one of the most successful European Commissioners ever – with arguably a greater claim than any figure apart from Delors himself to be considered a 'founding father' of the modern European Union – Margaret Thatcher chose not to reappoint him to the Commission when his term of office expired in January 1989. His own commitment to European solutions had begun seriously to outrun the tolerance of the prime minister, who expressed her growing **Euroscepticism** in the **Bruges speech** of September 1988. His specific advocacy of a greater degree of **tax harmonization**, where unanimity was still required in the Council, had also deeply irritated the British Chancellor of the Exchequer, Nigel Lawson, with whom he had open disagreements in the **Ecofin Council** during the UK **presidency** in 1988. Cockfield found himself caught up in a increasingly bitter internal battle over European policy in the Conservative party that was to cost not only him his job, but also Lawson, Howe and Thatcher their jobs within less than two years.

Co-decision procedure

First introduced by the 1992 **Maastricht Treaty**, 'co-decision' is a procedure by which the **European Parliament** and the **Council of Ministers** jointly enact legislation within the European Union. For a draft **legal act** to be adopted under co-decision, both institutions must agree to the text, in exactly the same form, and each has a veto over its adoption. In those policy areas where it applies – which have grown steadily over time and now encompass a majority of **legal bases** in the **Treaties** – co-decision establishes in effect a joint legislature between the Parliament and the Council. Under the **Lisbon Treaty**, which entered into force in December 2009, a combination of co-decision between these two institutions and **qualified majority voting** (QMV) within the Council is deemed to constitute the 'ordinary legislative procedure' of the Union (Article 294 TFEU). (By contrast, the simple consultation by the Council of the Parliament and/or the use of **unanimity** in the Council denotes a 'special legislative procedure'.)

The classic model of EU law-making involved the Council enacting legislation, after consulting the Parliament; the only serious leverage that the Parliament could exercise lay in its ability to delay its **opinion** on the legislative proposal tabled by the **European Commission**. This **consultation procedure** was the dominant mode of decision-making for many years and still remains in operation in certain politically sensitive policy fields, notably **tax harmonization** and **own resources**. The initial attempt to give the Parliament a more significant role in the legislative process was embodied in the **cooperation procedure** between the Council and Parliament, introduced by the 1986 **Single European Act**. This provided for a second reading of the Commission's proposal in each institution, with the Council only able to overturn the Parliament's position (where the Commission backed the latter) if it acted unanimously to do so. In the absence both of agreement between the two institutions and of unanimity within the Council for its own position, the proposal would lapse.

The co-decision procedure grew out of, and has now replaced, the less ambitious cooperation procedure. Co-decision allows either the Council or Parliament – not just the Council, as before – to reject the proposed legal act at any stage. It also provides more stages to the legislative process: whereas the cooperation procedure introduced a second reading, co-decision permits a further, final push for compromise, through a 'conciliation committee' of the two institutions, followed by a third-reading vote. Paradoxically, although there are more veto points in the process, the dynamic set-up is firmly directed towards agreement, with the successive readings and the conciliation committee designed to enhance the prospect of an eventual compromise being found.

Formally speaking, the co-decision procedure operates as follows. The **European Commission** submits a proposal to the Parliament and the Council, so starting the first reading of the legislative process. The first mover is the Parliament, which adopts a position on the proposal and communicates it to the Council. There is no time limit for the delivery of the Parliament's position. If the Council approves the Parliament's position, the act is adopted using the Parliament's wording. If the Council does not approve the Parliament's position, it may instead adopt its own position and communicate this to the Parliament. Again, there is no time limit for the Council to act at first reading.

Once the Council acts, the second reading begins, with a three-month period for a parliamentary response. If, within these three months, the Parliament either approves the Council's first-reading position or takes no decision, the act concerned is deemed to be adopted, on the basis of the Council's wording. If the Parliament rejects the Council's first-reading position by an absolute majority of its members, the act is deemed 'not to have been adopted' and dies. If the Parliament proposes, by an absolute majority, amendments to the Council's first-reading position, the text so amended is forwarded to the Council and the Commission, which both deliver opinions on these amendments.

The Council then has another three months in which to react to the Parliament's amendments. If the Council, acting by a qualified majority, approves all the Parliament's amendments, the act is deemed adopted. (Where the Commission has delivered a negative opinion on a Parliament amendment, the Council can only approve this amendment unanimously.) However, if the Council does not approve all the Parliament's amendments, the **presidency** of the Council and the President of the Parliament must jointly convene a conciliation committee within six weeks.

The conciliation committee, which consists of an equal number of representatives of each institution – currently 27 from each side, to match the number of member states – has to produce an agreed joint text within another six weeks. It acts by QMV among the Council representatives – its 27 members thus in effect simply replicating the Council – and by simple majority among the Members of the European Parliament (MEPs). The positions of the two institutions at second reading are used as the starting point for the committee's work and the Commission is asked to 'take all necessary initiatives' to help reconcile them. If the committee fails to approve a joint text within the six-week deadline, the proposal falls. If it does approve such a joint text, this then needs to be approved by both the Council, acting by QMV (which is by definition a formality) and the full Parliament, acting by a majority of the votes cast, again within six weeks. If either institution fails to approve the joint text, the proposal lapses. (The various deadlines of three months and six weeks referred to throughout the process can be extended by a maximum of one month and two weeks respectively, if either the Parliament or the Council so requests.)

Until the 1997 **Amsterdam Treaty**, legislation adopted under co-decision needed to complete a second reading. Since Amsterdam came into effect in May 1999, legislation may be adopted at first reading, if the Council agrees to the Parliament's amendments or if neither the Parliament nor Council wish to make any changes to the Commission proposal. This change was conceived as a practical improvement in the system, to enable uncontroversial proposals to be agreed more quickly. Over time, however, the possibility of negotiating 'first-reading agreements' between the Council and Parliament has altered the political dynamic of the co-decision procedure. Exploratory talks, very often leading to formal negotiations, between the two institutions (with the Commission present to facilitate agreement) are now the norm, in an attempt to see if it is possible to agree and then adopt a joint text at first reading, which then automatically becomes law.

The statistics point to a very significant rise in the share of co-decision legislation adopted at first reading, especially since 2004. According to the Parliament's own figures, from 1993 to 1999 (before Amsterdam), 61.4 per cent of relevant legislation was adopted at second reading and 38.6 per cent at third reading. In the 1999–2004 Parliament, 28.0 per cent was adopted at first reading, 50.1 per cent at second reading and 21.8 per cent at third reading. In the 2004–9 Parliament, a dramatic shift occurred: the respective figures were 72.0, 22.9 and 5.1 per cent. (The number of co-decision proposals tabled in each of the three time periods was 153, 403 and 454.)

The growing popularity of deals between the Parliament and Council at first reading has been attributed to many factors, some of which are procedural incentives. For example, there are no time limits at first reading, whereas there is a strict deadline of three to four months at second reading. Equally, the range of amendments that can be discussed at first reading is very wide, whereas only ones already adopted can be considered at subsequent readings. Moreover, to be adopted at first reading, amendments only need a simple majority in the Parliament, whereas they require an absolute majority at second reading. However, the primary driver of this phenomenon is political: the negotiation of first-reading agreements inevitably gives a substantial measure of latitude, and thus power, to the **rapporteur** in the Parliament and to the Council presidency, the two principal interlocutors in this exercise. Each is in a position of trust vis-à-vis their colleagues in (respectively) the relevant parliamentary committee and Council formation (in practice **COREPER**). Direct discussions between the rapporteur and a presidency representative (often the chairman of COREPER I) will be supplemented by 'trialogues' between a wider group on each side (including the Commission). In the Parliament's case, the negotiators usually include the chairman of the committee and 'shadow rapporteurs' designated by the various **political groups**. The parliamentary committee often has a vested interest in seeking and securing an agreement before the issue has to be considered in plenary, and then presenting it to their (non-specialist) colleagues as in effect a fait accompli. Within the Council, the presidency has an equal interest in pushing for first-reading agreements as a way of accelerating the law-making process and so maximizing the legislative achievements of its six-month term in office. Indeed, even the European Commission has an interest in such agreements, as the full, multi-reading process, played out in a string of plenary votes and Council positions, makes it more difficult in practice for the Commission to perform a role of 'facilitator' or 'honest broker' in the legislative dialogue. Indeed, once the conciliation committee is convened, the Commission loses its formal right to withdraw its legislative proposal, something it may still do, if it wishes, at first and second reading.

There has been considerable criticism of the rise of first-reading agreements. The relative informality of the negotiations makes it difficult for both Members of the European Parliament (MEPs) from other committees and for member-state governments other than the Council presidency to follow the discussion in detail. The leaderships of the political groups in the Parliament have expressed particular frustration at the way that first-reading agreements have further decentralized power in the institution and drained group meetings of much of their content. Outside interests and **national parliaments** equally feel excluded as decision-making occurs earlier and behind closed doors. The fact that first-reading negotiations take place in secret and that there is no 'paper trail' of formal voting on amendments in plenary makes the legislative process more opaque and less accessible. This is particularly ironic for the Parliament, which has long campaigned for greater transparency in the Council, and prides itself on holding its committee meetings in public, but has now in effect succumbed to importing some of the less attractive aspects of Council decision-making itself.

Not all parliamentary committees resort to first-reading agreements to the same degree. In the 2004–9 Parliament, the economic and monetary affairs committee used such agreements on 95 per cent of available opportunities (38 out of 40), whereas the transport committee did so only 39 per cent of the time (20 out of 52). However, only two committees came to first-reading agreements less than 50 per cent of the time. The environment committee, which had the largest number of co-decision measures before it (91 out of 454), concluded first-reading agreements on 63 per cent of possible occasions (57 out of 91).

In a further evolution of the concept of a first-reading agreement, since July 2009 there has been a tendency for some committees, notably the committee on economic and monetary affairs, to start negotiations with the Council only *after* the Parliament's amendments have been debated and voted upon in plenary, with the legislative proposal then immediately returned to committee *before* a formal first-reading vote takes place. The purpose of such a move may be to clarify which amendments enjoy the support of absolute majorities in plenary, where the committee itself is divided, or to put public pressure on the Council in advance of discussions. This approach was applied notably to the package of Commission proposals to enhance supervision of the financial services sector in July 2010 (with agreement reached with the Council two months later). The same idea of forcing a plenary vote on amendments and then returning the matter straight to committee was even applied *in the middle of* crucial first-reading negotiations with the Council on the 'Six Pack' of Commission proposals to strengthen aspects of the **Stability and Growth Pact** (SGP), in response to the ongoing **eurozone debt crisis**. The plenary voted on the amendments to the six legislative proposals in June 2011 and reached agreement with the Council three months later.

As first-reading agreements have become more common, the average length of time taken up in their negotiation has risen: from 11 months to 16 months between the 1999–2004 and 2004–9 Parliaments. The corresponding figure for second-reading agreements has also risen, from 24 to 30 months. The latter now tend to fall into one of two categories – either 'late' first-reading agreements, where the second reading is largely a formality or, conversely, particularly difficult disputes where each institution is testing the other to the very end, with the strong implicit threat of veto.

The Six Pack experience (referred to above) also reveals another interesting feature of the way co-decision currently works. The Parliament has become increasingly astute at exploiting the Commission's habit of putting forward several separate, but linked, legislative proposals on a subject, not all of which are formally to be decided by co-decision, to insist on their being adopted simultaneously, as a package, with the Parliament's agreement contingent on their all being handled as if co-decision applied. The former head of the Council's legal service, Jean-Claude Piris, has taken particular exception to this negotiating strategy, by which the Parliament has the chance in effect to exercise 'powers that were not conferred on it in the Treaties, therefore affecting the balance between the institutions' (*The Future of Europe: Towards a Two-Speed Europe?*, 2012). Such packages have recently given the Parliament additional leverage in law-making, not only on the Six Pack in 2011, but on the financial services' supervision package and the establishment of the **European External Action Service** (EEAS) in 2010. (In the first case, two of the six proposals were subject to the consultation procedure; in the second case, one of six proposals – the creation of the **European Systemic Risk Board** (ESRB) – was so; in the third case, easily the most important of the four legal acts in question – the Council decision to establish the EEAS itself – only required the Parliament to be consulted.)

The 1992 Maastricht Treaty first applied the co-decision procedure to 15 legal bases for various policies, including the **single market**, **free movement of persons**, **freedom of establishment**, **education policy**, **cultural policy**, health and **consumer policy**, **Trans-European Networks** (TENs) and aspects of **environment policy**. The 1997 Amsterdam Treaty extended the number of co-decision legal bases to 32, including **transport policy**, **development policy**, **non-discrimination**, fraud, some aspects of **social and employment policy**, and further aspects of environment policy. The 2001 Nice Treaty extended co-decision to cover a further five legal bases, including industrial policy, judicial cooperation in civil matters (within **Justice and Home Affairs** (JHA)), and arrangements for **European political parties**. Most recently, the Lisbon Treaty took this process a very significant step further, by introducing co-decision, from December 2009, to the **Common Agricultural Policy** (CAP), **Common Fisheries Policy** (CFP), **Common Commercial Policy** (CCP) and nearly all of JHA. Now, as part of the Union's 'ordinary legislative procedure', co-decision covers 83 of the 130 legal bases currently included in the Treaties.

Further reading: Richard Corbett, Francis Jacobs and Michael Shackleton, *The European Parliament*, 2011.

'Cohesion' and Cohesion Fund

The word 'cohesion' was introduced into the **Treaties** by the 1986 **Single European Act** (SEA), which added a new title on 'economic and social cohesion' – since widened to 'economic, social and territorial cohesion' (Articles 174–8 TFEU). Poorer member states feared that the completion of the **single market** would further strengthen the position of their more prosperous partners. As a quid pro quo for their acceptance of higher priority and faster decision-making for the single market, they insisted that the concept of cohesion, based on 'reducing disparities between the various regions and the backwardness of the least-favoured regions', should become an explicit objective of Community action. The various **structural funds** were to underpin this process, with measures to improve their coordination to be introduced.

In negotiating the 1992 **Maastricht Treaty**, the poorer member states were able to take this process a critical step further, by securing agreement that the Union would establish a special Cohesion Fund by December 1993. Its purpose is to 'provide a financial contribution to projects in the fields of environment and **Trans-European Networks** in the area of transport infrastructure' (Article 177 TFEU). A **protocol** to the treaty restricted access to the Cohesion Fund to member states with a per capita gross domestic product (GDP) of less than 90 per cent of the Union average – at the time Greece, Ireland, Portugal and Spain – whilst obliging them to pursue economic policies tending towards convergence, in preparation for full membership of **Economic and Monetary Union** (EMU). The fund finances up to 85 per cent of spending on eligible projects.

Expenditure from the EU **Budget** on the Cohesion Fund amounted to a total of some € 17 billion over the financing period 1993–9 and remained broadly static, at € 18 billion, for the period 2000–6. A review of beneficiaries' eligibility was undertaken in 2003, resulting in Ireland being excluded from 2004 and Spain's funding being phased out over several years. However, the **accession** of 12 new member states in 2004 and 2007, all with national incomes below 90 per cent of the Union average, necessitated a substantial increase in funding, which is now set at € 70 billion for the years 2007–13. EU spending on the Cohesion Fund amounted to € 7.6 billion in 2011. A Cohesion Report is published by the **European Commission** every three years, reviewing the operation of the fund.

Cold War

The Cold War is the term used to describe the long military and ideological competition between the United States and the Soviet Union – the two superpowers to emerge from the Second World War – that ran from the defeat of the Axis powers in 1945 to the collapse of Communism in central and eastern Europe in 1989–90. The phrase 'Cold War' was coined by the British essayist George Orwell in 1945 and was popularized by the American journalist Walter Lippmann in a book of the same title two years later.

The Cold War was prompted by the determination of Moscow to retain the territory it occupied at the end of the war – the **Baltic states** were incorporated into the USSR; Poland, Hungary, Bulgaria, Romania and Albania were converted into satellite states; Czechoslovakia was allowed a limited measure of democratic life until a Communist coup in 1948; and the eastern sector of Germany was instituted as a de facto state, the German Democratic Republic (GDR), in 1949. **Winston Churchill** spoke in Fulton, Missouri, in

1946 of an 'iron curtain' descending across Europe 'from Stettin in the Baltic to Trieste in the Adriatic'.

The US administration had initially planned to withdraw militarily from Europe as soon as practically possible after the war and displayed little interest in the idea of western European unification, looking to the development of the new global political and economic institutions – notably the **United Nations,** International Monetary Fund (IMF) and aborted International Trade Organization (ITO) – to structure the post-war order. Washington had hoped that all European countries (east and west), as well as the USSR, would be able to work together on a range of practical reconstruction issues in the UN **Economic Commission for Europe** (ECE), so avoiding the formation of political or military alliances in Europe or between Europe and the US. However, the complete refusal of the Soviet Union to accept the logic of this approach – combined with the huge economic problems and fragility of democracy evident in much of western Europe – forced a dramatic reappraisal of US policy in 1946–7.

In March 1947, resolutions were introduced into both houses of the US Congress advocating the creation of a '**United States of Europe**' as a counterpoise to Soviet domination in the east. The same month, President Harry Truman enunciated what soon became known as the **Truman Doctrine**, whereby the United States would 'support free peoples who are resisting attempted subjugation by armed minorities or by outside pressures'. This was followed three months later by the **Marshall Plan**, aimed at providing huge financial assistance to friendly European nations, matched by the path-breaking American insistence that this aid be administered by the recipient states through a new pan-European body, the **Organization for European Economic Cooperation** (OEEC). Washington was strongly supportive of the foundation of the **Council of Europe** in May 1949 and the drafting of the **European Convention on Human Rights** (ECHR) the following year. On the military front, the US concluded that it had no choice but to keep its troops in western Europe for as long as necessary. The US initiated the **Brussels Treaty** of March 1948 – so creating the 'Western Union' and a putative **European army** – and only widened this to include itself and Canada, through the **North Atlantic Treaty Organization** (NATO) in April 1949, when the Soviet blockade of Berlin in 1948–9 made its participation essential. The Soviet Union responded to the Marshall Plan and OEEC by creating **COMECON** in 1949 and then eventually matched NATO with the **Warsaw Pact** in 1955.

In the early years of the Cold War, the prospect of some kind of direct armed confrontation between the US and USSR seemed very real. Although the US and its European allies managed to beat off the Berlin blockade, the two superpowers were engaged soon after in a war in Korea (1950–53), though indirectly so in the case of the USSR. Nonetheless, Soviet air support for the North Koreans led many to fear a similar offensive against western Europe. However, ironically, the establishment and consolidation of a Soviet nuclear capability, starting in 1949, gradually generated a geo-political stalemate, based on a recognition that nuclear war would lead to 'mutual assured destruction'. Instead the Cold War confrontation became more evident in the arms race, space race, promotion of client states and subterranean activity by intelligence services. The United States did not intervene in autumn 1956 when Moscow clamped down brutally on the Hungarian uprising; in August 1961, when it sanctioned the construction of the Berlin Wall; or August 1968, when it suppressed the 'Prague Spring' in Czechoslovakia. In the latter case, Washington in effect accepted the **Brezhnev Doctrine** as the Soviet counterpoint to the Truman Doctrine. Conversely, the Soviet Union was cautious not to involve itself too directly in the Vietnam War (1959–75) – limiting itself to the supply of arms and some military advisers – so leaving it to the Americans to face defeat at the hands of local Communist insurgents, mirroring the ignominious retreat of the French from Indo-China in 1954.

The most serious challenges to this Cold War 'order' came when the Soviet Union overplayed its hand in Cuba in October 1962. Although US nuclear weapons were by now stationed in several western European countries, the attempted deployment of such weapons by the Soviet Union in Cuba, only a hundred miles from the US coastline, broke an implicit understanding about superpower 'spheres of influence', already under serious strain since the Cuban revolution in January 1959. Moscow reluctantly agreed to withdraw the missiles, after a week-long crisis during which the world genuinely seemed close to war.

The 1970s witnessed a striking thaw in tension between the US and USSR – which came to be known as *détente* – aided by the combined effects of domestic economic stagnation in the Soviet Union and the perception of American 'imperial overstretch' in Vietnam and elsewhere. The leaders of the two countries began to hold **summit** meetings, starting with Presidents Richard Nixon and Leonid Brezhnev in May 1972. Two arms control agreements, products of the SALT I and SALT II negotiations, were signed in 1972 and 1979. A human rights dialogue, one component of the **Conference on Security and Cooperation in Europe** (CSCE), led to the **Helsinki Final Act** of August 1975. East and West Germany established formal relations in 1972, encouraged by the *Ostpolitik* of Federal Chancellor Willy Brandt, which also saw normalization of relations with several other Warsaw Pact countries and the abandonment of any post-war German territorial claims. However, relations between the superpowers began to cool again, as Moscow unwisely became embroiled in an expansionist adventure in Afghanistan, starting in

December 1979, and reacted very negatively to the growth of the Solidarity trade union movement in Poland, prompted in part by the emergence of John Paul II as Pope.

The election of Ronald Reagan to the US presidency in November 1980 marked an important turning point in the history of the Cold War. Rather than seek to maintain the illusion of cooperation with the Soviet Union, Reagan was willing to confront the 'evil empire' both philosophically and practically. In this, he was able to draw on the support of the new British prime minister, **Margaret Thatcher**, whom Moscow dubbed the 'Iron Lady'. In a renewal of the arms race, the United States matched and exceeded Soviet spending on nuclear and conventional weapons, placing a growing financial burden on the USSR, a quarter of whose gross national product (GDP) was soon being spent on defence. The US deployed short-range and intermediate-range tactical nuclear weapons in western Europe and announced a 'Star Wars' project (the Strategic Defence Initiative) to counter the Soviet nuclear threat.

The emergence of Mikhail Gorbachev as Soviet leader in 1985 created the circumstances that were to bring this 'second Cold War' to a close. Against considerable resistance from established interests, Gorbachev embarked on a twin process of domestic economic reform, *perestroika*, and gradual political liberalization, *glasnost*, which in turn allowed a resumption of *détente*. A series of Reagan–Gorbachev summits culminated in a 1987 treaty to eliminate intermediate-range nuclear weapons from Europe. The Polish government recognized Solidarity in April 1989, allowing democratic elections in June, which the trade union movement won by a huge margin. A reformist-minded government in Hungary opened its frontier with Austria in August and the Berlin Wall was breached three months later – less than two and a half years after Reagan had, standing by the Brandenburg Gate, called on Gorbachev to 'tear down this wall'. The Soviet Union withdrew, defeated, from Afghanistan the same year.

The Cold War had a number of important consequences for European integration, especially in the immediate post-war years. The development of international institutions in western Europe, first of an intergovernmental and then of a supranational kind, were a direct product of the division of the continent into Soviet and non-Soviet blocs. From 1947 onwards, the United States played a particularly important role in promoting unification. It did this initially by sponsoring or assisting in the creation of the OEEC, Western Union and Council of Europe, and then, once the immediate objective of averting economic collapse and halting the advance of Communism had been achieved, by welcoming the thinking of **Jean Monnet** and others in favour of building an integrated European economy, with **sovereignty**-sharing institutions to underpin it.

Several key figures in Congress and the administration, such as Senator William Fulbright and Paul Hoffmann, chief administrator of the Marshall Plan, concluded that a high degree of integration would be necessary if Europe was to survive economically without permanent US support. As a Marshall Plan staff paper put it in July 1949: 'The basic disparity in Western Europe today is the fact that the particular size of the unit necessary for its continued, successful existence in the world economy is larger than the actual size of existing political units' (quoted in Max Beloff, *The United States and the Unity of Europe*, 1963). The prophetic conclusion drawn was that western Europe should develop 'a single, pervasive and highly competitive domestic market . . . of sufficient size and scope to support mass production for mass consumption. This requires the elimination of barriers to the **free movement** of goods, persons and ultimately capital.' The basic institutional needs would be an independent 'Intra-European Commerce Commission', with free-standing executive authority, and a judicial mechanism to adjudicate on disputes in a way that was binding on individual states.

Jean Monnet had spent much of the war in Washington and had been impressed by the role of independent regulatory agencies – notably the Interstate Commerce Commission – in the US system. It was only a short jump from the common analysis which he and US policy-makers increasingly shared about what needed to be done in Europe to a position of official US support for the creation of a **European Coal and Steel Community** (ECSC) in 1950 and subsequent efforts at supranational integration later in the decade, including even acceptance of the unsuccessful **European Defence Community** (EDC). The US regretted that the United Kingdom refused to take part in the ECSC process – and some in Congress even suggested that financial aid to Britain should be cut off until it agreed to take part – but the bigger prize of the 'economic unification and political integration of Europe', as one act of Congress put it, was too important to be held back by doubts in London. The British advocacy of a **free trade area** in Europe, as an alternative to the **customs union** and **common market** of the **European Economic Community** (EEC), found little echo in Washington. Maintained successively by the Truman, Eisenhower and Kennedy administrations, the momentum of US pro-Europeanism was broken only in the mid-1960s by a combination of Gaullist obstruction in Europe and the distracting effects of the Vietnam War in Washington.

The United States consistently favoured the sometimes faltering efforts of the member states of the European Community to put in place a closer degree of foreign policy coordination, which it correctly calculated would be pursued within an 'Atlantic framework'. It welcomed the development of **European Political Cooperation** (EPC) in the 1970s and 1980s, and did nothing to impede the inclusion of a more ambitious **Common Foreign and**

Security Policy (CFSP) in the 1992 **Maastricht Treaty**. However, in practice, the superpower confrontation made it impossible for western Europe to develop a common foreign policy that might diverge in any significant way from that of Washington. An appreciation of this reality helps explain why the attempt by French President **Charles de Gaulle** in the early 1960s to launch one was received with such caution and was eventually rebuffed by the other EC member states.

In 1969, Henry Kissinger wrote that American policy 'has urged European unity while recoiling before its probable consequences'. The end of the Cold War has permitted the European Union, if it wishes, to develop as a self-reliant, stable and independent partner to the United States. To do so, however, would require the Union to display a higher level of strategic ambition, a greater degree of political consistency and unity, and a much bigger willingness to finance military capabilities than events since 1990 so far – notably the Balkans crisis and Iraq war – suggest is likely to be forthcoming.

COMECON

The Council for Mutual Economic Assistance – known variously as COMECON or CMEA – was established by the Soviet Union in January 1949 to promote economic cooperation and integration between the Communist states of central and eastern Europe. In addition to the USSR, the founder members were Bulgaria, Czechoslovakia, Hungary, Poland and Romania – countries that had been prevented by Stalin from taking part in the **Marshall Plan** and from joining the parallel **Organization for European Economic Cooperation** (OEEC). Membership was later extended to Albania (1949–61), the German Democratic Republic (1950), and a number of non-European Communist states: Mongolia (1962), Cuba (1972) and Vietnam (1978). Although all decisions within COMECON had theoretically to be agreed unanimously among member states, the organization was dominated from the start by the Soviet Union, which hosted its headquarters in Moscow. It became a de facto international economic planning agency for the USSR, defining the specialization of production between Soviet bloc countries. In effect, COMECON was the economic equivalent of the military alliance embodied in the **Warsaw Pact**.

The first tentative contacts between COMECON and the European Community took place in 1976, at a time when the Soviet Union was still barely prepared to recognize the Community and when the latter in turn disputed COMECON's right to negotiate on behalf of its member states. Unsurprisingly, these contacts led to no concrete result and were broken off in 1980 following the Soviet invasion of Afghanistan. During the 1980s, the Community concluded bilateral commercial agreements (in most cases limited to specific sectors) with Bulgaria, Czechoslovakia, Hungary, Poland

and Romania. Negotiations with COMECON were resumed in 1986 and resulted in a mutual recognition agreement two years later.

The collapse of the Soviet empire in central and eastern Europe in 1989–90 completely transformed trading patterns between COMECON states and led to the strongest of their economies, the German Democratic Republic (GDR), becoming part of the European Community through **German reunification**. In June 1991, the remaining members of COMECON resolved to wind the organization up; this was formally accomplished in September 1991. Subsequently, all central and eastern European countries that had been COMECON members applied to join the European Union, concluded Europe Agreements with the Union, and eventually acceded to the Union in either 2004 or 2007.

Comitology

The word 'comitology', one of the least understood in the lexicon of EU decision-making, refers to the process by which the **European Commission** is empowered to adopt certain types of administrative law. The use of the Commission's powers in this field is routed through a complex web of official-level committees, comprised of national civil servants, which the Commission itself chairs. The role of these committees has given rise to disputes with a direct bearing on the balance of power between the member states and the institutions of the Union, and between the institutions themselves. Not yet fully assimilated into English, 'comitology' is a translation of the French *comitologie.* Its first recorded use was in C. Northcote Parkinson's book, *Parkinson's Law* (1958), and it was defined in his *In-laws and Outlaws* (1962) as the study of committees and how they operate ('the latest of the biological sciences').

From the start, the **Treaty of Rome** empowered the Commission to adopt law directly, without the involvement of any other institutions or representatives, on specific matters in a very small number of policy fields. Today, these relate to particular aspects of **competition policy** (Articles 105–6 TFEU) and **free movement of persons** (Article 45(3) TFEU). However, the treaty also envisaged that the Commission might, more routinely, be devolved the right to adopt what are now called 'delegated' or 'implementing' acts to fill in the details of **EU law** across a wider span of policies. The Commission was permitted to exercise 'powers conferred on it by the **Council** [**of Ministers**] for the implementation of the rules laid down by the latter' (Article 211 EEC, since repealed). These implementing powers – now normally entrusted to the Commission by the Council and **European Parliament** jointly under the **co-decision procedure** – involve the formal adoption of **legal acts** by the Commission and are akin to 'statutory instruments' in the United Kingdom. Each such measure – which may take the form of a Commission **directive**,

regulation or **decision** – is subject to the supervision and (sometimes) approval of one of over 250 'comitology committees', all of which are composed of national experts, representing the governments of the member states, with a Commission official in the chair. Although the subject matter of these committees is for the most part highly technical – for example, the authorization of seed types, food additives or the thickness of safety glass – the questions being decided upon are often of very great concern to interested parties, and the committees' executive-dominated mode of operation (with 'bureaucrat talking to bureaucrat') has prompted fears about the extent to which decision-making in this field is subject to adequate democratic control.

Even though in 2009, 1,808 implementing measures were adopted by comitology committees, the basic institutional concept underpinning them has long reflected a pattern of Community decision-making – based on a dialogue between the Commission and the member states – which prevailed from the 1950s to 1980s, before the European Parliament became a major player in the legislative process in its own right. As a result, the Parliament's attitude towards comitology has always been much less sanguine than that of the other institutions. It has fought a consistent campaign to open up the committees' proceedings, with a view to it being able to express a view on, and ideally exercise a veto over, impending comitology decisions. In 1987, it forced the Commission and Council to clarify the type and number of comitology committees. A Council decision in July that year identified three basic types of committee (the first of which still survives, but the second and third of which have since been superseded):

- *advisory committees*, in which the Commission needs simply to 'take the utmost account' of the committee's opinion on its proposal and inform it of whether and how that opinion has been taken into account. Such committees, which operate by simple majority and in effect give the Commission almost complete discretion, have mostly been used for relatively routine decisions, such as the awarding of small grants by the Commission;
- *management committees*, in which the Commission could adopt its proposal so long as the committee, acting by **qualified majority voting** (QMV), did not reject it. (The voting weight of each member state representative in the committee corresponded to that in the Council of Ministers.) Where no opinion was adopted, the proposal took immediate effect. Where the proposal was rejected, it was referred to the Council, which could, within three months, adopt an alternative by QMV; if it failed to do so, the original Commission proposal was then deemed adopted. Management committees were the earliest form of comitology committee, being used from 1961 for the detailed

implementation of the **Common Agricultural Policy** (CAP). They were subsequently used for similar decisions under the **Common Fisheries Policy** (CFP) and **structural funds.**

- *regulatory committees*, in which the Commission could only proceed if it obtained a qualified majority in favour of its proposal. Any proposal failing to secure positive approval was referred to the Council, which had three months in which to act (again by QMV). If the Council failed to act, the Commission proposal was deemed adopted. Some regulatory committees dealt with quite politically sensitive issues, such as the authorization of genetically-modified organisms (GMOs).

The choice of which type of committee to use in any particular case was determined on an ad hoc basis (in each piece of originating legislation) – a situation that was clearly unsatisfactory. In June 1999, the Council updated the 1987 comitology decision, in order to set out some (non-binding) criteria for the choice of committees in the originating legislation. Henceforth, the 'management' procedure would normally be used for measures related to the agricultural and fisheries policies, as well as for 'the implementation of programmes with substantial budgetary implications'. The 'regulatory' procedure was to be applied for 'measures of general scope designed to apply essential provisions of basic instruments' and 'measures designed to adapt or update certain non-essential provisions' of such instruments. In parallel, each committee was required to adopt rules of procedure and make many of its documents – draft proposals and the agendas and minutes of meetings – available to the public for the first time. The European Parliament was to be 'informed by the Commission of committee proceedings on a regular basis' and was given a one-month right of scrutiny – known as the *droit de regard* – to force the Commission to re-examine any proposal (under the regulatory committee procedure) that it believed would 'exceed the implementing powers' extended to the executive in the originating legislation.

Despite these modest efforts towards greater openness, the striking asymmetry in the positions of the Council and Parliament in the comitology process became more evident, and more difficult to defend, as successive treaty changes increased the use of the **co-decision procedure** in EU law-making. In the areas covered by co-decision, the Parliament enjoyed equal power to the Council in defining the content of the originating legislation, but still had no formal say over any implementing measures adopted under it. An attempt was made to address this inconsistency during the **Convention on the Future of Europe** in 2002–3. The resulting draft **European Constitution** proposed, in a change carried forward into the **Lisbon Treaty**, that co-decision be extended to cover legislation setting the rules on comitology itself. This means that, instead of the Council establishing the architecture and modalities of the committee system unilaterally (on the basis of a Commission proposal for a Council decision), regulations on the subject now have to be adopted jointly with the Parliament.

In a further, very important, concession to the Parliament, the European Constitution proposed to create, and the Lisbon Treaty has since instituted, a new category of administrative law over which the Parliament can exercise a veto. Certain types of important implementing acts, deemed to be of a 'quasi-legislative' character, were redefined as being 'delegated acts'. Such acts correspond to part of the comitology measures previously adopted through regulatory committees, namely those that make changes of 'general application to supplement or amend certain non-essential elements of the [originating] legislative act' (Article 290 TFEU). Where changes relate to 'essential elements', they still require new originating legislation. The Commission's use of delegated powers may be blocked by either the Council (acting by qualified majority) or the Parliament (by a majority of its component members); the delegation of such powers may also be revoked by either institution, at any time, for any reason, in the future.

The new régime for delegated acts came into effect automatically in December 2009, with the entry into force of the Lisbon Treaty. The two branches of the legislature simply define, on a case by case basis, the scope, content and practical arrangements for any delegation of power. To smooth the process, however, a 'common understanding' between the institutions, agreed in March 2011, has identified certain standard clauses for inclusion in delegated acts. As any draft delegated act now goes straight to the Council and Parliament, rather than via a regulatory committee, there is no longer any 'early warning' system to flag up likely problems with a draft proposal. It was agreed that the Council or Parliament would each aim to express any objections within two months of the proposal being published. In April 2011, the Parliament voted, for the first time, to reject a delegated act. A measure to authorize a particular type of breast milk substitute was opposed by 328 to 323 votes, with 26 abstentions; however, because the number of members voting against the Commission regulation fell below the absolute majority required (369 votes), the proposal could still proceed to adoption.

The new post-Lisbon arrangements on 'implementing acts' (or classic comitology), now defined in Article 291 TFEU, were set down in a regulation adopted by the Council and Parliament, by co-decision, in December 2010. Whilst the 'advisory' procedure continues to exist, the 'management' and 'regulatory' procedures were in effect merged, with the creation of a new 'examination' procedure. This latter procedure is henceforth to be used for implementing acts in the fields of the CAP, CFP, **environment policy**, financial services, taxation, and human, animal or plant safety. Other policy areas are usually subject to the advisory procedure, if implementing acts are required.

Under the examination committee, if the Commission secures a qualified majority in favour of an implementing act, it is immediately adopted. Conversely, if the committee votes against a proposal by QMV, it falls. In the case of rejection, the proposal proceeds not to the Council, as before, but to a new appeals committee, composed of member-state civil servants. This can in turn either approve or reject the proposal, again by qualified majority. However, where no opinion either way is delivered by the examination committee, the Commission can adopt the measure, unless an absolute majority of the member states votes against it or unless it falls within certain sensitive policy fields – notably taxation, financial services and human, animal or plant safety. The presumption is therefore that, in most policy fields and in the absence of a hostile qualified majority, the Commission will ultimately get its way. Both the Parliament and Council (not just the Parliament) now enjoy a general *droit de regard* at any time, even if not a right of veto.

It is as yet unclear whether the latest post-Lisbon changes to comitology – introducing the distinction between 'delegated' and 'implementing' acts, and reducing to two the number of committee types for handling the latter – will make any significant difference to the way the system operates in practice. Although nearly all the reforms that have occurred, starting in the mid-1980s, have pointed in the direction of greater openness and potential politicization of comitology decision-making, the reality is that this field has stubbornly remained a *chasse gardée* of technocrats and experts. Enjoying a **right of initiative** in this, as in all other aspects of EU law-making, the Commission has retained, and fully exploited, its strategic advantage in the comitology process, even if its preference for the use of advisory committees over other procedures has not always found favour with the other institutions. In any case, sometimes there can be no entirely objective way of determining which procedure should apply or indeed whether comitology should be used at all. The distinction between, for example, 'essential' and 'non-essential' elements of a law is ultimately subjective, as is the exact meaning of phrases such as 'measures of general scope' or 'substantial budgetary implications'.

In the traditional field of what are now called 'implementing acts', the Commission tends to be highly adept at enlisting the support of the national experts who serve on the various comitology committees and is quick to appreciate the need to make adjustments if they identify practical problems with proposed measures. References up to the Council have in the past only happened very rarely: in less than a quarter of one per cent of cases in most years. It is true that the committees sometimes fail to act, or indeed reject Commission proposals, if they are subject to intense lobbying or media scrutiny, as has happened recently on some decisions to authorize the use of

GMOs. In such cases, the recent change in the rules would appear to make it less likely that a Commission proposal will simply be adopted by default.

Since the Lisbon Treaty entered into force, it has become increasingly apparent that, unlike the Commission or Parliament, the Council is proving unexpectedly reluctant to see the systematic inclusion of the option of delegated acts in legislative texts. In certain (but not all) policy areas, the member states prefer to rely on implementing acts – where they can retain the traditional comitology committees – even if formally this usually gives them less power to exercise a veto. Alternatively, they seem to prefer that the originating legislation should go into greater detail and that any updates be made in the same form (rather than by delegated or implementing acts at all). This issue has already generated disputes in relation to various EU programmes in the external relations field and could feature prominently in consideration by the Council and Parliament of EU programmes in many policy areas for the 2014–20 financing period.

Finally, it is worth noting that special arrangements have applied to comitology in the financial services sector for some years. Following a report in February 2001 by Alexandre Lamfalussy, the former President of the **European Monetary Institute** (EMI), the Union developed three committees of national regulators for the banking, insurance and securities sectors, which were given the responsibility inter alia for proposing to the Commission the various comitology measures which the latter would then consider, and formally adopt, in a compressed timescale. This in effect reversed the traditional comitology procedure, whereby the Commission made proposals to the member states. In January 2011, these three committees were converted into EU **agencies** – the European Banking Authority (EBA), the European Insurance and Occupational Pensions Authority (EIOPA) and the European Securities and Markets Authority (ESMA) – with the power to propose either delegated or implementing acts (known as 'regulatory' or implementing technical standards respectively) to the Commission, on a similar basis. The delegated acts are subject to potential Council or Parliament veto in the normal way.

Further reading: Alan Hardacre and Michael Kaeding, *The Lisbon Treaty and the New Comitology: Delegated and Implementing Acts*, 2011; Roger Scully and Rinus van Schendelen (editors), *The Unseen Hand: Unelected EU Legislators*, 2003.

Committee of the Regions

The 1992 **Maastricht Treaty** established a new European Union advisory body, the Committee of the Regions. Originally proposed by Germany and

Spain – the first a federal state and the second a country with a significant degree of devolution – the creation of the Committee was a response to the growth of regional consciousness within the Union. The same treaty, in a parallel move, entrenched **subsidiarity** as a principle of **EU law**. Like the **European Economic and Social Committee** (EESC), the Committee of the Regions, 'acting in an advisory capacity', is meant to 'assist' the legislative and policy-making institutions of the Union – the **European Commission**, **Council of Ministers** and **European Parliament** – in their work (Article 13(4) TEU). The Committee superseded a 42-member 'consultative council' of regional and local authorities that had advised the European Commission from 1988 to 2004.

The Committee of the Regions is composed of 'representatives of regional and local bodies' who must either have been elected to such a body or be 'politically accountable to an elected assembly' (Article 300 TFEU). The exact size of the Committee, which may not exceed 350 members, and its composition by member state, is determined by the Council, acting unanimously, on a proposal from the Commission. There are currently 344 members, who are complemented by an equal number of alternates. The members and alternates of the Committee are appointed by the Council in line with proposals received from each member state. The size of the Committee has always mirrored that of the EESC (starting at 222 in 1994) and, though it may theoretically differ, the distribution by member state is currently the same. Like that of the EESC, the Committee's term of office was, until the **Lisbon Treaty**, four years. It has now been lengthened to five years, to correspond to the terms of the Commission and Parliament, even if these terms are not synchronized. Members of the Committee now elect their office-holders – notably the President, 28 Vice-Presidents and other members of its Bureau – every two and a half years, as in the Parliament. Members of the Committee are paid no salary, but receive travel and accommodation expenses.

Much of the detailed work of the Committee of the Regions is done in six committees, known in English as 'commissions' to avoid linguistic confusion, each comprising around 100 members. **Rapporteurs**, chosen to reflect the political balance within the Committee, are appointed to draft the opinions on the legislative proposals referred to the Committee and other reports. These opinions and reports are prepared in the commissions and then adopted in plenary meetings. Such plenaries take place six times a year, usually in the premises of the European Parliament, and adopt an average of around 60 opinions a year.

The members have formed **political groups** which are increasingly influential in the politics of the Committee. Currently there are four such groups: the European People's Party (EPP) Group, the Party of European Socialists

(PES) Group, the Alliance of Liberals and Democrats for Europe (ALDE) Group, and the European Alliance (EA) Group (formerly the Union for a Europe of Nations (UEN) Group).

Consultation of the Committee of the Regions, both by the European Commission and, since the Lisbon Treaty, by the European Parliament, is specifically required by the **Treaties** in respect of a series of policy areas with a direct bearing on regional and local government. These are economic, social and territorial **cohesion**, **Trans-European Networks** (TENs), health, education, culture, the environment, employment, vocational training and transport. (These fields were first defined in the Maastricht Treaty and extended by the 1997 **Amsterdam Treaty**.) Here, the Committee adopts opinions directed to the Commission, Council and Parliament. They must be delivered within any time limit set by the institutions, and in the absence of an opinion being received, the latter may act anyway (Article 307 TFEU). In addition, the institutions may consult the Committee whenever they wish, and the Committee itself may, on its own initiative, submit opinions or pass resolutions on other matters affecting regional interests.

The Committee of the Regions finds itself in competition with the regional committee of the European Parliament, as well as with other bodies that claim to represent regional interests within the Union. The Lisbon Treaty granted the Committee the right to take action before the **European Court of Justice** (ECJ) where it considers that the principle of **subsidiarity** has been infringed by EU legislative action (Protocol 2, Article 8).

The Committee of the Regions has its own secretariat (of some 500 staff), headed by a secretary general appointed by the Committee's Bureau for five years. Certain common services are operated jointly with the EESC. The two bodies share their headquarters, at 99–101 rue Belliard, and five other buildings in Brussels.

Common Agricultural Policy (CAP)

From its launch in the early 1960s, the Common Agricultural Policy quickly emerged as the most important European policy in terms of the number of people directly affected, its share of the European Community **Budget** and the extent of the powers transferred from national to European level. Its origins may be traced back to the original compact between France and West Germany when the **Treaty of Rome** was being drafted by **the Six**: guaranteed markets for French agricultural products in exchange for wider markets for German manufactured goods.

The objectives of the CAP were set out in Article 39 EEC, now Article 39 TFEU, and have remained unchanged in successive revisions of the **Treaties**. They are to 'increase agricultural productivity by promoting technical progress and by ensuring the rational development of agricultural production', to 'ensure a fair standard of living for the agricultural community', to 'stabilize markets', to 'assure the availability of supplies' and to 'ensure that supplies reach consumers at reasonable prices'. Underpinning these objectives were three essential principles, pointing in not entirely consistent directions: the **free movement** of agricultural products between member states, 'Community preference' vis-à-vis foreign producers, and 'financial solidarity' between member states, with all sharing in the costs arising from the policy.

That agriculture should be publicly subsidized was not in doubt in the late 1950s, since in common with all other European countries, the Six already supported their farming sectors in various ways. Serious food shortages after the Second World War, compounded by fears of a mass exodus from the countryside to cities (as after the First World War), underpinned a broad consensus in favour of high food prices in many countries. However, because of significant differences in the precise policies operating among the Six, the member states concluded that, as John Paxton wrote soon after, it was simply 'not possible to remove the obstacles to trade by applying to agriculture the same procedures as [applied to] manufactured goods'. Instead, they 'decided to abolish all existing national [agricultural] policies and to establish a Community policy' that would be centrally financed and have a dedicated policy towards trade with third countries (*The Structure and Development of the Common Market*, 1968).

In seeking to establish the basis for a common system, the Community opted critically for support by means of guaranteed prices for individual agricultural products, rather than by direct income support for farmers. This choice, which emerged from the Stresa Conference in July 1958, was to be made operational through a series of Community-wide 'market organizations' or 'régimes' for particular products (Article 40 EEC, now Article 40 TFEU). The first such arrangements were brought into effect in 1962, under intense pressure from the French government. The full CAP was applied to beef, veal and milk from 1964; to olive oil from 1966; to cereals, pork, eggs, poultry meat, rice, sugar, and oils and fats from 1967; to processed fruit and vegetables from 1968; and to wine, tobacco, flax and hemp from 1970.

Under the system that evolved, the **European Commission** would propose, and the **Council of Ministers** adopt, a guaranteed price for each product every year. If the price that could be obtained for that product within the Community fell below the agreed price, unsold produce would be purchased and taken into intervention and stored for future sale or disposal. If the produce could be sold outside the Union but only at a price below the agreed price, then the producer became entitled to an 'export refund' to cover the difference. Each product was further protected by the imposition of levies on competing imports. These arrangements were at the most interventionist end of the scale of options envisaged in Article 40, which said that the 'common organization of agricultural markets' could be established, depending on the product, either by common rules on competition, or 'compulsory coordination' of the various national markets, or by 'a European market organization'. The seeds were sown for what became in effect a miniature 'planned' economy in the agricultural sector.

The CAP had the desired effect fairly quickly in enabling the member states to achieve self-sufficiency in most temperate products, backed by relatively stable prices and a growth in farm incomes. It secured the latter at a time when agriculture was shrinking as a share of the European economy – a significant transition it facilitated without undue hardship – and personal expenditure on food (as a share of consumer spending overall) was falling in most industrialized countries.

However, the Commission also discovered that the repercussions of guaranteeing prices were more serious than it had anticipated, especially the inherent risk of overproduction. Its first attempt to reform the CAP, by unwinding some of the choices made at its foundation, came as early as December 1968, with the publication of the Mansholt Plan. Predicting a growing structural surplus in farm production, the Commission sought to reduce the number of people employed in agriculture and to encourage the formation of larger, more efficient units of production. Although the plan ran into serious resistance from the very vested interests that the CAP had itself already entrenched, some of the proposals were adopted in diluted form by the Council in 1972, and the basic design sketched in the document set the pattern for future efforts to adjust and contain the CAP, which were renewed a decade later.

It is easy to understand why the treaty objectives of the CAP, drawn up at a time when food shortages in western Europe were still a vivid memory, placed such emphasis on safeguarding and boosting agricultural supply. However, by the early 1980s, greater productivity, backed by technical progress, was resulting in huge, unsaleable surpluses of certain products, at an enormous cost to the Community Budget. The taxpayer was in effect paying twice over, first through higher prices and second through subsidized storage or disposal of unwanted produce. Moreover, as demographic change continued to shrink the agricultural workforce – from 20 per cent among the Six in 1958 to 4.5 per cent among the EU15 in 2000 – so the political imperative of defending the CAP receded. Added to this were growing pressures from international trading partners. Even though the Community became the world's largest importer of agricultural products, there were increasingly acrimonious trade disputes with third countries, notably the United States and Australia, and a growing awareness that subsidized exports were doing damage to other countries' export markets. Notorious episodes like the repeated sale of cut-price butter to the Soviet Union in the 1980s further damaged the credibility of the CAP with the public.

Against this backdrop, the Commission felt able in 1983 and 1985 to present proposals for a much more ambitious reform of the CAP than the Mansholt Plan had envisaged. These were designed to bring supply and demand into closer balance, cut back on open-ended price support, compensate farmers directly for their loss of income, and introduce new mechanisms (known as 'stabilizers') for reducing production still further in certain problem sectors. The latter included most notably milk quotas, agreed by the Council in 1984, which were applied at the level of individual holdings, within a framework of production limits for each member state. In February 1988, following significant overruns in CAP spending, EC heads of government, meeting in the **European Council**, agreed to extend quotas to other agricultural products and to introduce a voluntary 'set-aside' scheme. (In order to fight overproduction, farmers would receive compensation for leaving a part of their arable land fallow.) The specific needs of the rural economy were to be addressed by the various 'Leader' programmes, starting in 1991. They also agreed to an 'agricultural guideline' limiting the growth of CAP expenditure to just under three-quarters of future rises in the EC Budget overall.

The process was taken a critical stage further with the tabling of a round of even more radical reform proposals by Ray MacSharry, the Irish Commissioner responsible for agriculture, in 1991. The centrepiece of the measures was a move away from near-total reliance on price support towards direct income aids – the 'decoupling' of income from production – a shift which has been echoed in all subsequent CAP reforms. At a 50-hour 'marathon' session in May 1992, agriculture ministers agreed to cuts in the guaranteed support prices for cereals, beef and butter, in return for which new, flat-rate payments per hectare were introduced. These changes were flanked by measures to encourage early retirement from agriculture, the compulsory extension of set-aside (except for small producers), and schemes to encourage farmers to use less intensive production methods ('extensification'). One important advantage of 'decoupling' was that it helped make EU farm subsidies more compatible with the rules on agricultural support set by the World Trade Organization (WTO).

The logic of the MacSharry reforms was maintained seven years later, when, as part of the Santer Commission's Agenda 2000 programme, the European Council agreed in Berlin in March 1999 to accelerate 'decoupling' through further reductions in the support prices for cereals, beef and butter, matched by stronger moves towards direct income support. Agenda 2000 also reoriented the objectives of agricultural policy to place greater emphasis on the environment. It made an integrated rural development policy the 'second pillar' of the CAP, alongside its traditional market expenditure and new income support (the first pillar). As part of the seven-year financial perspectives for 2000–06, agricultural expenditure was effectively frozen in real terms and spending on rural development was increased from 5 to 10 per cent of the total. However, the impact of the 2004 enlargement forced CAP expenditure to grow by a quarter during the remainder of the seven-year period.

The 2000–06 financing arrangements also foresaw a midterm review of CAP priorities in 2002. This review, conducted by the Austrian Commissioner for agriculture, Franz Fischler, led in June 2003 to the 'Luxembourg agreement' among farm ministers, which envisaged further important reforms. The deal broadened the move to direct income support, so that progressively it would cover all sectors, began the process of merging all payments to producers into a 'single farm payment', based on land rather than production, and provided for an automatic transfer of part of CAP spending towards wider rural development ('modulation'), on a rising curve, year by year. It also instituted a special 'financial discipline' in 'pillar one' spending, whereby automatic cuts in payments would be made to compensate for any sign of likely overspending. The planned extension of CAP reform sector-by-sector was maintained with the 2004 'Mediterranean package' for olive oil, tobacco, hops and cotton, and the 2006–8 reforms for wine, sugar, and fruit and vegetables. The 2008 'health check' for the CAP continued in the same direction, with a gradual phasing out of milk quotas (by 2015), a further strengthening of the 'single payment' scheme and increased use of modulation.

The sums involved in CAP spending are substantial. In 2011, the twin pillars of the CAP – market expenditure and income support, on the one hand, and rural development, on the other – accounted for € 42.8 and € 12.6 billion respectively (out of a total Union Budget of € 126.5 billion). However, as a result of successive reforms and improved budgetary discipline, the share of total EU spending devoted to agriculture has been falling fairly steadily for some time. Whereas the CAP represented some 70 per cent of the Budget in 1980, the proportion declined to 60 per cent in 1990, 51 per cent in 2000 and 43 per cent in 2011. Its share of the Union's total GDP has fallen from 0.54 per cent in 1990 to 0.43 per cent today. The share of rural development in total CAP spending now represents almost a quarter – a target originally advocated by the **European Parliament** in the mid-1980s. State support for producers as a percentage of gross farm receipts in the EU dropped from 35 to 20 per cent during the period 1995–2010. (The comparable shares fell from 62 to 50 per cent in Japan and from 10 to eight per cent in the United States, but rose from 15 to 20 per cent in Russia and from six to 17 per cent in China.) The biggest CAP payments go to major landowners and to industrial food producers: the largest single subsidy to date was € 180 million, given to ICBPI, the clearing-house for a network of Italian banks in 2009. Future CAP reform may well involve the placing of a ceiling on the absolute level of support which can be received by any individual or company.

Among the five largest EU member states, all countries except the United Kingdom receive annual payments in excess of € 5.0 billion from the CAP (and in France's case as much as € 9.7 billion). However, Britain's receipts have always been proportionately much lower – amounting to only € 3.7 billion in 2009. If the average EU member state receives CAP payments of 0.43 per cent of GDP, the UK obtains payments of only 0.23 per cent. This discrepancy has been the single most important reason for Britain facing a disproportionately high gross contribution to the EU Budget – a problem reflected in the **British Budget dispute** and the **abatement** solution provided by the **Fontainebleau Agreement** in 1984. The UK's low CAP receipts are produced by its smaller and relatively more efficient agricultural sector – in part the result of an agricultural revolution two centuries ago – compounded by a history of access to 'cheap food', by virtue of the Empire and Commonwealth connection. Countries such as Australia and New Zealand resented the loss of British markets as a consequence of the UK's accession to the Community in 1973, a loss only partially compensated for by special arrangements for butter and lamb. In time, they became leading members of the Cairns Group of countries fiercely critical within the WTO of the Union's agricultural subsidies and export refunds.

CAP funding was for many years channelled through the European Agricultural Guidance and Guarantee Fund (EAGGF, more commonly known by its French acronym, FEOGA), which was set up in 1962 and divided into two sections in 1964 – the very large 'guarantee' section responsible for the price support of European agriculture (the largest single component of the Budget by far), and the smaller 'guidance' section assisting in the development of farm structures and of rural areas. From the start of the 2007–13 financing period, this system was replaced by two 'new' funds that correspond to the twin pillars of the reformed CAP: a European Agricultural Guarantee Fund (EAGF) to finance market measures and income support (encompassing most of the old EAGGF guarantee section) and a European Agricultural Fund for Rural Development (EAFRD), which took over the old EAGGF guidance section and the Leader programme plus some limited components of the previous EAGGF guarantee section. The two funds now fall under the 'preservation and management of natural resources' heading of the Union's Budget, which includes expenditure on agriculture, rural development, fisheries and the environment.

For several decades, the operation of the CAP was further complicated by the 'agri-monetary' system of so-called 'green currencies'. The breakdown in

1969 of the Bretton Woods international monetary system resulted in a degree of price instability that was in conflict with the treaty objective of 'stable markets' for agriculture. Accordingly, a method for converting CAP prices (set in the **European Currency Unit** (ECU)) into the national currencies in which farmers were actually paid ('green rates') was introduced, together with monetary compensatory amounts (MCAs) to be paid or levied on member states' trade in agricultural products, to prevent any exploitation of the difference between market rates and green rates. Initially introduced on a temporary basis, the agri-monetary system was a central feature of the CAP for over 20 years, and was eventually modified as part of the 1992 reforms. The new system, which applied to the bulk of CAP expenditure (as well as spending on the **Common Fisheries Policy** (CFP)), eliminated MCAs as incompatible with the **single market** and brought green rates and market rates into closer alignment. The creation of **European Monetary Union** (EMU) and the adoption of the **euro** by a majority of member states has significantly simplified this cumbersome system and reduced its costs.

The successive rounds of CAP reform have not altered the procedures under which the policy is adopted and managed. Within the Council, the CAP has been subject to **qualified majority voting** (QMV) since 1966 and was largely unaffected by the **Luxembourg Compromise**, at least where use of QMV did not challenge French interests. The meetings of agriculture ministers are themselves prepared by a Special Committee for Agriculture (of national agricultural officials), in effect bypassing **COREPER**. Within the Commission, each product covered by the CAP has its own 'examination committee' (previously known as management committee), operating under **comitology** procedures: a large volume of implementing legislation has been passed each year through this process. Until the **Lisbon Treaty**, the European Parliament could only give an opinion on draft CAP legislation – under the **consultation procedure** – without the right of **co-decision**. The powerlessness of the Parliament was compounded by the designation of much of CAP spending as **compulsory expenditure** within the Budget, so that its amendments could be overruled by the Council.

The cumulative effect of these arrangements was to maximize the prospect of CAP proposals being adopted, and to minimize the impact of non-agricultural forces, including for many years that of finance ministers, on decision-making within the EU. Agricultural policy became something of a self-contained *chasse gardée*, dominated by the 'iron triangle' (as American political scientists would call it) of national farm ministers, the Commission directorate-general for agriculture and agricultural lobbies organized at European level. The latter – notably the Committee of Agricultural Organizations of the EU (COPA) and the General Committee for

Agricultural Cooperation in the EU (COGECA) – have traditionally enjoyed privileged access to policy-makers. The imposition of the multiannual 'financial perspectives' from the late 1980s was a critical move in subjecting both the Commission and farm ministers to a serious measure of budgetary discipline in the CAP sphere.

More recently, the introduction of the Lisbon Treaty opens up the potential for the European Parliament to exercise significant influence over the CAP for the first time. Agricultural legislation is henceforth subject to co-decision between the Council and Parliament, and the abolition of the distinction between compulsory and non-compulsory expenditure makes the two institutions co-equal over the details of CAP spending. (The opportunity to install a de facto parliamentary veto on comitology decisions in the CAP sphere, however, was missed.) How far the changes brought in by the new treaty make a difference will depend ultimately on the internal politics of the Parliament itself. It is still an open question whether the Parliament's agriculture committee, in particular, will remain beholden to existing interests or become a more independent force in its own right – and also how effective that committee will prove now that it needs to compete directly with other committees (notably the environment and budgets committees) in the Parliament, which are less sympathetic to the farming sector. This new parliamentary landscape, so far largely untested, will be an important factor in determining the future power of the agricultural lobby in the EU system.

Further reading: Wyn Grant, *The Common Agricultural Policy*, 1997; Ann-Christina Knudsen, *Farmers on Welfare: The Making of Europe's Common Agricultural Policy*, 2008.

Common Commercial Policy (CCP)

The Common Commercial Policy is the formal name given to the external trade policy of the European Union. External trade is an area of exclusive **competence** of the Union and has been so since the foundation of the **European Economic Community** (EEC) in 1958. It was listed in the original **Treaty of Rome** in second place among the activities of the Community, after the removal of customs duties and of quantitative restrictions on trade between member states (Article 3 EEC). Since the countries were to be linked together in a **customs union**, it was clearly necessary for them to draw up common policies with regard to trading relations with the rest of the world. Since the **Lisbon Treaty**, this exclusive competence has been recognized in Article 3(e) TFEU.

The main elements of the CCP are set out in Articles 206 and 207 TFEU. Article 207 TFEU (previously Article 133 EC) specifies that the policy will be conducted on the basis of 'uniform principles' in relation to the setting of tariff rates – achieved through a **Common Customs Tariff** (CCT) – and the conclusion of trade agreements in goods and services, one of several forms of **international agreement** which may be undertaken by the Union. The CCP also encompasses export policy, the commercial aspects of intellectual property, foreign direct investment and measures of commercial defence.

The **European Commission** is entrusted with the role of negotiating trade agreements with third countries on behalf of the Union. It does this on the basis of authorization given by the **Council of Ministers**, to which it reports back regularly through meetings of the latter's **Trade Policy Committee** (otherwise known as the Article 207 Committee). On most external trade issues – whether specific trade agreements or legislation 'defining the framework for implementing' the overall policy – **qualified majority voting** (QMV) applies in the Council, where it was introduced (at least theoretically) as early as 1966. However, unanimity is still required for certain decisions relating to trade in services, intellectual property and foreign direct investment – specifically where trade agreements contain provisions for which, elsewhere in the Treaties, 'unanimity is required for the adoption of internal rules' (Article 207(4) TFEU). Previously, as a result of French negotiating success in successive rounds of treaty reform, trade in cultural and audiovisual services was still subject to unanimity: under Lisbon, it remains so only to the degree that 'agreements risk prejudicing the Union's cultural and linguistic diversity'. Similarly, unanimity is now required for trade in social, educational and health services, in so far as any 'agreements risk seriously disturbing the national organization of such services and prejudicing the responsibility of Member States to deliver them'. The limits of these various provisos have yet to be tested.

Initially, the **European Parliament** had no power in the external trade field: although it was consulted on **association agreements**, it did not even enjoy this courtesy on trade agreements, **cooperation agreements** or the legislative framework underpinning trade policy. Starting in 1964, the Parliament gradually acquired the informal right to be informed of progress in major negotiations, through the so-called Luns–Westerterp procedure. With the 1986 **Single European Act** (SEA) and 1992 **Maastricht Treaty**, the assent procedure, since renamed the **consent procedure**, gave the Parliament a formal veto over (successively) association agreements and any other international agreements which involved institutional frameworks, had important budgetary implications or amended acts which had already been adopted under the **co-decision procedure** between the Council and the Parliament. As a result of the Lisbon Treaty, co-decision itself now applies to legislation in the CCP field, whilst consent has been extended to trade agreements (except where unanimity applies in the Council). In addition, under Lisbon, the Parliament is now, for the first time, to be kept 'immediately and fully informed at all stages' of the negotiation of international agreements, including trade agreements (under Article 218 TFEU). The willingness in practice of the Commission and Council to keep the Parliament fully informed about negotiations, including the process by which negotiating mandates are defined at the start, is likely to have a significant bearing on its preparedness to exercise its new right of veto.

The European Commission represents the member states as a bloc in all international trade negotiations, whether these are conducted with individual third countries, groups of third countries or multilateral fora, notably the World Trade Organization (WTO), the successor body to the General Agreement on Tariffs and Trade (GATT). In its role as negotiator, the Commission is strengthened by the sheer size of the EU, which is the largest trading bloc in the world and still represents around 25 per cent of global GDP. As the EU has enlarged, its share of external trade has, by definition, declined. If the EU member states are treated as separate countries, their total share of global trade in goods and services rises to over 35 per cent.

Since its inception, the European Community, now Union, has been committed to the principle of free trade, based on the 'progressive abolition of restrictions on international trade . . . and the lowering of customs and other barriers', as Article 110 EEC, now Article 206 TFEU, has always put it. Since the 1960s, the EU has played an active role in successive rounds of international trade liberalization within the GATT, now WTO, framework. It has allowed preferential access to many poorer countries through the UN's Generalized System of Preferences (GSP) and negotiated trade and other agreements with over 120 third countries or groups of countries, many of which enjoy similar benefits. The EU currently has an average tariff of 6.7 per cent on non-agricultural imports from other WTO contracting parties. In the past, a relatively low average tariff overall concealed significantly higher tariffs in certain 'sensitive' sectors, such as textiles and consumer electronics, but this is now much less pronounced. Quantitative restrictions also applied for several decades in textiles, steel and motor cars, but they have now been removed. During the 1980s, there were fears that the completion of the **single market** within the EU might be matched by a more protectionist external trade policy and that common technical standards would be exploited to shut out imports. Fears of a 'Fortress Europe' have proved largely groundless, although some environmental and public health standards clearly do inhibit trade. Today, the only persistent source of protectionism within the EU remains the **Common Agricultural Policy** (CAP), where the combined impact of 'export refunds' (which cover the difference between the domestic and international price of a product) and import levies can be significant. Controversy also sometimes surrounds the use of certain 'trade defence instruments' (TDIs) – notably against the dumping or subsidization of imports by third countries – even if these attempt carefully to follow WTO rules.

In spite of substantial differences in their economic and commercial interests, member states have in general sought and achieved a high degree of coherence and consistency in the pursuit of a common external trade policy, accepting in good faith the obligation to act as one. Inevitably, there have been occasional lapses: for example, unilateral French restrictions on the importation of Japanese video recorders in the early 1980s (all of which had to be routed through Poitiers) and a Greek embargo on trade with FYR Macedonia a decade later. Both were lifted under threat of Commission action through the **European Court of Justice** (ECJ). However, even if national governments accept the disciplines of a common policy, they often engage in ferocious bargaining privately (and sometimes publicly) in advance of key trade decisions being taken. Disputes over the imposition of anti-dumping duties on Chinese textile and footwear imports in 2005–6 provided a glimpse of intensive, competitive coalition-building within the Council.

An important feature of external trade policy is its interaction with foreign policy more generally, especially given the potential use of trade and other sanctions as a political weapon. The development of the EU's **Common Foreign and Security Policy** (CFSP) has provided a formal mechanism for imposing trade embargoes on third countries. The Maastricht Treaty, in wording updated by the Lisbon Treaty, empowered the Council, in the event of a CFSP decision providing for the 'interruption or reduction, in part or completely, of economic and financial relations with one or more third countries', to take 'the necessary measures' by a qualified majority (Article 215(1) TFEU). It now does this on the basis of a joint proposal from the **High Representative** and the Commission, although there is no obligation on the part of the Council to consult the European Parliament. (Interestingly, this is the only provision in the **Treaties** where the Commission is required to make a legislative proposal as a result of a prior decision among governments, so contravening the general principle that the Commission's **right of initiative** is exercised entirely independently.)

Common Customs Tariff (CCT)

The Common Customs Tariff, also known as the common external tariff, provides the means whereby import duties are imposed on goods entering the European Union. A common tariff is a necessary feature of a **customs union**, although not of a **free trade area**. Without a common tariff, goods from third countries could enter the EU through the member state with the lowest import duties and then benefit from **free movement** within the Union as a whole. The CCT was thus introduced at the same time as the abolition of individual customs duties by the member states in July 1968. Provided for in Article 28 TFEU, the CCT is composed of a variety of different types of duty: normal, preferential, agricultural, anti-dumping and countervailing duties. These are set out in over a hundred **legal acts** and brought together in the so-called 'Taric' database, using an internationally agreed nomenclature. (Taric is an acronym for the French phrase *tarif intégré des Communautés européennes.*) Decided upon as part of the EU's external trade policy – which is officially known as the **Common Commercial Policy** (CCP) – the CCT is managed by the **European Commission** and the revenue it generates forms part of the Union's **own resources.**

The original **Treaty of Rome** contained a 49-page annex giving a precise list of the products to be subject to the CCT, with designated tariff rates varying between zero and 80 per cent, but mostly in the range of 10 to 25 per cent. Individual rates have subsequently been adjusted downwards, as a result of unilateral concessions or bilateral or multilateral trade negotiations. Except for some agricultural products, most rates are now located between zero and 7.5 per cent. In 2010, the trade-weighted CCT for industrial products stood at 1.6 per cent, whilst for countries with preferential agreements with the EU, it was only 0.3 per cent. A complete schedule of EU customs duties, running to almost a thousand pages, is published annually by the Commission.

'Common European home'

A crucial concept in the end of the **Cold War**, the phrase a 'common European home' was first used as a metaphor for the relationship between eastern and western Europe by Mikhail Gorbachev in 1985, soon after he became General Secretary of the Communist Party of the Soviet Union. In his book, *Perestroika: New Thinking for our Country and the World* (1987), Gorbachev argued that whilst 'the home is common . . . each family has its own apartment, and there are different entrances too. The concept of a "common European home" suggests above all a degree of integrity, even if its states belong to different social systems and opposing military-political alliances.' He noted that 'integrative processes are developing intensively in both parts of Europe', prompting 'the search for some kind of mutually advantageous cooperation' and making war potentially 'disastrous for Europe today'.

After becoming Soviet President in 1988, Gorbachev drew out the implications of the concept in increasingly radical terms. Speaking to the Parliamentary Assembly of the **Council of Europe** in July 1989 – a month after the rule of the Communist Party had in effect been ended in Poland by democratic election – he declared that the 'philosophy of the "common European home" rules out the probability of an armed clash and the very possibility of the use of force or threat of force – alliance against alliance, inside the alliances, wherever. This philosophy suggests that a doctrine of restraint should take the place of the doctrine of deterrence. This is not just a play on words, but the logic of European development prompted by life itself.'

Common Fisheries Policy (CFP)

The catching of wild fish at sea by hunter-gatherers constitutes the last non-leisure activity still carried out on a significant scale in Europe that dates back to prehistoric times. During the twentieth century, fishing at sea became increasingly efficient as boats progressed from sail-driven to engine-driven vessels, with a growing impact in depleting fish stocks, particularly in the North Atlantic. Although the Second World War resulted in a temporary halt to deep-sea fishing off the coast of western Europe, allowing a recovery of stocks, by the 1960s the latter were once more coming under strain.

The development of a Common Fisheries Policy by the European Community, now Union, represented an attempt to allow fish stocks to be exploited on a pan-European basis, whilst seeking to bring supply and demand into better balance. Article 38 TFEU, dating from the original **Treaty of Rome**, makes it clear that fish and fish products are to be considered as agricultural products. The CFP, established between 1970 and 1983, is based on the same principles as those of the **Common Agricultural Policy** (CAP). Its objectives are simultaneously to preserve fish stocks, protect the marine environment, ensure the economic viability of European fleets and provide consumers with quality produce. The policy was drawn up by **the Six** in the run-up to the Community's first **enlargement**, with a view to presenting the four applicant states – Denmark, Ireland, **Norway** and the United Kingdom, all of which had important fishing industries – with something of a fait accompli. It was partly the unpopularity of this initiative that resulted in the Norwegian electorate rejecting membership in a referendum in September 1972. (Whereas the overall vote showed 53.5 per cent of the electorate against membership, that figure rose to over 70 per cent in some areas with large fishing fleets.) The ironic consequence of Norway's decision not to join was to deny the Community use of one of its largest potential fishing grounds.

In principle, under the CFP, all fishing vessels are guaranteed access to all waters within the European Union. However, from the start, it was agreed that national coastal fishing rights should be retained for the first six nautical miles (9.6 kilometres) offshore, and the new member states managed to secure a temporary doubling of this right to 12 nautical miles (19.3 kilometres). Then, beginning in 1975, **Iceland**, followed by Norway, declared unilaterally that they enjoyed exclusive fishing rights of up to 200 nautical miles (322 kilometres) offshore, denying several member states access to areas which they had traditionally fished in the Atlantic. This was the third attempt by the Icelandic government in 80 years unilaterally to expand its fishing rights and it was largely successful, critically because of its threat (which the US administration declined to contest) to close the NATO anti-submarine warfare base in Kevlavik, from which operations to prevent Soviet naval intrusion into the Greenland–Iceland–UK gap were carried out. The **Council of Ministers** adopted a resolution in November 1976 accepting the Icelandic move and extending the EU's own fishing limit to 200 nautical miles from January of the following year. The new 'exclusive economic zones' (EEZs) were legitimized by the Convention on the Law of the Sea in 1982.

The adoption of this convention, combined with the fact that the fisheries arrangements agreed in advance of the 1972 **accession** treaty were initially put in place for only ten years, led to the renegotiation of the CFP in 1981–2. After a marathon bargaining session in January 1983, the Council of Ministers struck a deal, based on four pillars, which largely remains in place today. First, a new 'access régime' was put in place, which generalized the 12-mile limit to every coastal member state. However, in order to maintain the fiction of free and equal access to all waters, the limit was restricted to a (renewable) period of ten years; it was prolonged in the two subsequent reviews, in 1992 and 2002. Second, a new 'conservation régime' established an annual 'total allowable catch' (TAC) for each of the main species of fish and then divided this into quotas for each member state. The calculation of TACs and quotas was to be made 'in the light of the available scientific advice' and with a view to maintaining 'relative stability' of market share. (The notion of 'relative stability' was an important concession to Britain and Ireland, to help them retain their existing proportion of the total European catch.) Third, this conservation régime was reinforced by a series of 'technical measures', updated regularly, covering matters such as net sizes, by-catches and the minimum dimensions of fish to be caught. Fourth, an 'enforcement régime' was designed to ensure that TACs, quotas and other rules were honoured in practice. However, left primarily in the hands of the member states, enforcement was quickly to prove inadequate, even with the introduction of modern technology (such as satellite monitoring and on-board, closed-circuit television).

The CFP, as revised in 1983, did not solve the fundamental problem that the volume of fishing activity was still greater than the stocks available to be exploited and that this divergence was, if anything, growing. TACs and quotas had to be supplemented in 1986 by 'multiannual guidance programmes' (MAGPs), aimed at reducing the actual size of the Community fishing fleet, in the hope of better matching 'fishing effort' – namely 'days at sea', calculated as capacity multiplied by the activity of a fleet – with the limited available resources of fish. The development of the CFP was further disrupted by the withdrawal of **Greenland** from the Community in 1985 and the accession of Spain and Portugal the following year. The latter had a considerable impact on both the size and structure of the Community fleet and its catch potential.

The Spanish fleet's traditional interest in South Atlantic fishing resulted in the Community negotiating international fisheries agreements – first with coastal states in Africa, and subsequently with island states in the Indian and Pacific oceans – to open their waters to European vessels. Over time, the impact of these agreements was substantial: more than half the fish now eaten in the EU is imported from beyond Union waters. By 2009, the Union had 18 bilateral fisheries agreements with third countries, many involving the payment of financial compensation by the Union. The fact that several agreements permit the fishing of tuna, a species which has long been under extreme stress, has also been controversial.

The advent of international agreements created more space for the imposition of tougher reform measures at home. In the second CFP review, in 1992, the Council of Ministers adopted new regulations providing for strict limits on the number of vessels, through a licensing system for fishing boats, accompanied by structural measures to alleviate the impact of these measures on fishing communities. Greater emphasis was also laid on developing 'aquaculture', the official term for fish farming, which has since grown to represent almost a fifth of total fisheries production in the EU.

The Council adopted a third round of CFP reform in 2002. To address the continuing problems of overfishing, 'multiannual recovery plans' were introduced for endangered stocks, alongside 'multiannual management plans' for other stocks. The Commission was granted the power to take emergency measures for periods of six months in cases of serious threat to the conservation of maritime resources. EU financial aid was focused more on improving product quality, promoting selective fishing techniques, upgrading safety and working conditions on boats, and installing on-board, satellite-based vessel monitoring systems (VMS). An EU fishing register was established, backed by a 'scrappage fund', based on the principle that once public financing was accepted for the decommissioning of any vessel, the reduction in fleet capacity had to be permanent. Financial aid was also made available for the permanent transfer of EU vessels to third countries. A Community Fisheries Control Agency (CFCA), based in Vigo, Spain, was established in 2005, in order to coordinate the work of national inspection bodies in the sector.

Successive CFP reforms have failed, however, to close the gap between fishing capacity and resources. In a plain-speaking Green Paper in April 2009 – published in advance of the next decennial CFP review, due in 2012 – the European Commission conceded that 'the objectives agreed in 2002 to achieve sustainable fisheries have not been met'. Critical to this has been 'chronic overcapacity of which overfishing is both a cause and a consequence:

fleets have the power to fish much more than can safely be removed without jeopardizing the future productivity of stocks' – a situation which has prevailed 'for decades' and has been getting worse because of the introduction of larger, more productive vessels. Although the number of people working in the sector has been falling at the rate of around 3,000 per year (to just under a quarter of a million people today) and the number of vessels in the fishing fleet has been declining by over a thousand a year (to around 88,000), the effects have been more than offset by the growing number and productivity of large boats, especially in Spain, France and much of northern Europe. The number of vessels is no longer the problem: Greece and Italy have 20 and 15 per cent of the EU fleet respectively, but only five and 10 per cent of the tonnage, whereas Spain has 15 per cent of the fleet and 24 per cent of the tonnage. Unless and until the Union is willing to restrict the number, weight, length and/or power of the most productive vessels, the serious structural problems at the heart of the CFP are likely to remain unresolved.

A broader background factor is that, as the Commission puts it, 'unlike other industries', fishing 'benefits from free access to the natural resource it exploits and does not have to contribute to the public management costs associated with its activities'. A mechanism needs to be found for costing the externalities involved and charging them to producers. However, the political constraint is that fishing remains an important employer in certain peripheral regions of the Union where there are few alternative opportunities for work. The concentrated nature of the sector makes it more difficult to confront the vested interests involved.

A number of features of the CFP generate significant public disquiet and reflect the dysfunctionality of the current policy. Under the TAC system, national quotas are drawn up annually for particular species. In some fishing grounds, this often requires fishermen to discard by-catches of species for which quotas have already been met. The image of dead fish being thrown back into the sea at a time of overall fish shortage is highly damaging. In early 2011, the European Commission indicated that a different solution would need to be found to this problem.

A second issue is 'quota hopping', whereby fishermen from one member state are able to register ships in another in order to take advantage of its fishing quota (drawing on the principle of **freedom of establishment** enshrined in Article 49 TFEU). The **Factortame case** brought this problem to a head in the United Kingdom in the late 1980s (in relation to Spanish boats) and although the issue has become less acute since, it proved to be a significant irritant in relation to **Croatia**'s application to join the Union (reflecting Zagreb's fear that Italian and Slovenian boats would penetrate its territorial waters).

More generally, there are serious problems with the enforcement of CFP rules, which is a complex and costly process, open to fraud. Although the new CFCA coordinates cross-border collaboration between national inspection services, implementation and enforcement still fall to each member state individually, with differing levels of commitment to the identification and eradication of malpractice. National penalties for those breaking the rules remain inadequate and there is little political will to legislate for tough common penalties at supranational level. Poor supervision also undermines the reliability of the data on which scientific advice is based, making it more likely that unsustainable catch levels will be set.

The fisheries sector initially received funding from the CAP, but was given its own financing mechanism, the Financial Instrument for Fisheries Guidance (FIFG), in 1994. The FIFG was assigned € 1.1 billion over the 2000–06 financing period. It was then replaced by the European Fisheries Fund (EFF), which has a € 3.8 billion allocation for the years 2007–13.

Until the **Lisbon Treaty** entered into force in December 2009, decision-making on the CFP, like the CAP, was the preserve of the Council of Ministers, operating by **qualified majority voting** (QMV). Now the Council shares legislative power in these fields with the **European Parliament**, through the **co-decision procedure.** In parallel, the abolition of the distinction between **compulsory and non-compulsory expenditure** in the annual EU **Budget** means that the CFP, like the CAP, is no longer ring-fenced from other spending priorities, with the Council losing its monopoly of power in this field too.

Common Foreign and Security Policy (CFSP)

The founding **Treaties** made no reference to a European foreign policy as such, a field which was seen very much as the continuing preserve of national foreign ministries. The external aspects of Community action were nonetheless potentially very substantial: from the start, there was to be a **Common Commercial Policy** (CCP), an area of exclusive Community **competence** covering the whole of external trade relations with third countries, whilst the potential existed to evolve a common **development policy**, which was quickly institutionalized through the creation of a **European Development Fund** (EDF). In parallel, the **European Commission** was able to establish that the external aspects of any 'domestic' EC policy (such as transport or the single market) were matters of Community competence too (see 1971 **ERTA case**).

The first serious suggestion that the EU should develop a collective foreign policy came from French President **Charles de Gaulle**. In 1959, his government proposed that EC foreign ministers should begin to meet, on a quarterly basis, to discuss 'international policy'. The first such gathering took place in January 1960. This initiative was partly a response to his failure to secure the installation of a Franco-British-American 'politico-military directory' at the heart of the **North Atlantic Treaty Organization** (NATO). De Gaulle's thinking soon moved on to the much more ambitious idea of founding an intergovernmental 'political union' among **the Six**, covering foreign policy and defence, which would run in parallel to the existing Communities and potentially envelop them. Significant differences of opinion about the institutional form of this **Fouchet Plan**, as well as its relationship with the Atlantic Alliance, led to the collapse of negotiations in April 1962. Not only did this reverse upset existing arrangements – for example, the regular meetings of foreign ministers were discontinued – but the General moved onto an increasingly erratic path in foreign relations, culminating in France's withdrawal from the integrated military command structure of NATO in March 1966, so making the idea of a common Community position in foreign policy virtually inconceivable.

Following de Gaulle's departure from office in April 1969, efforts in the direction of greater foreign-policy coordination at European level were relaunched. Encouraged by the new French President, Georges Pompidou, the EC heads of government, meeting in The Hague in December 1969, invited their foreign ministers to make proposals for closer cooperation in this field. As a result, a system of **European Political Cooperation** (EPC) was instituted in October 1970, which saw foreign ministers meet on a half-yearly, then quarterly, basis, backed by a Political Committee of senior national officials. This new intergovernmental structure was gradually consolidated – for example, by the development in 1981 of the **Troika** of past, present and future **presidencies** of the Council to offer greater continuity in dealings with third countries, and the provision of informal staff support centrally by the Council secretariat – until such time as it was formalized in the first major treaty revision adopted at Community level, the 1986 **Single European Act** (SEA). The new treaty committed the member states to 'endeavour jointly to formulate and implement a European foreign policy' (Article 30 SEA). The European Commission was to be 'fully' associated, and the **European Parliament** 'closely' associated, with EPC.

The 1992 **Maastricht Treaty** built on the structures of EPC, converting them into a Common Foreign and Security Policy, which formed one of the two intergovernmental **pillars** of the new European Union (Articles J.1–11 TEU, since amended). CFSP was to be based on 'general guidelines' laid down by the **European Council** in areas where the member states had 'important interests in common'. In addition to issuing declarations, the **Foreign Affairs Council** (FAC) could make recommendations for these guidelines to the European Council; once agreed, the FAC was in turn responsible for translating them into 'joint actions' and 'common positions'. Joint actions would 'commit the Member States in the positions they adopt and in the conduct of their activity'. Although all these decisions were to be taken by **unanimity**, the Council could itself decide unanimously that joint actions and common positions, as well as any implementing measures, would be subject to **qualified majority voting** (QMV).

The rotating Council presidency would 'represent the Union' for the purposes of CFSP and was 'responsible for the implementation of common measures' under it, assisted by the other members of the Troika. Echoing the language of the SEA, the European Commission was 'fully associated' with this and other aspects of the CFSP process. Proposals for action could come from the Council presidency, any member state or the Commission. The European Parliament was given the right to be consulted on 'the main aspects and the basic choices' and to be 'kept regularly informed' of developments in this field, with its views 'duly taken into consideration'. (There is no obligation on the Council to consult the Parliament on specific decisions that relate exclusively to CFSP.)

The Maastricht Treaty foresaw that CFSP would 'include all questions related to the security of the Union, including the eventual framing of a common defence policy, which might in time lead to a common defence' (Article J.4(4) TEU). In the interim, the **Western European Union** (WEU) was invited to 'elaborate and implement decisions and actions of the Union which have defence implications'. Any decisions with 'military or defence implications' were always subject to unanimity, and any CFSP position had to be 'compatible' with NATO policy. The 1992 **Petersberg tasks** permitted the WEU to undertake out-of-area missions for humanitarian and rescue work, peacekeeping and crisis management, including peacemaking.

The member states were obliged to support CFSP 'actively and unreservedly in a spirit of loyalty and mutual solidarity' and to 'refrain from any action' which might 'impair its effectiveness'. Those sitting on the **United Nations** Security Council (UNSC) were required to 'concert and keep the other Member States fully informed' about activities in that forum, with the permanent members (France and the United Kingdom) obliged to 'defend the positions and the interests of the Union' (Article J.5(4), now 34 TEU).

Whilst the language of the Maastricht Treaty raised high hopes of what the new CFSP might deliver, the harsh reality of the Balkans crisis quickly revealed significant divergences among member states and a general lack of political will to act, especially if it might involve the use of force (see **Yugoslavia**). In 1993, a British academic, Christopher Hill, famously pointed to an emerging 'capability-expectations gap' in European foreign policy ('The Capability-Expectations Gap – or Conceptualizing Europe's International Role', *Journal of Common Market Studies*, Volume 31, Number 3, 1993). The progress registered in the early years of CFSP was more workaday, even if sometimes still significant: a strategy to prepare the former Communist countries of central and eastern Europe for eventual **accession** to the Union; the launch of the 'Barcelona Process' in the Mediterranean; the development of a new approach to post-Soviet Russia; an attempt to strengthen **Transatlantic relations** through the 'New Transatlantic Agenda'; the launch of the 'Asia–Europe Meeting' (ASEM) dialogue; and the continued deepening of relations with Latin America.

Further institutional strengthening of CFSP followed. The 1997 **Amsterdam Treaty** established the post of **High Representative** for CSFP within the Council secretariat to assist the presidency, whilst the institutional link between the WEU and the EU was formalized, with the Petersberg tasks henceforth defined as EU functions. (The High Representative was to be simultaneously Secretary General of the Council and of the WEU.) The European Council was empowered to launch 'common strategies', as well as provide 'general guidelines' for the FAC. Instead of having to veto a unanimous decision, a member state was given the option of engaging in 'constructive abstention' in the CFSP field. In return for abstaining, a member state would be absolved from applying the decision in question. If a third or more of member states abstain, no decision can be taken. (To date, no decision has ever been taken in the Council on the basis of constructive abstention.)

Following the Franco-British **Saint-Malo Declaration** in December 1998, the Cologne and Helsinki meetings of the European Council in June and December 1999 launched a formal defence dimension to the Union, superseding the WEU. This initiative was given treaty status in the 2001 **Nice Treaty**, known at first as the European Security and Defence Policy (ESDP) and since the **Lisbon Treaty** came into force in December 2009, as the **Common Security and Defence Policy** (CSDP). A **Political and Security Committee** (PSC) was established to prepare meetings of the FAC, with an **EU Military Committee** and Military Staff reporting to it.

The arrangements for CFSP that operate today draw extensively on the formulae developed and refined successively in the Maastricht, Amsterdam and Nice Treaties, but they also take them several steps further. Most notably, the position of High Representative has been significantly strengthened by the Lisbon Treaty, so that he or she, in addition to discharging existing functions, assumes the role of the Council presidency in CFSP (including chairing FAC meetings) and serves as European Commissioner for external relations (and indeed as first Vice-President of the Commission). The High Representative is assisted by a new **European External Action Service** (EEAS), which brings together the foreign-policy staff of the Commission and Council secretariat (as well as national diplomats on secondment) in an independent body 'equidistant' between the two institutions (Article 27 TEU).

The European Council now has the responsibility to 'identify the Union's strategic interests, determine the objectives of and define general guidelines for [CFSP], including for matters with defence implications' (Article 26(1) TEU). The European Council may henceforth adopt 'decisions', dispensing with the previous complex mixture of common strategies, joint actions and common positions. Like joint actions in the past, decisions defining actions by the Union commit the member states. The range of situations in which the Council may act by QMV has been widened and a ***passerelle* clause** has been introduced to permit (otherwise) unanimous decisions in this field, except those having military or defence implications (Article 31(3) and (4) TEU), to be taken by QMV in the future if the Council (unanimously) so chooses.

The Lisbon Treaty has added a new section on CSDP (Articles 42–6 TEU), which it defines as 'an integral part' of CFSP and says 'shall provide the Union with an operational capacity drawing on civilian and military assets'. Such operations may involve 'both national resources and Union instruments, together with the Commission where appropriate'. The treaty lengthens the list of Petersberg tasks on which such assets might be deployed. In addition, it incorporates a mutual defence clause (previously provided within the WEU by Article 5 of the 1954 Modified **Brussels Treaty**), which reads: 'If a Member State is a victim of armed aggression on its territory, the other Member States shall have towards it an obligation of aid and assistance by all the means in their power, in accordance with Article 51 of the United Nations Charter' (Article 42(7) TEU). Finally, the treaty allows a form of **enhanced cooperation** in defence, so that those member states 'whose military capabilities fulfil higher criteria and which have made more binding commitments to one another' may establish **Permanent Structured Cooperation in Defence** (PSCD). This possibility has yet to be activated. Giving a treaty base to the European Defence Agency (EDA) is also designed to promote the development of such capabilities, as well as cost-saving in procurement.

An important issue that the Lisbon Treaty sought to address is how the European Union marries together its trade and development policies, as well as the external aspects of domestic policies, such as environment and transport – usually decided by QMV and administered by the Commission – with classic foreign policy, usually determined by unanimity and traditionally administered by the Council itself. The 'triple-hatted' role of the High Representative and the special place occupied by the new EEAS, at the interface of intergovernmental and supranational concepts of Europe, is designed to help promote 'joined up' policy-making in this field.

Although the European Parliament only has the right to be consulted on the 'main aspects and basic choices' of CFSP and CSDP, it has exploited the fact that non-military CFSP spending, including the operation of the EEAS, must feature in the annual **Budget** (and thus be approved by the Parliament), in order to exercise an influence on foreign policy-making not directly foreseen in the Treaties. The High Representative and chairman of the PSC routinely appear before the Parliament's foreign affairs committee to discuss civilian crisis-management missions, whilst the Parliament is now informed about military missions through its special dialogue with the Council for access to confidential documents.

So far, the major national capitals have only been willing to endow CFSP with relatively modest funding (€ 272 million in 2011). All 'expenditure arising from operations having defence or military implications' is still financed directly by the member states, through the so-called 'Athena' mechanism, even if administrative spending on military operations is carried by the Union Budget (Article 41 TEU). The Athena mechanism was established in 2004 by Council decision and is updated every three years.

It is often argued that the unanimity requirement for EU foreign-policy coordination allows only for a 'lowest common denominator' approach, with the result that the Union has all too often failed to exercise an influence commensurate with its political and economic weight. Those who defend unanimity in CFSP argue, in return, that there is a balance to be struck between national **sovereignty** – of which foreign and defence policy is still a key expression – and the common interest. What might be for some critics a lack of cohesion is for others a welcome flexibility. Equally, they argue, there has to be a recognition that in CFSP and CSDP, there is a significant imbalance of power among the member states, which renders decision-making in this field very different from that in any other aspect of EU policy. To proceed with a major foreign-policy initiative in the face of opposition from one or more of those member states that are independently powerful in the area concerned – say Britain in Transatlantic relations, France in the Middle East, or Spain in Latin America – would be seriously problematic, if not counterproductive. To undertake a significant EU military commitment without the involvement of Britain and France might simply be technically impossible, whether or not it was politically wise.

In practice, within international institutions like the United Nations or multilateral negotiating fora like the **Organization for Security and Cooperation in Europe** (OSCE), the member states have held together increasingly well. CFSP procedures allow individual member states to continue to deal with essentially bilateral foreign policy issues in the way they wish – either with only limited reference to other member states or, conversely, by securing collective backing for them in the hope of multiplying their impact – whilst equally enabling issues to be dealt with on a common basis where there is a general political will that this be done. However, especially in such a sensitive field, procedures can of themselves neither engender such a political will nor substitute for it. Even if the new structures introduced by the Lisbon Treaty now provide a reasonably coherent framework for the development of a European foreign policy, its practical realization in coming years will still depend primarily on political calculations made in certain national capitals, rather than in Brussels. In recent years, for example, Paris, Berlin and London have chosen to use a CFSP framework to work together on the issue of Iranian nuclear reactors (as the 'EU 3'), but this modest success did nothing to prevent them splitting spectacularly in October 2011 over the admission of the Palestinian authority to UNESCO – when France voted in favour and Germany against, whilst the UK abstained.

In general, the reflex instinct of the larger member states is still to try to contain CFSP mainly to 'second order' issues, rather than allow the EU to find and assert its own identity as a player on the world stage. Confronted with this reality, the natural response of the Commission (and now the EEAS) has been to fashion the Union in the mould of what Asle Toje has called a 'small power'. Operating defensively within an international system defined by others, the default reaction of the Union collectively to major international crises – as opposed to that of certain member states individually – still tends to be one of either 'dependence or **neutrality**', with a marked reluctance to provide distinctive leadership on its own. Ironically, the public debate about CFSP barely takes account of this, being polarized, as Toje argues (see below), between 'those who see in the EU a nascent superpower' – a tendency witnessed, for example, in **Valéry Giscard d'Estaing**'s emphasis on a *Europe puissance* in his inaugural address to the 2002–3 **Convention on the Future of Europe** – and 'those who dismiss entirely its foreign policy efforts'. This false antithesis – reinforcing the 'capability-expectations gap' identified by Hill almost two decades ago – often makes it difficult to conduct a serious discussion about the problems and potential of CFSP.

Further reading: Federiga Bindi (editor), *The Foreign Policy of the European Union*, 2010; Stephan Keukeleire and Jennifer MacNaughtan, *The Foreign Policy of the European Union*, 2008; Alse Toje, *The European Union as a Small Power: After the Post-Cold War*, 2011.

Common market

The objective of 'establishing a common market' is the central policy commitment contained in the 1957 **Treaty of Rome** that created the **European Economic Community** (EEC) (Article 2 EEC, now incorporated in Article 3 TEU). Although the notion of a common market had already featured, for two specific sectors, in the 1951 **Treaty of Paris** establishing the **European Coal and Steel Community** (ECSC), it was generalized by the EEC to apply to the economy as a whole. The definition of the common market in the original Treaty of Rome is not precise, appearing to encompass not only the barrier-free movement of the factors of production – the so-called '**four freedoms**' – but also the flanking policies of a **customs union**, **competition policy** and some other components of the EEC. The idea of Europe's new common market quickly entered the political bloodstream and became synonymous with all three **European Communities** and the process of European integration itself. At the time of the first **enlargement** in 1973, for example, many people talked of the United Kingdom, Ireland and Denmark 'joining the Common Market' (usually spelt with initial capital letters). In the **British referendum on EC membership** in June 1975, the question posed was: 'Do you think that the United Kingdom should stay in the European Community (the Common Market)?'

On becoming President of the **European Commission** in 1985, **Jacques Delors** decided to relaunch the stalled process of building an integrated economy through a programme designed to complete the '**single market**' or 'internal market' by the end of 1992. In the 1986 **Single European Act** (SEA), the internal market was defined as comprising 'an area without internal frontiers in which the **free movement** of goods, persons, services and capital is ensured' (Article 8(a) EEC, now Article 26(2) TFEU). Once the title 'European Union' was introduced by the 1992 **Maastricht Treaty**, the twin uses of 'common market' – to denote either the internal economy or the Communities as a whole – were largely superseded by reference to the single or internal market on the one hand, and to the EU on the other.

Common Security and Defence Policy (CSDP)

Following the fall of the Berlin Wall in November 1989 and the end of the **Cold War**, the possibility that the European Community, soon to be Union, might take on an active security and defence role was mooted for the first time since the 1950s. The 1992 **Maastricht Treaty** converted the existing **European Political Cooperation** (EPC) into a more formal **Common Foreign and Security Policy** (CFSP), which was to 'include all questions related to the security of the Union, including the eventual framing of a common defence policy, which might in time lead to a common defence' (Article J.4(1) TEU, now Article 42(2) TEU amended). The **Western European Union** (WEU) was designated as 'an integral part of the development of the Union' and invited to 'elaborate and implement decisions and actions of the Union which have defence implications', which in practice corresponded to the so-called **Petersberg tasks** of humanitarian and rescue missions, peacekeeping, and crisis management, including peacemaking. It was made clear that any EU defence role had to 'respect the obligations' of those member states that were members of the **North Atlantic Treaty Organization** (NATO) and be 'compatible with the common security and defence policy established within that framework' (Article J.4(4) TEU, now Article 42(2) TEU).

A rapid series of developments almost a decade later finally gave substance to the Maastricht commitment that the EU should develop a defence dimension. The two largest military powers in Europe, Britain and France, agreed in principle, in the **Saint-Malo Declaration** of December 1998, that the Union 'must have the capacity for autonomous action, backed up by credible military forces' for use 'where the [NATO] Alliance as a whole is not engaged'. Soon after, at the Cologne and Helsinki meetings of the **European Council** in June and December 1999, EU heads of government decided to move beyond the WEU by launching a 'common European security and defence policy', which was formalized in the 2001 **Nice Treaty** as the European Security and Defence Policy (ESDP). They backed this with the so-called '**Helsinki Headline Goal**' for the rapid deployment by 2003 of up to 60,000 military personnel on EU-defined missions in pursuit of the **Petersberg tasks** of out-of-area humanitarian and rescue missions, peacekeeping, and crisis management, including peacemaking. However, faced with resource constraints, the European Council effectively abandoned the Helsinki Headline Goal in June 2004, adopting instead a more modest 'Headline Goal 2010', based on the notion of separate, smaller, multiple 'Battlegroups' of around 1,500 troops each. An **EU Military Committee**, composed of the 'chiefs of defence' of member states and their representatives in Brussels, was also established at Helsinki and began work in January 2001. It is supported by an EU Military Staff, composed almost entirely of officials seconded from the member states.

The **Lisbon Treaty**, which entered into force in December 2009, renamed ESDP as CSDP – which now forms 'an integral part' of CFSP, under Article 42(1) TEU – and strengthened the treaty references to it. CSDP should provide the EU with 'an operational capacity drawing on civilian and military assets' for use on 'missions outside the Union for peacekeeping, conflict prevention and strengthening international security in accordance with the principles of the **United Nations** Charter'. These 'Petersberg plus' tasks are listed in detail in Article 43(1) TEU and now include 'joint disarmament operations, humanitarian and rescue tasks, military advice and assistance tasks, conflict prevention and peacekeeping tasks, [and] tasks of combat forces in crisis management, including peacemaking and post-conflict stabilization'.

Article 42(2) TEU, as amended by the Lisbon Treaty, now states that CSDP 'shall include the progressive framing of a common Union defence policy', which 'will lead to a common defence, when the European Council, acting unanimously, so decides'. Such a decision would need to be ratified by member states 'in accordance with their respective constitutional requirements'

(Article 42(2) TEU). The treaty also commits the member states to 'undertake progressively to improve their military capabilities', working through the European Defence Agency (EDA), already established in July 2004 (Article 42(3) TEU).

Two other important changes were introduced by the Lisbon Treaty. First, with the winding-down of the WEU (which ceased to exist at the end of June 2011), the mutual defence clause contained in Article 5 of the 1954 Modified **Brussels Treaty** was in effect superseded by a comparable guarantee among EU member states. Article 42(7) TEU states: 'If a Member State is the victim of armed aggression on its territory, the other Member States shall have towards it an obligation of aid and assistance by all the means in their power, in accordance with Article 51 of the United Nations Charter.'

Second, a framework has been established for the creation of a vanguard group of member states 'whose military capabilities fulfil higher criteria and which have made more binding commitments to one another in this area with a view to the most demanding missions' (Article 42(6) TEU). To participate in this **Permanent Structured Cooperation in Defence** (PSCD) – in effect a tailored form of **enhanced cooperation** for defence – member states must meet a high standard of military capability (defined in detail in Article 1(b) of **Protocol** 10 of the **Treaties**) and they must inter alia undertake to participate in multinational forces, the main European defence equipment programmes and the work of the EDA. PSCD may be activated by a decision of the **Council of Ministers**, acting by **qualified majority voting** (QMV), on the basis of a request from a group of member states, however few, which claim to meet the necessary criteria. It will be open to other member states, on the same basis thereafter.

Since the advent of CSDP, the European Union has undertaken 14 civilian, six military, and three mixed civilian–military operations. Most civilian operations have been police, 'rule of law', peace monitoring or border assistance missions: for example, EUPM in Bosnia and Herzegovina since 2003; EUJUST LEX in Iraq since 2005; the Aceh Monitoring Mission in 2005–6; EUPOL COPPS in Palestine since 2006, EUBAM Moldovia–Ukraine in 2005–9; EUPOL Afghanistan in 2007–10; and EULEX Kosovo since 2008. Of the six military missions undertaken so far, two have been 'Berlin Plus' operations conducted jointly with NATO: Concordia in FYR Macedonia in 2003 and Althea in Bosnia and Herzegovina since 2004. Four have been autonomous, EU-led operations: Artemis and EUFOR RDC (both in the Democratic Republic of Congo) in 2003 and 2006; EUFOR Tchad/RCA (in Chad and the Central African Republic) in 2008–9; and Atalanta or EU NAVFOR Somalia (off the Somali coast) since 2008. In 2011, a total of about 6,000 troops were deployed in 16 ongoing CSDP missions.

Despite this ostensibly impressive catalogue, the reality so far is that, as

Asle Toje has written, 'the EU favours small-scale, low-intensity, pre- and post-crisis management operations – all of which are relatively low on the international agenda.' By contrast, the Union 'did not play a role in the great power politics of the past decade – whether it be in relation to Kosovo, Iraq, NATO's eastern enlargement, Darfur or Afghanistan' ('The European Union as a Small Power', *Journal of Common Market Studies*, Volume 49, Number 1, January 2011). That there was no suggestion that the Anglo-French led military intervention in Libya, beginning in March 2011, should be designated as a CSDP mission is a powerful testimony of this phenomenon, which is unlikely to change soon.

Decisions on CSDP matters (other than launching PSCD) are taken in the Council of Ministers by **unanimity** (Article 42(4) TEU). The **Foreign Affairs Council**'s discussions of such issues are prepared in the **Political and Security Committee** (PSC) and, as necessary, the EU Military Committee. CSDP actions are based on proposals made by the **High Representative** for CFSP or on initiatives coming from one or more member states. The **European Commission** as a whole has no **right of initiative** in this field, although where the High Representative proposes the combined use of national resources and Union policy instruments, the Commission's agreement is required. The **European Court of Justice** (ECJ) has no jurisdiction over CSDP issues, or indeed CFSP matters more widely (Article 275 TFEU).

The High Representative is obliged to keep the **European Parliament** informed about the 'main aspects and basic choices' of CFSP and ESDP. The Parliament in turn must hold a debate on CFSP and ESDP issues at least twice a year. There is no requirement that the Parliament be consulted on decisions in these fields, in the formal sense of the **consultation procedure** which applies for legislation in certain fields. However, in practice, considerable effort in made by the High Representative to ensure that the Parliament does not criticize EU action in this field, partly through fear that it might spill over into other areas of external relations – such as legislation in the fields of **Common Commercial Policy** (CCP) and **development policy**, or most **international agreements** – where it has a right of veto.

Denmark is the only member state to have sought and obtained an **opt-out** from CSDP. In order to secure **ratification** of the Maastricht Treaty, which was initially rejected by Danish voters, EU heads of government agreed at the Edinburgh European Council in December 1992 that Denmark 'does not participate in the elaboration and the implementation of decisions and actions of the Union which have defence implications'. In return, Copenhagen signalled that it would 'not prevent the other Member States from further developing their cooperation in this area'. This wording was subsequently incorporated in Protocol 22 to the Treaties.

In September 2011, the foreign ministers of five of the six largest member states – France, Germany, Italy, Poland and Spain – wrote to the High Representative, Catherine Ashton, suggesting that she 'examine all institutional and legal options' that were open, including PSCD, to develop 'critical CSDP capabilities', especially through the establishment of a 'planning and conduct' cell to provide stronger, more coherent way of organizing joint civil and military crisis management interventions. The British government remains strongly hostile to such an initiative, thus making it more likely that the possibility of PSCD will be invoked.

Further reading: Jolyon Howorth, *Security and Defence Policy in the European Union*, 2007.

'Communautization'

In European Union politics, an area of policy is said to have been 'communautized' or 'communitized' – with spelling a matter of personal preference – when it is brought within the ambit of the '**Community method**' of decision-making. The difference between communautized and non-communautized decision-making corresponds closely to that between **supranationalism and intergovernmentalism**.

The use of the word 'Community' in this context is important in that, following the 1992 **Maastricht Treaty**, a distinction had to be drawn between the traditional, so-called 'first' or European Community '**pillar**' of the European Union, established by the **Treaty of Rome**, which operated on a supranational basis, and the new, second and third pillars, for respectively **Common Foreign and Security Policy** (CFSP) and **Justice and Home Affairs** (JHA), where a form of intergovernmental decision-making was used. The 1997 **Amsterdam Treaty** transferred some areas of JHA policy into the first pillar, so 'communautizing' them. The **Lisbon Treaty** in turn has abolished the pillared structure, bringing the remainder of JHA within the Community method, whilst leaving important aspects of CFSP outside it.

'Community method'

The 'Community method' is a phrase used to denote the particular character of the system of law-making in which the institutions of the European Union have been engaged since the 1950s. The essence of the 'Community method' lies in its use of a free-standing set of institutions at European level to enact law that binds the member states, takes precedence over national legislation and is enforceable in courts, at both national and supranational levels.

The concept of the 'Community method' is most closely associated with the thinking of **Jean Monnet**, the French technocrat who played an influential role in the foundation of the **European Communities**, and is sometimes called the 'Monnet method'. He believed that the nations of Europe should move beyond **intergovernmentalism** as the dominant mode of cooperation – reflected in early post-war bodies such as the **Council of Europe** and the **Organization for European Economic Cooperation** (OEEC) – and instead espouse **supranationalism**, by seeking to make binding commitments through common institutions whose decisions would take precedence over national ones in certain fields. Such a concept was path-breaking at the time and the founding **Treaties** are still unique in establishing an international legal and institutional structure of this kind.

The model which Monnet attempted to establish was based on his idea that a strong executive – an 'independent European organization', as he called it, which took the form successively of a **High Authority** and the **European Commission** – would articulate and embody the common interest of all participating states. It would propose (and implement) legislation to be adopted in a **Council of Ministers** representing national governments, in which ideally no one country would be able to exercise a veto. The binding character of the laws so enacted would be guaranteed by a superior court at supranational level – a **European Court of Justice** (ECJ). In time, the legislative process should be widened to include a directly-elected **European Parliament**, working in parallel to the Council. In answer to an accusation by French President **Charles de Gaulle** in 1962 that the United States was the key driver in federating Europe, Monnet declared that 'this [institutional] method is the real "federator" of Europe'.

The political system established by the **Treaties** in the 1950s represented a compromise between the new Community method and traditional intergovernmental decision-making – in that the areas of Community **competence** were limited in scope and the Council still acted by **unanimity** in many fields, as if it were a classic intergovernmental or diplomatic body, even when enacting supranational law. Successive treaty changes introduced since the 1986 **Single European Act** (SEA) have strengthened the Community method, by extending Community **competence**, increasing the use of **qualified majority voting** (QMV) in the Council, and forcing the Council to share an increasing proportion of its legislative power with the European Parliament. The Community method remains a deep article of faith for orthodox pro-Europeans, who are highly suspicious of any procedures – such as those in the **pillars** established under the 1992 **Maastricht Treaty** – which are essentially intergovernmental in character. The 'depillarization' of the European Union by the **Lisbon Treaty** was therefore a development of both legal and symbolic importance. See also '**communautization**'.

Further reading: Renaud Dehousse (editor), *The 'Community Method': Obstinate or Obsolete?*, 2011.

Competence

The competence of the European Union is its right to act in a defined policy area. The **Treaties** specify the fields in which the Union enjoys competence, and in such fields, which cumulatively cover a very wide area of public policy, the EU institutions may adopt legally-binding measures – known as **legal acts** – and the legislation thus enacted enjoys **primacy** over national law. The competence of the Union takes two main forms: exclusive competence and shared competence with the member states. An additional category of 'supporting' competence complements that of member states without displacing it. Article 4 TEU states 'competences not conferred upon the Union in the Treaties remain with the Member States.'

Until the **Lisbon Treaty**, which entered into force in December 2009, the areas of EU competence had never been listed in one place and had to be deduced from a wide variety of treaty articles, with inevitable disputes – particularly between the **European Commission** and the **Council of Ministers** or individual member states – about the boundaries of the Union's exclusive competence in particular. The nature of EU competence and the areas subject to it are now set out in detail in Articles 2–6 TFEU.

In areas of exclusive competence, 'only the Union may legislate and adopt legally binding acts, the Member States being able to do so themselves only if so empowered by the Union or for the implementation of Union acts' (Article 2(1) TFEU). As Damian Chalmers and Adam Tomkins have put it, the mere existence of exclusive competence is 'sufficient to pre-empt Member State laws' and, in these fields, there is 'a complete surrender of law-making power by the Member States to the European Union' (*European Union Public Law*, 2007). As listed in Article 3 TFEU, the areas of exclusive competence are relatively few: the **customs union**, **competition policy** to the extent necessary for the functioning of the **single market**, monetary policy within the **eurozone**, **Common Commercial Policy** (CCP), the conservation of marine biological resources under the **Common Fisheries Policy** (CFP), and certain types of **international agreement**.

In the past, the European Commission had asserted that a number of other fields fell within the exclusive competence of the Union – notably the single market, the whole of competition policy, the **Common Agricultural Policy** (CAP) and **transport policy** – but this view was not shared by the **Convention on the Future of Europe** in 2002–3, which drafted the **European Constitution**, or by the two subsequent **Intergovernmental Conferences** (IGC) in 2003–4 and 2007, before the provisions on competence were finally embodied in the Lisbon Treaty.

In the policy areas where there is shared competence between the EU and the member states, which are much more numerous, both may legislate in any field, but the member states can only 'exercise their competence to the extent that the Union has not exercised its competence' (Article 2(2) TFEU). When the Union acts, it takes precedence and establishes what lawyers call an 'occupied field'. This process may be reversed, in the unlikely event that the Union 'has decided to cease exercising its competence'. In practice, in areas of shared competence, as Chalmers and Tomkins put it, member states 'retain a power to regulate matters falling within' the relevant field, 'but they must not create a conflict with the rules adopted by the European Union'. The areas of shared competence listed in Article 4 TFEU are not exhaustive, but the 'principal areas' cited are the single market, social policy, **cohesion**, the CAP and CFP (except the conservation of marine biological resources), **environment policy**, consumer protection, transport policy, **Trans-European Networks** (TENs), **energy policy**, the Area of Freedom, Security and Justice (FSJ), otherwise known as **Justice and Home Affairs** (JHA), and aspects of public health.

The listing goes on to cite **development policy**, humanitarian aid, **research and development policy** and space policy as further areas where there is deemed to be shared competence, but where its exercise by the Union 'shall not result in the Member States being prevented from exercising theirs'. In these particular areas, there is in effect a kind of parallel competence, where Union action does not pre-empt that of the member states.

A further and very prominent area of shared competence – **Common Foreign and Security Policy** (CFSP) – is only alluded to indirectly in Article 2 TFEU. A longer, free-standing article, grouped with the other CFSP provisions, makes it clear that Union competence in this field covers 'all areas of foreign policy and all questions relating to the Union's security, including the progressive framing of a common defence policy that might lead to a common defence' (Article 24 TEU).

It is also worth noting that in some areas of shared competence, the member states are specifically allowed by the Treaties to enact more stringent or protective measures than those provided in Union law, provided that these do not have discriminatory intent or effect. These fields include environment policy, consumer protection, public health and a particular aspect of social policy, namely health and safety at work.

The third category of competence cited in the Treaties – the intellectually rather unsatisfactory concept of a 'supporting' competence – allows the Union 'to carry out actions to support, coordinate or supplement the actions of the Member States, without thereby superseding their competence in these areas' (Article 2(5) TFEU). These fields remain ones of national competence, but with the Union able to take legally-binding measures only so long as they do 'not entail **harmonization** of the Member States' laws or regulations'. The areas cited in Article 6 TFEU are policy in relation to human health, industry, culture, tourism, education, vocational training, youth, sport, civil protection and administrative cooperation. Originally, the Constitution had foreseen the concept of 'complementary action', but this was diluted to suit some of the member states in the 2007 IGC.

Articles 2(3) and 5 TFEU require the member states to 'coordinate their economic and employment policies within arrangements as determined by the Treaty, which the Union shall have competence to provide'. Here, as Jean-Claude Piris has observed, 'the EU has only a competence of coordination, while the Member States retain the competence on substance' (*The Lisbon Treaty: A Legal and Political Analysis*, 2010). Although this area might better have been classified as a supporting (or complementary) competence, rather than as a shared one, 'it was decided politically within the Convention that the importance of the coordination done by the EU' made it difficult to present it in this way. Neither of the subsequent IGCs, Piris notes, 'corrected the work of the Convention on this point'.

Finally, implicit in the Treaties and established explicitly by rulings of the **European Court of Justice** (ECJ) is the doctrine of 'implied' competence, which means that where EU institutions have the power to regulate a matter internally, they may also act externally. The Court's keynote judgement in the **ERTA case** (*Commission* v *Council*, Case 22/70) in 1971 was reconfirmed in Opinion 1/76, which states: 'The power to bind the Community vis-à-vis third countries . . . flows by implication from the provisions of the Treaty creating the internal power and in so far as the participation of the Community in the international agreement is . . . necessary for the attainment of one of the objectives of the Community.' Furthermore, if the matter in question is the subject of formally established common rules, the Union's power to act externally becomes exclusive: individual member states may no longer act independently. Implied competence is of great importance in the field of external relations.

Competition policy

Since the 1951 **Treaty of Paris** establishing the **European Coal and Steel Community** (ECSC), the avoidance of anti-competitive behaviour by market operators has played a central part in the European integration process. The importance attached to this objective reflected, more than anything else, the deep interest in regulatory issues taken by **Jean Monnet**, the architect of the **Schuman Plan**, who drew on his own experience in the United States during the Second World War. US anti-trust legislation, shaped by the Sherman Act of 1890 and the Clayton Act of 1914, provided a powerful guide to how federal law might be used to forge a continental economy. The role and powers of the ECSC **High Authority**, of which Monnet served as the first president, were modelled in part on those of independent regulatory agencies in Washington, notably the Federal

Trade Commission (FTC) and the Interstate Commerce Commission (ICC).

When the **European Economic Community** (EEC) was founded in 1957, 'the introduction of competition rules was seen', as David Harrison has noted, 'as the essential counterpart of the merging of national markets so as to create one market'. The **Spaak Committee** sought to find a formula that would 'reconcile mass production and the absence of monopoly' within an integrated European economy. The key articles written into the **Treaty of Rome** on competition policy – Articles 85 and 86 EEC, now Articles 101 and 102 TFEU – were in effect highly condensed versions of US practice in the field. Once again, Monnet played an important role, influencing the French and other negotiators of the treaty, both directly and through his former colleague and trusted friend, **Pierre Uri**.

Article 101 TFEU prohibits and renders 'automatically void' any 'agreements between undertakings, decisions by associations of undertakings and concerted practices which may affect trade between Member States and which have as their object or effect the prevention, restriction or distortion of competition within the internal market'. Included under this heading are price-fixing and market-sharing arrangements, production controls and discriminatory contracts intended to place particular trading parties at a disadvantage. However, exempted from this general prohibition are agreements or practices that contribute to 'improving the production or distribution of goods or to promoting technical or economic progress, while allowing consumers a fair share of the resulting benefit'. In parallel, Article 102 TFEU prohibits 'any abuse by one or more undertakings of a dominant position within the internal market or in a substantial part of it . . . in so far as it may affect trade between Member States'. This latter provision is an almost direct transposition into European law of anti-trust rules in the US Sherman Act.

Articles 101 and 102 TFEU apply to all economic sectors except the **Common Agricultural Policy** (CAP) and the common **transport policy**, which have their own competition rules (adopted respectively in 1962 and 1968). These exemptions were driven by political considerations: the power of the agricultural lobby in the first case and the fact that the rail industry and much of the airline industry were state-owned at the time the **Treaties** were drafted in the second. The special arrangements for the coal and steel industries (Articles 65–6 ECSC) expired with the Treaty of Paris in 2002. Under Article 106 TFEU, publicly-owned undertakings, including monopolies of a commercial character, are bound by the rules of competition 'in so far as the application of such rules does not obstruct the performance . . . of the particular tasks assigned to them. The development of trade must not be affected to such an extent as would be contrary to the interests of the Union.' The treaty obligations here represented a compromise between the views of those member states (Germany and the Netherlands) which wanted to liberalize sectors such as energy, postal services and telecommunications, and others (France, Italy and Belgium) that preferred to protect state monopolies in these fields. In practice, the latter remained outside the writ of competition policy until, starting in the 1980s, a combination of progress in completing the **single market** and the general spread of privatization at national level weakened the hold of the state in such sectors. (The EU cannot prevent state ownership, as Article 345 TFEU specifies that 'the Treaties shall in no way prejudge the rules in Member States governing the system of property ownership.')

The **European Commission** has a general responsibility to enforce Articles 101 and 102 TFEU, in cooperation with the authorities of member states, and the right to conduct investigations either at their request or on its own initiative (Article 105 TFEU). The practical means whereby the Commission may discharge this responsibility were defined in a competition policy **regulation** passed by the **Council of Ministers** in February 1962 and updated periodically since. All agreements or actions that might fall foul of Articles 101 and 102 have to be notified by undertakings to the Commission, which is in turn empowered not only to request information from undertakings suspected of anti-competitive practices, but to carry out 'all necessary investigations', including examination and copying of business records, 'ask for oral explanations on the spot' and 'enter any premises, land and means of transport' owned by the undertakings under investigation.

The Commission is unusually powerful in the competition policy field. From 1962 onwards, the Council devolved to the Commission the right to adopt **decisions** in law without the need to consult it or any other Community institution. In addition, in respect of the enforcement of member states' obligations towards publicly-owned undertakings, the Treaty of Rome itself gave the Commission the right to take legally-binding action directly (Article 106 TFEU). However, in practice, even if it enjoys ample powers, the Commission has never found it easy to cope with the sheer volume of cases that it could potentially address. To lighten its growing workload and counter rising criticism of its handling of cases, the Commission chose voluntarily to dispense with the need to be informed of agreements between undertakings that together had less than a five per cent share of the relevant market within the Union. More controversially, it also allowed certain 'block exemptions' from normal competition policy rules for certain sectors – notably motor vehicle distribution and the operation of 'tied' bars and public houses – where exclusive distribution and franchise agreements could be maintained. In the same logic, it floated the idea in the early 2000s that the national competition authorities should be allowed to act on its behalf in delivering Union policy, as in effect service providers in the member states. Since 2003, these national authorities – now brought together in a 'European Competition Network' (ECN) – may individually apply EU competition rules (in respect of Articles 101 and 102 TFEU) in their entirety, on behalf of the Commission, under defined conditions.

The Commission (or the national competition authorities on its behalf) may impose fines on undertakings found to have supplied 'incorrect or misleading information' or to have failed to supply information on request. More importantly, they may also impose fines ranging from € 1,000 to € 1.0 million 'or a sum in excess thereof but not exceeding 10 per cent of turnover in the preceding business year' on undertakings found to have infringed Articles 101 or 102 TFEU, assessed with regard 'to the gravity and to the duration of the infringement'. Failure to supply information, submit to an investigation or abandon a prohibited practice may incur a 'periodic penalty payment' at rates ranging between € 50 and € 1,000 a day. These powers are absolute, subject only to a right of appeal of undertakings in the General Court of the **European Court of Justice** (ECJ).

The fines imposed on undertakings can be substantial. The Commission's landmark fines of the 1990s – of € 75 million against Tetra Pak in 1991 and € 102 million against Volkswagen in 1998 – now seem modest. In the years 2005–9, it imposed fines totalling nearly € 10 billion, in 39 cases involving over 200 companies. In May 2009, it imposed its biggest ever fine, € 1.06 billion, on the US chip-maker, Intel, for abusing its dominant position with regard to the sale and marketing of its central processing unit for computers. In December 2009, the Commission forced Microsoft to offer a choice of web browsers to all users of various Windows and Vista systems, who had previously been compelled to use Microsoft's own browser.

In its Continental Can ruling of 1973 *(Europemballage Corporation and Continental Can Co. Inc.* v *Commission,* Case 6/72), the ECJ established that a merger or acquisition may constitute an 'abuse of a dominant position' prohibited under Article 102 TFEU. Such an abuse may be proved even if the company cannot be shown actually to have exploited its market position to the detriment of competitors. The question of whether a merger might be potentially prejudicial to competition depends on the definition of the geographical market involved. With the widening and deepening of the single market, national markets have increasingly ceased to be the appropriate frame of reference within which to consider mergers, the vetting of which has now become an important part of EU competition policy.

Since September 1990, the Commission has enjoyed sole authority to vet large-scale mergers, defined in a 'merger control regulation' – which it took 16 years to agree in the Council and was most recently updated in 2004 – as those involving concerns with a combined annual turnover of at least € 2.5 billion, of which more than € 100 million is generated in each of at least three member states. In each of these states, the turnover of at least two of the concerns must exceed € 25 million. Overall, the Union-wide turnover of at least two of the concerns must exceed € 100 million. However, if each of the concerns generates two-thirds of its Union-wide turnover in one member state, the proposed merger is vetted not by the Commission but by the relevant national authorities. Commission decisions under the mergers regulation affect companies with a turnover of around € 50 billion in a typical year.

Market failure and market abuse need not only be the consequence of the activities of undertakings, whether privately or publicly owned; they can also flow from the activities of government. Thus a further major component of EU competition policy is the outlawing of government subsidies or 'state aids' to favoured national undertakings. The provision of financial assistance from public funds to commercial enterprises, public or private, that distort the conditions of competition within the Union are subject to strict rules laid down in Articles 107–9 TFEU (originally Articles 87–9 EEC). Article 107 states that 'any aid granted by a Member State or through State resources in any form whatsoever which distorts or threatens to distort competition by favouring certain undertakings or the production of certain goods shall, in so far as it affects trade between Member States, be incompatible with the internal market.'

State aids must in all circumstances be notified to the Commission, which can block them or, in the case of those already granted, insist upon repayment. To be approved, state aids must be of a specified amount and time-limited, and in the case of an enterprise in difficulties may be given only in conjunction with a restructuring programme. They may also be approved if they are given in response to emergency needs, are designed to 'remedy a serious disturbance' in a member-state economy, are linked to 'an important project of common European interest', promote cultural or heritage conservation, or encourage economic development in particularly disadvantaged regions.

Normally, the Commission takes about 450 decisions on state aids a year, some of which are inevitably controversial. A difficult balance sometimes has to be struck between the competing imperatives of efficiency and equity, or in judging whether a subsidy now may reduce the potential for market distortion in future. The long list given in the treaty of circumstances in which state aids may be granted provides plenty of scope for ingenious economic arguments driven by essentially political motives. As in competition policy more widely, the ECJ is the ultimate arbiter of the legality of contested state aids. The European Commission publishes a regular 'scoreboard' of state aids (other than for the CAP and transport), which, until recently, showed the total to be on a gradually downward path, falling to around 0.5 per cent of the Union's gross domestic product (GDP) in 2007 (€ 67.4 billion).

However, the economic and financial crisis that began in autumn 2008 has led to a sudden and spectacular increase in state aids, as a result of the need to subsidize the banking sector in particular. In 2008, the share of state aids in GDP jumped to 2.2 per cent (€ 280 billion), of which 1.7 per cent (€ 212 billion) related directly to the crisis. In 2009, the situation deteriorated badly. A 'temporary framework' for state aids in response to the crisis was adopted, although many with strings attached. This allowed the Commission to authorize over 40 major rescue schemes across the Union, with a total value of some € 4.6 trillion over the two-year period from October 2008 to October 2010, representing around 20 per cent of EU GDP. There is a legal obligation for the subsidies to be phased out as soon as economic recovery allows. Whilst some claim that this rapid reaction shows that the Union's state aids' régime is sufficiently flexible to respond to an enormous crisis, others fear that permanent damage has been inflicted on the integrity of the system.

From time to time, it is suggested that a new European agency or 'cartel office', independent of the Commission, should be set up to enforce competition rules, but this has so far been resisted by the Commission on the grounds that it already enjoys the necessary independence, but is equally able to assess the political dimension which inevitably arises in particularly controversial competition cases. Since the 1980s, a string of very active Commissioners for competition policy – Frans Andriessen, Peter Sutherland, Leon Brittan, Mario Monti and Neelie Kroes – have been instrumental in making competition policy much more effective at EU level, greatly reducing criticism of the Commission's performance. The shrewd decision to decentralize many actions under Articles 101 and 102 TFEU, making the national competition authorities both partners and subordinates of the Commission, has also greatly helped.

The **Lisbon Treaty** states that 'the competition rules necessary for the functioning of the internal market' are an area of exclusive European Union **competence** (Article 3(1)b TFEU). Maintaining arrangements set down in the original Treaty of Rome, legislation in the field is adopted by the Council, using QMV, after consulting the European Parliament. There has been relatively little pressure to extend **co-decision** between the Council and Parliament to this policy area. Since 1971, the Commission has drawn up an annual report on its activities in respect of competition policy for submission to, and debate in, the Parliament.

Further reading: Michelle Cini and Lee McGowan, *Competition Policy in the European Union*, 2008; Robert Lane, *EC Competition Law*, 2001.

Compulsory and non-compulsory expenditure

Compulsory and non-compulsory expenditure – sometimes also known as obligatory and non-obligatory expenditure – were technical terms used in relation to the European Union **Budget** before the entry into force of the **Lisbon Treaty** in December 2009. The distinction was introduced by the 1970 Budgetary Treaty and took effect from 1975. Compulsory expenditure was deemed to be spending which 'the budgetary authority is obliged to enter in the budget by virtue of a legal undertaking entered into under the Treaty or an act adopted by virtue of this Treaty'. All other expenditure was non-obligatory.

Although the difference between compulsory and non-compulsory expenditure was never entirely clear-cut – with the boundary between the two seemingly drawn as much for political as technical reasons – the distinction had an important bearing on the exercise of power within the annual **budgetary process**. Under the procedure that applied from 1975 to 2009, one arm of the joint budgetary authority, the **Council of Ministers**, had the final say on compulsory spending, whilst the other arm, the **European Parliament**, had the last word on non-compulsory spending. The Parliament's discretion over the latter was limited by a 'maximum rate' of increase in expenditure over the previous year, which could only be changed by agreement between the Council, acting by **qualified majority voting** (QMV), and the Parliament, with the support of a majority of MEPs and three-fifths of the votes cast. Within this constraint, the larger the share of non-compulsory expenditure in the Budget, the greater was the Parliament's power, which was directed as much at changing budgetary priorities as significantly increasing the overall amount of spending.

For some years, arguments between the Council and the Parliament over the classification of expenditure flared up on a regular basis. However, in 1982, the **European Commission**, which proposes the Budget, secured agreement with the two other institutions on which spending headings were deemed to fall into which category, and that each side of the budgetary authority would respect this division. This arrangement – struck largely at the Parliament's expense – held fairly consistently from then on.

Easily the most important element within compulsory expenditure was price support under the **Common Agricultural Policy** (CAP): this alone constituted 70 per cent of the Community Budget in 1975, when the compulsory/non-compulsory distinction took effect. Other 'unavoidable' expenditures were deemed to include transfers made to non-EU countries under various **international agreements** and refunds to member states. However, the salaries of Community officials and other administrative costs were considered discretionary, and thus did not feature as compulsory expenditure. Over time, the share of non-compulsory spending gradually rose, reflecting the evolution of EU policy priorities, from a quarter of the Budget in 1988 to a half in 2005. The Lisbon Treaty has made the Council and Parliament co-equal in the power they exercise within a simplified budgetary process, so rendering the distinction between compulsory and non-compulsory expenditure redundant.

Concentric circles

The idea of 'concentric circles' was frequently invoked during the early- to mid-1990s as a model of how Europe as a whole might develop in coming years. Characteristically this concept took one of two forms: a multi-tiered relationship between the European Union and other European countries, or a multi-tiered European Union itself.

In the first formulation, the member states of the European Union would occupy the central core; an intermediate circle of other countries would enjoy privileged links, along the lines of the **European Economic Area** (EEA) but with an enhanced status; and other European states with **association agreements** could make up a third circle. When commentators first talked of 'concentric circles' in these terms, there were natural candidates for the second and third tiers: several of the countries of the **European Free Trade Association** (EFTA) had yet to join the EU, and the states of central and eastern Europe were only just emerging into democracy. Such a formula promised conveniently to avoid the need for an early or wide **enlargement** of the Union and it offered the prospect of a potentially permanent 'privileged partnership' for certain countries, notably **Switzerland** or **Turkey**, which, for political reasons, might not wish or be able to join the EU. The **accession** of three EEA countries to the EU in 1995, followed by the inclusion of a dozen more new member states in 2004–7, effectively emptied the outer tiers of their potential membership at that time, rendering this concept of concentric circles largely redundant.

The second formulation of concentric circles has been used to sketch how the European Union itself might evolve internally. Various models have been offered at different times, mainly by commentators from **the Six** founding member states. In a typical variant, a central group or 'hard core' of member states would provide political leadership to the Union, engage in all common policies, and develop additional areas of **enhanced cooperation** as it chooses. A second circle would comprise member states that were involved in all the Union's common policies but preferred not to play a vanguard role. A third circle would comprise member states with **opt-outs** from some common policies. A final, outer circle might encompass non-member states which chose to participate in certain EU policies (through, for example, the EEA or **Schengen**).

In August 1994, French prime minister Edouard Balladur proposed a three-tier Europe along these lines. His 'organization of European integration' would be structured around: i) an inner group of EU member states, which would use the single currency and engage in closer defence cooperation; ii) other existing EU member states; and iii) an area beyond the EU enjoying a looser economic and security relationship with the Union. One central problem with his concept was that inner-core arrangements in defence would be very difficult to envisage without the participation of Britain, a country very unlikely to join stage three of **Economic and Monetary Union** (EMU). A decade later, a senior French European Commission official, François Lamoureux – a former confidant of **Jacques Delors** and author of the highly integrationist 'Penelope' project – vented frustration with the United Kingdom's attitude towards closer cooperation, by suggesting that the status of 'opt-out' countries within the Union could be formalized as a 'European rearguard'. His remarks were not well received within the Commission and he took early retirement soon after. See also '**variable geometry**', '**two-speed Europe**' and **Lamers–Schäuble paper**.

Conference on Security and Cooperation in Europe (CSCE)

Begun in July 1973, the CSCE, the first stage of which was concluded by the signing of the **Helsinki Final Act** on 1 August 1975, was an attempt to reconcile the conflicting interests of the Atlantic Alliance and the countries of the **Warsaw Pact** during the latter part of the **Cold War**. All European countries (except Albania) took part in the negotiations that resulted in the Final Act, together with the United States and Canada, a total of 35 states. Broadly, the countries of the Eastern bloc were interested in military security and in extending economic and technological cooperation with the West, while the countries of the West were interested in promoting human rights in the East.

These different priorities were reflected in the various 'baskets' into which the Final Act was divided – security and disarmament, on the one hand, and economic, scientific and technological cooperation and the protection of the environment, on the other. The former laid down certain principles for the conduct of relations between states: respect for **sovereignty**, non-interference in internal affairs, inviolability of frontiers, renunciation of force as a means of settling disputes, and respect for human rights.

The Helsinki meeting was succeeded by a series of CSCE follow-up meetings, held in Belgrade (1977–8), Madrid (1980–3), Vienna (1986–9) and Helsinki (1992). In between such meetings, expert groups discussed particular aspects of the subjects covered by the Final Act, notably human rights and the peaceful settlement of disputes. Linked to the CSCE were conferences on confidence- and security-building measures (CSBM: Stockholm, 1984–6) and on conventional forces in Europe (CFE: 1989–92). Of these follow-up meetings, the one that yielded the most substantial results was the meeting concluded in Vienna in January 1989, where a permanent mechanism for monitoring human rights was agreed by all 35 countries.

In November 1990, following the collapse of Communism in central and eastern Europe, the CSCE heads of government met in Paris for the first time since the 1975 meeting in Helsinki. The CFE Treaty was signed on 19 November and the **Charter of Paris** for a New Europe two days later. The Paris summit, originally proposed by Mikhail Gorbachev, gave the CSCE a formal institutional structure – which was officially renamed the **Organization for Security and Cooperation in Europe** (OSCE) in 1995 – and in effect marked the end of the Cold War.

Congress of Europe

Organized by the International Committee of the Movements for European Unity, the precursor of the **European Movement**, the Congress of Europe was a major international gathering of campaigners for closer European integration, held in The Hague from 7 to 11 May 1948. The meeting sought, on an all-party basis, to enlist public support and bring pressure to bear upon governments for institutional and other initiatives designed to unite the western part of the newly-divided continent. **Winston Churchill** served as president-of-honour of the event, which was attended by over 800 prominent politicians, lawyers and academics from almost every country in Europe. Among participants who were later to play an important part in the course of post-war European history were **Konrad Adenauer**, **François Mitterrand** and **Paul-Henri Spaak**.

The Congress adopted a 'Message to Europeans' which called for 'a united Europe, throughout whose area the **free movement** of persons, ideas and goods is restored'. This would be underpinned by a 'Charter of Human Rights', a Court of Justice to guarantee those rights, and a 'European Assembly where the live forces of all our nations shall be represented'. These ideas were worked out in more detail in a political report considered by the Congress, which prompted a number of specific resolutions, adopted unanimously.

The Congress, the name of which was a deliberate echo of the 1815 Congress of Vienna attended by the victorious powers at the end of the Napoleonic wars, represented perhaps the high-water mark of enthusiasm for European unity in the immediate post-war period. The commitment with which Churchill, in particular, approached the event – as part of what Michael Charlton (*The Price of Victory*, 1983) calls his 'powerful unofficial British foreign policy' at this time – guaranteed that it made a substantial impact across Europe. Several of the main ideas put forward in The Hague were taken up the following year in the statute of the **Council of Europe**, even if this organization was structured essentially on intergovernmental lines.

In 1988, 1998 and 2008, the European Movement organized major conferences in The Hague to commemorate the anniversary of the original Congress. The original documents from the 1948 event are available on the Movement's website.

Consent procedure

The 'consent' procedure gives the **European Parliament** a right of veto over certain important decisions assigned to, and taken by, the **Council of Ministers** or **European Council**. The Parliament expresses its view in a single reading between the Council agreeing its position and formally adopting it (with the Council acting in most cases by **unanimity**). Introduced as the 'assent' procedure by the 1986 **Single European Act** (SEA), this decision-making method initially required an absolute majority of the total membership of the Parliament to vote in favour of the proposal before the act in question could finally be adopted by the Council, and it applied to two areas of decision-making: the conclusion of **association agreements** with third countries (now Article 217 TFEU) and the **accession** of new member states (Article 49 TEU). Subsequent treaty changes have both extended the range of Council decisions subject to this form of parliamentary veto – whilst continuing to apply it mainly to either **international agreements** or quasi-constitutional issues – and loosened the absolute majority requirement among MEPs.

Since the **Lisbon Treaty** entered into force in December 2009 – substituting the name 'consent' for 'assent' – the procedure now applies to 14 other areas of policy or types of decision (the last nine of which were introduced by that treaty). They are: i) approval of international agreements which involve institutional frameworks, have important budgetary implications or (since Lisbon) cover policy areas where the **co-decision procedure** between the Council and Parliament applies (Articles 207 and 218 TFEU); ii) determination of a 'clear risk' of a serious breach of fundamental rights by a member state and/or the imposition of sanctions on that member state for a 'serious and persistent breach' of such rights (Articles 7(1-2) TEU and 354 TFEU – see **suspension**); iii) use of **enhanced cooperation** by nine or more member states (Article 329(1) TFEU); iv) adoption of a **uniform electoral procedure** for the European Parliament (Article 223(1) TFEU); v) adoption of anti-discrimination measures (Article 19(1) TFEU); vi) extension of **European citizenship** rights (Article 25 TEU); vii) use of the general ***passerelle*** **clause** to extend the areas subject to **qualified majority voting** (QMV) in the Council or co-decision between the Council and Parliament (Article 48(7) TEU); viii) use of **Article 352** TFEU, the so-called 'flexibility clause', which allows the Council to adopt measures not explicitly sanctioned by the powers contained in specific treaty articles; ix) adoption of implementing measures for the Union's **own resources** system (Article 311(4) TFEU); x) adoption of Multiannual Financial Frameworks (MFFs) (Article 312(2) TFEU); xi) aspects of criminal justice procedure and extension of categories of serious cross-border crime subject to EU definition and sanctions (Articles 82 and 83 TFEU); xii) establishment of, or extension of the powers of, a European Public Prosecutor's Office (Article 86 TFEU); xiii) accession by the Union to the **European Convention on Human Rights** (ECHR); and xiv) use of the **exit clause**, whereby a member state may leave the Union (Article 50 TEU).

The requirement for an absolute majority of MEPs has been significantly diluted since the SEA. The 1992 **Maastricht Treaty** allowed association agreements to be approved by a simple majority of votes cast in the Parliament, rather than by the absolute majority of Members previously required, but it maintained the status quo ante for decisions on the accession of new member states. In the 14 other fields listed above, only four have an absolute-majority requirement: the determination of a clear risk of, or actual breaches of, fundamental rights; the adoption of a uniform electoral procedure; the use of the general *passerelle* clause; and the adoption of MFFs. In the first case, a two-thirds majority of MEPs voting is also required, because of the extreme political sensitivity of the question.

When it was introduced, the notion of assent represented an important advance in parliamentary power. It gave the European Parliament a simple, unequivocal, 'up-down' capacity to reject proposals in a limited number of policy areas – at a time when the routine legislative process, in the form of either the traditional **consultation procedure** or the (then) new **cooperation procedure**, fell far short of this. However, with the development of the co-decision procedure, introduced by Maastricht, the Parliament was soon to enjoy a right of veto over an increasing proportion of routine EU legislation, acting in effect as a joint legislature with the Council in the fields where this applied. Co-decision was – and remains as part of the 'ordinary legislative procedure' – a more attractive formula from the Parliament's perspective, allowing it to propose amendments to specific clauses and to engage in a dialogue with the Council through several readings, rather than being forced to react to the latter's position, at the end of the law-making process, on a take-it-or-leave-it basis.

When the assent procedure was introduced, the Parliament asserted its position, by delaying its approval, or simply rejecting the Council's position, in a number of high-profile international agreements. It refused to endorse protocols to association agreements with Israel in 1988 (until concessions on exports from the West Bank had been secured) and with Syria and Morocco in 1992 (because of human rights abuses). The Parliament also held up the EU–Turkey customs union in 1995 until certain constitutional and legislative changes had been made by the Turkish government to guarantee freedom of speech. In recent years, there have been fewer examples of the Parliament's approval being withheld, which may reflect a growing willingness on the part of the Commission and Council to factor parliamentary sensitivities into their negotiations at an earlier stage. However, since Lisbon extended the need for consent to any international agreement where co-decision applies to the policy area in question – so broadening it to cover most agreements in the fields of external trade policy and all aspects of **Justice and Home Affairs** (JHA) – it has taken some time for the Commission and Council to adjust to the reality of sharing power with the Parliament in these fields. The latter's rejection in February 2010 of the SWIFT agreement on the sharing of financial data with the United States, negotiated before Lisbon came into effect and without effective parliamentary involvement, proved a striking case in point. There will now be pressure from the Parliament for more intensive dialogue between the two institutions before international agreements are submitted for its consent.

Consultation procedure

The **Treaties** provide for consultation with many different institutions and bodies under various EU decision-making procedures, but the expression 'consultation procedure' is usually reserved for the simplest form of one-stage consultation of the **European Parliament** by the **Council of Ministers**, in those policy areas where the latter acts on its own as the Union's legislature and the former is asked to give an **opinion** on a piece of draft legislation. Under the consultation procedure, the Council is under no obligation to take account of the view that the Parliament expresses (which takes the form of a resolution adopted in plenary). Equally, however, the Council cannot simply act in the absence of the Parliament's opinion, a principle established by the **European Court of Justice** (ECJ) in the 1980 'isoglucose' case (*Roquette Frères* v *Council*, Case 138/79). This in effect allows the Parliament to delay the adoption of legislation by the Council within a reasonable period, even if it cannot amend or veto it.

Consultation was the only method by which the Parliament was involved in the legislative process from the foundation of the European Communities until the 1986 **Single European Act** (SEA). Since then, consultation has been gradually supplemented and superseded by new procedures that give the Parliament much greater power. The SEA introduced the multi-reading **cooperation procedure** – whereby if the Parliament's amendments were endorsed by the Commission, they could only be rejected by the Council acting unanimously – and the **consent procedure** (initially known as the assent procedure) – which gives the Parliament a straight veto over a limited number of important Council decisions. The 1992 **Maastricht Treaty** went a significant step further than the cooperation procedure, by establishing the **co-decision procedure**, in effect making the Council and Parliament a co-equal joint legislature in the policy areas where it applies. Whereas amendments adopted by the Parliament under the consultation procedure only require a simple majority of votes to pass, those adopted under co-decision require (and the cooperation procedure previously required), at least at second reading, the support of an absolute majority of members.

Although the 1997 **Amsterdam Treaty** and 2001 **Nice Treaty** significantly broadened the range of issues subject to co-decision, it was the entry into force of the **Lisbon Treaty** in December 2009 which finally marked the 'tipping point' in favour of co-decision (over consultation) in EU law-making. Lisbon defined co-decision as part of the 'normal legislative procedure' of the Union and relegated consultation to the status of a 'special legislative procedure'; it also abolished the cooperation procedure. Today, the consultation procedure still applies to certain politically sensitive areas of law-making such as **tax harmonisation** and **own resources**, as well as many decisions in the fields of **Economic and Monetary Union** (EMU) and institutional reform. However, before the Lisbon Treaty, the consultation procedure applied to the **Common Agricultural Policy** (CAP), the **Common Fisheries Policy** (CFP), the **Common Commercial Policy** (CCP) and much of **Justice and Home Affairs** (JHA). Co-decision now applies in these four policy areas. Until December 2009, around 55 per cent of legislation coming to the Parliament was based on consultation, compared with less than 20 per cent since then. However, even in the past, consultation was less significant 'qualitatively' than it might appear quantitatively: although some consultation decisions are extremely important, many of those before 2009 were fairly routine matters concerning agriculture and fisheries. Much of the new keynote legislation enacted in the first decade of the 2000s already relied on co-decision: for example, the controversial services directive, the chemicals (REACH) regulation and the climate-change package, all adopted during the 2004–9 European Parliament.

Consumer policy

Although the original **Treaty of Rome** made no specific provision for a Community-wide policy to protect the interests of consumers, the **common market** itself, underpinned by a **competition policy**, was designed to widen consumer choice. The EC heads of government first agreed to develop a specific consumer protection policy in 1972, with the **European Commission** establishing a consultative committee for consumers in 1973 (now the Consumers' Consultative Council) and the **Council of Ministers** adopting its first Consumer Action Programme two years later.

The **legal base** for consumer policy was gradually put in place during the

1980s and 1990s. The 1986 **Single European Act** (SEA) obliged the Commission, in making legislative proposals for the completion of the **single market**, to 'take as a base a high level of protection' in the consumer protection field, as in health, safety and the environment (Article 114(3) TFEU). The 1992 **Maastricht Treaty** provided for the adoption of 'measures which support, supplement and monitor the policy pursued by the Member States' in consumer policy (Article 169(2) TFEU). Member states are allowed to maintain or introduce 'more stringent protective measures' – in line with a principle first laid down by the **European Court of Justice** (ECJ) in 1986 (*Commission* v *Denmark*, Case 302/86) – provided that such measures are not discriminatory or a 'disguised restriction' on trade between member states. Article 12 TFEU stipulates that 'Consumer protection requirements shall be taken into account in defining and implementing other Union policies and activities.'

The Consumer Action Programme led to Community legislation being adopted on unit pricing, standard quantities for pre-packaged products, labelling, misleading and comparative advertising, dangerous substances and the use of additives in foodstuffs. The controversial product liability directive in 1985 empowered consumers to bring proceedings against producers for damage without having to prove negligence on the part of the latter. Subsequent legislation has covered inter alia unfair terms in contracts, doorstep and distance selling, package holidays, timeshare property, consumer credit, toy safety, cosmetic products and medical devices.

In October 2008, the Commission put forward a proposal for a general consumer rights' directive, which consolidated much of the existing legislation in this policy field and updated it to reflect changing patterns of consumption, notably the growth of online shopping. A parallel 'Consumer Policy Strategy 2007–13', backed by funding of € 167 billion over the seven-year financing period, was aimed at reinforcing the retail dimension of the single market. In order to monitor the application of consumer policy measures, the Commission has sought to assist and develop national consumer bodies and promote more cooperation among them. The main Brussels-based consumers' lobby is the European Bureau of Consumers' Unions, known by its French acronym, BEUC. Information to consumers is made available through a network of European Consumer Information Centres (*Euroguichets*).

Convention on the Future of Europe

Established by the **European Council** meeting in Laeken, Belgium, in December 2001, the Convention on the Future of Europe met from February 2002 to July 2003 and drafted the **European Constitution**. In their Laeken Declaration, EU heads of government set out the role and composition of the Convention: its central task was to recommend possible treaty changes, in advance of an **Intergovernmental Conference** (IGC) to be convened soon after, and to do so on the basis of deliberations by 105 political figures, drawn from the EU institutions and the current and prospective member states.

The Laeken summit designated the former French President, **Valéry Giscard d'Estaing**, as the President of the Convention. (Guy Verhofstadt, the Belgian prime minister and president-in-office of the European Council, had unsuccessfully sought to install his outgoing Dutch opposite number, Wim Kok instead.) The former Italian and Belgian prime ministers, Giuliano Amato and Jean-Luc Dehaene, were appointed Vice-Presidents of the Convention. In addition, the Convention comprised 56 national parliamentarians, 28 representatives of governments, 16 Members of the **European Parliament** (MEPs) and two European Commissioners. Each member (other than the President and two Vice-Presidents) was matched by a substitute. There were also 13 observers from EU bodies not represented in their own right.

In accordance with the Laeken Declaration, the 'triumvirate' of Giscard, Amato and Dehaene, together with ten other *conventionnels*, formed a central Praesidium, whose task it was to 'lend impetus' to, and offer 'an initial working basis' for, the proceedings of the Convention. Both the Praesidium and the Convention as a whole were serviced by a 15-strong secretariat, based in the **Council of Ministers** and headed by John Kerr, a skilled negotiator and former UK permanent representative to the EU.

At the inaugural session of the Convention, held in the European Parliament on 28 February 2002, Giscard stressed the need for high ambition in the work ahead. Instead of simply proposing options or limiting themselves to adjustments to the existing **Treaties** – as several more minimalist governments would have preferred – he urged his colleagues to 'dream of Europe', develop a 'Convention spirit', and, critically, 'achieve a broad consensus on a single proposal for reform' which would 'open the way towards a Constitution for Europe'. Giscard's frequent public comparison of the new European Convention with the Philadelphia Convention which had drafted the US Constitution in 1787 made a big impact in the media and was largely taken at face value.

After an initial 'open, attentive listening' phase, as Giscard described it, the Convention moved to detailed discussion of specific reforms. It was already clear that, in Giscard's concept, the scope of any constitution would go beyond the purely institutional, covering the existing or future policies of the Union as well. Six working groups, of about 30 members each, started work in May, dealing with **subsidiarity**, the EU **Charter of Fundamental Rights**, the **legal personality** of the Union, the involvement of **national parliaments** in EU decision-making, the **competences** of the Union, and **European economic governance**. A further set of four working groups was established in July, dealing with the Union's external action, defence, simplification of legislative procedures, and freedom, security and justice. An eleventh working group was set up in November on social Europe.

The progress of the Convention was defined by three distinct developments in the autumn of 2002. The first was the initiative taken by Giscard and the Praesidium, on 22 October, in sketching out a fairly detailed outline of a new 'constitutional treaty'. This framework provided a list of potential treaty articles and offered some suggested content in respect of institutions, so in effect shaping the broad terms of the rest of the Convention's discussions. The plan was that the Union would be given a 'single institutional structure', by merging the existing **Treaties** into a single text, demolishing the separate **pillars** (between Community and Union activity) established by the 1992 **Maastricht Treaty**, and endowing the whole of the resulting Union with a **legal personality**. This basic concept survived into the Convention's eventual proposal for a 'Draft Treaty establishing a Constitution for Europe' the following July. Among other important reforms suggested in the Praesidium text were the creation of a new permanent **President of the European Council** and the inclusion of an '**exit clause**' by which member states could leave the Union. Giscard also opened up debates about whether there might be a 'Congress of the Peoples of Europe', as a kind of upper chamber mixing national and European parliamentarians, and whether the European Union should be given a new name, such as the '**United States of Europe**' or 'Europe United'. However, neither of these latter ideas found much support.

The second key development was the gradual delivery of the reports of the 11 working groups between September 2002 and February 2003, generating a regular flow of specific proposals to flesh out the overall structure suggested by the Praesidium. Among the more important proposals to be endorsed were that the **Charter of Fundamental Rights** should be incorporated into the new treaty, **qualified majority voting** (QMV) in the Council and **co-decision** between the Council and Parliament should become the general rule in EU law-making, **national parliaments** should be given a specific role in policing **subsidiarity**, the annual **budgetary process** should be simplified, with the Council and Parliament becoming co-equal in all respects, and the variety of **legal acts** that the Union adopts should be streamlined and reduced (see '**hierarchy of acts**').

The third development was the unexpected decision by France and Germany to significantly upgrade their governmental representation in the Convention. In October 2002, Berlin nominated the German foreign minister, Joschka Fischer; Paris sent its foreign minister, Dominique de Villepin, to the Convention two months later. (Three other foreign ministers were already members of the Convention and three more joined later, bringing the total to eight.) The arrival of Fischer and de Villepin prompted a series of Franco-German papers, culminating in a joint submission to the Convention on institutional reforms in January 2003, timed to coincide with the fortieth anniversary of the **Elysée Treaty**. This latter text endorsed the idea of a permanent President of the European Council, proposed the post of High Representative be transformed into a European foreign minister (taking in the role of Commissioner for external relations), and advocated the formal election of the President of the Commission by the European Parliament, on the basis of a European Council nomination made by QMV. It also supported the wider use of QMV in the Council of Ministers on policy questions, matched by greater co-decision with the Parliament. Although several smaller member states reacted badly to what they saw as a Franco-German attempt to rush the Convention into a particular outcome, the reality was that most points in the joint paper were subsequently accepted.

Drawing on the various inputs, the Praesidium began to circulate draft treaty articles from January 2003 onwards, opening the third phase of the Convention's work. Consideration in plenary sessions of groups of potential treaty articles generated over 2,500 amendments, slowing down the business of the Convention. At the same time, EU heads of government, meeting with Giscard in Athens in April, felt that the Convention process needed to be brought to a head and instructed him to conclude its deliberations by June. Back in Brussels, Giscard decided to accelerate the pace of work, whilst maladroitly redoubling efforts to promote some of his own personal hobby-horses. He proposed specific amendments to make the European Council a separate institution to the Council of Ministers, defined as the 'highest authority of the Union', with a Vice-President as well as President (jointly forming part of a wider Bureau of persons chairing various Council formations), and reporting to the 'Congress'. Other than making the European Council a separate institution, all of these ideas were rejected. One *conventionnel*, quoted by Peter Norman (see below), accused Giscard of 'trying to copy a president from the United States, a People's Congress from China and a Politburo from the Soviet Union'.

Giscard's amendments were a distraction from two of the most difficult institutional questions that still had to be addressed, both brought into focus by the imminence of **enlargement**. These issues – the method and weighting of votes under QMV in the Council and the size of the college of European Commissioners – had a capacity to pit large and small member states against one another. They had been ducked in the 1997 **Amsterdam Treaty** and caused considerable ill-will in the negotiation of the 2001 **Nice Treaty**. The Convention addressed these issues relatively late in the day. Despite great misgivings on the part of Spanish and Polish representatives, it eventually agreed on a 'double majority' system of QMV, where a measure would need to secure the support of at least half the member states, representing 60 per cent of the Union's population, to pass. Equally, under strong pressure from

Giscard, the Convention accepted that the number of Commissioners should be reduced to fewer than the number of member states: the proposal accepted was that the college be limited to 15 Commissioners, chosen on the basis of equal rotation among member states; in addition there would be non-voting or 'junior' Commissioners from all the other member states. Interestingly, these proved to be two of the relatively few areas where the Convention's proposals were rewritten by the subsequent IGC. The formulae later reached by the IGC in 2003–4 – and eventually carried forward into the **Lisbon Treaty** – provided for a QMV threshold of 55 per cent of member states and 65 per cent of population, and a Commission that would comprise two-thirds of the number of member states on a rotating basis. Critically, however, in the IGC text, the European Council could unanimously decide, if it wished, to 'alter the number' of Commissioners, so implicitly allowing it to keep the Commission at its existing size.

The final days of the Convention proved intense and chaotic, with tempers rising as the participants struggled to agree a text before the Thessaloniki European Council on 19–20 June. The Praesidium was widely criticized for the way it sought to control both the content and procedure of the endgame, even though it performed a critical role in trying to find the centre of gravity of the Convention as a whole. *Conventionnels* from smaller member states staged a revolt against the proposed wording in the draft treaty on the role of the President of the European Council, which they believed reflected a bias in favour of big-country power that had characterized Giscard's chairmanship throughout. New ideas, such as the introduction of ***passerelle* clauses** or the **citizens' initiative**, were introduced and endorsed at a late stage. From the chair, Giscard deemed Parts One and Two of the Convention's draft European Constitution to be adopted, without a final vote. (The first part dealt with general principles and institutional arrangements; the second incorporated the Charter of Fundamental Rights.) There was no time to consider in detail either Part Three, dealing with policy, or Part Four, addressing 'general and final provisions'. After Thessaloniki, the Convention was allowed to meet for three more weeks in order to finalize these outstanding portions of the text, which it did with relative ease. Eight Eurosceptic members of the Convention submitted a dissenting report.

In all, the Convention met in plenary session 26 times over 52 days during its 17-month life. The Praesidium met on 50 occasions and submitted 52 papers to the Convention. Over 6,000 amendments were tabled by individual members. The proceedings of the Convention were open to the public and broadcast live and its website attracted much higher traffic than that of any of the EU institutions. By any standards, the Convention was a path-breaking experiment in democratic discussion at EU level, and most immediately it made it politically impossible for any thorough-going treaty change in the future to occur without a routine IGC being prepared by a Convention. (Indeed the European Constitution foresaw this, and the subsequent Lisbon Treaty provides for this, as the 'ordinary revision procedure', in Article 48(2–5) TEU.)

The European Constitution produced by the Convention was a much more ambitious and coherent document than would ever have been drafted by an IGC on its own. Indeed, the IGC which met from October 2003 to June 2004 made relatively few changes to the text (other than on those difficult 'big versus small' country issues mentioned above). However, casting a very significant retrospective shadow over the Convention's proceedings is the reality that the Constitution – partly because of its title, partly because of its content and partly for completely extraneous reasons – became the first European treaty since the **European Defence Community** (EDC) in 1954 to fail to secure **ratification** in the member states. The rejection of the text in the **French and Dutch referenda** of May–June 2005 was a major body blow to the process of European integration and, ironically, made it much less likely that any further institutional reform on such a scale will ever be attempted again. A huge effort was required in 2007 to resuscitate the Constitution, in diluted form, as the Reform Treaty, later renamed the Lisbon Treaty. In fact, nearly all the major changes introduced by the Lisbon Treaty are to be found in the Constitution, and are thus products of the Convention, but only political experts now associate the treaty with the Convention. Giscard's proud hope that the *conventionnels* would be seen as the new **founding fathers** of the European Union – with he himself the most prominent among them – has been largely dashed.

Further reading: Guy Milton and Jacques Keller-Noëllet, *The European Constitution: Its Origins, Negotiation and Meaning*, 2005; Peter Norman, *The Accidental Constitution: The Making of Europe's Constitutional Treaty*, 2005.

Convergence criteria

Under the arrangements for **Economic and Monetary Union** (EMU), no EU member state may adopt the single currency, the **euro**, unless it has demonstrated 'a high degree of sustainable convergence', defined by reference to four criteria set out in Article 140 TFEU and in **Protocol** 13 to the **Treaties.** The first of the four convergence criteria is 'a high degree of price stability . . . apparent from a rate of inflation which is close to that of, at most, the three best performing Member States'. (The country's average inflation rate must not exceed that of the three best-performing states by more than 1.5 per cent over the previous year.) The second criterion is the 'sustainability of the government financial position', evident from the absence of a budget deficit or national debt position which is deemed 'excessive' by the **Council of Ministers** under the **excessive deficit procedure** (EDP; Article 126 TFEU and Protocol 12). The third criterion is observance of the 'normal fluctuation margins' provided for in the **Exchange-Rate Mechanism** (ERM) of the **European Monetary System** (EMS) 'for at least two years, without devaluing against the **euro**' on its own initiative. The fourth criterion, which relates to the sustainability of the convergence, specifies that a state's average long-term interest rate must not exceed by more than 2 per cent that of the three best-performing member states in terms of price stability, over the previous year. It will be noted that all the criteria are purely 'nominal' and relate to the performance of the national economies and not to their structure.

Under Article 140 TFEU, the **European Commission** and the **European Central Bank** (ECB) are required to make regular reports to the **Ecofin Council** on the economic performance of member states with reference to these four criteria. Together with other economic indicators, such reports enabled the **European Council** to decide in May 1998 that 11 member states would take part in the third stage of EMU, which began on 1 January 1999. In the case of seven of the 11 countries, the Council controversially abrogated its earlier decisions that their deficits or debt were excessive at the time. (Greece did not meet the convergence criteria, Denmark and the United Kingdom had permanent **opt-outs** from EMU stage three, and Sweden engineered failure to meet the criteria to avoid entry.) Six more countries have since entered stage three of EMU, starting with Greece in January 2001. The convergence criteria have been applied increasingly strictly in deciding on access, partly because the **Stability and Growth Pact** (SGP) and excessive deficit procedure have proved much less effective than expected in disciplining countries once they have joined. In May 2006, the European Commission refused to propose that Lithuania join the eurozone, on the grounds that its inflation rate was slightly above that required by the criteria.

Cooperation agreement

A cooperation agreement is one of several types of **international agreement** that may be concluded between the European Union and third countries or international organizations. More broad-ranging than a trade agreement but less ambitious than an **association agreement**, the concept of a cooperation agreement was not foreseen in the **Treaty of Rome**. Instead, such agreements evolved organically, relying on a range of ad hoc **legal bases**, as the **European Commission** and **Council of Ministers** sought to go beyond the limitations of pure trade agreements, without casually extending the prospect of deeper political relations or future **accession** implied by association. Cooperation agreements have come to be used primarily in the fields of **development policy** and economic, financial and technical cooperation of various kinds. They sometimes incorporate trade agreements too, under titles such as 'trade and cooperation agreements' or 'economic and trade cooperation agreements'. About 40 cooperation agreements are currently in force, with another 20 under negotiation. In addition, narrower, more sector-specific agreements – covering, for example, aspects of customs or taxation – have developed.

During the 1970s, 'first generation' cooperation agreements, usually lasting for only five years, were signed with many of the Maghreb and Mashreq states individually, as well as with the Gulf Cooperation Council. In the 1980s, more elaborate, 'second generation', agreements developed, providing for economic and other forms of cooperation over a wider field. Whilst still lasting for five years, these agreements contained a *clause évolutive*, allowing for cooperation to be extended into new policy fields by mutual consent. Agreements of this type, which normally allow for some financial assistance from the Union and often envisage cooperation in areas such as the environment or science and technology, were concluded with India, China, Pakistan and several countries in Latin America. More recently, however, still more ambitious third and fourth generations of cooperation agreements have emerged. These are similar to earlier agreements, but contain additional, more political, elements such as human rights clauses and joint undertakings in the fight against drug-trafficking or terrorism. Often known as 'partnership and cooperation agreements', 'framework cooperation agreements' or 'political dialogue and cooperation agreements', such agreements have been concluded with certain countries or groups of countries in the former Soviet Union, Latin America and Asia. Economic Partnership Agreements (EPAs) – a form of cooperation agreement based on reciprocal access to markets – are being negotiated with 39 of the 79 **ACP states.**

Some cooperation agreements are managed by a joint 'cooperation council', which brings together national government ministers, on the one side, and Commissioners and representatives of both the Council of Ministers and the member states, on the other. The presidency of a cooperation council rotates, on a six-monthly basis, between the two sides. Since the **Lisbon Treaty** came into force in December 2009, the **High Representative** for **Common Foreign and Security Policy** (CFSP) has the right to serve as president on the EU side, but has chosen to delegate that role to the six-month, rotating **presidency** of the (EU) **Council of Ministers** (which exercised it before). Meetings of each cooperation council are prepared at official level by a 'cooperation committee'. Meetings occur annually or biannually, with a total of about 10 per year. The question of whether a cooperation agreement is adopted in the Council on the basis of **qualified majority voting** (QMV) or unanimity depends on the legal base(s) underpinning each agreement (and whether it is a 'mixed' agreement to which the member states are also individual parties). Since the **Lisbon Treaty**, most cooperation agreements require the **consent** of the **European Parliament** before they can be finally concluded.

Cooperation procedure

The cooperation procedure was introduced by the 1986 **Single European Act** (SEA) as a means of strengthening the role of the **European Parliament** in the legislative process at European Community level (Article 252 EC, since repealed). It built on and (to some degree) replaced the traditional one-reading **consultation procedure** – under which the **Council of Ministers** obtained the Parliament's opinion on draft legislation, but could simply ignore it – by introducing a second reading, with the possibility that the Council might only be able to reject the Parliament's position by acting unanimously.

The cooperation procedure applied to a limited number of policy fields, notably the **single market**, the health and safety of workers, and some aspects of regional policy, and of **research and development policy**. It was superseded by the **co-decision procedure** in the 1992 **Maastricht Treaty** and 1997 **Amsterdam Treaty** (Article 251 EC, now Article 294 TFEU). Co-decision created a legislative dialogue between the Council and the Parliament of up to three readings, with the latter able to reject a proposal at each stage. Following Amsterdam, the cooperation procedure was retained for a very narrow range of issues, specifically related to **Economic and Monetary Union** (EMU), and was rarely employed (only once in the years 2004–9). Under the **Lisbon Treaty**, which came into force in December 2009, the cooperation procedure was finally abolished, with the four remaining treaty bases that still used it all being moved to co-decision.

Procedurally, the initial stage of the cooperation procedure was the same as that applying under consultation. The **European Commission** would communicate a draft legislative proposal to the Council of Ministers, which in turn invited the Parliament to give an opinion on the text. Once that opinion had been received by the Council, however, the two procedures diverged. Under the cooperation procedure, when the Council agreed its variant of the text, this opened a second round of dialogue with the Parliament, rather than the proposal simply becoming law. The Council's conclusion, adopted under **qualified majority voting** (QMV), was reached in the form of a 'common position' and this was sent back to the Parliament, accompanied by an explanation of the views of the Council and the Commission, for a second reading.

At this point, the Parliament could, by a simple majority, adopt the Council's common position or indeed fail to take any action on it. In either case, the Council could then proceed to the formal enactment of the proposal, as embodied in its common position. However, equally, the Parliament could seek either to amend the common position or reject it altogether, in each case by an absolute majority. If the Parliament voted to reject a common position, the Council had to act unanimously to have it reinstated. If, instead, the Parliament adopted amendments to the common position, the Commission was given the opportunity to re-examine its original proposal in the light of these amendments, and to forward the results of this re-examination to the Council, alongside the Parliament's amendments.

At its second reading, the Council could adopt the Commission's revised proposal by QMV. If it chose to amend it, however, the Council had to act by unanimity. Equally, it could adopt those amendments from the Parliament which the Commission had not incorporated in its revised proposal, again acting by unanimity. If it failed to take a decision within a deadline, the proposal fell (whereas under consultation, an unadopted proposal remains in abeyance).

Agreement to institute the cooperation procedure in the 1985 **Intergovernmental Conference** (IGC) was a concession to critics who feared that the proposed extension of QMV in the Council under the SEA would, without any corresponding increase in parliamentary power, widen the '**democratic deficit**' in Community decision-making. It could leave the Community in a situation where no individual parliament, whether at national or European level, could exercise any influence on legislative outcomes. The introduction of the cooperation procedure in July 1987 – matched by the parallel assent procedure, now known as the **consent procedure**, which gave the Parliament an 'up-down' veto in certain (admittedly, relatively few) areas where the Council acted by unanimity – began the Parliament's long march towards the exercise of significant legislative power.

Not only did the cooperation procedure give the Parliament a second chance to influence the substance of legislation, but it also changed the balance of power between the institutions, to the Parliament's advantage. The distinction it drew between the Council acting unanimously or by QMV, depending on the position of the Commission, was not new to the Treaties: it was already a condition of the consultation procedure that, if the Council diverged from the Commission's proposal, it would need to do so unanimously. However, for the first time, the Commission had a positive incentive to incorporate the Parliament's amendments into its text. By using the threat of outright rejection at second reading, or stressing the risk that the proposal might lapse if there was no agreement between the Parliament and the Council, the Parliament was in a strong position to get the Commission to respond positively to at least some of its requests. If the Parliament voted for an amendment by an absolute majority and secured the support of the Commission (by its incorporation in its revised proposal), there was now a strong presumption that it would find its way into the final text adopted by the

Council by QMV (and it could only be amended again by the Council acting unanimously). As a result, the cooperation procedure created a new, cross-cutting dynamic in the law-making process in favour of the Commission's proposal being agreed on the Parliament's terms. Conversely, it required the Parliament to exercise much greater discipline than in the past, in order to mobilize the absolute majority necessary either to amend or reject the Council's common position. One consequence was to encourage the two largest political groups, the Socialists and the centre-right European People's Party (EPP), to work more closely together, so blunting ideological dividing-lines within the Parliament.

The cooperation procedure was criticized for extending legislative power to the Parliament in an oblique and complicated way. Initially, institutional maximalists in the Parliament had pushed for a three-reading process, very similar to what eventually became co-decision, including the possibility of a 'conciliation committee' with the Council, reflecting the practice between the two chambers of the US Congress and the German parliament. At one stage in the SEA negotiations, a very simple reform was suggested, whereby the Council would henceforth deliberate on the legislative proposal as already amended by the Parliament, but this was rejected as potentially giving the Parliament too big an influence in framing the context of Council decision-making. It also touched the sensitivities of the Commission, which feared a dilution of its traditional brokerage role in legislative bargaining. In the IGC negotiations, the interests of the Parliament were only seriously defended by the Italian government, whose foreign minister, Emilio Colombo – co-author of the **Genscher–Colombo Plan** and himself a former President of the Parliament – threatened difficulties in national **ratification** if no significant moves were made in the latter's favour.

In the third edition of *The European Parliament* (1995), Richard Corbett, Francis Jacobs and Michael Shackleton showed that during the heyday of the cooperation procedure – the six and a half years from July 1987 to December 1993, when 332 pieces of legislation were subject to some 4,500 amendments under this process – the Parliament had, for the first time, a 'perceptible impact' on EC law-making. The Parliament's first-reading amendments were accepted by the Commission in 55 per cent, and approved by the Council in 43 per cent, of cases. On second reading, 44 per cent of the Parliament's amendments were accepted by the Commission and, critically, 24 per cent were approved by the Council. On second reading, the Parliament accepted the Council's common position in 39 per cent of the cases.

The Parliament successfully extracted concessions by threatening to reject the Commission's proposal on several occasions (for example, on motor car emissions in 1989), in effect overturning the previous positions of the majority and minority in the Council. It rejected the Council's common position in four instances, with the Council unable to muster the unanimity required to override the Parliament's vote in three of these four cases (for example, the benzene directive in 1988). The Commission chose pre-emptively to withdraw a proposed directive on sweeteners in foodstuffs in 1992, in the face of parliamentary opposition.

Further reading: David Earnshaw and David Judge, 'The Life and Times of the European Union's Cooperation Procedure', *Journal of Common Market Studies,* Volume 35, Number 4, December 1997.

Copenhagen criteria

Following the collapse of Communism in the former Soviet bloc in 1989–90, several central and eastern European countries expressed strong interest in joining the European Union. The Union responded by creating a new type of **association agreement**, called a Europe Agreement, as a staging post to eventual **accession**. At its meeting in Copenhagen in June 1993, the **European Council** (of EU heads of government) agreed that all countries with Europe Agreements 'that so desire shall become members of the Union'. The conditions of eligibility for accession, which became known soon after as the 'Copenhagen criteria', were listed in the meeting's conclusions as:

> *. . . stability of institutions guaranteeing democracy, the rule of law, human rights and respect for and protection of minorities . . . a functioning market economy, as well as the capacity to cope with competitive pressure and market forces within the Union; [and] the ability to take on the obligations of membership, including adherence to the aims of political, economic and monetary union.*

The first of these conditions is sometimes styled as the 'political criterion', the second the 'economic criterion', and the third the '*acquis* criterion', the last referring to the ability of the applicant state to take on the obligations of the whole of the ***acquis communautaire***. The conclusions go on to note that 'the Union's capacity to absorb new members, while maintaining the momentum of European integration, is an important consideration in the general interest of both the Union and the candidate countries.' This latter observation forms the basis of the subsequent claim, now accepted by all institutions, that the 'absorption capacity' of the Union itself constitutes in effect a fourth Copenhagen criterion.

The formal opinion drawn up by the **European Commission** on any applicant state must now assess its eligibility for membership in the light of the Copenhagen criteria. At the Luxembourg European Council in December 1997, it was decided that whilst compliance with the political criterion was a prerequisite for the opening of **enlargement** negotiations, the economic and *acquis* criteria could be evaluated in a 'forward-looking, dynamic way'. By definition, the absorption capacity of the Union was something that only the EU institutions themselves could assess.

COREPER

The Committee of Permanent Representatives – known by its French acronym COREPER, derived from *Comité des représentants permanents* – is the most important official-level body within the **Council of Ministers** and one of the strongest centres of power within the EU political system. Comprised of the Brussels-based ambassadors of the 27 member states, COREPER is tasked with preparing all meetings of the Council and acts as the 'junction box' which determines which items reach ministers for decision and in what form.

COREPER is descended from an ad hoc coordinating committee of national officials, established in March 1953 and known as COCOR (*Comité de coordination*), which prepared ministerial meetings in the **European Coal and Steel Community** (ECSC). Drawing on this experience, the 1957 **Treaty of Rome** already foresaw that the Council's rules of procedure should permit 'the creation of a committee composed of representatives of the member states' to assist the Council in its work (Article 151 EEC). In January 1958, only a week after the treaty entered into force, the foreign ministers of **the Six** decided to take advantage of this possibility. The new committee was to be composed of a senior official from each member state – to be known as a 'permanent representative' – who would follow daily Community business in situ on behalf of the minister and enjoy the support of a full diplomatic mission or **permanent representation** in Brussels. As Martin Westlake and David Galloway have written, the foreign ministers' decision 'that the permanent representatives should be high-ranking diplomats with ambassadorial status' proved important. 'Since the diplomats were primarily answerable to their foreign ministers, the creation of COREPER consolidated the preeminent role of the member states' foreign ministries in the early development of the European Communities' (*The Council of the European Union*, 2006).

As the volume of Council business grew, it was decided in 1962 to divide COREPER into two branches: deputy permanent representatives, dealing with routine legislative matters, would sit in COREPER I, whilst the permanent representatives themselves, focused primarily on foreign policy, finance, institutional and other cross-cutting issues, would sit in COREPER II. From the start, COREPER sanctioned the creation of Council working groups, under its control, to work on thematic issues or specific legislative proposals. (Today these working groups number between 100 and 150 at any given time.) However, again to ease its workload, some of COREPER's coordinating responsibilities were devolved to more specialist preparatory bodies within the Council system. One such body, the Special Committee for Agriculture (SCA), was established by the Council itself in 1960. Two others were already foreseen in the Treaty of Rome – the **Monetary Committee**, now known as the **Economic and Financial Committee**, and the Article 113 Committee, now called the **Trade Policy Committee** (or Article 207 Committee), for **Common Commercial Policy** (CCP) – and they gradually assumed increasingly important functions. The 1992 **Maastricht Treaty** established further committees in the fields of **Common Foreign and Security Policy** (CFSP) and **Justice and Home Affairs** (JHA). The CFSP body, now known as the **Political and Security Committee** (PSC), has emerged as especially significant, with the member states designating separate 'PSC ambassadors' in parallel to the permanent and deputy permanent representatives. These various specialist bodies exist alongside COREPER and are supposed to operate 'without prejudice' to the latter in preparing the work of the Council in their policy areas. However, in practice, they have acquired an increasing degree of independence and authority – with their conclusions often being rubber-stamped by COREPER – so diluting somewhat the previously exceptional influence exercised by permanent and deputy permanent representatives in Council decision-making.

The nature and role of COREPER was formalized in the 1967 **Merger Treaty**: 'A committee consisting of the Permanent Representatives of the governments of the Member States shall be responsible for preparing the work of the Council and for carrying out the tasks assigned to it by the latter' (Article 4 Merger, now Article 240(1) TFEU). The 1997 **Amsterdam Treaty** added that COREPER may also 'adopt procedural decisions in cases provided for in the Council's Rules of Procedure'. The Council's rules of procedure specify that these latter decisions may relate to the holding of Council meetings other than in Brussels or Luxembourg, the broadcasting of Council proceedings and publishing of votes, the use of the written procedure, the consultation of other institutions or bodies, and the extension of deadlines for such consultations (Article 19(1) RoP). The rules also require that 'All items on the agenda for a Council meeting shall be examined in advance by COREPER unless the latter decides otherwise' (Article 19(2) RoP).

The meetings of COREPER II and I are chaired respectively by the permanent representative and deputy permanent representative from the member state holding the rotating **presidency** of the Council. The chairmanship of the various committees reporting to COREPER varies: that of the SCA and Trade Policy Committee changes with the presidency, whilst the Economic and Finance Committee chooses its own chairman and the Political and Security Committee now has a permanent chairman designated from among its members by the **High Representative** for CFSP.

COREPER meets in Brussels every working week – COREPER II usually on Wednesdays and sometimes on Thursdays, and COREPER I on Wednesdays and sometimes on Fridays. These meetings are themselves prepared the previous day by (respectively) the **Antici and Mertens Groups** of mid-rank (but potentially high-flying) officials, often chosen personally by ambassadors. COREPER II deals with the work of the **Foreign Affairs Council** (FAC), the **General Affairs Council** (GAC), the **Ecofin Council** and the JHA Council. COREPER I covers the six other normal Council formations – dealing with the great bulk of the legislative output of the institution – and its chairman often leads for the Council side in negotiations with the Parliament under the **co-decision procedure.**

A COREPER meeting will characteristically be attended by about 150 officials, drawn from the 27 permanent representations, the Council secretariat and the **European Commission**. Its business will include reports on inter-institutional discussions, approval of the agendas of forthcoming Council meetings, and, most importantly, discussion in detail of the outstanding points of disagreement between the member states on all the specific items to be discussed at those Council meetings, with an attempt, led from the chair, to narrow remaining divergences so far as possible. Items may be inserted by COREPER on the Council's agenda as either 'A points' or 'B points', depending on whether agreement has already been achieved (the former) or further discussion is required (the latter). Sometimes items are included as 'false B points', when there is already agreement in practice, but for political reasons it is useful to hold a discussion among ministers. Research suggests that about half the items decided on in the Council are discussed at ministerial level at some point, even if in most cases decisions are taken unanimously, even when **qualified majority voting** (QMV) applies.

Coudenhove-Kalergi, Richard (1894–1972)

Born in Tokyo, the son of an Austro-Hungarian diplomat father and a Japanese mother, Count Richard Coudenhove-Kalergi was the best-known pioneer of the idea of a united Europe during the second quarter of the twentieth century. In Berlin and Vienna in the 1920s, Coudenhove-Kalergi began his campaign for what he called '**Pan-Europa**' in a long series of books and articles. In 1922, he wrote that 'either continental Europe, from Portugal to Poland, will amalgamate itself into a super-state or, already in the course of this century, it will perish politically.' The following year, he founded a 'Pan-European Union' and, in October 1926, he convened a 'Pan-European Congress' in Vienna, attended by some 2,000 people. This was followed by further congresses in Berlin (1930), Basle (1932), Vienna (1935) and New York (1943). He received the support and sympathy of many of the leading statesmen of the day – notably **Aristide Briand**, **Winston Churchill**, Thomas

Masaryk and Walter Rathenau – and of other figures in public life, such as the violinist Bronislaw Hubermann. Thomas Mann agreed to join the committee of the Pan-European Union, describing the concept in a letter to Coudenhove-Kalergi in 1926 as an 'idea that the world so stands in need of'.

As early as 1932, Coudenhove-Kalergi predicted the trauma that was to come, telling the Basle congress, 'Stalin is preparing a civil war, and Hitler a war between peoples.' In 1940, he emigrated to New York, from where he drew up a constitution for a **United States of Europe**, including a European constituent assembly, which he submitted to the foreign ministers of the European states opposed to the Axis powers. After the Second World War, he attempted to build the first foundations of such a structure, with the creation, at a meeting in Gstaad in July 1947, of a 'European Parliamentary Union', of which he served as secretary general. The existence of the European Parliamentary Union helped prepare the ground for the Parliamentary Assembly component of the new **Council of Europe**, established two years later. In 1952, he relaunched his Pan-European Union, which became a member organization of the **European Movement** (although it later broke away) and held its sixth congress in Baden Baden in 1954.

Coudenhove-Kalergi's vision of European integration – set out in his 1954 book, *An Idea Conquers the World* – was essentially political, in contrast to the more technocratic, economically-driven approach of **Jean Monnet** and his followers. Paradoxically this led him to sympathize with **Charles de Gaulle**, who, from a different standpoint, also viewed European integration in essentially political terms and whose principled opposition to the division of Europe brought about by the **Yalta Agreement** he much admired ('he draws no dividing line between politics and history'). Although Coudenhove-Kalergi's ideas enjoyed tacit or active support among many politicians and intellectuals of all parties and nationalities, he was never very successful in converting this into concrete action or attracting mass support.

Council of the Baltic Sea States (CBSS)

The Council of the Baltic Sea States is, as its names suggests, an intergovernmental forum for promoting cross-border cooperation in the Baltic Sea region. It was founded in Copenhagen in 1992, in response to a joint initiative of the German and Danish foreign ministers, Hans-Dietrich Genscher and Uffe Ellemann-Jensen. It comprises the governments of ten states of the Baltic Sea region – Denmark, Finland, **Norway**, Sweden, Estonia, Latvia, Lithuania, Germany, Poland and Russia – as well as of **Iceland** (which joined in 1995) and the **European Commission**, representing the European Union. Ten other countries have observer status – Belarus, France, Italy, the Netherlands, Romania, Slovakia, Spain, the Ukraine, the United Kingdom and the United States.

The CBSS's governing body is its Council, consisting of foreign ministers and chaired by a presidency that rotates annually among member states. A biannual Baltic Sea States Summit brings together heads of governments. The routine work of the CBSS is conducted by a 'committee of senior officials', drawn from the foreign ministries of member states, supported since 1998 by a small secretariat located in Stockholm. There are several expert groups and task forces focusing on specific issues. Among the problems addressed by the CBSS are barriers to trade and investment, environmental protection, nuclear safety, technology transfer, heritage protection and human trafficking. The CBSS has also played a role in trying to assist the development of the Russian enclave of Kaliningrad, involving the latter in its flagship higher education cooperation project, 'EuroFaculty', which promoted cooperation between universities in the three **Baltic states** between 1993 and 2005.

A Baltic Sea Parliamentary Conference (BSPC) has brought together national and regional parliamentarians from the region since 1991 and now provides a parliamentary counterpart to CBSS activity. The BSPC usually meets for two days each year in late summer, passing a resolution that is forwarded to the CBSS, with a seven-member standing committee meeting in the interim to prepare business. Included as participants in the BSPC are delegations from the **European Parliament** and the Parliamentary Assemblies of the **Council of Europe** and the **Organization for Security and Cooperation in Europe** (OSCE). The BSPC is serviced by the secretariat of the **Nordic Council** in Copenhagen. The Baltic Sea Parliamentary Conference is not to be confused with the Baltic Assembly, a joint parliamentary body for the three Baltic states, established in June 1994. Both the Nordic Council and the Baltic Assembly send delegations to the BSPC.

Council of Europe

Founded in May 1949 by the Treaty of London, the Council of Europe is an intergovernmental consultative organization, based in Strasbourg, France, with a current membership of 47 countries with a combined population of over 800 million people. The Council seeks to promote 'greater unity between its members for the purpose of . . . facilitating their economic and social progress, in particular by the maintenance and further realization of human rights and fundamental freedoms'. The first exclusively European political organization to be established after the Second World War, the Council of Europe pre-dates the European Union and is not an institution of the Union. The original idea of creating a 'Council of Europe' was put forward by the former British prime minister, **Winston Churchill**, in his **Zurich speech** of September 1946, and the body was set up in response to a resolution adopted by the **Congress of Europe**, which Churchill chaired, in The Hague in May

1948. Much of the Council's work has been concerned with human rights, education and culture, and more recently with citizenship, environmental protection, medical ethics and the fight against drugs, violence and organized crime. Following the collapse of Communism in 1989–90, the Council became very active in democracy-building and constitutional reform in those European countries that once formed part of either the Soviet bloc or the Soviet Union itself.

Membership of the Council of Europe is open to any European state that has a democratic system of government, accepts the principle of the rule of law and is able and willing to guarantee fundamental human rights and freedoms. The ten founder members were Belgium, France, Denmark, Ireland, Italy, Luxembourg, the Netherlands, Norway, Sweden and the United Kingdom. They were joined by Greece and Turkey later in 1949, by Iceland in 1950, and – in an act of reconciliation first suggested by Churchill – by the Federal Republic of Germany in 1951. (Controversially, the **Saarland** was also admitted as an observer.) Austria joined the Council in 1956, once Russian forces had withdrawn from its territory. Cyprus, Switzerland and Malta became members in the 1960s, Portugal, Spain and Liechtenstein in the 1970s, and San Marino and Finland in the 1980s. The first of the former Communist countries to join were Hungary (in 1990) and Czechoslovakia (1991). They have since been followed by Albania, Armenia, Azerbaijan, Bosnia and Herzegovina, Bulgaria, Croatia, Estonia, Georgia, Latvia, Lithuania, FYR Macedonia, Moldova, Poland, Romania, Russia, Serbia, Slovenia and Ukraine – as well as by **micro-states** Andorra and Monaco. Most recently, Montenegro joined as a separate state in May 2007. In addition, the Holy See (Vatican City) enjoys observer status – as do the United States, Canada, Japan and Mexico. The only unambiguously European state still outside the Council of Europe is Belarus, whose application has been pending since 1993.

The Council of Europe has three main institutions: the Committee of Ministers, comprised of foreign ministers or their ambassadors; the Parliamentary Assembly (formerly Consultative Assembly), with 318 members and 318 non-voting substitutes (plus 18 observers) nominated by the **national parliaments** of member states; and the Congress of Local and Regional Authorities of Europe, made up of councillors from sub-national layers of government. In parallel, the Council has created the European Court of Human Rights, also based in Strasbourg, which adjudicates on cases brought under the 1950 **European Convention on Human Rights** (ECHR). Since 1999, a Commissioner for Human Rights supplements this work by monitoring the human rights' situation in member states.

The Committee of Ministers adopts recommendations addressed to member states on the basis of consensus. (A simple or two-thirds majority voting is needed for decisions of a more administrative kind.) The Committee meets at foreign-minister level on average twice a year. The ambassadors of member states – formally speaking, permanent representatives and referred to as 'Ministers' deputies' – meet roughly monthly between the full meetings of the Committee and enjoy devolved decision-making power. Member states take it in turn to chair each meeting of the Committee, in the alphabetical order of their country in the English language.

Meeting in plenary session for one week, four times a year, the Parliamentary Assembly of the Council of Europe (PACE) adopts resolutions addressed to the Committee of Ministers. It also elects the judges of the European Court of Human Rights and the Commissioner for Human Rights from shortlists proposed by the Committee. The Assembly elects a President and 20 Vice-Presidents (on an annual basis). It has ten policy committees, which meet either in Strasbourg or Paris. One of the Assembly's biggest problems is the relatively poor attendance of its members, concealed to some degree by the presence of substitutes: in many votes, fewer than 100 members take part and very rarely are more than 200 present.

Over the last six decades, over 6,000 national parliamentarians have served as members of the Assembly. Although they sit in alphabetical order, most are also members of **political groups**. Members have been allowed to form groups under the Assembly's rules of procedure since 1965: to do so currently requires at least 20 members or substitutes of at least six nationalities. The five political groups at present are, from right to left: the European Democrat Group (EDG), with 86 members or substitutes; the European People's Party (EPP) Group (with 215); the Alliance of Liberals and Democrats for Europe (ALDE) Group (87); the Socialist Group (178); and the United European Left (GUE) Group (35). This group structure mirrors closely that of the **European Parliament**, although there is neither a Green group nor a hard-line Eurosceptic group in the Assembly. (Currently, 33 members or substitutes sit in no political group). The chairmen of political groups meet informally in a Presidential Committee and the full groups convene once a quarter during the Assembly's sessions. All the key office-holders of the Assembly come together in a Bureau. The work of the Assembly and the Committee of Ministers is coordinated through a joint committee. For its part, the Congress of Local and Regional Authorities, like the Assembly, adopts resolutions for consideration by the Committee of Ministers. It is a bicameral body, with one chamber for local representatives and another for regional representatives, nominated by the member states.

The Council of Europe has a secretariat of approximately 2,200 officials, headed by a Secretary General – who has been elected since 1965 by the Parliamentary Assembly from its own membership – and divided into six specialist directorates. The role of Secretary General entails a difficult political balancing act between the interests of the Committee of Ministers and the members of the Assembly – the first having no say in his or her election and the second sometimes feeling neglected by one of their own – and, perhaps as a result, no incumbent has ever managed to secure a second five-year term. The current Secretary General, whose term runs from 2009 to 2014, is Thorbjørn Jagland, a former prime minister of Norway. Among his more distinguished predecessors are Catherine Lalumière (of France) and Marcellino Oreja Aguire (of Spain). The Parliamentary Assembly now has its own Secretary General, also elected by members. The official **languages** of the Council of Europe are French and English, although interpretation is also provided from and into German, Italian and Russian (as working languages) at meetings of the Assembly and the Congress. The Council's annual budget – some € 217 million in 2011 – is adopted by the Committee of Ministers and comprised largely of contributions from member states, calculated on a formula reflecting each country's population adjusted by national income.

Critically, unlike the institutions of the European Union, those of the Council of Europe have no power to make law. Instead, agreements reached unanimously between member states may be embodied in conventions, which are then open for signature by individual states. Once adopted by a member state, a convention is binding on that country in the same way as any other international agreement adopted under any other treaty. Less formally, consensus reached in the Committee of Ministers on a subject may be embodied in a non-binding charter or code. There are now some 200 conventions, charters or codes.

In addition to the European Convention on Human Rights, the best known Council of Europe conventions are the 1954 European Cultural Convention, the 1979 Berne Convention on the protection of rare and endangered animals and plants, the 1981 Convention on data protection, the 1986 Convention on the legal personality of international non-governmental organizations (NGOs), the 1987 Convention on the prevention of torture, the 1990 Convention on measures to locate, freeze and confiscate assets associated with organized crime, the 1995 Convention on the protection of national minorities, the 2001 Convention on cyber crime, and the 2005 Convention on trafficking in human beings. Among the more prominent charters are the 1961 European Social Charter, the 1985 Charter on local self-government, and the 1992 Charter on regional and minority languages.

In its historical context, the institutional design of the Council of Europe was a compromise between those who advocated European integration along supranational lines and those who, although in favour of a wide measure of cooperation, preferred the member states to retain firm control of the process through strictly intergovernmental cooperation. The mixture of a parliamentary assembly and a ministerial committee reflected this duality, but the absence of direct law-making powers meant the balance was tilted firmly in the direction of member states. Paul Reynaud, the former French prime minister, commented at the time that the 'Council of Europe consists of two bodies, one of them *for* Europe, and the other *against* it.' **Paul-Henri Spaak**, President of the Consultative Assembly, was (subsequently) more damning, commenting that 'of all the international bodies I have known, I have never found any more timorous or more impotent.'

In its very early years, the Council succeeded in becoming the main forum for debate over the future of Europe: it was in the Council's Assembly in 1950, for example, that Churchill first called for the creation of a **European army** (during his time as a member from 1949 to 1951). However, as individual governments chose to ignore the Assembly's recommendations, enthusiasm began to wane, and by 1951, in creating the **European Coal and Steel Community** (ECSC), **the Six** embarked upon a more ambitious, explicitly supranational project.

The parting of the ways was especially painful for the British government, which had played such an important role in the creation of the Council of Europe, including the suggestion (of Foreign Secretary Ernest Bevin) that the body be based in Strasbourg as a symbol of Franco-German reconciliation. London attached high importance to what it saw as the necessary compromise (between European and national elements) at the heart of the Council of Europe: in an ingenious rearguard action which came too late, the 'Eden Plan' of March 1952 suggested that the new ECSC should be subordinated to the Strasbourg body, with the former's institutions operating as subdivisions of the latter's. This manoeuvre reached mildly comic proportions when, at British insistence, the Secretary General of the Council of Europe refused to host the inaugural session of the ECSC Common Assembly, unless he was able to provide its secretariat. After the ECSC's President, **Jean Monnet**, hired alternative premises in the city – with the opening session held in the Strasbourg chamber of commerce – the Council of Europe quietly backed down. The outcome of this symbolic trial of strength was a harbinger of things to come. Spaak resigned as President of its Consultative Assembly in order to become the first President of the new ECSC Common Assembly. The latter body, rather than the Consultative Assembly, was chosen to draw up the treaty for a **European Political Community** (EPC) – although a face-saving solution was later found in the form of an Ad Hoc Assembly which included some of the latter's members. By the end of the 1950s, the focus of attention had shifted decisively away from the Council of Europe and towards what was to become the European Community and, later, the European Union.

The Council of Europe has always had great difficulty accepting its eclipse by the EU institutions. This has been especially the case for the Parliamentary Assembly. Even today, members of the latter are often to be heard asserting that it has comparable legitimacy to the European Parliament and that EU activity in certain fields risks 'dividing Europe'. The Assembly has repeatedly sought to develop joint structures with the Parliament, but, with the exception of occasional meetings (for example, annually between the political group leaders in the two bodies), little has been achieved. Between 1953 and July 1999, this was logistically very difficult in any case, because the hemicycle of the Council of Europe's building in Strasbourg – the *Maison de l'Europe*, later the *Palais de l'Europe* – played host to the Parliament for its monthly plenary sessions. As a result, a pattern developed of the Parliament and Assembly seeking to meet at different times in Strasbourg – a process compounded by the fact that the former's committees meet in Brussels and the latter's in Paris and Strasbourg. Now that the Parliament sits in its own separate, bigger, purpose-built complex next to the *Palais*, it would be logically possible to develop closer links between the Parliament and the Assembly, but on the one occasion that they both convened in Strasbourg at the same time (by scheduling error), there was very little contact.

Moreover, the Council of Europe has suffered a wider identity problem from the fact the **European symbols** which it invented – a **European flag**, a **European anthem** and a Europe day – have all now been adopted by the European Union. In the first two cases, the EU transposed the existing symbols in their original form; in the third case, the Union in effect moved the date from 5 May, the anniversary of the signing of the Treaty of London in 1949, to 9 May, the anniversary of the **Schuman Plan** in 1950. There are thus now two competing Europe days, with the second increasingly displacing the first. The degree of resentment felt by the Council of Europe towards this process was revealed in the text of the institution's official history (*A European Story*, 1986): as the 'mother of European institutions', the Council condemned the creation of a rival Europe Day as a 'Freudian act of matricide' by the European Community.

Until the end of the 1980s, the political importance of the Council of Europe was limited to three main areas. First, it was a forum in which countries not belonging to the European Community could remain in touch with the integration process. Second, membership of the Council of Europe was an indispensable proof of democratic credentials for countries (like Portugal and Spain in the mid-1970s) seeking to regain their international respectability after periods of dictatorship. This aspect of the Council's role was reinforced by the decision to suspend the membership of Greece and Turkey during periods of military rule, and played an important part in the Council's re-emergence after the collapse of Communism. Third, the Council made steady and substantial progress in the field of human and fundamental rights, an area that was largely excluded from the European Community **Treaties** in their original form.

From 1989 onwards, the Council of Europe acted as a de facto ante-chamber for the countries of central and eastern Europe, many of which aspired to membership of the European Union. In response to their demands, for example, the Council set up a European Commission for Democracy through Law, based in Venice, in 1990, to advise on questions of legal and constitutional reform and the operation of democratic institutions. During this period, the Council also held two summit meetings of heads of government – in Vienna (October 1993) and Strasbourg (October 1997) – but the process has since become more occasional. The last such summit was held in Warsaw in May 2005. The eventual **accession** of ten former Communist countries to the European Union in 2004–7 and the extension of treaty status to the EU's **Charter of Fundamental Rights** by the **Lisbon Treaty** in 2009 appear to have gradually brought to a close the period of renewal that the Council of Europe enjoyed during much of the last two decades. In recent years, the Council of Europe and the EU have developed a number of jointly-funded programmes for institution-building and the development of civil society in south-eastern and eastern Europe, Turkey, Russia and the South Caucasus.

The big remaining uncertainty is how the Union's accession to the ECHR, also foreseen by the Lisbon Treaty, will operate in practice, and its implications for the relationship between the Council's and the Union's respective courts – the European Court of Human Rights and the **European Court of Justice** (ECJ) – and their jusrisprudence. An agreement reached by the Union and the Council of Europe in July 2011 envisages that the Union will, like all other contracting parties, provide a judge for the Court, elected by the Parliamentary Assembly, to which a delegation of Members of the European Parliament (MEPs) would be assigned for the purposes of the election. (The Parliament's 18-strong delegation will be the same size as those of the largest member states, whilst four MEPs will sit on the Assembly's committee on legal affairs.) The Union will also be entitled to sit on the Committee of Ministers of the Council of Europe and vote on some of the decisions it takes on ECHR issues.

In parallel to its core activities, the Council of Europe has provided the setting in which a number of quasi-autonomous intergovernmental activities take place, encompassing some or all of the Council's members. These are usually regulated by so-called 'partial agreements' among the member states, within a Council framework, often with each being assigned its own budget. The 'Venice Commission' referred to above is a case in point. On this basis, the Council operates two specialized loan facilities. The first is the Council of Europe Development Bank (CEB) – originally established in 1956 as the Resettlement Fund for National Refugees – which helps finance social housing and infrastructure, as well as providing aid for refugees and victims of natural and man-made disasters. Involving 39 of the Council of Europe's 47 member states, this Paris-based bank has assets of around € 20 billion. It recently provided a € 1.0 billion loan for the redevelopment of South Ossetia, following the brief war between Georgia and Russia (ironically, both Council of Europe members) over the territory in 2008. The Council of Europe's second loan facility is its more modest 'Eurimages' programme for the co-production, distribution, exhibition and digitization of European feature films and documentaries. Created in 1989 with some € 20 million in capital, the fund enables film companies to borrow against the anticipated revenue from successful ventures.

There are several other 'partial agreements'. In 1980, the Council of Europe took over the organization of the Pompidou Group, a Europe-wide forum for combatting the abuse and illicit trafficking of drugs. In 1992, the Council established the European Audiovisual Observatory, a think tank and information service dedicated to the promotion of the European television, film and multimedia industries. Since 1996, it has hosted the European Directorate for the Quality of Medicines (EDQM), the technical secretariat of the European Pharmacopoeia Commission. In 1990, the Council established the European Centre for Global Interdependence and Solidarity – which is known as the 'North–South Centre' and based in Lisbon – as a network of governments, parliamentarians, local authorities and NGOs engaged in the promotion of human rights, democracy and education worldwide. Likewise, in 1997, it created the European Centre for Modern Languages (ECML), based in Graz, Austria, as a training centre for teachers, authors and other professionals in the field of modern languages.

Further reading: Martyn Bond, *The Council of Europe: Structure, History and Issues in European Politics*, 2012.

Council of Ministers

The 1957 **Treaty of Rome** made the Council of Ministers the dominant decision-making body and pre-eminent political **institution** of the European Community. Comprised of ministers from the governments of the member states, the Council was initially the exclusive legislature and the budgetary authority of the new Community system. Once the **European Commission** had exercised its '**right of initiative**' and had made a formal proposal, it fell to the Council to decide whether it would be enacted, subject only (in most cases) to the requirement that the **European Parliament** be consulted. The Council also had the right to assign itself executive functions to implement legislation, even though in practice it rarely used this latter power, usually entrusting such responsibility to the Commission (under the **comitology** system). In the original institutional design of the late 1950s, the Council thus enjoyed an unusually extensive array of legislative, budgetary and even executive powers, all of which underlined its central position in Community politics.

The supremacy of the Council has declined in recent decades, as a result of two main factors. First, successive treaty changes have forced the Council increasingly to share its powers with the European Parliament. Although this shift started with the Budgetary Treaties of 1970 and 1975 – which made the Council and Parliament the 'joint budgetary authority' of the Community – it was only when the 1986 **Single European Act** (SEA) gave the Parliament a direct involvement in law-making that the latter's views began to be taken seriously by member-state representatives sitting in the Council and its preparatory bodies. The **cooperation procedure** introduced by the Single Act started a long process which has led – notably through the institution of the **co-decision procedure** between the Parliament and Council by the 1992 **Maastricht Treaty** – to a situation where today, under the **Lisbon Treaty**, the two institutions form a de facto joint legislature in most, although not all, policy fields. Article 16 TEU makes this point by stating that the 'Council shall, jointly with the European Parliament, exercise legislative and budgetary functions. It shall carry out policy-making and coordinating functions as laid down in the **Treaties**.' In parallel, the Council's ability to confer on itself executive powers to implement legislation directly has been significantly restricted; except in economic policy coordination, such powers must now be 'duly justified' and are subject to approval by the Parliament.

The second, parallel development eroding the dominance of the Council of Ministers over time has, ironically, been the increasing importance of the regular summit meetings of EU heads of state or government. The **European Council**, established in 1975, put in place a higher political authority than the Council among the member-state governments, and one which emerged during the 1980s and 1990s as a key agenda-setting and dispute-resolution forum within the Community political system. The Lisbon Treaty has taken this process further, by making the European Council an EU institution in its own right and by establishing a 'permanent' **President of the European Council**, separate to the traditional arrangements for chairing the Council of Ministers.

Although the Council of Ministers is the principal arena for the representation of national interests in the EU decision-making process, its acts are those of a fully-fledged Union institution, made on behalf of and in the name of the Union as a whole. In its capacity as the sole or joint legislature of the Union – on its own or with the European Parliament – the Council may adopt any of the three types of binding **legal act** provided for in the Treaties: **regulations**, **directives** and **decisions**. It may also issue non-binding recommendations to member states and adopt resolutions.

Articles 16 TEU and 237–43 TFEU set out in detail the composition and operating procedures of the Council. It is composed 'of a representative of each Member State at ministerial level, who may commit the government of that Member State in question and cast its vote' (Article 16(2) TEU). This wording, dating from the Maastricht Treaty, makes it clear (it was previously ambiguous) that it is ministers, not officials, who represent the member states in Council meetings. It also allows federal states, such as Belgium or Germany, to be represented if necessary by a minister from a provincial or *Land* government. The Council meets 'in different configurations, the list of which is adopted' by decision of the heads of government in the European Council (Articles 16(6) TEU and 236 TFEU).

The Council is currently divided into ten such distinct, subject-based, formations which operate in parallel. Until December 1999, there was no limit on the number of configurations in which the Council could meet: the number was initially capped at 16, and then reduced again in June 2002. The existence of the **Foreign Affairs Council** (FAC) and **General Affairs Council** (GAC) – comprised respectively of foreign ministers and a mixture of foreign and European affairs ministers – is now foreseen in the Treaties (under Article 16(6) TEU); each of these Councils meets once a month, usually back-to-back. The Council of Economics and Finance Ministers (**Ecofin Council**) and the Council of Agriculture and Fisheries Ministers also meet monthly. There are regular, but less frequent, meetings of the Justice and Home Affairs (JHA) Council, the Competitiveness Council (covering the single market, industry and research), the Environment Council, the Employment, Social Policy, Health and Consumer Affairs Council (ESPCO), the Transport, Telecommunications and Energy Council, and the Education, Youth and Culture Council. From time to time, joint or 'jumbo' Councils may be held to discuss issues that cross the boundaries of any one Council's responsibilities. In all, the Council has in recent years met on average about 80 times a year. The senior Council configuration has traditionally been the Foreign Affairs Council, but since the Lisbon Treaty, that role has been formally transferred to the General Affairs Council, which is now explicitly entrusted with a general coordinating role within the system – 'to ensure consistency in the work of the different Council configurations' (Article 16(6) TEU).

The chairmanship or '**presidency**' of the Council rotates every six months among the member states of the Union. Originally, the order of rotation was alphabetical, but now it is settled by a complex bargaining process, leading to a decision of the European Council (Article 236 TFEU). The 'president-in-office' is responsible for chairing all Council meetings other than the Foreign Affairs Council; since Lisbon, the latter role falls to the **High Representative** for **Common Foreign and Security Policy** (CFSP). The rotating presidency organizes the political business of the Council and represents it in meetings with other EU institutions and bodies. It is assisted in its work by the permanent 'general secretariat' of the Council, comprising some 3,200 officials, based entirely in Brussels and grouped into eight functional or policy-related directorates-general (plus a legal service). The Council secretariat is headed by a Secretary General, appointed for a four-year term. He or she is usually a former permanent representative, although the current Secretary General, Uwe Corsepius, who took office in June 2011, is unusual in having no prior direct Brussels experience. (He served previously as the European affairs adviser to the German Chancellor, Angela Merkel, in Berlin.)

In addition to providing routine logistical support, the Council secretariat prepares background papers, draws up the minutes of meetings, suggests compromise texts to the presidency, and ensures that the acts of the Council are properly transposed into legal form and duly published in the ***Official Journal***. The Council's legal service, which advises on the form and **legal base** of any proposal, carries considerable authority. The Council secretariat's influence on the content of decision-making is often inversely proportional to the size of the member state holding the presidency. The **permanent representations** (or embassies to the EU) of the five or six largest member states are usually sufficiently well staffed to be able to free themselves, if they wish, from reliance on the technical expertise and institutional memory of the Council secretariat. However, since the Council secretariat also services the European Council, even though the rotating presidency no longer chairs that body, the secretariat is now in a strong position to replace the presidency as the key institutional bridge between these two levels of decision-making among the member states.

National officials from the permanent representations meet together regularly to prepare the various decisions to be taken by the Council (and indeed European Council). There are two main layers to this process: **COREPER** and working groups. COREPER is an extremely important and powerful decision-making point within the Council system, and its role is recognized in Article 16(7) TEU: 'A Committee of Permanent Representatives of the Governments of the Member States shall be responsible for preparing the work of the Council.' It brings together the ambassadors of member states (COREPER II) and their deputies (COREPER I) to discuss the agenda of all forthcoming meetings of the Council. They decide what goes to the Council, in what form, and broker many of the key deals that make substantive discussion among ministers unnecessary. In certain policy areas, COREPER has either chosen to share its preparatory work with specialist committees or is obliged to do so by the Treaties – respective examples are the Special Committee for Agriculture (SCA) and the **Political and Security Committee** (PSC).

Working groups, made up of mid-rank civil servants from the permanent representations and (where necessary) domestic ministries, prepare the ground before items are taken to COREPER and then the full Council. The purpose of discussion in both tiers is to identify in precise detail the points of agreement and discord on any proposal, and to try to resolve remaining disagreements, so that the higher body (COREPER or the full Council) can focus on major points of dispute. Once a point has been settled at a lower level, the presidency will try to avoid it being reopened at a higher level. The power of mid-rank civil servants in this system is thus significant. Council agendas, set by the presidency, are divided into 'A points' and 'B points', the former being issues that have already been satisfactorily concluded at an official level. COREPER and the working groups are also serviced by the Council secretariat and chaired in most cases by the country holding the presidency. As in the full Council, the Commission is normally present at, and participates in, all their meetings.

The Council normally meets in Brussels, but for three months a year (in April, June and October) it meets in Luxembourg, as part of the 1965 agreement on the provisional location of various institutions, now codified in Protocol 6 to the Treaties (see **seats of EU institutions**). Meetings of the Council in Brussels take place in the Justus Lipsius building, named after a sixteenth-century Flemish humanist and scholar. In addition, the presidency normally convenes one 'informal' meeting of each Council in its own country during its six-month term, often over a weekend. (The informal meetings of foreign ministers are known as '**Gymnich meetings**'.) By definition, 'informals' are not official meetings of the Council and have no legal status. Often they are devoted to open-ended discussion of large or difficult issues on the Council's agenda, in the hope of finding new common ground. They rarely reach conclusions as such and normally issue no communiqués.

For the first 35 years of its existence, the Council met entirely behind closed doors. The Council's rules of procedure were only published for the first time in July 1979. Such a culture reflected the diplomatic norms of the national foreign ministries that dominated the Council system and the genuine fear that the process of deal-making and trading of concessions between member states would be made much more difficult if it had to be conducted in the public eye. However, at the time of the negotiation and **ratification** of the 1992 Maastricht Treaty, it became clear that it was simply no longer tenable for a legislative body in a democratic system to conduct all its business in private. In a spirit of greater transparency, the Council's rules were amended in October 1993 to provide that (unless a simple majority decided otherwise) its proceedings would henceforth be conducted in public whenever it acted 'as legislator', and to require the results of its votes on such matters (together with explanations of votes and formal statements) to be published. Since December 1999, the provisional agendas of meetings of the

Council and its preparatory bodies have also been published. Now Article 16(8) TEU states: 'The Council shall meet in public when it deliberates and votes on a draft legislative act. To this end, each Council meeting shall be divided into two parts, dealing respectively with deliberations on Union legislative acts and non-legislative activities.' The Council's rules of procedure now also allow it to vote to hold 'public debates on important issues affecting the interests of the European Union and its citizens' (Article 8(2) RoP). The public is given access to meetings, not physically, but through transmission of the relevant business 'by audiovisual means' (Article 7(3) RoP).

The gradual opening-up of the Council has resulted in much greater interest in the institution's voting procedures, practices and patterns. The Council has so far always taken decisions by one of three methods – **unanimity**, **qualified majority voting** (QMV) or simple majority voting. Where unanimity applies, abstentions by member states do not count (Article 238(4) TFEU). In cases of a simple majority, a majority of the component members of the Council (currently 14 out of 27) is required (Article 238(1) TFEU). Under QMV, each member state is assigned a number of votes which broadly reflects its relative size. To be adopted, a proposal must secure sufficient votes to reach a specific threshold – currently set at 255 out of 345 votes (or 73.9 per cent) – with the measure enjoying the support of a majority of the member states representing at least 62 per cent of the Union's total population (Article 3, Protocol 36 to the Treaties). The Lisbon Treaty will replace the current QMV system, introduced by the 2001 **Nice Treaty**, with a simpler 'double majority' voting arrangement, to take effect in 2014–17. Under this new system, the adoption of legislation will normally require the support of 55 per cent of the member states, representing at least 65 per cent of the population of the Union (Article 238 TFEU).

Until the Lisbon Treaty, the default position was that, except where otherwise prescribed, simple majority voting was used in the Council (Article 205(1) EC, now repealed). Under Lisbon, Article 16(3) TEU states that the Council shall 'act by qualified majority except where the Treaties provide otherwise'. However, in practice, in the past, the Treaties required either QMV or unanimity in nearly all areas, with a simple majority largely confined to procedural questions. In any case, for the first three decades of the Community's history, unanimity was the operating principle of the Council, even where theoretically a decision could be taken by a qualified or simple majority. The planned extension of QMV in 1966 – when the third stage of the 'transitional' phase of the Community's development came into effect – was overshadowed by an informal agreement, concluded in January of that year, known as the **Luxembourg Compromise**, which gave any member state a de facto right of veto on a matter that it considered to touch on a 'very important' national interest. This meant that votes were rarely, if ever, taken, except sometimes on detailed agricultural or budgetary issues, and an objection from any one member state – whether or not a 'very important' interest was really at stake – was usually enough to kill a proposal.

The 'veto culture' broke down fairly quickly after the introduction of the Single European Act, which came into effect in 1987, and since then the voting rules have been fairly scrupulously applied when any member state has insisted on this. However, voting actually occurs much more rarely in the Council than is necessary or indeed possible, as the presidency and Council secretariat very often seek to build a broader degree of consensus than required under QMV and attempt to avoid embarrassing member states, in the eyes both of their domestic public opinion and **national parliaments**, by subjecting them to visible defeat. Sometimes the presidency will simply assert to the Council that it is clear that a qualified majority exists, without taking any vote, so that the decision can be formally recorded as taken, without any evidence of dissent. This pervasive 'culture of consensus' in Council deliberations makes it more difficult, even with enhanced openness, to trace the precise dividing lines between member states in the positions they defend before decisions are finally adopted. (See the entry on **qualified majority voting** (QMV) for a more detailed analysis of the available evidence on voting in the Council.) The Council may act by written procedure (with the prior consent of all member states) or by 'simplified' written procedure (at the discretion of the presidency, mainly on procedural questions).

The gradual extension of co-decision by successive treaties since Maastricht – to the point where it now covers the great majority of the normal legislative work in the Union – has cast the Council in the role of an almost equal partner with the Parliament in a de facto joint legislature. Reflecting this change, co-decision has been designated by the Lisbon Treaty as the 'ordinary legislative procedure' (at least when it is combined with the use of QMV in the Council). Although the Council may have difficulty in admitting it, the institution is evolving in the direction of an upper chamber in a bicameral system, in which the Commission is the principal executive body and the European Council straddles the executive–legislative divide at a higher level. Since the 1950s, some enthusiasts for European integration have always hoped that the Council would one day be replaced by the Parliament, withering away to become an emasculated 'Chamber of States'. In practice, the permanence and vitality of the national interests represented in the Council has prevented this from happening, but equally the Council has come to share its legislative and budgetary power with an increasingly assertive Parliament. As a result, relations between the Council and the Parliament, which have never been easy, have if anything deteriorated over time.

In many ways, the Council was the big institutional loser from the many changes introduced by the Lisbon Treaty. In addition to the extension of co-decision with the Parliament, the two institutions were made completely equal in the budgetary process – by the abolition of their differing powers in respect of **compulsory and non-compulsory expenditure** – and the Parliament acquired a formal right of veto (under the **consent procedure**) over future Multiannual Financial Frameworks (MFFs). Even in the Council's modest executive function, the situation has changed to its disadvantage. Although the Council retains its (largely theoretical) responsibility for coordinating the economic policies of member states (under Article 121 TFEU) and it may still be entrusted with implementing powers in CFSP and other 'duly justified specific cases' (Article 291 TFEU), the reality is that in foreign policy, the coordinating function previously exercised by the presidency (and supported by the Council secretariat) has now shifted to the High Representative (supported by an independent **European External Action Service** (EEAS)), whilst in most domestic policy fields, any devolution of implementing power to the Council would require the approval of the Parliament in the authorizing legislation, which is most unlikely. In addition, although the Council retains its traditional role in **international agreements** – where it has the power to 'authorize the opening of negotiations, adopt negotiating directives, authorize the signing of agreements and conclude them' (Article 218(2) TFEU) – such agreements are now in most cases subject to a parliamentary consent.

Similar to full Council meetings, but distinct from them in law, are the gatherings of the 'Representatives of the Governments of Member States'. These take certain decisions which the Treaties specify as being for the member states acting collectively by 'common accord' (namely, unanimously, but with any abstentions counting against), rather than for the Council as an institution of the Union. The Representatives of Governments appoint the judges and advocates-general of the ECJ and General Court (Article 19(2) TEU), decide on the seats of the EU institutions (Article 341 TFEU) and conclude **Intergovernmental Conferences** (IGCs) under the 'ordinary revision procedure' for treaty change (Article 48(4) TEU). The right of Members of the European Parliament (MEPs) to put questions to the Council does not extend to matters decided on the basis of agreement between the governments of member states.

Previously known as the 'Council of the European Communities', the official title of the Council of Ministers has, since the entry into force of the Maastricht Treaty in November 1993, been the 'Council of the European Union'. The Council publishes an annual review of its work in the form of a report by its Secretary General.

Further reading: Fiona Hayes-Renshaw and Helen Wallace, *The Council of Ministers*, 2006; Daniel Naurin and Helen Wallace (editors), *Unveiling the Council of the European Union: Games Governments Play in Brussels*, 2008; Martin Westlake and David Galloway, *The Council of the European Union*, 2006.

Court of Auditors

Expenditure by the institutions of the European Union is subject to both internal and external controls. Internal controls are the responsibility of the Internal Audit Service of the **European Commission** and of similar services within other institutions. Since 1977, external controls have been the responsibility of the Court of Auditors – a separate institution composed of one appointee (or 'member') from each member state and a staff of about 900 people, based in Luxembourg.

External financial controls, of which the Court is the principal symbol, have been very substantially strengthened as the Community, now Union, has developed. Initially, responsibility for financial control was vested with a small Audit Board, composed for the most part of officials from the national audit offices or finance ministries of the member states. Under a Council decision in May 1959, the Audit Board – the members of which were appointed for a five-year period by the **Council of Ministers** – was required to draw up an annual report on the income and expenditure of the European Communities, a report that was forwarded to the Council and (from 1970) the **European Parliament**, along with the annual accounts prepared by the Commission, as part of the **discharge procedure**.

A number of developments – the **enlargement** of the Community in 1973, several well-publicized instances of fraud in the **Common Agricultural Policy** (CAP) spending, and the growth in the size of the annual **Budget** – reinforced a general feeling, especially among Members of the European Parliament (MEPs), that the Audit Board lacked the resources, independence and authority to do its job effectively. The Parliament was also interested in strengthening its own powers of oversight over Community expenditure, and the new, stronger 'Audit Office' for which it pressed was expected to work very closely with the Parliament's own committee on budgets (subsequently supplemented by a specific committee on budgetary control).

In July 1975, the representatives of the member states signed a new treaty on budgetary and financial provisions, which, inter alia, enhanced the budgetary powers of the Parliament. Under this treaty, which came into effect in 1977, important changes were made to external financial controls. The Audit Board was replaced by a Court of Auditors. The term of office of the members of the Court was extended from five to six years, and they were given the right to elect from among their own number a president for a renewable three-year term. The Council was required to consult the European Parliament on appointments to the Court. Since 1989, the Parliament's plenary has voted against a total of six nominees to the Court: in four instances, their governments have maintained the candidacies which have been confirmed by the Council; in two instances, the candidates have withdrawn.

The Court's composition and powers are set out in Articles 285 to 287 TFEU. It is tasked with examining 'whether all revenue has been received and all expenditure incurred in a lawful and regular manner and whether the financial management has been sound. In doing so, it shall report in particular on any cases of irregularity' (Article 287(2) TFEU). The remit of the Court extends not only to all Union institutions, bodies and **agencies**, but also to all national, regional and local bodies that receive or handle EU funds, both in the member states and elsewhere (for example, in developing countries). Since the definition of Union funds includes not only those entered in the annual Budget, but also the **European Development Fund** (EDF) and some of the lending activities of the **European Investment Bank** (EIB), the total volume of expenditure for which the Court is responsible is very large. In conducting its enquiries, the Court has the right to extract from any recipient of EU funds, 'at its request, any document or information necessary to carry out its task' (Article 287(3) TFEU). Its audit may be conducted either by scrutinizing records or engaging in on-the-spot checks.

The Court meets in four 'audit groups', each bringing together up to six members and dealing with a different area of EU activity. There are also two clusters of members dealing with horizontal issues. The Court adopts an annual work programme which its president presents early each year to the budgetary control committee of the European Parliament, although the approval of the Parliament is not a prerequirement of it proceeding.

The Court's findings are contained in an annual report on the execution of the general budget of the Union (for the previous year), adopted by a simple majority of its members each November. In recent years, the Court has, at the same time, issued separate, specific reports on the EDF and the individual agencies of the Union. The Court also produces special reports on particular subjects – it usually drafts about a dozen such reports each year on particular EU policies or programmes – and is required to give its opinion on any changes proposed by the Commission to the Union's Financial Regulation or to the system of **own resources**.

Central to the Court's annual report is a 'statement of assurance' which it provides to the Council and Parliament on the 'reliability of the accounts and the legality and regularity of the underlying transactions' (Article 287(1) TFEU). In 2011, for the 17th successive year, the Court was unable to provide an unequivocally positive statement of assurance on the legality and regularity of EU expenditure as reported by the Commission – the condition being that no more than two per cent of total spending should be subject to meaningful error. It found certain payments in 2010 under the CAP and **Cohesion Fund**, in particular, to be 'materially affected by error', although the problem was also witnessed, in varying degrees, in the fields of energy and transport. It estimated the likely error rate in payments at 3.7 per cent. For the fourth year, however, the Court was able to give an unqualified opinion that the accounts at least 'faithfully reflected overall revenue and expenditure for the year'.

The title 'Court' is a misnomer. It was chosen because several member states have similar bodies known by that name – such as the French and Belgian *Cours des comptes* and the Italian *Corte dei Conti* – but in fact the Court has no power to pass sentence, insist on repayment of misappropriated funds or impose any kind of sanction. The Court's powers are confined to drawing irregularities and shortcomings to the attention of the responsible authorities in the institution concerned, which may or may not act upon the Court's advice, and to the wider public. If no action is taken, all the Court can do is to highlight this failure in a subsequent report and withhold its approval of the institution's accounts for the financial year in question. The Court has persistently drawn attention to the reluctance of the Council, in particular, adequately to consider the Court's reports. The 1992 **Maastricht Treaty** gave the Court the full status of an EU institution, which allows it to bring actions in its own right against other Union institutions in the **European Court of Justice** (ECJ), in order to protect its prerogatives.

There is some evidence that the effectiveness of the Court of Auditors has been diminished by the fact that there is no consensus within the Union, or even among the members of the Court itself, on the proper role of an auditor. The narrow definition of auditing is concerned solely with the correspondence between the allocation of funds, the disbursement of those funds and the propriety of the accounting procedures. A broader definition would give the Court autonomous investigative powers and allow it to undertake 'value for money' auditing – along the lines of some enquiries conducted by the National Audit Office (NAO) in the United Kingdom and the Government Accountability Office (GAO) of the US Congress – but so far there has been a reluctance to allow the Court a more 'political' role of this kind, and the Court has not pressed for it.

Croatia

Croat enthusiasm for the creation of the Kingdom of Serbs, Croats and Slovenes (later **Yugoslavia**) in 1918 soon waned when they found themselves treated as a subject people within Greater Serbia. During the Second World

War, the German forces of occupation allowed a puppet state in Croatia a brief and inglorious independence, for which the Croats paid dearly in the period of Communist rule after 1945 (although Marshal Tito was himself half-Croat).

Amidst international misgivings, Croatia declared itself a sovereign state in June 1991, thereby prompting an armed conflict with Serbia and the expulsion of its own ethnic minority Serbs. The German government controversially recognized Croatia (and Slovenia) three weeks before the other EU member states and the **United Nations**, which waited until a ceasefire took effect in January 1992. A UN force, UNPROFOR, was deployed thereafter in an attempt to maintain peace. The conflict with Serbia continued sporadically until November 1995, and although Croatia ended by securing independent control over its own territory, about a quarter of its economy was destroyed and 16,000 of its citizens were either killed or went missing during the years 1991–5.

Croatia received assistance from the European Union from 1992 onwards and was admitted to the **Council of Europe** in 1996. It signed a Stabilization and Association Agreement with the Union in October 2001 and applied for membership in February 2003. The **European Council** granted candidate status to Croatia in June 2004, with **accession** negotiations opening in October 2005. Although the negotiations were frozen from January to September 2009 because of a border dispute with Slovenia, they accelerated soon after and were concluded in June 2011, with the European Council setting July 2013 as the date for Croatian accession, when the country will become the 28th **member state** of the union.

Cultural policy

Traditionally, cultural policy at European level was primarily the responsibility of the **Council of Europe**. Since the early 1950s, the Council of Europe has been very active in respect of the documenting and conservation of historic buildings, the safeguarding of minority cultures, the mounting of major exhibitions, the promotion of the role of culture in education, and the encouragement of cross-frontier cooperation in various fields of creative activity (for example, through the 'Eurimages' programme for the co-production and distribution of European films). To this end, as in other areas of the Council of Europe's work, various conventions have been drawn up. Since 1987, the Council of Europe has established a number of 'European cultural routes', centred upon themes such as the pilgrimage to Santiago de Compostela, the Vikings or the silk trade. At the level of symbolism, the Council of Europe was also responsible for instituting the **European anthem** and the **European flag**.

Within the European Union context, cultural policy was first formally recognized by the 1992 **Maastricht Treaty**: Article 167 TFEU refers to the contribution to be made 'to the flowering of the cultures of the Member States, while respecting their national and regional diversity and at the same time bringing the common cultural heritage to the fore'. This article does not, however, allow for 'any **harmonization** of the laws and regulations of the Member States'. In November 1992, the **Council of Ministers** drew up guidelines for the development of EU cultural policy, stressing that it 'should not supplant or compete with activities organized at national or regional level, but provide added value and promote interchange between them'.

Earlier references to cultural policy may be found in such EC documents as the 1973 Declaration on European Identity, the 1975 **Tindemans Report** on European Union, the 1983 **Stuttgart Declaration**, and the 1985 report of the Adonnino Committee for a People's Europe. From the mid-1980s onwards, a series of initiatives were taken, although some lacked legislative force because of the absence of a specific **legal base** for culture. They included the development of the European Capital of Culture scheme, efforts to translate and publish 'important works of European culture', the encouragement of commercial sponsorship for cultural activities, and the co-financing of four European Union orchestras. Other measures were, and continue to be, taken as part of the **single market** programme and the protection of intellectual property – for example, in relation to the tax treatment of second-hand goods, copyright, counterfeiting, export licensing for goods of cultural value, and régimes for lending, rental and resale rights.

After the entry into force of the Maastricht Treaty, action was focused on developing three specific cultural programmes, starting in 1996–7. These were the Ariane, Kaleidoscope and Raphael programmes, for respectively books and reading, contemporary arts (both visual and performing), and cultural heritage. They were superseded by a more ambitious framework programme for culture, aimed at creating a 'common cultural area' in Europe. Known as 'Culture 2000', the programme ran from 2000 to 2006; it was backed by € 167 million for the provision of grants in all artistic and cultural fields, notably for festivals, master classes, exhibitions, new productions, tours, conferences and translation. Its successor, the 'Culture 2007' programme, runs from 2007 to 2013, enjoys funding of € 400 million over this seven-year period, and places additional emphasis on cross-border mobility of artists and their output, as well as intercultural dialogue. The **European Commission** awards four prizes in the cultural field – for cultural heritage, contemporary architecture, music and literature. There is a significant crossover between EU cultural policy and audiovisual policy, as well as with the Union's policies for youth, sport and **languages**.

Customs union

A customs union is a territory within which there are no tariffs or quotas between participating countries – the distinguishing feature of a **free trade area** – and, where, in addition, a single set of tariffs and quotas is applied to goods entering the territory from outside. The expression is normally used to denote a territory within which two or more contiguous states have agreed to form such a union. As customs unions involve the setting of common tariffs and quotas, it is logical for them to evolve common external trade policies, although relatively few do. Customs unions are recognized as 'regional trading arrangements' within the World Trade Organization (WTO), and their members are exempt from the requirement to accord 'most favoured nation' treatment to non-members.

The European Union is a customs union with a common external trade policy, known as the **Common Commercial Policy** (CCP). From the outset, Article 9 of the **Treaty of Rome** (now Article 28 TFEU) stated that the **European Economic Community** (EEC) would be based upon 'a customs union which shall cover all trade in goods and which shall involve the prohibition between Member States of customs duties on imports and exports and of all charges having equivalent effect, and the adoption of a **common customs tariff** in their relations with third countries'.

Historically, customs unions have been both ends in themselves and means towards more political ends. In the nineteenth century, the best-known examples of customs unions were the Prussian-dominated *Zollverein* and the abolition of the restrictions on trade applied by the city-states of pre-unification Italy: before 1848, for example, there were no fewer than eight tolls payable at frontiers on goods being transported over the 240 kilometres from Milan to Florence. Both these examples are customs unions that were quite clearly an economic means to a political end. The **Belgo-Luxembourg Economic Union** (BLEU, 1921) and the Switzerland–Liechtenstein customs union (1924) are examples of arrangements with an essentially economic purpose. The League of Nations, through its Committee for **European Union**, attempted, without success, to foster the establishment of customs unions in Europe.

The period immediately after the Second World War gave rise to several proposals for new customs unions in western Europe. The French expressed an interest – partly as a means of containing Germany – in a customs union with Italy and the **Benelux** countries. Various combinations, with ingenious names like 'Fritalux' or 'Finebel', were suggested. The Scandinavian countries discussed the creation of a customs union among themselves, although both Sweden and Denmark were more interested in establishing themselves in continental markets. The Americans, both bilaterally and through the

Organization for European Economic Cooperation (OEEC), did their best to encourage the removal of barriers to trade within western Europe. The British, on the other hand, adopted a more cautious attitude: they were suspicious of the obviously federalist ambitions of some advocates of a European customs union – who argued that such a move would need to be underpinned by supranational institutions – and they feared that the United Kingdom's involvement would be incompatible with the system of Commonwealth preference and the sterling area upon which their trading arrangements were still largely based.

The failure of the **European Defence Community** (EDC) in 1954 prompted the pioneers of European integration to try economic means to secure their political objective, witnessed in the **Beyen Plan** of the following year. Drawing on the broad success of the **European Coal and Steel Community** (ECSC), they revisited the possibilities of economic integration on a more ambitious scale. In the resulting customs union and **common market** established by the Treaty of Rome, ambitious deadlines were set for the progressive elimination of customs duties and quantitative restrictions (quotas) on trade between member states (by 1970). Eighteen months ahead of schedule, the EEC's customs union was completed on 1 July 1968. It was an essential first step in building a more integrated European economy and was recognized internationally as a substantial triumph for the Community. Only with the 1985 programme to complete the **single market** by the end of 1992 was another step of comparable significance taken towards achieving a key objective of the Treaty.

The European Union has established customs unions with three **microstates** – Andorra, Monaco and San Marino – as well as with **Turkey** (1996). (Liechtenstein, **Iceland** and **Norway** are members of the **European Economic Area** (EEA), founded in 1994, which is a single market and free trade area, but not a customs union.) Other significant customs unions worldwide are those established by the Gulf Cooperation Council, Mercosur, the Andean Community, and various regional groupings in Africa. The countries of the North American Free Trade Area (NAFTA) have discussed the possible establishment of a customs union.

D

Danube Commission

With its headquarters in Budapest, the Danube Commission, founded under a Convention signed in Belgrade in August 1948, is responsible for all matters relating to navigation and shipping on the River Danube, including regulation of traffic, registration of vessels, maintenance of the waterway, safety and pollution. The member states – Austria, Bulgaria, Croatia, Germany, Hungary, Moldova, Romania, Russia, Serbia, Slovakia and Ukraine – undertake (where relevant) to maintain their stretches of the Danube in navigable condition and to allow free passage of each others' vessels. The Commission, which is modelled on the **Central Commission for Navigation on the Rhine** (CCNR), meets in ordinary session twice a year, with one representative (an ambassador) per member state. Expert groups addressing specific questions convene in the interim. The Commission elects a president, vice-president and secretary from among the 11 member states for a three-year term. Its secretariat, headed by a director-general, comprises some 30 employees. Its official languages are French, German and Russian.

Navigation of the 2,850 kilometre-long Danube was severely disrupted by the Balkans crisis (see **Yugoslavia**), with several bridges destroyed in 1999. The European Union contributed 85 per cent of the cost of the clearing of the river between 2000 and 2005, in a project administered by the Danube Commission. Use of the river quickly recovered, aided by increasing trade within the region, partly as a result of EU **enlargement**, and by improved interconnections with other waterways. In particular, the opening of the Nürnberg–Kelheim canal in September 1992, linking the Rhine and Danube rivers, has created in effect a single waterway stretching some 4,000 kilometres between Rotterdam on the North Sea and Sulina on the Black Sea.

Decision

A decision is one of three types of binding **legal act** which the institutions of the European Union may adopt, within the scope provided by the **Treaties**. The two others are **directives** and **regulations**.

Under Article 288 TFEU, a decision is 'binding in its entirety upon those to whom it is addressed'. The addressee may be the **institution** itself, any number of member states, or defined natural or legal persons. Decisions are not meant to have a general legislative character of the sort that applies equally to all categories of person – where a regulation would be more appropriate – but rather to address individual cases or situations. Equally, decisions differ from directives in being binding in their entirety: directives are binding only in respect of the result to be achieved, leaving member states some flexibility in how they achieve that result. Individual citizens may bring annulment proceedings against decisions in a way they may not against other types of act. The Treaties set out a number of specific areas in which decisions should be adopted, as well as allowing the institutions to choose between legal acts in other areas.

Proposed by the **European Commission**, decisions may be adopted either by the **Council of Ministers**, under the **consultation procedure**, or more frequently by the **European Parliament** and the Council acting jointly, under the **co-decision procedure**. (Under the **Lisbon Treaty**, co-decision forms part of the 'ordinary legislative procedure'.) The Council and Parliament may empower the Commission to adopt specific decisions to implement the detailed provisions of a directive or regulation, in accordance with the **comitology** process (in effect, administrative law). The Treaty also permits the Commission to adopt a limited number of decisions in its own right in aspects of **competition policy** (Article 106(3) TFEU). In the field of **Common Foreign and Security Policy** (CFSP), decisions may be proposed by the **High Representative** or the member states, for adoption by the Council.

Although many decisions taken by the EU institutions are relatively routine, certain Council decisions can be of great political importance, indeed of quasi-constitutional character. For example, decisions determine the **own resources** of the Union (normally every seven years), as well as electoral arrangements for the European Parliament (the 1976 European Elections Act, as amended). Both these decisions oblige member states to seek their **ratification** in accordance with national constitutional requirements, as if they were treaties.

de Gasperi, Alcide (1881–1954)

A leading post-war Italian Christian Democrat politician, Alcide de Gasperi is regarded as one of the '**founding fathers**' of the European Union. Born in the South Tyrol (or Trentino–Alto Adige) – now in north-eastern Italy, but then belonging to Austro-Hungary – de Gasperi studied philology in Vienna, before becoming a journalist and helping found the *Unione Politica Popolare del Trentino*. He was elected to the imperial parliament (Reichsrat) in Vienna in 1911, at the age of 30. After the First World War, South Tyrol was transferred to Italy and de Gasperi became an Italian citizen. His trans-frontier experience and early membership of a 'multinational' parliament profoundly affected his view of politics and Europe. A devout Catholic, and subsequently a member of *Opus Dei*, he was one of the founders of the *Partito Popolare Italiano* (PPI), securing election to the Italian Chamber of Deputies in 1921.

After the rigged general election in 1924, which saw Mussolini's Fascist party secure an absolute majority in the Chamber, most other parties, including the PPI, were dissolved. De Gasperi was arrested and imprisoned in March 1927 for his opposition to the new régime, but released 16 months later, after the intercession of Pope Pius IX, who secured for him a minor post in the Vatican library. From his sinecure as an archivist, de Gasperi was able to continue his political work subterraneously, both as a Christian Democrat writer and as a member of the Resistance. During the Second World War, he drew up the political programme of a new, specifically Catholic, political party, and in January 1943 outlined in *Le idee ricostruttive della Democrazia Cristiana* his concept for the structure of the post-Fascist Italian state. He guided the resulting party, *Democrazia Cristiana,* during the delicate period between the armistice and the constitution of the new state, serving as its first secretary.

In December 1944, de Gasperi became Italian foreign minister, and prime minister a year later. His position was confirmed when *Democrazia Cristiana* emerged as the largest party, with 35 per cent of the vote, in the elections for the constituent assembly held in June 1946. He then remained prime minister during the eight coalition governments that ruled Italy in the period up to August 1953 (including serving simultaneously as foreign minister in 1951–3). De Gasperi was central both in the post-war reconstruction of his country – where he steered through the new constitution in 1948 and gave his home region quasi-autonomous status – and in ensuring that Italy played a full part in both the Atlantic Alliance and in the movement towards European integration led by **Robert Schuman** and **Jean Monnet**. His determination to be pro-American and pro-European at the same time, echoing the position of **Konrad Adenauer** in West Germany, helped secure strong backing for his government in Washington and was rewarded with generous provision from the **Marshall Plan**. Equally, his preference for working with small centrist parties, rather than bringing the Socialists or Communists into government, paid dividends at the 1948 general election, when the DC was backed by 48 per cent of those voting.

In 1950–52, de Gasperi lent active support to the **Schuman Plan** to create a **European Coal and Steel Community** (ECSC) and was an enthusiastic supporter of the **Pleven Plan** for a **European Defence Community** (EDC). Indeed it was his suggestion, prompted by **Altiero Spinelli**, that the EDC Treaty (of which he was a signatory) should provide for an ambitious institutional review, based on the concept of a directly-elected assembly. This provision led to the parallel proposal for a **European Political Community** (EPC), so ironically contributing to the eventual abandonment of the EDC. In 1952, de Gasperi was awarded the **Charlemagne Prize** for his contribution to European unity. In 1954, he was elected President of the ECSC Assembly, the forerunner of the **European Parliament**. He died later that year and was the only one of the founding fathers not to witness the signature of the **Treaty of Rome** in 1957.

de Gaulle, Charles (1890–1970)

The wartime leader of the Free French, prime minister immediately after the Second World War, and both architect and first President of the Fifth Republic, Charles de Gaulle was France's most important twentieth-century political figure. During the years 1958 to 1969, he ended the chronic political instability which had plagued the Fourth Republic, by equipping France with modern political institutions, and restored his country's self-esteem in the wake of retreats in Indo-China and Algeria. His distinctive foreign policy, aimed at enhancing French prestige, saw in Europe an opportunity to develop a counterweight to the United States and a forum in which to assert French leadership in the world.

An unapologetic advocate of the nation state, de Gaulle was unsympathetic to the new European Community, built upon and administered by supranational institutions. He quickly sought to develop an alternative model, attempting to create an intergovernmental 'political union', based on his **Fouchet Plan** of 1961–2. When this initiative failed, de Gaulle promoted bilateral Franco-German cooperation, but as a substitute, rather than catalyst, for closer integration among **the Six**. In 1963 and again in 1967, he vetoed the United Kingdom's applications to join the Community. In 1965, he pursued an 'empty chair' policy to frustrate the extension of **qualified majority voting** (QMV) in the **Council of Ministers**, and froze the Community into acceptance of policies which served French interests, notably the **Common Agricultural Policy** (CAP). He challenged the Atlanticist perspective of the other five member states, by withdrawing from the integrated military command structure of the **North Atlantic Treaty Organization** (NATO) the following year. De Gaulle's 'shock diplomacy' forced the Community into a distorted mould from which it only gradually began to emerge in the 1970s.

Born in Lille in 1890, the son of a teacher, de Gaulle was raised in a strongly Catholic family, before entering the Saint-Cyr military academy outside Paris. Serving in the First World War, he was wounded, decorated and taken prisoner. In the 1920s and 1930s, he wrote several books on military history and strategy, irritating the army hierarchy with his criticism of its traditional warfare and his advocacy of new motorized techniques. In June 1940, de Gaulle was made both a general and the junior minister for defence in less than a week. Catapulted into the centre of a huge political crisis, he played a crucial role with **Jean Monnet** in convincing the new British prime minister, **Winston Churchill**, to support the idea of a de facto merger of the two countries, through a **Franco-British union**, in a last-ditch effort to avert French surrender to the Germans. He flew from London to Bordeaux on 16 June with the proposal, only to find that the retreating French government had already resigned, with Marshal Philippe Pétain replacing his ally, Paul Reynaud, the following day. De Gaulle returned to London, from where, on 18 June, he delivered a dramatic radio appeal, seeking to rally French resistance against the German invasion. With the support of few other mainstream political figures, he boldly established himself as leader of the 'Free French' and began waging an often lonely campaign to build up French forces, starting in the African colonies, against German control. In May 1943, the General moved to Algiers and, with the support of the National Council of the Resistance, began work on the formation of a provisional government to take over at the end of the war.

With the liberation of France in June–August 1944, the Allies chose to allow de Gaulle to become prime minister, rather than impose a military government on France. The general election in October produced a centre-left majority in the National Assembly, with the Communists the largest single political party. Although de Gaulle enjoyed great personal respect and his government did much to stabilize the country in difficult conditions (its national income was only 40 per cent of that in 1940), he suffered from having no party behind him and was frustrated in advancing his more ambitious plans. The new Assembly proposed to return in effect to the constitution of the Third Republic, with a weak executive, strong parliament, and *régime des parties* underpinned by proportional representation. The General was deeply opposed to this institutional settlement, with his reservations of principle decisively confirmed by the experience of power. He suddenly resigned as prime minister in January 1946 and proposed an alternative constitution – based on presidential and prime ministerial power, underpinned by a majoritarian electoral system – at Bayeux six months later. However, he found himself on the losing side of the referendum that endorsed the new Fourth Republic in October. He announced his withdrawal from politics, whilst allowing the creation (in 1947) of a new centre-right political party, the *Rassemblement du peuple français* (RPF), committed to continuing the struggle, in his name, for the kind of politics that his compatriots had rejected.

As the Fourth Republic proceeded, the early dominance of the centre-left gradually gave way to an advance of conservative forces, with the principal beneficiaries being first de Gaulle's own RPF, at the 1951 general election, and then the *Poujadistes* five years later. The highly fractured, and no less fractious, centre-ground found it more and more difficult to provide coherent government: there were 25 governments in 14 years, with none lasting more than 16 months. Political instability at home was matched by mounting tension in the colonies: defeat at Diên Biên Phu in May 1954 resulted in France leaving Indo-China, whilst independence movements became increasingly active in North Africa. The situation in Algeria, part of metropolitan France, deteriorated rapidly, with separatist terrorists and die-hard settlers refusing to compromise and Paris increasingly paralysed in the face of a growing crisis. Against the backdrop of an insurrection by army officers in Algiers and their threat to invade the mainland, the leaders of the governing parties turned to de Gaulle – who was now 67 years old and had held no political office for more than a decade – as the only political figure capable of finding a potential solution.

The General returned to power as French prime minister on 1 June 1958, determined not to repeat the mistakes of 1944–6 and to govern unequivocally on his own terms. He insisted on being given emergency powers for six months, a period he used to prepare a new constitution. Drafted by his trusty lieutenant, Michel Debré, and based on the principles set out at Bayeux, the text was approved in a popular referendum in October 1958. The new Fifth Republic gave the French President a substantially enhanced role, especially in foreign policy, whilst retaining his seven-year mandate. As importantly, it greatly strengthened the position of the prime minister in relation to the National Assembly, which would henceforth be elected in a single-member, double-ballot system, likely to promote a bipolar party system. The General was himself elected as President – by a college of national parliamentarians and local representatives – in January 1959. He appointed Debré as his premier.

The **Treaty of Rome** had come into effect on 1 January 1958, only five months before de Gaulle's own return to power. The General had refused to endorse the treaty during its negotiation and ratification, whilst Debré had bitterly opposed it. The language which the new President had used during his 'wilderness years' did not bode well for advocates of closer European integration. 'France cannot be France without greatness,' he had written on the first page of the first volume of his memoirs (*L'Appel*, 1954). Greatness implied a France 'sovereign, independent and free'. It was clear that in any struggle between **supranationalism and intergovernmentalism** in Europe, de Gaulle would decisively favour the latter.

Obliged to take some early and important decisions about France's relationship with the new **European Economic Community** (EEC), de Gaulle chose pragmatically to accept the existence of the latter, rather than abrogate the treaty, whilst seeking publicly to challenge the legitimacy of the '**Community method**' and to contain the Community's practical development to a limited number of policy areas which might be of advantage to France. He quickly concluded that France should respect the timetable for the first stage (due to begin in January 1959) of the EC's three-stage move to a **customs union** and **common market** by 1968. The need to meet this deadline, and the potential market consequences of failing to do so, were used to justify the government's so-called 'Pinay-Rueff' austerity and modernization plan of December 1958 (which involved a combination of devaluation and spending cuts). He used the logic of the EEC as a pretext to block the British idea ('Plan G') of creating a **free trade area** in Europe that would encompass both the Six and the other members of the **Organization for European Economic Cooperation** (OEEC). Equally, the development of the new **Common Agricultural Policy** (CAP), on which de Gaulle was determined to insist, would provide an opportunity to ease the process of transition in rural France. 'Had I been in power when the Treaty of Rome was signed,' de Gaulle later reflected (in 1965), 'things would probably have been different, but, in the event, I accepted the treaty as it was and, with my government, tried to draw out of it the best it had to offer.'

The new President launched his rhetorical assault on the Community's institutions in May 1960, when he offered an alternative vision of 'an organized cooperation between states, which might one day evolve into an impressive confederation'. Such a confederation, in which the central authority should have no binding power over its constituent parts, was in striking contrast to the 'Community method' favoured by **Jean Monnet**, **Robert Schuman**, René Pleven and several other Fourth Republic figures. In September 1960, de Gaulle declared that Europe's nation states were 'the only realities upon which one can build', unlike 'vaguely extra-national bodies', namely the Community institutions, 'which do not and cannot have . . . any political authority'. He went on: 'It is an illusion to believe that one could build something capable of effective action, which would be approved by the people, above and beyond the nation state.' Any other approach was 'to indulge in fantasy'.

The Europe which de Gaulle wanted to forge was intergovernmental rather than supranational, and geopolitical rather than economic. He subsequently claimed that it had been his ambition since the Second World War to bring together 'the states which border the Rhine, the Alps and the Pyrenees' as 'one of the three global powers and, if necessary one day, the arbiter between the Soviet and Anglo-Saxon camps' in world politics. A united Europe, capable of acting on the world stage, could be a useful platform from which a renascent France might project a far bigger influence than it could as one state acting alone. More immediately, it could help reconcile nationalist opinion at home to retreat and decolonization abroad, both in Indo-China and North Africa. However, any European entity would need to respect the right of each state to exercise a veto in decision-making, whilst seeing itself as independent from, not subservient to, the Atlantic Alliance.

De Gaulle's very first major foreign policy initiative was almost deliberately designed to provoke the Americans: his request in the summer of 1958 that the United States help France to develop nuclear weapons, in return for which Washington, London and Paris could form a co-equal 'politico-military directory' at the heart of NATO. When President Eisenhower rejected this proposal – unless France, like Britain, accepted the stationing of US nuclear weapons on its soil – de Gaulle proceeded with his independent nuclear deterrent anyway, the existence of which he announced publicly in November 1959, and the first testing of which took place in February 1960.

In March 1959, de Gaulle proposed to Bonn and Rome that the 'big three' within the EC should concert their foreign policies on a tripartite basis. The response of the German Chancellor, **Konrad Adenauer**, was non-committal, whilst that of the Italian prime minister, Amintore Fanfani, was even less positive, saying that Italy could only agree if the **Benelux** countries were included; the latter then insisted that the United Kingdom would need to be involved in some way too. As well as ensuring the participation of Europe's then most powerful international actor, British involvement was seen, especially in The Hague, as a vital guarantee that a commitment to NATO and the Atlantic Alliance would be given primacy in any new European profile on the world stage. Nothing came out of this early Gaullist démarche other than a commitment to hold informal quarterly meetings of the six EC foreign ministers to discuss 'international policy', starting in January 1960.

After these initial rebuffs, the General's thoughts returned to an idea which he had first voiced in 1953 for launching some kind of intergovernmental 'union of states' in Europe, to coordinate foreign policy and defence in particular, as an alternative to the supranational **European Defence Community** (EDC), which his 120 RPF deputies played an important part in defeating on the floor of the National Assembly in August 1954. This was the genesis of de Gaulle's Fouchet Plan for an intergovernmental political union, which would, as he put it privately to Adenauer in July 1960, 'not only be distinct from' the Community institutions, but 'hover over them with a view to bringing them under effective control'. The 'supranational structures established among the Six', he asserted, were 'tending inevitably and abusively to become irresponsible superstates' and needed to be 'subordinated to governments'.

De Gaulle managed to convince his fellow heads of government, at two EC **summit** meetings held in February and July 1961 – the first of their kind – to establish an intergovernmental committee to negotiate a new political union of the Six. Dealing with foreign policy, defence, economics and culture, the new 'union of states' would be structured on entirely intergovernmental lines, with new institutions to parallel those of the Community. However, the Dutch and Belgian governments objected not only to the institutional design of the proposed union, but to its deliberately uncertain relationship with NATO. The French proposed two drafts of the Fouchet Plan, in November 1961 and January 1962, the second of which was even more markedly intergovernmental than the first and gave the union even greater potential to act independently of the United States. The negotiations were suspended in April 1962 and never resumed.

As Miriam Camps wrote soon after, 'There was general agreement within the Six that Europe united could exercise a power and influence in the world that a divided Europe could not, but there was also a fear that the Europe envisaged by de Gaulle was not a Europe working in close and equal alliance with the United States, but a "third-force" Europe playing a dangerous power-game between East and West' (*European Unification in the Sixties: From the Veto to the Crisis*, 1967). These concerns were justified: de Gaulle told Adenauer privately in July 1960 that it was necessary 'to put an end to the American "integration" [of Europe] which the Atlantic Alliance currently entails, and which contradicts the existence of a Europe with its own personality and responsibility in international affairs'.

The failure of the Fouchet Plan was a major political reverse both for de Gaulle and for the new European Community. It led to a significant loss of political momentum at European level and heralded a period of growing instability in relations among the Six. There was a further hardening of de Gaulle's attitude towards closer integration, both rhetorically and practically – for example, the new meetings of heads of government and the quarterly meetings of foreign ministers were discontinued, at French insistence. Instead, the French President decided to press ahead with a strengthening of bilateral links with West Germany and, most dramatically, to veto British membership of the Community. The pattern of Community politics for the rest of the decade was being set.

Speaking at a press conference in the Elysée Palace in May 1962, four weeks after the collapse of the Fouchet negotiations, the French President intensified his verbal attack on the Community's institutions and philosophy. He satirized its functionaries as 'stateless people' and its technocratic jargon as a '*Volapük*' (an artificial international language akin to Esperanto). Five ministers from the pro-European, Christian Democrat MRP resigned from his government the following day. A month later, centrist and Socialist deputies staged a walkout of a National Assembly debate on European policy and a majority of deputies (296 out of 552) then signed a 'European Manifesto', protesting at the increasingly anti-European stance of the President.

De Gaulle ignored these reactions and was soon greatly strengthened by his successful granting of independence to Algeria – confirmed in a referendum he called in April 1962 – and victory in a second, equally critical, referendum he held, six months later, on the direct election of the French President by universal suffrage. Although the old parties of the Fourth

Republic all opposed this latter move, the General won the referendum by a substantial margin, disorientating his opponents. He then dissolved the National Assembly: in the November general election, aided by the new electoral system, his Gaullist party, now styled the *Union pour la nouvelle République* (UNR), came close to winning an absolute majority of seats. With the support of the *Républicains indépendants* – led by the young modernizer, **Valéry Giscard d'Estaing**, whom he appointed finance minister – de Gaulle was finally able to control the National Assembly.

As he registered these important domestic victories, de Gaulle's European strategy quickly moved onto a new track – that of trying to encourage bilateral arrangements at the heart of the Community, but outside its institutional structure, which would have the effect of excluding both the Benelux states and Britain from influence. He explored this approach with Adenauer during successful visits made by each leader to the other's country, in July and September 1962. Soon after, his foreign minister, Maurice Couve de Murville, visited Fanfani in Rome, to invite Italy to participate in a tripartite directory, reviving de Gaulle's idea of 1958–9. Italy once again rejected the idea, reluctant to see the Community divided into two tiers of member states. Somewhat surprisingly, the German government expressed fewer fears, agreeing the basic arrangements at a meeting of the two foreign ministers in December. As a result, when de Gaulle and Adenauer met in Paris on 22 January 1963, they were able to sign the **Elysée Treaty** on Franco-German Cooperation, which covered almost exactly the same territory as the failed Fouchet Plan: foreign policy, defence, economics and culture. The French and German leaders would meet at least twice a year, and other ministers usually at least quarterly, to 'reach, wherever possible, common positions' on issues of mutual concern.

A few days before the Elysée Treaty was signed, on 14 January 1963, the General used a press conference to declare that, as a result of 'very substantial problems', including a fundamental incompatibility both economically and politically between the UK and its partners, he believed that negotiations on British membership of the EC could not succeed. (In the process, he effectively ended the applications by Ireland, Denmark and Norway too.) Unlike Adenauer, de Gaulle saw the United Kingdom as a rival to his country's influence in Europe, and mistrusted the country's attachment to free trade and close association with the Americans. De Gaulle's veto shattered the hopes of all who wanted either a wider Europe or a deeper Europe – and, in very many cases, both. The ageing Adenauer looked as if he had fallen into a carefully laid trap, and the combination of the Elysée Treaty and the veto on UK entry soon after prompted serious criticisms of his handling of events and weakened his hold on power.

De Gaulle's European policy now became even more confrontational. He insisted very strongly on the need for the CAP to be put in place quickly, on

French terms, even threatening to leave the Community in October 1964 if his demands were not met. He gave expression to his increasingly strong personal and political antagonism towards **Walter Hallstein**, the German President of the European Commission. He opposed the Commission's plan to use the need for CAP financing as a pretext to introduce '**own resources**' to fund Community activities. In parallel, he took great exception to the prospect of **qualified majority voting** (QMV) being extended to a wider range of legislative decisions in the Council of Ministers in January 1966, some of which might not serve French interests. The 'empty chair' (or *chaise vide)* crisis followed during the second half of 1965, when French ministers, on the instruction of de Gaulle, refused to take part in meetings of the Council and the French permanent representative was withdrawn from Brussels. This episode was and remains the most serious breakdown in the day-to-day operation of the Community in its history. Whether or not the crisis was in part a populist tactic intended to help secure de Gaulle's re-election to the presidency of France in December 1965, in the first direct election to that post, is open to dispute. If so, it was not entirely successful, as the President was unexpectedly forced to a second ballot by his Socialist opponent, **François Mitterrand**, who used the negative image of de Gaulle's wrangling in Europe to some effect during the campaign.

None of France's partners among the Six shared the General's objections to developments in the Community, many of which had been specifically provided for in the Treaty of Rome. However, the 'empty chair' crisis resulted in a victory for the General, in the sense that the practice followed in the Council after the **Luxembourg Compromise** (of January 1966) – whereby discussion would simply continue and a vote be avoided on any QMV issue on which any one member state deemed a 'very important national interest' to be at stake – embodied the Gaullist view of how the Council should operate. The 'veto culture' thus established was to bedevil the Community until the **Single European Act** (SEA) was adopted 20 years later. Equally, the introduction of own resources was postponed; it was only agreed in 1970, after de Gaulle had left office.

During his last three years as President (1966–9), de Gaulle showed less interest in European developments, partly because he had succeeded in freezing the Community into a residual form – based on the rapid development of the CAP, the avoidance of majority voting in the Council and the exclusion of the United Kingdom from membership – with which he felt broadly comfortable, even if it was still more integrationist than he had originally hoped. Britain (together with Ireland, Denmark and Norway) made a second application to join the EEC in May 1967, only for this too to be rejected six months later. On 27 November, the French President declared that British entry 'would lead to the break-up of a Community which could not absorb so monumental an exception', namely 'a state which through its politics, economy and currency is not at present a part of Europe'. (The reference to Britain's currency was an allusion to the devaluation of sterling a week before.)

In February 1969, de Gaulle was willing to share his disappointment with the development of *l'Europe communautaire* in a private conversation with Christopher Soames, the son-in-law of **Winston Churchill**, who had recently been appointed British Ambassador in Paris. He went on to suggest that France and the United Kingdom should hold exploratory talks about the possible creation of a larger, looser grouping of countries, to be run by a directorate of the biggest countries, including Britain. A report of this discussion was circulated by the British Foreign Office to other governments, generating a major diplomatic row, known as the Soames affair.

Beyond Europe, the pattern of the General's foreign policy became equally, if not more, idiosyncratic. In March 1966, he announced that France was leaving the integrated military command of NATO. In June 1967, during the Arab–Israeli Six Day War, he was one of the few western leaders to condemn Israel and later referred to the Jews as 'an élite people: self-confident and domineering'. The following month, a visit to Montreal for the Expo 67 world's fair had to be abandoned when he was asked by the Canadian government to leave the country, after inciting Quebec to seek independence with the words '*Vive le Québec. Vive le Québec libre.*'

In May 1968, a sudden and dramatic outburst of student and industrial unrest engulfed France, bringing de Gaulle's government to the brink of collapse. After initial confusion and then contemplating resignation, the President managed to outmanoeuvre his critics by calling a snap general election. Relying once again on the choice between 'me or chaos' which had brought the General to power a decade earlier, the June 1968 election resulted in his UNR party winning an absolute majority in the National Assembly, the first such majority ever in republican history in France. Even if theoretically de Gaulle had never been stronger, the events of May had shown him, at the age of 77, to be increasingly tired and out of touch. He proved unable to rebuild momentum behind his government and when he called a referendum in April 1969 on a complex proposal for Senate and regional reform, some speculated that the initiative was designed to offer him an elegant opportunity to retire. When the proposition was defeated, he resigned immediately and played no further part in public life. De Gaulle died in November 1970, with his autobiography unfinished.

Further reading: Maurice Couve de Murville, *Une politique étrangère, 1958–1969*, 1971; Piers Ludlow, *The European Community and the Crises of the 1960s: Negotiating the Gaullist Challenge*, 2006.

Delors, Jacques (born 1925)
Born in Paris, the son of a messenger at the Banque de France, Jacques Delors left school at the age of 16. At the end of the Second World War, he followed his father into the bank, taking night classes at Paris University. A 'social Catholic' who eschewed both collectivism and individualism, he was briefly a member of the Christian Democrat MRP, became active in the Catholic trade union federation, the CFTC, and edited a journal, *Citoyen 60*, which advocated decentralization, social reform and European unification. During the 1960s, he worked for the French government's planning agency, the *Commissariat général du Plan*. With the resignation of **Charles de Gaulle** as French President in April 1969, Delors' background and philosophy made him the ideal choice as employment adviser to Jacques Chaban-Delmas, the modernizing Gaullist prime minister appointed by Georges Pompidou. He attracted considerable political and media attention as an advocate of Chaban's 'New Society', favouring a closer, more organized dialogue between business and labour, which he styled *la politique contractuelle*. He played an important part in the negotiation of collective agreements, known as *contrats de progrès*, in several of France's largest public enterprises. When Chaban was replaced as premier by the more orthodox Pierre Messmer in 1972, Delors left government service to teach economics at Paris University, whilst also establishing a discussion circle, *Échange et projets*, and serving on the general council of the Banque de France.

Two years later, in a move that was decisively to change his life, Delors joined the French Socialist party and became an adviser to **François Mitterrand**, who having been defeated by **Valéry Giscard d'Estaing** in the May 1974 presidential election, continued as de facto leader of the opposition. Delors was invited by Mitterrand to enter politics in his own right, being assigned a winnable position on the Socialist list for the first direct elections to the **European Parliament** in June 1979. After briefly serving as chairman of the Parliament's economic and monetary committee, he was called back to Paris in May 1981, when Mitterrand finally became French President, defeating Giscard in his bid for re-election. As finance minister in the new Socialist–Communist government, Delors quickly emerged as the anchor of fiscal rectitude in the first unambiguously left-wing administration in France for 45 years. With colleagues keen to experiment with 'Socialism in one country', Delors sought to contain public spending in an austerity budget in April 1982 and fought (unsuccessfully) to avert devaluation of the French franc within the **Exchange-Rate Mechanism** (ERM) of the **European Monetary System** (EMS). Realignments were conceded in October 1981, and February and June 1982. In March 1983, Delors won a crucial battle over the future direction of government policy, when Mitterrand chose to back him over the left in keeping the franc within the ERM and accepting in return the need for further austerity measures at home. In parallel, he convinced the German government to revalue the Deutschmark by 5.5 per cent, with the franc devalued by only 2.5 per cent.

After three and a half years in an exceptionally difficult job, from which he came close to resigning more than once, Delors was rewarded, in January 1985, by appointment as President of the **European Commission**, a post in which he was to serve for the next ten years. He took over from the low-key Gaston Thorn, a former prime minister of Luxembourg whose four-year term had been overshadowed by the **British Budget dispute** and a growing sense of **Eurosclerosis**. Although expectations of the potential of his new job were very low, Delors was to prove by far the most influential Commission President since the legendary **Walter Hallstein**, who held the post from 1958 to 1967, and he is now generally regarded as the most successful incumbent to date. His biographer, Charles Grant, has suggested that 'Delors did more than any individual since **Jean Monnet** to advance the cause of a united Europe.' In his new tasks, Delors was to bring to bear an exceptional combination of strategic vision, practical application and personal diplomacy which allowed him to quickly emerge as a master of Community politics.

Delors' decade-long presidency of the Commission was marked by a series of major political achievements, in all of which he was personally and deeply involved. Among the most prominent were the relaunch of the Community through the **single market** programme, set out in the **Cockfield White Paper** of June 1985; the negotiation of the **Single European Act** (SEA) in 1985, which quickly revitalized EC decision-making by extending **qualified majority voting** (QMV) in the **Council of Ministers**; the **accession** to the Community of Portugal and Spain in January 1986; the conclusion of two hard-fought, future-financing agreements, in 1988 and 1992, providing for substantial increases in the Community's **own resources**; the development of **Economic and Monetary Union** (EMU), the basic blueprint for which was provided by the **Delors Report** of April 1989, produced by a committee which he chaired; the negotiation of the **Maastricht Treaty** in 1991, establishing the European Union, institutionalizing EMU and launching a **Common Foreign and Security Policy** (CFSP); the promotion of a 'Social Europe', leading to the adoption of the EU **Social Charter and Social Chapter** in 1989 and 1992; the successful incorporation of East Germany into the Union, as part of **German reunification**, in October 1990; the development of the **European Economic Area** (EEA) in 1992–4; the **enlargement** of the Union to include three EEA states – Austria, Finland and Sweden – in January 1995; and the association of the ex-Communist countries of central and eastern Europe with the Union through Europe Agreements, concluded between 1991 and 1995, which prepared them for eventual membership a decade later.

The decisive strides made towards European integration during the Delors era may be attributed to several factors, all of which came together for the first time in the mid-1980s. The new debate about Eurosclerosis and the cost of '**non-Europe**' led to a growing willingness to consider pan-European policy solutions. The directly-elected European Parliament took the lead in defining that debate, as it strenuously made the case for 'more Europe', both in terms of policy deepening and institutional reform. The continuing break with Gaullism in France saw a new preparedness in Paris to think positively about the potential of Community action, driven by the timing of the French **presidency** of the Council in 1984 and reflected in Mitterrand's nomination of a French candidate for Commission President. However, more than anything else, the key factor in relaunching the Community was the striking ability of Delors himself to work actively with certain heads of government in pursuit of an increasingly ambitious agenda for Europe's future. In addition to his close (but sometimes strained) links with Mitterrand, Delors developed effective working relations with the German Chancellor, **Helmut Kohl**, the Italian prime minister, Benito Craxi, and – following his country's accession to the Community in 1986 – the Spanish premier, Felipe González. In doing so, he pioneered a new type of élite cooperation and bargaining among European leaders – driven out of the office of the President of the Commission – which was to reshape the politics of the Community, subsequently Union.

Delors' critical insight was to understand that the EC heads of government had the potential to commit their countries to a significantly more pro-European approach than their foreign, finance or other departmental ministers, who were too often trapped in sectoral positions dictated by national civil servants. He was one of the first people to appreciate that, rather than represent the apogée of defensive **intergovernmentalism**, the regular **summit** meetings of national leaders, held in the form of the **European Council**, offered a unique opportunity to mobilize strong, proactive leadership in favour of closer European integration. Although the European Council had existed since 1975, discussions at heads-of-government level had often tended to float above ordinary Community business, without much bearing on actual decisions, or non-decisions, in the Council of Ministers. Starting almost immediately, Delors sought to use European summit meetings to move beyond the limits of what was possible in the Council of Ministers, exploiting the political momentum of each successful initiative to justify taking further steps forward. He has subsequently said that the relaunch of Europe in 1985 'would not have been possible without the existence of the European Council'.

The new Delors agenda was focused initially on completion of the single market. A tour of capitals had revealed that this objective was more likely to command wide support among heads of government than three other initiatives he considered in detail – closer defence cooperation, institutional reform and EMU. At the March 1985 meeting of the European Council, Delors secured a commitment in principle to complete the single market by December 1992. This was followed up, at the Milan summit three months later, with two key breakthroughs: first, agreement to proceed with a radical programme of nearly 300 specific, single-market legislative measures, set out in the Cockfield White Paper; and second, the controversial decision to convene an **Intergovernmental Conference** (IGC) to draft treaty changes permitting greater use of QMV in the Council so that these measures could be more easily adopted. In effect, he was able to launch a second objective, institutional reform, on the back of the first. Together, the Milan IGC vote – taken against the wishes of the British, Danish and Greek governments – and the Single European Act which the IGC produced (signed in February 1986) brought about the early demise of the **Luxembourg Compromise** – an informal understanding whereby member states could delay, often indefinitely, the adoption of measures properly subject to majority voting. The end of the 'veto culture' made the Council more efficient in delivering the detailed legislative programme mandated by heads of government. An enormous growth in the Community's legislative output followed.

The 1985–7 experience was to set a pattern. Delors had struck upon a kind of 'virtuous' pro-European circle that was to generate increasingly impressive results. Correctly judging the mood of the key heads of government, the Commission President was repeatedly able to induce the European Council to agree some important new objective, often backed by a deadline, and then invite the Commission to make specific proposals, which would be endorsed in turn at a subsequent meeting of the European Council, leaving the once-dominant Council of Ministers to implement commitments that were now being defined at a higher level. The Commission, instead of being the servant of the Council of Ministers, became in effect a partner of the heads of government, pursuing common priorities and almost invariably enjoying the strong support of the European Parliament in the process.

This 'Delors method' was soon deployed to carry forward the next objectives which the Commission President set himself – an increase in the Community's own resources (the title of the accompanying White Paper was 'Making a success of the Single Act'), the development of a stronger social dimension at European level (to complement the single market), and moves towards a single currency (justified on the grounds that it would enable the full benefits of the single market to be realized). The 1988 German presidency of the Council offered Delors the opportunity, which he grasped, to persuade Chancellor Kohl to adopt a more positive position than his cautious finance ministry and Bundesbank on both future financing and EMU.

The Hanover European Council in June 1988 produced a deal that Germany would never have conceded in the Council of Ministers: the 'Delors I' financial package – whose multiannual character was the Commission President's own idea – doubled the **structural funds** and increased Germany's net contribution to the **Budget**, whilst Delors himself was invited to chair a committee, composed mainly of **central bank governors**, to propose moves towards a single currency. The resulting Delors Report sketched a route map that cleverly married the French and German positions on EMU. He then secured agreement at the Strasbourg summit in December 1989 to a start-date for an EMU IGC, successfully appealing to Kohl to override resistance from some of his ministers. At the same meeting, he emboldened Mitterrand to force the adoption of a new Social Charter against the lone opposition of British prime minister **Margaret Thatcher.**

The fall of the Berlin Wall in November 1989 brought new challenges and opportunities which Delors exploited to the full. One of the first European political leaders unequivocally to welcome the prospect of German reunification, he immediately mobilized the Commission to guarantee the practical logistics that enabled an enlargement of the Community to occur simultaneously with reunification on 3 October 1990. Delors quickly saw that a unified Germany would change the terms of the debate on Europe, encouraging the Bonn government to push for a stronger framework of political integration as a quid pro quo for the single currency. He backed efforts to convene an IGC on 'European Political Union' (EPU) to parallel the one on EMU. When the two tracks were brought together in the Maastricht Treaty, agreed in December 1991 and signed two months later, Delors achieved several of his outstanding goals, including a legally-binding timetable for EMU, the creation of a CFSP and the inclusion of a Social Chapter. Despite his strong belief that all member states should, if at all possible, advance at the same speed towards common goals – thus rejecting the view in some Franco-German circles that there should be a **two-speed Europe** or a Europe of **concentric circles** – Delors reluctantly proposed that the problem of winning UK acceptance of the new treaty be resolved in part by the concession of **opt-outs** from EMU and the Social Chapter. However, overall, Delors was disappointed with the Maastricht settlement, mainly because he resented another important concession to the British (which he had not proposed), namely the acceptance of a **'pillared' structure** for the new European Union, which left CFSP and **Justice and Home Affairs** (JHA) as areas of intergovernmental cooperation.

The European Councils of 1985–91, ending with the Maastricht summit of December 1991, proved to be consistently the most important events in the history of the European Community during that era. The agenda and outcomes of those meetings were defined, more than any other single factor, by the priorities and choices of Jacques Delors and his capacity to persuade many heads of government to follow his lead. The unusual ability of the various European institutions to work together in pursuit of ambitious objectives created a powerful 'motor of integration', with Delors personally at the fore. However, perhaps inevitably, a backlash set in. The **Maastricht ratification crisis** of 1992–3 saw the new treaty rejected in the first Danish referendum in June 1992 and come close to defeat in the **French referendum** held three months later. In September 1992 and August 1993, serious shocks were experienced within the ERM, as the financial markets tested the EMU design set out in the new treaty almost to breaking-point.

The award of the **Charlemagne Prize** to Jacques Delors in the summer of 1992 was to mark something of a watershed in his fortunes as Commission President. From then on, he was less ambitious and less effective than before, and often found himself on the defensive. He would normally have expected to retire as Commission President in January 1993, at the end of two four-year terms, but was asked to stay on for another two years, until the Commission's term was realigned as a five-year period, starting in January 1995, to reflect that of the Parliament. Although he successfully secured a second substantial increase in own resources in December 1992 – the 'Delors II' package agreed at the Edinburgh European Council was, he argued, the logical corollary of introducing the Maastricht Treaty – the deadline for the completion of the single market passed only a few days later with a general sense of anticlimax. Even if relations with neighbouring countries were stabilized through the advent of the EEA, the 1995 enlargement and conclusion of the Europe Agreements, these initiatives seemed tame by comparison to the battles of the past. They also unsettled some of Delors' closest supporters in Paris and Bonn, who were committed to the deepening, rather than widening, of the new European Union. Like many European leaders, Delors seemed unable to offer any contribution to avert or contain the developing tragedy in the Balkans during the years 1991–5 (see **Yugoslavia**).

Delors suffered too from a growing criticism of his style of management within the European Commission. During his tenure, he completely eclipsed most of his fellow Commissioners and the collegiality of the body visibly declined. Despite his formidable attention to detail and experience as a former civil servant, Delors displayed little interest in administrative structures or practices. He was happy to allow his ***cabinet***, headed by Pascal Lamy and François Lamoureux, to emerge as the effective power-centre of the system. Lamy, known as the 'Beast of the **Berlaymont**', used what Charles Grant called his 'élite squad of commandos, dedicated to enforcing the President's will', to short-circuit the traditional bureaucracy. Lamy quickly saw off his fellow compatriot, the veteran Secretary General, **Emile Noël**, and the latter's replacement, the former British Cabinet Office official, David Williamson, chose to confine himself to largely technical functions. Throughout the organization, directors-general and other senior officials were increasingly sidelined and became demoralized. Senior appointments were seen primarily as an opportunity to place loyalists or allies in positions from which they could assist the centre. Several of the long-run, structural shortcomings that eventually led to the **resignation of the Santer Commission** in 1999 were exacerbated or ignored during the Delors years.

Since leaving office in January 1995, at the age of 69, Delors has played only a modest role in public life, chairing a committee of UNESCO in Paris and serving as president of Notre Europe, a centre-left think tank (or *laboratoire des idées)* which he founded in 1996. He declined to enter the race for the French Presidency in May 1995, even though opinion polls suggested that he had a reasonable chance of winning election as the Socialist candidate against Jacques Chirac, and published his *Mémoires* in 2004. In retirement, Delors' own views have evolved in the direction of favouring a two-speed Europe of the kind he rejected as Commission President and of seeking to make EMU arrangements subject to closer political control.

Further reading: Helen Drake, *Jacques Delors: Perspectives on a European Leader*, 2000; Charles Grant, *Delors: The House that Jacques Built*, 1994; George Ross, *Jacques Delors and European Integration*, 1995.

Delors Report

The Delors Report of April 1989 – produced by an ad hoc committee of EC **central bank governors** chaired by **Jacques Delors**, President of the European Commission – stands out as one of the most important and far-reaching initiatives in European integration in recent decades. It established a detailed agenda for the achievement of **Economic and Monetary Union** (EMU) in Europe, and led directly to the convening in 1990 of the **Intergovernmental Conferences** (IGCs) which produced the **Maastricht Treaty** on European Union.

When Delors was appointed Commission President in January 1985, he considered launching a number of major policy initiatives to revitalize a stagnating European Community. These included the completion of the **single market**, the upgrading of foreign-policy cooperation – known as **European Political Cooperation** (EPC) – and the transformation of the **European Monetary System** (EMS) into a single-currency zone with a common central bank and joint monetary policy.

The minimum point of political agreement between the major member states lay with the first two proposals. Germany favoured deepening the single market and foreign-policy cooperation, but expressed scepticism about early moves towards EMU. The United Kingdom was keen on the single market, hostile to EMU and prepared to accept the further, limited, development of EPC. France strongly favoured monetary union, to contain and 'Europeanize' growing German economic power, could accept the development of EPC and might agree to early completion of the single market, especially under Delors' guidance. The net effect of this set of forces was agreement that the single market and EPC should have priority, with the EMU issue left open.

The 1986 **Single European Act** (SEA) reflected this compromise. It strengthened rights to **free movement** and set a 1992 deadline for the removal of all remaining internal barriers to the achievement of the single market. It gave a treaty base to a deeper form of EPC, but operating largely outside the normal EC institutions. On EMU, the text simply recalled the existing commitment to the 'progressive realization' of the concept, without defining it, acknowledged progress made so far through the operation of the EMS, and instituted an empty chapter heading in the **Treaties** available for further elaboration at some later date. Initial proposals on EMU floated by the **European Commission** during the 1985 Luxembourg IGC, which drafted the Single Act, did not secure British or German approval.

During the years 1986–7, little of any significance occurred on the EMS/EMU front, except the modest 'Nyborg–Basel' agreement of April 1987 to strengthen intra-marginal intervention among currencies participating in the **Exchange-Rate Mechanism** (ERM) of the EMS. However, during the German **presidency** of the **Council of Ministers** in January–June 1988, France and Delors both decided to renew pressure on the Community to actively consider EMU as a possibility. They were aided by three factors which had not applied at the time of the Single Act.

First, as the European economy continued its long expansion of the mid- to late-1980s, the EMS entered a period of growing stability, with fewer realignments, and this in turn generated increased confidence about Europe's practical capacity to institute a fixed exchange-rate régime. Second, Delors' personal standing rose substantially as a result of growing popular enthusiasm for the Commission's single-market programme, his association with successful implementation of the Single Act, and his adroit campaign to secure increased budgetary resources for the Community (leading to the 'Delors I' financial settlement at the Brussels European Council of February 1988).

Third, the natural and historic scepticism of the Bundesbank towards EMU was partly immobilized both by the fact that Germany held the presidency of the Council (which reduced that country's capacity to resist pressure for closer monetary integration) and by the personal determination of Chancellor **Helmut Kohl** and his foreign minister, Hans-Dietrich Genscher, to present a more positive, pro-European message to their European partners.

The latter were also keen to help **François Mitterrand**, who was seeking re-election as French President in May 1988 on a pro-European platform. They were aided by the fact that the President of the Bundesbank, Karl Otto Pöhl, was unusually confident that he could handle the EMU dossier without jeopardizing basic German interests. As Kenneth Dyson and Kevin Featherstone have written, the government in Paris sought to exploit the long-standing 'conflict between the Bundesbank's resistance to European monetary coordination and the federal government's commitment to realizing European union' (see below).

When Genscher suggested the creation of a 'committee of wise men' to possibly study moves towards EMU, in a personal memorandum in March 1988, Mitterrand and Delors skilfully exploited the opportunity to sign Kohl up to the concept. The four men agreed on a formula whereby a committee of central bank governors – to be chaired by the President of the Commission, rather than the more natural choice of President of the Bundesbank – would be mandated by the forthcoming Hanover meeting of the **European Council** in June 1988 to explore the practical ways of attaining EMU. This was a shrewd move on two counts. First, by giving the governors a pivotal role in the project from the start, the initiative sought to weaken their instinctive caution on monetary integration and tie them into any conclusions reached. (It also conveniently minimized the impact of finance ministers on the discussion.) Second, the task of the new committee would be to study *how*, rather than *whether*, EMU should be undertaken. It would take for granted the crucial issue of the desirability of EMU – just as the similar **Werner Report** had done almost two decades earlier.

Despite British resistance and Dutch reticence, the Hanover summit agreed to establish the Delors Committee, with the task of 'studying and proposing', in good time for their Madrid meeting in June 1989, 'concrete stages leading towards' EMU. The 12 central bank governors would serve on the committee in a personal capacity, together with three respected economists. The committee met eight times over the following ten months, and presented its unanimously-agreed, 43-page text – the *Report on Economic and Monetary Union in the European Community* – on 17 April 1989.

The Delors Report offered a comprehensive blueprint for moving towards EMU, in stages, on the basis of an independent European monetary institution, a common monetary policy, the irrevocable fixing of exchange rates and the eventual adoption of a single currency. The text argued that EMU would need to be formally underwritten by amendments to the **Treaty of Rome**, and suggested the calling of an early IGC to this end. It envisaged the Community moving together at one speed towards its EMU goal, with no firm deadlines being established in advance, so that progress could reflect growing economic convergence. The Delors conclusions represented a compromise between the

Franco-Italian desire to get the EMU process up and running as soon as possible, and the German belief that it should only take place once the participating countries' economies were ready for it. Given differences over whether the intermediate stages towards EMU should be long or short, the decision to fudge the issue of timing was fundamental to the report's political success.

The Delors Report was divided into three chapters. The first traced the history of EMU in Europe and pointed to crucial linkages between this project and the ongoing programme to complete the single market by the end of 1992. The second chapter identified the likely shape of EMU in a Community context, setting out the principal features of both monetary union and economic union (separately) and the basic political issues to be addressed. It then proposed a specific set of institutional arrangements for achieving the objective. The third chapter spelt out in detail the step-by-step approach to EMU – to which the committee was bound by its Hanover mandate – suggesting three discrete stages, beginning no later than July 1990, and progressing thereafter on a timetable which was deliberately left open.

The first stage would aim at greater convergence of economic performance through strengthened macro-economic policy coordination. New procedures would need to be put in place for that purpose. They would evolve against the backdrop of the completion of the single market, the creation of a single financial area, the inclusion of all EC currencies within the ERM, the removal of all impediments to the private use of the **European Currency Unit** (ECU), an enhanced role for the Committee of Central Bank Governors, and the possible creation of a European Reserve Fund (ERF) – to act as a precursor to a European System of Central Banks (ESCB) – promoting monetary coordination and managing both the EMS and a proportion of member states' reserves. The Community's **structural funds** would also be expanded and reformed to allow them to better promote regional adjustment in preparation for the potential shock of EMU on peripheral member states.

The second stage could begin once the Treaty of Rome had been amended to allow for the ESCB to be set up. This body would be created during this stage, replacing any ERF and absorbing all other existing EC monetary bodies, and gradually assuming a growing role in monetary policy. In parallel, the margins of fluctuation for currencies within the ERM would be narrowed.

The third and final stage would begin with a move to irrevocably fixed exchange rates and the assumption by the ESCB of exclusive control over monetary policy, becoming a European central bank in all but name. An external exchange rate policy would take effect and national reserves would be pooled. At some point later in this stage, a single currency would replace national currencies. The Council of Ministers would gain the right to impose binding limits on national budget deficits. Community structural funds might be further expanded and reformed as necessary.

To implement the three-stage move to EMU, the Delors Report advocated the introduction either of a single global set of amendments to the Treaty of Rome to cover all stages or of a series of mini-treaties before each stage. Either way, preparatory work should 'start immediately' on drafting the necessary amendments, with an IGC being called for the purpose. The Council of Ministers and central bank governors could, in the interim, begin work on measures to implement the first stage.

The publication of the Delors Report was a major political event in Community politics, prompting a widespread debate both about the merits of monetary union and the best means to achieve it. Most national capitals expressed broad support for the report's conclusions. The incumbent Spanish presidency of the Council was determined, under pressure from France and the European Commission, to get a clear commitment from heads of government to take the EMU process forward at the forthcoming Madrid European Council of June 1989. The main obstacle to agreement was the British prime minister, **Margaret Thatcher**, who was deeply sceptical of the idea of sterling entering the ERM under stage one of EMU, hostile to any decision to embark upon the first stage being construed as a commitment to the whole EMU process, and equally opposed to the convening of an IGC on EMU. However, under strong pressure from her Chancellor of the Exchequer, Nigel Lawson, and her Foreign Secretary, Geoffrey Howe – who secretly threatened to resign in tandem over the question – the prime minister announced her acceptance of stage one, and with it the perspective of sterling's entry into ERM, on condition that the second and third stages be left open and no IGC was called. The Delors Report, the European Council simply concluded, was 'a good basis for further work'. This compromise, unsatisfactory to most member states, lasted throughout the autumn, but at the Strasbourg meeting of the European Council in December 1989, it was agreed, on a proposal from President Mitterrand and against Britain's lone objection, to convene an IGC on EMU the following year. Thatcher, weakened in the interim by Lawson's resignation as Chancellor in October 1989 and suffering internal party turbulence after she replaced Howe as Foreign Secretary, found her negotiating strength draining away, leaving her in a minority of one.

The Delors Report differed in several important respects from the EMU arrangements finally adopted by the IGC that followed. Although the three-stage plan was maintained, a specific timeline was established for its completion, on the basis that full EMU would occur by default in 1999 for as many countries as met certain formal, strict **convergence criteria**. In effect, much greater priority was attached to macro-economic convergence as a precondition for entry than to the ongoing fiscal policy coordination in stage three which the report had envisaged. The Council of Ministers was not given the power to control national budgets; rather there would be a continuing obligation to keep budget deficits within limits, under the threat of fines. At its foundation, two member states (the United Kingdom and Denmark) were given the right to **opt out** of the system in perpetuity. The proposed ESCB was to be named the **European Monetary Institute** (EMI) in stage two and the **European Central Bank** (ECB) in stage three (although technically the ECB was still made part of a structure called the ESCB).

However, despite these differences, the Delors Report proved to be a document of seminal importance. Not only did it provide a credible route-map towards a single currency, it locked the central bank governors into the EMU objective – at a time when there was great caution about the project in many quarters – and in effect neutralized concerns in certain finance ministries, not least in Germany. The willingness of Bundesbank President Pöhl to work constructively with Delors on this blueprint changed the terms of the debate, outmanoeuvring critics generally and British opponents in particular. Thatcher is said to have been very disappointed by the performance of the Governor of the Bank of England, Robin Leigh-Pemberton, who had taken literally the notion that he was working on the committee in a 'personal capacity' and assumed that individual finance ministers and heads of governments would simply block any arrangement with which they were unhappy.

In April 1990, Mitterrand and Kohl suggested that the EMU IGC – due to meet for the first time in December that year, following German elections – should be parallelled by a similar conference to draft treaty amendments on the broader issues of 'European Political Union' (EPU). The impending prospect of **German reunification** had increased the political incentive for both the governments in Paris and Bonn to widen the European integration agenda in this way. At the 'Dublin II' European Council in June 1990, an EPU IGC was duly convened, also to begin work in December. The twin EMU and EPU IGCs led to agreement in December 1991 on the Maastricht Treaty. Thus in addition to its obvious importance as a catalyst for EMU, the Delors Report prompted a wider reform of Community institutions and policies of very great political significance.

Further reading: Kenneth Dyson and Kevin Featherstone, *The Road to Maastricht: Negotiating Economic and Monetary Union*, 1999.

Democratic deficit

The phrase 'democratic deficit', which is now used in a wide variety of political contexts, first developed in the late 1970s as a way of characterizing a significant shortcoming in the institutional structure of the then European Community, now Union. It refers specifically to a situation where powers transferred under the **Treaties** from national to European level might be subject to a lower degree of formal democratic control than before. Such a situation could arise in particular where decisions in the **Council of Ministers** are taken by **qualified majority voting** (QMV), thus depriving each **national parliament** of the formal power to force its government to veto any proposal, without there being a compensating increase in parliamentary power at European level. The effect is to increase executive power, at the expense of parliamentary control – even if any individual national executive henceforth has to share that enhanced power on a collective basis with other governments.

From 1966 onwards, this situation applied to legislation adopted in the Council in respect of, for example, the Community's agricultural, fisheries and external trade and competition policies. Here QMV coexisted – as indeed it still does for competition policy – with only the minimal **consultation procedure** with the **European Parliament**, whereby the latter could only give an opinion on draft legislation, rather than amend or block it. However, for many years, this proved to be more of a problem in theory than in practice, as de facto **unanimity** continued in the Council under the so-called **Luxembourg Compromise**, whereby member states collectively would decline to adopt laws that any one of their number considered might threaten its interests.

The 1986 **Single European Act** (SEA) changed the pattern of Community decision-making significantly: not only did it widen the range of policy areas subject to QMV in the Council, but in parallel, the political acceptability of use of the Luxembourg Compromise quickly collapsed. There was a lively debate about the need to give the **European Parliament** a real role in law-making for the first time, to offset the growing democratic deficit which greater use of majority voting in the Council would imply. The new **cooperation procedure** between the Council and Parliament, conceded in the SEA, was a first, rather modest, move in this direction. Relatively soon thereafter, the 1992 **Maastricht Treaty** attempted to address the problem more directly, by granting the Parliament a right of **co-decision** in the increasingly wide range of legislative matters decided by QMV in the Council – a process taken further in the 1997 **Amsterdam Treaty** and 2001 **Nice Treaty**.

Ironically, co-decision was not extended by any of these treaty changes to cover the agricultural, fisheries, external trade or competition policies, where what had once been a theoretical problem now became a real one. By the early 2000s, decision-making in these four areas accounted for about a fifth of new legislation in the EU (with the other four-fifths either being subject to unanimity in the Council or involving the Parliament in some meaningful way). In an attempt to address this issue, the **Convention on the Future of Europe** (2002–3) established the principle that wherever QMV was used in the Council, the Parliament should enjoy the power of co-decision. The aborted **European Constitution** attempted to apply this principle, which was carried through into the **Lisbon Treaty**. Hence the reference in both documents to co-decision and QMV as constituting the 'ordinary legislative procedure' of the Union. Since Lisbon, legislation on **competition policy** is now the only significant remaining field in which the Council decides by QMV but the Parliament is only consulted (Articles 103(1) and 109 TFEU).

The phrase 'democratic deficit' proved such an effective political weapon in the hands of advocates of greater parliamentary power that it increasingly came to be used to denote any situation where EU decisions might be taken without the direct involvement of parliamentarians. In some instances, the Parliament had a strong case, as in **comitology**, where the Commission and member states between them effectively controlled the adoption of 'implementing measures' (administrative law), even where the Parliament itself had co-decided the originating legislation. A less convincing claim was that the Council needed to be much more accountable to the European Parliament where it was engaged in essentially **intergovernmental** decision-making in areas of executive responsibility, as in large parts of **Common Foreign and Security Policy** (CFSP).

More recently, however, the notion of a democratic deficit has also been used to mount a wider, more general, critique of certain 'systemic' features of the Union that limit its effectiveness in offering democratic accountability, including aspects of the Parliament itself. Low turnouts in **European elections** are said to point to a major 'disconnect' between the public and the EU institutions, with the latter constituting, in Vernon Bogdanor's phrase, an 'alienated superstucture'. Some argue that the absence of meaningful transnational political parties denies the public Europe-wide ideological choices on a left–right, or indeed any other, basis. Simon Hix has claimed that, unlike at national level, 'there is no electoral contest for political leadership at European level or over the direction of the EU policy agenda' (*What's Wrong with the European Union and How to Fix It*, 2008). He has proposed that, to overcome this, the Commission President should be elected by national parliamentarians in a Europe-wide contest every five years, and that a majoritarian, winner-take-all principle be introduced for the allocation of spoils in the Parliament. The effect of both changes would be to move the Union in the direction of a structured competition between two coalitions, or even parties, along the lines of the politics in the United States.

Others continue to defend what some political scientists style the essentially 'consociational' character of EU institutions, with its deliberate blurring of differences and preference for consensus. This reflects a fear that only systematic compromise, enabling a very broad span of ideologies and national interests to be reflected in policy outcomes, can ensure that the EU enjoys the necessary degree of legitimacy. For any minority to be repeatedly defeated could risk alienating the publics (and potentially the governments) of particular member states to the point of crisis. There is thus a paradox at the heart of the new, wider debate about the democratic deficit in Europe: the best long-term means of increasing popular participation and interest in EU decision-making would appear to involve institutional changes that, in the short term at least, could weaken the already fragile legitimacy of the system.

Derogation

A derogation is a temporary waiver granted in **EU law** to a member state from an obligation applying generally to all member states. Most frequently, derogations are extended by one of the **legal acts**, notably **regulations** or **directives**, adopted under the **Treaties**. Usually the derogation will expire automatically after a number of years; in other instances, a derogation may be renewed, with it sometimes becoming permanent in all but name.

The granting of a derogation is sometimes foreseen in the wording of a treaty itself. For example, the 1986 **Single European Act** (SEA) introduced the possibility of derogations in respect of the achievement of the **single market**, although these 'must be of a temporary nature and must cause the least possible disturbance' to the functioning of the market (Article 27 TFEU). A specific type of treaty-sanctioned derogation applies when a **transitional period** is granted to a new member state in its **accession treaty**. The entrant may be given a period of grace during which it is allowed progressively to introduce and apply certain EU rules that otherwise might have damaging effects.

The most significant treaty-based derogation for *non-entrants* relates to the adoption of the single currency. Article 139 TFEU obliges the **Council of Ministers** to grant a derogation to any member state that does not meet the **convergence criteria** for entry into the third stage of **Economic and Monetary Union** (EMU). A treaty-based derogation differs from an '**opt-out**' in that a member state may enjoy an opt-out in perpetuity, as part of the deal struck at the time the treaty is negotiated. Thus the United Kingdom and Denmark enjoy exemptions as of right from stage three of EMU, whereas Sweden is in receipt, at least theoretically, only of a derogation. However, in political terms, after Sweden rejected **euro** entry in a referendum in September 2003, its derogation appears to have become a de facto opt-out, even if not a de jure one.

Development policy

In the complex negotiations that led to the signing of the **Treaty of Rome** in March 1957, one question proved especially difficult to resolve: how to reconcile the creation of a **customs union** in Europe with the traditional trading links, usually based on patterns of preferential access, which existed between several of **the Six** founding member states and their remaining overseas territories and colonies. The French government made the maintenance of such arrangements a precondition for signing any treaty, whereas Germany, which had lost all its colonies after the First World War, wished the new Community to be guided by as liberal an external trade régime as possible. The final flashpoint came over arrangements for the importation of bananas. The Bonn government withdrew from the negotiations for several days until it was accepted that it could continue to import bananas freely from Latin America, whilst France would maintain its discriminatory access in favour of its territories and colonies in Africa. A special **protocol** was annexed to the Treaty of Rome to give effect to this compromise.

The Treaty of Rome offered the 'non-European countries and territories' of the Community 'special arrangements for association', including (one-way) tariff-free access to the new customs union, so extending to them in effect some of the economic benefits of membership. It was also envisaged that financial aid for investment in the colonies would be provided in some form. The original list of the Community's **overseas countries and territories** (OCTs), contained in Annex IV to the treaty, included 18 French, Belgian, Dutch and Italian colonies. However, very soon after the treaty came into effect, the process of decolonization accelerated rapidly: most of France's African colonies were made autonomous within the 'French Community' in 1958 and achieved full independence two years later; the Belgian Congo became independent in 1960, whilst Burundi and Rwanda followed suit in 1962. The treaty's provisions on OCTs thus became largely redundant before they could even be implemented.

Notwithstanding this, the Community's fledgling development policy proceeded largely as originally planned, with essentially non-reciprocal trade preferences being extended to the former colonies, backed by the provision of financial aid through an intergovernmental **European Development Fund** (EDF). The latter is financed by direct contributions from the member states and still operates outside the EU **Budget**. (Article 132(3) EC, now Article 199(3) TFEU, obliges member states to 'contribute to the investments required for the progressive development' of the OCTs, but not of third countries.) The twin tracks of trade preferences and development aid were formalized in the Yaoundé and Arusha Conventions, signed with the 18 newly independent former colonies in 1963 and 1969. British accession to the Community in 1973 resulted in similar arrangements being put in place for

28 former British possessions, The new total of 46 recipient countries formed the 'African, Caribbean and Pacific Group of States' – known as the **ACP states** – in 1975.

With the Lomé Conventions (1975–2000) and Cotonou Agreements (since 2000), the number of ACP states has since risen to 79, whilst EDF funding has grown to € 22.7 billion over the period 2008–13 (the duration of the tenth EDF), backed by access to loans of € 3.6 billion from the **European Investment Bank** (EIB). In addition, the **European Commission** has evolved a substantial central 'development cooperation' policy, focused primarily on poverty reduction, food aid and adaptation to climate change. The primary vehicle for delivery of aid to third-world countries is the Development Cooperation Instrument (DCI), established in 2007, which spent € 2.2 billion in 2011. In parallel, the Commission spent € 0.8 billion on humanitarian aid in 2011. Substantial additional sums were provided to countries in the immediate vicinity of the Union under the **European Neighbourhood Policy** (ENP) and the pre-**accession** strategy (€ 1.4 billion each). Total spending by the EU institutions on development aid in 2011 was € 10.0 billion, of which the EDF represented € 3.5 billion.

Taken together, the European Union and its member states are by far the biggest donors of official development assistance worldwide, their contribution representing just over half of the total provided by participants in the Development Assistance Committee (DAC) of the **Organization for Economic Cooperation and Development** (OECD). However, only around a fifth of total European aid comes from the EU Budget or the EDF; the remainder is provided directly by the member states, either bilaterally or through international agencies (€ 41.8 billion in 2010). The proportion of the member states' total aid spent through Union structures varies widely – from only 7 per cent in Denmark to over 85 per cent in Greece. Both the Union and the individual member states make contributions to the various specialized **United Nations** aid agencies – notably the High Commission for Refugees (UNHCR) and the World Food Programme (WFP) – and the member states also make independent contributions to other multilateral aid agencies, most notably the World Bank and the International Development Agency (IDA). Together, the EU and its member states are the largest aid donors in sub-Saharan Africa, South America and southern Asia. Aid currently represents about 0.43 per cent of total EU gross national product (GNP) – a figure still a long way short of the United Nations target of 0.7 per cent, but steadily rising.

The Union's development policy has certain characteristics that set it apart from the policies of other major aid donors. First, aid is distributed more evenly across the range of recipient countries. The five largest beneficiaries of EU aid receive only 21 per cent of total aid, by comparison with 32 per cent of US aid and 42 per cent of Japanese aid. This underlines the fact that aid from the EU is disbursed with less regard for strategic or commercial factors. Second, more emphasis is laid on respect for human rights and the development of 'good government' in recipient countries. Third, the Union gives more aid than other donors to agricultural and rural development projects, which represent around half of total expenditure.

The Union is also the most important trading partner for the ACP states. Under the various EU–ACP agreements from Lomé onwards, all ACP industrial products and most ACP agricultural products have enjoyed free access to the Union market, on a non-reciprocal basis. This régime has deliberately been more generous than that offered to most other third-world countries. For many years, such an arrangement benefited from a 'waiver' from the 'most favoured nation' rule within the General Agreement on Tariffs and Trade (GATT). However, with the advent of the World Trade Organization (WTO) in 1995, the Union concluded that this situation would become unsustainable in the face of international criticism. In order to be WTO-consistent, the Cotonou Agreements have provided for full, reciprocal opening of trade, based on the removal of both tariff and non-tariff barriers, between the EU and the 39 (out of 79) ACP states that do not enjoy 'least developed country' (LDC) status. The Commission has been negotiating a series of Economic Partnership Agreements (EPAs) with these ACP states, ideally based on regional groupings, for this purpose.

The **legal base** for development policy was strengthened by the 1992 **Maastricht Treaty**, whilst stating that the Union policy 'shall be complementary to the policies pursued by the Member States', clearly putting the latter in a lead role. The **Lisbon Treaty**, which came into force in December 2009, rebalances the relationship somewhat, by declaring that the 'Union's development cooperation policy and that of the Member States complement and reinforce each other' (Article 208(1) TFEU). Both development policy and humanitarian aid are listed as areas of shared **competence** between the Union and the member states, but specifically where the exercise by the Union of its competence 'shall not result in the Member States being prevented from exercising theirs' (Article 4(4) TFEU). Decision-making on development policy is by **qualified majority voting** (QMV) in the **Council of Ministers** and by **co-decision** between the Council and the **European Parliament** (the ordinary legislative procedure). However, decisions specifically on the EDF are taken by **unanimity** among the member states and do not require the Parliament to be consulted.

Direct effect

Together with **primacy**, direct effect is one of the fundamental principles of **EU law**. Like primacy, it was implicit in the founding **Treaties** but was only made explicit by judgements of the **European Court of Justice** (ECJ). In the Van Gend en Loos case (Case 26/62), the Court ruled that the Treaties are not merely a compact between states entailing rights and obligations for those states and for the institutions established by them, but that they are the foundations of a 'new legal order of international law' entailing rights and obligations for individual citizens too. The Van Gend en Loos ruling stated that the 'subjects' of this order 'comprise not only Member States but also their nationals'. It went on:

> *Independently of the legislation of Member States, Community law ... not only imposes obligations on individuals but is also intended to confer upon them rights which become part of their legal heritage. These rights arise not only where they are expressly granted by the Treaty but also by reason of obligations which the Treaty imposes in a clearly defined way upon individuals as well as upon the Member States and upon the institutions of the Community.*

In other words, although the Treaties are international agreements concluded between sovereign states, they are, in the words of A. G. Toth, 'capable of generating legal effects in the member states without the need for any implementing measures, in the sense of conferring rights and in some cases obligations upon individuals which are enforceable in the national courts' (*The Oxford Encyclopaedia of European Community Law*, Volume I, 1990). These may involve legal relationships both between the member state and individuals ('vertical' direct effect) and between individuals themselves ('horizontal' direct effect).

The combination of primacy and direct effect has proved critical in the evolution of the EU as a qualitatively different type of legal order to that found, now or in the past, in the relationship between other democratic states internationally. That countries are bound by any treaties which they conclude with one another has long been a fundamental principle of international law, accepted even in the United States. What makes the European integration process so different and unique is that it has superimposed a new, supranational legal order onto a series of existing, separate, national orders. It has done this by establishing treaty-based rules that are interpreted and enforced by a single Court of Justice, whose judgements are binding on national governments and courts.

As Stephen Weatherill and Paul Beaumont have written, the 'cumulative effect of the two key principles of supremacy and of direct effect lends Community law immense practical vitality in domestic litigation. Direct effect ensures that an individual litigant is able to raise a relevant point of Community law before a national court; supremacy then ensures that the Community law will prevail over the national rule in the event of conflict' (*EU Law*, 1999).

Directive

A directive is one of three types of binding **legal act** which the institutions of the European Union may adopt, within the scope provided by the **Treaties**. The two others are **decisions** and **regulations.**

Under Article 288 TFEU, a directive is 'binding, as to the result to be achieved, upon each Member State to which it is addressed', but leaves 'to the national authorities the choice of form and methods'. A directive differs from a regulation in that it need not apply to all member states, is not binding in its entirety (but only in respect of the result to be achieved), and is not directly applicable, in that it does not automatically become part of a national legal system without implementing legislation. Normally, a directive will set a deadline for the necessary measures to be taken at the national level. It thus creates a framework of legal obligations on member states, to be met by methods those countries choose within a defined timescale. (It was for this reason that the aborted **European Constitution** proposed to change the word 'directive' to 'framework law'.)

Proposed by the **European Commission**, directives may be adopted either by the **Council of Ministers**, under the **consultation procedure**, or more frequently by the **European Parliament** and the Council acting jointly, under the **co-decision procedure**. (Under the **Lisbon Treaty**, co-decision forms part of the 'ordinary legislative procedure' of the Union.) In addition, the Council and Parliament may empower the Commission to adopt further directives to implement the detailed provisions of an original directive or regulation, through the **comitology** process (administrative law). (In certain aspects of **competition policy**, the Commission is permitted by Article 106(3) TFEU to adopt directives on its own.)

Directives tend to be the preferred vehicle for general legislation at EU level, in areas where a **harmonization** or **approximation** of national law, rather than strict uniformity, is sought by the political institutions. The Treaties list a number of policy fields where directives are deemed to be the appropriate legal act, notably **free movement** of goods, services, capital, and the health and safety of workers. In many other areas, the institutions are free in effect to choose between using directives and other instruments, as appropriate. The choice may depend on the complexity of legislative change envisaged, the flexibility of legal form permitted, and the specificity of outcome required. (Under comitology, Commission directives are most common in the environment, food safety and transport sectors.)

Even though directives are not directly applicable, this does not necessarily mean that they lack **direct effect**, under the principles established by the **European Court of Justice** (ECJ). Several cases have been brought before the Court to establish whether or not directives, once adopted but not correctly implemented in national law, confer rights on individual citizens. Rulings in the

Francovich and **Van Duyn cases** established that if the wording of a directive is sufficiently precise and unambiguous and the time limit for its implementation in national law has expired, it may be said to confer rights on individuals in their dealings with the state and to take precedence over national law.

Discharge procedure

Under Article 318 TFEU, the **European Commission** is required to submit annually to the **European Parliament** and the **Council of Ministers** 'the accounts of the preceding financial year relating to the implementation of the budget' and 'a financial statement of the assets and liabilities of the Union'. The decision to approve these accounts and release the Commission from its responsibility for management of the budget in question – a process known as giving or granting the 'discharge' – rests with the Parliament under Article 319 TFEU, acting with the aid of a recommendation from the Council and the annual report of the **Court of Auditors**. Until the 1970 Budgetary Treaty, the responsibility for granting the discharge lay with the Council; between then and the 1975 Budgetary Treaty, it rested jointly with the Council and Parliament.

The discharge procedure is an important element both in budgetary discipline and in the exercise of the Parliament's powers with respect to the annual **Budget.** It enables the Parliament to elicit explanations from the Commission about how monies have been spent and to insist on improvements in financial management for the future. The granting of the discharge has not infrequently been delayed, whilst additional assurances have been extracted from the Commission. The prospect of refusal is taken very seriously by the Commission. The then Budget Commissioner, Christopher Tugendhat, declared in 1977 that 'refusal to grant the discharge is a political sanction which would be extremely serious. The Commission thus censured would, I think, have to be replaced.' However, when the first instance of refusal actually occurred, in November 1984 (in relation to the 1982 accounts), it was only a few weeks before the mandate of the incumbent Commission, presided by Gaston Thorn, was due to expire anyway, so the issue of resignation did not arise. On the second occasion, in December 1998 (in relation to the 1996 accounts), a complex series of events ensued which led to the tabling of a censure motion within the Parliament in January 1999 and the **resignation of the Santer Commission** two months later. There was a lively debate at the time about the political consequences of a refusal of the discharge, with the Commission forced to argue that the discharge procedure and the censure motion were quite distinct mechanisms of accountability. Ironically, this argument helped embolden critics of the Commission to push for it to be censured or to resign.

In addition to granting discharge to the Commission's accounts, the

Parliament has decided to extend the same procedure for each of the other EU **institutions** and bodies, including all the Union's **agencies**. The fact that the Parliament grants discharge both to itself and to the Council – with an implicit asymmetry in relations – has generated tension between the two branches of the budgetary authority on this point. The Council has agreed to provide documents to the Parliament for the purposes of discharge, but it refuses to send a minister or its Secretary General for oral questioning.

Discrimination on grounds of nationality

Discrimination on grounds of nationality between citizens of the EU member states is prohibited under Article 18 TFEU in all policy areas covered by the **Treaties**. In addition, Article 45 TFEU specifically prohibits such discrimination in respect of employment, pay and working conditions, although it allows 'limitations justified on grounds of public policy, public security or public health' and exempts 'employment in the public service' from the non-discrimination principle. These treaty provisions are of great importance in relation to **free movement of persons** between the member states and **freedom of establishment** within them.

The meaning of the exemption for 'public service' employment was initially complicated by the fact that each member state has a different notion of what the public service encompasses. In response to a case involving the Belgian national railways, the **European Court of Justice** (ECJ) laid down its own definition: employment 'connected with the specific activities of the public service in so far as it is entrusted with the exercise of powers conferred by public law and with responsibility for safeguarding the general interests of the State, to which the specific interests of local authorities . . . must be assimilated' (*Commission* v *Belgium*, Case 149/79). This definition clearly includes national and local civil servants, the armed forces and the police as part of the public service, but appears to exclude many public-sector employees, especially those working in public enterprises. The ECJ has held that teachers, lecturers and (non-military) researchers do not fall within the scope of public service so defined and must not therefore be discriminated against. In *Commission* v *Luxembourg* (Case C-473/93), the Court ruled that Luxembourg's attempt to reserve all public-sector posts in health, education, transport, telecommunications and energy for its own nationals was illegal.

Independent of whether they are in the public service, the suppliers of services must not discriminate between European Union citizens. The fact that educational establishments cannot charge differential tuition fees to students from different member states is a reflection of this principle. Rules in Italy requiring officially-recognized tour guides to be Italian nationals had to be abandoned. In the case of a British citizen mugged on the Paris metro, who was denied the compensation for victims of criminal violence to which he would have been entitled had he been French, the ECJ ruled that, as a tourist, the individual was a recipient of services, and thus covered by the Treaties and entitled to the same protection and compensation as a French citizen (*Cowan* v *Le Trésor Public*, Case 186/87).

Dooge Committee

Otherwise known as the Ad Hoc Committee for Institutional Affairs, the Dooge Committee – chaired by James Dooge, an Irish Senator – was set up at the **European Council** meeting in Fontainebleau in June 1984. The creation of the committee followed a series of political initiatives which all pointed towards institutional and/or policy deepening within the Community: the **Genscher–Colombo Plan** of November 1981, the European Council's own **Stuttgart Declaration** of June 1983, and, most ambitiously, the **Draft Treaty establishing the European Union** (DTEU), tabled by the **European Parliament** in February 1984. The task assigned to the Dooge Committee was 'to make suggestions for the improvement of the operation of European cooperation in both the Community field and that of political, or any other, cooperation'. The committee was deliberately modelled on the **Spaak Committee** (of 1955–6), in the sense that its members were personal representatives of the heads of government and of the President of the **European Commission**. It presented an interim report in November 1984 and a final report in March 1985.

The committee called for a 'qualitative leap . . . demonstrating the common political will of the member states' and the eventual formulation of 'a genuine political entity' in the form of a **European Union**. Foreshadowing the 1992 **Maastricht Treaty**, this Union would act 'according to procedures which could vary depending whether the framework is that of intergovernmental cooperation, the Community **Treaties**, or new instruments yet to be agreed'. Among 'priority objectives', the committee endorsed the idea of the completion of the **single market** 'on the basis of a precise timetable' – an idea already being worked upon by the European Commission and enumerated three months later in the **Cockfield White Paper** – together with a strengthening of the **European Monetary System** (EMS). Under 'promotion of the common values of civilization', the committee supported measures to protect the environment, the introduction of a 'European social area, as the logical follow-on from an economically integrated, dynamic and competitive Community', and the projection of common cultural values.

The section on 'the search for an external identity' was more cautious. The recommendations amounted to a few practical measures for enhancing **European Political Cooperation** (EPC), including the creation of an EPC secretariat, the gradual incorporation of security issues into EPC, and greater efforts 'to draw up and adopt common standards for weapons systems and equipment'.

The final section on changes to the institutions and procedures was the most radical. A majority of the committee supported more frequent use of **qualified majority voting** (QMV) in the **Council of Ministers**, with the requirement for unanimity being applied only 'in certain exceptional cases'. In areas subject to QMV, the Council **presidency** would be obliged to put a matter to the vote within 30 days at the request of three member states of the Commission. The British, Danish and Greek representatives also accepted that more use would have to be made of majority voting, but wanted to grant the presidency greater discretion and to retain the practice laid down in the **Luxembourg Compromise** of allowing discussion to continue until unanimity was reached, whenever a member state considered that 'very important interests' were at stake.

The Dooge Committee proposed to reduce the number of Commissioners to one for each member state. The Commission President would be appointed by the **European Council**, and he or she would then propose to the governments the names of the other Commissioners. At the beginning of its term of office, the Commission 'should receive a vote of investiture on the basis of its programme' from the European Parliament. It also recommended that the Parliament should enjoy a right of **co-decision** with the Council, although in a way different from that eventually adopted in the Maastricht Treaty. The Parliament should also have the right to give its approval to all accession and **association agreements** (see **consent procedure**) and should have 'responsibility in decisions on revenue' as part of the annual **budgetary process.**

Finally, the committee recommended the calling of an **Intergovernmental Conference** (IGC) 'to negotiate a draft European Union Treaty'. When the report was considered at the Milan meeting of the European Council in June 1985, the proposal to convene an IGC was carried by majority vote, with the British, Danish and Greek representatives voting against. This IGC negotiated the **Single European Act** (SEA), which was signed in February 1986 and entered into force in July 1987.

The vote in the European Council was the final proof of what had become evident in the Dooge Committee's discussions and in their final report: a fundamental division between a minority who favoured only a minimalist approach to institutional reform and a majority prepared to go considerably further. Almost every page of the report contained footnotes and reservations, and the Danish and Greek representatives entered general reservations at the end. As an exercise in moving the Community forward, the Dooge Committee was only partially successful and cannot compare with the Spaak Committee. Nevertheless, many of its proposals were taken up either in the

Single Act or, at a later stage, in the Maastricht Treaty and subsequent treaty reforms.

Draft Treaty establishing the European Union (DTEU)

The DTEU, adopted by the **European Parliament** in February 1984, was an ambitious attempt to offer a comprehensive new institutional settlement for the then European Community. Largely the work of Italian federalist campaigner **Altiero Spinelli**, the draft treaty was the Parliament's principal contribution to a debate on reforming the founding **Treaties** which eventually led to the **Single European Act** (SEA) in 1986.

Spinelli believed that the 1979–84 European Parliament, the first to be directly elected, had a historic right and moral duty to act as a 'constituent assembly', in the sense of designing a constitutional order for a new political system. Working initially with friends and associates in the 'Crocodile Club' – established in July 1980 and named after the Strasbourg restaurant in which they first gathered – Spinelli was instrumental in setting up the Parliament's institutional affairs committee in January 1982. As the committee's principal **rapporteur**, he secured agreement on the drafting of a new treaty, the text of which was approved in outline in September 1983. This document was then submitted to constitutional experts and presented to the Parliament for final adoption – by 237 votes to 31, with 43 abstentions – the following February.

Article 1 of the draft treaty proclaimed the establishment of a **European Union**. The institutions of the new Union followed the established framework of the then Community, but with some very important innovations. The **European Commission** would have a five-year term – rather than a four-year one at that time – taking office six months after the **European elections**. The President of the Commission would, after designation by the **European Council**, put together a college of Commissioners. The new Commission would only take office after investiture by the Parliament. The **Council of Ministers** would be made up of 'representations' of the member states 'led by a minister who is permanently and specifically responsible for Union affairs'. The Council's proceedings would be held in public when acting as a 'legislative or budgetary authority'. The Council and Parliament together would 'jointly exercise legislative authority' in the Union, with either institution able to veto draft legislation. The **primacy** of Union law would be explicitly recognized.

A distinction would be drawn between 'common action' and 'cooperation', the first being supranational and the latter intergovernmental in character. Provision was made for activities to be transferred from the sphere of cooperation to common action, but not vice versa. The principle of **subsidiarity** was also to be recognized, whereby the Union 'shall only act to carry out those tasks which may be undertaken more effectively in common than by the member states acting separately'. Citizens of the member states would acquire a parallel **European citizenship**, whilst the Union should guarantee 'fundamental rights and freedoms' and penalize member states that might engage in their 'serious and persistent violation'.

The most controversial of the draft treaty's 87 articles came towards the end. Article 82 allowed for the text to enter into force once it had been ratified 'by a majority of the member states of the Communities whose population represents two-thirds of the total population'. By this provision, Spinelli sought to circumvent the established procedure for treaty revision set down in the **Treaty of Rome**, requiring the unanimous agreement of, and **ratification** in, all member states. (Spinelli maintained that the DTEU was an entirely new treaty, not an amendment to an existing one.) The implications of Article 82 were radical: either some member states could find themselves forced to join the new Union against their will or they might be effectively excluded from that Union, resulting in a dramatic move to a '**two-speed Europe**'. Either way, the idea was seen as a frontal assault on the notion of the 'constituent power of the member states', on an equal basis, as 'masters of the Treaties', as the German Federal Constitutional Court was subsequently to describe it.

The adoption of the DTEU proposal was a unilateral action by the European Parliament, in which the member-state governments played no part. As such, it was more an exercise in aspirational, rather than practical, politics. In the event, only the Belgian and Italian parliaments adopted resolutions calling for the DTEU to be ratified. More cautious expressions of support were received from some other parliaments. The draft treaty did, however, move the debate forwards, not least at a public level, building on the momentum established by the **Genscher–Colombo Plan** of November 1981 and the **Stuttgart Declaration** of June 1983. In a critical development, the French President, **François Mitterrand**, speaking to the European Parliament in May 1984, stated France's 'willingness to examine and defend your project, the inspiration behind which it approves', indicating his preparedness to support moves to convene an **Intergovernmental Conference** (IGC) to amend the Treaties. Ironically, such a conference was precisely what Spinelli and his colleagues had hoped to avoid, since the treaty amendments that an IGC would bring forward were subject to ratification (and, therefore, the possibility of a veto) in each member state. In the same speech, Mitterrand indicated a shift of France's position on the **Luxembourg Compromise**, which was frustrating use of **qualified majority voting** (QMV) in the Council: there should be a 'return to the Treaties' in the way governments approached law-making.

At the Fontainebleau meeting of the European Council, a month later, the heads of government decided to set up what became known as the **Dooge Committee**, to prepare detailed proposals on institutional reform. Reporting in March 1985, this committee endorsed the idea of drafting a new treaty, suggesting that it be guided 'by the spirit and method of the draft treaty voted by the European Parliament'. Three months later, by simple majority vote, the heads of government convened the IGC which proceeded to negotiate the 1986 **Single European Act** (SEA), introducing the first significant institutional amendments since the Communities were founded in the 1950s. Many of the reforms proposed in the DTEU – although not the proposal in Article 82 – were subsequently included in the successive treaty changes negotiated over the following quarter of a century, most notably in the 1992 **Maastricht Treaty** and the **Lisbon Treaty**, which entered into force in December 2009.

Further reading: Richard Corbett, *The European Parliament's Role in Closer EU Integration*, 1998.

Dunkirk Treaty

Signed on 4 March 1947, the Treaty of Dunkirk between the United Kingdom and France was the first post-war European security pact. Composed of only six articles, of which the second required the signatory states to provide each other with 'military and other support and assistance' in the event of an attack, the treaty was concluded for an initial period of 50 years, after which it was to remain in force unless either party gave a year's notice of withdrawal.

The Dunkirk Treaty was a 'regional arrangement' of the type encouraged by Article 52 of the **United Nations** Charter. As the preamble makes clear, it was directed against the possibility of 'a renewal of German aggression' and was prompted by the French government's sense of the country's vulnerability (the only other security pact France had at the time was with the Soviet Union). The treaty was widened to include the **Benelux** states by the signature of the more ambitious **Brussels Treaty** in March 1948. The following April, the **North Atlantic Treaty Organization** (NATO) in effect superseded the Brussels Treaty, although the latter remained formally in place and was updated to create the **Western European Union** (WEU) in October 1954.

E

Ecofin Council

The Council of Economics and Finance Ministers, widely known as Ecofin, is one of the principal configurations of the EU **Council of Ministers**. The finance ministers of the member-state governments meet on average once a month, usually on a Monday or Tuesday, to discuss the macro-economic situation in the member states, coordinate the economic policies of the member states (which they are obliged to regard 'as a matter of common concern' under Article 121(1) TFEU), determine the Union's position in international financial institutions (such as the International Monetary Fund), and adopt legislation in respect of **tax harmonization**, capital liberalization, the regulation of financial markets and the financing of the Union (**own resources**). The Ecofin Council also oversees the operation of **Economic and Monetary Union** (EMU), including respect for the **excessive deficit procedure** (EDP) and the **Stability and Growth Pact** (SGP), and the adoption of any realignments of non-**eurozone** currencies within the **Exchange-Rate Mechanism** (ERM). It is responsible for the adoption and **discharge** of the EU's annual **Budget** – with junior finance ministers and permanent representatives comprising a 'Budget Council' configuration of Ecofin – even if the adoption of the Multiannual Financial Framework (MFF) is now the preserve of the **General Affairs Council** (GAC). In preparing its decisions, the Ecofin Council is assisted by the **Economic and Financial Committee** (EFC), a high-level group of national officials from finance ministries and central banks, previously known as the **Monetary Committee**. Since January 2002, the finance ministers of the **eurozone** states have met in advance of the Ecofin Council to discuss EMU-related business. These meetings, which were initially informal and known as the 'euro-11', have since been formalized as the **Eurogroup**, whose status is now officially recognized by the **Lisbon Treaty**. The meetings of the Eurogroup finance ministers are prepared in turn by a Eurozone Working Group (EWG) of the EFC.

Economic Commission for Europe (ECE)

One of five regional commissions of the **United Nations**, the ECE was established in 1947, with its headquarters in Geneva, to promote cooperation between participating states in the process of post-war reconstruction. The division of Europe by the Iron Curtain largely prevented the ECE from fulfilling this role, which fell in the first instance to the **Organization for European Economic Cooperation** (OEEC), founded the following year to administer the **Marshall Plan** and the forerunner of today's Organisation for Economic Cooperation and Development (OECD). However, the inclusion of all European countries, as well as the United States and Canada, among its members gave the ECE another unique function – as the only major forum in which central and eastern European countries could work together with the West on a range of technical, industrial and economic issues throughout the **Cold War**. Operating in a difficult context, the ECE negotiated agreements, for example, on the network of 'E' roads linking all European countries and the **harmonization** of European road signs and signals, as well as developing less visible standards for transport, agriculture and the environment, and compiling reliable Europe-wide statistics in several sectors. The 1975 **Helsinki Final Act** of the **Conference on Security and Cooperation in Europe** (CSCE) sought to encourage signatory states to use the ECE to implement its provisions in specific areas.

Following the collapse of Communism in 1989–90, the ECE became a repository of practical advice and analysis for the transition to market economies. The organization greatly strengthened its linkages with the private sector, whilst continuing to elaborate norms, standards and conventions designed to facilitate international economic cooperation. The ECE now has 56 member states, including the countries of Central Asia (Kazakhstan, Kyrgyzstan, Tajikistan, Turkmenistan and Uzbekistan). It holds an annual plenary session, but most of the work is done in eight sectoral committees and various working parties and meetings of experts. The ECE's 220-strong secretariat is headed by an executive secretary. The body's working languages remain English, French and Russian. In addition to the European Union, it cooperates with over 70 intergovernmental and non-governmental organizations, some of a very specialized character, such as the European Flexible Bulk Container Association and the International Federation of Pedestrians.

Economic and Financial Committee (EFC)

The Economic and Financial Committee is the key official-level, advisory and preparatory body within the structure of the EU **Council of Ministers** for macro-economic, monetary and financial policy. Comprised of senior officials from the finance ministries and central banks of the member states, the EFC reports to the Council of Economics and Finance Ministers, the **Ecofin Council**. As such, it has a similarly privileged position to the **Political and Security Committee** (PSC) in enjoying direct access to ministerial discussion, in effect bypassing the Committee of Permanent Representatives, **COREPER**, even if it is meant to respect the latter's responsibility for preparing Council meetings.

Established under the 1992 **Maastricht Treaty**, by what is now Article 134 TFEU, the Economic and Financial Committee replaced the **Monetary Committee**, dating from the **Treaty of Rome**, which had broadly the same membership but a more limited remit. Beginning work at the start of stage three of **Economic and Monetary Union** (EMU), in January 1999, the new committee assumed the previous role of the Monetary Committee in preparing discussion on the Union's 'broad economic policy guidelines' (a recommendation to member states introduced in 1993), negotiating realignments within the **Exchange-Rate Mechanism** (ERM) and coordinating EU positions in international financial institutions, as well as providing general advice on any other business before the Ecofin Council. (The committee does not normally negotiate legislative texts, which would be dealt with in a Council working group.) In addition, however, the EFC enjoys a special role in respect of EMU. In the words of its statute, adopted by the Council, it provides 'the framework within which the dialogue between the Council and the **European Central Bank** (ECB) can be prepared and continued' at official level. It is also responsible for preparing Ecofin Council discussions on the application of the **Stability and Growth Pact** (SGP), including the **excessive deficit procedure** (EDP), and meetings of the **Eurogroup** (of **eurozone** finance ministers) held each month before Ecofin meetings.

Like the Monetary Committee before it, the EFC is comprised of 'experts possessing outstanding competence in the economic and financial field': two members (and two alternates) from each of the member states – one from the national administration and one from the central bank in each case – together with two members (and two alternates) from the **European Commission** and (now) the ECB. Echoing arrangements for its predecessor, the EFC elects its own chairman and vice-chairman for a (renewable) two-year term, its proceedings are 'confidential' (that is, secret), and it is serviced by the Commission, rather than the Council secretariat. Unlike the Monetary Committee, the EFC may choose to meet in one of two formations – either with or without the participation of the officials from the national central banks – depending on the business under discussion. The EFC has established a specialist subcommittee on government bond and bills markets, bringing together national officials responsible for issuing public debt.

The EFC has also spawned a Eurozone Working Group (EWG) of senior national officials from the eurozone states, for the purpose of preparing meetings of the Eurogroup. Under arrangements agreed between eurozone heads of government in October 2011, the EWG will henceforth prepare meetings of the new 'Euro Summit' too.

In December 2011, the heads of government of the 17 eurozone member states tasked a subgroup of the EWG – the Ad Hoc Working Group on a Fiscal Stability Union – with drafting a new intergovernmental treaty which, at German insistence, would oblige those states to engage in a more rigorous application of the SGP. This initiative followed the controversial refusal of the British prime minister, David Cameron, to support the more obvious route of amending the existing EU **Treaties** for the same purpose. The UK agreed to participate in the resulting negotiation, as an observer, even though it had no intention of signing the agreement, the **Fiscal Compact Treaty,** which it would subsequently draft.

Economic and Monetary Union (EMU)

The term 'Economic and Monetary Union' denotes the process by which a number of member states of the European Union (currently 17) have pooled their monetary **sovereignty**, by replacing their national currency with a single currency, the **euro**, and transferring responsibility for setting interest rates to a common monetary authority, the **European Central Bank** (ECB), of which their individual national central banks have in effect become subsidiaries.

Although EMU is the most ambitious of the European Union's current policies – and indeed one of the boldest economic experiments of all time – it was not mentioned as an objective in any of the founding **Treaties** in the 1950s. The goal of achieving some form of monetary union was first set at a **summit** meeting of the heads of government of **the Six** in The Hague in December 1969. Two months later, EC finance ministers agreed that the EMU objective should be the adoption of a single currency and commissioned the Luxembourg prime minister, Pierre Werner, to offer a blueprint for how this might be achieved. The **Werner Report**, delivered in June 1970, proposed a multi-stage move to a single currency by 1980, a target date subsequently endorsed by the Paris summit in October 1972. However, the Community's first major initiative towards EMU, a new currency management system known as the 'Snake' (and then the 'Snake in the Tunnel'), quickly hit serious problems – generated successively by acute dollar instability in the wake of the Vietnam War, the 1973–4 oil crisis and the continuing recession of the mid-1970s – and the attempt to forge a monetary union by 1980 had to be abandoned.

After a period of stasis, the idea of closer monetary integration was relaunched by **Roy Jenkins**, President of the **European Commission**, in October 1977. Jenkins enjoyed strong support from the French President, **Valéry Giscard d'Estaing**, and the German Chancellor, Helmut Schmidt, both of whom had been finance ministers at the time of the Werner Report. In January 1979, the remnant of the Snake in the Tunnel was replaced by a more ambitious **European Monetary System** (EMS), which, despite repeated realignments in its early years, gradually emerged as a source of stability and a 'framework for discipline' within the European economy. In March 1983, the decision by **François Mitterrand**, Giscard's successor as French President, to stay within the **Exchange-Rate Mechanism** (ERM) of the EMS, rather than give priority to domestic reflation, not only marked a significant turning-point in the economic policy of his Socialist–Communist administration (towards austerity), but also had the effect of reconfirming what was emerging as a long-term French aim of replacing the franc with a European currency.

As Commission President from January 1985, Mitterrand's former finance minister, **Jacques Delors**, sought consciously to generate support for a revival of EMU as a keynote Community policy. Amendments introduced to the **Treaty of Rome** by the 1986 **Single European Act** (SEA) made reference to EMU for the first time in a treaty text. Although EMU was primarily a political project, Delors took care to justify it firmly in economic terms. He argued that the efficiency and therefore the benefits of the **single market** could be maximized only if consumers, manufacturers, traders and investors were spared the risks and costs involved in currency fluctuation and exchange. Competition would be made keener if prices could be compared more clearly across borders, whilst the Union would be better able to advance its interests in international economic fora with a common currency, and Europe would itself be less vulnerable to large-scale external currency shocks.

In June 1988, the Hanover meeting of the **European Council** (of EC heads of government) commissioned Delors to work with national **central bank governors** on identifying the 'concrete stages' for a possible path to a single currency. The conclusions of the **Delors Report** of April 1989 – which proposed a three-stage move to EMU, underpinned by treaty changes – found favour with the leaders of all member states, apart from the British prime minister, **Margaret Thatcher**. The Madrid European Council in June 1989 decided, with Thatcher's reluctant acquiescence, to begin stage one of EMU, as proposed in the Delors Report, in July 1990, whilst leaving it to an **Intergovernmental Conference** (IGC) to draft the treaty changes necessary to define the subsequent stages in detail and set an end-date to the process. Six months later, in the face of Thatcher's lone opposition, the Strasbourg European Council decided to convene the IGC by the end of 1990.

The EMU IGC, which began work in December 1990, was addressing the most explicit transfer of sovereignty in the history of European integration: the shift from national governments to a new common central bank with the power to set interest rates, issue currency, and enjoy the associated right of 'seigniorage', the latter having been the exclusive prerogative of monarchs for literally thousands of years. From the start, the strongest proponents of EMU – the French government and the European Commission – made it clear that they wanted as many member states of the Union as possible (and ideally all member states) to participate in the single currency. However, in the absence of any willingness to establish a binding European fiscal policy – with national taxing and spending subordinate to a supranational macro-economic policy – it became logically necessary to limit the number of participating countries to those whose public finances were already capable of sustaining full membership in perpetuity in their own right. As a result, the question of which member states might qualify for membership – and how the assessment of their readiness would be made – lay at the heart of the business of the EMU IGC.

Simply stated, the Germans and most northern European countries preferred a 'narrow EMU' of fully compatible member states, with no deadline for the formation of the new currency zone. The French and most southern European countries pointed in the opposite direction, favouring a 'wide EMU' composed of as many economies as possible, with a clear deadline as to when the single currency would be adopted by all those that qualified. In the event, the outcome of the IGC was a compromise between the two schools: full EMU would take effect by a defined deadline and include as many countries, provided they constituted a majority of EU member states, as were able to meet certain fairly strict '**convergence criteria**' (relating to inflation, interest rates, exchange-rate stability and, more importantly, public deficits and debt).

The conclusions of the EMU IGC formed a key component of the 1992 **Maastricht Treaty**. The treaty defined EMU as 'the irrevocable fixing of exchange rates leading to the introduction of a single currency', backed by a single monetary policy, the primary objective of which would be to 'maintain price stability' (Article 3(b) EC, since repealed). There was only a limited strengthening of macro-economic coordination, with the overwhelming emphasis on the monetary dimension. A lengthy series of provisions – Articles 98–124 EC, now Articles 120–44, 219 and 282–4 TFEU – set out the specific institutional arrangements and policy obligations of stages two and three, including the successive creation of a **European Monetary Institute** (EMI) and a European Central Bank, the statutes of which were contained in **protocols** annexed to the treaty.

The United Kingdom and Denmark negotiated **opt-outs** from aspects of stage two and the whole of stage three, and were thus exempted from these provisions. The United Kingdom would 'not be obliged or committed to move to the third stage . . . without a separate decision to do so by its government and parliament'. Denmark was granted a similar opt-out at Maastricht, and a year later, at the Edinburgh European Council in December 1992, the country's definitive decision not to participate in the third stage was recognized.

The first stage of EMU began on 1 July 1990, as foreseen at Madrid, with the removal of exchange controls in eight of the (then) 12 member states (with the others to follow), the inclusion in principle of all currencies in the narrow band of the ERM (the United Kingdom joined in October 1990), and measures to encourage greater economic convergence among the member states. Once the **ratification** of the Maastricht Treaty was completed in November 1993, a clear legal framework was in place to govern the moves to stages two and three. However, in the interim, severe turbulence had developed on the currency markets, complicating the process. In September 1992, the UK and Italy were forced to suspend their membership of the ERM on '**Black Wednesday**', and, in August 1993, the permitted margin of fluctuation for currencies remaining within the ERM was widened to 15 per cent.

Despite these difficulties, the second stage of EMU began on 1 January 1994, with the newly created EMI, based in Frankfurt, gradually assuming a coordinating role among the national central banks, which were in turn to be made independent of their national governments during this period. Before the end of 1996, the **Council of Ministers** (meeting at the level of heads of government) was scheduled to decide, by **qualified majority voting** (QMV), whether a majority of countries satisfied the convergence criteria for membership, so that the transition to the third stage could be made by the qualifying states. The Council was also obliged to decide whether it was appropriate to begin the third stage, and, if so, when. Article 109(j)4 EC stated: 'If by the end of 1997 the date for the beginning of the third stage has not been set, the third stage shall start on 1 January 1999.' In the event, at its meeting in Madrid in December 1995, the European Council opted for January 1999 as the definitive starting-date for all participating countries. On 2 May 1998, the heads of government decided, on the basis of reports from the Commission and the EMI, that all member states except Denmark and the United Kingdom (which had opt-outs), Sweden (which did not wish to proceed and had engineered a technical failure to meet the convergence criteria) and Greece (which failed to qualify) would take part in stage three of EMU. They also appointed the President and other board members of the new ECB.

The single currency was originally specified as the **European Currency Unit** (ECU), but the European Council decided in Madrid in December 1995 to call it the **euro**. At the beginning of stage three, the 11 participating states adopted the 'irrevocably fixed' rates at which the euro was to be substituted for national currencies and took 'the other measures for the rapid introduction of [the euro] as the single currency' (Article 123 EC). The ECB became the sole issuing authority for euro banknotes and its approval was required for the issuing of euro coins by member states, the denominations and specifications of which are laid down by the Council of Ministers. Euro notes and coins entered into circulation on 1 January 2002. The area encompassing the member states using the single currency quickly became known as the **eurozone** or euro area.

At least every two years, or at the request of the member state concerned, the qualifications for entry of each country which has yet to qualify for stage three (but has no opt-out) are re-examined by the Council, on advice from the Commission and the ECB, and after consulting the European Parliament. On this basis, Greece was able to join in January 2001, adopting euro notes and coins two years later, even though it was subsequently revealed that Athens had falsified its national statistics to secure entry. Sweden voted against joining stage three in a referendum in September 2003 (by 55.9 to 42.0 per cent), establishing a de facto, even if not a de jure, opt-out for the country. Any new member state acceding to the Union is obliged to enter the single currency once it meets the convergence criteria. Of the ten countries that acceded to the EU in 2004, five have since been able to adopt the euro: Slovenia in January 2007, Cyprus and Malta in January 2008, Slovakia in January 2009 and Estonia in January 2011. (It has now become standard for stage-three entry and the adoption of euro notes and coins to occur simultaneously.) In May 2006, the Commission refused to support Lithuania's application to join the eurozone as the country's inflation rate was still marginally above the level required by the convergence criteria.

Once a member state enters the eurozone, it is still obliged to maintain its public finances at least within the parameters of those convergence criteria, by avoiding an 'excessive' deficit (Article 126(1) TFEU). A country's budget deficit should normally be no higher than three per cent of gross domestic product (GDP) in any year, and total government debt no greater than 60 per cent of its GDP (or diminishing towards it at a satisfactory rate). Under the **excessive deficit procedure** (EDP), if a state fails to meet these obligations, it can be penalized by the Council through a variety of sanctions, including the imposition of non-interest-bearing deposits or fines 'of an appropriate size' (Article 126(11) TFEU). However, the precise wording of the deficit and debt requirements is sufficiently imprecise as to allow the Council, if it wishes, to interpret transgressions more charitably. Although a **Stability and Growth Pact** (SGP), agreed at German insistence in June 1997, attempted to strengthen the operation of the EDP, it still proved possible for France and (ironically) Germany to prevent the Council from abandoning fiscal plans that generated excessive deficits in November 2003. As a result, the credibility of the system took a substantial blow, one from which it was unable to recover before the onset of the economic and financial crisis in 2008 itself led to a sudden, sharp deterioration in nearly all governments' public finances, rendering the EDP, and the SGP more widely, largely redundant.

A decade ago, the tensions at the heart of EMU were expected by many to become less acute as the new system bedded down. However, over time, they have in fact become more pronounced. Critically, the asymmetry between EMU's economic and monetary dimensions has not been resolved. EMU places monetary sovereignty in the hands of an independent, supranational body, the ECB, but leaves fiscal powers ultimately with the member states. Interest rates are therefore set with a view to the eurozone economy as a whole, whereas taxing and spending are still decided in national capitals, reflecting largely domestic considerations. This problem is compounded by the fact that the annual **Budget** of the European Union, at around one per cent of GDP, is too small to be an effective instrument of any collective or 'federal' macro-economic policy, and is almost certain to remain so. In addition, it has sometimes proved difficult for the ECB successfully to set a single interest rate for the whole of the eurozone when it still contains countries whose economies are not yet fully converged. Unduly low interest rates can induce excessive borrowing by both governments and individuals, as clearly occurred in several member states in the mid- to late-2000s.

The recent **eurozone debt crisis** – starting in Greece, Ireland and Portugal – has been in part a product of the increasingly painful mismatch between monetary and fiscal policies, as certain countries have grappled with the consequences of running up unsustainable budget deficits and national debts, without being able any longer individually to devalue their currencies as a short-term palliative. The question of how far member states should accept binding restrictions on their fiscal policies is thus at the heart of the current discussion about economic governance within the eurozone, just as it was debated (in a more theoretical way) at the time of the Delors Report, the EMU IGC and the adoption of the SGP. Delors himself has publicly regretted that the recommendation in his report that fiscal and monetary integration should be pursued hand in hand was largely sidestepped in the final text of the EMU IGC.

Reflecting a sense of urgency on this point, in March 2010, the **President of the European Council**, Herman Van Rompuy, was asked to chair a task force of EU finance ministers to suggest improvements in the operation of the SGP. Many of Van Rompuy's conclusions were (pre-emptively) tabled by the European Commission in the form of six legislative proposals on **European economic governance**. This 'Six Pack', enacted in October 2011 by the Council of Ministers and European Parliament, attempts to give greater teeth to the EDP and to institute, in parallel, closer advance scrutiny, also backed by the potential use of sanctions, of national government spending and macro-economic imbalances. The 'corrective arm' of the SGP is thus now matched by a more developed 'preventive arm', as the jargon has it.

The existence, growth and challenges of the eurozone bring into sharp relief the possibility of a **two-speed Europe**. The member states that participate in the third stage of EMU may be forced to – and some may well wish to – deepen their level of economic integration beyond that foreseen in other EU policies applying to all member states. This dynamic could affect not just fiscal policy, but financial services and structural reform questions as well. The agreement of a non-binding 'Euro Plus Pact' by the 17 eurozone countries in March 2011 – touching on such sensitive issues as wage indexation, retirement ages and the taxation of labour – was a sign of emerging pressures in this direction. Equally, the fact that six other member states (Bulgaria, Denmark, Latvia, Lithuania, Poland and Romania) immediately associated themselves with the new pact revealed their fears of isolation.

During the summer and autumn of 2011, the deepening of the eurozone debt crisis led to a decision to institutionalize previously informal meetings of the 17 eurozone heads of government, separate to the European Council. This new '**Euro Summit**' – which was agreed upon by heads of government in October 2011 and will convene at least twice a year (and almost certainly more frequently) – builds upon the experience of the eurozone finance ministers, who have met separately to the **Ecofin Council**, in the form of a **Eurogroup**, since 1998. The French President, Nicolas Sarkozy, had pressed hard for such a forum, initially against strong resistance from German Chancellor Angela Merkel, as a means of establishing a parallel framework to the EU institutions, organized essentially along intergovernmental lines. Germany, for its part, stressed the need to make the strictures of the SGP more rigorous among eurozone states. In the fourth quarter of 2011, Merkel advocated the adoption of changes to the EU Treaties which might have this effect. When the British prime minister, David Cameron, refused in December 2011 to allow a conventional treaty amendment to be negotiated, the eurozone states decided to proceed on their own – with at least the signatories of the Euro Plus Pact and possibly some other euro 'outs' – to draft and adopt an intergovernmental treaty outside an EU treaty framework, but using the EU institutions wherever possible. It remains to be seen how far the combination of the Eurogroup, Euro Summits and this new **Fiscal Compact Treaty** will alter the political and institutional dynamics of the Union, but the potential exists for them to make a significant impact in coming years.

Further reading: Michele Chang, *Monetary Integration in the European Union*, 2009; Paul de Grauwe, *Economics of Monetary Union*, 2007; Kenneth Dyson and Kevin Featherstone, *The Road to Maastricht: Negotiating Economic and Monetary Union in Europe*, 1999.

Education policy

Although a Community policy towards vocational training was foreseen in the **Treaty of Rome** (Articles 118 and 125 TFEU), it was not until the 1992 **Maastricht Treaty** that EU activity was broadened to include education policy as conventionally understood. Article 165 TFEU allows the Union to 'contribute to the development of quality education by encouraging cooperation between Member States and, if necessary, by supporting and supplementing their action'. It must do this whilst 'fully respecting the responsibility of the Member States for the content of teaching and the organization of education systems and their cultural and linguistic diversity'. Both vocational training and education are listed among the Union's areas of 'supporting' **competence** – rather than exclusive or shared competence – where it may adopt **legal acts** only so long as they do not involve the **harmonization** of the 'laws or regulations of the Member States'.

Article 165 specifies that Union action is to be aimed at 'developing the European dimension in education', especially by promoting the teaching of languages, student and teacher exchanges, mutual recognition of diplomas and periods of study, cooperation between educational establishments and distance learning, as well as by fostering cooperation with non-member countries and international organizations, such as the **Council of Europe**.

The Union's Lifelong Learning Programme, managed by the **European Commission**, enjoys funding averaging € 1.0 billion a year during the 2007–13 financing period. The biggest and best-known component is the Erasmus programme, with an annual budget of more than € 450 million and involving over 4,000 higher educational institutions in 33 countries. Since it was launched in 1987, over 2.5 million students and 250,000 teaching staff have participated in Erasmus exchanges. (230,000 students took part in the 2010–11 academic year). There are comparable programmes for secondary schools (Comenius), vocational training (Leonardo da Vinci) and adult education (Grundtvig). The Commission strongly supports efforts to modernize higher-education systems in member states, in tandem with the intergovernmental 'Bologna process', through the standardization of the length of degree courses and greater independence for universities in their financing, choice of students and hiring of academic staff. Policy-making is assisted by the Eurydice network, operational since 1980, which monitors education systems in 30 European countries.

In May 2009, education ministers adopted a 'strategic framework' for European cooperation in education and training (ET 2020), building on a similar initiative a decade earlier (ET 2010). These are in effect the educational dimensions of respectively the **Lisbon Strategy and Europe 2020**. The five main goals of ET 2020 are that at least 95 per cent of children should receive pre-school education, less than 15 per cent of 15-year-olds should have sub-standard literacy and numeracy skills, less than 10 per cent of pupils should leave school early, at least 40 per cent of 30–34 year olds should have higher-education qualifications, and at least 15 per cent of pre-retirement adults should undertake lifelong learning.

Elysée Treaty

The cornerstone of Franco-German cooperation in the post-war era – and an important underpinning of the 'Franco-German axis' within the European Union – is the Elysée Treaty, signed by French President **Charles de Gaulle** and West German Chancellor **Konrad Adenauer** on 22 January 1963 at the Elysée Palace in Paris. Otherwise known as the Franco-German Treaty, the document aimed to promote closer cooperation between the governments of the two countries in the fields of foreign policy, defence, education and youth. It provided for regular summits between government leaders (in principle at least twice a year) and for meetings of their foreign and defence ministers on a quarterly basis.

The Elysée Treaty is widely seen today as a significant catalyst for the development of European integration and as a powerful demonstration of the commitment of both countries to this process. Official commentary by both governments on the fortieth anniversary in 2003, for example, presented the treaty firmly in this light. At the time it was signed, however, the treaty was highly controversial and viewed by many pro-Europeans in other countries (and indeed in West Germany) as a questionable and potentially retrograde step.

The Elysée Treaty can only be understood in the context of the failure of de Gaulle's wider plan for an intergovernmental political union in Europe, the **Fouchet Plan** (of 1960–62), which had proposed cooperation among all of **the Six** along very similar lines. At one point in those negotiations, the five other EC member states proposed a counter-treaty that France rejected. The conclusion of a bilateral 'mini-Fouchet' with Germany was thus seen by many as a Gaullist *coup de théâtre* designed to camouflage the abandonment of the General's more ambitious project and to salvage something from the negotiations in a form that might lock Adenauer into a French concept of how Europe should develop.

Moreover, the Elysée Treaty was signed only eight days after de Gaulle's sensational veto of British membership of the Community. At his press conference making this announcement, on 14 January 1963, the French President paid a eulogistic tribute to Adenauer, taking advantage of his strong support for Franco-German cooperation – 'the very basis of the construction of Europe' – and implying that their impending meeting would lead to a closer 'organization' of their relations. When this happened, many despaired that the implication would be an attempt by France to dominate an unenlarged

Community, working on intergovernmental lines, with the German Chancellor cast in a passive and supporting role.

Representatives of Socialist parties in Europe issued a strong statement attacking the Elysée Treaty: inspired by an 'outworn concept of the absolute **sovereignty** of states' and implying the 'intention to establish an hegemony', they said, it would endanger the trust between partners and risk 'paralysing the functioning of the institutions of the Community'. To secure passage of the treaty through the Bundestag, the government in Bonn was forced, much to de Gaulle's annoyance, to add a preamble, insisting that the text was located in a wider commitment to the Atlantic Alliance and eventual UK entry into the Community. Criticism of Adenauer's handling of the whole episode within his own CDU party accelerated his retirement from the Chancellorship later that year.

In the event, the arrangements for closer cooperation set down in the Elysée Treaty proved of only limited significance. The impact of the new, regular meetings of Franco-German leaders and foreign ministers were constrained by the fact that – following the rebuff of the Fouchet Plan – de Gaulle himself decided to abandon similar meetings at EC level, a situation which continued for the remainder of his term of office. The only Community summit held between 1962 and 1969 was a symbolic one to celebrate the tenth anniversary of the **Treaty of Rome** in 1967. Bilateral Franco-German discussions in effect replaced European ones, but without a broader framework in which to multiply their influence. Once the General's successors, Georges Pompidou and **Valéry Giscard d'Estaing**, agreed to reactivate European summits, the countries began to work together more actively to shape a range of Europe-wide political initiatives – such as moves in the 1970s to peg currencies through the **Werner Plan** and **European Monetary System** (EMS) and introduce direct elections for the **European Parliament**.

Equally, the provisions of the Elysée Treaty on defence – including the proposed exchange of entire units and the development of joint armament programmes – remained largely a dead letter for many years. De Gaulle's decision to withdraw from the integrated military command structure of the **North Atlantic Treaty Organization** (NATO) in March 1966 divided France from Germany in this sphere. Only under President **François Mitterrand**, two decades later, did Franco-German military cooperation begin to gather speed. In 1987, French and German troops took part in joint manoeuvres for the first time. In January 1988, on the 25th anniversary of the Elysée Treaty, Mitterrand and the German Chancellor, **Helmut Kohl**, announced in Bonn that they planned to establish a Franco-German Security Council and develop a joint military capability (of 4,200 troops), known as the Franco-German Brigade, in parallel to but formally outside the NATO system. This brigade became the nucleus for the **Eurocorps**, open to other members of the **Western European Union** (WEU), which was created in 1991–3.

By contrast, in the educational field, progress was registered quite rapidly after the signature of the Elysée Treaty. At the first Franco-German summit in Bonn in July 1963, the two governments agreed to set up a 'Youth Bureau' – the *Office franco-allemand pour la jeunesse* (OFAJ) – with its headquarters at Bad Honnef, near Bonn. In subsequent decades, the Bureau was to oversee several million exchanges between French and German schoolchildren, many thousands of twinnings between schools, and the development of a significant student presence in each other's countries. The work of the Bureau was supplemented by initiatives in the field of language teaching and wider cultural cooperation in the 1980s.

At their Bonn meeting in January 1988, Mitterrand and Kohl broadened the cooperation foreseen in the Elysée Treaty to include economic policy. They announced the creation of a Franco-German Economic and Financial Council, under a separate protocol to the treaty. This protocol enjoins the Council every year 'to examine the broad outlines of the national budgets before their adoption by the governments and the vote in the national parliaments' and in general terms to coordinate French and German economic policies as closely as possible.

Further reading: Georges Henri Soutou, *L'Alliance incertaine: les rapports politico-stratégiques franco-allemands, 1954–1996*, 1996.

'Empty chair' crisis

See Luxembourg Compromise.

Energy policy

Since the coal industry was covered by the **European Coal and Steel Community** (ECSC) Treaty and nuclear energy by the **European Atomic Energy Community** (EAEC or Euratom) Treaty, the 1957 **Treaty of Rome** in its original form did not contain any reference to energy policy. As a result, the **legal base** for the development of a Community energy policy would depend on other provisions of a more general kind designed to promote the **common market**. In the negotiations leading to the 1992 **Maastricht Treaty**, it was proposed to introduce a specific title or chapter on energy into the **Treaties**, but differences of national interest prevented the unanimous agreement required. Instead, energy was simply added to the list of Union objectives (now Article 4 TFEU). Despite further discussion of the question in the subsequent **Intergovernmental Conferences** (IGCs), neither the 1997 **Amsterdam Treaty** nor the 2001 **Nice Treaty** included a section on energy. Policy towards the sector continued to rely on other treaty provisions, notably those added over time (starting in 1986) in relation to the **single market**, **environmental policy**, and **Trans-European Networks** (TENs), as well as (what is now) Article 122(1) TFEU, allowing the Union to take special measures when difficulties in the supply of products occur. All of these operated on the basis of **qualified majority voting** (QMV) in the **Council of Ministers**.

A first attempt at developing a comprehensive approach to energy issues at European level was made by the **European Commission** and **Council of Ministers** in April 1974, prompted by the unedifying and ill-coordinated scramble for energy supplies during the first oil crisis. A more considered statement on long-term energy goals was agreed by the Council in September 1986, when it was decided that the Community should seek to reduce its dependence on imported energy and encourage research into alternative sources of energy, backed by a strategy of maintaining minimum stocks to cushion the impact of emergencies.

During the 1990s, the opening up of energy markets, through greater cross-border trade and more competitive pricing, gradually emerged as the main focus of the Commission's activity in the energy field. The first of a series of 'internal energy market packages' was launched in 1996, challenging the interests of state-owned, monopoly producers in the gas and electricity sectors in particular. The legislation adopted sought to liberalize these sectors, by drawing a distinction between the ownership and operation of the network and supply to consumers, and putting in place independent regulators. Networks were opened up to competition, alternative suppliers were permitted to import and produce energy, and customers were allowed to choose between them. At the same time, serious efforts were made to promote greater energy efficiency, with energy labelling becoming compulsory throughout the EU for most appliances and cars. Energy-related projects, including the Joint European Torus (JET), became the second largest element in the Union's **research and development policy**. Commitments relating to energy were entered into at the UN Rio Earth Summit in 1992 and other international conferences. The 1994 Energy Charter Treaty, which came into effect four years later, sought to develop cooperation and reciprocal market access between the EU and the states of central and eastern Europe and the former Soviet Union. However, in August 2009, after years of foot-dragging, Russia indicated its definitive refusal to ratify the treaty, seriously limiting its value.

In the early 2000s, the emphasis of EU policy shifted towards diversifying energy sources – for both environmental and security reasons – by increasing the range of external suppliers of gas and oil, and by developing new, alternative energy sources or energy mixes. Indicative targets for the use of renewable energy were set in 2001, followed by a longer-term goal for each member state to produce over a fifth of its electricity from renewable sources by 2010. An EU Emissions Trading Scheme (ETS) was introduced in 2005, to exchange greenhouse-gas emission allowances between power plants and other large energy sources within the Union (which produce nearly half the latter's CO_2 emissions).

In March 2006, in response to growing concerns about the impact of climate change, the European Commission proposed a '20-20-20' initiative, linking energy and environmental policy more closely than before. Agreed by the Council and European Parliament in December 2008, it aims at reducing greenhouse-gas emissions by 20 per cent, increasing the share of renewables in energy consumption to 20 per cent, and improving energy efficiency by 20 per cent, all by 2020.

Liberalization of markets has continued in parallel: a second internal energy market package was brought forward in 2003, and since 2007, consumers have enjoyed, in nearly all member states, the right to choose their electricity and gas suppliers, without public service obligations being prejudiced. A third such package has introduced a pan-European regulatory structure for the Union, based on an Agency for the Cooperation of Energy Regulators (ACER) and a European Network of Transmission System Operator organizations (ENTSOs). The Commission is actively promoting the development of European grids – with substantial investment needed in interconnectors within and between member states – as well as the creation of a new 'mechanism for rapid solidarity' to help member states facing immediate supply shortages.

Despite efforts to develop new energy sources and improve self-reliance, the EU's dependence on third countries for its energy supply has been rising, rather than falling, in recent years and now stands at about half its total needs. The Union is particularly reliant on Russia, a situation exacerbated by its **enlargement** to include ten countries from the former Soviet bloc in 2004 and 2007. The EU imports just under a third of its oil and gas from Russia, with some new member states dependent on that country for all their gas supplies. In response, renewed efforts have been made to extend the geographic reach of EU energy policy eastwards, to try to tie in some other states of the former Soviet Union, notably through the 2004 Baku Initiative and the 2005 'Energy Community' Treaty. However, the impact of the sudden and dramatic gas dispute between Russia and the Ukraine in early 2009 – which left parts of Bulgaria, the Czech Republic and Slovakia without heating for two weeks – revealed the fragility of the situation. In July 2009, four EU member states – Austria, Bulgaria, Hungary and Romania – agreed to work with **Turkey** in developing the Nabucco gas pipeline to reduce European dependence on Russia.

A new treaty provision, Article 194 TFEU, introduced by the **Lisbon Treaty**, has finally resolved the question of the legal basis for energy policy. It states that a 'Union policy on energy shall aim, in a spirit of solidarity between Member States' – the latter phrase included at the request of the **Baltic states** and Poland – to 'ensure' the functioning of the energy market and security of supply within the Union, and to 'promote' the interconnection of energy networks, as well as energy efficiency, energy saving, and the development of new and renewable forms of energy. The Commission may propose measures to achieve these objectives, to be adopted by the Council and Parliament jointly under the **co-decision procedure**, with the Council acting by QMV. (Any measures involving **tax harmonization** require unanimity in the Council, with the Parliament simply consulted.) Action at EU level 'shall not affect a Member State's right to determine the conditions for exploiting its [own] energy resources, its choice between different energy sources and the general structure of its energy supply', even though, somewhat confusingly, measures impacting on the last two may be adopted by the Council unanimously under environment policy (Article 192(2)c TFEU).

Jean-Claude Piris, the former head of the Council legal service, notes that although many commentators 'have presented Article 194 TFEU as a major innovation establishing a new competence' for the EU in the energy field, in reality it simply makes the existing competence – established over time by the use of pre-existing treaty bases – 'clearer and more explicit'. The change 'symbolizes the growing importance attached to this area' by policy-makers in the Union and member states (*The Lisbon Treaty: A Legal and Political Analysis*, 2010).

Further reading: Janne Haaland Matláry, *Energy Policy in the European Union*, 1997.

Enhanced cooperation

Alternatively known as 'flexibility' or 'differentiated integration', enhanced cooperation allows a subset of member states of the European Union to develop a higher degree of integration than others in certain policy areas, on a voluntary basis, provided that certain strict conditions are met. A product of political battles before and after the 1992 **Maastricht Treaty**, enhanced cooperation was institutionalized in the late 1990s. It represents a departure from the previous orthodoxy that all member states should always move towards the same objectives at the same pace, one which was fundamental to the founding **Treaties**. Although the new arrangements for enhanced cooperation have been a source of lively political debate because of the theoretical issues they raise, they have so far only been invoked twice, in the fields of divorce law and patents.

Member states have always been free to engage in closer cooperation bilaterally, outside the EU framework, so long as the institutions or policies they develop do not undermine their common obligations within the Union. There are several examples of arrangements outside Union structures, sometimes encompassing non-member states, for collaboration for specific purposes. For many years, the **European Monetary System** (EMS) had no treaty basis, just as the **European Space Agency** (ESA) still lacks one today. The first serious example of a minority of EU member states deciding consciously to go further and faster than others in pursuit of an established Community goal was the **Schengen** Agreement of June 1985 'on the gradual abolition of controls at the common frontiers' of five member states. Formalized by the Schengen Convention five years later, this arrangement carried forward the logic of existing treaty provisions on **free movement** and the **single market** on a faster timescale, outside the treaty framework.

The success of the Schengen initiative fuelled frustration within the Union at a system which, because of the need for **unanimity** to effect treaty change, obliged the whole convoy always to move at the speed of the slowest ship – whether in defining new areas of cooperation or in allowing greater use of **qualified majority voting** (QMV) in the **Council of Ministers**. The outcome of the negotiation of the Maastricht Treaty reconciled these cross-pressures by extending a series of path-breaking '**opt-outs**' to the United Kingdom, Denmark and Ireland in areas – notably **Economic and Monetary Union** (EMU) and aspects of **Justice and Home Affairs** (JHA) – where it was politically impossible for all countries to move forward together.

After Maastricht, the traditional hostility of integrationists to '**variable geometry**' in Europe gradually evolved into acceptance of the possible benefits of differential arrangements between countries, so long as they were aimed at promoting closer integration among a vanguard and organized around certain general principles, rather than simply ad hoc opt-outs. In 1994, the then French prime minister, Edouard Balladur, proposed that an inner group form the centre of a Europe of '**concentric circles**', and in the **Lamers–Schäuble paper**, two leading German Christian Democrat parliamentarians argued that a 'hard core' of committed member states already existed and that it should pull ahead on its own. The case for greater flexibility was strengthened by the prospect of the progressive **enlargement** of the Union and the likely **accession** of some countries that might simply be unable, however willing, to match the pace set by the leaders.

Serious concerns were expressed, however, about the implications of such a process for the overall coherence and consistency of the Union – for example, in the homogeneity of **EU law**, the equitable sharing of financial burdens, and the guarantee of both fair competition and **non-discrimination**. The President of the European Commission, **Jacques Delors**, was particularly reluctant to abandon the concept that integration should encompass all member states moving in tandem, as were several countries that feared that they might be left behind. Franco-German advocates of a '**two-speed' Europe** were in effect forced to rein in their thinking and accept the logic of a more pragmatic régime, working within existing constraints. Equally, some in the Commission came to recognize that a measure of controlled flexibility, locked into the established EU institutions, might be preferable to the possible institution of new arrangements between ambitious governments, outside the Treaties.

These issues were addressed in the 1996 **Intergovernmental Conference** (IGC) that led to the **Amsterdam Treaty** of the following year. In the negotiation, several of **the Six** founding member states argued for some form of new flexibility arrangement to be given treaty status, although the United Kingdom, Spain, Portugal and the Scandinavian countries proved notably more cautious. A carefully-worded joint paper from the French and German governments in October 1996 provided a starting-point for the drafting of a text that might 'allow those Member States that are able and willing to advance more quickly than others' to do so.

The Amsterdam outcome, agreed in June 1997, attempted to reconcile the various positions, by formalizing the possibility of closer cooperation within a treaty framework, but only on the basis of very strict conditions. New articles were added both to the Maastricht Treaty and to the **Treaty of Rome** (Articles 40 and 43–5 TEU and Articles 11 and 11(a) EC, as they were respectively at the time), to permit member states 'which intend to establish closer cooperation between themselves . . . to make use of the institutions, procedures and mechanisms' of the European Union for this purpose. These arrangements were to apply both to the supranational EC '**pillar**' of the Union and that part of JHA, namely police and judicial cooperation in criminal matters, that remained intergovernmental. The field of **Common Foreign and Security Policy** (CFSP) was not touched, where the opportunity provided by Maastricht for the 'constructive abstention' of member states in Council decisions – permitting their selective non-participation in an agreed policy – was deemed sufficient.

Under Amsterdam, a group of countries could in effect 'borrow' EU institutions and decision-making processes, provided that closer cooperation was 'aimed at furthering the objectives of the Union', that it involved at least a majority of member states, did not penalize countries that chose not to participate, and was 'only used as a last resort'. Such cooperation could not fall within areas subject to the Community's exclusive **competence** (such as **Common Commercial Policy** (CCP) or monetary policy within the **eurozone**) – it had to operate 'within the limits of the powers conferred upon the Community', and must not distort trade or competition between the member states, nor entail any discrimination among nationals of the member states (Article 11 EC).

The Amsterdam Treaty also set out a complex decision-making process for agreement to proposed areas of closer cooperation. In the EC pillar, member states wishing to establish such cooperation would address a request to the **European Commission**, which would then submit a formal proposal to the Council of Ministers, or give its reasons for not doing so. In the JHA pillar, member states could make a proposal directly to the Council if the Commission declined to support it. In either case, the Council could then, acting by a qualified majority and after consulting the **European Parliament**, agree to the proposal. However, an 'emergency break' clause permitted any member state to insist that a vote should not be taken, and that the matter be referred to the **European Council** (of heads of government) for unanimous decision. Once established, closer cooperation would be open for other member states to join; indeed both the Commission and existing participants should 'ensure that as many Member States as possible are encouraged to take part'. Commentators quickly suggested that these arrangements were so restrictive that their actual use in practice would be virtually impossible.

In the negotiations leading to the 2001 **Nice Treaty**, the pro-flexibility member states renewed the charge, arguing strongly for easier use of the mechanism. The resulting agreement clarified that 'enhanced cooperation', as it was formally renamed, should be aimed specifically at 'reinforcing' the process of integration and must not undermine the single market or economic and social **cohesion**. It specified that henceforth a minimum of eight member states would need to take part. (Although eight states represented a majority at the time, they would not do so in the future.) The veto component of the 'emergency break' procedure was abandoned: if the issue went up to the European Council, there would be no unanimity requirement. The possibility of enhanced cooperation was extended to implementing acts under CFSP: these would need to be decided unanimously in the Council and could not have military or defence implications. Individual member states would make proposals for enhanced cooperation in the CFSP field directly to the Council, as they already did (before Nice) in the police and judicial cooperation area of JHA. It was also made clear that any acts arising from closer cooperation were excluded from the ***acquis communautaire*** and, therefore, need not be accepted by countries applying for accession to the Union.

In 2002–3, the **Convention on the Future of Europe** revisited these provisions once again, as did the ensuing IGC the following year. In the resulting proposal for a **European Constitution**, the parallel arrangements for enhanced cooperation in each of the three pillars were merged

(Articles I-44 and III-416–23 Constitution), reflecting the proposed abolition of the pillared structure of the Union. A minimum of only a third of member states would henceforth need to take part in any enhanced cooperation: nine countries in an EU of 27. The scope of cooperation would be extended to cover the whole of CFSP, not just implementing measures, even if unanimity was still required to trigger it in this field and the option would exist of special **'permanent structured cooperation' in defence** (PSCD).

Participants in an enhanced cooperation initiative would also benefit from the possibility of using ***passerelle* clauses**, allowing them (by a unanimous vote) to move decision-making to majority voting in policy areas – such as **tax harmonization** or social security – where unanimity still applied in the Council (for the full EU), and to apply **co-decision** between Council and Parliament, where the **consultation** procedure still applied (Article III-422 Constitution). The option of using *passerelle* clauses did not, however, extend to decisions with military or defence implications. Other than in CFSP, the assent – renamed **consent** – of the Parliament would also be required (with MEPs of all member states able to vote). Although this latter change might appear to make enhanced cooperation more difficult to invoke, it appealed to advocates of flexibility, by installing an additional safeguard against any moves to reverse or dilute integration in any field. All these changes, with one exception, were carried forward into the document that replaced the European Constitution, the **Lisbon Treaty** (Article 20 TEU and Articles 326–34 TFEU), which was agreed in 2007 and entered into effect in December 2009. The minimum number of member states needed to participate in an enhanced cooperation was reset at nine, as opposed to a third of member states (Article 20(2) TEU).

Until recently, the provisions for enhanced cooperation in the EU lay unused. Although there was discussion periodically of taking initiatives in the areas of corporate taxation and social security, in particular, no attempt was made, either by member states or by the Commission, to invoke enhanced cooperation during the first decade of its existence. Some attributed this to the stringent conditions for its use, whilst others noted that the fields where it might be needed – namely policies still requiring unanimity in the Council – had shrunk in number with each successive treaty change. Equally, the Commission's instinctive caution towards enhanced cooperation, still evident in discussions within the European Convention, made it reluctant to take the initiative in this field.

Finally, in the spring of 2010, a first attempt was made to use the enhanced cooperation mechanism, although in an unexpected field. Since 2006, a Commission proposal to facilitate 'cross-border' divorce had been blocked by Sweden in the Council, where unanimity is required for legislation on family law with cross-border implications, with no evident prospect of progress. Nine member states, subsequently joined by three more, requested that they be allowed to proceed on their own with passage of the **regulation** in question, under enhanced cooperation. (The measure was designed to permit couples of different nationalities, couples living apart in different EU states or couples living together in a country other than their home state, to choose which law applies if they separate, provided that it is the law of a country to which they have a close connection, by nationality or long-term residence.) As the proposal fell within an area of non-exclusive Union competence where no previous legislation had been adopted at EU level, the prospect of any interference with existing policies was minimal.

Initially, in January 2009, the Commission rejected the initiative. However, it shifted position later in the year, seemingly in response to the need of José Manuel Barroso and his college of Commissioners to secure reconfirmation in the European Parliament. In March 2010, the Commission proposed to the Council that it adopt a **decision** permitting 12 member states to engage in enhanced cooperation in 'the area of law applicable to divorce and legal separation'. This proposal secured the approval of the Council – with the 12 states concerned adopting it unanimously – and the **consent** of the Parliament within three months. It was then followed by the de facto resubmission by the Commission of the original proposal that had been blocked in the Council, now as a measure for adoption by the 12 member states participating in the enhanced cooperation. In this latter case, the Parliament was only consulted, because it is limited to that role in law-making relating to family law with cross-border implications.

Soon after, in December 2010, 12 member states asked the Commission to launch a second enhanced cooperation initiative, this time in the field of 'unitary patent protection'. As in divorce law, patents were a matter of non-exclusive Union competence, where no previous legislation had been adopted. Attempts to move beyond the existing intergovernmental European Patent Convention and establish a common patent within the EU had long stumbled on the issue of the language régime – where unanimity was required – with Italy and Spain refusing to accept that any new system should operate only in the three official languages (English, French and German) of the European Patent Office (EPO). All other member states (making 25 in all) joined the initiative, which was adopted by the Council in March 2011, having been approved by the Parliament a month before.

Further reading: Kenneth Dyson and Angelos Sepos (editors), *Which Europe? The Politics of Differentiated Integration*, 2010.

Enlargement

Enlargement is the process by which countries join the European Union. Article 49 TEU specifies that 'any European State' which respects human rights and the values of human dignity, freedom, democracy, equality and the rule of law 'may apply to become a member of the Union'. The applicant state 'shall address its application to the Council, which shall act unanimously after consulting the Commission and after receiving the consent of the European Parliament, which shall act by an absolute majority of its component members'.

In practice, the enlargement procedure runs as follows. An application is lodged by the country wishing to join the Union with the **Council of Ministers**. The **European Commission** delivers a formal opinion on the application – a process which, depending on the complexity of the case, may take several years – and the **European Parliament** is consulted. The Council – or now, in practice, the **European Council** (of heads of government) – acting unanimously, may then grant the applicant state 'candidate country' status. If it does so, negotiations begin between the applicant state, on the one side, and the **presidency** of the Council (representing the member states) and the Commission, on the other. The detailed negotiations are divided into subject-specific 'chapters' and are only completed when all chapters are closed. Once agreed, a draft Treaty of **Accession** is initialled by the applicant state and by representatives of the member states, and is submitted for approval by the European Parliament, where an absolute majority of its total membership must vote in favour, under the **consent procedure** (and thus a veto can be exercised). All signatory states proceed to the **ratification** of the accession treaty, 'in accordance with their respective constitutional requirements'. This always involves national parliamentary approval, and may also require a **referendum** in the applicant country, either for political reasons or because amendments to its domestic constitution are needed. Once ratification is complete, the treaty is formally signed and enters into force on an agreed date, with the country in question finally acceding to the Union.

The basic qualifications for membership of the Union are that the applicant country is a European state, that it is a stable democracy in which human and fundamental rights are respected and guaranteed, that it has a functioning market economy, and that it is able and willing to assume the practical obligations of membership, including adoption of the entirety of the ***acquis communautaire***. The European Council has given expression to these requirements in the **Copenhagen criteria**, agreed in June 1993. Since the **Lisbon Treaty** came into force, Article 49 TEU draws attention to these 'conditions of eligibility agreed upon by the European Council', which it says will be 'taken into account' by the Council in deciding on a country's admission.

No official definition exists of what is meant by a country being a 'European State' and there has never been, either geographically or culturally, a clearly defined eastern frontier of Europe. If membership of the **Council of Europe** is taken as the yardstick, it has long extended to countries whose claims to being European on geographic grounds at least are slight. To require applicant countries to be Christian would exclude **Turkey** and the Muslim republics in the western Balkans that emerged from the break-up of **Yugoslavia**. Morocco is so far the only country to have had an application rejected (in 1987) on the grounds that it was not a European state.

By contrast, the requirement that applicant states be democratic and respect human rights is more clear-cut. Such countries are in effect required to be parties to the Council of Europe's **European Convention on Human Rights** and to accept the right of individual petition under the Convention. They must now also accept the **Charter of Fundamental Rights**, given legal force by the Lisbon Treaty. Since the 1997 **Amsterdam Treaty**, there is provision for the **suspension** of certain membership rights if a member state engages in a 'serious and persistent' breach of fundamental rights. It was on the issues of democracy and human rights that the Community refused to conclude **association agreements** with the Spain of General Franco and the Portugal of Salazar and 'froze' the association agreement with Greece during the seven-year dictatorship of the Colonels (1967–74). In each case, such agreements were seen as a precursor to possible membership.

Since the first applications were received in 1961, 31 countries have applied to join **the Six** founding member states within the Community, now Union, and 21 have so far been admitted, in six rounds of enlargement between 1973 and 2007. The founding Six – Belgium, France, Germany, Luxembourg, the Netherlands and Italy – were joined by Denmark, Ireland and the United Kingdom in January 1973 (the Nine), Greece in January 1981 (the Ten), Portugal and Spain in January 1986 (the Twelve), and Austria, Finland and Sweden in January 1995 (EU 15). In May 2004, a 'big-bang' enlargement took place involving eight of the former Communist countries of central and eastern Europe – the Czech Republic, Estonia, Hungary, Latvia, Lithuania, Poland, Slovakia and Slovenia – together with Cyprus and Malta (EU 25). Finally, they were joined by Bulgaria and Romania in January 2007 (EU 27).

Croatia, which applied to join the Union in February 2003, will be admitted as the twenty-eighth member state in July 2013. Six other countries currently have applications pending. They are, in the order in which their applications were submitted: Turkey (1987), FYR Macedonia (2004), Montenegro (2008), Albania (2009), **Iceland** (2009) and Serbia (2009). Five of the six have so far been granted 'candidate country' status, the exception being Albania. Turkey has concluded a **customs union** with the EU, whilst all of the candidate countries have association agreements with the Union – whether by dint of membership of the **European Economic Area** (EEA), as in the case of Iceland, or through Stabilization and Association Agreements (SAAs) for the countries of the western Balkans. **Norway** withdrew its application to join the Union (twice), following negative **referenda** in 1972 and 1994, while **Switzerland** suspended its application in 1992, after the public rejected membership of the less ambitious EEA.

Further reading: Alfred Kellerman, Jaap de Zwaan and Jenö Czuczai, *EU Enlargement: The Constitutional Impact at EU and National Level*, 2001; Neill Nugent (editor), *European Union Enlargement*, 2004.

New EU member states, 1973–2007

Member state	*Date of application*	*Date of accession*
Ireland	31 July 1961 and 11 May 1967	1 January 1973
United Kingdom	9 August 1961 and 10 May 1967	1 January 1973
Denmark	10 August 1961 and 11 May 1967	1 January 1973
Greece	12 June 1975	1 January 1981
Portugal	28 March 1977	1 January 1986
Spain	28 July 1977	1 January 1986
East Germany	–	3 October 1990, as a result of **German reunification**
Austria	17 July 1989	1 January 1995
Cyprus	3 July 1990	1 May 2004
Malta	16 July 1990	1 May 2004
Sweden	1 July 1991	1 January 1995
Finland	18 March 1992	1 January 1995
Hungary	31 March 1994	1 May 2004
Poland	5 April 1994	1 May 2004
Romania	22 June 1995	1 January 2007
Slovakia	27 June 1995	1 May 2004
Latvia	27 October 1995	1 May 2004
Estonia	28 November 1995	1 May 2004
Lithuania	8 December 1995	1 May 2004
Bulgaria	16 December 1995	1 January 2007
Czech Republic	17 January 1996	1 May 2004
Slovenia	10 June 1996	1 May 2004

Applications for EU membership since 1962

Country	*Date of application*	*Status of application*
Norway	30 April 1962 and 11 May 1967(first application)	Suspended after vetoes by French President **Charles de Gaulle**, 14 January 1963 and 27 November 1967. Draft accession treaty rejected by referendum, 25 September 1972.
Turkey	14 April 1987	Unfavourable Commission opinion, 20 December 1989. Accepted as candidate country by European Council, 11 December 1999. Accession negotiations opened, 3 October 2005.
Morocco	20 July 1987	Rejected by the Council of Ministers as a non-European country.
Switzerland	20 May 1992	Suspended following rejection of European Economic Area (EEA) membership by referendum, 6 December 1992. EU membership rejected by referendum, 4 March 2001.
Norway	25 November 1992 (second application)	Draft accession treaty rejected by referendum, 28 November 1994.
Croatia	21 February 2003	Accepted as candidate country by European Council, 18 June 2004. Accession negotiations launched, 3 October 2005; completed, 30 June 2011. Accession treaty signed, 9 December 2011. Accession to take place on 1 July 2013.
Former Yugoslav Republic of Macedonia	22 March 2004	Accepted as candidate country by European Council, 16 December 2005. Accession negotiations yet to begin.
Montenegro	15 December 2008	Accepted as a candidate country by European Council, 17 December 2010. Launch of accession negotiations expected in June 2012.
Albania	28 April 2009	Application pending.
Iceland	17 July 2009	Accepted as candidate country by European Council, 17 June 2010. Accession negotiations launched, 27 July 2010.
Serbia	22 December 2009	Accepted as candidate country by European Council, 1 March 2012.

Environment policy

Although it was not referred to in the original text of the **Treaty of Rome**, environment policy became an area of Community action on the basis of a decision at the Paris **summit** of heads of government in October 1972. As environmental issues rose in political salience during the late 1960s and early 1970s, there was growing awareness that pollution could not always be addressed on a national basis, as was powerfully illustrated by the *Torrey Canyon* oil tanker disaster in March 1967. Responding to this mood, the **European Commission** submitted a communication on the environment in March 1972, and the Paris summit invited the EC institutions to establish a programme for action in this field, based on a precise timetable. The Commission presented a programme in April 1973, adopted by the **Council of Ministers** seven months later.

In the absence of a specific treaty base, the Commission proposed a series of legislative measures under Article 100 EC (now Article 115 TFEU), dealing with the approximation of laws, and Article 235 (now **Article 352** TFEU). Within less than three years, the Council unanimously adopted more than a dozen measures, including **directives** on water pollution, drinking and bathing water, vehicle emissions, dangerous chemicals and discharges, waste oils and detergents. As a part of this package, in 1975, the Council adopted a (non-binding) recommendation on the 'cost allocation and action by public authorities on environmental matters', a legal issue raised by the *Torrey Canyon* disaster, which in effect recognized the 'polluter pays' principle (now written into Article 191(2) TFEU).

In 1979, the Commission proposed a 'second generation of longer-term policies, aimed at promoting a qualitatively superior form of economic growth as a foundation for the future', with a special emphasis on the improved management of natural resources. The Council adopted further measures on water, air and noise pollution, CFCs, the control of waste, and the conservation of wild birds. It also adopted a **regulation** prohibiting the import of certain whale products, which consolidated public opposition to whaling in general. At the same time, the EU started to become a significant player on the international environmental scene and signed a number of European and international conventions, notably on wildlife and natural habitats, long-range trans-boundary air pollution, and the protection of the Mediterranean (Barcelona Convention, 1976) and the Antarctic (Canberra Convention, 1980).

Starting in June 1979, the directly-elected **European Parliament** – which included Greens from Germany and Belgium after 1984 – led a campaign for the recognition of environmental policy in the **Treaties** and the extension of **qualified majority voting** (QMV) to environmental legislation. The 1986 **Single European Act** (SEA) gave the Community explicit **competence** for environmental policy (Articles 130(r) to (t) EEC, now replaced by Articles 191–3 TFEU). It established a series of principles to guide such policy, namely 'that preventative action should be taken, that environmental damage should as a priority be rectified at source, and that the polluter should pay'. Environmental objectives would be pursued collectively 'to the extent' that they could 'be better attained at Community level than [that] of the individual member states' – the first allusion to the **subsidiarity** principle in the Treaties – whilst common measures should 'not prevent any Member State from maintaining or introducing more stringent measures compatible with this Treaty'. The latter provision arose from a judgement of the **European Court of Justice** (ECJ) in the 'Danish beer-case' (*Commission* v *Denmark*, Case 302/86). The Court ruled that a Danish law to the effect that beer and soft drinks could be marketed only in reusable containers was justified in terms of the protection of the environment, which was to be regarded as taking precedence over the obligation on member states under Article 34 TFEU not to enact measures restricting imports from other member states.

In an early example of a ***passerelle* clause**, the SEA permitted the Council to decide unanimously to allow QMV to be used in most aspects of environment policy, although in fact it never took advantage of this provision. The 1992 **Maastricht Treaty** simply made QMV the norm for environment policy and introduced the **co-decision procedure** between the Council and European Parliament for law-making in this field (Article 192 TFEU). **Unanimity** is still retained for any environmental decision having fiscal implications or affecting town and country planning, land use, water resource management or measures affecting a member state's energy sources and supply. However, a *passerelle* clause, dating from Maastricht, does allow any of these topics to be moved to QMV and co-decision if the Council unanimously so decides.

Environment policy has always been based on successive 'action programmes': the current programme, the sixth, was agreed in July 2002 and focuses on climate change. Emphasis is also laid on the importance of other policies being assessed in terms of their impact on the environment. The principle of preventive action was reinforced by the requirement laid down in a 1985 directive that all projects, public or private, above a certain cost should be the subject of an environmental impact assessment. In 1990, it was decided to establish a **European Environment Agency** (EEA) to help monitor the state of the environment.

Taking advantage of the use of QMV since 1993, the process of consolidating EU environmental legislation has continued in recent years. Among the more significant measures have been the 2000 water framework directive, the 2006 REACH package (dealing with the registration, evaluation and authorization of chemicals), and the 2006 and 2008 water framework directives. By contrast, efforts by the Commission to introduce a Union-wide carbon tax, which would still require unanimity, have foundered in the face of opposition from Germany, the United Kingdom and some other member states.

For the protection of the natural environment, the EU works very closely with international bodies and within guidelines laid down by international conventions. It has used its position as a major trading power to stamp out the trade in products derived from seal pups and continues to take similar action with respect to exotic birds and tropical hardwoods. The EU has been represented at successive UN conferences on the environment (starting at the Rio 'Earth Summit' in 1992) and on climate change (from Kyoto in 1997 onwards). Such diplomacy has been marked by both success and failure. In 1993–4, the Union played an important part in establishing a committee on trade and environment (CTE) within the new World Trade Organization (WTO), which is now at the heart of efforts to secure a legally-binding global agreement on climate change. However, although the Union has invested huge effort in meeting targets for the reduction in emissions of greenhouse gases under the Kyoto Protocol, including the creation of an emissions trading system (ETS), these have not in general been reciprocated by other advanced industrialized or emerging economies. The limitations of the Union's strategy of 'leading by example' became apparent at the UN's Copenhagen summit on climate change in December 2009. The outcome – a non-binding accord brokered directly by the United States and China, without significant EU involvement – was generally seen as a major political reverse. Despite difficulties of this kind, environmental protection in all its forms has been identified in opinion polls as an area in which there is a consistently very high level of public support for action at EU level.

Further reading: John McCormick, *Environmental Policy in the European Union*, 2001.

Equal treatment

Article 157 TFEU empowers the European Union to adopt legislation to apply the 'principle of equal opportunities and equal treatment of men and women in matters of employment and occupation', including 'equal pay without discrimination based on sex'. Each member state 'shall ensure that the principle of equal pay for male and female workers for equal work or work of equal value is applied'.

This principle of equal pay was enshrined in a directive adopted by the **Council of Ministers** in February 1975 and further enforced by a ruling from the **European Court of Justice** (ECJ) the same year, stating that this treaty article was of **direct effect** in cases of 'direct and overt discrimination' (*Gabrielle Defrenne* v *Sabena*, Case 43/75). The Court's 1995 ruling in the Kalanke case placed limits on positive action going beyond the removal of the disadvantages experienced by the 'under-represented sex' (*Kalanke* v *Freie Hansestadt Bremen*, Case C-450/93). However, in the 1997 Marschall judgement, the Court allowed, in the event of a male and female candidate possessing identical qualifications, priority to be given to the woman (*Marschall* v *Land Nordrhein Westfalen*, Case C-409/95).

In a 1990 judgement of the Court, the definition of pay in Article 157 TFEU as 'the ordinary basic or minimum wage or salary and any other consideration . . . which the worker receives' was held to include redundancy payments and payments under occupational pension schemes (*Barber* v *Guardian Royal Exchange Assurance Group*, commonly referred to as the 'Barber judgement', Case C-262/88). As with the Defrenne case, the Court ruled that its judgement was not of retroactive effect (except in respect of claims already submitted), but in view of the enormous potential financial implications of the ruling for employers and pension schemes throughout the member states, the governments added a **protocol** to the 1992 **Maastricht Treaty** stating that claims could not be made under the Barber ruling for periods of employment prior to May 1990.

Since equal pay was the only aspect of equal treatment specifically covered by the **Treaties**, a 1976 Council directive on access to employment, training, promotion and working conditions was enacted – under (then) Article 235 EEC, now **Article 352** TFEU – in order to broaden the scope of equal treatment in practice. 'Working conditions' were defined to include dismissal and, in a 1986 judgement, the Court ruled that compulsory retirement was a form of dismissal and thus covered by the requirements of equal treatment (*Marshall* v *Southampton and South-West Hampshire Area Health Authority*, Case 152/84). In *Dekker* v *Stichting VJV* (Case C-177/88), the ECJ ruled that refusal to employ someone on grounds of pregnancy constituted discrimination, and, in a second case, *Webb* v *EMO Air Cargo* (Case C-32/93), that pregnancy was inadmissible as grounds for dismissal.

In 1978, the Council adopted a directive on equal treatment in respect of social security schemes, including those for the self-employed. Although it was not possible to reach agreement on the equalization of pensionable ages for men and women, the directive allowed member states to continue applying their own rules to this and other sensitive matters. The ECJ has subsequently ruled that differential retirement ages for men and women are illegal under EU law, for instance, in *Commission* v *Italy* (Case C-46/07).

Equal treatment was addressed in the **Social Protocol** annexed to the Maastricht Treaty. The 1997 **Amsterdam Treaty** introduced a general provision that in 'all its activities, the Union shall aim to eliminate inequalities, and to promote equality, between men and women' (Article 8 TFEU). These changes to the Treaties allowed a range of new legislation to be passed on maternity protection, parental leave, social and occupational security, self-employment and the burden of proof in discrimination cases. In a case on a 2004 directive outlawing gender-based discrimination in the supply of goods and services (*ABC Test-Achats* v *Conseil des Ministres*, Case C-236/09), the ECJ ruled in March 2011 that a potentially indefinite **derogation** in respect of the treatment of insurance premia had to be abandoned in December 2012, when experience of the arrangement was due to be reviewed.

The *Test-Achats* ruling, which attracted great public interest because it ends the differential treatment of young male and female drivers for motor insurance, underlines how equal treatment has been a field in which, over several decades, legislation has been underpinned and reinforced by judicial rulings. However, the Commission reported in 2010 that women continue to earn on average 18 per cent less than men in the EU 27, with significant differences in the situation between member states. An Advisory Committee on Equal Opportunities was established in 1981.

Further reading: Helen Meenan, *Equality Law in an Enlarged European Union*, 2007.

ERTA case

The judgement given by the **European Court of Justice** (ECJ) in the ERTA case (*Commission* v *Council*, Case 22/70) in 1971 established that the exercise of European Community **competence** for any question of internal policy, as set out in the founding **Treaties**, automatically entailed an 'implied competence' for the external dimension of that policy as well. This 'parallelism' both limited the power of the member states to act individually in a range of areas – the external aspect of **transport policy**, in this specific case – and ensured that the **European Commission** would in future negotiate, on behalf of the **Council of Ministers**, at Community level, in these fields. The ERTA case was thus critical in establishing the role of the Commission in external relations.

In 1962, under the auspices of the UN **Economic Commission for Europe** (ECE), a large number of European countries, including most EC member states, had negotiated a European Road Traffic Agreement (ERTA). In the event, the ERTA Treaty, designed to regulate certain employment conditions in the road transport sector, failed to enter into force because insufficient ratifications were deposited. In 1969, the Council, on the basis of a proposal from the Commission, adopted a **regulation** on the issue; it was the first piece of Community legislation to be passed in this field and dealt entirely with matters internal to the Community. In parallel, discussions continued with non-member states about the possibility of an amended version of the aborted ERTA Treaty. In March 1970, the Council of Ministers agreed a joint negotiating position for all the member states in relation to the latest ERTA discussions. The European Commission challenged the Council's position, adopted by resolution, on the grounds that, since the **Treaty of Rome** made road transport a Community competence (and the 1969 regulation had formally exercised that competence), the Community as such and not the member states should henceforth undertake any negotiation with third countries, with the Commission acting on the Community's behalf.

The ECJ decided in the Commission's favour on the key issue at stake, even if the Commission actually lost the case on a technicality (namely that, as the ERTA negotiation had begun before the Council regulation was adopted in 1969, it would have been unreasonable for the other negotiating partners if responsibility had suddenly been transferred from the member states to the Commission in midstream). The ECJ ruled that the Community's authority to enter into agreements and sign treaties with third countries 'arises not only from an express conferment by the Treaty', as in **Common Commercial Policy** (CCP), 'but may equally flow from other provisions of the Treaty' or from legislation adopted under it. 'In particular,' it argued, 'each time the Community, with a view to implementing a common policy envisaged by the Treaty', such as transport policy, 'adopts provisions laying down common rules, whatever form these may take, the Member States no longer have the right, acting individually or even collectively, to undertake obligations with third countries which affect those rules.' Moreover, as and when 'such common rules come into being, the Community alone is in a position to assume and carry out contractual obligations towards third countries affecting the whole sphere of application of the Community legal system'.

The Court resolved a dispute between those who had argued that, as Trevor Hartley has put it, 'it would be illogical for the Union to have internal law-making power with regard to a certain topic and yet be unable to conclude international agreements in that field' and those who held that the Community possessed 'only such external powers as were expressly granted to it by the Treaties' (*Foundations of European Union Law*, 2010). The ERTA case thus established that the Community enjoyed 'implied competence' in the external field in all areas where it had explicit competence in the internal field.

EU law

The law of the European Union takes three basic forms: the **Treaties** concluded among the **member states**; legislation adopted under the Treaties by the EU **institutions**, in the form of **legal acts**; and case-law embodied in rulings of the **European Court of Justice** (ECJ).

Sometimes referred to as 'primary' legislation, the Treaties are the basis of the European Union's legal order. They serve as the Union's de facto constitution and provide the basis for the adoption of legislation. (The aborted **European Constitution** was itself a new treaty that attempted to combine and replace the Union's existing treaty texts.) The EU Treaties are dynamic, in that they not only establish a particular set of relations between the signatory states but also set out a programme of action for the future. They lay down a pattern of rights and obligations, not so much between the signatory states, as between the states and the Union thereby established. Indeed, some treaty articles confer specific rights upon individuals, as opposed to states – a principle known as **direct effect** – while others confer rights indirectly, by virtue of the obligations which they impose upon states. In both cases, such rights are enforceable at law. However, there are also articles that embody general principles that must first be translated into specific legislation before they can have legal effect. Many cases before the Court of Justice have centred upon the distinction that must be drawn between these different types of treaty commitment.

Implicit in the Treaties is the notion that they and legislation adopted under them enjoy **primacy** – that is, take precedence – over national law. Although this principle is not asserted formally in the Treaties, it has been upheld by the Court of Justice and is central to the operation of all the EU institutions. The power conferred by treaty upon the institutions to make law with a binding effect on and in the member states distinguishes the Union from other international organizations. The Treaties are self-contained, in that they provide procedures and institutions for enforcement, interpretation and the settlement of disputes without recourse to outside bodies. All these characteristics combine to make the EU Treaties profoundly different – in political significance, even if not in form – from other international treaties.

In a famous judgement in 1974, Lord Denning, then Master of the Rolls, described the impact of European law upon English law as like that of a 'rising tide', which, inexorably, makes its way up the broad estuaries into the very smallest creeks and inlets of national life (*Bulmer* v *Bollinger*). Based upon a continental tradition of civil law, EU law is indeed substantially different from English law, but this should not obscure the fact that it is also different from any other comparable body of law. It has some of the characteristics of international law, but of municipal law too; it is both public and private; and it relies on both enactment and precedent. It draws, however, upon a common heritage of principles – due process, equality before the law, the right to be heard, *non bis in idem* (not being tried twice for the same thing) – which serve to mitigate the unfamiliarity of its procedures.

The legislation adopted by EU institutions under the Treaties – often called secondary or derived legislation – is made up of three types of legal act: **regulations**, **decisions** and **directives** (Article 288 TFEU). Somewhat confusingly, the same article also allows the institutions to deliver recommendations and opinions, but since these do not have binding force, they are not part of EU law in a strict sense. In the course of 2011, the EU institutions adopted a total of 536 legal acts (plus 1,491 acts of administrative law under the **comitology** process). Once enacted, legislation (dating back to 1952) is stored in the CELEX (*Communitatis Europeae Lex*) database, divided into 17 subject areas, and made available online. In September 2011, the **European Commission** estimated that this database contains a cumulative total of about 8,400 regulations and 2,000 directives.

Until the European Union was created by the 1992 **Maastricht Treaty**, what we now call 'EU law' was, strictly speaking, Community law, since only the three **European Communities** had the power to pass legislation. After Maastricht, the intergovernmental **pillars** for **Common Foreign and Security Policy** (CFSP) and **Justice and Home Affairs** (JHA) were able to adopt legally-binding acts as well, although by different legislative procedures. As a result, the notion of European law widened to encompass both traditional Community law and new, special types of act emanating from the two additional pillars: common strategies, joint actions and common positions in CFSP; and common positions and framework decisions in JHA. The **Lisbon Treaty**, which entered into force in December 2009, has now abolished the Maastricht pillars, merging the European Union and the Communities into a single structure, named after the former but inheriting the **legal personality** of the latter. The special types of act introduced by Maastricht for CFSP and JHA have likewise disappeared. See also **legal base**, **legal certainty**.

EU Military Committee (EUMC)

The EU Military Committee advises and supports the **Council of Ministers** on defence and military matters, operating under the authority of the **Political and Security Committee** (PSC), which covers the whole range of **Common Foreign and Security Policy** (CFSP) issues. The creation of an EU Military Committee was agreed by heads of government at the Helsinki **European Council** in December 1999, and the new body was established by a Council decision in January 2001.

The EUMC is formally composed of the 'chiefs of defence' of the 26 EU member states that participate in the **Common Security and Defence Policy** (CSDP) activity within CFSP. (Denmark does not take part in EU decisions or actions with defence implications.) In practice, the committee usually meets at the level of the 'military representatives' (MilReps) of the member states to the Union, who are normally three-star flag officers based in Brussels with the same ambassadorial status as the **permanent representatives** who sit in **COREPER**. The committee chooses its own chairman, who is then formally appointed, on its recommendation, by the Council for a three-year term. This chairman must be a 'four-star flag officer', namely, a full general, admiral or air chief marshal, and should 'ideally' be a former chief of defence. The chairman's 'authority is derived from the EUMC to which he is responsible'. He or she has the right to participate in PSC and Council meetings whenever military matters are being discussed and also serves as the military adviser to the **High Representative** for CFSP.

From the outset, the EU Military Committee has been supported by an EU Military Staff (EUMS), currently numbering around 200 people, nearly all of whom are officers on secondment from the member states' armed forces. An EUMC Working Group assists the full committee on military capabilities and force planning issues. The chairman of the Military Committee gives 'directives and guidance' to the director general of the Military Staff (who is normally a three-star flag officer), on behalf of the committee. The military representatives who sit on the committee also serve as the official-level members of the steering board of the **European Defence Agency** (EDA). In order to promote effective cooperation with the **North Atlantic Treaty Organization** (NATO), the EUMS hosts a 'NATO Liaison Team' and maintains an 'EU Cell' at **Supreme Headquarters Allied Powers Europe** (SHAPE). More importantly, the MilReps from the 21 countries that are members of both the EU and NATO normally 'double hat' as their representatives in both bodies.

The EUMC is responsible for providing the PSC and Council with advice and recommendations on all military matters arising within the EU. It undertakes 'early warning, situation assessment and strategic planning' and manages the day-to-day aspects of any military operations undertaken by the Union. In the latter case, when an operation is thought to be necessary, the Military Committee will, at the request of the PSC, instruct the Military Staff to draw up and present 'strategic military options'. The committee then evaluates these options, before passing them on to the PSC, with its view on how best to proceed. The PSC in turn makes a recommendation to the Council, formalized in a proposal from the High Representative. The Council can only adopt a decision unanimously: abstentions do not count and any member state may engage in 'constructive abstention', whereby it is not obliged to participate in any resulting action (although so far the latter has never happened). Once the Council has endorsed the launch of an operation in principle, the EUMC will instruct a commander to submit an operational plan for approval by the PSC. Implementation lies with a 'committee of contributors', composed of those member states whose governments have agreed to be involved in the operation.

Given that, for the foreseeable future, most EU interventions are likely to be predominantly civilian in character, and very few entirely military, the issue of the coordination between the military and civilian sides of crisis management needed to be addressed. It was decided to create a parallel body to the EUMC, known as the Committee for Civilian Aspects of Crisis Management (CIVCOM), also reporting to the PSC (and whose chairman is chosen by the High Representative). CIVCOM has in turn been assisted (since 2008) by a 40-strong Civilian Planning and Conduct Capability (CPCC), which is in effect the civilian equivalent of the EUMS, but on a smaller scale. A Crisis Management and Planning Directorate (CMPD) acts as interface between these military and civilian structures. (The situation is further complicated by the fact that a separate crisis response staff exists within the **European Commission**, although the latter's work is confined to humanitarian aid and disaster relief.)

Whether these arrangements would work effectively in the event of the EU launching a large-scale operation still remains to be tested. Some defence experts fear that the complex administrative framework might simply blunt the impact of military advice, without relieving any tensions between the military and civilian aspects of any operation. Others worry that a major operation, however coordinated, would simply require more manpower at the centre than the current EU bodies comprise. The updated **Helsinski Headline Goal** – known as the 'Headline Goal 2010' – envisages the deployment of multiple, combat-ready 'battlegroups', usually of 1,500 troops each, outside the formal structures of NATO. The scale of the manpower available at the centre to coordinate such an operation is very limited, especially by comparison with SHAPE, the military command structure of NATO in Europe, which has about 4,500 staff.

Conscious of the complexity and potential weakness of the interface between military and civilian crisis management structures, in particular, several governments have called on the High Representative for CFSP, Catherine Ashton, to propose the creation of a stronger, more integrated, 'planning and conduct' cell that would render the system more coherent. The 'Weimar Triangle' of French, German and Polish defence ministers put forward such a suggestion in December 2010, supported by the Italian and Spanish ministers five months later. All five governments reaffirmed this view in a letter sent by their foreign ministers to the High Representative in September 2011. However, so far, no progress has been made in this direction, mainly because of strong opposition from the British government. The implication of the 'letter of the five' was that, if the United Kingdom could not agree, the provisions on **Permanent Structured Cooperation in Defence** (PSCD) – the equivalent of **enhanced cooperation** in the defence field, introduced by the **Lisbon Treaty** – should be invoked for this purpose, allowing a subgroup of states to go ahead on their own.

The fact that there is no reference in the **Treaties** to the EUMC and CIVCOM or their supporting structures, which have largely depended so far on ad hoc arrangements, reflects a strong desire on the part of London and some other national capitals to avoid any '**communautization**' of defence. Although all these bodies have been moved over from the Council secretariat to the new **European External Action Service** (EEAS), which is independent of both the Council and Commission, they have been placed under the direct authority and responsibility of the High Representative, rather than as a routine part of the rest of the organization. Somewhat incongruously, however, the Situation Centre (SITCEN), which exchanges intelligence between the member states and provides intelligence for crisis management purposes, is part of the normal EEAS structure, reporting to its corporate board.

The Council decision setting up the EU Military Committee refers to the latter as 'the highest military body established within the Council', echoing the words of the Nice European Council in December 2000. There is no provision in the current list of configurations of the Council of Ministers for a separate 'Council of Defence Ministers', although defence ministers did meet periodically before the number of such configurations was reduced to ten in June 2002 and met informally twice a year after that. In December 2010, the High Representative convened a meeting of the **Foreign Affairs Council** (FAC) which was held in two parts, the first comprised of defence ministers and the second of development ministers. So, in effect, a Council of Defence Ministers, chaired by the High Representative, has now been re-established, in all but name, as a subdivision of the FAC. The plan is for it to meet twice formally and twice informally in any given year.

Euratom

See **European Atomic Energy Community** (EAEC or Euratom).

Euro

Although the 1992 **Maastricht Treaty** (Article 32(3) EC) referred to the **European Currency Unit** (ECU) as the name of the single currency to be introduced in stage three of **Economic and Monetary Union** (EMU), EU heads of government decided, at the Madrid meeting of the **European Council** in December 1995, to call the new currency the 'euro'. The legal status of the euro (which is made up of 100 cents) was fixed a year later by the European Council in Dublin, with the technical arrangements set out in two **regulations** adopted in June 1997. It was decided that the words 'euro' and 'cent' would always be rendered in the singular and that 'euro' would begin with a small 'e'. The symbol € and code EUR were chosen to signify the new currency.

Eleven member states were deemed by the European Council on 2 May

1998 to meet the **convergence criteria** for entry into EMU stage three. The euro was formally introduced as the single currency for these countries on 1 January 1999, with its value in terms of each national currency 'irrevocably fixed' on the basis of the closing market rates of the previous day. The national currencies in question became non-decimal subdivisions of the single currency. The euro was immediately used for all transactions by the **European Central Bank** (ECB) and for all new issues of government bonds; it also replaced the ECU on a one-for-one basis in all areas of the Union's finances. Three years later, on 1 January 2002, euro notes and coins entered into circulation in a massive changeover, lasting for two months, in which the 11 national currencies were physically withdrawn.

Euro banknotes are issued by the ECB in accordance with a standard design, in denominations of five, ten, 20, 50, 100, 200, and 500 euro. Euro coins are issued by national authorities, with a standard design on the front, but with different national motifs on the reverse, in denominations of one, two, five, ten, 20 and 50 cents, and one and two euros. Although the Netherlands and Finland have attempted to limit the use of one and two cent coins for reasons of convenience – and there are serious concerns about the use of 500 euro notes for money laundering – all denominations are legally valid throughout the **eurozone**. In 2011, the ECB estimated that 14.2 billion notes and 95.6 billion coins, with a combined value of € 870 billion, were in circulation in the 17 EU member states using the euro. Between a quarter and a third of coins in circulation in any one eurozone state are currently thought to have been issued by another state.

Eurobarometer

Eurobarometer – an anglicization of the French word *Eurobaromètre* – is the name given to a range of surveys of public opinion carried out across the European Union by polling organizations on behalf of the **European Commission**. A general six-monthly survey has been conducted and published since 1973, composed of both 'tracking' questions, used to establish overall trends, and questions that relate to current issues. A standard sample of 1,000 people is used in each member state, except for Luxembourg (600 people), the United Kingdom (1,000 in Great Britain, 300 in Northern Ireland), and Germany (1,000 in the former West Germany, 500 in the former East Germany). The regular surveys are supplemented by about 20 special surveys each year on particular issues – such as the **euro**, **enlargement**, defence, animal welfare and drug abuse – or among particular sectors of society, such as the young or the self-employed. Some less broadly-based 'flash' surveys on current issues are conducted by telephone polling, and occasional 'qualitative' studies are undertaken with focus groups. Although the standard of Eurobarometer surveys is very high and the range of topics treated wide, there is little evidence that they play any significant role in shaping the debate or decision-making on major policy issues in the European Union.

Eurobonds

The word 'Eurobond' (spelt with a capital 'E') originated in the early 1960s, to denote international bonds denominated in the currency of a country other than the one in which it was issued. The first Eurobond was issued in July 1963 to finance the development of the new *autostrade* (motorway) network in Italy. Such bonds may be issued either by sovereign governments or private companies, enabling the issuer to tap a broader and more liquid market for its debt than a single, national jurisdiction might allow. A 'Eurodollar' market developed particularly rapidly in London and became an important catalyst for the City's emergence as the largest financial centre in Europe.

The word 'eurobond' (with a lower-case 'e') refers to a concept, yet to be realized in practice, whereby some or all of the 17 member states of the EU using the single currency, the **euro**, would issue sovereign debt collectively, underpinned by the joint and several liability of all those countries participating. Instead of separate national markets for central government debt – the largest of which, Germany's, was worth € 2.1 trillion in 2010 – there would be a combined market of up to € 7.8 trillion, almost as big as that of the United States (€ 10.3 trillion). All but the most financially solvent of the **eurozone** states would certainly pay a lower interest rate on their debt, whilst all smaller member states would automatically benefit from economies of scale through their involvement in much larger issues. (As a result of the second factor, countries such as Austria, Luxembourg and the Netherlands would enjoy reduced rates.) The process of issuing of government debt and the cost of servicing it would thus be simultaneously eased. The introduction of eurobonds was first advocated by the European Primary Dealers Association (EPDA) in September 2008, and popularized as a means of helping resolve the **eurozone debt crisis** by Bruegel, a Brussels-based think tank, in May 2010.

Eurobonds would almost certainly need to be issued by a central authority, whether the **European Commission**, a 'European Monetary Fund', or, more probably, a dedicated European debt office. The issuing body would receive the proceeds of the bonds, which would be passed on to participating governments. The process would also need to be subject to a high degree of conditionality. In return for access to eurobond issuance, any eurozone state would be forced to prove that it was on course to bring its annual budget deficit and accumulated national debt down to the thresholds imposed by the **excessive deficit procedure** (EDP) – of respectively three and 60 per cent of gross domestic product (GDP) – and then hold them at or below those levels. The power to refuse access to eurobond issues could itself become a powerful sanction against any state that failed to follow the rules, significantly increasing its costs of borrowing.

A specific variant of the eurobond concept is the idea of creating a eurozone 'redemption fund'. Under this scheme, each eurozone state would remain responsible for the repayment of national debt below a certain threshold – in November 2011, the German Council of Economic Experts (GCEE) suggested logically that this figure should be set at 60 per cent of GDP – and all pre-existing debt above that level would be mutualized, reissued as eurobonds and repaid over a period of 20 to 25 years. Eurozone states would be debarred from taking on any additional debt above the 60 per cent ceiling in the future.

The European Commission put both of these eurobond options forward in a Green Paper on (what it dubbed) 'stability bonds', in November 2011 – as well as a third, less ambitious, suggestion for the joint issuing of national bonds, without the assumption of joint liability. The Commission argued that the introduction of eurobonds had the potential 'quickly [to] alleviate the current sovereign debt crisis, as the high-yield Member States could benefit from the stronger creditworthiness of the low-yield Member States'. It stressed, however, that 'for any such effect to be durable', eurobonds 'would have to be accompanied by parallel commitments' to the 'budgetary and structural adjustment' necessary to ensure sustainable public finances.

Although the French President, Nicolas Sarkozy, endorsed the Commission's overall approach, both the German government and the Bundesbank strongly opposed it – at least as a means of dealing with the eurozone debt crisis – arguing, on 'moral hazard' grounds, that eurobonds would in effect shift the burden of debt repayment from miscreant to virtuous states (especially Germany) and provide no automatic guarantee against any repeat of bad behaviour. The German Chancellor, Angela Merkel, reacted vehemently to the Commission Green Paper, calling it 'extraordinarily inappropriate'. The Austrian, Dutch and Finnish governments also expressed reservations, although in more guarded terms. Partly to assuage Sarkozy, however, Merkel has conceded that eurobonds could be acceptable after the crisis is over, once all eurozone member states have stabilized their public finances at an appropriate level, but she maintains that they can play no part in the resolution of the crisis itself.

One complicating factor is that, according to the Commission, the EU **Treaties** currently lack a sufficiently strong **legal base** to permit the introduction of eurobonds, at least in their first two forms, as a Union initiative. The 'no bail-out' clause (Article 125(1) TFEU), introduced by the 1992 **Maastricht Treaty** as part of the three-stage move to **Economic and Monetary Union** (EMU), prohibits member states from assuming the liabilities of other member states, as well as debarring the Union collectively from doing so. Any treaty change to allow eurobonds would, of course, require unanimous agreement, thus allowing Germany (or any other member state) to exercise a veto. Even if an attempt were made to invoke **Article 352** TFEU – which authorizes the **Council of Ministers** to take action to 'attain one of the objectives set out in the Treaties' even where the latter 'have not provided the necessary powers' – such action can only be taken on the basis of **unanimity**.

Eurocommunism

During the 1960s and 1970s, Communism in western Europe went through an important change. An increasing number of Communist parties asserted their ideological independence from the Soviet Union, by renouncing the Leninist philosophy of violent revolution and dictatorship of the proletariat, accepting the legitimacy of democratic pluralism, invoking separate 'national roads to socialism' and envisaging the possibility of entering coalition governments with non-socialist parties within existing political systems. This tendency, pioneered by the Italian Communist party, the *Partito Comunista Italiano* (PCI) and supported by the Spanish Communists, the *Partido Comunista de España* (PCE) after the restoration of democracy in 1976–7, became known as 'Eurocommunism'. It was a European political movement to the extent that, like **Christian Democracy** after the Second World War, it developed simultaneously in several, mainly southern European, countries, and (ironically) also defined itself in contradistinction to the political situation on the other side of the Iron Curtain. Eurocommunism was more pro-European than traditional Communism and reflected a post-1968 emphasis on the situation of 'minority' groups, particularly young people and women, rather than traditional industrial workers. It probably reached its apogée in 1977, when the leaders of the Italian, Spanish and French Communist parties met in Madrid to identify a 'new way' in European politics. (The Portuguese and Greek Communist parties, by contrast, preferred to hold to their traditional Stalinist positions.)

As early as 1956, PCI leader Palmiro Togliatti had advocated the notion of 'polycentrism', which would in effect deny the Communist Party of the Soviet Union (CPSU) a dominant or guiding role in defining the international Communist movement. His party became the pioneer in accepting the logic of competition within a multi-party democracy. Togliatti's successor in the 1970s, Enrico Berlinguer, took the philosophy one stage further with his active support for an 'historic compromise' with the dominant Italian Christian Democrats. It was this prospect which induced the Red Brigades in 1978 to kidnap and subsequently murder Aldo Moro, the veteran Italian Christian Democrat leader, who was on his way to vote for the first government to include Communist ministers since 1947. The terrorists' strategy succeeded in that, with the kidnapping, the formation of the new government was halted, and after Moro's death, the Christian Democrats moved away from cooperation with the PCI.

When **François Mitterrand** became French President in May 1981, he invited members of the French Communist party, the *Parti communiste français* (PCF), to enter government alongside his own Socialist party; their acceptance implicated them in the economic crisis which followed. With the failure of the 'historic compromise' to take off in Italy and the resignation of PCF ministers in France in 1984, the credibility of Eurocommunism declined. The electoral appeal of Communist parties in western Europe receded, matched by the growth of the Greens (who broke on to the scene at the 1984 European elections). After the collapse of Communism in central and eastern Europe in 1989–90, such parties became mainly marginal forces (as in France or Spain) or reinvented themselves as mainstream Social Democrats (as in Italy).

Eurocontrol

The European Organization for the Safety of Air Navigation, known as Eurocontrol, is an intergovernmental body established to promote and facilitate cooperation among participating states in all aspects of air traffic control and air safety. Founded in December 1960, with its headquarters in Brussels, Eurocontrol operates the Upper Area Control Centre at Maastricht in the Netherlands. All the member states of the European Union participate in Eurocontrol, together with 11 other European countries.

Despite the obvious rationale for its existence, Eurocontrol had difficulty from the start in establishing itself as the single agency responsible for air traffic control in western Europe, let alone for the continent as a whole. Certain countries proved very reluctant, for political and sometimes military reasons, to surrender national control of their airspace and, in some cases, even to press ahead with the technical coordination of different systems. With Eurocontrol hamstrung by the requirement for unanimity in its decision-making, airspace remained subject to several autonomous administrations operating from various centres, with a relatively low degree of central coordination. A revised Eurocontrol Convention, introduced in June 1997, did allow the possibility that some decisions might be taken by majority vote within the organization.

Starting in March 2000, EU heads of government decided to break with the impasse that had characterized Eurocontrol decision-making and instead use the supranational law-making potential of the Union as the vehicle for integrating air traffic control in Europe. The **European Council** invited the **European Commission** to establish a high-level advisory group on the creation of a 'Single European Sky', whose report, issued in November 2000, recommended that the airspace above the EU be gradually moved from a system based on national boundaries to one of 'functional airspace blocks' which might cross such boundaries. In parallel, a distinction should be drawn, at both EU and national levels, between regulation and service provision. In effect, the EU would be established as the regulator of upper airspace in Europe, with Eurocontrol as the service provider. Equally, the member states would be obliged to separate national supervisory authorities from air navigation service providers.

The Commission proposed two sets of **regulations** to establish a new regulatory framework along these lines: these were adopted jointly by the **European Parliament** and the **Council of Ministers**, under the **co-decision procedure**, in March 2004 and October 2009. In parallel, in October 2002, the European Union joined Eurocontrol, alongside the member states, in its own right. Functional airspace blocks are to be put in place by December 2012, to 'enable optimum use of airspace, taking into account air traffic flows', although any single block cannot be created without the agreement of all the member states affected. Under **comitology** arrangements, the Commission has established and chairs a Single Sky Committee, composed of two representatives of each member state, which can issue instructions to Eurocontrol as the Union's service provider. However, Eurocontrol continues to exist separately, with a wider membership than the EU 27. Equally, the Single European Sky is established 'without prejudice to Member States' **sovereignty** over their airspace and to the requirements of the Member States relating to public order, public security and defence matters'. The arrangement does not cover military operations or training.

Eurocorps

Even before the end of the **Cold War** brought about a new security situation in Europe, there was growing pressure on western European countries to play a bigger role in their own defence, through a greater degree of burden-sharing with the United States within the **North Atlantic Treaty Organization** (NATO). Capitalizing on this mood, President **François Mitterrand** and Chancellor **Helmut Kohl** announced in January 1988 that they proposed to deepen bilateral Franco-German cooperation in the defence and security fields, building on the provisions of the 1963 **Elysée Treaty**, signed exactly a quarter of a century before. They set up a Franco-German Security Council and committed themselves to develop a joint military capability for specific tasks, in parallel to, but formally outside, the NATO system. Under French command, based in Müllheim, Germany, and comprising 5,000 mechanized infantry, the resulting Franco-German Brigade became operational two years later. In October 1991, following the collapse of Communism in central and eastern Europe, the French and German leaders invited other states within the revitalized **Western European Union** (WEU) to join them in the development of a wider, pan-European version of the brigade. The establishment of a 'European corps' of some 35,000 troops was agreed upon in La Rochelle the following May. Headquartered in **Strasbourg**, the new Eurocorps started work in October 1993.

Since the La Rochelle agreement, Belgium (1993), Spain (1994), Luxembourg (1996) and Poland (2008) have all joined France and Germany as full, 'framework' members of the Eurocorps, pledging the use of 11 brigades or almost 60,000 troops to the force. In addition, seven countries – Austria, Finland, Greece, Italy, the Netherlands, Turkey and the United Kingdom – have become associated or 'contributing' nations. (The fact that Austria and Finland are outside NATO, and Turkey is outside the European Union, gives the Eurocorps additional value as a structure in which they can cooperate.) Two components of Eurocorps – a 1,000-strong complement in Strasbourg and the existing Franco-German Brigade – are under the direct operational command of its headquarters. However, the rest of the six framework nations' contributions remain under local control, on the basis that member states 'transfer authority' to Eurocorps as necessary.

Formally speaking, Eurocorps is a free-standing body which does not report to any other international organization. In practice, however, it quickly became a facility at the disposal of NATO and the European Union. Under agreements concluded in January and May 1993, Eurocorps forces could be assigned to either NATO or the (now defunct) WEU, and since the development of the **Common Security and Defence Policy** (CSDP) within the **Common Foreign and Security Policy** (CFSP), Eurocorps is also available for EU missions. In 2001, Eurocorps was awarded the right to serve as a 'high readiness force' at the disposal of the NATO system. It has already performed this role for the land component of the NATO Response Force (NRF) several times, most recently in 2011. (Since 1995, NATO has had its own **Allied Rapid Reaction Corps** (ARRC).)

Eurocorps actions have so far been centred upon the '**Petersberg tasks**' of humanitarian and rescue work, peacekeeping, and crisis management, including peacemaking, rather than on defensive or offensive military engagement. These tasks were originally assigned to the WEU in 1992 but transferred to the EU by the **Amsterdam Treaty** in 1997. The principal Eurocorps deployments have been in Bosnia and Herzegovina (SFOR, 1998–2000), Kosovo (KFOR, 2000), and Afghanistan (ISAF, 2004–5).

Eurocrats

Conflating the words 'Europe' and 'bureaucrat', 'Eurocrat' is a mildly pejorative term used to denote an official of the European Union. It was reputedly coined by Richard Mayne, a British journalist working for **Walter Hallstein**, the first Secretary General of the **European Commission**, in the late 1950s.

The total number of permanent or temporary officials in the various institutions or bodies of the EU is currently about 48,000. This figure has grown fairly consistently – from around 9,000 in 1970 to 17,000 in 1980, 24,000 in 1990, and 32,000 in 2000. Over a quarter of all EU staff are employed in connection with interpretation and translation between the 23 official **languages** of the Union. Some 25,000 of the 48,000 total are employed by the largest single EU institution, the European Commission, and another 5,000 now work in various **agencies**. The **European Parliament** employs 6,500 people in its general secretariat and **political groups**, whilst the **Council of Ministers** has 3,200 staff, the **European Court of Justice** (ECJ) 2,000, the **Court of Auditors** 900, and the **European Economic and Social Committee** (EESC) and the **Committee of the Regions** some 1,300 between them. The new **European External Action Service** (EEAS) started work in 2011 with 1,500 staff in Brussels, and another 1,400 people, mainly local agents, in the field. In addition, individual Members of the European Parliament (MEPs) also retain around 2,000 personal assistants and researchers, funded from their parliamentary allowances; since July 2009, those employed in Brussels (around 1,500) enjoy the status of EU 'contract' staff.

The number of posts occupied by officials within the various EU institutions is set down in each year's **Budget**. The Commission struggles constantly with the two arms of the EU's joint 'budgetary authority' – the Council and the Parliament – over the number of posts that it is granted. By contrast, since 1970, the Council and Parliament have had a gentlemen's agreement that they can each determine the size of their own staff complements (within certain limits) without interference from the other institution. On this basis, the staff of the Parliament has grown more than twice as rapidly than the Council's in recent years.

Eurocrats are divided into hierarchical categories, reflecting the type of work undertaken, with these categories in turn subdivided into grades. Until recently, posts were divided into a four-tier 'ABCD' hierarchy, reflecting French administrative arrangements adopted in 1948. As a result of major reforms to the **staff regulations** of EU officials, proposed by then Commission Vice-President Neil Kinnock and adopted by the Council, these four categories were merged in April 2004 into two simpler and substantially overlapping groups: Administrators (AD) and Assistants (AST). To encourage flexibility and reward talent, there are now 14 grades on a single spine, rather than 22 on four seperate spines. The AD category runs from (the highest) grade 16 to (the lowest) grade 5, and the AST category runs from (the highest) grade 11 to (the lowest) grade 1. The two categories overlap between grades 11 and 5. A head of unit may be appointed at AD9 level or above, rather than at the equivalent of AD12 before.

EU staff fall into three categories, depending on ease of recruitment and the security of tenure which results. Permanent officials are normally selected by publicly-advertised, open competitions (or *concours* in French), and in return they enjoy job security for life, like civil servants in many national administrations. It is sometimes possible to transfer into a European institution from a national civil service without a competition (especially at AD14 level and above). Temporary officials, who are known as 'temporary agents' (from the French phrase *agents temporaries*) can be employed at the discretion of the institution, although often they too are chosen by open competition, and enjoy job security for as long as their services are required: many work for political groups in the European Parliament, some for the ***cabinets*** of Commissioners, and others for EU agencies or on specific projects for the Commission. Under the Kinnock reforms, for the first time, temporary agents can move over to become permanent officials within the institutions after at least ten years' service, on the basis of internal competitions, if they can find an appropriate post. Finally, 'contract staff', previously known as *auxiliaries*, are short-term appointees, who sometimes successfully use their positions to become temporary or permanent officials.

Where they relate to more than one post, open competitions for recruitment have traditionally been organized by 'language of origin', rather than by nationality. Written tests are followed by interviews. 'Reserve lists' are then drawn up comprising successful candidates who may subsequently be offered specific posts as they become available. Until recently, the holding of *concours* was a fairly haphazard process, reflecting the particular needs of individual institutions at any given time. However, following the creation of an inter-institutional European Personnel Selection Office (EPSO) in 2003, the Union has been moving towards holding fewer, more general, open competitions, but on a more predictable basis. In 2009, it launched an annual competition for 'graduate-level' recruitment at AD5 in all languages. The first competition attracted nearly 52,000 applicants for 308 places on the reserve list. Among candidates from the larger member states, Germans were proportionately the most successful, securing 47 places on the list, and Britons the least successful, winning only seven places (several of whom were dual nationals). Online testing is now used at the start of the recruitment process, screening out nearly a third of candidates, with less emphasis than before on knowledge of EU institutions and policies, and more on reasoning and core skills.

Only citizens of the member states may normally be employed in the EU institutions, unless (as in the case of translators or interpreters) shortages of skills among EU citizens require otherwise. Proficiency in at least two official languages has traditionally been required for all grades; under the 2004 reforms, this was supplemented by the need for an adequate working knowledge of a third language in advance of promotion. For many years, the upper age limit for recruitment was 35 years, but this was raised to 45 in the 1990s and has now been abolished, reflecting the EU's new opposition to age discrimination.

Under a **protocol** to the **Treaties**, employees of the institutions of the European Union – like the staff of most other international organizations – enjoy certain privileges and immunities. The most important of these is that they are exempt from national income tax on their salary and expenses wherever they work, although they remain resident for tax purposes in their country of origin for all other income. In return, Eurocrats pay a special income tax to the Union itself, deducted at source; this is applied at marginal rates rising from 13 to 51 per cent, and averages 22 per cent. The proceeds are paid to the EU Budget, where they are offset against member states' contributions. For many officials working outside their home country (by definition the great majority), the impact of this tax is largely neutralized by a 16 per cent 'expatriation allowance'. Conversely a special 'crisis levy', now set at 5.5 per cent of salary, has been applied since the early 1980s. Modest family, child and schooling allowances are also provided, as is health, accident and life insurance (on the basis of obligatory contributions amounting to 1.8 per cent of salary).

The salaries and other benefits of EU officials are set down in the staff regulations and are adjusted each year to take account of inflation. There is a multiple of 6.8 times from the bottom to top of the EU salary scale in gross terms and 5.1 times net: it starts at € 2,700 (monthly) gross and the same figure net for an AST1 (step 1), rising to € 18,400 gross and € 13,900 net for an AD16 (step 3), the level of the most senior director-general.

One of the biggest changes introduced by the 2004 reforms was to move the point of entry for officials down the salary scale by two grades. (For AD officials, the shift was from the equivalent of AD7 to AD5, and from AD11 to AD9.) As the Commission has put it, the 'spirit of the reform' was 'to change the structure of officials' careers by paying them less at the beginning, but offering more promotions and scope for higher salaries at the end of the career'. However, in parallel, the objective was to realize 'considerable financial savings in real terms'. It is logically impossible therefore that the higher number of grades to be climbed as officials move up the career pyramid can be offset by more rapid promotion, except for the most successful. Indeed, the Commission has calculated that within the first six years, the 2004 reforms saved a cumulative total of € 3.0 billion in the EU salary bill.

EU officials contribute 11.6 per cent of their gross income to a jointly-financed final-salary pension scheme. The standard retirement age is now 63 (raised from 60 in 2004), and the compulsory retirement age is 65 (with the possibility to apply to continue to the age of 67), although officials may retire earlier than 63 on a reduced pension. Pension rights are accumulated at the rate of 1.9 per cent of final salary for every year worked, up to a maximum of

70 per cent, with a special bonus for any years worked over the standard retirement age.

One of the most controversial features of any international organization is the question of national balance among its staff. Within the EU institutions, especially the Commission, informal quotas are used to ensure a broadly proportionate distribution of at least senior AD posts among the various nationalities; at lower levels, the outcome is more haphazard. Among the nearly 13,000 AD-level permanent and temporary officials working in the European Commission in 2009, 11.3 per cent were French (compared with 12.5 per cent of the total EU population), 10.8 per cent German (16.4), 9.9 per cent Belgian (2.1), 9.9 per cent Italian (12.0), 8.2 per cent Spanish (9.2) and 6.6 per cent British (12.3). In general, the higher up the hierarchy, the less unbalanced the ratios become. There is still a significant over-representation, at virtually every level, of people from the founding **Six**, other than Germany. Belgians do especially well, perhaps because of their multilingual skills and physical proximity to career openings in Brussels. The British have only half their proportionate 'entitlement' at AD level, and an even lower share among ASTs. With fewer good applicants possessing the necessary language skills than many other countries, the UK has pursued an alternative, defensive strategy of seeking to obtain a disproportionately high share of the most senior posts.

When the Community institutions were first established, a general sense of uncertainty about their prospects and power diminished the appeal of becoming a Eurocrat to many 'high-flying' national civil servants who might easily have secured such posts. As Michele Cini has written, whilst 'the French government encouraged the ablest of its staff to join the Commission' – Jean-François Deniau and François-Xavier Ortoli, both of whom later became Commissioners, being striking examples – 'other member states were unable to persuade their top-grade officials to leave national office for Brussels' (*The European Commission*, 1996). Many of those who joined the Commission early on were young, enthusiastic and highly international in their outlook – and equally keen to start a new life away from home, unencumbered by national loyalties. A pattern was set which has been repeated with each **enlargement**, as new cohorts of ambitious 'young internationalists' arrive in Brussels. The average age of the new officials recruited from the ten new member states after the 2004 enlargement was only 33, whereas that of existing staff was some 15 years older. About half of all Eurocrats will reach retirement age over the next decade and a half.

EUROFOR

EUROFOR, the European Rapid Operational Force, is an international rapid-reaction force for military peace support operations, consisting of land forces from four member states of the European Union – France, Italy,

Portugal and Spain. Announced at the Lisbon ministerial meeting of the **Western European Union** (WEU) in May 1995 and established 18 months later, EUROFOR has a permanent multinational command located in Florence. A treaty signed in July 2000 by the four contracting parties gave the organization a more permanent status and clarified its role and relationship with the WEU and the **North Atlantic Treaty Organization** (NATO). When the WEU merged into the European Union in 2000–2, EUROFOR became available to the European Union, as a vehicle for helping deliver the latter's new **Common Security and Defence Policy** (CSDP).

EUROFOR has a core command staff of about 100 officers in Florence, able to draw upon up to 25,000 troops as necessary. A EUROFOR battalion can be mobilized at three to five days' notice. A 'high-level inter-ministerial committee', composed of senior defence and foreign ministry officials from the participating states, is responsible for all aspects of the force's operations. By a decision of this committee, it may be placed at the disposal of the EU, NATO or the **United Nations**, in pursuit of the **Petersberg tasks** of peacekeeping, crisis management or humanitarian assistance. The relationship between EUROFOR and the EU is managed through the official-level **Political and Security Committee** (PSC) within the **Council of Ministers**. EUROFOR has so far been involved in relatively few missions: the most notable were Albania (2001) and FYR Macedonia (2003–4).

A similar European Maritime Force, EUROMARFOR, has been created for naval operations. Rather than having a permanent headquarters, EUROMARFOR is hosted by the country holding its rotating command. EUROFOR is not to be confused with 'EUFOR', an acronym for 'European Union force' used as a prefix to identify certain specific missions under CSDP, such as EUFOR-RDC, the European Force in the Congo (2006). See also **Eurocorps**, **Allied Rapid Reaction Corps** (ARRC).

Eurogroup and Euro Summit

Soon after the designation of the 11 members states which would participate in stage three of **Economic and Monetary Union** (EMU) on 2 May 1998, the finance ministers from these countries began gathering informally in advance of full meetings of the **Ecofin Council**. This inner grouping – which first met at the Château de Senningen in Luxembourg on 4 June 1998 – was initially known as the 'euro-11' (and then the 'euro-12', following the admission of the Greek drachma to the **eurozone**). In September 2004, EU finance ministers designated this forum the 'Eurogroup', and chose one of their number – the Luxembourg prime minister and finance minister, Jean-Claude Juncker – as its chairman. (This post took effect in January 2005, running for two-year periods, rather than rotating with the six-monthly **presidency** of the **Council of Ministers**.) Representatives of the **European Commission** and **European Central Bank**

(ECB) were invited to participate in Eurogroup meetings, but (controversially) the finance ministers of member states outside the eurozone were not. Meetings of the Eurogroup are prepared, at official level, by senior civil servants from the relevant member states, who convene in the Eurogroup Working Group (EWG) of the EU **Economic and Financial Committee** (EFC).

The position of the Eurogroup has been formalized by the **Lisbon Treaty**, which entered into force in December 2009 (where it is styled the 'Euro Group'). A **protocol**, annexed to the treaty, states that the ministers from member states 'whose currency is the euro shall meet informally. Such meetings shall take place, when necessary, to discuss questions related to the specific responsibilities they share with regard to the single currency.' They would henceforth elect a president for a period of two and a half years, by simple majority of the eurozone states. The revised duration of the term of office appears to have been designed to enable it to run concurrently with the post of **President of the European Council** also introduced by the Lisbon Treaty. (These provisions were carried forward from the aborted **European Constitution**.) Juncker was formally elected as President of the Eurogroup, under the Lisbon Treaty, in January 2010.

From early on, Juncker has argued consistently in favour of giving the Eurogroup a small, independent secretariat, rather than relying on the EFC, Commission and Council secretariat for logistical support. He favours representation of the Eurogroup in its own right in some international economic fora, notably the International Monetary Fund (IMF), in parallel to the European Union. More ambitiously, only a few months after his election to the French Presidency in May 2007, Nicolas Sarkozy began to argue that the heads of government from Eurogroup countries should hold separate, regular 'eurozone summits', ideally before meetings of the full European Council. The German Chancellor, Angela Merkel, forcibly rejected the idea in January 2008, fearful that summit leaders might second-guess the monetary policy of the ECB and that such an arrangement would promote a '**two-speed Europe**'. However, with the onset of the economic and financial crisis, Sarkozy managed to convene the first eurozone summit in October 2008 in Paris, during the six-month French **presidency** of the Council, so establishing an important precedent. From then on, under continuing French pressure and in response to the growing **eurozone debt crisis**, the full-time President of the European Council, Herman Van Rompuy, was induced to call eurozone summits – officially known as 'informal meetings of heads of state and government of the euro area' – in May 2010, and March and July 2011.

Shortly after the July 2011 gathering, Chancellor Merkel abandoned her principled opposition to eurozone summits, proposing jointly with Sarkozy, at a bilateral meeting in August 2011, that they should take place at least twice a year and constitute the core of a reinforced system of **European economic**

governance, under Van Rompuy's chairmanship. Both Van Rompuy and Merkel, unlike Sarkozy, were initially said to be keen to avoid back-to-back meetings of the eurozone leaders with the European Council, for fear that they might drain the latter of political substance, in the way that Eurogroup finance ministers' meetings have increasingly done to the Ecofin Council. However, van Rompuy eventually agreed to such meetings being held (usually) on a back-to-back basis, so long as the European Council, involving all 27 member states, was held first.

Merkel's resistance to Sarkozy's campaign for eurozone summits was weakened inter alia by the refusal of the new British prime minister, David Cameron, to attend such meetings and to act as a counterpoise to French thinking, as she had wished. Cameron's predecessor, Gordon Brown, had sought and secured guest status at the first summit in October 2008, reflecting the size of the UK economy. Brown even exercised influence on the wording of the communiqué issued by the eurozone leaders on that occasion. Prior to that, he had been extremely discomforted by his exclusion from the Eurogroup finance ministers' meetings and fought unsuccessfully for the UK's inclusion. His request was rebuffed by the (then) French finance minister, Dominique Strauss-Kahn, with words that subsequently proved ironic: 'Gordon, in a marriage, you don't admit strangers to the bedroom.'

The new arrangements were formalized at a further eurozone summit, held in effect in two parts – on 23 and 26 October 2011. The conclusions stated that henceforth there would be 'regular Euro Summit meetings', comprising the heads of state or government of eurozone countries, together with the President of the European Commission. It was agreed that these meetings 'would take place at least twice a year' and be held 'if possible . . . after European Council meetings'. A 'President of the Euro Summit' was to be designated 'at the same time as the European Council elects its President and for the same term of office'. Until the next such appointment was made in Spring 2012, 'the President of the European Council [would] chair the Euro Summit meetings'. Behind the scenes, Van Rompuy argued strongly that, for the integrity of the system, the two posts of President of the European Council and President of the Euro Summit should always and automatically be held by the same person, and that he or she need not come from a eurozone member state. The French President took the opposite position. The final wording was ambiguous on these points and will still need to be tested in practice.

The October 2011 eurozone summit also made important changes to the operation of the Eurogroup. The communiqué stated that, at the expiry of Juncker's mandate in July 2012, a decision would be taken on whether his successor 'should be elected [from] among members of the Eurogroup or be a full-time President based in Brussels'. It went on: 'Clear lines of responsibility and reporting between the Euro Summit, the Eurogroup and the preparatory bodies will be established.' The Presidents of the Euro Summit, Eurogroup and Commission will meet 'at least once a month', inviting the President of the ECB to join them, if appropriate. In parallel, the EWG would be upgraded, becoming the preparatory body for both the Euro Summit and the Eurogroup, and drawing on a strengthened EFC staff. The EWG would also have a full-time, Brussels-based chairman, elected at the same time as the person chairing the EFC (and by implication potentially the same individual). Reflecting the EWG's growing importance, a special subgroup of this body was tasked in December 2011 with negotiating the new intergovernmental treaty among the eurozone states (with its membership enlarged to include representatives of all other member states and the **European Parliament**). Meeting in January 2012, this sub-group devised the intergovernmental **Fiscal Compact Treaty** that was signed by 25 of the 27 EU member states on 2 March 2012. (The new treaty recognized the existence of the Euro Summit, whilst avoiding the question of whether meetings of the latter should be held before or after European Councils.)

Before it became associated with the eurozone, the term 'Eurogroup' was previously used, from 1968 to 1993, to denote a framework for defence cooperation between European members of the integrated military command of the **North Atlantic Treaty Organization** (NATO). Defence ministers of the European countries belonging to NATO, with the exception of France and Iceland, decided to set up an informal twice-yearly meeting in order to coordinate their positions more closely on security issues and thus to strengthen Europe's contribution to the Atlantic Alliance. The ministerial meetings of this Eurogroup, the chairmanship of which rotated annually, were prepared by an ad hoc committee of ambassadors, supported by a staff group, both located at NATO headquarters in Brussels. The framework spawned a series of subgroups, dealing with cooperation in operational concepts, tactical communications, logistics and joint training.

Euro-myths

'Euro-myths' is a general term, invented in the early 1990s, to characterize stories about the plans of 'barmy Brussels bureaucrats', usually representing a threat to the national way of life, that regularly feature in the British press. As a form of subversive, anti-bureaucratic humour, Euro-myths have extraordinary resilience and vitality, especially in such an adversarial political and media culture as Britain's. The most effective accusations are often those which mix wit or wordplay with half-truth to make their point. A good example was the story, '*Nein, nein, nein: Brussels says number's up for 999*', published in 2005, which claimed that Britain would have to drop its historic emergency telephone number in favour of the Europe-wide alternative, 112, when in fact the two numbers could be used in parallel. Any attempt to set such a story straight is almost always less arresting than the original claim, so its chances of being reported are slight. In the case of a 1994 EU regulation on the permissible size, weight and curvature of bananas for sale, which often occasions amusement, it is rarely, if ever, mentioned that the UK had similar restrictions of its own, dating from before the country joined the European Community, for both bananas and cucumbers.

The London office of the **European Commission** – which devotes part of its website to the issue – published 40 letters in national newspapers in a two-year period in an attempt to correct reports as diverse as that smokers would be banned from applying for jobs, yogurt was to be renamed as 'fermented milk pudding', and cows would have to sleep on mattresses. Although not exclusively a British phenomenon – there was recently a groundless fear in Italy that the EU was about to ban the hazelnut spread Nutella – the abundance and variety of Euro-myths in the United Kingdom greatly exceed anything to be found in any other member state. They are both a symptom and a cause of the low esteem in which the institutions of the European Union, especially the Commission, are generally held in Britain.

Europa

In ancient times, 'Europa' was both a person and a geographical expression. The myth of Europa is well known: the daughter of Agenor, King of Tyre, she attracted the attentions of Zeus. In order to seduce her, he transformed himself into a bull and, having enticed her onto his back, carried her away to Crete. There she eventually married the King of Crete and bore several sons, one of whom was King Minos, the builder of the labyrinth.

Geographically, Europa originally denoted the mainland of Greece, as opposed to the islands. As Greek colonization extended north and west, so the territory known as Europa was similarly extended, in contradistinction to Asia and Libya (North Africa). This tripartite division of the known world was the one adopted by Herodotus and later by the Romans. The growth of the Roman Empire brought with it a further extension of Europa as far as the Rhine to the north, the Straits of Gibraltar to the south and the British Isles to the west.

Europe's eastern frontier was always more problematic, as indeed it has remained. In the absence of an obvious geophysical feature, most ancient geographers settled on the River Don as the frontier. Only centuries later did the Ural Mountains become the accepted eastward limit of Europe.

Neither myth nor geography can shed much light on the origin of the word 'Europa'. Some etymologists have traced it back to a Semitic word, *Erib,* meaning darkness (namely, the direction in which the sun set). But if the word is of Greek origin, it means 'broad-faced' (possibly an attribute of the moon goddess), and there the trail goes cold.

Europe des patries

The phrase *'Europe des patries'* – variously translated in English as a 'Europe of nation states' or 'Europe of homelands' – is associated with French President **Charles de Gaulle** and encapsulates a model of European integration in which states are the essential building-blocks and remain pre-eminent in decision-making. The concept reflects a strong preference for **intergovernmentalism** over **supranationalism** in the building of Europe. It is difficult to trace any explicit use by de Gaulle of the phrase *'Europe des patries'* and indeed he claimed at least twice towards the end of his presidency that he had never employed it. The General's preference was instead for a *'Europe des États'* – a 'Europe of states'. The phrase was, however, used by his first prime minister, Michel Debré, as early as January 1959 and on several subsequent occasions.

European anthem

A special orchestral arrangement by Herbert von Karajan of the main theme of the last movement of Beethoven's Ninth Symphony – his setting of Friedrich Schiller's 'Ode to Joy' for choir, soloists and orchestra, composed in 1824 – was adopted in January 1972 by the **Council of Europe** as the European anthem. The *Ode an die Freude* was written by Schiller in 1785 as a 'celebration of the brotherhood of man'. Like the **European flag**, the anthem was appropriated for the use of the Community institutions, by the Milan **European Council** of EC heads of government in June 1985, following a recommendation of the Adonnino Committee for a People's Europe. See also **symbols of the Union.**

European army

The concept of a European army – in the form of a free-standing military capability existing at pan-European level and controlled by an independent supranational authority – was first given serious voice by **Winston Churchill**, the former British wartime prime minister, on 11 August 1950. He successfully moved a resolution in the Consultative Assembly of the **Council of Europe** calling for 'the immediate creation of a unified European army, subject to proper European democratic control and acting in full cooperation with the United States and Canada'.

The background to Churchill's proposal was the outbreak of the Korean War on 25 June 1950 and the worsening situation in central and eastern Europe, as the Communist parties strengthened their hold. He envisaged a European army as offering a security framework in which the new Federal Republic of Germany would be able to rearm without alarming its neighbours. In a letter to President Truman two days after his Strasbourg speech, Churchill wrote that such an army – in which the 'British, and I trust, the Americans, will be strongly represented' – was necessary to avoid continental

Europe becoming a neutral 'no-man's land between Britain and its American air bases, and the Soviet armies'. The following month, Washington proposed instead that German divisions be allowed to serve within the **North Atlantic Treaty Organization** (NATO), founded the previous year. (In the event, West Germany did not become a member until 1955.)

Despite American hesitation, Churchill's speech appears to have influenced the thinking of **Jean Monnet** and the French prime minister, René Pleven, who, two months later, tabled the so-called **Pleven Plan** for a **European Defence Community** (EDC), with a European army directed by autonomous supranational institutions akin to those being created from the new **European Coal and Steel Community** (ECSC). When Churchill became prime minister for a second time in October 1951, he maintained the position of the outgoing Labour government and declined to join **the Six** in negotiations for an EDC. Although Churchill remained committed to doing 'everything possible' to promote a European army, he no longer saw it as having an Anglo-American component. The EDC Treaty was signed in May 1952, but growing hostility to the idea in France led to its eventual rejection by the National Assembly in August 1954. The following year, the existing, intergovernmental **Brussels Treaty** Organization was upgraded into the **Western European Union** (WEU).

Following the EDC rebuff, the idea of a European army disappeared from mainstream political discourse in Europe for more than three decades. Only with the end of the **Cold War** did the concept of a distinctive European military capability revive, and then in a highly constrained, intergovernmental format, lacking the supranational character of the proposals in the early 1950s. The 1992 **Maastricht Treaty** provided for the new European Union to address security issues for the first time, through its **Common Foreign and Security Policy** (CFSP). It envisaged 'the eventual framing of a common defence policy, which might in time lead to a common defence'. The WEU was to be 'developed as the defence component of the European Union' (Declaration on WEU). In parallel, in October 1991, France and Germany announced the creation of a joint **Eurocorps** open to other WEU countries. Subsequently the WEU was itself superseded by the Union's **Common Security and Defence Policy** (CSDP), which was made part of CFSP by the 2001 **Nice Treaty**. See also **Permanent Structured Cooperation in Defence** (PSCD).

European Atomic Energy Community (EAEC or Euratom)

Usually known as Euratom, the European Atomic Energy Community was established by **the Six** under a treaty signed in Rome on 25 March 1957, the same day as the better-known **Treaty of Rome** founded the **European Economic Community** (EEC). The object of Euratom, in the words of Article 1 EAEC, was to create 'the conditions necessary for the speedy establishment and growth of nuclear industries'. The principal means were a 'nuclear **common market**' involving the free movement of specialized materials and equipment, a **common customs tariff**, **free movement of capital** for investment in nuclear energy, freedom of employment for specialists in the sector, promotion of research and investment, nuclear inspection, the sharing of information, and cooperation with third countries. Like the EEC Treaty, the Euratom Treaty was concluded for an unlimited period and is still in operation.

After the failure of the **European Defence Community** (EDC) in August 1954, it became clear that if the impetus of European integration were to be maintained, progress would need to be made on some less politically controversial front. The **Spaak Committee**, established by the **Messina Conference** in June 1955, proposed that the Six launch a combination of a general **common market** and **customs union**, drawing on the **Beyen Plan**, and an atomic energy community along the lines of the existing **European Coal and Steel Community** (ECSC). Accordingly, two parallel treaties were drafted (among others by **Pierre Uri**), of which the text on atomic energy was thought by many at the time to be the more important.

The enormous potential of atomic energy was fully appreciated in the early 1950s, as was the possible damage that could be done if fissile materials were to fall into the wrong hands. It was also realized that, like coal and steel in an earlier generation, the possession of nuclear weapons could be decisive in the event of war and the French were nervous about any possibility of nuclear weapons being held in German hands. Western Europe's reliance on the Middle East for its energy needs was underlined in the most dramatic way possible when, as a result of Egyptian president Gamal Abdel Nasser seizing control of the Suez Canal in July 1956, petrol rationing had to be introduced (see **Suez crisis**). All these factors pointed in the direction of a common effort on the part of the Six to develop atomic energy.

The institutions of Euratom were set up on the same quadripartite model that had served for the ECSC and were to be applied in parallel to the EEC (Article 2 EAEC). They comprised an independent executive commission, a legislative council and a supervisory parliamentary assembly, with legal disputes adjudicated by a court. The assembly and court were common to all three Communities – in the form of the **European Parliament** and **European Court of Justice** (ECJ) – but Euratom initially had its own Brussels-based Commission and its own Council. The 1965 **Merger Treaty** replaced the latter two institutions (from July 1967) with the common **European Commission** and EC **Council of Ministers**. As was the case with the EEC Commission provided for under the Treaty of Rome, the Euratom Commission was less able than the ECSC's High Authority to exercise power independently of the Council. The **legal acts** used by Euratom and the EEC were to be the same, namely **decisions**, **directives** and **regulations**.

Rather than having six members, the college of the Euratom Commission was comprised of only five individuals, as Luxembourg had no national nuclear programme. The first President of the Euratom Commission resigned for reasons of health soon after taking office. His successor, Etienne Hirsch, was a distinguished technocrat from the French Fourth Republic, but he soon clashed repeatedly with the new French President, **Charles de Gaulle**, who was deeply suspicious of Euratom's pretensions. From having been the prime advocate of cooperation in the nuclear field in 1956–8, attempting to replicate its own domestic atomic energy commission at supranational level and channel research funding into its national programme, France became extremely cautious of Euratom. De Gaulle in effect prevented it developing in a number of key areas – notably those with any military implications or which might involve cooperation with the United States – and as political attention shifted to the development of the EEC, momentum behind Euratom waned.

However, under the Euratom Treaty, the European Commission has continued to undertake important, if largely unsung, work in promoting cooperation, safety, security and waste management in the nuclear field. Its safeguard system helps ensure that civil nuclear materials are not diverted from the uses for which they are intended. The Euratom Supply Agency, established in 1960 and based in Luxembourg, is tasked with ensuring a 'regular and equitable supply' of nuclear fuels for users within the European Union. It has first option on the acquisition of EU-produced ores and special fissile materials, as well as an exclusive right to conclude contracts for the supply of such materials from inside or outside the Union.

The European Commission's Joint Research Centre (JRC) was established under Article 8 EAEC, which provides for a Joint Nuclear Research Centre. The JRC undertakes original research in a wide range of scientific fields, including nuclear safety, remote sensing by satellite, materials research, information technology and systems engineering. It has eight institutes spread over five sites, in Ispra (Italy), Petten (the Netherlands), Karlsruhe (Germany), Geel (Belgium) and Seville (Spain). Since 1995, the JRC has been required to compete for research contracts, including those put out to tender by the Commission itself. It has also been able to participate in 'research networks' with other public or private institutes in the member states.

Euratom initially established the Joint European Torus (JET) project, based at Culham, Oxfordshire (United Kingdom), which opened in 1983 and is one of only four large-scale nuclear fusion projects in the world and the largest 'tokamak' reactor in existence. JET is now managed by the UK Atomic Energy Authority (UKAEA), on behalf of the partners in the European Fusion Development Agreement (EFDA) – which brings together Euratom and national research bodies – with a view to developing nuclear fusion as a cleaner, safer, more efficient source of nuclear energy than nuclear fission. The successor project to JET is the International Thermonuclear Experimental Reactor (ITER), to be built at Cadarache in south-west France. Because of the scale and cost of ITER, the EU is undertaking the project in consortium with the governments of the United States, Japan, China, India, Russia and South Korea. As the host party, however, the Union will contribute 45 per cent of the total cost, with the other partners paying only nine per cent each.

During the drafting of a **European Constitution** by the **Convention on the Future of Europe** in 2002–3, there was a discussion about whether the EAEC Treaty should be merged into the proposed single text replacing the other treaties. However, it was decided to keep Euratom as a separate Community to the Union, based on a free-standing treaty, and this principle was maintained when the text of the **Lisbon Treaty** was finally agreed.

European Bank for Reconstruction and Development (EBRD)

The European Bank for Reconstruction and Development, based in London, was established in May 1990 to promote structural reform and the transition to market economies in the countries of central and eastern Europe and the former Soviet Union. It is not to be confused with the **European Investment Bank** (EIB) or the **European Central Bank** (ECB).

The first distinctively 'post-**Cold War**' institution in Europe, the EBRD was created as a response to the collapse of Communism in central and eastern Europe. In October 1989, French President **François Mitterrand** proposed the creation of a specialized development bank to promote economic restructuring and the liberalization of markets in the region, which would in turn help to underpin the transition to democracy. Less explicitly, the French government perhaps hoped to create a 'European' body that would counterbalance potential American economic and political influence. Many Western governments were initially sceptical, arguing that assistance could as effectively be directed to the region through bilateral channels or through established international agencies, such as the International Monetary Fund (IMF), the World Bank or the EIB. However, with strong German support, the proposal was endorsed by the Strasbourg meeting of the **European Council** in December 1989. It was agreed that membership of the EBRD would be open to non-European countries – notably the United States, Canada, Mexico, Japan, South Korea, Israel and Egypt – but that the member states of the European Community, the Community itself and the EIB would together hold a majority shareholding (51 per cent). The US is the largest single shareholder (with 10 per cent), followed by France, Germany, Italy, Japan and the United Kingdom (with 8.5 per cent each).

The Strasbourg decision resulted in the EBRD being given a mandate 'to foster the transition towards open market-oriented economies and to promote private and entrepreneurial initiative in the central and eastern European countries committed to and applying the principles of multi-party democracy, pluralism and market economies'. In April 1990, Jacques Attali, special adviser to President Mitterrand, and widely credited as the originator of the idea, was appointed as president of the EBRD (against opposition from the US and Japan, but with British support in exchange for French backing for London as the EBRD's headquarters). The EBRD began operations a year later.

In May 1990, the EBRD had a membership of 32 lender and eight borrower countries. The latter, known as its 'countries of operation', were initially Bulgaria, Czechoslovakia, East Germany, Hungary, Poland, Romania, the former Soviet Union (including the **Baltic states**) and the former **Yugoslavia**. The disintegration of various countries subsequently increased the number of recipients to 29 today (with the number of lenders remaining at 32). The Czech Republic became a lender country in 2007, having previously been only a borrower; Turkey migrated in the opposite direction in 2008.

The EBRD operates according to sound commercial principles and seeks to complement the private sector, not compete with other sources of finance. The EBRD's subscribed capital was doubled in April 1997 to 20 billion ECUs (now euro), and its lending – which is usually in the range of € 5.0 to 250 million – may not exceed this amount. At least 60 per cent of lending in any country must be to private-sector projects. The EBRD deals directly with project sponsors as well as with governments, and offers loans at near-market rates, representing up to 35 per cent of any project. It may also take equity stakes or offer loan guarantees. In 2010, it signed 386 projects worth over € 9.1 billion. The EBRD is both a merchant bank, dealing with commercially competitive borrowers, and a development bank, promoting the development of infrastructure in recipient countries, with a commitment to respect the environment. The EBRD plays an important part in improving nuclear safety: it manages the Chernobyl Shelter Fund, created in 1997, and contributed € 135 million in 2008 (in a grant from its profits) to the decommissioning of the plant. In 2006, the EBRD decided that it would phase out lending to the countries of central and eastern Europe which had joined the EU, in order to concentrate on some of the former Soviet republics and the Balkans. This process should be complete by 2015. In May 2011, the **Group of Eight** (G8) summit in Deauville invited the EBRD to begin operations in North Africa, following the events of the 'Arab spring'. It is expected that lending in the region might amount to about € 3.0 billion per year.

The EBRD has a board of governors, comprising one governor (usually the finance minister), plus an alternate, from each member state. The governors elect the bank's president, who manages its day-to-day business, under the guidance of a board of directors. Jacques Attali, the first president, was forced to resign in June 1993, following a media campaign against alleged profligacy. His immediate successors were Jacques de Larosière (1993–8), a former managing director of the IMF, and Horst Köhler (1998–2000), who later became IMF managing director and then German President. Jean Lemierre and Thomas Mirow, the two presidents since 2000, have been lower-profile figures, perhaps reflecting the declining visibility of the bank.

The EBRD holds an annual meeting each April or May, usually rotating between London and one of the 34 cities in which it has regional offices in countries of operation. The bank employs 1,500 staff and its four official languages are English, Russian, German and French. It publishes an annual *Transition Report*, which gives a unique overview of the process of economic reform in the countries to which it lends.

European Central Bank (ECB)

The core institution of **Economic and Monetary Union** (EMU) in Europe is the European Central Bank, which sets monetary policy for those EU member states that have adopted the single currency, the **euro**. Based in Frankfurt, the ECB was established by the 1992 **Maastricht Treaty** and came into operation on 1 June 1998, seven months before the start of stage three of EMU, when monetary **sovereignty** was pooled for participating states. The precursor to the ECB was the **European Monetary Institute** (EMI), created in January 1994, which operated for most of stage two of EMU.

Under Article 282(1) TFEU, introduced by the Maastricht Treaty, the ECB and the national central banks of all the EU member states together constitute a 'European System of Central Banks' (ESCB). Under Article 127 TFEU, the 'primary objective' of the system, which binds only stage-three members, is 'to maintain price stability' and its 'basic tasks' are to 'define and implement the monetary policy of the Union', to conduct foreign exchange operations, to hold and manage the official foreign reserves of the participating member states, and to promote the 'smooth operation of payment systems'. It should also contribute to the 'smooth conduct' of national policies for 'the prudential supervision of credit institutions and the stability of the financial system'. Overall, it acts 'in accordance with the principle of an open market economy with free competition'.

Under Article 128 TFEU, the ECB has the 'exclusive right' to authorize the issue of euro banknotes, which may be issued by either the ECB itself or the national central banks. The ECB's approval is required for the issuing of euro coins by member states, the denominations and specifications of which are laid down by the **Council of Ministers** – in practice, the **Ecofin Council** (Council of Economic and Finance Ministers) – after consulting the ECB and European Parliament.

A statute setting out the detailed structure and role of the ESCB and ECB is annexed as a **protocol** to the **Treaties.** Under Article 30 of that Statute, states participating in stage three of EMU are required to provide the ECB with foreign reserve assets of up to € 50 billion, each state being compensated by an equivalent claim on the ECB.

Under Article 282 TFEU, the ESCB is itself 'governed by the decision-making bodies of the European Central Bank' – in other words, the national central banks of EMU stage-three members are legally subordinate to the ECB. Under Articles 130–31 TFEU, they must also have been made legally independent of their individual national governments. Under Article 14 of the statute, they are obliged to 'act in accordance with the guidelines and instructions of the ECB'.

Only EMU stage-three central banks are allowed to participate in the ECB's decision-making bodies: the Governing Council and Executive Board. The Governing Council brings together the national **central bank governors** of the **eurozone**, together with the six members (President, Vice-President and four others) who comprise the (separate) Executive Board. The six members of the Executive Board are 'persons of recognized standing and professional experience in monetary or banking matters', serving for a non-renewable term of eight years. They are appointed by the **European Council**, which decides by using **qualified majority voting** (QMV), on a recommendation from the Council of Ministers, after consulting both the Governing Council of the ECB and the **European Parliament**, which has decided to institute public hearings (Article 11(2), ECB Statute). Before the Lisbon Treaty, they were appointed by the 'common accord' of the heads of government, rather than by QMV in the European Council. The six individuals become full-time employees of the ECB for the duration of their mandate.

The key decisions of the ECB are taken by its Governing Council, which 'shall formulate the monetary policy of the Union including, as appropriate, decisions relating to intermediate monetary objectives, key interest rates and the supply of reserves' (Article 12, ECB Statute). The Executive Board's role is to 'implement monetary policy in accordance with the guidelines and decisions laid down by the Governing Council'. The Executive Board may give instructions to the national central banks for this purpose. Equally, the Governing Council may delegate certain powers to the Executive Board. The Executive Board is 'responsible for the current business of the ECB'.

The Governing Council is required to meet at least ten times a year, and in practice it meets at least monthly and often every two weeks. The president-in-office of the Ecofin Council and a member of the **European Commission** are able to participate in its meetings, but without the right to vote. Within the Executive Board, each of the six members has one vote and the body, if it needs to vote, also acts by simple majority. The President of the ECB chairs both the Governing Council and the Executive Board, and has a casting vote in the event of a tie.

The Governing Council normally acts by simple majority, the quorum being two-thirds. Initially, each member state and each individual on the Executive Board had one vote. However, as the number of eurozone countries grew, the larger member states concluded that the 'one state, one vote' principle would become unsustainable. The issue was highlighted in 2002–3, when the German and French central bank governors were in effect outvoted by a coalition of smaller countries in their attempt to raise interest rates. The European Council changed the voting system in 2003 to one in which the five largest eurozone members collectively now have four votes between them (rotating annually), with the others (currently 12) having 11 votes between them. The categorization of states is determined by an assessment (at least every five years) of their gross domestic product (GDP) and volume of financial assets. Once the eurozone exceeds 21 member states, a three-tier system will be introduced. (For a more detailed analysis of ECB voting, see Simon Hix and Bjørn Høyland, *The Political System of the European Union*, 2011.) Certain decisions in the Governing Council allow votes to be weighted in accordance with participating states' share of the ECB's capital. In such cases, a majority is at least half the shareholders and two-thirds of the subscribed capital.

To differentiate the combination of the ECB and the national central banks of the eurozone countries (represented on the Governing Council) from the wider ESCB, the ECB decided to introduce the term 'Eurosystem' to refer specifically to the former. However, the central bank governors of all 27 EU member states, whether inside or outside the eurozone, meet together in an advisory General Council of the ECB. This latter body also sits in its entirety on the General Board of the **European Systemic Risk Board** (ESRB), created in January 2011. The ESRB is responsible for providing 'macro-prudential oversight of the financial system' as a whole and early warning of threats to its stability.

Legally-binding acts adopted by the ECB take the form of **regulations** and **decisions**. The Bank may also make recommendations and deliver opinions (both of which are non-binding). In certain circumstances, it may impose fines on undertakings that do not comply with its regulations and decisions (Article 132 TFEU). The ECB is required to draw up an annual report to the European Council, the Council of Ministers, the European Parliament and the Commission (Article 284(3) TFEU). It has a general right to be consulted on all legislation, European or national, in its areas of competence (Article 127 TFEU).

So far, there have been three presidents of the ECB. Under a heavily-criticized 'political agreement' within the European Council in May 1998, the outgoing EMI president, Wim Duisenberg (1935–2005), was appointed to head the ECB on the understanding that he would 'not wish' to serve the full eight-year term. He resigned in November 2003 and was replaced, as previously agreed, by a 'French citizen', namely Jean-Claude Trichet, the outgoing governor of the Banque de France. Trichet served for the following eight years, exercising great influence on the development of the institution and its policies. There was a widespread anticipation that he in turn would be replaced by Bundesbank president Alex Weber – partly as a means of reassuring German public opinion during the evolving **eurozone debt crisis** – until ironically the latter's increasingly explicit criticism of ECB policy led to uncertainty enveloping the succession. In April 2011, Weber suddenly announced his resignation from the Bundesbank and thus the ECB Governing Council, leaving the way open for the only other obvious contender, Mario Draghi, governor of the Italian central bank, to be appointed as the ECB's third President, starting in November that year. Jürgen Stark, a highly influential German member of the ECB Executive Board, followed Weber in resigning in September 2011.

The point of dispute that led to the departure of Weber and Stark did not relate to the ECB's core function of delivering low inflation. During its first 13 years of existence, the Bank's price stability objective was realized with striking success. Despite major economic instability within and outside the Union at different points during this period, inflation across the eurozone averaged 2.0 per cent – thus almost exactly meeting the 'less than 2.0 per cent, but close to 2.0 per cent' target the Bank had set itself. The ECB even surpassed the Bundesbank's achievement in Germany for the years before the single currency. The relatively strong performance of the euro on currency markets during this period – rising from a low of $ 0.9 in 2001 to a high of $ 1.6 in 2008, and then only falling back to $ 1.3 over the next three years – was a reflection, more than anything else, of ECB success in containing inflation.

As Trichet himself pointed out at a special retirement event in the Frankfurt opera house in October 2011, his eight years as ECB President can be divided neatly into two four-year phases. From 2003 to 2008, the Bank 'had to preserve stability after the bursting of the dot-com bubble and in the face of high and volatile oil and energy prices', he said. 'We fought hard to preserve the fiscal governance of the euro area, at a time when the three major countries [Germany, France and Italy] wanted to weaken the **Stability and Growth Pact**.' Proving itself 'fiercely independent', the Bank chose, starting in December 2005, to increase its interest rate ('refinancing rate') – by a long series of 11, mainly quarter-point, moves – from 1.0 to 3.25 per cent, in the face of some criticism by governments and markets. The final decision to raise the rate by 0.25 per cent in July 2008, immediately before the developing crisis was decisively worsened by the bankruptcy of Lehman Brothers, aroused particular controversy.

However, quickly thereafter, the Bank's interest-rate policy went into reverse, with its refinancing rate lowered back to 1.0 per cent by six moves in six months. The second four years of Trichet's term were dominated by an economic and financial 'crisis of a new kind', as he put it, the 'epicentre' of which – unlike the oil, sovereign debt or Asian crises of previous decades – was 'the financial system of the advanced economies'. The Bank's interest-rate policy was loosened throughout 2009, falling to 0.25 per cent in May that year – a level at which it stood for the subsequent 23 months. (The premature raising of the rate to 0.75 per cent, in two moves in April and July 2011, had to be partially reversed, to 0.5 per cent, in November 2011.)

In response to the twin crises in banking liquidity and government finances in the eurozone, the ECB has been forced by circumstance to take on a series of new roles, adopting what Trichet called 'non-standard measures' – as opposed to focusing simply on interest-rate adjustments (or 'standard measures'). These new functions have been increasingly contested in Germany and by some monetary economists, even if most policy-makers believe they have been necessary to avert a much deeper recession.

The ECB began to provide large amounts of money to the commercial banks at low interest rates for relatively short periods of time. In June 2009, it supplied € 422 billion in a one-year 'refinancing operation' to bolster liquidity in the financial sector and encourage bank lending, followed by a further € 75 billion in September and € 97 billion in December that year. In June 2010, the ECB launched a 'Covered Bond Purchase Programme' (CBPP), by which it bought up bank debt worth € 62 billion in the first 18 months of operation. More controversially, the Bank decided to exploit its routine 'open market operations' – which are used by central banks to smooth the path of interest rates and signal the direction of monetary policy – to purchase the sovereign debt issued by the governments of eurozone states in financial difficulty. It did this by intervening in secondary markets, rather than direct purchases, in order to avoid violating the 'no bail-out' provision and ban on the monetary financing of budget deficits in Articles 123(1) and 125(1) TFEU. The ECB's 'Securities Market Programme' (SMP) was instituted in parallel to the Greek bail-out in May 2010 and, following the subsequent Irish and Portuguese bail-outs, it purchased around € 75 billion of government debt over the following year. That figure then rapidly escalated during the second half of 2011, to € 211 billion, as the programme was extended to the purchase of Italian and Spanish bonds, in order to forestall 'contagion' spreading from the periphery towards the core of the eurozone.

The twin threads of ECB action – to support both commercial banks and governments – came together at the end of 2011, when it made available three-year loans to banks at a 0.25 per cent interest rate, not only to inject additional liquidity into the financial system, but to enable the banks to purchase government bonds, which offered higher yields. The latter operation was known among market-makers as a 'Sarkozy trade', after the French President, who had advocated it as another indirect means of overcoming the treaty restrictions on the ECB as a lender of last resort. In December 2011, 523 banks borrowed € 489 billion from the ECB on this basis, although only a small proportion of this sum appears to have been used to purchase bonds. By the end of February 2012, some 800 banks were drawing on support worth some € 525 billion.

Further reading: Karl Kaltenthaler, *Policymaking in the European Central Bank: The Masters of Europe's Money*, 2006.

European citizenship

The 1992 **Maastricht Treaty** amended the original **Treaty of Rome** to create citizenship of the European Union. Under Article 20 TFEU, 'every person holding the nationality of a Member State shall be a citizen of the Union'. The 1997 **Amsterdam Treaty** added the proposition, designed to reassure doubters, that 'Citizenship of the Union shall complement and not replace national citizenship.' Articles 20–24 TFEU set out the rights appertaining to citizenship: 'to move and reside freely within the territory of the Member States'; to vote and stand for election in municipal and **European elections** in the member state in which he or she resides; to receive protection from the diplomatic and consular authorities of any member state in any country in which the member state of which he or she is a national is not represented; and to petition the **European Parliament**, refer matters to the **European Ombudsman**, and to write to any EU institutions in any of the official **languages** of the Union and have such correspondence answered in the same language. Under Article 25 TFEU, these rights, now also replicated in the **Charter of Fundamental Rights**, may be strengthened or supplemented by the **Council of Ministers** without further treaty change. Acting unanimously on a proposal from the **European Commission** and after obtaining the **consent** of the European Parliament, the Council may recommend such changes to the member states for approval 'in accordance with their respective constitutional requirements'. (In subsequent rounds of negotiation for treaty change, suggestions have been made for the extension of the rights of Union citizenship into new fields, but so far, no such extensions have been agreed.)

In a declaration annexed to the **Treaties**, it is specified that 'the question whether an individual possesses the nationality of a Member State shall be settled solely by reference to the national law of the Member State concerned.' States may forward to the Council **presidency** details of those categories of person who are to be considered their nationals for the purpose of establishing their claim to citizenship of the Union. This was particularly important for the United Kingdom, which in the British Nationality Act 1981 defined several distinct categories of British national; of these, only British citizens, British subjects with the right of abode and those who are British Dependent

Territories citizens by virtue of a connection with Gibraltar are entitled to citizenship of the Union.

The development of European citizenship was one of several initiatives first advocated in the 1970s and 1980s, in the context of a 'People's Europe', in order to give citizens of member states a livelier sense of having a common European identity. When the Maastricht Treaty was passed, opponents of the text suggested that the inclusion of citizenship, strongly advocated by the Spanish government, was a significant move towards the creation of a European state. Although it is true that the idea of citizenship is normally associated with a state (but not exclusively: we may speak of 'Commonwealth citizens'), the form of citizenship so far extended by the treaty represents no more than a very modest enhancement of the rights which nationals of member states already enjoyed. The most important of these, the right to move and reside freely anywhere in the Union, drew on the existing treaty rights of **free movement of persons** and of **freedom of establishment**. It is quite significantly restricted by various provisions designed to prevent people of inadequate means from becoming a burden on the social security system of the member state where they choose to reside. The new right to vote in local and European elections pointedly does not extend to general elections. This suggestion was firmly resisted by countries with large numbers of potential voters possessing the nationality of another member state (for example, over 10 per cent of the population of Luxembourg is Portuguese).

Further reading: Elizabeth Meehan, *Citizenship and the European Union*, 2000.

European Coal and Steel Community (ECSC)

The European Coal and Steel Community was established by the **Treaty of Paris** in April 1951. The first of the three **European Communities** – the others being the **European Economic Community** (EEC) and the **European Atomic Energy Community** (EAEC or Euratom) – the ECSC was based upon the **Schuman Plan** of 1950. On 9 May 1950, **Robert Schuman,** the French foreign minister, proposed that French and German coal and steel production should be 'pooled' and placed under a common supranational authority, an initiative that owed its origin to **Jean Monnet**. In the event, not only France and West Germany, but also Belgium, Italy, Luxembourg and the Netherlands, decided to take part, thus forming **the Six**. The ECSC Treaty was concluded for a period of 50 years (Article 97 ECSC), whereas the EEC and Euratom Treaties (the **Treaties of Rome**) were of indefinite duration. The ECSC Treaty expired on 23 July 2002.

The coal and steel industries were chosen as the two industries essential to the waging of war. If they were placed under a common supranational authority, war between the signatory states would be, in Schuman's words, 'not only unthinkable, but materially impossible'. Coal was by far the largest source of energy at that time, and both coal and steel were essential to economic recovery. The experience already gained from the economic cooperation that was a condition of the economic aid received under the **Marshall Plan** suggested that recovery would be more rapid if European countries abandoned the elaborate pre-war system of tariffs and quotas. The elimination of such restrictions on trade, by the creation of a '**common market** for coal and steel' products among the Six, was a prime objective of the ECSC Treaty, backed by a common policy on imports and measures to enforce competition and harmonize state aids. The remit of ECSC policy covered inter alia, as Ernst Haas has put it, 'the production, pricing, marketing and distribution of coal and steel, as well as the forms of organization adopted by the enterprises engaged in these pursuits' (*The Uniting of Europe: Political, Social and Economic Forces 1950–1957*, 1958). Ownership of the coal and steel industries in signatory states was not affected as such, but the terms and conditions of business were subject to a high degree of both regulation and liberalization. This model was to prove broadly successful: trade in coal and steel products between the Six rose rapidly throughout the 1950s, while the extensive use of the Community's powers to break up cartels and monopolies kept price rises lower than they would otherwise have been.

The ECSC Treaty, which after ratification came into effect in July 1952, provided for four main institutions: a Special **Council of Ministers**; a **High Authority** (of which Monnet served as the first president); a Common Assembly, composed of 78 members nominated from the **national parliaments** of member states; and a Court of Justice for the settlement of disputes. The treaty thereby established the basic institutional framework that was later used for the more ambitious EEC: the ECSC's High Authority was the prototype of the **European Commission**, and the Common Assembly developed into the **European Parliament**. The High Authority was more powerful, admittedly in a more limited field, than the Commission was to prove in the cross-sectoral common market launched in 1958. The routine legislative process was that, subject in some cases to approval by the Council, the High Authority had the right to take binding **decisions** and also to adopt recommendations (rather akin to **directives** today) which were 'binding as to the aims to be pursued' but left it to member states or operators as to how these should be achieved. The other ECSC institutions, Haas suggested, were 'primarily designed as checks upon the power of the High Authority rather than initiators of action'. Overall, there was 'no possible neat division into legislative, executive and judicial organs. The High Authority both legislates and administers, while the Council of Ministers legislates as well as controls the primary legislator. The Assembly tends toward controlling but certainly cannot legislate. Only the Court is clearly and solely a judicial agency.'

Although by 1958, the two other Communities had been created, the institutions of the ECSC remained legally separate until the **Merger Treaty** of 1965. All were based in Luxembourg, a 'provisional' arrangement that was to have lasting consequences for the **seats of the EU institutions.** A **protocol** on relations with the **Council of Europe** was annexed to the ECSC Treaty. It called upon governments to recommend to their national parliaments that the members appointed to sit in the ECSC Common Assembly should be chosen from among the representatives to the Consultative Assembly of the Council of Europe. Both the Common Assembly and the High Authority of the ECSC were required to forward annual reports on their activities to the Council of Europe. The motive behind these provisions seems to have been to answer the criticism that the ECSC and the Council of Europe, in spite of their very different structures and areas of responsibility, might develop on the basis of mutual jealousy. The protocol made it clear that the Council of Europe was regarded at the time as the senior partner, although in practice that relationship was quickly to be inverted as the Six deepened their cooperation.

Both the structure of the ECSC and the range of powers exercised by its institutions embodied many compromises and ambiguities. Monnet's original preference was for an entirely independent sovereign authority, rather akin to the **European Central Bank** (ECB) in respect of monetary policy today, but the **Benelux** countries – drawing on their experience of a **customs union** – insisted that this body should be overseen by governments acting through a Council of Ministers. As Haas hints above, the Common Assembly's powers of control were to be exercised over the High Authority, not over the Council. While many of the objectives of the ECSC were consistent with free-market philosophy – the common market for coal and steel was based on **free movement** and competition – the institutions were also given powers of a more *dirigiste* character: to control imports, for example, or to set prices and place limits on production in the event of a crisis in the coal or steel industries. The ECSC was financed not by contributions from national governments, but by a levy on the production of the industries concerned (a primitive form of **own resource**). The hybrid nature of the ECSC's institutions and the tension between the different economic philosophies underpinning its role were to set a pattern for the later EEC.

The British attitude to the Schuman Plan and to the establishment of the ECSC was ambivalent. On the one hand, there was genuine enthusiasm for the prospect of a lasting reconciliation between France and Germany; on the other, deep scepticism about the precedent that would be set by, and the potential loss of **sovereignty** entailed in, entrusting significant powers to a supranational structure. The discussion exposed national instincts that remain very powerful over 60 years later. When the French government attempted to make acceptance of the principle of a High Authority a condition of taking part in the discussions on the plan, the British government was placed in an awkward position. As well as institutional concerns, the prime minister, Clement Attlee, and his Labour colleagues had ideological reasons to avoid committing Britain to the project: he had only recently nationalized the country's coal and steel industries and was very sensitive to a hostile reaction within the trade-union movement to the idea that these sectors might now escape domestic political control. Herbert Morrison, deputy prime minister, later recalled that the proposal for talks was put to London 'without prior consultation and with a request for an immediate reply'. Morrison's own instinct was clear: 'we cannot do it, the Durham miners won't wear it' (quoted in Bernard Donohue and G. W. Jones, *Herbert Morrison: Portrait of a Politician*, 1973).

In the Consultative Assembly of the Council of Europe, Conservative pro-Europeans, led by Harold Macmillan, put forward an alternative proposal that would have brought the planned ECSC arrangements under the auspices of the Council of Europe and greatly reduced their supranational character. This proposal attracted little support, and the Six signed the Treaty of Paris on 18 April 1951. A year later, this approach was reiterated, in slightly different form, as official British government policy by Anthony Eden, once again Foreign Secretary after the Conservatives had returned to power. The 'Eden Plan' was an attempt, as he put it whilst addressing the ECSC Common Assembly in September 1952, 'to suggest the means, and promote the action, by which two trends to European unity, the supranational and intergovernmental, could be linked together'. The only outcome was agreement that the assemblies of the Council of Europe and ECSC should meet together annually to discuss the progress of the latter. Although the Treaty made no provision for associate membership of the ECSC, the United Kingdom concluded an **association agreement** with the Six in December 1954.

The non-participation of the United Kingdom in the ECSC rankled with many on the continent and to some it was a great disappointment. *The Economist* noted on 15 December 1951:

> *In French and Benelux eyes, Britain is still regarded as the missing component, without which the Schuman community is in danger of German domination. In German eyes, Britain is the industrial competitor which, while urging Germany to sacrifice its national commercial preponderance to the common interest of the western European community, has itself retained its industrial independence.*

That commentary was written in the middle of the **ratification** of the ECSC Treaty by the national parliaments of the Six, a process which did not command unanimous support. The French National Assembly voted by 377 to 232 votes for the Treaty in December 1951 – with the Communists, Gaullists and some Socialists opposing it – whilst in Germany the following month, the majority was 378 to 143, with most SPD members in the Bundestag voting against. Ratification in Italian and the Benelux parliaments was less problematic.

The supranational institutions provided for, however modestly, under the ECSC Treaty marked a decisive break with the classic model of integration, based on **intergovernmentalism** and typified by previous pan-European bodies such as the Council of Europe and the **Organization for European Economic Cooperation** (OEEC). The significance of this shift was not lost upon German Chancellor **Konrad Adenauer**, who in a speech to the Bundestag in 1952 spoke of the 'political meaning' of the ECSC being 'infinitely larger than its economic purpose . . . For the first time in history, countries want to renounce part of their sovereignty, voluntarily and without compulsion, in order to transfer it to a supranational structure.' For the United States, John Foster Dulles, the incoming Secretary of State, welcomed the Schuman initiative as 'brilliantly creative', adding that it could 'go far to solve the most dangerous problem of our time, namely the relationship of Germany's industrial power to France and the West'. The ECSC and its supranational apparatus were also a decisive step beyond the post-war proposals for the internationalization of the Ruhr and the **Saarland**, although the latter helped to create the climate of opinion in which the Schuman Plan could find acceptance.

In practice, the day-to-day work of the ECSC proved more prosaic than its path-breaking institutional significance might imply. Although Monnet spoke confidently in June 1953 of the new Community as 'the first expression of the Europe that is being born', he appears to have become bored by the detailed operation of the coal and steel sectors and took the occasion of the rejection of the **European Defence Community** (EDC) by the French National Assembly to resign as President of the High Authority in November 1954; he was succeeded by a series of largely unknown technocrats. In any case, partly as a result of Monnet's success thereafter as advocate of the relaunch of European integration in new fields, the ECSC was soon overshadowed by the development of the EEC. The new Economic Community generalized to all sectors of the economy some of the key features which the ECSC had pioneered – including **non-discrimination**, abolition of intra-Community tariffs or 'charges having equivalent effect', elimination of 'quantitative restrictions' on the **free movement of goods**, and prohibition of subsidies, state aids and restrictive practices of various kinds.

Although the ECSC's practical achievements were not inconsiderable – facilitating a quadrupling of trade in steel products among the Six, for example, during the first decade of its existence – it failed to gain much credit for its work. A psychological turning-point came in March 1959, when the High Authority sought to use its emergency powers in the coal industry – one of the few areas where it was unable to act unilaterally – but proved incapable of persuading the Council of Ministers to declare the 'state of manifest crisis' that was a necessary precondition for this. (France, Germany and Italy all opposed the move.) During the 1960s, the ECSC largely disappeared from political consciousness among political and media élites in Europe, a process speeded by the merger of the High Authority into the European Commission in 1967. In October 1962, however, the press was interested in the appointment as a member of the High Authority of Karl-Maria Hettlage, previously a German junior minister in Adenauer's government, who was exposed as a former SS officer and associate of Albert Speer.

In the 1970s, the Commission used its powers under the ECSC Treaty to restructure the Community's steel industry, through the so-called Davignon Plan (1977), which entailed quantitative limits on production, minimum prices and financial aid for industrial redevelopment. These powers were invoked again to effect further restructuring in the wake of recession and stiffer competition from central and eastern Europe. The ECSC Treaty's provisions for aids to miners' housing and retraining helped mining communities adjust to the decline of the coal industry. However, nothing was done under the ECSC Treaty that could not, with modest adjustments, be brought within the ambit of the **Treaty of Rome** when the ECSC Treaty expired in 2002. As part of a transition over several years, the 2001 **Nice Treaty** provided for the transfer of the ECSC's outstanding funds to a new EU coal and steel research fund, whilst the rest of its activities were integrated into the existing policies of the European Union.

Further reading: Edmund Dell, *The Schuman Plan and the British Abdication of Leadership in Europe*, 1995; Alan Milward, *The Reconstruction of Western Europe 1945–51*, 1984.

European Commission

The European Commission is the principal executive body of the European Union. It is headed by a college of 27 Commissioners, who are political appointees nominated by the governments of the member states (through the **European Council**) and confirmed collectively by the **European Parliament**, to which they are responsible. Appointed to office for five years, the Commission is unique among international bureaucracies both in its explicitly political character – organizations of this kind are traditionally headed by a secretary general accountable to governments – and by virtue of its extensive combination of activities and responsibilities, which include not only the classic administrative functions of an executive, but also certain legislative and quasi-judicial roles too. Although the term 'European Commission', as used in the **Treaties**, refers only to the college of Commissioners, who collectively decide the institution's position on all matters, in practice it also denotes the 25,000 European civil servants (*fonctionnaires*) who work for the Commission, over three-quarters of whom are based in **Brussels**, the official **'seat' of the institution**.

Under Article 17(1) TEU, the primary task of the European Commission is to 'promote the general interest of the Union and take appropriate initiatives to that end'. For this purpose, it 'shall ensure the application of the Treaties, and of measures adopted by the institutions pursuant to them'. This function, with reference to which the Commission is sometimes referred to as the 'guardian of the Treaties', empowers it to take action – ultimately, by referring the matter to the **European Court of Justice** (ECJ) – if another institution or, under Article 258 TFEU, a member state is in default of its treaty obligations (see **reasoned opinion**).

The Commission also enjoys the **'right of initiative'** in proposing legislation to the **Council of Ministers** and European Parliament, and such legislation 'may only be adopted on the basis of a Commission proposal, except where the Treaties provide otherwise' (Article 17(2) TFEU). The Commission is then involved at every stage of the legislative process, with the right to amend or withdraw its proposal (Article 293(1) TFEU). On proposals subject to **qualified majority voting** (QMV) in the Council, the Commission's decision on whether to support any proposed amendments at first or second reading determines whether the vote on those amendments itself is by QMV or **unanimity** in the Council (Articles 293(1) and 294(9) TFEU).

The Commission exercises 'coordinating, executive and management functions, as laid down in the Treaties' in respect of EU policies, established in law, that need to be administered from the centre. Among the more complex of these are the **Common Agricultural Policy** (CAP) and the operation of the **structural funds**. In the field of **competition policy**, it enjoys an autonomous right to take decisions, subject only to potential challenge in the ECJ (Article 105 TFEU). In other fields, mostly under the so-called **comitology** system, the Commission is entrusted with the ability to adopt administrative law in its own right. The Commission also proposes and executes the annual EU **Budget**: it draws up a draft Budget with the help of estimates prepared by the other institutions; it is then responsible for implementing the Budget (once it has been adopted by the Council and the Parliament jointly) and submitting accounts at the end of each financial year, as part of the **discharge procedure**.

On issues such as **Common Commercial Policy** (CCP) and **development policy**, as well as the external aspects of domestic policy – such as transport, energy and the environment – the Commission represents the Union in its dealings with third countries and international organizations. Article 17(1) TEU states that except in the field of **Common Foreign and Security Policy**

(CFSP), the Commission 'shall ensure the Union's external representation'. Although the Council of Ministers is responsible for concluding the bilateral and multilateral **international agreements** to which the Union is a party, it is the Commission that normally negotiates these on the Council's behalf (Articles 207(3) and 218 TFEU), other than in the field of CFSP.

Underpinning the use of all these powers is what until recently was called in the Treaties the Commission's 'own power of decision', that is, the right to decide for itself on the substance and timing of its actions. The question of whether the Commission submits or alters a legislative proposal or brings an action before the ECJ is a matter entirely at its own discretion. This qualifies the Commission as an autonomous political institution, rather than a simple bureaucracy. The Commission's Annual Work Programme (AWP), published each autumn, sets out its broad priorities and detailed plans for legislative and non-legislative initiatives during the year ahead.

Although very extensive, the Commission's powers within the EU decision-making process are in fact less than those of the **High Authority** of the **European Coal and Steel Community** (ECSC), upon which the Commission is modelled. This is apparent not least in the choice of its name: 'Commission' – the ordinary French word for a committee – has none of the grandeur of 'High Authority', and was accordingly used by the drafters of the **Treaties of Rome** as less politically provocative. From 1958 until 1967, the ECSC's High Authority and the two Commissions of the **European Economic Community** (EEC) and the **European Atomic Energy Community** (EAEC or Euratom) led separate lives, but from July 1967 they were brought together as the single Commission of the European Communities under the 1965 **Merger Treaty**. The 1992 **Maastricht Treaty** formally named this institution the European Commission.

By the time the Merger Treaty was being negotiated, the EEC Commission under its first President, **Walter Hallstein**, had aroused the antipathy of French President **Charles de Gaulle**. The General took strong exception to what he saw as the Commission's pretensions to resemble a European government. Some of these were purely symbolic – such as Hallstein's insistence on receiving the credentials of foreign diplomats accredited to the Communities – whilst others had real institutional and policy substance, notably his determination to ensure that the treaty provisions on the Community's funding through free-standing **own resources** and the use of **qualified majority voting** (QMV) in the Council were put into effect. De Gaulle denounced the Commission in a number of well-publicized press conferences, with matters coming to a head in the 'empty chair crisis' of 1965, when the French government boycotted meetings of the Council for six months, leading to the **Luxembourg Compromise** of January 1966.

Whatever hostility the Commission may have aroused on the part of the larger member states, the smaller countries have always attached great importance to its role as the guardian and guarantor of a broader European interest. The involvement of the Commission in all areas and at every level of Union activity is seen as an important safeguard against the formation of any 'directorate' of the large states. This is why, for example, in the QMV procedure, a distinction is drawn between the majority necessary in the Council to adopt a Commission proposal and the majority needed when there is no such proposal. It also explains why the smaller states strongly supported **Roy Jenkins** when, as Commission President, he sought to ensure (against French opposition) that he and his successors should have the right to attend international economic summits on behalf of the Community as a whole. More recently, the current Commission President, José Manuel Barroso, has fought to safeguard the Commission's responsibility to 'ensure the Union's external representation' at policy-specific international summits – for example, on the environment – against potential encroachment by the new **President of the European Council**, Herman Van Rompuy, who, alongside the **High Representative**, has the same responsibility for external representation specifically in regard to CFSP.

Presidents of the European Commission

Period in office	*President*	*Country of origin*	*National political affiliation*	*Number of Commissioners*
1958–67	Walter Hallstein	Germany	Christian Democrat	9
1967–70	Jean Rey	Belgium	Liberal	14
1970–72	Franco Maria Malfatti	Italy	Christian Democrat	9
1972–3	Sicco Mansholt	Netherlands	Socialist	9
1973–7	François-Xavier Ortoli	France	Gaullist (UDR)	13
1977–81	Roy Jenkins	United Kingdom	Labour	13
1981–5	Gaston Thorn	Luxembourg	Liberal	14
1985–95	Jacques Delors	France	Socialist	14 then 17
1995–9	Jacques Santer	Luxembourg	Christian Democrat	20
1999–2004	Romano Prodi	Italy	Centre-left (L'Ulivo)	20 then 30
2004–	José Manuel Barroso	Portugal	Centre-right (PSD)	25 then 27

Historically, the Commission has been seen as, and has sought to serve as, the anchor for the integrity and coherence of the Union system as a whole, strongly defending the '**Community method**'. When Barroso maladroitly sought to convene a personal 'mini-summit' of selected national leaders in May 2007 in Sintra, Portugal, to discuss the possible relaunch of the **European Constitution**, he unleashed widespread criticism from those heads of government who were to be excluded. The meeting had to be abandoned, at least in its original form, on account of – as his spokesman ironically put it – the 'unexpected success' of the initiative. Since the onset of the **eurozone debt crisis**, the ten member states outside the **eurozone** have looked to the Commission to defend the interests of the **euro** 'outs' and prevent the emergence of a **two-speed Europe**.

The fact that the Commission is appointed, rather than directly elected, sometimes gives rise to criticism. However, it is precisely the fact of the Commission's *not* being elected that allows the present institutional balance to be maintained – a balance broadly satisfactory to the governments of all the member states, especially those of the smaller states. The procedure under which an incoming Commission must now secure the approval of the European Parliament is thought to give the institution greater democratic legitimacy, while falling well short of conferring on it an entirely independent political mandate.

The emphasis on the Commission's independence in the Treaties relates less to its mandate than to its freedom from outside pressure. Article 17(3) TEU states that, in carrying out its responsibilities, 'the Commission shall be completely independent', that its members 'shall be chosen . . . persons whose independence is beyond doubt', and that they 'shall neither seek nor take instructions from any Government or other institution, body, office or entity' – including, by implication, the European Council of heads of government (of which the Commission President is also a member in his own right), the Council of Ministers or the European Parliament. In dealing with Commissioners, member states are obliged in turn to 'respect their independence' and must 'not seek to influence them in the performance of their tasks' (Article 245 TFEU). On appointment, Commissioners commit themselves to remain strictly independent, in an oath sworn before the ECJ in Luxembourg. They are not allowed to undertake any outside role during their term of office, although they may remain members of a political party and attend party events. They may stand as candidates for election, taking leave of absence for the duration of the campaign and forcing a temporary reassignment of portfolios. Such candidacies used to occur very rarely – only five times between 1958 and 1999 – but in the Prodi (1999–2004) and first Barroso (2004–9) Commissions, a total of seven Commissioners sought 'electoral leave', all but one of them (Viviane Reding) subsequently leaving the college.

Individually, Commissioners may be dismissed by the President of the Commission or by the Court, on application from either the Council or the Commission itself (Articles 17(6) TEU and 245 TFEU). Collectively, the Commission may be dismissed by the European Parliament, through the passage of a censure motion with a two-thirds majority (Article 17(8) TEU). So far, no censure motion has ever been passed, but the voluntary **resignation of the Santer Commission** pre-empted the near certain adoption of such a motion in March 1999.

When the European Commission was established in 1958, Commissioners were nominated for a four-year term by 'common accord' of the governments of the member states (Article 158 EEC). There were two Commissioners for each of the three largest member states (France, Germany and Italy) and one for each of the three **Benelux** countries. This basic pattern was maintained, with successive rounds of **enlargement**, until the mid-1990s. Since then, both the term of office and method of selection of the college have changed. The Maastricht Treaty extended the Commission's term from four to five years, starting in 1994–5, in order to align it with that of the European Parliament, and made the Commission 'subject as a body to a vote of approval by the European Parliament' (then Article 214(2) EC). The 1997 **Amsterdam Treaty** provided for a separate, earlier vote of approval on the Commission President (Maastricht allowed the Parliament only to be consulted), whilst the 2001 **Nice Treaty** shifted decision-making on these appointments from 'common accord' of the member states to QMV within the Council. (The very involvement of the Parliament in the appointment process had been extracted by the Parliament, starting in February 1981, when it chose to hold a unilateral vote on the newly-appointed Commission of former Luxembourg prime minister Gaston Thorn.) Since 2004, each member state has nominated one Commissioner (see below).

Today, the appointment process, as set out in Article 17(7) TFEU, works as follows. 'Taking into account the elections to the European Parliament' every fifth year, the European Council, acting by QMV, nominates a candidate for the post of President of the European Commission. This candidate then needs to be 'elected by the European Parliament by a majority of its component members'. (Until the Lisbon Treaty, the word 'approved', rather than 'elected', was used, and only a simple majority, rather than an absolute majority, of the Parliament was required.) If the nominee for President fails to secure the required majority, the European Council will, within one month, propose a new candidate on the same basis.

Once the nominee for President has been endorsed by the Parliament, he or she consults with the member-state governments on the appointment of the other Commissioners. The Council of Ministers (rather than the European Council) proceeds to adopt, 'by common accord with the

President-elect . . . the list of other persons whom it proposes for appointment as members of the Commission'. They are 'subject as a body to a vote of consent by the European Parliament' by simple majority. Once this approval has been obtained, the Commission is formally 'appointed by the European Council, acting by a qualified majority'.

The closer involvement of the Parliament in the installation of the new Commission has made the process increasingly political. The successive nominees for Commission President have been forced to explain to the Parliament in advance, in greater and greater detail, their intended policies in office. This process reached an apogée in July 2009, when in seeking a second term, José Manuel Barroso chose to present a substantial personal manifesto to the Parliament – a 41-page set of 'Political Guidelines for the next Commission' – and make himself available to each of the **political groups** for interview. Candidates for Commission President have also faced greater ideological resistance from MEPs: Jacques Santer confronted serious opposition from the left in July 1994 (with 260 votes in favour, 238 against and 23 abstentions), as did Barroso to a lesser degree in both July 2004 (431 in favour, 251 against and 44 abstentions) and September 2009 (382 in favour, 219 against and 117 abstentions). The centre-right EPP had asserted in the spring of 2004 that, if it was reconfirmed as the largest political group in the Parliament after the June **European elections**, someone from its own 'political family' should be nominated by heads of government as Commission President. When this happened, with the choice of Barroso, some of the left drew the logical conclusion that they had little reason to support him. Five years later, seeking a second term, Barroso took care to try to present himself as an all-party candidate, rather than just an EPP nominee.

A further important factor in politicizing the appointment process has been the emergence of parliamentary hearings as the key determinant in practice of whether, once nominated, any individual Commissioner-designate actually takes up his or her post. Hearings are an invention of the Parliament itself, written into its rules of procedure and activated for the first time in 1994, as a means of screening individual Commissioners – and thus disaggregating the confirmation process – before the plenary votes on the proposed team as a whole. Each Commissioner-designate goes before one or more of the Parliament's 20 committees for an extended interview (usually lasting three hours), in which, after an opening statement, their background, policy views and intentions in office are all explored through questioning from the floor. In advance of each hearing, the 'candidate' answers a written questionnaire covering some of the same ground.

The hearings process first became politically significant in September–October 2004, when parliamentary committees started to refuse to endorse certain nominees. Formally speaking, the committees do not have a right of veto – they are simply reporting, through the Parliament's Conference of Presidents (comprising the leaders of political groups), to the plenary – but, in reality, any failure by a Commissioner-designate to clear the hearings' hurdle seriously damages, if not kills, his or her candidacy. The refusal of the Parliament's civil liberties committee to approve Rocco Buttiglione, the sitting Italian minister for European affairs, as commissioner for **Justice and Home Affairs** (JHA), on account of his expressed views on gay rights and the role of women, made a huge political impact and forced Barroso to withdraw his team. The vote on the proposed Commission had to be deferred for a month, from October to November 2004. Buttiglione withdrew and Barroso took the opportunity to force out another nominee who had underperformed in the hearings (Igrida Udre from Latvia) and to reshuffle a third (László Kovács from Hungary, who was moved from the energy portfolio to taxation). The 2009 hearings process proved less brutal, but still involved the loss of one Commissioner-designate, Rumiana Jeleva, the sitting Bulgarian foreign minister. As a result of the hearings process, as Richard Corbett, Francis Jacobs and Michael Shackleton argue, the suitability of nominees for the post of Commissioner is now 'better and more publicly scrutinized than before, and their personalities and views are becoming clearer at an earlier stage', just as 'benchmarks are being established to judge subsequent Commission performance' (*The European Parliament*, 2011).

Despite the great importance assumed by the hearings and the need for parliamentary approval of the Commission before taking office, the Treaties still give the Council complete control (as before the Maastricht Treaty) over the filling of any vacancy among Commissioners caused by death or retirement. By convention, a 'mini-hearing' of the new Commissioner is held, but only after the appointment has already been made by the Council. Only in the case of the need to choose a new President of the Commission in mid-term is there an obligation to secure the approval of the European Parliament.

The size of the college of Commissioners has grown over time. Initially, there were nine Commissioners. For a brief period after the entry into force of the **Merger Treaty** in 1967 there were 14, but this was reduced back to nine in 1969 and then raised to 13 in 1973, with the first enlargement (two Commissioners for the United Kingdom, and one each for Denmark and Ireland). The total gradually increased to 20, with the successive **accessions** of Greece, Portugal, Spain (two Commissioners), Austria, Finland and Sweden in 1981, 1986 and 1995. However, in advance of the entry of 12 new member states in 2004–7, it was agreed that the five largest member states would give up their second Commissioner from the end of the 1999–2004 Commission. It was widely thought at the time that there were not enough jobs of broadly equivalent weight to provide work for 20 Commissioners, let alone 27. The Nice Treaty provided that, in return for each member appointing only one

Commissioner, the voting weights in the Council of Ministers would be adjusted to reduce the over-representation of the smaller states for the purpose of calculating a qualified majority. Moreover, once the number of member states reached 27, the number of Commissioners would be reduced (from the start of the next new Commission) to fewer than the number of member states, with Commissioners 'chosen according to a rotation system based on the principle of equality' (Protocol 10). This situation was due to arise on 1 November 2009, but because of a delay in the confirmation of the second Barroso Commission and the imminence of the entry into force of the Lisbon Treaty (a month later), no action was taken.

The Lisbon Treaty provides that, from 2014, the number of Commissioners should be only two-thirds the number of member states – again based on the principle of equal rotation – although a let-out clause allows the European Council, acting unanimously, to set this reduction aside (Articles 17(5) TEU and 244 TFEU). In the event, this waiver was invoked immediately that the new treaty entered into force. In order to secure a 'yes' vote in the second **Irish referendum** on the Lisbon Treaty in October 2009, it was agreed among the governments that the principle of 'one state, one Commissioner' would be maintained indefinitely, and a decision of the European Council to that effect was taken in December 2009.

Traditionally, the allocation of portfolios within the college was decided, not always entirely amicably, by the Commissioners themselves, on a proposal from the President. In recent years, however, the President has been much freer to assign the portfolios among colleagues without their agreement, both by dint of his or her formal powers 'to decide on the internal organization of the Commission' and to force the resignation of colleagues (Article 17(6) TEU), and because of the need to put together a credible team that will survive the hearings in the Parliament. Until the hearings process was launched in 1994, the allocation of portfolios was normally left until after the Commission had taken office; since then it has had to precede the Parliament's confirmation of the college. Inevitably, the composition of the Commission is a complex political balancing act, one that ideally needs to take account not only of the talents and expertise of the individuals concerned, but of the competing preferences and interests of the governments of large and small member states, as well as differing economic and ideological philosophies. The Commission President is now helped by the fact that, since the Nice Treaty, he or she has a formal veto over the nomination of any individual to the college: in 2009, Barroso allegedly refused to agree to at least one individual proposed by a member state. The withdrawal of Commissioners-designate after hearings in 2004 and 2009 may encourage greater 'quality control' at the start of the nomination process by Commission Presidents in the future. The President is free to appoint one or more

Vice-Presidents, in addition to the High Representative for CFSP, who automatically enjoys this status (Article 17(6)c TEU).

Of the more than 200 Commissioners (including members of the High Authority) who have held office since 1952, about one third had previous experience of ministerial office in their country of origin before going to Brussels, and over two-thirds had been politicians in some form. If anything, recent Commissions have been more 'political': the last three Commission Presidents have been former prime ministers and 24 of the 27 current Commissioners have held ministerial or parliamentary office. Some Commissioners return from Brussels to hold high national office: Romano Prodi became Italian prime minister for a second time; Claude Cheysson and Michel Barnier became French foreign ministers; Peter Mandelson became de facto deputy prime minister in Britain; and Dalia Grybauskaité was elected President of Lithuania. More often, however, appointment to the college marks the beginning of the end of a politician's career. This may partly explain why, controversially, in addition to a generous monthly salary – of around € 20,000 per month after tax, with Vice-Presidents and the President receiving slightly more – Commissioners also enjoy the cushion of a 'transitional allowance' for up to three years after their term of office expires, in order to dissuade them from immediately taking outside positions which might involve conflicts of interest. (The allowance is set at between 40 and 60 per cent of their previous salary, depending on length of service.) A code of conduct requires former Commissioners to submit for approval any appointment they take up within 18 months of leaving office.

The college of Commissioners meets weekly, normally on Wednesdays, and although Article 250 TFEU allows decisions to be taken by simple majority, in practice all major decisions are taken by consensus, with the Commission operating on the basis of collective responsibility. However, the principle of collective responsibility is not entirely matched by the equivalent principle of 'ministerial responsibility' to be found in government departments at national level. Each Commissioner may be given responsibility for one or more, or even parts of several, of the 33 directorates-general (DG), plus other ancillary services, into which the Commission is divided. This means that, in some cases, there is no clear and exclusive relationship between the Commissioner and his or her services (although there has been an effort to reduce such overlaps in recent years). The interface between each Commissioner and his or her services is managed by a small ***cabinet*** (or private office), and the various *cabinets* together provide a political framework through which policy differences within the Commission are brokered. The director-generals, directors and heads of unit are often at one remove from this process, adding to a sense of the political and administrative structures being separate and detached.

The most senior official in the Commission's administration is the Secretary General, who has his or her own directorate-general, known as the secretariat general. In the early days, the Secretary General was a very powerful political player within the system: the first office-holder, **Emile Noël**, exercised a legendary influence over Commission decision-making during much of his nearly 30 years in post. However, as the Commission has expanded and become more diverse – with the number of Commissioners rising from nine to 27 over the last 40 years, and the number of officials rising from 9,000 to 25,000 today – the role of the Secretary General and his or her secretariat general has evolved in a more routine and bureaucratic direction. In addition to servicing the formal needs of the meetings of the college, they provide a range of horizontal administrative services, including managing the logistics of inter-institutional relations. However, it is the President's *cabinet*, rather than the secretariat general, that now leads the discussion within the Commission when there are major differences of viewpoint to be overcome. The current Secretary General, Catherine Day, appointed in 2005, is the second Irish citizen in a row to hold the post, following David O'Sullivan.

Some of the difficulties confronted by the Commission are a simple product of its multinational character. As David Spence has written (see below), cultural diversity 'has its costs – difficulties in communication; different, possibly incompatible, assumptions about how to deal with superiors and subordinates; incongruent expectations about how to manage conflicts; and culturally-defined differences' in coordinating units and services. The specific **language** régime in the EU institutions also requires many Commission documents to be translated into all 23 official and working languages, even if most meetings held in the Commission use English, French or German, or a mixture of the three. At a more immediate level, Commission staff in Brussels are dispersed into 70 different buildings in Brussels, whilst 18 of the 33 directorates-general have at least some staff based in Luxembourg. Whilst the Commissioners and their *cabinets* are located in the **Berlaymont**, most of their detailed policy staff in the DGs are usually somewhere else.

The Commission is generally perceived to have a poor record in respect of its own internal organization. As long ago as 1979, the Spierenburg Report identified a number of failings, including low motivation among officials, over-elaborate hierarchies of authority, absence of career planning, and inflexible responses to changing priorities, all compounded by the rivalry and intrigue often found in international bureaucracies, especially in relation to appointments and promotions (see **Eurocrats**). Very little action followed from this report. Change was only forced by the serious crisis, based on evidence of poor financial management and fraud in some areas, that led to the dramatic resignation of the Santer Commission in 1999. Since then, the Commission has moved to professionalize its management and improve rotation and promotion prospects among its staff. The 2004 Kinnock reforms provided the first comprehensive overhaul to the Union's internal **staff regulations** in almost 40 years. The Commission has also increasingly sought to use **agencies** to provide advice, administer certain policies, conduct risk assessment and contribute to the compliance and enforcement of **EU law**.

The case for the Commission – the boldest of all the institutional experiments embodied in the founding Treaties – must ultimately rest on whether it works, and whether the Union would work better if radical changes were made to its role. On the whole, despite shortcomings, the Commission does work. The very rapid progress made in developing common policies in Europe since the 1950s could not have been achieved without the Commission acting as a motivator, monitor and proposer of compromises, nor without the longer-term view of a common European interest that the Commission provides. It has been an important, independent anchor for the complex process of melding together diverse national interests and traditions in Europe, as well as a powerful safeguard against the dominance of a few, larger countries in the Union – a tendency which finds easier expression in some of the other EU institutions.

Further reading: Michelle Cini, *The European Commission: Leadership, Organisation and Culture in the EU Administration*, 1996; Liesbet Hooghe, *The European Commission and the Integration of Europe*, 2002; Neill Nugent (editor), *At the Heart of the Union*, 1996; Neill Nugent, *The European Commission*, 2001; Edward Page, *People who Run Europe*, 1997; Andy Smith, *Politics and the European Commission*, 2006; David Spence with Geoffrey Edwards (editors), *The European Commission*, 2006; Anne Stevens with Handley Stevens, *Brussels Bureaucrats? – The Administration of the European Union*, 2001; Martin Westlake, *The Commission and the Parliament: Partners and Rivals in the European Policy-Making Process*, 1994.

European Communities

The phrase 'European Communities' is used to denote the three Communities that were created in the 1950s through the adoption of corresponding **Treaties** by **the Six** founding member states of today's European Union. The Communities are the **European Coal and Steel Community** (ECSC), established by the **Treaty of Paris** in April 1951; the **European Economic Community** (EEC), widely known at the time as the '**Common Market**', established by the **Treaty of Rome** in March 1957; and the **European Atomic Energy Community** (EAEC or Euratom), established by a parallel Treaty of

Rome. The EEC and Euratom Treaties, which were signed at the same time, are together known as the *Treaties* of Rome, whereas the EEC Treaty is itself conventionally known as the *Treaty* of Rome.

From the 1965 **Merger Treaty** onwards, the three Communities shared the same institutions while remaining legally distinct, and they always had the same membership, from the Six (in 1951–72) onwards. In the 1992 **Maastricht Treaty**, the European Economic Community was officially renamed the 'European Community' (EC), and the title of the EEC Treaty was correspondingly adjusted to read the 'Treaty establishing the European Community'. However, the EC, ECSC and Euratom remained separate entities within the wider European Union also established by the Maastricht Treaty, whose formal title is the Treaty on European Union (TEU). When the ECSC Treaty expired in July 2002, after 50 years, ECSC activities were continued under the EC Treaty, leaving only two Communities in existence.

The **Lisbon Treaty**, which came into force in December 2009, ended the distinction between the European Community and the European Union. The EEC Treaty, subsequently EC Treaty, has now been renamed the Treaty on the Functioning of the European Union (TFEU). The intergovernmental '**pillars**' for **Common Foreign and Security Policy** (CFSP) and **Justice and Home Affairs** (JHA) established by the Maastricht Treaty, separate to the Communities, have been abolished. The Union and the EC are now joined in a single, legally consistent, structure. However, the same arrangement has yet to be applied to the Euratom Treaty, so the European Atomic Energy Community continues as the only remaining 'Community', in parallel. The EAEC is legally separate to the Union, but since it has the same membership and shares the same institutions, it is to all intents and purposes part of the Union and is generally regarded as such.

The word 'Community' is said to have appealed to **Jean Monnet** and **Robert Schuman**, the two **founding fathers** most closely involved in creating the ECSC in 1950–51, because it conjured up a sense of 'togetherness' and joint action in a common enterprise. Richard Mayne describes how Monnet sought to secure the widest use of the word in the 1950s: 'the first report of the **High Authority** [of the ECSC] . . . was significantly entitled *The Activities of the European Community*, with the words "coal and steel" quietly omitted' (*The Community of Europe*, 1962). However, having been central to the nomenclature of European integration for over 60 years, the word is now becoming mainly one of historical interest. In addition to the survival of the Euratom Community, it still features in concepts such as '**communautization**' and the '**Community method**', essentially designed to draw a distinction between supranational and intergovernmental models of integration or cooperation.

European Constitution

From start of the Communities, the **Treaties** have served as a de facto constitution for Europe and they continue to do so today. The **European Court of Justice** (ECJ) recognized them in 1986 as the 'basic constitutional charter' of the Union (*Les Verts – Parti Écologiste* v *European Parliament*; Case 294/83). However, starting in the late 1970s, the suggestion began to gain ground that the specifically institutional elements of the Treaties – whether in existing or amended form – should be abstracted from the other provisions and embodied in a separate document. The proposed **Draft Treaty establishing the European Union** (DTEU), adopted by the **European Parliament** in February 1984, was an early exercise in this direction, even if it would have significantly altered the balance of power between the institutions. Once the **Charter of Fundamental Rights** was adopted in December 2000, it was suggested that this text too should be incorporated into any constitution.

The argument for a constitution of the sort originally envisaged rested on the proposition that greater clarity was needed in the institutional arrangements of the Union. The constitutional elements in the Treaties were widely scattered and would benefit from being brought together into a coherent, intelligible whole, with repetitions excised, the language brought up to date, and the substance made consistent with the case law of the ECJ. This might diminish the alienation and bewilderment thought to be characteristic of public attitudes to the Union. In particular, it might serve to provide clear-cut answers to questions about the division of responsibility between the Union and national, regional, or local authorities, and thereby help to safeguard the principle of **subsidiarity**.

An adjunct to this argument was the (logically separate) suggestion that in future only the constitution of the Union need be subject to the very strict rules for Treaty amendment (notably the need for unanimity among all the governments and ratification in all the **national parliaments** of the member states). The non-constitutional provisions of the Treaties could be amended under a simpler, faster procedure. This would, it was suggested, circumvent the impending problem of amending the Treaties once enlargement almost doubled the number of member states.

Those who opposed the idea of a constitution tended to argue that it would be a decisive step in the direction of transforming the Union into some form of 'state'. They asserted that constitutions embody and assign **sovereignty**, whereas treaties are agreements between sovereign states. Either the use of the word 'constitution' would be a misnomer or it would be an accurate description of a qualitative change that was itself undesirable. Critics also pointed to the practical difficulty of distinguishing between the constitutional and non-constitutional elements in the existing Treaties, to the problems such a distinction might pose for the homogeneity of the law contained in or flowing from the Treaties, and to the possibility that the fragile consensus upon which some provisions were based might fall apart, if the text were to be disassembled.

Despite these difficulties, the **European Commission** joined the European Parliament in calling for a constitution, in order to improve the transparency and legitimacy of EU institutions. In 2000, at the Commission's request, the **European University Institute** (EUI) in Florence prepared a model 'Basic Treaty' of only 95 articles (the different EU Treaties in force at the time contained over 700 articles). This text was published, with commentaries, in Kim Feus (editor), *A Simplified Treaty for the EU*, in 2001. It demonstrated, in the words of Guy Milton and Jacques Keller-Noëllet (see below), that it was 'perfectly possible, simply by a reordering and rationalization of the current treaties, to create a constitution for Europe, without any changes to the Union's existing institutions, powers and procedures'. Meanwhile, several major European political figures declared themselves in favour of drafting a constitution. These included the French and German Presidents, Jacques Chirac and Johannes Rau, who expressed this view in speeches made respectively to the Bundestag in June 2000 and European Parliament in April 2001.

Pressures for a new, more ambitious approach to treaty reform intensified after the messy outcome of the **Intergovernmental Conference** (IGC) that drafted the **Nice Treaty**. The long and bad-tempered **European Council** meeting (of EU heads of government) in Nice in December 2000 resulted both in a commitment to undertake a further round of treaty change and in a general willingness to experiment with a more open method of negotiation for the future. During the second half of 2001, the Belgian **presidency** of the **Council of Ministers** pushed hard for a Convention – comprised of representatives of the European Parliament, European Commission, member-state governments and **national parliaments** – to be called before the next IGC and for the latter to discuss a wide range of issues. The **Laeken Declaration**, adopted by the European Council in December 2001, convened a **Convention on the Future of Europe**, which opened the following February. A section of the declaration entitled 'Towards a Constitution for European citizens' posed the question of whether the changes to be discussed 'might not lead in the long run to the adoption of a constitutional text in the Union'. It was left to the members of the Convention to provide an answer.

At the very first meeting of the Convention, its chairman, former French President **Valéry Giscard d'Estaing**, invited his colleagues to 'open the way towards a Constitution for Europe'. With the evident support of most of the *conventionnels*, this approach was quickly accepted. The constitutional template which found favour was not, however, that of a succinct synthesis of EU institutional provisions, appropriately amended or updated – as had originally been suggested by the EUI and others – but rather an amalgamation of all the existing treaty provisions, relating both to institutions and policy, into one, new, continuous document that would need to be ratified in its entirety from scratch. However, it was agreed that explicitly 'constitutional' provisions would be gathered together in a distinctive opening section. (In discussion, it was also decided to exempt the **European Atomic Energy Community** (EAEC or Euratom) from this process.)

The final product of the Convention, the Draft Treaty establishing a Constitution for Europe, in effect proposed to merge the 1957 **Treaty of Rome** (the Treaty establishing the European Community), the 1992 **Maastricht Treaty** (the Treaty on European Union), both as subsequently amended, along with 15 other treaties and acts, into a single text. This new draft treaty, presented in sections between May and July 2003, was divided into four parts: the first set out the Union's general principles and broad institutional arrangements, the second reproduced and gave treaty status to the Charter of Fundamental Rights, the third provided details of both the internal and external policies of the Union and of the latter's 'functioning' (which encompassed detailed institutional issues and budgetary and financial matters), and the fourth set out certain 'general and final provisions'. As Jean-Claude Piris has written, a non-specialist, reading just the 60 articles in Part I of the document, running to around 30 pages, was able to gain 'a reasonably clear idea of what the Union is, of what it does, and how it does it'. The more specialist reader 'would have been able to find almost everything in a single document', rather than struggle with a complex multiplicity of sources (*The Lisbon Treaty: A Legal and Political Analysis*, 2010).

The European Constitution proposed a large number of important institutional changes, by comparison to the institutional order that it aimed to supersede. The **'pillared' structure** of the Union, established by the Maastricht Treaty, would be abolished, with the 'communautization' of all remaining intergovernmental aspects of **Justice and Home Affairs** (JHA) and the extension of **legal personality** to all Union activities. The post of **High Representative** for **Common Foreign and Security Policy** (CFSP) would be upgraded, as a 'Union Minister for Foreign Affairs', merging its existing role with those of the European Commissioner for external relations and the Council presidency in the CFSP field. The European Council would be made a separate EU institution, chaired by a full-time **President of the European Council**, appointed for a 30-month term (renewable once). Within the Council of Ministers, the use of **qualified majority voting** (QMV) would be broadened, especially to cover the JHA field. In parallel, the legislative and budgetary powers of the European Parliament would expand: **co-decision** between the Council and Parliament would henceforth include inter alia the **Common Agricultural Policy** (CAP), **Common Fisheries Policy** (CFP) and the **Common Commercial Policy** (CCP), as well as the remaining areas of JHA subject to the **consultation procedure**. The combined use of QMV in the Council and co-decision between the Council and Parliament would be dubbed the 'ordinary legislative procedure' of the Union. The two institutions would become co-equal in all aspects of the **budgetary process**, with a single reading and the abolition of the distinction between **compulsory and non-compulsory expenditure**. Reform of the **comitology** process would introduce a new distinction between delegated and implementing acts (the first of which could be vetoed or rescinded by either the Parliament or Council).

The Charter of Fundamental Rights would be given treaty status and the Union empowered to accede to the **European Convention on Human Rights** (ECHR). Union **competence** would be established or extended in the fields of policy, sport, public health, **energy policy** and intellectual property rights. Responsibility for policing the **subsidiarity** implications of draft EU law would be entrusted to **national parliaments**. A '**citizens' initiative**' would enable one million members of the general public to invite the European Commission to come forward with a specific legislative proposal. Any member state wishing to leave the Union would be permitted to take advantage of an '**exit clause**'. The process of amending the Treaties would itself be modified, so that a Convention would precede an **Intergovernmental Conference** (IGC), unless the European Parliament decided otherwise. A new 'simplified revision procedure' would also allow the European Council, acting unanimously, to adjust the policy responsibilities of the Union, without convening either an IGC or Convention, although ratification by all member states would still be required.

All the proposals listed above – other than the naming of High Representative as Union Minister for Foreign Affairs – were subsequently to feature in the **Lisbon Treaty**, the successor document to the European Constitution, which was signed in December 2007 and entered into force in December 2009, after ratification in the 27 member states. These reforms thus now form part of the institutional architecture of the Union. However, in drafting the Lisbon Treaty, a number of other proposals contained in the European Constitution were either dropped or watered down, mainly in order to indicate that the whole 'constitutional concept', as the European Council put it in June 2007, was no longer relevant. Most importantly, the attempt to merge the existing Treaties into a single, new document with the title of 'constitution' was discarded. Instead, the Lisbon Treaty embodies a series of amendments to the Maastricht Treaty (TEU) and the Treaty of Rome, the latter of which is now renamed the Treaty on the Functioning of the European Union (TFEU). Equally, the provisions to give the **symbols of the Union** treaty status and to assert the **primacy** of Union law were also abandoned. The text of the Charter of Fundamental Rights was taken out of the main body of the treaty, even if a cross-reference still signals that it now has full treaty status. Finally, although for different reasons, the introduction of a reformed system of qualified majority voting within the Council – based on the need to obtain a 'double majority' of population and states – was deferred until 2014.

In retrospect, it is clear that the (potentially misleading) characterization of the treaty prepared by the Convention on the Future of Europe as a 'constitution' was a serious political miscalculation. It raised fears and expectations that made it difficult to conduct an intelligent discussion about the actual contents of the text. Its ratification quickly ran into major difficulties and eventually had to be discontinued. Of the 25 EU member states at the time, 15 decided to ratify the treaty exclusively by the national parliamentary route (14 of which successfully completed that process), whilst nine decided to use **referenda**, with one (the Czech Republic) waiting to choose between the two. Of the nine referenda, two (in Denmark and Ireland) would have followed from national constitutional requirements, although in the event they were never held. Seven countries chose the referendum route for domestic political reasons, mainly because the move to a European Constitution was widely seen as highly significant. Although the new treaty was passed comfortably in Spain and Luxembourg in February and July 2005, the **French and Dutch referenda** in May and June 2005 resulted in 'no' votes by decisive margins (with respectively 54.7 and 61.6 per cent of the two populations rejecting the treaty). The shock delivered by these twin outcomes was so dramatic that the referenda planned in three other states – Poland, Portugal and the United Kingdom – were abandoned.

Further reading: Jean-Claude Piris, *The Constitution for Europe: A Legal Analysis*, 2006.

European Convention on Human Rights (ECHR)

Among the first acts of the General Assembly of the **United Nations** was the adoption of the Universal Declaration of Human Rights, in December 1948. This declaration, although comprehensive, did not set out a means whereby respect for human rights could be enforced. When the **Council of Europe** was established the following year, 'maintenance and further realization of human rights and fundamental freedoms' were listed among its basic objectives and quickly came to constitute its central task. This priority reflected a determination among mainstream political leaders in many countries to build institutional safeguards against any reversion to Fascism or the triumph of Communism in post-war western Europe. To this end, a Convention for the Protection of Human Rights and Fundamental Freedoms – otherwise known as the European Convention on Human Rights – was drawn up by the Council of Europe in 1949–50 and signed in Rome on 4 November 1950. Although less comprehensive than the Universal Declaration, the Convention was more ambitious in that it both required signatory states to accept certain duties of observance and set up specific machinery for the enforcement of the rights set down therein. The Convention came into force on 3 September 1953.

The Convention has been amended several times since 1953 and various **protocols** have been added to it. It consists of 59 Articles. Among the rights guaranteed are: the right to life, liberty and security of person; the right to a fair trial, with the possibility of having the sentence reviewed by a higher tribunal; respect for privacy and family life; freedom of thought, conscience and religion; freedom of expression; freedom of the press; freedom of peaceful assembly and association; freedom from torture, inhuman or degrading treatment, slavery or forced labour; prohibition of the death penalty (since 2003); the right to leave or return to one's own country; and the elimination of discrimination in the enjoyment of rights and freedoms guaranteed under the Convention. As C. A. Gearty has commented, 'some of these rights are crystal clear, others are very vague; some are unequivocal, others are heavily qualified' ('The European Court of Human Rights and the protection of civil liberties', *Cambridge Law Journal*, Volume 52, Number 1, March 1993). The text was produced relatively quickly and was designed to secure the broadest measure of support among the national parliamentarians and ministers who adopted it in the Council of Europe.

Several member states of the Council of Europe have chosen to incorporate the Convention into their domestic law or to make reference to it in their constitutions. Whether or not they do so, they have been obliged since 1958 to 'ensure that their domestic legislation is compatible with the Convention' by whatever means. The United Kingdom gave effect in domestic law to the rights contained in the Convention by its Human Rights Act of 1998. The Convention was never intended to supplant national measures for the protection of human rights, but rather to provide an additional guarantee at the international level. Exhaustion of national remedies is a precondition for bringing proceedings under the Convention.

The European Court of Human Rights established by the Convention is based in Strasbourg, France. There are as many judges as there are member states of the Council of Europe (currently 47). They are chosen – a third of them at a time in elections held every three years, for a non-renewable nine year term – by the Parliamentary Assembly of the Council of Europe from lists of names, three for each vacancy, submitted by the signatory states. One of the three candidates for each vacancy is recommended to the full Assembly by the latter's committee on legal affairs, and this recommendation is usually, but not always, followed in the election. When the European Union accedes to the Convention, as foreseen by the **Lisbon Treaty**, it will be entitled to a judge nominated and elected on the same basis.

All applications are addressed directly to the Court, and sifted by a panel of three judges. They may be brought by persons, groups or private organizations, or by one state against another. The complainant must show that all domestic legal remedies have been exhausted – and for this reason, the Court does not see itself as a 'court of appeal' – whilst the complaint must be brought within six months of the final decision by the national courts or authorities concerned. Cases accepted as admissible are normally heard by a chamber of seven judges. Once the facts have been established, provision exists for a 'friendly settlement' between the parties. If this is not accepted, the Court formally adjudicates. Exceptionally, cases may be brought before a Grand Chamber of 17 judges, either on appeal or by virtue of their importance. A judge from the state in which the case originated always sits in the Grand Chamber, to ensure a proper understanding of that state's legal system. Responsibility for monitoring the enforcement of the Court's decision (decisions of the Grand Chamber are final) rests with the Committee of Ministers of the Council of Europe. All signatory states to the Convention are required to recognize the right of individual application to the Court and the Court's jurisdiction over all inter-state cases.

The Court receives around 5,000 complaints every year. Of these, about two-thirds are eliminated as clearly inadmissible. Of those that are investigated further, about 10 per cent are declared admissible. Only three inter-state cases have ever been referred to the Court: on methods used to interrogate terrorist suspects in Northern Ireland; on the Turkish invasion of northern Cyprus; and on the Russian invasion of South Ossetia. The number of judgements delivered by the Court averaged only one a year during the Court's first decade, but the figure is now more than 20. The procedure outlined above was introduced in November 1998 and was designed to speed up the Court's work. Under the previous two-tier procedure – which involved a European Commission on Human Rights, as well as a Court – it could take up to six years for a case to be decided.

Before 1998, acceptance of the judgements of the Court by the member states of the Council of Europe was ultimately voluntary, relying on what the President of the Court referred to at the time as 'the traditional good faith required of the signatories to an international agreement'. However, Article 46 of the Convention now reads: 'The High Contracting Parties undertake to abide by the final judgement of the Court in any case where they are parties.' The Court's judgement is transmitted to the Committee of Ministers, whose responsibility it is to 'supervise its execution'. If the Court has ruled against a member state, it invites that country to inform it of the measures it is taking to comply with its obligations. If the Committee of Ministers is dissatisfied by the response, it will usually pass a resolution on the matter. The limitation of such a system lies in the fact that governments are being asked to react to the behaviour of one of their own number and that, in any case, there are no specific sanctions to induce the right response.

As a result, a new Protocol 14 to the Convention, which took effect in June 2010, has added a further mechanism for promoting compliance. If it 'considers that a High Contracting Party refuses to abide by a final judgement', the Committee of Ministers may, by a two-thirds majority, vote to 'refer to the Court the question of whether that Party has failed to fulfil its obligations' and, should the Court find that the country is so failing, 'it shall refer the case to the Committee of Ministers for consideration of the measures to be taken'. There is still no indication of precisely what these measures might be, but for the first time the route of sanctions is explicitly envisaged. The ultimate sanction would, of course, be expulsion from the Council of Europe, a possibility which has always existed under Articles 3 and 8 of its Statute. (In 1970, Greece was threatened with expulsion but chose instead to withdraw voluntarily, returning after the end of military rule.) Any country that aspires to membership of the European Union may also be conscious that the perception of a negative human rights' record could significantly complicate negotiations for **accession**, as to some degree **Turkey** has recently found.

Over the years, rulings of the Court have forced important changes in domestic law and practice in Council of Europe member states: for example, 'on abortion law in the Federal Republic of Germany, on detention on remand in Austria, on the status of illegitimacy in Belgium, and on surveillance, contempt of court, and correspondence of prisoners, in the United Kingdom' (James Fawcett, 'European Convention on Human Rights', in Vernon Bogdanor (editor), *The Blackwell Encyclopaedia of Political Science*, 1991). More recently, however, there has been growing concern about the reluctance, or even refusal, of some member governments to abide by the rulings of the Court. Russia has been developing a record of frequent dispute with the Court. In recent years, Italy and Slovakia have expelled third country nationals, in defiance of Court rulings preventing such action on the grounds that the individuals concerned would be at risk of persecution, torture or execution. The attitude in many member-state judiciaries, let alone among executives, can be surprisingly relaxed. For example, Lord Hope, a member of the Supreme Court of the United Kingdom, said in an interview in August 2010: 'We are not obliged to follow what [the Court in] Strasbourg says in every case. Our task, when presented with their judgements, is to see whether we can apply them within our system. There are instances when we say [that] we cannot do that, that their principles cannot be applied here, or that they have been insufficiently explained . . .' Formally speaking, under the

1998 Human Rights Act, the UK Supreme Court (previously the judicial committee of the House of Lords) and some lower courts can issue a 'declaration of incompatibility' if domestic legislation contradicts the rights guaranteed by the ECHR. However, the declaration has no legal effect unless the UK Parliament amends the law in question.

The Council of Europe's human rights activities have increased over time, not only as a result of new accessions to the Council, but also because the Convention on Human Rights itself has been supplemented by other conventions, such as the 1989 Convention for the Prevention of Torture and Inhuman or Degrading Treatment or Punishment. In 1997, the member states decided to create the new post of Council of Europe Commissioner for Human Rights, mandated to monitor and foster the observance of human rights in member states, and to assist those states in the implementation of the Council's standards in this field. Unlike the Court, the Commissioner does not act upon individual complaints; rather he or she visits individual countries to evaluate the situation and makes general and specific recommendations to the Committee of Ministers and the Parliamentary Assembly for improvement. The post of Commissioner took effect in 1999 and the office-holder is elected for a six-year term by the Assembly. The current appointee (for the years 2006–12) is Thomas Hammarberg, previously a Swedish diplomat and secretary general of Amnesty International.

Further reading: Ed Bates, *The Evolution of the European Convention on Human Rights*, 2010; Steven Greer, *The European Convention on Human Rights: Achievements, Problems and Prospects*, 2006; Francis Jacobs, Robin White and Clare Ovey, *The European Convention on Human Rights*, 2010.

European Council

The European Council brings together the 'heads of state or government' of the member states of the European Union, together with the President of the **European Commission**, in regular **summit** meetings that provide the most visible and politically potent face of EU activity to be found in any forum. Although it has developed separately from the **Council of Ministers** – and was made a free-standing institution to the Council by the recent **Lisbon Treaty** – the European Council is in effect the top tier of the Council system, at the apex of collective decision-making among the governments of the member states of the Union. The European Council – not to be confused with the Strasbourg-based **Council of Europe** – is the key arena for agreeing new policy objectives and resolving disputes among member states. Its meetings, sometimes characterized by intense media interest and high political drama, have been central to nearly all of the most important policy and institutional developments within the EU in recent decades.

It is ironic that, given the significance of the European Council today, the founding **Treaties** made no reference to this or indeed to any other form of summit structure for the **European Communities**. The first meeting of government leaders was held in Paris in February 1961, at the suggestion of French President **Charles de Gaulle**, who wished to advance his plans for a European political union along intergovernmental lines; a further summit followed in Bonn in July that year. When negotiations on de Gaulle's **Fouchet Plan** collapsed in 1962, France turned away from summitry. The only meeting of heads of government to be held during the remainder of the General's term of office was a largely ceremonial session in May 1967, to mark the tenth anniversary of the signing of the **Treaty of Rome**.

De Gaulle's successor, Georges Pompidou, quickly reactivated the summit process, using it as a means to give new vitality to the Community. 'Conferences of heads of state or government', as they were then called, were held in The Hague (in December 1969), Paris (in October 1972) and Copenhagen (in December 1973). Two meetings followed in Paris in September and December 1974, at the invitation of Pompidou's successor, **Valéry Giscard d'Estaing**, during France's tenure of the six-month, rotating **presidency** of the Council. During the years 1972–4, both Pompidou and Giscard suggested that the holding of summits should be put on a more regular and formal footing, in what the latter chose to style a 'European Council'. Initially, the notion of upgrading the role of national leaders in this way encountered considerable scepticism among strong integrationists, notably within the **Benelux** countries, who feared that it might herald a move towards greater **intergovernmentalism** along Gaullist lines. However, the support extended by **Jean Monnet** to Giscard's proposal in 1974 helped reassure doubters. Monnet argued that 'what is lacking more than anything else in European affairs is authority. Discussion is organized; decision is not' (*Memoirs*, 1978). Regular summits could enhance both the authority of the European institutions and their capacity to act. He described the choice to be made as 'the most important decision for Europe since the Treaty of Rome'.

In the event, in return for agreeing to formalize and regularize summitry, the doubters were to be compensated by the promise of direct elections to the **European Parliament** (finally achieved in June 1979) – a concession first suggested by Monnet himself. Almost casually, this compromise set in train, admittedly at different speeds, what were to prove to be two of the most important institutional developments in the history of the Union. At the second Paris summit in December 1974, fellow leaders agreed that Giscard's new forum would convene from the following year. Although the words 'European Council' were not used in the conclusions, the term was reiterated so frequently (especially by the French President himself) that it became widely accepted. The body held its first meeting in Dublin in March 1975 and established itself rapidly as a central component of Community decision-making.

Member states are free to nominate as their lead representative in the European Council either their head of government (prime minister) or head of state (in effect, president, if directly elected and exercising executive responsibilities). Hence the description of the meeting as being one of 'heads of state or government'. In addition, the President of the **European Commission** was invited to attend European Council meetings from the start. The existence and composition of the European Council was first recognized in a treaty text by the 1986 **Single European Act** (SEA), amended by the 1992 **Maastricht Treaty**, which defined its membership and chairmanship in this way:

> *The European Council shall bring together the Heads of State or Government of the Member States and the President of the Commission of the European Communities. They shall be assisted by the Ministers for Foreign Affairs and by a Member of the Commission. The European Council shall meet at least twice a year, under the chairmanship of the Head of State or Government of the Member State which holds the Presidency of the Council.* (Article 4 TEU)

This situation prevailed until December 2009, when the Lisbon Treaty entered into force. The analogous wording, introduced by Lisbon, no longer provides for the members of the European Council to be 'assisted' by their foreign ministers and by a member of the Commission (Article 15(2–3) TEU). Instead, if 'the agenda so requires, [they] may decide each to be assisted by a minister and, in the case of the President of the Commission, by a member of the Commission'. In the place of the foreign ministers collectively, the **High Representative** for the **Common Foreign and Security Policy** (CFSP) will 'take part' in the European Council's work. More importantly, the chairmanship of the European Council is no longer provided by the rotating presidency of the Council, but by a specially-chosen **President of the European Council**, who serves for a term of 30 months, renewable once, and who is also a full member of the European Council in his or her own right. The first person chosen to hold this post, the outgoing Belgian prime minister, Herman Van Rompuy, immediately secured agreement that foreign ministers would only attend a maximum of one European Council meeting a year. (The heads of state or government are now unaccompanied, other than by officials from the Council secretariat and the permanent representative of the member state holding the rotating presidency of the Council.)

In practice, most countries have chosen to send the prime minister as their lead representative to the European Council, the notable exceptions being France and Romania (consistently), Finland (intermittently), and

Poland and the Czech Republic (occasionally). In Cyprus, the head of state is also head of government (as in the United States). Where there is cohabitation between a directly-elected president and a prime minister who each come from different political parties, there can be friction on the question of which of the two attends. When this issue first arose in France in 1986, **François Mitterrand** insisted that the president should continue to represent the country, regardless of whether the same party controlled the bifurcated executive branch. In Poland, cohabitation resulted in each of three permutations being used at different times – with either the president or prime minister attending, or on one occasion, both attending – but with the reversion to one-party rule, the prime minister now represents the country.

Since 1988, the President of the European Parliament has also been invited to address each formal meeting of the European Council at the start of proceedings – although he or she does not take part in subsequent business, unless asked to do so, as has occurred occasionally when discussions have concerned institutional reform. (Article 235(2) TFEU states that the 'President of the European Parliament may be invited to be heard by the European Council'.) This speech used to be largely a formality, but one interesting effect of **enlargement** has been to increase the relative political potential of a scene-setting intervention of about 20 minutes' length, made at the beginning of a meeting at which nearly 30 other people may be hoping to take the floor, some only for a very few minutes.

The Paris agreement in December 1974 envisaged that the European Council would meet three times a year. After some variation, a pattern emerged of meetings being held routinely in June and December – in each of the two presidency countries at the end of their respective terms of office – with a third meeting (usually in the spring) in Brussels. The Single European Act spoke cautiously of the body meeting 'at least twice a year'. Although the European Council did meet only twice in 1986 and 1987, the three-meeting norm quickly reasserted itself – but with the third meeting being held either in the spring or autumn, and not necessarily in Brussels. In 1990, for the first time, four meetings were held, and in 1991 one (of the three meetings that year) was deemed to be an 'informal' gathering, namely without conclusions. In 1999, no fewer than six European Council meetings were held, with two of them 'informals' and only one in Brussels.

In order to reassert some discipline in the way Council presidencies practised EU summitry, two sets of decisions were taken soon thereafter. First, heads of government decided in December 2000 (in Nice) that, from 2002 onwards, they would hold at least one European Council in Brussels during each six-month presidency, and that all meetings would take place in that city from whenever the number of member states rose to 18 or more (as it did in May 2004). Second, in June 2002 (in Seville), they agreed to meet four times a year, with additional meetings allowed under exceptional circumstances. The standard pattern that emerged during the 2000s was one of quarterly summits, held in March, June, October and December. However, as the decade progressed, the number of meetings began to rise again, partly driven by the economic and financial crisis, with seven in 2008 and eight in 2009. The UK presidency in 2005 managed to convene one of its two meetings at Hampton Court, outside London, establishing a precedent (followed by two subsequent presidencies) that informal summits need not be held in Brussels, whilst the Czech presidency brought leaders together in Prague in April 2009 to meet the new US President, Barack Obama.

With the appointment of a 'permanent' or full-time President of the European Council under the Lisbon Treaty, the tendency towards holding more, rather than fewer, European Councils has intensified, but in a more structured way. Van Rompuy prefers to schedule about six meetings a year, but with several of them lasting only for a day, eschewing the classic two-day event. He also prefers the meetings to be clearly focused, in advance, on one or two specific policy items. The purpose appears to be to drive forward a continuous agenda, which he sees it as his responsibility to ensure is implemented.

As the European Council has developed, its procedures and working methods have become more formal, and this process has been decisively confirmed now that, since the Lisbon Treaty, the body is an EU institution in its own right. It was only in December 2009 that the European Council adopted any internal rules of procedure. Until June 2002, the definition of its agenda was also fairly casual: the head of government of the presidency country would simply send a short letter to his or her colleagues some days before each meeting, identifying the likely topics for discussion. Since then, first the presidency country, now the President of the European Council, has been obliged to issue an 'annotated' agenda at least four weeks before the meeting, based on discussion in the **General Affairs Council** (GAC) and bilateral contacts with individual governments. In a gesture towards openness, the first version of this draft agenda is made available to the public, even if subsequent revisions are not.

The Lisbon Treaty specifies that it is the responsibility of the General Affairs Council to 'prepare and ensure the follow-up to meetings of the European Council, in liaison with the President of the European Council and the Commission' (Article 6 TEU). However, performing this role successfully is greatly complicated by the fact that foreign ministers, who often (but not always) sit in the GAC, no longer participate in the European Council: they are represented instead by the High Representative, who is in turn not a member of the GAC. Conversely, the President of the European Council does not sit in the GAC. Van Rompuy has agreed to attend an informal

'GAC lunch' before each European Council meeting, but has so far declined to take part in any formal discussion within the Council, arguing that this confuses his institutional status.

The process of drafting the conclusions of European Council meetings has also evolved over time, as has their content and style. The purpose of conclusions is to embody points of agreement among the member states on the policy issues under discussion at the meeting and offer joint statements on significant international events. They may review progress towards established policy goals, set new objectives, establish targets and deadlines, and/or commit the member states to support specific legislative action in a particular field. Responsibility for drafting conclusions used to rest with the presidency country, which would sometimes spring surprises on the heads of government at the last moment. It was thus decided (again in June 2002) to try to negotiate and agree as much of the draft text as possible in **COREPER**, the Committee of Permanent Representatives (composed of the member states' ambassadors to the EU), during the month running up to each summit meeting. On this basis, a pre-final version of the conclusions is submitted for ministerial consideration at the GAC meeting held a few days before the European Council itself. After that, no draft conclusions are produced until a final text is presented by the President to the European Council during its meeting. The first draft of the conclusions is usually circulated in English, even when there is a French presidency.

Over time, there was a pronounced tendency for the length of the European Council conclusions to become longer, more diffuse and more anodyne, as the rotating presidency of the Council sought to use them as a vehicle for broadcasting progress towards their goals, however modest. Whereas the Hague summit in 1969 encapsulated a series of key strategic initiatives in a succinct three-page communiqué, the text issued at the end of the Helsinki European Council in December 1999 ran to 62 pages. The average length of conclusions in the 2000s was around 25 pages. In 2007, the French President, Nicolas Sarkozy, captured the mood when he said that most such texts were 'as empty as they were long', displayed an '*ennui mortel*' and seemed 'incomprehensible even to the people who drafted them'. Since Van Rompuy has been President of the European Council, he has made a conscious, and largely successful, effort to produce much tighter summit conclusions, with fewer broad-ranging declarations and more emphasis on specific announcements or tasking.

From its inception, the de facto role of the European Council quickly emerged as that of the key arena for setting new policy objectives within the Community system and resolving major policy disputes between the member states. In performing these functions, it was filling something of a political vacuum. In the decade from 1975 to 1985, the Council of Ministers acted almost entirely by **unanimity** and had become mired in inertia, whilst the European Commission had lost political confidence and the European Parliament was limited to an essentially advisory role. A formal remit for the European Council was set out for the first time in the **Stuttgart Declaration** of June 1983. This stated that the body would provide 'general political impetus to the construction of Europe', would issue 'general political guidelines' on policy questions, initiate cooperation in new areas of activity and express the common position of member states on foreign-policy questions. The Maastricht Treaty stated the European Council's role succinctly as being to 'provide the Union with the necessary impetus for its development and . . . define the general political guidelines thereof'. The Lisbon Treaty has strengthened the second part of this sentence to read: 'define the general political directions and priorities' of the Union (Article 15(1) TEU). Maastricht also required the European Council to 'define the principles of and general guidelines for' the Union's CFSP. This too has been adjusted to read: 'The European Council shall identify the Union's strategic interests, [and] determine the objectives of and define general guidelines for [CFSP], including for matters with defence implications. It shall adopt the necessary decisions' (Article 26 TEU).

There has traditionally been a tendency for European Council meetings to give priority, not to long-range thinking or bold initiatives, but to immediate, practical issues on which the member states are divided and where decision at lower levels in the Council, whether official or ministerial, has proved impossible. Such issues may be both intrinsically complex and politically sensitive, and by the time they reach the European Council, they may well be urgent too. As a result, meetings have often been dominated by a single issue, sometimes legislative in character, with less urgent matters addressed only in a *pro forma* way. Since he became President of the European Council, Van Rompuy has sought to escape from this syndrome, stressing that the institution should focus on charting the overall direction of the Union, rather than engaging in short-term crisis resolution, and that it should avoid becoming enmeshed in resolving disputes over the detailed content of legislation. In his view, the latter responsibility devolves to the sectoral Councils and the rotating presidency.

Van Rompuy is helped by the fact that, in general, the growth of **co-decision** between the Council of Ministers and the European Parliament has made it more difficult for heads of government to simply act as the final 'court of appeal' on EU legislation, as they cannot now determine the outcome of the law-making process without the agreement of another institution. However, from time to time, the European Council has performed this role quite dramatically, as it did on the climate change package in December 2008, when the settlement agreed by heads of government was simply accepted by the Parliament.

The Lisbon Treaty states unequivocally that the European Council 'shall not exercise legislative functions' (Article 15(1) TEU). This represents a change of philosophy and marks a further step in defining the Council of Ministers as the legislative component of the whole Council system (and, by implication, recognizing the Council of Ministers as one branch of a joint legislature with the Parliament). The Stuttgart Declaration in 1983 had foreseen that the European Council might itself take legislative decisions, if it wished, acting as a configuration of the Council of Ministers. That practice has now been formally ended, although in reality its invocation was relatively rare. If a routine decision of a legislative character was agreed in the European Council, it was usually taken politically by heads of government and then confirmed legally at a subsequent meeting of the Council of Ministers at a lower level, after any final redrafting.

However, this pattern was disrupted and confused by the tendency in successive treaties (until the Lisbon Treaty) to specifically reserve certain formal decisions to the 'Council meeting in the composition of heads of state and government'. The consequences were sometimes laborious: for example, the June 2008 summit meeting had to been convened in two parts: a meeting of the Council of Ministers to approve Slovakia's entry into stage three of **Economic and Monetary Union** (EMU), followed by the conventional European Council meeting to discuss all other items of business.

The Lisbon Treaty has simplified this situation, by assigning the adoption of a number of specific **legal acts** directly to the European Council. There are now over 30 references in the Treaties to such decisions, usually to be taken either by unanimity or **qualified majority voting** (QMV). Examples of decisions requiring unanimity in the European Council are the use of various ***passerelle* clauses** – to allow extensions in the use of QMV in the Council and co-decision between the Council and Parliament – and the determination of whether a 'serious and persistent breach' of fundamental values might exist in a member state (see **suspension**). Most decisions taken by QMV concern senior appointments or nominations within the institutions – for example, of the President of the European Council, the High Representative, and members of the European Commission and the Executive Board of the **European Central Bank** (ECB). In addition, a small category of decisions require 'consensus' – in these cases, no legal act is adopted, but abstention is in effect a negative vote, unlike under unanimity – whilst a few procedural questions can be settled by simple majority (for example, adoption of the institution's rules of procedure).

In any case, whatever the formal decision-making method, there has traditionally been a very strong desire within the European Council that it act, wherever possible, on the basis of consensus. This applies especially wherever general objectives or new policy goals are being defined. The instinct was recognized in the Lisbon Treaty, which introduced a requirement that except where the Treaties specifically provide otherwise, 'decisions of the European Council shall be taken by consensus' (Article 15(4) TEU). Indeed, historically, there have been very few occasions where minorities have been overridden in summit meetings. The most notable instances concern the United Kingdom during the period when **Margaret Thatcher** was prime minister (1979–90). The UK, Denmark and Greece were defeated in a formal vote on the convening, at Milan in June 1985, of the **Intergovernmental Conference** (IGC) that led to the Single European Act. Likewise, the UK was unable to prevent the convening of the IGC on EMU and the adoption of the **European Social Charter** at the Madrid and Strasbourg summits in June and December 1989. Britain also found itself isolated and defeated over the setting of a date for the second stage of EMU at the 'Rome II' summit in October 1990. This latter defeat acted as a catalyst for the events that led to Thatcher's resignation less than a month later.

The only significant recent occasion of involuntary majority decision-making in the European Council appears to have been in Brussels in June 2007. The German Chancellor, Angela Merkel, who was chairing the meeting, threatened to call a vote to convene the IGC that replaced the **European Constitution** with the 'Reform Treaty', now the Lisbon Treaty, in the face of deep Polish objections, in effect forcing Warsaw to accept a detailed negotiating mandate for the IGC which included specific arrangements on voting rights in the Council.

European Council meetings have usually take place over two days, often beginning on the late afternoon of a Thursday and ending on Friday afternoon. If agreement has proved particularly difficult, they might stretch into Saturday. However, since becoming President of the European Council, Van Rompuy has sought to move to a situation where about half of summit meetings follow the traditional, two-day pattern, and the rest are simply one-day meetings, avoiding the need for heads of government to stay overnight in Brussels. This shift corresponds to his vision of the summits forming a more regular and more routine part of the political life of national leaders, where they together define and drive forward the ongoing political agenda of the Union. Hence also his desire to limit attendance at European Council meetings, by excluding foreign ministers, partly in order to make the summit experience more personal to its participants, especially given the expansion in the number of people attending with **enlargement**. The regularity of European Councils already forces national leaders to invest considerable personal time and political capital in EU issues, whether they wish to or not. The approach adopted by Van Rompuy is likely to make this even more the case.

Comprised of presidents and prime ministers who enjoy powerful political legitimacy of their own – either by dint of direct election or by commanding majorities in their national parliaments – the European Council is not collectively accountable in any meaningful sense to any other political body within the EU. Since December 1981, however, the person chairing the European Council has reported the outcome of each meeting to the European Parliament. The process was begun by Thatcher as president-in-office, confirmed in the Stuttgart Declaration and formalized in the Maastricht Treaty. Since the Lisbon Treaty entered into force, the report back to the Parliament is undertaken by Van Rompuy as President of the European Council (Article15(6)b TEU). He has chosen not only to appear formally in the Parliament's plenary session, but to give an informal briefing to its Conference of Presidents (comprising the leaders of **political groups**) immediately after each summit ends.

When the decision was taken to make the European Council a free-standing institution, there was a discussion about whether to give it a separate administrative structure to that of the Council of Ministers. It was decided that, for both political and practical reasons, it would be better to retain a fused structure. Article 235(4) TFEU thus provides that the 'European Council shall be assisted by the General Secretariat of the Council'. The President of the European Council has a personal ***cabinet***, but otherwise relies on the same officials who prepare meetings of the GAC, the Foreign Affairs Council, the various sectoral Councils and COREPER. See also **Eurogroup and Euro Summit**.

Further reading: Simon Bulmer and Wolfgang Wessels, *The European Council: Decision-Making in European Politics*, 1987; Béatrice Taulègne, *Le Conseil européen*, 1993; Jan Werts, *The European Council*, 2008; Martin Westlake and David Galloway, *The Council of the European Union*, 2006.

European Court

The phrase 'European Court' may refer to either the **European Court of Justice** (ECJ) in Luxembourg or the European Court of Human Rights in Strasbourg, depending upon the context. The European Court of Justice, an institution of the European Union, adjudicates on disputes arising from the interpretation or application of the EU **Treaties** or legislation adopted under them. It is now assisted by a General Court, previously known as the Court of First Instance, and a Civil Service Tribunal. The European Court of Human Rights, an institution of the intergovernmental **Council of Europe**, is concerned solely with cases brought under the **European Convention on Human Rights** (ECHR).

Judgements of the ECJ, like the supranational law to which they relate, are binding on the EU member states and are respected by national courts as such. EU law is deemed to enjoy both **primacy** over national law and **direct effect** within the member states. The only area of uncertainty relates to any direct conflict between the ruling of the ECJ and that of a national constitutional court, something which the ECJ has so far taken care to avoid.

By contrast, the legal status of rulings of the European Court of Human Rights depends on their acceptance by the governments of the individual member states of the Council of Europe, with the ultimate sanction that a country which systematically refused to implement them could be expelled from the organization. Many states have incorporated the ECHR into either their constitutions or domestic legislation in some form, which reduces the prospect of negative rulings. Moreover, since 1998, member states have accepted in principle that they will 'abide by the final judgement of the Court in any case where they are parties', even if in practice they do not always fulfil this commitment.

European Court of Human Rights

See **European Convention on Human Rights** (ECHR).

European Court of Justice (ECJ)

The European Court of Justice is the final arbiter of disputes arising from the European Union **Treaties** or legislation adopted under them. The Court was one of the four Community **institutions** established in 1951 under Article 7 of the **European Coal and Steel Community** (ECSC) Treaty. Since the **Treaty of Rome** was adopted in 1957, it has been entrusted with the responsibility to 'ensure that in the interpretation and application of the **Treaties** the law is observed' (Article 220 EEC, now Article 19(1) TEU). The Treaties lay down the structure, jurisdiction and powers of the Court – which is formally known as the Court of Justice of the European Union and is based in Luxembourg – whilst its detailed organization and procedures are set out in a Statute, annexed to the Treaties as a **protocol**.

The Court consists of 27 judges, one from each member state, appointed by the governments of the member states (as opposed to the **European Council**) for a six-year term. To promote continuity, half the judges retire every three years and they may be reappointed. They are assisted by eight **advocates-general**, also chosen for six years, who make 'reasoned submissions' in open court on cases that are particularly complex or raise new points of law. The President of the Court is elected by the judges from among their number, for a three-year term, and may be re-elected. The judges and advocates-general are required to be 'persons whose independence is beyond doubt and who possess the qualifications required for appointment to the highest judicial offices in their respective countries or who are jurisconsults of recognized competence' (Article 253 TFEU). The Court sits as a Grand Chamber of 13 judges (chaired by the President) or in smaller chambers of three or five judges each. For particularly important institutional cases, the 'full Court' of 27 judges may convene. The senior official of the Court is the Registrar.

The Court has four main areas of jurisdiction. First, an action may be brought against a member state, either by the **European Commission** or by another member state, for failure to fulfil a treaty obligation (Articles 258–60 TFEU). In both cases, the Commission is required to deliver a '**reasoned opinion**', having given the state concerned an opportunity to submit observations. If the Court finds the state to be in breach of a treaty obligation, the latter is required 'to take the necessary measures to comply with the judgement of the Court'. Failure to comply may result in the imposition of 'a lump sum or penalty payment'.

Second, the Court has an important function of judicial review (Article 263 TFEU). It is empowered to 'review the legality' of legislation (and any other acts having legal effect) adopted by the various EU institutions and bodies. Actions in this field may be brought by the Commission, the **Council of Ministers** or the **European Parliament**, or by a member state. (Some other institutions and bodies are allowed to bring actions specifically in order to protect their own prerogatives.) Individuals or organizations ('natural or legal persons') may also bring such actions in respect of acts addressed to them personally or of direct concern to them. The Court may declare the act void and require the offending institution to take the 'necessary measures' (Articles 264 and 266 TFEU). Cases of this kind are most commonly brought because of alleged inadequacies in the **legal bases** of the acts in question.

Third, the Court rules on cases relating to the '**failure to act**' by certain EU institutions (Article 265 TFEU). If the Commission, Council or Parliament fails to act and in so doing infringes a requirement laid down in the Treaties, a member state or another EU institution (Commission, Council, Parliament or **Court of Auditors**) may bring an action before the Court 'to have the infringement established'. Individuals may bring such actions on the same basis under 'judicial review' (above). Once again, the Court may require the offending institution to take the 'necessary measures'.

Fourth, the Court may give '**preliminary rulings**' on the meaning of EU law (Article 267 TFEU). In the event of a question of treaty interpretation or the validity or interpretation of acts of the EU institutions or bodies being raised before a national court, that court may request the ECJ to give a preliminary ruling. The Court's ruling must be sought when such a question is raised before a national court against whose decisions there is no final appeal. This procedure is used to resolve questions of incompatibility between national law and Union law.

Certain of the ECJ's responsibilities are devolved to a General Court – known until the **Lisbon Treaty** as the Court of First Instance (CFI) – which, under Article 256(1) TFEU, has the 'jurisdiction to hear and determine at first instance' specific classes of case. The CFI, also composed of a judge from each member state appointed for six years, was established in October 1988, under provisions of the 1986 **Single European Act** (SEA), as a means of relieving an overburdened ECJ of certain types of action, often involving complex issues of fact, that were taking up a disproportionate amount of its time. The jurisdiction of the CFI has always been restricted to cases brought by individuals or organizations, as opposed to EU institutions or member states, seeking to annul Union acts or establish a failure to act. At first, this role was limited to disputes between the institutions and their employees (involving interpretation of the **staff regulations**) and to cases relating to **competition policy** and the ECSC. Similar actions in relation to 'trade defence instruments' (TDIs) and intellectual property were transferred from the ECJ to the CFI in 1994. Rulings of the General Court may be appealed against in the ECJ within a two-month deadline, but only with respect to points of law. The General Court is not empowered to give preliminary rulings. Some critics argued that the creation of a two-tier system, with different judges, would add unnecessary complexity to the ECJ system, with the risk of competing jurisprudence. In the event, the system appears to have worked satisfactorily. In 2001, a specialist court comprising seven judges, known as the Civil Service Tribunal, was established specifically to deal with legal disputes involving the staff regulations. It currently hears about 120 cases a year and its rulings may be appealed against in the General Court.

The ECJ's procedures are based almost wholly on written submissions from the contending parties. At the start of proceedings, each case is given a number by the Registrar: since the introduction of the Court of First Instance in 1988, the ECJ's cases are prefixed with a 'C' and those of the CFI (now General Court) with a 'T' (derived from the French *Tribunal*). One of the Union's official **languages** is chosen as the procedural language for the case, but otherwise the normal rules on the use of official languages apply. French and English are the working languages. The governments of member states and Union institutions may choose to intervene in actions in which they are not directly involved. The court's rulings, published periodically in *European Court Reports*, are composed of two parts: the reasoning (which will normally draw upon the submission of the advocate-general) and the judgement itself. Judgements are delivered in the name of the Court as a whole; dissenting opinions (if any) are not recorded. The only authentic text of a judgement is the one in the language of the case.

The position of the Court of Justice is an exceptionally powerful one, in that there is no appeal against its rulings, which are binding with effect from the date of delivery. The Court can strike down as illegal the legislative acts of member states or Union institutions, and it is a source of law in its own right. Since both the Union's founding Treaties and the legislation adopted under them are neither sufficiently precise nor sufficiently comprehensive to cover all legal eventualities, the Court has, over the years, been able to play a major part in shaping the corpus of **EU law**. Nevertheless, springing as it does from a variety of legal traditions, the Court has had to bring about a synthesis of these traditions with respect both to its mode of operation and the substance of its judgements. As a supreme court, the ECJ is not formally bound by precedent. However, the self-evident need for consistency, coherence and equality of treatment ensures that precedents are taken into account, although no point of law is ever settled by reference to precedent alone. The precedents that have guided the Court in a given judgement are cited in the reasoning.

The ECJ's power to interpret EU law is exercised in the light of the fundamental purposes of the Treaties and the internal logic of particular policies. This has led the Court to play an important 'integrationist' role in its own right – similar to that of the United States Supreme Court with respect to the US Constitution. The Court has worked within a tradition of interpretation that allows the 'ultimate purpose' of a piece of legislation to be taken into consideration. This means that it is regarded as legitimate, with respect to a particular text, to take not only the exact purport of the words into account, but also anything that may usefully and convincingly be adduced about the intention behind those words. As a result, the Court has tended to give a 'dynamic', rather than a strictly literal, interpretation of treaty provisions, and this factor has proved a key element in some of the Court's most noteworthy judgements.

Such an approach is consistent with the 1969 Vienna Convention on the Law of International Treaties, which states that a 'treaty shall be interpreted ... in the light of its object and purpose.' Interpretations may be incidental to a judgement or embodied in a preliminary ruling.

Underpinning the Court's judgements and EU law as a whole are certain fundamental doctrines, some of them familiar in national law and others arising from the unique nature of the Union. Among them are the autonomy of EU law – its separateness from national law and the independence of the law-making and law-enforcing Union institutions – and its **primacy** over national law. This was expressed in the Court judgement in the Van Gend en Loos case in 1963 (Case 26/62): 'The Community constitutes a new legal order of international law, in favour of which the States within certain areas have limited their sovereign rights...' The duties of national courts to apply EU law were spelt out the following year in *Costa* v *ENEL* (Case 6/64). In this judgement, the Court emphasized that EU law cannot be 'overridden by domestic legal provisions . . . without being deprived of its character as Community law and without the legal basis of the Community itself being called into question'. The ECJ did much to introduce the principle of **proportionality** into the Union's legal framework: it and the parallel principle of **subsidiarity** were given treaty status by the 1992 **Maastricht Treaty** (Article 5 TEU).

The number of cases brought before the ECJ has increased spectacularly since 1970. In that year, only 79 cases were brought, but by 1985 the number had increased to 433. It is now running at an annual average of around 600 – 631 in 2010 – of which over half are requests for preliminary rulings (385 in 2010). Even though some cases can be disposed of in groups and others do not result in the Court having to give a final judgement, the backlog of cases pending has remained high (799 in 2010), despite the creation of the General Court, which itself now deals with over 600 cases a year. (In 2010, the General admitted 636 new cases and had 1,300 cases pending.) A preliminary ruling or a direct action usually takes about 16 months to be delivered, with appeals usually requiring slightly less time (15 months). A small number of urgent preliminary rulings are given each year (five in 2010) in an average of two months.

Under Articles 105 to 107 of the 1992 Agreement establishing the **European Economic Area** (EEA), the ECJ (together with the **European Free Trade Association** (EFTA) Court and the courts of final appeal in the EFTA countries) is required to transmit its judgements on matters covered by the EEA Agreement to the EEA Joint Committee, which is responsible for ensuring the 'homogeneous interpretation of the Agreement'.

Further reading: Karen J. Alter, *The European Court's Political Power: Selected Essays*, 2009; Renaud Dehousse, *The European Court of Justice: The Politics of Judicial Integration*, 1998; Alec Stone Sweet, *The Judicial Construction of Europe*, 2004.

European Currency Unit (ECU)

A 'European Unit of Account' (EUA) was first introduced by the European Payments Union (EPU), an offshoot of the **Organization for European Economic Cooperation** (OEEC) in the 1950s. Like that of the US dollar at the time, the value of EUA was defined as equivalent to 0.888 grammes of fine gold. (The equal value of the two units continued until President Richard Nixon abandoned the gold standard in August 1971, with the dollar falling by 7.9 per cent soon after.) The EUA was used as a neutral denominator for the annual **Budget** of the European Communities and other book-keeping purposes. When the **European Monetary System** (EMS) was established in January 1979, the European Currency Unit was brought into service and it replaced the EUA three months later at parity. The name drew on the *écu*, a medieval French coin, first issued in 1266, which bore a shield on one face. (The name of the Portuguese escudo was of the same origin.)

Like its predecessor, the ECU was constituted as a 'basket' of national currencies, each currency's weighting within the basket being fixed as a percentage in line with each country's share of the Union's gross national product (GNP) and internal trade. The composition of the ECU was frozen in November 1993 at the start of stage two of **Economic and Monetary Union** (EMU). Currency movements against the dollar were reflected in the central rate of the ECU, which in turn could be used to give cross-rates for or between the national currencies of the member states.

The ECU established itself in international money markets as a stable alternative to the dollar, the Deutschmark and pound sterling. It was also used as a denomination for bank deposits and travellers' cheques, and for book-keeping in respect of transactions involving several currencies. For example, European railways used the ECU when each company's share of revenue from the sale of international tickets was being calculated. The ECU was backed by the **European Monetary Cooperation Fund** (EMCF) and its successor, the **European Monetary Institute** (EMI), to which countries participating in the EMS made available 20 per cent of their gold and dollar reserves. With the exception of some five and 50 ECU gold and silver coins minted in Belgium in 1987 to commemorate the thirtieth anniversary of the **Treaty of Rome**, the ECU was not legal tender in any part of the Union.

Proposals for the use of a 'hard ECU' as a common European currency were put forward in 1989–90 by Nigel Lawson and John Major, successive UK Chancellors of the Exchequer, in discussions on the possible design of EMU. The idea was that the ECU should be allowed to circulate alongside national currencies and float against them within the EMS. It would be 'hard' in the sense that it could not be devalued. If it found sufficient support with the public, it might evolve over time into a single currency. The idea was not adopted.

The 1992 **Maastricht Treaty** gave the ECU a central role in the third and final stage of the process leading to EMU. It required the 'irrevocable fixing' of exchange rates between national currencies and the ECU, which was specified as the single currency. The ECU would cease to be a basket currency and become a currency in its own right, with the **European Central Bank** (ECB) as the issuing authority. In spite of the treaty references to the ECU as the single currency, the Madrid meeting of the European Council in December 1995 decided to name the new currency the **euro.** In January 1999, the euro replaced the ECU on a one-to-one basis for all purposes.

European Defence Community (EDC)

With the outbreak of the Korean War in 1950, British and American demands for West German rearmament became more insistent. In August 1950, the former British prime minister, **Winston Churchill**, put forward a resolution in the Consultative Assembly of the **Council of Europe** that called for the creation of a **European army** under the authority of a European defence minister and subject to democratic control by the Assembly. The resolution was passed by 89 votes to five, with 29 abstentions. In this European army, Churchill said, 'we would all play an honourable and active part'.

On 24 October 1950, influenced by the thinking of **Jean Monnet**, the French government put forward a proposal to create among **the Six** a European Defence Community, within which a rearmed West Germany could be contained. The proposal, known as the **Pleven Plan** – named after the then French prime minister, René Pleven – was for 'the creation, for our common defence, of a European army tied to political institutions of a united Europe'. The army, to which member states would second units, would operate under a single commander. The institutional structure would follow the 'quadripartite' formula developed for the **European Coal and Steel Community** (ECSC), with a Council of national ministers, a nine-member Commission, a parliamentary assembly and a Court of Justice. In the detailed intergovernmental negotiations – which culminated in the signature of a Treaty establishing a European Defence Community in Paris on 27 May 1952 – it was agreed that of the army's 40 divisions, 14 would be French, 12 German, 11 Italian and three from the **Benelux** countries, and that they would be mixed so that no corps could consist of troops solely of one nationality. There was to be one uniform and one flag, and senior officers would be drawn from all nationalities and be responsible to the institutions of the EDC. The Community would have its own budget and make provision both for common procurement and joint training.

The EDC proposal quickly ran into problems. Although Churchill, as opposition leader, had favoured a European army in the summer of 1950, the British government proved sceptical of the EDC project. The Foreign Secretary, Ernest Bevin, told the House of Commons in November 1950 that 'Europe is not big enough, it is not strong enough and it is not able to stand by itself' in military affairs. The 'new paradox [is] that European unity is no longer possible within Europe alone but only within the broader Atlantic community'. Moreover, when Churchill returned to power in October 1951, he did not reverse the position of the Labour government. Meanwhile, in Washington, securing West German participation in the **North Atlantic Treaty Organization** (NATO) was seen as more important than creating an independent European defence capability, whatever assurances were given that the new Community would operate as part of the Atlantic Alliance. As Theodore White wrote: 'The United States Army wanted German troops, flesh and blood soldiers, quickly, not a long philosophical discussion about the creation of a new superstate' (*Fire in the Ashes*, 1954).

A further difficulty was that the EDC proposal was not self-contained. It was complemented by a parallel discussion about the possible creation of a **European Political Community** (EPC), justified on the grounds that a federal army would need to be made accountable to federal institutions. At the suggestion of the Italian prime minister, **Alcide de Gasperi**, the EDC Treaty included provisions (in Article 38) for further institutional developments, based on a new 'federal or confederal structure'. Specifically, and perhaps unwisely, the text left it to the newly-established ECSC Assembly, the forerunner of the **European Parliament**, to fill in the details of the powers and composition of the proposed EDC Assembly, as part of what could be a broader institutional rationalization of the emerging Communities (ECSC and EDC). The ECSC Assembly was enlarged with some members of the Consultative Assembly of the **Council of Europe** forming a special 'Ad Hoc Assembly' for this purpose. At the request of the foreign ministers of the Six, this new assembly began its deliberations before the EDC Treaty had been ratified. In March 1953, it proposed an ambitious complementary draft treaty designed to institute an EPC on highly integrationist lines.

In both Germany and France, the process of ratification of the EDC Treaty proved 'involved and turbulent', as F. Roy Willis has described it (*France, Germany and the New Europe, 1945–1967*, 1968). The Bonn government confronted intense opposition to the treaty from the Social Democrats in both houses of parliament, as well as a complicated case in the Federal Constitutional Court. Communist extremists staged a riot outside the Bundestag during the ratification debate. The Chancellor, **Konrad Adenauer**, had to use the most dramatic of language to rally support: 'Germany's position today is more perilous than it has ever been before throughout her long history. Germany is divided and torn, disarmed and defenceless, bordered by a colossus which is trying to enslave and swallow her ... We are at the crossroads of slavery and freedom.' If the EDC Treaty were to be rejected, 'the gradually brightening future of the German people, and of Europe, would be plunged into darkness again' and 'the Soviet Union would be done the greatest imaginable service'.

Meanwhile, in France, attitudes towards the EDC Treaty had soured. Although the original Pleven Plan had been supported by 348 votes to 224 in the National Assembly in October 1950, by the time the new conservative prime minister Antoine Pinay signed the treaty a year and a half later, concerns about revived German influence and a loss of national sovereignty had become more pronounced. As Tony Judt has written, the growing public debate 'revealed the extent of French reluctance to countenance German rearmament under any conditions' (*Postwar: A History of Europe since 1945*, 2005). The Gaullists in the National Assembly had been strengthened by the June 1951 general election and the continued hostility of the powerful

Communist Party towards defence cooperation was as strong as ever. The government in Paris was forced to propose a number of additional **protocols** to the draft treaty designed to safeguard French interests, by for example deferring for several years the time when any French troops might serve under German command. These were discussed inconclusively at conferences held in Rome in February 1953 and Brussels in August 1954.

The French Socialists, by now out of government, and the centre-left Radicals found themselves increasingly divided on Europe. There was also a rising tide of popular discontent with growing national humiliation abroad: Diên Biên Phu had fallen in May 1954 and the Tunisian crisis was sapping French morale, whilst problems in Algeria were escalating. In the end, the new Radical prime minister, Pierre Mendès-France, refused to make ratification of the EDC Treaty a matter of confidence for the survival of his two-month-old government. In Judt's words, he 'rightly calculated that it would have been imprudent to stake the future of his fragile coalition . . . on an unpopular proposal to rearm the national enemy'. On 30 August 1954, the National Assembly finally voted by 319 votes to 264, with 43 abstentions, to postpone discussion of the treaty sine die, thus effectively killing it. Both the Socialists and Radicals divided almost equally for and against the text. Its victorious opponents – predominantly Communists and Gaullists – sang the *Marseillaise* in the chamber. Twenty-three members of the government failed to take part in the vote, including the interior minister, **François Mitterrand**.

The failure of the EDC was the first serious setback for the proponents of European unification. However, less than a year later, in June 1955, the Six met at the **Messina Conference** to explore whether progress could be made instead on the economic front, drawing on the **Beyen Plan** for a general **common market** and **customs union**. Meanwhile, only a month after the National Assembly's vote, the British government convened a meeting in London of representatives of the six EDC signatory states, together with the United Kingdom, United States and Canada, to discuss defence cooperation in Europe. A ministerial conference in Paris in October 1955 led to the strengthening of the intergovernmental **Western European Union** (WEU), through the adoption of the Modified **Brussels Treaty**, and the entry of West Germany into NATO, on the basis that it would finally be allowed to rearm.

Further reading: Edward Fursdon, *The European Defence Community: A History*, 1980.

European Development Fund (EDF)

The European Development Fund is the principal instrument by which the European Union provides development aid to the 79 **ACP states**, mostly former colonies of the member states, as well as the Union's 21 **overseas**

countries and territories (OCTs). Its purpose is to promote 'the objectives of poverty eradication, sustainable development and the gradual integration of the ACP countries into the world economy'.

So far there have been ten EDF 'cycles', each covering an average period of five years. For sake of convenience, they correspond with the periods of the successive agreements concluded between the European Community, now Union, and the ACP states. After an initial start-up phase, the European Community negotiated the Yaoundé I and II Conventions with the developing countries concerned (corresponding to the second and third EDFs; 1964–75), followed by the Lomé I to IV (and revised Lomé IV) Conventions (the fourth to eighth EDFs; 1975–2000). More recently, the Cotonou Agreement (ninth EDF) ran from 2000 to 2007, and the current, revised Cotonou Agreement (tenth EDF) covers the period from 2008 to 2013. The ninth and tenth EDFs were allocated €13.5 billion and €22.7 billion respectively, with a further €3.6 billion currently available for loans, guarantees and risk capital from the **European Investment Bank** (EIB). The EDF was assigned € 3.5 billion in the year 2011.

The EDF system was launched at the start of the **European Economic Community** (EEC) in 1958, as a hard-fought concession to France during the negotiation of the **Treaty of Rome**. Its initial role was to grant technical and financial assistance to certain African countries that were still colonies at the time. In order to offer national capitals maximum control over its operation, the EDF was, and indeed remains, an intergovernmental arrangement, funded by separately-negotiated contributions from the member states, although its resources are managed by the **European Commission** and EIB. Since 1973, the Commission has argued strongly that the monies spent on the EDF should derive from the Union's **own resources** and feature as a normal part of its **Budget**. Its latest attempt to secure the 'budgetization' of the EDF was rejected by the **European Council** in December 2005.

The separate arrangements for financing the EDF have not prevented the emergence of additional spending for **development policy** in the EU Budget itself, notably through the Development Cooperation Instrument (DCI), worth € 2.2 billion in 2011. However, policy coherence is complicated by the need for different administrative rules and decision-making structures for these two types of aid. Whereas spending from the EU Budget is governed by the general Financial Regulation, the EDF expenditure is governed by its own regulation and rules set out in each successive agreement.

As there is no specific legal base for the EDF in the **Treaties**, the successive agreements have been concluded on an intergovernmental basis within the EU and with the third countries involved. Decisions are taken between the representatives of the member states, meeting within the **Council of Ministers**, rather than by the Council itself. Such agreements then need to be ratified by all EU member states, as well as two-thirds of the ACP countries.

European Economic Area (EEA)

The European Economic Area is a **free trade area** and **single market** encompassing 30 countries – namely, the 27 member states of the European Union, together with **Iceland**, Liechtenstein and **Norway**. It was established by an **association agreement**, which was concluded under (what is now) Article 217 TFEU, was signed in Oporto on 2 May 1992, and came into effect on 1 January 1994. The EEA is not a **customs union**: the Union's **Common Customs Tariff** (CCT) does not encompass the three other members of the EEA, and the latter do not participate in its external trade policy – known as the **Common Commercial Policy** (CCP) – with third countries.

The EEA was designed to provide a means by which the members of the **European Free Trade Association** (EFTA) could be brought within the EU's rapidly deepening single market, whilst choosing to remain outside the Union itself. However, the advent of the EEA was complicated, and its significance diminished, by the fact that three EFTA countries which were founder signatories of the EEA – Austria, Finland and Sweden – chose to join the EU very soon after, in January 1995, and a fourth, **Switzerland**, had to renounce its signature when EEA membership was narrowly rejected by popular referendum in December 1992 (by 50.3 to 49.7 per cent). Thus EFTA now only boasts four member states, and only three of these are members of the EEA.

The EEA Agreement consists of 129 articles of general provisions, 49 protocols covering specific issues, and 22 annexes listing in detail those portions of existing EU legislation that henceforth apply throughout the EEA. With very few exceptions, the agreement takes precedence over other bilateral or multilateral agreements to which the signatory states are party. Article 121 specifies that it should not affect other regional cooperation arrangements such as the **Nordic Council**, the customs union between Switzerland and Liechtenstein, and certain cross-border agreements between Austria and Italy.

The EEA owes its origin to the mutual desire on the part of the member states of EFTA and the EU to integrate their economies more completely, on the basis of a structured relationship, without full membership by the former of the latter. Although each of the individual EFTA states already had a bilateral free trade agreement with the Community – with the last barriers to trade in industrial goods removed in January 1984 – all parties expressed a desire in the 1984 Luxembourg Declaration to extend their cooperation still further, by building what they called an *espace économique européen*.

The need to forge new arrangements was given greater urgency by the Community's decision in 1985 to undertake its ambitious programme to complete the single market by 1992. The first steps were to simplify the formalities governing trade, and in 1986 negotiations began to extend the use of the EC's Single Administrative Document (SAD) to the EFTA states. The accession of Spain and Portugal to the Community in the same year was used as an opportunity to adjust and extend the free trade agreements into new fields, such as scientific and technological cooperation. In 1987, the Community asserted the so-called 'Interlaken principles', which made it clear that the single market programme would enjoy priority in the event of a conflict of interest with EFTA, and implied that the latter could not expect indefinitely to enjoy the economic benefits of free trade with the Community unless institutional relations were strengthened. In a speech to the **European Parliament** in January 1989, **Jacques Delors**, the then President of the European Commission, expressed the Community's willingness to move towards 'a new, more structured partnership with common decision-making and administrative institutions'. Eighteen months later (in June 1990) negotiations for the EEA began.

The fundamental purpose of the arrangements set out in the resulting EEA Agreement is to allow the **free movement** of goods, persons, services and capital throughout the EEA. The provisions in the agreement on the **free movement of goods** (Articles 8 to 27 and 53 to 65) apply to nearly all industrial goods and certain agricultural products. Some 800 items of Union legislation on the free movement of goods were listed in the annexes to the agreement from the start. **Free movement of persons** (Articles 28 to 35) covers all employed and self-employed persons, with the exception of those in the public service. The entire ***acquis communautaire*** in this field was integrated into the agreement. Similarly, **free movement of services** (Articles 36 to 39) was extended throughout the EEA, as was (with only minor exceptions) **free movement of capital** (Articles 40 to 45). The various annexes listing relevant EU laws are updated automatically as the Union adopts new legislation in the fields in question.

By way of complement to the **four freedoms**, the EEA Agreement prohibits **discrimination on grounds of nationality**. Union rules in relation to **competition policy**, including state aids, serve as the model for similar obligations applying in the EFTA signatories. State monopolies of a commercial character have had to be adjusted or progressively eliminated, with some exceptions for those maintained on the sale of alcohol. The participating EFTA states are able to take part in a wide range of the Union's programmes – notably in the fields of research and development, environment, energy, transport, and cultural and educational policy – including the work of **agencies** and expert groups set up under these policies. In return, the EFTA states make a proportionate annual contribution towards the operational and administrative costs of the various Union programmes and agencies in which they participate. The contribution is currently set at 2.6 per cent of the total, amounting to around € 300 million, and affects over 200 lines in the Union's annual **Budget**. In addition, these states are also providing € 1.8 billion over the period 2009–14, in the form of an 'enlargement fund' for development projects in the new member states, together with Greece, Portugal and Spain.

The institutional structure established by the EEA Agreement represents an unusual amalgam of components of the EU and EFTA systems. An EEA Council is composed of ministerial representatives of the governments of the signatory states, together with the European Commission (Articles 89 to 91). It meets at least twice a year, with the purpose – akin to that of the **European Council** within the EU – of giving 'political impetus' to the EEA and 'laying down the general guidelines' of its action. The EEA Council's decisions are 'taken by agreement' between the Union, as one party, and the three participating EFTA states, as the other party, with its presidency rotating every six months between a country on either side. The Council is supported by an EEA Joint Committee, composed of senior officials, which meets at least once a month and takes routine decisions on the same basis. An EEA Joint Parliamentary Committee, composed of Members of the European Parliament (MEPs) and parliamentarians from the participating EFTA states, holds at least two general sessions a year and passes non-binding resolutions. At the level of '**social partners**', an EEA Consultative Committee, composed of members of the **European Economic and Social Committee** (EESC) and the EFTA Consultative Committee, may also offer advice (Article 96).

The monitoring of obligations arising from the EEA Agreement is performed by the Commission in the Union and by an EFTA Surveillance Authority in the participating EFTA states. An EFTA Court was established to adjudicate on disputes, working in cooperation with the **European Court of Justice** (ECJ). The original idea of giving these responsibilities (with respect to the EFTA signatories) to the European Commission and the ECJ had to be abandoned when the latter gave an opinion in December 1991 that such an arrangement was illegal by infringing the autonomy of the Community's legal order.

The institutions of the EEA have no independent constitutional or sovereign authority. The EEA Agreement requires them to work in parallel with the Union institutions, on the basis of consultations and the exchange of information. **Legal acts** of the Union on matters covered by the EEA are transposed into the annexes of the EEA Agreement by decision of the Joint Committee, with a view to ensuring both legal consistency and uniform application. Article 107 of the Agreement allows national courts and tribunals in EFTA states to seek rulings in the ECJ on the interpretation of EEA rules; such rulings are binding.

Legally, the EEA Agreement was and remains the most ambitious and comprehensive treaty ever concluded by the European Union with any third countries. The main areas of Union policy remaining outside the EEA are actions in the spheres of **Common Foreign and Security Policy** (CFSP) and **Justice and Home Affairs** (JHA), as well as external trade and **development policy**, monetary and fiscal policy, and most of the **Common Agricultural Policy** (CAP) and all of the **Common Fisheries Policy** (CFP).

Overall, the political effect of the EEA has been to export both the freedoms and obligations of **EU law**, on an ongoing basis, to countries that have become economically interdependent with the Union, without those states having any meaningful say in Union decision-making. The three EFTA countries within the EEA are in effect 'policy-takers' rather than policy-makers. One critic, former Norwegian prime minister Jens Stoltenberg, characterized the resulting situation as one of 'fax democracy', with his own country, Iceland and Liechtenstein simply being informed of new binding legislation decided by EU institutions in which they are not represented. In practice, the three states attempt to influence legislation upstream and are invited to comment on draft proposals before the Commission tables them. However, as EFTA Secretary General Kare Bryn commented in October 2008, once a proposal is sent to the EU **Council of Ministers** and the European Parliament, 'our ability to [exercise] influence is plus or minus zero'.

Countries acceding to the European Union are obliged to join the EEA, but those joining EFTA may choose whether or not to do so. EEA membership in turn makes accession to the Union a near certainty for any country that wishes to join. As a result of EEA membership, it will automatically have adopted a very large part of the *acquis communautaire*. However, since 1995, the only EFTA country to seriously contemplate EU membership, at least initially, was Switzerland – ironically not itself a member of the EEA. (The assumption was that Liechtenstein would follow Switzerland in whichever path it chose.) Although the Swiss government decided that membership should be a 'strategic goal', pro-European campaigners forced a premature referendum in March 2001, with the governing coalition cornered into advocating a 'no' vote. The Swiss people then rejected EU membership by 76.8 to 23.2 per cent, in effect shutting off the option for the foreseeable future.

At that time, neither Norway nor Iceland were interested in membership, for a variety of historic, cultural or economic reasons. However, starting in autumn 2008, the international economic and financial crisis put such extreme pressure on Iceland that a lively debate about its joining the Union quickly sprang up. After several political parties and trades unions came out in favour, the Icelandic government applied for membership in July 2009. The European Commission gave a positive opinion on the application seven months later and the European Council granted Iceland candidate status in June 2010. On **accession** to the Union, Iceland would leave EFTA. Only two EEA members would then remain outside the Union.

European Economic Community (EEC)

The European Economic Community was established by **the Six** under the **Treaty of Rome**, which was signed on 25 March 1957 and entered into force on 1 January 1958. The Treaty of Rome was the most important of the three founding **Treaties** of the **European Communities**, with the EEC encompassing the creation of a **customs union** and a **common market** – now usually known as the **single market** or internal market – based on the **free movement** of goods, services, persons and capital. The EEC also enjoyed exclusive **competence** for external trade policy, known as the **Common Commercial Policy** (CCP), and aspects of **competition policy**, as well as sharing competence with the member states in several other fields. The latter included agriculture and fisheries – leading to the **Common Agricultural Policy** (CAP) and **Common Fisheries Policy** (CFP) – **development policy**, **transport policy**, **regional policy** and **social policy**. Successive amendments to the Treaty of Rome – contained notably in the 1986 **Single European Act** (SEA), 1992 **Maastricht Treaty**, 1997 **Amsterdam Treaty**, 2001 **Nice Treaty** and the 2007 **Lisbon Treaty** (which entered into force in December 2009) – have significantly widened the competence and altered the institutional arrangements originally foreseen for the EEC.

With the entry into force of the Maastricht Treaty in November 1993, the EEC was officially renamed the European Community, itself part of a broader European Union. The official title of the Treaty of Rome was shortened from 'Treaty establishing the European Economic Community' to 'Treaty establishing the European Community'. The European Community **pillar** of the new European Union, established by Maastricht, continued to enjoy **legal personality**, whereas the Union itself did not. The Lisbon Treaty finally merged the European Community and the European Union, with the totality now known by the latter name and enjoying **legal personality**. The Treaty of Rome changed its title once again, to Treaty on the Functioning of the European Union (TFEU). Despite the successive changes of nomenclature, the EEC established in 1958 remains the core of today's European Union. For the origins of the EEC, see **Beyen Plan**, **Messina Conference** and **Spaak Committee**.

European economic governance

The development of **Economic and Monetary Union** (EMU) in Europe posed the question of how far the pooling of monetary **sovereignty**, with the adoption of a single currency and single monetary policy, should be matched by a higher degree of macro-economic policy coordination at European level – and, if so, in what form. The 1989 **Delors Report**, which provided the initial blueprint for EMU, foresaw a more balanced relationship between the economic and monetary sides of the project than was finally agreed in the 1990–91 **Intergovernmental Conference** (IGC) which negotiated the EMU component of the 1992 **Maastricht Treaty**. In October 1990, shortly before the EMU IGC discussion was about to begin, the French President, **François Mitterrand**, had used the phrase '*gouvernement économique éuropéen*' to characterize the political counterpoise he envisaged to the potential power of an independent **European Central Bank** (ECB). In the IGC negotiations, it became clear that, in the French view, the **European Council** and **Ecofin Council** should set strategic economic guidelines, ideally backed by an external exchange-rate policy for the single currency, and that they should have a much bigger role than the **European Commission** in policing any rules on the member states' levels of budget deficit and national debt among EMU member states.

In the event, the German finance ministry and Bundesbank, with strong Dutch and British support, managed to secure a more 'monetarist' outcome to the negotiations, with a fully independent ECB, an enforcement role led by the Commission, and fiscal coordination limited essentially to governments respecting the deficit and debt ceilings, set at respectively 3 and 60 per cent of gross national product (GNP). The quid pro quo was German agreement to the French desire for the absolute irreversibility of the EMU process and an acceptance that full membership should automatically proceed for as many countries as met certain **convergence criteria** by a stated date.

The governments of France and some Mediterranean countries, as well as elements on the left in northern Europe, were never wholly happy with the Maastricht settlement. In 1996–7, they successfully fended off efforts by the German CDU/CSU finance minister, Theo Waigel, to install a stronger variant of the **Stability and Growth Pact** (SGP) that would have made the debt and deficit limits more automatically applicable in law. Once stage three of EMU began in 1999, proposals began to resurface for a more explicit, centralized economic policy-making process at EU level to offset the alleged 'deflationary' bias of ECB policy-making. This could be based on a mixture of greater synchronization of budgetary policies, a more flexible approach to deficits in times of downturn, a more active external exchange-rate policy for the **euro**, and/or greater openness to **tax harmonization** (or at least the avoidance of 'fiscal dumping').

After the election of Gerhard Schröder as German Chancellor in October 1998, the new, left-wing German finance minister, Oskar Lafontaine, aligned Berlin behind calls for a more active European economic policy of this kind.

However, once he resigned the following year, traditional Franco-German differences on the issue began to reassert themselves. Although Paris and Bonn conspired to ensure that the **excessive deficit procedure** (EDP) was in effect suspended when they both started to move above the 3 per cent budget deficit limit in 2003 and tabled a joint paper to a working party on 'economic governance' that was set up within the **Convention on the Future of Europe** in 2002–3, little followed from either move, other than the eventual codification of the existence of the **Eurogroup** of **eurozone** finance ministers in the **Lisbon Treaty**. It was only with the onset of the economic and financial crisis in autumn 2008 that the situation changed. Heads of government were forced to expand greatly the lending activities of the **European Investment Bank** (EIB), put the state aids régime of EU **competition policy** into temporary abeyance, in order to help rescue the banking sector, and finally envisage the possibility of bailing out the public finances of certain eurozone states.

The new French President, Nicolas Sarkozy, quickly took advantage of the crisis to relaunch the idea of a European economic government – or 'governance' as it was increasingly known, following the Convention. He presented this in essentially institutional, rather than policy, terms – based on the convening of regular meetings of eurozone leaders to confront the crisis. Despite resistance from Angela Merkel, Schröder's successor as German Chancellor, Sarkozy was able to exploit the French **presidency** of the **Council of Ministers** to hold the first-ever eurozone summit meeting, admittedly outside the European Council framework, in Paris in October 2008. Merkel and some others still declined to make such meetings a routine feature of EU decision-making. Once the Lisbon Treaty came into effect in December 2009, the new **President of the European Council**, Herman Van Rompuy, likewise resisted French efforts to institutionalize eurozone summits, although he was forced to concede them in May 2010 and March and July 2011. He argued that if Europe needed an 'economic government', the full European Council already constituted one.

After some agonizing, the German government finally accepted that the developing eurozone debt crisis merited enhanced 'economic governance', but only if the concept denoted primarily a mixture of a tougher SGP and more systematic structural reform of national economies. In March 2010, the European Council tasked Van Rompuy with chairing a special task force of finance ministers to prepare measures to improve the 'preventive' and 'corrective' arms of the pact. Seven months later, the Ecofin Council agreed arrangements for a new 'European semester', covering the period January to June each year, during which the Commission would produce an Annual Growth Survey, which would provide the basis for two sets of commitments to be undertaken by member states: Stability and Convergence Programmes (SCPs) on the budgetary front, and National Reform Programmes (NRPs) in respect of domestic structural reform. These would be adopted in a two-stage process at the March and June European Council meetings each year. When President Sarkozy met Chancellor Merkel in Deauville, France, in October 2010, their summit communiqué opened with the words: 'France and Germany agree that economic governance needs to be reinforced.'

The Van Rompuy task force conclusions, published later the same month, envisaged a significant strengthening of the SGP in general and the EDP in particular, including more automatic sanctions for those transgressing the rules, as well as the development of a new 'excessive imbalances procedure'. These arrangements were formalized in a 'Six Pact' of legislative proposals, submitted pre-emptively by the Commission in September 2010 and adopted by the Council and Parliament in October 2011. In parallel, Merkel proposed, and Sarkozy accepted, the idea of a 'competitiveness pact' for deeper structural reform within the eurozone. Eventually agreed at the March 2011 European Council as the 'Euro Plus Pact', this committed the 17 eurozone member states to 'translating EU fiscal rules as set out in the Stability and Growth Pact into national legislation', and to undertaking less specific reforms to phase out wage indexation, increase retirement ages and lighten the taxation of labour. (Six other member states – Bulgaria, Denmark, Latvia, Lithuania, Poland and Romania – associated themselves with the pact.)

With all these moves in play, Merkel was finally willing to accede to Sarkozy's wish that eurozone summits be institutionalized in some form. At a bilateral meeting in the Elysée Palace in August 2011, she accepted that a **Euro Summit**, as the new configuration would be called, should occur at least twice a year. The first such meeting was held in October 2011, back-to-back with the European Council. However, even if Sarkozy had succeeded in creating a deeper structure for eurozone governance, its policy substance seemed increasingly to be on terms set in Berlin. As Wolfgang Münchau, writing in the *Financial Times* in early 2011, was one of the first to discern, the character of European economic governance was becoming 'a French concept with German content', corresponding to long-term Bundesbank and German finance ministry goals.

European Economic and Social Committee (EESC)

The European Economic and Social Committee is one of two unelected EU advisory bodies – the other being the **Committee of the Regions** – which 'assist' the **European Commission**, **Council of Ministers** and **European Parliament**, by 'acting in an advisory capacity' in many policy fields. The Committee is composed of 'representatives of organizations of employers, of the employed, and of other parties representative of civil society' (Article 300 TFEU). It was established by the **Treaty of Rome** in March 1957 – unlike the Committee of the Regions, which dates from the 1992 **Maastricht Treaty** –

and its inclusion in the Community's institutional structure reflects the fact that five of **the Six** founding member states (the exception being West Germany) possessed comparable nominated bodies at national level. The specific design of the EESC owes much to the French *Conseil économique et social* which featured in the constitutions of both the Fourth and Fifth Republics.

The exact size of the Committee, which may not exceed 350 members, and its composition by member state are determined by the Council, acting unanimously, on a proposal from the Commission. The EESC and the Committee of the Regions both have the same number of full members, currently 344, who are appointed by the Council on the basis of a list of nominees proposed by each member-state government. (The EESC started life in 1958 with 101 members.) The distribution between member states is as follows:

France, Germany, Italy and United Kingdom	24
Spain and Poland	21
Romania	15
Austria, Belgium, Bulgaria, Czech Republic, Greece, Hungary, Netherlands, Portugal and Sweden	12
Denmark, Finland, Ireland, Lithuania and Slovakia	9
Estonia, Latvia and Slovenia	7
Cyprus and Luxembourg	6
Malta	5

The terms of office of both Committees were, until the **Lisbon Treaty**, four years. They have now been lengthened to five years, to correspond with those of the Commission and Parliament, even if the terms are not synchronized. The Committee elects its President, two Vice-Presidents and other office-holders every two and a half years, as in the Parliament. Members of the EESC are paid no salary, but receive travel and accommodation expenses.

Although members sit alphabetically and vote in a personal capacity, the politics of the EESC has long been dominated by the interaction of its three groups of members – employers, employees and 'various interests' – whose status is entrenched in the Committee's rules of procedure. The employers (Group I) and employees (Group II) tend each to vote and act as blocs, often giving the representatives of 'various interests' (Group III) a decisive say in any contested outcome. However, the members of the latter group represent diverse, and often diverging, interests – such as farmers, consumers, cooperatives, professional bodies and the self-employed – and therefore have more difficulty in acting as a coherent force. Members from Groups I and II are generally appointed by national governments on the basis of recommendations from their employers' organizations and trade unions, whereas the members from Group III are often closer to the views of the ruling parties in the countries nominating them. In practice, most governments present roughly equal numbers of members from each of the three groups, even though they are under no legal obligation to do so.

By mutual agreement, the presidency of the EESC rotates between the three groups, and the Committee is managed by a 39-member Bureau also composed on a tripartite basis. The Committee conducts its advisory work by means of six 'sections' covering different areas of EU activity, together with a hybrid committee on consultative change. Typically, when a legislative proposal is received from the Commission, the relevant section will set up a small study group from among its members, with a **rapporteur** tasked with preparing a draft opinion, including, where appropriate, suggested amendments to the proposal. The draft opinion prepared by the study group, which attempts to act by consensus, is then put to the section, which can amend it. Once adopted by the section, the opinion is placed on the agenda of the next two-day plenary session of the Committee, for final adoption. The Committee holds nine plenary sessions a year. Amendments to an opinion are admissible from any member at either section or plenary stage. The Committee delivers an average of 210 opinions a year.

There has been talk periodically of abolishing the EESC. For a long time after the first direct elections in 1979, the European Parliament was particularly critical of the Committee's continued existence, especially when the latter started to publicize itself, rather maladroitly, as 'the other European assembly'. The fact that Germany, the United Kingdom, Denmark and Sweden do not have national committees of this type reduced the effectiveness of any claim that it was indispensable. However, its prospects of survival were greatly increased when the Maastricht Treaty instituted the parallel Committee of the Regions, leaving the Economic and Social Committee intact. Now the bigger threat is to the EESC's relevance, rather than its existence, through its evident marginalization from the formal dialogue between management and labour which the Commission has been promoting actively at EU level since the mid-1980s (see **social partners**). In response, the Committee has chosen to present itself as a wider 'bridge between Europe and organized civil society' and vehicle for greater participatory democracy, emphasizing the diversity of its Group III members, rather than the special status of those from Groups I and II. The EESC has also taken a series of ad hoc initiatives – notably the creation of thematic 'observatories' covering the single market, the labour market, sustainable development and the Lisbon Strategy for economic reform – designed to promote exchange of information and best practice with 'stakeholders' at large.

The EESC is sometimes referred to as 'EcoSoc', echoing the acronym of a similar body, the Economic and Social Council, within the **United Nations** system. Since 2002, the Committee has chosen to style itself as the 'European' Economic and Social Committee, to differentiate itself both from the UN body and similar organizations at national level with which it cooperates closely.

The EESC has its own secretariat (of some 700 staff), headed by a secretary general appointed by the Committee's Bureau for five years. Certain common services are operated jointly with the Committee of the Regions. The two bodies share their headquarters, at 99–101 rue Belliard, and five other buildings in Brussels.

European elections

Elections to the **European Parliament**, known as European elections, are held every five years, by direct universal suffrage, in accordance with the provisions of Article 14(3) TEU. They are the only democratic, transnational elections to be organized anywhere in the world and currently involve around 386 million potential voters (the only larger free electorate being in India). The first European elections took place in June 1979; before that date, the Members of the European Parliament (MEPs) were nominated by and from the **national parliaments** of the member states.

Since the 1992 **Maastricht Treaty**, every EU citizen has enjoyed the right both to vote and to stand as a candidate in European (and local) elections in whichever member state they reside, even if they are not nationals of that state. European elections take place over an agreed four-day period around the second weekend in June, allowing member states to vote on a Thursday (the Netherlands and United Kingdom), Friday (Czech Republic and Ireland), Saturday (Czech Republic, Cyprus, Italy, Latvia, Slovakia and Malta) or Sunday (when all other countries hold their elections, including Italy for a second day). No results are announced until all polling stations have closed on the Sunday evening. The timing of the European elections may be adjusted by up to one month by the **Council of Ministers**, acting unanimously, but until now efforts to move the elections from June to May, as some member states would like, have consistently failed. In the most recent European elections, held on 4–7 June 2009, 736 MEPs were elected from 170 different national political parties in the 27 member states.

The founding **Treaties** envisaged that elections to the Parliament would be held on the basis of a **uniform electoral procedure**, but it has proved impossible for the member states, with their diverse political traditions, to agree on such a scheme, which also requires **unanimity** in the Council of Ministers. The 1997 **Amsterdam Treaty** loosened the requirement to allow elections to be held (alternatively) 'in accordance with principles common to all Member States'. Accordingly, in decisions taken in June and September 2002 – amending the 1976 European Elections Act, which first set down minimum common arrangements – the Council established certain common principles which member states must now follow in designing their national systems for the quinquennial European elections.

First, the European electoral system must be one of proportional representation (PR), 'using the list system or the single transferable vote' (STV). Second, member states 'may authorize voting based on a preferential list system'. Third, they 'may establish constituencies . . . or subdivide [their] electoral area in a different manner, without affecting the essentially proportional nature of the voting system'. Fourth, they 'may set a minimum threshold for the allocation of seats. At national level this threshold may not exceed five per cent of the votes cast'.

The practical effect of the first of these principles is to limit the PR electoral systems that can be used to the following modes of election: i) a national list system, with or without preferential voting, and with or without a national threshold; ii) a regional list system, with or without preferential voting; and iii) an STV system, which by definition involves several multi-member constituencies. A fourth system of proportional representation – the 'additional member system' (AMS) of single-member constituencies with a national top-up list, used in Germany for the Bundestag and in Britain for regional elections – may or may not be allowed: no member state has so far sought to use it for European elections. Table 1 shows the electoral systems employed in the member states at the last European elections, in June 2009.

In national or regional list systems, political parties present slates of candidates and electors vote for a single list. The number of candidates elected from each list is determined by a mathematical formula – usually named after a leading mathematician, such as d'Hondt, Droop, Hagenbach-Bischoff, Hare-Niemeyer, Saint Lagüe or Schepers – which rewards parties in varying degrees of proportionality. The d'Hondt system is the most common seat-allocation method in use for European elections (and indeed more widely) – operating in 17 of the 27 member states – and one which tends to favour larger parties over smaller ones, whilst still ensuring a good measure of proportionality. (Formally, to allocate seats under d'Hondt, the total number of votes for each party list is divided by two, then by three, then by four (and so on), as each position is allocated, with the highest remaining number winning, until all the available positions are taken.)

Under national or regional list systems, candidates are elected in the order in which they appear on a party's slate, unless preferential voting between candidates is permitted. In this latter case, candidates may be elected in a different order, and the ease of this will depend on the number of votes needed to break the rank order of the list.

Under STV, a member state is divided up into a series of multi-member constituencies. Each party is likely to run more than one candidate in each constituency, but is under no obligation to do so. The elector expresses his or her preferences between individual candidates in order, and to secure election, any candidate must obtain a pre-established quota of votes. This quota is

Table 1: European Parliament – Electoral systems in member states (2009)

Member state	*Number of MEPs (2009)*	*Number of constituencies*	*Type of PR system*	*Preferential voting?*	*Minimum threshold*
Austria	17	1	National list	Yes	4%
Belgium	22	4	Regional list	Yes	None
Bulgaria	17	1	National list	Yes	None
Cyprus	6	1	National list	No	None
Czech Republic	22	1	National list	Yes	5%
Denmark	13	1	National list	No	None
Estonia	6	1	National list	No	None
Finland	13	1	National list	Yes	None
France	72	8	Regional list	No	5%
Germany*	99	1	National and regional lists	No	5%
Greece	22	1	National list	No	3%
Hungary	22	1	National list	No	5%
Ireland	12	4	STV	Yes	None
Italy**	72	5	Regional list	Yes	None
Latvia	8	1	National list	Yes	None
Lithuania	12	1	National list	Yes	5%
Luxembourg	6	1	National list	Yes	None
Malta	5	1	STV	Yes	None
Netherlands	25	1	National list	Yes	None
Poland	50	13	Regional list	No	5%
Portugal	22	1	National list	No	None
Romania	33	1	National list	No	5%
Slovakia	13	1	National list	Yes	5%
Slovenia	7	1	National list	Yes	None
Spain	50	1	National list	No	None
Sweden	18	1	National list	Yes	4%
UK – Great Britain	69	11	Regional list	No	None
UK – Northern Ireland	3	1	STV	Yes	None

* Germany has a single national constituency, although MEPs may be elected from either national or regional lists.

** Italy has five electoral districts, but seats are allocated on the basis of parties' national vote.

Source: European Parliament.

obtained by dividing the total number of valid votes by the number of seats plus one, and adding one to the result obtained. Votes are redistributed until the required number of candidates is elected.

Some countries use lists for European elections but not national ones: Germany uses AMS for national parliamentary elections and list systems for European elections; France and Britain use non-PR, majoritarian systems for national parliamentary elections, but list systems for European elections. By contrast, the STV system is used for national elections in Ireland and Malta (as well as for the Senate in Australia).

Of the 27 EU member states, 25 currently use some form of list system in European elections. Twenty states use national lists, whilst four – Belgium, France, Italy and the mainland of the United Kingdom – use regional list systems, although in Italy the allocation of seats is determined by each party's national vote. One member state, Germany, uses a mixture of both national and regional lists. Two member states, Ireland and Malta, and one region of the United Kingdom, Northern Ireland, use STV.

In terms of preferential voting, an STV system automatically allows 'voter choice' between candidates. Among the 25 countries with national or regional list systems, 14 make some provision for preferential voting between candidates, whilst 11 – including France, Germany, Poland, Spain and the United Kingdom – do not. In Luxembourg, electors are permitted to split their preference votes between candidates on different party lists, in effect replicating the high degree of voter choice allowed under STV.

In terms of minimum thresholds before votes are converted into seats, STV and regional list systems automatically provide a de facto threshold; this is sufficiently high to obviate the need for a formal threshold of five per cent or less. In national list systems, 12 countries stipulate formal thresholds, eight of them at five per cent. In some cases, the consequences can be significant: in Germany, such a threshold denied seven political parties representation in the European Parliament in 2009. In those smaller member states which use national lists but without applying a formal threshold – Denmark, Estonia, Finland, Latvia, Luxembourg, the Netherlands, Portugal and Slovenia – there is in effect a (sometimes relatively high) threshold in each, generated automatically by the number of seats at stake. But in the two large member states, Italy and Spain, which allocate seats on the basis of the national vote but where there is no formal threshold, the result is that the effective threshold to representation is very low.

In the absence of a uniform electoral system, there are also significant variations in the detailed arrangements for participation in European elections in the member states – especially in relation to the minimum age for standing as a candidate (which varies between 18 and 25 years), residence requirements for both candidates and voters, and the voting rights (in their home country) of citizens living abroad. In seven member states, only political parties may nominate candidates, whilst in five countries, candidates are required to provide a deposit. There are also divergences in the handling of vacancies which may arise among Members: in most member states, a seat goes to the next unelected candidate on the relevant party's list, whilst in some others, substitutes may be designated.

Table 2 shows the results of the seven European elections held to date, in terms of the relative strengths of the main political tendencies in the European Parliament, usually reflected in the strength of the various **political groups**, since 1979. As can be seen, the first 'direct elections' to the European Parliament in 1979 led to a broad centre-right majority, compounded by the effect of the (then) single-member, first-past-the-post electoral system in Britain, which gave the Conservatives an exaggerated victory nationally. The 1984 and 1989 European elections saw a significant advance of the left and the emergence of Green representatives for the first time. In 1994, the pendulum began to swing back again to the centre-right, a process since continued in the 1999, 2004 and 2009 contests.

Table 3 shows the results specifically in the United Kingdom (excluding Northern Ireland), by seats won and percentage share of the vote. It is clear that, since the introduction of proportional representation in 1999, there has been a marked fracturing of the traditional party system in Britain, with the growth of new forces that were shut out by the first-past-the-post system and are largely unrepresented at Westminster. Together, the Conservative and Labour parties commanded over 70 per cent of the vote at the four European elections from 1979 to 1994. In the three elections since then, their percentage share has fallen successively to 63.8 (1999), 49.3 (2004) and 43.4 (2009). The UK Independence Party, Greens and British National Party together won 31.3 per cent of the vote and 17 seats (out of 69) in 2009. In the British general election a year later, however, they secured 6.0 per cent of the vote and only one seat.

Table 4 shows the turnout in all EU member states, by election. Overall, turnout has fallen slowly over time – from 62 to 43 per cent – against the backdrop of significant national variations. The UK turnout has been consistently well below the average, whilst in Germany, Greece, Italy, the Netherlands and Spain, it has fallen considerably. Voting is notionally compulsory in Belgium and Luxembourg, and was regarded as a civic duty in Italy until recently. The turnout figures are also affected by the fact that national, regional or local elections are sometimes held on the same day as European elections, making overall comparisons more difficult. Luxembourg normally holds its general election on the same day as the European elections.

European elections have often been described as 'second order' elections, in the sense that the interest and behaviour of voters are closer to those observed in local elections or by-elections at national level than to a general election, as the British experience since 1999 would seem to testify. European elections do not result in the choice of a recognizable executive, in a way that general or presidential elections do in member states. In effect, European elections are more akin to midterm Congressional elections in the United States: interestingly, for the last 40 years, turnout in the latter elections has consistently been lower than the current level of participation in European elections (37.8 per cent in 2010, for example). Opinions differ on whether the relatively low turnout in European elections is a reflection of the perceived lack of importance of the contest or simply a leading indicator of a more general public detachment from, and disillusionment with, parliamentary systems in many Western democracies, which is likely to grow over time.

European elections in the member states are rarely, if ever, decided on European issues, let alone on the question of the balance of power in the European Parliament. Most parties make only half-hearted attempts to focus the electorate's attention on such questions, and then only if opinion polls suggest that this might be politically advantageous. Nor do they get much help from the media, most of which prefer the much more familiar parameters of domestic political debate, attempting to highlight party splits, personality clashes, and the discomfort of the sitting government. Perhaps crucially, many of the issues in which the average elector is interested – for example, taxation, social security, housing, local transport and education – are only occasionally or indirectly dealt with in the Parliament, the legislative agenda of which broadly reflects the way in which the Treaties are framed. European elections are thus largely made up of 27 national campaigns, with local variants in particular regions. Nor do the results provide much evidence of Europe-wide political trends, since losses for one political party in one country are very often compensated for by gains for a related party in another.

Broadly speaking, parties that do well in any national contest may expect to do well in European elections held either at the same time or a few months afterwards. This phenomenon helped the British Conservatives in 1979 and Silvio Berlusconi's *Forza Italia* in 1994. Governing parties may also expect to do badly if European elections fall within the period of midterm unpopularity, although in June 2009 parties of the left in power performed consistently much worse than those from the centre-right in power (falling by nine per cent on average, compared with two per cent). Before the UK adopted PR for European elections in 1999, the swings that resulted from the phenomenon of midterm unpopularity were particularly marked in that country, generating Conservative and Labour landslides in the 1979 and 1994 elections respectively.

Further reading: Michael Bruter and Yves Déloye (editors), *Encyclopedia of European Elections*, 2007; Juliet Lodge, *The 2009 Elections to the European Parliament*, 2010.

Table 2: Results of European elections: Percentage share of main political groups, 1979–2009 (*Number of seats in italics*)

Political group or tendency	*1979*	*1984*	*1989*	*1994*	*1999*	*2004*	*2009*
Christian Democrats	26.3%	25.3%	23.4%	27.5%	37.2%	36.7%	36.0%
(currently EPP Group)	*108*	*110*	*121*	*156*	*233*	*288*	*265*
Socialists	27.3%	30.0%	34.7%	34.9%	28.8%	27.6%	25.0%
(currently S&D Group)	*112*	*130*	*180*	*198*	*180*	*217*	*184*
Liberals	9.8%	7.1%	9.5%	7.8%	8.0%	12.7%	11.4%
(currently ALDE Group)	*40*	*31*	*49*	*44*	*50*	*100*	*84*
Conservatives	15.4%	11.5%	6.6%	–	–	–	7.3%
(currently ECR Group)	*63*	*50*	*34*	–	–	–	*54*
Gaullists and others	5.4%	6.7%	3.9%	9.3%	4.8%	5.5%	–
(no longer a separate group)	*22*	*29*	*20*	*53*	*30*	*43*	–
Greens	–	4.6%	5.8%	4.1%	7.7%	5.5%	7.5%
(currently Greens/EFA Group)		*20*	*30*	*23*	*48*	*43*	*55*
Far left/Alternative left	10.7%	9.4%	10.6%	8.3%	6.7%	5.2%	4.8%
(currently GUE Group)	*44*	*41*	*55*	*47*	*42*	*41*	*35*
Hard Eurosceptics	–	–	–	3.4%	2.6%	2.8%	4.2%
(currently EFD Group)	–	–	–	*19*	*16*	*22*	*31*
Others (including far right)	5.1%	5.3%	5.6%	4.8%	4.3%	3.9%	3.8%
	21	*23*	*29*	*27*	*27*	*31*	*28*
Total number of seats	410	434	518	567	626	785	736

Table 3: Results of European elections in Great Britain 1979–2009 (by seats and percentage share of the vote)

Political Party	*1979*	*1984*	*1989*	*1994*	*1999*	*2004*	*2009*
Conservatives	60	45	32	18	36	27	25
% share	50.6	40.8	34.7	27.6	35.8	26.7	27.7
Labour	17	32	45	62	29	19	13
% share	33.0	36.5	40.1	44.0	28.0	22.6	15.7
Liberal Democrats	0	0	0	2	10	12	11
% share	13.1	19.5	6.7	16.6	12.7	14.9	13.7
UK Independence Party	–	–	–	0	3	12	13
% share	–	–	–	1.0	7.0	16.2	16.5
Greens	–	–	0	0	2	2	2
% share	–	–	14.9	3.2	6.3	6.2	8.6
British National Party	–	–	–	–	0	0	2
% share	–	–	–	–	1.1	4.9	6.2
Scottish National Party	1	1	1	2	2	2	2
% share	1.9	1.7	2.7	3.2	2.7	1.4	2.1
Plaid Cymru	0	0	0	0	2	1	1
% share	0.6	0.8	0.8	1.0	1.9	1.0	0.8
Others	0	0	0	0	0	0	0
% share	0.8	0.7	0.3	3.4	4.5	6.1	8.7
Number of seats (GB)	78	78	78	84	84	75	69

Table 4: Turnout at European elections by member state, 1979–2009

Member state	*1979*	*1981*	*1984*	*1987*	*1989*	*1994*	*1995–6*	*1999*	*2004*	*2007*	*2009*
Belgium	91.36		92.09		90.73	90.66		91.05	90.81		90.39
Denmark	47.82		52.38		46.17	52.92		50.46	47.89		59.54
France	60.71		56.72		48.80	52.71		46.76	42.76		40.63
Germany	65.73		56.76		62.28	60.02		45.19	43.00		43.30
Ireland	63.61		47.56		68.28	43.98		50.21	58.58		58.64
Italy	85.65		82.47		81.07	73.60		69.76	71.72		65.05
Luxembourg	88.91		88.79		87.39	88.55		87.27	91.35		90.75
Netherlands	58.12		50.88		47.48	35.69		30.02	39.26		36.75
United Kingdom	32.35		32.57		36.37	36.43		24.00	38.52		34.70
Greece		81.48	80.59		80.03	73.18		70.25	63.22		52.61
Portugal				72.42	51.10	35.54		39.93	38.60		36.78
Spain				68.52	54.71	59.14		63.05	45.14		44.90
Austria							67.73	49.40	42.43		45.97
Finland							57.60	30.14	39.43		40.30
Sweden							41.63	38.84	37.85		45.53
Cyprus									72.50		59.40
Czech Republic									28.30		28.20
Estonia									26.83		43.90
Hungary									38.50		36.31
Latvia									41.34		53.70
Lithuania									48.38		20.98
Malta									82.39		78.79
Poland									20.87		24.53
Slovakia									16.97		19.64
Slovenia									28.35		28.33
Bulgaria										29.22	38.99
Romania										29.47	27.67
EU total	61.99		58.98		58.41	56.67		49.51	45.47		43.00
Number voting (million)	120.8		122.3		143.3	152.9		143.4	156.0		163.5

Source: European Parliament.

European External Action Service (EEAS)

The idea of creating a 'European foreign service' first emerged during the **Convention on the Future of Europe** that drafted the **European Constitution** in 2002–3. The central concept was that the existing directorates-general and other units covering EU external relations within both the **European Commission** and the general secretariat of the **Council of Ministers** should be merged into a single, free-standing service that would report to a new European foreign minister. This move would eliminate overlap between institutions and create a coherent centre of expertise comparable to a traditional foreign ministry at national level. The new service might deal both with **Common Foreign and Security Policy** (CFSP) and some other aspects of external policy, the contours of which would need to be settled.

In the event, the Convention devised only the most general of blueprints for the new foreign service, which it called an 'external action service' to avoid offending the sensitivities of the foreign ministries of certain larger member states. The arrangements set out in the Constitution, which survived into the **Lisbon Treaty**, provided that the 'Union Minister for Foreign Affairs', renamed (for the same reason) the **High Representative**, 'shall be assisted by a European External Action Service', comprising officials of the relevant departments of the Council and the Commission, as well as staff 'seconded from national diplomatic services' of the member states (Article 27(3) TEU). The question of how far beyond CFSP the EEAS should stretch – and whether, in particular, it should encompass **Common Commercial Policy** (CCP), **development policy**, **enlargement** and humanitarian aid – was left deliberately vague.

The process of developing the EEAS was bound to be complex and difficult. The new body was intended, unusually and quite deliberately, to straddle the treacherous boundary between **supranationalism and intergovernmentalism** in the EU institutions. The weaving together of these two philosophies, reflecting the differing assumptions of the Commission and Council in external relations, contradicted the classic method of creating new bodies rooted in one or other tradition. Moreover, unlike virtually all previous EU bodies, it would also be built out of components of two existing and continuing 'parent' institutions, drawing on very different corporate cultures, with all the potential to provoke 'the mother of all bureaucratic battles', as one senior official, Robert Cooper, accurately predicted before the event.

The precise organization of the EEAS was eventually determined by a **decision** of the Council of Ministers, adopted in July 2010, after a lengthy tussle between the Council, Commission and **European Parliament**. In a unique decision-making method, the proposal was made by the High Representative, subject to the formal consent of the Commission, after receiving an **opinion** from the Parliament. Soon after, other necessary legislative measures – notably amendments to the EU's Financial Regulation and **staff regulations** – were adopted, on which the Parliament enjoyed **co-decision** with the Council, as well as special budgetary provision for the EEAS, where the Parliament's approval was also required. The Parliament skillfully made it clear that its agreement to these latter acts was contingent on it having an effective say on aspects of the initial Council decision on the EEAS. As a result, in effect, all three institutions had to give their simultaneous authorization to the EEAS package before it could be enacted in its entirety.

When detailed negotiations on the EEAS' structure started in October 2009, fully six years had passed since the signature of the European Constitution. Previous talks had been interrupted twice – first by the abandonment of the Constitution itself, following its defeat in the **French and Dutch referenda** of May–June 2005, and then, a second time, after the initial rejection of the Lisbon Treaty in the first **Irish referendum** in June 2008. In the event, the Commission and Council were able to agree fairly rapidly that the EEAS should be 'equidistant' organizationally between its two parent institutions, that it should enjoy autonomy in budgetary and personnel matters, and that its policy staff should have 'single desk' responsibility for geographic areas or thematic issues. Although the service would report to the High Representative, it would also assist the **President of the European Council** and the President of the Commission in 'ensuring the Union's external representation' in CFSP and non-CFSP issues respectively.

The most difficult question to be answered was precisely which staff, from which directorates-general of the Commission and the Council, should be transferred into the EEAS. It made obvious sense for those parts of the two institutions' directorates-general for external relations, which dealt with CFSP and the general coordination of external policy, to merge and form the core of the new service. Conversely, the Commission argued successfully that it should retain its staff dealing with CCP and enlargement. It was also agreed that the Commission's DG for development policy would be divided, with the policy and 'programming' staff going to the EEAS and those officials responsible for coordination and budget execution (together with EuropeAid and ECHO, the humanitarian aid office) remaining in the Commission. The latter's 140 delegations to third countries and international organizations were transferred into the EEAS, as 'Union delegations'. However, although all staff in the field would report formally to the head of delegation – the EU ambassador, appointed by the High Representative and located in the EEAS – they would actually be employed by either the EEAS or the Commission, depending on the corresponding division of responsibility in Brussels. The civilian and military crisis management staffs would join the EEAS, but with a direct reporting line into the High Representative.

The EEAS became fully operational in January 2011. It is organized into four main clusters of activity, three of which report to a four-man 'corporate board' of senior officials, headed by the Secretary General, Pierre Vimont, previously French ambassador to the United States. The first cluster deals with the core policy work of the service and is composed of six functional and geographical DGs, subdivided into 11 directorates and 40 units. These are the 'single desks' at the heart of the system. In addition to global and multilateral issues, and crisis response and operational coordination, the seven DGs cover the Americas, Africa, Asia and the Pacific, the Middle East and 'Southern Neighbourhood', Russia, the Eastern Neighbourhood and the Western Balkans.

The second cluster within the EEAS covers horizontal political activity, notably the operation of the **Political and Security Committee** (PSC), which prepares all meetings of the Foreign Affairs Council (FAC), and the Situation Centre (SITCEN), which exchanges intelligence between the member states, as well as strategic planning, legal affairs, and relations with the other EU institutions and bodies. The third cluster deals with internal organizational issues – such as administration, finance, audit and inspection – including the deployment of staff in the Union delegations around the world.

The fourth cluster, reporting directly to the High Representative, encompasses the military and civilian 'crisis management' structures previously contained in the Council secretariat. These cover the operation of the **EU Military Committee** (EUMC) and EU Military Staff (EUMS), and their civilian equivalents – the Committee for Civilian Aspects of Crisis Management (CIVCOM) and the Civilian Planning and Conduct Capability (CPCC) – together with the Crisis Management and Planning Directorate (CMPD), which acts as an interface between the two sides. In addition, the three CFSP **agencies** – the European Defence Agency (EDA), the European Union Satellite Centre (EUSC) and the EU Institute for Security Studies (EUISS) – also report directly to the High Representative, who chairs their governing boards.

The volume of staff brought into the EEAS from the Commission was at least three times as many as those joining from the Council secretariat. Whereas the Commission had almost 1,100 policy staff (centrally and in delegations) dealing with EEAS-type work, the Council had less than 300 (or 500, including the EUMS). The gap is to be made up in part by diplomats on secondment from national foreign ministries – initially around 200 – where there is particularly strong competition from some of the smaller member states to secure positions within the new service. As a result of a concession secured by the European Parliament, national officials will be able to stay on secondment to the EEAS for up to ten years (rather than for four years, as initially planned). Conversely, established EU officials must constitute at least 60 per cent of all policy staff. The Parliament also gained a political commitment from the High Representative that the heads of EU delegations in strategically or politically important countries, as well as EU Special Representatives, will appear in closed meetings of the Parliament's foreign affairs committee for de facto hearings before they take up their appointments. The EEAS currently has a permanent establishment plan of 1,500 staff, a third of whom are based in delegations around the world. In addition, another 1,400 people are locally employed. By contrast, the national foreign ministries of the 27 member states collectively boast around 94,000 officials.

Further reading: Michael Emerson et al., *Upgrading the EU's Role as Global Actor*, 2011.

European Financial Stability Facility (EFSF) and European Stability Mechanism (ESM)

Devised at high speed by EU finance ministers at an emergency meeting of the **Ecofin Council** on 9 May 2010 – coinciding ironically with the 60th anniversary of the **Schuman Plan** – the European Financial Stability Facility is currently the principal EU 'bail-out' fund available 'to provide temporary financial assistance' to member states within the **eurozone**. Regulated by the intergovernmental EFSF Framework Agreement, which required **ratification** by **national parliaments**, this 'special purpose vehicle' takes the form of a Luxembourg-registered company, owned by the governments of the 17 eurozone member states. Drawing on 'guarantee commitments' from member states of € 780 billion, subscribed using the same key as their share of the paid-up capital of the **European Central Bank** (ECB), the EFSF has a lending capacity of € 440 billion. National guarantees range in size from Germany's € 221 billion (27.1 per cent) to Malta's € 704 million (0.1 per cent). The EFSF can issue bonds or other debt instruments in order to provide loans to countries in difficulty, subject to conditions negotiated on its behalf by the **European Commission**, 'in liaison' with the ECB and the International Monetary Fund (IMF).

The EFSF was incorporated in June 2010 and the Framework Agreement entered into force two months later. The facility is governed by a board comprising senior officials (or junior ministers) from the finance ministries of the eurozone states, with the Commission and ECB enjoying observer status. The board is headed by the chairman of the EU's **Economic and Financial Committee** (EFC); its chief executive, Klaus Regling, was previously a senior Commission official. The EFSF receives treasury management and other administrative support from the **European Investment Bank** (EIB), whilst the German debt management office, the DMO, and (since January 2012) the ECB are used as its agents for market operations.

During the course of the **eurozone debt crisis**, the EFSF has so far been activated to assist two countries – Ireland, with € 17.7 billion of loans in November 2010, and Portugal, with € 26.0 billion of loans in May 2011. In each case, such financing forms part of a broader package of support, with parallel loans from the International Monetary Fund (IMF) and the **European Financial Stabilization Mechanism** (EFSM). The latter is a smaller (€ 60 billion), treaty-based fund covering all member states, administered by the Commission, which uses the EU **Budget** as collateral for money raised on the financial markets. In the course of 2011, the EFSF raised some € 16 billion on the capital markets in two issues each for Ireland and Portugal, and it expects to raise another € 10 billion in 2012.

All loans extended by the EFSF are subject to strict conditionality. The applicant state negotiates a macro-economic 'adjustment programme' with the Commission, which acts as agent for the eurozone 17 for this purpose. Any such programme needs to secure the unanimous approval of both the EFSF board and the **Eurogroup** of finance ministers, before being embodied in a memorandum of understanding with the country concerned. The Commission monitors compliance closely, with the possibility of the payment schedule being delayed or halted if plans for fiscal consolidation and structural reform falter.

The heads of government of the eurozone member states decided at a summit in Brussels in July 2011 to increase EFSF resources from € 440 billion to € 780 billion, whilst keeping maximum lending at the first figure: the 'over-guarantee' of 165 per cent is intended to ensure the facility's 'triple A' rating in the markets. The eurozone summit also agreed to reduce the interest rate on EFSF loans and extend their maturities, as well as to widen the role of the facility, so that in future it could finance the recapitalization of financial institutions, including in countries without adjustment programmes, and intervene in secondary markets (on the basis of ECB analysis) in order to try to limit the risks of financial contagion between member states. All these changes were also carried forward into the design of the new European Stability Mechanism (ESM), which is intended as the long-term replacement for both the EFSF and EFSM. An ESM Treaty was concluded among the 17 eurozone states in July 2011, with a view (originally) to its entry into force in June 2013, since brought forward to July 2012. A revised version of the treaty was signed in February 2012.

The ESM will be an intergovernmental organization established under public international law, directed by a Board of Governors, comprising the finance ministers of the eurozone states and chaired either by the President of the Eurogroup or by one of their (other) colleagues, elected for a two-year term. The Board of Governors will appoint a managing director (for a five-year term, renewable once), who will chair a Board of Directors comprised of senior national officials (like the current EFSF board). The ESM Treaty will enter into force once member states representing 90 per cent of its subscribed capital have ratified the text. The ESM will have an effective lending capacity of € 500 billion, equivalent to the EFSF and EFSM combined, based on a capital stock of € 700 billion, comprised of € 80 billion in paid-in shares and € 620 billion in callable shares. (By contrast, the EFSF is based entrirely on guarantees.) The European Council has agreed that, as with the EFSF, the Commission and ECB should be invited to perform certain ESM-related tasks, and that, in addition, the **European Court of Justice** (ECJ) should be asked to adjudicate on any legal disputes arising under the ESM Treaty.

Both the changes to the EFSF agreement and the ESM Treaty itself required ratification by the **national parliaments** of the eurozone states – a process which put governments on the defensive in several countries. In Finland, demands had to be resisted that the Greek government put up state assets as collateral for future EFSF or ESM loans. In Germany, the creation of a special subcommittee of the budget committee of the Bundestag was conceded, following a parallel ruling by the Federal Constitutional Court in Karlsruhe about the need for parliamentary control over specific lending decisions. In Slovakia, the governing coalition was seriously divided about the merits of ratification, with the parliament first rejecting the EFSF/ESM package in October 2011 and then only endorsing it after the government agreed to call an early general election. The changes to the EFSF agreement were ratified by all national parliaments by mid-October 2011, whilst the ESM Treaty still needed to be endorsed by all parliaments at the time that it was revised and resubmitted for signature in February 2012.

The decision to establish the ESM was itself a product of German insistence that, for any bail-out mechanism to be fully consistent with the Treaties, it needed to be a public body grounded in a specific **legal base**. Article 125(1) TFEU – the so-called 'no bail-out clause' dating from the 1992 **Maastricht Treaty** – precludes the Union from being 'liable for' or assuming the financial commitments of governments or other public authorities in the member states, or indeed one member state assuming the liabilities of any other. In December 2010, the European Council agreed to a request made by Chancellor Angela Merkel that Article 136 TFEU (on economic coordination within the eurozone) be amended with the following addition: 'The Member States whose currency is the euro may establish a stability mechanism to be activated if indispensable to safeguard the stability of the euro area as a whole. The granting of any required financial assistance under the mechanism will be made subject to strict conditionality.' This amendment is designed to enable both the ECJ and the Karlsruhe court to conclude that the Treaties are not being breached by the operation of the EFSF or ESM (see **Karlsruhe judgements**).

The deepening of the eurozone debt crisis during the second half of 2011 led to further initiatives to strengthen the bail-out mechanisms. In October, eurozone heads of government agreed to try to 'leverage' the resources of the EFSF by various technical means, including 'partial risk protection' (of 20 to 30 per cent) to undepin national debt issues. In December, they also agreed that (assuming that the ratification could be completed in time) the ESM Treaty should come into force a year earlier than planned, in July 2012, and then run alongside the EFSF and EFSM for 13 months, before replacing them (as planned) from June 2013. The unanimous decision-making method of the ESM ('mutual agreement rule') would be amended to allow for countries with 85 per cent of subscribed capital to take 'urgent' decisions when the 'financial and economic sustainability' of the eurozone was under threat. (It was always anticipated that technical and procedural questions would require an 80 per cent majority.) The purpose of this change is clearly to prevent the governments or parliaments of small eurozone states from preventing the adoption of urgent measures in crisis conditions.

European Financial Stabilization Mechanism (EFSM)

Like the bigger **European Financial Stability Facility** (EFSF), the European Financial Stabilization Mechanism was devised at an emergency meeting of EU finance ministers on 9 May 2010, in response to the developing **eurozone debt crisis**. Given legal form two days later as a **regulation** of the **Council of Ministers**, under Article 122(2) TFEU, the EFSM is a treaty-based financial support facility, which permits the European Union to borrow up to € 60 billion for the purpose of 'on-lending' to any member state 'which is experiencing, or is seriously threatened with, a severe economic or financial disturbance caused by exceptional occurrences beyond its control'. Given that some commentators doubted whether the running up of an excessive deficit by a eurozone state genuinely constituted an act beyond its control, as required by Article 122(2), the regulation helpfully specifies that the recent international economic and financial crisis has indeed led to 'a severe deterioration of the borrowing conditions of several Member States beyond what can be explained by economic fundamentals'.

EFSM funds are raised on the capital markets by the **European Commission** and guaranteed by the Union's annual **Budget** (€ 126.5 billion in 2011), up to the limit of unused **own resources** in any year. Like EFSF loans, funding from the EFSM is made available to recipients on the basis of strict conditionality. The Commission agrees a macro-economic 'adjustment programme' with the member state concerned. On this basis, the Commission makes a proposal for a **decision** to the Council, to be adopted by **qualified majority voting** (QMV), and followed by a memorandum of understanding with the state in question. Progress in meeting the provisions of the adjustment programme are reviewed by the Commission at least every six months, with the possibility for the Commission to propose and the Council adopt revisions, as necessary. So far, EFSM funding of up to € 48.5 billion has been made available to Portugal and Ireland (but not Greece) as part of their 'bail-out' packages: Ireland may receive € 22.5 billion and Portugal € 26.0 billion over a three-year period. (By the end of 2011, a total of € 28.0 billion had been disbursed.)

The EFSM complements an existing EU balance of payments' support facility, always foreseen in the **Treaty of Rome** (Article 108 EEC, now replaced by Article 143 TFEU), but which was only given legislative form in July 1988 (as a Council regulation) and used for the first time in October 2008. Since 1999, this 'facility providing medium-term financial assistance for Member States' balance of payments' has been confined to countries that have yet to adopt the **euro**. Its funding, set at € 12.0 billion in February 2002, was increased to € 25.0 in December 2008 and doubled to € 50.0 billion in May 2009. The recipients so far have been Hungary, Latvia and Romania, which received credit lines of € 6.5, 3.1 and 5.0 billion (in October 2008, January 2009 and March 2009) respectively. Access to this facility requires a Commission proposal, followed by a Council **decision**, based on a memorandum of understanding between the Union and the state concerned, setting out the conditions for receipt.

European flag

The European flag – a circle of twelve five-pointed gold stars on a dark blue background – was devised originally by the **Council of Europe** for its own use. Adopted by the Consultative Assembly in October 1955 and Committee of Ministers two months later, it was first flown at the Château de la Muette in Paris immediately thereafter. For many years, the Council of Europe sought to promote use of the flag by other European institutions, but without success. In April 1983, however, the European Parliament advocated adoption of the flag by the then European Community and, following the report of the Adonnino Committee for a People's Europe, heads of government agreed to its general use by the Community institutions at the Milan **European Council** in June 1985. Since then, the European flag has become the most visible symbol of the European Union. The aborted **European Constitution** provided for the flag to be designated as one of the '**symbols of the Union**' (Article I-8 Constitution). However, the successor **Lisbon Treaty** dropped this section of the original text and currently the symbols have no legal standing (although they are referred to in the European Parliament's rules of procedure).

Correctly described in heraldic terminology as 'on a field azure, a circle of twelve mullets or, their points not touching', the European flag triumphed over two alternative designs. The first was a very colourful proposal by Count **Richard Coudenhove-Kalergi**'s **Pan-Europa**, a golden disc representing the sun of Apollo on a blue background with a red cross superimposed, emblematic of Europe's Graeco-Christian heritage. The second was the flag of the **European Movement**, a large green capital 'E' on a white background. A variant of this flag was used by the **European Commission** until 1985. The Turks, then as now members of the Council of Europe, objected on principle to any design incorporating a cross, but did not realize that a circle of twelve gold stars is also a Christian symbol: the Virgin Mary's halo (Revelation 12.1).

The present design was ultimately the work of Paul Lévy, the Council of Europe's director of information in the early 1950s. He drew on a number of concepts suggested by a colleague, Arsène Heitz, including an elegant design for a circle of stars, with one larger star in the middle. Lévy originally proposed 15 stars, reflecting the number of members of the Council at the time. The Germans objected on the grounds that this number included the **Saarland**, an observer member, whose separate status they did not wish to promote. France and Italy objected to 14 and 13 stars for various reasons. Lévy then suggested twelve stars, which had the advantage of representing 'perfection and entirety, as embodied in the twelve apostles, months of the year or signs of the zodiac', as he put it later. The fact that there were twelve stars and twelve member states of the European Community at the time the latter adopted the flag in 1985 was thus entirely coincidental. It was never proposed, either by the Council of Europe or the EC, to follow the example of the Stars and Stripes in the United States and add a star for each new accession. Fliers of the flag and users of the symbol should note that the gold stars must have their single points uppermost.

European Free Trade Association (EFTA)

EFTA was established by the Stockholm Convention of January 1960 as a **free trade area** (for industrial products) among seven western European countries which were unwilling or unable to join the recently formed **European Economic Community** (EEC). Austria, Denmark, **Norway**, Portugal, Sweden, **Switzerland** and the United Kingdom – known as 'the Seven', to distinguish them from '**the Six**' EC member states – accepted the logic of developing a more integrated European economy, but rejected the concepts of a **customs union** and **common market**, based on **supranational** institutions and law, embodied in the **Treaty of Rome** of March 1957. EFTA came into effect in May 1960.

In a rearguard action to prevent the EEC being formed, the United Kingdom had led an unsuccessful effort to forge a broader free trade area among all the members of the **Organization for European Economic Cooperation** (OEEC), to which both the Six and the Seven belonged. The foundation of EFTA in 1960 was a delayed response, on a more modest scale, to the failure of this alternative strategy. Had French President **Charles de Gaulle** not chosen to veto British membership of the Community in 1963 and 1967 (and with it in effect that of two other EFTA states, Denmark and Norway), it is likely that the Association would have quickly withered away. Instead it developed cautiously during the years from 1960 to 1973, when Britain eventually secured membership of the Community. Full free trade in industrial products was achieved within EFTA in 1966, Iceland joined in March 1970, and the individual EFTA countries concluded bilateral free trade agreements with the Community in 1973. Tariffs between the EEC and EFTA were eliminated four years later.

However, the **accession** of most of the more significant EFTA states to the Community, subsequently Union, gradually ended their membership of the Association. The UK and Denmark left EFTA in 1973, Portugal in 1986, and Austria and Sweden in 1995. Although Finland joined EFTA in 1986, having been an associate member since 1961, it departed to join the EU nine years later. Only Iceland, Norway and Switzerland were left – along with Liechtenstein, which joined in 1991.

Before the departure of Austria, Sweden and Finland in January 1995 – sometimes referred to in EU circles as the 'EFTAn **enlargement**' – there was already very strong pressure within EFTA to upgrade and deepen its relations with the EU, with the specific aim of gaining full access to its developing **single market**. Negotiations led to agreement in May 1992 on the creation of a joint **European Economic Area** (EEA), which came into effect in January 1994. It was intended that, to the extent that EFTA was retained, it would act as a coherent forum for the four non-EU members of the EEA. However, the rejection by one of the four, Switzerland, of its proposed membership of the EEA – in a **referendum** held in December 1992 – created an unexpectedly complex situation, with EFTA now able to speak for only three or its members on EEA issues (namely Iceland, Liechtenstein and Norway).

Not only did this outcome make the web of relations between the institutions of the EU, EEA and EFTA unusually complicated (even by European standards), but it specifically weakened EFTA's continuing rationale as a separate body. As a result, since the early 1990s, EFTA has spent much time negotiating bilateral free trade agreements, first with the countries of central and eastern Europe, and then since the latter's accession to the EU, with another 16 third countries or trade blocs around the world. (Even though the total population of the EFTA countries is only 12.6 million, their combined GDP amounts to almost one trillion US dollars.) In parallel, Switzerland has been forced to engage in bilateral negotiations with the EU to catch up with arrangements already operating throughout the EEA.

The Stockholm Convention originally established only one EFTA institution, an entirely intergovernmental council. The EFTA Council is composed of one representative of each member state and usually meets once a month at official level and twice a year at ministerial level (in June and December). Decisions are normally reached by consensus, with each member state having one vote. The presidency of EFTA rotates on an annual basis. Specialist standing committees, composed of officials, advise the Council. Over time an EFTA Parliamentary Committee (of national parliamentarians) also evolved: it now has two formations, for EEA and non-EEA affairs, with the former acting as the EEA side of its joint parliamentary committee with the **European Parliament**. An EFTA Consultative Committee now also provides a forum for the '**social partners**' to discuss issues of special concern to business and labour.

The advent of the EEA also involved the creation of two entirely new EFTA bodies, both with quasi-supranational characteristics. An EFTA Surveillance Authority performs a role comparable to that of the **European Commission** as 'guardian of the treaties', in ensuring that Liechtenstein, Iceland and Norway act in ways consistent with their obligations under the EEA Treaty. An EFTA Court adjudicates on disputes arising under the EEA Treaty, in the same way that the **European Court of Justice** (ECJ) does so for the EU treaties. Originally the plan had been to entrust these twin roles to the European Commission and ECJ respectively, but the ECJ gave an opinion to the EU **Council of Ministers** in December 1991 that such an arrangement would be illegal, as the EU constitutes an autonomous legal order and its institutions cannot exercise power over or on behalf of non-member states. The curious result is that EFTA now exercises responsibilities from which one of its members, Switzerland, is excluded.

EFTA is serviced by a 100-strong secretariat, based in Geneva, with offices in Brussels and Luxembourg. The Geneva headquarters service the EFTA Council and handle relations with non-member states. The Brussels office leads on EEA and EU affairs, including the work of the EFTA Surveillance Authority, whilst the Luxembourg-based staff organize the work of the EFTA Court and engage in statistical cooperation with **Eurostat**, as part of a joint European Statistical System. See also **supranationalism and intergovernmentalism**.

European Investment Bank (EIB)

Established in 1958 by the **Treaty of Rome** – under Articles 129–30 EEC, now Articles 308–9 TFEU – the European Investment Bank assists in the financing of capital investment in EU member states and third countries. Since 1992, the EIB has been the largest multilateral lender in the world, surpassing even the World Bank.

Within the Union, the EIB focuses on financing projects in less developed regions of member states and projects which 'are of such a size or nature' that they cannot be wholly funded by the countries involved (Article 309 TFEU). The EIB Statute, annexed by **protocol** to the **Treaties**, states that it may 'grant finance, in particular in the form of loans and guarantees to its members or to private or public undertakings' within the Union, 'to the extent that funds are not available from other sources on reasonable terms'. It may also 'grant financing for investment to be carried out, in whole or in part, outside the territories of Member States' (Article 16 of EIB Statute).

The EIB's capital is subscribed by the member states. The Bank was originally provided with one billion EUA in subscribed capital in 1958, a figure that was doubled with the first **enlargement** of the Community in 1973. Further enlargements and the widening of the Union's policy responsibilities saw the capital of the EIB increase further, from 14 billion ECU in 1981 to € 165 billion in 2004. In 2009, it was decided to increase the sum once again to € 232 billion, so that the Bank could undertake additional activity in the face of the severe economic downturn. The EIB committed itself to increase its lending by two-thirds in 2009–10, provided that it could find suitable projects, as part of the European Economic Recovery Plan adopted by the European Council in December 2008. By the end of 2010, it had provided € 61 billion in loans as part of this programme.

The Bank uses its subscribed capital to borrow funds on the capital markets of the member states. The funds so raised are then loaned to private enterprises or public authorities at highly competitive rates of interest. Under Article 16 of the EIB Statute, the 'aggregate amount outstanding at any time of loans and guarantees granted by the Bank shall not exceed 250 per cent of its subscribed capital' and other funds. This means that at the moment the EIB can extend loans or guarantees up to a total value of around € 600 billion.

When the EIB was created, Germany and the Netherlands insisted that the Bank be established as a body separate to the **European Commission**, operating under the control of the member states, with a measure of independence in its lending priorities, and using funds raised on the money markets, rather than from the Community Budget. As EIB activity is underwritten by the member states, the Bank can take advantage of the high credit ratings of the latter. Although the EIB operates on a non-profit-making basis (Article

309 TFEU), it usually shows a surplus on its operations (of € 2.1 billion in 2010). Its capital adequacy ratio stands at 35 per cent. As far as possible, EIB loans are granted only on the basis that other sources of finance are also used. They do not normally exceed 50 per cent of total investment costs and are conditional upon adequate financial guarantees. Neither the EIB nor a member state may impose conditions requiring funds to be spent within a specified member state. Equally, no investment may be undertaken within a member state without that country's prior agreement.

EIB lending has risen rapidly in recent years, reflecting both the growth in the Bank's subscribed capital and increasing demand for its products. The EIB lent € 48 billion in 2007, € 57 billion in 2008, € 70 billion in 2009 and € 72 billion in 2010. It has established a series of 'priority objectives' for its lending, notably projects related to greater **cohesion** and economic convergence; innovation in pursuit of the Union's Lisbon Strategy and Europe 2020 goals; promotion of human capital; development of **Trans-European Networks** (TENs); environmental sustainability and diversity of energy supply; and encouragement of small and medium-sized enterprises (SMEs). Some 85 per cent of EIB lending takes place within the territory of the Union. The main priorities in 2011 were industry, energy, transport and water and waste treatment.

Many of the most significant projects part-financed by the EIB in recent years have been in the transport sector, notably the Spanish high-speed rail network, where € 25 billion has been made available in loans over the period 2002–15. A wide range of smaller projects have also received EIB support, including the Crossrail urban rail link and upgrading of the M25 orbital motorway in London (€ 1.1 billion and € 450 million respectively), urban transport in the Paris region (€ 600 million), the Westmetro project in Finland (€ 450 million), improvements to the Polish road network (€ 450 million) and the new terminal at Dublin airport (€ 260 million).

The Bank's extra-EU activities began in 1962 and now extend to some 120 countries around the world, accounting for over a tenth of total lending (€ 8.8 billion in 2010). They are grouped into the four 'external mandates': the current or potential **enlargement** countries of south-eastern Europe; the countries of the **European Neighbourhood Policy** (ENP), as well as Russia; the **ACP states** (with separate arrangements for South Africa) and the **overseas countries and territories** (OCTs) of the Union; and the countries of Asia and Latin America. Within the ENP mandate, there is a Facility for Euro-Mediterranean Investment and Partnership (FEMIP), established in 2002. Following the 'Arab spring', it was decided in May 2011 to increase EIB lending in the Mediterranean region to € 6.0 billion over the period 2011–13.

The finance ministers of the member states act as the Board of Governors of the EIB. They appoint a Board of Directors – composed of one director from each member state, plus one from the European Commission – which serves for a five-year term. The directors propose, and the governors appoint, a president and eight vice-presidents, who together form a Management Committee, with a six-year term. The governors may, acting unanimously, increase the capital subscribed by the member states.

Unlike the **European Central Bank** (ECB), the EIB is not an institution of the European Union, even though, like the ECB, it enjoys **legal personality** in its own right (Article 308 TFEU). It is a body whose existence is sanctioned by the Treaty, but unlike a variety of other such bodies – the **European Economic and Social Committee** (EESC), the **Committee of the Regions**, the **Ombudsman** and the European Data Protection Supervisor – it is not covered under Article 1 of the EU's Financial Regulation. The EIB is not subject to the EU's annual **budgetary process** and there is no provision for it to be formally responsible to the **European Parliament** in any way. This has led to criticism that the Bank's activities are subject to insufficient scrutiny, especially given the increasing scale of its lending. The headquarters of the EIB are in Luxembourg. The Bank has over 2,000 staff, including those engaged in project appraisal. It has offices in 13 member states of the Union, as well as five local offices in various ACP states.

European League for Economic Cooperation (ELEC)

In May 1946, Paul van Zeeland (1893–1973), a former prime minister and future foreign minister of Belgium, and Joseph Retinger (1888–1960), a leading pro-European Pole in exile, established 'an élite group' of 'acknowledged economic experts' – as Walter Lipgens put it in *A History of European Integration,* Volume 1, 1982 – to argue the case for closer economic unity in post-war Europe. Initially known as the *Ligue indépendante de cooperation européenne,* ELEC adopted its present name two years later, at the time of the **Congress of Europe** in The Hague. Many of ELEC's early members were prominent economists, business leaders and centre-right politicians who had served in governments-in-exile in London. The League was organized on a national basis – with sections in the United Kingdom, France and the **Benelux** countries – and played an important part in preparing the intellectual ground for the creation of the **European Communities** in the 1950s. The organization continued in subsequent decades and still exists today, with 16 national chapters and a small central staff in Brussels.

European Monetary Cooperation Fund (EMCF)

The European Monetary Cooperation Fund was set up in April 1973, by a **regulation** of the **Council of Ministers**, as part of the European Community's first attempt to achieve **Economic and Monetary Union** (EMU), following the 1970 **Werner Report.** Its remit was to promote the progressive narrowing of fluctuation margins between Community currencies, encourage intervention in those currencies on the exchange markets, and facilitate settlements between central banks, leading to a concerted policy on reserves. The **central bank governors** of the EC member states comprised the EMCF's Board of Governors; they met at least four times a year and acted by unanimity.

By the mid-1970s, after the failure of the 'Snake' and the 'Snake in the Tunnel', it was clear that the initial EMU project was moribund and the EMCF fell into disuse. However, the fund was revived when the **European Currency Unit** (ECU) was introduced in 1979 as part of the new **European Monetary System** (EMS). Participating member states agreed to deposit 20 per cent of their gold and dollar reserves with the EMCF, which issued ECUs in exchange. Interventions by central banks on the exchange markets as part of the **Exchange-Rate Mechanism** (ERM) were regulated by the fund, which was also able to offer short-term credits to help member states' balance of payments. At the beginning of stage two of EMU in January 1994, the EMCF was wound up and its functions were taken over by the **European Monetary Institute** (EMI). They were transferred to the **European Central Bank** (ECB) in June 1998, when the latter was created, seven months in advance of EMU stage three.

European Monetary Institute (EMI)

The European Monetary Institute was the precursor to the **European Central Bank** (ECB), operating for all but the last seven months of stage two of **Economic and Monetary Union** (EMU), namely from 1 January 1994 to 30 May 1998. Established under Article 117 EC, introduced by the 1992 **Maastricht Treaty** and repealed as redundant by the **Lisbon Treaty** in 2009, the EMI formalized and assumed the role of the (pre-existing) Committee of **Central Bank Governors** – which brought together the heads of the monetary authorities of the EU member states – and built on their work by performing additional tasks. The Institute's central function was to 'prepare the instruments and the procedures necessary' for the move to EMU stage three (in January 1999), which would see the transfer of monetary **sovereignty** among participating countries to the new ECB and the replacement of their individual national currencies by a single currency. In June 1998, the Council of the EMI became in effect the Governing Council of the ECB, encompassing the central bank governors of (only) stage-three members. (Governors from member states outside stage three join them in the ECB's General Council, which is advisory and technical in character.)

Under Article 117 EC, the EMI's specific responsibilities were to strengthen cooperation between the national central banks and improve the coordination of the monetary policies pursued by them, to 'monitor the functioning' of the **European Monetary System** (EMS), assume the tasks of the **European Monetary Cooperation Fund** (EMCF), and 'facilitate the use' and 'oversee [the] development' of the **European Currency Unit** (ECU), which subsequently became the **euro**.

The EMI, acting by a two-thirds majority of its Council, was empowered to draw up opinions or recommendations 'on the overall orientation of monetary policy and exchange-rate policy' and on 'policies which might affect the internal or external monetary situation', in particular the functioning of the EMS. It could also make recommendations to member states 'concerning the conduct of their monetary policy'. It had a general right to be consulted on any EU legislation which might bear on its areas of activity. A more detailed Statute for the EMI was annexed as a **protocol** to the Treaty (this too was repealed in 2009). The Institute was based in Frankfurt and built up a staff of around 200 officials as the embryo ECB. Its two presidents were Alexandre Lamfalussy, a Hungarian-born Belgian economist, who had previously served as director general of the **Bank for International Settlements** (BIS), and (from July 1997) Wim Duisenberg (1935–2005), the former Dutch finance minister and central bank governor who became the first President of the ECB.

European Monetary System (EMS)

The European Monetary System was created in January 1979, in order to promote 'a zone of monetary stability in Europe' and to strengthen cooperation between member-state governments and national central banks with respect to monetary policy. Its principal instrument was the **Exchange-Rate Mechanism** (ERM), which linked the value of national currencies through a grid of central exchange rates against a new basket currency, the **European Currency Unit** (ECU), backed by intervention both bilaterally and centrally through the **European Monetary Cooperation Fund** (EMCF). The EMS ceased to exist formally with the move to stage three of **Economic and Monetary Union** (EMU) in January 1999, when 11 countries adopted the **euro** as Europe's single currency. However, the Exchange-Rate Mechanism survives in the form of 'ERM II', which provides a comparable framework for limiting the fluctuation between the euro and certain member-state currencies outside the **eurozone**.

The EMS was proposed by **Roy Jenkins** in October 1977, during his first year as President of the **European Commission**, after the failure of the earlier attempt to achieve EMU through the path suggested by the 1970 **Werner Report**. With strong support from West German Chancellor Helmut Schmidt and French President **Valéry Giscard d'Estaing**, the creation of the EMS was sanctioned by heads of government through a resolution of the **European Council** in Brussels in December 1978, and by an agreement between central banks in March 1979 (replacing the previous 'Snake' and 'Snake in the Tunnel').

Although the EMS initially had no legal foundation, all member states chose to participate in it from the start. Their currencies formed part of the ECU and they deposited 20 per cent of their gold and dollar reserves with the EMCF. However, founding member states were free to decide whether to join the ERM and over what timescale. Countries acceding afterwards were given considerable latitude in practice, even if in theory it was a political obligation to join, as part of the ***acquis communautaire***. The pound sterling did not enter the ERM until October 1990 (and left in September 1992 on **Black Wednesday**). The Greek drachma did not join until March 1998, and the Swedish krona has never been part of the ERM in either of its forms.

The existence of the EMS was acknowledged in law by the 1992 **Maastricht Treaty**. With the move to a single currency, the ECU was substituted by the euro; the functions of the EMCF were taken over by the **European Monetary Institute** (EMI) for (all but the last seven months of) stage two of EMU (1994–9) and are now exercised by the **European Central Bank** (ECB) in stage three.

Further reading: Piers Ludlow, *The Making of the European Monetary System: A case study in the politics of the European Community*, 1982; Horst Ungerer et al., *The European Monetary System: Developments and Perspectives*, IMF Occasional Paper, 1990.

European Movement

The all-party European Movement is the principal international, membership-based organization campaigning in favour of closer European integration. Founded in October 1948, it brought together a large number of post-war groups in western Europe active in the European cause. Its first presidents-of-honour were the French Socialist leader Léon Blum, **Winston Churchill**, **Alcide de Gasperi** and **Paul-Henri Spaak**. The Movement's immediate precursor, the International Committee of the Movements for European Unity, organized the **Congress of Europe**, held in The Hague in May 1948, and played an important part in the creation of the **Council of Europe**, the College of Europe and the European Cultural Centre. At that time, some of the Movement's younger members campaigned actively to promote the abolition of national borders. The *New York Times* reported in August 1950 that 300 students mobbed the Franco-German frontier post at Wissembourg, carrying banners proclaiming 'We demand a European government and parliament'.

In recent years, the European Movement has been less obviously active or influential, although it continues to organize conferences and educational events aimed mainly at the general public. The central body, now known as the European Movement International, has its headquarters in Brussels; in addition, there are 44 national chapters in individual European countries. The central organization receives a subsidy, amounting to € 430,000 in 2010, from the **European Commission**. Some national chapters also receive public funds, but many are dependent on membership fees and donations. The European Commission also subsidizes the Union of European Federalists (to the sum of € 110,000 in 2010), as well as the more critical Statewatch (€ 68,000).

European Neighbourhood Policy (ENP)

The concept of a European Neighbourhood Policy was first put forward by the **European Commission** in March 2003, in advance of the **enlargement** of the European Union the following year. It was seen as a way of grouping together and rendering consistent EU policies towards two sets of proximate countries with which the Union wished to have close economic and political relations, but to which it did not intend to offer the prospect of **accession**. The first group comprises the 'new neighbours' to the Union's east and south-east – the six former Soviet republics of Armenia, Azerbaijan, Belarus, Georgia, Moldova and Ukraine – which are now covered by the 'Eastern Partnership', launched at a special summit in Prague in May 2009. The second group involves ten of the 16 countries covered by the existing Euro-Mediterranean Partnership (Euromed), established in November 1995 and involved since July 2008 in the Union for the Mediterranean (UfM). These are the Maghreb states of Algeria, Libya, Morocco and Tunisia; the Mashreq states of Egypt, Jordan, Lebanon and Syria; and both the Palestinian Authority and Israel. This second relationship is increasingly known as the 'Southern Partnership' and was upgraded in March 2011 as a 'Partnership for Democracy and Shared Prosperity', following the 'Arab spring'. For a variety of political reasons, the ENP relationship is in partial or complete abeyance with four countries (Belarus, Algeria, Libya and Syria). The ENP does not cover Russia (subject to a separate 'strategic partnership'), the applicant or potential applicant countries (currently **Turkey** and the seven countries of the western Balkans), the members of the **European Free Trade Association** (EFTA) or the western European **micro-states**.

The main purpose of the ENP is to create a zone of stability, security and prosperity in the immediate vicinity of the Union, in most cases by helping the individual partner countries in their transition to democracy and market economics. The strategy to the east is designed to avoid the external borders of the Union replacing the former Iron Curtain as a dividing line, with the 'new Eastern Europe' becoming too dependent on Russia. In respect of the Euromed states, the hope is that closer links may help erode divisions and promote peace in the Middle East. In both cases, there is a desire to limit illegal immigration, not only by agreed joint action, but by helping narrow the economic divergences which help generate population flows in the first place.

The ENP has both bilateral and multilateral components. Bilaterally, all ENP partners already have **association agreements** or partnership and cooperation agreements (a form of **cooperation agreement**) with the EU, usually covering a wide range of issues, including political and security questions, market access, the environment, transport and energy. Building on these, a specific ENP Action Plan, setting out a range of reform commitments over a three to five year period, is negotiated for each country, with the Union providing financial and technical assistance in return. Commitments in respect of democracy, human rights and the rule of law usually prove the most problematic dimension of this process. (Belarus, Algeria, Libya and Syria do not have Action Plans.) The European Commission, which is responsible for negotiating these agreements on behalf of the **Council of Ministers**, publishes an annual progress report on each country. Multilaterally, ministerial meetings are held each year, at various levels, between the two groups of partners (separately) and the European Union. A second Eastern Partnership was held in Warsaw in September 2011. A parliamentary dimension has already been established for the Mediterranean side, in the form of the Euro-Mediterranean Parliamentary Assembly (EMPA), and a parallel body, known as the 'Euronest' Parliamentary Assembly, is being developed for the Eastern Partnership countries. The absence of democracy in Belarus has significantly complicated the launch of the latter.

Since January 2007, financial support for both Mediterranean and Eastern partners has been provided through the European Neighbourhood and Partnership Instrument (ENPI). This encompasses not only the ENP, but also the 'strategic partnership' with Russia, and funding for applicant and potential applicant countries (Croatia, FYR Macedonia, Albania, Bosnia and Herzegovina, Montenegro, Serbia and Kosovo). The ENPI replaced TACIS for the Eastern neighbours and Russia, and MEDA for the Mediterranean partners. Over the EU's current seven-year financing period (2007–13), some € 12 billion has been assigned to the ENPI, an increase of a third in real terms compared with the previous period (2000–6).

European Organization for Nuclear Research (CERN)

Normally known by its original French acronym, CERN (*Conseil Européen pour la Recherche Nucléaire*) dates from a July 1953 convention drawn up under the auspices of the **United Nations** and is not formally associated with the European Union. CERN has 20 member countries (18 from the EU, together with **Norway** and **Switzerland**) and is dedicated to 'sub-nuclear research of a pure scientific and fundamental character'. Originally focused on study of the atomic nucleus, it has broadened its research to cover high-energy particle physics, with a view to 'finding out what the universe is made of and how it works'.

Based in Geneva, CERN has the most advanced experimental facilities for particle physics in the world, including six accelerators and a decelerator. The centrepiece is a circular tunnel, 27 kilometres in circumference and located 100 metres underground, which sits astride the Franco-Swiss border, between Geneva airport and the Jura mountains. From 1989 to 2000, this tunnel housed the Large Electron Positron (LEP) storage ring. Since 2008, it has hosted the Large Hadron Collider (LHC), the most powerful such machine in the world. The LHC is designed to recreate the conditions that prevailed immediately after the Big Bang, by colliding two beams of sub-atomic particles ('hadrons') head-on at very high energy (a combined force of up to 14 trillion electron volts). Nine days after its launch in September 2008, the LHC had to close for 14 months, following a leak of helium into the system caused by a faulty electrical connection between two of its 5,000 magnets.

CERN is supported financially by direct contributions from its member states, with an annual budget of one billion Swiss francs and a staff of about 2,500 people. In addition to its 20 members, six countries, together with the **European Commission** and UNESCO, have observer status, whilst some 8,000 scientists from nearly 600 universities and research institutes around the world (half the world's particle physicists) use CERN's facilities. The world wide web was invented at CERN in 1990 by one of its scientists, Tim Berners Lee, as a means of sharing research among scientists in different locations. The address of the world's first website, launched in 1991, was *http://info.cern.ch*. In a move that proved to be of huge significance, the organization announced in 1993 that use of the web would be free.

European Parliament

The European Parliament is currently composed of 754 Members – from 2014, it will have 751 Members – elected in Union-wide **European elections** held every five years. One of the five main **institutions** of the European Union, the Parliament has its official 'seat' in Strasbourg, France, but its committees and **political groups** meet in Brussels, the capital of Belgium, and its secretariat is divided between Brussels and Luxembourg (see **seats of EU institutions**). Although the Parliament had only modest beginnings as the Common Assembly of the **European Coal and Steel Community** (ECSC) in 1952, it now has very significant legislative, budgetary and supervisory powers, and in many policy areas it acts as part of a joint legislature with the **Council of Ministers**.

Article 7 of the 1951 **Treaty of Paris** establishing the ECSC made provision for four institutions: a **High Authority** (later to become the **European Commission**), a Special **Council of Ministers**, a **European Court of Justice** (ECJ) and a Common Assembly. The Assembly was to 'consist of representatives of the peoples of the States brought together in the Community' and to exercise 'supervisory' powers (Article 20 ECSC). Its 78 MEPs were to be nominated by the **national parliaments** of **the Six** from among their own members, in accordance with procedures laid down individually by each member state. France, Italy and West Germany had 18 members, Belgium and the Netherlands had 10, and Luxembourg four.

However, even at this early date, it was foreseen that the Members of the European Parliament (MEPs) would one day be elected directly by the public, rather than nominated, and under Article 21(3) ECSC, the Assembly was empowered to draw up 'proposals for elections by direct universal suffrage in accordance with a **uniform** [**electoral**] **procedure** in all Member States'.

The powers of the Common Assembly were relatively modest, other than that, by a two-thirds majority, the chamber could pass a motion of censure on the High Authority, forcing its members to resign 'as a body'. The Assembly was also able to put forward proposals for amendments to the annual budget proposed by the High Authority and to require the latter to answer oral or written questions. The Assembly discussed the annual report that the High Authority was required to lay before it by each February.

In common with the other institutions of the ECSC, the Assembly's headquarters and its secretariat (originally 37 people) were established in Luxembourg. However, Luxembourg was unable to offer the necessary facilities for the plenary sessions of the Assembly, which was required to work in the four official **languages** used among the Six: French, German, Italian and Dutch. In July 1952, the ECSC foreign ministers decided that the Assembly's plenary sessions should be held in Strasbourg, where the Consultative Assembly of the **Council of Europe** already met. **Jean Monnet**, the first President of the ECSC **High Authority**, relates in his *Memoirs* how the Secretary General of the Council of Europe sought to assert responsibility for organizing the first session of the Assembly, as part of an attempt to 'take over our parliamentary and ministerial institutions'. In the event, the session was organized, under Monnet's guidance, by the administrations of the six national parliaments, and opened on 5 September 1952. To underline its separate identity, the Assembly met not on the premises of the Council of Europe, but in the Strasbourg chamber of commerce. **Paul-Henri Spaak** was elected its first President by 38 votes to 30, the MEPs voting along party lines, even though political groups had not yet been formed.

The first important change in the status and composition of the Assembly was brought about by the entry into force, on 1 January 1958, of the **Treaties of Rome** establishing the **European Economic Community** (EEC) and the

European Atomic Energy Community (EAEC or Euratom). These two treaties provided for each new Community to have an Assembly, and – as with the Court of Justice and the **European Economic and Social Committee** (EESC) – the remit of the already existing ECSC Assembly was expanded to cover all three Communities, under the 'Convention on certain institutions common to the European Communities' signed in Rome at the same time as the EEC and Euratom Treaties. The number of MEPs was almost doubled, to 142, but since no progress had been made with direct elections, they were still nominated by national parliaments.

At the Assembly's first plenary session, in March 1958, the former French prime minister and foreign minister, **Robert Schuman**, was elected its President, after members refused to endorse an Italian figure pre-selected by member-state governments in the Council as part of a wider package of appointments. The powers of the Assembly, as set out in the EEC and Euratom Treaties, were broadly similar to those laid down in the ECSC Treaty, except that they were now described as 'advisory' – in respect of legislation – as well as 'supervisory' – in respect of the European Commission (Article 137 EEC, since revised).

At its first session, the Assembly also adopted the name 'European Parliamentary Assembly', in place of the old 'Common Assembly'. Four years later, in March 1962, it changed its name in French and Italian to 'European Parliament' ('Parliament' was already used in the Dutch and German versions of the Treaties). 'Assembly' continued to be used in English for official purposes (often with dismissive intent) until the change to 'Parliament' was formalized by the **Single European Act** (SEA) in 1986.

Under the Treaty of Rome, the Parliament inherited the powers of the Common Assembly, including a right to dismiss the Commission on the basis of a censure motion carried by a two-thirds majority of votes cast, representing more than half the total number of MEPs (Article 144 EEC, now Article 234 TFEU). The Parliament was empowered, like other institutions of the Community and the governments of member states, to bring an action in the Court of Justice against either the Commission or the Council for '**failure to act**' (Article 175 EEC, now Article 265 TFEU). However, critically, the Parliament's role in relation to Community legislation remained marginal: its powers were limited to the giving of opinions and the submission of amendments on draft legislation proposed by the Commission, and only then on those items which the Council was obliged to refer to it. The limitations of what is now known as the **consultation procedure** generated deep frustration among MEPs. Although the Parliament succeeded in inducing the Council to consult it on a wider range of legislative matters than was strictly necessary, the reality was that the Council was not required to incorporate any of the Parliament's amendments in the legislation finally adopted and it rarely did so.

European Parliament – Composition by member state, 1958–2014

Member state	*1958*	*1973*	*1979*	*1984*	*1987*	*1994*	*1995*	*2004*	*2007*	*2009*	*2011**	*2014*
Austria							21	18	18	17	19	19
Belgium	14	14	24	24	24	25	25	24	24	22	22	22
Bulgaria									18	17	18	18
Cyprus								6	6	6	6	6
Czech Republic								24	24	22	22	22
Denmark		10	16	16	16	16	16	14	14	13	13	13
Estonia								6	6	6	6	6
Finland							16	14	14	13	13	13
France	36	36	81	81	81	87	87	78	78	72	74	74
Germany	36	36	81	81	81	99	99	99	99	99	99	96
Greece				24	24	25	25	24	24	22	22	22
Hungary								24	24	22	22	22
Ireland		10	15	15	15	15	15	13	13	12	12	12
Italy	36	36	81	81	81	87	87	78	78	72	73	73
Latvia								9	9	8	9	9
Lithuania								13	13	12	12	12
Luxembourg	6	6	6	6	6	6	6	6	6	6	6	6
Malta								5	5	5	6	6
Netherlands	14	14	25	25	25	31	31	27	27	25	26	26
Poland								54	54	50	51	51
Portugal					24	25	25	24	24	22	22	22
Romania									35	33	33	33
Slovakia								14	14	13	13	13
Slovenia								7	7	7	8	8
Sweden							22	19	19	18	20	20
Spain					60	64	64	54	54	50	54	54
United Kingdom		36	81	81	81	87	87	78	78	72	73	73
Total	142	198	410	434	518	567	626	732	785	736	754	751

* 18 additional members entered the Parliament in December 2011.

Source: European Parliament.

The Treaties also made only very modest provision for involving the Parliament in the negotiation and conclusion of **international agreements** with non-member countries or international organizations (usually negotiated by the Commission, on the basis of a mandate laid down by the Council). In 1964, the Dutch foreign minister, Joseph Luns, then president-in-office of the Council, wrote to the Parliament to express the Council's willingness to involve the Parliament in the discussions preceding the opening of negotiations for new **association agreements** and to keep Parliament informed of the progress of such negotiations. This became known as the 'Luns procedure'. Nine years later, with the support of the Commission, this courtesy was extended to all trade agreements, in what became known as the Luns–Westerterp procedure. At that time, **cooperation agreements**, since they were not provided for in any of the Treaties, were concluded on the basis of Article 235 EEC (now **Article 352** TFEU), under which consultation of the Parliament was mandatory anyway.

As noted above, the ECSC Treaty (Article 23) required the High Authority to answer oral or written questions from Members of the Common Assembly. A similar provision was included with respect to the Commission in the Treaty of Rome (Article 197 EEC), but it was not until 1973 that the Parliament made provision in its plenary agendas for a dedicated question time to the Commission. The Council, which was not under a similar treaty obligation to answer MEPs' questions, agreed of its own volition in 1960 to reply to questions on matters that the Council had already considered, but again no regular question time was instituted until 1973. In 1975, it became possible to put questions to the foreign ministers meeting in **European Political Cooperation** (EPC).

Until the Single European Act, the only really significant increase in the Parliament's powers came in relation to the annual **Budget**, and even here they were difficult to use in practice. The switch, under the 1970 Budgetary Treaty, from a system of contributions by member states to one that gave the Community its **own resources** was accompanied by measures to increase the Parliament's say in the allocation of expenditure (although not in revenue-raising). A second Budgetary Treaty, signed in 1975, gave the Parliament the right to reject the Community Budget and to grant **discharge** (or sign off the accounts) of the Commission. In reality, however, rejection of the Budget, like dismissal of the Commission, was a 'nuclear' option which it was difficult to deploy constructively. In attempting, more prosaically, to amend the Budget, the Parliament was greatly limited by the fact that – because of a deliberate distinction between **compulsory and non-compulsory expenditure** – it could not in practice influence either the level or content of the overwhelmingly predominant component of spending at that time, the **Common Agricultural Policy** (CAP).

With the **accession** of Denmark, Ireland and the United Kingdom to the Communities in 1973, the number of MEPs was further increased from 142 to 198. In line with the practice followed in other member states, British MEPs were appointed to reflect the strength of the political parties in the lower chamber, although the MEPs could be drawn from either house of parliament. This gave the Conservatives 18 of the UK's entitlement of 36 seats, the Labour party 17, and the Liberals one. However, the Labour party's official policy was in favour of renegotiating the 'Tory terms' of British entry into the Community and, pending the results of such a **renegotiation**, against participating in the Community institutions. Accordingly, the party refused to take up the seats allocated to it. Not until after Labour was re-elected and the **British referendum on EC membership** held in June 1975 did the party occupy the 18 seats to which they were by then entitled.

The shifts within the UK delegation served to emphasize the extent to which the European Parliament, at this stage in its development, was merely an outgrowth of national politics in the member states. The practice of nominating MEPs from national parliaments meant that the Parliament's composition was constantly changing to take account of successive national general election results. During the period of the nominated Parliament (1952–79), a total of about 750 national parliamentarians served as MEPs – some for a few months, others for many years (the average length being about five years) – all exercising a 'dual mandate' as members of two parliaments at once.

The situation began to change in the mid-1970s. As part of a political deal among the EC heads of government that also saw the establishment of the **European Council** as a regular and permanent structure for future **summit** meetings, the Paris summit of December 1974 decided that direct elections to the European Parliament should be held 'as soon as possible'. The heads of government called upon the Council of Ministers to take a decision on the matter in 1976, with a view to direct elections being held 'at any time in or after 1978'. The Paris communiqué added that 'the competence of the European Assembly will be extended, in particular by granting it certain powers in the Communities' legislative process.' Both the British and the Danish governments declined to commit themselves to the introduction of direct elections.

In January 1975, after two years of discussion, the European Parliament adopted the Patijn report on direct elections, the one subject (at the time) in relation to which the Parliament, rather than the Commission, enjoyed a **right of initiative** (Article 138(3) EEC, now Article 223(1) TFEU). The report proposed that the number of MEPs be increased to 355, that each member state's allocation of seats be strictly related to its population (although Luxembourg, as a special case, would be left with the six seats it had had ever since 1958), and that the elections should be held on the same day in all member states. In the European Elections Act, a **decision** adopted by the Council in September 1976, the Parliament's recommendations on these points were largely ignored: the total number of MEPs was fixed at 410; the four large member states (France, Germany Italy and the United Kingdom) would – in spite of population variations amounting to several million people – each have the same number of MEPs (81); and because of different national traditions with regard to the day of the week upon which voting normally took place, member states were left free to choose any date within a four-day period (from Thursday to Sunday).

The parliamentary term was fixed at five years. MEPs could be members of their national parliaments, but could not be government ministers, Commissioners, European civil servants, judges of the Court of Justice, members of the **Court of Auditors** or the EESC, or directors of the **European Investment Bank** (EIB). (Membership of the **Committee of the Regions** has since also been added to the list of incompatible functions.) The choice of electoral system and many other arrangements were left to the discretion of individual member states, pending the introduction of a uniform electoral procedure, for which the Act set no deadline.

At the Rome meeting of the European Council in December 1975, the date for direct elections was fixed as May or June 1978. However, difficulties in passing the enabling legislation in the United Kingdom meant that the Copenhagen meeting of the European Council in April 1978 had to postpone the elections for one year until 7–10 June 1979. (The terms of the 'Lib–Lab pact' required the Labour government to attempt to introduce a regional list system of proportional representation, a proposal rejected by the House of Commons, as a result of a Labour backbench revolt.)

The June 1979 European elections, the first international elections in history and involving an electorate of more than 190 million people (exceeded only by that of India), attracted a Community-wide turnout of 62 per cent. This overall figure concealed substantial differences: participation ranged from 91 per cent in Belgium, where voting is notionally compulsory, to 32 per cent in the United Kingdom. At its first session, in July 1979, the new European Parliament elected Simone Veil, a former French minister and Holocaust survivor, as its President.

Although the heads of government had declared in 1974 that, in parallel to direct elections, the Parliament would gain an enhanced role in the legislative process, no such reform was introduced in July 1979. However, as many advocates had predicted, the process of direct elections did give the

Parliament greater visibility and authority. As importantly, the elections generated a body largely composed of full-time MEPs, as opposed to the necessarily part-time members in the Parliament that preceded it. It would clearly be more difficult for the Council and the Commission simply to ignore the Parliament's views, and MEPs would have the time, the tenacity and the expertise to insist on their views being taken seriously. Five months after direct elections, for the first time in its history, the Parliament used its power under Article 203(8) EEC (now Article 314(7) TFEU) to reject the Community Budget. The potential importance of the Parliament was further underlined by the ECJ's ruling in the 'isoglucose' case in 1980 that a Council decision was void unless the opinion of the Parliament had been not merely sought, but actually obtained. This judgement (*Roquette Frères* v *Council*, Case 138/79) implied that, within reason, the Parliament could prevent the Council from acting unless and until it had delivered its opinion.

The first directly-elected Parliament, running from 1979 to 1984, set the pattern for its successors in several ways. It showed a real determination not only to use its powers to the full, but to increase them wherever possible, if possible by radically reforming the Community's whole institutional structure. In April 1982, the Parliament tightened its control over Community spending by deferring its grant of discharge to the Commission for the year 1980. In September 1982, the Parliament resolved to bring an action in the ECJ against the Council of Ministers for the latter's 'failure to act' in developing a common **transport policy**. The Parliament adopted a **Draft Treaty establishing the European Union** (DTEU) in February 1984, an exercise spearheaded by **Altiero Spinelli**, as well as a host of other resolutions on institutional questions. For the first time, a report was given to the Parliament by the prime minister of the member state holding the rotating six-month **presidency** of the Council of Ministers (**Margaret Thatcher** in December 1981). In parallel, the Parliament sought, with only modest success, to resolve the practical difficulties arising out of having three places of work, and decided in July 1981 no longer to hold any plenary sessions in Luxembourg. The political interest in, and excitement of, the directly-elected Parliament's first term was real and has only occasionally been matched in subsequent years.

The accession of Greece in 1981 and of Portugal and Spain in 1986 increased the size of the Parliament from 410 to 518 MEPs. In July 1990, it was decided to admit 18 'observers' from the former East Germany, initially to be appointed by that country's *Volkskammer* and later by the Bundestag. These observers had speaking rights in committees and political groups, but not in plenary sessions, and could neither vote nor hold office. This was obviously only a temporary solution. **German reunification** meant that the country now had a population some 20 million people greater than that of the next largest member state, and there was a lively debate about whether this should be reflected in its number of MEPs in the Parliament. The suggestion that the German delegation be increased by 18 members (from 81 to 99) aroused strong opposition in France, and the matter was not resolved until the Edinburgh European Council in December 1992. At the same time, the opportunity was taken to adjust the overall allocation of seats, with effect from the following European elections in June 1994, increasing the overall number of MEPs from 518 to 567. Following the accession to the Union in January 1995 of Austria, Finland and Sweden (with 21, 16 and 22 members respectively), the size of the Parliament increased again to 626 seats.

The subsequent enlargements of the Union in 2004 and 2007 took the size of the Parliament first to 785 members (in June 2004) and then, as part of an overall scaling down, back to 736 members (in June 2009). As a result of a change introduced by the Lisbon Treaty, the Parliament's size will be set definitively at 751 members from June 2014. Because the entry into force of Lisbon (in December 2009) followed, rather than preceded, the 2009 European elections, it was agreed that the 18 additional MEPs assigned to 12 under-represented member states by that treaty should be allowed to take their seats, without the corresponding reduction of three seats foreseen for Germany taking effect before June 2014. The adoption of a new **protocol** to the **Treaties** to this effect was proposed by Spain (which stood to gain four MEPs) and adopted by the member states in June 2010; the text completed its **ratification** in November 2011 and took effect the following month. As a result, there are now 754, rather than 736 or 751, MEPs.

The process by which the European Parliament has, over 60 years, acquired a significant degree of power has been long and complex (and is dealt with in the detailed entries in this *Companion* on the various legislative procedures referred to below). **Winston Churchill** suggested in August 1950, when addressing the Consultative Assembly of the Council of Europe, that 'Building up a European Parliament must be gradual . . . It should roll forward on a tide of facts, events and impulses, rather than by elaborate constitution-making.' In practice, the growth in powers of the Parliament created soon after Churchill spoke has depended on both the logic of events and a conscious strategy of seeking and exploiting institutional change. The Parliament's rise has paralleled that of the European Community, now Union. As the latter has grown in responsibility and influence, so the need for a parliamentary dimension, to improve the accountability and legitimacy of the integration process, has become apparent. In this sense, the Parliament has been an institution 'condemned to succeed' with the passage of time.

It is now clear that the powers of the European Parliament, as laid down in the founding Treaties, were directed primarily 'against' the Commission, because it was assumed that the Commission would develop into something approaching a European government. Yet, in practice, the principal tension to emerge fairly quickly within the system was not between the Parliament and the Commission, but between the Parliament and the Council. Indeed, the Parliament and the Commission have very often found themselves on broadly the same side of the argument, usually in favour of more ambitious common European solutions than the Council would naturally support. It was therefore quite rational that both the Parliament and the Commission should advocate two sets of institutional changes that would alter the balance in Council–Parliament relations to the advantage of the latter: first, the sharing of the Council's initial legislative monopoly with the Parliament through some form of 'co-decision' between the two institutions, and second, the exercise, wherever possible, of the Council's legislative power by **qualified majority voting** (QMV), rather than **unanimity**, in order to undermine the veto position of the most reluctant states. Some governments have more or less consistently supported the Parliament in these ambitions. Italy, Germany and the **Benelux** states have usually been on the Parliament's side, whereas Britain, France and Denmark have been variously ambivalent or openly hostile.

The first significant extension of the Parliament's legislative power vis-à-vis the Council came with the introduction of the **cooperation procedure**, since abolished, and of the assent procedure, now known as the **consent procedure**, by the Single European Act. The cooperation procedure provided that where, in a second reading, an absolute majority of MEPs voted for an amendment approved of by the Commission, the change would be included in the Council text unless all member states were opposed (Article 149(2) EEC, now repealed). Thus a sort of 'reverse veto' was instituted in the Council, to Parliament's advantage. The consent procedure was much simpler: by an absolute majority (and in most cases, later, by a simple majority), the Parliament could veto a certain category of important Council decision. Although these new procedures, which entered into force in July 1987, applied in only limited fields, they established the Parliament for the first time, at least in the eyes of the Council, as a serious political player and were to prove a decisive staging post in the institution's long march to legislative power.

The 1992 Maastricht Treaty introduced the **co-decision procedure** (Article 189(c) EC, now Article 294 TFEU), which extended the cooperation procedure to allow the Parliament an opportunity to negotiate directly with the Council in a 'conciliation committee' and a right of veto at the final stage if agreement could not be reached. The remit of co-decision (and indeed consent) has been progressively extended by the successive treaty changes since Maastricht, embodied in the 1997 **Amsterdam Treaty**, the 2001 **Nice Treaty**, and the 2007 **Lisbon Treaty**, which entered into force in December 2009. Lisbon designated a combination of co-decision and QMV (in the

Council) as the 'ordinary legislative procedure' of the Union (and repealed the cooperation procedure). Under Lisbon, the Council and Parliament also finally enjoy equal powers to amend or reject planned expenditure in the Budget, whilst the Parliament's consent must be obtained before nearly all international agreements are concluded by the Council. The position of the Parliament vis-à-vis the Commission has also been strengthened. Under successive treaty changes, from Maastricht to Lisbon, the Parliament must now give its approval before the President and other members of the Commission take office, in two separate votes, as well as retaining the power to dismiss them en bloc. The Parliament may also veto delegated acts adopted by the Commission (see **comitology**). The term of office of the Commission has been lengthened from four to five years, to make it concurrent with that of the Parliament.

As Herman Van Rompuy, the **President of the European Council**, recently summarized the situation: 'The European Parliament is now *incontournable*: virtually no legislation can be adopted without the approval of Parliament, nor any budget, no financial framework, no international agreement, no delegation of powers to the Commission, no appointment of the Commission, no choice of a President of the Commission.' He added with only slight exaggeration: 'Only I am chosen without Parliament's approval!'

Of all the institutions of the European Union, the Parliament is the one that has changed the most since its foundation, whether in terms of its status, powers or composition. However, in respect of its internal organization, it has changed relatively little. The organizational structure of the Parliament is laid down in its rules of procedure, with respect to which the Parliament is sovereign under Article 232 TFEU. A President is elected for two and a half years at the beginning and at the midpoint of every five-year term. Since July 1979, the Parliament's 14 Presidents have been:

1979–82	Simone Veil (France, Liberal)
1982–4	Pieter Dankert (The Netherlands, Socialist)
1984–7	Pierre Pflimlin (France, Christian Democrat)
1987–9	Lord (Henry) Plumb (United Kingdom, Conservative)
1989–92	Enrique Baron (Spain, Socialist)
1992–4	Egon Klepsch (Germany, Christian Democrat)
1994–7	Klaus Hänsch (Germany, Social Democrat)
1997–9	José María Gil-Robles (Spain, centre-right)
1999–2002	Nicole Fontaine (France, centre-right)
2002–4	Pat Cox (Ireland, Liberal)
2004–7	Josep Borrell (Spain, Socialist)
2007–9	Hans-Gert Pöttering (Germany, Christian Democrat)
2009–12	Jerzy Buzek (Poland, centre-right)
2012–	Martin Schulz (Germany, Social Democrat)

The first four elections for the post of President of the Parliament were fiercely contested, running to between two and four ballots, often with a high degree of drama. For most of the period since 1989, however, there has been an agreement between the two largest political groups, the European People's Party and the Socialists, to share the post of President between them on a rotating basis. This big-group 'duopoly' did not apply in the 1999–2004 Parliament, when an EPP–Liberal deal was struck: in July 1999, the French RPR politician, Nicole Fontaine, beat the Socialist former President of Portugal, Mario Soares, in a single ballot, whilst in January 2002 an Irish Liberal, Pat Cox, beat a British Socialist, David Martin, on the third ballot.

Under the Parliament's rules, its President is required to 'direct all the activities of Parliament and of its bodies', as well as 'to open, suspend and close sittings', maintain order and put matters to the vote. The President represents the Parliament 'in international relations, on ceremonial occasions and in administrative, legal or financial matters'. The President may lead delegations from the Parliament taking part in conciliation meetings with the Council, either on legislation or the annual Budget. (He or she is also responsible for declaring the Union's annual Budget adopted, under Article 314(9) TFEU.) Since June 1987, the President of the Parliament has been able to address the European Council at the start of its meetings.

Fourteen Vice-Presidents of the Parliament are elected every two and a half years at the same time as the President, but the political groups normally agree upon the slate of candidates in advance and table a joint list. The President and Vice-Presidents make up the Bureau of the Parliament (together with five Quaestors, specifically elected to defend members' interests, who attend in an advisory capacity). The principal task of the Bureau is to take 'financial, organizational and administrative decisions' (Rule 23), including the appointment of the Parliament's Secretary General. Vice-Presidents share with the President the task of presiding over plenary sessions of the Parliament. A body known as the Conference of Presidents (Rule 25) is composed of the President and the leaders of the Parliament's seven political groups. It is responsible for more political 'decisions on the organization of Parliament's work', including the drawing up of the Parliament's agenda, the operation of its committees, legislative planning and relations with both other EU institutions and national parliaments. It is enjoined under the rules to 'endeavour to reach a consensus on matters referred to it', but, if necessary, it may take votes, with each leader's vote being weighted to reflect the size of his or her political group. The fact that the President of the Parliament chairs both the Bureau and the Conference of Presidents, and sets their agendas, is an important source of his or her day-to-day power.

The Secretary General of the Parliament is a political appointee, usually with an administrative background, who runs the Parliament's administration, prepares its budget and acts as de facto political adviser to the President. There have only been seven Secretaries General in the six decades of the Parliament's history, with the last three – Julian Priestley (1997–2007), Harald Rømer (2007–9) and Klaus Welle (since 2009) – all having served as secretaries general of political groups at some stage before appointment. Because the Parliament started as a very small body and has grown relatively quickly, the Secretary General is still administratively responsible for every aspect of its many activities, from personnel, finance and security to research, committee work and plenary business. In the US House of Representatives, by contrast, such functions are divided between a Clerk, Parliamentarian, Sergeant-at-Arms, Chief Executive Officer and Librarian of Congress.

The Parliament currently has about 5,000 permanent staff, as well as 1,000 temporary staff employed on behalf of the political groups. Approximately half the Parliament's permanent staff are based in Brussels and half in Luxembourg, where formally the administration is headquartered and where a lot of 'back-office' services are located. The overall operating budget of the Parliament was € 1.6 billion in 2011. The Parliament has been able to take advantage of a 'gentlemen's agreement' with the Council and Commission, struck in April 1970, whereby it is allocated up to 20 per cent of the administrative expenditure of the Union institutions in each year's Budget.

Much of the daily political business of the Parliament is conducted in its 20 standing committees. Each committee elects its own officers – a chairman and four vice-chairmen – every two and a half years. In practice, the candidates for these posts and the number of places in each committee allocated to each of the political groups are decided by agreement among the groups themselves on the basis of the d'Hondt system of proportionality. There are currently 20 committees, listed in the order they appear in the Parliament's rules of procedure, with their number of members in parentheses:

I	Foreign affairs	(76)
II	Development	(30)
III	International trade	(31)
IV	Budgets	(43)
V	Budgetary control	(30)
VI	Economic and monetary affairs	(48)
VII	Employment and social affairs	(49)
VIII	Environment, public health and food safety	(69)
IX	Industry, research and energy	(61)
X	Internal market and consumer protection	(41)

XI	Transport and tourism	(47)
XII	Regional development	(50)
XIII	Agriculture and rural development	(44)
XIV	Fisheries	(25)
XV	Culture and education	(31)
XVI	Legal affairs	(25)
XVII	Civil liberties, justice and home affairs	(60)
XVIII	Constitutional affairs	(24)
XIX	Women's rights and gender equality	(35)
XX	Petitions	(35)

The foreign affairs committee is the only committee to have subcommittees: two, which deal respectively with human rights and defence and security (with 31 members each). The decision on the number, size and composition of committees is taken by the plenary of the Parliament, on a proposal from the Conference of Presidents. Under Rules 184 and 185, the Parliament may also set up special committees or temporary committees of inquiry, the latter in order 'to investigate alleged contraventions of Union law or instances of maladministration in the implementation of Union law'. Since the Maastricht Treaty, the status of committees of inquiry has been recognized in law (Article 226 TFEU).

The Parliament's 20 policy committees (and two subcommittees) meet at least once, and often twice, a month in Brussels, for between two and four half-days at a time, as well as occasionally in the margins of plenary sessions in Strasbourg. There is a presumption in favour of committees meeting in public, although they are free to convene in private and sometimes do so on sensitive matters. Commission representatives attend and often take part in committee meetings. At least once in each presidency, the president-in-office of the relevant Council configuration will attend a meeting of the appropriate parliamentary committee. At all meetings, full interpretation is provided, documents are available in all official **languages** and full minutes are kept, although there is no verbatim transcript of proceedings. Committee meetings are increasingly streamed live on the Parliament's website.

For many MEPs, work in one or more committees constitutes the core of their political engagement in the Parliament. Assignment to a committee that corresponds to a member's interest is highly prized. Positions on some of the more prestigious or legislatively active committees – such as the foreign affairs and environment committees respectively – are much sought after. Such committees have tended to grow in size over time, as a result of the pressure for membership. In the larger political groups at least, the heads of national party delegations tend to control committee assignments. In order to exercise significant policy influence within the Parliament, members will seek to become the spokesman or 'coordinator' of their political group on a committee (in the larger groups, the coordinator is usually elected by his or her colleagues) or seek appointment as the Parliament's **rapporteur** (or the group's 'shadow rapporteur') on a specific piece of legislation.

The office-holders and political group coordinators meet regularly to decide on the appointment of rapporteurs, on whether to open 'first-reading' negotiations with the Council under the co-decision procedure, and on how to handle relations with other bodies within the Parliament. As well as sharing common policy interests and enthusiasms, they often develop a strong bond of mutual respect and trust. The rapporteur system also promotes a general tendency towards compromise, as the member chosen to articulate the committee's view will usually seek a position acceptable to a broad majority, for fear of criticism or defeat. Committees also have a strong vested interest in holding together, as it maximizes their chances of securing the support of the political groups and plenary for any given position. If the coordinators of the various groups all defend the same position on a particular proposal, it is very difficult for those outside the committee to push a different line.

Contacts between the European Parliament and other parliaments outside the EU are maintained through a system of 40 bilateral or multilateral inter-parliamentary delegations, each with its own officers. In most cases, meetings are held alternately in the Union and in the country or countries concerned. Inter-parliamentary delegations take the form of 'joint committees' with the parliaments of those countries linked to the Union by **association agreements**. There has been a growing tendency in recent years to establish relations with groups of countries: here the delegations take the form of 'joint parliamentary assemblies', as with the countries of Latin America (Eurolat) and the Eastern and Southern Neighbourhoods (Euronest and Euromed). The biggest and oldest of these multilateral fora is the ACP–EU Joint Assembly, which is composed of one representative of each of the 79 **ACP states** and an equal number of MEPs. It meets for a week-long session twice a year, once in the Union and once in an ACP state. In April 2010, the European Parliament opened a small liaison office in Washington DC, in order to promote closer links with the US Congress.

For most of the year, the Parliament works in a monthly cycle: two weeks during which the committee meetings take place, one week kept as far as possible free of committee meetings so that the political groups can meet; and a fourth week spent in Strasbourg for the monthly plenary session. This cycle is suspended between mid-July and late August for a summer recess and disrupted in the autumn because there is usually a second part-session in either September or October, originally to deal with the annual Budget (when it had two readings) and now simply to fulfil the treaty requirement that '12 periods of monthly sessions' be held in Strasbourg (Protocol 6 to the Treaties, introduced by the Amsterdam Treaty). Other meetings – whether of the Conference of Presidents, the Bureau, inter-parliamentary delegations or other bodies – have to be fitted into this cycle, together with (since 1993) additional, two-day 'mini-plenary' sessions held between four and six times a year in Brussels. In addition to the summer recess and short breaks for Christmas and Easter, about five weeks are left open for external visits by inter-parliamentary delegations or for members to spend time in their regions. The need to secure meeting rooms and interpretation normally means that the timing of most meetings needs to be fixed well in advance. In spring 2011, the Parliament set its meeting schedule two years in advance for the first time: the calendar of plenary sessions is adopted by the plenary itself, on a proposal from the Conference of Presidents (often with amendments), whilst the Conference of Presidents itself is empowered to decide on the timing of all other meetings. Although the Parliament meets in plenary session only between 60 and 65 days a year, the total number of days consumed in parliamentary business overall is one of the highest in the world, at 156 days in 2011.

Article 229 TFEU requires the Parliament to hold an annual session, which begins on the second Tuesday in March. This obligation determines the pattern of the calendar in the first half of the year. In a year in which European elections are held, the European Elections Act specifies that the newly-elected Parliament shall meet on the first Tuesday after one month has elapsed since the last day of polling (a Sunday). An ECJ ruling in 1964 established that the Parliament, whether or not it is actually sitting, is in continuous session: this ruling allows MEPs' privileges and immunities to apply throughout the year. Technically, therefore, the plenary sessions in Strasbourg and Brussels are 'part-sessions' of an annual session, although they are normally referred to simply as plenary sessions (as in Protocol 6 above).

The business of a plenary session consists for the most part of debates on reports adopted in committee and brought forward for consideration by the Parliament as a whole. The report is presented by the committee's rapporteur; the representatives of each of the political groups are given precedence in the debate that follows; the responsible Commissioner is normally expected to intervene, especially if the Commission wants to comment on the proposals for amendment to a legislative proposal contained in the report; other MEPs may take part in the debate, within the limit of the speaking-time allocated to their political groups for the day or, after that, by catching the President's eye. Provision exists for less controversial or important reports to be taken with only a short introduction or without debate.

Other regular items on the plenary session agenda include statements by the Commission and/or the Council on major issues, usually followed by a debate; question time with the Commission and the Council; 'question hour' with the President of the Commission (introduced in 2009); a report by the **President of the European Council** after each summit meeting of heads of government (introduced in 2010); and, at the beginning and end of every six-month rotating presidency of the Council, presentation or a report by the prime minister or foreign minister of that country on its programme of work. An hour is set aside for debates on breaches of human rights in third countries (previously there were debates on 'topical and urgent subjects' for three hours). Special events in the Parliament's annual calendar include the 'State of the Union' address by the President of the European Commission each September (introduced in 2010), the adoption of the Union's Budget in October or November, a six-monthly debate with the **High Representative** on **Common Foreign and Security Policy** (CFSP), and annual debates with the Presidents of the **European Central Bank** (ECB) and the **Court of Auditors** on the presentation of these institutions' annual reports. Heads of state are periodically invited to address the Parliament in a formal session. During the 2004–9 European Parliament, about a fifth of plenary time was spent on debating legislation, another fifth on discussing own-initiative reports, a quarter on Commission or Council statements, a tenth on questions of various kinds, and a tenth on voting or explanations of votes.

The Parliament's views on legislation are expressed in the form of reports composed of three parts: a draft legislative resolution, which simply states whether the Parliament approves, rejects or amends the Commission proposal; the draft amendments (if any) to the proposal; and an explanatory statement. A report may also contain, for reference, opinions drawn up by committees other than the one primarily responsible. Non-legislative reports contain only a draft resolution and explanatory statement. In neither case does the explanatory statement have any formal standing.

Voting in plenary sessions is normally by show of hands, but the numbers are often checked electronically by a system requiring MEPs to use voting cards. At the request of a political group or 40 members, and on the final vote on a legislative proposal, votes are taken by electronic roll-call. Only in these latter cases will the record attached to the daily minutes show how individual members voted. The quorum is a third of the Parliament's total membership, but votes are valid and voting may continue however few MEPs are present until the President, on request, formally establishes that the meeting is inquorate. A verbatim record (traditionally known as 'the Rainbow', from the variously coloured sheets upon which it was once typed) of speeches in the original language of delivery is published daily on the Parliament's website and in its final form translated into the official languages and annexed to the ***Official Journal***.

An MEP is normally a full member of one of the Parliament's 20 committees and a substitute member of another. He or she may also be a full member of one of the Parliament's inter-parliamentary delegations. In an average month, an MEP will spend three nights in Strasbourg at one of the Parliament's plenary sessions, and between five and ten nights in Brussels at committee meetings, additional plenary sessions, delegation meetings, or meetings of his or her political group. Persistent absentees (assessed on the basis of participation in roll-call votes in plenary) are liable to have their daily allowances (when they do appear) cut by half.

Members may submit both written and oral questions to the Commission and the Council, and written questions to the President of the European Council, the High Representative and the ECB. No limit is placed upon the number of written questions that an MEP may ask. The questions are forwarded to the relevant institution through the President of the Parliament, and are supposed to be answered within six weeks and published in the *Official Journal*. 'Priority questions', limited to one per MEP per month, are defined as those requiring immediate answer but 'no detailed research'; for these the deadline is only three weeks. A total of 30,511 written questions were submitted in the 2004–9 European Parliament. The number of written questions to the Commission, in particular, has been rising sharply recently, with over 10,000 questions requiring answer in 2010.

Each MEP may submit one oral question to the Commission for answer at the monthly question time in plenary. In practice, interest in the question time process is quite limited, and an effort to institute a monthly 'question hour' with the Commission President in 2009 has been only partially successful. More popular are 'oral questions with debate', in response to which a resolution may be tabled and voted upon. Such questions may be tabled by a committee, a political group or 40 MEPs, and they allow the Parliament to explore topical issues in greater depth than is possible at normal question time. The decision whether or not to place such a question on the agenda rests, like other agenda issues, with the Conference of Presidents, which usually timetables a handful each month.

Since the Amsterdam Treaty, the Parliament is required, having sought the opinion of the Commission and 'with the approval of the Council acting unanimously, [to] lay down the regulations and general conditions governing the performance of the duties of its Members' (Article 190 EC). An early attempt to define this 'Members' Statute' in 1999 failed, when the Council and Parliament were unable to reach agreement, partly because **unanimity** was required in the Council. However, after the Nice Treaty introduced QMV on the issue, agreement was eventually reached on a Statute, which was adopted in June 2005 and took effect at the beginning of the next Parliament, in July 2009. Until then, MEPs' salaries were paid from member-state exchequers at whatever level applied to the national parliamentarians from the country in question. This meant that there were very wide discrepancies in pay, depending on which member state the MEP came from – the highest gross figure being Italy, at over € 10,000 a month, and the lowest Bulgaria, at less than € 1,000. The Statute has changed this by providing for a common salary for MEPs, paid for from the Parliament's own budget and set at 38.5 per cent of that of a judge in the European Court of Justice – the Parliament had originally wanted a rate of 50 per cent – a gross figure of € 7,957 per month in 2011. The salary is automatically subject to the same 'Union tax', deducted at source, as applies to EU officials (see **Eurocrats**), so reducing it to € 6,201. Member states are free to top up the marginal rate of tax to the equivalent of the rate that would apply if the sum were paid domestically, provided there is no double taxation. Instead of receiving national parliamentary pensions, MEPs elected in 2009 and thereafter receive a pension calculated at 3.5 per cent of their salary for each year served, up to a maximum of 70 per cent.

There has always been a common system for expenses and allowances for MEPs, which are also paid from the Parliament's own budget, indexed for inflation and calculated in euro. Following criticism of the generous, flat-rate mileage allowance for members' official travel (that had applied since 1979), the system was reformed in July 2009 to reimburse MEPs on a 'costs incurred' basis, based on the production of receipts. They are allowed to claim up to a ceiling represented by the club-class air fare or first-class rail fare for the sector involved, or for the use of a car at the rate of € 0.49 per kilometre. For all official meetings within the Union, members are paid an attendance allowance (intended to cover food and board), worth € 304 a day, as long as they have 'signed in' for the day in question. (Outside the Union, the daily allowance is half that figure.) MEPs can also claim travel costs, up to a maximum of about € 4,300 a year, for attendance in an official capacity (that is, on the basis of a formal invitation) at meetings, conferences or other events anywhere in the world.

In terms of logistical and staff support, MEPs are entitled to free, furnished office accommodation on the European Parliament's premises in Brussels and Strasbourg, together with an office or 'general expenditure' allowance, paid automatically, of € 4,300 a month. They each have a credit line at their disposal for a further € 19,300 a month to employ research staff and assistants. As a result of reforms adopted in 2009, most assistants are now employed directly by the Parliament and in no case may payments to them be routed through members. Unless they were retained on a date set retrospectively in 2008, MEPs may no longer employ members of their family. When they leave office, members receive a transitional allowance of no less than six months' pay and of no more than 20, with the latter requiring 20 years' service.

The Members' Statute, echoing the European Elections Act, specifies that MEPs 'shall be free and independent' and 'shall vote on an individual and personal basis. They shall not be bound by any instructions and shall not receive a binding mandate.' MEPs enjoy certain immunities, which are set out in Articles 8 to 10 of the Protocol 7 on the privileges and immunities of the European Union, annexed to the Treaties. MEPs 'shall not be subject to any form of inquiry, detention or legal proceedings in respect of opinions expressed or votes cast by them in the performance of their duties' (Article 8). Within their own member states, MEPs enjoy immunities from arrest and legal proceedings similar to those extended to national MPs; elsewhere in the Union, they enjoy 'immunity from any measure of detention and from legal proceedings', except when found in flagrante delicto (Article 9). Only the Parliament itself can waive the immunity of an MEP, and it normally does so if the case relates to a period before the member was elected to the Parliament or to matters that do not directly concern his or her political activities. The Parliament's rules of procedure oblige members to record their financial interests in a register kept for this purpose, and to declare such interests when taking part in a debate on a matter connected with them.

The June 2009 European elections saw 736 MEPs elected from 170 national political parties in the 27 member states. Just over half of those elected (50.4 per cent) were new to the Parliament, repeating the pattern of very high turnover among members that has been evident at successive contests. Discounting the effect of enlargement, the highest rate for re-election of incumbents since 1989 was 54.0 per cent in 2004 and the lowest, 42.5 per cent in 1994. There are substantial variations in incumbency between national delegations, with German, British and Irish MEPs traditionally enjoying a high average length of service, and Italian MEPs a very low one. Large member states with high incumbency rates tend to boast MEPs who exercise disproportional influence in the Parliament, provided that the members sit in large political groups: the German CDU/CSDU and SPD members, as the largest national delegations in both the EPP and Socialist groups, tend to secure an unusually high number of key appointments in the Parliament, as a result. Only one member, the former President of the Parliament, Hans-Gert Pöttering, has served continuously since the first direct elections in 1979, and only six others since 1984.

The political background of MEPs varies considerably from one country to another. In recent Parliaments, just over a third of MEPs have previously served as members of their national parliaments and about a fifth have held ministerial office. (The current figures are respectively 36 and 17 per cent.) There are significant national variations: whereas five of the seven Slovenian MEPs in 2011 were former ministers, there were none in either the German or Dutch delegations, and only two among British MEPs. Many more members have held, or still hold, office at local or regional level as councillors, mayors or members of regional assemblies.

The list of well-known people who have been elected as MEPs since 1979 includes several former or future heads of state or government – notably Giulio Andreotti, Silvio Berlusconi, Willy Brandt, Jacques Chirac, Bettino Craxi, **Valéry Giscard d'Estaing**, Vytautas Landsbergis and Mario Soares. The roster can be misleading, however, in that some individuals have simply headed their party lists for the elections and then resigned from the Parliament at an early opportunity, whilst others have used membership of the Parliament as a political retirement job, taking little part in its activities. The former Polish and Belgian prime ministers, Jerzy Buzek and Guy Verhofstadt – elected respectively as President of the Parliament and leader of the Liberal (ALDE) group in July 2009 – were unusual in fitting neither category. In most countries there is a much less sharp distinction than in the United Kingdom between a national or local political career and a career in the European Parliament. Although some British former MEPs have become MPs and gone on to be ministers, to date no British Commissioner has been an MEP: all have come from the House of Commons or, in two cases, the House of Lords.

To the 'elder statesman' can be added a discernable group of 'rising stars' – younger members who cut their teeth in the Parliament and then move on to national politics. Nick Clegg, Geoff Hoon, Chris Huhne, Alexander Stubb, Cecilia Malmström and Ana Palacio might be considered recent examples of this pattern. Serving as an MEP can be a springboard to higher political office, especially in the smaller member states. Between 1979 and 2009, 122 members left the Parliament to become national ministers (indeed, in two cases, heads of state). Equally, since 1958, 34 MEPs have gone on to serve as European Commissioners. The current (second) Barroso Commission contains seven former MEPs (in a college of 27 members).

Within any national parliament, a broad consensus tends to exist about its role in the political system and, by extension, about the role of an individual parliamentarian. Historically, such a single, shared vision has been less evident to date in the case of the European Parliament, which draws on 27 distinct national traditions, some more focused than others on holding the executive to account. However, with the passage of time, it has become clear that a distinguishing feature of the European Parliament is that, unlike nearly all of the national parliaments in the Union, its principal political function is not to sustain a government in power. There is no compliant 'governing majority' which sees its task as to adopt proposals from the executive as a matter of course. Majorities in the Parliament have to be built, issue by issue, through explanation, persuasion and negotiation. Equally, a higher proportion of the Parliament's work is devoted to technical issues that need not provoke party-political divisions. These forces, together with the prevailing culture of compromise in committees – where the rapporteur system is oriented towards the idea of finding or building a consensus – tend to promote a much less confrontational style of political behaviour than is routinely found in many national capitals. Still in evidence too is a feeling, dating back to the Parliament's uncertain beginnings, that in order to have any influence within the system, its actions should, wherever possible, command a very wide measure of support within the house. To that has been added, more recently, a desire in some quarters to assert a 'pro-European' majority of the larger political groups to marginalize populists and Eurosceptics. Successive treaty changes, starting with the Single European Act, have reinforced the tendency towards left–right compromise, by requiring the Parliament to act by an absolute majority of its members in its formal legislative dialogue with the Council of Ministers.

However, the triumph of consensus politics, which is inevitably far from complete, does come at a political price. It has blunted the edge of partisan debate and created habits of mind that serve to render issues less clear-cut and therefore less arresting to the public. The indifference of the media towards the Parliament and low turnout in European elections are, at least in part, encouraged by these aspects of its political culture. There are many who believe that, unless the Parliament can establish itself as the forum in which distinct and competing views on the big issues affecting Europe's future are addressed and debated, rather than merely homogenized, it will always fail to capture the attention and earn the respect of both national political élites and the wider public.

Further reading: Richard Corbett, Francis Jacobs and Michael Shackleton, *The European Parliament*, 2011; Simon Hix, Abdul Noury and Gerard Roland, *Democratic Politics in the European Parliament*, 2007; David Judge and David Earnshaw, *The European Parliament*, 2008; Amie Kreppel, *The European Parliament and Supranational Party System*, 2002; David Marquand, *Parliament for Europe*, 1979; Julian Priestley, *Six Battles that Shaped Europe's Parliament*, 2008; Martin Westlake, *A Modern Guide to the European Parliament*, 1994.

European Political Community (EPC)

In October 1950, the French government proposed – through the **Pleven Plan** – that a **European Defence Community** (EDC) should be created, with a **European army** under the control of supranational institutions similar to those planned for the new **European Coal and Steel Community** (ECSC). Article 38 of the resulting Treaty to establish a European Defence Community, which was signed in May 1952, envisaged that the new Community should have an assembly 'elected on a democratic basis'. Proposals for the precise powers and composition of this EDC Assembly, as part of a 'subsequent federal or confederal structure' which would wrap together the ECSC and EDC, were to be worked out in detail by the recently-created ECSC Assembly, the forerunner of the **European Parliament**. In September 1952, the foreign ministers of **the Six** set this work in hand, by inviting the ECSC Assembly 'to draft a treaty constituting a European Political Authority', even though the EDC Treaty itself had yet to be ratified. The proposals contained in the resulting text – formally entitled the Draft Treaty embodying the Statute of the European Community – became known as the European Political Community (EPC).

That the task of drafting this institutional design for Europe should be entrusted to the ECSC Assembly aroused the jealousy of fellow national parliamentarians sitting in the Consultative Assembly of the **Council of Europe**. The latter body had played an important part in raising the issue of a European army, through its path-breaking resolution of August 1950, proposed by **Winston Churchill**. The problem was resolved by temporarily enlarging the ECSC Assembly to include nine additional members of the Consultative Assembly (giving a total of 87 members). The enlarged ECSC Assembly, known as the 'Ad Hoc Assembly', met in Strasbourg during the autumn and winter of 1952–3, under the presidency of **Paul-Henri Spaak**. Much of the detailed work was undertaken by the Assembly's 26-strong constitutional committee (and four subcommittees), meeting under the chairmanship of Heinrich von Brentano (1904–64), a rising CDU politician who was appointed German foreign minister in 1955. Half the members of the Ad Hoc Assembly were Christian Democrats, reflecting both their strength in **national parliaments** at the time and the fact that no Communists participated in the ECSC Assembly.

The draft treaty was adopted by the Ad Hoc Assembly on 10 March 1953, by 50 votes to nil, with five abstentions. The ostensible unity in the assembly in favour of the treaty was somewhat misleading. The representatives of a number of major political parties within the Six did not support the text. The French Socialists, led by Guy Mollet, were among those abstaining – on the grounds that the treaty was too integrationist to allow the United Kingdom to join. The French Gaullists and German Social Democrats boycotted the vote: the first in opposition to the treaty's federalist aspirations; the second because they opposed the linkage with the EDC. The Communists – who were major political forces in Italy and France – were unable to vote by dint of not being members; they would mostly have opposed the treaty, if they could.

Article 1 of the draft treaty proposed to establish 'a European Community of a supranational character . . . founded upon a union of peoples and states, upon respect for their personality and upon equal rights and duties for all'. This European Community was to be equipped with a bicameral Parliament, with a lower house (or 'People's Chamber') composed of 'deputies representing the peoples united in the Community', and an upper house (or Senate) made up of 'senators representing the people of each state'. The former were to be directly elected every five years, the latter would be chosen by national parliaments from among their members. The lower chamber would have 268 members and the upper chamber 87. (The choice of this number of Senators suggests that the Ad Hoc Assembly expected that it would be carried forward as the Senate.) In principle, France, Germany and Italy would have 63 deputies and 21 senators each. However, France was to benefit from seven additional deputies 'in order to take into account its overseas departments and territories'. The Parliament would hold two sessions every year.

The administration of the Community was to be put in the hands of a powerful European Executive Council. Its president, elected by the Senate, would appoint the other Executive members, of whom no more than two could be of the same nationality. Members of the Executive were to be known as 'Ministers of the European Community'. The Executive as a whole would need to receive a vote of confidence from both chambers of the Parliament, either of which had the power to dismiss it. However, if the People's Chamber voted by a majority of less than three-fifths to dismiss the Executive, the latter could then choose either to resign voluntarily or to dissolve the Chamber. (The second option could be overruled only by a vote of the Senate to dismiss the Executive.)

A Council of National Ministers would be responsible for 'harmonizing the action of the European Executive Council with that of the governments of member states'. It was to be composed of one member from each government, with a presidency rotating among them every three months. The Court of Justice of the ECSC would act as the judicial authority for the new Community, which was also to be equipped with an advisory Economic and Social Council, drawing on the role of similar bodies in all the founding member states other than West Germany. Laws were to require the assent of both chambers. The Senate would be empowered to request a second reading. The president of the European Executive Council was to be responsible for promulgating laws duly adopted, and the Council would enjoy the power to issue 'regulations to ensure the implementation of the laws of the Community'.

The proposed Community would take over the powers and functions of both the ECSC and the EDC, as well as pursue its own specific objectives. Prominent among these would be the establishment of 'a **common market** among the member states, based on the **free movement** of goods, capital and persons'. The budget of the Community would be made up of what are now called '**own resources**' (to include taxes levied by the Community), as well as contributions from member states, fixed by unanimous agreement in the Council of National Ministers.

As a project, the draft treaty was extremely ambitious, for although the basic institutional structure of the EPC reflected the 'quadripartite' scheme already in place under the ECSC Treaty, there were many very striking differences in terms of the balance of power between the institutions. The extensive powers of the 'Ministers' in the European Executive Council were a substantial advance on those of the ECSC **High Authority**, and completely overshadowed those of the Council of National Ministers. The relation between the two bodies affords a very instructive comparison with the powers of the **European Commission** and the **Council of Ministers** as set out in the **Treaty of Rome** only four years later. Similarly, to take only one example, the right of the European Executive Council to dissolve the Parliament was far in excess of anything contemplated before (or since) in Commission–Parliament relations.

In September 1953, the draft treaty was submitted to an **Intergovernmental Conference** (IGC) whose task it was to reconcile the aspirations of the Ad Hoc Assembly with the more pragmatic instincts of some of the member-state governments. Unfortunately for advocates of the text, the departure of **Robert Schuman** as French foreign minister in January that year – extracted by the Gaullists as a condition for supporting the government of René Meyer – shifted the French position in a less sympathetic direction. Schuman's successor, Georges Bidault, argued that, in the EPC design, the Senate should be composed of national ministers, rather than parliamentarians, and that, in parallel, each government should retain a right of veto over the decisions of the European Executive Council. The IGC discussions proved more protracted than expected, weakening in turn the momentum for ratification of the EDC Treaty during the first half of 1954. Discussions on the EPC Treaty were simply abandoned when, on 30 August, the French National Assembly finally voted against the EDC Treaty, by refusing to place ratification of the latter on its plenary agenda.

Jean Monnet wrote of the failure of the EPC initiative: 'The constitution-makers were . . . insufficiently [cautious] when they imagined that European unity would begin with the establishment of a federal political system . . . [they] proposed to go too fast, without waiting for the force of necessity to make it seem natural in the eyes of Europeans' (*Memoirs*, 1978).

Further reading: Richard T. Griffiths, *Europe's First Constitution: The European Political Community 1952–1954*, 2000; Jean-Claude Masclet, *L'Union politique de l'Europe*, 1997.

European Political Cooperation (EPC)

European Political Cooperation refers to the process by which, between 1970 and 1993, the member states of the (then) European Community discussed and coordinated their positions on foreign affairs. Based on regular meetings of foreign ministers, EPC procedures existed informally until they were given treaty status by the 1986 **Single European Act** (SEA). They were replaced by the **Common Foreign and Security Policy** (CFSP) provisions of the 1992 **Maastricht Treaty**, which currently operate.

Cooperation in foreign policy had not been foreseen in the founding **Treaties**. Ad hoc meetings of foreign ministers developed from 1960, but the failure of the **Fouchet Plan** – the proposal by French President **Charles de Gaulle** to create an intergovernmental political union focused on foreign and defence policy – led to the abandonment of this practice, at French insistence. Following the General's departure from office in 1969, governments began to explore once again the potential of organized consultation and, where possible, common action in the foreign-policy field. At The Hague summit in December 1969, heads of government invited foreign ministers to make proposals for closer cooperation. A committee of senior officials, chaired by the Belgian diplomat, Viscount Étienne Davignon, who later became a European Commissioner, met to discuss possible modalities.

The Davignon Report of October 1970 – also known as the Luxembourg Report – recommended that foreign ministers should meet every six months. This formation would be known as the 'Conference of Foreign Ministers meeting in Political Cooperation', to distinguish it from the existing **General Affairs Council** (GAC). Senior officials from national foreign ministries would form a Political Committee, meeting four times a year, to prepare the ground. The president-in-office of the **Council of Ministers** would chair the EPC process and submit an annual report on it to the **European Parliament**. Six-monthly 'colloquies' would be held with the relevant committee of the Parliament. These proposals were described in the Davignon Report as 'the first practical endeavours to demonstrate to all that Europe has a political vocation'. They were adopted by foreign ministers later in October 1970 and put into effect the following month.

A second Davignon Report was commissioned by the Paris summit in October 1972. Also known as the Copenhagen Report and agreed in July 1973, it increased the frequency of foreign ministers' meetings to four times a year, invited ministers to consult in the margins of formal EC Council meetings in the interim, and allowed the Political Committee to meet more often than quarterly, with the latter's de facto working groups given formal status. The report also institutionalized a regular exchange of encrypted messages known as the 'COREU' (*Correspondence européenne*) system, designed to ensure a serious flow of information between the foreign ministries. In parallel, it strengthened the involvement of the member states' embassies in each others' capitals, as well as of missions accredited to international organizations, in the supply of that information.

From the start, the main feature of EPC was its intergovernmental character, with consensus decision-making on all matters. Civil servants in the country holding the rotating **presidency** of the Council were in the driving seat, rather than any central institution. Cooperation took place largely outside the Community framework: the Commission had no right of initiative, the foreign ministers were not subject to the procedures laid down in the **Treaty of Rome** for decision-making in the Council, and recourse could not be had to the **European Court of Justice** (ECJ). It was not until 1976 that foreign ministers meeting in political cooperation were prepared to answer written questions from the European Parliament. However, the range of subjects included in EPC embraced, in the words of the second Davignon Report, 'all important foreign policy questions [which] concern European interests . . . where the adoption of a common position is necessary or desirable'.

The so-called London Report on EPC, adopted in October 1981, made further improvements to the procedures, including a process for automatic consultation at times of crisis, greater involvement of the Commission, the institution of the **Troika** – of past, present and future presidencies of the Council – to provide continuity, and the creation of a small secretariat in all but name, hosted by the Council in Brussels, to help the Troika in its work. (The failure of other leaders to accept a suggestion by French President Georges Pompidou in 1971 that Paris should host any central EPC staff meant that it had been operating with none at all.) Importantly, the London report also envisaged 'security' being dealt with for the first time in the context of EPC, even if Ireland, as a neutral country, had severe reservations.

When EPC was finally given treaty status – in Title III of the 1986 Single European Act – the provisions essentially codified procedures that already existed. EPC would remain outside the normal ambit of the Community institutions, although the Commission was to be 'fully associated' and the Parliament 'closely associated' with it. The signatory states expressed their readiness 'to coordinate their positions more closely on the political and economic aspects of security' (Article 30(6) SEA). The EPC secretariat was formalized and expanded to about 20 persons in total.

In practice, by the early to mid-1980s, EPC operated at a number of distinct levels. Operationally, as an evolution of the COREU system, each member state had a 'European correspondent' in its national capital and collectively the 'Group of European Correspondents' was tasked with ensuring the smooth functioning of the system. At a policy level, upwards of 20 working groups, covering both geographical areas and horizontal issues, would meet regularly, initially in national capitals and subsequently in Brussels. They would prepare the monthly meetings of the Political Committee, which had emerged as the key junction-box of the system. Composed of national 'political directors', it negotiated joint positions and prepared ministerial decisions – the forerunner of today's **Political and Security Committee** (PSC). Foreign ministers themselves would meet in political cooperation twice during each six-month Council presidency and hold one informal **Gymnich meeting** each spring and autumn. They would also discuss and adopt EPC positions in the margins of General Affairs Councils, as necessary. Heads of government would do the same at their regular **European Council** meetings.

During its 23-year existence, EPC addressed, with varying degrees of success or failure, nearly all of the main foreign policy issues facing the EC partners at the time – whether on East–West relations, the Middle East, South and Southern Africa, Cyprus, Afghanistan, Poland, Libya, human rights, non-proliferation or terrorism. The record was mixed. The EC's early ability to forge a joint approach on human rights proved important in the run-up to the **Helsinki Final Act** of the **Conference on Security and Cooperation in Europe** (CSCE) in August 1975. After member states had reacted in disarray to the war in October 1973, the Venice Declaration on the Middle East in June 1980 managed to serve as a reference point for the peace process for some years. Achieving a common stance on South Africa in the mid-1980s, after much dispute, helped build pressure on the apartheid regime. Regular consultations between member states certainly encouraged a general convergence of policy over time. However, the EPC process failed to respond to Henry Kissinger's call in April 1972 for 1973 to become the '**Year of Europe**', based on a new transatlantic partnership, or to cope with the renewal of the **Cold War**, caused by hardening attitudes in Moscow – from the Soviet invasion of Afghanistan in December 1979, through the imposition of martial law in Poland in December 1981, to the shooting down of the Korean airliner in September 1983. In the last case, the Greek presidency of the Council prevented foreign ministers from agreeing a declaration even condemning the Soviet action. Only the coming to power of Mikhail Gorbachev in November 1984 helped renew momentum in East–West relations and ease transatlantic tensions.

Further reading: Simon Nuttall, *European Political Cooperation*, 1992.

European political parties

Although parliamentary institutions have existed at a pan-European level for over six decades, the development of transnational structures encompassing members of like-minded national political parties has proved to be a relatively tentative and slow process. Initially, the only such bodies were the **political groups**, limited to parliamentarians, in the Parliamentary Assembly of the **Council of Europe** and (more substantially) the **European Parliament**. However, during the 1960s and 1970s, loose confederations of national parties gradually evolved at European level, in parallel to the political groups, often with the positive encouragement and support of the latter.

The emergence of transnational party activity was initially driven by the centre and centre-right of European politics, where **Christian Democracy** was a strong force in uniting many of the continental politicians most committed to closer European integration. The European Union of Christian Democrats (EUCD) was created in 1965, evolving from a looser network of youth activists known as the *Nouvelles équipes internationales*. With the prospect of the introduction of direct elections to the European Parliament, the EUCD spawned the first self-styled 'European political party', the European People's Party, in 1976. In parallel, a broader range of Christian Democrat, Conservative and Gaullist parties coalesced to form the European Democrat Union (EDU), in 1978. On the left, a 'liaison bureau' for Socialist parties within the European Community was created in 1957; it became the Confederation of Socialist Parties in the EC in 1974 (as part of the Socialist International). A Federation of Liberal and Democrat Parties was formed in 1976, whilst – after the first **European elections** in 1979 – a European Free Alliance (EFA) of 'nationalist, regionalist and autonomist' parties was founded in 1981, and a Europe-wide coordinating body for Green parties was established three years later.

With the exception of the EPP, none of these various organizations yet described themselves as European political parties, nor did they have direct membership or a common manifesto that was (even at least theoretically) binding on constituent parties. However, as the institutional reform debate gathered pace during the 1980s, there was a growing appreciation, in the European Parliament and beyond, of the 'federalizing' potential of promoting European parties, especially if the institutions and resources of the European Community could themselves be used as a spur. As David Marquand wrote before the first direct elections in 1979: 'The Community's chances of moving beyond the narrow limits of the present ***Europe des patries*** depend crucially on the emergence of a *Europe des partis*, in which the political forces that matter at the national level are bound together by the need to fight for power at the Community level' (*A Parliament for Europe*, 1978).

The first visible impact of a transnational political party came when the EPP began, in the mid-1980s, to convene 'party summits' before each meeting of the **European Council**. The prime ministers and opposition leaders from the EPP member parties, together with sympathetic Commissioners, met to discuss some of the items on the agenda of the European Council, sometimes attracting media attention in the process. Such meetings played a part in solidifying support among centre-right leaders for **Economic and Monetary Union** (EMU) in the years from 1989 onwards, but otherwise their influence was difficult to discern. However, on the back of these meetings, a number of EPP-led governments pushed for some more formal recognition to be given to the existence and role of European political parties in law. The negotiations leading to the 1992 **Maastricht Treaty** resulted in agreement to a new Article 138(a) EC, which stated that: 'Political parties at European level are important as a factor for integration within the Union. They contribute to forming a European awareness and to expressing the political will of the citizens of the Union.' This is now Article 10(4) TEU, with the first sentence having been dropped by the **Lisbon Treaty**.

Soon after the Maastricht Treaty had been signed, the Confederation of Socialist Parties converted itself into the Party of European Socialists (PES), in November 1992, and began to hold party summits before European Council meetings. They were followed by the Liberals, who became the European Liberal, Democrat and Reform (ELDR) Party in December 1993, and by the EFA the following year. The Greens established a European Federation of Green Parties (EFGP) in June 1993, but still eschewed the idea of forming a transnational party. Since then, the Socialists and Liberals have joined the EPP in organizing party summits before the meetings of the European Council. In recent years, moreover, both the EPP and PES have attempted to convene 'pre-Council' meetings, bringing together the relevant ministers, Commissioners and spokesmen in the European Parliament, in advance of individual meetings of the **Council of Ministers**, in its various configurations. Efforts in a similar direction have begun to develop within the European Commission. All main European political parties hold periodic congresses – which gather together delegates from each of the member parties, together with transnational office-holders, and act as the sovereign bodies of the parties – and have councils and (narrower) presidencies of key office-holders that meet in between.

Exploiting the Maastricht reference to European political parties, the political groups in the European Parliament began to put pressure on the **European Commission** to come forward with a legislative proposal that would formally provide for the registration of individual parties and offer them a measure of state funding. In the absence of an explicit legal base for a 'party statute' of this kind, the Commission was hesitant to respond, but in 2001 it eventually agreed to move in this direction, on the basis of a pilot project in the Union's annual **Budget**. It was also conscious of the desirability of separating out the funding of political groups from that of parties – an issue brought to a head in 2000, when the **Court of Auditors** stated that it believed the groups' increasing cross-subsidization of the parties to be illegal.

The Commission's proposed **regulation**, relying on Article 235 EC (now **Article 352** TFEU) and thus requiring unanimous agreement in the Council of Ministers, quickly ran into difficulties. There were disagreements among member states about how to verify the democratic nature of parties seeking recognition, the electoral and transnational thresholds to be met for a party to qualify as 'European', and the rules regarding the acceptance of donations or sponsorship from outside persons or bodies. With negotiations stalled, both the Commission and the Parliament suggested that the 2000 **Intergovernmental Conference**, leading to the **Nice Treaty** the following year, should provide a clear **legal base** for the introduction of legislation in this field, ideally backed by the use of **qualified majority voting** (QMV), rather than unanimity, in the Council. The Nice Treaty duly made this change, by adding a second paragraph to the original Maastricht Treaty article. Now Article 224 TFEU, this allows the Council and the Parliament, using QMV and the **codecision procedure**, to 'lay down the regulations governing political parties at European level . . . and in particular the rules regarding their funding'. Drawing on this new provision, it proved possible to agree an initial regulation in November 2003, in time for the 2004 European elections, with a range of outstanding issues left to a second regulation that was eventually adopted in December 2007.

To register as a 'political party at European level', the body in question must be a political party or an alliance of political parties, and must observe the principles on which the European Union is founded – in effect, respect for democracy and fundamental rights – but need not support the existence of the Union itself. A European political party must also enjoy parliamentary representation – defined as Members of the European Parliament (MEPs) or members of **national parliaments** or regional assemblies – in at least a quarter of member states (currently seven countries) or have received at least three per cent of the votes cast, in a quarter of the member states, at the most recent **European elections**. The registration process is administered by the European Parliament, whose Bureau (composed of its President and 14 Vice-Presidents) is responsible for settling the practical arrangements.

Eight European political parties were established under the initial regulation, starting in 2004. Seven of these parties still operate: the European People's Party (EPP), corresponding to the EPP Group in the European Parliament; the Party of European Socialists (PES), corresponding to the Group of Socialists and Democrats (S&D) in the Parliament; the European Liberal Democrat and Reform (ELDR) Party and the European Democratic Party (EDP), reflecting different strands within the ALDE (Liberal) Group in the Parliament; the European Green Party (EGP) and European Free Alliance (EFA), reflecting the two wings of the Greens/EFA Group in the Parliament; and the Party of the European Left (EL), corresponding to the GUE component of the GUE/NGL Group in the Parliament. The eighth party was the Alliance for a Europe of Nations (AEN), corresponding to the UEN Group in the Parliament, which ceased to exist in 2009. Its place has been taken by the Alliance of European Conservatives and Reformists (AECR), corresponding to the new ECR Group in the Parliament. In addition, there are two parties which do not correspond to political groups in the European Parliament (and indeed have virtually no support there): the EU Democrats (EUD), a Eurosceptic party which has been registered since 2006; and the European Christian Political Movement (ECPM), registered since 2010.

Financial support for European political parties is made available in the European Parliament's annual budget: funding has risen from € 6.5 million in 2004 to € 17.4 million in 2011. Under the distribution key, 15 per cent of the total money is given to the parties in equal shares, as a lump sum (€ 211,000 in 2010), with the remaining 85 per cent provided proportionately, on the basis of the number of MEPs who choose positively to affiliate to each party (representing an increment to a party of € 18,000 per additional MEP in 2010). The amounts awarded in 2010 ranged from € 5.0 million granted to the EPP (backed by 262 MEPs) to € 210,000 for the ECPM (backed by one MEP). However, each party is obliged to raise at least 15 per cent of its overall annual spending from outside sources, with no single donation exceeding € 12,000. Overall, about half of party funding is spent on central administration (mainly salaries and rent) and a quarter on meetings of various kinds. Even though the parties have been allowed since 2008 to spend money on European election campaigns – provided that they do not directly or indirectly subsidize national parties or candidates – virtually nothing was spent on such campaigning in 2009.

The 2007 regulation on European political parties also provides for the possibility of each party creating a parallel political foundation (or think tank), with separate, additional funding offered on the same basis as that of the parties. Eight such political foundations were immediately established in

2008, joined by a ninth in 2009. The financing available for such political foundations has risen rapidly, from € 5.0 million in 2008 to € 11.4 million in 2011. The largest recipients are the EPP and PES foundations, the Centre for European Studies (CES) and the Foundation for European Progressive Studies (FEPS), with € 3.3 million and € 2.2 million in funding respectively in 2010.

The financial independence guaranteed by EU funding has removed the biggest single stumbling-block to the launch and survival of European political parties. However, such parties still have a long way to go before they approximate, at transnational level, to the role played by national parties within their own domestic political systems. The absence of either Europe-wide constituencies for European elections or the selection of national candidates for those elections at European level means that the new European political parties still lack the key defining feature of political parties as traditionally understood: the capacity to decide who runs for election and thus holds office. Their inability to gain hold of the nomination process is itself a reflection of the fact that party political activity in Europe remains firmly organized around national (and sometimes regional) issues, personalities and media reporting. As the former British minister for European affairs, Denis MacShane, has put it: 'If in America, the watchword is "all politics is local", in Europe, it might be "all politics is national" or trouble ensues.'

At the moment, transnational parties can offer little in the way of an independent career structure to the aspiring politician, with the most important posts held either ex officio or by virtue of behind-the-scenes agreements between national parties. They have at best limited direct memberships, whilst their policy programmes do not bind their national affiliates and usually attract limited media interest. In most cases, the five-yearly manifestoes of European parties tend towards the lowest common denominator acceptable to their national affiliates and avoid radical or eye-catching commitments. The European parties, although more substantial than before, still serve primarily as fora for the exchange of ideas and for the provision of various kinds of mutual support. The development of pre-summit and pre-Council meetings is an important attempt to move transnational parties towards the role of policy coordination at European level – and this process could have significant long-term implications – but, for the moment, the energies of politicians and the attention of the electorate seem to remain firmly focused at the level of the member states.

Further reading: Simon Hix and Christopher Lord, *Political Parties in the European Union*, 1997.

European political parties and foundations

In 2010, there were ten registered European political parties, encompassing – as full, associate or observer members – 254 national political parties from within, and 73 from outside, the EU (or 327 parties in total).

European People's Party (EPP), founded in 1976 and incorporated as a European political party in 2004. Membership: 46 full member parties from within the EU; six associate member parties from outside the EU; two observer parties from within, and 18 from outside, the EU (72 parties in total). Supporting MEPs: 265. Affiliated European political foundation: *Centre for European Studies* (CES).

Party of European Socialists (PES), founded in 1992 and incorporated as a European political party in 2004. Membership: 31 full member parties from within, and one from outside, the EU; one associate party from within, and ten from outside, the EU; one observer party from within, and four from outside, the EU (48 parties in total). Supporting MEPs: 173. Affiliated European political foundation: *Foundation for European Progressive Studies* (FEPS).

European Liberal, Democrat and Reform Party (ELDR), founded in 1993 and incorporated as a European political party in 2004. Membership: 33 full member parties from within, and 14 from outside, the EU; one associate party from outside the EU; seven observer parties from within, and one from outside, the EU (56 parties in total). Supporting MEPs: 74. Affiliated European political foundation: *European Liberal Forum* (ELF).

European Green Party (EGP), founded and incorporated as a European political party in 2004. Membership: 29 full member parties from within, and seven from outside, the EU; two observer parties from within, and seven from outside, the EU (45 parties in total). Supporting MEPs: 46. Affiliated European political foundation: *Green European Institute* (GEI).

Alliance of European Conservatives and Reformists (AECR), founded and incorporated as a European political party in 2010. Membership: 11 full member parties from within the EU. Supporting MEPs: 44. Affiliated European political foundation: *New Direction – Foundation for European Reform* (ND).

Party of the European Left (EL), founded and incorporated as a European political party in 2004. Membership: 15 full member parties from within, and four from outside, the EU; 11 observer parties from within the EU (30 parties in total). Supporting MEPs: 27. Affiliated European political foundation: *Transform Europe* (TE).

European Democratic Party (EDP), founded and incorporated as a European political party in 2004. Membership: seven full member parties from within, and one from outside, the EU (eight parties in total). Supporting MEPs: 16. Affiliated European political foundation: *Institute of European Democrats* (IED).

European Free Alliance (EFA), founded in 1981 and incorporated as a European political party in 2004. Membership: 33 full member parties and eight observer parties from within the EU (41 parties in total). Supporting MEPs: seven. Affiliated European political foundation: *Centre Maurits Coppierters* (CMC).

EU Democrats (EUD), previously Alliance for a Europe of Democracies, founded and incorporated as a European political party in 2005. Membership: four full member parties from within the EU. Supporting MEPs: one. Affiliated European political foundation: *Organization for European Interstate Cooperation* (OEIC).

European Christian Political Movement (ECPM), founded in 2005 and incorporated as a European political party in 2010. Membership: ten full member parties from within, and ten outside, the EU (20 parties in total). Supporting MEPs: one. Affiliated European political foundation: *European Christian Political Foundation* (ECPF).

European Regional Development Fund (ERDF)

Although the original preamble to the **Treaty of Rome** contained a commitment to 'reducing the differences between the various regions and the backwardness of the less-favoured regions', regional policy developed relatively slowly in the Community. Agreement was not reached on the establishment of the European Regional Development Fund until 1972; it came into operation three years later. The creation of the ERDF was in part a concession to the United Kingdom, to coincide with its **accession** to the Community, in the belief that receipts from the Fund would help compensate for the bias in the annual **Budget** towards agricultural spending. In the event, the ERDF began on a very small scale and was initially shared between member states on the basis of fixed quotas.

The role of the ERDF was defined by the 1992 **Maastricht Treaty** as being 'to help to redress the main regional imbalances in the Community through participation in the development and structural adjustment of regions whose development is lagging behind and in the conversion of declining industrial regions' (Article 176 TFEU). In common with the other EU **structural funds**, the ERDF is directed towards particular objectives, first drawn up in 1988 and revised in 2000 and 2007, reflecting the starting dates of various multiannual financing periods. In practice, the fund is used mainly for promoting infrastructure, investment and innovation. Only projects chosen by the **European Commission** as qualifying for assistance may receive ERDF aid, which must complement, not substitute for, assistance from national sources, in accordance with the principle of **additionality**.

From 1988 to 2006, the ERDF was concerned mainly with Objectives 1 and 2 of the structural funds: underdeveloped regions (defined as those with a per capita GDP of less than 75 per cent of the European average) and those particularly affected by the decline of traditional industries such as coal, steel, shipbuilding and textiles. The problems of inner cities were also addressed. Assistance from the ERDF was given in the form of grants within 'Community Support Frameworks' agreed with member states on the basis of development plans. In addition, the 'Interreg' initiative was designed to promote cooperation between regions across national boundaries.

In the Objective l regions, ERDF assistance could not exceed 75 per cent of the total cost of a project, and could not be less than 50 per cent of the total cost met from public funds. In Objective 2 regions, these figures were reduced to 50 and 25 per cent respectively. More than 80 per cent of the structural funds – which amounted to almost € 213 billion over the years 2000–6 – was allocated to Objectives 1 and 2. The amount spent on the ERDF during that period was € 123 billion.

For the period 2007–13, there are now three Union objectives for all the structural funds: i) the 'convergence' objective, previously Objective 1 (absorbing 81.5 per cent of the funds); the 'regional competitiveness and employment' objective, previously Objective 2 (15.9 per cent); and iii) the 'European territorial cooperation' objective (2.5 per cent). Funding is still reserved primarily for regions whose GDP is below 75 per cent of the Union average, and the co-financing ceilings remain as before. All three objectives are covered by different aspects of the ERDF, with the third representing essentially an upgrading of the existing Interreg programme. The first objective covers 84 regions in 17 member states, with a total population of 170 million people; the second covers 168 regions in 19 member states, with a population of 314 million. The third objective covers cross-border regions encompassing a population of 182 million. The ERDF receives € 201 billion over the 2007–13 financing period, out of a total for all the structural funds of € 347 billion. In addition, some € 75 billion is to be spent on ERDF projects by national governments. EU spending on the ERDF amounted to € 25.2 billion in 2011. The ERDF is complemented by the **Cohesion Fund**, which amounts to € 70 billion over the same seven-year period.

The development of the ERDF, the growing importance of the regional factors in how the other structural funds are spent, and the establishment of the **Committee of the Regions** in 1993, have encouraged a trend for regional and local authorities to establish their own direct links with the Commission, instead of being obliged to operate through national government departments. Some commentators have seen the growth of 'multilevel governance' as a significant new force in EU decision-making, whilst others view it as largely symbolic or presentational.

European Social Fund (ESF)

The oldest of the European Union's **structural funds**, the European Social Fund was established mainly at the instigation of Italy, the poorest country of **the Six**. Article 162 TFEU states that the objective of the ESF is 'to render the employment of workers easier and to increase their geographical and occupational mobility within the Union, and to facilitate their adaptation to industrial changes and to changes in production systems, in particular through vocational training and retraining'. The ESF is administered by the

European Commission, assisted by a committee of 'representatives of governments, trade unions and employers' organizations' (Article 163 TFEU).

The ESF is concerned mainly with combatting long-term unemployment, with special measures to assist people under the age of 25, and with helping workers adapt to technological change. As with the other funds, ESF assistance is directed more towards programmes than towards individual projects. Only organizations financially supported by a public authority may apply for ESF aid, which is, in nearly all cases, intended to complement aid from national sources, in accordance with the principle of **additionality**. Particular attention is paid to people with special difficulties in finding and remaining in work, such as migrant workers, women and the disabled. Supplementing the projects brought forward by member states is the Union's own EQUAL programme, designed to promote transnational cooperation in the elimination of discrimination and inequalities in the labour market.

ESF funding started from a low base but was substantially increased in 1988, reflecting the record (12 per cent) unemployment in the European Community in the mid-1980s. Some € 76 billion is provided for the ESF during the current seven-year EU financing period (2007–13), with an additional € 38 billion foreseen in spending on ESF projects by national governments and € 3.8 billion by the private sector (bringing the total to € 117.5 billion). EU spending on the ESF amounted to € 8.8 billion in 2011.

European Space Agency (ESA)

Established in 1975, the ESA brought together the European Space Research Organization (ESRO) and the European Space Vehicle Launcher Development Organization (ELDO). The ESA is not a European Union body, although a framework agreement for cooperation between the two organizations was signed in 2004, resulting in the Union becoming a member in its own right. In addition to the Union, the ESA has 18 member countries (16 EU member states, plus **Norway** and **Switzerland**), whilst Canada has associate status. Headquartered in Paris, the Agency runs a research and technical centre in Noordwijk (The Netherlands), a research institute in Frascati (Italy), an operations centre in Darmstadt (Germany), and an astronaut centre in Cologne. It has about 2,000 staff and a budget of € 3.99 billion (in 2011).

Most of the ESA's work has been centred upon giving Europe its own launch capability, and then in launching satellites for communications, broadcasting, meteorology and space research from a site in Kourou, French Guiana. The Ariane series of launch vehicles was developed by the ESA, as was the Giotto space laboratory, which studied Halley's Comet, and the Hubble Space Telescope (jointly with NASA). The ESA is a participant in the manned International Space Station project with the United States. Its most ambitious current project is Galileo, a navigational system using some

30 satellites, which was begun in July 2004. Most of the funding for the ESA comes from participating states, although some revenue is earned from the launching of satellites on behalf of commercial interests. The European Union itself is now the biggest budget contributor to the Agency (19.5 per cent) and all the new member states (from the 2004–7 enlargements) intend to join in the near future (the Czech Republic having already done so).

The increasingly close cooperation between the ESA and EU has led to discussion of whether the Agency should be folded into the Union. The EU began to develop a putative space policy of its own in 1999, agreeing a common strategy with the ESA the following year. The **Convention on the Future of Europe** (2002–3) proposed to make space policy an area of shared **competence** between the Union and member states. This provision, included in the draft **European Constitution**, was carried forward into the **Lisbon Treaty**, which entered into force in December 2009. It allows the Union 'to draw up a European space policy', which 'may take the form of a European space programme' and involve the forging of 'any appropriate relations' with the ESA (Article 189 TFEU). However, Union space policy may not involve the harmonization of national laws; as in **research and development policy**, the exercise of the Union's competence 'shall not result in Member States being prevented from exercising theirs' (Article 4(3) TFEU).

European Stability Mechanism (ESM)

See **European Financial Stability Facility** (EFSF) and European Stability Mechanism (ESM)

European Systemic Risk Board (ESRB)

In October 2008, the **European Commission** invited Jacques de Larosière, the former Managing Director of the International Monetary Fund (IMF), and seven other leading economists and policy-makers to report on the implications of the serious crisis developing in the financial markets for the future regulation of those markets in the European Union. The 85-page de Larosière report, published four months later, recommended the upgrading of existing arrangements for the supervision of the banking, securities and insurance sectors into a fully-fledged 'European System of Financial Supervision' (ESFS). This would also involve the creation of a 'European Systemic Risk Council' (ESRC) to offer a 'financial stability early-warning system' for the Union as a whole. The ESRC would replace the Banking Supervision Committee of the **European Central Bank** (ECB) and whilst operating in conjunction with the ECB, would be formally independent of it. The main conclusions of the report were accepted by the EU institutions and, accordingly, three new supervisory **agencies** – the European Banking Authority (EBA), the European Securities and Markets Authority (ESMA), and the

European Insurance and Occupational Pensions Authority (EIOPA) – were established in January 2011, together with (under a slightly adjusted title) the European Systemic Risk Board.

Established by a **regulation** of the **Council of Ministers** and **European Parliament**, adopted in November 2010 under the **co-decision procedure**, the ESRB is responsible for 'macro-prudential oversight of the financial system' within the Union, issuing warnings (to the EU institutions, member-state governments and/or the European or national supervisory authorities) about systemic risks to the economy and recommendations about how to forestall or minimize their potential impact. The ESRB is governed by a 37-member General Board, composed largely of high-level, ex officio figures – notably the President and Vice-President of the **European Central Bank** (ECB), the 27 national **central bank governors** (the General Council of the ECB), and the heads of the three supervisory authorities. The President of the ECB chairs the General Board (initially for a five-year term, pending a review of arrangements). One deputy chairman is elected for a five-year term (currently the Governor of the Bank of England), whilst the other is automatically the person who already chairs the joint committee of the three supervisory authorities. A subgroup of the General Board acts as a Steering Committee, responsible for day-to-day business. Warnings may be adopted by a simple majority of members of the General Board and recommendations by a two-thirds' majority. Any decision to render a warning or recommendation public also requires a two-thirds' majority. Although the ESRB has no legislative power, its recommendations to the European Commission may include requests that draft legislation be introduced (see **right of initiative**). Two advisory committees support the work of the ESRB, whose 20-strong secretariat is provided by the ECB in Frankfurt. The ESRB publishes an annual report to the Council and Parliament, which its President presents in person at a parliamentary hearing. He or she also has regular, confidential discussions with the bureau of the Parliament's committee on economic and monetary affairs.

'European Union'

Although the concept of a 'European Union' had been in wide use for decades, the words were not included in any of the founding **Treaties** of the **European Communities** in the 1950s. However, the preamble to the **Treaty of Rome** opened with the words 'Determined to lay the foundations of an **ever closer union** among the peoples of Europe', a deliberate echo of the 'more perfect union' referred to in the Constitution of the United States. The commitment to create a European Union was first officially endorsed at the Paris **summit** of October 1972, at which the heads of government of the member states, the 'driving wheels of European construction', confirmed their intention of 'converting their entire relationship into a European Union before the end of this decade'. This objective was reaffirmed at the Copenhagen summit the following year. However, it was not until the 1992 **Maastricht Treaty** – the formal title of which is the Treaty on European Union (TEU) – that such a union was brought into existence.

'European Union' and similar phrases are to be found in many documents that mark the successive stages of the debate about European integration. The wording has tended to oscillate between some variant of 'union' and the more modest notion of a 'united Europe'. Of the pre-war proposals, the best known were the **Pan-Europa** of **Count Richard Coudenhove-Kalergi** and the plan for a European Federal Union put forward in 1929 by **Aristide Briand** in the League of Nations. (The League itself established a committee for European Union.) The aborted draft Treaty establishing the **European Political Community** (EPC) of 1953 described the proposed arrangement as being 'founded upon a union of peoples and states'. After the abandonment of that text, the resolution adopted by the foreign ministers at the **Messina Conference** in 1955 talked only of 'the setting up of a united Europe'. Six years later, however, heads of government spoke confidently in Bonn in July 1961 of 'the will for political union already implicit in the treaties' and their desire to 'enable a statutory character to be given to the union of their peoples'. Various drafts of the ensuing **Fouchet Plan** in 1961–2 envisaged a European Political Union or a European Union. After that initiative failed, however, the 1969 summit in The Hague reverted only to advocating 'a united Europe'.

Magniloquence apart, the first serious attempt to define what European Union might actually mean was made in the 1975 **Tindemans Report**, drafted for the **European Council** by the then Belgian prime minister, Leo Tindemans. It identified the essential components of European Union as 'a united front to the outside world'; 'a common economic and monetary policy', backed by common policies for industry, agriculture, energy and research; and regional and social policies that would allow 'the solidarity of our peoples to be effective and adequate'. Above all, the European Union was to be founded upon 'institutions with the necessary powers to determine a common, coherent and all-inclusive political view, the efficiency needed for action, the legitimacy needed for democratic control'. Although little concrete action followed from the Tindemans Report, there was no dissent at the time from its broad definition of the elements which a European Union might comprise. It entered into the general appreciation of what ***les finalités politiques*** of European integration might entail.

Eight years after Tindemans, the member states reaffirmed the Paris summit commitment in the 1983 **Stuttgart Declaration** (formally known as the Solemn Declaration on European Union) in response to the proposals in the

Genscher–Colombo Plan. The Declaration said that 'European Union is being achieved by deepening and broadening the scope of European activities so that they coherently cover . . . a growing proportion of member states' mutual relations and of their external relations.' Heads of government undertook to review progress within five years, and to 'decide whether the progress achieved should be incorporated in a Treaty on European Union'.

The most ambitious scheme of the early 1980s was the **Draft Treaty establishing the European Union** (DTEU) proposed by the **European Parliament** in February 1984, at the instigation of **Altiero Spinelli**. In the DTEU, the new European Union would take over the whole of the ***acquis communautaire*** and its institutions would assume the functions already carried out by the institutions of the Community. Unlike the arrangements later agreed in Maastricht, the Union would have its own **legal personality** and be based predominantly on the '**Community method**'.

In the preamble to the 1986 **Single European Act** (SEA), the member states once again reaffirmed their commitment to European Union as expressed at the Paris summit. The SEA envisaged parallel arrangements for the European Communities, on the one hand, and a strengthened, formalized system of **European Political Cooperation** (EPC) for foreign policy, on the other. The latter had its own decision-making procedures, based essentially on **intergovernmentalism**. This model, employing what would later become known as separate '**pillars**', was refined and developed in the European Union actually established five years later under the Maastricht Treaty.

In the late 1980s, a widespread view emerged among heads of government and finance ministers that Europe should adopt a single currency, by establishing an **Economic and Monetary Union** (EMU). The Madrid European Council in June 1989 agreed to hold an **Intergovernmental Conference** (IGC) on this subject, planned for late 1990. However, the fall of the Berlin Wall and the collapse of Communism accelerated pressure, led by France and Germany, for wider institutional reform and deeper integration in other policy spheres. It was thus decided at the 'Dublin II' European Council in June 1990 that the EMU IGC would be paralleled by a second IGC on 'European Political Union', although the meaning of the words 'political union' was not clearly defined. These simultaneous discussions on monetary and political union made it natural that the resulting agreement in Maastricht should be called the Treaty on European Union.

Early in the life of the **Convention on the Future of Europe** (2002–3), its President, **Valéry Giscard d'Estaing**, raised the question of whether the phrase 'European Union' should be retained as the title of any successor structure embodied in a **European Constitution**. He suggested a variety of alternatives, including a '**United States of Europe**'. However, there was no enthusiasm for change. It now looks certain that European Union will remain the title of the form of regional cooperation established in Europe for the foreseeable future.

European University Institute (EUI)

Founded in 1976, the European University Institute is a postgraduate university offering doctoral degrees in the social sciences and humanities (and both doctoral and Master's degrees in law). It is located in more than half a dozen buildings, based on the Badia Fiesolana in the village of Fiesole, north of Florence. There are four academic departments – political and social sciences, history and civilization, economics, and law – as well as an interdisciplinary Robert Schuman Centre for Advanced Studies, which specializes in policy issues and EU-related questions. Having boasted only around a hundred academics and students in the early 1980s, the EUI has grown to encompass almost a thousand scholars today. Although it is one of the smallest universities in Europe, it is one of the largest specialist social-science research centres in the world.

The issue of whether there should be a 'European university' is a longstanding one in EU politics. Although the 1951 **Treaty of Paris** specified that 'an institution of university status shall be established', no such body was in fact created. Instead, EC heads of government agreed in July 1961 to support 'the establishment by Italy of a European university in Florence, to the intellectual life and financing of which the six governments will contribute'. Negotiations began in 1970, with agreement reached in April 1972 to set up an exclusively postgraduate college focused on issues largely related to European integration. The buildings and land for the project were donated by the Italian government.

Like the College of Europe in Bruges, the EUI is not a European Union body; but unlike Bruges, the Institute is not a private body either. It has its own legal personality, independent of the **Treaties**. EU member states and other countries can contract into the EUI by signing its founding intergovernmental convention. The Institute is financed by a mixture of direct contributions from contracting states and funding from the EU **Budget**, the latter having gradually increased as a proportion over time. Of the Institute's € 52.0 million budget in 2010, some € 24.9 million came from governments, € 8.3 million from the European Commission, and the remainder from other sources (including € 9.4 million in external research funding). In addition to its teaching and research activities, the EUI has since 1984 been the repository of the historical archives of the European Communities and it also administers the EU's Max Weber programme to train about 40 postdoctoral Europeans in the skills required to be good teachers and researchers.

The EUI is headed by a President, appointed by the Institute's High Council, comprised of representatives of the contracting states (on which the EU

Council of Ministers and **European Commission** sit as observers). The President chairs an Academic Council, which appoints academics and students, and a Research Council (of outside academics), which oversees the Institute's research programmes. The President is assisted by a Secretary General, who is supported in turn by an administrative staff of some 140 people. The Institute's full- or part-time teaching complement is largely comprised of academics on five-year professorships and shorter fellowships of various kinds. Full professorships (of which there are currently 52) may normally be renewed only once, up to a maximum of eight years, in order to promote rotation. Although the Institute has its own **staff regulations**, these are very similar to those of the European Union. As a result, EUI staff are rewarded on the same pay scales as EU civil servants, with their salaries exempted from national taxation, but subject to a (lower) special tax at source (see **Eurocrats**).

No tuition fees are required from students admitted to the Institute who are nationals of EU member states sponsoring the Institute. Fees for those from other countries are around € 12,000 per year, but in some cases special scholarships are available. Each year, sponsoring governments also award grants to some 150 students from their countries to cover their maintenance costs for up to four years (the duration of the Institute's doctoral programme). The deadline for applications for admission to the EUI is at the end of January each year, with a second round at the end of April, if there are still unfilled places.

Euroscepticism

Euroscepticism is the modern term, dating from the late 1980s, used to denote intellectual objection and resistance to the process of European integration. It is most commonly (although not exclusively) to be found among Conservatives in Anglo-Saxon countries, notably the United Kingdom, where there is an entrenched culture of national exceptionalism in both the House of Commons and the national press. The term was initially associated with the European policy of **Margaret Thatcher** towards the end of her term as British prime minister (1979–90), but it is now applied more widely.

Eurosceptics are 'sceptical' towards specifically the institutional structure of the European Union and the assumptions of **supranationalism** and sovereignty-sharing which underpin it. Whilst usually professing to be in favour of European states working more closely together on issues of common concern – what Thatcher described as 'willing and active cooperation between independent sovereign states' – they believe that such cooperation should ideally be organized along intergovernmental lines, with as few legally binding commitments or constraints imposed from the centre as possible. Eurosceptics are critical of the extension of the '**Community method**', especially as embodied in successive changes to the EU **Treaties**, and are fearful of the process of '**ever closer union**', believing that continued integration can or will result in the development of a European state. As such, Euroscepticism shares many of the features of Gaullism in the 1960s, and it is no coincidence that Margaret Thatcher and **Charles de Gaulle** are the two national leaders to have stood out most strongly against the deepening of Community institutions over the last half century. Both resisted attempts to widen Community **competence**, opposed the ambitions of the **European Commission**, sought to maintain unanimous decision-making in the **Council of Ministers**, and talked of the development of a European 'superstate' in Brussels.

More an attitude of mind than a detailed political philosophy, Euroscepticism can be held with varying degrees of intensity. In Britain, it is possible to identify at least three main strains, which may be termed pragmatic, principled and absolutist Euroscepticism. *Pragmatic Eurosceptics* tend to the view that the European integration process has, at any given moment, gone as far as it should, without their having any clear intention or plan to reverse it. The hostility of the British Conservative party leadership in opposition (1997–2010) to each of the three successive EU Treaties negotiated by the then Labour government, without giving any commitment to renounce them once the party returned to power, is a good example of pragmatic Euroscepticism in practice.

Principled Eurosceptics tend to be economic liberals who argue strongly that a combination of treaty changes and rulings by the **European Court of Justice** (ECJ) have, over time, changed the character of the Community, now Union. They are often prepared to accept a limited degree of sovereignty-sharing for the original, mainly economic, purposes of the Community – notably the development of a Europe-wide **single market**, **competition policy** and external trade policy – but they have serious reservations about many of the policies adopted since 1989. The best statement of principled Euroscepticism is to be found in Thatcher's **Bruges speech** of September 1988, in which she said that, whilst the **Treaty of Rome** had been 'intended as a charter for economic liberty', this philosophy was being undermined by initiatives such as the development of **Economic and Monetary Union** (EMU) and a 'Social Europe'. Many principled Eurosceptics believe that there should be a **referendum** on Britain's continuing membership of the Union, whereas pragmatic Eurosceptics would prefer to accept the status quo and hold referenda only on future treaty changes that might transfer further powers from member states to the EU level.

Absolutist Eurosceptics reject the very concept of supranational decision-making, which they believe is undemocratic and illegitimate, and want to see Britain leave the European Union. They argue that democracy and legitimacy can only come from electoral mandates obtained within a single, cohesive political community, organized at the level of the nation state (as the default locus of any 'demos'). Even the degree of sovereignty-sharing embodied in the original Treaty of Rome was therefore unacceptable, let alone the extensions introduced by subsequent treaties. Only a small minority of Conservative politicians are absolutist Eurosceptics; this position is represented rather by the UK Independence Party, which gained around 16 per cent of the vote in both the 2004 and 2009 **European elections**, but less than a fifth of that figure at the British general elections in each of the following years.

It follows that in any referendum on continued British membership of the Union, the pragmatic Eurosceptics would vote in favour, the deep Eurosceptics would vote against, and the principled Eurosceptics would divide between the two camps. Conversely, on a referendum on further transfers of competence, all Eurosceptics would vote against. This helps explain why the Conservative party leadership is currently against the first, 'in or out', type of referendum and in favour of the second, and equally why it would be very unlikely to agree to any treaty change that had to be put to the public in a referendum at all.

Although Euroscepticism in its current form developed in Britain, from the early 1990s onwards, it began to spread to a number of other EU member states and the United States. The use of referenda to ratify the **Maastricht Treaty** in 1992–3, the aborted **European Constitution** in 2004–5 and the **Lisbon Treaty** in 2008–9 prompted the growth of Euroscepticism in Denmark, France, the Netherlands and Ireland, in particular. The *souveraintiste* position of the narrowly-unsuccessful 'no' campaign in the **French referendum on the Maastricht Treaty** in September 1992 was a powerful example of this process, which fed into the strong performance of the 'Europe of Nations' list, led by Jimmy Goldsmith and Philippe de Villiers, in the 1994 European elections. Similar Eurosceptic arguments were used by the successful 'no' campaign in the first **Irish referendum** on the Lisbon Treaty in June 2008, led by businessman Declan Ganley. However, the force of Euroscepticism has tended to recede in these countries after each referendum, even if it remains a residual factor, whereas in Britain it is a powerful continuing feature of day-to-day politics.

Following the **enlargement** of the EU to central and eastern Europe in 2004–7, Euroscepticism has recently become a component in the politics of the Czech Republic – where President Václav Klaus has echoed Thatcherite language on sovereignty – as it has to a lesser extent in Poland. During the recent **eurozone debt crisis**, Eurosceptic tendencies have also become apparent in certain smaller member states, notably Finland and Slovakia, where there has been a marked reluctance to contribute to the bail-outs for Greece, Ireland and Portugal. In the United States, a strand of Euroscepticism has found favour among some neo-conservative journalists and academics, with its principal redoubt being the Margaret Thatcher Center for Freedom at the Heritage Foundation in Washington DC.

Further reading: Anthony Forster, *Euroscepticism in Contemporary British Politics*, 2002; Cécline Leconte, *Understanding Euroscepticism*, 2010.

'Eurosclerosis'

The word 'Eurosclerosis' was coined by Malcolm Baldridge, US Commerce Secretary, in a speech delivered in Venice in 1983. Echoing the analysis of economists at the **Organization for Economic Cooperation and Development** (OECD) that unemployment was becoming increasingly a 'European phenomenon', Baldridge argued that the countries of western Europe were falling behind their Pacific Rim rivals because they had more rigid labour markets, less efficient product markets, and a mixture of subsidies and protectionism in less dynamic sectors. Whereas the downturn in the United States was essentially cyclical, that in Europe had a stronger structural component and might herald the start of a period of sustained low growth. The idea of Eurosclerosis instantly caught the media's attention and played into the parallel debate about the costs of '**non-Europe**', resulting from the continuing existence of barriers to the **free movement** of goods, services and capital in the European Community. It provided powerful support for the argument that completion of the **single market** should become the Community's central policy goal in the mid-1980s.

Eurostat

Eurostat is the statistical office of the European Union. Based in Luxembourg, with a staff of some 700 officials, the body was originally established in 1953 as the statistical division of the **European Coal and Steel Community** (ECSC), becoming a directorate-general of the **European Commission** in 1958. It has since evolved into one of the largest and most comprehensive statistical organizations in the world, covering all aspects of EU activities. Eurostat publishes a variety of economic indicators, including notably the Harmonized Index of Consumer Prices (HICP) and other data on which the operation of the monetary policy of the **European Central Bank** (ECB) depends. Its Intrastat system is critical to calculations of internal trade within the **single market**. Detailed statistics from Eurostat – in areas such as taxation, employment, trade, industry, agriculture, energy, transport, tourism and general demography – are now often essential to policy-makers. The annual *Eurostat Yearbook* and *Key Figures on Europe* are especially useful.

Since Eurostat is heavily dependent on information supplied by the EU member states, not all of it equally comprehensive and reliable, the organization has played an important role in seeking to ensure the consistency and comparability of data supplied. It is at the centre of a European Statistical

System (ESS), incorporating the statistical offices, ministries, agencies and central banks that collect official statistics in EU member states and the countries of the **European Free Trade Association** (EFTA).

In 2003, the director-general of Eurostat, Yves Franchet, together with two other senior officials, were removed from office, and over 50 contracts with outside suppliers were cancelled, following revelations of fraud and financial mismanagement. It was alleged that, during the years 1996–2001, a system of double accounting had been used in part of the organization, with the value of certain contracts deliberately inflated and up to five million euro of payments to suppliers routed through unofficial bank accounts. In parallel, some companies owing money to Eurostat had been allowed, either deliberately or inadvertently, to get away with substantial non-payment. A series of legal cases and internal investigations followed, but the eventual outcome was inconclusive.

Euro Summit

See **Eurogroup and Euro Summit**.

Eurozone

The term 'eurozone' or 'euro area' denotes the territory covered by those member states within the European Union which use the **euro**, the single currency introduced as part of stage three of **Economic and Monetary Union** (EMU). Eleven of the (then) 15 EU member states were deemed to meet the **convergence criteria** for stage-three membership on 2 May 1998 and adopted the euro on 1 January 1999, forming the eurozone. (The United Kingdom and Denmark had formal **opt-outs** and Sweden subsequently established a de facto one.) Six more member states have since joined the eurozone: Greece in 2001, followed between 2007 and 2011 by five of the ten new member states that acceded to the Union in 2004. The finance ministers of the 17 eurozone countries meet as the **Eurogroup**, an arrangement formalized by the **Lisbon Treaty**. At present, the member states within the eurozone encompass 328 million citizens, out of a total EU population of 500 million (representing respectively 21.6 and 28.4 per cent of global GDP).

In advance of any country joining the eurozone, the value of its currency must be 'irrevocably fixed' in terms of the euro, backed by the force of law. When the single currency was being established, the irrevocable fixing was determined at market rates the day before the euro was adopted – on 31 December 1998 for 1 January 1999 – with a substantial gap (three years) before notes and coins were introduced. (The value of the euro was the same as the **European Currency Unit** (ECU) that preceded it.) Since Greece joined in 2001, it has become customary to fix the exchange irrevocably some five months before entry. Since Slovenia joined in 2007, it has been standard practice for a country to enter the eurozone and introduce euro notes and coins on the same day.

EU member states within the eurozone

Member state	*Previous currency*	*Irrevocably fixed exchange rate*	*Date of irrevocable fixing*	*Date of adoption of euro*	*Date of introduction of euro notes and coins*
Euro-11					
Austria	Schilling	13.7603	31 Dec 1998	1 Jan 1999	1 Jan 2002
Belgium	Franc	40.3399	31 Dec 1998	1 Jan 1999	1 Jan 2002
Finland	Markka	5.94573	31 Dec 1998	1 Jan 1999	1 Jan 2002
France	Franc	6.55957	31 Dec 1998	1 Jan 1999	1 Jan 2002
Germany	Deutschmark	1.95583	31 Dec 1998	1 Jan 1999	1 Jan 2002
Ireland	Punt	0.787564	31 Dec 1998	1 Jan 1999	1 Jan 2002
Italy	Lira	1,936.27	31 Dec 1998	1 Jan 1999	1 Jan 2002
Luxembourg	Franc	40.3399	31 Dec 1998	1 Jan 1999	1 Jan 2002
The Netherlands	Guilder	2.20371	31 Dec 1998	1 Jan 1999	1 Jan 2002
Portugal	Escudo	200.482	31 Dec 1998	1 Jan 1999	1 Jan 2002
Spain	Peseta	166.386	31 Dec 1998	1 Jan 1999	1 Jan 2002
Subsequent entrants					
Greece	Drachma	340.750	19 Jun 2000	1 Jan 2001	1 Jan 2003
Slovenia	Tolar	239.640	11 Jul 2006	1 Jan 2007	1 Jan 2007
Cyprus	Pound	0.585274	10 Jul 2007	1 Jan 2008	1 Jan 2008
Malta	Lira	0.42930	10 Jul 2007	1 Jan 2008	1 Jan 2008
Slovakia	Koruna	30.1260	8 Jul 2008	1 Jan 2009	1 Jan 2009
Estonia	Kroon	15.6466	13 Jul 2010	1 Jan 2011	1 Jan 2011

A number of countries and territories outside the European Union have made arrangements for the euro to be used as the local currency, even if officially they do not form part of the eurozone. Three western European **micro-states** – Monaco, San Marino and Vatican City – replaced their domestic currencies (the Monaco franc, San Marino lira and Vatican City lira respectively) at the same time as France and Italy adopted the single currency in 1999. They have agreements with the Union whereby they can issue euro coins (but not notes). A fourth micro-state, Andorra, did not have its own domestic currency, so effectively imported the euro from France and Spain in 1999, but is now negotiating a similar agreement to that enjoyed by the three others. Elsewhere, Montenegro and Kosovo have both adopted the euro as their domestic currencies. Certain **overseas countries and territories** (OCTs) of the Union, all of them French possessions, also use the euro – Mayotte (off the coast of Madagascar), Saint Pierre Miquelon (Newfoundland) and the French Southern and Antarctic Territories – as do the British sovereign base areas (SBAs) of Akrotiri and Dhekelia in Cyprus. (The SBAs are neither OCTs nor do they form part of the territory of the United Kingdom for the purposes of its EU membership.) The French overseas departments (Réunion, Guadeloupe, Guiana and Martinique), being an integral part of France, use the euro. Some 175 million other people inhabit countries whose currencies are pegged to the euro, mainly in the Francophone currency unions in Africa.

Eurozone debt crisis

One of the many consequences of the global financial crisis that became endemic in the autumn of 2008 was a very rapid and substantial deterioration in national public finances across the European Union. The fiscal position of most member states had in fact improved significantly during the mid-2000s: the average budget deficit in the Union declined from 2.4 to 0.9 per cent of gross domestic product (GDP) in the years 2005–7, and the average national debt from 62.8 to 59.0 per cent. The **eurozone** states saw falls from 2.5 to 0.7 per cent, and from 70.0 to 66.2 per cent, respectively. However, the general contraction of the economy – in 2009, GDP fell by an average of 4.3 per cent – automatically generated much lower tax revenues and higher public expenditure. This problem was greatly compounded by the substantial one-off cost of 'bailing out' and recapitalizing the commercial banks in many countries, whose balance sheets were under great strain because of large-scale lending to households and companies over the previous decade. Starting in October 2008, state support for 40 major rescue schemes in the financial sector across the Union amounted (in their first two years) to over € 4.6 trillion, representing 20 per cent of EU GDP, and peaking at an astonishing 30 per cent. In effect, excessive private borrowing was being transformed into public expenditure on an historically unprecedented scale.

Any EU member state that had failed to reduce its deficit and debt levels during the relatively benign years of the mid-2000s quickly found itself in a potentially exposed position, especially if the option of depreciating its national currency had been removed by adoption of the single currency. The upward appreciation of the **euro** by 30 per cent during the years 2002–7 compounded such pressures, with differences in unit labour costs between member states becoming increasingly pronounced. Starting in late 2008, yields on the sovereign debt issued by individual countries within the eurozone began to diverge markedly from their previous pattern of broad convergence on the value of German bonds, as markets started to price government debt issues separately, depending on the fiscal situation, general economic outlook, and fragility of the banking sector in each country. The consequences of what Herman Van Rompuy, **President of the European Council**, was to call a 'sleeping pill' taken by some European countries after they joined the single currency were about to become apparent.

What is now generally known as the 'eurozone debt crisis' began as a series of specific national debt crises in three member states – Greece, Ireland and Portugal, in that order – when, for different reasons, their governments became incapable of raising capital on the financial markets. Faced with the prospect of the first sovereign default in any advanced economy since the Second World War, the European Union and the International Monetary Fund (IMF) agreed jointly to bail out each of these three countries, by providing them with substantial interest-bearing loans, in return for national adjustment programmes to correct their public finances. Following the Greek bail-out in April 2010, the Union and IMF decided to establish a general support facility for states in severe difficulty: this was used for Ireland in November 2010 and Portugal in May 2011. However, the successive bail-outs failed to contain the crisis, the impact of which appeared to become cumulative, generating increasing fears for the longer-term sustainability of the public finances of certain larger, less peripheral, eurozone states, notably Italy and Spain, and leading to discussion of the possible collapse or break-up of the single-currency area as a whole.

As this wider eurozone debt crisis deepened, a vigorous discussion broke out about how both to halt 'contagion' between countries and to prevent any repeat of the situation in the future. The German Chancellor, Angela Merkel, insisted that further legal measures be adopted at EU level to oblige states to correct their public finances on a continuing basis. Some others, whilst broadly accepting the German case, placed the emphasis on other possible solutions – including the mutualization of debt by issuing **eurobonds** or the **European Central Bank** (ECB) becoming a lender of last resort to governments – ideas which Merkel rejected as a matter of principle. The

French President, Nicolas Sarkozy, used the crisis to push for the creation of separate eurozone structures, in parallel to the Union, accentuating the likelihood of a **'two-speed' Europe** in which France and Germany would be dominant.

The situation in Greece, which represents only two per cent of the overall eurozone economy, was the immediate trigger for the debt crisis. Against the trend of generally improving public finances in the mid-2000s, the country's deficit had already risen in 2005–7, from 5.2 to 6.4 per cent of GDP, with its debt edging up from 100.3 to 105.0 per cent – as Athens took advantage of much lower interest rates, following Greece's entry into stage three of EMU in 2001, to sustain a higher level of state provision than justified by the country's tax revenues or productivity growth. (Greek private and corporate debt remained relatively modest by international standards, even as government finances deteriorated.) However, the scale of the problem was not fully apparent at the time: indeed the country report for Greece issued by the **Organization for Economic Cooperation and Development** (OECD) in May 2007 painted a relatively benign picture of an economy on a likely path of continued growth and declining deficits. The warning lights began to flash in the summer of 2009, when the **European Commission** began to suspect that the figures supplied by the Greek government were defective. In November 2009, following the electoral defeat of the centre-right New Democracy government which had been in power for the previous five years, it became clear that the fiscal position in Athens was much worse than previously understood. The best estimate of the country's annual budget deficit for 2009 was revised upwards from around 7.0 per cent of GDP to 12.7 per cent, then to 13.6 per cent, and finally (during the course of 2010) to 15.4 per cent. The national debt was recalculated as standing at over 125 per cent of GDP and rising rapidly.

The initial reaction to news of the Greek situation was one of confusion and dismay. Most policy-makers took the view that any default by Greece would carry systemic risks to the whole European economy, given the high exposure of French and German banks in particular to Greek sovereign and private debt, as well as hugely damaging the credibility of **Economic and Monetary Union** (EMU) as a project. (France and Germany together had Greek debt holdings of some € 90 billion). However, the most obvious alternative – namely that the government in Athens be offered some kind of financial support by the Union or its member states – was initially resisted by Germany as contrary to the 'no bail-out' philosophy and provisions of the EMU rules established in the 1992 **Maastricht Treaty**. These reservations were given added weight by the revelation that Greece had in fact been deliberately under-reporting its deficit and debt situation, both to qualify for the single currency in 2001 and subsequently. The suspicious upward revision of its GDP by almost a quarter in 2007 now took on new meaning.

After a period of hesitation, the **Eurogroup** (of eurozone finance ministers) decided in March 2010 to explore with the IMF the possible creation of a joint financial safety net that could be used to assist Greece or any other eurozone state that might need emergency support to stave off default on its sovereign debt. The French government was sceptical about IMF involvement, whereas the German government and the ECB insisted that, if such a rescue facility were established, an external guarantee of financial rigour of the kind offered by the IMF would be important. In parallel, to assuage German concerns, the March 2010 European Council meeting invited its President, Herman Van Rompuy, to chair a task force (of the finance ministers of the 27 EU member states) to recommend stronger arrangements for ensuring fiscal discipline in the eurozone member states, including by strengthening the **Stability and Growth Pact** (SGP), in the future.

Following many weeks of growing turbulence on the financial markets, on 23 April 2010, the government in Athens finally requested financial support from the Union. The following day, in the margins of the IMF–World Bank spring meetings in Washington, Dominique Strauss-Kahn, the Fund's managing director, offered to finance a third of any sum jointly provided by the Union and IMF. Initial discussion suggested the creation of a bail-out facility of some € 45 billion, but on 2 May, the Eurogroup and the IMF agreed on the provision of loans to Greece amounting to € 110 billion, spread over three years, conditional upon the country adopting a severe domestic reform programme. Of this total, € 80 billion would be provided by the eurozone member states in bilateral loans (pooled by the Commission) and € 30 billion on a multilateral basis by the IMF, with € 45 billion of the total to be made available for use in the first year. The loans would be released in tranches, on the basis of strict conditionality, based on a regular assessment by the Commission, ECB and IMF – a combination which rapidly became known as the '**troika**' – of progress in delivering domestic reform. The agreed reforms required a reduction of the Greek budget deficit to 3.0 per cent of GDP over four years, based on immediate tax increases and spending cuts, and backed by broader structural reform, involving notably a rise in the pensionable age and a programme of state asset sales. A general strike on 5 May prompted widespread rioting in Athens, leaving three people dead.

The reaction to the Greek bail-out was nowhere near as positive as European leaders had expected. Not only was the country's debt downgraded to junk status, with bond yields rising to over 15 per cent, but fear began to spread through the markets that the Greek situation might be replicated in other peripheral eurozone states. The heads of government of the (then)

16 countries within the zone convened in emergency session on Friday, 7 May in Brussels to discuss the situation. They instructed the Commission immediately to design some kind of 'stabilization mechanism' that could allow for future bail-outs, if necessary. The **Ecofin Council** (of all 27 EU finance ministers) met two days later, on Sunday, 9 May – ironically the 60th anniversary of the **Schuman Plan**, which had launched the post-war European integration process on a supranational path – to look at and adopt the new facility.

After a lively and intricate debate about modalities, conducted against the need to agree something credible before the markets opened for business the following day, the Ecofin Council announced the creation of a triple-barrelled 'crisis fund'. This would offer the possibility of up to € 750 billion in loans from three sources: € 440 billion from a new **European Financial Stability Facility** (EFSF), € 60 billion from a new **European Financial Stabilization Mechanism** (EFSM), and € 250 billion from the IMF. Established as a Luxembourg-registered company, formally outside the EU structure, the EFSF is owned by the governments of the 17 eurozone member states and underpinned by guarantees offered by those governments using the same key as their share of the paid-up capital of the ECB. By contrast, the EFSM is a treaty-based financial support facility, which permits the European Commission, on behalf of the Union, to borrow up to € 60 billion, guaranteed by the Union's annual **Budget**, for 'on-lending' to member states in difficulty. (The relatively modest size of the Union Budget prevented it from taking on a bigger role.) At the time, the € 750 billion total figure was seen as enormous, and was meant to be. As the (then) French finance minister, Christine Lagarde, was quoted as saying soon after: 'The only thing the markets understand is money. We had to get real, which meant get big. If you don't have a big number on the board, they will think you are really just a bunch of amateurs.'

Following agreement in May 2010 on both the EU–IMF Greek bail-out and these more structured rescue facilities for use in future cases, several important initiatives were taken by different players and institutions at European level. In late May, the European Commission put forward proposals to strengthen upstream macro-economic coordination at EU level, pulling together and reforming a variety of existing mechanisms into a more coherent 'European semester'. This provided for a six-month cycle during the first half of each year, whereby a new Annual Growth Survey, to be published by the Commission in January, would lead to the adoption at the March and June European Councils of country-specific Stability or Convergence Programmes for budgetary alignment (the former for eurozone states; the latter for those outside the single currency), as well as National Reform Programmes (NRPs) for structural reform. The European semester was agreed in the Ecofin Council in September 2010 and activated four months later. Building on this, the recommendations of the Van Rompuy task force, published in October 2010, foreshadowed a significant strengthening of the SGP in general, and the **excessive deficit procedure** (EDP) in particular. However, in an attempt to retain its **right of initiative**, the Commission pre-empted the Van Rompuy conclusions with its own, near-identical, proposals for six specific legislative measures, known as the 'Six Pack', which were eventually adopted a year later.

At a controversial bilateral summit in Deauville, France, also held in October, President Sarkozy and Chancellor Merkel agreed that automatic financial sanctions should apply for any country failing to take the necessary measures under the EDP, backed (although this idea was later abandoned) by the threat of suspension of the voting rights in the Council of any states in 'serious violation of the basic principles' of EMU. They also concluded that a permanent rescue facility should replace the EFSF and EFSM in due course and that 'private-sector involvement' (PSI) should routinely feature in bail-outs, with the commercial banks accepting a write-off of part of their bond holdings. Although the Deauville deal played badly with several other member states, appearing to prejudge decision-making in wider EU and eurozone bodies – in a poignant coincidence, the Van Rompuy task force was actually meeting in Luxembourg at the time the Deauville communiqué was issued – it reflected the reality that a more assertive display of Franco-German leadership was becoming essential to address the crisis, even if within that partnership, power was shifting decisively in favour of Berlin. The arrangements for the permanent bail-out facility, known as the **European Stability Mechanism** (ESM), were subsequently agreed among the 17 eurozone states in the first half of 2011 and formalized by an intergovernmental treaty signed in July that year.

Germany also made it clear that it expected that a reliable **legal base**, rooted in the EU **Treaties**, be put in place for the future ESM, to guard against any hostile rulings by its own Federal Constitutional Court (see **Karlsruhe judgements**) or the **European Court of Justice** (ECJ). After initial scepticism in several quarters, the **European Council** accordingly agreed in December 2010 to Merkel's specific request that Article 136 TFEU be amended to enable eurozone states to 'establish a stability mechanism to be activated if indispensable to safeguard the stability of the euro area as a whole'. The granting of any assistance under this permanent mechanism would be made 'subject to strict conditionality'.

Soon after, Berlin also insisted on stronger commitments by eurozone states to general structural reform, beyond the traditional areas of EU **competence**, through an intergovernmental 'competitiveness pact' covering such sensitive issues as wage indexation, retirement ages and the taxation of labour. Later redubbed the 'Pact for the Euro' and finally the 'Euro Plus Pact', this agreement was adopted by all 17 eurozone member states (and eight others) in March 2011. Barroso and Van Rompuy buried their earlier differences in the handling of the eurozone crisis to negotiate a joint text for the pact, to ensure its acceptability to the widest number of member states, even at some cost in the clarity of content. Among the commitments undertaken in the Euro Plus Pact are that signatories will transpose the EU's deficit and debt rules into national legislation in a way which is 'sufficiently strong, binding and durable' to be effective (even though **EU law** on the matter is already supposed to enjoy **primacy** in the member states).

In the interim, Ireland became the beneficiary of the second national bailout to be financed by the EU and IMF. Whereas the Greek debt crisis was generated essentially by unsustainable public spending, matched by inadequate tax revenues and the continued prospect of low growth, the Irish crisis was driven by excessive private-sector borrowing during the early- to mid-2000s, powered (once again) by interest rates that were lower than justified by economic fundamentals, as well as by imprudent tax breaks for construction. An asset bubble followed, in which the country's principal commercial banks lost over € 100 billion through bad loans extended to property owners and developers. Several Irish banks went bankrupt in 2008–9 and had to be nationalized. Outstanding debt owed collectively by, the government, banks, individuals and the corporate sector rose to over 500 per cent of GDP, the highest in the industrialized world. Under pressure from the ECB, the government chose to offer a complete guarantee to all depositors and shareholders in the country's banks, a commitment which would need to be met in part from current or future state spending. Ireland's budget deficit rose from a mere 0.1 per cent of GDP in 2007 to a startling 32.4 per cent in 2010, with the level of national debt escalating from 25.0 to 96.2 per cent over the same three-year period.

The Fianna Fáil-led government of Brian Cowen requested support from the Union on 21 November 2010. A week later, the Eurogroup agreed an € 85.0 billion Irish rescue package, subsequently endorsed by the Ecofin Council as a whole. The EU and IMF jointly agreed to extend € 67.5 billion in loans to Ireland over three years, at an interest rate of 5.8 per cent. The total sum was divided between € 22.5 billion each from the EFSM and the IMF, and € 17.7 billion from the EFSF. In addition, three non-eurozone countries – the United Kingdom, Sweden and Denmark – provided bilateral loans to Ireland of € 3.8 billion, € 600 million and € 400 million respectively. Of the € 85.0 billion total, € 17.5 billion would be contributed by the Irish government itself, partly from its national pension reserve. Some € 10 billion of the facility was to be used for immediate recapitalization of the country's banks and € 25 billion to ease their liquidity.

The third country to require a bail-out was Portugal, whose budget deficit suddenly jumped from 3.5 to 10.1 per cent of GDP between 2008 and 2009, and whose national debt was on a sharply rising curve – from 63.9 per cent of GDP in 2006 to 93.0 three years later. With sluggish growth, a widening trade deficit, bond yields rising to nine per cent and a governing Socialist party in revolt against austerity measures, the Portuguese prime minister, José Sócrates, requested support from the Union on 6 April 2011. Almost six weeks later, on 16 May, it was granted three-year loans totalling € 78 billion, divided equally between EFSF, EFSM and IMF sources (each of which contributed € 26 billion). Of the total, € 12 billion was to be devoted to support for the country's banks. In return, the government undertook to reduce its budget deficit from 9.1 per cent of GDP in 2010 (a figure originally expected to come in at 9.8 per cent) to 3.0 per cent in 2013.

The Greek, Irish and Portuguese debt crises quickly had a significant impact on the fortunes of the governments of each country. Irresistible opportunities arose for opposition parties to discomfort the incumbent administrations, bringing two of them down. In Ireland, the life of the Fianna Fáil-led administration was effectively ended by the crisis and resulting bail-out: in November 2010, taking advantage of opposition from Fine Gael, the junior coalition partner, the Greens, were able to force an early general election as the price for their support for austerity measures. The contest in February 2011 led to a Fine Gael victory, although ironically the Greens lost all their seats. In Portugal, immediately following the bail-out deal, Sócrates' retrenchment programme was rejected by the country's parliament, forcing a general election a month later, in June 2011, which led in turn to victory for the opposition centre-right. Although Portugal's sovereign debt was quickly downgraded to junk status, the process of budgetary adjustment initially proved more rapid than expected.

Meanwhile, in Greece, where the Socialist government of George Papandreou had a majority of only two votes in its parliament, the situation continued to deteriorate during the remainder of 2010 and throughout 2011. GDP fell by a total of 10 per cent over those two years. The administration in Athens experienced increasing difficulty in meeting the ambitious reform targets that it had agreed in May 2010, not least in the face of strong public resistance, led by the trade unions. After briefly easing, bond yields on Greek debt continued on an upward path. The government's fiscal adjustment schedule had to be revised, so that the budget deficit would be reduced to three per cent by 2014 at the earliest, rather than 2013, and national debt – expected to peak at about € 340 billion or 166 per cent of GDP in 2012 – would only fall back below its 2009 level by 2020 at the earliest (when it would still represent 120 per cent of GDP). It became clear that there was no realistic prospect of the country returning to the financial markets to raise new debt in the foreseeable future (whereas Ireland hoped to do so by 2014).

The growing appreciation of the sheer intractability of the Greek problem led to a reappraisal of policy. In July 2011, a special eurozone summit agreed in principle to provide a second bail-out package to Greece, comprised of EFSF/ESM and IMF loans of up to € 130 billion (the exact details of which had still to be worked out). Such support would be contingent not only on continued fiscal consolidation but, at German insistence, on an agreement between the Greek government and its private-sector creditors whereby the latter would accept a 'voluntary bond exchange' reducing the nominal value of their sovereign debt by 50 per cent. It was foreseen that this PSI – which still had to be negotiated with the international banks through the Washington-based Institute for International Finance (IIF) – might cut Greece's debt by up to € 100 billion. It was also agreed to reduce the interest rate charged on loans to Greece from 5.0 to 3.5 per cent and to lengthen their term from seven and a half to 15 years. These concessions were also extended to Ireland and Portugal, on a broadly comparable basis, even if initially, the French government resisted any reduction in the interest rate on loans to Ireland unless Dublin agreed to raise its low level of corporation tax. Eventually a compromise was reached whereby Ireland agreed to look more positively at the possible creation of a 'common consolidated corporate tax base' across the Union, even if it would not increase the rate (see **tax harmonization**).

After an initially positive reaction, the decisions taken by the July 2011 eurozone summit proved inadequate to reassure the financial markets, which were in a brittle state as a parallel political drama played out in Washington between the Obama administration and Congress over raising the ceiling for the US national debt. Rather than narrow, as expected, the spread of Greek over German bonds widened to over 20 per cent during the summer. A continuing exodus of capital from Greek banks gathered even greater speed, eventually reaching around 17 per cent of GDP for the whole year. At the same time, a much broader concern began to take hold about the possibility of containing the crisis. Commentators began to speculate seriously about whether Greece's continued use of the euro was sustainable – with huge implications for its banking system and those of several other economies – and fear became widespread of a deeper potential domino effect or 'contagion' between states, reaching closer to the heart of the eurozone. Ironically, the very success of the **single market** in promoting the interpenetration of economies meant that a catastrophic loss of confidence in one state could now generate or exacerbate a simultaneous fiscal and banking crisis in other states, requiring each of them in turn to seek further public support for their financial sectors, so worsening their fiscal situations, prompting the need for further bail-outs.

Such a prospect began to shape market perceptions of the two next most vulnerable eurozone economies, Italy and Spain. Objectively, the public finances of each country were in somewhat better shape than in the three states already in receipt of bail-outs. Although Italy had a national debt of 119 per cent of GDP (the second highest after Greece) in 2010, its budget deficit was only 4.6 per cent (1.4 per cent below the eurozone average and lower than in Austria or the Netherlands). Conversely, at 60 per cent, Spain's national debt was the fifth lowest in the eurozone in 2010, even if its budget deficit was the third highest, at 9.2 per cent. (Offsetting their respective national debts, Spain's private-sector debt was relatively high and Italy's relatively low.) However, whatever mitigating factors might be cited, the perception developed that low productivity in each country, underpinned by severe domestic political constraints on structural reform, would make it impossible for them to grow their way out of stagnation, so building up further, serious fiscal problems for the future. Italian bond yields moved from 2.0 per cent in mid-2010 to peak at 7.8 per cent in November 2011, whilst Spanish bonds moved from 2.0 to 6.1 per cent over the same period. In both cases, the problem was exacerbated by a national tradition of issuing relatively short-term bonds, which meant that the two governments had to tap the markets frequently, often for substantial amounts of money. (Italy and Spain were expected to refinance around € 320 billion and € 140 billion of sovereign debt respectively in 2012.)

The governments in both Rome and Madrid proved unable to withstand the pressures of this situation. In Italy, after teetering on the brink of collapse for several months, the centre-right coalition of Silvio Berlusconi lost its parliamentary majority in November 2011, as a result of stresses caused by successive rounds of budget savings (of 3.5 per cent of GDP), as well as resistance to structural reforms (with the retirement age due to be raised to 67 by 2026) and the continued rise in yields on Italian sovereign debt. The prime minister was forced to resign as a quid pro quo for approval of the final package by the lower chamber, which aimed to move Italy to a balanced budget within three years. Berlusconi's government was replaced by a caretaker administration composed of unelected technocrats, led by a former European Commissioner, Mario Monti (see **Monti Report**). In Spain, the Socialist government of José Luis Zapatero chose to call an early general election in November 2011, which it knew it was almost certain to lose to the opposition Partido Popular, rather than persist in its efforts to address the crisis.

The prospect that Italy or Spain might need to be bailed out also exposed the potential limitations of the existing EU–IMF support facility. Although the latter was still far from fully employed, its collective firepower of € 750 billion would fall far short of the scale of support required if contagion finally spread to these two countries. Even the IMF only had approximately € 300 billion of possible future lending available for crises in any part of the world. Twin debates emerged about the desirability of significantly boosting the size of the EFSF–EFSM facility, including by bringing forward the ESM, and of strengthening the lending capacity of the IMF. French pressure to increase the joint capacity of the EFSF–EFSM from € 500 million to over € 1.0 trillion was resisted by Germany, although eurozone heads of government agreed (in October 2011) to review this question in March 2012. However, in the face of continuing market pressure, the same leaders decided, in December 2011, that eurozone member states (and others willing to contribute) should extend bilateral loans of up to € 200 billion to the IMF for future eurozone support. By routeing this funding indirectly through the IMF, it was hoped to elicit matching funds from other non-European, especially Asian, members of the Fund. However, the United States indicated that it would not participate in this process, given the scale of its own domestic fiscal crisis and the fact that over three-quarters of IMF lending was already going to European countries.

By October 2011, Chancellor Merkel had concluded that further treaty changes were needed to strengthen the operation of the SGP, building on the legislation adopted in the Six Pack. Although several other leaders expressed caution about the risks of having to secure **ratification** of such changes in **national parliaments** and possibly by **referendum** too, the eurozone summit on 26 October invited Van Rompuy to 'identify possible steps' to 'strengthen the economic union and make it commensurate with the monetary union'. Working with the Presidents of the Commission and Eurogroup, he would explore the 'possibility of limited treaty changes', reporting back in December, with a view to final agreement three months later.

However, the glide-path to identifying and agreeing such a treaty reform was to be severely disrupted by a spectacular flare-up in Greece. When, immediately after the eurozone summit, prime minister Papandreou sought the endorsement of the Greek parliament for the country's second bail-out package and associated consolidation measures, it became clear that his Socialist party was seriously divided on the matter, whilst the opposition was determined to try to force both his resignation and an early general election as the price of any agreement. The political and economic stresses of retrenchment were proving almost impossible to manage, whilst the Commission's decision to establish a permanent 'monitoring capacity' for the bail-out on the ground in Athens, in conjunction with the ECB and IMF, crystallized the image of a country increasingly governed from Brussels, Frankfurt and Berlin.

In a frantic attempt to buy time before the looming parliamentary vote, on 31 October, Papandreou suddenly proposed that the Greek electorate should decide on the package in a referendum, to be held in January 2012, in a 'supreme act of democracy and patriotism'. The reaction of stunned foreign leaders and financial markets was uniformly hostile, whilst support from within the government and Socialist party (neither of which he had consulted in advance) was at best lukewarm. On 2 November, Papandreou was in effect summoned by President Sarkozy and Chancellor Merkel to the annual **Group of Twenty** (G20) summit in Cannes, France, where he received an unequivocal message that all other eurozone states and the IMF regarded the referendum as a dangerous distraction, delaying what everyone else considered to be a done deal. He was also told that Greece could not expect to receive any further funding from the existing bail-out programme unless and until it had unequivocally endorsed the new one. The next tranche of funding, worth € 8.0 billion, was due in mid-November.

There was widespread media speculation that Greece would be forced to leave the eurozone, and perhaps the European Union, if it voted against the package. Sources close to Merkel and Sarkozy raised the stakes by briefing about possible expulsion and the need for any referendum, which would need to be held in December at the latest, to address the wider issue of Greece's continued membership of the eurozone, in order to maximize the chances of a 'yes' vote. At a joint press conference with the French President, Merkel said that 'in essence, the referendum is about nothing else but the question, does Greece want to stay in the eurozone: yes or no?', whilst Sarkozy added that it had been a 'mistake' to admit Greece to the single-currency area. The shift in the terms of debate was dramatic and sharp. Only a few days before, the European Commission had reassuringly indicated that the Treaties 'do not permit either departure or expulsion from monetary union', whilst the established position of the ECB's legal service was that 'a Member State's exit from EMU, without a parallel withdrawal from the EU, would be legally inconceivable' and 'while perhaps feasible through indirect means, [its] expulsion from the EU or EMU would be legally next to impossible' (*ECB Legal Working Paper Series*, Number 10, December 2009).

Faced with a political crisis that was now spiralling out of control, Papandreou offered to resign as prime minister, but only so long as the bail-out package was endorsed by the Greek parliament, with the support of the opposition, and a caretaker government was appointed until new elections could be held. On 4 November, the outgoing prime minister won parliamentary approval for the package, on this basis. After several days of frenzied manoeuvring among political leaders in Athens, a cross-party coalition, headed by a non-party technocrat, Lucas Papademos, former Vice-President of the ECB, eventually took office. However, although 'successfully' resolved in a technical sense – Papandreou even claimed that the referendum switchback had been a 'useful shock' to the system – the Greek drama was widely seen as a huge and wholly avoidable political own goal, one that had not only further shaken market confidence in that country's willingness and ability to stay the course of reform, but had also exposed the fragility of the EU-level decision-making process on EMU issues. At a more immediate and practical level, it also made negotiation with the international banks of a 50 per cent 'hair cut' on Greek debt more complicated. When EU heads of government met in Brussels in December, they were forced to give a definitive assurance that similar PSI requirements would not be applied to any future bail-outs with countries other than Greece.

The backwash from the Greek turmoil also made it significantly more difficult to conduct the inevitably tense discussion about how to satisfy Chancellor Merkel's insistence that the legal status of the SGP be further upgraded. Continuing market turbulence and media excitement during the autumn meant that the October eurozone summit was retrospectively presented as a relative failure. The forthcoming December European Council was now, like all the earlier summits of 2011, widely cast as a 'make or break' moment in the ongoing eurozone crisis. In visits to national capitals, Merkel floated the idea that the European Commission should be given the power to take member states to the **European Court of Justice** (ECJ), with the latter able to strike down national budgets, so circumventing the current role of the **Council of Ministers** in threatening to fine recalcitrant states. She privately described the existing EDP as ineffective, both because the Council was reluctant to impose fines and because any fines would only make the fiscal situation of the offending country worse. However, as the autumn proceeded, she softened her stance and accepted that the transposition into the Treaties of the provisions of the Six Pack and greater automaticity in the threat of sanctions by the Council, together with a commitment to transpose 'balanced budget' obligations into domestic constitutional law, were probably as much as could realistically be achieved for now.

In a manoeuvre which aroused similar irritation to their Deauville démarche, Merkel and Sarkozy – increasingly dubbed 'Merkozy' by the media and styled the 'royal couple' by at least one fellow leader – attempted to preempt the report being drafted by Van Rompuy, by holding a bilateral summit at the Elysée Palace four days before the European Council in December. They jointly endorsed the idea of a substantial new eurozone treaty – to be adopted either by the Union as a whole (Germany's strong preference) or by the 17 eurozone states on their own (a solution actively canvassed by France) – to upgrade and strengthen the existing EDP arrangements. A key part of this would be to establish a lower limit for a cyclically-adjusted budget deficit, instituting a sort of European 'golden rule' that would need to be transposed into national constitutions. However, Van Rompuy, supported by the Commission and the ECB, recommended a little-known route that required only the most minimal treaty change possible, namely an amendment to **Protocol** 12 of the Treaties (on aspects of the EDP), which (quite unusually) could be adopted unanimously by the European Council without any need for national parliamentary ratification. This approach would be complemented by a more intensive use of law-making possibilities within the existing Treaties, if necessary through **enhanced cooperation.**

In a delicious reversal of fortune, at the summit meeting on 9 December, Merkel was virtually isolated in opposing use of Protocol 12 – holding out for a wider, conventional treaty reform involving an **Intergovernmental Conference** (IGC) – until the British prime minister, David Cameron, insisted that he could not agree to this solution unless a series of ill-prepared, late demands on the regulation of financial services were immediately met 'in full'. Since the same British conditions applied to any wider treaty change, Van Rompuy declared that (as he later reported) 'there was no alternative but to go down the route of a separate treaty among the 17 eurozone members, though open to others', which would exist in parallel to the Union – an exercise over which Britain could, by definition, exercise no influence. The result was less a British 'veto' than a decision by the other member states to move away from a framework in which the UK could insist on its negotiating points.

Cameron ignored the advice given to him by Philip Stephens in the *Financial Times* earlier the same week to eschew the illusion that Britain could somehow 'lead a powerful new alliance' of euro 'outs' and to take care not to 'attach conditions to British acquiescence in treaty changes' applying only to the eurozone. The Germans and the Commission immediately moved to sign up as many of the 'outs' as possible to the principle of participating in the new, intergovernmental treaty, so outmanoeuvring France. The six signatories of the Euro Plus Pact outside the eurozone quickly signalled their willingness to do so, and the other three – the Czech Republic, Hungary and Sweden – declared that they would decide after consulting their national parliaments. Ironically, the only reason Cameron would have needed to secure national parliamentary approval for a Protocol 12 change – and uniquely within the Union – was because of the requirements of the new European Union Act that he himself had insisted upon passing in the UK earlier in the year to reassure Eurosceptics in his own Conservative party. In addition to isolating Britain, the prime minister's 'veto' managed to generate resentment that, in order to avoid facing down his own party in a parliamentary vote, he had chosen to ignore the common European interest at a moment of great need. The only person remotely satisfied with the outcome was President Sarkozy, who saw in any intergovernmental treaty a potential opportunity to escape some of the constraints of the '**Community method**' in the political and legal management of the eurozone. In the event, the resulting text, the **Fiscal Compact Treaty**, negotiated in January 2012, drew heavily on the EU institutions, even if it took an intergovernmental form.

If Merkel secured only part of what she had originally hoped for in pushing for treaty change, and in a different form, she had nonetheless, throughout the autumn of 2011, strongly and successfully resisted pressure to resort to a range of other ambitious solutions which had been put on the table by various governments and experts. These included the possible mutualization of some or all of the outstanding eurozone sovereign debt, by issuing joint eurobonds through a European debt office or 'European Monetary Fund', or allowing the ECB to act as a lender of last resort to governments (it already did so to banks), able to purchase unlimited amounts of sovereign debt, as in the United States or the United Kingdom. Both of these options – the first advocated by the Commission, the second by Sarkozy – would have required treaty change, but not of a kind the German Chancellor was prepared to countenance. She also reacted coolly to the suggestion made by the outgoing President of the ECB, Jean-Claude Trichet, that a new European finance ministry should take on a variety of tasks currently performed by the Commission, the Ecofin Council and Eurogroup. Such a body could, as Trichet proposed, be given responsibility for policing member-state budget deficits and national debts within the eurozone, including administering preventative action.

As the dramatic politics in the second half of 2011 indicated, the eurozone debt crisis was beginning to have a significant impact on the operation of the EU institutional system. The **Lisbon Treaty**, which entered into force in November 2009, had already upgraded the role of the regular EU summit meeting, the European Council. This body had become a separate institution from the Council of Ministers, with its own full-time President. The crisis further reinforced the importance of meetings of heads of government as the prime forum in which policy disputes were resolved and a sense of overall direction was set within the Union system. The invention of the new post of President of the European Council quickly proved its worth too: had the six-monthly, rotating **presidency** of the Council of Ministers still chaired summit meetings, there would have been severe discontinuity in the conduct of business at the highest level, especially as four of the six presidencies in the years 2009–11 were held by member states outside the eurozone. Already there was widespread and sometimes justified criticism of the absence of a 'centre that could hold' in the crisis – with competing roles for the Presidents of the European Council, Council of Ministers, Commission, ECB and Eurogroup – but immobilism in the European Council would have almost certainly tested this problem to breaking point.

However, as the crisis unfolded, the integrity of the European Council as a single body also found itself under strain. There were pressures for it to splinter into inner and outer groupings, as President Sarkozy insisted that summit meetings specifically of the leaders of the 17 eurozone states be convened. With some reluctance, Van Rompuy held ad hoc eurozone summits in May 2010, March 2011 and July 2011. After initial resistance from Merkel to the institutionalization of such meetings, Sarkozy finally secured her support for them to become a regular feature of decision-making in July 2011, an arrangement formalized as the '**Euro Summit**' when all eurozone leaders met again three months later.

Underpinning the emergence of eurozone summits as a new forum of European decision-making was the growing importance of subsidiary eurozone structures, notably the Eurogroup of finance ministers and the Euro Working Group (EWG) of key officials. In effect, a new 'shadow system' was being established at all levels: the European Council shadowed by the Euro Summit; the Ecofin Council by the Eurogroup; and the **Economic and Financial Committee** by the EWG, of which technically at least it remained a subdivision. So, even within the Council, the traditional EU bodies will find themselves fighting to retain predominance in coming years, as the eurozone states and the media focus on the 'core' grouping at each level as potentially the key locus of decision-making. The Eurogroup and EWG already have separate presidencies from the Ecofin Council and EFC respectively. Van Rompuy has struggled to ensure that the Euro Summit should always be chaired by the President of the European Council – to ensure coherence and 'keep the two configurations as close as possible, in a spirit of trust', as he has put it – but the result so far is that there is no formal obligation for this joint chairmanship to apply. Van Rompuy has also sought to establish a pattern that Euro Summits should normally follow, rather than precede or be held separately from, European Council meetings, as Sarkozy preferred: the only commitment, for the moment, is that this pattern will be respected 'if possible'.

For its part, the European Commission has found itself on the defensive throughout the crisis, partly because the principal bail-out mechanism created in May 2010, the EFSF, is intergovernmental in character, operating through national guarantees, rather than as an independent central fund, organized along supranational lines. Equally, the modest size of the Union's annual Budget (at one per cent of collective GDP), together with the treaty bar on the monetary financing of budget deficits (constraining the ECB), has left national capitals firmly in the driving seat of policy. Although the Commission has not been entirely marginalized – it has succeeded, for example, in exploiting its right of initiative to embed some solutions in EU law (as in the Six Pack), just as it forms part of the 'troika' with the ECB and

IMF that controls the release of bail-out funds – in the end, its margin of manoeuvre is severely limited by the Council's specific responsibility for coordinating the economic policies of the member states (Article 121 TFEU) and its responsibilities in respect of EMU.

A different Commission President might have insisted on playing a more assertive leadership role, but José Manuel Barroso has found it difficult to break out of the pattern he established during his first term in office (2004–9) of rarely moving beyond the mid-point of the positions of the largest member states. Although Barroso asserts defiantly that the Commission is the 'real economic government' of Europe, it is clear that a mixture of the European Council, eurozone summits, the Eurogroup and the ECB (and not least their supporting civil servants) has already assumed that role. In autumn 2011, Barroso did confront Berlin by advocating the adoption of eurobonds, but then only under an implicit threat that some in the Parliament might push for a motion of censure against the Commission if it refused to act.

A further, potentially very important, consequence of the eurozone crisis is the growing and very visible intermingling and interdependence of the national and European levels in EU politics. The fates of the governments of the five member states most affected by the crisis to date – Greece, Ireland, Portugal, Italy and Spain – have all been directly and dramatically shaped by the crisis in ways already described. None of the five governing parties or coalitions survived in power. Even in other countries, not directly in the firing line, the solutions to the crisis adopted at EU level have proved highly controversial, destabilizing sitting governments. In Slovakia, approval of adjustments to the EFSF agreement divided the governing coalition, and after their initial rejection by the country's parliament in October 2011, led to the calling of an early general election. In Finland, the same question was a key issue in the April 2011 general election and made the subsequent formation of a new government extremely difficult.

The growing interdependence of national and European politics within the eurozone is a reflection, ironically, of the success of EMU and the single market in creating a set of economic forces that now transcend national frontiers and operate on a continental scale. However, whilst the barrier-free European economy is increasingly transnational (backed by a supranational monetary policy within the eurozone), responsibility for macro-economic policy and the organization of political accountability in Europe remain primarily national: in short, monetary union is not mirrored by a fiscal or political union. As the eurozone crisis plays out, the near impossibility of maintaining this mismatch has become more and more apparent. Different players have advocated different ways of resolving this tension – whether through the break-up of the eurozone, the mutualization of public debt, the imposition of de facto federal control of national budgets or the emergence of the ECB as a lender of last resort for governments. However, none of these radical options has been adopted. Instead, the centre of gravity of policy-making at European level has sought simultaneously to avoid any national default, the departure of any eurozone state, the development of a bigger Union Budget, the institution of a supranational bail-out fund, the transfer of responsibility for imposing fiscal discipline from collective action by governments to an independent central authority, the possibility of the systematic financing of national debt and deficits by the common central bank, or the adoption of genuinely binding commitments to thorough-going domestic economic reform. Although there has been movement in some of these directions – notably through greater central coordination of national fiscal policies – every step has been cautious, ambiguous and uncertain in its effects. It remains to be seen whether the pragmatic, piecemeal approach so far adopted will eventually resolve the current crisis – by far the biggest political, as well as economic, crisis to face the European Union in its six-decade history – or prevent it from happening again in some form in the future.

Further reading: Michael Mitsopoulos and Theodore Pelagidis, *Understanding the Crisis in Greece: from Boom to Bust*, 2011.

'Ever closer union'

The words 'ever closer union' have featured as the first indent of the preamble of the **Treaty of Rome** since its signature in March 1957. The member states declared themselves 'determined to lay the foundations of an ever closer union among the peoples of Europe'. Since the 1992 **Maastricht Treaty**, the phrase has also appeared in the last indent of the preamble of the Treaty on European Union (TEU), where the member states are 'resolved to continue the process of creating an ever closer union among the peoples of Europe, in which decisions are taken as closely as possible to the citizen in accordance with the principle of **subsidiarity**'.

Critics of the European Union often cite the commitment to an 'ever closer union' as evidence that its architects intended European integration to be not only a one-way process – which is indisputable – but one without limit, thus leading progressively to the creation of a federal state. Defenders of the Union point out, in return, that the 'ever closer union' is envisaged 'among the peoples', rather than among the states, of Europe. This suggests that the intermingling of interests and identities which integration promotes is expected to proceed on a voluntary basis, with the grain of public opinion, rather than against it. In any case, they note, the preambles of the **Treaties** have minimal legal standing: the limits of integration are defined later in those texts and depend on the powers (or **competence**) which the member states themselves choose to confer upon the Union.

The implicit ambiguity of the words 'ever closer union' would appear to be deliberate. Jean François Deniau (1928–2007), a member of the French delegation to the negotiation of the Treaty of Rome (and subsequently a European Commissioner), claims to have authored the preamble of the treaty. He writes in his memoirs that the phrase 'succeeded in escaping from the quasi-religious debate between a federal Europe and a Europe of nations or states. *Vive le mouvement.* We might not know exactly where we were going, but at least we were on the way' (*Survivre*, 2006).

Excessive deficit procedure (EDP)

One of the **convergence criteria** to be met by member states under the provisions on **Economic and Monetary Union** (EMU), introduced by the 1992 **Maastricht Treaty**, is the avoidance of 'excessive' deficits in levels of planned or actual public expenditure in relation to revenue (Article 126 TFEU). This requirement applies both in advance of entry into stage three of EMU – the adoption of the single currency and a single monetary policy – and thereafter. The 'reference values' for this purpose, defined in **Protocol** 12 to the **Treaties**, are that net borrowing by national, regional and local government, plus social security funds, should normally be no more than three per cent of a country's gross domestic product (GDP) in any year, and total government debt no more than 60 per cent of its GDP. However, the wording of this obligation is deliberately evasive: there are exemptions if a state's annual budget deficit has 'declined substantially and continuously' and comes close to three per cent or if the excess is only 'temporary' and still close to three per cent, whilst the national debt ceiling can also be exceeded if the level 'is sufficiently diminishing and approaching [60 per cent] at a satisfactory pace' (Article 126(2) TFEU). The question of whether the budget deficit 'exceeds government investment expenditure' may also be taken into account, as may 'all other relevant factors, including the medium-term economic and budgetary position of the Member State' (Article 126(3) TFEU).

Under the EDP, as set out in Article 126 TFEU, the **European Commission** has an obligation to 'monitor the development of the budgetary situation and of the stock of government debt' in each country, 'with a view to identifying gross errors' and preparing a report on any member state that fails, or looks likely to fail, to stay within the three per cent and 60 per cent limits. Member states are required to report their planned and actual levels of deficits and debt 'promptly and regularly' to the Commission. Any report from the Commission on a member state is discussed first in the **Economic and Financial Committee** (EFC) of senior national officials. Thereafter, the

Commission takes an official view on whether a member state has an excessive deficit. If the Commission concludes that such a deficit exists, it will address an opinion to the **Council of Ministers** to that effect. The **Ecofin Council** (of EU finance ministers) then considers the opinion and decides formally whether an excessive deficit exists. If the existence of such a deficit is confirmed by the Council, the latter will make recommendations to the member state in question about how to remedy the situation.

If a member state that has entered stage three of EMU ignores these recommendations, sanctions may be applied. The Council may give it notice to take defined deficit-reduction measures 'within a specified time limit'. If this fails to elicit the required response, the Council may follow up by more concrete action, notably the obligation to make 'a non-interest-bearing deposit of an appropriate size' available to the Union until the excessive deficit is corrected or the imposition of 'fines of an appropriate size'. (Withdrawal of lending facilities from the **European Investment Bank** (EIB) is also listed as a possible sanction against the state in question.) Under Article 126(13) TFEU, decisions taken by the Council under the EDP are adopted by **qualified majority voting** (QMV), excluding any vote by the state under consideration. The EDP is considered to be an element of the **Stability and Growth Pact** (SGP) – a set of political and legal commitments first adopted in June 1997 – which guides member states in their approach to the fiscal obligations of membership of stage-three of EMU.

Of the 27 EU member states, only Luxembourg has not so far, at some time since the system came into operation, been found to have an excessive deficit. At the time of writing, in December 2011, all but four member states – Estonia, Finland, Luxembourg and Sweden – have excessive deficits, including 14 of the 17 **eurozone** states. However, at no stage has any sanction been applied to any state for having annual deficit above three per cent of GDP or a national debt above 60 per cent. A pattern of flexible interpretation of the rules has been evident from the start. In what was a surprisingly uncontroversial move, the outstanding Council decisions to the effect that excessive deficits existed in Austria, Belgium, France, Germany, Italy, Portugal, Spain, Sweden and the United Kingdom were all abrogated in May 1998, as part of the decision to move to stage three of EMU. Then, in November 2003, the French and German governments succeeded in preventing the Council adopting a recommendation from the Commission that they both reduce their deficits by 0.5 per cent of GDP the following year. Germany's move to the 'laxist' camp significantly reduced the authority of the Commission in seeking to enforce the EDP, which was in effect held in 'abeyance', and it weakened the position of other fiscally orthodox eurozone member states – notably Austria, Belgium, Finland, Luxembourg and the Netherlands – in holding the line. The Commission brought an action against the Council in the **European Court of Justice** (ECJ). However, in its ruling of July 2004 (Case C-27/04), the Court found that since no formal decision had been taken by the Council, the Commission's action was inadmissible.

Ironically, the effects of the November 2003 non-decision were concealed by the general improvement in public finances which accompanied the buoyant growth in much of the European economy during the mid-2000s: the average budget deficit in the eurozone states fell from 2.5 to 0.7 per cent of GDP, and the average national debt from 70.0 to 66.2 per cent, over the three years to 2007. When the Commission produced a proposal to strengthen the operation of the EDP in September 2004, it secured little support from governments.

Once the economic and financial crisis hit the European economy in 2008–9, it was clear that the EDP had already become a largely technical exercise without significant political effect. Public finances among the eurozone states deteriorated rapidly, with budget deficit and national debt levels rising to averages of 6.0 and 80.2 per cent of GDP respectively by 2010. The scale of the economic downturn was so great that the application of sanctions against offending countries would have been politically impossible, as well as simply exacerbating the crisis. There were specific cases where greater fiscal discipline in the mid-2000s would have made a difference – notably in Greece and Portugal, the two countries which ran deficits above 3.0 per cent in 2007 and triggered the **eurozone debt crisis**. However, the fact that four additional countries ran up deficits above 3.0 per cent in 2008, and eight more in 2009, said relatively little about the previous management of their public finances.

As a result of the developing eurozone debt crisis, the EU heads of government concluded, under pressure from Germany and the European Commission, that renewed efforts should be made to strengthen the SGP in general, and the EDP in particular. In March 2010, the **President of the European Council**, Herman Van Rompuy, was invited to chair a 'task force' of EU finance ministers (in effect the Ecofin Council), in order to design strengthened arrangements for '**European economic governance**'. The Commission, sensing that its **right of initiative** in legislative matters was being circumvented, issued similar proposals to those emerging within the Van Rompuy task force, in September 2010. The Commission's package of five **regulations** and one **directive** quickly became known as the legislative 'Six Pack' on economic governance. These measures were adopted, after long negotiations in the Council – and in four cases jointly with the Parliament, where the **co-decision procedure** applied – in October 2011.

The key change introduced by the Six Pack to the EDP was to alter the decision-making procedure in the Council, so that henceforth a 'reverse' qualified majority will apply to votes on Commission recommendations on measures to be taken to correct a member state's excessive deficit. In future, the Commission proposal will be adopted unless a qualified majority in the Council actively opposes it. In the words of the Commission, this should make 'the enforcement of the rules stricter and more automatic' and thus 'more dissuasive and credible'. However, the initial decision in the Council to find that a member state's deficit is 'excessive' remains by positive QMV, as foreseen in Article 126(13) TFEU.

The assessment of whether an excessive deficit exists has also been made more stringent, by taking greater account of accumulated national debt. If a member state has a debt level above 60 per cent of GDP, even if its budget deficit is below three per cent, it will be deemed to run an excessive deficit, unless it is reducing that debt by at least one-twentieth each year (averaged over three years). Finally, the sanctions available for particularly serious cases of non-compliance with the rules are specified as a non-interest-bearing deposit of 0.2 per cent of the member state's GDP, which could then be converted into a fine. However, the imposition of such sanctions remains subject to conventional QMV.

In parallel to these reforms, the impact of which has yet to be tested, the Six Pack has established a new mechanism for guiding each member state's fiscal situation before it falls into an excessive deficit. This process, adopted under Article 121(4) TFEU, aims to strengthen (what is now known as) the 'preventive arm' of the SGP – as opposed to the latter's 'corrective arm', namely the EDP. Henceforth, each member state will be assigned a 'medium-term budgetary objective' by the Council (on the basis of a Commission proposal). This will include an 'expenditure benchmark', in effect capping the country's annual rise in public spending at a rate consistent with its overall economic growth prospects. If a member state consistently fails to follow this expenditure path, it may be subject to sanctions (in the form of a non-interest-bearing deposit of 0.2 per cent of GDP, adopted by reverse QMV).

A third component of the Six Pack is the introduction of a new 'excessive imbalances procedure', which aims to provide an 'early warning system', based on a scoreboard of ten indicators, of emerging stresses within individual eurozone economies. The idea is to look at issues other than deficits and debt, such as developing asset bubbles or trade imbalances, which can have a major impact on the stability of eurozone economies but were largely ignored in the 2000s. Based on Article 121(6) TFEU, this procedure is intended to allow the Council, on the basis of a Commission recommendation, to force any state to adjust its economic policies, on the basis of a Corrective Action Plan, or face a sanction for non-compliance (of a non-interest-bearing deposit of 0.1 per cent of GDP, which may be converted into a fine).

Exchange-Rate Mechanism (ERM)
Introduced as part of the **European Monetary System** (EMS) in January 1979, the Exchange-Rate Mechanism was devised as a means of minimizing fluctuations among the currencies of EC member states. Each participating currency was given a central exchange rate against the **European Currency Unit** (ECU), which in turn allowed a grid of bilateral central rates to be established covering all participating currencies. Each currency was allowed to fluctuate against the others by an agreed margin around these bilateral central rates: if it approached its top or bottom limit, a 'divergence indicator' was triggered and national central banks would intervene on exchange markets to bring the two currencies back into line. They would do this by bilateral intervention or coordinated multilateral intervention through the **European Monetary Cooperation Fund** (EMCF). Other measures, notably adjustments in short-term interest rates, might also be taken by the national monetary authorities. If a currency could not be held within its agreed margins, a realignment of the central rates could be negotiated between all the governments and central banks, through the EC **Monetary Committee.**

The ERM was the successor to two similar, but less successful, systems for limiting currency fluctuations – known as the 'Snake' and the 'Snake in the Tunnel' – which operated from 1971 onwards, following the 1970 **Werner Report** on **Economic and Monetary Union** (EMU). When the ERM was launched in 1979, eight currencies took part: the Belgian and Luxembourg francs, the French franc, the Danish krone, the Deutschmark, the Dutch guilder, the Italian lira and the Irish punt. Only five of these had survived in the previous Snake in the Tunnel. The pound sterling did not participate, nor did the Greek drachma (after Greece joined the Community in 1981). The Spanish peseta joined the ERM in June 1989, the pound sterling in October 1990, and the Portuguese escudo in April 1992. All currencies were allowed to fluctuate within a margin of 2.25 per cent on either side of their bilateral central rates (the 'narrow band'), except the peseta, lira, escudo and pound sterling, which took advantage of a 'broad band' of 6 per cent, which could be negotiated on entry.

Currency speculation on an unprecedented scale on 16 September 1992 – known as '**Black Wednesday**' – caused the pound sterling and the lira to leave the ERM and the peseta to be devalued by five per cent. This speculation was prompted, at least in part, by the possibility of a 'no' vote in the **French referendum on the Maastricht Treaty** four days later. In the recriminations that followed, Germany, the country whose currency and monetary policy had in effect become the anchor of the system, was blamed for maintaining high interest rates whilst refusing to revalue its currency. Conversely, the United Kingdom was criticized for having chosen unilaterally to bring the pound into the ERM at an unsustainably overvalued exchange rate. Almost a year later, on 2 August 1993, further large-scale speculation came close to destroying the ERM. The wide band was increased to 15 per cent and extended to all participating currencies (although the Germans and the Dutch agreed bilaterally to retain the narrow band between their two currencies). On this basis, the majority of currencies were able to move back to their pre-August 1993 alignments. The Austrian schilling joined the ERM in January 1995 and the Finnish markka in October 1996, whilst the lira rejoined in November 1996. The Greek drachma joined in March 1998. The Swedish krona has never joined the ERM and the pound has not rejoined.

During the early history of the ERM, realignments occurred relatively frequently, as the system grappled with high inflation and economic divergences across Europe. From March 1979 to April 1986, there were nine realignments, six of which involved three or more currencies. The dramatic realignment crisis of March 1983, when French President **François Mitterrand** chose to abandon Socialist economic policies in favour of monetary stability, proved to be a critical turning-point. From then on, the pursuit of a *franc fort* by France strengthened the central role of Germany within the system. Between May 1986 and August 1992, a 'harder ERM' emerged: during this period, there were only three realignments (one of which involved three currencies). This second phase was shattered by the events of 1992–3. With the new, very broad bands of 15 per cent, there was hardly any need for further realignments.

Before 1992, the ERM was widely credited with having achieved its primary goal of creating monetary stability among participating states, and in particular with having helped to shield their economies from the side effects of fluctuations in the value of the dollar. The ERM removed the temptation to engage in competitive devaluation. It also contributed to economic convergence by serving to lessen interest-rate differentials and in general acted as an external discipline of which member states were able to take advantage in the fight against inflation. In effect, by locking onto the Deutschmark – the only currency never to have been realigned downwards – the other participants were importing the twin features of German monetary policy: a hard currency and a priority for low inflation. Competitiveness would henceforth be achieved through 'disinflation', rather than devaluation. The effects were impressive, with the average inflation rate of ERM members falling from 12 per cent in 1980 to 4 per cent in 1993.

The instability which hit the EMS during 1992–3 was fuelled by the growing association (in the eyes of markets and commentators) of any currency's successful narrow-band ERM membership with its prospects of qualifying as a first-wave entrant to stage three of EMU, when the single currency would be adopted. Ironically, the countdown to EMU, sanctioned by the 1992 **Maastricht Treaty**, helped destabilize the ERM and made it a much looser arrangement. This came at a time when the core roles of the

Deutschmark and Bundesbank monetary policy were rendered much more complicated by the side effects of **German reunification**. The situation was resolved by accelerating the move to EMU, whilst downgrading the exchange-rate stability priority for those countries whose performance otherwise (in respect of inflation, interest rates and public finances) pointed to the sustainability of membership.

As the ERM has been part of the ***acquis communautaire*** since 1979, all states acceding to the European Union since that date have been expected to join it, although not necessarily immediately. In practice, however, Sweden has refused to do so, without sanction. Observance of the 'normal fluctuation margins' within the ERM for at least two years is also one of the formal **convergence criteria** that must be met by a member state before it can proceed to stage three of EMU.

In 1997, the impending move to stage three (by 11 of the 13 member states within the ERM in January 1999) prompted EU finance ministers and **central bank governors** to assess the future of the ERM. A new 'ERM II' – still officially called the Exchange-Rate Mechanism – was set up to govern the relationship between the **euro**, the single currency which succeeded the ECU, and other currencies within the EU. A resolution adopted by the **European Council** in Amsterdam in June 1997 provided that currencies outside the **eurozone** would be permitted to fluctuate within 15 per cent of their central rate against the euro. (They may request a narrower band on an ad hoc basis.) Supported by the **European Central Bank** (ECB), intervention to support a currency at the margin is now 'automatic and unlimited', provided that this does not conflict with the ECB's goal of price stability. (Intra-marginal intervention is also still possible.) As a result, ERM II differs from the original ERM in two key respects: it accepts a wide fluctuation band as normal, but backs it with a stronger commitment to intervene from the centre. The Amsterdam European Council resolution also stated that membership of ERM II was 'voluntary', although those legally committed to join the single currency 'can be expected to join the mechanism' within an undefined timescale. An agreement between the ECB and national central banks in September 1998 (updated in March 2006) elaborates the detail of the ERM II arrangements.

Initially, the membership of ERM II was very limited. The Danish krone and Greek drachma were the only two participating currencies from 1999 to 2000, and the Danish krone was alone from 2001 to 2004. However, the accession of ten new member states to the EU in May 2004 gave new vitality to membership. The Estonian kroon, Lithuanian litas and Slovene tolar joined ERM II in June 2004; the Latvian lats, Cypriot pound and Maltese lira followed suit in May 2005; and the Slovak koruna entered in November 2005. (Slovenia, Cyprus, Malta, Slovakia and Estonia have subsequently moved to stage three, adopting the euro.) In March 2007, the first realignment within ERM II took place, with an 8.5 per cent revaluation of the Slovak koruna, being negotiated by member-state governments and national central banks through the EU **Economic and Financial Committee** (EFC), the successor to the Monetary Committee.

Those EU currencies still outside the mechanism are the Polish zloty, Czech koruna, Hungarian forint, Bulgarian lev and Romanian leu, as well as the pound sterling and Swedish krona. These currencies may float freely or pursue some other exchange-rate arrangement, such as a 'crawling peg' or using another currency (such as the dollar) as an anchor. In recent years, Hungary has tried to act as if it were part of ERM II, the Czech Republic has pursued a managed float, with the euro as a reference, and Poland has allowed a free float.

Exit clause

Introduced by the **Lisbon Treaty**, the so-called 'exit clause' provides member states for the first time with a formal mechanism by which they may leave the European Union. Article 50 TEU states: 'Any Member State may decide to withdraw from the Union in accordance with its own constitutional requirements.' Once the state in question officially notifies the **European Council** (of heads of government) of its intention to leave, the **European Commission** will, on the basis of 'guidelines' given by the European Council and a mandate from the **Council of Ministers**, seek to negotiate an agreement with that country on 'the arrangements for its withdrawal, taking account of the framework for its future relationship with the Union'. If an agreement is reached, it will then need to be confirmed by the Council of Ministers, after obtaining the **consent** of the **European Parliament**. If no agreement is possible, the **Treaties** automatically cease to apply to the state in question two years after it gave its original notification of intention to leave.

The Council acts by **qualified majority voting** (QMV) in taking decisions on this issue, although a 'super majority' is required. Under the 'double majority' system introduced by the Lisbon Treaty (Article 238 TFEU), 72 per cent of member states, representing at least 65 per cent of the Union's population, must vote in favour of any proposal (as opposed to 55 per cent of states, representing at least 65 per cent of the population, normally). The departing member state is debarred from participating in discussions or decisions on its exit, whether in the Council of Ministers or the European Council, although in the European Parliament, it would appear that its Members may still vote on the matter. If the country involved subsequently wishes to rejoin the Union, it may do so, but its application will be dealt with under the routine **accession** procedure, a process which might take some years.

So far, no member state has ever sought to leave the European Union, although **Greenland** – which is a part of the territory of Denmark, but enjoying a high degree of devolution – was allowed to withdraw in July 1986, following a **referendum** on the question. In practice, any country that wished to secede could always do so, quite legally, under the Vienna Convention on the Law of Treaties, simply by revoking its accession treaty. However, without orderly arrangements for departure, any exit from the Union would, as Andrew Duff has written, 'be an ad hoc exercise . . . almost certain to leave the departing country's relationship with its erstwhile partners in a sorry state' (*The Struggle for Europe's Constitution*, 2005). Until the **Convention on the Future of Europe** in 2002–3, there had been scarcely any mainstream debate about a possible 'exit clause', although in May 1994, Alain Lamassoure, then French minister for European affairs, had advocated 'a right of secession, with a procedure and a status for any state which decided to leave the Union'. Some strong integrationists – as well as the relatively few Eurosceptics – who participated in the Convention, took the view that a formal process for departure should be written into the proposed **European Constitution**. The draft presented to the Convention contained such a provision, which – although opposed by 41 members of the Convention and attracting 35 amendments – survived largely unchanged into the final text. It was then transposed into the Lisbon Treaty, which entered into force in December 2009.

Many commentators argue that the right to leave the European Union is an important factor in preventing the latter ever developing into a federal state. No federation in the democratic world provides formally for the possibility of secession. In its ruling on the Lisbon Treaty in June 2009, the German Federal Constitutional Court stated: 'The right to withdraw underlines the member states' **sovereignty** and shows . . . that the current state of development of the European Union does not transgress the boundary towards a state within the meaning of international law. If a member state can withdraw . . . the process of European integration is not irreversible.'

F

Factortame case

The Factortame case *(R* v *Secretary of State for Transport, ex parte Factortame Ltd,* Case 213/89) was a landmark ruling by the judicial committee of the House of Lords (now the Supreme Court), following a reference to the **European Court of Justice** (ECJ), by which for the first time in British history an Act of Parliament was declared void in the United Kingdom courts on the grounds that it contravened **EU law.** The case served to underline both the **primacy** of European law and the importance attached by the ECJ to the removal of any impediment to an individual's power to assert rights arising from such law.

The case arose when Factortame, a Spanish-controlled fishing company, sought judicial review of certain provisions of the British Merchant Shipping Act 1988, which prevented foreign ships registered as British vessels from fishing in UK waters. The system of quotas and total allowable catches under the **Common Fisheries Policy** (CFP) made it attractive to seek British registration, and until the 1988 Act the rules for such registration were relatively lax. The plaintiff alleged that the new restrictions were both discriminatory and contrary to its right to **freedom of establishment** under the **Treaties**. The High Court of Justice of England and Wales granted Factortame an order that the relevant part of the Act be disapplied. However, both the Court of Appeal and the House of Lords took the view that a British court had no power to order a waiver from the provisions of the Act. The House of Lords then referred the case to the ECJ, as it was required to do under Article 234 EC, now Article 267 TFEU, which states that a court 'against whose decision there is no judicial remedy under national law' must make such a reference when its judgement depends on a question of EU law.

The European Court ruled in June 1990 that unless a power of waiver existed at national level, the effectiveness of European law would be impaired. As a result, the House of Lords then ruled in favour of Factortame and the relevant part of the Merchant Shipping Act was struck down. In the ruling, the Lords stated that the provisions of the European Communities Act 1972 giving precedence to European over domestic law in the UK had the same effect as if such provisions had been replicated in every subsequent Act of Parliament. It was open to Parliament to rescind or qualify that provision, but it needed to do so explicitly. It follows that, as Trevor Hartley has written, 'Union law will always prevail [in the UK] unless Parliament clearly and expressly states in a future Act that the latter is to override Union law' (*The Foundations of European Union Law*, Oxford, 2010).

Failure to act

In parallel to provision for the judicial review of the legality of legislative or administrative acts taken by the EU **institutions** (Article 263 TFEU), the **Treaties** provide a mechanism by which the *inaction* of the institutions, in defiance of a treaty obligation, can also be challenged. Under Article 265 TFEU, the individual EU institutions or a member state can bring an action before the **European Court of Justice** (ECJ) alleging the failure to act of another institution or body. Originally, only the **European Commission** and the **Council of Ministers** were subject to potential proceedings for failure to act (Article 175 EEC), but subsequent treaty changes have broadened that obligation very considerably. Article 265 TFEU now reads:

> *Should the* ***European Parliament****, the* ***European Council****, the Council, the Commission or the* ***European Central Bank****, in infringement of this Treaty, fail to act, the Member States and the other institutions of the Union may bring an action before the Court of Justice to have the infringement established. This Article shall apply, under the same conditions, to bodies, offices and* ***agencies*** *of the Union which fail to act.*

In the eyes of the European Court, proceedings taken to force the adoption of an act are simply the equal and opposite of proceedings which may be taken to annul an illegal act. The ECJ has ruled that Articles 263 and 265 'merely prescribe one and the same method of recourse', subject to the so-called 'unity principle' in the way they are handled.

The institution or body concerned must first be 'called upon to act' by the plaintiff, and thereafter it has two months within which to 'define its position'. If it does not, an action may be brought within a further two months. An institution or body that is found by the Court to have failed to act 'shall be required to take the necessary measures' (Article 266 TFEU).

Very few actions have ever been successfully brought under Article 265. This is partly because the Treaties tend to give the European Commission considerable discretion over how it uses its powers. Equally, the obligation on any institution merely to 'define its position' may, in the way the Court has chosen to interpret this requirement, obviate the need for the actual adoption of a **legal act** on the matter in question.

The most important case so far was that brought by the **European**

Parliament in 1983 against the Council for the latter's failure to enact a common **transport policy**, as required by Articles 3, 74 and 75 EEC at the time (*European Parliament* v *Council*, Case 13/83). In May 1985, the Court found partially in the Parliament's favour: it agreed that the Council had failed to act in respect of specific rules for international transport (such as non-resident carriers) referred to in the **Treaty of Rome**, but ruled that the general obligation to establish a common transport policy was insufficiently precise to be enforceable, and that it would be inappropriate for the Court to attempt to spell out what it might mean in practice. In effect, an institution could not be held to have failed to act where it was free to adopt a discretionary act. Rather, a failure to act needed to relate to defined measures that were sufficiently precise 'to allow the Court to determine whether their adoption, or failure to adopt them, is lawful'. Moreover, the ECJ added that an institution need only take action to fulfil its obligations within 'a reasonable period', unless an exact deadline is specified; it also declined to clarify what consequences follow if no action is taken. The Council's subsequent willingness to pass transport legislation seems to have had as much to do with its acceptance that **qualified majority voting** (QMV) should apply in this area – formally it had been introduced in 1966 but was then quickly frustrated by the **Luxembourg Compromise** – as with the Court's ruling.

In practice, there seems to be no sanction for the Court to impose in the case of failure to act. The obligation on an institution to 'take the necessary measures' to comply with an ECJ ruling does not specify the form or content of such measures. Equally, the Court's power under Article 260 TFEU, introduced by the Maastricht Treaty, to impose a 'lump sum or penalty payment' on a member state found to be in default of its treaty obligations does not extend to the Council as the collective embodiment of the member states, or to the other institutions.

Federalism and confederalism

Federalism can be defined as a multi-layered system of government in which the highest level enjoys exclusive **competence** in one or more policy fields, and in which some decisions at that level can be taken without the unanimous agreement of all the component parts. Confederalism, by contrast, is a multi-layered arrangement in which the highest level enjoys exclusive competence in no area, and all decisions at that level have to be taken unanimously.

The two concepts are closely linked, in that historically confederations have often evolved into federations, although the one is not a precondition for the other. The United States before 1789 was a confederation; since its Constitution took effect in that year, it has been a federation. **Switzerland** moved from confederal to federal status in 1848, even if it still styles itself officially as a confederation. The confederal German Bund established in 1815 became the federal North German Bund in 1867 (with the expulsion of Austria and the new dominance of Prussia), and a notionally federal structure was maintained under the Weimar Republic after the First World War. The distinction in German between a confederation of states, a *Staatenbund*, and a federal state, a *Bundesstaat*, was well established in the nineteenth century.

Today, eight of the ten largest countries in the world by area are federations – even if not all of them are democracies – reflecting the convenience of the federal structure as a means of combining coherence and diversity in a single political system. As early as 1885, A. V. Dicey wrote in *The Law of the Constitution* that federalism was 'a political contrivance intended to reconcile national unity and power with the maintenance of states' rights'. Smaller countries with federal structures tend also to be marked by a variety of linguistic communities, each of which needs to be accommodated within a system that allows them the necessary degree of autonomy. Federalism is not always successful in holding such divergent groups together, as the recent experiences of Czechoslovakia and **Yugoslavia** testify (although in both of these latter cases, the components of the federation were escaping from an undemocratic past).

Within federations, the distribution of power between the centre and the component parts – usually states, regions or provinces – varies considerably from case to case and may change substantially over time. The areas reserved to the central government normally include at least defence, foreign policy, external trade, citizenship, immigration and the management of the currency. The degree of centralization of policies for taxation, public spending, policing, transport, education, welfare and the environment will depend on a variety of political, geographic and cultural factors (including linguistic issues). Most federations have a single currency, a central bank to administer a common monetary policy, a supreme court to uphold certain common rights and to adjudicate in disputes between levels of government, and a bicameral parliament in which the upper chamber is composed of representatives of the states, regions or provinces.

Within the European Union, Germany, Austria and Belgium currently have federal systems of government. As its title suggests, in 1949, the new Federal Republic of Germany was given a more distinctively federal character than its Weimar predecessor, to guard against any recurrence of the concentration of power that had marked the intervening Third Reich. (Its ten *Länder* were supplemented by six from the former German Democratic Republic through **German reunification** in October 1990.) Austria was re-established with nine *Länder* after the Second World War. Belgium moved from being a unitary state to a federal one through a succession of constitutional reforms between

1970 and 1993, in order to absorb the deepening linguistic divide within the country. (Under the Belgian system, three regions and three linguistic communities operate in parallel.)

In recent decades, in response to the growth of regionalism, several unitary states within the EU have chosen to devolve significant powers either to a general regional structure (as in France and Italy) or to specific regions or 'nations' with separate historic or linguistic identities (as in the United Kingdom and Spain). Formally speaking, however, devolution can be revoked by the central government, without formal constitutional impediment, although politically this might be very difficult in practice. Devolution is logically quite distinct from federalism, although – as in the Belgian case – the one may lead to the other. Under devolution, as Vernon Bogdanor has written, 'the powers of the subordinate legislature are conferred by the centre which retains residual constitutional authority, whereas under a federal system the powers of both the centre and the provinces are determined by the [country's] constitution' (*The Blackwell Encyclopaedia of Political Science*, 1987).

Notions of federalism exercised a powerful influence upon many of the pioneers of European integration in the 1940s and early 1950s. In continental Europe, the two world wars had done much to discredit the nation state as the basis for international relations. Federalist ideas, ambitions and assumptions were important in the thinking of individuals such as **Jean Monnet** and **Altiero Spinelli**, and they are to be found throughout the founding **Treaties** of the **European Communities**. The architects of these treaties hoped to create a new type of international organization that would move beyond traditional, non-binding cooperation between nation states that remained entirely sovereign. In effect they wanted to institute a novel multi-level system of government on a continental scale, in which sovereignty would be shared between the nation state and a new tier of authority located above it. It is precisely this characteristic which made – and still makes – the European Communities, now the European Union, quite different to any other international organization or any other sovereignty-sharing experience among democracies to date. In particular, high importance was attached to the creation of free-standing European institutions whose actions would have the force of law and whose policy remit would include some areas of exclusive **competence**, and where member states might decide on some issues together by majority voting, with relations between the levels of government regulated by an independent judicial authority. The role of the **European Commission**, the legislative power of the **Council of Ministers**, the creation of a **European Court of Justice** (ECJ) and provision for a directly-elected **European Parliament** all reflected this.

The architects of the Treaties appreciated, however, that it would not be possible – either politically or practically – to jump from totally independent nation states to a federal system in one move. As **Robert Schuman** put it in May 1950, Europe would 'not be built in a day or as a single structure', but rather through 'practical achievements [*réalisations concrètes*] that first create a sense of common purpose [*une solidarité de fait*]'. Certain features both of the nation state and of confederalism would need to coexist with the federal component of the new system, even if over time the latter should become more important. Hence the acceptance that, for example, the areas of Community competence would be limited, that **unanimity** among member states might continue in several major fields of Council decision-making, and that the power of the **European Parliament** should (at least initially) be heavily circumscribed.

From the start, the Communities represented a hybrid structure and one which political commentators found hard to define. The mixture of federal and confederal elements resulted in its often being described as '*sui generis*' or unique, defying conventional political science categorization. As Murray Forsyth has put it (see below), the new system perhaps most closely approximated those confederations which became federations over time: it was located on 'the spectrum between interstate and intrastate relations' and might be styled a 'contractual union of states'. The attempt to define the European Union as 'of federal type' in the draft **Maastricht Treaty** was defeated when the words were removed at British insistence.

In analysing the European institutions, the concepts of **supranationalism and intergovernmentalism** are closely linked with those of federalism and confederalism respectively. There has been a constant tension between supranational and intergovernmental philosophies and forces. The institutional history of the European Union is essentially the process by which the federal or supranational character of the new political system has grown more pronounced over time – through extensions of Community competence, the rise of majority voting in the Council of Ministers and the gradual sharing of the latter's legislative power with the European Parliament, all supported by the self-assured assertion of judicial authority by the ECJ. This process has not been without resistance, whether on the part of civil servants in national governments, major political figures – notably French President **Charles de Gaulle** in the 1960s and British prime minister **Margaret Thatcher** in the 1980s – or indeed swathes of the general public, witnessed in the outcomes of several **referenda** on Europe since 1992.

Further reading: Murray Forsyth, *Unions of States: The Theory and Practice of Confederation*, 1981; Kalypso Nikolaidis and Robert Howse (editors), *The Federal Vision*, 2001.

Finalités politiques

The phrase *finalités politiques* is sometimes used in EU political discourse to denote the ultimate goals of the European integration process and/or the institutional form which this process might take. For example, Anna Lindh, then Swedish foreign minister, noted in a speech to the **European Parliament** in March 2001: 'There will certainly be a debate on the long-term political goals of the Union – *les finalités politiques* – on constitutional issues, on a federation, on the division of responsibility between the Union's institutions and between the Union and the member states, and on the relationship between **enlargement** and deepening.'

Notwithstanding Lindh's use of the phrase, the notion of *finalités politiques* was invoked much more frequently in the first 30 years of the European integration than it has been in recent decades. This is probably due to two factors: the European Union's institutional structure is now more 'complete', as a result of successive treaty reforms starting in the mid-1980s, and the default language for discussion of such issues in political and academic circles is increasingly English, rather than French.

Fiscal Compact Treaty

The Fiscal Compact Treaty – formally known as the Treaty on Stability, Coordination and Governance in the **Economic and Monetary Union** (EMU) – is an intergovernmental agreement concluded outside the **Treaties** of the European Union, binding its signatories in their approach to macroeconomic policy-making in respect to EMU. It was negotiated in January 2012 and signed on 2 March 2012 by all 17 members of stage three of EMU, together with eight of the 10 member states that are currently outside the **eurozone** (the two exceptions being the Czech Republic and United Kingdom). The text is due to enter force on 1 January 2013, once it has been ratified by at least 12 of the 17 eurozone signatories. Any eurozone state failing to ratify the treaty will forfeit access, from March 2013, to any future emergency funding it may need from the **European Stability Mechanism** (ESM), created in response to the **eurozone debt crisis.**

The 'fiscal compact' at the heart of the treaty – the phrase was first used by Mario Draghi, the new President of the **European Central Bank** (ECB), speaking in the European Parliament in November 2011 – is a commitment by signatories that 'the budgetary position of the general government of [each] Contracting Party shall be balanced or in surplus'. This general obligation is specifically defined as meaning that the country's annual, cyclically-adjusted, 'structural deficit' will not exceed 0.5 per cent of its gross domestic product (GDP). This reference value would normally, by definition, be lower than the 3.0 per cent budget deficit ceiling already set down in the 1992 **Maastricht Treaty** and operationalised in the existing **excessive**

deficit procedure (EDP). However, where a country's overall national debt level is 'significantly below' the 60 per cent ceiling foreseen in the Maastricht Treaty, the annual deficit may rise to 1.0 per cent of GDP.

States with deficits above 0.5 per cent will follow a convergence path towards this goal negotiated with the EU institutions, on the basis of a proposal tabled by the **European Commission** and adopted by the **Council of Ministers**. Countries with national debts above 60 per cent of GDP must reduce them at a rate of (at least) one-twentieth per year. In 'exceptional circumstances', notably 'periods of severe economic downturn', these figures may be adjusted by the Council. Disputes relating to the application of the treaty may be taken to the **European Court of Justice** (ECJ), which is empowered, on behalf of the signatory states, to impose fines of up to 0.1 per cent of GDP on countries that fail to abide by certain of its obligations.

The 25 signatories to the Fiscal Compact Treaty undertake to support proposals or recommendations made by the Commission, when the latter considers that a state is 'in breach of the deficit criterion in the framework of an excessive deficit procedure', unless there is a qualified majority against them. In effect, this commitment helps underpin the move to so-called 'reverse' **qualified majority voting** (QMV) in the EDP and the **Stability and Growth Pact** (SGP) more widely, introduced for certain Council decisions by the 'Six Pack' legislation adopted in autumn 2011. The treaty also formalizes the existence of the new **Euro Summit,** established by the eurozone states in September 2011. These meetings 'shall take place when necessary, and at least twice a year', with the eight non-eurozone signatories able to attend at least once a year. The President of the Euro Summit will be appointed by simple majority of the eurozone heads of government 'at the same time as the European Council elects its President and for the same term of office'. (However, as the latter appointment is made by QMV, there is a potential asymmetry in the decision-making methods for the two posts.) The signatories to the treaty commit to transpose the central principles of the fiscal compact into national law, where such provisions must be 'of binding force and permanent character, preferably constitutional'. They also state their 'aim of incorporating the substance' of the treaty into 'the legal framework of the European Union' within five years.

Fontainebleau Agreement

The Fontainebleau Agreement of June 1984 marked the conclusion of the long-running **British Budget dispute** – a five-year argument over the size of the United Kingdom's net contribution to the **Budget** of the European Community. In recognition of the unusually low level of UK receipts from, compared with contribution to, the Budget, the **European Council** meeting (of heads of government) in Fontainebleau, outside Paris, agreed to grant

Britain a significant **abatement** – or rebate – on its payments towards the Community's **own resources**. The British prime minister, **Margaret Thatcher**, only secured the deal after a tense period of diplomatic brinkmanship: at one point, the UK in effect threatened to withhold payments to the Budget, and two earlier summits (in December 1983 and March 1984) were allowed to fail, as lower offers were refused. One meeting prompted the Greek Socialist prime minister, Andreas Papandreou, to say that 'it would be a great relief if Britain left the Community.'

Under the Fontainebleau formula, which is calculated annually, the UK gross contribution to the EU Budget is reduced by 66 per cent of the difference between its 'unabated' contribution and its receipts, subject to a number of technical qualifications. The resulting abatement is financed by the other member states in proportion to the size of their gross national income (GNI), the reference indicator used for budgetary calculations in the Union. To offset distortions, four other net contributors – Austria, Germany, the Netherlands and Sweden – benefit from a reduction of three-quarters in their share of the UK abatement (a kind of 'rebate on the rebate'). These countries also make lower contributions to the EU's system of **own resources** at source. In practice, approximately 60 per cent of the UK abatement is financed by France, Italy and Spain (in that order).

The Fontainebleau Agreement was generally regarded as a significant negotiating success for Thatcher and her Conservative government. It has since generated an average annual refund to the UK exchequer of some € 3.6 billion, totalling € 92.5 billion (in nominal terms) over 26 years. In 2010, Britain made gross payments to the EU Budget of € 18.5 billion, obtained receipts of € 6.6 billion, and enjoyed an abatement of € 3.6 billion.

When the UK secured the Fontainebleau deal, it was the poorest of the net contributors (with 90 per cent of average GDP per head), whereas now it is one of the richest (with 110 per cent). France and some other countries, supported at times by the **European Commission**, have used this change as an argument to try to reopen the abatement issue. However, as the technical origin of the British Budget problem lies in the unusual mismatch between the country's contributions and receipts, ironically, any rise in Britain's relative prosperity actually has the potential to make the problem more acute. In any case, because **unanimity** is still required in the Council for nearly all decisions on own resources and 'future financing' issues, the Fontainebleau deal has survived the move to multiannual 'financial perspectives' within the Union, starting in 1988. Successive British governments have declared the existing arrangement to be non-negotiable. When the financing of the most recent Multiannual Financial Framework (MFF) was being settled, the then British prime minister, **Tony Blair**, told the House of Commons in June 2005: 'The UK rebate will remain and we will not negotiate it away. Period.'

In fact, the current 2007–13 MFF deal, struck in December 2005 at the end of Blair's second and last UK **presidency** of the **Council of Ministers**, did involve a number of concessions by Britain. Blair came under huge pressure to excuse the new, poorer member states from central and eastern Europe from payment of their share of the abatement. The calculation of the latter has traditionally taken into account all expenditure internal to the Union, but he agreed that spending on the **structural funds** (including the **Cohesion Fund**) in the new member states would be exempted. As a result, the UK abatement should be about € 10 billion lower over the whole seven-year period than would otherwise be the case (some € 41 billion, rather € 51 billion), with the impact peaking 2011–13.

In its proposals (in June 2011) for the financing of the next MFF, covering the years 2014–20, the European Commission recommended that the existing UK abatement should be replaced by a series of annual lump-sum payments, the amounts of which would be agreed in advance. The 'correction mechanisms' for three of the four other member states currently benefiting from adjustments would also be replaced: Britain would receive € 3.6 billion a year, Germany € 2.5 billion, the Netherlands € 1.05 billion, and Sweden € 0.3 billion. Such an arrangement, the Commission argues, would be consistent with the Fontainebleau principle that 'any Member State sustaining a budgetary burden which is excessive in relation to its relative prosperity may benefit from a correction at the appropriate time.'

Foreign Affairs Council (FAC) and General Affairs Council (GAC)

The Foreign Affairs and General Affairs Councils are configurations of the EU **Council of Ministers** composed of member states' foreign ministers (FAC) and a mixture of their foreign and European affairs ministers (GAC). Usually, both Councils meet monthly, often back-to-back. The FAC addresses issues arising in the European Union's **Common Foreign and Security Policy** (CFSP) and other external policy areas, notably external trade policy, known as **Common Commercial Policy** (CCP), **development policy** and humanitarian aid. The **Lisbon Treaty** states that the FAC will 'elaborate the Union's external action on the basis of strategic guidelines laid down by the **European Council** [of heads of government] and ensure that the Union's action is consistent' (Article 16(6) TEU). The FAC meets periodically in the composition of defence or development ministers.

The principal task of the GAC, by contrast, is to attempt to provide some central political coordination within the Council system – to 'ensure consistency in the work of the different Council configurations' – as well as to 'prepare and ensure the follow-up to meetings of the European Council'. Article 2(2) of the Council's rules of procedure specifies that the GAC 'shall be responsible for overall coordination of policies, institutional and administrative questions, horizontal dossiers which affect several of the EU's policies, such as the Multi-annual Financial Framework (MFF) and **enlargement**, and any dossier entrusted to it by the European Council'. Meetings of both the FAC and GAC are prepared by **COREPER** II, with the **Political and Security Committee** (PSC) in practice taking the lead on most CFSP business. A General Affairs Group (GAG) feeds into COREPER on institutional questions.

From June 2002 to December 2009, when the Lisbon Treaty entered into force, the two Councils operated as one, as the 'General Affairs and External Relations Council' (GAERC). Before the 1992 **Maastricht Treaty**, there was a third formation, known as 'Foreign Ministers meeting in [**European**] **Political Cooperation**' (EPC), but once CFSP replaced EPC, this became unnecessary. All of these meetings were chaired by the foreign minister of the member state holding the rotating **presidency** of the Council, who was informally known as the 'president-in-office of the Council'. In an important innovation, the Lisbon Treaty has entrusted the chairmanship of the FAC to the **High Representative** for CFSP, although the foreign minister of the presidency country may still chair the GAC, with the latter now styled 'President of the Council'. Although notionally all Councils are and always have been equal, the existence and role of both the FAC and GAC is now specifically provided for in the **Treaties**. (The existence of other Council formations, such as the **Ecofin Council** (finance ministers) or the Agriculture Council, are defined by the European Council in a decision renewed periodically.) The High Representative, Catherine Ashton, convened back-to-back meetings of the FAC in the specific composition of defence and development ministers in December 2010, and intends to hold such meetings on a regular basis in the future.

When foreign ministers go to Brussels or Luxembourg for meetings of the FAC and GAC, they are usually accompanied by junior ministers specifically tasked with European affairs. Very often, the former take the lead in the FAC and the latter in the GAC, although there is no hard and fast rule. The rapid development of CFSP had made it more difficult for foreign ministers to find the time to involve themselves in the detailed coordination of Union business, across sectors, or specifically institutional issues, except on the most important or pressing of matters. However, the lower the level of ministerial representation in the GAC, the greater its potential difficulty in impacting on the work of more 'senior' configurations of the Council or in preparing that of the European Council.

Fouchet Plan

The Fouchet Plan of 1961–2 was an important, if unsuccessful, diplomatic initiative by the then French President, **Charles de Gaulle**, to alter the emerging institutional balance of the European Community away from the supranational model of the **founding fathers** and towards a looser, intergovernmental approach based on cooperation among 'sovereign' nation states. By proposing to create a new 'union of states', to parallel the existing Community in the foreign policy and defence sphere, the Fouchet Plan ostensibly offered to complete some of the unfinished political business left open by the failure of the **European Defence Community** (EDC) in 1954, and which the **Treaty of Rome** in 1957 had been careful to avoid. However, by casting this new political cooperation in a strictly intergovernmental mould, and then going on to suggest that some existing EC functions might be subsumed within the new Union, the plan raised the spectre of the progressive erosion of the supranational character of the Community and the frustration of its 'federal' institutional dynamic. Such institutional concerns were compounded by parallel fears that de Gaulle would attempt to use any putative European foreign and defence policy to promote the continent's independence from the Atlantic Alliance and US strategic interests. The General's desire to give Europe a stronger, more distinct voice on the international stage was seen as part of a wider Gaullist threat to Western stability and security.

In their reactions to the Fouchet Plan, the governments of **the Six** founding member states revealed both differing approaches to Europe's institutional design and competing visions of Europe's place in the world. As the French position hardened in the face of growing opposition, the Dutch and Belgian governments asserted that negotiations should be deferred until pro-Atlanticist Britain had been admitted to the Community. The discussions reached deadlock in April 1962 and were suspended, never to be resumed. The Fouchet debate revealed a deep clash between two competing concepts of European unity – based on **supranationalism and intergovernmentalism** – and its acrimonious failure set the Community on an unstable path until the resignation of de Gaulle seven years later.

In September 1960, at a press conferences in the Elysée Palace, the French President set out a plan for closer political cooperation in Europe which, in its scope and institutional form, echoed closely ideas he had developed during his 'wilderness years' of the Fourth Republic. He declared that 'ensuring regular cooperation between the states of western Europe is something which France considers desirable, possible and practicable in the political, economic, cultural and defence fields.' To promote this, he proposed 'regular organized concertation between governments', based on a new intergovernmental structure, meeting at the levels both of heads of government and foreign ministers, answerable to an assembly of national parliamentarians, and enjoying public endorsement by means of a 'solemn European referendum' to give this undertaking 'the popular support and participation which is essential to it'. The emphasis on strong ministerial or executive authority based on a direct mandate from the electorate – an important feature of

Gaullism and one which the General had already succeeded in embodying in the new Fifth Republic – would now be replicated at European level. The implication was that this structure would operate separate from, but in parallel to, the existing European Community.

To carry this initiative forward, de Gaulle invited other leaders to the first-ever EC **summit** meeting, which he hosted at the Quai d'Orsay in Paris on 10–11 February 1961. The day before the meeting, de Gaulle met with the German Chancellor, **Konrad Adenauer**: they decided to recommend to the four other leaders that they all agree immediately to hold such summits on a regular basis from now on. During the full meeting of the Six, however, the Dutch refused to accept this proposal, although they were willing to agree to de Gaulle's fall-back position: the creation of a special 'committee of representatives of the six governments', under French chairmanship, to draw up 'concrete proposals' for such summits in the future and other 'methods by which closer political cooperation could be organized'. The new group was to report to a second summit meeting in the early summer.

The 'Intergovernmental Committee on Political Union' met between March 1961 and April 1962, under the chairmanship of Christian Fouchet, a former Gaullist deputy then serving as French ambassador to Denmark. During the initial discussions, the German, Italian and Luxembourg governments proved broadly, if cautiously, supportive of the French démarche, with Belgium remaining neutral. They accepted that regular summit meetings could act as the focal point of closer political cooperation, so long as the existing, separate role of the EC was not threatened and the position of the **North Atlantic Treaty Organization** (NATO) was not jeopardized. From the start, however, the Dutch government proved much more reluctant. With the full backing of foreign minister Joseph Luns, the Dutch representative argued that any moves towards a European foreign policy should, as a matter of principle, be firmly rooted in existing Community structures, and would need to be underpinned by a clear and unequivocal commitment to the Atlantic Alliance. The best guarantee of the latter would be for negotiations to await British membership of the Community, an application for which seemed imminent. For the Dutch, building 'political Europe' in any form was less important than sustaining US leadership of Europe, which might be prejudiced by the emergence of a separate European identity in external affairs.

At the second EC summit, held in Bad Godesberg on 18 July 1961, an ambiguous communiqué allowed both Paris and The Hague to claim movement in their directions. The General secured agreement that the Six would henceforth hold regular summit meetings and that foreign-policy co-operation should be deepened and 'ultimately' be embodied in institutions. Equally, however, the summit expressed the desire to root political union in a strong Atlantic Alliance, to allow 'the accession to the EC of other European states', and to study some of the wider institutional reform ideas advocated by strong pro-Europeans, including implicitly the merger of the executives of the three existing Communities and direct election of the **European Parliament**. A spirit of optimism was captured in the headline of *Le Monde* the following day: 'Political Europe is Born'.

The mandate of the Fouchet committee was renewed and negotiations resumed in September 1961. The committee was now charged specifically with devising and submitting 'proposals on the means which will enable as soon as possible a statutory character to be given to the union of [the] peoples' of Europe. This delphic phraseology concealed, however, very different emphases among the member states. In written submissions, Germany and Italy were prepared to accept de Gaulle's logic of an intergovernmental structure for a future union, whilst Belgium and Luxembourg preferred a 'political community' to mirror the EC, based on an independent executive commission. The Dutch offered no written contribution. France decided to wrest the initiative by tabling a draft treaty, which (it rightly calculated) would immediately become the practical basis for discussion.

Drawn up by the foreign ministry in Paris and submitted on 2 November 1961, the first Fouchet Plan ran to 18 articles and some 1,500 words. The French 'Draft Treaty for the establishment of a Political Union', as Murray Forsyth has written, 'may be said to represent the nearest approach to the founding text of a classic confederation that has been made in post-war Europe' (*Unions of States: The Theory and Practice of Confederation*, 1981). It envisaged the creation of a 'union of states, hereafter called the Union' which, operating in parallel to the existing EC, would adopt a common foreign policy, a common defence policy, and policies for close cooperation in science and culture. The Union's defence policy would be conducted 'in cooperation with other free nations', tacitly accepting the importance of NATO.

The new Union would be governed by a Council representing national governments, all of whose decisions would be taken unanimously. (Abstention of up to two states would not prevent a decision being taken, and decisions would only be binding upon those participating in them.) The Council would meet every four months at the level of heads of government, and at least once in the intervening period at the level of foreign ministers. Each meeting of heads of government would elect a President from among their number, who would hold office for a two-month period either side of the next meeting. The Council would be serviced by a new body, a European Political Commission, to be based in Paris and composed of senior officials on secondment from their national foreign ministries. The existing Brussels-based **European Commission** would be bypassed for this purpose. The draft treaty also contained provisions for a 'general review' of its operation three years after entering force. The purpose of this review would be, in an ambiguous phrase, 'the gradual establishment of an organization centralizing, within the Union, the European Communities'.

The reaction of France's partners to the draft treaty was mixed. Although ambivalent, West Germany, Italy and Luxembourg suggested they could do business on the basis of the proposal, whilst seeking additional guarantees in respect of NATO and the integrity of the existing EC. The Netherlands, by contrast, stated that the whole proposal was unacceptable. In a critical development, Belgium moved from the neutral camp into a stance of clear opposition, aligning itself firmly with the Dutch. **Paul-Henri Spaak**, returning as Belgian foreign minister after four years as Secretary General of NATO, was decisive in this. In addition to principled objections to intergovernmentalism, Spaak seems to have decided to penalize de Gaulle for two positions France had taken in other negotiations: its opposition to President Kennedy's ideas for a multilateral nuclear force in Europe and its foot-dragging in NATO negotiations on a joint Western response to the Soviet construction of the Berlin Wall in August 1961.

Working in tandem, the Dutch and Belgian delegations raised the stakes. They indicated that, in addition to their serious reservations about the institutional form of the proposed Union and its defence provisions, they believed that the United Kingdom should participate directly in the political union discussions, and if it could not, that negotiations should be deferred until it had entered the Community. Following the Bad Godesberg summit, the British prime minister, Harold Macmillan, had applied for membership on 10 August 1961, a move quickly followed by Ireland, Denmark and Norway. Entry negotiations opened two months later, in Paris, on 10 October, just before the submission by France of the first Fouchet Plan. 'From that moment on,' as Jean-Claude Masclet has written, the Netherlands and Belgium 'posed the problem of political union as a choice between two alternatives: either a supranational system [without Britain] or a looser régime with British participation' (*L'Union politique de l'Europe*, 1994). Ideally, of course, both countries would have preferred a third option: a supranational system including Britain. The first and third alternatives were out of the question so far as de Gaulle was concerned (and were not supported by Britain either). The second also posed acute problems for France, in so far as it required Paris to decide its definitive attitude to UK membership, and it risked ensuring that the new Union would be more firmly tied to NATO than de Gaulle wished.

During the autumn, the negotiations failed to make progress. In response, the French government tabled a revised version of the Fouchet Plan on 18 January 1962. To widespread astonishment, this text was characterized not by concessions, but by a significant hardening of position. Crucial changes accentuated the intergovernmental character of the proposed Union and enhanced its ability to act independently of the United States. The French President himself appears to have been central to the shift, ignoring efforts by the Quai d'Orsay to narrow differences. De Gaulle may well have taken fright at the dangers of the new British linkage in the negotiations, with the potential for France to be forced to admit Britain to the Community in return for Dutch and Belgian agreement to the Plan. Equally, the belligerence of Luns and Spaak suggested that once Britain was admitted to the EC, London's potential to exercise leadership against France could be substantial.

Slightly more succinct than its predecessor, the revised Fouchet Plan contained several important changes. It proposed the creation of a network of 'Committees of Ministers' for the various policy areas of the Union, building a structure which could over time supersede the existing EC Council of Ministers. It included economics as one of the areas of cooperation within the Union, taking the latter directly into the central policy field of the EC. Defence policy was no longer to be conducted 'in cooperation with other free nations', thus removing any implicit reference to NATO. Finally, the review scheduled for three years after the treaty came into force would now simply deal with 'simplifying, rationalizing and coordinating' cooperation among the member states, rather than fusing the Union and EC. The separate Union structure could thus remain a permanent feature, gradually acquiring new powers.

The second Plan prompted the formation of a brief-lived, but highly damaging, anti-French front among the other member states, significantly increasing the chances that the negotiations would fail. The three countries which had previously broadly supported France – Italy, Luxembourg and, most crucially, West Germany – all indicated that they could not accept a Union along the lines now envisaged in Paris. The Italians played a particularly important role in preparing a counter-proposal, signed jointly by 'the Five', which contradicted French thinking on several vital points. This text envisaged a 'European Union' of both 'states and of European peoples', whose activities would not prejudice the powers of the existing Community. Economics would not feature as an area of cooperation, being left entirely to the EC. A common defence policy would be adopted within the framework of (or to strengthen) the Atlantic Alliance. The dual structure of Council and Committees of Ministers would be retained, but decisions could be taken by **qualified majority voting** (QMV) where the Council unanimously sanctioned it. A Secretary General 'independent of the member states' would be appointed to service the Union, with his own secretariat of supranational officials. The European Parliament would be consulted formally on some Union decisions before they were taken. The **European Court of Justice** (ECJ) would be given the task of settling any disputes between member states on Union questions. The biggest surprise came at the end: the proposed review after three years would be automatic and have several highly integrationist goals, including the greater use of QMV, direct election of the European Parliament, and the merger of the Union and Community into 'an organic institutional framework'.

The agreement by the Five on a counter-treaty was a major diplomatic defeat for France. In a rearguard effort to retrieve the situation, the General engaged in active bilateral diplomacy with the German and Italian heads of government, Konrad Adenauer and Amintore Fanfani, with some success in breaking up the unity of the other states. Elaborate attempts were made by Paris to neutralize each of the new propositions in the counter-treaty. When the EC foreign ministers met in Paris on 17 April 1962, it was clear that Luns and Spaak had been deeply irritated by de Gaulle's approaches to the Germans and Italians, which they saw as presaging their own exclusion from the power politics of any future Union. They simply declared that it would be best if the Fouchet negotiations were suspended until it was unmistakably clear that the United Kingdom would be joining the EC. Spaak explained that, for Belgium and Holland, political union required one of 'two possible safeguards: either the adoption of the **Community method**, or the counterweight provided by Britain'. Given French refusal to countenance the former, 'Britain must be one of the members of the inadequate union which people wish to impose on us.' Neither of the Belgian or Dutch conditions being met, he said, 'it is better to leave things as they are.'

The French foreign minister, Maurice Couve de Murville, then offered one final concession, which involved little real risk to France: if negotiations continued, the final draft treaty, when agreed, could be submitted to the British for their approval. Only if London accepted the text – it could hardly do otherwise without undermining its own EC membership bid – would the Treaty be signed by the Six. Spaak and Luns rejected this offer, noting that it did not in any way guarantee British membership. The meeting broke up, without agreement and issuing no communiqué.

The shock delivered to the Community by the Fouchet débâcle was severe. Although in Bad Godesberg the EC heads of government had expressed their intention to meet regularly, they did not in fact reconvene for six years, and then only for a formal session to mark the tenth anniversary of the Treaty of Rome. Foreign ministers suspended their quarterly meetings too. A period of stagnation set in, with de Gaulle announcing France's veto of the first British application to join the Community in January 1963, the Community becoming increasingly bogged down at French insistence in complex negotiations on the financing of the **Common Agricultural Policy** (CAP), France in effect threatening to leave the Community in October 1964 unless agreement was reached on the CAP and, finally, France boycotting the Council of Ministers, during the second half of 1965, in order to prevent the automatic introduction of QMV planned for January 1966. The 'empty chair crisis' was only resolved by the **Luxembourg Compromise**, which allowed unanimity to prevail wherever important national interests were at stake, so frustrating EC decision-making for the next two decades.

Further reading: Georges-Henri Soutou, 'Le général de Gaulle, le plan Fouchet et l'Europe', in *Commentaire*, Number 52, Winter 1990–91.

Founding fathers

The 'founding fathers' of the European Union are generally taken to be a series of leading political and administrative figures who played a decisive role in the creation of the three **European Communities** in the 1950s. They are conventionally accepted as being **Jean Monnet**, a leading civil servant during the French Fourth Republic, and **Robert Schuman**, **Konrad Adenauer**, **Alcide de Gasperi**, and **Paul-Henri Spaak**, the prime ministers or foreign ministers of France, Germany, Italy and Belgium respectively. Monnet, Schuman, Adenauer and de Gasperi all played a significant role in the creation of the first supranational organization in Europe – the **European Coal and Steel Community** (ECSC) in 1951–2 – and Monnet, Adenauer and Spaak in establishing the **European Economic Community** (EEC) and **European Atomic Energy Community** (EAEC or Euratom) in 1957–8.

The founding fathers shared a deep distrust of nationalism. Schuman and de Gasperi came from border regions – Lorraine and South Tyrol – and led in effect multinational lives. Spaak had been arrested during the First World War, Adenauer and Schuman during the second, and de Gasperi between the wars. Schuman, Adenauer and de Gasperi were leading Christian Democrats and strong Catholics, with only Spaak a Socialist. The fact that the first three came from the centre-right of politics reflected the relative weakness of the democratic left in Europe during the 1950s and its much greater scepticism towards European integration. Monnet was unusual in that he did not come from a border area, was neither elected nor imprisoned, had no party attachment, professed no religious commitment, and spent the First World War in Britain and the Second World War in both Britain and the United States.

A number of lesser figures can also make a claim for inclusion in the pantheon of founding fathers. Three stand out: Johan Willem Beyen, the Dutch liberal foreign minister in the mid-1950s, whose **Beyen Plan** proposed the creation of a **common market** and **customs union** in Europe after the failure of the **European Defence Community** (EDC) in 1954; **Pierre Uri**, the French Socialist economist who assisted Monnet in the drafting of the

Schuman Plan in 1950 that led to the ECSC and who contributed to the **Treaties of Rome** establishing the EEC and EAEC (Euratom); and **Walter Hallstein**, the German Christian Democrat junior foreign minister who helped draft the latter treaties and then became the first President of the **European Commission.**

The historian Alan Milward has satirized the founding fathers as modern-day 'European saints', seen by their 'servants on earth', notably by **Eurocrats** and others in Brussels, as 'men who held fast to their faith in European unity and through the righteousness of their beliefs and the single-mindedness of their actions overcame the doubting faithlessness of the world around them' (*The European Rescue of the Nation State*, 1992). There is certainly a tendency in many circles to romanticize the motivations of the founding fathers, some of whose actions were either forced by necessity or served their short-term political convenience. The advocacy by Schuman and Monnet of the pooling of Franco-Germany sovereignty in the coal and steel sectors, for example, was an ingenious solution to the acute problem which the government in Paris faced of how to reconcile deeply hostile French parliamentary and public opinion to the reindustrialization of Germany, which the Americans, British and Germans themselves felt to be essential to the economic survival of western Europe. However, the willingness of these leaders to look beyond the confines of their national borders and political systems, as well as their ability to foresee the unexpected potential of common action through supranational institutions, marked them out decisively from many of their contemporaries, whose vision was still confined to the logic of the nation state, and it has justifiably given them a special place in the history of post-war Europe.

Four freedoms

The 'four freedoms' that underpin the **single market** are the '**free movement** of goods, persons, services and capital'. Set out in Articles 26, 28–37 and 45–66 TFEU, these freedoms, which have been realized in varying degrees within the European Union over the last half century, are fundamental to the new European legal order which the architects of the **Treaty of Rome** sought to establish and they provide the central justification for that treaty to be seen as a liberalizing document.

The sheer ambition of the goal of removing all barriers to the free movement of goods, persons, services and capital in Europe – in effect covering all potentially mobile factors of production – has ensured that a huge amount of energy has been expended on legislative action in these fields since 1958. The most comprehensive effort in this regard was embodied in the 1992 single market programme, set out in the **Cockfield White Paper** of 1985. Where the necessary legislation has proved politically impossible to enact, the jurisprudence of the **European Court of Justice** (ECJ), based on the principle of **direct effect**, has helped ensure that member states cannot maintain discriminatory measures against citizens exercising the four freedoms.

The draft **European Constitution** would have untied the four freedoms from the single market specifically and added a fifth to this list, by stating: 'The free movement of persons, services, goods and capital, and **freedom of establishment** shall be guaranteed within and by the Union, in accordance with the Constitution' (Article I-4(1) Constitution). Under the **Lisbon Treaty**, the freedom of establishment – the right to practise a trade or profession – remains a subset of the other freedoms.

The phrase 'four freedoms' does not appear as such in the **Treaties**: it gained currency because President Franklin D. Roosevelt, in his State of the Union address to the US Congress in January 1941, had spoken of the world being 'founded upon four essential human freedoms': freedom of speech, freedom to worship, freedom from want, and freedom from fear. See also **free movement of capital, free movement of goods, free movement of persons, free movement of services.**

Further reading: Catherine Barnard, *The Substantive Law of the EU: The Four Freedoms*, 2010.

Franco-British union

In June 1940, in an attempt to avert the imminent surrender of France to Germany, **Jean Monnet**, then working in London as chairman of the Franco-British Committee for Economic Coordination and reporting to the prime ministers of both countries, proposed that the British and French governments should make a declaration proclaiming the 'indissoluble union' of the two countries, which would 'no longer be two nations but one'. This Franco-British union would entail the creation of 'joint organs for defence, foreign, financial and economic policies', based on a single war cabinet, the pooling of the two countries' armed forces and mutual citizenship.

The detailed plan – which initially included proposals for a **customs union** and common currency – was prepared by Jean Monnet, working with a British colleague on the Coordination Committee, Arthur Salter. Following his arrival in London, the drafting team was widened to include **Charles de Gaulle**, the new French under-secretary for defence, as well as René Pleven, working at the French embassy, Robert Vansittart, permanent secretary of the Foreign Office, and Desmond Morton, private secretary to prime minister **Winston Churchill**. The final text they agreed envisaged 'the real, complete, immediate and enduring unity of the two countries acting in all things as one, without regard to separate interests', with this being the 'indispensable condition for any hope of victory' against Germany. The plan was quickly approved by Churchill and his War Cabinet on 16 June, and communicated to the French government of Paul Reynaud, which had retreated from Paris to Bordeaux. However, the intervention came too late to keep France in the war. The divided French cabinet, which by then included Marshal Philippe Pétain as deputy premier – who derided the idea of union as like being 'wedded to a corpse' – was incapable of responding. On 17 June, the prime minister resigned and soon after, the French surrender was complete. The following day, de Gaulle broadcast from London to the French people, pleading that the 'flame of French resistance' be kept alive and establishing himself as de facto leader of a government in exile. This dramatic episode forms the first chapter of Monnet's *Mémoires* (1976).

Francovich case

The **Treaties** provide little guidance on the remedies available to those who suffer from the non-implementation or mis-implementation of **EU law**. After a period in which the **European Court of Justice** (ECJ) accorded member states a high degree of autonomy, based on existing remedies in domestic law, it began to insist on the rights of the individual citizen, independent of arrangements at national level. In the Francovich case *(Francovich and Bonifaci* v *Italy,* Cases C-6/90 and C-9/90), the Court established the so-called 'state liability' principle, whereby an individual who suffers damage as a consequence of the failure by a member state to implement a piece of EU legislation may claim compensation from the authorities of that state.

Mr Francovich was an employee of an Italian firm that went bankrupt. A 1980 directive on the protection of employees (from non-payment of salaries they were owed) in cases of insolvency had not been given effect in Italian law. The ECJ ruled in 1991 that Mr Francovich could claim appropriate damages from the Italian state for the financial loss he had suffered, even though Italy had not transposed the directive in question. It held that:

> *. . . the full effectiveness of Community rules would be impaired and the protection of the rights which they grant would be weakened if individuals were unable to obtain compensation when their rights are infringed by a breach of Community law for which a Member State can be held responsible . . . It follows that the principle of State liability for harm caused to individuals by breaches of Community law for which the State can be held responsible is inherent in the system of the Treaty.*

The Francovich ruling followed from earlier judgements – notably in the Van Gend en Loos and Costa cases – which established that European legislation conferred rights and duties directly upon the citizens of the member states (see **direct effect**). It reinforced the general treaty obligation laid upon states to 'take any appropriate measure, general or particular, to ensure fulfilment of the obligations arising out of the Treaties or resulting from the acts of the institutions of the Union' (Article 4(3) TFEU).

Freedom of establishment

Freedom of establishment – the right to practise a trade or profession – is guaranteed for the nationals of the member states throughout the European Union by Articles 49 to 55 TFEU, which cover both employed and self-employed persons. Although not listed as one of the '**four freedoms**', the freedom (or right) of establishment is a central principle of the **single market** and is critical to both the **free movement of persons** and **free movement of services**. Article 49 prohibits 'restrictions on the freedom of establishment of nationals of a Member State in the territory of another Member State' and guarantees non-discrimination towards such persons. Nationals of one member state enjoy 'the right to take up and pursue activities as self-employed persons and to set up and manage undertakings' in another member state, 'under the conditions laid down for its own nationals by the law of the country where such establishment is effected . . .'. A critical component of freedom of establishment is the **mutual recognition of qualifications**, provided for in Article 53 TFEU, substantial progress towards which has been achieved in recent years. Article 51 excludes 'activities . . . connected, even occasionally, with the exercise of official authority' from the scope of freedom of establishment.

The basic legislation on freedom of establishment was identified by the **European Commission** in a 'general programme' set out in 1961. (There was a parallel general programme for promoting the free movement of services.) On this basis, proposals were brought forward on particular sectors of economic activity, not including the professions, since progress first had to be made on the mutual recognition of qualifications. In the mid-1970s, a number of judgements of the **European Court of Justice** (ECJ) helped to accelerate the process of removing national restrictions on freedom of establishment: for example, doctors from one member state have been able to practise in any other since 1976. The ECJ has held that any natural or legal person may establish multiple professional bases or branches in different member states, and buy or rent whatever property may be required for that purpose. Any citizen of the Union may thus 'participate, on a stable and continuous basis, in the economic life of a Member State other than his State of origin and to profit therefrom . . .'. With some exceptions, it is now the case that nationals of the member states are entitled to practise a trade or profession anywhere in the Union and indeed throughout the **European Economic Area** (EEA).

Free movement

Although the concept of the free movement has its origins in economic theory, the **founding fathers** of the **European Communities** saw it as a legal tool to achieve a political end, namely the '**ever closer union** among the peoples of Europe' asserted in the preambles to the **Treaties**. What quickly became known as the '**four freedoms**' – the rights of cross-frontier 'free movement of goods, persons, services and capital' (Article 26(2) TFEU) – were central to the obligations and policies set out in the original **Treaty of Rome** and they have been at the heart of the European integration process ever since. The free movement principle was given effect by the adoption of supranational law, binding on the member states, to be adjudicated by a **European Court of Justice** (ECJ), which quickly asserted the principles of the **primacy** and **direct effect** of Community law. The existence of a separate, supranational legal order became the most striking difference between the creation of a **common market** (or **single market**) in Europe and efforts to establish a parallel **free trade area**, through the **European Free Trade Association** (EFTA), which was based on intergovernmental cooperation. See also **discrimination on grounds of nationality, freedom of establishment, free movement of capital, free movement of goods, free movement of persons, free movement of services.**

Free movement of capital

When the **Treaty of Rome** was negotiated in 1956–7, not only did each member state have its own national currency, but, under the Bretton Woods system, the exchange rates between those currencies were fixed and controls were maintained on capital movements between states, in part to sustain such parities. The only exception to this pattern among **the Six** was the **Belgo-Luxembourg Economic Union** (BLEU), whereby the two countries' currencies were interchangeable. The new treaty tried to square the circle between the liberalizing economic logic of the new **common market** and the continued political imperative of national control of economic policy. Capital movements lay at the heart of this tension and the wording on it in the treaty required especially careful drafting.

The original treaty provisions (Articles 67–73 EEC) were very cautiously worded. They required the member states to 'progressively abolish' all restrictions on capital movements and end discrimination based on the nationality or location of the investment 'to the extent necessary to ensure the proper functioning of the common market'. Member states had to be 'as liberal as possible in granting such exchange authorizations as are still necessary'. They would 'endeavour to avoid' introducing new restrictions and promote further liberalization to the extent that the economic situation allowed. The treaty explicitly recognized that capital movements could 'lead to disturbances in the capital market' in member states and that safeguard measures might need to be taken, with the approval of the **European Commission**. Awareness of the complexity of the relationship between capital movements and currencies was also reflected in Article 106 EEC (on balance of payments), which stated that one member state would authorize payments in another's currency 'to the extent that the movement of goods, services, capital and persons between Member States has been liberalized pursuant to this Treaty'.

All the treaty references above have since been superseded by more ambitious and less equivocal language. First, the 1986 **Single European Act** (SEA) added a general reference to the **single market**, which it defined as 'an area without internal frontiers in which the **free movement of goods**, services, persons and capital is ensured in accordance with the provisions of the Treaties' (now Article 26(2) TFEU). Then the 1992 **Maastricht Treaty** repealed Articles 67–73 and 106 EEC, substituting the current Articles 63–6 TFEU. The first of these articles prohibits 'all restrictions' on the movement of capital and on payments, both between member states and with third countries. Restrictions may be retained specifically for reasons of taxation, prudential supervision, and public policy or security, for example, to fight money laundering. The reference to a link between capital movements and currencies was removed, in the context of the creation of an **Economic and Monetary Union** (EMU).

Decision-making in the **Council of Ministers** on capital movements was initially conducted by **unanimity** and theoretically switched to **qualified majority voting** (QMV) in January 1966. However, the operation of the **Luxembourg Compromise** prevented the adoption of any substantial legislation in this field until a **directive** was adopted by QMV in 1988 requiring most capital movements to be freed by July 1990 (with **transitional periods** for Spain, Portugal, Ireland and Greece). Member states were allowed to take 'protective measures' in the event of 'short-term capital movements of exceptional magnitude'. The Maastricht Treaty introduced **co-decision** between the Council and the **European Parliament** for legislation on capital movements, as it did for all other single market measures.

The free movement of capital is a necessary, but not a sufficient, condition for a 'perfect' market for capital to exist within the European Union. So long as differing exchange rates continue between **eurozone** and non-eurozone member states, variations in the price of capital may distort the conditions of competition. Equally, all remaining national restrictions in the financial services sector would need to be removed.

Free movement of goods

Perhaps the most fundamental of the '**four freedoms**', the free movement of goods is central to the **common market**, now known as the internal or **single**

market, established by the **Treaty of Rome** in March 1957. The treaty listed the free movement of goods as the first substantive policy responsibility of the new **European Economic Community** (EEC). Today, Article 26(2) TFEU defines the single market as 'an area without internal frontiers in which the free movement of goods, persons, services and capital is ensured in accordance with the provisions of the Treaties'.

The mechanics of **free movement** were set out in specific treaty articles dealing with the common market and **customs union**, which drew on principles pioneered earlier in the 1950s in the **European Coal and Steel Community** (ECSC). Article 28(1) and 30 TFEU prohibit the imposition of 'customs duties on imports and exports and of all charges having equivalent effect' between member states. Articles 34 and 35 TFEU prohibit quantitative restrictions (quotas) and 'all measures having equivalent effect' between member states. The principle of **non-discrimination** must apply. Article 36 TFEU provides for certain exceptions from the free movement principle. It allows member states to prohibit or restrict imports 'on grounds of public morality, public policy or public security' – as well as the protection of the 'health and life of humans, animals or plants', of national treasures or of 'industrial and commercial property' – provided that such limitations do not 'constitute a means of arbitrary discrimination or a disguised restriction on trade' between member states.

In practice, the introduction of the customs union for industrial goods progressed quickly, as the striking growth in intra-Community trade during the 1960s attests. There was an annual increase of 28 per cent during the decade 1958–68, twice the rate of increase with non-EC countries in Europe. The elimination of tariffs and quotas proved relatively unproblematic, helped by the fact that, by the time the EEC Treaty came into force (in 1958), most formal quotas on trade between **the Six** had already been removed. Although some national authorities, wishing to protect their domestic markets, attempted to substitute national tax measures for tariffs, it was usually obvious that these constituted 'charges having an equivalent effect'. (Article 110 TFEU imposed a parallel prohibition of discriminatory taxation.) The Treaty of Rome laid down a 12-year **transitional period** during which the removal of internal customs duties and quotas was to be effected (by 1970), and in the event this process was accomplished 18 months ahead of schedule. This allowed the Community's **Common Customs Tariff** (CCT) to be applied from July 1968.

The problem plaguing the free movement of goods lay, rather, in the tenacity, and indeed growth, of domestic technical standards – justified on (sometimes dubious) health and safety, consumer protection or environmental grounds – which had the effect of compartmentalizing the European market, often quite severely. Whilst many of these **non-tariff barriers** to trade could reasonably be considered to be 'measures having an equivalent effect' to quantitative restrictions, the fact that the Treaty of Rome made no explicit reference at the time to environmental and consumer protection (at least) enabled some governments to argue that restrictions in these fields were consistent with Community law. In the agricultural field, the operation of the complex 'agri-monetary' system compounded a growing focus on the protection of human, animal and plant health to justify the continuation of border controls, complicating the cross-frontier movement of goods. In 1974, the **European Commission** observed that the situation on non-tariff barriers was deteriorating and had 'reverted to a position comparable to that at the beginning of the 1960s'.

In the interim, the Commission had been making very slow progress in its attempts, sector by sector, to secure agreement to new, common Europe-wide specifications to enable goods to circulate freely throughout the Community. Its ambitious but laborious **harmonization** programme had become bogged down, because of its inherent complexity and the need for unanimous decision-making in the **Council of Ministers**. Under Article 100 EEC (now Article 115 TFEU), any member state could simply block a change that might threaten the vested interests of its producers.

This unhappy situation led to a number of cases in the **European Court of Justice** (ECJ) concerned with the key question of what exactly was meant by the treaty references to measures having 'equivalent effect' to quantitative restrictions. Fortunately for the Commission, the Court ruled consistently in favour of a maximum degree of freedom of movement for goods. In the Dassonville case in 1974 (Case 8/74), the Court found that 'All trading rules enacted by Member States, which are capable of hindering, directly or indirectly, actually or potentially, intra-Community trade are to be considered as measures having an effect equivalent to quantitative restrictions.' There was no need for evidence of the actual existence of an obstacle to the free movement of goods between member states, merely that the national measure concerned *might* have such an effect. Building on this, the ECJ ruled, in the so-called '**Cassis de Dijon case**' in 1979 (Case 120/78), that a national measure – in this case a rule on the minimum alcoholic content of liqueurs – could have an effect equivalent to a quantitative restriction on imports even if the requirement applied equally to goods produced both at home and in any other member state. The result was that, as a general principle, a product lawfully manufactured and on sale in one EU member state could be imported into another without restriction, through a de facto mutual recognition of technical standards.

Despite this flurry of judicial activity, it was unlikely that the problem of non-tariff barriers could be adequately addressed through court rulings alone, especially given the inventiveness of some governments in creating restrictions and the rapid evolution of products in the market. Renewed efforts were made by the new European Commission which took office in January 1985, under President **Jacques Delors**. It addressed this issue as its top priority, securing a commitment from heads of government, meeting in the European Council, to complete a barrier-free **single market** by the end of 1992.

The **Cockfield White Paper** identified the remaining non-tariff barriers to the free movement of goods, dividing them into technical barriers (differing product specifications), physical barriers (frontier controls, customs formalities) and fiscal barriers (see **tax harmonization**). Many of them were simply bureaucratic: the **Kangaroo Group** published a list of the 46 documents needed by the driver of a semi-articulated lorry travelling from West Germany to Italy via Austria. The White Paper also highlighted the continuing need to move to **qualified majority voting** (QMV) for Council decision-making in this area. The **Single European Act** (SEA), signed the following year, introduced a new Article 100(a) EEC (now Article 114 TFEU) allowing the use of QMV. Other measures were also taken, such as the introduction of the so-called Single Administrative Document (SAD), to ease the crossing of internal frontiers, the abolition of road haulage quotas (under the Community's new common **transport policy**), the simplification of transit procedures, and the removal of animal and plant health controls from the point of entry to offices inside member states. Frontier controls affecting the free movement of goods were in effect removed in time for the scheduled completion of the single market on 1 January 1993.

Further reading: Peter Oliver et al, *Free Movement of Goods in the European Union*, 2010.

Free movement of persons

In principle, any EU citizen meeting certain minimum requirements has the right to travel to, and to reside, study or work in, any other EU member state. Several articles in the **Treaties** underpin this entitlement to individual **free movement**. Because an open labour market was an essential component in the creation of a **common market**, the right to free movement was originally foreseen for 'workers' or those establishing businesses. Article 45 TFEU, dating from the original text of the **Treaty of Rome** in 1957, says that 'Freedom of movement for workers shall be secured' within the Union. It also abolishes **discrimination on grounds of nationality** in employment, except in the public service and in the case of 'limitations justified on grounds of public policy, public security or public health'. Article 49 extends the same principle of free movement to the self-employed, as part of **freedom of establishment**, whilst Article 56 reinforces this right by prohibiting restrictions on the cross-border provision of services. Subsequent treaty changes have widened the scope of individual free movement to cover all citizens, and not just workers, the self-employed or providers of services. Article 26(2), introduced by the 1986 **Single European Act** (SEA) defines the **single market** as 'an area without internal frontiers in which the **free movement** of goods, persons, services and capital is ensured'. The provisions on **European citizenship**, introduced by the 1992 **Maastricht Treaty**, took this a step further. Article 21(1) states: 'Every citizen of the Union shall have the right to move and reside freely within the territory of the Member States, subject to the limitations and conditions laid down in the Treaties.'

The practical attainment of the right of individual free movement was hindered for many years by insistence on the use of **unanimity** within the **Council of Ministers** on all matters in this field. The treaty required decisions relating to social security to be taken unanimously, whilst the **Luxembourg Compromise** frustrated the use of **qualified majority voting** (QMV) in all other dimensions. Nonetheless, the details of the right of workers (and their families) to move and reside freely within the member states with a view to taking up or seeking employment were set out in a regulation and a directive adopted in 1968, whilst rulings of the **European Court of Justice** (ECJ) gradually widened the definition of workers, the self-employed and service providers, whilst limiting the grounds on which member states could exclude individuals from access to their territory (see for example, the **Van Duyn case**). However, as late as 1982, the Court maintained the principle that the Treaties 'guarantee only the free movement of persons who pursue or are desirous of pursuing an economic activity', rather than citizens more widely (*Levin* v *Staatssecretaris van Justitie*; Case 53/81).

The debate in the mid-1980s about the completion of the single market and the potential adoption of treaty reform, culminating in the passage of the Single Act and the demise of the Luxembourg Compromise, changed the context in which free movement of persons was seen. As A. G. Toth has argued, the principle 'assumed a constitutional significance going beyond the establishment of a common market' and became instead 'the visible manifestation' of the '**ever closer union** among the peoples of Europe', to which the preambles of the Treaties refer (*The Oxford Encyclopaedia of European Community Law*, Volume II, 2005).

The Council adopted three linked directives in 1990 on the right of residence for students, retired people and individuals of independent means. These measures and some existing legislation relating to persons from the three traditional economic categories were consolidated and extended by a new EU 'residence directive', adopted in 2004. The result is that any European citizen may visit and stay in a member state other than his or her own for a period of up to three months, subject only to possession of a valid passport or identity card, before 'right of residence' rules apply. After that, the citizen may reside anywhere in the Union so long as he or she is covered by health insurance and is in receipt of welfare benefits or other income sufficient 'to avoid becoming a burden on the social assistance system of the host Member State'. Regardless of nationality, any family members in immediate descending or ascending order may accompany the citizen and may also stay in the member state in question if the citizen dies.

A **transitional period** of up to seven years permitted existing member states to restrict the free movement of workers from the eight central and eastern European countries that acceded to the Union in 2004. A similar period is currently running for workers from Bulgaria and Romania, which joined in 2007.

According to **Eurostat**, in 2008, 11.4 million EU citizens resided in a member state other than their own, mostly in Germany (2.5 million), Spain (2.1 million), the United Kingdom (1.6 million), France (1.3 million) and Italy (0.9 million). The highest percentage of non-nationals from other EU member states was in Luxembourg (36.6 per cent), followed by Cyprus (10.3 per cent), Ireland (8.9 per cent) and Belgium (6.2 per cent). EU citizens account for just under 40 per cent of migrants resident within the territory of the EU 27.

Free movement of services

The freedom to provide services within the European Union is different from **freedom of establishment** in that it is concerned with performance of services anywhere within the Union, without the provider of the service having his or her place of business established in the country where the service is performed. The **single market** is defined in Article 26(2) TFEU as comprising 'an area without internal frontiers in which the free movement of goods, persons, services and capital is ensured in accordance with the provisions of the **Treaties**'.

Article 56 TFEU requires member states to remove all restrictions on freedom to provide services with respect to citizens of the Union. The freedom may also be extended to nationals of non-member countries. Article 57 makes it clear that the Treaty provisions on services are supplementary to those relating to goods, persons and capital, and identifies four types of service in particular: industrial, commercial, professional and craft industries. Special considerations apply to transport, banking and insurance under Article 58(2). Member states are able to impose restrictions on public policy grounds (provided they are non-discriminatory) and to exclude services involving the exercise of official authority.

A 'general programme', launched by the **European Commission** in 1961, identified the restrictions to be removed, notably those based on nationality, residence, qualifications and procedures for the cross-border transfer of funds to pay for the service. It was followed by legislation on particular professions, helped partly by rulings of the **European Court of Justice** (ECJ). However, it was not until the late 1980s, when substantial progress was finally made in enacting legislation for the single market generally, as well as the **mutual recognition of qualifications**, that freedom to provide services across national boundaries began to become a reality. Although there has been a very substantial expansion in the service sector in recent decades – to the point where it now represents some 70 per cent of economic activity in the Union – non-tariff barriers in the sector have remained unusually stubborn.

In March 2000, the Lisbon meeting of the **European Council** invited the Commission to bring forward a new strategy for the services sector. The Commission reported in July 2002 and published a draft services directive in January 2004. After three years of intensive discussion and negotiation, the 'Bolkestein directive' – as it was sometimes called, after its author, Frits Bolkestein, the free-market Dutch Commissioner for the single market – was eventually adopted in December 2006, taking effect three years later. The directive's liberalizing thrust proved highly unpopular in trade union circles and the text was watered down before final adoption. Fears about its likely effect featured in the **French referendum on the European Constitution** in May 2005, boosting the 'no' vote.

The directive consolidates case law on both the freedom to provide services and the freedom of establishment, and simplifies administrative procedures for producers and consumers alike. In principle, the directive covers all services, other than those sectors for which there is specific EU legislation (such as financial services or transport) or which are explicitly excluded by the Treaties (notably certain social services, healthcare provided by the state, and the work of professionals, such as notaries and bailiffs, acting on behalf of governments).

Free trade area

A **free trade area** (FTA) is a form of regional trade arrangement under which two or more countries remove tariffs and quantitative restrictions (quotas) on products originating in each other's territories, while retaining separate tariff and other trade arrangements with third countries. A **customs union**, by contrast, denotes a deeper level of economic integration, in that participating countries adopt a common external tariff and sometimes a common external trade policy. The European Union is a customs union, with its own **Common Customs Tariff** (CCT) and **Common Commercial Policy** (CCP), provided for in the **Treaty of Rome**. In addition, the Union seeks to promote the **free movement**, not only of goods, but also of services, capital and persons in a **single market**.

Before the **European Economic Community** (EEC) was founded in 1958, there was a lively debate about whether the next step towards European integration should take the form of a customs union or a free trade area. The founding **Six** member states chose the former route, whilst (in response) the United Kingdom and six other countries subsequently created a free trade area in industrialized goods, known as the **European Free Trade Association** (EFTA). Although EFTA's membership grew at first, most of its members subsequently joined the EU with successive **enlargements**, and the Association now encompasses only **Iceland, Norway, Switzerland** and Liechtenstein (see **micro-states**). The first three of these countries are also members, alongside the 27 EU member states, of the **European Economic Area** (EEA), created in 1992.

Since then, two other European free trade areas have been established, both following the end of Communism in central and eastern Europe: the Baltic Free Trade Area (BAFTA) and a **Central European Free Trade Agreement** (CEFTA). BAFTA was established by the three **Baltic states** in 1994 and ceased to exist when they joined the EU ten years later. CEFTA included the four **Visegrád** states, as well as Slovenia, Bulgaria and Romania, until they successively joined the EU in 2004 and 2007. The organization continues, with its membership having shifted to the south and east: it now encompasses seven Balkan states, plus Moldova.

Free trade areas are not without difficulties. In order to avoid deflections of trade, they require complex and heavily-negotiated 'rules of origin' to determine whether items traded between their constituent territories qualify for tariff- and quota-free access. In practice, FTAs almost invariably provide exceptions from such tariff- and quota-free rules for 'sensitive' products, notably in the agricultural sector. The rules of the World Trade Organization (WTO), which generally prohibit preferential arrangements, require FTAs to include 'substantially all' trade in goods. The application of this criterion has proved contentious, and many FTAs have not been formally approved by the WTO.

French and Dutch referenda on the European Constitution

On 29 May and 1 June 2005, France and the Netherlands, two of **the Six** founding member states of the European Communities, held **referenda** on the **ratification** of the **European Constitution**. In each case, the electorate renounced the position of both the government and principal opposition parties, voting to reject the proposed treaty by a decisive margin. In France, 54.7 per of those casting ballots opposed the Constitution and 45.3 per cent supported it, on a turnout of 69.3 per cent. In the Netherlands, the margin of defeat was even wider: with 61.6 per cent voting against the text and only 38.4 per cent in favour, on a turnout of 62.8 per cent. In the earlier ratification votes in the two countries' **national parliaments**, less than a tenth of members had opposed the treaty in either case.

The French referendum of Sunday, 29 May 2005 was the third national vote to be held on a European issue since the foundation of the Fifth Republic: President Georges Pompidou had put the question of the **enlargement** of the Community (to include the United Kingdom, Ireland and Denmark) to a referendum in April 1972, whilst President **François Mitterrand** sought public approval for ratification of the **Maastricht Treaty** in September 1992. The very close outcome in the **French referendum on the Maastricht Treaty** – when 51.05 per cent voted in favour and 48.95 per cent against, on a 69.8 per cent turnout – had already alerted the political élite to the dangers of choosing the referendum route for any future treaty ratification. In 2003, President Jacques Chirac allegedly sought agreement among EU heads of government collectively to avoid holding referenda on the Constitution if possible. However, once the British prime minister, **Tony Blair**, unexpectedly conceded such a referendum in April 2004 – ironically in part because his position at home had been greatly weakened by division with France over the Iraq war – it became increasingly difficult for Chirac to resist calls to hold a popular vote in France too. Repeating the mistake of Mitterrand in 1992, he also calculated that the referendum could be exploited to divide his opponents and give a midterm boost to his own standing as president.

Following centre-right defeats in the 2004 regional and **European elections**, Chirac used his traditional address to the nation on 14 July to announce that a referendum on the Constitution would be held during the second half of the following year. Opinion polls soon showed the 'yes' camp commanding a clear majority, a position sustained throughout the remainder of 2004. After the Spanish electorate endorsed the Constitution by a wide margin (76.7 to 17.2 per cent, with 6.0 per cent of ballots left blank) in February 2005, Chirac decided to accelerate the timetable for his own referendum, bringing it forward to May.

The overall alignment of the parties in France on the European Constitution differed to that on the Maastricht Treaty 13 years earlier. Whilst the more extreme parties remained unremittingly hostile to closer European integration, the views of the mainstream left and right had largely reversed, partly reflecting the question of which party controlled the Elysée. In 2005, the Gaullist UMP was united in its support for the Constitution, whereas its predecessor, the RPR, had been bitterly divided over Maastricht. Conversely, the Socialist party was much less convinced of the merits of the Constitution than those of Maastricht. Although the Socialist leadership won a clear mandate for a 'yes' position in an internal ballot of party members, an active dissident group, led by former prime minister Laurent Fabius, exploited growing disenchantment with the EU as a force for economic liberalization in France to press for a 'no' vote. (Fabius himself was assumed to be seeking opportunistically to broaden his populist appeal in advance of the Socialist party's nomination for the 2007 presidential election.) At a time of 10 per cent unemployment, the opponents of the Constitution were able to tap into a rich seam of working-class and lower middle-class disquiet about the future, epitomized in widespread opposition to the 'Bolkestein directive' to promote **free movement of services** and fears of workers from central and eastern Europe undercutting French wages in coming years. This mood was compounded by an attempt by some on the right – notably Jean-Marie Le Pen's *Front national* and Philippe de Villiers' conservative MPF – to convert the referendum into a de facto poll on Turkey's putative membership of the Union.

From March 2005 onwards, the opinion polls showed a growing majority of the French public against the constitutional treaty and the government found itself on the defensive throughout the referendum campaign. The final opinion poll predicted the result almost precisely. In making their case, Chirac and his prime minister, Jean-Pierre Raffarin, were handicapped by their deep unpopularity and the fact that few outside the President's own party wanted the referendum to be seen as a vindication of his leadership. To some degree, Chirac was still bedevilled by the consequences of the dramatic political events of April 2002, when he was re-elected on the second ballot of the presidential election, against Le Pen, with 82.2 per cent of the vote. Chirac's three interventions during the campaign – in a youth debate, at a Franco-German-Polish summit meeting, and in a televised address to the nation – had little effect. There was no single event – like the head-to-head televised debate between President Mitterrand and Philippe Séguin, the leader of the 'no' camp, in 1992 – which acted as a focal point for the contest.

In the event, the outcome of the French referendum showed a high degree of unity and loyalty among UMP and centrist UDF voters, between 75 and 80 per cent of whom voted 'yes'. The supporters of all other parties voted 'no', including a majority of both Socialists and Greens – by between 55 and 60 per cent – even though the leadership of the latter parties supported the Constitution. The margin of rejection among voters to the left and right of the mainstream parties was much bigger, rising to as high as 95 per cent. Demographically, the richer and older the voters, the more likely they were to vote 'yes'. In the most affluent parts of Paris, three-quarters of voters supported the Constitution, whereas two-thirds or more rejected it in towns in industrial decline. Interestingly, despite their reliance on the **Common Agricultural Policy** (CAP), 70 per cent of farmers rejected the treaty. A similar, but much less pronounced, pattern of voting had already been evident in the Maastricht referendum in 1992. The general view was that the shift in the intervening years reflected two continuing and linked trends:

first, the declining hold of the traditional parties and their leaders on French public opinion, most vividly illustrated in the failure of the Socialist presidential candidate to qualify for the second ballot in April 2002; and second, the emergence of a powerful constituency of 'outsiders' in French politics – to be found mainly, but not entirely, to the left and right of the (shrinking) mainstream parties – who often see themselves as victims of globalization and view the European Union as a vehicle for spreading insecurity through the **single market** and free trade. Overall, the French referendum result was both a product of, and a further catalyst for, what Gilles Ivaldi (see below) has called 'the centrifugal electoral dynamics of French politics'.

The most immediate impact of the French referendum was to strengthen opponents of the European Constitution in the referendum due to be held in the Netherlands three days later, on Wednesday, 1 June. The context of this second vote differed from that of the first in at least two important respects. First, whereas France had a history of populist hostility towards European integration dating back many decades – first seen in Gaullist and Communist opposition to the **European Defence Community** (EDC) in the 1950s – **Euroscepticism** was a relatively new phenomenon to the Dutch. Second, whereas French public opinion often resisted economic liberalization within the EU, Dutch opinion was much less hostile in principle to such reform. The growing sense of insecurity in the Netherlands related less to the prospect of economic reform than to issues of cultural identity, immigration and crime. (Perhaps for this reason, the question of Turkish membership featured more prominently in the Dutch campaign than in the French.)

Equally, there were important similarities. Both France and the Netherlands were facing periods of fiscal retrenchment, leaving their centre-right governments deeply unpopular at midterm. In both countries, all the mainstream 'establishment' parties supported a 'yes' vote, with the political élite even more solidly behind the treaty in The Hague than in Paris. The only organized Dutch political forces to oppose the text were the Maoists, Christian fundamentalists, and supporters of Pim Fortuyn and Geert Wilders. As in France, the Dutch campaign revealed growing concerns about the country's declining influence in an enlarged European Union and a fear of its seeming inability to shape its own future. As the campaign proceeded, there was, like in France, a significant shift from the 'yes' to the 'no' camps: opinion polls showed a fall in support for the Constitution from 73 per cent in November 2004 to less than half that figure immediately after the French vote. The outcome in France made it easier for the Dutch public to vote against the Constitution without fear of the potentially negative consequences of rejecting it on their own. As in France, there was evidence of a growing cultural and social divide in democratic politics, as the public began to fracture into three distinct components: a successful élite group, which feels broadly comfortable with internationalization and Europe; a 'squeezed middle', which increasingly expresses its resentments and discontents by voting for populist or nationalist parties and against Europe; and a disconnected, marginal, often immigrant, underclass, which does not participate in the political process in any meaningful way at all.

Taken together, the French and Dutch votes constituted a major event in the political history of the European Union. They ended the prospect of the constitutional treaty, in its original form, securing ratification in all 27 member states. Planned referenda in six more member states were abandoned. The outcome of the French and Dutch votes also redoubled the determination of political leaders to avoid a situation in the future where treaty changes might raise the expectation of ratification by referendum. However, contrary to widespread expectations at the time – including the view of Commission President José Manuel Barroso in September 2005 that he could not see 'any magic formula that would bring [the text] back to life' – the constitutional project did not die. After a long 'period of reflection', the institutional reform process was relaunched in summer 2007, driven by a determination by the new German Chancellor, Angela Merkel, to see some elements of the Constitution survive. The German and French governments, in a coordinated move, indicated that they could not envisage any further enlargement of the Union taking place unless and until a treaty of some form were in place. This was an ironic turn of events, given that some French and Dutch voters had opposed the Constitution in the hope of halting the enlargement process.

The resulting Reform Treaty, subsequently renamed the **Lisbon Treaty**, entered into force in December 2009. Ratification of this latter treaty followed the parliamentary route in both France and the Netherlands. In France, the new French President, Nicolas Sarkozy, had run on an electoral platform which specifically included a commitment to adopt a 'simplified' treaty without a referendum. In the Netherlands, the government of Jan Peter Balkenende insisted, with the support of the United Kingdom, on the removal from the original constitutional text (which it had negotiated) of those elements – such as treaty status for the '**symbols of the Union**' or the explicit assertion of the **primacy** of the **EU law** – which could be portrayed by critics as giving the Union the features of statehood. On this basis, the Dutch parliament agreed that a second referendum was not necessary to ratify the Lisbon Treaty.

Further reading: Paul Hainsworth, 'France says No: the 29 May 2005 Referendum on the European Constitution', *Parliamentary Affairs*; Volume 59, Number 1, January 2006; Gilles Ivaldi, 'Beyond France's 2005 Referendum on the European Constitutional Treaty', *West European Politics*, Volume 29, Number 1, 2006.

French referendum on the Maastricht Treaty

On 20 September 1992, in the eighth **referendum** to be held since the foundation of the Fifth Republic in 1958, the French public voted, by the narrow margin of 51.05 to 48.95 per cent, on a 69.8 per cent turnout, to approve the **ratification** of the **Maastricht Treaty** on European Union. The referendum was the second to be called by a French President on a European treaty, following that of Georges Pompidou in April 1972 on the **enlargement** of the Community to include the United Kingdom, Ireland and Denmark.

The Maastricht referendum was announced by President **François Mitterrand** on 3 June 1992, the day after a referendum in Denmark had rejected the same text. In the confident expectation of a decisive victory, Mitterrand saw this initiative – for which there was no constitutional necessity – as a means both of restoring political momentum behind the Maastricht settlement and of dividing the centre-right opposition in the run-up to parliamentary elections due the following March. However, as the campaign progressed, it became increasingly a domestic plebiscite on Mitterrand's own waning and unpopular hold on power after 11 years in the Elysée. The tightening of the margin between the two sides – with opinion polls at one stage predicting a 'no' majority – meant that, when the reporting 'black-out' on such polls started on 13 September, there were increasing fears that the government could lose the vote.

The referendum campaign pitted the mainstream political establishment against a coalition of outsiders. The 'yes' campaign comprised the bulk of the Socialist party, the centrist UDF, the leadership of the Gaullist RPR, most business leaders and the main national newspapers. Mitterrand evidently hoped that the alignment of the pro-European UDF with his own Socialist party, which had also underpinned ratification of the treaty in the French parliament, might outlive the campaign and relieve some of the pressures on his minority government, but this failed to materialize. Conversely, the 'no' camp encompassed the Communist party (PCF) and left-wing trade unions, Socialist dissidents led by Jean-Pierre Chevènement, Jean-Marie Le Pen's *Front national*, the conservative *souveraintistes* of Philippe de Villiers, and a substantial block of dissident Gaullists, led by former ministers Philippe Séguin and Charles Pasqua.

The articulate Séguin quickly emerged as the de facto leader of the 'no' camp, appearing alongside Mitterrand – and by satellite, German Chancellor **Helmut Kohl** – in a high-profile televised debate on the treaty. By contrast, the RPR leader, Jacques Chirac, was uncharacteristically self-effacing during the campaign: although potentially the biggest beneficiary of a Mitterrand defeat, he felt compelled to support the treaty and did not want to accentuate his party's divisions in public.

One of the principal issues of the campaign was the question of German power and whether Maastricht would accentuate or contain it. The opponents of the treaty argued that **Economic and Monetary Union** (EMU) would institutionalize deflationary economics, pioneered by the Bundesbank, and that extensions of Community **competence** and **qualified majority voting** (QMV) in the **Council of Ministers** would prevent France from defending its national interest. Advocates of the treaty argued the reverse: that EMU was a French strategic goal which involved sharing monetary **sovereignty** that would otherwise be exercised by Germany alone, and that **German reunification** required the creation of a stronger European framework which could, in Byron Criddle's words, 'reconfirm the continued binding of the German leviathan' (see below). Former prime minister Michel Rocard argued graphically that the treaty was necessary to 'save Germany from its demons', with former President **Valéry Giscard d'Estaing** adding that a 'no' vote 'would ensure German predominance in Europe'.

During the final week of the referendum campaign, rising tension and uncertainty about the result helped generate acute instability on the (already volatile) currency markets, culminating in the dramatic events of 16 September, '**Black Wednesday**', when the pound sterling and Italian lira were ejected from the **Exchange-Rate Mechanism** (ERM) of the **European Monetary System** (EMS), and the Spanish peseta was devalued by five per cent. The disruptive impact of German reunification on the ERM had made existing parities unsustainable, but for various reasons the member states refused a realignment, until one was in effect forced upon them by events.

The narrow 'yes' majority – a '*petit oui*' of 548,775 votes out of a total of 25.79 million cast – was a serious political disappointment for Mitterrand and it highlighted the continued lack of consensus on European issues in France, where a substantial, populist minority of left and right had long opposed closer integration. In the event, around 80 per cent of Socialists and 60 per cent of UDF supporters voted 'yes', but only 40 per cent of Gaullists and 20 per cent of Communists did so. Had Chirac not given grudging support to the treaty, it would almost certainly have been defeated. The lasting impact of the referendum in France was to shift political discourse in a more Eurosceptic direction, as European issues – which had become the preserve of ministers, civil servants and the business élite in Paris during the 1970s and 1980s – were once again opened up to wider public debate. The narrowness of the result, together with the monetary crisis of Black Wednesday, made ratification substantially more difficult to achieve in the United Kingdom. The **Maastricht ratification crisis** begun with the Danish referendum on 2 June 1992 was thus exacerbated by the French President's tactical manoeuvre, which backfired badly.

Further reading: Byron Criddle, 'The French Referendum on the Maastricht Treaty, September 1992', *Parliamentary Affairs*, Volume 46, Number 2, 1993.

Functionalism and neo-functionalism

Functionalism and neo-functionalism are theories of integration which featured prominently in writing about the prospects and practice of European unification from the 1940s to the 1980s. The theories had both 'positive' and 'normative' characteristics. Although they purported to explain how institutional integration would develop, or was already developing, in practice – essentially on a 'modular' basis, policy sector by policy sector – they worked from differing assumptions about the conditions necessary for legitimate government at supranational level, and thus offered contrasting blueprints for how decision-makers might go about 'building Europe'.

Functionalism denotes a form of integration between states which is based upon practical cooperation in well-defined areas with a minimum of institutional apparatus. It involves no institutional blueprint and is driven by economic, social and technical imperatives, rather than by political forces. Functionalist thinkers, notably David Mitrany, writing during and after the Second World War, envisaged a future in which a series of apolitical, technocratic agencies would operate at international level to address a range of specific questions – such as the coordination of policy on air traffic control, postal services or refugees – that required a measure of common management to be effective.

Functionalists believed that, as states acquired the habit of working together on technical issues, the number of areas in which they would be willing to cooperate would gradually widen, with joint action spilling over from one sector to another. Through this process, the notion of **sovereignty** and the constraints of the nation state would gradually be superseded, with common policies developing pragmatically at continental or global levels. In *A Working Peace System* (1943, updated 1966), Mitrany foresaw the emergence of a new order which would 'overlay political divisions with a spreading web of international activities and agencies, in which and through which the interests and life of all the nations would be gradually integrated'.

Although functionalism does not preclude the incremental development of a free-standing political system at international level, it sees this as only one possible long-term outcome, rather than an inevitable one. The integrative dynamic of practical experience and learning by citizens could lead over time to an 'accumulation of partial transfers' of loyalty, bringing about a 'translation of the true seat of authority' and a new sharing of sovereignty. However, it views as potentially dangerous any premature transition to **federalism** without a corresponding community of values and opinion to underpin it. As Paul Taylor has put it, 'the functionalist argument [is] that sovereignty is vitally dependent upon the loyalties of citizens; that institution is sovereign which attracts popular loyalties' ('The Concept of Community and the European Integration Process' in Michael Hodges (editor), *European Integration*,

1972). This view was given additional credence by the writings of the distinguished polymath social scientist, Karl Deutsch. Having examined the creation and survival of federal or unitary nation states in European history, Deutsch argued in 1957 that legal and institutional frameworks were much less important than the existence of a common sense of community at mass level. A decade later, he concluded that the progress of institutional unification in Europe had 'not been matched by any corresponding integration of mutual behaviour' (*France, Germany and the Western Alliance*, 1967).

Neo-functionalism accepts the logic of functionalist 'spillover' between policy areas, taking it several steps further. It argues that a federal political system can evolve on a modular basis and will be guided at least as much by the choices and preferences of political élites as by technical necessities or public opinion. Neo-functionalist writers in the 1950s and 1960s – notably American political scientist Ernst Haas and his student, Leon Lindberg – asserted that the benefits of, and interests created by, integration in any one policy sector would quickly create strong political pressures – notably from organized special interests and civil servants – for a further deepening in contiguous policy areas. National political leaders would respond positively to such demands, and the development of joint policies would be accompanied by the creation of supranational political institutions to exercise democratic control over the process. Haas defined political integration as 'the process whereby political actors in several distinct national settings are persuaded to shift their loyalties, expectations and political activities towards a new and larger centre, whose institutions possess or demand jurisdiction over the pre-existing national states. The end result of a process of political integration is a new political community, superimposed over the pre-existing ones' (*The Uniting of Europe: Political, Social and Economic Forces, 1950–57*, 1958).

Haas argued that the **European Coal and Steel Community** (ECSC) had already shown that the 'initiation of a deliberate scheme of political unification, to be accepted by the key groups that make up a pluralistic society, does not require absolute majority support, nor need it rest on identical aims on the part of all participants.' Instead, the ECSC offered a 'multitude of different advantages to different groups', which increasingly tended to organize on a multinational basis and to favour further integration wherever it might help them. Popular attitudes towards European integration were less important than the reality of sovereignty-sharing among an increasingly wide span of political actors.

In *The Political Dynamics of European Economic Integration* (1963), Lindberg argued that the effect of spillover would be to move decision-making over time from a diplomatic search for the lowest common denominator, or simply splitting the difference, to an 'upgrading [of] common interests', with 'the participation of institutions or individuals with an autonomous role that permits them to participate in actually defining the terms of the agreement'. Although the integration process would be far from smooth, participants would ultimately 'prefer to resolve crises by expanding their mutual obligations', as Philippe Schmitter has put it, rather than contracting them ('spill-back') or avoiding decisions altogether ('Neo-Functionalism', in Antje Wiener and Thomas Diez (editors), *European Integration Theory*, 2009).

The credibility of the Haas–Lindberg analysis came under strain as the political momentum behind first the ECSC, and then the EEC, stalled in the course of the 1960s. As the Communities entered a period of stasis lasting two decades, neo-functionalism became increasingly unfashionable. Nowadays, it is often contrasted with the theory of 'liberal intergovernmentalism', most closely associated with Andrew Moravcsik, which developed in the 1990s. The latter sees sovereign state actors, as opposed to oblique bureaucratic or business forces, as the key drivers of the pace and form of European unification. The EU integration process, Moravcsik writes, 'can best be understood as a series of rational choices made by national leaders. These choices respond to constraints and opportunities stemming from the economic interests of powerful domestic constituents, the relative power of each state in the international system, and the role of institutions in bolstering the credibility of interstate commitments' (*The Choice for Europe: Social Purpose and State Power from Messina to Maastricht*, 1998). Whereas neo-functionalism assumes a gradual process of growing interdependence which steadily transforms the nature of relations between states, the liberal intergovernmental model focuses on the grand bargains struck between leaders, often at **summit** meetings, to explain major steps in European integration. The two perspectives need not, however, be seen as incompatible, as liberal intergovernmentalism attaches too little importance to the routine 'Europeanization' and *engrenage* (or meshing-in) of national élites through their engagement in EU business, whilst neo-functionalism fails to account for the sudden step-changes that periodically occur in deepening the Union's policies or institutions, usually under the impact of one or two particularly influential heads of government.

G

General Affairs Council

See **Foreign Affairs Council** (FAC) **and General Affairs Council** (GAC).

Genscher–Colombo Plan

The Genscher–Colombo Plan was a bilateral initiative taken in November 1981 by the German and Italian foreign ministers, Hans-Dietrich Genscher and Emilio Colombo, in which they proposed the adoption of a 'draft European Act' to supplement the **Treaty of Rome.** Their plan envisaged a 'common foreign policy' and 'coordination of security policy', based on the further development of **European Political Cooperation** (EPC). The **European Council** (of EC heads of government) would be recognized as the 'organ of political guidance' within the Community, with its (then) rotating president-in-office reporting every six months to the **European Parliament**. The latter body would be consulted before the appointment of the President of the **European Commission** and before further **enlargement** of the Community.

According to the plan, the various formations of the **Council of Ministers** would be widened to include regular meetings of ministers of justice and culture, and potentially of ministers in other policy areas not covered by the **Treaties.** 'Decisive importance' was attached to adhering to the Council voting procedures set down in the Treaties, with an obligation on any member state to explain in writing why it might be attempting to block a decision requiring **qualified majority voting** (QMV), by invoking the **Luxembourg Compromise**. States would have the chance to defer a Council decision at two successive meetings, but, after that, by implication, a vote would be taken.

Reactions among the member states to the Genscher–Colombo Plan were generally cautious. France – which had yet to embark on the vigorously pro-European policy that would later characterize its new President, **François Mitterrand** – displayed little public enthusiasm for the Bonn–Rome initiative, still less for its obvious exclusion from the exercise. The French minister for European affairs, André Chandernagor, spoke mischievously of some politicians trying to build Europe 'from the roof down'. The United Kingdom was fearful of the budgetary implications of extending Community activity into new policy areas and also, with Denmark and Greece, it was concerned about any potential watering-down of the Luxembourg Compromise. The position even of Germany was uncertain, as Chancellor Helmut Schmidt's commitment to the proposals co-authored by his foreign minister – who was also leader of his (Liberal) FDP coalition partner – sometimes looked half-hearted.

In the event, the European Council, meeting in London in November 1981, received the Genscher–Colombo text 'with satisfaction' and requested the foreign ministers to study it and report back in due course. During long negotiations among EU ambassadors in Brussels, it was agreed to downgrade the document from a draft legislative text to a mere declaration without binding effect. On this basis, the 'Solemn Declaration on European Union' – usually known as the **Stuttgart Declaration** – was adopted at the European Council meeting in that city 18 months later. The long-term significance of the Genscher–Colombo Plan and the Stuttgart Declaration that followed lay in the degree to which – together with the Parliament's more ambitious **Draft Treaty establishing the European Union** (DTEU) in February 1984 – they helped define a new agenda for institutional reform in Europe. The main points in the Genscher–Colombo Plan were eventually agreed in the **Intergovernmental Conferences** (IGCs) that drafted the 1986 **Single European Act** (SEA) and 1992 **Maastricht Treaty**.

German reunification

The 1949 Basic Law (*Grundgesetz*) or constitution of the Federal Republic of Germany (FRG) made provision for the eventual reunification of the divided Germany, without specifying in detail how this might be achieved. In the event, after the fall of the Berlin Wall on 9 November 1989, the FRG and the German Democratic Republic (GDR) agreed in early 1990 that the individual *Länder* of the GDR – Brandenburg, Sachsen, Sachsen-Anhalt, Thüringen, Mecklenburg-Vorpommern and the city of East Berlin – would join the FRG under Article 23 of its constitution, adding almost 17 million people to the latter's population. However, this meant a de facto **enlargement** of the European Community of a kind not provided for in the **Treaty of Rome**. In April 1990, the **European Council** meeting in Dublin decided that the territory of the former GDR would be incorporated into the Community on German reunification. The two Germanies consulted very closely with the Community institutions before reunification was finally and formally achieved under the Unification Treaty *(Einigungsvertrag)* on 3 October 1990.

Many of the most contentious issues were settled in the preparatory State

Treaty *(Staatsvertrag)*, which came into effect on 1 July 1990. In this text, the two Germanies agreed that **EU law** would apply in the former GDR with effect from reunification and that the GDR would progressively align its policies with Community practices and objectives. A **protocol** to the Treaty of Rome already allowed trade between the two Germanies to be regarded as 'internal trade' and thus not subject to the **Common Customs Tariff** (CCT), in line with the constitution of the FRG. Particular articles of the State Treaty dealt with the application of the **Common Agricultural Policy** (CAP), monetary reform and the transition to a market economy.

On the Community side, the reunification of Germany prompted a comprehensive appraisal of the ***acquis communautaire*** and the identification of measures that would have to be modified to take account of the former GDR's special circumstances or applied only after a transitional period. A temporary committee of the **European Parliament** was set up for this purpose. An analysis was also made of the GDR's international obligations as set out in various treaties and agreements. In the institutional field, the only major change consequent upon reunification was an increase in the number of German seats in the European Parliament. With effect from the date of reunification, 18 'observers' from the former GDR were added to the Parliament, with speaking rights in committees but without the right to vote. Initially, these observers were chosen by the GDR parliament, the *Volkskammer*, but later by the Bundestag. In 1991, the European Parliament voted – by 241 votes to 62 (38 of whom were French) – in favour of increasing the number of German members from 81 to 99, with effect from the 1994 **European elections**. This decision was controversial in some member states, and it was not endorsed until the Edinburgh meeting of the European Council in December 1992. (The French government used opposition in the French National Assembly as a pretext for forcing the Parliament to build a new hemicycle and offices in Strasbourg: see **seats of EU institutions**.) German representation in other institutions was not increased, with the weighting assigned to Germany for the purposes of **qualified majority voting** (QMV) in the **Council of Ministers** left unchanged.

The absence of a treaty formally ending the Second World War, the special status of Berlin, the presence of Russian troops in the GDR, the de facto incorporation of the former GDR into the **North Atlantic Treaty Organization** (NATO) and anxieties over a reunited Germany's eastern frontier with Poland gave rise to negotiations in July and August 1990, known as the 'Two plus Four' talks (referring to the two Germanies, plus France, the United Kingdom, the United States and the USSR). Agreement was reached on the ending of the Allies' special status in Germany, on a new German–Polish Treaty, on the granting of full **sovereignty** to a reunited Germany, including the right to join NATO, and on the withdrawal of Soviet forces from German soil. The last of the 550,000 Russians (350,000 soldiers plus civilian employees and families) left Germany in mid-1994, at a cost to the German taxpayer of about 13 billion Deutschmarks (€ 6.6 billion)

Although the GDR was economically the most advanced of the COMECON states, it was very backward by comparison with the FRG. This meant that the reunited Germany found itself with some of both the richest and poorest regions in the European Union. Levels of pollution in the GDR were particularly high, and the whole fabric of the country was in a poor state of repair. Dealing with these problems was to demand huge resources for many years to come. The initial loss of population from east to west was stemmed in part by the (controversial) decision to make Berlin once more the capital of Germany.

An important and largely unforeseen side effect of German reunification was the de facto breakdown of the **Exchange-Rate Mechanism** (ERM) of the **European Monetary System** (EMS) in September 1992. The German government's choice of financing the costs of reunification mainly by additional borrowing, rather than higher taxes, and its determination to maintain international confidence in the Deutschmark forced the Bundesbank to adopt higher interest rates. This in turn required other member states to keep their own interest rates high, so that their currencies could remain within the permitted narrow band of fluctuation against the German currency. By September 1992 the strain had become too great, and the pound sterling and the Italian lira were driven out of the ERM on **Black Wednesday**. Germany was widely criticized for pursuing an essentially domestic interest-rate policy, with little or no regard for the wider European responsibilities that flowed from its anchor role within the ERM.

Politically, German reunification was a very substantial triumph for Chancellor **Helmut Kohl**. The uncertainty surrounding it meant that his calmness and fixity of purpose suddenly became very attractive to the German electorate, and his CDU–CSU party did very well in the first all-German elections of December 1990, the European elections of June 1994 and the national elections four months later. Over the longer term, reunification consolidated Germany's position as the most influential member state of the Union.

Further reading: Jeffrey Anderson, *German Unification and the Union of Europe*, 1999.

Giscard d'Estaing, Valéry (born 1926)

Born into a comfortable upper middle-class family – his father was a senior civil servant and his mother allegedly a descendant of Louis XV – Valéry Giscard d'Estaing served in the French army, at the age of 18, during its advance into Germany in 1944–5. He returned to Paris to study at the École

Polytechnique and then become one of the first graduates of the new élite French civil-service training school, the École Nationale d'Administration (ENA), created by **Charles de Gaulle** as prime minister in 1945. Like his father, Giscard was appointed an *inspecteur des finances*. After spells in the Banque de France, the finance ministry and the office of premier Edgar Faure, he was elected to the French National Assembly in 1956, in effect inheriting his grandfather's constituency of Puy-de-Dôme in the Auvergne. He quickly took over part of an amorphous conservative party, the CNIP, which he relaunched as the *Républicains indépendants*, and accepted office under de Gaulle, now French President, first as junior (1959–62) and then, at the age of 35, as full finance minister (1962–6). He was the first product of ENA to hold high office in France.

Giscard was one of the few conservatives outside the Gaullist party to survive and indeed prosper during the first half of the 1960s, protected both by his loyalty to the General and his ministerial status. However, de Gaulle's unexpectedly poor performance in the December 1965 presidential election prompted the President to replace the technocratic Giscard as finance minister with his former prime minister and personal loyalist, Michel Debré. From then on, Giscard drifted away from de Gaulle, presenting himself increasingly as an internal critic within the majority, espousing a '*oui, mais...*' position towards the government, and eventually and controversially advocating a 'no' vote in the 1969 referendum that precipitated the President's resignation.

In return for his support in the resulting presidential election, de Gaulle's successor, Georges Pompidou, invited Giscard to return to the finance ministry, where he served throughout the new President's term, from June 1969 until the latter's early death in April 1974. During the Pompidou years, Giscard was able to express more openly his strong interest in, and increasing commitment to, common action at European level. He presented his party as the 'centrist and European component of the majority' and supported early moves towards **Economic and Monetary Union** (EMU), working in tandem with Raymond Barre, the French European Commissioner responsible for monetary affairs at the time of the **Werner Report**. In 1971, France entered the 'Snake', linking European currencies on a flexible basis, but the system proved unworkable at a time of growing dollar instability during the Vietnam War.

In May 1974, Giscard ran for the French Presidency – against the official Gaullist (UDR) candidate, former prime minister Jacques Chaban Delmas – presenting himself as both an ally of, and alternative to, Gaullism in power and as the standard-bearer of 'change without risk'. With the support of dissident agriculture minister Jacques Chirac, Giscard knocked Chaban out of the contest on the first ballot and then proceeded to defeat Socialist rival

François Mitterrand by a narrow margin on the second ballot, so becoming the third President of the Fifth Republic. As a reward, Giscard appointed Chirac as his prime minister, but the two quickly fell out. Chirac resigned as premier in 1976, to be replaced by Barre, and he refounded the UDR as the RPR, effectively committing himself to displace Giscard as President. Chirac was elected to the new post of Mayor of Paris in 1977 against a Giscardian candidate, so establishing a powerful political base. Giscard reacted by merging the RI and the *Centre démocrate* (the former Christian Democrat MRP of **Robert Schuman**) into a new centre-right grouping, the UDF.

During his time at the Elysée, Giscard proved a reformist President in domestic affairs, liberalizing divorce and abortion law, and lowering the age of voting from 21 to 18. In international policy, he continued Pompidou's work in relaunching Europe and promoting multilateral cooperation after the stasis of de Gaulle's later years. He worked very closely with the new German Chancellor Helmut Schmidt (1974–82) – whom he knew well from their years as finance ministers together – using Franco-German cooperation as an engine to push forward European integration at a time of considerable economic difficulty across the continent. He was directly responsible for the initiative that transformed the system of occasional European Community **summits** into the new **European Council** in 1974–5, and accepted the idea of introducing direct elections to the **European Parliament** as a quid pro quo. At the international level, he was the key mover in the parallel development of the **Group of Seven** (G7) summits among the leaders of the major Western economies. Giscard and Schmidt backed the attempt by **Roy Jenkins**, as President of the **European Commission**, to relaunch EMU in 1977, leading to the foundation of the **European Monetary System** (EMS) in December 1978. He was an active advocate of the creation of the **European Currency Unit** (ECU) in March 1979, although he less successfully proposed that the Community become an *espace judiciaire européen*, an early precursor to cooperation in **Justice and Home Affairs** (JHA). These initiatives, although seen as modest at the time, were significantly to shape the political dynamics of Europe in the longer term. To assuage Gaullist sensitivities, they were presented as part of a strategy to build a 'European confederation', which would offer France a renewed opportunity for international leadership.

The first President of the Fifth Republic to be voted out of office after a single term, Giscard was unexpectedly defeated by Mitterrand in May 1981, in a closely fought replay of the 1974 contest. Just as Giscard had been elected seven years before because of his own and Chirac's disloyalty to the mainstream Gaullists, so Chirac's decision to run in the first ballot against Giscard in 1981 – and his refusal to support him unequivocally on the second ballot – accounted for the incumbent President's narrow defeat. Giscard initially withdrew from political life, still only 58 years old, but after a period of reflection, chose to return to the National Assembly in 1984 – where he served as chairman of its foreign affairs committee from 1987 to 1989 – and became president of the Auvergne regional council two years later.

Giscard remained active in the European debate, becoming a strong advocate of moves to create a single currency and working with Helmut Schmidt in retirement on the project. Giscard was always thought to evince a characteristically French distaste for the supranational pretensions of the European Commission and Parliament, preferring a more intergovernmental approach to advancing integration wherever possible. It was therefore a matter of some surprise when he sought and secured election to the European Parliament in 1989, on a joint RPR–UDF list. He was quickly chosen as leader of the Liberal group (ELDR), but in late 1991, he suddenly left to join the much bigger, centre-right EPP Group – allegedly in expectation that he might emerge as the latter's candidate for the post of President of the Parliament. He resigned from the Parliament two years later.

Although Giscard continued to offer advice from the sidelines as an elder statesman, the election of Chirac as French President in 1995 seemed at first to mark the de facto end of his political career. However, refusing to accept defeat at the hands of his rival, he intervened decisively in a national debate in 2000 that led to a constitutional amendment to reduce the President's term of office from seven to five years. In 2001, he also opposed the **Nice Treaty**, which Chirac had heralded as a French negotiating success, claiming that it failed to address the main institutional issues facing the Union, whilst reducing France's relative voting weight in the **Council of Ministers.**

These disputes weakened Chirac and ironically led to a new modus vivendi emerging between the two men who had dominated French centre-right politics throughout the last quarter of the twentieth century. In December 2001, Chirac pushed successfully for Giscard – who by now was serving somewhat incongruously as a member of the EU's **Committee of the Regions** – to be appointed as chairman of the new **Convention on the Future of Europe**, which was to look at further institutional change, including the possible drafting of a **European Constitution.** Giscard quickly adopted a maximalist interpretation of the mandate extended to the Convention by the Laeken Declaration and committed it to the drafting of a full constitutional text. He provided forceful, if controversial, leadership to the Convention process (in 2002–3), proposing his own wording for several sections. Giscard's instinctive preference for intergovernmental structures was reflected in his successful advocacy of the new post of **President of the European Council** and insistence that the European Council itself be recognized formally as a separate EU institution to the Council of Ministers, as well as in his equally unsuccessful espousal of a 'Congress of the Peoples of Europe', composed jointly of European and national parliamentarians. Giscard tried to get the European

Council referred to in the text of the constitution as the 'supreme body' of the Union. When challenged in the Convention about his assertion that there was an 'emerging consensus' in favour of a permanent President of the European Council, even though most speakers had opposed the initiative, he replied coolly: 'Yes, but I can discern a future consensus for it.'

The rejection of the European Constitution in the **French referendum** of June 2005 came as a major political and personal blow to Giscard, potentially depriving him of his claim to be a new '**founding father**' of the European Union. Once again, he refused to accept defeat, commenting memorably that 'the French people have made a serious mistake which will need to be corrected.' Although the subsequent **Lisbon Treaty** comprised much of the constitutional text, most political leaders had an interest in presenting it as quite distinct and less ambitious. Giscard launched a vigorous campaign against this interpretation, claiming that it was 'the same letter in a new envelope'. In doing so, he was once again proving to be a political figure of extraordinary resilience and longevity.

Poignantly, in July 2007, on the same day as *Le Monde* reported Giscard commenting on the Reform Treaty (as the Lisbon Treaty was initially known), the newspaper reprinted an account of a debate held in the French National Assembly exactly 50 years before. The only unambiguously enthusiastic voice in favour of the ratification of the **Treaty of Rome** was reported to be the same Giscard, then only 30 years old, who, in his maiden speech, had declared prophetically: 'I hope that we will pursue two objectives: the construction of an economic and, in due course, political entity on a continental scale; and, in parallel, the continued assertion of the vocation of our country to enlighten and perhaps lead this process.' In later life, he described the building of the European Union as 'the greatest success of the twentieth century in Europe'.

Valéry Giscard d'Estaing served as president of the **European Movement** at international level from 1989 to 1997 and was awarded the **Charlemagne Prize** in 2002. He published his memoirs, *Le Pouvoir et la Vie,* in three volumes in 1988, 1991 and 2006.

Further reading: Samy Cohen and Marie-Claude Smouts (editors), *La Politique extérieure de Valéry Giscard d'Estaing*, 1985; J. R. Frears, *France in the Giscard Presidency*, 1981.

Greenland and the Faeroes

Greenland is an island of over two million square kilometres – an area larger than France, Germany, Italy, Spain and the United Kingdom put together – with a population of only 50,000 people. The island was a Danish colony until 1953, when it became an integral part of Denmark itself. In January

1973, as part of Denmark, Greenland joined the European Community. In May 1979, Greenland was granted a substantial measure of home rule within Denmark, including the right to hold a **referendum** on whether to remain inside the Community. The vote was held in February 1982, with a majority in favour of withdrawal. A treaty was accordingly signed in March 1984 'amending, with regard to Greenland, the Treaties establishing the European Communities', and the island's departure took effect in July 1986. Since then, Greenland has been one of the **overseas countries and territories** (OCTs) of the European Union. Unlike other OCTs, it does not benefit from the **European Development Fund** (EDF), but instead receives an annual payment by way of compensation for access to its fishing grounds. Greenland also qualifies for assistance from the **structural funds**.

The Faeroes are a small group of islands in the North Atlantic, enjoying internal autonomy under Danish sovereignty. They have opted to remain outside the European Union. However, the islands' trade is covered by free trade arrangements within the **European Economic Area** (EEA).

Group of Seven (G7) / Eight (G8) / Twenty (G20)

Following the economic crisis of 1973–4, the finance ministers of the world's six largest Western industrialized countries – the United States, Japan, France, Germany, Italy and the United Kingdom – began to meet informally, at the suggestion of US Treasury Secretary George Schultz, as the 'Library Group'. The following year, the heads of government of this 'Group of Six' (G6), as they quickly became known, held their first **summit**, as invitees of French President **Valéry Giscard d'Estaing** at Rambouillet, outside Paris. They agreed to institutionalize the meeting as an annual 'Western economic summit': each country would hold the presidency in turn for a calendar year and host the summit sometime between May and July. Canada joined the group in 1976, making it the Group of Seven (G7). The following year, the President of the **European Commission** and the prime minister of the member state occupying the rotating **presidency** of the **Council of Ministers** were invited to participate as permanent guests of the G7 leaders. (An account by **Roy Jenkins** of how, as Commission President, he overcame Giscard's opposition to Community involvement may be found in his *European Diary* (1989).) The fact that no fewer than six of the participants at the summits – four national leaders and two Community representatives – came from Europe meant that the latter's interests were more than adequately represented.

In parallel to the annual summits, the finance ministers of the G7 countries continued to meet separately on a regular basis, discussing macro-economic coordination and producing, for example, the Plaza and Louvre accords on currency stabilization in 1985 and 1987. From 1994 to 1997, Russia was invited to participate in some sessions of G7 summits as a guest – forming the so-called 'P8' of 'G7 plus one'. At the suggestion of US President Bill Clinton, Russia became a full member of the new Group of Eight (G8) in 1998. Since then, a distinction has been drawn between the G8 and G7 processes, the first operating at the level of heads of government (and increasingly other ministers) and the second specifically at the level of finance ministers. The governors of national central banks, including the President of the **European Central Bank** (ECB), are now invited to the meetings of the G7 finance ministers. At official level, the G7 meetings are prepared by 'deputies' and the G8 summits by 'sherpas' (and 'sous-sherpas').

During the last decade, the annual presidency of the G8 has emerged as a much more publicly visible role, fuelled by the growing controversy around globalization issues. The fact that G8 countries represent only 14 per cent of the world's population, whilst still generating over 55 per cent of global output (a figure expected to fall to a quarter in 2050), has exposed it to attack. The disruption by violent protests at the G8 summit in Genoa in 2001 led to a reappraisal of the group's direction, with the G8 process now addressing a broader set of issues and the country in the chair undertaking many more activities than before. During the 2000s, the G8 presidencies and summits played an important part in launching the Global Health Fund, promoting action to relieve the position of heavily indebted third-world countries, and evolving specific programmes to encourage development in sub-Saharan Africa. G8 summits began increasingly to involve other international leaders. Participants at the summit at Gleneagles in July 2005 were joined, for part of their proceedings, by the leaders of China, India, Brazil, Mexico and South Africa – the 'outreach five' or 'G8 plus five' – as well as by the heads of several international organizations. This dialogue has been continued, in varying forms, at subsequent meetings. A tier of G8 'departmental level' ministerial meetings was developed (including foreign, finance, environment, development, energy, employment, home affairs and science ministers) and a series of special 'expert groups' were formed (on issues such as health, nuclear safety and intellectual property). The speakers of the national parliaments of the G8 member states began to meet each autumn in the country of the presidency. Since 2007, they have included the President of the **European Parliament** as a permanent guest.

As the democratic experience in Russia became increasingly problematic in the 2000s, so that country's membership of the G8 proved more controversial. During his 2008 US presidential election bid, the Republican candidate, Senator John McCain, called for Russia's expulsion, arguing that the G8 should again become 'a club of leading market democracies: it should include Brazil and India, but exclude Russia'. However, the intra-G8 problem of Russia was quickly overtaken, from the autumn of 2008 on, by the sudden impact of the international economic and financial crisis in challenging the status and relevance of the whole G7/G8 process as the principal framework for discussion of global economic issues. The pre-existing, but little-known, Group of Twenty (G20), comprising both industrialized and emerging-market economies, rapidly developed as a forum that usefully encompassed a much wider range of actors.

The G20 emerged as an offshoot of G7 meetings. In September 1999, the Canadian finance minister, Paul Martin, secured the support of his colleagues for the creation of such a forum, which met for the first time three months later. In addition to the finance ministers and central bank governors of the G8 countries and the European Union (which was designated from the start as a full participant), the G20 embraces those of Argentina, Australia, Brazil, China, India, Indonesia, Mexico, Saudi Arabia, South Africa, South Korea and Turkey. Together, the G20 countries represent over two-thirds of the world's population and generate almost 90 per cent of global output. The Managing Director of the International Monetary Fund (IMF) and the President of the World Bank are permanent guests at G20 meetings and a variety of other international organizations are usually invited. The G20 is chaired on a rotating basis by a country drawn from a different regional grouping each year: South Korea in 2010, France in 2011 and Mexico in 2012. Like the G7 and G8, the G20 has no permanent secretariat; responsibility for servicing its meetings rests with the country in the chair.

Since the onset of the economic and financial crisis in 2008, G20 finance ministers have met at least twice, rather than once, per year. At the suggestion of US President George W. Bush, G20 heads of government have held regular summits and there have been annual meetings of foreign ministers too. The first G20 summit took place in Washington in November 2008, while two were held in 2009 (London and Pittsburgh) and 2010 (Toronto and Seoul). From 2011, the pattern has reverted to one summit per year. The summits and ministerial gatherings are prepared at official level by meetings of 'deputies' and working groups. In 2009, a G20 parliamentary speakers' meeting was held, in addition to the G8 meeting, for the first time.

The advent of G8 summits was initially heralded as an unambiguously positive development in world affairs, with great media excitement surrounding the meetings. This process reached its apogée at the London summit in April 2009, hosted by the (then) British prime minister, Gordon Brown, which attempted to address the economic crisis, creating inter alia a Financial Stability Board (FSB), which operates in parallel to the **Bank for International Settlements** (BIS) in Basle. The Pittsburgh meeting, five months later, decided that the G20 would replace the G8 as the principal forum for worldwide economic cooperation. However, since then, enthusiasm for the G20 has waned, as successive meetings have failed to deliver on the early promise of the new system. In response to the Japanese earthquake and nuclear safety crisis in March 2011, it was G7 finance ministers who took the lead in defining the international economic response, with concerted intervention to stabilize the yen.

Following the introduction of the **Lisbon Treaty** in December 2010, the prime minister of the member state holding the rotating presidency of the Council ceded his or her place (as one of the Union's two representatives) at G8 and G20 summits to the occupant of the new post of **President of the European Council**. By mutual agreement, the President of the European Commission leads the EU delegation to the G20 meeting, and the President heads the delegation of the European Council to the G8 one. (This division of labour reflects the fact that the business of G20 summits tends to be primarily political, whereas that of G8 meetings is predominantly economic.) The **High Representative** for the **Common Foreign and Security Policy** (CFSP) now represents both the Council of Ministers and European Commission at meetings of foreign ministers. For meetings of finance or other ministers, the representatives of the rotating presidency continue to attend, alongside the relevant Commissioners and (where appropriate) the ECB. The formal exclusion of certain major European economies from the G20 process has been a source of controversy in the countries concerned. However, Spain (the world's ninth largest economy) and the Netherlands (the 16th largest economy) have so far been invited to four G20 summits as 'outreach' guests.

The G7, G8 and G20 are to be distinguished from a variety of other groupings using a 'G' prefix, notably the G10 nations within the IMF and the G77 group of developing countries at the **United Nations** (UN). The member states of the **Organization for Economic Cooperation and Development** (OECD) met in the 1990s as the G24, and today they are sometimes referred to as the G30.

Gymnich meetings

The EU member state which occupies the rotating **presidency** of the **Council of Ministers** usually programmes several 'informal' meetings of ministers, at which discussions can be held in a relaxed atmosphere without the need to take decisions or adopt conclusions. By convention, these meetings are held on the territory of the presidency country and are an opportunity for that member state to showcase activities during its six-month term. Since April 1974, foreign ministers have met informally every spring and autumn in the presidency country at gatherings known as 'Gymnich meetings' or 'Gymnichs'. They are named after Schloss Gymnich, near Bonn, where the first such event was held. Often these meetings are devoted to one or more major themes. For example, in September 2007, the Portuguese presidency's

Gymnich meeting in Viana do Castelo provided foreign ministers with an opportunity to take stock of the **Intergovernmental Conference** (IGC) negotiating what became the **Lisbon Treaty**. The March 2010 meeting, hosted by the Spanish presidency in Córdoba, enabled foreign ministers to review progress in establishing the new **European External Action Service** (EEAS). The Córdoba Gymnich was the first to be attended by the **High Representative** since the latter became responsible, under the Lisbon Treaty, for chairing the **Foreign Affairs Council** (FAC). After some initial resistance, it was accepted that the High Representative, rather than the foreign minister of the presidency country, should chair Gymnich meetings as well as the FAC itself.

H

Hallstein, Walter (1901–82)

Walter Hallstein was the first President of the **European Commission** and, other than **Jacques Delors**, the most influential holder of that office to date. Pursuing an academic career until becoming an adviser to **Konrad Adenauer** in 1950, Hallstein led the German delegation in the discussions on the **Schuman Plan** and was appointed a junior minister in the foreign ministry in 1951. He developed the 'Hallstein doctrine', by which (between 1955 and 1967) West Germany refused to have diplomatic relations with countries that recognized East Germany as a state. He represented the Federal Republic at the **Messina Conference** in June 1955 and was actively involved in the negotiations that led, two years later, to the signing of the **Treaties of Rome** establishing the **European Economic Community** (EEC) and the **European Atomic Energy Community** (EAEC or Euratom).

In 1958, Hallstein was rewarded for his European commitment and expertise by being chosen as the first President of the new EEC Commission, a post in which he remained for nine years. He was also the first German to head a major international body after the Second World War; the appointment was seen by some, in the words of *The Economist* at the time, as a 'trophy of national rehabilitation'. With an ambitious view of the potential of the Commission as an institution, he quickly became a central figure in the politics of European integration. Working in tandem with his talented Secretary General, **Emil Noël**, Hallstein built the Commission up from a small central secretariat into something approaching the embryonic European government which he thought it should be.

Hallstein set a rapid pace in presenting measures to create a **customs union** and **common market**, in accordance with the three stages of the 'transitional phase' of the Community's planned development from 1958 onwards. Equally, the decisions he took with his Vice-President responsible for agriculture, Sicco Mansholt, had a decisive impact on the shape of the emerging **Common Agricultural Policy** (CAP). Under Hallstein's presidency, it was agreed that the Commission in Brussels would serve all three European Communities, rather than just the EEC (see **Merger Treaty**). His activist vision was, as he put it soon after taking office, that 'unification of [Europe's] economies is a political act leading to political union.' He was one of the first to argue that the founding **Treaties** had 'set in motion a process far more ambitious than the modest words "economic integration" would suggest', with the emerging Community 'a federation in the making'.

Hallstein's vigorous advocacy of the Commission's authority and independent policy role soon brought him into conflict with some national politicians wary of the pretensions of supranational institutions, notably the French President, **Charles de Gaulle**. The dialectic between Hallstein and de Gaulle was to become one of the most vivid features of European politics in the mid-1960s. The General was consistently irritated by the minor governmental symbolism which Hallstein promoted, such as his insistence that the Commission receive the credentials of ambassadors accredited to the Community. However, he also became increasingly opposed to Hallstein's larger objectives, such as moving as quickly as possible to a system of **own resources** for the Community **Budget** and insisting that **qualified majority voting** (QMV) be applied to important areas of decision-making within the **Council of Ministers**, as the Treaties foresaw from January 1966.

The conflict came to a head during the second half of 1965, with the so-called 'empty chair crisis', when France boycotted meetings of the Council and its preparatory bodies. The crisis was resolved by the **Luxembourg Compromise** of January 1966. Hallstein's authority never fully recovered from this bruising confrontation: as F. Roy Willis wrote soon after, 'In the struggle with de Gaulle, he was to lose not only the battle for **supranationalism** but his own job too' (*France, Germany and the New Europe, 1945–1967*, 1968). At the special summit to mark the tenth anniversary of the Treaties of Rome, in May 1967, the French President allegedly refused to acknowledge him. Hallstein resigned the following month, when the Merger Treaty took effect – de Gaulle having secured German acquiescence in his departure – and retired from public life in 1972. He was followed as Commission President by a series of short-lived incumbents – Jean Rey, Franco Maria Malfatti and Sicco Mansholt together occupied the post for a total of only six years – who were more modest in their political style and more careful in their handling of heads of state or government.

Further reading: Walter Hallstein, *United Europe: Challenge and Opportunity*, 1962, and *Europe in the Making*, 1972; Wilfried Loth et al., *Walter Hallstein: The Forgotten European?*, 1998.

Harmonization

The **free movement of goods** within the **common market** was one of the fundamental objectives of the **Treaty of Rome.** However, differences between national product standards meant that free circulation was difficult to achieve, and such standards allowed member states too much scope for introducing or maintaining 'technical' barriers to trade on (sometimes spurious) scientific or health and safety grounds. With the removal of tariffs and quotas on trade between the EC member states – achieved in 1968 under Articles 9 and 34 EEC, now Articles 28, 34 and 35 TFEU – product standards became the key residual instrument for protectionism within the Community. Throughout the 1960s and 1970s, the **European Commission** sought to draw up common standards, a process usually known as harmonization, but referred to in the Treaty as 'approximation' (or in French, *rapprochement*). Article 100 EEC referred to the 'approximation of such laws, regulations or administrative provisions of the Member States as directly affect the establishment or functioning of the common [now internal] market'. This wording is still maintained in Article 115 TFEU, as well as in the newer, parallel, Article 114 TFEU – introduced by the 1986 **Single European Act** (SEA) – which talks of approximating such laws and other provisions that 'have as their object the establishment or functioning of the internal market'. Together, **Articles 114 and 115** constitute the legal base for harmonization.

Although, from the start, harmonization was supported in principle by industry and indeed governments, for many years progress proved very slow. The Commission became locked into a pattern of proposing extremely detailed draft legislation of a kind which sometimes prompted ridicule and was only rarely adopted. The difficulty of securing agreement was exacerbated by the fact that, before the Single European Act introduced **qualified majority voting** (QMV) in this field, agreement in the **Council of Ministers** had to be unanimous. Encouraged by the judgement of the **European Court of Justice** (ECJ) in the **Cassis de Dijon case** in 1980 (Case 120/78), the Commission eventually decided to adopt a 'new approach', based on mutual recognition, as a precursor to relaunching the **single market** more widely. The new approach, agreed by the Council in a resolution in May 1985, worked from the presumption that a product legally on sale in one member state could be freely sold in any other. The aim henceforth was to set only minimum common standards, on the basis of health and safety requirements, and to leave the technical details to be worked out by specialist bodies in consultation with manufacturers (notably through the CEN and CENELEC systems). Harmonization along such lines became one of the essential foundations of the comprehensive single market programme set out in the

Cockfield White Paper of June 1985 and has remained central to Commission thinking on the integration of the European economy ever since.

Heath, Edward (1916–2005)

Edward Heath was the prime minister who secured the accession of the United Kingdom to the European Community in January 1973, an achievement which seems all the greater with the passage of time. A lifelong advocate of Britain's active involvement in the process of European integration, Heath was elected a Conservative MP in 1950 and made his maiden speech in the House of Commons on the **Schuman Plan**, arguing for British participation in the proposed **European Coal and Steel Community** (ECSC), against the mainstream view in all political parties at the time. Following the decision of his political mentor, Harold Macmillan (British prime minister 1957–63), to launch Britain's first application to join the European Community in 1961, Heath was entrusted, as Lord Privy Seal, with responsibility for leading the negotiations for entry. After a promising start, these discussions were brought to an abrupt end by the veto of French President **Charles de Gaulle** in January 1963. Speaking in response to an event which delivered a serious blow to pro-Europeans in Britain and was to keep his country out of the Community for a decade, Heath declared, with the quiet determination that characterized his approach to the issue:

> *We in Britain are not going to turn our backs on the mainland of Europe or on the countries of the Community. We are part of Europe by geography, tradition, history, culture and civilization. We shall continue to work with our friends in Europe for the true unity and strength of this continent.*

The Conservatives lost power to Labour in October 1964 and Heath was elected leader of his party nine months later, as a 'young modernizer' committed to a more technocratic style of politics. After five difficult years in opposition, in which he suffered constant attacks from the right wing of his party, Heath unexpectedly led the Conservative party to victory at the June 1970 general election. One of his government's first acts was successfully to reactivate the stalled negotiations that had followed the UK's second application for Community membership, made by the previous Labour government of Harold Wilson in 1967.

The strong personal rapport which Heath rapidly established with de Gaulle's successor, Georges Pompidou, was an important component in bringing entry negotiations to a successful conclusion. Heath understood the importance of personal relations in foreign policy and used this to full effect with the French President. A critical summit between the two men in Paris in May 1971, held without the prior knowledge of a sceptical Quai d'Orsay, allowed the essential breakthrough to occur, after which detailed arrangements were agreed relatively quickly. Speaking with Heath in the same room of the Elysée Palace as de Gaulle had pronounced his veto eight years before, Pompidou uttered the crucial words that, in his judgement, 'it would be unreasonable to think that agreement between Britain and the European Community will not be reached' in the the ensuing months.

Heath signed the UK's accession treaty on 22 January 1972, at a ceremony in the Palais d'Egmont in Brussels. As he approached the building, at what he later described as the 'proudest moment of my life', a protester threw ink over him and he had quickly to be eased into the suit of one of his officials. The prime minister then forced Community membership through a divided House of Commons, against the backdrop of an increasingly vociferous and polarized national debate. Now opposition leader for the second time, Wilson opportunistically objected to the 'Tory terms' negotiated by the Heath government and, in doing so, unleashed a growing tide of anti-Europeanism in his party and more widely. The Conservatives relied on a revolt by Labour pro-Europeans, led by **Roy Jenkins**, to secure passage of the bill to effect entry – in a parliamentary struggle lasting four months and requiring more than a 170 hours of debate – with the majority for membership falling at one stage to only eight votes. EC membership was to prove one of few unambiguous achievements of a government bedevilled by domestic unrest, whether in Ulster, on pay and prices, or on its attempted reform of trade-union power. There is little doubt that, as the Chancellor of the Exchequer, Anthony Barber, later commented, British accession to the Community was 'brought about primarily through the perseverance of one man' determined to change the political future of his country.

Heath's government was defeated in the early general election he called in February 1974, following a bitter industrial relations dispute with the coal miners; he then failed to dislodge Wilson's minority Labour government in a second election in October of the same year. Four months later, he lost the leadership of the Conservative party to **Margaret Thatcher**, who challenged him from the right. The issue of Europe played little part in Heath's downfall, which was generated by a mixture of his electoral record – a failure to win three of the four general elections he had contested as party leader – and a growing sense that the managerial politics he represented had run its course. Heath was the first former Conservative leader to refuse to follow a convention by which, in declining to criticize publicly his successor, he would enjoy elder statesman status within the party. Mrs Thatcher's policies in general, and especially her growing lack of enthusiasm towards Europe after she became prime minister in May 1979, provided Heath with many pretexts for differing with the woman who had supplanted him as leader and whom he openly despised.

In May 1970, in a speech to the British Chamber of Commerce in Paris, just before the election that brought him to power, Heath had said that it would not be in the interests of the Community if it were to be enlarged without the 'full-hearted consent of the parliaments and peoples of the new member countries'. This proposition was extensively cited by opponents of British membership, notably in the Labour party, to strengthen the case for holding a **referendum** on the question, even after the country had joined. When Wilson returned to power in February 1974, he put in place a largely cosmetic process of '**renegotiation**' of the terms of entry, which in turn led to the referendum that confirmed British membership in June 1975. Although they were opposed to the referendum in principle, both Heath and Thatcher campaigned for a 'yes' vote – alongside the leaders of the Labour and Liberal parties – with varying degrees of enthusiasm. (See also **British referendum on EC membership**.)

Despite Heath's commitment to Europe, he wrote little on the subject. The only comprehensive expression of his thinking was given in his Godkin lectures at Harvard University in 1970, published later that year as *Old World, New Horizons*. He published his autobiography, *The Course of my Life*, in 1998.

Further reading: Uwe Kitzinger, *Diplomacy and Persuasion: How Britain joined the Common Market*, 1973; Con O'Neill, *Britain's Entry into the European Community*, 2000.

Helsinki Final Act

Signed in Helsinki on 1 August 1975 by the 35 states that participated in the 1973–5 **Conference on Security and Cooperation in Europe** (CSCE) – including the United States and the Soviet Union, as well as nearly all countries of Europe on both sides of the Iron Curtain – the Final Act was the most significant joint declaration by East and West during the **Cold War**. Together with the **Charter of Paris** for a New Europe, which was signed on 21 November 1990 and in effect ended the Cold War, the Final Act is the legal basis for today's **Organization for Security and Cooperation in Europe** (OSCE), which encompasses 56 states (all European countries plus the United States, Canada and the central Asian republics of the former USSR).

The Helsinki Final Act set out ten key 'principles guiding relations between participating states'. These included the inviolability of frontiers, the territorial integrity of states, respect for human rights (including explicitly freedom of thought, conscience, religion or belief), self-determination of peoples and non-intervention in the internal affairs of other states. The first two principles were presented by Soviet leaders as a recognition of the USSR's territorial gains in central and eastern Europe after the Second World War, whilst the last three were used by foreign critics and internal dissidents to highlight the hypocrisy of the Soviet régime. Interpretation of the Final Act thus became a lively ideological battleground until the collapse of Communism in Europe in 1989–90.

Helsinki Headline Goal

The Anglo-French **Saint-Malo Declaration** of December 1998 proposed that the European Union should possess the 'capacity for autonomous action, backed up by credible military forces', operating alongside, but outside, the formal structures of the **North Atlantic Treaty Organization** (NATO). Six months later, at the Cologne meeting of the **European Council**, the EU heads of government collectively endorsed this Anglo-French objective as part of a new **Common Security and Defence Policy** (CSDP), which was later incorporated into the 2001 **Nice Treaty**. The Helsinki European Council in December 1999 reiterated the 'determination to develop an autonomous capacity to take decisions and, where NATO as a whole is not engaged, to launch and conduct EU-led military operations in response to international crises'. This process, the summit conclusions noted defensively, 'will avoid unnecessary duplication and does not imply the creation of a **European army**'.

The so-called 'Helsinki Headline Goal', set at that meeting, was that the EU member states should, on a voluntary basis, be able to deploy, at 60 days' notice and for a period of at least a year, up to 60,000 self-sustaining troops, capable of undertaking all the **Petersberg tasks** (of humanitarian and rescue work, peacekeeping, and crisis management, including peacemaking). The target date for the achievement of this ambitious objective was 2003. In practice, in order to sustain up to 60,000 troops in the field for a year, the member states needed to put more than twice that number of personnel at the disposal of the new force. Various 'capabilities conferences' in 2000–1 elicited a commitment to about 100,000 troops and 5,000 police for the 'Helsinki Force Catalogue'. Although the European Council adopted a 'European Capabilities Action Plan' in December 2001 to advance this process and a number of modest ESDP missions were launched in 2003, foreign ministers admitted that progress was 'limited and constrained by recognized shortfalls'.

In face of these difficulties, an updated and more modest Headline Goal was agreed by the European Council in June 2004, setting a revised timetable, whereby the Union would 'be able by 2010 to respond with rapid and decisive action, applying a fully coherent approach to the whole spectrum of crisis management operations'. This new commitment also took account of the EU's European Security Strategy (agreed in December 2003) and the de facto expansion of the Petersberg tasks implied by it (to include joint disarmament operations, the combatting of terrorism and security sector reform). Accordingly, the new 'Headline Goal 2010' encompasses a wider range of objectives than its predecessor. Equally, the vehicle for its delivery has shifted from the notion of a single force of 60,000 troops – a figure originally chosen because it would give the EU the capacity to wage an actual war – to that of a series of separate, smaller units, usually of only 1,500 troops each. Each of these 'Battlegroups' needs to be combat-ready and capable of deployment in all terrains, within five to 30 days for stand-alone operations for an initial duration of 30 days (and, if resupplied, of 120 days). Fifteen Battlegroups were put at the Union's disposal by January 2007, involving in some way all 26 of the EU member states involved in ESDP. They include a Nordic Battlegroup, under Swedish command, and a 'Weimar Battlegroup' encompassing France, Germany and Poland. To date, no Battlegroup has been deployed.

When the original Helsinki Headline Goal was set, the EU's prospective military capability was often referred to as the 'European rapid reaction force'. That title was never officially adopted, although in 2001 the EU did create a specific Rapid Reaction Mechanism, now called Stability Instrument, for certain urgent civilian crisis management interventions. Within NATO, the **Allied Rapid Reaction Corps** (ARRC) is a 'high readiness force' of a military kind, and NATO has awarded the same status to **Eurocorps**, of which six EU member states are full members. Both the ARRC and Eurocorps can be used for EU military missions by mutual consent.

'Hierarchy of acts'

A translation of the French *hiérarchie des actes*, this is the name given to the idea of drafting a coherent list of the different types of legislative act and the law-making procedures for their adoption within the European Union, with a view to the inclusion of such a list in the **Treaties**. Sometimes known as a 'hierarchy of norms', the proposal draws on a reform introduced in France by the constitution of the Fifth Republic adopted in 1959.

At present, a variety of different types of **legal acts** may be adopted at EU level under a range of procedures, depending upon the **legal base** and the subject matter in question. A 'hierarchy' would lay down different categories of legislation, ranging from the most important (namely the Treaties themselves and amendments thereto) to the most trivial (certain implementing decisions under **comitology**), and specify the appropriate legislative procedure for each. In so doing, it would attempt to define in one place the role of the various institutions in the EU law-making process and establish a clear order of precedence between the acts in question.

A 'Declaration on the Hierarchy of Community Acts' was annexed to the 1992 **Maastricht Treaty**, with a view to the issue being taken up in the subsequent **Intergovernmental Conference** (IGC) in 1996. However, the proposal did not feature in the texts of either the 1997 **Amsterdam Treaty** or 2001 **Nice Treaty**, partly because of disagreements over how far the **co-decision pro-**

cedure should be extended, but it was addressed obliquely by the **Convention on the Future of Europe** in 2002–3. Whilst falling short of a clear hierarchy, the text of the **European Constitution** proposed some adjustments to the nomenclature of legal instruments, in order to make their nature clearer. (The relevant provisions were contained in Title V, Chapter I, of the Constitution.) Some of these changes survived into the **Lisbon Treaty**, agreed by the member states in June 2007, as well as the definition of the co-decision procedure as the 'ordinary legislative procedure' of the Union.

High Authority

The executive institution of the **European Coal and Steel Community** (ECSC), established in 1952, the High Authority was the forerunner of the **European Commission.** Its first president (1952–4) was **Jean Monnet**, who resigned after the failure of plans to create a parallel **European Defence Community** (EDC). Under the 1965 **Merger Treaty**, the High Authority was amalgamated (with effect from July 1967) with the Commissions of the two other Communities created in 1958: the **European Economic Community** (EEC) and **European Atomic Energy Community** (EAEC or Euratom).

Within its relatively narrow field – essentially the production, distribution and pricing of coal and steel – the High Authority was attributed more extensive powers than the Commission would subsequently enjoy in relation to the cross-sectoral **common market** launched in 1958. The first example of a free-standing, supranational organization in Europe, the High Authority was able to take binding **decisions** which in many cases the ECSC's Special Council of Ministers could not block or overturn. As Ernst Haas wrote in his classic account of the politics of the ECSC, the 'balance of "federal" as against "intergovernmental" powers seems to point to the conclusion that in all matters relating to the routine regulation of the common market [for coal and steel], the High Authority is independent of governments' (*The Uniting of Europe: Political, Social and Economic Forces 1950–1957*, 1958).

Further reading: Dirk Spierenburg and Raymond Poidevin, *The History of the High Authority of the European Coal and Steel Community*, 1994.

High Representative

During the mid-1990s, a number of diplomats and policy advisers in France and Germany suggested that the European Union's **Common Foreign and Security Policy** (CFSP) should be given a more 'human face and voice' by creating the post of Secretary General for CFSP, akin to similar roles in the **United Nations** and the **North Atlantic Treaty Organization** (NATO). Although this idea was discussed in the negotiations which led to the 1997 **Amsterdam Treaty**, it was not taken up in the final text. Instead, the existing position of Secretary General of the **Council of Ministers** was given the additional title of 'High Representative' for CFSP, with responsibility for 'contributing to the formulation, preparation and implementation of policy decisions, and, when appropriate and acting on behalf of the Council at the request of the **presidency**, through conducting dialogue with third parties' (Article 26 TEU, now repealed). The traditional functions of the Secretary General in managing the Council system were devolved to a new Deputy Secretary General. The Council was given the power to appoint 'Special Representatives' on specific CFSP issues.

At its meeting in Cologne in June 1999, the **European Council** appointed Javier Solana, outgoing Secretary General of NATO, as High Representative for CFSP. Four months later, Solana was also made Secretary General of the **Western European Union** (WEU), as part of the progressive takeover of the WEU by the EU which led to the development of a **Common Security and Defence Policy** (CSDP) as part of CFSP. In the process, he became head of two former WEU bodies – the EU Satellite Centre and EU Institute for Security Studies (EUISS) – which were converted into EU **agencies**. The staff resources within the Council secretariat for external relations were expanded significantly to reflect the needs of this new position.

The new High Representative faced challenges on at least two fronts. Within the Council, he would inevitably find himself in competition with the rotating presidency in representing the Union in its CFSP relations with third countries and international organizations, including in the negotiation of **international agreements**, and in implementing CFSP decisions. (The presidency remained formally responsible for all of these, with the 'assistance' of the High Representative, under provisions of Articles 18 and 24 TEU, now repealed.) In parallel, the High Representative also needed to develop an effective modus vivendi with the **European Commission**, which already had a Commissioner for external relations, as well as Commissioners for **development policy**, humanitarian aid, **enlargement** and the Union's **Common Commercial Policy** (CCP) for external trade. The Commissioner for external relations was entitled to make proposals in the CFSP field (alongside the member states) and could be invited to undertake negotiations on behalf of the Council (instead of the presidency). Equally, if the High Representative ignored the trade or development angles of foreign policy, there was a serious risk of incoherence in Union action externally. In the event, Solana's experience and diplomatic skills enabled him quickly to master the political and bureaucratic quicksand of the EU system, to develop an effective division of labour with his institutional colleagues. He established the practice that he could and would make proposals to the Council, with the support of both the presidency and Commission, and share with the presidency responsibility for negotiating with third countries. His good relations in particular with Chris

Patten, the Commissioner for external relations from 1999 to 2004, enabled the Union to strengthen its profile and action on a number of CFSP issues, including the Middle East and Afghanistan. However, their partnership was overshadowed by the political divisions within the EU – dividing what US Defense Secretary Donald Rumsfeld called '**old and new Europe**' – and between the Union and the United States, before, during and after the 2003 Iraq War.

The question of the respective roles of the High Representative and Commissioner for external relations featured prominently in the **Convention on the Future of Europe** (2002–3), which drafted the aborted **European Constitution**. The Laeken Declaration of EU heads of government in December 2001 asked the Convention to look at how the 'synergy' between the two posts could be strengthened. The Convention discussion – initially conducted in a working group chaired by the former Belgian prime minister Jean-Luc Dehaene – pitted intergovernmental and supranational views of how CFSP should develop against one another. Some *conventionnels* wanted to retain the status quo, underpinned by practical improvements in coordination between the posts. Others wanted to transfer CFSP from the Council to the Commission, with the post of High Representative simply abolished. In between, there was a wide span of opinion which favoured combining the two posts in some way – possibly taking in the CFSP functions of the Council presidency as well – to create a single, upgraded position of either 'external representative' or 'foreign minister' for the Union.

The final form of this merged position was defined in a paper submitted jointly to the Convention by the French and German governments in January 2003, which came in at the more ambitious end of the spectrum. The Franco-German proposal envisaged a new 'Union Minister for Foreign Affairs', who would be appointed by the European Council, acting by **qualified majority voting** (QMV), with the approval of the President of the European Commission. The European foreign minister would replace the two existing posts (of High Representative and Commissioner for external relations) and assume the previous function of the Council presidency on CFSP. Given the different natures of the two institutions, he or she would sit in both, chairing the **Foreign Affairs Council** (FAC) and serving as a Vice-President of the Commission. He or she would be supported logistically by a 'European diplomatic service' drawn from the relevant departments of the Commission and Council. This proposal was then included – with only modest changes, such as calling the diplomatic service a **European External Action Service** (EEAS) – in the final draft of the Constitution.

The new 'double-hatted', or more accurately 'triple-hatted', post of European foreign minister was meant to parallel and, to some degree, offset the other major institutional innovation which the Convention proposed – the creation of a permanent post of **President of the European Council**. The latter individual, as well as having responsibility for chairing the European Council and trying to 'drive forward its work', would 'at his or her level . . . ensure the external representation of the Union' on CFSP issues, 'without prejudice to the powers of the Union Minister for Foreign Affairs' (Article I-22 Constitution). It was not clear whether the words 'at his or her level' – implying that the President of the European Council would deal with heads of state and government, whilst the High Representative would meet foreign ministers – meant that the second post was subordinate to the first. Another interesting feature was that no explicit attempt was made to conflate the external roles of the new President of the European Council with that of the President of the European Commission, whose institution would continue to 'ensure the Union's external representation' in non-CSFP areas.

The ambiguity of this new 'diarchy' or even 'triarchy' at the top of EU foreign policy reflected a political compromise between those, notably in the larger member states, who wanted the President of the European Council to be a strong, assertive figure with a major domestic and international role in profiling the Union, and those who feared the intergovernmental potential of the new position and saw his or her function as primarily that of bringing greater continuity and coherence to the management of the day-to-day business of heads of government.

Despite their path-breaking character, the innovations contained in the Constitution in the CFSP field survived virtually unscathed into the **Lisbon Treaty**, which finally entered force in December 2009. The only significant change was that, to assuage national diplomatic and parliamentary sensitivities following the rejection of the Constitution in the **French and Dutch referenda** of May–June 2005, the words 'Union Minister for Foreign Affairs' were dropped and the existing title of High Representative was retained (even if the role of the post was still very significantly enhanced).

At the time of the Convention discussion, it was assumed that Javier Solana would wish to become the first European foreign minister, and indeed, in June 2004, the European Council signalled its intention to appoint him to that post, once the Constitution had been ratified. In the event, however, it was only five years later that an appointment could be made to the combined post of High Representative and Vice-President of the Commission. By that time, Solana had expressed the desire to retire, after a decade in office, and the search began for a suitable alternative. The choice was intimately bound up with the parallel question of who would be appointed as the first President of the European Council. Several background factors bore on the choices to be made: the preference of Europe's centre-right governments that one of their number should hold the European Council post; the preference of heads of government more generally that the first incumbent of the latter position should not be too dominant a figure (so inhibiting the candidacy of the former British prime minister **Tony Blair**); and the positive desire of centre-left governments to secure the post of High Representative for one of their own. Most importantly, it became apparent that the French President, Nicolas Sarkozy, and the German Chancellor, Angela Merkel, believed that – especially if Blair was not going to become President of the European Council – the position of High Representative should initially go to a British candidate, not least in order to ensure effective cooperation between the Foreign Office and the new EEAS, under a possible Conservative government in the future.

During late October and early November 2009, there was increasing speculation that the one candidate who would meet all criteria was the British Foreign Secretary, David Miliband, and that he had been informally offered the job by the French and German governments. After some days of uncertainty about his intentions, Miliband publicly ruled this option out. When the (then) British prime minister, Gordon Brown, went to Brussels for an informal meeting of the European Council on 19 November 2009, at which the appointments were to be decided, he allegedly had the names of three other current or former Labour ministers in his pocket – Peter Mandelson, Geoff Hoon and Catherine Ashton. When Fredrick Reinfeldt, the Swedish prime minister who was chairing the European Council meeting, asked Brown if he wished to name a candidate for High Representative, he offered Ashton for the post. Her selection was acceptable to the Socialist prime ministers, with whom Brown discussed the question at the 'pre-summit' meeting of the Party of European Socialists (PES) earlier the same day. It also fitted with the immediate political needs of the Commission President, José Manuel Barroso, who saw the practical advantages of appointing an incumbent Commissioner – Ashton had replaced Mandelson as Commissioner for external trade the previous year – and who needed to retain at least the same number of women in his new college of Commissioners, if problems in confirmation by the **European Parliament** were to be avoided.

The post which Ashton took up on 1 December 2009 is unique, and potentially very powerful, in several ways. She is the only person in the EU system to sit simultaneously, as of right, in the European Commission, the Council of Ministers and the European Council: she is a member of the first; she chairs a configuration of the second, the Foreign Affairs Council; and she attends the third. Moreover, in chairing the FAC, the High Representative not only controls both its agenda and the follow-up to its decisions, but she also submits many of the proposals for action which it considers. The High Representative is thus in the unusual position of tabling texts on which she is simultaneously responsible for negotiating compromises. Although most of the decisions to be taken by the FAC require **unanimity**, when they are implementing an existing CFSP position or acting on a mandate from heads of government, they may be taken by QMV. Equally, the High Representative heads the new EEAS, putting at her disposal, in one, independent body – separate from both Commission and Council, and reporting directly to her – the staff who previously served in the foreign policy directorates-general of those two institutions, as well as the separate military staff located within the Council secretariat.

The list of both formal responsibilities and practical resources assigned to the High Representative is formidable. In addition to chairing the FAC (Article 18(3) and 27(1) TEU), she conducts and implements the Union's CFSP, as defined by the Council and European Council (Articles 18(2), 24(1) and 26(3) TEU), and ensures the consistency of the whole of the Union's external action beyond CFSP, drawing on his or her role as a Vice-President of the Commission (Article 18(4) TFEU). The High Representative 'shall represent the Union' on CFSP matters and 'conduct political dialogue with third parties on the Union's behalf' (Article 27(2) TEU). She proposes to the Council the Union's negotiating mandate for international agreements relating 'exclusively or principally' to CFSP and may be chosen by the Council to conduct those negotiations (Article 218(3) TFEU). As Commission Vice-President, she does the same on non-CFSP external relations questions in her domain. The High Representative coordinates the position of the Union and member states in international organizations and at international conferences, including presenting the EU position at the **United Nations** (Article 34 TEU). She issues declarations and statements on behalf of the Union, averaging about one per day, on the whole range of CFSP issues. In all of this, the High Representative is 'assisted' by the EEAS, reporting exclusively to her (Article 27(3) TEU). The Union's 140 delegations (or de facto embassies) in third countries are placed 'under the authority' of the High Representative (Article 221(2) TFEU), as are the Union's Special Representatives, whose appointment she proposes to the Council (Article 33 TEU). The High Representative chairs the governing boards of the Union's three CFSP agencies: the European Defence Agency (EDA), the European Union Satellite Centre (EUSC) and the EU Institute for Security Studies (EUISS). Finally and importantly, the **Political and Security Committee**, which prepares Council discussions on CFSP and directs crisis management operations, is now chaired by a representative of the High Representative, as are most of the Council's 16 working groups in the CFSP field (European Council decision of 1 December 2009).

A great deal of time and energy was devoted during Ashton's first year or so in office to working out how her various roles could be exercised in a coherent way and to managing the politics and practical logistics of establishing the EEAS. This process attracted considerable criticism in the media and certain national capitals, notably Paris. In a potential rebuff, Ashton was forced to concede that the rotating presidency of the Council and other Commissioners, rather than officials of her choice, would routinely substitute for her, respectively in her Council and Commission functions, when she could not attend meetings herself. One area of complexity, where things are still in flux, is the relationship between the High Representative, President of the European Council and President of the European Commission for the Union's external relations at the highest level. Article 17(1) TEU states that, with the exception of CFSP 'and other cases provided for in the Treaties', the Commission 'shall ensure the Union's external representation'. Barroso is determined to protect the Commission's rights, not only in external trade and development policy, but in other areas too – such as the external aspects of environment, energy, transport or economic policy – where the boundaries between CFSP and wider external policy are often unclear. The evolution of foreign policy in national capitals towards 'globalization' and 'soft power' issues is making this interface increasingly blurred.

However, despite start-up problems and inevitable turf fights, the fact remains that, so long as the High Representative retains the trust and confidence of the Foreign Affairs Council, she is potentially in an exceptionally strong position to exercise such power and influence as the Union commands in the foreign, security and defence policy fields. The Lisbon Treaty has, in a complex but sophisticated way, endowed the EU with the institutional mechanisms it needs to underpin a strong and effective policy in CFSP, including CSDP. However, the key political question is whether, in coming years, the foreign and defence ministers of the larger member states, in particular, will be prepared to share their still considerable power and exposure with a European office-holder who now has the potential to emerge, not only as the 'face and voice' of European diplomacy, as originally envisaged in the 1990s, but as a major player, and thus rival, on the international scene in his or her own right.

Human rights

See **European Convention on Human Rights** (ECHR), **Charter of Fundamental Rights.**

I

Iceland

A Danish possession from 1380, Iceland was granted devolution in 1874 and became wholly independent in 1944. With a population of 320,000, the island has the lowest population density of any European country. The Icelanders claim to have the oldest parliament in the world, the Althing, dating from 930.

In spite of its remoteness, the legacy of British and United States occupation during the Second World War led Iceland to participate actively in European organizations from the late 1940s onwards, becoming a member of the **Organization for European Economic Cooperation** (OEEC), the **Council of Europe**, the **North Atlantic Treaty Organization** (NATO), the **Western European Union** (WEU) and the **European Free Trade Association** (EFTA), as well as the **Nordic Council**.

In common with other EFTA states, Iceland concluded a free trade agreement with the European Community in 1973, and it became a signatory to the agreement establishing the **European Economic Area** (EEA) in May 1992. Although there was a continuing debate in Iceland about possible membership of the Community, now Union, the particular structure of the local economy, with its heavy reliance on fishing and fish products, made this option seem inappropriate for many years. Even if membership of the EEA means that Iceland is bound by EU legislation in the **single market** and several other policy fields, and indeed makes a contribution towards the Union's **Budget**, it does not involve acceptance of the **Common Fisheries Policy** (CFP). The fishing sector alone accounted for about three-quarters of the island's export earnings until the 1990s and still represents over a third. Successive 'cod wars' (between 1952 and 1976) with the United Kingdom, also Iceland's largest export market, flowed from its unilateral determination to extend its fishing zone from three to 200 nautical miles.

From the early 1990s, Iceland made a strategic decision to diversify its economy, by promoting the development of financial services, high-technology manufacturing and tourism. Sustained economic growth generated a relatively high national income, and allowed the government to lower taxes (moving to a single rate of income tax, set at 22.75 per cent), whilst maintaining generous levels of agricultural support and social welfare. By the mid-2000s, however, Iceland's position began to cause concern. As an extremely small, open economy, increasingly dependent on financial services, the country looked potentially vulnerable to external economic shocks. In early 2007, the foreign minister publicly speculated about the possibility that, as a safeguard, Iceland might seek to adopt the European single currency without becoming a member of the European Union – a possibility that was quickly dismissed by both the **European Commission** and **European Central Bank** (ECB).

When the international economic and financial crisis hit Iceland in September 2008, the country found itself with an external debt of eight times its national income. In a matter of a few days, its three largest banks collapsed, its stock exchange fell by 90 per cent, and its currency (the króna) depreciated by a third. The centre-right prime minister, Geir Haarde, spoke of impending 'national bankruptcy'. Against the backdrop of a 15 per cent contraction in GDP, a centre-left coalition won an early general election, held in April 2009, following the resignation of Haarde on health grounds and scenes of rioting outside the parliament. The successor government, led by Jóhanna Sigurðardóttir, entered office committed to seeking early entry into the European Union – a process greatly facilitated by its membership of the EEA. Iceland applied to join the Union in July 2009, was accepted by the **European Council** as a candidate country a year later, and opened accession negotiations a month after that.

A cloud has been cast over Iceland's entry prospects by its continuing difficulty in resolving the so-called 'Icesave dispute' with the Netherlands and United Kingdom. In the collapse of Landsbanki in September 2008, over 300,000 British and Dutch depositors lost € 3.8 billion in savings. As the money was covered by EU deposit-protection legislation, adopted in 1994, applying in Iceland through its membership of the EEA, the British and Dutch governments reimbursed their citizens and began negotiations to retrieve the outstanding amount from the Icelandic government. Successive agreements between the governments for Iceland to repay the sum over up to 30 years were opposed by the country's president, Ólafur Ragnar Grímsson, who forced the issue to two referenda, held in March 2010 and April 2011, when the deals were rejected by wide margins. On the second occasion, prime minister Sigurðardóttir declared that 'the worst option has been chosen'. In June 2011, the EFTA Surveillance Authority asked the Icelandic government to begin making repayments within three months. The matter is now before the EFTA Court, which settles EEA-related disputes involving the three EFTA countries that are members of the EEA.

Institutions

The seven institutions of the European Union are the **European Commission, European Council, Council of Ministers, European Parliament, European Court of Justice** (ECJ), **European Central Bank** (ECB) and **Court of Auditors.** The composition, role and evolution of each of the institutions is described in detail in separate entries in this *Companion.* The official title of the Council of Ministers is the Council of the European Union, whilst that of the ECJ is the Court of Justice of the European Union. A number of other bodies are provided for in the **Treaties** but do not enjoy the status of institutions, notably the two advisory bodies – the **European Economic and Social Committee** (EESC) and **Committee of the Regions** – and the **European Investment Bank** (EIB).

Four of today's seven EU institutions featured in the original **Treaties of Rome**, signed in March 1957: the Council of Ministers, Commission, Parliament (then called the Assembly) and Court of Justice. However, at that time, only the Assembly and Court were common to all three **European Communities** (by dint of a parallel convention signed by the member states). There were two Commissions – one for the **European Economic Community** (EEC) and another for the **European Atomic Energy Community** (EAEC or Euratom) – alongside the existing **High Authority** for the **European Coal and Steel Community** (ECSC), dating from 1952. There were also three separate Councils of Ministers, one for each Community. The 1965 **Merger Treaty**, which entered effect two years later, finally amalgamated these bodies into a single Commission and single Council, acting on behalf of all the Communities and later the Union.

The Assembly changed its name, on its own initiative, to the European Parliament in 1962, but this was only recognized in the **Treaties** by the 1986 **Single European Act** (SEA). The Court of Auditors was created by the 1975 Budgetary Treaty, but only given the status of an institution by the 1992 **Maastricht Treaty**, which also established the ECB, to which such status was extended from the outset. The European Council (of EU heads of government) was established in 1975, formally recognized by the SEA, and made an EU institution in its own right by the **Lisbon Treaty**, which came into effect in December 2009. The decision to remove the European Council from the ambit of the Council of Ministers was seen by many as far from necessary: as the instigator of the European Council in the mid-1970s, **Valéry Giscard d'Estaing** succeeded in gaining the approval of the 2002–3 **Convention on the Future of Europe** for his idea of 'upgrading' the body to institutional status, and the proposal, contained in the draft **European Constitution**, survived into the Lisbon Treaty. See also **seats of EU institutions.**

Intergovernmental Conference (IGC)

Intergovernmental Conferences are special meetings of representatives of the governments of the member states of the European Union, convened to draft and agree amendments to the **Treaties**. They convene at the request of the **Council of Ministers**, in accordance with Article 48(4) TEU. Their conclusions must be reached 'by common accord' (that is, unanimously) among the member states and must then be submitted to **national parliaments** (and, in some cases, electorates, by **referendum**) for **ratification** on the basis of domestic constitutional requirements. Traditionally, only member-state governments or the **European Commission** could propose treaty amendments, but under the **Lisbon Treaty**, the **European Parliament** may do so too.

There have been eight significant revisions of the Treaties since 1958, all agreed through IGCs: the 1965 **Merger Treaty**, the 1970 and 1975 Budgetary Treaties, the 1986 **Single European Act** (SEA), the 1992 **Maastricht Treaty**, the 1997 **Amsterdam Treaty**, the 2001 **Nice Treaty**, and the 2007 **Lisbon Treaty**, which entered force in December 2009. The growing frequency of IGCs reflects the fact that, during the 1980s and 1990s, they became, in effect, the 'constitutional conventions' of the European Union – even if their membership was limited to ministers and civil servants. From being essentially procedural mechanisms for endorsing treaty changes on which there was already a consensus among member states (as, for example, on successive **accession** treaties), they quickly emerged as genuine political arenas in which competing visions of the institutional structure and policy direction of the Union were articulated. Once it became established (at the Milan European Council in June 1985) that the convening of an IGC required the approval of only a simple majority of the member states, advocates of treaty change sought to invoke such conferences with increasing enthusiasm. Then, once any negotiation was under way, there was a clear presumption in favour of agreeing on some reform, with strong pressure on hesitant member states to compromise. So far, no IGC ever convened has failed to agree a text.

As the IGC developed as a regular and important forum for constitutional change within the Union, criticism grew about its obvious lack of transparency. If the EU were simply an international organization like any other, it would be possible for governments to alter its founding treaties, at will, behind closed doors. The fact that the Union adopted binding law – which was gradually entering into the fabric of domestic political life – made this increasingly difficult. There were defensive efforts to dispel the air of secrecy surrounding the process by appointing a Reflection Group to prepare the 1996–7 IGC (which drafted the Amsterdam Treaty). However, the Council was sufficiently nervous about this experience that it chose not to repeat it before the 2000 IGC (which drafted the Nice Treaty), with the Commission in response appointing its own 'Group of Independent Experts' for this purpose. In the event, the widespread dissatisfaction with the outcome of the Nice negotiation led member-state governments to accept that the next IGC – convened to deal with 'Nice leftovers', just as the previous one had been called to address 'Amsterdam leftovers' – should at least be preceded by a broader gathering of political stakeholders at European level, to be held in public. In 1999–2000, a meeting of this kind, known as a Convention, had already brought together, on a one-off basis, members of national parliaments and governments, as well as of the European Parliament and the Commission, to draft the (then) non-binding **Charter of Fundamental Rights**. At the Laeken European Council in December 2001, the heads of government agreed to use the same 'Convention method' to prepare the next IGC, due to be held in 2004. The resulting **Convention on the Future of Europe**, held in 2002–3, drafted the **European Constitution**, which eventually became, in diluted form, the Lisbon Treaty.

The European Constitution proposed, and the Lisbon Treaty maintains, that, henceforth, IGCs will normally be preceded by Conventions. The treaty provides an 'ordinary revision procedure' whereby the **President of the European Council** will 'convene a Convention composed of representatives of the national Parliaments, of the Heads of State or Government of the Member States, of the European Parliament and of the Commission' (Article 48(3) TEU). The Convention 'shall examine the proposals for amendments and shall adopt by consensus a recommendation' to the IGC that follows. The European Council may, however, dispense with holding a Convention 'should this not be justified by the extent of the proposed amendments', provided that the European Parliament agrees, through the **consent procedure**. This latter provision gives the Parliament a veto over the non-holding of a Convention, and in return for its consent, it may seek to extract concessions about the substance of the negotiation in the IGC.

The holding of Conventions before IGCs was advocated by some of the more integrationist member states, as well as by the European Commission and European Parliament, as a means of promoting maximalist outcomes in the treaty reform process. The experience of how the 2003–4 IGC endorsed many of the provisions of the European Constitution – which itself was much more ambitious than anything an IGC would have proposed in 2002–3 – appears to have confirmed the validity of this assumption. In theory, of course, any text agreed in a Convention may still be rejected, in whole or in part, by an IGC. As the German Federal Constitutional Court stated in its ruling on the Lisbon Treaty in June 2009, the new arrangement is 'constitutionally unobjectionable as long as the member states are not legally bound by the results achieved by the Convention, and as long as they can freely decide which Treaty amendments they ultimately wish to agree under international law'. (See **Karlsruhe judgements.**)

A more significant change introduced by the Lisbon Treaty may prove to be the possibility allowed to the European Council (under Article 48(6) TEU) of invoking a 'simplified revision procedure' that enables amendments to be made, without either a Convention or an IGC, to the treaty provisions relating specifically to the internal policies of the Union. EU heads of government may, acting unanimously, amend any of the 172 articles of part three of the **Treaty of Rome**, now known as the Treaty on the Functioning of the European Union (TFEU), including the institutional rules for the **single market** and **Economic and Monetary Union** (EMU), so long as they do not extend the **competence** of the Union (Article 48(6)3 TEU). However, their decision must then, like the results of an IGC, be approved by the member states individually, 'in accordance with their respective constitutional requirements' (Article 48(6)2 TEU), meaning that, in practice, this may not differ greatly from the old IGC-only practice. In December 2009, the European Council used this option for the first time, when it put forward, at the insistence of the German government, an amendment to Article 136 TFEU that would give a treaty base to the **European Stability Mechanism** (ESM) that is being established, on an intergovernmental basis, for the member states within the **eurozone.**

Further reading: Derek Beach, *The Dynamics of European Integration: Why and When EU Institutions Matter*, 2005; Thomas Christiansen and Christine Reh, *Constitutionalizing the European Union*, 2009; Paul Thurner and Franz Urban Pappi, *European Union Intergovernmental Conferences*, 2009.

Intergovernmentalism

See **supranationalism and intergovernmentalism.**

Inter-Institutional Agreement (IIA)

Although adjustments to the powers of, and relationship between, the **institutions** of the European Union can formally be made only by treaty amendment – usually involving the convening of an **Intergovernmental Conference** (IGC) and always requiring **ratification** of any resulting text in the member states – a more flexible method has evolved for sketching in the detail of their day-to-day relations, where the institutions consider it useful to do so. Since the 1992 **Maastricht Treaty**, an increasingly complex web of tripartite Inter-Institutional Agreements has grown up between the **European Commission, Council of Ministers** and **European Parliament**, starting in the field of the EU **Budget** (where joint declarations had previously been used) and spreading more widely. Although such agreements are adopted formally by each institution, they are not **legal acts** and as such are not justiciable (although the **European Court of Justice** (ECJ) may refer to them in its reasoning). They are rather high-level statements of political intent and the relevance of their provisions depends on the will of each of the institutions to consider itself bound by them on a continuing basis.

Characteristically, the Commission will take the lead in proposing an IIA and come forward with a draft text as the basis for negotiation. As an IIA is not a legal act, the Commission's **right of initiative** does not apply: in preparing the IIA on **Better Law-Making** (2003), for example, the Parliament's negotiators rejected the Commission draft and offered an alternative that then became the base text. On behalf of the European Commission, IIAs are negotiated by individual Commissioners and the outcome is then approved by the full college. For the Council, the **presidency** undertakes the negotiation, subject to approval by **COREPER** and a full Council meeting. Within the Parliament, the mandate to negotiate an IIA is extended to a group of members by the **Conference of Presidents**, with the outcome subject to the latter's approval, followed by an opinion from the Parliament's constitutional affairs committee and then formal endorsement in plenary.

The IIA on Better Law-Making (2003) was negotiated by a special structure created for the purpose, the 'high-level inter-institutional working group', which met several times at official level, and once at political level. However, despite hopes that this framework might offer a regular forum for dialogue on inter-institutional issues of various kinds, including the possible negotiation of future IIAs, it quickly fell into disuse.

The multi-annual financial perspectives for the EU have until now been agreed through successive IIAs on budgetary discipline (covering seven-year periods and agreed in 1993, 1999 and 2006). The **Lisbon Treaty** requires these agreements, henceforth known as Multiannual Financial Frameworks (MFFs), to take the form of Council **regulations**, subject to the Parliament's approval (under the **consent procedure**). In addition to Better Law-Making, the most important IIAs in the institutional field have provided for the statute of the European **Ombudsman** (1993), the rights of the Parliament's committees of inquiry (1994), the Parliament's involvement in the **comitology** process (1994 and 2006), arrangements for the codification and recasting of existing legislation (1994 and 2001), and common guidelines for ensuring the quality of drafting of legislation (1998). In total, over 100 IIAs have been concluded between the three institutions.

Separately, any two of the three institutions may conclude bilateral agreements, which are sometimes confused with tripartite IIAs. Notable among these are the successive Commission–Parliament codes of conduct (1990 and 1995) and Framework Agreements (2000, 2005 and 2010) that guide their overall relations, as well as a series of seven Commission–Parliament agreements on comitology (from 1988 to 2007), and a Parliament–Council agreement on access to sensitive information in the field of **Common Security and Defence Policy** (CSDP) (2002).

The Lisbon Treaty has introduced an explicit reference to IIAs into the body of the Treaties and permits them, for the first time, to be 'binding' on the three institutions. A new treaty article reads: 'The European Parliament, the Council and the Commission shall consult each other and by common agreement make arrangements for their cooperation. To that end, they may, in compliance with the Treaties, conclude interinstitutional agreements which may be of a binding nature' (Article 295 TFEU).

Internal market

See **single market.**

International agreements

Agreements of various kinds are routinely concluded between the European Union and third countries (whether individually or in groups) or international organizations. They characteristically take one of four forms: trade agreements, **cooperation agreements, association agreements** or 'sector agreements'. The overall arrangements for the negotiation and conclusion of international agreements are set out in Article 218 TFEU, previously Article 300 EC.

Trade agreements follow directly from the Union's exclusive **competence** in the field of external trade policy, known as the **Common Commercial Policy** (CCP), and are negotiated under Article 207 TFEU, previously Article 133 EC.

Cooperation agreements have evolved mainly in the fields of **development policy** and economic, financial and technical cooperation of various kinds. They rely on Articles 209 and 211–12 TFEU (previously Articles 179 and 181–181(a) EC), as well as the 'all-purpose' **Article 352** TFEU, previously Article 308 EC. Some cooperation agreements now range very widely, including policies for the environment or human rights. (Specific **legal bases** in these policy areas may be added in these cases.) Joint trade and cooperation agreements (TCAs) are often negotiated as single texts.

Association agreements allow the Union to develop deeper relations with particular countries – using Article 217 TFEU, previously Article 310 EC – and usually include inter alia elements that would otherwise be covered by trade or cooperation agreements. In some cases, association agreements may envisage, or be followed by, the **accession** of the partner countries to the Union itself.

As their name implies, *sector agreements* relate to individual policy areas – relations in the fields of customs, taxation or fisheries, for example – and are based on the relevant treaty article(s) for the policy areas in question.

International agreements are usually negotiated by the **European Commission**, on the basis of a mandate laid down by the **Council of Ministers** and are subject to the latter's approval. It is the responsibility of the Council, not the Commission, to 'authorize the opening of negotiations, adopt negotiating directives, authorize the signing of agreements and conclude them' (Article 218(2) TFEU). The process starts with the Commission recommending to the Council that a negotiation be opened; the former then conducts the negotiation on the latter's behalf. If the negotiation is successful, the Commission initials an agreement and then proposes to the Council that it first sign and then formally conclude the agreement. In the specific case of trade agreements, however, negotiations are conducted under the continuous oversight of a special Council committee, now known as the **Trade Policy Committee** (previously the Article 133 Committee). In other cases, the Council may designate 'a special committee in consultation with which the negotiations must be conducted' (Article 218(4) TFEU).

Within the Council, trade agreements have been subject to **qualified majority voting** (QMV) since 1966, whereas the decision-making method for cooperation and sector agreements depends on their specific legal base, automatically requiring unanimity whenever Article 308, now Article 352, is invoked. Association agreements required **unanimity** until the **Lisbon Treaty**, which provides for QMV, unless they touch on policy areas, like taxation, still decided unanimously in the Council. Where a text is a so-called 'mixed agreement' – one which includes areas that fall within the parallel **competence** of the Union and the member states, as is often the case for cooperation and association agreements – it will also need to be ratified separately by each of the member states, in effect giving them a veto over the outcome, even if QMV applies in the Council.

For many years, the position of the **European Parliament** in respect of international agreements was very weak. It had no formal right to be consulted on trade agreements, although from 1973 onwards it was kept abreast of negotiations through the informal Luns–Westerterp procedure. On association agreements and on some cooperation and sector agreements, it could at best give only an opinion, under the **consultation procedure**. However, since the 1986 **Single European Act** (SEA), the Parliament has progressively increased its powers in the external field. The SEA gave it a right of veto – initially called the assent procedure, and now termed the **consent procedure** – over association agreements. This right was extended by the 1992 **Maastricht Treaty** to cover any other international agreements which involved institutional frameworks, had important budgetary implications or amended acts which had already been adopted under **co-decision** between the Council and the Parliament. Significantly, the Lisbon Treaty has recently extended the need for the Parliament's consent to include any agreement in any policy where co-decision, now called the 'ordinary legislative procedure', applies. This covers nearly all trade agreements and most cooperation and sector agreements.

Before the Lisbon Treaty, the various types of agreement listed above were, strictly speaking, all concluded by the European Community, rather than by the European Union, because the latter lacked formal **legal personality**. This meant that such agreements could not cover policy in the fields of the (then) intergovernmental **pillars**, established by the Maastricht Treaty, for **Common Foreign and Security Policy** (CFSP) and **Justice and Home Affairs** (JHA). The Maastricht Treaty did allow for international agreements in the CFSP and JHA fields (under the then Articles 24 and 38 TEU), which quickly became increasingly common. Usually, such agreements were negotiated for the Council by its own rotating **presidency** (rather than by the Commission, even if the latter assisted it), and were then agreed unanimously in the Council, with no obligation on the latter to consult the European Parliament. The Lisbon Treaty, which abolished the pillared structure of the Union, has significantly altered the situation in both the CFSP and JHA areas, but in differing ways: in the first, the **High Representative**, rather than the Council presidency, now takes the lead in negotiations; in the second, the negotiating procedure mirrors that for existing international agreements concluded under Article 218 TFEU. The significance of the changes made to decision-making on international agreements by Lisbon, both in the JHA field and more widely, was thrown into sharp relief by the 'SWIFT affair' – concerning an EU–US agreement on the transfer of data relating to the banking transactions of individual Europeans – in 2009–10.

Ioannina Compromise

The Ioannina Compromise was a special arrangement – agreed by the foreign ministers of the European Union, at a **Gymnich meeting** in Ioannina, Greece, on 26–27 March 1994 – designed to provide a 'safety catch' to allow member states which found themselves likely to be narrowly outvoted in the **Council of Ministers** the opportunity for continuing discussion. If countries representing a number of votes close to the 'blocking minority' opposed the adoption of acts by **qualified majority voting** (QMV), the Council would do its utmost to reach, within a reasonable timescale, a satisfactory solution that could be agreed by a bigger majority.

The agreement in Ioannina brought to an end an awkward episode during which British prime minister John Major, supported by Felipe González of Spain, campaigned to dilute the impact of the impending **accession** to the

Union of Austria, Finland and Sweden on the capacity of existing member states to exercise a blocking minority in the Council. This 'EFTAn **enlargement**', like previous enlargements, simply extrapolated the established pattern of voting weights, which significantly over-represented smaller member states, at the expense of larger ones. The share of votes commanded by the five largest member states in the Council was set to decline from 63.3 to 55.2 per cent, even though they still represented some four-fifths of the Union's population. Major was under significant political pressure from Eurosceptic critics within his own Conservative party, who argued that the existing QMV threshold was a vital safeguard which should not be eroded. Following the Ioannina meeting, the accession treaty for the three applicant countries (plus Norway, which subsequently rejected membership in a **referendum** for the second time) was finalized and sent for **ratification** in all the existing member states and the new entrants.

Formalized through a **decision** of the Council on 29 March 1994 (updated on 1 January 1995 to reflect the non-membership of Norway), the Ioannina Compromise provided that – even though the new QMV threshold would now be 62 votes out of 87 (rather than 54 out 76, before enlargement), with a blocking minority of 26 votes, rather than the 23 – the Council would nonetheless, if between 23 and 25 votes were cast against a proposal, 'do all in its power to reach, within a reasonable time and without prejudicing obligatory time limits laid down by Union law . . . a satisfactory solution that could be adopted by at least 65 votes'. (Since there is no obligatory time limit on the Council in respect, critically, of the adoption of a common position at first reading, at least, under the **co-decision procedure**, that particular proviso was of little significance.) The decision went on to commit the Council **presidency** to undertake, 'with the assistance' of the **European Commission**, 'any initiative necessary to facilitate a wider basis of agreement in the Council'. The members of the Council expressed their willingness to support this process.

The Ioannina Compromise was conceded as a temporary expedient, pending a full-scale review of the operation of QMV during the 1996 **Intergovernmental Conference** (IGC). However, in the event, the IGC sidestepped this awkward question, with Declaration 50 to the 1997 **Amsterdam Treaty** simply rolling the Ioannina Compromise forward until the next enlargement took effect (which was in 2004). The issue of 'big country versus small country' power in the Council was finally addressed when the voting weights for QMV were adjusted by the 2001 **Nice Treaty**. The relative position of the middle-sized member states was weakened and a population threshold was introduced for the first time. Under these arrangements, which still apply, a qualified majority needs to meet a triple hurdle: in the current Union of 27 member states, the majority is normally attained when 255 (out of 345) votes out are cast in favour of a proposition (73.9 per cent), and the countries in favour represent at least a majority of the member states and comprise at least 62 per cent of the total population of the Union. There is no provision any longer for the Ioannina safety-catch, as the Council decision of 1994–5 embodying the agreement was rendered void.

The title 'Ioannina Compromise' was redolent, intentionally or not, of the **Luxembourg Compromise**, by which any member state had in practice been able to postpone indefinitely a QMV decision being taken by the Council between 1966 and 1987, if it felt that a 'very important national interest' was at stake. During the rather fewer years it applied – from the 1995 enlargement to the entry into force of the Nice voting rules in 2003 – the Ioannina arrangement proved much less problematic. It was deployed only very occasionally and never held up discussion for more than a few days. However, awareness of its potential use was a factor that the Council presidency might sometimes take into account in its private calculations of whether a qualified majority yet existed for a proposal.

The **Lisbon Treaty** maintains the current system of QMV until November 2014, but after that date moves to a 'double majority' voting system of the kind favoured notably by the largest single member state, Germany. A qualified majority will normally be constituted by 55 per cent of member states, representing at least 65 per cent of the Union's population. Under pressure from the Polish government, a declaration to the treaty provided that, once the treaty had been ratified, a new Council decision would be adopted immediately that would in effect revive the Ioannina Compromise from 2014 onwards – and on much more generous terms than the original arrangement. This decision – which was adopted by the Council in December 2007 and entered into force with Lisbon two years later – states that if a group of member states representing only three-quarters of either the number of states or the population required to form a blocking minority 'indicate their opposition to the Council adopting an act by a qualified majority, the Council shall discuss the issue'. From April 2017, the percentages required are set even lower – at 55 per cent of the population or number of member states required to form a blocking minority. The decision goes on to repeat the original language of Ioannina, in saying that the Council will 'do all in its power to reach, within a reasonable time and without prejudicing obligatory time limits laid down by Union law, a satisfactory solution to address concerns raised by the members of the Council' in a minority. On the face of it, this 'Ioannina-*bis*' mechanism, as it is sometimes called in Brussels circles, is potentially a much more radical concession than the original Ioannina Compromise.

The resuscitation of Ioannina in this form was a last-minute offer to the then Polish President, Lech Kaczynski, at the June 2007 European Council meeting in Brussels and was in effect his country's price for accepting the Lisbon Treaty at that meeting. His brother, the then Polish prime minister, Jaroslaw Kaczynski, hailed the new arrangement as a 'strong mechanism' that would 'significantly strengthen our position after 2017', claiming that it would only require one other large member state 'or two smaller countries' to join Poland, in order to be able to 'block decisions' under QMV in the Council. How significant the change will really prove, after 2014 and 2017, remains unclear. Jean-Claude Piris, then head of the Council's legal service, pointed out in 2009 that both the original and the new Ioannina decisions specifically require the member states to respect the Council's rules of procedure, and that the latter currently allow a simple majority of member states to force a vote on any proposal at any time. So, in practice, much will depend on the attitude of the member states at the time when these new arrangements come into effect later this decade.

Irish referenda on EU Treaties

Between 1972 and 2009, Ireland held eight **referenda** on European Union issues, more than any other member state. The electorate was invited to vote not only on the **accession** treaty in June 1972, but on each subsequent revision to the **Treaties** of any substance. The first four referenda resulted in positive outcomes, with the 'yes' vote falling gradually from 83.1 per cent on accession to 61.7 per cent on the **Amsterdam Treaty**, 27 years later. This period was one in which Ireland enjoyed a high level of economic growth and was a major net recipient of EU funding, averaging over € 2 billion per year (peaking at 6.3 of GDP in 1991). However, soon after the Amsterdam vote, the previously benign national mood towards the Union became more critical. The country's fifth referendum, held on the **Nice Treaty** in June 2001, unexpectedly resulted in a 53.9 per cent 'no' vote, on a low turnout. After an assurance was extended to Ireland by the other member states about its continued **neutrality**, this outcome was reversed in a further referendum, held in November 2002, which generated a 62.9 'yes' vote, on a higher turnout. The same pattern was repeated seven years later over the **Lisbon Treaty**, the successor to the aborted **European Constitution**. In the intervening years, Ireland's net receipts from the EU Budget had shrunk by three-quarters, to only just over half a billion euro per year. In June 2008, 53.4 per cent of those voting rejected the treaty, and once again, the result had to be reversed – after certain additional assurances were extended to Ireland, this time in a legally-binding form – in a second ballot, held in October 2009, which elicited a 67.1 per cent 'yes' vote. In 2009, Ireland became a net contributor to the EU **Budget** for the first time.

Referenda in Ireland, 1972–2009

Treaty	*Date*	*'Yes' vote (per cent)*	*'No' vote (per cent)*	*Turnout (per cent)*
Accession Treaty	10 May 1972	83.1	16.9	70.9
Single European Act	26 May 1987	69.9	30.1	44.1
Maastricht Treaty	18 June 1992	69.1	30.9	57.3
Amsterdam Treaty	22 May 1998	61.7	38.3	56.2
Nice Treaty	7 June 2001	46.1	53.9	34.8
Nice Treaty	19 October 2002	62.9	37.1	48.5
Lisbon Treaty	12 June 2008	46.6	53.4	53.1
Lisbon Treaty	2 October 2009	67.1	32.9	59.0

Ireland's habit of routinely holding referenda on European treaties flows from a ruling of the country's supreme court in 1987. In *Crotty* v *An Taoiseach*, the court found (by a margin of three to two) that the **Single European Act** (SEA), by giving a legal basis to **European Political Cooperation** (EPC), could limit the freedom of Ireland to pursue its own foreign policy and was thus incompatible with the country's constitution. It could only be ratified if the constitution was modified to make the two documents consistent. As Article 46 of that constitution obliges the government to hold a referendum on any amendments proposed thereto, public approval by popular vote became necessary before the treaty could be ratified. Since then, as a precautionary move, Irish governments have consistently proposed constitutional amendments and called referenda on any treaty changes where this situation might arise. (Since 1972, there have been a total of 28 referenda on constitutional amendments on all subjects, 21 of which have passed.)

There is a continuing debate in Ireland about whether some of the referenda held on successive EU treaties have been legally necessary, since the government's decision to change the constitution and hold a popular vote is taken on the basis of the advice of its law officers, rather than precise criteria established by the supreme court itself. The court has indicated only that anything which might 'alter the essential scope and objectives' of the Communities, now Union, would require constitutional amendment. By implication, extensions of **qualified majority voting** (QMV) in the **Council of Ministers** or of **co-decision** between the Council and the **European Parliament** do not, of themselves, meet this criterion. In the specific case of the Single Act, the court said that the 'possible ultimate objective of a form of European political union between the Member States . . . as an addition to the existing economic union between them' justified the need for a change in the constitution. Some lawyers doubt whether the Amsterdam and Nice Treaties, most notably, were sufficiently far-reaching in their extensions of Union **competence** to require referenda to be held.

The political risk to any government in Ireland from the automatic holding of referenda on significant EU treaties (or indeed on any other matter) has been compounded by the effects of a second judgement by the supreme court. In *McKenna* v *An Taoiseach* (1995) – a case brought by Irish Green MEP Patricia McKenna in advance of the 1996 referendum on divorce – the court ruled that no state funds could be spent by the government in advocating an amendment to the constitution. The use of public money in favour of a particular outcome, it argued, 'infringes the concept of equality which is fundamental to the democratic nature of the state'. The law was subsequently changed to give the 'yes' and 'no' sides in constitutional referenda equal time on domestic television and radio. Given that all main political parties in Ireland, except Sinn Féin, have consistently supported successive EU treaties, the effect of these developments was to greatly strengthen opponents of the treaties. Since 1995, two of the three treaties put to a vote have been rejected, at least first time round.

The twin constraints of the *Crotty* and *McKenna* judgements have led some to suggest that the government should be more cautious in assuming that EU treaties need constitutional amendments for passage and, if it uses referenda, seek to hold them as consultative votes under another provision, Article 27, of the constitution. The latter route would give the government greater control over the wording of the question, allow public money to be spent in favour of a 'yes' vote, and free the broadcast media of the need to treat both sides equally.

Further reading: Brigid Laffan and Jane O'Mahony, *Ireland and the European Union*, 2008.

J

Jenkins, Roy (1920–2003)

The Oxford-educated son of a Labour Cabinet minister, Roy Jenkins was himself elected a Labour MP in 1948. He rose rapidly at Westminster, emerging as a prominent advocate of 'Gaitskellism', Europe and social reform. In 1965, Jenkins was appointed as Home Secretary in the first government of Harold Wilson, moving on to become Chancellor of the Exchequer in November 1967, after the politically damaging devaluation of sterling. Although the government's unexpected defeat by the Conservatives under **Edward Heath** in the June 1970 election was partly attributed to Jenkins' stern management of the economy, he was elected deputy leader of the Labour party soon after. Wilson's opportunistic hostility to the 'Tory terms' negotiated by the Heath government for British **accession** to the European Community forced Jenkins increasingly into internal opposition to Wilson's leadership and the mainstream of his party. He led 69 pro-European Labour MPs in defying the party whip in October 1971, when the House of Commons endorsed the decision to join the Community, and he resigned as deputy leader the following year.

When Labour was returned to government in February 1974, Jenkins was reappointed as Home Secretary, failing to secure the Foreign Office because of his pro-European views. He became the leading Labour figure in the cross-party 'Britain in Europe' campaign for a 'yes' vote in the **referendum** in June 1975, which followed the largely notional **renegotiation** of the terms of membership by the second Wilson government (see **British referendum on EC membership**). He contested the Labour leadership on Wilson's sudden resignation in spring 1976, coming third out of six candidates, behind James Callaghan and Michael Foot.

Passed over a second time for the post of Foreign Secretary, Jenkins accepted nomination as President of the **European Commission** – in succession to French Gaullist François-Xavier Ortoli – a position he held from January 1977 until January 1981. Despite an unpromising economic backdrop and a general perception of stagnation in the European project, Jenkins' presidency was marked by steady efforts to relaunch the Community and enhance the Commission's standing. Against strong opposition from French President **Valéry Giscard d'Estaing**, he succeeded in ensuring that he and his successors could attend **summits** of the **Group of Seven** (G7) industrialized nations. His most enduring achievement was to resuscitate the concept of **Economic and Monetary Union** (EMU) – following the failure of the **Werner Plan** and the 'Snake' earlier in the 1970s – by proposing the creation of a new **European Monetary System** (EMS) in a seminal speech made at the **European University Institute** (EUI) in Florence in October 1977. By contrast, Jenkins failed to provide any significant impetus to the linked problems of reform of the **Common Agricultural Policy** (CAP) and the emerging **British Budget dispute**, although he successfully helped prepare the ground for the EC's second **enlargement** to include Greece in 1981.

Jenkins did not seek renomination to the Commission in 1981, by which time Conservative leader **Margaret Thatcher** had become British prime minister. He chose instead to return to domestic politics, securing election once again as an MP (1982–7) and leading the new Social Democratic party that split away from Labour and sought unsuccessfully to 'break the mould' of two-party politics in Britain. Jenkins published a *European Diary* (1989) covering his four years as Commission President. Suavely written, it provides a fascinating insider's account of life at the top of the Community institutions, with its extraordinary mixture of great issues and petty intrigue. Jenkins' character sketches of the politicians with whom he dealt are especially entertaining. In retirement, Jenkins wrote a set of well-received memoirs, *A Life at the Centre* (1991), as well as accomplished biographies of two British prime ministers, William Gladstone and **Winston Churchill**. He was elected Chancellor of Oxford University in 1987, a role in which he served until his death in January 2003, when he was succeeded by Chris Patten, then European Commissioner for external relations.

Juste retour

The concept of *juste retour* became current in the period 1979–84, when the **British Budget dispute** was a dominant issue on the political agenda of the then European Community. The principle of 'fair return' implied that, in broad terms and over time, the **contributions and receipts** of any member state to and from the Community **Budget** should broadly balance. It was asserted by prime minister **Margaret Thatcher** and popularized in her demand 'to have our own money back', in a struggle over Britain's net contribution that eventually led to the **abatement** established by the **Fontainebleau Agreement** of June 1984. Strictly applied, the principle of *juste retour* would neutralize any redistributive effect of the Budget between member states and is clearly incompatible with the proposition that some countries should be net beneficiaries of it. A more realistic understanding takes account not only of a member state's contributions but also its relative prosperity and the extent to which other (non-spending) policies help create certain collective goods, such as **free movement**, the **single market** or external trade policy, from which that country may gain significant advantage. The existence of an abatement and its de facto extension from the United Kingdom to cover four other countries – Austria, Germany, the Netherlands and Sweden – suggests that the principle is more easily conceded in practice than in theory.

Justice and Home Affairs (JHA)

There was no provision in the founding **Treaties** for any form of common policy at Community level in the field of Justice and Home Affairs. For many years, cooperation in this area was largely confined to the intergovernmental **Council of Europe** and the Hague Conference on private international law. The Council of Europe adopted conventions on a range of issues – such as extradition (1957), mutual assistance in criminal matters (1959) and the suppression of terrorism (1977) – and hosted the 'Pompidou Group' on drug trafficking.

Starting in 1976, the interior ministers of the EC member states, joined soon after by ministers of justice, began to meet regularly, outside the formal structure of the **Council of Ministers**, in a framework known as the **Trevi Group**. Their discussions focused initially on the growth of international terrorism and gradually widened to include organized crime and police cooperation more generally. In December 1977, French President **Valéry Giscard d'Estaing** proposed to heads of government that they create an *espace judiciaire européen* – variously translated as a 'European legal area' or 'European judicial space' – which would develop a common framework for all those legal matters with a Community dimension. It might both guarantee the citizens of the member states a common corpus of basic legal rights and promote practical cooperation between police forces, immigration officers and judicial authorities. However, a number of governments, including notably the Dutch, insisted on maintaining existing cooperation through the Council of Europe.

By the mid-1980s, the Community's commitment to complete the **single market**, including the **free movement of persons**, prompted a growing recognition that the member states would need to work much more closely together if the planned relaxation of internal frontiers (and the parallel shift of emphasis to external frontiers) was to be successfully achieved. This challenge was given added urgency by the decision in June 1985 of five of the (then) ten member states to proceed further and faster on their own, by signing the **Schengen** Agreement to create a frontier-free zone. Annexed to the

1986 **Single European Act** (SEA) were several non-binding declarations which foresaw the need for joint action by governments in the fields of cross-border crime and immigration. Seven intergovernmental conventions were agreed during the years 1987–91, but several ran into ratification difficulties in **national parliaments.**

The 1992 **Maastricht Treaty** attempted to consolidate and rationalize the various ad hoc arrangements that had sprung up, by instituting an intergovernmental '**pillar**' for cooperation in the JHA field (then Articles K.1 to K.9 TEU). Nine areas of 'common interest' were identified within this 'third' pillar of the new European Union, including policy on external borders, asylum, immigration, treatment of third-country nationals, judicial cooperation in civil matters, and police and judicial cooperation in criminal matters. The Union was empowered to adopt two novel types of act – common positions and framework decisions – as well as traditional conventions requiring ratification by national parliaments. As in the parallel 'second' pillar for **Common Foreign and Security Policy** (CFSP), the decision-making process for JHA deliberately eschewed the classic '**Community method**' of the first, original pillar. The **European Commission** was forced to share its **right of initiative** with the member states (and in some cases had no right of initiative at all), whilst the **European Parliament** and the **European Court of Justice** (ECJ) were in effect excluded. A special coordinating committee of senior national officials, initially known as the K.4 Committee, was to assist the Council in its work: decision-making within the latter was to be exclusively by **unanimity**. As in CFSP, operational costs arising from JHA action were to be borne either by the annual **Budget** of the Union or directly by member states in proportion to their gross national product (GNP), although administrative expenditure was always charged to the Budget. The only aspect of JHA exempted from the intergovernmental method was visa policy, where normal Community procedures were to be used from the start, even including (for some aspects) **qualified majority voting** (QMV) in the Council.

The institutional balance struck by the Maastricht Treaty was not to last long. As soon as the Conservative government of John Major in Britain had been replaced by the new Labour administration of **Tony Blair**, the 1997 **Amsterdam Treaty** began a process of 'communautizing' JHA that was eventually to be completed in the **Lisbon Treaty** 12 years later. Amsterdam transferred asylum and immigration policy, as well as judicial cooperation in civil matters, into the Community pillar, where they joined visa policy (Articles 61–9 EC). Decision-making in some of these areas was moved to QMV in the Council and **co-decision** between the Council and the Parliament, either immediately or five years later (in 2004). In other fields that were communautized, a ***passerelle* clause** allowed the Council, acting unanimously, to switch to QMV and co-decision at some stage in the future, if it wished. This *passerelle* clause was invoked in December 2004 for certain aspects of policy on visas, asylum and immigration. The ECJ was empowered to act in respect of most JHA matters falling within the Community pillar and to give **preliminary rulings** on issues that remained in the JHA pillar. The '**Schengen** *acquis*' – comprising essentially the 1985 Schengen Agreement and 1990 Schengen Implementing Convention – were also recognized by the Lisbon Treaty and incorporated into the Community pillar. As a result of all these changes, the only policy that remained in the original intergovernmental pillar for JHA was police and judicial cooperation in criminal matters.

The Amsterdam Treaty also made the creation of an 'Area of Freedom, Security and Justice' (AFSJ) the principal, all-embracing objective of cooperation in the JHA field. Within this rubric, the concept of 'freedom' was understood to encompass not only the free movement of persons and questions bearing on visas, asylum and immigration, but also human and fundamental rights, and **non-discrimination** policy. 'Security' covered measures taken against terrorism and other forms of organized or serious crime, whilst 'justice' was concerned with equal access to justice, judicial cooperation, the cross-border enforcement of judgements in civil matters, the definition of particular categories of offence and the sentences such offences carry, as well as mutual assistance in criminal matters.

The component elements of an AFSJ were set out by the European Commission and endorsed at a meeting of the **European Council** in Vienna in December 1998. Ten months later, the heads of government held a special meeting in Tampere, Finland, to establish the first of (so far) three five-year programmes for future action in this area. The provisions of the Amsterdam Treaty, the new presentational emphasis on AFSJ and the launch of the Tampere programme all combined, together with the huge political impact of the terrorist attacks of 11 September 2001, to generate new ambition and intensity to EU activity in the JHA field. The Tampere programme (1999) has since been followed by the Hague and Stockholm programmes (2004 and 2009).

In the meantime, the **Convention on the Future of Europe** (2002–3), in drafting the text of the **European Constitution**, rapidly concluded that the intergovernmental pillars established by the Maastricht Treaty should be demolished. It proposed that the Commission's right of initiative, QMV in the Council, co-decision between the Council and the Parliament, and full jurisdiction for the ECJ should all become the norm throughout JHA policy, and that traditional **legal acts** – **decisions**, **regulations** and **directives** – should replace the special JHA acts that previously applied. These proposals were carried forward with relatively few changes into the Lisbon Treaty, which entered into force in December 2009 (Articles 67–88 TFEU). The biggest shifts in decision-making were in police and judicial cooperation and in legal immigration, where QMV and co-decision now apply for the first time.

The main areas of JHA still subject to unanimity post-Lisbon are passports and identity cards, family law, the establishment of a European Public Prosecutor's Office, any extension of the lists of areas of crime or criminal procedure subject to EU jurisdiction, and aspects of cross-border activity by police. A special safeguard was introduced by the Lisbon Treaty in the form of an 'emergency break', whereby in two sensitive areas where QMV now applies – legislation on i) the admissibility of evidence, the rights of individuals in criminal procedure, and the rights of victims of crime; and ii) 'the definition of criminal offences and sanctions in areas of particularly serious crime' – any member state which considers that a proposal 'would affect fundamental aspects of its criminal justice system' may refer the matter to the European Council, suspending the legislative process for up to four months. If there is no consensus among heads of government on what to do, any nine or more member states may move rapidly to adopt the measure in question under **enhanced cooperation** (Articles 82(3) and 83(3) TFEU). The same 'accelerator' mechanism is available in two areas where unanimity applies: the creation of the European Public Prosecutor's Office (Article 86(1) TFEU) and police cooperation in the prevention, detection and investigation of criminal offences (Article 87(3) TFEU).

The United Kingdom, Ireland and Denmark enjoy **opt-outs** from EU policy in the field of JHA. Introduced by the Amsterdam Treaty, these opt-outs initially applied only to those aspects of JHA which the same treaty simultaneously communautized. However, as Lisbon extended the Community method to the whole of JHA, the scope of the opt-outs was correspondingly broadened. Formally speaking, the UK and Ireland may 'opt in' to the negotiation of any measure before it is adopted or may accept the measure at any time after it has been adopted. In a one-off concession added to the Lisbon Treaty at a late stage, the UK is specifically exempted for a five-year period (expiring in November 2014) from the authority of the Commission and ECJ in the field of police and judicial cooperation (previously covered by the old JHA pillar before its abolition). Equally, the UK may signal that it wishes to withdraw from the whole of cooperation in this field until six months before the expiry of the same five-year period (Article 10, Protocol 36 to the Treaties). The situation is even more complicated and unsatisfactory for Denmark, because there is no arrangement for it to opt into JHA measures, even though it is a member of the Schengen area. Ad hoc agreements in international law have to be negotiated for this purpose.

K

Kangaroo Group

Subtitled 'the movement for free movement', the all-party Kangaroo Group brings together politicians and business leaders to campaign for the removal of remaining **non-tariff barriers** to trade between EU member states. Founded by members of the first directly-elected **European Parliament**, led by British Conservative Basil de Ferranti (1930–88) and German Social Democrat Dieter Rogalla, and named after a kangaroo because of the animal's ability to leap over barriers, the group quickly proved one of the most successful single-issue lobbies ever established at European level. It played an important part in providing the rationale and political impetus for the **single market** programme embodied in the **Cockfield White Paper** in 1985. Having achieved its key objective of putting the completion of the single market at the heart of the Community's political agenda, the group gradually became a less visible force. It still organizes events of various kinds, including regular speaker-meetings in the Parliament, often advocating liberalizing measures in advance of their being proposed by the **European Commission.**

Karlsruhe judgements

The German Federal Constitutional Court (*Bundesverfassungsgericht*), based in Karlsruhe, has been called upon to deliver two important rulings about the compatibility of European Union **Treaties** with the Basic Law (*Grundgesetz*) or constitution of the Federal Republic. Although the 'Karlsruhe judgements' of 1993 and 2009 found that the **Maastricht Treaty** and the **Lisbon Treaty** respectively were compatible with the German constitution, some of the grounds used by the court to justify this conclusion cast doubt on the democratic legitimacy of the EU institutions in their current form and challenged the automatic **primacy** of **EU law.**

The first Karlsruhe judgement, delivered on 12 October 1993, arose from a case brought by opponents of the Maastricht Treaty, led by Manfred Brunner, formerly *chef de* **cabinet** to Martin Bangemann, the senior German member of the **European Commission** at the time. The action (*Brunner* v *European Union Treaty*) sought to challenge both the treaty itself and certain amendments to the Basic Law that were a precondition to German **ratification** of the text. In its ruling, the Federal Constitutional Court declared that, so long as the Union lacked certain attributes of statehood, it remained a *Staatenverbund* (association of states) rather than a *Bundesstaat* (federal state). The Maastricht Treaty, it said, 'establishes an association of states for the creation of an **ever closer union** among the peoples of Europe . . . rather than a federal state, based upon the people of one state of Europe'. Even if the Union was on a path of 'gradual further integration', the source of legitimacy within the Union still remained primarily the institutions of the nation state, specifically through the explicit prior authorization by **national parliaments** of the extent to which **sovereignty** was shared at supranational level. Although 'the democratic foundations upon which the Union is based [should be] extended concurrently with integration' – most obviously through the granting of greater legislative powers to the **European Parliament** – it was important that 'a living democracy' be 'maintained in the member states while integration proceeds'.

The Karlsruhe court saw Community law as essentially a more developed form of normal public international law, rather than as a separate and distinct 'new legal order' of the kind identified by the **European Court of Justice** (ECJ) in the Van Gend en Loos case (Case 26/62). It stated that 'the authority of [Union law] is derived from the member states and has binding effect on German sovereign territory only by virtue of the German command to apply the law (*Rechtsanwendungsbefehl*)'. The validity and application of EU law in Germany flowed from the country's 'act of consent', which could itself be revoked. As a result, Germany was 'maintaining its status as a sovereign state in its own right, as well as the status of sovereign equality with other states'. As the 'limited individual powers' transferred to the Union were conferred, rather than ceded without condition, the Union could have 'no exclusive **competence** for jurisdictional conflicts' which might arise between EU and national levels. The Federal Constitutional Court thus asserted, by implication, that the ECJ did not possess the ultimate power to determine its own field of discretion – known in German as *Kompetenz-Kompetenz* – and that instead the former court could override the latter, at least within Germany, on any matter where it deemed that the EU institutions were exceeding the powers conferred on them. For this purpose, the court said that it retained the right to review all **legal acts** adopted at EU level and warned that it would monitor closely the use of Article 235 EC, now **Article 352** TFEU – a potentially 'competence stretching' provision by which the **Council of Ministers** may adopt measures for which there is no other explicit **legal base** – to ensure that de facto treaty changes were not introduced by the back door. Equally, any attempt to exploit this article to harmonize national laws in the fields of education, vocational training, youth, culture or public health – where the Maastricht Treaty only allowed 'supporting and supplementary' action at EU level (under what are now Articles 165–8 TFEU) – would be ruled illegal on German territory. This somewhat unexpected judgement, which posed serious constitutional questions and aroused concern in both Bonn and Brussels, nonetheless enabled Germany to complete its ratification of the Maastricht Treaty – the last member state to do so.

The second Karlsruhe judgement, delivered on 30 June 2009, addressed similar issues raised in six cases brought by various citizens against the Lisbon Treaty and amendments to the Basic Law introduced to underpin it, as well as against a parallel law to give operational effect to the new Lisbon procedures for national parliamentary scrutiny over the **subsidiarity** implications of draft EU law – known as the 'Act extending and strengthening the rights of the Bundestag and the Bundesrat in European Union matters'.

The Federal Constitutional Court's ruling in 2009 – comprising 421 paragraphs over 63 pages – starts from the same premise as the judgement it delivered 16 years earlier, but draws out its implications in greater detail and more clear-cut terms. It asserts that Germany is allowed by its constitution to join a *Staatenverbund*, but not a *Bundesstaat* or *Staatsverband* (federation), and defines the former as a 'close long-term association of states which remain sovereign, an association which exercises public authority on the basis of a treaty, whose fundamental order is, however, at the disposal of the member states alone and in which the . . . citizens of those states remain the agents of democratic legitimation'. As such, the member states, as the constituent authority of the Union, 'remain permanently the masters of the Treaties' and the autonomy enjoyed by the Union in certain policy fields 'is independent but derived, namely accorded by other legal entities'. The Basic Law 'does not grant the bodies acting on behalf of Germany', notably the federal parliament, 'powers to abandon the right to self-determination of the German people, in the form of Germany's sovereignty under international law, by joining a federal state'. It therefore 'prohibits the transfer of competence to decide on its own competence' – *Kompetenz-Kompetenz* – to a higher level and requires that membership of the Union be reversible. Departure from the Union would not be 'secession from a *Staatsverband* . . . , but merely withdrawal from a *Staatenverbund* which is founded on the principle of reversible self-commitment'. German participation in the European integration process is desirable and acceptable so long as it respects the 'inalienable' or 'non-transferable constitutional identity' of the Federal Republic, and with it the 'constituent power of the member states as the masters of the Treaties'. It is important to avoid 'dynamic treaty provisions of a blanket character' that could lead to a higher degree of integration than foreseen and agreed to by the constituent authority, and 'suitable national safeguards' are needed to prevent this.

In its own words, the Federal Constitutional Court – in a way consistent with 'the Basic Law's openness towards European law' (*Europarechtsfreundlichkeit*) – 'reviews whether legal instruments of the European institutions and bodies remain within the limits of the sovereign powers conferred on them'. It also reviews whether the 'inviolable core content of the constitutional identity of the Basic Law' is respected. These ultra vires and 'identity' tests are 'incumbent on the Federal Constitutional Court alone' and 'can result in . . . Union law being declared inapplicable in Germany'. As Jean-Claude Piris has written, such an arrangement 'is hardly compatible' with the obligation on the ECJ, under Article 19(1) TEU, to 'ensure that in the interpretation and application of the Treaties the law is observed' (*The Lisbon Treaty: A Legal and Political Analysis*, 2010).

The Karlsruhe court, whilst upholding the Lisbon Treaty and amendments to the Basic Law flowing from it, ruled unconstitutional the 'Act extending and strengthening the rights of the Bundestag and the Bundesrat in European Union matters'. It stated that the law needed to be amended to provide additional, ex ante parliamentary safeguards against unintended or unauthorized increases in Union competence. Before the German federal government could agree to certain decisions (mainly of a quasi-constitutional character) requiring unanimity in the Council of Ministers, the explicit approval of the German parliament would henceforth be required.

The passage of domestic laws would now be mandatory in advance of: i) the use of the Article 352 TFEU (see above); ii) the use of the new general ***passerelle* clause** (Article 48(7) TUE), allowing for the extension of **qualified majority voting** (QMV) in the Council and/or the extension of **co-decision** between the Council and Parliament; and iii) the use of three specific provisions to widen EU competence in the field of police and judicial cooperation in criminal matters (Articles 82(2), 83(1) and 86(4) TFEU) and one relating to the **European Investment Bank** (EIB) (Article 308 TFEU). Concurrent resolutions in the two houses of parliament would also be needed before the use of specific *passerelle* clauses in five fields (with legislation required in a sixth field). These new safeguards would apply in addition to those EU decisions – such as increases in **own resources**, the accession by the EU to the **European Convention on Human Rights** (ECHR) or the extension of **European citizenship** rights – where EU decisions already needed to be approved in each member state 'in accordance with their respective constitutional requirements'. Following the June 2009 court judgement, the German government rushed through amendments to the Act to provide for these changes: adopted by the Bundestag and Bundesrat on 8 and

18 September respectively, they enabled the Federal Republic to ratify the Lisbon Treaty a week later.

The June 2009 ruling also sharpened the Federal Constitutional Court's general analysis of the institutional structure of the Union, in a way that heightened the discomfort of many traditional advocates of a more politically integrated Europe, not only in Germany. Given that the EU is not a state, the court argued, 'it is not therefore required to develop democratically [a] system of European institutions analogous to that of a state'. The Council of Ministers, it said, 'is not a second chamber, as it would be in a federal state, but the representative body of masters of the Treaties'. Likewise, the European Parliament 'is not a body of representation of a sovereign European people', but rather one of the 'peoples of Europe organized in their states'. As such, its composition 'need not do justice to equality' between member states in terms of equal representation for the same number of votes cast – one of the grounds for the challenge to the domestic constitutionality of the Lisbon Treaty in the court. Instead, 'representation in the European Parliament does not take as its reference point the equality of the citizens of the Union, but nationality.' The court noted that the composition of all the EU institutions was defined on this basis, whereas ironically this is 'an absolutely prohibited distinction' in the policies of the Union: 'this contradiction can only be explained by the character of the European Union as an association of sovereign states.'

The court argued that, given the Union's present state of development, the Bundestag remained 'the body of representation of the German people' at 'the focal point of an interweaved democratic system', whilst the European Parliament provided a 'sufficient level of legitimation' in the current 'system of conferred powers'. However, an unacceptable **democratic deficit** would exist if 'the legislative competences which are essential for democratic self-determination were [to be] exercised mainly at Union level', making the Union correspond to 'the federal level of a federal state'. Such a situation would require the German government to work to reform the system – to close the gap between power and legitimacy at supranational level – and, the court noted almost casually, 'if the worst comes to the worst, even to refuse to participate further in the European Union'. The court indicated what the key remaining legislative competences of the Federal Republic would need to be, speaking of the need to retain 'sufficient space for the political formation of the economic, cultural and social circumstances of life'. Areas in which the Federal Republic must retain 'substantial national scope of action' included nationality and citizenship, the use of force, deployment of troops, criminal law, fiscal policy, welfare policy, education, the family, language, religion, and freedom of speech, press and association. Finally, the court also expressed the view that the Lisbon Treaty 'considerably curtailed' the position of national parliaments, by extending the range of QMV decisions in the Council and by 'communautizing' a number of policy fields (notably police and judicial cooperation in criminal matters).

Cumulatively, the 1993 and 2009 Karlsruhe judgements marked an important shift in the jurisprudence of the Federal Constitutional Court. Until 1993, the principal issue of concern to the court in respect of Community law was the question of whether, at supranational level, it yet guaranteed an 'application of fundamental rights which in substance and effectiveness [was] essentially similar to the protection of fundamental rights required unconditionally by the Basic Law'. It located this issue in the wider process of institution-building at supranational level, which it welcomed as consistent with the Basic Law, including the development of a 'democratically legitimated parliament directly elected by general suffrage' and possessing legislative power. The court's first *Solange* (or 'so long as') ruling of 1974 concluded that the necessary guarantees on fundamental rights did not yet exist, noting that, at this stage of the 'continuing integration process, which is still in flux', the Community 'still lacks in particular a codified catalogue of fundamental rights'. By 1986, however, the second *Solange* ruling suggested that practical guarantees had now developed sufficiently, mainly through decisions of the ECJ, to excuse the German court from needing to review European legislation on these grounds. In both cases, it was clear that the court saw itself as having only a 'provisional' role in adjudicating on Community law and that, once fundamental rights were firmly assured, it would recognize, for all practical purposes, the primacy of the Treaties and legislation adopted under them.

This debate helps account for the fact that the strongest political pressure in Europe for the inclusion of some kind of **Charter of Fundamental Rights** in the Treaties came from pro-European forces in Germany, partly in the hope of closing off any possibility that the Karlsruhe court might involve itself systematically in questions of European law. German politicians, especially Social Democrats, led efforts in this direction, with Chancellor Gerhard Schröder securing agreement from other EU heads of government to the drafting of a (then non-binding) Charter in October 1999, and Roman Herzog, the country's recently-retired president, chairing the Convention that drew it up.

In hearing the cases against the Maastricht and Lisbon Treaties, the court could have invoked (respectively) either its second *Solange* ruling or the fact that the Lisbon Treaty would make the Charter legally binding, in order to argue that the practical need to intervene on matters of Community or Union law no longer applied. In 2009, such a ruling would have been consistent with the first *Solange* judgement, which specifically stated that reference of cases to the German Constitutional Court would only be 'admissible and necessary' for 'as long as the integration process has not progressed so far that' an adequate catalogue of fundamental rights had been codified in European law. Instead, the court chose to go down a different path, asserting a new philosophy of defensive judicial activism, no longer focused on fundamental rights, but on the broader question of policing the boundary between Union and national competence. This approach went further than the 1974 ruling, which had stated that the 'legal difficulty' in question arose 'exclusively' because of the Community's level of development. The 1993 and 2009 rulings suggest that, in the eyes of the court, the problem is now inherent in the nature of the European Union itself, regardless of how complete its institutional structure might be.

Kohl, Helmut (born 1930)

The son of a Bavarian finance ministry official, Helmut Kohl was born into a conservative, Catholic family in Ludwigshafen, now in Rhineland-Palatinate. He grew up during the Nazi era, was briefly called up to the youth wing of the air force, and became active in the new Christian Democratic Union (CDU) immediately following the Second World War. After taking a doctorate in politics at Heidelberg university in 1958, he returned to Ludwigshafen, where he worked in industry, became a local councillor and secured election to the *Land* parliament. Kohl served as Minister President (regional prime minister) of Rhineland-Palatinate from 1969 to 1976, establishing himself as a national figure. He was elected chairman of the CDU in 1973, running as the party's candidate for Chancellor in the 1976 Bundestag elections. The party's margin of defeat was sufficiently narrow for him to survive as CDU leader. He eventually become Chancellor six years later, at the age of 52, when the (Liberal) Free Democrat Party (FDP) switched coalition partners – from the Social-Democrat SPD to the CDU – in midterm. Despite his initial reputation as a *Provinzler* – an orthodox, regional party loyalist of limited vision – Kohl steadily emerged as the dominant force in German politics, winning four successive elections as Chancellor, in 1983, 1987, 1990 and 1994. He served as head of government for 16 years, longer than any figure since Bismarck, and decisively shaped the future of his country as the architect of **German reunification**, following the fall of the Berlin Wall.

On entering government in October 1982, Kohl chose to maintain the *Ostpolitik* towards East Germany defined by his SPD predecessors Willy Brandt and Helmut Schmidt. He also proved a staunch supporter of the Atlantic Alliance, firmly backing the deployment of Cruise and Pershing missiles in Germany. Although the policy of rearmament against the Soviet renewal of intermediate nuclear weapons had begun under Schmidt, it had proved highly divisive within the SPD and provoked, as Kohl himself put it, 'one of the most dramatic debates in German post-war history'. In domestic policy,

Kohl followed conservative economic policies, reducing taxes and containing public expenditure. A convinced pro-European in the tradition of **Konrad Adenauer**, Kohl worked effectively with his foreign minister, Hans-Dietrich Genscher – the FDP leader who had already served for eight years in the same post under both Brandt and Schmidt – to maintain a strong place for Germany in the politics of the European Community. He quickly established excellent personal relations with **François Mitterrand**, the French President with whom 13 of his 16 years in office overlapped. Despite hailing from different political families, Kohl and Mitterrand viewed national and European politics in very similar terms, combining a powerful instinct for survival at home with a deep aversion to nationalism abroad. The two leaders took bilateral Franco-German cooperation to a new level of intensity: the picture of the two men standing hand-in-hand on the seventieth anniversary of the Battle of Verdun is one of the most iconic images of European politics in the 1980s.

Kohl and Mitterrand worked closely with **Jacques Delors**, President of the **European Commission** from 1985 to 1995, to ease the European Community through the most dramatic period of deepening in its history. Whilst Kohl himself rarely took the lead in proposing new policies, he supported most of the initiatives advanced by Delors or Mitterrand, whether they served Germany's immediate interest – such as the completion of the **single market** – or required an additional German financial sacrifice – as in the case of increased **own resources** or the development of a **cohesion** policy. The German Chancellor used his country's **presidency** of the **Council of Ministers** in the first half of 1988 to move beyond its instinctive reluctance to reform the **Common Agricultural Policy** (CAP) and to escape the traditional caution of the Bundesbank towards closer monetary integration. In a major shift of policy, Kohl accepted the French objective of reviving **Economic and Monetary Union** (EMU), so that a single European currency might evolve within a defined timescale. The Hanover meeting of the European Council in June 1988 commissioned the **Delors Report**, which established the basic blueprint for EMU. Bilaterally, Kohl used the occasion of the 25th anniversary of the **Elysée Treaty** in January 1988 to establish a Franco-German Brigade of 5,000 infantry, which subsequently evolved into the **Eurocorps**. Kohl and Mitterrand were jointly awarded the **Charlemagne Prize** in 1988 in recognition of their work.

As Anthony Glees has written, 'Kohl's political career and the whole of West German political life' were reshaped by the time-lagged consequences of 'one single event' – the advent of Mikhail Gorbachev as Soviet leader in March 1985. But for this, Kohl might now be 'remembered as one of the least distinguished heads of government of the Bonn Republic' (*Reinventing Germany: German Political Development since 1945*, 1996). Although Kohl's coalition was returned to office with a reduced majority in the January 1987 Bundestag election, the CDU registered its (until then) lowest-ever share of the vote (at 34.4 per cent), and the standing of both the Chancellor and his party continued to decline thereafter. In the June 1989 **European elections**, the CDU fell behind the SPD for the first time in two decades and there was a 7 per cent vote for the far-right Republicans. This situation was spectacularly transformed by the dramatic events which led to the fall of the Berlin Wall on 9 November 1989 and the collapse of the Communist dictatorship within the German Democratic Republic (GDR). It was Gorbachev, in Glees' words, who 'encouraged the East German people to think about making political and economic changes to their system' and 'refused to sanction the use of force to subsequently restrain them'. On a visit to the Federal Republic in June 1989 marked by 'Gorbymania', the Soviet president said that the Wall 'could disappear once the conditions that generated the need for it disappeared' and that 'everything was possible' in Germany.

Kohl reacted to the seismic events of autumn 1989 with a combination of tough-mindedness and clear thinking that impressed both his compatriots and the wider international community. He quickly identified the need for German reunification – at a time when several leaders, notably the British prime minister, **Margaret Thatcher**, and initially even his great ally, President Mitterrand, expressed serious doubts – and shrewdly drew on the unequivocal support of the US President, George H. W. Bush, to manoeuvre Gorbachev into supporting a development which followed logically from his previous positions. Although his initial proposals were cautious – thinking first in terms of a confederation, rather than expansion of the Federal Republic – Kohl encouraged people in both German states, especially the GDR, to think of a unified country as their natural home, so reawakening a sense of common national pride that had been unrealized since the war. More pragmatically, he promised to fund the costly withdrawal of the 385,000 Soviet troops based in the GDR, in return for the new Germany's membership of NATO. Kohl's only significant error was to suggest briefly that the line of the post-war Polish–German border might open for renegotiation. (Both the West and East German parliaments subsequently passed resolutions confirming their acceptance of the existing border.)

The huge problems and uncertainties posed by German reunification gave rise to a political climate in which Kohl's qualities of dignity, reliability and sense of purpose were shown to particular advantage. Whilst his controversial decision to insist on the substitution of the Deutschmark for the Ostmark at parity raised the immediate cost of restructuring the East German economy, it helped to maintain the self-respect of ex-GDR citizens and prevent their mass exodus to the west. A German unity fund of almost € 60 billion was established to ease the transition (although the net transfer to the East

German economy over the subsequent 20 years would eventually amount to some € 1.6 trillion). On 12 September 1990, following the 'Two plus Four' talks, a reunification treaty was signed by the two German states and the four Allied powers that had occupied the country after the Second World War – the United States, Soviet Union, United Kingdom and France. The treaty took effect on 3 October, which became the 'Day of Unity' in Germany. Two months later, Kohl's coalition government was re-elected with a 134-seat majority in the first all-German elections since the 1930s – a political outcome which 18 months earlier would have seemed inconceivable.

At European level, Kohl argued strongly in favour of anchoring Germany's renewed strength as a united country in a process of deeper **sovereignty**-sharing. As he put it succinctly: 'There will be no Fourth Reich. This united Germany will be part of a peaceful Europe.' With Mitterrand, he put forward proposals for the institutional reform of the European Community and they worked together on building EMU and 'European Political Union' (EPU) in tandem. These twin tracks were sanctioned by the two Dublin European Councils of April and June 1990 and led eventually, after parallel **Intergovernmental Conferences** (IGCs), to agreement on the **Maastricht Treaty** in December 1991. However, despite the best efforts of Kohl and Mitterrand, the issue of the rebirth of German power still featured prominently in the **French referendum** on the treaty in September 1992. Kohl even appeared, by satellite from Bonn, to support Mitterrand in the main televised debate of the campaign, arguing that the popular vote was a 'moment of destiny' for both countries and Europe as a whole. The text was only endorsed by a very narrow margin, with many doubting that the new Germany – a single country of over 80 million inhabitants, located in the centre of the European continent and no longer confronted by the Soviet Union to its east – could or would be simply the old West Germany writ large.

During the second half of his 16-year chancellorship, most of Kohl's energy was absorbed in dealing with the multiple consequences, domestic and foreign, of the reunification process. He set out consciously, and largely successfully, to steer the enlarged Federal Republic on a course that maintained as much as possible of the moderate, law-based, internationalist political culture of the previous four decades. He stressed that he wanted to see the 'Europeanization of Germany', rather than the reverse. When, in September 1993, the **Lamers–Schäuble paper**, authored by two leading CDU figures, raised the possibility of formalizing a '**two-speed Europe**', spearheaded in effect by Germany and France, Kohl pointedly refused to be drawn down that route. Although the Chancellor believed deeply in Franco-German cooperation – and had used it to great effect – he did not see it as a substitute for continued closer integration across the continent as a whole. Kohl understood the importance of the Union as a system in which the interests of all member states, however small, were respected. He also maintained the German commitment to EMU defined at Maastricht, even when the disciplines of the **convergence criteria** compounded problems in financing the reconstruction of the old GDR economy (which involved a net transfer from west to east of some 4.5 per cent of GDP per year). Kohl made little effort to push for the new **European Central Bank** (ECB) to be located on German soil until such time as fears that domestic opinion was turning against the single currency made it necessary to argue the case for Frankfurt. Even the eastward move of the country's capital, starting in 1991, from Bonn to Berlin – a distance as far as from London to Bonn – was carried off without inducing national soul-searching or arousing nationalist excitement. A more pragmatic, populist politician might have handled each of these challenges differently.

The CDU–CSU–FDP coalition secured a fourth, this time very narrow, re-election in the Bundestag election of October 1994, but lost its majority in the upper chamber, the Bundesrat, soon after. The events of 1989–90 had marked an economic, as well as political, turning-point for Germany: growth in the Federal Republic averaged only two per cent in the 1990s, compared with almost twice that figure during the previous decade. The domestic electorate became increasingly restless and critical of the long-serving Chancellor, even if his international stock remained high. Within the European Union, the retirements of Mitterrand and Delors in 1995 denied Kohl the easy relationship he had enjoyed with like-minded leaders of real influence. The mood within the CDU became less pro-European, with the party removing the reference to creating a '**United States of Europe**' from its statutes in 1995. In December 1996, Kohl wrote a joint letter with Mitterrand's successor, Jacques Chirac, on EU institutional reform, which set much of the agenda for the IGC negotiating the 1997 **Amsterdam Treaty**. However, the level of the ambition was much more modest than in the Kohl–Mitterrand initiatives of the recent past: for example, pressure from the *Länder* constrained the Chancellor in the degree of **communautization** he could accept in the field of **Justice and Home Affairs** (JHA). 'No one wants a centralized superstate' in Europe, he declared defensively, 'it does not and will not exist'.

Kohl's ability to survive in power was partly based on continuing respect for his accomplishment in reuniting Germany and partly on his ruthless success in outmanoeuvring, marginalizing or eliminating rivals within the CDU. Over the years, he had deployed this skill against a series of figures – including regional premiers Ernst Albrecht and Lothar Späth, and CDU secretary general Heiner Geissler – who are now largely forgotten outside German political circles. The result was that, towards the end of his political career, Kohl had left his party without any obvious successor.

In the Bundestag election of September 1998, Kohl finally lost power to the

SPD, whose leader, Gerhard Schröder, duly replaced him as Chancellor. When he addressed the CDU parliamentary group for the last time as party leader, he allegedly made a long plea for the party to maintain its European commitment, only to be interrupted by a backbencher shouting, to applause, 'we have had enough of this'. Kohl remained in parliament until 2002, a period during which he grappled with the revelation that in the 1990s he had been aware of illegal funding for the CDU to the tune of more than € 2.0 million euro. Kickbacks from the sale of German armaments to Saudi Arabia and the privatization of the Elf Aquitaine oil company in France had been channelled to the party through secret Swiss bank accounts. Whilst there was no evidence of personal enrichment by Kohl himself, the former Chancellor refused to answer questions about the scandal. He was fined € 150,000 in an out-of-court settlement with prosecutors in February 2001. Kohl's replacement as CDU leader, Wolfgang Schäuble, took responsibility for the scandal and resigned. The episode left Kohl looking an increasingly isolated figure, although ultimately it was impossible for the scale of his historical achievement in reuniting Germany to be eclipsed.

In retirement, Kohl's personal life was further overshadowed by the illness and suicide of his wife, who had developed an extreme allergy to light, and by recurrent health problems of his own. He married again in 2008, his new wife a civil servant 34 years his junior. He has so far published three volumes of memoirs, covering the years 1930–82, 1982–90 and 1990–94. The European Council awarded him the status of Honorary Citizen of Europe in December 1998, an honour only previously bestowed on **Jean Monnet**. The longest serving German Chancellor since Bismarck and the architect of Germany's renewed unity, Kohl was described by George H. W. Bush in 2006 as 'the greatest European leader of the second half of the twentieth century'.

L

Lamers–Schäuble paper

In September 1994, a paper entitled *Reflections on European Policy*, drawn up by two senior German Christian Democrat (CDU) parliamentarians, Karl Lamers and Wolfgang Schäuble, suggested that there was and should be a 'hard core' of member states of the European Union 'oriented to greater integration and closer cooperation'. It called for this group to be further strengthened in order 'to counteract the centrifugal forces generated by constant **enlargement**'. The group of countries in question was thought to be composed of Germany, France and the **Benelux** countries (namely **the Six** founding member states, with the exception of Italy). The paper asserted that among the most precise and demanding preconditions for membership of the hard core was meeting the **convergence criteria** for the third stage of **Economic and Monetary Union** (EMU), described as 'the cornerstone of political union'.

Although the Lamers–Schäuble paper emphasized that the EU hard core 'must not be closed to other member states' – and indeed should be open to any partner 'able and willing to meet its requirements' – the use of the phrase caused considerable irritation both in certain national capitals and within the European institutions. The concept was criticized by opponents of a **two-speed Europe**, notably **Jacques Delors**, President of the European Commission. The German Chancellor, **Helmut Kohl**, pointedly declined to endorse the Lamers–Schäuble position, whilst the foreign minister and leader of the Liberal FDP, Klaus Kinkel, said that it was 'laden with too many concepts that do not fit with our European policy'. The discussion exposed divisions among governments about the struggle to meet the convergence criteria and whether a wider Europe need be at the expense of a deeper Europe. 'If the ideas expressed in the CDU's proposal were to be put into practice,' the Italian foreign ministry said in a statement, 'we would evidently risk a break-up of Europe, which is completely unacceptable.'

In a special reference to the United Kingdom, the Lamers–Schäuble paper said that the existence of a hard core (and the intensification of

Franco-German cooperation implicit in it) did not imply 'the abandoning of hopes that Great Britain will assume its role in the heart of Europe and thus in its core'. In a speech in Leiden a few days later, British prime minister John Major set out his counter-case for 'a multi-speed, multi-layered, multi-track Europe'. He argued that one or several core groups should be allowed to emerge, pursuing various policies on a flexible and non-exclusive basis. Lamers responded by arguing in London that his 'firmly-held belief ... borne out by the entire course of European integration' was that 'if a smaller group of countries presses ahead with particularly intensive and far-reaching economic and political integration, this group as core has a centripetal or magnetic effect' on others.

It is interesting to note that the political difficulty that Lamers and Schäuble confronted in arguing explicitly for a 'hard core' within the EU was compounded by problems in translating the original German phrase, *feste Kern*. The word *fest* means 'solid' or 'firm': to translate it as 'hard' in English can introduce associations of exclusiveness and of lack of sympathy towards outsiders not present in the original. In French, it was translated as *noyau dur*, the primary meaning of *noyau* being the stone of a fruit, bringing with it less negative associations of durability and germination.

Languages

The rules governing the use of languages in the institutions of the European Union are decided by the **Council of Ministers**, acting unanimously, under Article 342 TFEU. As Article 217 of the original **Treaty of Rome**, this was the legal base for the very first legislative act of the **European Economic Community** (EEC), Council **Regulation** 1/1958 of 15 April 1958, which specified Dutch, French, German and Italian as 'the official languages and the working languages' of the institutions of **the Six** and gave them equal status. There was no treaty obligation on the Council to allow each member state to designate its own language, but once the pattern was set, it became politically impossible to reverse. Successive **enlargements** have since increased the number of languages to 23 (with the regulation amended on each occasion accordingly).

The number of languages used in the EU institutions is fewer than the number of member states, because several languages are shared by at least two countries. German has official language status in no less than five member states – Germany, Austria, Belgium, Luxembourg and part of Italy – and it is actually spoken in 12 EU countries in all. Both French and English are official languages in three member states – in France, Belgium and Luxembourg in the first case, and in the United Kingdom, Ireland and Malta in the second. Dutch, Finnish, Greek and Swedish are all official languages in two member states. The two countries that use English, in addition to the UK, have both chosen to invoke their domestic languages: Maltese became as an official EU language with Malta's accession in 2004, and Irish (Gaelic) was made an official language in 2007, 34 years after Ireland joined the Community. Because Irish is the only official language not spoken by a majority of the country's population – only 1.7 million out of 4.2 million Irish citizens are able to do so – it was agreed that the obligations for its use at EU level could be less stringent than normal.

The European Union is in fact unique among international organizations in permitting each member state to import its own official language. Many other international bodies operate only in English and French, including notably the **Council of Europe** and **North Atlantic Treaty Organization** (NATO), whilst the **United Nations** uses six languages: English, French, Spanish, Russian, Arabic and Chinese. The traditional explanation for this divergence is that, unlike other bodies, the EU makes binding supranational law, overriding the authority of **national parliaments**. As such, texts for adoption need to be completely comprehensible and accurate in advance in all the countries to which they will apply. However, in practice, it is unlikely that, had the EU been founded with 27 member states, rather than six, the language régime would have been so generous. The fact that only four languages were needed at the start meant it was relatively easy to establish the pattern. By contrast, when the Council of Europe was founded in 1949, its ten members already used at least eight languages between them.

In practice, the requirements for language use in the EU institution take some account of the sensitivity of the issues under discussion and the degree of political-level involvement in proceedings. This makes the day-to-day arrangements less rigid than they might at first appear. The institutions are allowed to 'stipulate in their rules of procedure which of the languages are to be used in specific cases' and non-institutional bodies are free to choose their language régime completely. Most institutions work on the basis that all official documents should be available in all languages, at any of their formal meetings, and that full interpretation should be provided in and out of all languages at such meetings. However, arrangements for preparatory or informal meetings, as well as the circulation of working papers, are more flexible. For example, whereas discussions in a full meeting of the Council of Ministers will be conducted in all languages, those in **COREPER** and the Council's working groups take place largely in English, French or German. Similarly, in the **European Commission**, the preparatory meetings of *chefs de* ***cabinets*** are held in English and French, whilst the full meetings of the college of Commissioners may use all languages. By contrast, in the **European Court of Justice** (ECJ), a specific language is chosen for each case, usually that of the applicant. Although the Court's decisions are published in all languages, only the version set out in the 'language of the case' is definitive.

Pressure from Spain to allow regional languages (Catalan, Galician and Basque) to be officially recognized at EU level has led several of the EU institutions to reach agreements for their limited use, outside Regulation 1/1958, notably in correspondence with citizens. In the latter context, the 1997 **Amsterdam Treaty** had widened the provisions on **European citizenship** to give every citizen of the Union the right to use any of the official languages in correspondence with the EU institutions and to receive a reply in the same language. However, this concession was largely cosmetic, as the right in question had already been established in the 1958 Council regulation.

The 23 languages currently in use at EU level give rise to no fewer than 506 possible language combinations: the formula is n^2-n, where n equals the number of languages in use. Each additional language adds a further 2(n-1) combinations. The resource allocation implications are significant. The Commission's translation service, which is based in Luxembourg, has an output of about a million pages a year. Over a quarter of the officials working in the Union's institutions are employed in connection with interpretation and translation in some way: the **European Parliament** is the largest single employer of interpreters in the world, and the Commission of translators. In 2011, some 30 per cent of the Parliament's staff (1,800 people) and budget (€ 488 million) were directly or indirectly devoted to language questions.

Legal act

Article 288 TFEU lists five different types of legal act which the institutions of the European Union may adopt. These are **regulations**, **decisions** and **directives** – all of which are legally binding – and **recommendations** and **opinions**, which are not. The first three types of act are also sometimes referred to in the budgetary sphere as 'basic acts', in that they can constitute a sufficient **legal base** for authorizing the inclusion of appropriations in the annual EU **Budget**. The distinction between these various types of act is fundamental to an understanding of **EU law**. In some cases, the choice of legal instrument in respect of particular actions is specified in the **Treaties**, whilst in others it is left to the discretion of the institutions – normally the **European Commission**, which enjoys the **right of initiative** in proposing EU legislation.

A regulation is a legal act of 'general application'. It is 'binding in its entirety and directly applicable in all Member States'. A decision is meant to be narrower in scope, although nonetheless 'binding in its entirety upon those to whom it is addressed', which may be the institution itself, any number of member states, or defined natural or legal persons. A directive is 'binding, as to the result to be achieved, upon each Member State to which it is addressed', but leaves 'to the national authorities the choice of form and methods'.

The essential legal difference between a regulation and directive is that whereas the latter must be transposed into national law (usually by a deadline) before entering into force, the former is directly applicable and therefore usually has immediate **direct effect**. The key political difference is that a regulation will normally be used when the institutions wish or need to secure a strictly uniform outcome across member states, whereas use of a directive allows for greater flexibility and sensitivity in the **harmonization** or approximation of national laws.

By contrast, recommendations and opinions 'have no binding force': they are essentially statements of view by institutions, similar in effect to resolutions. Unlike regulations, directives and those decisions that are addressed to all member states, recommendations and opinions of the institutions do not need to be published in the ***Official Journal***.

The typology of legal act set out above did not apply to measures adopted in the intergovernmental '**pillars**' for **Common Foreign and Security Policy** (CFSP) and **Justice and Home Affairs** (JHA) that were provided for in the 1992 **Maastricht Treaty**. Here, there were special types of act: common strategies, joint actions and common positions in CFSP; and common positions and framework decisions in JHA. Under the **Lisbon Treaty**, which entered into force in December 2009, the Maastricht pillars were abolished and these special types of act were discontinued.

The **Convention on the Future of Europe** in 2002–3, tasked with drafting a **European Constitution**, addressed the long-standing question of whether the EU should establish a formal **hierarchy of acts**, listing all possible instruments in diminishing order of importance, with a view to simplifying and clarifying matters. In the event, the text of the draft Constitution (Article I-33) went some way in this direction. It would sensibly have renamed regulations as 'European laws' and directives as 'European framework laws', so clarifying their essential nature. Decisions would have retained their current name, as 'European decisions'. However, in the Lisbon Treaty, which otherwise took over large parts of the Constitution, the existing nomenclature for legal acts was maintained, mainly to assuage political sensitivities in the Netherlands and United Kingdom.

In addition to the legal acts adopted by the Council on its own or by the Council or Parliament together, the Commission may also adopt delegated or implementing acts, under **comitology**, to fill in the detail of the originating legislation. Such Commission regulations, decisions and directives are full legal acts, even if their scope is much narrower.

In recent decades, the volume of substantive EU legislation has grown – as the Union's range of activities has widened and the use of **qualified majority voting** (QMV) has become the norm in the Council – whilst the use of comitology has declined. In 1970, the Council adopted 345 legal acts: 249 regulations, 71 decisions and 25 directives. In addition, the Commission adopted 3,561 comitology acts: 2,426 regulations, 435 decisions and three directives. By comparison, in 2011, the Council adopted on its own or jointly with the Parliament a total of 536 legal acts: 167 regulations, 333 decisions and 36 directives. (Of these, 56 regulations, 28 decisions and 24 directives were enacted under the **co-decision procedure** with the Parliament.) In addition, under comitology, the Commission adopted 1,491 measures: 1,066 regulations, 356 decisions and 69 directives.

Legal base

Unlike a state, which claims to have unlimited legal powers in its territory – but like all other organizations established under international law – the European Union exercises authority only in so far as it has been specifically attributed powers or '**competence**' by the contracting parties, namely the member-state signatories to the **Treaties**. This 'principle of conferral' is set out in Article 5 TEU, which states that 'the Union shall act only within the limits of the competences conferred on it by the Member States in the Treaties to obtain the objectives set out therein. Competences not conferred on the Union . . . remain with the Member States.'

It follows that all binding **legal acts** of the European Union must have a 'legal base', in that they must derive directly from a specific provision in one of the Treaties that justifies action in the field in question. In general, treaty articles are drafted in such a way as to lay down, not only the subject matter covered, but also the nature and the extent of the powers conferred upon the Union in that field. The legal base for any legislative proposal, in the form of reference to one or several treaty articles, is usually specified in the preamble of the text submitted by the **European Commission**. As A. G. Toth has written, the **European Court of Justice** (ECJ) 'will declare void, for lack of competence, an act which does not have a proper legal basis in a relevant Treaty provision or in another measure itself adopted under the Treaties' (*The Oxford Encyclopaedia of European Community Law*, Volume I, 1990).

The question of which legal base is chosen by the Commission is clearly important as a safeguard against any deliberate or inadvertent transgression of EU competence. The ECJ has determined that the Commission's choice of legal base (and any changes made to it during the legislative process) must rest on objective factors open to review (*Commission* v *Council*, Case C-440/05). The question is also politically significant in that it can determine the decision-making method which applies to the proposal under consideration: if a treaty base allowing **qualified majority voting** (QMV) in the **Council of Ministers** is chosen over one that needs **unanimity**, this can seriously affect the prospect of adoption and the content of any agreement reached. Likewise, how far, and in what way, the **European Parliament** is involved, flowing from the legal base chosen, may have important consequences. Before the Lisbon Treaty made

QMV in the Council and **co-decision** between the Council and Parliament the 'ordinary legislative procedure', there were regular disputes between the institutions about the choice of legal bases of proposals, precisely because of the way this would impact on their relative power in the law-making process. The Parliament, in particular, might seek to replace a legal base requiring unanimity in the Council and mere **consultation** (of the Parliament) with one where QMV and co-decision applied (or at least add such a base, for future reference), whilst some member states in the Council might seek to do the opposite – conscious that, if the Commission felt that the legality of the proposed act was being undermined, it could ultimately withdraw it. As the remaining areas where unanimity and consultation have shrunk in number, this may be less of a problem in the future, but it will still continue in some fields.

Legal certainty

The concept of 'legal certainty' is accepted as a general principle of law in most democratic political systems. It requires law to be coherent, unambiguous, accessible, and clear with respect to scope, purpose, effect and validity. Equally the law needs to be consistently applied by state bodies. Although nowhere defined in the **Treaties**, legal certainty has been recognized by the **European Court of Justice** (ECJ), since at least 1961, as a general principle of **EU law**. The **legal acts** adopted by the EU institutions and any national acts derived from them must respect the principle, and they may be challenged in the courts if they do not.

Apart from the bureaucratic inconvenience involved, legal ambiguity or contradictory administrative requirements can significantly inhibit trade and investment, and lead to costly disputes. A substantial number of legal cases relate to the allegedly 'retroactive' application of new EU rules by member states to activities completed before or whilst those rules are promulgated. Others concern the 'legitimate expectations' that such rules may generate, only for these to be called into question by seemingly contradictory subsequent acts. As the European Court has ruled, the 'requirement of legal certainty must be observed all the more strictly in the case of a measure liable to have financial consequences in order that those concerned may know precisely the extent of the obligations which it imposes on them' (Case 115/94; *Opel Austria* v *Council*).

Legal personality

From the start, the **Treaty of Rome** stated that the **European Economic Community** (EEC) 'shall have legal personality' (Article 210 EEC, later Article 281 EC). Identical provisions were written into the Treaties establishing the **European Coal and Steel Community** (ECSC), which has now lapsed, and the **European Atomic Energy Community** (Euratom or EAEC). As a result of legal personality, the three **European Communities** enjoyed certain rights and obligations both within the national legal systems of the member states and beyond. In the international sphere, these rights – dependent on their recognition by others – included the rights to make treaties and conclude other agreements with third countries, to join international organizations and to set up new ones, to conduct diplomatic relations and establish diplomatic representation, and to bring international claims and participate in the settlement of disputes. On this basis, over time, the EEC, subsequently renamed the European Community, entered into treaties or agreements with the majority of countries in the world, and the **European Commission** (on behalf of the Community) opened delegations in 135 countries. (Indeed, in areas of *exclusive* Community **competence**, such as external trade policy, the member states could no longer conclude treaties or agreements with third countries; in areas of *shared* competence, both the Community and member states would jointly negotiate 'mixed agreements'.)

With respect to national law, the Community was given 'the most extensive legal capacity accorded to legal persons' under the national laws of member states (by Article 212 EEC, later Article 282 EC, and identical provisions in the other founding **Treaties**). They could 'in particular' acquire or dispose of property and be a party to national legal proceedings (represented by the European Commission); by implication, they could also conclude contracts under public and private law. Although the 1965 **Merger Treaty** gave the three Communities common institutions, and although the 1992 **Maastricht Treaty** made them a component part of the European Union, they retained their distinct legal personalities. Until the entry into force of the **Lisbon Treaty** in December 2009, the European Union itself, by contrast, did not possess explicit legal personality.

Certain member states, notably Britain and France, had opposed the granting of legal personality to the new Union in the negotiation of the Maastricht Treaty. However, somewhat confusingly, the latter treaty invited the Union to 'assert its identity on the international scene' and allowed it (by the then Articles 24 and 38 TEU) to conclude treaties and agreements with third countries in the two Union fields which lay outside the domain of the Community '**pillar**', namely **Common Foreign and Security Policy** (CFSP) and the external aspects of **Justice and Home Affairs** (JHA). Starting in 1993, these articles were used to underpin peacekeeping and crisis management operations (in CFSP) and mutual assistance in criminal matters (in JHA). So, whatever the theoretical position, the Union gradually came to act in its own right in the international sphere. Many lawyers argued that, in any case, even if the Union was not granted explicit international legal personality, it could still acquire it in practice, simply by conducting foreign relations with third parties and being accepted as an equal partner by its interlocutors. This process had already occurred with several other international organizations, notably the **United Nations** and its various bodies. The Lisbon Treaty, by merging the European Union and the European Community, has extended explicit legal personality to all the activities of both, thus resolving the essential ambiguity on this point. (The only remaining complication is that Euratom is still a separate Community.)

Although the abolition of the distinction between EC and EU action in international affairs would ensure greater simplicity, consistency and legal clarity in the Union's relations with third countries, it was long resisted by the British government, on the grounds that it would undermine the intergovernmental pillars established at Maastricht. However, advocates of legal personality for the Union succeeded in winning the support of the **Convention on the Future of Europe** (2002–3), partly because such a move was seen as a precondition for merging the existing treaties and replacing them with a **European Constitution**. The Convention set up a working group on legal personality, chaired by the former Italian prime minister Giuliano Amato, which concluded that there was 'a very broad consensus (with one member against) that the Union should in future have its own explicit legal personality. It should be a single legal personality and should replace the existing personalities.' The Lisbon Treaty has carried forward that provision of the Constitution (except with regard to Euratom), even if the treaties are no longer merged. Article 281 EC has been replaced by Article 47 TEU, which states that 'The European Union shall have legal personality' (Article 282 EC has become Article 335 TEU).

In the long struggle over the European Constitution and later the Lisbon Treaty, the question of legal personality often became entangled in a debate about whether its formal extension to the Union would represent a qualitative change in the nature of the latter, converting it into some kind of 'state'. Whilst legal personality may be a necessary condition for statehood, it is not a sufficient one, as the experience of the Communities themselves testify. Many international organizations of an intergovernmental character, such as the International Monetary Fund (IMF) and the World Bank, have international legal personality. As Philippe de Schoutheete and Sami Andoura have argued, the existence of legal personality 'has no relation, positive or negative, to the intergovernmental or the supranational character of the organization concerned'. They note that the Universal Postal Union, which enjoys such personality, 'was founded in 1874 at a time when the concept and the word "supranational" would have been meaningless' (*In Studia Diplomatica*, Volume LX, 2007, 1).

The International Court of Justice (ICJ) ruled in 1947, in respect of the United Nations, that 'whereas a State possesses the totality of international rights and duties recognized by international law, those of an entity such as [an international organization] must depend upon its purposes and functions as specified or implied in its constituent documents and developed in practice.' The 1986 Vienna Convention on the Law of Treaties refers to international organizations as 'subjects of international law distinct from States'. As A. G. Toth has written, 'States (and only States) enjoy legal personality ipso facto, which personality is original in nature and plenary or unlimited in scope.' As a result, 'international organizations enjoy international legal personality but, in contrast to States, their personality is derivative in nature and functional (limited) in scope' (*Oxford Encyclopaedia of European Community Law*, Volume I, 1990).

Reflecting this, Toth notes, Community (now Union) membership of those 'international organizations and conferences which admit sovereign States only . . . is necessarily restricted to less than full membership, often to observer status'. For example, the Union's right to bring an international claim does not extend to the ICJ, as only states may be parties to cases in that court. The status that the EU enjoys in other international organizations depends ultimately on the internal rules of each of the bodies concerned. The question of whether the EU might at some point be admitted as a member of the UN in its own right – an issue which particularly exercises those fearing the consequences of the granting of legal personality to the Union – is thus primarily a matter for the UN itself, which (under Article 4 of its Charter) currently admits only states as members.

Lisbon Treaty

The Lisbon Treaty is the most important reform to the founding **Treaties** of the European Union to have been adopted since the 1992 **Maastricht Treaty**. Signed on 13 December 2007, it entered into force on 1 December 2009, following **ratification** in the 27 EU member states. The Lisbon Treaty replicates many, but not all, of the provisions of the **European Constitution**, which had been drafted by the 2002–3 **Convention on the Future of Europe**, but the ratification of which was abandoned following negative popular votes in the **French and Dutch referenda** of May–June 2005 (by respectively 54.7 and 61.6 per cent of those voting).

The European Constitution would have combined and replaced all existing treaties – other than the Treaty establishing the **European Atomic Energy Community** (EAEC or Euratom) – with a single text. Instead, the Lisbon Treaty has imported a complex series of amendments into the two principal treaties governing the institutions and policies of the Union: the 1992 **Maastricht Treaty**, known as the Treaty on European Union (TEU), and the 1957 **Treaty of Rome**, known (since Maastricht) as the Treaty establishing the European Community and renamed by Lisbon as the Treaty on the Functioning of the European Union (TFEU).

Among the most important changes introduced by the Lisbon Treaty were the creation of a post of 'permanent' **President of the European Council** and the upgrading of the existing position of **High Representative** for **Common Foreign and Security Policy** (CFSP). The **European Council** was made a separate institution to the **Council of Ministers**, with its new President chosen for a 30-month term, renewable once (Article 15 TEU). The High Representative combined his or her existing functions with those of the **presidency** of the Council in the CFSP field – including responsibility for chairing of the **Foreign Affairs Council** (FAC) – and of the European Commissioner for external relations (Article 27 TEU). A new, free-standing **European External Action Service** (EEAS) – composed of the CFSP officials from the Commission, Council secretariat and national diplomatic services – was established, reporting to the High Representative.

The **pillared structure** of the Union, established by the Maastricht Treaty, was abolished and the whole of the resulting, merged entity, called the European Union, was given **legal personality** (Article 47 TEU). In the process, all remaining intergovernmental aspects of **Justice and Home Affairs** (JHA) were 'communautized' (essentially covering police and judicial cooperation in criminal matters), with the United Kingdom widening its **opt-out** from Union action in the JHA field. The range of policy areas subject to **qualified majority voting** (QMV) in the Council was broadened, notably in JHA. The legislative and budgetary powers of the European Parliament were expanded, with 'co-decision' henceforth including inter alia the **Common Agricultural Policy** (CAP), **Common Fisheries Policy** (CFP) and the **Common Commercial Policy** (CCP), as well as the remaining areas of JHA, which had previously been subject to the **consultation procedure**. The combination of QMV in the Council and co-decision between the Council and Parliament was designated as the 'ordinary legislative procedure' of the Union (Article 294 TFEU). The Parliament and Council became co-equal in all aspects of the **budgetary process**, with the abolition of the distinction between **compulsory and non-compulsory expenditure**, which had operated particularly to the Parliament's disadvantage (Article 314 TFEU). The **comitology** process was reformed, with a new distinction introduced between delegated and implementing acts, and the Parliament and Council each enjoying a right of veto in the former (Article 290 TFEU).

Under the Lisbon Treaty, the **Charter of Fundamental Rights** was recognized as having 'the same legal value as the Treaties' – even if the United Kingdom and Poland obtained a de facto opt-out from some of its legal effects in their territories (**Protocol** 30) – whilst the Union is empowered to become a signatory to the **European Convention on Human Rights** (ECHR) (Article 6 TEU). New areas of **competence** were established for the Union in the fields of space policy (Article 189 TFEU) and sport (Article 165 TFEU), whilst its competence in some other areas was strengthened, notably in public health (Article 168 TFEU), **energy policy** (Article 194 TFEU), and intellectual property rights (Article 118 TFEU). **National parliaments** were given a specific responsibility for policing the **subsidiarity** implications of draft EU law (Article 12(b) TEU). Under a '**citizens' initiative**', any petition proposing a new draft law and receiving one million signatures will have to be considered by the **European Commission** (Article 11(4) TEU). An '**exit clause**' was introduced, to allow member states to leave the Union (Article 50 TEU). The procedure for future treaty reform was altered so that a Convention will automatically precede an **Intergovernmental Conference** (IGC), unless the European Parliament considers that it is not necessary (Article 48 TEU). Equally, a new 'simplified revision procedure' may be invoked directly by heads of government to make changes specifically to the policy responsibilities of the Union set out in the Treaty on the Functioning of the European Union. In these circumstances, no Convention or IGC will be convened, but the unanimous agreement of, and ratification by, all member states will still be necessary.

Formally speaking, the Lisbon Treaty was drafted by an Intergovernmental Conference which held 24 meetings between July and October 2007, during the Portuguese presidency of the Council. In practice, however, the mandate of the IGC had been defined in advance at the previous meeting of the European Council in June 2007, with German Chancellor Angela Merkel in the chair. This mandate was extremely detailed and reflected weeks of preparatory work by the German presidency. It was also highly prescriptive, declaring itself 'the exclusive basis and framework for the work of the IGC that will be convened'. Member states would abandon the 'constitutional concept, which consisted in repealing all existing Treaties and replacing them by a single text'; strike out planned references to the **symbols of the Union** and of the **primacy** of Union law; abandon the title of 'Union Minister for Foreign Affairs' for the upgraded High Representative post; make it clear that 'competences not conferred upon the Union in the Treaties remain with the Member States'; and remove the Charter of Fundamental Rights from the main body of the text, whilst still ensuring that it enjoyed treaty status. These and other changes were designed primarily to reassure public opinion in countries that had rejected the constitution – and those that might have done so, if referenda had been held there – that the reforms now envisaged did not entail any 'state-like' characteristics. In total, about 350 changes were made to the constitutional text by the IGC; where no changes were introduced, the provisions of the latter were simply rolled forward automatically into the Lisbon Treaty.

Ratification of the Lisbon Treaty proceeded more smoothly than that of the European Constitution, partly because the latter's provisions had been diluted and partly because the new French President, Nicolas Sarkozy, had taken office in April 2007 with an explicit mandate to negotiate a 'simplified' treaty to succeed the constitution, without holding another **referendum**. Indeed, he argued that any second referendum defeat would be both 'catastrophic for Europe' and risk France's 'exclusion from European integration'. However, in Ireland – where the holding of referenda on European treaties has become routine – the electorate rejected the text in June 2008 (by 53.4 to 46.6 per cent), repeating their initial reaction to the **Nice Treaty** seven years earlier (although on a significantly higher turnout). A series of 'assurances' were then negotiated for Ireland, guaranteeing that each member state would retain a European Commissioner and that nothing in the treaty would affect the country's rights in regard to taxation, 'Ireland's traditional policy of **neutrality**' or the provisions of the Irish constitution in relation to the right to life, education and the family. Agreed by the European Council in June 2009, these assurances – which will be formalized in law by inclusion in a protocol to be attached to the next accession treaty – enabled the Irish government to call a second referendum in October 2009, with the public finally endorsing the treaty by a margin of 67.1 to 32.9 per cent (see **Irish referenda on EU Treaties**). The Irish situation prompted concern that an early general election in Britain might lead to any majority Conservative government seeking to reopen UK ratification, especially as both the Czech and Polish presidents, Václav Klaus and Lech Kaczynski, decided to delay signing the Lisbon Treaty until after the second Irish referendum result. As the price for his signature, Klaus secured agreement that the Czech Republic would be given the same legal guarantee on the Charter of Fundamental Rights as Britain and Poland, at the time of the next significant treaty revision.

Further reading: Paul Craig, *The Lisbon Treaty: Law, Politics and Treaty Reform*, 2010; Jean-Claude Piris, *The Lisbon Treaty: A Legal and Political Analysis*, 2010.

Luxembourg Compromise

The Luxembourg Compromise was an informal arrangement, arrived at by **the Six** member states of the European Community in January 1966, whereby decisions which the **Treaties** foresaw being taken by **qualified majority voting** (QMV) in the **Council of Ministers** could be postponed until unanimous agreement had been reached. Its effect was to create a de facto national veto over all key decisions, and for almost two decades it stalled progress in many important areas of policy. Although some commentators occasionally claim that the Luxembourg Compromise still exists, in reality it disappeared during the course of the 1980s and no longer has any significant bearing on the way the European Union functions. QMV now applies in all areas where it is provided for in the Treaties. A member state can no longer veto a proposal unless unanimity is explicitly specified as the decision-making method.

The Luxembourg Compromise resolved an acute crisis in the Community's development, which had two linked but distinct components. The first was the rejection by France in June 1965 of a series of key **European Commission** proposals – on the financing of the new **Common Agricultural Policy** (CAP), the introduction of EC '**own resources**', and the widening of the budgetary powers of the **European Parliament**. The second was the outright refusal by France to accept that, when the so-called 'third stage' of the transitional phase of the Community's development came into effect in January 1966, QMV should, as the Treaty of Rome specified, automatically be introduced for the first time on a significant range of issues in the Council of Ministers.

So long as these important problems remained unresolved, the French President, **Charles de Gaulle**, instructed his ministers to boycott all Council meetings during the second half of 1965 – a period which coincided with his own scheduled re-election to office at home (for the first time by universal suffrage) at the end of the year. The policy of the *chaise vide* – or 'empty chair' – as it became known, effectively immobilized Community decision-making and delivered a severe psychological body-blow to the advocates of closer European integration.

Although the 1965 crisis developed initially around the CAP/EC financing package, it escalated spectacularly in September of that year when de Gaulle chose to broaden the issues at stake to include the planned shift to greater majority voting in the Council and, as a subsidiary question, the growing independence of the Commission as a free-standing political authority. The French President had long been hostile towards what he considered the dangerously federal implications of majority voting, having asserted at the time of his 1961–2 Fouchet Plan that 'there is no way that a foreign majority can constrain recalcitrant nations' in the Community. Now he reiterated this position with growing precision, speaking of 'certain mistakes or ambiguities in the **Treaties** setting up the economic union of the Six. That is why the crisis was, sooner or later, inevitable.'

According to de Gaulle, the fact that majority voting was to be introduced at all was the result of the **Treaty of Rome** having been negotiated in 1957, towards the end of the Fourth Republic, when France had been weak and before 'we had decided to take our destiny into our own hands'. To accept QMV now would leave France 'exposed to the possibility of being overruled' on issues of importance and would greatly strengthen the relative position of the Commission – 'this embryonic technocracy, for the most part foreign' – in the Community system. The prospect of majority voting caused the French government particular concern in the field, most obviously, of the **Common**

Agricultural Policy (CAP). However, its introduction in respect of the **right of establishment** of foreign nationals, the **free movement of capital**, aspects of **transport policy**, and the development of a **Common Commercial Policy** (CCP) for external trade also raised grave misgivings in Paris.

As the autumn of 1965 proceeded, it became clear that no agreement between de Gaulle and the other member states was likely at least until the December presidential election in France was out of the way. In the event, that contest proved a catalyst for compromise. The shock to de Gaulle of failing to win an outright victory on the first ballot against a pro-European Socialist, **François Mitterrand**, was compounded by the impressive performance of the centrist third candidate, Jean Lecanuet, who ran on an even more integrationist platform. The government's resolve on European affairs began to weaken, with prime minister Georges Pompidou predicting just before the second ballot against Mitterrand, two weeks later, that France might resume negotiations with her partners soon after the election. This did indeed occur, and the 'empty chair' component of the crisis ended.

Two special Council meetings were held in Luxembourg during January 1966 (without the Commission in attendance). At the first – on 17–18 January – the five other member states stood out against French demands on QMV, but progress was confirmed towards a settlement on CAP financing, and agreement that the introduction of own resources should be postponed (until 1970) and with it greater budgetary powers for the European Parliament. At the second meeting – on 28–29 January – the Council agreed, by a set of non-binding conclusions entered in its minutes, on a formula in respect of majority voting. This was the essence of what became known as the Luxembourg Compromise.

The Council conclusions stated that if one member state considered that 'a very important national interest' was at stake – often referred to as a 'vital' national interest – then the Council would endeavour to reach, within a reasonable period, solutions that could be adopted unanimously. The French delegation considered that when very important interests were at issue, discussion 'must be continued' until unanimous agreement was reached. However, this more maximalist formulation – which is the one most widely associated with the Compromise – was not accepted by the five other member states. The Council conclusions simply noted that there was a difference of opinion on what precisely would happen when a complete resolution of a dispute within the Council could not be achieved.

If France accepted defeat on the precise formulation of the Luxembourg Compromise, it won its basic objective – which was to create a firm presumption within the Council in favour of unanimous voting remaining the norm after 1966, even where QMV was explicitly provided for in the Treaties and no 'very important national interest' had been identified. The working assumption became that, since any country could invoke the Compromise at any time, there was little point in pressing a proposal whenever strong objections were raised by one of the member states. Discussion which failed to elicit the necessary degree of compromise in the Council was simply stalled, sometimes to the point where the Commission would withdraw the proposal in despair. (A good example of an area where majority voting was foreseen from 1966 but did not apply in practice, is the free movement of capital. No progress was made in agreeing any liberalization proposals between 1966 and 1986, as a direct consequence of the assumption that a qualified majority, even if attained, would be insufficient to secure the adoption of directives.)

In a limited number of areas – specifically certain technical decisions on the CAP and the adoption of the Community's annual **Budget** – QMV was in fact used after 1966. It was necessary to the continued operation of the Community and broadly suited the interests of France. But the parameters of this shift were very clearly understood. The position was sufficiently clear for the British government to state, in its 1971 White Paper on UK **accession**: 'All the countries concerned recognize that an attempt to impose a majority view in a case where one or more members considered their vital interests to be at stake would imperil the very fabric of the Community . . . [In such cases], it is Community practice to proceed only by **unanimity**.'

From time to time, attempts were made to encourage the Council to broaden the scope of majority voting, but always without success. The most notable followed the election of **Valéry Giscard d'Estaing** as French President in May 1974. Anxious to move the Community forward from its institutional impasse, he secured an ostensibly radical commitment by the heads of government at the Paris summit in December 1974 'to renounce the practice which consists of making agreements on all questions conditional on the unanimous consent of the member states'. In practice, however, this declaration changed nothing. Matters blocked on routine policy grounds by one member state continued simply not to get adopted. It was not necessary for the Luxembourg Compromise to be invoked formally – recourse was had to it perhaps only ten times in the 15 years after 1966 – for decision-making on literally hundreds of Commission proposals over these years to be stillborn. This pervasive immobilism within the Council prevailed until the early 1980s, when for a variety of reasons the previous 'veto culture' steadily began to erode. The crucial turning-point occurred in May 1982, when Britain invoked the Compromise on an agricultural issue where ironically its position was pitted against the vested interest of France, once the arch-defender of the veto.

The UK government, attempting to pursue its claim for a reduction in its net contribution to the Community Budget by other means (see **British**

Budget dispute), announced that it could not agree to the adoption of the annual settlement on agricultural prices (to which it had already acquiesced at official level). The reaction in the Council was almost uniformly hostile, with only Denmark and Greece supporting the previously accepted principle that it was entirely up to the country in question to determine what its own 'very important national interest' in any matter might be. All other member states indicated that the Compromise should only be invoked if the 'interest' at stake related directly to the substance of the proposal being considered. In this case, they argued, it did not. The prices package was then adopted by a qualified majority vote against an attempted UK veto. In entries to the minutes, five countries – all the original parties to the Luxembourg Compromise except France – then indicated that their preference was henceforth that majority voting should be used wherever the Treaties so provided.

In the event, the British timing of its agricultural prices démarche could not have been worse. At the end of 1981, a new institutional reform agenda had started to emerge within the Community, encouraged by the integrationist German and Italian foreign ministers. The resulting **Genscher–Colombo Plan** for a draft 'European Act' had included passing proposals to limit the Luxembourg Compromise to genuine cases of 'vital' interest. The UK episode of May 1982 decisively hardened attitudes in favour of a substantial change in decision-making practice. This mood found a ready echo in the European Commission and, more importantly, in the now directly elected European Parliament, which was looking for a 'democratic' issue on which to cut its teeth. Guided by its specially formed committee on institutional affairs (which began work in January 1982), the Parliament became increasingly insistent on the need for the Council strictly to follow treaty provisions on voting. It even launched a legal action in the **European Court of Justice** (ECJ) against the Council for '**failure to act**' in respect of a common transport policy, where use of majority voting was foreseen.

Reflecting this renewed interest in institutional issues and responding specifically to the Genscher–Colombo Plan, the European Council in Stuttgart of June 1983 agreed a 'Solemn Declaration on European Union', the so-called **Stuttgart Declaration**. On the question of voting, the document stated that the 'application of the decision-making procedures laid down in the Treaties is of vital importance in order to improve the EC's capacity to act.' It stopped short, however, of defining the limits of the Luxembourg Compromise – precisely because there was no agreement on what they were. All governments entered parallel statements about the Luxembourg Compromise, setting out their various interpretations of the practice.

During the first half of 1984, when France occupied the presidency of the Council, the attitude of the government in Paris towards maintaining the veto evolved considerably. Whereas prime minister Pierre Mauroy had vigorously defended the Luxembourg Compromise soon after the Stuttgart Declaration, by the following summer his President was striking a very different note. **François Mitterrand** confirmed a significant shift in his country's position in a keynote speech to the European Parliament in May 1984. The President asked: 'How can the complex and diversified entity which the Community has become be governed by rules like those of the old Diet of the Kingdom of Poland, where every member could block decisions? It is time we returned to a more normal and promising way of doing things . . . The more frequent practice of voting on important questions heralds a return to the Treaties.' Mitterrand's remarks were greeted with sustained applause: France's break from the Gaullist conception of the Council was becoming more and more explicit.

Propelled by growing French enthusiasm, the institutional reform debate gathered speed in the course of 1984, with agreement at the Fontainebleau European Council in June to create a special committee of personal representatives of the heads of government – the **Dooge Committee** on Institutional Affairs – to suggest possible amendments to the Treaty of Rome. Even the British position began to shift, albeit slightly. In the run-up to Fontainebleau, London suggested, in a paper entitled *Europe: The Future*, that QMV should henceforth be respected where provided for in the Treaties, with the veto remaining when genuine national interests were at stake, on the basis of a clear justification to the Council. The Dooge Committee reported in March 1985, but was unable to agree on the key issues of majority voting and the Luxembourg Compromise. However, France moved into the German and Benelux camp in arguing for more majority voting to allow the completion of the **single market**. Ireland also resiled from its previous support for the Compromise, leaving only Britain, Denmark and Greece as unequivocal advocates. The seven member states (out of ten) now favouring change supported the call for an **Intergovernmental Conference** (IGC) to draft treaty changes to widen the field of QMV.

The newly-appointed President of the European Commission, **Jacques Delors**, correctly saw this shift as one of great significance. He skilfully argued that the Commission's developing objective of completing the single market by December 1992 – endorsed by the Brussels European Council in March 1985 – could be achieved only by an extension of QMV, with the implicit abandonment of the Luxembourg Compromise. Britain responded with an important concession. It proposed that, where the European Council had set an objective, there would be a political understanding that the Compromise should not apply. In the event, the British proposal proved insufficiently ambitious to satisfy the Germans, French and Italians. At the Milan European Council of June 1985, there was stalemate on both the future of the veto and the extension of majority voting by treaty reform. The minority camp argued for retention of the Compromise in certain circumstances and against the calling of an IGC to widen the field for majority voting. The majority camp held the opposite view, against the Compromise and for an IGC.

The impasse was resolved by a highly controversial decision to convene an IGC to draft amendments to the Treaty of Rome. Against spirited opposition from the United Kingdom, Denmark and Greece, the Italian presidency decided to push the issue to a vote, arguing that only a simple majority was necessary, under (then) Article 236 EEC, to convene an IGC. Opposing governments suggested that unanimity should apply to this decision because vital national interests might be at stake. The presidency replied that they could not be since the calling of an IGC was in itself a purely procedural decision neutral between member states. Only the outcome of the IGC could raise such questions, and there the right of veto was safeguarded because agreement to treaty amendments would require the approval of all governments and **ratification** by their national parliaments. This interpretation prevailed, marking a further very significant splintering of the 'veto culture' on which the survival of the Luxembourg Compromise depended.

The subsequent **Single European Act** (SEA), negotiated by the IGC that met during autumn 1985 and signed in February 1986, sanctioned a substantial widening of QMV on the single market and other issues (the health and safety of workers, aspects of **research and development policy**, and **environment policy**). At the time, the implications for the Luxembourg Compromise of this change were unclear. Some commentators, especially in countries long opposed to the Compromise, argued that its days were now clearly numbered. Others, mainly in the United Kingdom, held that although majority voting would now certainly become the norm in any area where it was formally provided for, the residual right to invoke the Compromise would remain in any case where a vital national interest was legitimately threatened. It was claimed that the Single Act would make no particular difference to whether the Compromise survived.

The British prime minister, **Margaret Thatcher**, reported to the House of Commons on her return from the Luxembourg European Council in December 1985 that the 'Luxembourg Compromise ... is unaffected'. As late as February 1990, the British Foreign Secretary, Douglas Hurd, told the House of Commons' foreign affairs committee that the Compromise was 'alive and well', fully available to any government. There had, he claimed, been several occasions when use of it had 'hovered over a discussion'. In France, during ratification of the **Maastricht Treaty** in 1992, several Gaullist deputies even asserted that the Compromise was the cornerstone of French membership of the Community and should be codified in law. Giscard d'Estaing administered a dose of reality when he warned them that the issue of the veto was 'no longer meaningful today'.

In practice, the Luxembourg Compromise effectively died with the Single European Act. The growing reluctance of member states either to invoke it or to accept its invocation by others was greatly accelerated once the Single Act entered into force in July 1987. Since that date, there has been only one known attempt to use the Compromise, and that failed. In 1988, the Greek government objected to the size of the proposed devaluation of the 'green drachma' in an otherwise agreed agricultural prices settlement, pleading a vital national interest. The United Kingdom, Denmark, France, Ireland and Portugal accepted that discussions should continue; other delegations objected. The European Commission and the Greek government subsequently agreed a devaluation by bilateral negotiation, which was then accepted by the Council. However, when the Commission's interpretation of this deal was quickly disputed by Athens, which again threatened to use the veto, other member states refused to make any concessions, and the Greek government, completely isolated, had to give in. The following year, in similar circumstances, the Greeks chose not to press the point. (The last successful invocation of the Compromise was in June 1985, when the German government blocked a Council decision to reduce agricultural prices for cereals and colza.)

Throughout its life, the Luxembourg Compromise was never accepted by either the European Commission or the **European Court of Justice** (ECJ). The Commission used its exclusion from the January 1966 Council meeting to argue that it had never been a party to the agreement. It subsequently denounced the Compromise on many occasions. The Court, for its part, has frequently ruled that resolutions or declarations of political will by the Council or the member states collectively cannot prevail against the rules contained in the Treaties. In 1988, the Court held (in *UK* v *Council*, Case 68/86) that 'the rules regarding the manner in which the Community institutions arrive at their decisions are laid down in the Treaty and are not at the disposal of the Member States or of the institutions themselves.' This view is now accepted in the Council itself.

See also **Ioannina Compromise.**

Further reading: Miriam Camps, *European Unification in the Sixties: From the Veto to the Crisis*, 1967; John Newhouse, *Collision in Brussels: The Common Market Crisis of 30 June 1965*, 1967; Jean-Marie Palayret et al. (editors), *Visions, Votes and Vetoes: The Empty Chair Crisis and the Luxembourg Compromise Forty Years On*, 2006.

M

Maastricht ratification crisis

The **Maastricht Treaty** was the first European treaty to run into significant difficulties in securing **ratification** since the **European Defence Community** (EDC) was rejected by the French National Assembly in August 1954. In one country – Denmark – the public voted against the treaty in a referendum; in a second – France – the government came very close to suffering a similar defeat; and in a third – the United Kingdom – the government almost resigned after losing a critical vote in the House of Commons. The Maastricht ratification crisis engulfed the European Union from June 1992 for over a year.

On its signature in February 1992, the widespread assumption was that the ratification of the Maastricht Treaty would be largely a formality. However, almost immediately, growing hostility denied it the necessary five-sixths majority for ratification in the Danish parliament, the *Folketing*. This early sign of **Euroscepticism** was unexpectedly confirmed in the popular **referendum** which followed on 2 June, when the Danish electorate rejected the treaty, by 50.7 to 49.3 per cent of the vote. A referendum was held in Ireland, on 18 June, where the treaty passed with a 69.1 per cent 'yes' vote. After initial hesitation, EU foreign ministers decided to press ahead with ratification, even though technically the text could only enter into force if Denmark were to reverse its position.

The day after the Danish referendum, the French President, **François Mitterrand**, surprised many by announcing that the Maastricht Treaty would be submitted to a popular vote in his country too, even though there was no constitutional requirement to this effect. Commentators speculated that he was seeking to divide the opposition, where the centre-right RPR and centrist UDF parties supported the text, but Gaullist dissidents within the RPR, as well as the populist *Front national*, did not. In the event, the build-up to the referendum in France was accompanied by acute turbulence on the currency markets. The vote took place on 20 September, four days after the events of **Black Wednesday** forced both the British pound and the Italian lira out of the **Exchange-Rate Mechanism** (ERM) of the **European Monetary System** (EMS). The French electorate voted by only a tiny margin – of 51.05 to 48.95 per cent – in favour of the treaty.

By now, the Danish government was insisting on a series of 'clarifications' as the condition for holding a second referendum. These demands were specified in a paper entitled *Denmark in Europe*, issued on 30 October. At the Edinburgh meeting of the **European Council** in December, Denmark was granted a permanent **opt-out** from stage three of **Economic and Monetary Union** (EMU), it received certain reassurances on **European citizenship**, and the country's non-participation in 'decisions and actions of the Union which have defence implications' was formally recognized. A second Danish referendum was held on 18 May 1993, with the treaty securing a positive vote of 56.8 per cent.

It was in the United Kingdom that ratification confronted the most serious problems. The result of the April 1992 general election gave John Major's Conservative government a much smaller majority than before, and left a minority of Conservative MPs who were deeply hostile to European integration in general and the treaty in particular very well placed to cause difficulty. The Labour party, although not opposed to the treaty in principle, was fiercely critical of the UK opt-outs from the **Social Chapter** and single currency, and sought to use this as a pretext for maximizing the government's discomfort. The passage of the bill through the House of Commons was to prove slow and acrimonious.

The government secured an early second reading for the Maastricht Treaty Bill before the first Danish referendum, but then chose to postpone the critical committee stage until after the situation in Denmark had clarified. This turned out to be a mistake. In the interim, Black Wednesday and the close French referendum result hugely emboldened Eurosceptic critics of the treaty. The government only won a 'paving motion' to proceed to committee stage by three votes (with Liberal Democrat support) in November 1992. The committee stage then took 23 days over five months, with 163 hours of debate and 600 amendments. After passage at third reading, the text moved to the Lords, where the former prime minister, **Margaret Thatcher**, led Conservative dissidents in calling (unsuccessfully) for a referendum. 'I personally would never have signed this treaty,' she declared.

Although the government managed to obtain majorities for the treaty in both houses, it had been forced to concede that before it formally ratified the text, it would allow a separate vote in the Commons on the question of whether to ratify in the absence of British participation in the Social Chapter. This vote took place on 23 July 1993 amid high drama. A rebellion by 24 Conservative MPs – cynically designed to face the government with the prospect of having to ratify the treaty on a basis it could not accept (namely, with the UK having to embrace the Social Chapter) – left the government defeated by 324 to 316 votes. This was the most serious parliamentary defeat suffered by a Conservative administration in more than a century. The Foreign Secretary, Douglas Hurd, signalled that the government could and would, if necessary, simply ratify the existing text (on behalf of the United Kingdom as a state), regardless of any majority in the Commons, which legally it had the right to do. After the defeat, John Major immediately called a vote of confidence to reverse the previous result. The following day, with the support of all his potential successors in the Cabinet, he survived this vote by threatening to dissolve Parliament and call an immediate general election.

The last member state to ratify the treaty was Germany, where anti-Maastricht campaigners had succeeded in referring the text to the German Federal Constitutional Court in Karlsruhe. The legal arguments were not resolved until a ruling in favour of ratification on 12 October 1993, allowing the treaty to enter into force the following month (see **Karlsruhe judgements**).

Further reading: David Baker, Andrew Gamble and Steve Ludlam, 'The Parliamentary Siege of Maastricht 1993', *Parliamentary Affairs,* Volume 47, Number 1, 1994.

Maastricht Treaty

Formally entitled the Treaty on European Union (TEU), the Maastricht Treaty introduced the most important set of changes to Community institutional arrangements since the signature of the **Treaty of Rome** in March 1957. The treaty was the product of a year-long negotiation in two **Intergovernmental Conferences** (IGCs), starting in December 1990 and concluding at the **European Council** meeting in Maastricht, the Netherlands, on 9–10 December 1991. Formally signed in Maastricht on 7 February 1992, the treaty entered into force in November 1993, after unexpected delays in its **ratification** by several member states. A number of the treaty's key provisions have subsequently been amended by the **Amsterdam**, **Nice** and **Lisbon Treaties**.

The twin IGCs leading to Maastricht – one on **Economic and Monetary Union** (EMU) and the other on 'European Political Union' (EPU) – were conducted in parallel by the successive Luxembourg and Dutch **presidencies** of the **Council of Ministers**. The EMU IGC was set in train by a decision of the European Council, meeting in Madrid in June 1989, at which the **Delors Report** on EMU was discussed. The EPU IGC was sanctioned a year later in Dublin, drawing on proposals for closer political integration put forward by French President **François Mitterrand**, German Chancellor **Helmut Kohl** and the Belgian government in April 1990, following the collapse of Communism in central and eastern Europe.

The EMU IGC, conducted by finance ministers, saw disagreements about the pace of progress towards monetary union, the rules by which it should be governed, and the institutions needed to manage it. The arrangements finally agreed provided for EMU to develop in three stages – of which the first had already begun in practice in 1990 – culminating in the adoption of a single currency and a common monetary policy in the third stage. The German, Dutch and British governments insisted on full EMU being open only to countries that met stringent **convergence criteria**, with the new monetary policy maintained by a fully independent **European Central Bank** (ECB). Arguments for a substantial degree of macro-economic policy coordination to parallel monetary union were resisted. In addition, Britain and Denmark, the two member states that wished to take separate decisions on any future transition to the single currency, secured **opt-outs** in perpetuity. The new EMU system was set out in additions to the Treaty of Rome (Articles 102(a)–9 EC, now Articles 123–44 TFEU).

The EPU IGC, conducted by foreign ministers, was responsible for the basic structure of the Maastricht Treaty itself. The first part (or 'title') of the text which they agreed contained a series of 'common provisions' which in effect established the new treaty as a parallel document to the existing **Treaties** and provided a portmanteau framework into which they could fit. It proclaimed the establishment of the European Union, which was 'founded on the European Communities, supplemented by the policies and forms of cooperation established by this Treaty' (Article A TEU, now superseded by Article 1 TEU). It set out the objectives of the Union, made the Communities' institutions its institutions, and required the Union to respect fundamental rights, **subsidiarity** and the 'national identities' of its Member States (Articles B–F, now 2–6 TEU). On British insistence, reference in the draft text to the Union being 'of a federal type' was removed (see **federalism and confederalism**) and the Union was denied **legal personality**.

The second section of the Maastricht Treaty contained a series of detailed amendments to the Treaty of Rome, which had established the **European Economic Community** (EEC), now to be called the European Community (EC). As well as setting out arrangements for EMU, it extended Community **competence** to, or deepened existing competence in, a variety of other policy areas – notably **education policy**, culture, vocational training, **Trans-European Networks** (TENs), industry policy, **consumer policy**, **environment policy** and **development policy**. It established **European citizenship** and elaborated the principle of subsidiarity. It made provision for a more powerful **European Parliament** – with a new **co-decision procedure** for legislation to be adopted jointly by the Parliament and the Council, an extension of the **consent procedure**, and an enhanced say in the appointment of the President and members of the **European Commission**. The treaty empowered the Parliament to appoint an **Ombudsman** and formalized its right to set up **committees of inquiry**. It also gave the Parliament the right to be consulted on appointments to the **Court of Auditors** – which acquired the full status of an **institution** – and to the Executive Board of the ECB. A consultative **Committee of the Regions** was established by the treaty, which also gave the **European Court of Justice** (ECJ) the right to fine defaulting member states.

The third and fourth sections of the Maastricht Treaty contained amendments to the existing **European Coal and Steel Community** (ECSC) and the **European Atomic Energy Community** (EAEC or Euratom) Treaties. Importantly, the fifth and sixth sections set up the so-called intergovernmental '**pillars**' of the Union, covering a new **Common Foreign and Security Policy** (CFSP) – the successor to **European Political Cooperation** (EPC) – and cooperation in the fields of **Justice and Home Affairs** (JHA). (CFSP was dealt with in Articles K–K.9 TEU, now Articles 23–46 TEU, and JHA in Articles J-J.11 TEU, now Articles 67–89 TFEU.) The seventh section contained general provisions, transposed and adapted from those formerly in the Treaty of Rome, on **enlargement** (Article 49 TEU), treaty amendment (Article 48 TEU) and **ratification** (Article 54 TEU). The treaty was concluded for an unlimited period (Article 53 TFEU).

Annexed to the Maastricht Treaty were 17 **protocols**, including the Statutes of the ECB and its immediate precursor, the **European Monetary Institute** (EMI), details of the **excessive deficit procedure** (EDP), arrangements for the British and Danish **opt-outs** on EMU, the so-called Social Protocol for the UK (see **Social Charters and Social Chapter**), the non-retroactive applicability of the Barber judgement on **equal treatment**, and a set of undertakings on **cohesion** to benefit the poorer member states. Also annexed to the treaty were 33 non-binding declarations, of which the most important were those on the role of **national parliaments**, the '**hierarchy of acts**' and the future role of the **Western European Union** (WEU).

In effect, the Treaty on European Union performed two quite distinct functions. The first, fifth, sixth and seventh sections constituted a new arrangement in parallel to the existing EC, EAEC and ECSC Treaties. However, at the same time, the second, third and fourth sections (and most of the protocols) amended those latter three treaties. This complex structure reflected differences in the legal status between the new Union and the existing Communities: the Communities possessed legal personality and adopted **legal acts**, whereas the Union did not. The difficulty of understanding this relationship was compounded by the linguistic ambiguity in the fact that the totality of the Union and the Communities together were henceforth to be known as the Union. (The description of European citizenship as 'citizenship of the Union' even though it featured in the amendments to the EC Treaty highlighted this confusion.)

Soon after it had been signed, the Maastricht Treaty began to run into political difficulty in the member states. However ably drafted, a text covering so many heterogeneous issues – some very important and sensitive, others quite trivial – which had been negotiated largely behind closed doors and took a form unintelligible to the general public, could hardly be expected to win many friends. The period during which it was due to be ratified also coincided with a low point in the Community's fortunes. Against the backdrop of the Balkans crisis (see **Yugoslavia**) and rows over the Uruguay Round of world trade talks, there was a general impression of Europe having lost its way. **Referenda** were held to ratify the treaty in Denmark and Ireland (as on the Single Act) and in France (for the first time). The unexpected rejection of the text by the Danes on 2 June 1992 was followed by only a very narrow endorsement in the **French referendum** on 20 September, called unnecessarily by President Mitterrand in an attempt to disorient his political opponents at home. The **Maastricht ratification crisis** of 1992–3 induced acute monetary instability, revealed popular discontent with European integration and helped propel the rise of **Euroscepticism**.

Further reading: Kenneth Dyson and Kevin Featherstone, *The Road to Maastricht: Negotiating Economic and Monetary Union in Europe*, 1999; Finn Laursen and Sophie Vanhoonecker (editors), *The Intergovernmental Conference on Political Union*, 1992.

MacDougall Report

In April 1975, the **European Commission** invited an expert group of seven economists to prepare a report on the role of public finance in European economic integration. Their report, generally known as the MacDougall Report after the group's chairman, Donald MacDougall (1912–2004), former chief economic adviser to the British government, ran to some 70 pages and was published in May 1977. It studied the role of public finance both in unitary states (France, Italy and the United Kingdom) and in federations (Australia, Canada, Germany, Switzerland and the United States), with particular emphasis on its redistributive effects, the allocation of responsibility for revenue-raising, and the scope for counter-cyclical fiscal policy to promote long-term growth. It attempted to draw lessons from the study of spending and taxing at national level for a European Community that might seek to move in the direction of closer economic integration, including **Economic and Monetary Union** (EMU).

The report identified three potential scenarios beyond the status quo in Europe: 'pre-federal integration', federation with a small European-level public sector, and federation with a large European-level public sector. When the report was written, total spending by the Community institutions represented about 0.75 per cent of the combined gross domestic product (GDP) of the member states. The first scenario would involve raising the expenditure figure to between 2.0 and 2.5 per cent of combined GDP, the second to between 7.5 and 10 per cent, and the third to between 20 to 25 per cent. On this basis, more than a third of a century later, the European Union would still be regarded as well short even of the 'pre-federal' stage: in 2011, total expenditure from the EU **Budget** accounted for only one per cent of the Union's GDP.

The central assumption of MacDougall's thinking was, as he explains in his memoirs (*Don and Mandarin*, 1987), that the successful adoption of EMU in Europe would require 'extremely powerful' equilibrating mechanisms, through transfer payments, to prevent intolerable disparities developing – in terms of growth, employment and living standards – between the regions and countries within a single currency zone. In a view echoed by French economist Robert Marjolin, under whose chairmanship he had worked on an earlier report for the Commission in 1973, MacDougall believed that EMU 'could be achieved only when there was a much larger Community budget' and that the economic component was as important as the monetary one.

Although the MacDougall Report was widely discussed on publication, little concrete action flowed from it, other than to redouble the Commission's determination to see the system of '**own resources**' for the Community, which was agreed in 1970, put into effect as soon as possible (1980). Although widely shared at the time, the report's Keynesian premise – that an integrated European economy, and indeed a sustainable supranational political system underpinning it, would need to be characterized by a relatively high level of government spending – fell increasingly out of favour. MacDougall failed to foresee the new emphasis in the 1980s and 1990s on the twin strategies of reviving the European economy through supply-side liberalization, based on completion of the **single market**, and of attempting to develop a single currency without any significant degree of 'fiscal federalism'. This error was perhaps understandable, since the EU scarcely existed as a 'regulatory state' in the early to mid-1970s and the most systematically developed Community policy at that time, the **Common Agricultural Policy** (CAP), was heavily dependent on public expenditure. Ironically, the experience of the CAP itself led national finance ministries to exercise extreme caution in sanctioning other policies that might have significant spending implications at European level.

Majority voting

See **qualified majority voting** (QMV).

Marshall Plan

The Marshall Plan was the name given to the European Recovery Programme (ERP) under which the United States gave financial assistance totalling over $13 billion to promote the economic recovery of Europe after the Second World War. The programme ran from 1948 to 1951 and benefited 16 countries, with just under two-thirds of the resources going to Britain, France, West Germany and Italy, in that order. After a period of intractable stagnation, the Marshall Plan coincided with the fastest economic expansion in European history, with output rising by 35 per cent in four years. Although economists argue about how far the plan generated this spectacular revival directly, most view it as a powerful catalyst that relieved huge imbalances and laid the foundation for two decades of high growth across much of the continent. Together with existing bilateral programmes for Greece and Turkey, Marshall Fund money also played a critical part in stemming the advance of Communist parties in western and south-eastern Europe.

Immediately after the war, the US government had rejected the suggestion of its Treasury Secretary, Henry Morganthau, that Germany should be forced to pay massive reparations to the countries it had invaded. Instead, limits were imposed on its industrial production, especially of coal and steel. In the event, these restrictions compounded growing problems of low demand, broken infrastructure and agricultural crisis across Europe. Prompted by a realization that many countries were simply too enfeebled by war to recover economically without assistance – and concerned by the increasing success of Communist parties, notably in France and Italy – President Harry Truman undertook a major shift of policy. In an initiative seen in Washington as akin to a 'New Deal for Europe', his administration resolved to make available substantial US financial support for the reconstruction of the continent. The offer was extended by Secretary of State George Marshall in a speech at Harvard University on 5 June 1947. A key feature was that the recovery programme should be 'a joint one, agreed to by a number of, if not all, European nations'; it would be open to any country in Europe and would supersede bilateral aid offered by the United States on a piecemeal basis until then.

As a result of pressure from the Soviet Union, the countries of central and eastern Europe (even those which, like Czechoslovakia, had at first responded favourably to the American offer) declined to attend the conference in Paris in July 1947 at which the ERP was to be worked out in detail. At the conference, participants were told that the programme would aim at 'the speediest possible reactivation of the European economic machine and ... its restoration to a self-supporting basis'. Two conditions of great importance for the process of European unification were laid down: that the European countries needed to begin dismantling barriers to trade among themselves, and that a European organization must be set up to oversee the process of economic recovery. This latter condition led to the establishment of the **Organization for European Economic Cooperation** (OEEC) in 1948, a body which brought together the recipients of the Marshall Fund, plus the United States and Canada. The OEEC was transformed into the **Organization for Economic Cooperation and Development** (OECD) in 1961.

Reactions to the American proposals were mixed. Particularly among the parties of the left, some interpreted the Marshall Plan as US economic imperialism on a bold scale. All kinds of forebodings were expressed, solicitously encouraged by Stalin's USSR. General Marshall himself was accorded a prominent place in Soviet demonology. Conversely, there was concern within some of the nations that had suffered German occupation at Washington's determination to put the German economy back on its feet. Nor was the plan uncontroversial within the United States: it required prodigious efforts by the administration to secure the approval of the project from a sceptical Congress. The original European request for $22 billion was scaled down to $17 billion when Truman communicated the plan to Capitol Hill. The final figure voted through was $4 billion lower. However, the $13 billion that resulted still represents the equivalent of about ten times that amount in today's prices.

In the end, the conviction and perseverance of a few figures in Washington – Marshall himself and his State Department colleagues Dean Acheson, William Clayton and George Kennan – were rewarded with the determined support of a number of key Europeans, notably the British, French and Belgian foreign ministers, Ernest Bevin, Georges Bidault and **Paul-Henri Spaak**. Together these far-sighted individuals made the Marshall Plan happen. Moscow responded by announcing a 'Molotov Plan' for its own satellite states, leading to the creation of **COMECON** in 1949.

As the **Cold War** deepened, it became increasingly clear that significant military, as well as economic, support from the United States would be necessary to contain the advance of the Soviet Union and promote the closer integration of western Europe. The US sponsorship of the **Brussels Treaty** in March 1948 and the decision to create the **North Atlantic Treaty Organization** (NATO) 13 months later were the result. The Berlin Blockade of June 1948 to May 1949 brought the Soviet challenge into vivid relief. The Marshall Plan and NATO can thus be seen as parallel, successive efforts towards the same objective by different means.

Further reading: Greg Behrman, *The Most Noble Adventure: The Marshall Plan and the Reconstruction of Post-War Europe*, 2008; Charles L. Mee, *The Marshall Plan: The Launching of Pax Americana*, 1984.

Member state

There are currently 27 member states of the European Union. These are **the Six** countries which founded the three **European Communities** in the 1950s – through signature of the **Treaty of Paris** in April 1951 and the two **Treaties of Rome** in March 1957 – and the 21 countries that have subsequently joined them, by signing **accession** treaties, in six successive rounds of **enlargement** between 1973 and 2007.

The member states of the Union, grouped together cumulatively by order of accession, are:

The Six: 1952–72
- Belgium
- France
- Germany
- Luxembourg
- The Netherlands
- Italy

The Nine: 1973–80
- Denmark
- Ireland
- United Kingdom

The Ten: 1981–5
- Greece

The Twelve: 1985–94
- Portugal
- Spain

EU 15: 1995–2004
- Austria
- Finland
- Sweden

EU 25: 2004–6
- Czech Republic
- Cyprus
- Estonia
- Hungary
- Latvia
- Lithuania
- Malta
- Poland
- Slovakia
- Slovenia

EU 27: since 2007
- Bulgaria
- Romania.

The territory of a member state may change over time. France originally included Algeria, until the latter's independence in 1962. The process of **German reunification** in 1990 led to the addition of six new *Länder* to the existing Federal Republic of Germany. Conversely, a member state may choose to designate only part of its territory for the purposes of membership of the Union: since 1986, Denmark has not included **Greenland**, for this purpose, following a **referendum** in the latter territory in which a majority of the inhabitants voted to leave the Community. Parts of member states that are not included in the EU, most frequently remaining colonies, are usually designated as **overseas countries and territories** (OCTs) of the Union.

So far no member state has split in two whilst already within the EU, although the question of whether a region seceding from an existing member state would need, if it wished, to rejoin the Union from scratch has been posed in regard to Scotland, Flanders and Catalunya. If any such new state wished to have representation in the EU institutions – most notably, a member of the **European Commission**, votes in the **Council of Ministers** and seats in the **European Parliament** – as opposed to being simply a territory within the Union, then a treaty change, agreed unanimously by the governments of the existing member states and ratified in their **national parliaments**, would be required. No member state has so far ever sought to leave the Union, but the Lisbon Treaty introduces a formal process for this, for the first time, through the so-called '**exit clause**' (Article 50 TEU).

Merger Treaty

The 1965 Merger Treaty, which entered into force in July 1967, was the first amendment to the **Treaty of Paris** and **Treaties of Rome**. The purpose was to create a set of common European institutions – a single **Council of Ministers** and a common **European Commission** – serving all three **European Communities**. This move was seen as an important step towards the complete amalgamation of the three Communities, and had been advocated by strong integrationists, including notably the **Action Committee for a United States of Europe** (ACUSE), throughout the early 1960s. Article 32 of the Merger Treaty referred in passing to a 'Treaty establishing a Single European Community', something that was never to be drawn up.

Formally speaking, the new 'Council of the European Communities' (Article 1) replaced the Special Council of Ministers of the **European Coal and Steel Community** (ECSC), and the Councils of the **European Economic Community** (EEC) and the **European Atomic Energy Community** (EAEC or Euratom). Similarly the new 'Commission of the European Communities' replaced the **High Authority** of the ECSC and the Commissions of the EEC and Euratom (Article 9). It was not necessary to provide for the amalgamation of the **European Parliament** or the **European Court of Justice** (ECJ) in the Merger Treaty, since the 1957 'Convention on Certain Institutions Common to the European Communities' – signed in parallel to the Treaty of Rome and having the same legal status – had already stipulated that one body in each case would exercise the functions set out in the original **Treaties**. The Merger Treaty provided for a common **Budget** of the Communities to replace the three separate budgets (Article 20). It also created a 'single administration' composed of the officials of the three original Communities (Article 24). Its essential provisions having been incorporated into other treaties, the Merger Treaty was repealed in 1999 by Article 9(1) of the **Amsterdam Treaty**.

Basic statistics on the member states of the European Union

Member state	*Date of EC/EU membership*	*Population (million, 2010)*	*Gross domestic product (billion euro, 2010)*	*GDP per capita* (thousand euro, 2010)*	*Member of eurozone*	*Member of Schengen area*	*Member of NATO*	*Number of Members of the European Parliament (2011)*	*Number of votes in Council of Ministers*
Austria	1995	8.4	286	32.4	yes	yes	no	19	10
Belgium	1952	10.7	354	30.4	yes	yes	yes	22	12
Bulgaria	2007	7.6	36	11.2	no	no	yes	18	10
Cyprus	2004	0.8	17	25.0	yes	no	no	6	4
Czech Republic	2004	10.5	145	20.5	no	yes	yes	22	12
Denmark	1973	5.5	234	31.9	opt-out	yes	yes	13	7
Estonia	2004	1.3	14	16.5	yes	yes	yes	6	4
Finland	1995	5.3	180	29.7	yes	yes	no	13	7
France	1952	64.4	1,933	27.4	yes	yes	yes	74	29
Germany	1952	82.0	2,477	30.1	yes	yes	yes	99	29
Greece	1981	11.3	227	22.5	yes	yes	yes	22	12
Hungary	2004	10.0	97	16.2	no	yes	yes	22	12
Ireland	1973	4.4	156	32.6	yes	no	no	12	7
Italy	1952	60.0	1,556	25.7	yes	yes	yes	73	29

Latvia	2004	2.3	18	13.2	no	yes	yes	9	4
Lithuania	2004	3.5	27	14.9	no	yes	yes	12	7
Luxembourg	1952	0.5	40	70.2	yes	yes	yes	6	4
Malta	2004	0.4	6	21.2	yes	yes	no	6	3
Netherlands	1952	16.5	588	34.2	yes	yes	yes	26	13
Poland	2004	38.1	354	16.0	no	yes	yes	51	27
Portugal	1986	10.6	173	20.7	yes	yes	yes	22	12
Romania	2007	21.5	122	11.6	no	no	yes	33	14
Slovakia	2004	5.4	66	19.0	yes	yes	yes	13	7
Slovenia	2004	2.0	35	21.9	yes	yes	yes	8	4
Spain	1986	45.8	1,051	25.7	yes	yes	yes	54	27
Sweden	1995	9.3	345	31.6	no	yes	no	20	10
United Kingdom	1973	61.6	1,697	29.2	opt-out	no	yes	73	29
EU *27*		499.7	12,257	25.6				754	345
Eurozone *17*		327.8	9,176	27.7					
United States		310.1	10,997	37.9					
Japan		127.6	4,169	27.3					
China		1,312.5	4,246	3.2					

Sources: European Central Bank (ECB) and Eurostat.

* Figures on a purchasing power parity basis.

The Merger Treaty had the effect of consolidating the Communities' activities in **Brussels.** Under pressure from the Luxembourg government, which sought compensation for the loss of the ECSC from its territory, the member states signed a separate agreement on the 'provisional location' of the institutions. This required the Council of Ministers to meet in Luxembourg during three months each year (in April, June and October) and for certain directorates-general of the Commission to be based there. It also stipulated that the secretariat of the European Parliament would remain in Luxembourg, together with the Court of Justice and the **European Investment Bank** (EIB). See also **seats of the EU institutions**.

Messina Conference

On 30 August 1954, after a long period of uncertainty in Paris, the French National Assembly finally rejected the treaty that would have established a **European Defence Community** (EDC). Both the EDC and parallel moves to establish a **European Political Community** (EPC) were abandoned in consequence. The governments of **the Six**, still keen to reaffirm their commitment to European integration and to extend its scope beyond the relatively narrow confines of the **European Coal and Steel Community** (ECSC), decided to explore what could be done to make their economies more economically interdependent. On 1–3 June 1955, the ECSC foreign ministers met in Messina, Sicily, to consider memoranda drawn up by the various governments. They drew notably on ideas for a general **common market** and **customs union** contained in the **Beyen Plan**, presented by the Dutch foreign minister of the same name two months earlier. The Messina Conference decided to set up an intergovernmental committee, under Belgian foreign minister **Paul-Henri Spaak**, to consider possible options in more detail. The **Spaak Committee**, which met between July 1955 and the following April, presented its report to the foreign ministers in Venice on 29–30 May 1956. Its recommendations were largely drafted by the French economist, **Pierre Uri**, a close associate of **Jean Monnet**. They were used as the basis for negotiating two new treaties, one establishing a **European Economic Community** (EEC) and the other a **European Atomic Energy Community** (EAEC or Euratom). The twin **Treaties of Rome** were signed ten months later, ratified soon after, and came into effect on 1 January 1958.

The significance of the Messina Conference is that, at a low point in the history of European integration, there was still enough energy and enthusiasm among the Six to allow two very complex and far-reaching treaties to be negotiated in a remarkably short time. The United Kingdom was invited to participate in the conference and in the resulting Spaak Committee but sent only an under-secretary from the Board of Trade, who was subsequently instructed to withdraw from the discussions. The story of Britain's non-involvement is told in Michael Charlton's *The Price of Victory* (1983) and Hugo Young's *This Blessed Plot: Britain and Europe from Churchill to Blair* (1999).

Micro-states

The term 'micro-states' is used by political scientists and students of international relations to denote very small sovereign states. There are five such states in western Europe – Andorra, Liechtenstein, Monaco, San Marino and Vatican City – ranging in population from 900 (Vatican City) to 80,000 (Andorra). Several micro-states are located wholly within the territory of a member state of the European Union, but none has sought to join the Union in its own right. The Union has established particular relations with each of them: the **euro** is now the currency of all except Liechtenstein, whilst only Andorra is not a de jure or de facto member of the **Schengen** zone. Monaco is the only micro-state not to have joined the **Council of Europe**, whilst all belong to the **United Nations** and all participate in the **Organization for Security and Cooperation in Europe** (OSCE). None of the micro-states belongs to any defensive alliance.

Mitterrand, François (1916–96)

One of eight children, François Mitterrand was born into a staunchly Catholic family in Angoulême, south-west France, and studied at the forerunner of *Sciences-Po* in Paris, before serving in the army at the start of the Second World War. He was awarded the *Croix de guerre* and taken prisoner before France fell to the Germans in June 1940. After escaping captivity, Mitterrand took an administrative post in the Vichy régime, from which he also operated in the Resistance, under the assumed name of 'Morland'. He unsuccessfully sought to enter the entourage of the Free French leader, **Charles de Gaulle**, visiting him in Algiers in 1943. When France was liberated the following year, he briefly became secretary general of the ministry for prisoners of war, at the age of only 27.

Mitterrand soon decided to enter politics professionally, securing election as a deputy from the Nièvre in 1946: he was to serve, with only brief interruption, as either a deputy or senator for the area until he became French President in May 1981. Cunning, complex, secretive and intellectually gifted, Mitterrand was quickly appointed a junior minister in 1947, and six years later became the leader of his small centrist party, the UDSR, displacing the more conservative René Pleven, who as prime minister had first proposed the **European Defence Community** (EDC). He served in both centre-left and centre-right administrations during the 1950s, in almost a dozen different ministerial roles, emerging as a prominent figure in the politics of the Fourth Republic. Although frequently accused of opportunism, Mitterrand's views evolved in an increasingly left-wing direction, even as the centre of gravity of French politics was moving to the right. The critical turning-point was his resignation from the centre-right government of Joseph Laniel in 1953 over its policies in the North African colonies. He consistently supported efforts towards closer European integration, having attended the **Congress of Europe** in The Hague in 1948. However, as interior minister in August 1954, Mitterrand, like many other members of the government, absented himself from the crucial vote that killed the EDC Treaty. Eight of his USDR deputies voted in favour of the EDC, and ten against.

Mitterrand strongly resisted the return to power of **Charles de Gaulle** in May 1958, entering a period of opposition to the new hegemony of the Gaullists and their allies that was to last for 23 years. He condemned the constitution of the Fifth Republic as a '*Coup d'État permanent*' – the title of a book he published in May 1964 – and stood against the General in the first direct election for President in December 1965. His unexpected success in forcing de Gaulle to a second ballot and then winning 45 per cent of the vote was seen as a vindication of his controversial strategy of acting as a *rassembleur* of what he called the 'democratic and socialist left'. Unlike many, he quickly understood that, under the majoritarian electoral system that de Gaulle had introduced for parliamentary and presidential elections, party politics would become increasingly bipolar and victory would go to the less divided of the two camps. However, he seriously mishandled the events of May 1968, calling on de Gaulle to hold a snap presidential election in which he, Mitterrand, intended to run. Instead, the General dissolved the National Assembly and secured the largest single-party majority in French political history. As a result, Mitterrand was unable to run against Georges Pompidou in the sudden 1969 presidential election. Ironically, the failure of any of the three competing left-wing candidates to reach the second ballot confirmed that only the kind of alliance of the left that he had engineered in 1965 could possibly defeat the centre-right.

Mitterrand took over and relaunched the Socialist party in 1971, and ran again for the French presidency in May 1974, as the candidate of a united left, following Pompidou's death in office. Although Mitterrand led on the first ballot, he was narrowly defeated on the second by **Valéry Giscard d'Estaing**, the incumbent finance minister and conservative reformer. Mitterrand acted in effect as leader of the opposition throughout Giscard's presidency, although he provided broad support for the latter's European policy. He weathered the collapse of the Union of the Left in 1976 and was able to take advantage of the internecine conflict that developed between Giscard and his first prime minister, the Gaullist dissident Jacques Chirac, who rapidly emerged as his principal rival on the centre-right.

On his third attempt, at the age of 64, Mitterrand succeeded in gaining the

French presidency, in May 1981, at the end of Giscard's seven-year term. In doing so, he is the only candidate to date to have defeated an incumbent President seeking re-election. Mitterrand then dissolved the National Assembly to convert his presidential majority into a parliamentary one. In government, his Socialist–Communist coalition quickly faced difficult economic conditions, exacerbated by the costs of implementing its own ambitious programme of nationalization and social reform. The value of the French franc came under increasing strain, forcing three realignments within the **Exchange-Rate Mechanism** (ERM) of the **European Monetary System** (EMS) – in October 1981, and February and June 1982. Problems came to a head in March 1983, when, against the backdrop of a crisis meeting of EC finance ministers in Brussels, the French President was forced to choose in effect between consolidating domestic finances at home and leaving the ERM. To the dismay of the left, Mitterrand opted for consolidation, and the resulting 'priority to Europe' heralded the start of the *franc fort* policy – of attempting to maintain the established parity with the Deutschmark – which was to last until France adopted the single currency, at the start of stage three of **Economic and Monetary Union** (EMU), 16 years later.

France's six-month **presidency of the Council of Ministers** during the first half of 1984 offered Mitterrand an opportunity to develop a more expansive approach to Europe, one he used actively to end the political deadlock that bedevilled the Community at the time. He and his foreign minister, Roland Dumas, engaged in a tour of capitals which brought the responsibilities of holding the Council presidency to a new level of intensity. Meeting six times with both the German Chancellor, **Helmut Kohl**, and the British prime minister, **Margaret Thatcher**, Mitterrand played a key role in resolving the long-running **British Budget dispute**, culminating in the **Fontainebleau Agreement** of June 1984 which gave the United Kingdom an annual **abatement**. He also acknowledged the need to limit the 'veto culture' in the Council, imposed until then, at French insistence, by the **Luxembourg Compromise**. He accepted the inevitability of at least modest reform of the **Common Agricultural Policy** (CAP) and loosened France's remaining objections to the **enlargement** of the Community to include Spain and Portugal. By offering his respected finance minister, **Jacques Delors**, for appointment as President of the **European Commission** from January 1985, he helped galvanize the executive leadership of the Community. He accepted Delors' recommendation in favour of completion of the **single market** by 1992 as the principal objective for coming years, so putting both France and Europe on a more liberalizing path. When he lost his domestic parliamentary majority in the March 1986 National Assembly elections, Mitterrand used European and foreign policy to maintain his profile and credibility during a two-year period of *cohabitation* with Gaullist premier Jacques Chirac (who thus served two successive Presidents). Mitterrand attached increasing importance to deepening Franco-German cooperation, developing stronger links with Chancellor Kohl, reflected in the launching of the **Eurocorps** and the Franco-German Security Council in January 1988.

Re-elected to a second presidential term in May 1988, defeating Chirac on the second ballot, Mitterrand moved quickly to consolidate his emerging position as an elder statesman of European politics. He worked closely with Delors to promote joint ideas for a single currency and a Social Europe – leading to the presentation to heads of government of the **Delors Report** on EMU in April 1989 and their adoption of a Community **Social Charter** in December 1989, at the end of his second presidency of the Council of Ministers. The only substantial resistance to this process came from Thatcher, who expressed her, essentially intergovernmental, alternative vision in the **Bruges speech** of September 1988. However, the dramatic fall of the Berlin Wall in November 1989 – opening up a wider collapse of Communism in central and eastern Europe – briefly disrupted the new 'Delors–Kohl–Mitterrand axis' at the heart of the Community system. The French President initially shared the British prime minister's instinctive hostility to the prospect of **German reunification**, allegedly claiming – as detailed in official British government records of meetings between the two leaders – that Kohl was gambling 'on the national adrenalin of the German people', 'Germany could win more ground than Hitler ever did' and that 'Europe would have to bear the consequences'.

Mitterrand visited East Berlin in December 1989 in circumstances that prompted criticism in the Federal Republic. In declarations that Kohl subsequently called 'destructive to the process of radical change', he said that the collapsing régime could 'count on France's solidarity with the GDR' and that their two countries still had 'a great deal to do together'. He seemed initially to wish to promote a renewal of Socialism in an independent, probably neutral, East Germany, rather than facilitate the rebirth of a single, united, pro-western German state, at the heart of a reunited Europe. (For a fascinating account of this episode and Mitterrand's general approach to the issue, see Michael Sutton, *France and the Construction of Europe, 1944–2007*, 2007.)

However, unlike Thatcher, Mitterrand quickly recognized the basic unsustainability of his position, moving to trade French support for German unity as a means of locking Kohl into EMU, against the doubts of the Bundesbank. He also accepted that deeper political integration of the Union – with more **qualified majority voting** (QMV) in the **Council of Ministers** and greater legislative powers for the **European Parliament** – might be a necessary concomitant to reunification, in order to help dissolve the enhanced power of a reunited Germany in a wider **sovereignty** pooled at European level. Mitterrand's joint proposals with Kohl on 'European Political Union' (EPU), submitted to the 'Dublin I' meeting of the European Council in April 1990, defined many of the contours of the negotiations that led, after the fall of Thatcher, to the 1992 **Maastricht Treaty.**

Mitterrand's acceptance of political union marked a significant shift in the official French position towards European integration and aroused some controversy at home. He wrongly calculated that he could exploit domestic divisions on Europe to disorient the Gaullist opposition. However, his decision to call the **French referendum on the Maastricht Treaty** in September 1992 represented a serious unforced error of judgement, compounding the difficulties occasioned by his unsuccessful appointment of Edith Cresson as prime minister (1991–2). The treaty was approved by only a very narrow margin – of 51.05 to 48.95 per cent – and the President found himself on the defensive thereafter. Pierre Bérégovoy, Cresson's successor as premier (1992–3), committed suicide after the centre-right won an overwhelming majority in the March 1993 National Assembly elections. Mitterrand's last two years as President were marked by a second period of *cohabitation* – with the new centre-right prime minister, Edouard Balladur, emerging as a rival to Chirac – as well as growing concerns about his health. It was revealed that the President had been suffering from prostate cancer since 1981, despite repeated official statements that he was in good health. Further discomfort was added by new accusations concerning Mitterrand's Vichy past – about which de Gaulle had been excoriating in private conversation in the 1960s – and the uncovering of his illegitimate daughter, Mazarine Pingeot.

At the beginning of his third and final French presidency of the Council of Ministers, in January 1995, Mitterrand made a dramatic speech in the European Parliament, in which, departing from his prepared text to offer some valedictory personal advice to Europe's new political élite, he declared that the biggest threat facing the Union was the rise of nationalism, and that ultimately *'le nationalisme, c'est la guerre'*. War had not only defined Europe's past, but it could be Europe's future too, unless political leadership made that impossible. This was to prove to be his last major public pronouncement.

After his retirement in May 1995, at the age of 78, Mitterrand published three short books (two posthumously) – *Mémoire à deux voix* (1995), *Mémoires interrompus* (1996) and *De l'Allemagne, de la France* (1996) – which attempted to clarify some of the more controversial episodes in his political life, notably his employment under the Vichy régime and initial hostility to German reunification.

Monetary Committee

The Monetary Committee was established in 1958, under Article 105 EEC of the **Treaty of Rome,** as an official-level advisory and preparatory body to the

EU **Council of Ministers** in the economic and financial field. It comprised senior officials from national finance ministries and central banks, as well as from the **European Commission** (which provided its secretariat). The advice of the Monetary Committee was sought on all major legislative or non-legislative issues before the Council of Economics and Finance Ministers – the **Ecofin Council** – and its chairman (chosen by his peers, rather than rotating every six months with the Council **presidency**) often attended the meetings of that Council to present reports and comment on issues under discussion. The Monetary Committee oversaw economic policy coordination within the Union and coordinated its positions in international financial institutions, notably the International Monetary Fund (IMF). It played an increasingly important role in the operation of the **European Monetary System** (EMS): from the mid-1980s onwards, meetings of the Committee, rather than of ministers, served as the negotiating forum which determined parities when currencies were realigned within the **Exchange-Rate Mechanism** (ERM) or when new currencies joined. The Committee's importance, otherwise shielded by the secrecy of its proceedings, was thrown into sharp relief on 16–17 September 1992, when it met in an emergency, overnight session on **Black Wednesday**, to suspend the pound sterling and Italian lira from the ERM and devalue the Spanish peseta.

During stage two of **Economic and Monetary Union** (EMU), from 1994 to 1998, the Monetary Committee assisted the Ecofin Council in monitoring progress towards economic convergence by the member states, and gave advice on which countries met the various **convergence criteria**. The reports that it presented to the Council on this matter were independent of those drawn up by the Commission and the **European Monetary Institute** (EMI). The Monetary Committee was replaced by a new **Economic and Financial Committee** (EFC) at the beginning of stage three of EMU in January 1999.

Monnet, Jean (1888–1979)

'If a united Europe is created in our time,' wrote American journalist Theodore White in the 1950s, 'then Jean Monnet will probably be revered centuries hence as its patron saint.' Never a member of any political party or elected to any public office, Monnet was a technocrat of exceptional vision and ambition, reshaping the thinking of the political leaders with whom he worked, by offering innovative practical solutions to seemingly intractable problems. More than those of any other single figure, his ideas were to define the contours of European integration after the Second World War.

Born in Cognac, south-west France, Monnet left school at 16 and worked as a salesman in his family's brandy business, travelling widely in France, Canada and several other countries at a young age. During the First World War, he identified the danger posed by France and Britain competing for crucial raw materials: he proposed and then ran an Anglo-French Supply Commission, based in London, which helped coordinate the flow of essential resources between the Allies. In appreciation of his services, Monnet was appointed in 1919, at the age of 31, as deputy secretary general of the newly established League of Nations and awarded an honorary knighthood by the British government. He was soon disillusioned by the League's laborious decision-making, where strict **unanimity** was the rule: 'I saw the power of one country to say "no": I realized that goodwill was not enough – among men or nations' (quoted in Anthony Sampson, *The New Europeans*, 1971). In 1923, Monnet chose to resume his career in business. Over the next decade and a half, he rescued the family firm, worked in US banking, reorganized the Swedish match industry, and advised on the financing of railways in China, where he lived for two years.

Following the outbreak of the Second World War, Monnet was appointed chairman of the Franco-British Committee for Economic Coordination in London, reporting to the prime ministers of the two countries. As France retreated in the face of the German advance of June 1940, he persuaded **Winston Churchill** to forward to his French counterpart, Paul Reynaud, a draft declaration proclaiming an 'indissoluble' **Franco-British union**. By the time the proposal was received in France, however, the government was incapable of offering a response. He spent the next three years of the war in Washington, working as a British civil servant, where he once again coordinated the purchase of war supplies. He became highly influential in White House circles: 'There isn't a smarter fellow in town than Jean Monnet,' said Treasury Secretary Henry Morgenthau at the time. He played a key role in developing the Lend-Lease scheme, which in effect gave war materials to Britain before the US entered the war in 1941, and in helping to plan industrial production during the conflict. He suggested the phrase 'arsenal of democracy' which President Franklin D. Roosevelt used to such effect in describing the US role. In 1943, Monnet joined the French Committee of National Liberation, headed by General **Charles de Gaulle** in Algiers, which evolved into the provisional government once France was liberated. He spent the rest of the war between Algiers and Washington.

With his impressive international experience and ability to operate at the highest level of government, Monnet was the obvious choice to head the *Commissariat général au Plan*, established by de Gaulle's post-war administration of 1944–6. As chief French planner, he was not only to play an important role in the country's economic recovery during the Fourth Republic – based in part on his 'Monnet Plan' which set investment targets and channelled funds to basic industries that had been shattered in the war, providing a framework through which US aid from the **Marshall Fund** could operate – but he was also to become, in François Duchêne's words, 'the first man to propose **European union** in a form governments had to take seriously'. Monnet's crucial skills lay in his ability to see how thorny national problems might be solved by imaginative joint action at international level – pioneering what Alan Milward was later to call 'the European rescue of the nation state' – and equally to understand how state power could be harnessed to promote a dynamic market economy. He also believed that 'all great ideas are simple' and brought to bear 'that rare kind of intelligence that is always able to select the essential', as Max Kohnstamm put it (*Jean Monnet: The Power of Imagination*, 1982).

For Monnet, the best way to break any logjam of vested interests was to reformat the problem in a new context, so that traditional positions made less sense. It was this instinct which led him, in the spring of 1950, to suggest to **Robert Schuman**, the French foreign minister, that French and German coal and steel production should be pooled. He saw that, however strongly it was opposed by French public opinion, the reindustrialization of Germany was inevitable and indeed desirable, given the inability of the United States to carry the burden of post-war reconstruction of Europe on its own. By merging the two industries under supranational control, the French fear of German dominance could be assuaged and the opportunity created of rationalizing and modernizing production in a way that national factors might otherwise make impossible. Monnet's appreciation of how a 'coal and steel pool' in Europe could help resolve simultaneously a range of US, German and French problems helps explain why Washington welcomed the initiative with great enthusiasm.

Supported by his trusted associate, **Pierre Uri**, Monnet was the key draftsman of the historic declaration, delivered by Schuman at the Quai d'Orsay on 9 May 1950, outlining the French government's **Schuman Plan** for the creation of a **European Coal and Steel Community** (ECSC). Monnet chaired the intergovernmental negotiations that drafted the ECSC Treaty and then agreed to serve (from 1952) as the first President of its executive **High Authority**, the forerunner of the **European Commission**. The negotiation of the ECSC brought into relief Monnet's institutional design, which was decisively to shape the future of European integration: this hinged on the idea of supranational law, proposed, adopted, executed and interpreted by free-standing European institutions enjoying a superior authority to those of the member states. The concept of the High Authority was a product of Monnet's time in Washington, where he had come to value the role of independent regulatory agencies, appointed by politicians but placed outside their daily control.

Once again attempting to 'change the context' of an intractable problem, Monnet believed that the ECSC solution which he had developed for the question of German reindustrialization could and should be replicated by

the Six for the parallel issue of German rearmament – a process he considered unavoidable following the North Korean invasion of South Korea in June 1950. In October that year, only five months after the Schuman Plan, he convinced French premier René Pleven to propose the creation of a **European Defence Community** (EDC). The **Pleven Plan** drew on the political momentum created by **Winston Churchill**'s endorsement of the concept of a **European army** in the Consultative Assembly of the **Council of Europe**. When the EDC proposal eventually came to nothing, after four years of negotiation and attempted **ratification**, a deeply disappointed Monnet resigned from the ECSC High Authority in November 1954. Already in his mid-sixties, he chose to devote his remaining years to freelance campaigning on behalf of closer European unity. He created an **Action Committee for the United States of Europe** (ACUSE), bringing together representatives of mainstream political parties and trade unions, and provided intellectual and moral support to those – notably the **Benelux** foreign ministers – who were looking for innovative ways of relaunching Europe after the EDC rebuff. In 1955, he strongly endorsed the **Beyen Plan** (for a **common market** and **customs union**) that led to the **Messina Conference** later that year and the negotiation in 1956–7 of the **Treaty of Rome**, establishing the **European Economic Community** (EEC).

Two principal ideas underpinned Monnet's tireless campaigning on behalf of Europe: that unity would be built not on the basis of visions and generalities, but through finding workable solutions to real problems – the *réalisations concrètes* to which Schuman referred in his May 1950 declaration – and that common institutions, making binding law, rather than intergovernmental cooperation, were the key to building a durable European structure. He believed that it was only through institutions, as repositories of experience and shared values, that human beings could accumulate a wider understanding and transmit it to future generations. He would often quote the Swiss philosopher, Henri-Frédéric Amiel, who wrote: 'Each man's experience starts again from the beginning. Only institutions grow wiser; they accumulate collective experience, and owing to this experience and this wisdom, men subject to the same rules will not see their own nature changing, but their behaviour gradually transformed.'

Monnet's vision of Europe diverged radically from that of his contemporary and compatriot, Charles de Gaulle, who returned to power in France in May 1958. The years that followed saw an intellectual and practical battle between the 'Monnet' or '**Community method**' – advocated notably by Commission President **Walter Hallstein**, in which free-standing supranational institutions would defend a common European interest and in which no one government should be able to enforce its view – and the Gaullist concept of a ***Europe des patries***, in which the nation state remained central to identity and power. Monnet's Action Committee vigorously opposed de Gaulle's insistence on **intergovernmentalism**, as well as his hostility to British membership of the Community. Monnet's experience of living in London and various American cities had convinced him that there need be no contradiction between Atlanticism and 'Europeanism', and that a notion of Europe that drew on Anglo-Saxon culture would be stronger and more likely to succeed. However, in the immediate term, it was de Gaulle's view that held sway.

Monnet was unusual among the **founding fathers** of the new European Community in having an instinctive distaste for party politics and a general mistrust of politicians, especially because of their reluctance to take a long-term view. He saw that the successful development of European unity would depend as much on enlightened public administration and informal networks of the powerful, across party lines, as on the building of a new democratic polity, even if he was broadly in favour of the latter. Monnet also looked firmly beyond mainland Europe for inspiration: he was deeply affected by his time in the United States, which taught him the potential of ambitious federal action on a continental scale. De Gaulle even referred dismissively to him once as 'a great American', rather than Frenchman, although in fact they both shared a desire that Europe and America should develop as a 'partnership of equals', but by very different routes. Equally, Monnet respected British pragmatism, believed that the country's 'deeply democratic' instincts could help solidify the new European institutions, and remained confident that the best way of convincing the United Kingdom to play a full part in the unification of Europe was to create structures that both mattered and worked. A few days after becoming President of the ECSC High Authority in August 1952, Monnet had visited London. He was greeted by Roger Makins, the deputy under secretary for Europe at the Foreign Office, with the words: 'Now that you are a fact, we shall deal with you.'

After the disappointments of the 1960s, Monnet was relieved when de Gaulle's successor, Georges Pompidou, chose to promote **enlargement** of the Community and a broader relaunch of political integration, culminating in the Paris Summit of October 1972 and British entry three months later. In 1974, Monnet strongly supported Pompidou's own successor, **Valéry Giscard d'Estaing**, in proposing the creation of the **European Council**, as a forum for regular discussion among EC heads of government. Unlike some integrationists, he clearly saw the potential of such **summits**, which they feared might 'reintergovernmentalize' the Community, to do precisely the opposite – namely, to give renewed political impetus and direction to a Europe sorely lacking in executive authority. He subsequently described the creation of the

European Council as 'the most important decision for Europe since the Treaty of Rome'. One of the early actions of this new body (in April 1976) was to confer upon Monnet the title of 'honorary citizen of Europe' – a status that guaranteed his position as *primus inter pares* among the founding fathers.

Monnet's account of his own life, published in French in 1976 (*Mémoires*) and translated into English two years later (*Memoirs*), remains an invaluable source-book for the history of European politics in the three decades following the Second World War. When he died in March 1979, his funeral was attended by the French President and German Chancellor. In November 1988, on the centenary of his birth, Monnet's body was transferred to the Pantheon.

Further reading: Douglas Brinkley and Clifford Hackett, *Jean Monnet: The Path to European Unity*, 1992; François Duchêne, *Jean Monnet: the First Statesman of Interdependence*, 1994; Eric Roussel, *Jean Monnet*, 1996.

Monti Report

On the 60th anniversary of the **Schuman Plan**, 9 May 2010, Mario Monti – a former European Commissioner for competition policy, who was then serving as president of Bocconi University in Milan and has subsequently become Italian prime minister – delivered a report to José Manuel Barroso, President of the **European Commission**, on the operation and completion of the **single market** in the European Union. The 107-page Monti Report – *A New Strategy for the Single Market* – had been commissioned by Barroso in October 2009, soon after his reconfirmation as Commission President by the **European Parliament**, as a means of underlining that further progress in this field would be an important priority for his second five-year term in office.

The report, written in large part by Monti himself, argued that, whilst the single market in goods had been largely complete for some years, important 'missing links' remained in the **free movement** of services, capital and people, where 'market construction' was often still needed. It also stressed that, even where the single market was ostensibly complete, regular 'market maintenance' was required. Product innovation and other factors meant that it faced a 'new frontier' needing constant attention, notably in the fields of the digital economy and e-commerce.

Some of Monti's more eye-catching proposals were in the area of a citizen's right to live and work throughout the Union, echoing the focus of the Adonnino report on a People's Europe a quarter of a century before. He identified as particular problems the non-portability of pensions and health insurance rights, and the need for greatly increased **mutual recognition of professional qualifications** (where, he noted, only seven out of 800 professions allow automatic mutual recognition in all 27 member states). For citizens seeking to live in countries other than their own, there should be mutual recognition of official documents (to avoid translation difficulties when seeking to register as a foreign resident) and a 'European free movement card', which would 'contain in a single document all the information a European citizen may require' to live and work in another member state.

Given that some 2,500 pieces of EU legislation had already been adopted in the single market sphere, the report noted that 'a new wave of **regulations** and **directives**' was unlikely to be required in many sectors. Where legislation was needed, there should – reversing the pattern of the original 1992 single market programme – be less use of directives and more of regulations, mainly in order to maximize **legal certainty** and reduce problems in transposition. In some cases, the best way of completing the single market might lie not in **harmonization** or even mutual recognition, but in the creation of a '28th régime' that could run alongside the 27 existing national standards – for example, in health insurance rights. Under such a system, if businesses or citizens see the single market as 'their main horizon, they can opt for a standard and single legal framework valid across member states; if they move in a predominantly national setting, they will remain under the national régime.' The 28th standard could also act as a reference-point for the future convergence of national rules.

More generally, the tone struck by Monti was rather downbeat. He argued that, despite the single market's successes and the fact that it remained 'Europe's best endogenous source of growth and job creation', the outlook for its further completion was less propitious than in the recent past. For various reasons, the Union was experiencing both 'integration fatigue' and 'market fatigue', whilst **enlargement** had diversified the number of interests and perspectives on the single market within the Union. There were now distinct, and often conflicting views, among the 'continental social market economies', the Anglo-Saxon countries, the Nordic states and the new member states from central and eastern Europe. Although the new entrants constituted 'a remarkable potential political engine [for the] further development of the single market', enlargement had also generated growing 'suspicion, fear and sometimes open hostility' to continued liberalization among citizens of some of the older member states. This had been witnessed in public resistance to the services directive – even though it was expected to boost EU gross domestic product (GDP) by up to 1.5 per cent – and the outcome of the **French referendum on the European Constitution** in May 2005.

Monti suggested that future progress on the single market would be maximized by engaging in deliberate 'consensus building', so that member states with 'different cultural traditions, political preferences and concerns' could each find in the measures proposed something of appeal, including by drawing on elements outside the traditional definition of the market. He proposed that they accept a grand 'package deal' that would relaunch market liberalization, whilst deepening certain other policies, including in the fields of employment, the environment, the regions, transport and taxation. The inspiration for this approach was probably that of **Jacques Delors**, who, as Commission President from 1985 to 1995, used the 1992 single market programme as a basis for launching **Economic and Monetary Union** (EMU), Social Europe and **cohesion** policy.

Monti noted that completion of the single market in the 2010s could be 'particularly crucial for the solidity of the **euro** and for monetary union to deliver [its] promised economic benefits' and would serve 'as a vector to enhance total factor productivity and competitiveness in euro-area economies'. Ironically, two decades earlier, the argument made for EMU invoked the opposite line of causation – namely that a single currency would itself be a powerful means of realizing the full benefits of the single market.

Multiannual Financial Framework (MFF)

See **budgetary process**.

Mutual recognition of professional qualifications

The mutual recognition of professional qualifications, provided for in Article 53 TFEU, is an essential aspect of **freedom of establishment** – and thus of the wider rights of the **free movement of persons** and **free movement of services** – within the European Union. The purpose is to ensure that qualifications (of comparable standard) obtained by professionals in any one member state are recognized in all other member states, so enabling individuals to practise freely throughout the **single market**.

Initially, the **European Commission** sought to make progress in this field by gradually bringing forward specific proposals to harmonize standards for each of the many 'regulated' professions – thought to number over 800, from auctioneers to zoo-keepers. However, since the requirements and structure of regulation have traditionally varied greatly between the member states – with certain professions regulated in some countries but not in others (for example, osteopathy), and some professions allowed to regulate themselves – this sectoral approach proved very slow. Twelve directives were eventually adopted (between 1977 and 1993) to establish both mutually-agreed minimum training requirements and the mutual recognition of qualifications in such fields as medicine, nursing, midwifery, pharmacy, dentistry, veterinary practice, engineering and architecture – although in the last case, it took 15 years before the relevant legislation was finally enacted in 1985. As A. J. Toth has written, such directives 'created a system of automatic and unconditional recognition' of diplomas and certificates between member states, with each country giving them 'the same effect in its territory as the qualifications that the Member State itself awards' (*The Oxford Encyclopaedia of European Community Law*, Volume II, 2005).

Although the sectoral approach may be suited to particularly sensitive sectors and has the advantage of offering complete **legal certainty**, the laborious and time-consuming process of securing agreement led the Commission, encouraged by rulings of the **European Court of Justice** (ECJ), to bring forward horizontal proposals covering as many of the other, remaining professions as possible. The first such directive – covering both employed and self-employed persons, and providing for the mutual recognition of all qualifications requiring a three-year university degree and, where appropriate, the necessary professional training – was adopted by the **Council of Ministers** in 1988. A second directive, relating to professions regulated below degree level, was adopted four years later. A specific directive for crafts and tradespeople, such as hairdressers and construction workers, was adopted in 1999. These directives guarantee the right of mutual recognition of qualifications, whilst dispensing with the prior definition of common minimum training requirements between the member states: if one member state believes that the standard applied in another is less rigorous than its own, it can require any individual to undergo an additional aptitude test or 'adaptation period' before his or her qualifications are recognized. In 2005, existing EU law in this field (both sectoral and horizontal) was consolidated into a single professional qualifications directive, coming into effect two years later. The mutual recognition of qualifications applies to citizens of the European Union and other countries of the **European Economic Area** (EEA); it does not extend to third-country nationals resident in the Union.

The practical operation of the mutual recognition principle has not been without difficulty or controversy, especially in the medical field. Some national, regional or local authorities are ill-equipped to verify that a citizen from another EU member state has the necessary qualifications to practise. The Commission is planning to introduce a digital 'European professional card' for individuals, containing certain basic information, and to promote electronic access by governments to each other's documents proving the professional qualifications of individuals. A recent case of a German doctor who administered a lethal overdose of a drug to a patient on his first day in practice in the United Kingdom has also exposed the need for member states to be freer to insist on minimum domestic language and communication skills in certain professions, without this being exploited as a form of disguised protectionism. The House of Lords' EU committee noted in October 2011 that the 2005 professional qualifications directive 'strikes the wrong balance between facilitating mobility and ensuring patient safety' in the medical field. The Commission is currently considering whether to propose an amendment to the directive to permit the imposition of additional language tests before medical professionals come into contact with patients.

N

National parliaments

Although there is a widespread perception that national parliaments have only become involved in EU decision-making in recent years, the founding **Treaties** provided from the start that they should feature in at least four ways.

First, a limited number of important decisions taken unanimously by the **Council of Ministers** and **European Council** (or by 'common accord' of the member states) have always required the separate approval by the member states individually, 'in accordance with their respective constitutional requirements', before they can take effect. In practice, this means that certain agreements reached at EU level have formally to be confirmed by each of the national parliaments (and sometimes by **referenda** too). This requirement applies specifically to the **ratification** of new treaties embodying changes to existing ones (Article 48 TEU) or providing for the **accession** of member states (Article 49 TEU), as well to changes in the Union's system of **own resources** (Article 311 TFEU).

The **Lisbon Treaty**, which entered force in December 2009, has extended the range of decisions over which national parliaments have a say, by instituting a right for any individual parliament to block the use of certain ***passerelle* clauses**, provided it expresses its opposition within a period of six months. In addition, two member states, Germany and the United Kingdom, have recently introduced a unilateral requirement that their national parliaments will need to give explicit approval in advance, sometimes by law, for the use of *passerelle* clauses and the 'competence-stretching' **Article 352** TFEU.

Second, whenever a **directive** – a **legal act** of the Union which is binding on the states 'as to the result to be achieved', but does not itself have **direct effect** – is adopted, the text usually sets out certain general propositions which may require transposition, in whole or in part, into more detailed provisions of national law. The legislation in each member state to transpose the directive will itself usually need to be passed by the national parliament in question (although in some cases the government may be able to meet its obligation by administrative action). Here, however, the national parliament has no discretion: it must faithfully reflect the intention of the EU legislature and is only a free agent to the extent that it may add provisions that are not inconsistent with the directive (a temptation known as 'gold-plating').

Third, until direct elections were introduced in June 1979, the **European Parliament** was composed of delegates from the national parliaments – just as the Parliamentary Assembly of the **Council of Europe** (PACE) and the **NATO Parliamentary Assembly** still are. Although the nominated Members of the European Parliament (MEPs) had limited influence at that time – until 1987, the Parliament had no formal legislative power of any kind, although it could reject the annual **Budget** and dismiss the **European Commission** – their presence meant that each national parliament included a group of members who were well informed about Community affairs, as well as offering an obvious channel for inter-parliamentary dialogue. Direct election ended this situation – other than for a dwindling band of 'dual mandate' members – and indeed gave rise to a new sense of rivalry between MEPs and national parliamentarians.

Finally, government ministers sitting in the Council of Ministers have always been responsible to their national parliaments for decisions taken at EU level. In practice, this responsibility became more important following the move to a directly-elected European Parliament, as fewer and fewer national Members of Parliament (MPs) were connected to the EU political process. Each member state has evolved slightly different arrangements, but normally they involve national parliaments attempting to scrutinize European legislation before it is adopted, as well as ministers reporting back after key meetings of the Council and answering questions or participating in debates on EU issues. In the British House of Commons, for example, in addition to a set of committees which scrutinize draft European legislation, the prime minister reports to the full chamber after each meeting of the European Council, whilst the Foreign Secretary opens a general debate every six months on overall EU policy. In recent years, the German Chancellor has begun to appear in the Bundestag after European Councils, and in March 2011, that chamber in effect adopted a mandate binding the government in advance of Angela Merkel's attendance at that month's summit. The French government has given an undertaking that it will not let a matter be decided by a vote in the Council until the National Assembly and Senate have had an opportunity to express their views.

At the time when all important decisions in the Council were subject to a national veto, whether because **unanimity** was the formal decision-making method or because of the operation of the **Luxembourg Compromise**, national parliaments were in turn – by virtue of the control they could potentially exercise over individual members of the Council – in an unusually strong position. At least in theory, each national parliament could force its minister to veto any item under consideration. The ability or willingness to exercise this power depended, of course, on the specific relationship between the parliament and government in each member state. Moreover, ironically, the 'veto culture' in the Council meant that relatively few controversial measures were proposed by the European Commission – and even fewer had a realistic chance of securing the simultaneous consent of all governments. However, the gradual extension of **qualified majority voting** (QMV) in the Council (starting in 1987), together with the sharing of the Council's legislative power with the directly-elected Parliament through the **co-decision procedure** (introduced in 1993), has both increased the Commission's ambition and significantly diluted the potential ability of any one national parliament to block a piece of legislation, except in those fields where unanimity still applies.

Even when unanimity does apply in the Council, blockage of a decision by national parliaments is very rare, although not unknown. An example occurred in Britain in November 1996, when a European standing committee of the House of Commons refused to authorize the government to agree to the legislative measures underpinning the new **Stability and Growth Pact** (SGP). As the government feared that it did not have enough votes to override this obstruction on the floor of the House, the necessary legislation was held up in the Council until the May 1997 general election resulted in a change of government in the UK. More recently, in autumn 2011, there was a significant risk that several national parliaments – notably in Germany, Finland and Slovakia – might refuse to endorse changes to (or impose additional conditions on the operation of) the **European Financial Stability Facility** (EFSF) and its successor body, the **European Stability Mechanism** (ESM), key tools in the Union's response to the **eurozone debt crisis**. The Slovakian parliament voted first to reject, and then to approve, the measures within three days in October 2011, with the government agreeing to call an early general election in between. However, in each country, approval was finally given to texts which, in any case, were formally separate treaties between the 17 **eurozone** states, rather than EU legislative proposals.

The structures and effectiveness of national parliaments' scrutiny procedures for the examination of law emanating from the Union vary enormously. All parliaments now have committees specializing in European affairs. The first was the Danish *Folketing*'s 'Market Committee', established in the early 1980s: the notion of a 'national scrutiny reserve' first became a feature of business in the Council at that time as a result. In Ireland and Spain, these are joint committees of the upper and lower houses. In Belgium, Germany, Greece and Ireland, specific provision is made for the (non-voting) involvement of MEPs in the work of such committees. In some cases, there is a general EU affairs committee, addressing horizontal issues, whilst consideration of individual proposals is left to the normal subject-specific committees of the parliament. In other cases, the EU committee will itself have a series of specialized sub-committees for this purpose. In the British case, the House of Lords follows the latter pattern, whilst the House of Commons has a *sui generis* arrangement of limited effectiveness: a Commons select committee on EU legislation sifts and directs specific proposals to one of three themed European standing committees which normally vote along party lines.

In some parliaments, scrutiny is at best rudimentary; in others, it is very rigorous. The most intense is probably provided by the European affairs committee of the Danish *Folketing* – the successor body to the Market Committee – which meets weekly and can vote formally to bind any minister negotiating in the Council, and on occasion make it necessary for that minister to check back with the chairman of the committee in Copenhagen to discuss an evolving negotiation. The Finnish 'Grand Committee' is developing in a similar direction, reflecting the need to secure parliamentary approval before all major positions taken in the Council of Ministers or European Council. The eurozone debt crisis is resulting in certain national parliaments insisting on detailed scrutiny of individual EFSF/ESM decisions, through the relevant committees: in Germany, the Federal Constitutional Court has forced the Bundestag and Bundesrat to establish special mechanisms to this end, including a special, nine-member, subcommittee of the Bundestag's budget committee, meeting in secret. Following a different path altogether for the parliamentary oversight of European affairs is the comprehensive, thoughtful work in Britain of the House of Lords' select committee on the EU, whose reports are sometimes influential by virtue of the quality of their analysis, rather than any implicit threat to the government. To the extent that any consistent pattern can be discerned, it is probably that those national parliaments that are least likely to generate majority governments are in turn the ones best placed, if they wish, to hold their executives to account in routine EU decision-making.

The national parliamentary committees for European affairs are brought together with a group of MEPs every six months in a body known as the 'Conference of Parliamentary Committees for Union Affairs' or COSAC (originally an acronym for *Conférence des organes spécialisés dans les affaires communautaires*). Stemming from a joint initiative of the French National Assembly and the European Parliament in November 1989, COSAC meets once every six months, under the chairmanship of the parliament of whichever country is holding the rotating **presidency** of the Council of Ministers, and discusses current issues of European integration; each parliament has a delegation of six members and conclusions are normally drawn up by consensus, although some procedural decisions can be taken by a three-quarters' majority vote. In between full COSAC meetings, there are meetings of the chairmen of the relevant national scrutiny committees. Operating on the same principle are conferences of the chairmen of the foreign policy and defence committees in national parliaments, known respectively as COFACC and CODACC.

COSAC grew out of the 'Conference of Presidents of National Parliaments' – now known as the EU Speakers' Conference (EUSC) – a parallel body, founded in 1975, which brings together the presidents or speakers of the national parliaments of the member states, together with the European Parliament. (The presidency of the EUSC rotates annually, based on whichever member state held the Council presidency during the second six months of the previous year. Each annual meeting of the EUSC is prepared by a meeting of the secretaries general of the relevant parliaments.) A similar but separate structure, meeting every other year, embraces the presidents and speakers of all the parliaments of the 47 members of the **Council of Europe**, as well as the Parliamentary Assembly of the Council of Europe itself and the European Parliament.

A growing awareness of the limitations of national parliamentary involvement in an era of QMV and co-decision, together with the political consequences of several negative votes in referenda to endorse new treaties, has led to a renewed willingness to seek a way of deepening the involvement of national parliaments in the EU decision-making process. Two declarations were appended to the 1992 Maastricht Treaty, the one enjoining the European Parliament and national parliaments to step up contacts and the exchange of information, the other inviting governments to ensure that 'national parliaments receive Commission proposals for legislation in good time for information and possible examination' and supporting the idea of further inter-parliamentary meetings, along the lines of the 1990 'Assizes'. A legally-binding **protocol** on the role of national parliaments was annexed to the 1997 **Amsterdam Treaty** and this was strengthened in the 2001 **Nice Treaty**. The protocol recognizes the position of COSAC, which may communicate to the EU institutions 'any contribution which it deems appropriate', and lays down a six-week minimum period – now extended by the Lisbon Treaty to eight weeks – for legislative proposals to be considered by national parliaments. (This period runs from the date of the proposal's receipt by national parliaments in all **languages** to the date of the item being placed on the agenda of the Council.)

Under the Lisbon Treaty, the potential involvement of national parliaments in routine EU decision-making has been further strengthened in several ways – although, conversely, continued extensions of QMV, co-decision and Union competence exercise a strong countervailing force, by limiting the range of policy areas where any individual national parliament can prevent the adoption in the Council of policies of which it might disapprove. In addition to introducing the right of veto for national parliaments over certain *passerelle* clauses (see above), the Lisbon Treaty adds a new paragraph on their role to the Treaties (Article 12 TEU) which lists the aspects of their contribution 'to the good functioning of the Union' and adds new rights in the process. National parliaments now have the right to be informed directly by the EU institutions of legislative proposals, rather than only to receive such information through their governments. They are given a specific monitoring role in respect of aspects of **Justice and Home Affairs** (JHA), including explicitly over the activities of Europol and Eurojust.

Most importantly, national parliaments are given a formal role under Lisbon in 'seeing to it that the principle of **subsidiarity** is respected' in the EU law-making process (Article 12(b) TEU). The existing protocol to the Treaties on subsidiarity and **proportionality** has been amended to allow (each component chamber of) any national parliament to send a 'reasoned opinion' stating that it does not consider that a draft proposal respects the principle of subsidiarity. In a system in which two votes are assigned to each parliament, a total of a third of parliamentary votes (18 votes out of 54) can force the Commission to review its proposal (the so-called 'yellow card'). If a simple majority of parliamentary votes (28 out of 54) objects to the proposal (on a co-decision matter) and the Commission chooses to maintain its proposal, the subsidiarity issue must be settled in the Council or Parliament before either can proceed to a first reading: a vote by either 55 per cent of the member states in the Council or a simple majority of the Parliament, upholding the subsidiarity objection, results in consideration of the measure being terminated ('orange card'). (This system is described in greater detail in the entry on subsidiarity in this *Companion*.) Between December 2009, when the Lisbon Treaty came into force, and February 2012, 112 reasoned opinions were received from national parliaments objecting to legislative proposals on grounds of subsidiarity (in respect of a total of 254 proposals). The largest number (from nine chambers) related to a Commission proposal on the residence rights of seasonal workers from third countries. Measures in the fields of **social and employment policy** and **free movement of persons** appear to attract particular interest. However, at the time of writing, neither the yellow nor orange card thresholds had been reached on any proposal. In addition, under the Lisbon Treaty, any member-state government may now introduce an action before the **European Court of Justice** (ECJ) 'on behalf of [its] national Parliament or a chamber thereof' if the latter considers subsidiarity to have been infringed.

In advance of the introduction of this formal subsidiarity check, the European Commission decided in September 2006 to institute a mechanism by which any of the 40 national parliamentary chambers in the Union were given an informal right to comment on legislative proposals or major communications at the same time as they are sent to the Council and Parliament. This 'Barroso initiative' covers all aspects of any proposal or communication, not simply its subsidiarity implications. The results of this consultation may influence the Commission's thinking before it submits a proposal or allow it to amend a proposal once the text has been put forward. In 2011, 36 of the 40 chambers issued a total of 558 opinions on the Commission's various proposals and communications, most of which were positive, as well as 64 reasoned opinions on subsidiarity. The number of submissions has more than doubled in two years, with the upper chambers in bicameral systems generally more active than the lower chambers.

The European Parliament was, for many years, sceptical of the recognition of national parliaments as a force in EU decision-making, seeing them as potential allies of the Council in defending a broadly intergovernmental vision of Europe. This attitude prevailed even though many MEPs were themselves former national parliamentarians (150 of the 518 elected in 1989, for example). However, more recently, the balance of opinion among MEPs has shifted decisively in favour of a strategy of inclusion, rather than exclusion. The European Parliament was impressed by the constructive attitude taken by the national parliamentarians who participated in the Convention which drafted the **Charter of Fundamental Rights** in 1999–2000. The Parliament pushed hard for this 'Convention method' to be repeated for the drafting of a **European Constitution**. The resulting **Convention on the Future of Europe** in 2002–3, 56 of whose 105 members were national parliamentarians, endorsed the most integrationist treaty text ever proposed by an EU body. National parliamentarians even resisted the temptation to create some form of second chamber, in parallel to the European Parliament. This self-restraint was even more remarkable given that the Convention's own president, **Valéry Giscard d'Estaing**, strongly favoured the institution of a 'Congress' of national parliamentarians, which would meet regularly to hold the **European Council** (of heads of government) to account.

Efforts by the European Parliament to deepen relations with national parliaments have taken many forms. In 2003, it invited each of the national parliaments to establish a small representative office in its premises in Brussels: starting with the Danish *Folketing*, this offer has since been taken up by all but the Maltese and Slovakian parliaments. Most national parliaments now have between one and three staff permanently based in Brussels, promoting a two-way flow of information and practical contacts among parliamentarians. The European Parliament is also used as the base for a small secretariat for COSAC, COFACC and CODACC (it is composed of four seconded national parliamentary officials and one European Parliament official). During the 'reflection period' debate that followed the failure of the European Constitution, the European Parliament instituted a series of three-monthly 'joint parliamentary meetings' (JPMs) in Brussels, bringing together several hundred MEPs and MPs. These have since been continued, on a six-monthly basis, on policy themes agreed between the European Parliament and the national parliament of the member state holding the presidency of the Council of Ministers; they are co-chaired by the presidents of those parliaments.

In addition, 'joint committee meetings' are held between some individual European Parliament committees and the chairmen of, or a small delegation from, the corresponding committees in national parliaments. The Hungarian parliament invited seven sets of national committee chairmen to meetings in Budapest during the Hungarian presidency in the first half of 2011. Equally, some individual national parliamentary committees visit the European Parliament for bilateral dialogues, just as some EP committees visit member-state capitals to discuss national business in situ. Discussions of this kind are underpinned by an electronic system for the inter-parliamentary exchange of documents (IPEX), so that all parliaments can keep abreast of the state-of-play in the consideration and adoption of all major EU legislation.

The impact and effectiveness of all the various forms of involvement by national parliaments in EU decision-making depend ultimately on the willingness of national MPs themselves to become engaged in such work. Traditionally, there have been few career advantages in making a significant commitment to the 'European scrutiny' process. To be meaningful, this activity is inevitably time-consuming and specialist, whilst much of it is of limited interest to the media or to constituents. As a result, it rarely increases the likelihood of ministerial preferment and sometime attracts individuals with either a very strong enthusiasm for, or antipathy against, the European Union, whose views are not always taken seriously by governments. The key question is whether, over time, the growing power of the Union and the greater opportunities for involvement in its business will create a rising curve of interest among the 9,571 parliamentarians in member-state capitals in the substance of European policy and its 'mainstreaming' as part of their daily work. They will receive only modest encouragement from their governments in this process, as the latter appreciate that in an era of QMV and co-decision, it is increasingly difficult for ministers or civil servants to make public commitments about the outcome of EU law-making, without running the risk of embarrassment through compromise or defeat.

NATO

See **North Atlantic Treaty Organization**.

NATO Parliamentary Assembly

Founded in July 1955 as the Conference of Members of Parliament from the member countries of the **North Atlantic Treaty Organization** (NATO) – and known as the North Atlantic Assembly from 1966 to 1990 – the NATO Parliamentary Assembly brings together 257 members of the **national parliaments** of the 28 NATO member states. The US Congress has 36 members, whilst the French, German, Italian and United Kingdom parliaments have 18 each. (Members are chosen from both the upper and lower chambers and may not include serving ministers.) Associate membership has been extended to parliamentarians from 14 other countries, including Russia. A ten-strong delegation from the **European Parliament** has observer status.

The role of the Assembly, which was not provided for in the 1949 Treaty of Washington and which remains formally independent of NATO, is to provide a parliamentary forum for the discussion of defence and security issues, and to 'foster mutual understanding among Alliance parliamentarians of the key security challenges facing the transatlantic partnership'. The Assembly played an important role in preparing the ground for the expansion of NATO membership to the countries of central and eastern Europe. The Assembly meets in plenary session twice a year in different NATO or associated countries, but its five committees and their subcommittees meet more frequently. The president and five vice-presidents are elected annually: together with one representative per member state, they serve on a steering committee that decides the agenda and organizational questions. The Assembly's opinions are expressed in the form of recommendations, resolutions and declarations. The Assembly is serviced by a 30-strong international secretariat based in Brussels.

Neutrality

A neutral state is one that adopts an attitude of impartiality between belligerents. The rights and duties of neutral states were laid down in 1907 in two conventions signed in The Hague. Briefly, a neutral state must neither assist nor hinder a belligerent; its territory (including its airspace and its territorial waters) is inviolable and must be defended; it must not allow recruiting activities on behalf of the belligerents on its territory, although it is under no obligation to prevent its nationals from volunteering to fight on one side or the other; it must not trade with a belligerent, although its nationals may do so as private individuals; and although the sick and wounded of a belligerent may transit the territory of a neutral state, any active members of a belligerent state's armed forces must be interned if they enter the territory of a neutral state (special provisions apply to warships undergoing essential maintenance and reprovisioning in a neutral port). Some states are permanent neutrals in respect of all armed conflicts, other states declare themselves neutral in respect of particular conflicts (as Ireland did in the Second World War). Neutrality is to be distinguished from non-belligerency, which means favouring one side in a conflict without formally taking part in it.

Switzerland has been neutral since the Congress of Vienna in 1815. Within the European Union, neutrality was scarcely an issue until the 1992 **Maastricht Treaty** introduced a **Common Foreign and Security Policy** (CFSP), with the explicit possibility of a 'common defence' at a later stage. At that time, only one member state out of 12 (Ireland) was neutral; all others were members of the **North Atlantic Treaty Organization** (NATO), even if France had chosen to leave the latter's integrated military command structure in 1966. With **enlargement**, however, the number of formally neutral member states has grown, and today only 21 of the 27 EU member states are also within NATO. Neutrality is an explicit provision of the constitutions of Austria (dating from 1955) and Malta (1987), whilst Cyprus, Finland and Sweden, like Ireland, are considered to be neutral by virtue of long-standing foreign policies.

As the end of the **Cold War** gradually redefined what 'neutrality' meant for European states, it became easier for neutral countries – now increasingly referred to as 'post-neutrals' – to accept the legitimacy of common European action in the security and defence field. After some initial scepticism, they have accepted the development of a **Common Security and Defence Policy** (CSDP) within the CFSP, whilst seeking both to contain its defensive component and to stress its autonomy from NATO. In this, they have been helped by the right of any country to excuse itself from CFSP/CSDP obligations through 'constructive absention'. In practice, nearly all the neutral states have participated in recent EU crisis management operations in third countries, including in the Balkans and the Democratic Republic of Congo, and all of them provide forces for the EU's Battlegroups, under the **Helsinki Headline Goal**. Ironically, the only EU member state not to participate in CSDP is Denmark, a member of NATO.

Nice Treaty

The origins of the Treaty of Nice, signed on 26 February 2001, are to be found in a **protocol** on 'the institutions with the prospect of **enlargement** of the European Union' annexed to the 1997 **Amsterdam Treaty**. This text acknowledged that certain reforms essential to the success of enlargement had not been secured in the negotiation of the Amsterdam Treaty and stated that another **Intergovernmental Conference** (IGC) would need to be convened, under Article 48 TEU, 'at least one year before the membership of the European Union exceeds twenty'. The protocol specifically linked a reduction in the size of the **European Commission** to a 'reweighting' of votes under the system of **qualified majority voting** (QMV) in the **Council of Ministers**.

In the trade-off being suggested, the large member states would lose their second Commissioner in return for greater voting power in the Council. In parallel, the smaller member states might be reassured by other institutional changes – such as a widening of the fields of QMV and of **co-decision** between the Council and **European Parliament** – designed to strengthen the '**Community method**'.

This debate was bound to take the Union into a particularly sensitive series of questions related to the balance of power within the Council and between the EU institutions as a whole. Given that the institutional changes being envisaged would themselves have a direct bearing on the position of the applicant states, the **European Council** decided in Cologne in June 1999 to accelerate the discussion and convene the planned IGC in 2000. The specific agenda for the IGC was settled at the Cologne and Helsinki European Council meetings in June and December 1999. In addition to addressing the difficult 'Amsterdam leftovers' referred to above, the IGC was invited to draw up any other amendments to the **Treaties** which were thought to be necessary for enlargement or desirable for the smooth implementation of the Amsterdam Treaty (which only entered into force in May 1999). Preparatory work for the IGC would be undertaken within the Council system itself, rather than by an outside Reflection Group of the kind which met before the 1996–7 IGC that drafted the Amsterdam Treaty. The new IGC formally opened on 14 February 2000, with an official-level meeting (composed mainly of the permanent representatives of the member states) taking place approximately once a fortnight, which in turn reported to the **General Affairs Council** (GAC) monthly.

The text eventually agreed at an awkward and lengthy meeting of the European Council, held in Nice on 7–11 December 2000, introduced a large number of amendments to the Treaties on many aspects of the Union's institutions and procedures, often only tangentially related to enlargement. Even more than the Amsterdam Treaty which preceded it, the Nice Treaty lacked a powerful, central, non-institutional theme of the kind which had justified and explained to the public the purpose of the 1986 **Single European Act** (SEA) in completing the **single market** or of the 1992 **Maastricht Treaty** in creating a single currency. Instead, the Nice Treaty seemed like the product of 'a largely incomprehensible demarcation dispute between people with a vested interest' in EU decision-making, as the British think-tanker, Heather Grabbe, aptly described it at the time, and failed to engage the interest of even the political class in most member states.

The IGC process leading up to the Nice summit was also less well managed by the successive Portuguese and French **presidencies** of the Council than some previous negotiations, with Paris deciding in July 2000 in effect to start the discussion from scratch again. The situation during the French presidency was complicated by *cohabitation* and mutual mistrust between the Gaullist President, Jacques Chirac, and his Socialist government, led by Lionel Jospin, with sometimes different negotiating priorities and approaches being pursued at different levels. France was accused both of aggressively pushing certain issues that reflected its own interests and of working secretly behind-the-scenes with a limited number of other member states, rather than seeking an open compromise acceptable to all. The climate of tension was further fuelled when the presidency responded to criticism by declaring that it 'preferred failure to an unsatisfactory agreement'.

A further contributory factor was the relatively little time that the foreign (and other) ministers in the General Affairs Council found themselves devoting in practice to discussing and settling IGC issues over successive months – a pattern which had already been apparent, in less acute form, during the negotiation of the Amsterdam Treaty. As a result, a number of particularly sensitive issues were left unresolved, and with which heads of government were forced to grapple at the last minute. When the Nice European Council convened on 7 December, there was no certainty as to whether a deal would be struck. Confusion continued right up until the last moment, with a text finally emerging at 4.40 a.m. on the fifth day of the meeting – making the Nice European Council by far the longest summit in the Union's history.

As during the negotiations leading up to the Amsterdam Treaty, it was the 'big versus small country' power questions of the weighting of votes within the Council and the size of the Commission that proved most divisive and difficult to resolve. The difference this time was that, three years later, the member states were under even greater pressure to find a solution. In the IGC discussion, a range of proposals had been discussed, including the idea of moving to a 'double majority' of states and population. Chirac was particularly strongly opposed to this suggestion, because it would explicitly decouple the voting strengths of Germany and France in the Council for the first time and might play badly with domestic public opinion.

The complex formula on QMV eventually agreed at Nice (Article 205 EC) had three components. First, votes in the Council were reweighted slightly in favour of the largest member states, at the expense of most of the others, especially middle-sized countries. The share of Germany, France, Italy and the United Kingdom each rose from 11.5 per cent of the EU 15's total votes (10 votes each out of 87) to 12.2 per cent (29 votes each out of 237). However, as the immediate effect of enlargement (starting in 2004) would be to dilute the position of the larger states in a bigger pool of predominantly small states – with a new total of 321 votes for 25 member states, and 345 votes for 27 – the effects of this reweighting would be fairly effectively concealed. Second, the threshold for the attainment of the qualified majority in the Council – set at

255 out of 345 votes in an EU of 27 states – was in effect raised from 71.3 to 73.9 per cent of all votes, the highest it had ever been (having started at 70.6 per cent in 1958). Third, for the first time it was stipulated that any qualified majority had to include a minimum number of countries – a simple majority of member states – representing a certain proportion – at least 62 per cent – of the total population of the Union.

These last innovations pointed in opposite directions. Although the need for a simple majority of states had always been an unstated feature of the QMV system in the past, the impending enlargement could make it possible to achieve a qualified majority with only a minority of states, so it was now thought useful to make this condition explicit, in order to reassure smaller member states. Conversely, the 62 per cent population requirement was designed to safeguard the position of larger states: until then, the minimum population needed for a qualified majority had fallen, with successive enlargements, from 70.5 per cent in 1973 to 58.2 per cent in 2000. Although the 62 per cent criterion effectively broke the absolute equality of France and Germany in the Council, this feature could be presented by Chirac as marginal to the operation of the system as a whole.

The Nice voting system took effect in January 2005 and still applies (Article 3, **Protocol** 36 to the Treaties). Under the **Lisbon Treaty**, QMV will be replaced in 2014–17 by a new, simpler 'double majority' voting system, whereby legislation will normally be adopted if it commands the support of 55 per cent of the member states, representing at least 65 per cent of the population of the Union (Article 238 TFEU).

The solution found on the composition of the European Commission was more straightforward. It was agreed that, starting in 2005, the Commission would include 'one national of each of the Member States', in effect removing the second Commissioner from each of five largest countries (Article 213 EC). Moreover, once the Union had expanded to comprise 27 member states, the number of Commissioners (in the next new Commission) would be reduced to fewer than the number of member states, with Commissioners 'chosen according to a rotation system based on the principle of equality' (Protocol 10). This situation was due to arise on 1 November 2009, but because of a delay in the confirmation of the second Barroso Commission and the imminent entry into force of new arrangements under the Lisbon Treaty (on 1 December), no action was taken.

At Nice, as at Amsterdam, the EU member states were able to agree to some extensions of QMV in Council decision-making and to greater use of co-decision between the Council and Parliament. QMV would henceforth be extended to 38 additional provisions of the Treaties, including decisions on anti-discrimination policy, financial assistance to member states, **international agreements** on services and intellectual property, and judicial cooperation in civil matters. It was also to apply, on a deferred basis, to asylum and immigration policy and aspects of the **free movement of persons** (after May 2004), and to the **structural funds** and the EU's Financial Regulation (after January 2007). In the institutional field, QMV was extended to the nomination and appointment of the President and other members of the European Commission, to the appointment of the members of the **Court of Auditors** and of the advisory **European Economic and Social Committee** (EESC) and **Committee of the Regions**, and to the appointment of the Secretary General and Deputy Secretary General of the Council. Reinforcing moves made in the Amsterdam Treaty, the position of the Commission President was further strengthened by virtue of provisions making him or her responsible for the allocation of portfolios and clarifying that 'a Member of the Commission shall resign if the President so requests.' The extension of co-decision in the Nice Treaty was more modest than many in the European Parliament had hoped for. It was conceded in only five areas, including industrial policy, judicial cooperation in civil matters and arrangements for **European political parties.**

Following the 'Haider affair' in Austria, in 1999–2000, the Amsterdam provision on the possible **suspension** of the rights of a member state engaged in 'serious and persistent breaches' of fundamental rights was modified to allow 'a clear risk' of such a breach to be grounds for investigation, with the Council acting by a four-fifths majority, after receiving the **consent** of the Parliament. Likewise, the Amsterdam arrangements for '**enhanced cooperation**' among member states were overhauled, making them potentially easier to use, and extended both to **Common Foreign and Security Policy** (CFSP) and **Justice and Home Affairs** (JHA). In the CFSP field, the new **Common Security and Defence Policy** (CSDP), established by the heads of government at the Cologne and Helsinki European Council meetings in June and December 1999, was given treaty status.

Among other changes introduced by the Treaty were an increase in the maximum size of the European Parliament, set at 732 rather than 700 members, ceilings on the size of the European Economic and Social Committee (EESC) and the Committee of the Regions, set at 350 members each, and a strengthening of the reference to the role of European political parties introduced by the Maastricht Treaty. The statute of the **European Court of Justice** (ECJ) was updated in a protocol annexed to the Treaties. A declaration called for one European Council meeting in each presidency to be held in Brussels with effect from 2002, and for all such meetings to be held there once the number of member states reached 18. The **Charter of Fundamental Rights** was 'solemnly proclaimed' jointly by the Council, Parliament and Commission at the Nice summit, but at least five member states, led by the United Kingdom, prevented it from being given treaty status.

Although the Nice Treaty allowed some useful 'tidying up' of EU institutional arrangements, the outcome seemed rather ragged and messy. Advocates of deeper institutional reform, especially among the more maximalist member states and Members of the European Parliament (MEPs), quickly expressed their dissatisfaction. This potential problem was already acknowledged in a declaration, agreed at Nice, on the 'Future of the Union', which committed the Swedish and Belgian presidencies of the Council in 2001 to encourage 'wide-ranging discussions with all interested parties', including the applicant states, on further institutional changes, with a new IGC to be called in 2003. Four topics in particular were identified for debate: the division of competences between European and national authorities; the role of **national parliaments**; the legal status of the Charter of Fundamental Rights; and the simplification of the Treaties. The declaration spoke of 'the need to improve and to monitor the democratic legitimacy and transparency of the Union and its institutions, to bring them closer to the citizens of the Member States'.

So just as so-called 'Amsterdam leftovers' had led to the Nice Treaty, now a set of 'Nice leftovers' would in turn generate a further round of institutional reform. The Laeken Declaration, adopted by heads of government in December 2001, only 12 months after they had agreed the Nice Treaty, set the European Union on a more ambitious path that led successively to the **Convention on the Future of Europe** (2002–3), the aborted **European Constitution**, and eventually the adoption of the Lisbon Treaty.

Further reading: David Galloway, *The Treaty of Nice and Beyond: Realities and Illusions of Power in the EU*, 2001.

Noël, Émile (1922–96)

Émile Noël was the first Secretary General of the **European Commission** and the most influential occupant of that post to date. Born in Constantinople, Noël was educated at the École Normale Supérieure in Paris, before joining the staff of the newly-founded **Council of Europe** in 1949. Working on the Council's political committee, he became involved in drafting (by the special 'Ad Hoc Assembly' in 1952–3) the aborted Treaty for a **European Political Community** (EPC). When Guy Mollet, President of the Council's Consultative Assembly, was nominated French prime minister in January 1956, he invited Noël, a fellow French Socialist, to join him in the government, as his deputy *chef de* ***cabinet***. Opposed to the country's policies in Algeria, Noël was given lead responsibility for Europe, developing close links with other strongly pro-European French technocrats in Paris, notably **Jean Monnet** and **Pierre Uri**. Critically, Noël coordinated the position of the French delegation (led by Robert Marjolin) to the negotiations that drafted the **Treaties of Rome** founding the **European Economic Community** (EEC) and the **European Atomic Energy Community** (EAEC or Euratom) in 1956–7. As a result of this work, he was invited to become Secretary General of the new European Commission under its President, **Walter Hallstein**, who had negotiated the same texts on the West German side.

On taking up his duties in the Commission in Brussels in January 1958, Noël found himself, at the age of only 35, at the epicentre of the new organization of Europe. He quickly established himself as Hallstein's right-hand man – 'the éminence grise to the éminence grise' as one colleague memorably described him – and as an individual who 'knew everyone, knew everything and said as little as possible'. Robert Lemaignen, one of France's first European Commissioners (1958–62), commented of Noël: 'It would have been hard to find a person better fitted for his post.' The Secretary General 'looks after the inner workings of the Commission, prepares its discussion and its agenda, draws up its minutes – he attends all its meetings, even the most confidential – and puts its decisions into proper legal shape . . . Many of these tasks demand absolute discretion and perfect tact. Noël fulfilled them perfectly' (*L'Europe au berceau, souvenirs d'un technocrate*, 1964).

When Hallstein stepped down as President in 1967, on the entry into force of the **Merger Treaty**, Noël continued as Secretary General of the single Commission serving all three Communities, a post he retained until his retirement in 1987, at the (then) compulsory age of 65. During his nearly three decades in post, Noël became increasingly central to the design and evolution of the administrative structures and working methods of the institution. He oversaw the growth of the Commission staff from zero in 1958 to some 3,500 in 1966, before the Merger Treaty took effect, and 15,000 20 years later. His presence also ensured that French became the working language of the Commission, a dominance only seriously challenged in recent years. He successfully encouraged the French government to place some of its best and brightest officials at the Commission's disposal. However, notwithstanding his exceptional negotiating and political skills, Noël left the emerging Commission structure open to multiple criticisms, many of which were voiced in the Spierenburg Report, instigated by **Roy Jenkins** as Commission President in 1979. He modelled administrative arrangements perhaps too closely on those of the domestic civil service in Paris, underestimating the need for innovation and flexibility in a multinational and multilingual environment.

The highly effective political 'tandem' which Noël established with Hallstein was not fully replicated in his dealings with the latter's successors: some Presidents proved too short-lived or lacking in authority to serve as the powerful public protagonist he needed as an ally, whilst others, like Jenkins, were wary of the influence he sought to exercise behind the scenes. Ironically, the close of Noël's career was marred by tension with his compatriot **Jacques**

Delors (from 1985), whose *chef de **cabinet***, Pascal Lamy, sought successfully to circumvent his dominance by building up the power of the President's staff. Subsequent Secretaries General have tended to be more modest figures, reluctant to allow themselves to be seen as strong political actors in their own right.

Noël served in retirement as the first President of the **European University Institute** (EUI) in Fiesole, near Florence (1987–93). His reputation and administrative skills helped to launch this new body on a rising curve of credibility in the world of postgraduate social science. True to his reputation for discretion, he chose to write no memoirs, denying future generations a potentially incomparable account of the practical politics of European integration at the highest level.

Non-discrimination

The **Treaties** contain two articles, dating from the original **Treaty of Rome**, which outlaw specific types of discrimination: Article 18 TFEU prohibits **discrimination on grounds of nationality** and Article 157 TFEU requires 'equal pay without discrimination based on sex', as well as '**equal treatment** of men and women in matters of employment and occupation' more generally. The 1997 **Amsterdam Treaty** significantly widened the potential scope of European Union action to encompass 'discrimination based on sex, racial or ethnic origin, religion or belief, disability, age or sexual orientation' (Article 19 TFEU). Since the 1992 **Maastricht Treaty**, the rights set out in the **European Convention on Human Rights** (ECHR) – including the prohibition of 'discrimination on any ground' (Article 14) – have been recognized as 'general principles' of **EU law** (Article 6 TEU), whilst those specifically guaranteed by the Union's **Charter of Fundamental Rights** were given legal effect by the **Lisbon Treaty** in December 2009.

The adoption of legislation under Articles 18 and 157 TFEU involves **qualified majority voting** (QMV) in the **Council of Ministers** and **co-decision** between the Council and the **European Parliament**. By contrast, legislation brought forward under Article 19 TFEU can only be passed by **unanimity** in the Council, with the **consent** of the Parliament (unless it involves only 'incentive measures' and does not seek to harmonize national legal provisions).

'Non-Europe'

The concept of 'non-Europe' – a phrase first employed in the **Albert–Ball Report** of 1983 and popularized by the **Cecchini Report** five years later – was used to denote the economic price to be paid by citizens for the absence of a fully-functioning **single market** in Europe. The fragmentation of markets along national lines – whether as a result of technical standards, regulatory requirements or frontier controls – was preventing an optimum allocation of resources, raising prices and limiting consumer choice. Identifying the 'cost of non-Europe' became an important tool in generating political support for the 1992 single market programme, whose measures often impacted adversely on producers in individual, protected national markets. In sectors where the single market remains to be completed – notably services, public purchasing and the digital economy – the problem of 'non-Europe' remains. More recently, however, the phrase 'non-Europe' has been applied increasingly to any policy area where the absence of coordinated action at European level may prevent some collective good being realized – for example, in the fields of energy security or climate change – or where a European 'added value' could be realized by greater pooling of national spending at supranational level – for example, in development aid.

Non-tariff barriers

A non-tariff barrier is an obstacle to trade arising not from the imposition of tariffs, levies or quantitative restrictions (quotas), but from different product specifications and standards, discriminatory public purchasing policies, restrictive pricing or distribution agreements, patent or copyright difficulties, and major discrepancies in the tax structure. The establishment of the **customs union** in 1968 effectively removed tariffs, levies and quotas from intra-Community trade, and the need to remove remaining non-tariff barriers was the prime purpose of the **single market** programme (launched in 1985, originally for completion in 1992). Non-tariff barriers afford many means of resorting to covert protectionism and their removal is also a priority for other bodies committed to free trade, notably the **Organization for Economic Cooperation and Development** (OECD) and the World Trade Organization (WTO). See also **Cassis de Dijon case.**

Nordic Council

The five countries that participate in the Nordic Council – Denmark, Finland, **Iceland**, **Norway** and Sweden – have a long history of contact of various kinds: as colonies or possessions of each other, as unions brought about by conquest or intermarriage, and as trading partners. Norway, a Danish possession until 1814, gained its independence from Sweden in 1905; Finland, formerly Swedish, was a Grand Duchy within the Russian Empire and became independent in 1917; Iceland secured dominion status under the Danish Crown in 1918 and independence in 1944. Denmark, Norway and Sweden established the Nordic Inter-Parliamentary Union in 1907, and in 1919 the Norden Association, a private body, was set up to promote cultural contacts. In 1938, the Danish foreign minister proposed the creation of a Nordic Council but the idea was not taken up until after the Second World

War. In the late 1940s, unsuccessful attempts were made to establish both a Nordic Customs Union and a Nordic Defence Union; progress was made with a Nordic Passport Union (completed in 1958). In August 1951, at the suggestion of the Danish prime minister, Hans Hedtoft, the Nordic Inter-parliamentary Union endorsed the idea of a Nordic Council, and by the end of 1952, the parliaments of Denmark, Iceland, Norway and Sweden had approved an agreement establishing the institutions of the Council and defining the scope of cooperation between the signatory states; because of Soviet hostility, Finland did not join until 1955.

The Nordic Council consists of 87 parliamentary representatives: 20 chosen by each of the national parliaments of Denmark, Finland, Norway and Sweden, and seven from Iceland. They are joined by an unspecified number of ministerial representatives, who have no voting rights. Special provision is made within the Danish delegation for representatives of the autonomous communities of **Greenland and the Faeroes** and within the Finnish delegation for the Åland Islands. The Council has six standing committees, but meets in plenary session only twice a year, the signatory states taking turns to host the meetings and act as president. Votes are taken by simple majority, but on measures affecting particular states, only the representatives from those states may vote. Decisions, in the form of recommendations, are communicated to the governments.

In March 1962, the Nordic Council was given more formal status with the signing of a Treaty of Cooperation between the five Nordic states in Helsinki. The fields of cooperation were defined as comprising juridical, cultural, educational, economic, employment and communications policy, building on existing arrangements for the free movement of citizens and the passport union. With the revision of the Helsinki Treaty in February 1971 came the establishment of an intergovernmental Nordic Council of Ministers, in which each country has one vote and decisions (other than on procedural matters) are taken unanimously. Although they do not take legal form, 'the decisions of the Council of Ministers are binding on each country' (Article 63), unless they require national parliamentary approval. The revised treaty added environmental protection to the areas of Nordic cooperation. Small secretariats were established for the Nordic institutions in Copenhagen.

Since 1974, all five governments have had ministers specifically responsible for cooperation through the Nordic Council of Ministers. Regular contact is maintained between government departments at official level in 14 specialist 'committees of senior officials' and a variety of working groups. The Council of Ministers oversees the work of the Nordic Investment Bank, the Nordic Fund for Technology and Industrial Development, the Nordic Cultural Fund and a number of joint development projects in the third world. It also provides the forum through which the five governments can coordinate their positions in other international bodies – even if this is limited by the fact that two of the five (Norway and Iceland) are outside the European Union, and another two (Finland and Sweden) outside the **North Atlantic Treaty Organization** (NATO).

Although well established and with substantial achievements to its credit, the machinery of Nordic cooperation has proved disappointing in certain respects. Determined efforts to establish a Nordic Economic Union came to nothing: a **customs union** was achieved only within the **European Free Trade Association** (EFTA) in 1960; security coordination has been limited to discussion of a Nordic 'nuclear-free zone'; and attempts to address the cultural, legal and technical challenges of certain complex issues – for example, satellite broadcasting – by intergovernmental agreement has proved inconclusive. Conversely, following the collapse of the Soviet Union, the institutions successfully encouraged the development of new political machinery for cooperation in adjacent areas, in the form of the **Council of the Baltic Sea States** (CBSS), the **Barents Euro-Arctic Council** (BEAC) and the **Arctic Council**. Some of the committees and working groups of the Nordic Council of Ministers now include representatives of the Baltic states.

Nordic cooperation is sometimes put forward as a model for wider European cooperation as an alternative to the more ambitious, supranational, law-based model followed by the European Union. Its limitations, however, are clear, in spite of the advantages the Nordic countries enjoy by virtue of a substantial degree of cultural, linguistic and economic homogeneity.

North Atlantic Treaty Organization (NATO)

On 17 March 1948, Belgium, France, Luxembourg, the Netherlands and the United Kingdom signed a 50-year agreement on economic, social and cultural collaboration and collective self-defence known as the **Brussels Treaty** or 'Western Union'. Three months later, the beginning of the Berlin blockade marked a further deterioration in relations between the United States and the Soviet Union, and in July talks began in Washington between the United States, Canada and the Brussels Treaty powers on a new, wider collective security alliance to be known as the North Atlantic Treaty Organization and covering the whole of the North Atlantic area. Formal negotiations began in December 1948 and the draft Treaty was published three months later. Five more countries (Denmark, **Iceland**, Italy, **Norway** and Portugal) were invited to sign the treaty, and – in spite of intense opposition from the Soviet Union, which claimed that the text contravened the United Nations Charter – the signing ceremony took place in Washington DC on 4 April 1949. The treaty entered into force on 24 August 1949.

The NATO Treaty contains only 14 articles. The commitment to collective security is to be found in Article 5, which states:

> *The Parties agree that an armed attack against one or more of them in Europe or North America shall be considered an attack against them all, and consequently they agree that, if such an armed attack occurs, each of them, in exercise of the right of individual or collective self-defence recognized by Article 51 of the Charter of the United Nations, will assist the Party or Parties so attacked by taking forthwith, individually, and in concert with the other Parties, such action as it deems necessary, including the use of armed force, to restore and maintain the security of the North Atlantic area.*

The North Atlantic Treaty differed from the Brussels Treaty in that, within NATO, the 'action' to be taken by allies in response to one of their number being attacked need not involve use of armed force. Equally it only applied to aggression within the 'North Atlantic area', which comprises the territory of any of the signatory states in Europe or North America, the territory of Turkey, and 'the islands under the jurisdiction [of any of the signatory states] in the North Atlantic area north of the Tropic of Cancer'. This explains why, for example, NATO did not become involved in the Falklands war of 1982. On 2 October 2001, the North Atlantic Council, NATO's highest decision-making body, decided that, since the terrorist attacks on the World Trade Center in New York and the Pentagon in Washington DC on 11 September were 'directed from abroad', they were covered by Article 5.

The headquarters of NATO were initially located in London (at 13 Belgrave Square) and then, from 1952, in Paris (first in the Palais de Chaillot and then, from 1960, at the Porte Dauphine). Following the decision of President **Charles de Gaulle** to withdraw France from NATO's integrated military command structure in March 1966, they were transferred to the outskirts of Brussels the following year. In parallel, the location of the military command structure in Europe, **Supreme Headquarters Allied Powers Europe** (SHAPE), was moved from Rocquencourt, outside Paris, to Casteau, north of Mons, in Belgium. France finally rejoined the integrated military command structure in April 2009.

Since its foundation, the membership of NATO has increased from 12 to 28 states. Greece and Turkey joined in 1952, West Germany in 1955 and Spain in 1982. The Soviet Union sought to join in 1955 but this was rejected. Because membership proved a divisive issue in Spain, it had to be confirmed by a referendum held four years later, in March 1986, and the country refrained from participating in the integrated military command structure for a further decade. With the end of the **Cold War** and the collapse of **Communism** in Europe in 1989–90, NATO faced pressure to widen its membership to include many of the countries of central and eastern Europe that had previously been members of the **Warsaw Pact**. The same developments forced a reappraisal of NATO's role and structure, accompanied by cuts in national defence budgets.

Starting with the NATO summit in Rome in November 1991, the organization began actively to develop closer relations with the former Warsaw Pact countries, as well as some former republics of the Soviet Union, with a view to possible membership in the longer term. NATO created a joint consultative body on security issues, the North Atlantic Cooperation Council (NACC), which by 1996 encompassed 24 non-NATO members, and in January 1994, it launched the Partnership for Peace, a programme of 'practical bilateral cooperation' on a tailored basis with individual countries, 12 of which have subsequently joined NATO. The NACC evolved into the Euro-Atlantic Partnership Council (EAPC) in 1997 and, at the same time, NATO invited the Czech Republic, Hungary and Poland to begin accession talks. In March 1999, these three countries became the first former Warsaw Pact states to enter NATO. The experience enabled the Washington summit in April 1999 to develop the concept of a 'Membership Action Plan' (MAP), which is now a precondition for each country seeking to join the organization. On this basis, nine more countries have since become members: Bulgaria, Romania, Slovakia, Slovenia and the three **Baltic states** in March 2004, and Albania and **Croatia** in April 2009.

Russia has strongly opposed the eastern enlargement of NATO, despite the latter's efforts to minimize damage to bilateral relations through a NATO–Russia Permanent Joint Council, created in 1998, and other initiatives. Some in Moscow claim that there was a commitment given by the United States, at the time of **German reunification** in 1990, that NATO 'would not move a centimeter to the east' after the Cold War, as former Soviet president Mikhail Gorbachev put it in April 2009. However, those involved on the US and European sides of the 'Two plus Four' negotiations at that time deny this.

From 1990 onwards, the greatly reduced threat of a direct armed attack on the NATO states suggested that new thinking was required about the future role and tasks of the organization. The defensive strategies of the era of superpower confrontation, during which NATO forces were never actually deployed (except on practice missions), seemed of declining relevance. James Baker, the US Secretary of State at the time, began to conceive NATO as a possible mechanism for the projection of 'soft power'. This dovetailed with a greater likelihood that NATO countries would be under pressure to undertake peacemaking, peacekeeping, humanitarian or counterterrorist activities outside the traditional 'North Atlantic area'. A lively debate ensued about whether NATO forces could be used legally 'out of area', even in defence of its members' extraterritorial interests. The Alliance's 'New Strategic Concept', agreed at the NATO summit in Rome in November 1991, identified the need for 'enhanced flexibility and mobility' in the armed forces: the creation of an **Allied Rapid Reaction Corps** (ARRC) followed in 1995. Although the

1991–2 Gulf War involved 12 of NATO's then 16 members, there was no request for the intervention to be conducted under a NATO aegis.

Soon thereafter, the mood changed markedly, and NATO quickly found itself cast in the front line of major international disputes, with the Balkans crisis acting as the catalyst. Although still 'within area', NATO became involved in enforcing the UN arms embargo and economic sanctions against the Federal Republic of **Yugoslavia** in June 1993, through Operation Sharp Guard. Then, after diplomatic efforts failed to resolve the complex pattern of conflicts in the region, notably the civil war in Bosnia-Herzegovina (culminating in the Srebrenica massacre in July 1995), NATO accepted a UN mandate to intervene militarily to end the fighting. The rapid success of the air campaign which NATO launched in August 1995, Operation Deliberate Force, led to the Dayton peace agreement of December that year. By way of follow-up on the ground, NATO put in place an Implementation Force (IFOR) of some 60,000 troops, with a 32,000-strong Stabilization Force (SFOR) succeeding it in December 1996. (The latter handed its mandate over to the European Union's Operation Althea in December 2004.) A further NATO military operation was seen in Kosovo, where a 78-day air campaign was waged in 1999 and some 14,000 troops have been deployed in the Kosovo Force (KFOR) since then. In addition, three operations took place in FYR Macedonia in 2001–3.

Today, in addition to its ongoing role in Kosovo, NATO has land and air forces deployed 'out of area' in Afghanistan, Iraq and on the African continent, whilst naval forces are active in the Mediterranean and off the Horn of Africa. The International Security Assistance Force (ISAF) in Afghanistan, which at its peak comprised some 130,000 troops from 47 countries, was put under NATO leadership in August 2003. In parallel, there is a small NATO training mission in Iraq. NATO forces have been assisting the African Union, by providing airlift, for its peacekeeping missions in Somalia (AMISOM) and, until recently, Sudan (AMIS). In the Mediterranean, since October 2001 – as part of NATO's response to the attacks of 11 September – Operation Active Endeavour has coordinated maritime surveillance designed to detect and deter potential terrorist activity. Since 2008, Operations Allied Provider, Allied Protector and Ocean Shield have involved at-sea counter-piracy activities in the Gulf of Aden and off the coast of Somalia. In March 2011, following passage of UN Security Council Resolution 1973, NATO took control of the no-fly zone over Libya and began enforcing an arms embargo at sea against the régime of Colonel Gaddafi, through Operation Unified Protector. In recent years, the Alliance has also provided assistance to a number of countries hit by natural disasters, including Pakistan after the earthquake of October 2005.

Ultimate decision-making power within NATO resides in the North Atlantic Council. Each member state designates a permanent representative (or ambassador) to NATO, who is supported by a political and military staff of varying size. The NAC meets weekly at permanent-representative level, usually on a Wednesday, and convenes periodically at ministerial level too. NAC ministerial meetings may bring together defence ministers, foreign ministers or heads of government. With respect to the latter, there have been 25 NATO summits since 1949, nine of them since 1999. The NAC is chaired by the NATO Secretary General and operates by consensus (votes are never taken). It is the only NATO body to derive its authority explicitly from the North Atlantic Treaty and it has the sole responsibility for setting up any subsidiary bodies within the organization.

Reporting to the NAC, on the civilian side, are the Defence Planning Committee (DPC) and the Nuclear Planning Group (NPG). Chaired by the Secretary General, both bodies are formally comprised of the defence ministers, but they more routinely meet at permanent-representative level. They are only open to countries within NATO's integrated military command structure (currently all 28 members). The DPC provides policy guidance to the organization's military bodies, and its work is in turn prepared by a number of subordinate committees (notably the Defence Review Committee (DRC), which oversees the 'force planning process' within NATO and other issues related to the operation of the integrated military structure). The NPG discusses specific policy issues related to nuclear forces, including in NATO's words, 'the safety, security and survivability of nuclear weapons, communications and information systems, deployment issues and wider questions of common concern, such as nuclear arms control and nuclear proliferation'. Both the DPC and the NPG are empowered to take decisions with the full authority of the NAC, as necessary.

The senior military body within NATO, whose authority also formally derives from the North Atlantic Council, is the Military Committee. Composed of the member states' military representatives (MilReps) to NATO – who in practice operate in parallel to the permanent representatives and are for the most part national chiefs of staff – the Committee 'is responsible for recommending to NATO's political authorities those measures considered necessary for the common defence of the NATO area and for the implementation of decisions regarding [its] operations and missions'. The Military Committee appoints its own chairman for a three-year term. It usually meets each Thursday, to follow up on the NAC meeting the previous day.

Responsible to the Military Committee were, traditionally, the two NATO strategic commands for different parts of the 'North Atlantic area': Allied Command Europe (ACE) and Allied Command Atlantic (ACA or ACLANT), headed respectively by Supreme Allied Commanders Europe (SACEUR) and Atlantic (SACLANT). However, these have been superseded by two new commands organized on functional, rather than geographic, lines: Allied Command Operations (ACO), which is responsible for all of NATO's military operations, and Allied Command Transformation (ACT), which performs other, more horizontal, tasks, such as training and research. The two commands are still physically located at SHAPE in Casteau, near Mons, and at what is now called HQ SACT, in Norfolk, Virginia.

The post of Secretary General quickly emerged as a key post in the NATO structure. Usually a former senior minister in one of the member states, the Secretary General is appointed for a four-year term and not only chairs the organization's key bodies, but acts as its public face to the outside world. Among the more notable of the 12 Secretaries General to date have been **Paul-Henri Spaak** (during the years 1957–61), Joseph Luns (1971–84) and Javier Solana (1995–9), the last of whom moved on to become the EU's first **High Representative** for **Common Foreign and Security Policy** (CFSP). Willy Claes (1994–5) had to resign over a domestic Socialist party financing scandal in Belgium involving the purchase of military helicopters. The current Secretary General, appointed in August 2009, is Anders Fogh Rasmussen, a former prime minister of Denmark. For a reason that is not entirely evident, 10 of the 14 deputy secretaries-general since 1952 have been Italians.

Some 4,000 people are based at NATO headquarters in Brussels. About 1,200 officials, who are either recruited directly or seconded from national governments, work on a NATO International Staff, providing policy support and secretariat functions, whilst around 500 nationals are seconded to NATO's International Military Staff. In addition, some 2,000 diplomatic and military officials work on the staffs of the member states' permanent and military representatives to NATO, together with about 300 in the missions of partner countries. (In parallel, some 4,500 people are employed or stationed at SHAPE.) NATO's civil and military budgets are based on national contributions: the United States currently provides 22 per cent of total funding, Germany 16 per cent, and France and the United Kingdom 12 per cent each.

A measure of democratic supervision of the NATO system is provided by the **NATO Parliamentary Assembly**, which was founded in 1955 – in an initiative separate to the North Atlantic Treaty – and meets in plenary session twice a year. It is composed of 257 members from the **national parliaments** of NATO member states, including 36 US senators and congressmen. A ten-strong delegation from the **European Parliament** has observer status.

The 28 members of NATO spent a total of $994 billion on defence in 2011, over two-thirds of which ($690 billion) was represented by spending by the US Pentagon. The alliance had 3.5 million men and women serving in its armed services, compared with 5.7 million in 1990.

Historically, linkages between NATO and the European Union have been weak. In 1993, Robert Hunter, the then US ambassador to NATO, famously remarked that the two organizations were 'living in the same city, but on different planets'. The fact that not all EU member states are within NATO – only 21 states are currently members of both bodies – has complicated the development of a formal interface, although since the 1991 **Maastricht Treaty**, the development of the EU's defence role must 'respect the obligations' of those member states within NATO and be 'compatible with the common security and defence policy established within that framework' (Article 42(2) TEU). Despite fears that the emergence of the EU's **Common Security and Defence Policy** (CSDP) would lead to competition or duplication between the roles of the two structures, the opposite seems to have happened. The end of the Cold War has undermined classical notions of **neutrality**, with the CSDP offering 'post-neutral' states within the EU an opportunity to engage in an external military role through the **Petersberg tasks** (of humanitarian and rescue missions, peacekeeping, and crisis management, including peacemaking). In practice, NATO's ARRC works closely with the European Union, whilst the latter's Battlegroups (as well as the six-nation **Eurocorps**) are available for use in NATO, as well as EU, missions. The 'Berlin Plus' Framework Agreement of March 2003 formalized operational arrangements for NATO–EU cooperation in this field. EU forces took over from NATO in FYR Macedonia (in 2003) and Bosnia and Herzegovina (in 2004) – as specifically Berlin Plus exercises – whilst the two organizations currently work together in Kosovo and Afghanistan, as well as off the Horn of Africa.

At a political level, the High Representative for CFSP now has a standing invitation to attend all NATO ministerial meetings, whilst the NATO Secretary General is invited to take part in the EU **Foreign Affairs Council** (FAC) and meetings of defence ministers, as and when relevant issues are on the agenda. At an administrative level, the permanent representatives to the NAC and the EU **Political and Security Committee** (PSC) meet together regularly. For reasons of practical convenience, the military representatives of the 21 NATO states within the Union normally 'double hat' as members of both the **EU Military Committee** (EUMC) and the NATO Military Committee. Since 2005–6, the EU Military Staff has hosted a 'NATO Permanent Liaison Team' on its own premises and maintained an 'EU Cell' at SHAPE.

The issue of EU–NATO cooperation featured prominently in a review of the NATO 'Strategic Concept' undertaken by a group led by the former US Secretary of State, Madeleine Albright, in 2009–10. The NATO Summit in Lisbon in November 2010 – attended by the **President of the European Council**, the President of the European Commission and the **High Representative** – adopted an updated concept, based on the propositions that NATO should embrace a wider range of future partners (from Australia and New Zealand to China and India), deepen its role as a forum for the political and strategic (as well as military) aspects of **transatlantic relations**, address new security threats (including cyber-attacks and energy security issues) and promote the modernization of capabilities among its members.

The 2011 Libyan crisis revealed the extent to which NATO has changed since the fall of the Berlin Wall. The Swedes and four Arab countries participated in the seven-month operation, using the full NATO decision-making system – from which Germany, Poland and many other Alliance members chose to absent themselves. After brief involvement, even the United States too was happy to retreat from military engagement, leaving a limited number of European countries to handle a problem in their own region. Yet, as one NATO insider has put it, 'If America now expects Europe to sort out its backyard, there is a risk that European nations in turn may be less enthusiastic about engaging in global operations when called upon to do so by Washington.' Whether a 'regionalized' NATO would be stronger in meeting future challenges seems doubtful.

Further reading: Julian Lindley-French, *The North Atlantic Treaty Organization*, 2006.

Norway

A Danish territory from 1521, Norway was ceded to Sweden in 1814, after Denmark supported France in the Napoleonic wars. (By contrast, Denmark was allowed to retain **Iceland, Greenland and the Faroes**.) In 1905, Norway declared independence from Sweden and invited a Danish prince to become its king. After German occupation in the Second World War, Norway became a founder member of the **North Atlantic Treaty Organization** (NATO), the **Council of Europe**, and the **European Free Trade Association** (EFTA). In 1962 and again in 1967, Norway applied for membership of the European Community, at the same time as the United Kingdom. In response to the second application, a draft **accession** treaty was successfully negotiated. However, in September 1972, 53.6 per cent of Norwegian voters opposed entry in a **referendum**, partly because of tensions over the new **Common Fisheries Policy** (CFP). It was the first 'no' vote on Europe to be delivered by the public in either a member state of, or applicant country to, the Community.

In common with other EFTA states, Norway concluded a free trade agreement with the Community in 1973 and became a signatory to the agreement establishing a **European Economic Area** (EEA) in May 1992. Reflecting an increasingly high level of economic integration with western Europe (the Community being easily Norway's biggest trading partner), the Labour government of Gro Harlem Brundtland soon took the view – prompted by the fact that Austria, Sweden and Finland had already applied for membership –

that Norway should seek once again to join the Community. The application was forwarded to the **Council of Ministers** in November 1992, a generally favourable opinion was given by the **European Commission** in February 1993, and entry negotiations were completed in March the following year. With one of the largest merchant fleets in the world, Norway expressed particular interest in the development of an EU maritime policy.

Membership of the Union proved still to be controversial in Norway, especially in rural areas. Emotionally, many people remained attached to national independence, preferring regional cooperation (the country has always been active in the **Nordic Council**) to political integration on a continental scale. Church groups campaigned against membership, on the grounds that the breaking of the state monopoly on the sale of alcoholic drinks would disrupt society. Although the two main political parties – the Labour party and centre-right Høyre – both campaigned officially in favour of membership, the Norwegian people rejected it for a second time, by a margin of 52.5 per cent to 47.5 per cent, in a referendum held on 28 November 1994.

Following the accession of Austria, Sweden and Finland to the Union in January 1995, Norway was left as one of only three non-EU member states – along with **Iceland** and Liechtenstein – within the EEA, as well as the only mainland Scandinavian country outside the Union. As an EEA member, Norway is bound by EU legislation in the **single market** and several other policy fields, and makes a contribution towards the Union's annual **Budget**. It joined the **Schengen** Agreement in December 1996, along with Iceland, and now participates in several other EU bodies and programmes, notably Europol, Frontex, the European Defence Agency (EDA) and the Union's Battlegroups. Norway currently contributes € 340 million per year in funding and adopts over two-thirds of EU legislation – making it 'the most integrated outsider', with 'extensive Europeanization' of public policy, in the words of a recent government-sponsored report on relations with the Union (*Outside and Inside: Norway's Agreements with the EU*, 2012).

In recent years, the impressive economic success of Norway – with the increasing exploitation of oil and natural gas reserves, which began in the 1980s – has, if anything, lessened pressure on the country to join the Union. Norway is now the third largest oil exporter in the world and enjoys the second highest GDP per capita (after Luxembourg). It has consistently run substantial trade and budget surpluses. Since 1995, government revenues from oil have been saved in a sovereign wealth fund, which is now the second largest in the world (behind China and the United Arab Emirates), with assets worth over € 350 billion. Unlike Iceland, Norway was able to weather the international economic and financial crisis of 2008–9 with relative ease, with its economy still growing and its currency, the krona, rising in value as a safe haven.

O

Official Journal

The *Official Journal of the European Union*, normally referred to as the 'OJ', is published every working day in three distinct volumes or segments – the 'L', 'C' and 'S' series – and in all 23 official **languages** of the Union. It is produced by the Publications Office of the European Union in Luxembourg – a directorate-general of the **European Commission** – and is accessible on the Union's EUR-Lex website.

The L (legislation) series contains the texts of all **legal acts** adopted by the EU institutions. It is accompanied by a regularly-updated compendium, the *Directory of European Union Legislation in Force*, divided into 20 main subject areas, which currently lists over 25,000 measures, running to some 170,000 pages (in English). Publication of all legislative acts in the *Official Journal* is an 'essential procedural requirement' under Article 297 TFEU, which also provides for them to enter into force 'on the date specified in them or, in the absence thereof, on the twentieth day following their publication'. Care is taken to ensure that the date of publication of each issue of the *OJ* is, in fact, the date upon which the issue is actually available in all the official languages from the Publications Office.

The C (communications) series contains a wide range of other material. This includes the texts of legislative proposals from the **European Commission**, opinions thereon delivered by other institutions, **Inter-Institutional Agreements** (IIAs) and other declarations or statements of importance, lists of cases brought before the **European Court of Justice** (ECJ) and General Court (previously known as the Court of First Instance), key extracts from the latter's rulings, notices of major tenders opened by the institutions, details of competitions for the recruitment of civil servants, and information on the daily value of the **euro**. The minutes of sittings of the **European Parliament** are also published in the C series, with the verbatim report of proceedings in an annex.

Since 1978, there has also been an S (supplement) series, concerned mainly with invitations to tender for public works contracts, under EU rules for public purchasing. It covers contracts within the member states and the

European Economic Area (EEA), as well as projects eligible for aid from the **European Development Fund** (EDF).

The L and C series are available in printed and electronic forms (both online and on CD-ROM). A special CE version of the C series, available electronically, provides an extended range of documents. The S series is published only in electronic form, as Tenders Electronic Daily (TED). Online access to the *OJ* is free, whereas hard-copy and CD-ROM versions of the various series are available by subscription through the official publications offices of member-state governments (such as the Stationery Office in the United Kingdom).

'Old' and 'new' Europe

Although first used by Karl Marx in the *Communist Manifesto* (1848), the distinction between 'old' and 'new' Europe was popularized by the (then) US Defence Secretary, Donald Rumsfeld, in January 2003. At a press conference in Washington DC, he asserted that the prospect of a US-led invasion of Iraq was dividing European countries into two camps, with 'old' Europe opposing military action and 'new' Europe supporting it, in a context where the continent's 'centre of gravity' was 'shifting to the east'.

In reaction to a joint statement by French President Jacques Chirac and German Chancellor Gerhard Schröder that they would work together to oppose any US-led military action in Iraq, Rumsfeld said that, whilst these two countries had been a 'problem', 'vast numbers of other countries in Europe [are] not with France and Germany on this. They are with the United States . . . You are thinking of Europe as Germany and France. I don't. I think that is old Europe.' Rumsfeld's characterization prompted a lively reaction among politicians and the media in France and Germany, with French finance minister Francis Mer saying he was 'profoundly vexed' by such language.

Whichever countries qualified for 'old' or 'new' status, the dividing-line identified by Rumsfeld proved real. On 30 January, eight days after his remarks, the prime ministers of Britain, Spain, Italy, Portugal, Denmark, Poland and Hungary, together with Czech President Václav Havel, co-authored a letter to the *Wall Street Journal* expressing support for the US administration. Six days after France's veto of a second UN Security Council resolution on Iraq on 10 March 2003, President George Bush met with prime ministers **Tony Blair**, José María Aznar, Silvio Berlusconi and José Manuel Barroso in the Azores to assert an allied position in favour of invasion.

When the six-week invasion of Iraq began on 20 March, the European Union was evenly divided on the issue, with six of the (then) 15 EU member states backing the US action and six opposing it. The supporters were Denmark, Italy, the Netherlands, Portugal, Spain and the United Kingdom, all of which had centre-right governments at the time, except Britain. The six opponents were Austria, Belgium, France, Germany, Greece and Sweden, which had a more diverse range of parties in power. By contrast, seven of the eight central and eastern European countries that joined the EU in May 2004 supported the invasion (the exception being Slovenia), as did Bulgaria and Romania. All the countries supporting the action subsequently sent troops to Iraq to assist in reconstruction.

Ombudsman

The institution generally known as the Ombudsman is of Scandinavian origin (the first Ombudsman was appointed in Sweden in 1809). The Ombudsman acts as an intermediary between the citizen and the public authorities, local or national. A majority of European Union member states now have an Ombudsman, the role having been introduced in several countries in recent decades. The exact title of the post is subject to many variations: in the United Kingdom, the Ombudsman is known as the Parliamentary Commissioner for Administration; in France, simply as the *Médiateur*; in Greece, as the Citizen's Advocate; in Spain, as the Defender of the People. The precise duties of the Ombudsman also vary, but broadly speaking they are directed towards the investigation of complaints brought by individuals against the authorities. The Ombudsman is required to be both impartial and independent of government.

The idea that there might be a European Community Ombudsman was first put forward in the 1970s, but it was not until the 1992 **Maastricht Treaty** that the initiative was finally agreed. The treaty introduced a new provision (now Article 228 TFEU) requiring the **European Parliament** to appoint, now elect, an Ombudsman 'empowered to receive complaints from any citizen of the Union or any natural or legal person residing or having its registered office in a Member State concerning instances of maladministration in the activities of the Union institutions, bodies, offices or agencies', with the exception of the **European Court of Justice** (ECJ) acting in its judicial role. The use of the word 'maladministration' to describe the subject of the Ombudsman's investigations means that within the EU institutions the remit is similar to that of the Ombudsman in the United Kingdom. 'Maladministration' covers both incompetence and deliberate wrongdoing – whether it be undue delay, failure to follow agreed procedures, discrimination or inconsistency of treatment. The European Code of Good Administrative Behaviour, adopted by the EU institutions in September 2001, provides guidance for what is normally expected of officials.

The Ombudsman may make investigations either on his own initiative or on the basis of complaints brought to his attention, either directly or through a Member of the European Parliament (MEP), except in relation to matters that are or have been the subject of legal proceedings. In line with the pattern in most member states, the Ombudsman has no powers of sanction. The results of his investigations are forwarded to the European Parliament and the institution concerned. His five-year term of office coincides with that of the Parliament and he may be dismissed only by the ECJ, at the request of the Parliament. He is required to submit to the Parliament an annual report 'on the outcome of his inquiries'.

The Parliament decided to choose the Ombudsman by election every five years. Those applying need the declared support of a certain number of MEPs (currently 40) and are then screened by the petitions committee of the Parliament, which decides which candidates may go forward to a vote in plenary. There are up to three rounds of voting in plenary, with the top two candidates on the second ballot going through to the third. The first three elections for Ombudsman (1995, 1999 and 2003) were closely contested, with the left-of-centre candidate winning on each occasion. Since then the incumbent has been re-elected twice, once by a wide margin (2005) and once more narrowly (2010). Both holders of the post to date, Jacob Söderman (1995–2003) and Nikiforos Diamondouros (since 2003), have been former national Ombudsmen (for Finland and Greece respectively), although this is not a formal requirement. In office, they have promoted the development of a European Network of Ombudsmen to compare best practice and, on occasion, facilitate the transfer of cases between European, national and regional levels. The office of the Ombudsman, with a budget of € 9.3 million, is located in the premises of the Parliament in Strasbourg, where 63 staff are employed.

The Ombudsman has access to all files held by EU institutions except on 'duly substantiated grounds of secrecy'. Access to material 'originating in a Member State' and classified as secret is given only with the permission of that member state; access to non-secret material may be given if the relevant member state is so informed. Member states are laid under a general obligation to provide, through their **permanent representations**, any information that may help to clarify instances of maladministration by Union institutions or bodies, unless such information is secret. The Ombudsman and his staff are, in turn, laid under an obligation not to divulge any information secured in the performance of their duties.

Although the Ombudsman received 2,667 complaints in 2010 – almost twice the number submitted in 2000 – only 12 per cent (323) led to formal inquiries. In a large number of cases, the Ombudsman was able to transfer the case to his national homologue or another organization, or advises the complainant that there appeared to be no grounds for suspecting maladministration. Of the 326 cases investigated and closed in 2010, maladministration was found in 40 cases (12 per cent), with another 179 cases (55 per cent) settled on a friendly basis between the institution and the individual concerned. Of the 40 cases of maladministration, all but seven were closed 'with critical remarks', signalling that the institution or body concerned in effect refused to accept the Ombudsman's recommendation. A majority of the inquiries conducted (65 per cent) related to the **European Commission**, whilst 10 per cent involved the European Personnel Selection Office (EPSO), 9 per cent concerned the European Parliament and 6 per cent the **Council of Ministers**. The most common allegation of maladministration dealt with by the Ombudsman now relates to alleged lack of transparency by the institutions (over a third), whereas a decade ago, accusations of unfairness in competitions for staff vacancies or tendering for contracts predominated.

Opt-out

When a member state of the European Union is allowed not to participate in a policy provided for in the **Treaties**, it is said to have an 'opt-out'. At the moment, three member states – the United Kingdom, Denmark and Ireland – enjoy formal exemptions from certain EU policies in this way. An opt-out differs from a **derogation** in that the former is envisaged as being permanent, rather than temporary, and it needs to be included in a treaty text, normally through a **protocol**. A derogation can feature either in a treaty – usually for a **transitional period** following the **accession** of a new member state – or in a normal **legal act**, adopted by the institutions.

The United Kingdom and Denmark have de jure opt-outs from stage three of **Economic and Monetary Union** (EMU). As such, they do not have to adopt the **single currency** or the common monetary policy defined by the **European Central Bank** (ECB), and they are not bound by the **Stability and Growth Pact** (SGP). Both countries' opt-outs were provided for in protocols to the 1992 **Maastricht Treaty**. In addition, Sweden has acquired a de facto opt-out from stage-three membership, following rejection of entry in a **referendum** (in September 2003) and the government's persistent refusal to join the **Exchange-Rate Mechanism** (ERM).

The United Kingdom, Ireland and Denmark enjoy opt-outs from EU policy in **Justice and Home Affairs** (JHA). These arrangements originate in the '**communautization**', by the 1997 **Amsterdam Treaty**, of part of the intergovernmental **pillar** for JHA established by the Maastricht Treaty. In return for transferring policy on visas, asylum, immigration and judicial cooperation in civil matters, together with the **Schengen** *acquis*, into the Community pillar, the three countries were given the right to decline to participate in all policies in these fields. With the subsequent abolition, by the **Lisbon Treaty**, of the remnant of the JHA pillar – covering notably police and judicial cooperation in criminal matters – this right was recently extended to cover the rest of the JHA field. The UK and Ireland, which normally act together because they have maintained a 'common travel area' since 1923, have a right to 'opt-in', on a case-by-case basis, to most legislation adopted by the other member states in JHA. Indeed, through Lisbon, the UK has even acquired a retrospective right to opt out of any existing legislation by which it had previously been bound.

The Maastricht Treaty also gave the United Kingdom an opt-out from the **Social Chapter** (introduced by that treaty), meaning that in certain areas of employment and social policy the other member states could proceed to adopt legislation – some of it decided by **qualified majority voting** (QMV) in the **Council of Ministers** – without Britain either taking part in the process or being bound by the law which resulted. In 1997, the incoming Labour government of **Tony Blair** chose to end this opt-out: the Amsterdam Treaty transposed the relevant protocol into the main body of the treaty text (now included in parts of Articles 151–9 TFEU) and extended its coverage to include the UK.

More recently, in Protocol 30 to the Treaties, introduced by the Lisbon Treaty, the United Kingdom and Poland have secured certain 'legal clarifications' in relation to the impact in their countries of the EU **Charter of Fundamental Rights**, which the treaty makes legally binding. These safeguards fall some way short of a formal opt-out and their significance has yet to be tested in the courts. The Czech President, Václav Klaus, made it a condition of his signing the treaty in November 2009 that Protocol 30 be extended to cover the Czech Republic at the time of the next significant treaty revision.

The UK, Polish and Czech demands in relation to the Charter of Fundamental Rights form part of a wider pattern in recent years of member states seeking to secure additional 'assurances' or 'guarantees' that certain treaty provisions will not affect their constitutions, laws or national practices. Such commitments have usually been elicited after the **ratification** of a new EU treaty has been rejected in a national referendum, in the hope of making it possible to submit the text to the electorate for a second vote soon thereafter.

Denmark started this process, when the Maastricht Treaty was initially rejected in a referendum in June 1992. At the Edinburgh European Council in December that year, the EU heads of government extended several assurances in the form of a 'decision', taken in their collective names (rather than by an EU institution), the legal validity of which was questioned at the time. (Formally, they concluded an interpretative agreement in public international law, under Article 31 of the Vienna Convention on the Law of Treaties.) They agreed that the concept of **European citizenship**, introduced by the Maastricht Treaty, did 'not in any way take the place of national citizenship', and that the question of whether an individual possessed the nationality of a member state would 'be settled solely by reference to the national law' of the member state in question. Any legal uncertainty resulting from this assurance was resolved when the same wording was subsequently transposed into the Amsterdam Treaty (Protocol 22 to the

Treaties). Likewise, the heads of government confirmed that Denmark was under no obligation to join the **Western European Union** (WEU) and accepted that the country 'does not participate in the elaboration and the implementation of decisions and actions of the Union which have defence implications', although conversely it would 'not prevent the other Member States from further developing their cooperation in this area'. Following the demise of the WEU, this situation has now been carried forward to apply to Denmark's involvement in the EU's **Common Security and Defence Policy** (CSDP): for example, Denmark is the only member state not to participate in the **European Defence Agency** (EDA). On its election in September 2011, the government of Helle Thorning-Schmidt indicated its intention to hold a referendum to end Denmark's opt-outs in JHA and CSDP, but not EMU.

Ireland has also had recourse to assurances on two occasions, following the referenda which rejected the **Nice Treaty** in June 2001 and the Lisbon Treaty in June 2008. These assurances made it easier to hold repeat votes in October 2002 and Ocober 2009 respectively, each generating a 'yes' majority. On the first occasion, the Irish government sought and secured a non-binding declaration from other EU heads of government about the country's freedom to pursue its own security and defence policy within the European Union. The Seville European Council of June 2002 declared that the EU respected Ireland's 'tradition of military **neutrality**' and reiterated that nothing in the treaty would 'involve the establishment of a **European army**', 'impose any binding mutual defence commitments' or prevent any country taking 'its own sovereign decision, in accordance with its constitution and its laws' on whether to commit troops in any EU defence operation.

The assurances sought by Ireland over the Lisbon Treaty went substantially further than those of 2002. The European Council agreed in June 2009 that, once the Lisbon Treaty entered into force, it would adopt a decision, under Article 17(5) TEU, to ensure that 'the Commission shall continue to include one national of each Member State'. It also confirmed, by way of a decision of the heads of government – similar to the interpretative agreement concluded to meet Danish concerns in December 1992 – that 'nothing in the Treaty of Lisbon makes any change of any kind, for any Member State, to the extent or operation of the Union's **competences** in relation to taxation', that the treaty 'does not prejudice the security and defence policy of Member States, including Ireland's traditional policy of neutrality', and that the provisions of the Irish constitution in relation to the right to life, education and the family would not be affected by the Charter of Fundamental Rights becoming legally binding. The last three assurances, the European Council promised, will be formalized in EU law by inclusion in a protocol to be adopted in parallel to the next **accession** to the Union (in practice, that of **Croatia**).

Ordinary legislative procedure

See **co-decision procedure, qualified majority voting** (QMV).

Organization for Economic Cooperation and Development (OECD) / Organization for European Economic Cooperation (OEEC)

The Organization for Economic Cooperation and Development (OECD) is a Paris-based intergovernmental organization established to promote economic cooperation between industrialized states, to coordinate development assistance to the third world, and to provide a forum for the resolution of problems affecting international economic policy and world trade. The OECD was founded as the Organization for European Economic Cooperation (OEEC) in 1948, at the insistence of the United States, in order to oversee the coordinated implementation of the European Recovery Programme established under the **Marshall Plan** by its European recipients. Washington was determined that the European countries themselves should take a lead role in the reconstruction of their own continent. The OEEC was path-breaking in being the first pan-European body to be created after the Second World War, before either the **North Atlantic Treaty Organization** (NATO) or the **Council of Europe**. However, it now seems much less significant than it did at the time, because its mission, in the words of Leon Lindberg and Stuart Scheingold, was simply to 'rebuild', rather than 'transcend' the nation state – in contrast with the subsequent **European Communities** (*Europe's Would-Be Polity: Patterns of Change in the European Community*, 1970).

The founding members of the OEEC were Austria, Belgium, Denmark, France, Greece, Iceland, Ireland, Italy, Luxembourg, the Netherlands, Norway, Portugal, Sweden, Switzerland, Turkey, the United Kingdom, and the British, French and American zones of occupied Germany. The Federal Republic of Germany joined the OEEC in 1949, and the United States and Canada became associate members in 1950. Spain joined the OEEC in 1959. All important decisions were taken by a Council, representing the member states, which could act only by unanimity (abstentions not counted), with each country having one vote. However, Robert Marjolin, the French technocrat colleague of **Jean Monnet** who served as the first Secretary General of the OEEC (1948–54), directed the body towards a more ambitious role than this purely intergovernmental framework might have suggested.

A significant early achievement of the OEEC was the creation of a European Payments Union (EPU), which operated from 1950 to 1958. It allowed participating states to settle their bilateral trading accounts on a multilateral basis, using the **Bank for International Settlements** (BIS) as a clearing house, so reducing the transaction costs to trade. Credit was automatically extended by surplus countries to deficit countries within certain limits.

As Herbert Grubel has written, 'this automatic credit was equivalent to a pooling of international reserves because deficit countries did not have to employ reserves useful for financing trade with the rest of the world in settlement with Union partners' (*The International Monetary System*, 1977). To facilitate payments, the EPU developed the European Unit of Account (EUA), the forerunner of the **European Currency Unit** (ECU) and thus ultimately of the **euro**. Backed by OEEC-sponsored measures to liberalize import restrictions within Europe, the EPU facilitated a more than doubling of trade among OEEC countries in the years to 1958, when current account convertibility was restored among the participating states.

During the mid-1950s, the OEEC was the forum in which **the Six** began the discussions on creating a **common market** and **customs union** that led to the **Messina Conference** and the **Treaty of Rome**. In response to the prospect of the **European Economic Community** (EEC), the United Kingdom made a counter-proposal in February 1957, only a month before the signature of the EEC Treaty, that a **free trade area** (limited to manufactured goods) be established among the OEEC states, including the Six. In this way, the British government hoped to avoid exclusion from continental markets while retaining Commonwealth preference for agricultural products. Although this initiative did not stop the Six proceeding with their more ambitious supranational plans for the EEC, the OEEC agreed to appoint a committee, under the chairmanship of Reginald Maudling, then President of the Board of Trade in London, to examine the proposal (known as 'Plan G'). Initially, it looked as though the West German government of **Konrad Adenauer** might be willing to support the British concept in some form, but following the return to power in France of **Charles de Gaulle** in June 1958, the project quickly ran into the sand. The Six decided to accelerate the creation of the planned customs union, with its own external tariff, whilst the OEEC members outside the EEC considered the possibility of founding a rival organization among themselves instead. The legacy of the work of the Maudling Committee was the **European Free Trade Association** (EFTA), established in 1960, comprising seven countries – Austria, Denmark, Norway, Portugal, Sweden, Switzerland and the United Kingdom.

The new EEC–EFTA division effectively split the OEEC, occasioning wry remarks about Europe being 'at sixes and sevens'. As a result, the OEEC was refounded and renamed, with the United States and Canada as full members, under the OECD Convention signed in Paris in December 1960. Henceforth the body was to be open in principle to all Western market economies and its scope was widened to include relations with developing countries, although the body's intergovernmental character remained unchanged. Japan joined the OECD in 1964, Finland in 1969, Australia in 1971 and New Zealand in 1973.

During the economic crises of the 1970s, the OECD fostered the setting up of the International Energy Agency (IEA), which joined the existing Nuclear Energy Agency (both co-located with the OECD), as well as the **Group of Seven** (G7) leading industrialized economies. In response to the collapse of Communism, it was the OECD member states – meeting as the 'Group of 24' – that founded the **European Bank for Reconstruction and Development** (EBRD) in May 1990. The Czech Republic, Hungary, Poland, Slovakia, Mexico and South Korea joined the OECD between 1994 and 2000, bringing its total membership to 30 states. In May 2007, Estonia, Slovenia, Israel, Russia and Chile opened accession negotiations.

Today, the OECD remains an important force in the field of international economic cooperation. Its many reports on member countries' economic performance and major policy issues are authoritative and influential. It is a prime compiler of comparable economic data and, producing over 300 reports a year, the world's single largest economic publisher. It administers a series of technical cooperative ventures, notably the international export credits régime, and hosts the International Transport Forum (IFT), the successor to the European Conference of Ministers of Transport (ECMT). Above all, the OECD is an arena in which the sharing of best practice and mobilization of peer pressure can act as a powerful incentive to improve policy worldwide.

The OECD has a secretariat of some 2,500 officials, many of the more senior of whom are professional economists or civil servants on secondment from national governments. Operating in English and French, the secretariat is divided into 15 directorates, working out of the Château de la Muette and surrounding buildings in Paris. The organization has spawned over 220 committees and working groups focusing on issues of various kinds. The subject matter ranges from the very general, such as the OECD economic policy committee or global forum on governance, to the highly specific, such as its working group on the harmonization of regulatory oversight in biotechnology.

The OECD Council, like its OEEC predecessor, takes decisions that are supposed to be binding on member states. It can also make recommendations – which are much more numerous – and adopts a variety of declarations, understandings arrangements, principles and guidelines. The OECD can enter into agreements with non-member states and international organizations. However, unlike the European Union, the OECD has no supranational machinery for the enforcement of decisions or the resolution of disputes which might arise under them, nor do its workings create a body of law enjoying **primacy** over national law. From time to time, OECD conventions are adopted which may, if member states choose, be given treaty status in international law (for example, the 1999 OECD anti-bribery convention). The OECD also lacks a parliamentary body responsible for general supervision of its activities, although it does attempt to involve national parliaments in its work in an ad hoc way. Formally, the European Union enjoys only observer status within the OECD's decision-making bodies, although in practice it operates as if it were a member in most respects – in parallel to the individual member states – not least because the Union enjoys exclusive or shared **competence** in nearly all the policy areas covered by OECD activity.

Further reading: Robert Marjolin, *Architect of European Unity: Memoirs 1911–1986*, 1989; Richard Woodward, *The Organization for Economic Cooperation and Development*, 2009.

Organization for Security and Cooperation in Europe (OSCE)
Set up under the **Charter of Paris** of November 1990, the OSCE is an intergovernmental organization that undertakes a wide range of activities designed to promote democracy and human rights, defuse internal and cross-border conflicts, encourage security cooperation and fight international crime. In recent years, it has been especially active in the countries of the former **Yugoslavia** and of the Caucasus. The OSCE developed from an earlier, looser negotiating framework, the **Conference on Security and Cooperation in Europe** (CSCE), which first brought together the countries of the Atlantic Alliance and **Warsaw Pact** and was responsible for agreeing the 1975 **Helsinki Final Act**. Membership of the OSCE includes virtually every European country, as well as the central Asian republics once part of the Soviet Union, together with the United States and Canada. In total, it encompasses 56 states across the northern hemisphere, spanning a territory from Vancouver to Vladivostok.

Decision-making within the OSCE is the responsibility of a Ministerial Council (of foreign ministers), assisted by a Permanent Council which meets weekly at ambassador level, and both operate by unanimity. The post of 'chairman-in-office' of the Council rotates annually among member states. The need for unanimity among 56 countries complicates the process of finding agreement, a problem compounded by the absence of an officially-sanctioned 'core' grouping of key states akin to the Security Council within the **United Nations**. Although occasional **summits** of heads of government are held – most recently, after a decade-long gap, in Astana, Kazakhstan, in December 2010 – they are largely symbolic affairs. A parallel OSCE Forum for Security Cooperation deals with military and security issues, but it has been largely bypassed on major issues: for example, it played no role in the 'Meseberg initiative' for an EU–Russia security dialogue, launched by German Chancellor Angela Merkel and Russian President Dmitry Medvedev in June 2010. The OSCE has a secretariat of over 400 staff, based in Vienna, together with another 750 international and 2,400 local staff in the field, engaged in missions of various kinds in around 20 countries.

A number of OSCE institutions underline the shift that took place in Paris in 1990 from securing commitments in respect of human rights and democratic reform to trying to ensure that such commitments are honoured in practice. The OSCE structure includes a Parliamentary Assembly of 320 national parliamentarians – which met for the first time in Budapest in July 1992 and is serviced by its own secretariat in Copenhagen – and a Court of Conciliation and Arbitration, based in Geneva, which attempts to resolve disputes between signatories. The OSCE has a Representative on Freedom of the Media (based in Vienna), an Office for Democratic Institutions and Human Rights (ODIHR), formerly known as the Office for Free Elections (Warsaw), and a High Commissioner on National Minorities (The Hague). Election monitoring is one of the Organization's most high-profile activities.

The European Union is not a member of the OSCE, enjoying only observer status. However, the Paris Charter was signed by **Jacques Delors** as President of the **European Commission** and the position taken by the member states of the Union within the OSCE is now discussed collectively as part of the EU's **Common Foreign and Security Policy** (CFSP). Since the entry into force of the **Lisbon Treaty** in December 2009, the positions of the Union may be represented, at their respective levels, by the **President of the European Council** and the **High Representative** for CFSP, both of whom attended the Astana summit.

Further reading: David Galbreath, *The Organization for Security and Cooperation in Europe*, 2007.

Overseas countries and territories (OCTs)

The 21 overseas countries and territories of the European Union are the scattered remains, most of them very small islands, of the British, French and Dutch overseas possessions. When the **Treaty of Rome** was signed in March 1957, 18 additional French, Belgian, Dutch and Italian colonies were listed as OCTs, but these all obtained independence soon after and became **ACP states** and beneficiaries of the European Community's **development policy**.

Articles 198–204 TFEU set out the legal framework for the association of the OCTs with the Union, the purpose of which is 'to promote the economic and social development of the countries and territories and to establish close economic relations between them and the Union as a whole'. Since its departure from the Community in 1986, **Greenland** (although it remains part of Denmark) is now also counted among the OCTs.

The OCTs may be listed in four groups:

British OCTs in the Caribbean: Anguilla, Bermuda, the British Virgin Islands, the Cayman Islands, Montserrat, the Turks and Caicos Islands; in the south Atlantic: the Falkland Islands, Saint Helena and its dependencies, South Georgia and the South Sandwich Islands; in the Pacific: Pitcairn, the British Antarctic Territory and the British Indian Ocean Territory.

French OCTs in the Pacific: French Polynesia, New Caledonia and its dependencies, Wallis and Futuna Islands; French Southern and Antarctic Territories. French OCTs also include the 'territorial collectivities' of Mayotte off the coast of Madagascar, and St Pierre and Miquelon (Newfoundland). The French overseas departments (Réunion, Guadeloupe, Guiana and Martinique) are an integral part of France and so of the European Union. They benefit from various forms of special assistance under Article 349 TFEU, together with Madeira, the Azores, and the Canary Islands.

Dutch OCTs in the Caribbean: Aruba and the Netherlands Antilles.

Danish OCT: Greenland.

Not only are the OCTs extremely diverse in respect of geography, resources, climate, population, population density and prosperity, but the provisions governing their status in relation to the Union – and hence the applicability of **EU law** – also vary from one OCT to another, even among those historically associated with the same member state. In general terms, EU law is applicable only to member states' European territory, not to their OCTs. However, member states apply to their trade with the OCTs the same treatment as they apply to each other, and the OCTs apply to every member state the treatment applied to the state with which they have special relations. Moreover, since citizens of the Danish, Dutch and French OCTs (and of the Falkland Islands among British OCTs) are nationals of the parent country, they also enjoy **European citizenship**.

Underlying some of these legal and commercial issues is the broader question of whether or not the OCTs should enjoy a privileged relationship with the Union. At the very least, it would be illogical were their position to be less advantageous than that of ACP states, the great majority of which are former colonies. Accordingly, the Union takes care to ensure that the periodic renegotiations of its principal trade-and-aid instruments do not result in the OCTs being left behind, and as far as possible the OCTs' interests are taken into account in decisions on the **Common Commercial Policy** (CCP) and on the **European Development Fund** (EDF). In the negotiations which led to the ninth and tenth EDFs – the original and revised Cotonou Agreements – it was agreed that € 175 million and € 286 million respectively should be set aside for the OCTs during the 2000–07 and 2008–13 financing periods respectively. The OCTs are also eligible for loans from the **European Investment Bank** (EIB).

Own resources

Article 201 of the **Treaty of Rome** (now Article 311 TFEU) foresaw that, after an initial period in which the annual **Budget** of the **European Economic Community** (EEC) would be financed by direct contributions from the member states, a system of 'own resources' would be introduced, with revenues accruing to the Community automatically, as of right, without further national approval. (The **European Coal and Steel Community** (ECSC), founded in 1952, was already funded by a direct levy on industrial production in the two sectors concerned (under Articles 49–50 ECSC).) Financing through own resources, which was agreed in 1970 but only took full effect a decade later, sets the (now) European Union apart from all other international organizations and is an important symbol of its independence from the member states. Because of their political sensitivity, decisions in this field are taken in the **Council of Ministers** by **unanimity** and subject to ratification by all **national parliaments.** It is also an area in which the **European Parliament** enjoys only a right of **consultation**, by contrast with its much more extensive powers on the expenditure side of the Budget. These institutional arrangements remain in place under the **Lisbon Treaty**, although implementing measures on own resources now require the **consent** of the Parliament.

The Council of Ministers has taken a series of formal **decisions** defining the precise operation of the own resources system – notably in April 1970, May 1985, June 1988, October 1994, September 2000 and June 2007. Its 1970 and 1988 decisions established initially three, then four, main sources of income for the Community, now Union. The first source is the revenue from the **Common Customs Tariff** (CCT), levied by the member states on imports (other than agricultural products) from non-EU countries. The second is a mixture of agricultural duties, levied specifically on imports of agricultural products from non-EU countries, and sugar levies paid by sugar producers to finance export refunds for that product. The third source of EU income is a proportion of member states' revenues from **value-added tax** (VAT), levied at a common rate. The so-called 'fourth resource', introduced in 1988, is a contribution based on each member state's gross national income (GNI), again levied at a common percentage rate. The proportion of EU revenue represented by the first two sources – 'traditional own resources' (TOR) – as well as by VAT, has declined significantly over the last two decades: in 2011, the 'fourth resource' accounted for 74.7 per cent of income, and TOR and VAT for only 13.3 and 10.9 per cent respectively. (The respective amounts were € 94.5, € 16.8 and € 13.8 billion. Together with other income of € 1.4 billion, they added up to, and matched planned spending of, € 126.5 billion in that year.)

The origins of TOR lie in the Council's 1970 own resources decision, which officially assigned to the Community the revenues derived from two early common policies – the **customs union** and the **Common Agricultural Policy** (CAP). The CCT was introduced in 1968, whilst 'agricultural revenues' had been in place since 1962 (they were renamed 'agricultural duties' and 'sugar levies' in 1994). In recent years, the difference between duties imposed on agricultural and non-agricultural products has almost entirely disappeared, and in June 2007, the Council merged them into a single resource.

The 1970 decision also foresaw the intoduction of the third resource, which could consist of up to one per cent of national revenue from VAT, applied to a uniform or harmonized 'base' (a method of calculation which takes account of discrepancies in revenue caused by different VAT rates and coverage in each country). The Budget was to be financed from these three sources of revenue from January 1975, but delays in passing the measures required to establish a uniform VAT base (notably the sixth VAT directive) meant that the new system only became completely operational in 1980. By the Council decision of May 1985, the VAT limit (or 'call in' rate) was raised from 1.0 to 1.4 per cent, to boost Community income.

By 1987, however, it was clear that revenue was simply inadequate to finance both existing policies, the costs of which were overshooting, and new policies agreed at the time of the 1986 **Single European Act** (SEA). This problem was compounded by the gradual erosion of customs duties and agricultural levies, owing to tariff reductions and concessionary trade agreements. Accordingly, the **European Commission** submitted a set of proposals – known as the 'Delors I package' – that provided inter alia for the institution of the 'fourth' own resource, based initially on gross national product (GNP). This was seen as both fairer than other resources and better able to place the Budget on a secure, long-term footing. The Delors I proposals were agreed by the **European Council** in February 1988 and the new system of own resources was adopted by the Council four months later, coming into effect in January 1989.

For the first time, the Council's 1988 decision instituted an overall ceiling on the volume of own resources – and thus an upper limit on possible EU expenditure – expressed as a percentage of the Union's total GNP. This ceiling was initially set at 1.20 per cent of GNP, rising to 1.27 per cent in 1999. In June 2007, when GNI replaced GDP as the EU's preferred indicator, the 1.27 per cent figure was converted to 1.24 per cent of GNI, and was reduced to 1.23 per cent from 2010. Member states were initially allowed to retain 10 per cent of the revenue to cover the costs of collection of TOR; this was increased to 25 per cent in 2001. With respect to the VAT resource, it was specified that the uniform base for the assessment of VAT should not exceed 55 per cent of any member state's GNP. This was to safeguard the interest of poorer countries, since revenue from VAT, as a turnover tax, is not a wholly accurate indicator of relative national income. In 1994, the VAT base was limited to 50 per cent of any member state's GNP. In 2000, the call-in rate was reduced from 1.4 per cent of the uniform VAT base to 0.75 per cent (in 2002) and 0.5 per cent (in 2004), as part of a deliberate shift from the third to the fourth resource. The 2007 decision further reduced this rate to 0.3 per cent.

Special arrangements have been devised for certain net-contributor member states under the own resources system. Since the **Fontainebleau**

Agreement of June 1984, the United Kingdom has received an annual **abatement**. Since September 2000, Austria, Germany, the Netherlands and Sweden have each benefited from a 75 per cent reduction in their share of paying for the UK abatement. Since June 2007, these four countries have also been allowed to make lower rates of VAT contribution, and the Netherlands and Sweden to make lower rates of GNI contribution. In June 2011, the Commission proposed that the arrangements for the UK, Germany, the Netherlands and Sweden should be replaced from 2014 by annual lump-sum reductions to the GNI-based contributions paid by member states, totalling € 7.5 billion.

In addition to own resources, the Union has several other sources of revenue, which usually add up to between one and two per cent of total annual income. These include fines imposed on companies in breach of **competition policy** or other rules, contributions from non-EU countries towards certain EU programmes, a special Community tax levied on the remuneration of EU officials (see **Eurocrats**), interest on bank balances and late payments, reimbursement of unused grants, and balances carried forward from previous years.

It is not widely appreciated that the European Union receives certain tax revenues as of right. Although TOR are in effect a form of EU tax, they are sufficiently technical and discreet that they avoid arousing political controversy. Since they are not levied directly on the individual citizen, their existence is virtually unknown. Likewise, the fact that a share of national VAT receipts is directed to the Union is not indicated on bills given to customers.

Periodically, the suggestion is made that a completely new 'Union tax' should be introduced, for example, in the form of an indirect tax on carbon use (as already applies in some member states) or a 'Tobin tax' on financial transactions. In June 2011, in response to pressure from the European Parliament, the European Commission proposed that a Union-wide financial transactions tax (FTT) should feature as part of the own resources system, with a corresponding reduction of reliance on the GNI-based resource, to finance the post-2013 Multiannual Financial Framework (MFF). Two-thirds of the proceeds of the FTT – set at 0.1 per cent on trades of bonds and shares and 0.01 per cent on derivatives – would be directed to EU finances, raising about 23 per cent of total EU revenue by 2020. Whilst this initiative received the support of the French and German governments, it was quickly rejected by the United Kingdom and Luxembourg, with Finland, Sweden and the Czech Republic expressing serious reservations as well. The Commission also proposed that the existing VAT-based resource should be overhauled in the direction of becoming a genuine and more important Union tax. However, as both proposals will require unanimous endorsement in the Council, their adoption remains highly uncertain. See also **British Budget dispute**, **Fontainebleau Agreement**.

European Union revenue, 1971–2010: own resources by type as a percentage of total revenue

Type of own resource	1971	1975	1980	1985	1990	1995	2000	2005	2010
National contributions:	**70.7**	**37.7**	**46.4**	**62.4**	**63.0**	**71.1**	**78.4**	**81.0**	**80.9**
– VAT-based own resource			46.2	54.0	62.8	52.1	38.0	15.0	9.8
– GNP/GNI- based own resource					0.4	18.9	40.5	66.2	
– Direct funding by member states	70.7	37.7							
Traditional Own Resources:	**28.6**	**57.7**	**49.7**	**36.4**	**26.2**	**19.3**	**16.5**	**13.1**	**12.3**
– Agricultural duties	13.6	7.0	9.7	3.9	2.5	1.1	1.3	1.7	0.0
– Sugar levies	2.7	1.1	2.9	3.7	2.0	1.8	1.3	0.9	0.2
– Customs duties	12.3	49.5	37.1	28.8	24.6	18.5	15.7	15.0	16.2
– Retained for collection					-2.9	-2.1	-1.8	-4.4	-4.1
Total revenue (million EUA, ECU or euro)	**3,573**	**6,298**	**15,903**	**28,813**	**46,469**	**75,077**	**92,724**	**107,091**	**127,795**

Source: European Commission

P

Padoa-Schioppa Report

In April 1986, a group of eight independent experts, led by Italian central banker Tommaso Padoa-Schioppa (1940–2010), was asked by **Jacques Delors**, President of the **European Commission**, to prepare a report on the economic consequences of two key decisions taken the previous year: to admit Spain and Portugal to the European Community and to attempt to complete a **single market** by the end of 1992. Its 150-page report, entitled *Efficiency, Stability and Equity: A Strategy for the Evolution of the Economic System of the European Community*, was published in April 1987, and in book form, with a preface by Delors, later in the same year.

The Padoa-Schioppa Report reviewed progress in integrating the European economy, assessing inter alia the development of **free movement** (of goods, services, capital and people), **competition policy**, macro-economic coordination, and the operation of the **Common Agricultural Policy** (CAP) and the **structural funds**. It painted a very mixed picture, regarding both sectors and member states, and predicted that the 'opening of the market in the enlarged Community will have distributive effects that are likely to be stronger and more disruptive than those experienced in the Sixties, when trade integration proceeded among less heterogeneous countries and in a context of faster economic growth.'

The report strongly supported the development of mutual recognition of technical standards, rather than full **harmonization**, as the best way of progressing the single market. It favoured action to remove distortions of trade in the steel, textile and agricultural sectors. For the first time since the **MacDougall Report** a decade earlier, the redistributive effects and potential of the Community **Budget** were assessed. The report recommended an increase in the structural funds, with priority given to peripheral regions and to those dependent on declining industries, as well as a reform of the system of **contributions and receipts** among member states to take greater account of their relative prosperity. (The significant increase in EC **own resources** that was agreed in 1988 involved a 'fourth resource' based on relative gross national income (GNI), reflecting this approach.)

Padoa-Schioppa also used the report to press the case for **Economic and Monetary Union** (EMU), arguing that 'capital mobility and exchange-rate fixity together leave no room for independent monetary policies.' This foreshadowed his argument elsewhere that the Community was attempting to pursue an 'inconsistent quartet' of policy objectives, involving open trade, complete **free movement of capital**, fixed exchange rates and the retention of independent monetary authorities at national level. In a view which was to exercise considerable influence in EU political circles and appeared vindicated by the currency crises of 1992–3, he posited that these four objectives could 'be reconciled only by transforming the fourth element into monetary union, or by eroding the first three in varying degrees'.

Padoa-Schioppa subsequently served as an executive director of the new **European Central Bank** (ECB) from 1988 to 2005, and as Italian finance minister from 2006 to 2008, under prime minister Romano Prodi.

Pan-Europa

One of several 'macro-nationalisms' (such as Pan-Slavism or Pan-Africanism), Pan-Europa is an idea most closely associated with the name of Count **Richard Coudenhove-Kalergi** and is noteworthy as a forerunner of the idea of a United Europe (see '**European Union**') in the interwar years. Under Coudenhove-Kalergi's scheme, the best prospect for world peace lay in the emergence of very large units encompassing, in most cases, many independent states or nations. The idea of Pan-Europa was linked to the widely held belief that, if it were to succeed, the **League of Nations** would have to be underpinned by strong regional groupings. There were to be five of these: the British Empire, Pan-Europa, Pan-America, China and Japan, and the Soviet Union. Pan Europa was to be brought into being by a conference convened by Italy (which was on more or less friendly terms with all the great powers), Switzerland, Spain, the Netherlands or one of the Scandinavian countries (which had been neutral in the First World War). English would be the common language. This scheme clearly cut across several contemporary macro-nationalisms organized on straightforwardly ethnic lines (notably the Pan-Germanism developed under the Second Reich and taken to catastrophic extremes under the Third). Pan-Europa gave its name to Coudenhove-Kalergi's organization, the Pan-European Union, and was the title of his best-known book (1923).

The Pan-European Union still exists as an international discussion circle and pressure group, revived by Otto von Habsburg (1912–2011), son of the last Austro-Hungarian emperor, in 1972. Largely comprised of supporters or sympathizers of **Christian Democracy**, the Pan-European Union was underpinned by the formation of an all-party 'intergroup' of the same name in the European Parliament during the period of von Habsburg's membership of that institution. On 19 August 1989, it organized a 'Pan-European picnic' outside Sopron, Hungary – on the Austro-Hungarian border – during which the Iron Curtain was breached for the first time. In a critical moment in the collapse of Communism in central and eastern Europe, the Hungarian authorities allowed the barbed wire fence between the two countries to be cut open for a period of three hours. In addition to Hungarians, some 680 East Germans on holiday in the country chose to flee to the West that afternoon, and the opening continued in place thereafter.

Passerelle clause

Passerelle clauses are provisions in the **Treaties** that permit, in certain cases, the **European Council** (of EU heads of government) or the **Council of Ministers** to alter the decision-making procedures of the Union in a more integrationist direction – specifically, by replacing **unanimity** with **qualified majority voting** (QMV) in the Council and by introducing **co-decision** with the European Parliament – without the need to go through the normal process of treaty reform, including the convening of an **Intergovernmental Conference** (IGC). The triggering of a *passerelle* clause always itself requires unanimity and in many cases is subject to either approval or rejection by the **European Parliament** and/or **national parliaments**. There have been seven *passerelle* clauses in the Treaties to date, six of which currently apply, but only one of which (now abolished) has ever been used.

Since the introduction of the **Lisbon Treaty** in December 2009, there is now a general, 'horizontal' *passerelle* clause (Article 48(7) TEU), allowing the European Council to decide to move to QMV and co-decision in any policy areas or legislative procedures where they do not currently apply, other than 'decisions with military implications or those in the area of defence'. To activate this clause, the European Council needs to act by unanimity, after obtaining the **consent** of the European Parliament. More likely to object are national parliaments, any one of which has the power to block the decision, providing that it 'makes known its opposition within six months' of being notified by the European Council of the latter's intention to act.

The Lisbon Treaty also provides for four new, sector-specific *passerelle* clauses, which have slightly different arrangements from those foreseen in the general clause. These relate to the possible introduction of QMV for aspects of **Common Foreign and Security Policy** (CFSP) (Article 31(3) TEU) and the Multiannual Financial Framework (MFF) (Article 312 (2) TFEU), the possible use of both QMV and co-decision for family law with cross-border implications (Article 81(3) TFEU), and the possible introduction of either QMV or co-decision in policy fields already subject to

enhanced cooperation where they would not otherwise apply. In each case, although unanimity in the Council is required, the need for the consent of the European Parliament is dropped, and, other than for family law, national parliaments have no right of veto.

Before Lisbon, there were already three *passerelle* clauses of a similar kind, two of which survive. The latter relate to the fields of environment policy (Article 192(2) TFEU), introduced by the 1992 **Maastricht Treaty**, and **social and employment policy** (Article 153(2) TFEU), introduced by the 1997 **Amsterdam Treaty**. Once again, in each case, the Council can extend the scope of QMV and co-decision to additional aspects of those policies, acting by unanimity, but without the European Parliament needing to give its consent or national parliaments being able to block the move. The Amsterdam Treaty also allowed the Council to move to QMV and co-decision in most of those aspects of **Justice and Home Affairs** (JHA) which it simultaneously 'communautarized'. This last *passerelle* clause is the only one to have been invoked to date: in December 2004, the Council decided to move to QMV and co-decision for certain aspects of policy on visas, asylum and immigration, starting the following month. However, this clause was repealed by the Lisbon Treaty, which abolished the remaining intergovernmental **pillar** for JHA and brought the whole of policy in this field within the ambit of the '**Community method**'.

In the same spirit, even if they are not normally described as *passerelles*, there are several other treaty articles that allow the Council to extend the scope of the Union's **competence**, acting by unanimity and usually only with the consent of the European Parliament. **Article 352** TFEU, sometimes called the 'flexibility clause', has since 1958 (originally as Article 235 EEC) offered a **legal base** for the adoption of measures not explicitly sanctioned by the powers contained in specific treaty articles, but which might nonetheless be deemed desirable by the institutions and member states in pursuit of their broader objectives. More recently, three treaty articles were introduced by the Lisbon Treaty that allow the Council the possibility of broadening the Union's competence in judicial cooperation in criminal matters (Articles 82(2), 83(1) and 86(4) TFEU).

The *passerelle* clauses have always been controversial. Critics object in principle to it being possible for a transient coalition of states, admittedly acting unanimously, to permanently alter decision-making procedures without needing to secure a separate treaty change. This has been a particular concern to national parliamentarians, who would otherwise be called upon to enact legislation to ratify such treaty changes. The German Federal Constitutional Court, in its June 2009 ruling on the Lisbon Treaty (see **Karlsruhe judgements**), broadly endorsed this approach, specifying that use of the general *passerelle* clause and the specific *passerelle* on family law would need to be authorized by an act of the German parliament, and that use of any of the other five *passerelles* would require prior approval by an affirmative resolution of some kind. (The Court also stated that use of Article 352 TFEU and the three JHA articles referred to above would require acts of parliament.) Similarly, in October 2007, during the Lisbon ratification process, the British government conceded that any *passerelle* clause could only be used with the explicit approval of both Houses of Parliament. In June 2008, the House of Commons' foreign affairs committee recommended that such approval should be embodied in law, a position endorsed by the new Conservative–Liberal Democrat coalition government in May 2010. Legislation to this effect was enacted in July 2011.

Permanent representation

Each member state of the European Union maintains an embassy in Brussels, the purpose of which is to manage the country's dealings with the various institutions of the Union, most especially its direct involvement in the legislative process through the **Council of Ministers**. These bodies exercise considerable influence on decision-making, not only in Brussels but in national capitals. Their task is to represent and interpret the views of the member states within the Union institutions, while communicating back to national capitals accurate and complete information on developments in Brussels as the basis for domestic policy on European issues.

These embassies are officially known as permanent representations, and are often referred to as national representations. Only member states have representations to the Union; the embassies of other countries accredited to the Union are known as missions. The permanent representations to the Union are separate from the delegations to the **North Atlantic Treaty Organization** (NATO) or the bilateral embassies to Belgium also maintained by member states in Brussels. The UK permanent representation to the EU is often referred to by the acronym **UKREP**.

Each of the representations is headed by a permanent representative, or ambassador, who is normally a senior official of the country's foreign ministry. The ambassadors and their deputies meet together weekly in **COREPER**, the powerful Committee of Permanent Representatives that prepares all Council meetings and operates as a central brokerage-point between member states in the Union's legislative process. They sit beside ministers in meetings of the Council, and are second in importance only to heads of government and foreign ministers in their country's influence on European issues.

In addition to ambassadors and their deputies – and, since 2001, parallel member-state representatives to the Union's **Political and Security Committee** (PSC) – permanent representations are composed of administrative-grade officials, drawn from both the country's foreign ministry and (increasingly) domestic government departments. The overall complement of any representation depends on the size of the country, its physical proximity to Belgium and whether or not it is currently (or soon will be) occupying the rotating **presidency** of the Council. During the six-month presidency, all representations are larger than at other times. The biggest member states now have representations of between 100 and 200 staff, about two-thirds of whom come from domestic government departments.

While ambassadors and their deputies normally devote most of their time to meetings of COREPER and the full Council and to high-level communication with their foreign ministries, the day-to-day work of the national representations on most policy issues is conducted at the less senior level of counsellors and first secretaries. These mid-rank civil servants take part in all working groups of the Council, reporting the details of the discussions to their domestic departments, and then seek to convert the instructions they receive back from their national capitals into workable negotiating positions. Their task is to identify and hold the line on the issues that matter at home so that they can be resolved at a higher, more political level – namely in COREPER or the full Council – and to settle as many uncontroversial, technical points as possible.

There is a fundamental conflict of interest at the heart of the role that permanent representations play. On the one hand, they are guided by an operational imperative within the Council, as a Union institution, to discharge its business efficiently and to resolve differences. The culture of the Council, especially since the extension of **qualified majority voting** (QMV) by successive treaty changes, is biased towards splitting differences and doing deals. On the other hand, each permanent representation knows that its very *raison d'être* is to defend and advance the particular position of its own member state. Without the clear articulation of individual, often divergent, national interests, the Council would lose its essentially intergovernmental character and become little more than an adjunct to the **European Commission**. Member states guard that role for the Council, in what they perceive as both their individual and collective interests, and are keen to ensure that decisions, so far as reasonably possible, should not offend particular national sensitivities, especially their own. Individual representations that fail to acknowledge this necessity would quickly lose the confidence of their national capitals and so forfeit the ability to speak authoritatively on behalf of their ministers.

With the growing legislative power of the **European Parliament**, an increasing proportion of permanent representations' staff time is now being devoted to following, and trying to influence, activities in the Parliament's committees and plenary. Although each permanent representation has long had a small, dedicated unit for parliamentary liaison, effective influence depends on the officials covering specific policy issues being able to devote serious effort to intervening with Members of the European Parliament (MEPs), from both their own country and others. The heavy burden of day-to-day Council work and a lack of experience in lobbying, rather than in diplomatic bargaining between states, often make this difficult in practice.

Permanent Structured Cooperation in Defence (PSCD)

The **Lisbon Treaty** allows an inner core of EU member states to push ahead, on a voluntary basis, with a higher degree of military integration. Articles 42(6) and 46 TEU provide that, as part of the **Common Security and Defence Policy** (CSDP), a group of member states 'whose military capabilities fulfil higher criteria and which have made more binding commitments to one another' may, 'with a view to [undertaking] the most demanding missions', constitute 'permanent structured cooperation' in defence.

Some commentators have envisaged PSCD as a potential defence equivalent of the **eurozone** or **Schengen**, whilst others fear that it may presage a '**two-speed Europe**' in this field. Its origins lie in a Franco-German proposal to the **Convention on the Future of Europe** (in 2002–3), which drafted the aborted **European Constitution**. Paris and Berlin signalled their desire to put in place a mechanism that would allow a core group of countries to go 'further and faster' in the defence field, in much the same way as **enhanced cooperation**, introduced by the 1997 **Amsterdam Treaty**, already allowed for such moves in policies other than defence. This proposal was seen by several current or future member states – including the United Kingdom, various 'neutrals' and some enlargement states – as problematic. As Jolyon Howorth has written, they saw 'two main dangers': first, that an 'exclusivist' PSCD might be 'restricted to a small band of self-selected countries'; and second, that it 'would be seen as an alternative' to the **North Atlantic Treaty Organization** (NATO). In September 2003, a compromise was reached between the Union's three largest member states at a meeting in Berlin. The UK, in a 'desire to mend fences with its European allies' after the divisions of the Iraq War (see '**old' and 'new' Europe**), agreed to the principle of PSCD 'in exchange for explicit commitments . . . that the scheme would be as inclusive as possible and that it would work in harmony with NATO' (Jolyon Howorth, 'A European Union with Teeth?', in Nicolas Jabko and Craig Parsons (editors), *The State of the Union*, Volume 7, 2005). Access to PSCD and the content of the cooperation that resulted was to be defined primarily in terms of defence 'capacity', notably the ability to contribute or take part in the battlegroups being developed under the 1999 **Helsinki Headline Goal**.

Under the arrangements proposed in the Constitution, which are now included in the Lisbon Treaty, the member states participating in PSCD are required to demonstrate the ability to meet a high standard of defence capability – which is defined in detail in Article 1(b) of **Protocol** 10 of the treaty – and they must undertake to participate in multinational forces, the main European defence equipment programmes and the work of the European Defence Agency (EDA). They must also make a commitment to 'bring their defence apparatus into line with each other as far as possible', to cooperate in meeting any agreed levels of investment in defence equipment, and to 'take concrete measures' to enhance the general 'availability, interoperability, flexibility and deployability' of their forces. The EDA is tasked with assessing regularly the contributions made by member states to common capabilities.

PSCD, which has yet to be activated, may be established by the **Council of Ministers**, acting by **qualified majority voting** (QMV), on the basis of a request from a group of member states, however few, which claim to meet the criteria set out above. (There is currently no independent means of verifying their attainment of the criteria.) Once established, access to the arrangement will then be open to other member states, provided they meet the criteria, on the basis of a QMV vote by existing participants in the Council. Countries may be suspended, on a similar basis, if they cease to fulfil the criteria, and they may withdraw, for any reason, at any moment.

As Jean-Claude Piris has written (*The Lisbon Treaty: A Legal and Political Analysis*, 2010), this 'swift and simple procedure is quite remarkable when compared with the conditions for launching' enhanced cooperation in the rest of the **Common Foreign and Security Policy** (CFSP), allowed since the Amsterdam Treaty. The two systems differ in two key respects: first, there is no minimum number of member states that need to take part before PSCD can be activated, whereas nine are required (since the Lisbon Treaty) for enhanced cooperation in CFSP to be used; and second, the move to PSCD is sanctioned in the Council by QMV, whereas enhanced cooperation in CFSP (not more widely) requires **unanimity**. However, in both PSCD and enhanced cooperation in CFSP (although again not more widely), participating countries can, if they wish, deny access to new entrants.

In September 2011, the foreign ministers of five of the six largest EU member states – France, Germany, Italy, Poland and Spain – wrote a letter to Catherine Ashton, the Union's **High Representative** for CFSP, inviting her to 'examine all institutional and legal options available to member states, including Permanent Structured Cooperation, to develop critical CSDP capabilities'. It was the first time that the possible move to PSCD had been invoked. The five governments also advocated the creation of a joint civil–military 'planning and conduct' cell for the coordination of EU crisis management operations.

Petersberg tasks

At a meeting in Petersberg, near Bonn, on 19 June 1992, the member states of the **Western European Union** (WEU) issued a declaration that marked an important stage in the post-**Cold War** evolution of European security and defence. The Petersberg Declaration identified three broad categories of future WEU out-of-area activity that went beyond those arising from the general mutual defence commitment contained in the 1948 **Brussels Treaty**: humanitarian and rescue tasks, peacekeeping, and crisis management, including peacemaking. The Petersberg Declaration also looked forward to the enlargement of the WEU, and defined the rights and obligations of members, associate members and observers.

The three so-called 'Petersberg tasks', would, under the 1997 **Amsterdam Treaty**, be increasingly carried out by the WEU acting as the 'operational capability' of the European Union, under the latter's **Common Foreign and Security Policy** (CFSP). Amsterdam gave the Petersberg tasks treaty status and defined them as 'humanitarian and rescue tasks, peacekeeping tasks and tasks of combat forces in crisis management, including peacemaking' (then Article 17(2) TEU). It also foresaw the possibility that 'closer institutional relations' between the EU and WEU would lead to the integration of the WEU into the Union, 'should the Council so decide'. At the Cologne meeting of the **European Council** in June 1999, the heads of government declared that the EU would take over those WEU functions which were 'necessary' for it 'to fulfill its new responsibilities in the area of the Petersberg tasks'. The 2001 **Nice Treaty** consolidated this process by establishing an EU **Common Security and Defence Policy** (CSDP) as part of CFSP.

The **Lisbon Treaty**, which entered into force in December 2009, has widened the range of EU tasks in this field. CSDP missions 'outside the Union for peacekeeping, conflict prevention and strengthening international security in accordance with the principles of the **United Nations** Charter' may 'include joint disarmament operations, humanitarian and rescue tasks, military advice and assistance tasks, conflict prevention and peacekeeping tasks, [and] tasks of combat forces in crisis management, including peacemaking and post-conflict stabilization' (Article 43(1) TEU). These 'Petersberg plus' tasks, as they might be called, are thus at the heart of the EU's emerging defence policy.

Petitions

See **citizens' initiative and petitions.**

Pillars and 'pillared structure'

The expression 'pillars' springs from a metaphor commonly used to describe the structure of the European Union as it was established by the

1992 **Maastricht Treaty** (then Article 1 TEU). The Union was said to resemble the pediment of a temple and to rest upon three pillars: i) the existing **European Communities**, founded in 1952 and 1958; ii) the **Common Foreign and Security Policy** (CFSP), which grew out of **European Political Cooperation** (EPC) formalized by the 1986 **Single European Act** (SEA); and iii) new arrangements for cooperation in the field of **Justice and Home Affairs** (JHA). The first pillar was itself composed of three Communities: the **European Community**, formerly known as the **European Economic Community** (EEC), the **European Atomic Energy Community** (EAEC or Euratom), and the **European Coal and Steel Community** (ECSC), which expired in 2002.

The first (EC) pillar was and indeed remains unambiguously supranational in character, passing **legal acts** that are binding on the member states. The **European Commission** proposes draft legislation which, once enacted by the **Council of Ministers** and (in most cases) the **European Parliament**, is justiciable in the **European Court of Justice** (ECJ). By contrast, the second and third pillars operated on an essentially intergovernmental basis, with the Commission, Parliament and Court playing subordinate or marginal roles. Moreover, whereas, in the first pillar, the Council decides largely by **qualified majority voting** (QMV), in the second and third pillars, it did so mainly by **unanimity**. Action in the second and third pillars also resulted in agreements between governments which either did not take legal form or, where they did – as common strategies, joint actions or common positions in CFSP, and common positions or framework decisions in JHA – were outside the purview of the ECJ and, in some cases, required simultaneous ratification or enactment in national law.

The relatively clear-cut boundary between **supranationalism and intergovernmentalism** set out in the Maastricht design – heralded at the time as a considerable negotiating success for the British prime minister, John Major – was progressively eroded in the years that followed. Integrationists dissatisfied with the pillared structure attempted to extend the '**Community method**' to CFSP and JHA, so establishing a greater 'unicity' in the EU institutional system. The 1998 **Amsterdam Treaty** transferred asylum, visa and immigration policy from the third to the first pillars, with JHA coming to signify a policy area straddling both pillars. The shrunken second pillar was left to cover essentially criminal law enforcement and renamed 'police and judicial cooperation in criminal matters' (PJC). The involvement of the Commission and Parliament in the second and third pillars was also somewhat increased.

Opponents of the Union's pillared structure were to score a major victory when the **Convention on the Future of Europe** (2002–3) drafted a **European Constitution** that proposed to merge the second and third pillars into the first. The resulting mono-pillar European Union, organized on a supranational basis, would encompass all activity previously undertaken in the three separate pillars, whilst retaining specific safeguards to replicate certain intergovernmental features of CFSP (such as the non-involvement of the ECJ). With minor adjustments, this outcome was embodied in the **Lisbon Treaty**, and as a result, the pillared structure of the Union was abolished when the new treaty came into force in December 2009.

Further reading: Eileen Denza, *The Intergovernmental Pillars of the European Union*, 2002.

Pleven Plan

The Pleven Plan was the original proposal for a **European Defence Community** (EDC) among **the Six**. Put forward by French prime minister René Pleven in the National Assembly on 24 October 1950, the plan was controversial principally because it provided for a rearmed Germany to contribute units to a defence force under a unified supranational command. Although the initial concept was approved in the Assembly by 343 votes to 225, the resulting EDC Treaty was eventually rejected by the same body four years later, in August 1954. Pleven said that the inspiration for his proposal was the call by **Winston Churchill**, made in the Consultative Assembly of the **Council of Europe** in August 1950, for the creation of a **European army**.

Political groups

Members of the **European Parliament** (MEPs) sit neither in national delegations nor in alphabetical order, but in groups formed on the basis of party political affiliation. The existence of such groups dates back to the very beginnings of the European Communities, featuring in the Common Assembly of the **European Coal and Steel Community** (ECSC), and was confirmed at the inaugural meeting of the Parliament in March 1958. This seating practice still sets the Parliament apart from all other international assemblies (other than the **Benelux** Inter-parliamentary Council). Even though political groups have since evolved in other bodies – notably the Parliamentary Assembly of the **Council of Europe** (PACE), the EU **Committee of the Regions** and (until its recent demise) the Assembly of the **Western European Union** (WEU) – the members still sit physically either by national delegation or in alphabetical order.

For the formation of a political group, Rule 29 of the European Parliament's rules of procedure requires a minimum number of members: currently 25 MEPs from seven or more states. Each group is required to deposit its name, the signatures of its members and the names of its officers with the President of the Parliament. Until 1999, the larger the number of members, the fewer the nationalities needed to form a group (29 MEPs from one EU member state, as opposed to 14 MEPs from four member states, were able to do so). The principle now established is that, in order to ensure a genuinely transnational character for each group, its members should come from a significant proportion of the member states. The threshold was set at one fifth of states in July 2004 and then raised to one quarter five years later, to make it consistent with the parallel precondition for coalitions of national parties to register and receive funding as **European political parties**.

The Parliament's rules of procedure say very little about the role of the political groups, but this belies their real significance in shaping the politics and behaviour of the institution. As Richard Corbett, Francis Jacobs and Michael Shackleton have argued, the groups are 'of central importance in the work of the Parliament' (*The European Parliament*, 2011). They 'play the decisive role in choosing the President, Vice-Presidents and committee chairs. They set the parliamentary agenda, choose the **rapporteurs** and decide on the allocation of speaking time. They have their own staff, receive considerable funds from the Parliament and often influence the choice of Parliament's top officials.' Frequently it is deals struck between the political groups – none of which has ever individually commanded a majority of members on its own – which determine the Parliament's position on the issues before it. Members outside a political group are thus in effect denied the opportunity to occupy any significant jobs or exercise any meaningful power, except in the latter case when the balance of forces is evenly divided in a committee or plenary vote.

By mutual agreement and long-standing practice, each group receives a proportionate share of the various political posts in the Parliament, apportioned by a mathematical formula known as the d'Hondt system, which somewhat over-represents larger groups. (The posts in question are notably the 14 Vice-Presidencies of the Parliament, and the chairmanships and vice-chairmanships of its 22 committees and subcommittees and 40 interparliamentary delegations.) Moreover, within each committee, the d'Hondt system is normally used to apportion between groups the various rapporteurships for legislative proposals and own-initiative reports. Speaking time in plenary session debates is also largely assigned on the same basis.

Each political group is automatically entitled to its own funds from the Parliament's budget – for administrative and promotional, although not explicitly electoral, purposes – as well as to employ a secretariat composed of individuals recruited directly by the group but paid by the institution. (Such staff members are appointed as temporary agents or contract staff, rather than permanent officials, of the Parliament.) The funds available to the groups and the number of people in their secretariats are once again broadly proportionate to the respective size of each group, with the figures recalculated at the beginning of each year.

In 2011, the combined budgets of the seven political groups amounted to € 54.8 million – a figure set informally (since 1988) at three per cent of the Parliament's overall budget. Their secretariats totalled 1,004 individuals (made up of 409 policy advisers and 595 other staff), adding another € 122.2 million in staff salary costs, charged directly to the Parliament's personnel budget. (In 1982, by contrast, the groups had only 285 staff.) The groups characteristically divide their spending between administrative costs (less than a fifth), meetings and invitations to guests (about a third) and promotional material, advertising and the internet (up to a half). They may, and usually do, carry over around a quarter of their allotted budget to the following year. Other direct and indirect costs of the groups in 2011 – charged directly to the Parliament's budget and covering back-office support of various kinds – amounted to another € 77.5 million. Cumulatively, funding on this scale – a total of € 254.8 million, representing some 13 per cent of the Parliament's budget – renders the political groups among the most generously resourced political organizations in the democratic world, alongside the party appointees in the US Congress – where some 2,500 individuals work either for the majority and minority staffs on committees or for the party leaderships in the two houses.

The various political and financial advantages enjoyed by political groups in the Parliament explain why, in a body of 736 members, in which 170 national political parties are currently represented, only a very few MEPs sit as genuine independents. However, even these *non-inscrits* (or non-attached members) have their own budget, secretariat and share of speaking time, although the first two allocations are less generous than for a comparably-sized political group.

The power structure within the political groups, especially the larger ones, tends to be fairly decentralized, with relatively weak leaderships. Although the chairmen or chairwomen of the groups are elected by their colleagues, their power of patronage – and so, ultimately, their ability to enforce discipline – is usually limited. The assignment of jobs is at best shared with the heads of the national delegations of which the group is composed, and in some cases the latter have established effective control. Questions of patronage are complicated by the absence of a coherent career structure within the Parliament, by the need to take nationality as well as ability into account, and by the operation of the d'Hondt system of proportionality in the allocation of spoils. The leaders of groups do not normally control who is chosen as the chairmen of the Parliament's committees or even the group spokesmen ('coordinators') on those committees. (In the larger groups, the former are selected by agreement among national delegation leaders and the latter by the individual members of the committees, themselves chosen by the same national delegation leaders.) The most important posts in the Parliament, including those of group leaders, usually go to members from the largest delegations in each of the political groups. The German MEPs are especially well placed to secure key positions: not only do they constitute the largest single national delegation in the Parliament (with 99 members), but (at present) they represent the largest individual contingents in four of the seven political groups.

The many constraints on group leaderships may help explain why relatively few major politicians have aspired to chair their political groups, and why occupying such posts has so far rarely proved a springboard to major office in other European institutions or at national level. Since direct elections were introduced in 1979, for example, only one group leader has so far been appointed as a European Commissioner: Martin Bangemann, who led the Liberal group in 1979–84. His better known successor, the former French President **Valéry Giscard d'Estaing** (Liberal chairman in 1989–91), described the same group as 'quite impossible to lead'. Hans-Gert Pöttering, the long-serving chairman of the centre-right EPP Group (1999–2007) who became President of the European Parliament (2007–9), later joked that 'a special place in purgatory' had been reserved for group leaders.

Over the years, the size and composition of the various political groups have fluctuated greatly, depending on the outcome of **European elections** and shifting alignments between national parties. Groups have been formed only to disappear, or to reappear under a different name, or to survive with a significant change of membership. All current groups have changed their names at least once: the Liberals, for example, have been successively the Liberal Group (1953–76), the Liberal and Democratic Group (1976–85), the Liberal Democratic and Reformist Group (1985–94), the Group of the European Liberal, Democratic and Reform Party (ELDR) (1994–2004), and now the Group of the Alliance of Liberals and Democrats for Europe (ALDE).

The long-run development of the political groups has been marked first by diversification and fragmentation, and then, more recently, by a measure of consolidation. In the ECSC Common Assembly (from 1953 to 1958), only three 'political families' in continental Europe – Socialists, Christian Democrats and Liberals – were represented as political groups, with the Communists either excluded or refusing to sit. The period of the nominated Parliament of **the Six** (1958–72) saw the emergence of a Gaullist group (European Democratic Union) composed exclusively of French MEPs who left the Liberals in 1965 (when the rules were changed to allow mono-national groups). With the first enlargement in 1973, an Anglo-Danish European Conservative Group (ECG) and a Franco-Italian Communist group were formed, bringing the total number of political groups to six, in a Parliament of 198 members. The Gaullists rebranded themselves as the Group of European Progressive Democrats, and in 1979, at the time of the first direct elections, the Christian Democrats were renamed the Group of the European People's Party (EPP Group), whilst the Conservatives became the European Democratic Group (EDG).

Although the more than doubling in the number of MEPs in 1979 (to 410) offered an opportunity to increase substantially the threshold necessary to form a group (originally 17 members, but reduced in 1965 to 14), a vigorous rearguard action by MEPs from smaller political parties prevented this from happening. The number of groups increased, as new parties from left and right secured election for the first time. A 'Technical Coordination Group' was formed in 1979 by left-wing independents who would otherwise have needed to sit as *non-inscrits*: this evolved into the Rainbow Group, comprised largely of Greens and regionalists, five years later. A new European Right Group, the nucleus of which was the French *Front national*, emerged in 1984. The Communists abandoned the struggle to keep their pro-Moscow and **Eurocommunist** wings together and split into two groups in 1989, known respectively (and ironically) as the Group of the United European Left and the Left Unity Group. The Rainbow Group also lost its Greens, who established themselves as a separate group. As a result of these complex manoeuvres, by July 1989, there were ten political groups in the Parliament, whereas before direct elections, in early 1979, there had been six.

This striking pattern of fragmentation gradually reversed during the 1990s. In May 1992, the European Democratic Group of Conservative MEPs joined the EPP Group as allied members (with the name of the latter being adjusted to EPP–ED Group in July 1999 for the decade until they left). In parallel, the EPP began to work with the Socialist Group – the latter renamed Group of the Party of European Socialists (PES) in 1993 – to force through rule changes that would make it more difficult to form small groups. In July 1994, the European Right Group ceased to exist, falling below the new, more stringent threshold. The Group of the United European Left collapsed, after most of its Italian Communist members left to join the Socialists: the Left Unity Group survived and renamed itself the (with a slight difference in the order of the words) the Group of the European United Left.

Although two new groups sprang up in July 1994 – the Eurosceptic Europe of Nations Group (led by Jimmy Goldsmith) and the Forza Europa Group, comprised largely of members from Silvio Berlusconi's new *Forza Italia* party – neither found it easy to survive. Forza Europa quickly sought to join another group and, after a period with the Gaullists, its members eventually entered the EPP Group in June 1998 – against resistance from some Christian Democrat true believers who opposed the strategy of widening the EPP into a 'catch all' coalition of the centre-right being pioneered by Wilfried Martens, as president of the EPP party and leader of the EPP Group, and Klaus Welle, successively secretary general of both party and group. In the face of these changes, the Europe of Nations Group proved unable to hold together. Its moderates merged with the remnant of the Gaullist group – which had been successively renamed Group of the European Democratic Alliance (EDA) and the Union for Europe Group – when the latter's French members left to join the EPP Group in July 1999, so creating the Union for a Europe of Nations (UEN) Group. The deepest Eurosceptics from the old Europe of Nations Group managed to form a separate Europe of Democracies and Diversities (EDD) Group, thanks to the entry to the Parliament of the UK Independence Party. Since then, the Parliament has had a moderately Eurosceptic group (starting with the UEN) and a hard-line Eurosceptic group (starting with the EDD) to the right of the EPP in the hemicycle. To complete the picture, on the left, the Green and Rainbow groups – the latter now known as the Group of the European Radical Alliance (ERA) – decided to remerge, forming the Group of the Greens/European Free Alliance, a name which persists to this day. As a result of all these changes, there were only seven political groups in July 1999, rather than ten a decade before.

The process of growing consolidation was confirmed when some *non-inscrit* members from the Italian Radicals and the *Front national* – sharing few obvious 'political affinities' of the kind required by the Parliament's rules – unsuccessfully sought to create a new technical group in 1999. The attempt was rejected by a majority of the Parliament, in an act whose legality was later upheld, under challenge, by the Court of First Instance (now known as the General Court) in October 2001.

Despite the enlargement of the Union to include 12 new member states in 2004–7 – and with it the arrival of some 60 new national parties in the European Parliament – the political group configuration established in 1999 has persisted, with only modest changes, since then. All seven political groups that existed in July 1999 have survived, although with some changes of name and composition. The EDD Group became first the Independence and Democracy (ID) Group and later the Europe of Freedom and Democracy (EFD) Group. When, in July 2009, the British Conservative and Czech ODS MEPs left the EPP Group (as it once again became), they took over and renamed the UEN Group as the Group of European Conservatives and Reformists (ECR). The Irish secretary general of the UEN Group even continued in post, although his own national political party, Fianna Fáil, took the opportunity to leave the UEN to join the Liberal ALDE Group. The PES Group was restyled as the Group of the Progressive Alliance of Socialists and Democrats (S&D Group), in response to a demand from its Italian members.

In 2007, various parties of the far right, otherwise sitting as *non-inscrits*, briefly succeeded in reconstituting the old European Right Group (of 1984–94), under the new title of the Group of Identity, Tradition and Sovereignty

(ITS). However, this combination collapsed after only six months, when its Italian and Romanian members fell out over immigration policy.

Looking back over the more than three decades since the first direct elections to the Parliament, certain trends are clear. The first is the gradual accretion of the two largest groups – the centre-right EPP Group and Socialist group (under its different names) – at the expense of most of the smaller groups. The share of members in the 'big two' groups has risen from half in 1979 to over 60 per cent today, having peaked at almost two-thirds (before the Conservatives separated from the EPP). Among the smaller groups, only the Liberals in the middle have found it easy to survive and prosper, rising from 8.8 per cent 30 years ago (when it was only the fifth largest group) to 11.54 per cent today. The three biggest of the seven groups in the Parliament have consistently represented over 70 per cent of the MEPs since 1999.

The 'bipolarization' of the Parliament was greatly promoted by the merger during the 1990s of most of the mainstream centre-right into a single group, mirroring the longer-standing homogeneity of the Socialists. The largest centre-right parties from the five biggest countries sat in three different groups until 1998; they all sat in the EPP–ED Group from 1999 to 2009, and four of the five are still in the EPP Group today. Encouraging a 'tripolarization' of the Parliament was the adoption of proportional representation in the United Kingdom. Until then, the Liberals were significantly under-represented in the Parliament, and the overall balance between left and right was seriously affected by the use of the simple majority, first-past-the-post electoral system in Britain. Under this system, the British Liberal Democrats – the largest such party in Europe – failed to win any seats in European elections until 1994, while the spectacular swings to which the system was prone resulted in the number of British Conservative MEPs dropping from 60 to 18, and Labour MEPs increasing from 17 to 62, in the 15 years from 1979 to 1994.

The consolidation of the group system has coincided with the growing power of the European Parliament as an institution. Some commentators believe that these two trends are linked. Most of the powers granted to the Parliament since 1987, notably under the **co-decision** and **consent procedures**, require it to act by an absolute majority of its total membership, rather than simply a majority of those voting. Whilst there was speculation in the late 1990s that a stronger pattern of left–right confrontation was emerging in the Parliament, the incentive for the two largest groups to cooperate to secure absolute majorities, as well as the marked reluctance of the Liberals to enter any consistent alliance with either of the principal groups to their left or right, appears to have held this dynamic in check.

Collusion between the main political groups, although not always publicly evident, is particularly important in underpinning the Parliament's day-to-day operations. Through the regular, closed meetings of the Conference of

Presidents, group leaders act as de facto business managers, performing the function of the 'usual channels' in a Westminster-type system. If the two largest groups are able to agree, they can dominate every aspect of the institution's workings, from setting its agenda of business in plenary to changing its internal structures and rules. Indeed the first draft of the Parliament's plenary agendas, ostensibly proposed by the monthly meeting of committee chairmen, is often the product of bargaining behind the scenes between the EPP and S&D Groups. Equally, deals between the two groups often determine senior staff appointments: the Parliament's last three Secretaries General have served in similar roles in political groups at an earlier stage in their careers.

Political Groups in the European Parliament
At present, the 754-strong European Parliament has seven political groups. In diminishing order of size, the composition, budget and staff of these groups are as follows (February 2012):

EPP Group: Group of the European People's Party (Christian Democrats).
271 MEPs from 41 Christian Democratic and other centre-right and centre parties from 26 member states, representing 35.9 per cent of the Parliament. They include, in diminishing order of size, the Christian Democratic Union (CDU) and Christian Social Union (CSU) of Germany (34 and 8 MEPs respectively), *Forza Italia* and other Italian parties (29 and 6), the French UMP (29), Polish Civic Platform and PSL (26 and 3) and Spanish *Partido Popular* (25). Budget for 2011: € 20.4 million. Staff: 139 policy advisers; 202 others.

S&D Group: Group of the Progressive Alliance of Socialists and Democrats.
190 MEPs from 31 Socialist, Social Democratic and Labour parties in all 27 member states, representing 25.2 per cent of the Parliament. They include the German SPD (23), Spanish PSOE (21), Italian Democrats (21), French PS (14) and British Labour party (13). Budget for 2011: € 14.4 million. Staff: 101 policy advisers; 143 others.

ALDE Group: Group of the Alliance of Liberals and Democrats for Europe.
85 MEPs from 28 Liberal and centrist parties in 20 member states, representing 11.3 per cent of the Parliament. They include the German FDP (12), British Liberal Democrats (12), Italian *Lista Di Pietro* (7), French *Mouvement démocrate* (6) and Dutch D66 and VVD (6). Budget for 2011: € 6.4 million. Staff: 50 policy advisers; 71 others.

Green Group: Group of the Greens/European Free Alliance.
58 MEPs from 13 ecological and six regionalist parties in 14 member states, representing 7.7 per cent of the Parliament. They include the *Europe écologie* from France (15), *Die Grüne* from Germany (14) and three parties from the United Kingdom: the Greens (2), the Scottish National Party (SNP) (2) and Plaid Cymru (1). Budget for 2011: € 4.0 million. Staff: 35 policy advisers; 48 others.

ECR Group: Group of European Conservatives and Reformists.
53 MEPs from ten parties in nine member states, representing 7.0 per cent of the Parliament. They include the British Conservatives and Official Ulster Unionists (25 and 1), Polish Law and Justice (11) and Czech ODS (9). Budget for 2011: € 3.7 million. Staff: 34 policy advisers; 47 others.

GUE/NGL Group: Confederal Group of the European United Left/Nordic Green Left.
34 left-wing MEPs from 16 parties in 13 member states, representing 4.5 per cent of the Parliament. They include the German *Die Linke* (8), left-wing parties from France and Portugal (5 each), the Czech KSCM (4) and Sinn Féin (which has two Members, one each from Ireland and Northern Ireland). Budget for 2011: € 2.6 million. Staff: 24 policy advisers; 35 others.

EFD Group: Europe of Freedom and Democracy Group.
33 MEPs from nine parties in eight member states, representing 4.4 per cent of the Parliament. They include the UK Independence Party (13) and the Italian Northern League (9). Budget for 2011: € 2.2 million. Staff: 24 policy advisers; 32 others.

In addition, 30 predominantly right-wing MEPs sit individually as *non-inscrits* (non-attached or independent members), without the benefits of membership of a political group. Representing 4.0 per cent of the Parliament, they include members of the Austrian Freedom Party, Belgian *Vlaams Belang*, French *Front national*, Hungarian Jobbik, the British National Party and Northern Irish Democratic Unionist Party (DUP). The budget for the *non-inscrits* in 2011: € 1.2 million, based on an allocation of approximately € 45,000 per member. Staff: three policy advisers; 17 others.

Political and Security Committee (PSC)

The Political and Security Committee reports to the EU **Council of Ministers** on matters relating to the Union's **Common Foreign and Security Policy** (CFSP), including its **Common Security and Defence Policy** (CSDP). Composed of national representatives of ambassadorial rank, the PSC usually meets twice weekly in Brussels and has, in practice, largely displaced **COREPER**, the Committee of Permanent Representatives, as the key preparatory body for meetings of the **Foreign Affairs Council** (FAC) – even if it must work 'without prejudice' to COREPER's formal role in preparing meetings of the Council.

The PSC, which is often referred to by its French acronym 'COPS', derives from an earlier 'Political Committee', which brought together 'political directors' from national capitals for monthly meetings under **European Political Cooperation** (EPC). The 1992 **Maastricht Treaty**, which replaced EPC with CFSP, formalized and enhanced the role of the Political Committee, so that it would 'monitor the international situation', 'contribute to the definition of policies' and scrutinize 'the implementation of agreed policies'. Although the Political Committee was renamed the PSC at the Helsinki European Council in December 1999, these original functions were maintained (as they are today, under Article 38 TEU). The organizational aspects of the PSC's work were codified in a Council decision in January 2001, whilst the **Nice Treaty**, soon thereafter, broadened the committee's formal remit to include exercising, 'under the responsibility of the Council, political control and strategic direction of crisis management operations' – which includes EU military operations – and taking decisions, on the Council's behalf, when authorized to do so, in this field. In effect, the PSC acts as an intermediary between the **EU Military Committee** (which reports to the PSC) and the FAC (to which the PSC reports), in the management of military operations by the Union.

The PSC was chaired by the rotating **presidency** of the Council until the **Lisbon Treaty** entered into force in December 2009. The **High Representative** for CFSP, currently Catherine Ashton, chooses the official who chairs the committee, as her 'representative', placing it to a significant degree under her control. Conscious of the political meaning of this power, the FAC has insisted, in a decision of December 2009, that the High Representative must 'ensure that the person he or she intends to appoint . . . will enjoy the confidence of the Member States'. The first PSC chairman under the new system, Olof Skoog, was in effect elected by the members of the PSC before being appointed by the High Representative in November 2010. Mr Skoog, previously Swedish representative to the PSC, became an official of the **European External Action Service** (EEAS) on his appointment. The High Representative may herself chair the PSC at any time and is expected to do so in a major military crisis. However, she cannot act without the agreement of the PSC specifically on military crisis management issues.

Positive and negative integration

Writing in the Royal Institute of International Relations' journal, *The World Today*, in January 1968, John Pinder drew a distinction between what he called 'positive' and 'negative' integration in Europe. Negative integration involved the removal of restrictions or barriers to activity across Europe, in effect creating an open space in which the **free movement** of goods, services, capital and people could be achieved. Positive integration involved the adoption of active policies to harmonize national arrangements and/or replace them with common European ones, sometimes supported by sufficient spending at Community level. The creation of a **customs union** and **common market** were examples of negative integration, whilst the development of the **Common Agricultural Policy** (CAP) and **regional policy** were instances of positive integration. However, both negative and positive integration depended on binding supranational law.

The belief that negative integration would lead over time to positive integration has been a key assumption of those believing in the 'spillover' theory of integration, even before the distinction was formally drawn by Pinder (see **functionalism and neo-functionalism**). The achievement of one European policy was expected to generate support for complementary policies that would further deepen interdependence. For the first 30 years of the Community's development, such spillover effects were relatively limited. In the 1990s, however, the logic of completing the **single market** encouraged greater regulation of consumer, environmental and social standards at European level, and built critical political momentum for the creation of a single currency and common monetary policy through **Economic and Monetary Union** (EMU). It did not, by contrast, significantly increase support for greater **tax harmonization** or higher levels of public expenditure at the European Union level.

The juxtaposition of 'positive' and 'negative' political phenomena had been made fashionable by the Oxford philosopher, Isaiah Berlin, in his essay, 'Two Concepts of Liberty', in 1958. Pinder's analysis cleverly drew on this distinction a decade later to add conceptual depth to discussion of European integration and identify possible pathways for the future evolution of the European Community.

'Precursors' of European integration

The idea of '**European Union**' may be traced back through several centuries. Of the most frequently cited proposals, the first was motivated by the need to offer more effective resistance to the Turks. The other proposals were prompted by the desirability of avoiding war and, to a lesser extent, of promoting commerce.

In 1463, Antoine Marini, a Frenchman in the service of George, King of Bohemia, drew up a *Traité d' alliance et confédération entre le Roy Louis* XI, *Georges Roy de Bohême et la Seigneurie de Venise, pour résister au Turc.* This alliance was to be overseen by an assembly voting by simple majority (meeting for the first five years in Basle, Switzerland, then in a French city, then in an Italian one), and a court of justice for the settlement of disputes. It would be equipped with its own army. Its budget would be drawn largely from the dues paid to the Church. For this and for other reasons, the plan met with strong opposition from the Pope and was not adopted.

More fully worked out and more influential was the 'Grand Design' of the Duc de Sully (1560–1641), who in his *Mémoires* (1638 and 1662) attributed it to Henri IV. Under this proposal, developed in 1600–7, the eleven monarchies (five elective, six hereditary) and four republics which made up Europe from the Atlantic to the Balkans and the border with Russia, would come together in a *Conseil de l'Europe* composed of six provincial councils (in Danzig, Nuremberg, Vienna, Bologna, Constance, and one other city), and a 40-member *Conseil général* meeting in a different city every year. The larger states would send four representatives; the smaller, two. The *Conseil général* would be responsible principally for the peaceful settlement of border and religious disputes, but would also have a role in promoting trade, notably through the removal of customs barriers. In his speech to the Congress of Europe in May 1948, **Winston Churchill** declared that, 'After this long passage of time, we are all the servants of the Grand Design.'

A little after the Grand Design, the Moravian scholar, Amos Comenius (1592–1670), proposed in his *Panegersia* (1645, published 1666) a transnational peace plan based on mergers between national bodies. Learned societies would amalgamate to form a 'Council of Light', ecclesiastical courts would establish a Europe-wide 'Consistory', and national tribunals a Court of Justice.

Peace was also the main preoccupation of the English Quaker William Penn (1644–1718), whose *Essay towards the Present and Future Peace of Europe* was written in 1692–4. He envisaged a 'General Diet', meeting either every year, or every two or three years as necessary, composed of the representatives of sovereigns, with a mandate to resolve, by secret ballot, disputes upon which ambassadors were not able to reach agreement. A state which did not accept the Diet's decisions would be compelled to do so (and pay an appropriate indemnity) by the other states acting in concert.

Similar to Penn's proposal was the *Projet de Paix perpétuelle* (1712) of the Abbé de Saint-Pierre (1658–1743). Based upon a system of *arbitrage perpétuel*, peace would be secured by a '*Union Européenne . . . une Societe, une Union permanente et perpétuelle entre les Souverains*' represented by 24 deputies meeting as a Congress or Senate in a free city. In addition, the Congress would be responsible for ensuring that the laws governing trade were '*égales et reciproques pour toutes les nations, et fondées sur l'equité*'. The Congress would oversee all bilateral treaties between European sovereigns, which would be valid only if endorsed by at least three-quarters of the deputies. The Abbé's project was widely discussed in its day, attracting both commendation from Rousseau and ridicule from Voltaire.

Most of these proposals were directed towards linking the separate political authorities (the sovereigns or sovereign republics) within a finely drawn framework of supranational institutions. From this political union would flow the benefits in which the authors of the proposals were chiefly interested: peace and free trade. The same consequences might follow from a different kind of political union, as was proposed by many theorists, now largely forgotten, during that brief period when Napoleon held sway over a substantial part of western Europe. The first proposal marking a decisive break with this tradition – by virtue of the fact that economic integration was to be the principal engine of unity, rather than the consequence – was made by the French political economist, Saint-Simon (1760–1825), who published his *De la réorganisation de la Société européenne* in 1814. He envisaged a *parlement européen*, to which would be elected, for every million electors capable of reading and writing (60 million people was his estimate), a businessman, a scholar, an administrator and a magistrate, making a total of 240 deputies. This parliament, with its own extraterritorial capital, would have the power to raise taxes and the responsibility for directing large-scale public works, drawing up a moral code, and guaranteeing liberty of conscience and of worship.

Many other writers, including Goethe, Burke, Kant and Hugo (see **United States of Europe**), have touched on the idea of European union. The fullest anthology can be found in Denis de Rougemont, *Vingt-huit siècles d'Europe*, 1961. See also **Europa, Aristide Briand** and **Richard Coudenhove-Kalergi**.

Further reading: Pierre Gerbet, 'Précurseurs de l'Europe unie', in Pierre Gerbet et al. (editors), *Dictionnaire historique de l'Europe unie*, 2009.

Preliminary ruling

Article 267 TFEU allows national courts and tribunals to refer to the **European Court of Justice** (ECJ) requests for rulings on points of **EU law**. Such references are mandatory in the case of courts against whose judgements there is no possibility of appeal in national law. (In the United Kingdom, this definition includes both the new Supreme Court and its predecessor, the judicial committee of the House of Lords.) Preliminary references relate essentially to the interpretation of the **Treaties** or acts of the EU **institutions** or other bodies taken under them. They constitute a step in proceedings before a national court, in which a judgement will be given by the latter in due course. The national court must propose precisely which point of EU law should be the subject of the European Court's ruling, and it must be a point directly relevant to the outcome of the case. The Court is careful in its preliminary rulings to address only the points specifically raised, which are normally on the substance or the applicability of EU law, and to deal only with the facts of the case as established by the national court. In the Court's own words in 1977, the effect of such rulings is to 'ensure that Community law is interpreted and applied in a uniform manner in all Member States' (*Hoffmann-La Roche* v *Centrafarm*, Case 107/76).

Presidency

The presidency of the **Council of Ministers** rotates among the member states of the European Union every six months. The relevant minister from the presidency country chairs each of the sector-specific Council formations – whether of agriculture or finance or environment ministers – and the foreign minister usually chairs the **General Affairs Council** (GAC), which has a coordinating function within the Council system. The foreign minister is thus president-in-office of the Council as a whole. Before the **Lisbon Treaty** entered into force in December 2009, the foreign minister also chaired the **Foreign Affairs Council** (FAC), just as the head of state or government chaired the **European Council**. These responsibilities now fall to the **High Representative** for **Common Foreign and Security Policy** (CFSP), and the full-time **President of the European Council**, posts currently held respectively by Catherine Ashton and Herman Van Rompuy. The member state holding the presidency occupies two seats in the Council of Ministers, one as president, one as a national delegation. The positions it adopts in these two guises need not be identical.

The presidency is responsible for managing the business of the Council during its six-month term. It convenes meetings, establishes their agendas, drafts compromise texts from the chair, prepares conclusions, and calls votes where **qualified majority voting** (QMV) applies. Under Articles 1–3 of the Council's rules of procedure, the presidency announces its planned schedule of Council meetings seven months before it takes office, presents indicative agendas for these meetings at the start of its term, and supplies more detailed draft agendas two weeks before each meeting. The presidency speaks for the Council before the **European Parliament**, the **European Economic and Social Committee** (EESC), the **Committee of the Regions** and other EU bodies (on all issues other than CFSP, although the High Representative may invite the presidency to act as a substitute in this latter field). The presidency replies on behalf of the Council to oral and written questions posed in the Parliament, and both presents its prospectus to the Parliament at the beginning of each term and reports back on its achievements at the end of that term.

When the heads of government decided in June 1981 to institute this report-back to the Parliament, it was agreed that they would undertake it in person, and it fell to **Margaret Thatcher** to inaugurate the process at the end of the British presidency in December 1981. The new practice was confirmed in the **Stuttgart Declaration** of June 1983 and has been consistently followed ever since. (In recent years, heads of government have increasingly sought to present the six-month programme to the Parliament at the beginning of the term as well.) In June 2010, it was decided to maintain this arrangement, even though the President of the European Council would now also report to the Parliament on each of the meetings he chairs. In addition, the head of state of the presidency country will sometimes address the Parliament 'in solemn session' at some point during the six-month period.

Each presidency usually tries to progress a number of distinctive priorities, reflecting its own national perspective, during its term in the chair. In practice, advancing such agendas has never been easy, especially for small member states, partly because of the brevity of the period in office and partly because of the pressure on the presidency to act as an honest broker, in the interests of the Union as a whole. However, the division between the European Council and the Council of Ministers, formalized by the Lisbon Treaty (which makes them separate institutions with different chairs) has made it even more difficult. The presidency has become more of a facilitator, and less of a player in its own right, than in the past. The Belgian prime minister, Yves Leterme, was quoted in December 2010, at the end of his six-month tour of duty, as saying that the task of the presidency was now 'to keep all four wheels on the vehicle' rather than to become a fifth wheel in its own right. Equally, he suggested, the position of the prime minister of the presidency country had changed from that of 'team captain' to one of 'team manager'.

During the passage of the **single market** programme (1985–92), it started to become common to assess presidencies very largely on the basis of their legislative output. The resulting pressure to deliver results – a process hugely facilitated by the extension of majority voting under the 1986 **Single European Act** (SEA) and subsequent treaty changes – helped to revitalize the Council of Ministers as an efficient decision-taking body. The pattern established in the late 1980s and 1990s has since been maintained. Characteristically, presidencies now work intensively to try to ensure that the Council reaches agreement on as many of the major outstanding 'dossiers' facing the Union as possible. Since the 1997 **Amsterdam Treaty** allowed the Council and Parliament to agree legislation at first reading under the **co-decision procedure**, there has been a growing desire on the part of presidencies to accelerate the law-making process, sometimes to the irritation of any member states less enthusiastic about the measures in question.

Until the Lisbon Treaty entrusted this task to the permanent President of the Council and the High Representative, the country holding the presidency represented both the European Council and Council of Ministers in the EU's dealings with third countries. The prime minister of the presidency country attended **Group of Eight** (G8) and **Group of Twenty** (G20) summits, whilst the foreign minister spoke for the Union at the **United Nations** General Assembly (UNGA), with both often attending bilateral summits. These figures were able to attain an international exposure which their national positions might only sometimes merit. A powerful example of this was the attention commanded by the Luxembourg foreign minister, Jacques Poos, at the time of the Gulf crisis in 1991. The Spanish government, which held the first presidency under the Lisbon Treaty (January–June 2010), had difficulty in grasping the power shift which was occurring and famously announced the holding of an EU–US summit in Madrid, only to find the Obama White House disavow it on the grounds that the rotating presidency was no longer its interlocutor. The President of the European Council, Herman Van Rompuy, has secured agreement in principle that bilateral summits between the EU and third countries (or groups of countries) on European soil will now take place in Brussels, rather than in the country of the presidency. (So far, the rotating presidency has continued to chair ACP–EU ministerial meetings, as well as association and cooperation councils, but only on behalf of the High Representative, who could exercise these roles at any time if she wished to.)

The change in external representation introduced by Lisbon, plus the fact that since May 2004 meetings of the European Council have normally been held in Brussels, means that both the prestige and financial burden to a member state of holding the presidency is declining. In 2001, it was estimated that the average cost of a presidency was about € 75 million, with each meeting of the European Council outside Brussels costing around € 20 million to host. The 2008 French presidency set the all-time record, at over € 150 million.

Until January 1993, the presidency of the Council was held by the member states in alphabetical order, each state's position in the order being determined by the country's name in its own language. This had the disadvantage that when there was an even number of member states, it was always the same countries which held the 'shorter' presidency in the second half of the year, which includes the summer and Christmas holiday breaks. Agreement was reached to reverse each annual pair of presidencies, so that Danmark would precede Belgique, Ellas (Greece) would precede Deutschland, and so on. However, this cycle itself came to an end in 1998, when, in preparation for **enlargement**, a new arrangement was laid down providing that each **Troika** (the last, current and next) of presidencies would include one large and two small member states. This arrangement had in turn to be abandoned in 2004, once there were too few large member states to sustain it. Now a list of future presidencies is drawn up and adopted which takes account of the 'diversity and geographical balance' of the member states.

In December 2004, the Council agreed on the order of its future presidencies until June 2020. Over the period between January 2012 and June 2020, the presidency will be held by the member states as follows:

2012	Denmark Cyprus	2017	Malta United Kingdom
2013	Ireland Lithuania	2018	Estonia Bulgaria
2014	Greece Italy	2019	Austria Romania
2015	Latvia Luxembourg	2020	Finland
2016	Netherlands Slovakia		

In September 2006, the Council imported an arrangement, initially put forward in the **European Constitution**, that, in place of the traditional rolling Troika, presidencies would henceforth be grouped into fixed, 18-month 'Trios', with a common programme for their joint period in the chair. Poland, Denmark and Cyprus form such a trio from July 2011 to December 2012. The following Trio, from January 2013 to June 2014, comprises Ireland, Lithuania and Greece. Other than encouraging countries to think further in advance about the priorities of their presidencies – and perhaps to dilute some of their more domestically-focused aspirations – there is little evidence so far of the Trio system making any significant impact on the operation of the Council. Interestingly, in an early sign of potential tension between the Council presidency and the High Representative, an offer by the Polish–Danish–Cypriot Trio to draft a joint 18-month programme on all aspects of external relations – so that **Common Commercial Policy** (CCP), **development policy**, humanitarian aid and CFSP, could be presented to the outside world as a coherent whole – was rejected by the High Representative as an infringement on her area of **competence**.

Further reading: Ole Elgström, *European Union Council Presidencies: A Comparative Perspective*, 2003; Martin Westlake, 'Why Presidencies still matter', *Österreichische Zeitschrift für Politikwissenschaft*, Volume 36, Number 2, 2007.

President of the European Council

From its inception in 1974, a key feature of the **European Council** (of heads of state or government) was that each of the EU's regular summit meetings was chaired by the prime minister or president of the member state holding the rotating six-month **presidency** of the **Council of Ministers**. The **Lisbon Treaty**, which entered into force in December 2009, has ended this system. Instead, the European Council now chooses its own president, by **qualified majority voting** (QMV), for a 30-month term, renewable once. In November 2009, Herman Van Rompuy, then prime minister of Belgium, was chosen to perform this role; he took office the following month.

The creation of the new post of President of the European Council was the outcome of a lively debate, pitting large member states against small, at the time of the **Convention on the Future of Europe**, which elaborated a draft **European Constitution** in 2002–3. During the first half of 2002, the Spanish and British prime ministers, José María Aznar and **Tony Blair**, together with French President Jacques Chirac – known as the 'ABC group' – began advocating the idea of a full-time or 'permanent' president of the European Council, chosen by his or her peers for a term of either five or two and a half years. They argued that the system of twice-yearly rotation was becoming increasingly problematic, given both the scale of the job and the fact that **enlargement** meant that in future it was unlikely that any government leader would ever serve as president-in-office for more than one six-month term (the role coming round only once every 14 years in an EU of 27 member states). To operate effectively, the Council system needed a stronger point of coordination and continuity at the highest level. It was assumed that the person chosen for the job would be a current or former head of government, who would resign all other responsibilities once appointed.

The concept crystallized in an ambitious proposal put forward by the British Foreign Office, whereby the new office-holder might chair not only the quarterly summit meetings, but the **General Affairs Council** (of foreign or European affairs ministers) as well, and supervise the work both of some individual sectoral Councils and of the **High Representative** for **Common Foreign and Security Policy** (CFSP). A more cautious formulation followed in a package of proposals for the constitution tabled jointly by Paris and Berlin at the Convention in January 2003 (which also envisaged the creation of a European foreign minister and wider use of QMV and **co-decision**). The key role of the new President of the European Council would be to prepare the quarterly EU summit meetings, ensure the implementation of their conclusions, and represent the Union (at head of government level) at bilateral and multilateral summit meetings with third countries around the world.

Just as they had been sceptical of the creation of the European Council in the first place, so the small member states and many more federally-minded figures in the **European Parliament** and **European Commission** expressed doubts about the creation of a permanent president whom they feared might 'intergovernmentalize' the Union. When the Convention first discussed the subject in January 2003, few speakers expressed strong support for the idea, whilst in April, seven (of the then 15) member states – immediately dubbed the 'seven dwarfs' – publicly opposed it. (The only small member state to offer support was Denmark.) Some critics voiced the counter-demand that if such a post were created, it should be merged with that of President of the European Commission, creating a true 'European President'. Others suggested that European Commissioners should be allowed to chair individual formations of the Council of Ministers, to help 'communautize' the latter. However, as a result of tenacious support from the Convention's chairman, former French President **Valéry Giscard d'Estaing**, as well as backing from the official representatives of all the large member states, the initial concept was retained. Giscard even attempted (unsuccessfully) to institute a post of Vice-President of the European Council, as part of a proposed *bureau* of Council members that would coordinate and drive forward the Council system as a whole.

In the end, the Convention decided to accept the post of President of the European Council, with a remit broadly along the lines recommended in the Franco-German paper. The office-holder would chair, 'drive forward' and 'ensure the preparation and continuity' of the work of the European Council.

In doing so, he or she would 'endeavour to facilitate cohesion and consensus' in its proceedings and work 'in cooperation with the President of the Commission, and on the basis of the work of the General Affairs Council'. It was not specified that the person chosen need be a current or former member of the European Council, only that the post was incompatible with the continued holding of any national office. The Convention's proposal was accepted unchanged by the subsequent **Intergovernmental Conference** (IGC) in 2003–4, and was carried through into the Reform Treaty, subsequently redubbed the Lisbon Treaty, in 2007 (Article 15 TEU).

Although it was clear to all that the new post of President of the European Council would offer great potential to its occupant, both in terms of visibility and influence, there was equally, from the start, considerable uncertainty about how exactly the role would function and develop in practice. One inevitable ambiguity was the relationship between the new position and the existing presidency of the Council of Ministers, which would continue to rotate for all other Councils (except the Foreign Affairs Council) on a six-monthly basis. Some commentators envisaged an important crossover between the two presidencies, whilst others saw them as firmly distinct. Similarly, the precise relationship between the Presidents of the European Council and of the European Commission, especially in providing overall executive leadership to the Union, was unclear – as was the specific relationship in the field of CFSP between the President of the European Council and the (upgraded) High Representative, although here the model asserted was akin to that between a head of government and a foreign minister. The answer to such questions was always likely to depend as much on the temperament and style of the first one or two individuals to hold the new office, as on any precise institutional template that could be defined in advance.

The issue of who should be appointed as President of the European Council came to a head as soon as it finally became clear, in autumn 2009, that all 27 member states would ratify the Lisbon Treaty. The unpredictability of the Lisbon ratification situation over the previous summer had largely detached the question of who might get the new European Council job from the renomination of José Manuel Barroso for a second term as Commission President. Instead, the identity of the occupant of the new post of President of the European Council became linked to the choice of High Representative, where a parallel vacancy existed (once it became apparent that the incumbent, Javier Solana, did not wish to move into the more substantial variant of the position introduced by the Lisbon Treaty).

A period of intense, but discrete, bargaining about these two posts took place among the member-state governments during late October and November 2009. The process was overseen by Fredrik Reinfeldt, the Swedish prime minister and president-in-office of the European Council, who found it difficult to make any headway for some time. On 10 November, he commented pointedly about names for the post of President of the European Council: 'I have not asked anyone to confirm that they will be a candidate as of now, and I will not unless there is a clear majority in favour of them getting the position. [We are in] a very tense situation, where there are prime ministers and top people who already have jobs. I have to be sure before I ask them to be candidates.' Ironically, Reinfeldt's own name was mentioned at one point as a possible contender, complicating matters, whilst the other sitting prime ministers thought to be interested included Paavo Lipponen from Finland, and each of the three **Benelux** prime ministers – Jan Peter Balkenende of the Netherlands, Herman Van Rompuy of Belgium and Jean-Claude Junker of Luxembourg. An informal meeting of the European Council was called for 19 November to settle the two appointments.

Among former premiers, the name most often mentioned, and the one exciting most media attention, was that of Tony Blair, whose potential candidacy had been on the table since his retirement as British prime minister, after a decade in power, in June 2007. In October that year, the new French President, Nicolas Sarkozy, had publicly supported Blair's possible appointment as a 'smart move' for Europe, describing him as 'a remarkable man' and 'the most European of the British'. Sarkozy then tried to sign up the German Chancellor, Angela Merkel, to the idea, but she proved much more cautious. In a widely noted move, Sarkozy invited Blair to address the congress of his UMP party in January 2008. However, when the question arose again in October 2009, the Blair candidacy failed to gain traction. The Italian prime minister, Silvio Berlusconi, was alone in declaring his support, as others held back. It became clear that changes in those holding office, resentments dating from the Iraq War and fears of big-country dominance of the Union, compounded by Blair's continued stature as an international figure, all counted against him. Most heads of government, it seemed, did not want to be overshadowed by a personality who was still better known and more highly respected on the world stage. Blair also failed to secure any strong backing from leading Socialist or Social Democrat leaders or political parties across the Union: the Party of European Socialists made it clear that they were more interested in one of their number being appointed to replace Solana as High Representative. A more concerning feature was a sense in certain quarters that any UK candidate, however able, might be inappropriate because of the country's non-participation in certain key EU policies. A senior French diplomat was quoted as saying: 'The UK is not in the **eurozone** or in **Schengen**, and has a number of **opt-outs**. These are not advantages [to Britain] in the search for a candidate.'

Sarkozy and Merkel met privately and decided that, whilst they would jointly support one candidate, it could not be Blair. They pointedly failed to endorse him in their subsequent public statements. As the French President commented laconically to the press: 'The names that come out of the hat first are not necessarily the ones that get chosen.' Instead, Paris and Berlin made it known that they would welcome any British decision to nominate a candidate for the post of High Representative, with the expectation it would be the Foreign Secretary, David Miliband, or another leading Labour figure.

The eventual choice of Herman Van Rompuy as the first President of the European Council came as an almost complete surprise to anyone beyond a close circle of Brussels insiders. Having served as prime minister for only a year, little known outside Belgian politics, and defined by a deliberately modest and low-key style, Van Rompuy represented the polar opposite of the 'Blair option'. His appointment was initially thought to represent something of a failure of nerve by European leaders and it occasioned hostile media coverage in many quarters. The parallel selection of Catherine Ashton as High Representative, who was very much in the same understated mould, reinforced this perception.

Although Van Rompuy took up office on 1 December 2009, he chose only to assume his functions fully, one month later, at the end of the Swedish presidency of the Council. In office, he has brought a quiet determination to his new role, which has already had a significant impact on the way the European Council, itself made a separate institution to the Council by the Lisbon Treaty, operates in practice. From very early in his term, Van Rompuy used the revised treaty wording on the composition of the European Council to extract agreement from the heads of government that their foreign ministers, who had attended every summit since the European Council was invented in 1975, should no longer attend such meetings. If the professed objective was to make the summit process a more personal and less bureaucratic experience for heads of government, the political consequence has been to shift power over EU policy-making in national capitals away from foreign ministries towards the offices of the prime ministers themselves. Foreign ministers, already downgraded by the enhanced role of the High Representative, now attend only one summit a year, the September European Council devoted to foreign policy, and even that is not guaranteed.

The pattern of summit meetings has also changed. Van Rompuy seeks to convene European Councils on a more regular basis than before. There is a treaty obligation to hold four meetings a year: he held six in 2010, and envisaged the same number for 2011 from the very start. In return, meetings are shorter, with about a half lasting only a single day. He wants heads of government to see the summits in Brussels as a routine part of their regular governmental business, rather than as special meetings requiring an overnight stay. Reflecting the same approach, as many meetings of the European Council as possible now have a specific policy theme, whilst their conclusions are much shorter and more focused than before. Conclusions now tend to be between five and ten pages long, whereas previously the 'presidency conclusions', as they were then called, routinely ran to 20 or 30 pages. (The limit case, at 62 pages, was reached in Helsinki in December 1999.)

In his own words, Van Rompuy sees the European Council as a forum that 'brings the Union's highest executive leaders around the table . . . to establish political priorities, set the Union's strategic course and take responsibility in crisis situations'. He wishes it to be as intimate a grouping as practically possible in a Union of 27 member states. In his first annual report, Van Rompuy wrote: 'With about 30 people around an oval table, one can see eye-to-eye, or just about . . . Only trust between persons can establish a shared sense of direction.' On another occasion he has said that, since 'nearly halving its size', he has managed to move the European Council back towards Giscard's original concept of a 'fireside chat' and away from the 'massively larger and therefore more formal event' that each summit had become: 'it is now actually possible to look each other directly in the eye, rather than needing a pair of binoculars! This change helps to build trust and find consensus.'

As Van Rompuy sees it, the role of President of the European Council – which he prefers to call 'full-time', rather than 'permanent' – is 'to prepare, chair and lead the meetings of the European Council, to seek consensus among the members, and to make sure that the decisions we take are subsequently put into practice'. The latter phrase is particularly significant: there is no reference in the treaty article on the functions of the post (Article 15(6) TEU) to its holder being responsible for ensuring the follow-up to European Council actions, other than in ensuring 'continuity'. However, in practice, Van Rompuy has understood that the heads of government increasingly look to him, rather than (as in the past) the President of the Commission, to ensure, as he puts it, 'the better preparation and follow-up' of European Council meetings. 'On paper,' he notes, 'I have no greater powers than any previous incumbent. But three small changes – of being full-time, longer-term and actually chosen by my fellows – cumulatively make a big difference.'

The Lisbon Treaty specifically states that the European Council does 'not exercise legislative functions' (Article 15(1) TEU), in order to draw a distinction between its role and that of the Council of Ministers. Van Rompuy has accordingly made it clear that he does not want the European Council to see its role – one it has often played in the past – as that of resolving legislative disputes that are blocked at a lower level in the Council. Instead, he envisages the European Council as more of a strategic, executive body, with its President driving forward an agreed agenda, promoting 'joined up' policy-making among the EU institutions, and ensuring that what the heads of government want actually happens. (In this model, the day-to-day executive remains the Commission, taking its cues from the heads of government.)

To the extent that the President of the European Council gets involved in law-making – as in the European Council's task force on **European economic governance**, involving finance ministers, which Van Rompuy was asked to chair in spring 2010 – it seems to be more in order to help design proposals, than to enact them, so arguably usurping the exclusive **right of initiative** of the Commission. Hence the determination of José Manuel Barroso in turn to pre-empt this process, by insisting that the Commission put forward six legislative proposals in this field in September 2010, even before the Van Rompuy task force had completed its work, let alone the European Council endorsed it. With time, it should become clear whether the involvement of the President of the European Council in the design of the system of economic governance in 2010–11 was an exceptional necessity or has set a precedent which will be repeated in other fields.

If the tension between Van Rompuy and Barroso over economic governance suggests that there could be an incipient power struggle over aspects of domestic policy, there is little evidence of a comparable boundary dispute in foreign policy. The Lisbon Treaty states that the President of the European Council 'shall, at his level and in that capacity, ensure the external representation of the Union' on CFSP, 'without prejudice to the powers of the High Representative' (Article 15(6) TEU), and this has so far been respected fairly scrupulously by both Van Rompuy and Ashton. The former has organized some strategic foreign policy discussions in the European Council and met with heads of state and government from and in third countries, whilst the latter has confined herself essentially to dialogue with foreign ministers. Indeed, Van Rompuy has been very cautious to date in asserting an external role, as became apparent during the Libya crisis in March 2011, when he was reluctant to speak for the Union, even when Ashton was being criticized for her lack of visibility. By contrast, he has firmly asserted his rights vis-à-vis the rotating presidency of the Council of Ministers in the external field, which (despite the instincts of some member states) no longer plays a representational role externally. Van Rompuy has insisted that henceforth all bilateral and multilateral EU summits on European soil will take place in Brussels, rather than in the presidency country. Equally, he cut a deal with Barroso that the two of them would jointly represent the Union in the **Group of Eight** (G8) and **Group of Twenty** (G20) annual summits, with the prime minister of the presidency country no longer attending (unless they happen to represent a G8 or G20 country in their own right).

Primacy

The primacy or supremacy of **EU law** over national or domestic law was implicit in the founding **Treaties**, but not explicitly stated by them. Together with **direct effect**, it is one of the fundamental principles of EU law. A parallel may be found in Article 27 of the 1969 Vienna Convention on the Law of

International Treaties: 'A party may not invoke the provisions of its internal law as justification for its failure to perform a treaty.'

The principle was formally established by the judgements of the **European Court of Justice** (ECJ), notably in the *Costa* v *ENEL* case (Case 6/64) in 1964. Although the Costa ruling related to a commercial dispute of token financial importance, its constitutional significance was considerable: it is sometimes compared to that of *Marbury* v *Madison* (1803), which established the right of the Supreme Court to strike down federal laws in the United States. The Court ruled that:

> *By contrast with ordinary international treaties, the EEC Treaty has created its own legal system which, on the entry into force of the Treaty, became an integral part of the legal systems of the Member States and which their courts are bound to apply . . . The law stemming from the Treaty, an independent source of law, could not . . . be overridden by domestic legal provisions, however framed, without being deprived of its character as Community law and without the legal basis of the Community itself being called into question. The transfer by the States from their domestic legal systems to the Community legal system of the rights and obligations arising under the Treaty carries with it a permanent limitation of their sovereign rights against which a subsequent unilateral act incompatible with the concept of the Community cannot prevail.*

The Court asserted that the nature of the integration process sanctioned by the Treaties necessarily required the primacy of supranational law for it to function. If national law could be upheld against EU law, member states could in effect simply ignore the intended obligations of membership, so undermining the logic of **free movement** and a **single market** within the Union. The 'force of Community law', the Court ruled, 'cannot vary from one State to another, in deference to subsequent domestic laws, without jeopardizing the attainment' of treaty obligations. In *Commission* v *Italy* (Case 48/71), the ECJ declared that Community law must be 'fully applicable at the same time and with identical effects over the whole territory of the Community without the Member States being able to place any obstacles in the way' and that 'no provision whatsoever of national law may be invoked to override' the supranational law of the Community.

Implicit in these judgements was the proposition that European law enjoyed primacy over national *constitutional* law. This was asserted explicitly by the ECJ in its ruling in the *Internationale Handelsgesellschaft* v *EVGF* case (Case 11/70), in which it stated that the validity of a Community legal act 'cannot be affected by allegations that it runs counter to either fundamental rights as formulated by the constitution of [a] State or the principles of a national constitutional structure'. Whereas the primacy of Community law over non-constitutional provisions of national law was widely acknowledged, the German, French and Italian constitutional courts refused to accept that supranational law could take precedence over the constitutions of member states, as the Community exercised powers conferred upon it by those states which could theoretically be revoked. The uncertainty over what might happen in the event of a direct clash between EU law and a national constitution remains to this day, in part because the ECJ has sought, in practice, to avoid adjudicating in such situations.

However, with the passage of time, nearly all other constitutional courts in the member states have, one by one, asserted that they have the ultimate right to determine the law within their own jurisdictions: for example, the Danish court did so at the time of ratification of the 1992 **Maastricht Treaty**, the Spanish court in its ruling on the **European Constitution** in 2004, and the Polish and Hungarian courts at the time of their countries' **accession** to the Union the same year.

In their rulings on the **Lisbon Treaty**, several courts took the opportunity to underline the point. In December 2007, the French *Conseil constitutionnel* reconfirmed 'the place of the Constitution at the summit of the domestic legal order' and stressed that no treaty may contain 'a clause running counter to the Constitution' or which might 'adversely affect the conditions essential for the exercise of national **sovereignty**'. In November 2008, the Czech constitutional court declared that, in the event of a conflict between the national and European constitutional orders, the provisions of the national constitution 'must take precedence'. Finally, in a significant judgement delivered in June 2009, the German Federal Constitutional Court stated bluntly that the 'Federal Republic of Germany does not recognize an absolute primacy of the application of Union law, which would be constitutionally objectionable' (see **Karlsruhe judgements**).

The issue has remained live in part because the European Constitution had attempted to assert the primacy of European law for the first time in a treaty text. Article I-6 stated: 'The Constitution and law adopted by the institutions of the Union in exercising **competences** conferred on it shall have primacy over the law of the Member States.' However, following the rejection of the text in the **French and Dutch referenda** of May–June 2005, the Dutch, British and several other governments argued that this provision should be dropped, partly because of its implications for national constitutional law. In June 2007, the **European Council** decided that it would not feature in the Constitution's successor, the Reform Treaty, which later became the Lisbon Treaty. Instead, a non-binding declaration simply recalls the primacy of European law 'under the conditions laid down by the . . . case-law' of the ECJ. Equally, the treaty now states that the Union must respect member states' 'national identities, inherent in their fundamental structures, political and constitutional, inclusive of regional and local self-government' (Article 4(2) TEU), so making reference indirectly to their various constitutions.

In the United Kingdom, the primacy of European law was established in domestic legislation by the European Communities Act 1972, which provides that European law must be recognized and enforced by British courts, and that any question about the 'effect' of the Treaties or law adopted under them must be decided 'in accordance with the principles of any relevant decision' of the ECJ. The British government drafted this provision to help resolve a potential conflict between the implications of accession to the Community and the sovereignty of Parliament, which has traditionally served as the fundamental principle of the British constitution. In effect, the presumption is that EU law now takes precedence over national law in the UK unless Parliament expressly states that the latter is to override the former. The consequences of this were witnessed in the outcome of the **Factortame case** in 1990, when an inadvertent discrepancy of this sort arose.

The absence of a written constitution – and thus of a separate constitutional court – in Britain has meant that there has been no judicial resistance in this country against the assertion of the primacy of EU law. However, in July 2011, the British government secured the passage of domestic legislation which inter alia recognized that Parliament was sovereign, at least in common law, by the inclusion of this clause: 'It is only by virtue of an Act of Parliament that directly applicable or directly effective EU law . . . falls to be recognized and available in law in the United Kingdom.'

Further reading: Karen J. Alter, *Establishing the Supremacy of European Union Law*, 2001; European Parliament, *National Constitutional Law and European Integration: A Study*, 2011.

Proportionality

The concept of proportionality was established as a general principle of **EU law** by the **European Court of Justice** (ECJ) during the 1960s, culminating in a landmark case, *Internationale Handelsgesellschaft* v *EVGF* (Case 11/70), in 1970. The idea of proportionality, which has long existed in German public law, is essentially that the legislative or administrative means adopted to fulfil an objective should be no more than the minimum required to achieve that end. In the words of Damian Chalmers and Adam Tomkins, 'proportionality consists of numerous, related principles: measures must be appropriate; they must be necessary in order to achieve legitimate objectives; when there is a choice between several appropriate measures, recourse must be had to the least onerous; and the disadvantages caused must not be disproportionate to the aims pursued' (*European Union Public Law*, 2007).

Proportionality was recognized, alongside **subsidiarity**, in amendments introduced by the 1992 **Maastricht Treaty**. Article 5(4) TEU now states that 'the content and form of Union action shall not exceed what is necessary to achieve the objectives of the **Treaties.**' A **protocol** on the application of the principles of subsidiarity and proportionality, originally annexed to the 1997 **Amsterdam Treaty**, requires each institution to 'ensure constant respect' for these principles in the law-making process and specifies that draft legislation must 'contain a detailed statement making it possible to appraise compliance' with them.

Whilst the ECJ has proved cautious in embracing the subsidiarity, it has continued to be active in developing and applying the proportionality test. This may be partly because, whereas the Court introduced the proportionality principle on its own, subsidiarity was in effect imposed on it by a political authority, the heads of government, through treaty change. As Takis Tridimas has argued, the proportionality test enables the Court 'to review not only the legality but also, to some extent, the merits of legislative and administrative measures'. As such, it is 'often perceived as the most far-reaching ground of review, the most potent weapon in the arsenal of the public law judge', even if it is often applied flexibly (*The General Principles of EU Law*, 2006).

Further reading: Evelyn Ellis (editor), *The Principle of Proportionality in the Laws of Europe*, 1999.

Protocol

Most of the European Union's **Treaties** have annexed to them protocols and declarations. A protocol has legal force equal to that of the main body of the treaty, and usually sets down detailed provisions or clarifications on matters touched on in the treaty to which it is attached. For example, the Statutes of the **European Court of Justice** (ECJ), the **European Central Bank** (ECB) and the **European Investment Bank** (EIB) are annexed to various treaties by protocols, as are statements on the application of **subsidiarity**, the role of **national parliaments** and the arrangements for formal **opt-outs** from treaty undertakings by individual member states.

By contrast, a declaration accompanying a treaty has no legal force, although it may still have political importance, by giving a clear indication of the intention of those adopting the treaty or making a common commitment to future action. Declarations are annexed not to the treaty itself, but to the 'Final Act' of the **Intergovernmental Conference** (IGC) which has negotiated it. They are characteristically shorter and more numerous than protocols – for example, the **Lisbon Treaty** that replaced the planned **European Constitution** has 14 protocols and 65 declarations – and they may be adopted either by the Conference itself (all member states) or by one or more individual member states. The larger the number of signatories to a declaration, the more politically important the text is likely to prove.

For a member state with serious concerns about some aspect of a proposed treaty, securing a declaration from fellow member states often indicates that it has been defeated in an attempt to obtain a protocol. In negotiating the Lisbon Treaty in 2007, for example, the British government sought protocols on the application of the **Charter of Fundamental Rights** and the status of national foreign policies within **Common Foreign and Security Policy** (CFSP); in the event, it secured a protocol on the first and a declaration on the second. Conversely, member states may seek the transposition of an existing legislative act into a treaty protocol to give it enhanced legal force and make it more difficult to change. For example, in 1997, the French government successfully sought to convert the 1992 decision (of representatives of the member states) on the **seats of the EU institutions** into a protocol to the **Amsterdam Treaty**. In 2007, the Polish government sought to update the Council decision embodying the **Ioannina Compromise** (on blocking minorities in the Council) and convert it into a protocol to the Lisbon Treaty; instead it secured a declaration setting out the text of a further decision to be taken by the Council, once Lisbon entered into force, in respect of the situation after 2014. In parallel, some the more ambitious components of the original draft European Constitution that were in effect downgraded in the Lisbon negotiations are now reflected in declarations annexed to the Treaties: for example, on the **primacy** of EU law over national law (by the IGC) and on the **symbols of the Union** (by 16 member states).

Q

Qualified majority voting (QMV)

Qualified majority voting is the most widely used method of voting in the EU **Council of Ministers**. The other main methods are simple majority voting, where half plus one of the member states are needed to constitute a majority, and **unanimity**, where all member states that cast a vote must support a proposal for it to be adopted, but abstentions are not counted. Simple majority voting is used mainly for procedural matters in the Council, whilst unanimity is retained mostly for matters of high sensitivity for the member states, where defeat could be seriously problematic.

For the purposes of QMV, the 1957 **Treaty of Rome** assigned to each member state a proportionate or 'weighted' number of votes, broadly reflecting the size of its population, as well as defining the total number of assenting votes (or threshold) necessary for a measure to be adopted in the Council. These figures have been updated with each **enlargement** of the Union.

The accompanying table shows, from 1958 to the present day, the number of votes assigned to each member state (in diminishing order of size) and the share that each state has represented of the total, as well as the total number of votes assigned to all states collectively, the 'qualified majority' threshold required for the passage of a measure, and the 'blocking minority' needed to frustrate it. It also gives the 'official' percentage share of the total EU population represented by each member state in 2010. The total number of votes necessary for a measure to be adopted under QMV is currently 255 out of 345 possible votes (or 73.9 per cent). An abstention is equivalent to a vote against.

The 2001 **Nice Treaty** added two further requirements, namely that the qualified majority encompass at least half the member states (currently 14 out of 27) and that it represent 'at least 62 per cent of the total population of the Union' (Article 3, **Protocol** 36 to the **Treaties**). The population requirement is technically only invoked when a member state requests that a 'check' be made, but in practice it is taken into account by the Council secretariat in calculating for the **presidency** whether a qualified majority has been attained.

Evolution of voting weights in the Council of Ministers since 1958

Member State	*EU 6*		*EU 9*		*EU 10*		*EU 12*		*EU 15*		*EU 25*		*EU 27*		*Population in 2010*	*Share of EU population*
	Number and percentage of votes														*× 1,000*	*per cent*
Germany	4	23.5%	10	17.2%	10	15.9%	10	13.2%	10	11.5%	29	9%	29	8.4%	82,002.4	16.41%
France	4	23.5%	10	17.2%	10	15.9%	10	13.2%	10	11.5%	29	9%	29	8.4%	64,350.8	12.88%
UK			10	17.2%	10	15.9%	10	13.2%	10	11.5%	29	9%	29	8.4%	61,576.1	12.32%
Italy	4	23.5%	10	17.2%	10	15.9%	10	13.2%	10	11.5%	29	9%	29	8.4%	60,045.1	12.02%
Spain							8	10.5%	8	9.2%	27	8.4%	27	7.8%	45,828.2	9.17%
Poland											27	8.4%	27	7.8%	38,135.9	7.63%
Romania													14	4.1%	21,498.6	4.30%
Netherlands	2	11.8%	5	8.6%	5	7.9%	5	6.6%	5	5.7%	13	4%	13	3.8%	16,485.8	3.30%
Greece					5	7.9%	5	6.6%	5	5.7%	12	3.7%	12	3.5%	11,260.4	2.25%
Belgium	2	11.8%	5	8.6%	5	7.9%	5	6.6%	5	5.7%	12	3.7%	12	3.5%	10,750.0	2.15%
Portugal							5	6.6%	5	5.7%	12	3.7%	12	3.5%	10,627.3	2.13%
Czech Rep.											12	3.7%	12	3.5%	10,467.5	2.09%
Hungary											12	3.7%	12	3.5%	10,031.0	2.01%
Sweden									4	4.6%	10	3.1%	10	2.9%	9,256.3	1.85%
Austria									4	4.6%	10	3.1%	10	2.9%	8,355.3	1.67%
Bulgaria													10	2.9%	7,606.6	1.52%
Denmark			3	5.2%	3	4.8%	3	3.9%	3	3.4%	7	2.2%	7	2.0%	5,511.5	1.10%
Slovakia											7	2.2%	7	2.0%	5,412.3	1.08%
Finland									3	3.4%	7	2.2%	7	2.0%	5,326.3	1.07%
Ireland			3	5.2%	3	4.8%	3	3.9%	3	3.4%	7	2.2%	7	2.0%	4,450.0	0.89%

Lithuania											7	2.2%	7	2.0%	3,349.9	0.67%
Latvia											4	1.2%	4	1.2%	2,261.3	0.45%
Slovenia											4	1.2%	4	1.2%	2,032.4	0.41%
Estonia											4	1.2%	4	1.2%	1,340.4	0.27%
Cyprus											4	1.2%	4	1.2%	796.9	0.16%
Luxembourg	1	5.9%	2	3.4%	2	3.2%	2	2.6%	2	2.3%	4	1.2%	4	1.2%	493.5	0.10%
Malta											3	0.2%	3	0.9%	413.6	0.08%
Total	**17**		**58**		**63**		**76**		**87**		**321**		**345**		499, 665.1	**100.00%**
QMV	12		41		45		54		62		232		255		See footnote 1	
QMV threshold	70.6%		70.7%		71.4%		71%		71.3%		72.3%		73.9%		See footnote 2	
Blocking minority	6		18		19		23		26		90		91		See footnote 3	
Share of large member states	70.5% of votes		68.8% of votes		63.6% of votes		63.3% of votes		55.2% of votes		52.8% of votes		49.3% of votes		6 out of 27 22.2% number of MS	70.4%

Source: Jean-Claude Piris, *The Lisbon Treaty: A Legal and Political Analysis*, 2010. (Reproduced with the permission of Cambridge University Press).

1) Until 31 October 2014, any member state may request a check that the qualified majority equals at least 62 per cent of the total EU population.
2) From 1 November 2014, the qualified majority equals at least 55 per cent of member states (15) representing at least 65 per cent of the total EU population.
3) From 1 November 2014, the blocking minority must include at least the minimum number of member states representing more than 35 per cent of the total EU population, plus one (4) or 45 percent of member states (13).

(The member states have to report their populations annually, so that the Council can take a decision on the numbers each December.) The arrangements for the use of QMV in the Council apply *pari passu* to the **European Council** (of EU heads of government).

A small number of treaty articles require a 'super majority' of some kind to be attained. Such 'reinforced QMV', as it is sometimes called, applies to (the relatively few) cases where the Council is permitted by the Treaties to take a decision by QMV without there being a proposal from either the **European Commission**, using its **right of initiative**, or (since the **Lisbon Treaty**) from the **High Representative** for **Common Foreign and Security Policy** (CFSP). Proposals may be tabled by the member states in two fields – CFSP and police and judicial cooperation in criminal matters – a hangover from the pre-Lisbon situation when these policy areas were separate **pillars** for intergovernmental cooperation within the Union. The **European Parliament** has the right to propose legislation in three fields: the adoption of the 'statutes' for both the European **Ombudsman** and Members of the European Parliament (MEPs), and the adoption of a **uniform electoral procedure** for the Parliament itself. In all these cases, the threshold for the adoption of a measure in the Council is still 255 votes, but these votes must be cast by at least two-thirds (currently 18), rather than half, of the member states.

In addition, a four-fifths majority is required in the Council in determining whether there is a 'clear risk of a serious breach' by a member state of the fundamental values on which the Union is based (Article 7(1) TEU). On this and associated voting on the possible **suspension** of certain membership rights, the member state in question is not counted in the calculation of whether the necessary majority exists (Article 354 TFEU). Member states with **opt-outs** in certain policy areas, notably **Economic and Monetary Union** (EMU), **Common Security and Defence Policy** (CSDP) and **Justice and Home Affairs** (JHA) – do not normally vote in the Council in areas where they are not affected, although this principle does not apply in the European Parliament to members from such states.

The QMV system arose as a direct consequence of the enormous disparity in size of population among the Community's founding member states. It was an attempt to reconcile the interests of Luxembourg, with barely a third of a million inhabitants, with those of France, Italy and West Germany, each with populations of over 50 million. Giving every member state a single, equal vote in every circumstance was clearly not an option – although that is the effect wherever unanimity is required – but equally the smaller states needed some safeguards against the larger countries automatically getting their way. The issue had already been grappled with once before, in the design of a voting system for the Special Council of Ministers in the **European Coal and Steel Community** (ECSC), established by **the Six** in 1952. In the ECSC Council, there were in fact two intermediate possibilities between simple majority voting and unanimity – namely, voting by a two-thirds majority and by a five-sixths majority – and, in certain circumstances, any country producing more than 20 per cent of the Community's total coal and steel output (in practice, France and Germany) could unilaterally veto a majority vote.

The architects of the Treaty of Rome decided to institute a new system, in which the power relationship between the member states would be framed in a quite different way. A total of 17 votes in the Council were distributed as follows:

France	4	Belgium	2
Italy	4	The Netherlands	2
West Germany	4	Luxembourg	1

For a measure to be adopted, a threshold of 12 assenting votes had to be attained (and these needed to be cast by at least four member states if the Council was acting in the absence of a Commission proposal). This meant that, for most legislation decided by QMV, the three largest member states could, acting together, always secure a qualified majority, but that if they were divided, any two of them needed the support of the two biggest **Benelux** states to win. In effect, Belgium and the Netherlands were treated as if they together constituted a fourth large member state.

Since that time, despite successive **enlargements**, one feature of the QMV system has remained constant. The blocking minority has stayed more or less constant at just below 30 per cent of available votes, although it has fallen slightly over time (from 29.4 per cent in 1958 to 26.1 per cent since 2007). Equally, QMV continues to favour small states – now formalized as the principle of 'digressive proportionality' – but the relative position of large countries has become steadily weaker. **German reunification** significantly increased the discrepancy between the largest member state and the smallest, whilst the proportion of small member states within the Union has grown since 1995, as a result of enlargement. Whereas five of the Union's 12 member states were 'large' in the years 1986–94, only six out of 27 can now be characterized in this way. The three **Baltic states** have a collective population which is roughly one-twelfth the size of Germany's, yet they enjoy a combined weighting under QMV of 17 votes, compared with only 29 for Germany. Today, although the six largest member states still represent 70 per cent of the EU's total population, they command only 49 per cent of the votes in the Council.

The introduction by the Nice Treaty of the 62-per-cent-population requirement – together with some reweighting of votes away from medium-sized countries – was a response to this situation, and followed a difficult discussion during the 1990s on the question of 'big versus small' country power. Already, in the final stage of the enlargement negotiations with Austria, Finland and Sweden, the British government had held out for the 'blocking minority' (then 23 out of 76 votes) to be held constant numerically, even though the three entrants would increase it to 26 votes out of 87. The resulting **Ioannina Compromise** of March 1994 provided that, if between 23 and 25 votes were cast against a proposal, the Council would 'do all in its power to reach, within a reasonable time and without prejudicing obligatory time limits laid down by Union law, . . . a satisfactory solution that could be adopted by at least 65 votes' (the old qualified majority threshold). The member states avoided a bruising battle on the issue in the **Intergovernmental Conference** (IGC) that negotiated the 1997 Amsterdam Treaty, but eventually had to face it in the IGC that led to Nice. The final compromise was agreed four days into the longest meeting of the European Council ever held.

The Lisbon Treaty provides that the current method of calculating a qualified majority in the Council will be replaced, from November 2014, by a new system based on a 'double majority' of both states and population, with the traditional national weightings abandoned. The pre-Nice IGC had considered such a 'double majority' option as a substitute for either QMV or unanimity, but rejected it (mainly because of opposition from the French government, which held the Council presidency at the time). The **Convention on the Future of Europe** in 2002–3 took a more positive view, incorporating into its draft **European Constitution** the proposal that eventually survived, in amended form, into the Lisbon text (Article 238 TFEU). The Convention recommended that legislation should be adopted if it commanded the support of at least half of the member states, representing 60 per cent of the population of the Union. The subsequent IGC in 2003–4 raised the respective thresholds to 55 per cent of member states and 65 per cent of population – the formula contained in the Lisbon Treaty. Where the Council acts other than on the proposal of the Commission or High Representative, the support of 72 per cent of the member states, representing at least 65 per cent of the EU population, will be required. A 'double majority' arrangement of this kind was advocated particularly strongly by Germany, the most populous member state, and conversely it was resisted by Spain and Poland, which feared their relative loss of weight compared with the four larger member states.

Several last-minute concessions were made to Poland, which held out longest against the change, threatening to veto the whole treaty. It was agreed to defer the introduction of the 'double majority' system to November 2014 and then to allow any member state, between that date and March 2017, to request that the previous Nice system of QMV still be used in adopting legislation (Article 3, Protocol 36). Equally, it was agreed to resuscitate the Ioannina Compromise in new form. From 2014, states representing three-quarters of either the number of states or the size of population required to form a blocking minority (and from April 2017, states representing only 55 per cent of each of these thresholds) will be able to force the Council to continue to discuss a proposal, even if a qualified majority already exists for its passage. (A Council decision to this effect was adopted in December 2007 and entered into effect, alongside Lisbon, two years later.) It remains to be seen how significant this concession will prove.

The policy areas covered by QMV in the Treaties have grown over time, to the point where they now cover about three-quarters of decision-making in the Council. QMV and **co-decision** between the Council and Parliament are together defined in the Lisbon Treaty as constituting the 'ordinary legislative procedure'. Initially, from 1958 to 1965, relatively few policy fields were subject to QMV – most importantly, the establishment of a **customs union** and **competition policy** – although votes on procedural questions could be taken by simple majority. The prospect of automatically changing the voting system to QMV in certain areas in January 1966 was a key cause of the 'empty chair crisis', during which French President **Charles de Gaulle** instructed his ministers to boycott Council meetings during the second half of 1965. France refused to accept the planned extension of QMV to inter alia the **Common Agricultural Policy** (CAP), the **right of establishment** of nationals of other member states, the **free movement of services**, the **free movement of capital**, aspects of **transport policy**, and the development of a **Common Commercial Policy** (CCP) for external trade. The impasse was eventually resolved by the **Luxembourg Compromise** in January 1966, whereby the member states agreed that if any one government considered 'a very important national interest' to be at stake in a QMV vote, the Council would endeavour to reach, within a reasonable period, solutions that could be adopted unanimously. The French government asserted that, in such cases, discussion 'must be continued' until unanimous agreement was reached.

Although the Luxembourg Compromise was contested, with the five other member states rejecting France's interpretation, its impact was to prove highly significant. In practice, since any country could invoke the Compromise at any time, the political will to push proposals that encountered any significant resistance quickly dissipated, and unanimous voting remained the norm after 1966, even where no 'very important national interest' was evident. The Council developed the habit of simply discontinuing discussion of proposals with which any one state had serious difficulties, effectively immobilizing Community decision-making. (Some decisions on the CAP and the annual **Budget** of the Community were taken by QMV, especially when these corresponded to French interests.)

The Community only managed to break free of the 'veto culture' two decades later, when the 1986 **Single European Act** (SEA) widened the field of QMV to include the Community's flagship **single market** programme, as well as the health and safety of workers, aspects of **research and development policy**, and **environment policy**. The political momentum generated by the combination of the single market programme and the Single Act rapidly led to the Luxembourg Compromise falling into disuse. After July 1987, an expectation gained hold that the formal voting provisions of the Treaties would be applied more literally, especially as the Council's rules of procedure were amended to enable a simple majority of member states to insist that a QMV vote be held. This revision of the rules marked the first occasion on which the Council as a body had formally provided itself with a mechanism for triggering a vote. Henceforth QMV was accepted as the decision-making method wherever it was foreseen by the Treaties. The subsequent Maastricht, Amsterdam, Nice and Lisbon Treaties have progressively generalized the use of QMV to the position of predominance in Council business which it holds today.

In practice, only a minority of issues to be settled by QMV in the Council actually come to a vote in which any dissent is expressed. This is partly because the QMV process, rather than divide the Council into sharply opposed camps, as one might expect, characteristically promotes the search for the lowest common denominator formulae which can command the widest basis of agreement. The attitude of most states in the Council is that, in the end, they wish to be on the winning side. Although forming part of a blocking minority can be a particularly effective means of extracting concessions, being left as part of a defeated minority is deeply unattractive from a negotiating standpoint, since there is always a risk of securing few, if any, concessions at all.

In those many cases where a qualified majority can be found, the presidency may still seek to avoid a formal vote, simply saying that it believes the necessary threshold has been attained, and that a decision is deemed to have been taken unless anyone objects. In such circumstances, it would normally only be a minority country which believed that the QMV threshold could not be reached in an open vote that would have any incentive to challenge the presidency's judgement. Since ministers often face domestic political costs for being seen to have been defeated in the Council, it is convenient for member states with less than a blocking minority to fall in behind the majority view before the final text is adopted.

Following the SEA, some academics and other commentators began to seek evidence of the outcome of Council votes and of whether there were any consistent patterns or alignments among the member states. Until the

Council agreed to publish the results of voting in 1994, this work was extremely difficult. Since then, this has become an increasingly lively area of research. Two schools of interpretation have sprung up: 'qualitative' researchers tend to emphasize the continued 'culture of consensus' in Council decision-making, even after the demise of the Luxembourg Compromise and the substantial extension of QMV by successive treaty changes, whereas quantitative researchers focus on evidence of patterns of alignment or conflict between member states – whether on geographical, distributional or left–right ideological lines.

The distinction between these two schools – pitting a 'Council of consensus' against a 'Council of conflict', as Sara Hagemann has neatly put it – has become the dominant dividing-line in the expanding literature on Council decision-making in recent years. Quantitative research tends to revolve around a 'rational choice' assumption that member states' positions are driven by a conscious definition and articulation of their interests and preferences. Qualitative analysis, by contrast, stresses the force of more 'organic' factors, such as the internal culture and informal norms and assumptions of the institution itself.

There are several problems with the data on which quantitative analysis depends. Evidence of the positions of the member states is still restricted to the final vote in the Council, rather than what may have happened earlier, in discussions in working groups and **COREPER**, or in dialogue with what is now, in most QMV fields, the other branch of the legislature, namely the European Parliament. There is no easy-to-access record of member states' preferences at the beginning of the decision-making process or of their positions at each of the successive stages (not to speak of any decisions which never reach a vote). However, the research to date, summarized in a series of essays edited by Daniel Naurin and Helen Wallace (see below), has thrown up a number of very interesting insights.

Dorothee Heisenberg and Sara Hagemann, studying the periods 1994–2002 and 1999–2006 respectively, have concluded that over three-quarters of legislative acts adopted in the Council under QMV are agreed unanimously. Hagemann's research suggests that the ratio of dissenting decisions since 1999 – expressed either by a negative vote or abstention – has varied between 18 and 32 per cent. However, she notes that, when dissenting statements entered into the Council minutes are included, the range goes up to 33–49 per cent, on a rising curve over time. Mikko Mattila has calculated that in about a third of cases of dissent since 2004 (by a negative vote or abstention), only one member state expresses opposition; that in another third, two to three member states do so; and that in a final third, the opposition involves four or more member states. The broad conclusion suggested by these figures is that between a third and a half of legislative acts, at the time they are formally voted on by QMV in the Council, confront significant opposition in some form by one or more member states (in most cases by three or fewer).

Research has also been conducted on whether there are any discernable patterns of alignment among the member states in their recorded votes in the Council. Several studies suggest a North–South divide – although whether this is primarily driven by differing distributional interests (between net contributors to, and net recipients from, the EU Budget), levels of economic development, or 'liberal versus interventionist' attitudes to European policy is unclear. For example, Robert Thomson and others found a North–South correlation in about a third of votes in the Council in 1999–2000. Research by Hagemann for 1999–2006 suggests that ideological divisions, on a left–right scale, were also clearly discernible before enlargement in 2004 – with nearly all member states that experienced a change of government shifting position in the expected direction – but that this pattern then became less pronounced after that date. Somewhat counter-intuitively, the changes of government in several of the Six founding member states – Belgium and Luxembourg (in 1999), Italy (2002) and France and the Netherlands (2003), all from left to right – showed a particularly marked impact on those countries' voting positions in the Council.

Attempts have also been made to identify which member states work most closely together in COREPER and Council working groups on QMV issues. Interview-based surveys conducted by Daniel Naurin and Rutger Lindahl in 2003 and 2006 suggested that diplomats from Germany, France and the United Kingdom – followed by Sweden, the Netherlands, Denmark and Spain – are the most 'networked' in their relations with partners. Cooperation maps can be drawn up showing the frequency of bilateral dialogue. In broad-brush terms, these show France closely interlinked with both Germany and the Mediterranean countries, Germany interlinked with both France and the countries of central and eastern Europe, and Britain associated especially closely with Ireland, the Netherlands and the Scandinavians. As Naurin and Lindahl have noted, Germany and France are each 'number one on [their lists] of most frequently mentioned cooperation partners'. Germany was already at the intersection of the northern and southern camps before enlargement; since 2004, its 'bridge-building role is even more striking' as it sits 'at the crossroads between North, South and East'.

Further reading: Daniel Naurin and Helen Wallace (editors), *Unveiling the Council of the European Union: Games Governments Play in Brussels*, 2008; Martin Westlake and David Galloway, *The Council of the European Union*, 2006.

R

Rapporteur

A feature of many continental parliamentary systems, a rapporteur is the member of a committee who is given responsibility for drawing up a report on a draft law or any other matter referred to that committee. The rapporteur leads discussion on the item in the committee, collects the views of his or her colleagues, and drafts a text for adoption by a majority of the committee, proposing (where appropriate) formal amendments to a legislative proposal. The rapporteur then becomes responsible for presenting the committee's report to the full chamber and for advising members on other amendments tabled to it. The job of rapporteur is obviously attractive whenever the subject of the report is politically important, and rapporteurships are normally allocated among members by agreement between the political parties or groups represented in the committee. Although there is scope for the rapporteur to inject his or her own personal preferences into the report, the need to gain majority support both in committee and in the full chamber imposes a significant constraint on his or her freedom of action. On a contentious matter, the art of being a successful rapporteur often lies in identifying the centre of gravity of the Parliament and positioning the report a little to one side of that in the direction of the author's own views.

The system of rapporteurships is used in the **European Parliament** and in most other international parliamentary bodies, notably the Parliamentary Assemblies of the **Council of Europe** and **North Atlantic Treaty Organization** (NATO), and (until its recent demise) the Assembly of the **Western European Union** (WEU). Within the European Union, it is also used in the **European Economic and Social Committee** (EESC) and **Committee of the Regions**. The use of rapporteurs in the French and Italian parliaments was important in determining its adoption at European level in the early years.

In the European Parliament, nearly 2,000 rapporteurships are assigned in each five-year term, about half of which are to steer through the institution's position on legislative proposals from the **European Commission**. The coordinators (or spokesmen) of the various **political groups** on each of the Parliament's 20 committees agree among themselves on the assignment of rapporteurships between the groups and then recommend this to the full committee. Traditionally each group is given a certain number of points each year, proportionate to its relative size, which it can use to bid for reports in a rolling auction that continues throughout the year. The coordinator of the group that wins a particular report is then normally free to decide which of his or her colleagues will serve as its author. If a member is an acknowledged expert on the subject in question (perhaps having authored a report on an allied issue before), the prospect of that individual being designated as rapporteur may enable his or her group to purchase the report more cheaply. On issues of great institutional significance, such as the Parliament's positions on treaty reform, 'co-rapporteurs' are often appointed from the two largest political groups (EPP and S&D Groups). Equally, by convention, the rapporteurships for certain annual reports – notably the Parliament's position on the EU **Budget** and its reaction to the Commission's **competition policy** report – rotate among the largest groups in turn.

The growth in the Parliament's legislative power, through the extension of the **co-decision procedure**, has greatly increased the political significance of the post of rapporteur on any piece of draft law. The rapporteurships on the chemicals and services directives (2004–6), as well as on packages of measures on the environment and energy (2008–9), financial services (2009–10) and macro-economic surveillance (2010–11), have been among the most influential positions available to any members in recent years. Political groups that do not hold the rapporteurship on a major proposal have taken to designating 'shadow rapporteurs' to monitor developments and act as a counterpoise to the official rapporteur. The rapporteur will not only be subject to intensive lobbying from outside interests, but often now engages in detailed discussions with the Council and the Commission – otherwise known as 'trialogues' – about the amendments he or she is thinking of proposing to the committee. The consequential recent rise of first-reading agreements between the Council and Parliament under co-decision has further strengthened the leverage of rapporteurs in the legislative process, to the advantage of Parliament's committees and at the expense of the chamber as a whole.

Ratification

In international law, ratification is the confirmation of an international agreement. Originally, this entailed formal approval by the sovereign of an agreement entered into on his or her behalf by an agent; in those rare instances of agreements concluded between sovereigns on the basis of direct negotiations (such as the 'Holy Alliance' of 1815 between Russia, Prussia and Austria) ratification was not necessary. Although in a number of countries, including the United Kingdom, ratification remains a formal prerogative of the head of state, the term is now most frequently used to denote parliamentary approval of an international agreement.

Most major agreements contain a ratification clause. This may specify that the agreement will not enter into force until all signatories have ratified it, or allow for entry into force as soon as a certain number of signatories have ratified it among them. All the **Treaties** on which the European Union is based are of the former type, and the same provisions apply to any amendments to them. Articles 54 TEU and 357 TFEU provide that the Treaties 'shall be ratified by the High Contracting Parties in accordance with their respective constitutional requirements' and enter into force 'on the first day of the month following the deposit of the instrument of ratification by the last signatory State to take this step'. These instruments of ratification are deposited with the Italian government, which hosted the signature of the **Treaties of Rome** in March 1957.

The 'constitutional requirements' of all member states currently involve parliamentary approval for any EU treaty in some form, whether by simple or 'super' majorities. In some cases, in addition to parliamentary approval, endorsement will be sought by popular **referendum**. The reason for this varies from country to country. In one member state, Denmark, a referendum is required by the constitution if a treaty both transfers powers to the Union and falls short of securing a five-sixths majority in the Danish parliament. Had the **Maastricht Treaty** obtained this super-majority, the narrowly-lost Danish referendum of June 1992 would not have taken place. In other countries, the government will sometimes decide to call a referendum for domestic political reasons. For example, the **French referenda** on the Maastricht Treaty and the **European Constitution** (in September 1992 and May 2005 respectively) were political initiatives, rather than products of a constitutional requirement. The Dutch referendum on the European Constitution in June 2005 fell into the same category. The successive **Irish referenda** on each treaty change have reflected the government's decision to amend the constitution, as a precautionary move, given that any amendment to the Irish constitution itself automatically requires popular approval by referendum.

Ratification of EU treaties has become significantly more difficult with the passage of time. European integration is more controversial than in the past, there are more member states, and more governments have felt the need to secure public approval for treaties by referenda. At the time that the ratification of the European Constitution was aborted after the French and Dutch votes in 2005, four member states had held and another six planned to hold

Constitutional requirements for ratification of EU Treaties in member states

Unicameral legislatures	
Bulgaria	Simple majority in the National Assembly
Cyprus	Simple majority, with a one-third quorum, in the House of Representatives
Denmark	Simple majority, with a 50 per cent quorum, in the *Folketing*. Five-sixths majority of all members or a referendum if the treaty involves a transfer of powers
Estonia	Simple majority in the *Riigikogu*
Finland	Ratification directly by the President, unless the treaty affects the constitution, in which case a two-thirds majority of all members of the *Eduskunta* is required
Greece	Three-fifths majority of all members of the parliament. Absolute majority of all members if the treaty involves a transfer of powers
Hungary	Two-thirds majority of all members of the National Assembly
Latvia	Simple majority in the *Saeima*
Lithuania	Simple majority, with a 40 per cent quorum, in the *Seimas*
Luxembourg	Simple majority in the Chamber of Deputies
Malta	Simple majority in the House of Representatives
Portugal	Simple majority in the Assembly of the Republic
Slovakia	Three-fifths majority in the National Council
Slovenia	Two-thirds majority of all members of the National Assembly
Sweden	Three-quarters majority in the *Riksdag*

Bicameral legislatures	
Austria	Two-thirds of all members, with a 50 per cent quorum, in each chamber, the *Nationalrat* and *Bundesrat*
Czech Republic	Simple majority in each chamber, the Chamber of Deputies and Senate. Three-fifths majority of all members in each chamber if the treaty involves a transfer of powers
France	Simple majority in each chamber, the National Assembly and Senate. President may submit the ratification bill to a referendum. If a change to the constitution is deemed necessary before the treaty is ratified, either a two-thirds majority of a joint session of the two chambers (Congress) or approval in a referendum is required
Germany	Simple majority in each chamber, the Bundestag and Bundesrat
Ireland	Simple majority in each chamber, the *Dáil* and Senate. If a change to the constitution is deemed necessary before the treaty is ratified, a referendum is required
Italy	Simple majority, with a 50 per cent quorum, in each chamber, the Chamber of Deputies and Senate
Netherlands	Simple majority in each chamber, the *Eerste* and *Tweede Kamer*
Poland	Simple majority, with a 50 per cent quorum, in each chamber, the *Sjem* and Senate. Two-thirds majority if the treaty involves a transfer of powers
Romania	Two-thirds majority in a joint session of the two chambers, the Chamber of Deputies and Senate
Spain	Absolute majority of all members of the lower chamber, the Congress. Simple majority in the upper chamber, the Senate
United Kingdom	Simple majorities in each chamber, the House of Commons and House of Lords
Multicameral legislature	
Belgium	Simple majorities in the two federal chambers, the Chamber of Representatives and Senate, and the five regional and linguistic chambers

Sources: European Parliament; House of Commons' Library; Thomas Christiansen and Christine Reh, *Constitutionalizing the European Union*, 2009.

referenda (most of them without any constitutional obligation to do so). By contrast, before the Maastricht Treaty, only Denmark and Ireland had ever held referenda to approve a European treaty change – as opposed to **accession** to the Community. Both votes were on the **Single European Act** (SEA), in February 1986 and May 1987 respectively.

However, even in the era of exclusively parliamentary ratification, approval of treaties was not always plain sailing. The French National Assembly famously rejected the **European Defence Community** (EDC) Treaty in August 1954, killing with it the proposed **European Political Community** (EPC). Even the ratifications of the **European Coal and Steel Community** (ECSC), the **European Economic Community** (EEC) and **Euratom** were contested in the parliaments of some of **the Six.** On the ECSC Treaty, for example, the majority in the French National Assembly was 376 to 240, with 11 abstentions, and that in the German Bundestag, 232 to 142, with three abstentions. On the Treaty of Rome, the vote was 341 to 235 in the French National Assembly, and 311 to 144, with 54 abstentions, in the Italian Chamber of Deputies. Opposition parties in the three biggest founding countries were distinctly lukewarm throughout: the German Social Democrats were initially very sceptical about European integration, a position which had eased to one of abstention by 1957; whilst outright hostility was maintained by the strong Communist parties in both Italy and France, and by the increasingly ascendant Gaullists in France. Had the German Social Democrats been in power throughout the 1950s – many had expected them to win the 1949 federal elections, rather than the Christian Democrats – or had the Gaullists come to power in France before 1958, the course of European integration might have been very different.

When negotiations take place to draft amendments to the Treaties, some of the more integrationist advocates of treaty change usually suggest that a ratification formula should be incorporated that would allow the new text to enter into force even if some contracting parties had failed to ratify it. This is an attempt to induce any laggards to move with the majority, for fear of being left out. So far, all efforts in this direction have been resisted in the various **Intergovernmental Conferences** (IGCs), with such moves denounced in certain quarters as a deliberate attempt to create a **two-speed Europe**.

Reasoned opinion

The **European Commission** has the power, under Article 258 TFEU, to bring actions in the **European Court of Justice** (ECJ) against member states which it believes have 'failed to fulfil an obligation under the **Treaties**'. The first stage of this process is a 'letter of formal notice' to the member state in question. The second is a 'reasoned opinion', in which the Commission sets out in full its appreciation of the circumstances of the case and the grounds for the legal action. At either of these stages, the matter may be settled before it reaches the Court. Only as a last resort and only in a minority of cases – if the member state concerned 'does not comply with the opinion within the period laid down by the Commission' – will the Commission bring an action in the Court.

The Commission is also obliged, under Article 259 TFEU, to give a reasoned opinion if one member state brings an action against another before the ECJ for the other's alleged failure to fulfil a treaty obligation. In such cases, the Commission delivers its opinion once each of the states has submitted its case and its observations on the other party's case. If the Commission fails to deliver its opinion within three months of that time, the case will proceed to the Court anyway.

Referendum

None of **the Six** founding member states held popular referenda to approve their countries' membership of the **European Communities** in the 1950s, relying entirely on parliamentary **ratification** and handling the EC **Treaties** like any other international treaties. The first referendum on a Community-related question was held by French President Georges Pompidou in April 1972, to seek endorsement for **enlargement** to include Denmark, Ireland, **Norway** and the United Kingdom from January 1973. Three of the four enlargement countries also held referenda, with Norway rejecting membership in September 1972. (The United Kingdom held a referendum two and a half years after it had become a member state, in June 1975.)

In one of the three new entrants, Ireland, there was an obligation for any change to the country's constitution to be put to the people in a referendum. Accordingly, subsequent modifications to the EC Treaties with a bearing on that constitution could be ratified following a popular vote. As a result, **Irish referenda** have been held on every substantial treaty change, starting with the 1986 **Single European Act** (SEA). The Danish constitution requires that any treaty involving a transfer of powers from national to supranational level be ratified either by a five-sixths majority in the *Folketing* or by referendum: so far, on three occasions – the Single Act, the 1992 **Maastricht Treaty** and the 1997 **Amsterdam Treaty** – the Danish government has used the referendum route.

In addition to Ireland and Denmark routinely holding referenda, four other member states – France, Luxembourg, the Netherlands and Spain – have so far staged popular votes on proposed treaty changes: France on the Maastricht Treaty in September 1992, and all four on the **European Constitution** in 2005 (with 'no' votes delivered in France and the Netherlands on the latter). Had the Constitution not been abandoned thereafter, no fewer than four other countries – the Czech Republic, Poland, Portugal and the United Kingdom – as well as Ireland and Denmark, would have held referenda on the text. Most of the applicant states held **accession** referenda before the enlargements of 1995 and 2004, with all but one (Norway again, in November 1994) voting in favour. However, neither Bulgaria nor Romania held referenda before their accession in 2007. Two member states outside the **eurozone** have voted on stage three (full) membership of **Economic and Monetary Union** (EMU) – Denmark in September 2000 and Sweden in September 2003 – with both rejecting entry. Since 1992, the electorates of five EU member states – Denmark, France, Ireland, the Netherlands and Sweden – have rejected pro-integrationist positions recommended to them by their governments in referenda. Since 1972, a total of 44 referenda have been held by current or prospective member states on issues related to European integration.

See also **French referendum on Maastricht Treaty, French and Dutch referenda on European Constitution**.

Further reading: Sara Binzer Hobolt, *Europe in Question: Referendums on European Integration*, 2009:

Referenda held on European issues since 1972

Country	*Issue*	*Date*	*%Yes*	*% No*
France	EC enlargement	21 April 1972	67.7	32.3
Ireland	EC accession	10 May 1972	83.0	17.0
Norway	EC accession	25 September 1972	46.5	53.5
Denmark	EC accession	2 October 1972	63.3	36.7
United Kingdom	Continued EC membership	5 June 1975	67.2	32.8
Greenland	Continued EC membership	23 February 1982	48.0	52.0
Denmark	Single European Act	27 February 1986	56.2	43.8
Ireland	Single European Act	26 May 1987	69.9	30.1
Italy	EP as constitutional convention	18 June 1989	88.1	11.9
Denmark	Maastricht Treaty	2 June 1992	49.3	50.7
Ireland	Maastricht Treaty	18 June 1992	69.1	30.9
France	Maastricht Treaty	20 September 1992	51.0	49.0
Switzerland	EEA membership	6 December 1992	49.7	50.3
Liechtenstein	EEA membership	13 December 1992	55.8	44.2

Referenda held on European issues since 1972

Country	*Issue*	*Date*	*%Yes*	*% No*
Denmark	Maastricht Treaty	18 May 1993	56.8	43.2
Austria	EU accession	12 June 1994	66.4	33.6
Finland	EU accession	16 October 1994	56.9	43.1
Sweden	EU accession	13 November 1994	52.2	46.9
Norway	EU accession	28 November 1994	47.5	52.5
Liechtenstein	EEA membership	9 April 1995	55.9	44.1
Ireland	Amsterdam Treaty	22 May 1998	61.7	38.3
Denmark	Amsterdam Treaty	28 May 1998	55.1	44.9
Denmark	Euro membership	28 September 2000	46.8	53.2
Switzerland	EU membership	4 March 2001	23.2	76.8
Ireland	Nice Treaty	7 June 2001	46.1	53.9
Ireland	Nice Treaty	19 October 2002	62.9	37.1
Malta	EU accession	10 March 2003	53.6	46.4
Slovenia	EU accession	23 March 2003	89.6	10.4
Hungary	EU accession	12 April 2003	83.8	16.0
Lithuania	EU accession	10–11 May 2003	91.0	9.0
Slovakia	EU accession	16–17 May 2003	92.5	6.2
Poland	EU accession	7–8 June 2003	77.4	22.5
Czech Republic	EU accession	13–14 June 2003	77.3	22.7
Sweden	Euro membership	14 September 2003	42.0	55.9
Estonia	EU accession	14 September 2003	66.8	33.2
Latvia	EU accession	20 September 2003	67.5	32.3
Romania	EU accession and NATO accession	18–19 October 2003	89.7	8.8
Spain	European Constitution	20 February 2005	76.7	17.2
France	European Constitution	29 May 2005	45.3	54.7
Netherlands	European Constitution	1 June 2005	38.4	61.6
Switzerland	Schengen membership	5 June 2005	54.6	45.4
Luxembourg	European Constitution	10 July 2005	56.5	43.5
Ireland	Lisbon Treaty	12 June 2008	46.6	53.4
Ireland	Lisbon Treaty	2 October 2009	67.1	32.9

Sources: European Commission; Foreign and Commonwealth Office; House of Commons' Library; *Journal of Common Market Studies.*

Regulation

A regulation is one of three types of binding **legal act** which the institutions of the European Union may adopt, within the scope provided by the **Treaties**. The other two are **decisions** and **directives.**

Under Article 288 TFEU, a regulation is an act of 'general application' and is 'binding in its entirety and directly applicable in all Member States'.

Regulations differ from decisions in being of general application, rather than addressed to one or more member states, or defined natural or legal persons, or to the institution adopting the measure itself. They apply to all citizens in all member states. Regulations differ from directives in three respects. First, regulations are of general application, whereas directives impose obligations on the member states (individually or collectively). Second, regulations are binding in their entirety, whereas directives are binding only in respect of the result to be achieved. Third, as a consequence, unlike directives, regulations are directly applicable: that is, they enter into the legal system of all member states automatically and simultaneously, without any need for national implementing legislation. In practice, some regulations may need further clarification through implementing measures at national level, but if so, such measures cannot interfere with the direct applicability of a regulation itself or be used to slow down or distort its application. Taken together, these various features render regulations the most powerful legislative tool at the disposal of the EU institutions.

In addition to their direct applicability – which relates to the way they become operative – regulations also enjoy **direct effect**, in accordance with the principles established by the **European Court of Justice** (ECJ). This means that regulations may create rights and obligations for individuals that are enforceable in national courts, whether between the member state and individuals ('vertical direct effect') or between individuals themselves ('horizontal direct effect'). The Court has ruled that 'a regulation has direct effect and is, as such, capable of creating individual rights which national courts must protect' (Leonesio case, Case 93/71).

Proposed by the **European Commission**, regulations may be adopted either by the **Council of Ministers**, under the **consultation procedure**, or more frequently by the **European Parliament** and the Council acting jointly, under the **co-decision procedure**. (Under the **Lisbon Treaty**, co-decision forms part of the 'ordinary legislative procedure'.) The Treaties specify very few policy areas in which the regulation is the legal act that needs to be used. Conversely, there are many areas where the institutions are free in effect to choose between regulations, directives and decisions, as appropriate. In practice, from the start of the Community, regulations were used as the primary instrument to realize some of the core objectives of the **Treaty of Rome**, notably in the fields of the **Common Customs Tariff** (CCT), **competition policy** and agriculture. Where the institutions wanted quickly to establish certain uniform, common rules, regulations provided an effective means of doing so. In areas where this was less necessary or where political sensitivity pointed to a more flexible approach, directives proved more appropriate.

In two specific policy areas – aspects of competition policy and the free movement of workers (Articles 106(3) and 45(3) TFEU) – the European

Commission is permitted to adopt regulations in its own right, without reference to the other institutions. More routinely, the European Commission may also adopt regulations, as delegated or implementing measures, under powers granted to it by the Council and Parliament. Much of the day-to-day management of the **Common Agricultural Policy** (CAP), in particular, is carried out by means of Commission regulations under **comitology**.

Renegotiation

In June 1971, the Conservative government of **Edward Heath** successfully completed negotiations for British **accession** to the European Community, only a year after entering power. The opposition Labour party, which had applied for membership as recently as 1967 when it was in government, had since become seriously divided on the issue. Although its leader, Harold Wilson, had declared as prime minister in 1969 that his government 'intended to advance' membership 'with all the means in their power', he now chose to reject the basis on which entry had finally been secured. In October 1971, a majority of Labour MPs voted against British membership, and the following year, Wilson committed any future Labour administration to hold a **referendum** after a 'renegotiation' of the 'Tory terms' of membership.

Although the United Kingdom joined the Community on 1 January 1973, Labour unexpectedly won the (early) general election held in February 1974. Wilson returned to power, initially as head of a minority administration. His manifesto had committed Labour to submit the results of a renegotiation to the British people 'through a general election or a consultative referendum'. The new government started the process of renegotiation and secured re-election by a narrow margin in October 1974, before the discussions with its European partners were complete. The following January, Wilson confirmed that a referendum would be held.

The renegotiation of entry terms was conducted by Whitehall both with the **European Commission** and with other member-state governments in the **Council of Ministers**. It covered a range of issues, aimed at securing most importantly some modest alleviation of UK contributions to the Community **Budget** and essentially cosmetic changes to the **Common Agricultural Policy** (CAP). The government also sought (often ambiguous or unnecessary) reassurances in respect of control over the **free movement of capital**, the possible extension of **value-added tax** (VAT), the Community's formal commitment to **Economic and Monetary Union** (EMU), the expansion of development policy, and decision-making over regional policy and **tax harmonisation.**

The renegotiation was completed at the first meeting of the **European Council** of EC heads of government, held in Dublin on 10–11 March 1975. The following week, on the basis of the summit outcome, the Cabinet voted by 16 votes to seven in favour of recommending a 'yes' vote in the consequent referendum. This position was endorsed in the House of Commons on 9 April, by an overall majority of 226, although slightly more Labour MPs voted against the new terms of membership than in favour. Ministers opposed to the result were allowed by the prime minister to campaign and vote against continued membership in the referendum held on 5 June 1975, in a highly unusual 'agreement to differ' within the government. In this, they enjoyed the support of many grass-roots Labour activists: a special party conference on 26 April embarrassingly rejected the new terms. (See **British referendum on EC membership.**)

The renegotiation exercise cast an unfortunate shadow over the early years of Britain's membership of the Community. Despite a two-to-one majority for continued membership in the June referendum, the uncertainty which renegotiation generated – conducted under the unsettling threat of withdrawal – meant that, for two and a half years, the issue was to distract ministers and absorb the attention of European partners in what was ultimately a complex operation in internal party management and political survival. It confirmed fears about the half-hearted nature of British commitment to the Community, symbolized by the fact that from January 1973 until July 1975 the Labour party sent no representatives to the (nominated) **European Parliament**. Nor did the outcome resolve the divisions within the Labour party, except in the short term. After losing power in May 1979, the party swung decisively against the EC, and four years later ran on a platform of withdrawal.

Further reading: David Butler and Uwe Kitzinger, *The 1975 Referendum*, 1976; Con O'Neill, *Britain's Entry into the European Community*, 2000.

Research and development policy

The possibility of a European-level policy for industrial research and development was foreseen, in some form, in each of the founding **Treaties** of the three **European Communities** established in the 1950s. A resolution adopted by the **Council of Ministers** in January 1974 was the first attempt to introduce a coherent overall strategy, based primarily on the coordination of national research policies and the identification of projects of common interest. A series of sectoral, civilian research initiatives were proposed by the **European Commission** and adopted by the **Council of Ministers** in the 1980s – notably ESPRIT for information technology, RACE for communications technology, and BRITE for industrial materials and production techniques. An intergovernmental Eureka programme, initiated by French President **François Mitterrand**, attempted to offer a European response to some of the civilian research spin-offs from the US Strategic Defence Initiative (SDI) or 'Star Wars' project. In 1984, these separate Community programmes were brought together for the first time in a 'multiannual framework programme' (FP). This more coordinated approach was underpinned by new treaty provisions on 'research and technological development' introduced by the 1987 **Single European Act** (SEA) and the 1992 **Maastricht Treaty.**

The objective of research policy is to strengthen the Union's 'scientific and technological bases' to create a 'European research area' in which 'researchers, scientific knowledge and technology circulate freely', thus promoting a more competitive economy (Article 179 TFEU). Under Article 180 TFEU, four EU activities are specified: promoting cooperation with and between companies, research centres and universities; promoting cooperation with non-member countries and international organizations; dissemination of research findings; and improving the training and mobility of researchers in the member states. Article 181 TFEU states that the 'Union and the Member States shall coordinate their research and technological development activities so as to ensure that national policies and Union policy are mutually consistent.' Since the Maastricht Treaty, Articles 182–6 TFEU have provided for EU research to be undertaken within a multiannual framework programme, enacted jointly by the Council and the **European Parliament** under the **co-decision procedure**. Initially, the Council acted by unanimity for framework programmes (even though co-decision applied), but since the 1997 **Amsterdam Treaty**, it uses **qualified majority voting** (QMV).

As the 'framework programme' approach proved increasingly successful, the duration of each programme was increased – from four to five, and now seven years – and the budgetary provision for it, initially modest, grew substantially. Whereas the second FP received € 5.4 billion in funding over five years (1987–91), the fourth received € 14.9 billion (1994–8), and the budget for the current, seventh programme – known as 'FP7' – has risen to € 50.5 billion over seven years (2007–13).

FP7 is divided into four priority areas. The 'cooperation' strand promotes transnational collaborative research in ten main areas, backed by funding of € 32.4 billion. The 'ideas' strand supports cutting-edge research by individuals or teams, drawing on € 7.5 billion, dispensed by a European Research Council (ERC). The 'people' strand increases mobility among, and promotes the career development of, researchers throughout the Union, backed by € 4.75 billion. The 'capacities' strand seeks to strengthen research capabilities, including infrastructure, drawing on € 4.1 billion. The FP7 also contributes € 1.75 billion towards the research activities of the Commission's Joint Research Centre (JRC), which falls under the aegis of the **European Atomic Energy Community** (EAEC or Euratom).

Unlike the **structural funds**, resources devoted to research are not subject to national quotas, with project sponsors applying directly to the Commission. As a general rule, only projects at the 'pre-competitive' stage are eligible for assistance and they must involve cooperation between partners in at least three member states (one of whom may be an external 'associated' country). There has been a good deal of criticism of the bureaucratic complexity surrounding the administration of EU research projects; designed mainly to minimize the prospects of fraud, such requirements are alleged to stifle academic creativity and lock researchers into patterns of inquiry determined too far in advance. See also **education policy**, **European Organization for Nuclear Research** (CERN).

Resignation of Santer Commission

On 15 March 1999, Jacques Santer, President of the **European Commission** and former prime minister of Luxembourg, resigned with all 19 of his fellow Commissioners, in the wake of revelations of fraud and financial mismanagement within the institution. This was the first, and so far only, time that a college of Commissioners has left office collectively by resignation. However, in accordance with Article 201 EC, now Article 234 TFEU, they remained in place to deal with current business until the **Council of Ministers** formally proposed, and the **European Parliament** approved, the appointment of a successor body, with the new Commission taking office in September 1999. The interim Commission President was Manuel Marín, former Spanish foreign minister, and his successor was Romano Prodi, former Italian prime minister, who served from 1999 to 2004.

A year before, in March 1998, the European Parliament had refused to approve the accounts (or grant the '**discharge**') for the 1996 **Budget**, reflecting its dissatisfaction with the general standard of financial management in the Commission and the lack of clarity and accountability in the fight against fraud. In December 1998, approval was again withheld because of the inability of Commission President Santer to convince the Parliament that action was being taken to address its concerns. A **censure motion** was tabled against the Commission and debated the following month. By this time, there was increasing criticism of the performance of individual Commissioners, notably of former French prime minister Edith Cresson, but none of the college showed any willingness to accept personal responsibility for the situation. Rather than force one or more of his colleagues to resign individually, which might have nipped the crisis in the bud, Santer decided to stand behind the principle of collective responsibility, ultimately to his own cost. (Allegedly, he came under huge behind-the-scenes pressure from French President Jacques Chirac not to act against Cresson.)

Although the censure motion was not adopted, the price for the Commission was that the main **political groups** in the Parliament insisted on the creation of a 'Committee of Independent Experts' (CIE) to report on the situation. The five-strong committee, chaired by André Middelhoek, a former president of the EU **Court of Auditors**, met between 2 February and 15 March 1999 – a fast-track timetable dictated by the Parliament's desire to see results before the **European elections** due in June that year. Its mandate was to 'examine the way in which the Commission detects and deals with fraud, mismanagement and nepotism', review 'practices in the awarding of all financial contracts', and 'establish to what extent the Commission, as a body, or Commissioners individually, bear specific responsibility' for any abuses. As the committee's work progressed, new revelations entered the public domain and pressure mounted for heads to roll, creating a growing sense of crisis around the Commission.

In the event, the first part of the CIE's report – which was published on 15 March, as foreseen, and dealt with specific allegations against the Commission – was more damning than many had expected. Rather than pull its punches, the committee provided a forensic account of serious irregularities that the Commission could find little way to excuse or justify. The college of Commissioners met within hours of the report becoming public and chose to resign en bloc. Had they not resigned, they would certainly have been dismissed by passage of a censure motion at the next plenary session of the Parliament.

The fall of the Santer Commission was the culmination of growing dissatisfaction with the Commission's administrative performance over many years. As early as 1979, the Spierenburg Report had identified several important failings: low motivation among officials, over-elaborate hierarchies of authority and inflexible responses to changing priorities, all compounded by the usual rivalry and intrigue witnessed in international bureaucracies over appointments and promotions. Very little action had followed from this report.

During the 1990s, awareness of these problems had been highlighted by anecdotal reports of financial irregularities in the administration of certain programmes. Several investigative journalists and Members of the European Parliament (MEPs) took the lead in bringing such questions to a wider audience. Several of the dossiers they had exposed were examined in detail by the CIE, the oldest concerning the 1989 European Year of Tourism (EYT). The Commission had been conspicuously slow to address the allegations of corruption in the allocation of external contracts for the EYT, even though by 1999 no fewer than 76 organizations or individuals were the subject of criminal proceedings or internal inquiries. Irregularities were also at the heart of the second and third dossiers investigated by the CIE, the MEDA programme (for development assistance to Mediterranean countries) and the European Community Humanitarian Office (ECHO). The CIE also examined irregularities in the awarding of contracts in the fields of vocational training and nuclear safety, as well as in the Commission's own security services. There were also alleged instances of personal favouritism by six Commissioners: the hiring by Mrs Cresson of her personal dentist as an expert scientific adviser to the Commission occasioned particular ridicule, when it was revealed that he received € 136,000 for 24 pages of work over an 18-month period.

Cases of favouritism apart, the CIE's report revealed a fairly consistent pattern within the Commission. An understaffed organization was constantly being invited to take on new responsibilities, resulting in excessive use of, and reliance on, external contractors. Ignorance of the details of how programmes were being managed was evident at the highest levels. Internal procedures for investigating irregularities were opaque and cumbersome. Financial controls were inadequate. Most serious of all, responsibility was so widely diffused as to be extremely hard to attribute: as the Committee remarked, 'it is becoming difficult to find anyone who has even the slightest sense of responsibility.'

The CIE published a second report, analysing potential reforms to the Commission, in September 1999. The Prodi Commission quickly committed itself to carrying forward the reform process, publishing a White Paper, *Reforming the Commission*, in March 2000. The fight against fraud was stepped up, with the quasi-independent and newly-empowered European Anti-Fraud Office, OLAF, taking on an increasingly assertive and confident role. The administrative reform priorities were to make internal responsibilities within the institution clearer, improve efficiency, avoid administrative overload, increase transparency and accountability, and improve staff recruitment, training and management. Under Prodi, the number of directorates-general and size of Commissioners' ***cabinets*** were reduced, a new internal audit service and an inter-institutional European Personnel Selection Office (EPSO) were created, and a 'code of good administrative behaviour' was drawn up. Changes to the Financial Regulation and **staff regulations**, both requiring legislative action, were also introduced. The improvements in the staff regulations, known as the 'Kinnock reforms', were designed inter alia to increase mobility within senior management, encourage faster promotion of the most able officials, and allow responsibility to be taken at lower levels within the organization.

Further reading: Michelle Cini, *From Integration to Integrity: Administrative Ethics and Reform in the European Commission*, 2007; Julian Priestley, *Six Battles that shaped Europe's Parliament*, 2008.

Right of initiative

Within the European Union, the expression 'right of initiative' denotes the general rule that the **European Commission** enjoys the exclusive power to propose legislation under the **Treaties**. With few exceptions, only the Commission can choose to submit draft **legal acts**, and it remains free to withdraw or modify such texts at almost any time. In practice, the object, character and timing of the specific proposals that the Commission tables may reflect requests from, and commitments it makes to, the **European Council**, the **Council of Ministers** or the **European Parliament** – and may spring from lobbying by individual governments or interest groups over many years – but normally, without the Commission's willingness to initiate the legislative process, no law can be passed. As such, the right of initiative is perhaps the most jealously guarded of the Commission's prerogatives.

The concept of the exclusive right of initiative derives from the view of **Jean Monnet** and other **founding fathers** that the Commission (and its precursor, the **High Authority**) should be an independent supranational authority, acting as a kind of 'embryonic government' committed to the common European interest. They believed that joint action at European level could only work successfully on the basis of draft legislation being brought forward and promoted by a body whose interests were distinct from, and ideally neutral between, those of the individual member states. As such, the Commission's right of initiative is unique, distinguishing the institution not only from other international bureaucracies, but also from the executives of other democratic political systems. As Giandomenico Majone has written: 'The Commission's monopoly of legislative and policy initiative – its agenda-setting power – has no analogue either in parliamentary or in presidential democracies' (*Dilemmas of European Integration*, 2005). Where there is a separation of powers (between the executive and legislative branches), as in the United States, only legislators can introduce draft bills. Where there is a 'fused' system of government, as in most of Europe, the government may sometimes have the formal right to introduce legislation, but parliamentarians are certainly not debarred from doing so.

The Commission usually takes care not to exercise its right of initiative in a capricious or cavalier way. Before formally submitting a draft proposal, it often takes extensive soundings among interested parties and may issue a consultation document in the form of a Green or White Paper. The proposal will also figure in the Commission's Annual Work Programme (AWP). The Commission will give careful thought not only to the detail of the draft but also to its **legal base** in the Treaties, since this may affect whether **qualified majority voting** (QMV) or **unanimity** is used in the Council, and thus the chances of the proposal being adopted. All but the simplest proposals are discussed collectively by the Commissioners at one of their weekly meetings before being agreed. Once adopted by the Commission, proposals are published in the ***Official Journal***.

In addition to routine legislation, the right of initiative enjoyed by the Commission applies to the EU's annual **Budget** and to **international agreements** other than in the field of **Common Foreign and Security Policy**

(CFSP). In the former case, the Commission forwards to the Council and Parliament a draft Budget based on its own expenditure estimates and on those drawn up by other institutions. In the latter case, the Commission submits to the Council 'recommendations', which once agreed form the basis of the Commission's negotiating mandate (Article 218(1) TFEU).

There is a recurrent debate about whether the Commission's right of initiative should be shared with other institutions and/or with member states. Some in the European Parliament have pushed for the Commission to be obliged to propose legislation if the Parliament demands it. Since the 1992 **Maastricht Treaty**, the Parliament may, 'acting by a majority of its component Members, request the Commission to submit any appropriate proposal on matters on which it considers that a Union act is required for the purpose of implementing the Treaties' (Article 225 TFEU). The Commission is under no obligation to respond positively to such a request, but the five-yearly framework agreement negotiated between the two institutions currently provides that the Commission will 'report on the concrete follow-up to any request . . . within three months' and will give 'detailed explanations of the reasons' if it decides not to submit a proposal. The Treaties now provide that in three specific areas, the Parliament, rather than the Commission, makes a legislative proposal to the Council: the adoption of the 'statutes' for both the European **Ombudsman** and Members of the European Parliament (MEPs), and the adoption of a **uniform electoral procedure** for the Parliament. (In addition, the Parliament proposes the detailed arrangements for the operation of its own Committees of Inquiry, subject to the **consent** of both the Council and Commission.)

In the intergovernmental **pillars** established by the Maastricht Treaty and abolished by the **Lisbon Treaty** in December 2009, the member states, as well as the Commission, could submit initiatives or proposals to the Council. In CFSP, this right is now shared between the **High Representative** and the member states (Article 30(1) TEU), whilst in that part of **Justice and Home Affairs** (JHA) which were still intergovernmental at the time Lisbon took effect – namely, police and judicial cooperation in criminal matters – one quarter of the member states or the Commission may submit initiatives or proposals to the Council and Parliament (Article 76 TFEU). Previously, Article 34(2) TEU had allowed an initiative to come from any one member state.

S

Saarland

The 'Saarland question' was a long-standing dispute about whether this resource-rich, Franco-German border territory should be returned to Germany (after both the First and Second World Wars) or instead be administered as a separate entity under international supervision but de facto French control. The absence of a formal peace treaty establishing definitive post-war frontiers after 1945 meant that France and West Germany were obliged to find a way of deciding this thorny issue bilaterally. In the end, the disagreement was resolved in favour of Germany in 1955, on broadly amicable terms.

The traditional economic importance of the Saarland, one of the smallest German states, resided in the richness of its coalfields, running along the frontier of north-eastern France, and upon which the steelworks of Lorraine largely depended. For this reason, the French government insisted at the end of the First World War that the Saarland coalmines be given to France as compensation for the loss of those in northern France, and that the territory be governed for 15 years by an international commission under the auspices of the League of Nations. Under this arrangement, a plebiscite was to be held in 1935 and the local population – who had retained their German nationality – voted in favour of the Saarland being restored to Germany. This outcome greatly annoyed the French and gave a significant boost to the Hitler régime in Berlin.

At the end of the Second World War, the Saarland lay within the French zone of occupied Germany. In 1947, the authorities in France decided unilaterally to erect a customs barrier between the Saarland and the rest of this zone and moved to integrate the territory economically into France, whilst extending to it the prospect of a high degree of political independence. A local referendum endorsed this approach, with 83 per cent of Saarlanders voting in favour of the 'Franco-Saar economic union'. Given the weakened state of West Germany, there was resigned acceptance of the legitimacy of this outcome in many circles, although the new government in Bonn refused to let the issue die entirely. In 1950, France even ensured that the Saarland was admitted as an associate member of the **Council of Europe**.

During the early 1950s, three important developments changed the picture. First, the development of the new **European Coal and Steel Community** (ECSC) gradually eased the tensions surrounding the Saarland, now that its resources were to be placed under supranational control. Second, under the influence of **Robert Schuman**, the French government moved to advocate the 'Europeanization' of the Saarland – following an initiative to this effect in the Council of Europe in 1952. Third, as the uncertainties of the French Fourth Republic contrasted increasingly unfavourably with the political stability and 'economic miracle' of the new Federal Republic, support for the (re)integration of the Saarland into West Germany grew steadily within the territory itself.

The 'Europeanization' option quickly ran into difficulties. As the territory was to be administered by the abortive **European Political Community** (EPC), the credibility of this approach suffered from the demise in 1954 of the **European Defence Community** (EDC), on which the EPC depended. However, in the interim, German Chancellor **Konrad Adenauer** had come round to the concept, and the two governments resorted to the idea of using the new, post-EDC **Western European Union** (WEU) to oversee the Saarland as an autonomous European territory.

In return for agreeing that West Germany could join the **North Atlantic Treaty Organization** (NATO) in 1955, France secured agreement to a further referendum on the territory's future, in the confident expectation that 'Europeanization' under WEU auspices would be accepted. To assuage German concerns, this vote was meant to be the first stage of a two-part process. Saarlanders would first vote on the WEU proposal, and then – if and when a formal peace treaty between Germany and the Allies was ever signed – a separate and final decision would be taken at a later date. However, when it voted in October 1955, the Saarland rejected the WEU proposal, with 68 per cent of the electorate voting against. Soon after, a majority in the Saarland assembly supported the alternative option of joining the Federal Republic and Franco-German negotiations quickly settled the terms. The Saarland became the tenth *Land* of the Federal Republic in January 1957, with its economy fully integrated three years later.

In retrospect, the settlement of the Saarland dispute was seen as both a symbol of, and a catalyst for, growing Franco-German cooperation. It was made possible in part by the fact that the original cause of the dispute, the coalfields, had been effectively internationalized by the development of the ECSC. 'Paradoxically,' as F. Roy Willis observed, 'the failure of Europeanization of the Saar was to prove an encouragement to European integration . . . By 1956, it was clear that the way to European unity lay in economic integration, and creation of a "European territory" would have been a fruitless diversion' (*France, Germany and the New Europe, 1945–1967*, 1968).

Saint-Malo Declaration

At a Franco-British summit held in Saint-Malo in December 1998, the leaders of Europe's two most important military powers committed themselves to the development of an independent military capability for the European Union, operating alongside, but outside, the formal structures of the **North Atlantic Treaty Organization** (NATO). In their joint declaration, French President Jacques Chirac and British prime minister **Tony Blair** agreed that the Union 'must have the capacity for autonomous action, backed up by credible military forces' for use 'where the [NATO] Alliance as a whole is not engaged'. These forces could comprise either 'European capabilities pre-designated within NATO's European pillar or national or multinational European means outside the NATO framework'.

Acceptance of an independent EU military capability represented a significant change of position by the United Kingdom, which had previously insisted that any EU action in the defence field should in effect require prior US consent, through the NATO system. The US Secretary of State, Madeleine Albright, responded by asserting that 'three Ds' should govern any EU–NATO interface: there should be no duplication of what NATO was already doing effectively, no decoupling of the EU from the US, and no discrimination against non-EU countries within NATO.

The Saint-Malo Declaration was a seminal moment in the development of an EU defence capability, although all sides stressed that it did not presage the creation of a '**European army**'. It led directly to decisions taken by EU heads of government, at the Cologne and Helsinki meetings of the **European Council** in June and December 1999, to launch a 'common European security and defence policy' and to adopt the so-called '**Helsinki Headline Goal**'. The first was formalized in the 2001 **Nice Treaty** and is now known as the **Common Security and Defence Policy** (CSDP); the second committed member states, on a voluntary basis, to being able to deploy, at 60 days' notice and for a period of at least a year, military forces numbering 50,000 to 60,000 personnel, on EU-defined missions in pursuit of the **Petersberg tasks**. The latter commitment proved unworkable and has been superseded by the creation of a system of smaller EU Battlegroups.

Sapir Report

In July 2002, Romano Prodi, the President of the **European Commission**, invited an 'independent high-level study group', led by Belgian economist André Sapir, to 'review the entire system of EU economic policies' and to propose a new strategy for delivering growth in an enlarged Union. The group was composed of eight academics and central bankers, supported by three rapporteurs drawn from Commission staff. Presented in July 2003, the 183-page Sapir Report – entitled *An Agenda for a Growing Europe: Making the*

EU Economic System Deliver – recommended that the Union simplify and clarify its often-competing economic policy objectives, deepen the **single market**, promote greater labour market flexibility and make a number of radical reforms to 'refocus' the EU **Budget**. The latter included significantly reducing spending on the **Common Agricultural Policy** (CAP), increasing investment in infrastructure, education and research, and focusing the **structural funds** on low-income member states, especially new entrants. The Sapir Report noted: 'As it stands today, the EU Budget is an historical relic. Expenditures, revenues and procedures are all inconsistent with the present and future state of EU integration.' It also favoured loosening the requirements of the EU's **excessive deficit procedure** (EDP) to permit **eurozone** countries greater freedom to exceed the deficit and debt ratios (of respectively three and 60 per cent of gross national product).

The report's various proposals set off a lively internal battle within the European Commission, with the Commissioners for agriculture, regional policy, and economic and monetary policy all publicly disowning it. Pro-CAP governments and existing recipients of structural fund spending attacked the 'liberal' logic of Sapir's analysis, whilst national central banks expressed concern about its proposed dilution of the **Stability and Growth Pact** (SGP). As a result, Prodi was forced to distance himself from the report's conclusions, despite their evident appeal to many outside observers.

Schengen

Even in committing themselves to complete the **single market** in the mid-1980s, the member states of the European Union were divided on whether the principle of the **free movement of persons** should be confined to their own citizens – thus justifying the maintenance of limited internal border controls to distinguish between EU and non-EU nationals – or whether it should apply to everyone, regardless of citizenship, with such checks no longer required at all. In the latter case, increased reliance would be placed instead, away from the frontier, on spot checks of identity cards, residence permits, visas and other documentation, as well as strengthened controls at the EU's external borders. Because of the need for **unanimity** in the **Council of Ministers** on this sensitive question, it was impossible to move beyond the status quo.

The impasse was broken by a path-breaking decision by five of the (then) ten member states – France, Germany and the three **Benelux** states – to conclude their own treaty, known as the Schengen Agreement, on the 'gradual abolition of controls at their common frontiers'. This agreement was signed on 14 June 1985 on board a boat in the River Moselle, at the junction of French, German and Luxembourg territory, off the village of Schengen in Luxembourg. Its 33 articles were divided into short-term measures, such as the easing of frontier formalities and closer cooperation between border police, and longer-term objectives, notably the strengthening of external frontiers and greater **tax harmonization**, all designed to create a single territory without internal borders.

Although the agreement entered into force in March 2006, the actual abolition of internal frontier controls was made contingent on the resolution of a number of complex issues related to external frontiers and a common régime for the granting of visas, asylum and immigration rights to third-country nationals.

The Schengen Agreement was thus followed by a Schengen Implementing Convention, signed in the same village five years later, on 19 June 1990. The latter's 142 articles established an Executive Committee to take collective decisions (by unanimity) and set out to establish common procedures among the five signatories for visas, asylum and immigration, as well as extending cooperation in the control of drugs and firearms, and creating the Schengen Information System (SIS), by which personal data could be exchanged digitally between national authorities. In parallel, the 'Schengen five' concluded the Dublin Convention on the admission of asylum seekers with the (then) seven other member states of the Union.

National parliamentary ratification of the twin Schengen and Dublin Conventions took much longer than expected – five and seven years respectively – with the Schengen area finally taking effect in March 1995. In the interim, the 1992 **Maastricht Treaty** made many of the policy areas covered by the 'Schengen *acquis*', as it became known, part of the new intergovernmental pillar for **Justice and Home Affairs** (JHA), with visa policy itself 'communautized' and subject to **qualified majority voting** (QMV) in the **Council of Ministers** from January 1996. Thus the Schengen arrangements were increasingly being superseded by progress within the EU institutional structure. At the same time, the number of Schengen members grew: Italy joined in 1990 and Austria in 1995; they were to be followed by Greece in 2000, and Denmark, Finland and Sweden in 2001.

The logical conclusion was drawn from these trends when the 1997 **Amsterdam Treaty** included a **protocol** 'integrating the Schengen *acquis* into the framework of the European Union'. The Schengen Agreement and Convention were both given the force of Community law, but with the United Kingdom and Ireland granted **opt-outs** from the system. (Each country may apply to 'opt in' to any decisions on an ad hoc basis, as both have to the SIS and its successors, SIS I and SIS II.) In effect, Schengen was 'retro-fitted' onto the EU system as a form of **enhanced cooperation**. The protocol states that the 'signatories to the Schengen agreements are authorized to establish closer cooperation among themselves' in areas defined by the Council and using 'the institutional and legal framework' of the Union

(**Protocol** 19 to the Treaties). However, unlike other areas of enhanced cooperation, acceptance in full of the Schengen *acquis* was made a condition for any applicant country's future admission to the Union. In 2003, the Council of Ministers adopted a **regulation** on asylum (often called 'Dublin II'), which in effect replaced the original Dublin Convention.

Because Denmark, Finland and Sweden were members of the 'Nordic Passport Union' with **Iceland** and **Norway**, the latter two countries were admitted at the same time as the three others (in March 2001), as 'associate' members of Schengen. The same status was accorded to **Switzerland** in December 2008 (following a national **referendum** on membership). Of the five **micro-states** in western Europe, Monaco is treated as if it were part of France, whilst Liechtenstein has negotiated associate membership of Schengen, which will soon be implemented. The Vatican City and San Marino have open borders with Italy, even if they have no formal Schengen status. Andorra retains borders with both France and Spain and has no Schengen status.

Nine of the ten member states that acceded to the European Union in 2004 joined Schengen in December 2007, the exception being Cyprus, where the division of the island has complicated the possibilities of free movement. Bulgaria and Romania, which joined the Union in 2007, have yet to be accorded Schengen membership, although they are keen to secure it as soon as possible. In all, 22 of the 27 existing EU member states are now fully within the Schengen area, with three other countries enjoying associate status. The 25-state Schengen area currently encompasses over 400 million inhabitants.

Under the Schengen Borders Code, a regulation adopted jointly by the Council and **European Parliament** in March 2006, Schengen states may temporarily reimpose border controls 'in the event of a serious threat to their public policy or internal security'. The **European Commission** and other member states must be informed of any such action. At least eight EU member states have so far taken advantage of this right, mainly to police persons entering their territory in advance of sporting championships, summit meetings or other major public events.

In April 2011, a surge of illegal immigrants from Tunisia to Italy in the wake of the 'Arab Spring' led the French authorities to reinstate spot checks on the Franco-Italian border. After a brief stand-off, the French President, Nicolas Sarkozy, and Italian prime minister, Silvio Berlusconi, jointly advocated an overhaul of the Schengen *acquis*, to dilute the absolute right to free movement for non-European citizens. Keen to avoid unilateral action by individual member states, the Commission announced that it could support a tightening of the régime to allow, in certain circumstances, a 'coordinated and temporary reintroduction of controls, based on objective criteria and respecting the **Community method**'. In September 2011, the Commission outlined proposals to allow the reintroduction for up to six months of 'some internal border controls as a last resort', sanctioned at EU level, when a member state had lost control of its external frontier or was subject to exceptional migratory pressures. Even before the details of this change could be worked out, the Danish prime minister, Lars Løkke Rasmussen, announced that his centre-right coalition government intended permanently to reinstate certain aspects of border controls, a move which took effect in July 2011. However, Rasmussen was defeated in a general election two months later, and his centre-left successor, Helle Thorning-Schmidt, quickly reversed this initiative.

Further reading: Ruben Zaiotti, *Cultures of Border Control: Schengen and the Evolution of European Frontiers*, 2011.

Schuman, Robert (1886–1963)

Although he was born in Luxembourg and was a German citizen until the age of 33, Robert Schuman made his political career in France. The child of a French-speaking father – who came from Lorraine, then under German rule – and a Luxembourg mother, he was brought up as a strong Catholic and educated in Luxembourg and Metz, before studying law in various German cities. After Alsace-Lorraine was returned to France at the end of the First World War, Schuman sought election to the National Assembly as a Christian Democrat, and then served as a representative for the Moselle department continuously from 1919 to 1962 (with the exception of the years 1940–45). Only two decades after entering parliament did he secure a government post – under Paul Reynaud, immediately before the fall of France to Germany in June 1940. After briefly being trapped in the Pétain government, he resigned ministerial office and was arrested by the Gestapo soon after. He spent the remainder of the Second World War first under house arrest and then in hiding as a member of the Resistance.

Schuman resumed his parliamentary career in 1945, quickly becoming a central figure in the *Mouvement républican populaire* (MRP), which was to occupy a pivotal place in the complex and unstable coalition politics of the Fourth Republic (1946–58). He served as finance minister (1946–7), prime minister (1947–8) and foreign minister (1948–53) in a dozen successive governments. On the right wing of the centrist MRP, his anti-Communist and pro-European views made him an increasingly mainstream figure during the first half of the short-lived republic.

Schuman's comparatively long run as foreign minister under six different prime ministers gave him an opportunity to shape French external policy at a critical juncture. He negotiated French participation in the **Council of Europe** and the **North Atlantic Treaty Organization** (NATO), securing the headquarters of both bodies on French soil in the process. He also grappled with the thorny question of how to reconcile a sceptical France with the re-emergence of Germany, especially once the United States and Britain supported both the lifting of limits on the latter's industrial production and its integration within the Atlantic Alliance. As François Duchêne has written, Washington saw 'West Germany's revival as the key to the West European economy and to the **cold war** balance with the Soviet Union. French governments could only delay the process and seemed unable to devise alternatives' (in David Bell, Douglas Johnson and Peter Morris (editors), *French Political Leaders*, 1990).

It was in part to resolve this dilemma that Schuman responded so positively to the innovative suggestion by **Jean Monnet**, then head of the French *Commissariat général au Plan*, that France and Germany should aim to integrate their coal and steel industries in a common European framework, with a new supranational authority exercising legal control of the pooled resources. Drawing on his wartime thinking, Monnet worked up this concept in March–April 1950, seeking unsuccessfully to interest the then prime minister, Georges Bidault. He then approached Schuman, for whom it offered a timely solution to an immediate problem. The latter knew that he would be under strong pressure to agree to raise the ceilings on German production at a Franco-British-American foreign ministers' meeting, scheduled for 11 May in London, but was seriously constrained by having promised parliament that controls would not be lifted.

After securing the support of Bidault and the cabinet on the morning of 9 May, Schuman announced the proposal publicly in what was to prove a landmark speech the same afternoon. The proposal became known as the **Schuman Plan** (see entry below) and his speech as the 'Schuman declaration'. Reflecting Monnet's philosophy of encouraging the incremental or 'modular' integration of Europe, starting in the economic sphere, Schuman memorably declared: 'Europe will not be built in a day or as a single structure: it will be built upon practical achievements [*réalisations concrètes*] that first create a sense of common purpose [*une solidarité de fait*].' Schuman's claim to be regarded as one of the **founding fathers** of the European Union rests on the fact that his proposal in May 1950 led directly to the **Treaty of Paris** of the following year, establishing the **European Coal and Steel Community** (ECSC) among **the Six**. Having originated the concept, it was appropriate that he should be among the treaty's signatories.

Schuman and Monnet capitalized on the momentum of the ECSC initiative by encouraging the French prime minister, René Pleven, to put forward a proposal to create a parallel **European Defence Community** (EDC). This would have offered another supranational framework within which a rearmed Federal Republic of Germany could be contained. However, this move turned out to be a strategic miscalculation. The growth of the Gaullists within the National Assembly (from June 1951) undermined support for the plan in Paris, and ratification of the resulting treaty had to be postponed. Schuman was himself a victim of this process, being forced to leave the foreign ministry as the delayed consequences of the 1951 election worked through. As Philip M. Williams put it: 'In January 1953, René Meyer purchased precarious RPF [Gaullist] support for his new cabinet by sacrificing Schuman and equivocating on the **European army**' (*Crisis and Compromise: Politics in the Fourth Republic*, 1964). Eventually the EDC Treaty was rejected in a parliamentary vote in August 1954.

The historian Robert Turner has summarized Schuman's political contribution as a minister in the following terms:

> *For a brief period, following the exclusion of the PCF from government [in 1947] and before the resurgent nationalism of the classic right and the Gaullist movement asserted itself, there was a fragile consensus among the parties of government in favour of European integration. Schuman seized the opportunity and exploited it to the full with a personal commitment born of his devout Catholicism and personal experience of the transient nature of national frontiers.* (in Bell, Johnson and Morris, op cit).

Schuman held ministerial office once again, in 1955, as minister of justice. From 1955 to 1961, he served as President of the **European Movement**, and from 1958 to 1960 as the President of the first **European Parliament** (then composed of national parliamentarians) after the signature of the **Treaty of Rome**. He was awarded the **Charlemagne Prize** in 1958.

The anniversary of the Schuman declaration on 9 May is now celebrated each year by the EU institutions as 'Europe Day' and is designated a holiday within the European Union institutions. The section of the aborted **European Constitution** relating to the '**symbols of the Union**' (Article I-8 TECE) stated that 'Europe Day shall be celebrated on 9 May throughout the Union.'

Since 1988, the Institut Saint Benoit in Montigny-les-Metz has been engaged in an unusual, and so far unsuccessful, campaign to have Schuman beatified within the Catholic Church. The Bishop of Metz has quoted Pope Jean Paul II as saying in 2004 that 'in the case of a politician, it is necessary to proceed with great rigour and demand a miracle' before such a status can be conceded.

Further reading: Raymond Poidevin, *Robert Schuman, Homme d'État*, 1986; Robert Rochefort, *Robert Schuman*, 1968.

Schuman Plan

After the Second World War, deep suspicion existed of German motives in much of continental Europe, especially within those countries that had been occupied. Attitudes in Paris were no exception. Suggestions that the post-war German authorities should pay substantial reparations were overridden by President Harry Truman. Instead, the initial policy adopted was one of containing German economic and political might by imposing quantitative restrictions on its industrial production, notably of coal and steel, and by refusing to allow the country to rearm. Successive French governments accepted, indeed insisted on, this approach, even as it became apparent from 1947 onwards that it was not working. Attempts at the unilateral containment of German power were adding to a growing economic crisis across the continent and weakening resistance to Communist advance.

The United States and United Kingdom began to advocate strongly the easing of restrictions on Germany, placing the French in a difficult position. One solution alighted upon in Washington was to try to internationalize the 'German problem', by creating new economic and security frameworks in which the defeated power could more easily find a place. The successive proposals for the **Marshall Plan** in 1947, a programme of large-scale financial assistance for the reconstruction of Europe, and the **North Atlantic Treaty Organization** (NATO) in 1948, designed to create a single defence structure embracing the US and European countries, were in part driven by such thinking. The French government strongly supported both initiatives, although it did not wish the new Federal Republic to contribute troops to NATO.

As the decade ended, Europe experienced growing economic recovery, partly as a result of the Marshall Plan, and political space began to open up for Franco-German relations to evolve in a more positive direction. Under the influence of **Jean Monnet**, then head of the French *Commissariat général au Plan*, thinking in Paris took the 'internationalization' strategy of the Marshall Plan and NATO one critical step further.

On 9 May 1950, **Robert Schuman**, the French foreign minister, outlined an ambitious concept for the pooling of French and German coal and steel resources and production, under a common supranational authority 'open to the participation of the other countries of Europe'. Speaking in the *Salon de l'Horloge* of the Quai d'Orsay in Paris, 'almost exactly five years after the unconditional surrender of Germany', Schuman argued that 'the immediate establishment of common bases of industrial production' would 'end Franco-German hostility once and for all' and 'make war not only unthinkable but materially impossible'. It would serve as 'the first decisive act in the construction of Europe' and 'the first step in the federation of Europe'. (Earlier drafts of the speech had asserted more confidently in its opening paragraph that 'Europe should be organized on a federal basis': see **federalism**.) The 'Schuman declaration', as it quickly became known, set a template that was to suit the governments in Paris and Bonn as they sought to build a new relationship. The most powerful symbol of Franco-German reconciliation after the war, it was the basis for the first of the three **European Communities**, the **European Coal and Steel Community** (ECSC). The

Treaty of Paris, establishing the ECSC, was signed in April 1951 and took effect in July 1952.

The proposal for a 'coal and steel pool' which Schuman announced in May 1950 was largely the work of Monnet and his trusted adviser, **Pierre Uri**, who had developed the project in complete secrecy over the previous weeks. Even if the announcement was wholly unexpected, the idea itself was not entirely new. In April 1949, the annual conference of the **European Movement** had suggested that new European institutions should manage coal, steel, electricity and transport on a continental scale. Later that year, some members of the Consultative Assembly of the **Council of Europe** had argued for a European steel authority and a pooling of natural resources more widely. What was so remarkable about the Schuman Plan was that a strategy of interdependence was being put forward, in great detail, by the government of a major European country whose entire political history pointed in the opposite direction. As F. Roy Willis has written, 'Schuman broke completely with the foreign policy that since Richelieu's time had been based on the axiom that the weakness of Germany is the strength of France, and thereby made possible an entirely new approach' to a whole series of problems and disputes (*France, Germany and the New Europe, 1945–1967*, 1968).

Central to the Schuman Plan was the creation of 'an independent supranational institution', as he was to describe it three months later in the Council of Europe, formally outside the control of individual national governments. The resulting **High Authority** of the ECSC became the forerunner of the **European Commission**. Speaking in the same debate, Harold Macmillan, the future British prime minister, said that 'by far the most significant aspect of M. Schuman's initiative is the political. It is not, in its essentials, a purely economic or industrial conception; it is a grand design for a new Europe. It is not just a piece of convenient machinery; it is a revolutionary, almost mystical, conception.' However, it was precisely the **supranationalism** inherent in the Schuman Plan that led both the Labour government in 1950 and the Conservative government that came into office the following year to reject the idea of British participation – a decision which the US Secretary of State at the time, Dean Acheson, later described as 'the greatest mistake of the post-war period'.

Further reading: John Gillingham, *Coal, Steel and the Rebirth of Europe, 1945–1955*, 1991.

Seats of EU institutions

From the very creation of the **European Communities**, the question of where their **institutions** should be located has been a divisive and problematic issue. The founding **Treaties** provided that the member-state governments would decide 'by common accord' – that is, unanimously – 'the seat of the institutions' of each Community (Articles 77 ECSC, 216 EEC and 189 Euratom). The use of the word 'seat' in the singular implies that the intention was that all institutions for each Community should be based in one location, and at the very least that any individual institution should be in one place. **Jean Monnet** proposed that there should be a single 'European district' for this purpose, a kind of capital territory along the lines of the District of Columbia or Canberra. In June 1958, the **European Parliament** voted to support this concept, expressing a preference between possible cities. In a first round of voting, **Strasbourg** emerged, by one vote, as the favourite over **Brussels**, followed by Nice, Milan, Luxembourg, Paris and several other cities. In the second and final round, Brussels came out nine votes ahead of Strasbourg, followed by Milan, Nice and Luxembourg.

The governments of the member states were much less enthusiastic. The location of the emerging institutions quickly fragmented from 1952 onwards between Brussels, Luxembourg and Strasbourg, with no formal 'capital of Europe' being designated. After a long period in which the institutions were located on an ad hoc basis in these three cities, the governments decided in April 1965 on a provisional assignment, and in December 1992, at the Edinburgh meeting of the **European Council**, on a definitive assignment of institutions between these places of work. The Edinburgh agreement was subsequently updated, transposed and given treaty status as a **protocol** to the 1997 **Amsterdam Treaty**. As a result, any change to the allocation can now only be made by further treaty change, involving **ratification** by the **national parliaments** of all member states.

The Edinburgh agreement states that the **Council of Ministers** has its 'seat' in Brussels, but holds its April, June and October ministerial meetings in Luxembourg. The seat of the **European Commission** is in Brussels, with certain departments (known as directorates-general) based in Luxembourg. The advisory **European Economic and Social Committee** (EESC) and **Committee of the Regions** are also located in Brussels. Luxembourg is the seat of the **European Court of Justice** (ECJ), the **Court of Auditors** and the **European Investment Bank** (EIB). The Amsterdam protocol reiterates this list and adds that the **European Central Bank** (ECB) is based in Frankfurt.

The most complex, controversial and unsatisfactory situation relates to the **European Parliament**, where the Edinburgh decision and the successor protocol condemn the institution to a peripatetic tri-centric existence. The protocol states that, 'The European Parliament shall have its seat in Strasbourg, where the 12 periods of monthly plenary sessions . . . shall be held. The periods of additional plenary sessions shall be held in Brussels. The committees of the European Parliament shall meet in Brussels. The general secretariat of the European Parliament and its departments shall remain in

Luxembourg.' The origins and implications of this outcome are analysed in greater detail below.

The Edinburgh agreement also contained a commitment to give priority in the siting of new bodies to member states other than Belgium, France and Luxembourg. On this basis, the European Council in Brussels in October 1993 was able to take decisions on the location of a number of other bodies and **agencies**. Of these, the most important were the **European Monetary Institute** (EMI) and its successor, the ECB (in Frankfurt), Europol (The Hague) and the European Environment Agency (EEA) (Copenhagen). Other new agencies were to be located in London (the European Medicines Agency), Turin, Lisbon, Ireland and Spain. In a declaration annexed to the decision, it was agreed to move the European Centre for the Development of Vocational Training from Berlin to Thessaloniki.

The Edinburgh decision did not extend to meetings of the European Council, which was not at that stage a formal EU institution (although it has become one under the **Lisbon Treaty**). Until heads of government decided in 2002 – in a declaration accompanying the **Nice Treaty** – that at least one of their European Council meetings per **presidency** would be held in Brussels, it was normal for the one or both meetings every six months to take place in the country of the presidency. They also decided that once the EU exceeded 18 member states – as it first did in 2004 – European Council meetings would normally be held in Brussels, as they now are.

The history which led to today's messy allocation of institutions between the three main cities is an interesting one. When the **European Coal and Steel Community** (ECSC) was created in 1952, its **High Authority** was located in Luxembourg on an ad hoc basis. Both the ECSC Council and Court were also established there. Luxembourg was a last-minute compromise between the competing claims of The Hague, Turin and Liège. As Luxembourg could not offer facilities for the ECSC Common Assembly – the forerunner of the European Parliament – the latter borrowed the building in Strasbourg used by the Consultative Assembly of the **Council of Europe** for its plenary sessions. Given that there was a substantial overlap among the national parliamentarians who served as members of the two assemblies, this arrangement had some practical advantages. Staff of the ECSC Assembly, however, were still to be based in Luxembourg, like other officials of that Community.

Six years later, the **European Economic Community** (EEC) and Euratom were established. Until the 1965 **Merger Treaty**, the three Communities had separate Councils of Ministers and separate Commissions (that of the ECSC continuing to be known as the High Authority), but from 1958 the Court of Justice and the European Assembly (as the ECSC Common Assembly was now called) served all three Communities. The EEC and Euratom Commissions were based in Brussels, , where the three Councils also met. The committees of the European Assembly began meeting in Brussels, but the latter's staff remained in Luxembourg, and plenary sessions continued to be held in Strasbourg.

This complicated situation was brought to a head by the Merger Treaty, which formally amalgamated the institutions of the three Communities. Luxembourg, fearing it could lose everything to Brussels, fought hard to retain its privileged status, largely successfully. Strasbourg, too, wanted to keep the plenary sessions of the Assembly, even though they had originally been held there only for reasons of convenience. The resulting decision on 'the provisional location of certain institutions and departments of the Communities' annexed to the Merger Treaty (in April 1965) asserted that 'Luxembourg, Brussels and Strasbourg shall remain the provisional places of work of the institutions of the Communities.' To compensate Luxembourg for the loss of the ECSC Council, it was decided that in the months of April, June and October, the unified Council would meet in that city. The ECJ would remain in Luxembourg, as would the staff of the European Parliament, as the Assembly was by then calling itself. The EIB would be based in Luxembourg, as would certain Commission directorates-general (again to compensate it for the loss of the ECSC High Authority). No specific mention was made of the committees or plenary sessions of the Parliament.

From 1967, the European Parliament began of its own volition to hold some of its monthly part-sessions in Luxembourg; this practice continued throughout the 1970s, against the opposition of the French government. Between 1968 and 1979, 77 plenaries were held in Strasbourg and 58 in Luxembourg. However, the position of Luxembourg was seriously weakened in July 1979, after the first direct elections, when the new 434-member Parliament could find nowhere big enough in the city to meet. Members of the European Parliament (MEPs) – most of whom were new to the job – quickly became used to the idea of holding their plenary sessions exclusively in Strasbourg, especially when individual office accommodation soon became available in the latter. In July 1981, not long after an additional chamber was completed in Luxembourg, the Parliament voted to hold all plenary sessions in Strasbourg and all committee meetings in Brussels.

In a rearguard action, Luxembourg challenged the legality of the Parliament's decision in the ECJ, but lost. The Court ruled (in February 1983) that the Parliament had the right under the Treaties 'to adopt appropriate measures to ensure the due functioning and conduct of its proceedings' and that, since the Parliament had held plenaries in Luxembourg since 1967 of its own volition, it was free to abandon the practice at any time (*Luxembourg* v *Parliament*, Case 230/81). The governments' right under the **Treaties** to determine the seat of the institutions was unaffected. The Court's decision also allowed the Parliament to transfer a small number of administrative staff to Brussels in the interests of 'due functioning', but the great majority were obliged to remain in Luxembourg. From then on, the battle in the Parliament over its location became one between Strasbourg and Brussels, rather than between Strasbourg and Luxembourg.

Since the early 1980s, opinion in the European Parliament has been fairly evenly divided about the respective merits of Strasbourg and Brussels – often, but not always, with a small majority in favour of Brussels – and this has weakened the institution in pushing for a clear resolution of the problem of its multiple locations. In general, MEPs from centre-right parties – especially in France, Germany and Italy – have tended to be more sympathetic to Strasbourg, and those from the left and/or the newer member states more sympathetic to Brussels. Over time, advocates of Brussels developed a multiple strategy, based on promoting staff transfers to Brussels from Luxembourg, constructing new buildings in Brussels and encouraging the holding of 'mini-plenaries' in that city. They have hoped eventually to achieve their goal by a process of incremental change.

In October 1985, the Parliament adopted a resolution, by 132 votes to 113, with 13 abstentions, calling for the construction of a new 600-seat hemicycle that would enable some additional sessions to be held in Brussels. This move was promptly challenged in the ECJ by the French and Luxembourg governments; the Court handed down an ambiguous ruling that in effect confirmed the status quo. In January 1989, the Parliament adopted, by 222 votes to 176, with four abstentions, a report calling for a substantial transfer of staff from Luxembourg to Brussels, to reflect its operational needs, and reasserting the right to hold occasional sessions outside Strasbourg. This move was challenged immediately by both the Luxembourg and the French governments, but this time, the Court ruled in favour of the Parliament. Following this judgement, nearly all the policy-based staff in the Parliament were transferred to Brussels, resulting in significant cost savings.

In the early 1990s, the conflict escalated. Advocates of Brussels secured agreement in the Parliament to hold two mini-plenaries in Brussels in 1991, initially as 'enlarged Bureau' meetings or as 'meetings of the Conference of Presidents open to all MEPs', without votes. Similar mini-plenaries were scheduled for 1992. In return, the French government threatened to block all decisions on the siting of new EU institutions, bodies and **agencies** (such as the ECB and EEA) unless the member states definitively declared Strasbourg to be the seat of the Parliament. This demand was initially opposed by Belgium and Luxembourg, but was eventually agreed at the Edinburgh European Council, aided by the UK presidency. The British Foreign Secretary, Douglas Hurd, reversed London's traditional hostility to a multi-centre Parliament, arguing (somewhat perversely) that its physical dispersion could help offset the impact of the new powers it received under the **Maastricht Treaty**, being ratified at the same time.

The fact that the Parliament was not consulted in any way on the Edinburgh deal played badly among MEPs and further strengthened the supporters of Brussels. The Parliament, in voting its calendars for 1992, 1993 and 1996, deliberately scheduled only 11 Strasbourg sessions each year (rather than the 12 foreseen in the Edinburgh decision), and only ten for 1994, a European election year. Once again, the French government took the Parliament to court; in October 1997, the ECJ upheld the proposition that the heads of government were entitled to specify the number of monthly sessions to be held in Strasbourg (*France* v *Parliament*, Case C-345/95).

Meanwhile a separate dispute broke out over buildings. In January 1992, the Parliament signed a lease with developers for the construction of the first phase of what was to become a huge new hemicycle building and office complex, known as the *Espace Léopold*, which it would rent in Brussels. The French government retaliated by announcing that it would construct a comparable new building in Strasbourg and, in parallel, orchestrated the National Assembly into threatening to block the agreement allowing Germany (and certain other member states) to have extra MEPs (from June 1994) unless the Parliament's authorities signed a contract to lease these new Strasbourg premises as well. Egon Klepsch, the pro-Strasbourg President of the Parliament, eventually signed the contract in early 1994, amid some controversy.

Since the mid-1990s, the situation has largely been one of stalemate, but with events gradually moving in Brussels' favour. The number of two-day mini-plenaries in Brussels has risen from four to five per year, with other short 'micro-plenaries' occasionally being held. In 1999, to the acute irritation of the city of Strasbourg, the Parliament voted to shorten its monthly plenary from five to four days. The French government chose not to contest the decision before the ECJ. Brussels continues to grow: it now occupies 50 per cent of the combined surface of parliamentary buildings, compared with 30 per cent in Strasbourg and 20 per cent in Luxembourg. Over half of all parliamentary officials are now based in Brussels. All the **political group** secretariats have moved fully from Luxembourg to Brussels. The Parliament has gradually purchased all of the main buildings it occupies in both Brussels and Strasbourg (although not in Luxembourg), one advantage of which is that it can now dispose of its facilities as it chooses. However, conversely, the advocates of Brussels suffered one very major reverse: the inclusion of the Edinburgh decision as a protocol to the Amsterdam Treaty was an important strategic success for the French government.

In April 2000, the European Parliament proposed that, in any future treaty reform, the Parliament itself should be given the right to decide, by an absolute majority of its members, where it meets. However, the subsequent 2001

Nice Treaty and the draft **European Constitution** did not include this proposal. The **Convention on the Future of Europe** (2002–3) was unable to agree to it, partly because of divisions among the MEPs on the Convention. An alternative suggestion that decisions on the seats of the institutions should be taken by the Council of Ministers, acting by **qualified majority voting** (QMV), did not find favour either. The word 'Union' was simply substituted for 'Community' in the existing treaty reference, which now (after the Lisbon Treaty) reads: 'The seat of the institutions of the Union shall be determined by common accord of the governments of the Member States' (Article 341 TFEU).

In reaction to the disappointments of the early to mid-2000s, the pro-Brussels lobby changed tack, taking its case more aggressively to the public. The (then) Swedish MEP, now European Commissioner, Cecilia Malmström, launched a petition in favour of the European Parliament having one seat in Brussels. Supported by Scandinavian, Dutch and British MEPs, in particular, the initiative attracted 1.27 million signatures. The 'one seat' campaign, which continues, argues that the Parliament's basic effectiveness and legitimacy are damaged by the dispersion of its political activities over two sites and the location of part of its secretariat in a third. The need to travel to Strasbourg one working week in four for a full plenary session forces the Parliament to continue to organize its business on the basis of an outdated monthly cycle unlike that of any other legislature in the democratic world. Such an arrangement dates from an era when MEPs were national parliamentarians and wanted to concentrate their European activities into a single week abroad. Moreover, the monthly move from Brussels to Strasbourg and back is expensive, environmentally damaging and exposes the Parliament to public criticism as a 'travelling circus'. The campaign calculates the net cost of holding plenaries in Strasbourg, rather than Brussels, at some € 160 million per year – or just under 10 per cent of the Parliament's annual budget – and the additional CO_2 emissions generated at around 18,000 tonnes per year. It also argues that the willingness of the media to cover parliamentary proceedings is reduced by the cost and inconvenience of sending correspondents to Strasbourg from Brussels, where the European press corps is mainly based. More generally, the Parliament is denied the symbolic advantage of there being a single building, like the US Capitol, clearly associated in the public mind with the idea of democratic control exercised at federal level.

The defenders of the status quo have not sought to counter these arguments directly. Whilst some still stress the importance of the Strasbourg site as a historic symbol of Franco-German post-war reconciliation, most argue more pragmatically that, without the willingness of the French government to change its position on Strasbourg, it is pointless expending political capital on a situation which the Parliament itself cannot change. When the ceiling of the Strasbourg hemicycle collapsed in August 2008, the French authorities accepted the logic of the full plenary sessions being held in Brussels, as an emergency measure, for several months. However, when the Parliament itself voted in March 2011 to in effect reduce the number of plenary sessions for 2012 and 2013 from 12 to 11 – by holding two two-day sessions in the same week in October – the government in Paris immediately announced that it would challenge this decision in the ECJ, declaring that the status of Strasbourg as the seat of the Parliament was non-negotiable. The margin of the 'anti-Strasbourg' majority – a vote of 357 to 255, with 41 abstentions – suggested that, after a period of quiescence, the issue had revived with a vengeance. This was confirmed in voting on the **discharge** the 2009 and 2010 Budgets, when the Parliament noted that 'real savings could be achieved if [it] had only one workplace in a single location'.

Sforza, Carlo (1872–1952)

Count Carlo Sforza had the unusual distinction of serving as foreign minister of Italy both before (1920–21) and after (1947–51) the Fascist period. His *Makers of Modern Europe* (1930) and *Europe and Europeans* (1936), written during his years of exile, were influential contributions to the pro-European cause before the Second World War. In the latter, he wrote 'There is in Europe but one big obstacle – the tendency of those groups who continue to consider criminal any cession, however trifling, of a parcel of our different national sovereignties on behalf of some idea or organization vaster and more complex than our present states.' Sforza was a well-known figure in the United States, where he delivered a series of lectures published as *The Totalitarian War and After* in 1941. Together with **Alcide de Gasperi**, Sforza did much to restore Italy's international reputation in the late 1940s; his pro-European, pro-American stance helped to set the pattern for Italian post-war foreign policy. As foreign minister, he was closely involved in Italy's participation in the **Marshall Plan** and signed the treaties establishing the **Council of Europe**, the **North Atlantic Treaty Organization** (NATO) and the **European Coal and Steel Community** (ECSC), on behalf of his country.

Single currency

See **euro**, **eurozone**, **Economic and Monetary Union** (EMU).

Single European Act (SEA)

The 1986 Single European Act, which came into force in July 1987, was the first substantial revision of the **Treaties** on which the then **European Communities** were based. The new treaty was a response by EC heads of government to the demands for institutional reform that had emerged within the Community institutions in the early 1980s. There was pressure in several quarters for greater use of **qualified majority voting** (QMV) in the **Council of Ministers**, the granting of meaningful legislative powers to the **European Parliament**, an extension of the field of Community **competence**, and a strengthening of the existing, informal arrangements for foreign policy cooperation. Such moves were witnessed in the 1981 **Genscher–Colombo Plan** (which resulted in the 1983 **Stuttgart Declaration**), the European Parliament's proposal for a **Draft Treaty establishing the European Union** in 1984, and the general argument that the forthcoming **enlargement** of the Community (to include Portugal and Spain) made institutional changes more urgent.

With the advent of **Jacques Delors** as President of the **European Commission** in January 1985, it became clear that the ambitious attempt to relaunch the Community to which he was committed could only be achieved if decision-making procedures were updated. In particular, it was unlikely that the specific legislative programme set out in the **Cockfield White Paper** for the completion of the **single market** by 1992 could be adopted without at least some extension of QMV. The Milan meeting of the **European Council** in June 1985, which endorsed the Cockfield strategy, also considered the final report of the **Dooge Committee**, which had been set up the previous year. Among the committee's recommendations was that an **Intergovernmental Conference** (IGC) should be convened to consider amendments to the founding Treaties. Against British, Danish and Greek opposition, this was agreed in Milan.

The first meeting of the IGC took place the following September and negotiations proceeded rapidly. The IGC met six times at ministerial level over a three-month period, with 12 preparatory meetings of officials. At the Luxembourg meeting of the European Council in December, political agreement was reached among the heads of government on all but a few points: these were left to be resolved by foreign ministers later in the month.

The first part of the resulting Single Act contained a small number of common provisions, of which the most important gave formal recognition to the **European Council**, the forum which had brought together EC heads of government for regular **summits** since 1975 (Article 2 SEA). The second part set out a variety of additions and amendments to the Treaties. The third part was a new, separate treaty text formalizing the procedures for intergovernmental cooperation in the foreign policy sphere, known as **European Political Cooperation** (EPC). (This third section drew heavily on an informal British proposal from 1984 that had been artfully repackaged as a Franco-German initiative.) The overall document was called the *Single* European Act – a translation of *acte unique* in French – to underline the proposition that, despite its composite character, the text should be regarded, for political purposes, as a coherent whole. The fear among some member states was that the agreement underlying it might fall to pieces if the document was picked apart when submitted to **national parliaments** for **ratification.**

The Single Act introduced a number of new treaty articles extending Community competence in the areas of **cohesion** policy, the health and safety of workers, **research and development policy**, and **environment policy**. The most important change was the extension of QMV in the Council to legislation on the single market, the health and safety of workers, aspects of research and development policy, and environment policy. This process was reinforced by strengthening the **legal base** for the single market and setting 31 December 1992 as the legal deadline for its completion. The most contentious point in the negotiation was whether QMV should cover the health and safety of workers, with most of the founding **Six** strongly favouring such a move and the British equally strongly opposing it (until conceding it at the very end).

The Single Act also significantly increased the power of the European Parliament, by instituting both the assent procedure (now known as the **consent procedure**) and the **cooperation procedure** in a limited number of policy fields. The changes in the Council and Parliament were linked, in that the new cooperation procedure was applied to several of the areas to which QMV was extended. This was widely welcomed, as the abolition of the national veto on any subject meant that, without any increase in the Parliament's power, there could be no meaningful parliamentary input of any kind into law-making, at either national or European level. However, such a link was not conceded in other areas where QMV already applied, notably agriculture, fisheries, external trade or **competition policy**.

Other provisions in the Single Act created a Court of First Instance – now called the General Court – to relieve pressure on the **European Court of Justice** (ECJ), clarified arrangements for the exercise of implementing powers by the Commission under **comitology**, and made the first reference in a treaty to the existence of the **European Monetary System** (EMS) and the longer-term objective of **Economic and Monetary Union** (EMU). Most of the changes made to the operation of the EC institutions have since been modified, superseded or supplemented by the **Maastricht**, **Amsterdam**, **Nice** and **Lisbon Treaties**, as has the third section on European Political Cooperation, which is now replaced by arrangements for a **Common Foreign and Security Policy** (CFSP).

By January 1986, the draft Single Act was ready for signature. In all but two countries, this gave rise to no difficulty. The Italian government made its acceptance conditional upon approval by the European Parliament, which was forthcoming despite some early misgivings; conversely the Danish parliament voted to reject the Act on the grounds that it gave too many new powers to the European Parliament. The member states were not prepared to reopen the negotiations, so nine of the then Twelve – that is, all except Denmark, Greece and Italy – signed the SEA in Luxembourg in February 1986. In a referendum on 27 February, the Danish people voted in favour of the Act, and the following day a second and final signing ceremony took place in The Hague. However, the Act was not ratified in all the member states in time for it to enter into force by the target date of January 1987. The last member state to ratify was Ireland, where a **referendum** had to be held on 26 May 1987, following a supreme court ruling that the text was inconsistent with the Irish constitution, which therefore needed amendment. The SEA came into force five weeks later.

At the time, the agreement on the contents of the SEA fell short of the hopes of many in the Parliament and Commission. The outcome was initially described by Delors in December 1985 as a 'great disappointment' (although, as a result of an interpretation error, some listeners misunderstood the meaning of his words in French, '*une grande déception*'). However, he and others soon chose to put a more positive gloss on the text, as its potential to revive the Community became apparent. The provisions on QMV and the cooperation procedure proved to be of great political and institutional importance, with implications far beyond anything that could have been achieved on the basis of a 'gentlemen's agreement' of the kind that the British government originally favoured as an alternative to treaty change. The momentum generated by the Single Act quickly led to the demise of the **Luxembourg Compromise** in the Council and the emergence of the Parliament as a significant legislative player. The political impact of the 1992 goal, underpinned by QMV, enabled Delors to justify proposing a substantial increase in Community **own resources** for non-agricultural spending (part of the so-called 'Delors I package', under the rubric of 'Making a Success of the Single Act'), and to develop plans for both a 'Social Europe' and single currency to complement the logic of the single market.

Further reading: Andrew Moravcsik, 'Negotiating the Single European Act' in Robert Keohane and Stanley Hoffman (editors), *The New European Community: Decisionmaking and Institutional Change*, 1991.

Single market

The central policy commitment contained in the **Treaty of Rome**, signed in March 1957, was the establishment of a unified or **common market**, governed by a single set of rules, across the member states of the **European Economic Community** (EEC). Although the definition of the common market, provided for in the original Article 2 EEC, was not entirely precise – with it seeming to encompass the parallel **customs union** and other flanking policies of the Community – at its heart was the concept of **free movement** for the factors of production, based on the removal of internal barriers to trade, within what later began to be called a 'single' or 'internal' market.

The idea of creating a common market was not new. In the years immediately after the Second World War, the proposition that the economic recovery of western Europe would be accelerated if countries refrained from re-erecting barriers against each other's goods found many supporters. It was fundamental to US policy in Europe and the thinking behind the **Marshall Plan**. Paul Hoffman, the head of the American Economic Cooperation Administration, which supervised the disbursement of Marshall aid, called for the creation of a 'single large market' in western Europe in a speech in Paris in October 1949. However, neither the **Organization for European Economic Cooperation** (OEEC) nor the European Payments Union (EPU) (which it spawned) made significant progress in integrating the European economy on a continental scale.

The **Schuman Plan** of 9 May 1950 proposed a radical new way of uniting markets, by developing a set of common, binding rules which would be administered by an independent organization and underpinned by the authority of supranational law. The resulting **European Coal and Steel Community** (ECSC) was the first attempt to create a common market of this kind, but it only applied to two, admittedly strategically very important, sectors, and involved a relatively high degree of central management and control. By the end of the decade, after several reverses, **the Six** agreed to broaden the common market to encompass the economy as a whole: the new EEC foresaw 'the approximation of such laws, regulations or administrative provisions of the Member States as directly affect the establishment or functioning of the common market' (Article 100 EEC, now, with some rewording, Article 115 TFEU). The market would be based on what became known as the '**four freedoms**': the free movement of goods, services, capital and people.

Over the decade from 1958 to 1968, during which restrictions on trade were gradually being dismantled, trade among the member states of the Community grew at an average annual rate of 28 per cent. Even if this represented the acceleration of a trend which had already began in the 1950s, as part of the general post-war recovery, the rate of increase was fully twice that experienced in trade with non-Community countries in Europe. However, although the customs union was completed, as planned, by 1 July 1968, the single market had to wait longer. The **European Commission**, responsible for proposing draft legislation, chose to follow the laborious path of enforced **harmonization**, aiming to replace the full array of national laws in any individual sector with a single set of new common rules. Very often, this approach became bogged down in technicalities, a problem compounded by the need for **unanimity** when adopting the proposed legislation within the **Council of Ministers.**

After a second decade of slow progress, the logjam began to break in the early 1980s. The 1979 '**Cassis de Dijon**' ruling by the **European Court of Justice** (ECJ) prompted the Commission to move away from a strategy of complete harmonization towards the simpler route of 'mutual recognition' of existing national standards, wherever circumstances allowed. This was matched by a growing feeling among industrialists that market fragmentation along national lines was hampering the ability of European firms to compete internationally. Within the newly elected European Parliament, the **Kangaroo Group** took the lead in identifying the missing gaps in the single market and campaigning for them to be closed. The Parliament sponsored the **Albert–Ball Report**, which argued that there was a serious economic cost to '**non-Europe**'. Fortunately, the new President of the European Commission, **Jacques Delors**, taking office in January 1985, believed that the Community was badly in need of a bold, imaginative idea upon which to focus its energies. The project that seemed to command the widest support in national capitals was a concerted effort to complete the single market. Later that spring, the **Cockfield White Paper** identified the legislative measures needed to achieve this goal and the **European Council** set a deadline of December 1992 for their adoption, representing the lifespan of two four-year Commissions.

In parallel with the moves towards completing the single market, intergovernmental negotiations led to agreement on treaty reforms in the 1986 **Single European Act** (SEA). Given previous experience, it was generally recognized that the ambitious legislative programme set out in the Cockfield White Paper could not be completed unless decision-making was speeded up by greater use of **qualified majority voting** (QMV) in the Council. Accordingly, a new Article 95 EC (now **Article 114** TFEU) was added to the Treaty of Rome to allow single market measures to be agreed, not by unanimity, as under the original Article 94, but by qualified majority, the only exceptions being 'fiscal provisions, . . . the **free movement of persons** [and] the rights and interests of employed persons'. Another new article gave legal status to the 1992 deadline, and defined the single market as 'an area without internal frontiers in which the free movement of goods, persons, services and capital is ensured' (Article 14(2) EC, now Article 26(2) TFEU). The Single Act came into force on 1 July 1987.

The publicity surrounding the single market programme aroused great interest within the business community and some excitement more widely. Many member-state governments mounted 'awareness' programmes to ensure that their own businesses were prepared for the more intense competition likely to flow from it. Successive **presidencies** of the Council began to compete with each other to see how many items of single-market legislation could be agreed within each six-month period. By December 1992, some 260 out of the original list of 282 measures set out in the Cockfield White Paper had been adopted, although a number of these had not yet been transposed into national law and many had yet to enter into force.

Today, although the single market for goods is largely complete – with defence procurement and public purchasing being exceptions – there are still significant barriers affecting the free movement of services, capital and people. These tend to be of a technical nature when it comes to services and capital, reflecting differing national economic interests – notably in the financial services, healthcare, audiovisual and transport sectors – whereas they are often more obviously political when it comes to limitations on the '**freedom of establishment**' underpinning the free movement of citizens. Incomplete safeguards for intellectual property, the limited degree of **tax harmonization** and the rapidly evolving needs of the digital economy further complicate the situation. In May 2010, the **Monti Report** addressed some of these issues and 11 months later, the European Commission came forward with an action plan, known as the 'Single Market Act', which aimed to fill some of the remaining gaps through 12 specific legislative measures for adoption by the end of 2012. The Commission has estimated that the full implementation of the existing services directive, adopted in 2006, could boost EU GDP by up to 1.5 per cent and increase foreign direct investment (FDI) by a fifth.

Despite its shortcomings, the European Union's single market ranks as the largest common economic space within the industrialized world, comprising almost half a billion consumers, trading around four trillion euro in goods and services within the Union each year. It has contributed significantly to the prosperity and integration of the European economy, by reducing production costs, widening consumer choice and increasing competition. The European Commission estimates that, during the 2000s alone, the single market increased the Union's gross domestic product (GDP) by almost two per cent and created some 2.5 million jobs. Until the onset of the recent economic and financial crisis, trade within the EU was increasing at a rate of over 10 per cent per annum.

Six, The

'The Six' refers to the six countries – Belgium, France, Italy, Luxembourg, the Netherlands and West Germany – that formed the **European Coal and Steel Community** (ECSC) in 1951 under the **Treaty of Paris**, and then went on to found the **European Economic Community** (EEC) and the **European Atomic Energy Community** (EAEC or Euratom) under the two **Treaties of Rome** signed in March 1957. 'The Six' is a direct translation of the French *les*

Six. As membership of the **European Communities** widened through **enlargement**, the Six became the Nine in 1973 (adding Denmark, Ireland and the United Kingdom), the Ten in 1981 (Greece), and the Twelve in 1986 (Portugal and Spain). After the accession of Austria, Finland and Sweden in 1995, the phrase 'EU-15' began to be used in English, although *les Quinze* continued in French. The recent enlargements to include ten additional countries in 2004 (Cyprus, the Czech Republic, Estonia, Hungary, Latvia, Lithuania, Malta, Poland, Slovakia and Slovenia) and two more in 2007 (Bulgaria and Romania) have led to use of 'EU-25' and 'EU-27' in English (and *les Vingt-Cinq* and *les Vingt-Sept* in French).

In the pre-1973 literature on European integration, 'the Six' was often used to distinguish the member states of the Community from 'the Seven', the then countries that made up the **European Free Trade Association** (EFTA) at the time. At the height of the struggle between the two different visions of European integration which these organizations embodied – essentially of **supranationalism** versus **intergovernmentalism** – Europe was described as being 'at sixes and sevens'. Today, one tends to speak of the 'founding six' or the 'original six' when referring to the Six. The countries concerned still tend to be more strongly committed to the '**Community method**' than many of the member states that have joined more recently. Most of the leading post-war governmental leaders within the Six, with the notable exception of **Charles de Gaulle**, have been strong supporters of deeper European integration. The Six have all been members from the start of the **eurozone** and the **Schengen** group, and are often cited as potential or actual participants in any 'hard core' of a **two-speed Europe**. However, the rejection of the **European Constitution** in the **French and Dutch referenda** of May–June 2005 revealed a growing uncertainty among the electorates (and to some degree the political élites) of the Six about their place within the new, wider European Union which was emerging.

Social Charters and Social Chapter

The original *European Social Charter* was adopted in Turin in October 1961 by the member states of the **Council of Europe** and entered into force in 1965. Seen by its advocates at the time as a counterpart for economic and social rights to the 1950 **European Convention on Human Rights** (ECHR), the Charter listed 19 basic rights which all signatories accepted. Revisions to the Charter in 1988, 1991 and 1995 extended the number of rights to 31, but loosened the obligation to observe them. Signatories must now respect a 'compulsory nucleus' of six out of nine specified rights, and a total of 16 rights in all.

Unlike the ECHR, the European Social Charter has never been backed by judicial machinery for enforcement. Instead, observance is monitored by a committee of experts appointed (for a six-year term) by the Committee of Ministers of the Council of Europe. The latter's Parliamentary Assembly may also submit its views on the conclusions of experts. The Committee of Ministers may decide, by a two-thirds majority, to make 'necessary recommendations' to signatory states if they appear to be in default of obligations under the Charter. The impact of the Charter is thus vitiated by the feebleness of the enforcement procedures, which are heavily weighted in favour of governments.

The European Community's *Social Charter* – formally, the Charter on the Fundamental Social Rights of Workers – was adopted as a non-binding declaration by heads of government at the **European Council** meeting in Strasbourg in December 1989, with the support of all member states except the United Kingdom. It represented a significant move by **Jacques Delors**, as President of the **European Commission**, to develop a 'Social Europe' to complement his programme for completing the **single market** by 1992 and (to a lesser extent) ease left-wing fears about the 'monetarist' implications of the possible introduction of a single currency. The government of **Margaret Thatcher** asserted that the EC Charter did not prioritize job creation or respect the diversity of national practices and traditions in an area of policy that it believed should, in accordance with the principle of **subsidiarity**, be determined primarily by member states individually.

The scope of the EC Charter was very broad, covering freedom of movement, **equal treatment** for men and women, living and working conditions, social security, vocational training, health and safety, special measures for young people, the elderly, and the disabled, and the right to information, consultation and participation in the workplace. Despite UK objections, the adoption of the Charter was backed up soon after by the presentation by the European Commission of a 'Social Action Programme' of 47 proposals for legislation. In 2001, most of the rights contained in the EC Charter were incorporated in the broader **Charter of Fundamental Rights**, with the latter becoming legally binding in the Union through the **Lisbon Treaty** in December 2009.

The *Social Chapter* of the 1992 **Maastricht Treaty** was designed to make it easier to take forward the legislative agenda set out in the Social Action Programme. As Britain sought and secured an **opt-out** from this text, it was included not in the main body of the treaty, but rather as a **protocol**, with an 'Agreement on Social Policy' (concluded among the 11 other member states) attached. The agreement widened the scope of employment policy at EU level and extended **qualified majority voting** (QMV) in the **Council of Ministers** to important aspects of it. The United Kingdom was excluded from decision-making under the agreement and freed from the obligation to apply any legislation resulting from it. However, following the election of the Labour government of **Tony Blair** in 1997, Britain chose to rescind its opt-out, with the **Amsterdam Treaty** transposing the agreement into the main body of the treaty (as parts of Articles 151–9 TFEU) and applying it to all member states. The most prominent pieces of legislation adopted under the Social Chapter during its relatively brief lifetime (1993–7) were the directives on works councils (1994), parental leave (1996) and part-time work (1997).

Social and employment policy

Since the **European Coal and Steel Community** (ECSC) was founded in 1952, there has always been a social and employment dimension to the policies of the **European Communities**, now Union. The 1951 **Treaty of Paris** contained provisions aimed at safeguarding the wages of those employed in the coal and steel sectors and promoting the re-employment of those made redundant. The 1957 **Treaty of Rome**, establishing the **European Economic Community** (EEC) went further, entrusting the **European Commission** with the task of 'promoting close cooperation between Member States in the social field', particularly in matters relating to 'employment, labour law and working conditions, basic and advanced vocational training, social security, prevention of occupational accidents and diseases, occupational hygiene, [and] the right of association, and collective bargaining between employers and workers' (Article 118 EEC, now Article 156 TFEU). However, the **legal base** for the adoption of binding Community-level rules in these fields was unclear and any action required **unanimity**. The Treaty of Rome also asserted the principle of **equal treatment** between men and women in respect of pay (Article 119 EEC, now Article 157 TFEU) and established a **European Social Fund** (ESF) for worker training and retraining.

Few substantive measures were agreed under Article 118 EEC during the first quarter-century of the Community's existence. However, the arrival of **Jacques Delors** as President of the European Commission in 1985 marked a significant turning-point. He argued strongly that the Commission's flagship project, completion of the **single market** by 1992, should be matched by a parallel definition and levelling-up of employment rights at European level. This drive towards a 'Social Europe' was accepted by most heads of government, with the exception of British prime minister **Margaret Thatcher**. Delors ensured that, as a quid pro quo for the introduction of **qualified majority voting** (QMV) in the **Council of Ministers** on single market legislation in the 1986 **Single European Act** (SEA), the same decision-making method, together with a stronger legal base, would be provided for health and safety at work. A conscious policy of promoting the **social partners** at European level was also launched, with the Commission invited by the SEA to 'develop the dialogue between management and labour at

European level which could, if the two sides consider it desirable, lead to relations based on agreement' (Article 118(b) EEC, now Article 155(1) TFEU, reworded).

Delors maintained the momentum of Social Europe by proposing a non-binding European **Social Charter** – which was adopted by the **European Council**, meeting in Strasbourg in December 1989 in an eleven-to-one vote, in which Thatcher was defeated – and a 'Social Action Programme' of 47 items of legislation to give substance to the aspirations contained in the Charter. Soon after, the **Intergovernmental Conference** (IGC) that led to the 1992 **Maastricht Treaty** agreed to further strengthen the social provisions in the **Treaties** – both by making Union **competence** more explicit and widening the field of QMV – through adoption of what became known as the 'Social Chapter'. Thatcher's successor as prime minister, John Major, negotiated an **opt-out** for the United Kingdom from the Social Chapter, which stood as a **protocol**, annexed to the Treaties, for five years, until Major's own successor, **Tony Blair**, ended this anomaly in the 1997 **Amsterdam Treaty** (which incorporated the protocol as parts of Articles 151–61 TFEU).

As a result of this troubled and complex history, different aspects of social policy are subject to different decision-making methods within the EU institutions. QMV in the Council and **co-decision** between the Council and **European Parliament** (the 'ordinary legislative procedure') apply to legislation relating to the health and safety of workers, working conditions, information and consultation of workers, the integration of persons excluded from the labour market (and social exclusion more widely), and equality between men and women with regard to the labour market and treatment at work. However, **unanimity** in the Council and mere **consultation** of the European Parliament still apply to matters dealing with social security and the social protection of workers, redundancy, the 'representation and collective defence of the interests of workers and employers, including co-determination', and the conditions of employment for third-country nationals. QMV and co-decision can be used for measures promoting the 'modernization of social protection systems', provided that they do not touch on social security or the social protection of workers.

A unique (and surprisingly uncontroversial) feature of social policy decision-making is that, since the Amsterdam Treaty, it has been possible for the recognized social partners at European level to negotiate bilateral agreements which can then, provided that they correspond to a Union competence in the social policy field, be enacted in law. Use of this route requires the Commission to agree to make a proposal for adoption by the Council (Article 155 TFEU). The European Parliament has no standing whatever in such a process, not even being consulted on such measures.

Social partners

By origin a French expression (*partenaires sociaux*), 'social partners' denotes what in English are traditionally known as 'the two sides of industry', namely management and labour. Within the European Union, the **Economic and Social Committee** (ESC) – with its nominated representatives from employers, employees and 'various interests' – was, from the 1950s onwards, an institutional expression of the corporatism implicit in the idea of social partners. Since 1965, recognized bodies representing the social partners have been consulted directly by the **European Commission** on policy initiatives and relevant legislative proposals.

The European Commission and the **Council of Ministers** currently recognize six 'industry-wide' organizations as social partners at EU level. These are Business Europe (previously UNICE), the European Trade Union Confederation (ETUC), the Centre of Employers and Enterprises providing Public Services (CEEP), the European Association of Craft, Small and Medium-Sized Enterprises (UEAPME), the European Confederation of Executives and Managerial Staff (CEC), and *Eurocadres* (of professional and managerial staff).

In 1970, the Commission proposed, and the Council established, an EC Standing Employment Committee, which brought together the social partners, as well as the Commission and Council, for periodic meetings to discuss policy issues of mutual interest. In January 1985, the incoming President of the Commission, **Jacques Delors**, convened a meeting with business and trade-union leaders at Château Val Duchesse in Brussels, to launch a new 'social dialogue'. Soon after, the 1986 **Single European Act** (SEA) invited the Commission to 'endeavour to develop the dialogue between management and labour at European level which could, if the two sides consider it desirable, lead to relations based on agreement' (Article 118(b) EEC, since deleted). Subsequently, the 1997 **Amsterdam Treaty** formalized an obligation on the part of the Commission to 'take any relevant measure to facilitate' the dialogue between management and labour, and to consult both before submitting legislative proposals in the field of **social and employment policy** (Article 154 TFEU). It also allowed them to develop 'contractual relations, including agreements' which they would negotiate bilaterally, on their own. Such 'bipartite' or 'autonomous' agreements could be implemented either by the parties themselves – 'in accordance with the procedures and practices specific to management and labour and the Member States' – or, provided that they corresponded to a **competence** of the EU in the social policy field, they could be enacted in law. The latter route requires the Commission to agree to make a proposal for adoption by the Council (Article 155 TFEU). The **European Parliament** is simply informed of such agreements, being neither consulted on them nor a party to them.

Over the last quarter-century, over 300 bipartite agreements of various kinds have been negotiated by the social partners, often in specific sectors. Recent examples of voluntary agreements across the economy as a whole are those concluded on telework (2002), stress at work (2004) and harassment and violence at work (2007). Economy-wide agreements transposed by the Council into law have become less common over the last decade. Earlier examples include the directives on parental leave (1996), part-time work (1997) and fixed-term work (1999). Examples of where the social partners were unable to reach agreement include temporary agency work, information and consultation of employees, and European works councils.

Institutionally, the bipartite social dialogue at EU level takes place through a 64-member Social Dialogue Committee (SDC), with 32 representatives each from management and labour. Created in 1992, the SDC meets three to four times a year and may establish working groups on specific issues. When attempting to conclude an agreement, each side appoints a formal negotiating team and works from a negotiating mandate approved by its respective organizations. If successful, the outcome is formally adopted by the SDC and then submitted for approval to the signatories' decision-making bodies.

In March 2003, the Council abolished the Standing Employment Committee, which was generally thought to have become moribund, and replaced it with a 'Tripartite Social Summit for Growth and Employment'. Co-chaired by the President of the Commission and the **President of the European Council**, the Social Summit is held at least once a year, immediately before the spring meeting of the **European Council** (of heads of government). The management and labour sides each send a delegation of ten representatives. The current Council **presidency** and next two presidencies are also present. The secretariat is provided by the Commission.

Sovereignty

If sovereignty in relation to states is defined as an exclusive and comprehensive right of independent action, then it must follow that the member states of the European Union remain sovereign only in the sense that they could secede from the Union if they so wished. First under the **Treaty of Paris** (in 1952) and then under the **Treaty of Rome** (in 1957), the signatory states committed themselves to creating, in the words of the preamble of the latter treaty, an '**ever closer union** among the peoples of Europe', and established independent supranational institutions enjoying exclusive or shared **competence** in defined areas of policy. These institutions were endowed with a capacity for making laws which implicitly possessed both **primacy** and **direct effect** in the signatory states. The Treaty of Rome (unlike the Treaty of Paris) was concluded for an indefinite period. (See **supranationalism and intergovernmentalism**.)

It is often said that in signing the **Treaties**, the member states 'pooled' or 'merged' their sovereignty, in the sense that they thereby committed themselves to exercising their sovereignty in common in certain specified fields. Although attractive politically, such a notion is not consistent with the definition of sovereignty given above, under which the joint exercise of sovereignty is a contradiction in terms. In legal terms, it is more helpful to regard member states as having *delegated* their powers within defined limits to the institutions of what is now the European Union, albeit for an indefinite period. Such a delegation has occurred with respect to both internal and external actions. Article 5(2) TFEU speaks of the 'principle of conferral', whereby the Union 'shall only act within the limit of the competences conferred upon it by the Member States in the Treaties' and competences not so conferred 'remain with the Member States'.

In the British context, in particular, where there is no written constitution, the word 'sovereignty' is often used to refer to what might more accurately be described as 'parliamentary sovereignty'. This may be defined as the exclusive and comprehensive right of a **national parliament** to make laws within the national political system. However, as the EU Treaties constitute in effect a pan-European constitutional framework, national parliaments have lost their exclusive right to make laws that are binding upon their citizens. In any conflict between a law passed by a national parliament and one passed by the EU institutions, the latter automatically takes precedence, so long as national courts consider themselves so bound. It follows that parliamentary sovereignty can only be said to exist either in those policy areas where the EU has no competence or to the extent that a national parliament could pass a law forcing the member state in question to leave the Union.

That membership of the European Union entails a significant 'loss of sovereignty' is perhaps the most basic, but also one of the most powerful, of the arguments deployed by anti-Europeans in debates about EU treaty changes. It has played an important part in campaigns against various treaties in the United Kingdom, Denmark and more recently Ireland. It is often countered by the assertion that what really counts is not so much formal notions of sovereignty, such as state or parliamentary sovereignty, but the practical capacity of a country to defend or advance its own interests in an increasingly interdependent world. In pursuit of the latter, it may make sense to forego the legal cloak of sovereignty in order to retain the reality of its substance.

Especially for a small member state with little independent influence in the world, the transfer of sovereignty to a larger entity in whose decision-making process it will have some standing, may represent a net increase in that country's political power. Even for large member states, the ability to develop common policies on a continental scale can offer countries access to a 'collective good' that it could not generate on its own. The combined strength, whether economic or political, offered by the EU's **single market**, single currency or external trade policy, for example, has long been seen by many as justifying the loss of sovereignty that common binding rules entail. The rise of new challenges in an era of globalization – such as climate change, energy security, migration, terrorism and other forms of international crime – provides a further justification for action of this kind.

Most treaties curtail the freedom of action of their signatory states in certain specific areas. To take only the most obvious example, the Washington Treaty establishing the **North Atlantic Treaty Organization** (NATO) obliges the signatory states to come to the aid of any NATO member threatened by aggression, and if necessary to go to war. All treaties embodying obligations entail some loss of sovereignty; however, in international law, a capacity freely to enter into obligations laid down by treaty is part of the definition of a sovereign state. What makes the Treaty of Rome and its successor treaties qualitatively different from other treaties is the fact that the supranational political institutions they create are able to draw up and adopt laws that are binding upon the signatory states themselves. Moreover, the range of subjects affected goes well beyond those external actions with which most international treaties are concerned.

Further reading: Stanley Hoffmann, 'Reflections on the Nation State in Europe Today', in Hoffmann, *The European Sisyphus*, 1995; Noel Malcolm, *Sense on Sovereignty*, 1991.

Spaak, Paul-Henri (1899–1972)

His father a playwright and mother a Socialist senator, Paul-Henri Spaak was the most influential Belgian politician of the mid-twentieth century, serving as prime minister three times, including the period immediately before the Second World War, and as foreign minister for a total of 13 years. His time in government included three decisive periods in post-war history, on all of which he left a distinctive mark: the years in which new international institutions were established (1945–9), those leading up to the signing of the **Treaties of Rome** (1954–7), and those when French President **Charles de Gaulle** attempted to halt the logic of supranational integration in Europe (1961–6). From 1957 to 1961, Spaak served as Secretary General of the **North Atlantic Treaty Organization** (NATO), then based in Paris. A keen advocate of European integration, he was also a committed Atlanticist and a strong supporter of British membership of the emerging **European Communities**.

Captured by the Germans whilst attempting to join the Belgian army during the First World War, Spaak was consigned to a prison camp at the age of 17. He then became a Marxist, republican lawyer in Brussels, before being elected as a Socialist deputy in 1932. The combination of his obvious talent and a continuing moderation in his political views led to appointment to government and rapid promotion – as successively transport, foreign and prime minister within only three years (1935–8). Having controversially advocated Belgian neutrality before his country's invasion by Nazi Germany, as foreign minister, he famously faced down both the German authorities and King Leopold III, and became a central member of Belgium's government-in-exile in London.

After the war, Spaak was chosen as prime minister once again and led the campaign to prevent the king's return to power. Both as premier and then foreign minister, he also showed a determination to contribute to the design of a new world order way beyond the power-base conventionally offered by Belgian politics. He actively supported all efforts to construct international institutions, helping create **Benelux** and backing the **United Nations**, the **Marshall Plan**, NATO and the **Council of Europe**. He was the first president of the UN General Assembly in 1946 and chaired the Ministerial Council of the **Organization for European Economic Cooperation** (OEEC) in 1948. Out of power, he became President of the Consultative Assembly of the Council of Europe in 1949–51, a post from which he resigned in protest against the United Kingdom's rejection of the **Schuman Plan**.

Like **Jean Monnet**, Spaak believed deeply that supranational institutions were the next logical step in the uniting of Europe. Coming from a small country that had suffered twice in his own lifetime from the consequences of Franco-German enmity, Spaak's advocacy of 'federal' solutions at European level was logical – and indeed quickly became conventional wisdom in the Benelux countries. From 1952 to 1954, he was the first President of the Common Assembly of the **European Coal and Steel Community** (ECSC), serving opposite Monnet, who was President of its **High Authority**. Deeply disappointed by the failure of the **European Defence Community** (EDC), Spaak used his return to government in 1954 to push hard for a rapid revival of discussions among **the Six** about **sovereignty**-sharing in the economic field. He chaired the **Spaak Committee** (1955–6) set up by the **Messina Conference** in June 1955 to undertake the detailed preparatory work for what became soon after the **European Economic Community** (EEC) and **European Atomic Energy Community** (EAEC or Euratom). His firm leadership of this group in the direction of drafting specific treaty texts proved a decisive development and, given the rapid creation of the Communities thereafter, established his clear claim to be one of the **founding fathers** of the European Union.

After his time as Secretary General of NATO, Spaak returned to Belgian politics once again, as deputy prime minister and foreign minister, and quickly played a critical role in extricating Belgium from its damaging decolonization crisis in the Congo. Working closely with his Dutch colleague,

Joseph Luns, he chose to confront de Gaulle in 1961–2 over his design for an intergovernmental Europe, in the form of the **Fouchet Plan**, uttering the memorable phrase *l'Europe sera supranationale ou ne sera pas* ('Europe will be supranational or it will not be'). He led international criticism of the French President's decision to veto British membership of the Communities and supported **Walter Hallstein** in the struggle with the General over the powers of the **European Commission** and the extension of **qualified majority voting** (QMV) in the **Council of Ministers** – the 'empty chair crisis' – that led to the **Luxembourg Compromise** in January 1966. Both on the Fouchet Plan and during the empty chair crisis, he helped forge an alliance of 'the Five' against France, seriously constraining de Gaulle.

Spaak left office later in 1966, after the Socialists were ejected from government in Belgium. He then resigned from parliament when his party opposed the offer by the new centre-right administration that Brussels host NATO, after de Gaulle expelled the organization from Paris. Despite his significant impact in promoting or defending European integration at critical moments, Spaak left the political stage disappointed by the faltering path of the ambitious project to which he was devoted. He wrote in 1967:

> *The Europe that we wanted, the Europe whose position in the world we intended to restore, the Europe that we hoped to make the equal of the United States and the Soviet Union, is no longer realisable . . . My earlier enthusiasms, I can now appreciate, were illusions. We have not known how to halt the decline which has been Western Europe's penalty for the follies of the two world wars that originated among us.*

Spaak's memoirs, *Combats inachevés*, were published in two volumes in 1969 (and in English as *The Continuing Battle: Memories of a European* in 1971).

Spaak Committee

One of the decisions of the **Messina Conference** in June 1955 – a meeting of the foreign ministers of the **European Coal and Steel Community** (ECSC) – was to set up 'a committee of government delegates', chaired by Belgian foreign minister **Paul-Henri Spaak**, to make proposals for closer economic integration among **the Six**. Drawing on proposals such as the **Beyen Plan**, the Spaak Committee met between July 1955 and April 1956. It presented its final report to the ECSC foreign ministers, meeting at the Fondazione Cini in Venice, on 29–30 May 1956.

The 135-page Spaak Report – which subsequently provided the basis for the two treaties establishing the **European Economic Community** (EEC) and the **European Atomic Energy Community** (EAEC or Euratom) – was largely drafted by the French economist **Pierre Uri**, a close confidant of **Jean Monnet**. It addressed three main issues: the creation of a **common market**, a joint policy for nuclear energy, and treatment of certain priority economic sectors, including non-nuclear energy, transport and telecommunications. The report answered questions put by the Messina Conference about the choice between establishing a general common market and engaging in selective sectoral integration. Influenced by the sometimes difficult experience of the ECSC, it recommended the former, cross-sector approach, backed by a **customs union** and common external tariff.

The foreign ministers accepted the report after only a brief discussion, the single proviso being that the **overseas countries and territories** (OCTs) of the signatory states should be included in any new economic unit (a concession to France). The report dealt only cursorily with institutional questions, proposing a model broadly similar to that already established for the ECSC, with an independent executive commission, a stronger (legislative) council of national ministers, a supervisory parliamentary assembly, and a court responsible for adjudicating legal disputes.

Although the United Kingdom government had sent an observer to the Messina Conference and agreed to participate in the early sessions of the Spaak Committee, it decided in November 1955 to leave the process. Officially, its position was that the customs union towards which the Six were obviously moving was incompatible with Britain's preferential trading arrangements with the Commonwealth. Equally, the UK, which was already financing atomic research programmes with the United States and Canada, was reluctant to prejudice such cooperation through Euratom.

Against the background of the **Suez crisis** and the abortive Hungarian uprising of November 1956, it became increasingly clear that the Six were determined to move ahead as rapidly as possible with the new project. Only ten months after the Venice meeting, the EEC and Euratom Treaties were signed in Rome. For this reason, the work of the Spaak Committee is often referred to as a critical turning-point in the history of European integration. Its success is in part attributable to the fact that it was composed not of cautious, mid-rank officials but of independent-minded people who, by virtue of their experience and seniority, enjoyed the confidence of government leaders.

Spinelli, Altiero (1907–86)

Born in Rome, Altiero Spinelli was a lifelong advocate of **federalism**. A journalist and a leader of the young Communist movement in Lazio, he was arrested in 1927 and spent ten years in prison and a further six in 'confinement'. During the Second World War he was interned on the island of Ventotene, in the Gulf of Gaeta, along with some 800 others hostile to Mussolini's régime. In June 1941, Spinelli and a small group of federalists completed a 'manifesto', the final version of which was written on cigarette papers and concealed in the false bottom of a tin box. It was circulated clandestinely within the Resistance and adopted as the programme of the *Movimento Federalista Europeo*, which Spinelli founded in Milan in August 1943, following his release.

The Ventotene manifesto reflected Spinelli's disillusionment with orthodox Communism and his growing view, reflecting his reading *in confino* of leading Anglo-Saxon federalist theorists and professional economists – notably James Madison, Philip Lothian, William Beveridge and Lionel Robbins – that, as John Pinder has put it, 'the cause of war was not, as the Marxists claimed, capitalism, but absolute national **sovereignty**' which could be constrained within a post-war federal European structure, in which 'a democratic Germany should occupy a worthy place' (see below). The Ventotene manifesto argued that the eventual defeat of Germany should not be used by the Allied powers to restore the nation state in its old form, in a pattern consistent with their traditional geopolitical and economic interests. Instead, to prevent the resurgence of the 'ideology of national independence', the opportunity presented by the turmoil and uncertainty accompanying the end of the war must be seized to establish a 'European Federation . . . a free and united Europe'. Chief among the tasks of such a federation would be social reconstruction, ending the pre-eminence of the Catholic Church and the abandonment of corporatism. Advocates of federalism should prepare a set of new institutions as the moulds into which the 'incandescent lava' of popular feeling could be allowed to pour, there to cool and settle.

After the war, Spinelli resumed his career in journalism, from which he exercised a growing influence on the thinking of policy-makers in Rome about European integration. His writings also attracted the attention of **Jean Monnet**, who invited him to draft several speeches, including his address to the inaugural session of the Common Assembly of the **European Coal and Steel Community** (ECSC) in 1952. At this time, Spinelli was the lead advocate of the idea – put forward in 1950–52 by the Italian Christian Democrat prime minister, **Alcide de Gasperi** – that there should be a directly-elected assembly to underpin the planned **European Defence Community** (EDC). This was the genesis of the ambitious proposal for a **European Political Community** (EPC), which ironically contributed to the non-ratification of the EDC. Although equally disappointed, Spinelli diverged in his reaction to the failure of the EDC from that of Monnet and several other **founding fathers**, in arguing that the sectoral approach to integration had reached its limits. He distanced himself from the creation of the new **European Economic Community** (EEC) in 1957–8 and subsequently wrote a book, *The Eurocrats: Conflict and Crisis in the European Community* (1966), which criticized the **European Commission** for becoming the servant of the **Council of Ministers**, rather than the true driving force for integration. He taught at the Bologna campus of Johns Hopkins University and founded the *Istituto per Affari Internazionali* in 1967.

With the decline and departure of **Charles de Gaulle** as President of France, ending a period of stasis in the Community's development, Spinelli began to re-engage in practical politics, working first with the Italian foreign minister, Pietro Nenni, as a political adviser in Rome, and then accepting nomination in 1970 as one of Italy's (then two) members of the European Commission, with responsibility for industrial policy and the environment. He used his position in the Commission to argue strongly for institutional reform, proposing that a working party of independent experts be tasked with providing an assessment of the functioning of the Community. The resulting **Vedel Report** (of March 1972) proposed a range of reforms, notably an increase in the legislative power of the **European Parliament**, that were to become increasingly mainstream with the passage of time. He also effected a personal reconciliation with the *Partito Comunista Italiano* (PCI), which he had originally joined in 1924, but from which he had been expelled as too moderate in 1937. Now a pioneer of **Eurocommunism**, the PCI invited him to stand, as an independent of the left *(Indipendente di Sinistra)*, on its list for the 1976 Italian general election. Resigning as a Commissioner, he served on the foreign affairs committee of the Chamber of Deputies and was chosen as a nominated Member of the European Parliament (MEP).

In June 1979, Spinelli was elected to the European Parliament in the first direct elections, once again as an independent of the left, where he quickly made an impact through force of character and tenacity of argument. He campaigned vigorously for wide-ranging reforms to the Community institutions, first through an informal, all-party group known as the 'Crocodile Club' (named after the Strasbourg restaurant in which the group was founded in July 1980), and then, from January 1982, in the Parliament's committee on institutional affairs, established at his instigation and of which he became general **rapporteur** and later chairman. He wished to see the Parliament assume the role of a constituent assembly, which would adopt a draft **European Constitution**, to be submitted in turn for endorsement at the next European elections in June 1984. The text eventually adopted by the Parliament in February 1984 – the **Draft Treaty establishing the European Union** (DTEU) – was the principal monument to this final period of Spinelli's life. Although the proposal did not in the end command sufficient support outside the European Parliament to be adopted, there are many who have argued – among them **Jacques Delors**, who became Commission President in 1985 – that without the impetus which the Draft Treaty provided, the **Single European Act** (SEA), signed soon after, could never have been brought into being. Many of the ideas contained in the DTEU found their way into subsequent treaties.

Spinelli himself was more modest about his achievements. He was disappointed by what he saw as the lack of ambition of the Single Act and was openly critical of Delors' pragmatism. He died in May 1986 before their (largely unexpected) impact in revitalizing the European project could become apparent. The successive dashing of his hopes for a post-war European federation, a European Political Community and a constituent assembly troubled him. He saw himself as an outsider, battling not only the forces of nationalism, but also those of bureauractic realpolitik which he felt had distorted the Community institutions. He allegedly commented that Monnet had the 'great merit of having built Europe and the great responsibility for having built it badly'. The irony that his own thinking was given a particularly cool reception in the United Kingdom, even though British intellectuals had been perhaps his principal source of inspiration, was not lost on him either.

In his autobiography, *Come ho tentato di diventare saggio* ('How I Sought to Become Wise'; published posthumously in 1988), Spinelli compares himself to the fisherman in Ernest Hemingway's *The Old Man and the Sea,* who catches a huge fish after a long struggle, only to find on reaching the shore that, lashed to the side of his boat, his catch has been largely eaten away during the voyage home.

Further reading: John Pinder, 'Altiero Spinelli's European Federal Odyssey', *The International Spectator*, December 2007.

Stability and Growth Pact (SGP)

The Stability and Growth Pact, adopted by the Amsterdam meeting of the **European Council** in June 1997, is a set of political commitments and **legal acts** designed to strengthen discipline in the public finances of member states participating in, or aspiring to membership of, stage three of **Economic and Monetary Union** (EMU).

The Pact owes its origins to dissatisfaction in the German Bundesbank and finance ministry with aspects of the final deal struck in the **Intergovernmental Conference** (IGC) on EMU in 1990–91. Both bodies had sought and failed to secure unequivocally binding budgetary rules in the EMU provisions of the 1992 **Maastricht Treaty**. Although their position enjoyed broad support in the **Monetary Committee** at EU level, it was in effect overridden by German Chancellor **Helmut Kohl** in a bilateral deal with French President **François Mitterrand**. The flexibility allowed by the treaty in the interpretation by the **Council of Ministers** of whether a member state, even once it had met the **convergence criteria** used to assess entry to stage three, might subsequently be running an 'excessive deficit' led Theo Waigel, the German finance minister, to renew the charge on this point once the treaty had been ratified. The **excessive deficit procedure** (EDP), like the convergence criteria before that, requires member states to meet or come close to certain 'reference values', namely a government deficit of 3 per cent of gross national product (GDP) and national debt of 60 per cent of GDP. If they fail to do so, the Council may (on the basis of a proposal from the **European Commission**) apply sanctions against offending states – notably, in the form of non-interest-bearing loans or fines – although in practice no such sanctions have ever been administered.

In November 1995, Waigel proposed a 'Stability Pact for Europe', in which the Union would commit itself to more ambitious deficit and debt targets, backed by automatic sanctions to be administered by an independent body (a 'Stability Council'), with the resulting arrangements to be confirmed by treaty change. However, the SGP eventually adopted in 1997 fell short of the Waigel plan on all counts. Its centrepiece was simply a European Council resolution – committed to 'safeguarding sound government finances' as a means to 'strengthen the conditions for price stability' – in which the member states, the Council and the Commission set out how they proposed to engage in the prompt and vigorous implementation of the excessive deficit procedure. In parallel, two Council **regulations** attempted to tighten up the 'surveillance' procedure within the EDP, under Article 126 TFEU, and limit the discretion enjoyed by the institutions in the event of a member state moving away from the existing deficit and debt targets.

In practice, the adoption of the SGP was to exercise very little constraint on member states' budgetary policies. From the early 2000s, the Council began to turn a blind eye to Commission recommendations for greater fiscal responsibility as they approached the three per cent deficit threshold. The (then) President of the Commission, Romano Prodi, aided this process by noting casually in October 2002 that the SGP was 'stupid' in attempting to penalise countries already in financial difficulty. The decisive turning-point came the following year, when France and (ironically) Germany fought very hard to prevent the spirit of the SGP and the formal provisions of the EDP from being applied to their own excessive budget deficits. The Commission had proposed that member states reduce their deficits by 0.5 per cent in 2004 to bring the figures below the three per cent target. In November 2003, the **Ecofin Council** was unable to agree on whether to act against both countries, with the **presidency** finally proposing to postpone application of the rules for a temporary period. Italy and the United Kingdom supported France and Germany, whilst most smaller member states opposed the bending of the rules.

Although public finances in the EU member states subsequently improved during the mid-2000s, driven by buoyant growth, the SGP in general, and the EDP in particular, never recovered as a disciplining force. As Pascal

Lamy, a European Commissioner at the time, put it succinctly, 'the instrument of credibility had been destroyed.' The fiscal position of many member states was subsequently overwhelmed in any case by the global economic and financial crisis, starting in the autumn of 2008. The magnitude of the downturn generated average deficits among eurozone states of 6.0 per cent of GDP or above in 2009 and 2010, with only three countries – Estonia, Finland and Luxembourg – registering deficits of below 3.0 per cent in either year.

As a response to the developing **eurozone debt crisis**, the European Council decided in March 2010, at German insistence, to broaden and deepen the components of the SGP, as part of a general strengthening of '**European economic governance**'. A package of six legislative measures was adopted for this purpose by the Council in October 2010 (in four cases jointly with the **European Parliament** under the **co-decision procedure**). As part of this 'Six Pack', the existing EDP, which now represents the 'corrective arm' of the SGP, was made more stringent, with sanctions meant to apply more automatically. In parallel, a more coherent 'preventative arm' was put in place to try to avoid any member state's fiscal situation deteriorating to the point of an excessive deficit in the first place. A 'medium-term budgetary objective' would be assigned to the economy of each eurozone state, including an 'expenditure benchmark' for its future public spending trajectory. An 'excessive imbalances procedure' has also been instituted, to provide an early warning system for other emerging stresses within economies. In each case, sanctions may be imposed on eurozone states by the Council for non-compliance, as in the EDP. (Further details of the Six Pack changes are set out in the entry on the EDP in this *Companion*.)

Further reading: Mathieu Segers and Femke Van Esch, 'The Political Logic of the Budgetary Rules in EMU and the SGP', *Journal of Common Market Studies*, Volume 45, Number 5, December 2007.

Staff regulations

The European Union, like most international organizations, has detailed internal regulations which set out the terms and conditions on which its staff are employed. In the case of the institutions and bodies of the EU, the 'Staff Regulations of officials and the conditions of employment of other servants of the European Communities', running to some 120 pages in English, have the force of law. They establish the rules for the recruitment, promotion, remuneration and retirement of officials, as well as the respective rights and obligations of employees and employers. These arrangements take precedence over the national employment legislation applying in the member state in which the employee is based and may be less generous than such laws. Although the staff regulations apply equally in principle to all the EU institutions and bodies, their detailed application in each case is often subject to internal implementing decisions that may lead to variations in practice.

The original staff regulations for the **European Economic Community** (EEC), adopted in December 1961, drew heavily on French and Belgian administrative practices of that time. This can be seen in the importance attached to the definition of the formal role and responsibilities of the official, to his or her recruitment by open competition, and to the principle that as many staff as possible (from the top of the organization to the bottom) should enjoy the status of permanent officials – unlike in Germany, say, with its firm distinction between *Beamte* (officials) and *Angestellte* (clerks). The staff regulations of the various Communities were consolidated into a single text in March 1968, following the 1965 **Merger Treaty**, and have been amended frequently since.

In April 2004, significant changes were introduced to the staff regulations through the so-called 'Kinnock reforms', proposed by the (then) Vice-President of Commission, Neil Kinnock. In particular, these reforms attempted to increase vertical and horizontal mobility within the bureaucracy, by reducing the number of hierarchical categories among officials (from four to two) and making it easier for senior posts to be held by staff of more junior grades. They also lowered the average grade at which new entrants were recruited and increased the retirement age for officials. (Further details on the staff regulations and changes made to them by the Kinnock reforms can be found in the entry on **Eurocrats**.)

Enacted in the form of **regulations**, under Article 336 TFEU, the staff regulations were, until the **Lisbon Treaty**, adopted by the **Council of Ministers**, using **qualified majority voting** (QMV), with the **European Parliament** called upon to give only an **opinion** under the **consultation procedure**. Since Lisbon entered into force in December 2009, the Council now acts jointly with the Parliament under the **co-decision procedure**. The staff regulations are justiciable in a special EU Civil Service Tribunal, which forms part of the **European Court of Justice** (ECJ).

Structural funds

The structural funds are the principal means by which financial aid is directed towards the less-developed regions of the European Union. Article 175 TFEU lists the structural funds as the **European Social Fund** (ESF), the **European Regional Development Fund** (ERDF) and the 'guidance' section of the European Agricultural Guidance and Guarantee Fund (EAGGF) of the **Common Agricultural Policy** (CAP). (Often the Financial Instrument for Fisheries Guidance (FIFG) of the **Common Fisheries Policy** (CFP) is grouped together with the EAGGF.) However, in terms of day-to-day Union business, the structural funds are now usually taken to denote the ESF, the ERDF and the **Cohesion Fund**. In total, the three latter funds will receive € 347 billion over the seven-year financing period from 2007 to 2013, compared with € 213 billion for the years 2000–06. The total for 2007–13 is divided as follows: ESF, € 76 billion; ERDF, € 201 billion; and the Cohesion Fund, € 70 billion. Additional funding is contributed by the member states. The share of EU spending represented by these funds has been growing over time: from 13 per cent in 1985 to over 38 per cent today.

The ESF was foreseen in the original **Treaty of Rome** (Articles 123–8 EEC) and was put into effect from 1960 onwards. Its purpose is to 'improve employment opportunities for workers' through Community programmes for vocational training and retraining, as well as the promotion of geographical and occupational mobility (Article 162 TFEU). The ERDF was agreed in 1972 and introduced three years later, in parallel with the first **enlargement** of the Community (1973), with a view to providing capital assistance for productive investment and infrastructure in the regions. The fund was given treaty status by the 1986 **Single European Act** (SEA), which stated its purpose as being 'to help redress the main regional imbalances' of the Community, by contributing to the 'structural adjustment of regions whose development is lagging behind' and to the 'conversion of declining industrial regions' (Article 176 TFEU).

The **accession** of Greece in 1981 and of Portugal and Spain in 1986 led to a new emphasis in Community politics on 'economic and social cohesion' in general and on 'reducing disparities between the various regions and the backwardness of the less-favoured regions', in particular, as the Single Act put it (Article 174 TFEU). Several governments argued that the programme for the completion of the **single market** by 1992 would increase still further economic divergences between 'core' regions over those on the periphery, unless financial assistance was provided for the modernization of the latter. Integrated Mediterranean Programmes (IMPs) were set up in 1985 to give special help to Greece and the Mediterranean regions of France and Italy. More importantly, between 1987 and 1993, the overall funding for the structural funds was doubled in size, as part of the 'Delors I' future financing settlement.

The 1992 **Maastricht Treaty** set out the role of the structural funds in greater detail (in Articles 174–8 TFEU) and required the creation of a Cohesion Fund by December 1993. The Edinburgh European Council in December 1992 agreed to double the structural funds again over the period 1994–9, as part of the 'Delors II' financial settlement. In parallel, significant changes were made to the way the structural funds were administered. From 1989, funding was assigned to five horizontal objectives:

Objective 1	Assisting underdeveloped regions.
Objective 2	Assisting regions affected by the decline of traditional industries.
Objective 3	Combatting long-term unemployment (defined as more than 12 months) and the integration of young people (under-25s) into the labour market.
Objective 4	Helping workers adapt to technological change.
Objective 5	(a) Structural reform of agriculture, and (b) Helping rural areas.

Of these, Objective 1 was by far the most important, absorbing two-thirds of total funds. The enlargement negotiations with Austria, Finland and Sweden (leading to their accession in 1995) resulted in the creation of a sixth objective, designed primarily for assistance to the Arctic regions. By the mid-1990s, just over half of the Union's population lived in areas covered by Objectives 1, 2, 5(b) and 6. The **European Commission** proposed to reduce this figure to at most 40 per cent. As a result, with further enlargement, many regions would lose their eligibility for assistance from the structural funds.

Proposals for the further reform of the structural funds were included in the Commission's Agenda 2000 programme, which was adopted by the **European Council** in Berlin in March 1999. The criteria for eligibility were modified and the seven objectives were reduced to three:

Objective 1	Assisting underdeveloped regions, namely those with a per capita GDP less than 75 per cent of the Union average.
Objective 2	Helping areas facing structural difficulties.
Objective 3	Education, training and employment in areas not covered by Objective 1.

Just under 70 per cent of structural fund money was allocated to Objective 1 regions, with transitional relief for regions that were to lose their assisted area status. Each member state was given a quota of structural fund receipts: for the 2007–13 period, Poland is due to receive almost 20 per cent of total funds (€ 67.3 billion), Spain just over 10 per cent (€ 35.2 billion) and the Czech Republic nearly eight per cent (€ 26.7 billion). On a per capita basis, the 12 member states that joined the Union in 2004 and 2007 all feature among the top 15 recipients (with Greece, Portugal and Spain being the other three).

Maps must be drawn, and periodically redrawn, to define which areas qualify for assistance. This is undertaken by the Commission, in consultation with member states. Currently, Objective 1 regions cover approximately 22 per cent of the Union's total population, including the whole of Greece, Ireland (except Dublin), Portugal (except Lisbon), most of Spain, the French overseas territories, southern Italy, Sardinia, Sicily, all the former East Germany (except Berlin), and parts of Finland, Sweden and the United Kingdom.

Financial assistance from the structural funds, which is always given in the form of grants, is intended to complement assistance given at the national level, in accordance with the principle of **additionality**. The normal ratio involves 85 per cent of money coming from the EU Budget, matched by a 15 per cent national contribution. In certain cases, assistance may also be given in the form of loans from the **European Investment Bank** (EIB). In August 2011, in response to the **eurozone debt crisis**, the Commission proposed that the 85:15 per cent ratio be diluted from 2012 to a 95:5 ratio for six member states – Greece, Ireland and Portugal, which are in receipt of 'bail-out' loans from the **European Financial Stability Facility** (EFSF) and **European Financial Stabilization Mechanism** (EFSM), as well as Hungary, Latvia and Romania, which are taking advantage of the EU's 'balance of payments' loan facility for non-**eurozone** countries. Total annual receipts from the structural funds should not exceed four per cent of a member state's GDP. Six per cent of structural fund aid is reserved for initiatives devised and administered directly by the Commission itself, such as Interreg III (for cross-border projects), Leader Plus (for rural areas), and URBAN (for inner cities).

Stuttgart Declaration

The Stuttgart Declaration, formally known as the Solemn Declaration on **European Union**, was a wide-ranging statement concerning the institutions and policies of the European Community issued by the **European Council** meeting in Stuttgart on 17–19 June 1983. It represented the first serious attempt by heads of government to address the question of institutional reform and to push forward the 1972 objective of converting the Community into some form of 'European Union'. In terms deliberately reminiscent of the 1972 Paris summit, national leaders restated their determination to 'transform the whole complex of relations between their states into a European Union', envisaging for the first time the future adoption of a new treaty on the subject. It also attempted to codify the evolving role of the European Council in decision-making, as well as suggesting that the position of the **European Parliament** be enhanced, that European monetary cooperation be strengthened, and that the general scope of Community action be further broadened.

The Stuttgart Declaration represented a delayed response by the member states collectively to the **Genscher–Colombo Plan**, submitted by the German and Italian foreign ministers in November 1981 and the text of which it echoed in a number of respects. In external relations, the Declaration stressed the importance of developing the existing pattern of **European Political Cooperation** (EPC) and of joint action in respect of 'the political and economic aspects of security', although it fell short of endorsing the 'common foreign policy' proposed by the Genscher–Colombo text. It explained the European Council's role in promoting closer integration, declaring that henceforth it would be able to act 'in its capacity as' the **Council of Ministers** in any area of Community responsibility – something which was, in fact, legally invalid at the time, since action still required the latter's separate and subsequent endorsement. It confirmed that the president-in-office of the European Council would report to the European Parliament at least once every six months.

The Stuttgart Declaration obliquely challenged the continued operation of the **Luxembourg Compromise** – by which unanimity prevailed in practice for many decisions that were supposed to be taken in the Council by **qualified majority voting** (QMV) – by asserting that 'the application of the decision-making procedures laid down in the **Treaties** is of vital importance in order to improve the EC's capacity to act.' It did not endorse the proposal in the Genscher–Colombo Plan to establish new Councils for policy areas not provided for in the Treaties. It was generous, however, in its acknowledgement of the growing role of the European Parliament. It took up the Genscher–Colombo proposal to engage in non-binding consultation with the Parliament before the President of the **European Commission** was appointed and before new member states were admitted to the Community. It was agreed that, in practice, the **consultation procedure** would be extended to include all 'significant' **international agreements**.

Beyond institutional issues, the Declaration sought to intensify Community activity across a broad range of pressing economic policy issues in order to counteract the effects of the recession confronting Europe at the time. It spoke of adopting an 'overall economic strategy' to combat unemployment and inflation, and to promote convergence among national economies. It proposed a strengthening of the **European Monetary System** (EMS), including the development of a European Monetary Fund. Significantly, it identified the 'completion of the internal market' – one of the first official statements to use this phrase – as well as the 'development of an industrial strategy', as key Community objectives. It asserted that European Union was being achieved 'by deepening and broadening the scope of European activities so that they coherently cover . . . a growing proportion of member states' mutual relations', a process it evidently welcomed.

The Stuttgart Declaration was a statement of political intent – not a formal Council decision, let alone the treaty text that the Genscher–Colombo Plan had envisaged. It was criticized in the European Parliament and elsewhere both for its caution and the unenforceable character of its commitments. (The Parliament's much more ambitious **Draft Treaty establishing the European Union** (DTEU) was proposed the following year.)

However, the striking fact is that several of the Declaration's provisions were given legal force three years later in the 1986 **Single European Act** (SEA). The two exercises were linked by the commitment at the end of the Declaration to decide within five years on 'whether the progress achieved [in the interim] should be incorporated in a Treaty on European Union'. The Fontainebleau European Council of June 1984 set up both the **Dooge Committee** and the Adonnino Committee on a People's Europe. At the Milan European Council a year later, an **Intergovernmental Conference** (IGC) was convened, by a controversial majority vote, to negotiate the treaty changes which were to become the Single Act.

In retrospect, it is clear that the Stuttgart Declaration ended a long period in which institutional and policy deepening within the Community had been stalled. It marked an important turning-point, at the highest political level, in favour of closer integration, beginning a process which generated a series of very important reforms in the years to follow.

Subsidiarity

Subsidiarity is the principle that decisions should be taken at the lowest level consistent with effective action within a political system. Held to be a guiding principle of **federalism**, it has also been widely invoked in recent years as a means of limiting the European Union's **competence**. The 1992 **Maastricht Treaty** introduced a subsidiarity clause into the **Treaty of Rome** (Article 5 EC), since updated by the **Lisbon Treaty** (Article 5(3) TEU), which now reads:

> *Under the principle of subsidiarity, in areas which do not fall within its exclusive competence, the Union shall act only if and in so far as the objectives of the proposed action cannot be sufficiently achieved by the Member States . . . but can rather, by reason of the scale or effects of the proposed action, be better achieved at Union level.*

Subsidiarity is one of three principles of **EU law**, each now enjoying treaty status, which relate specifically to the extent and use of the Union's competence. The two others are 'conferral', whereby 'the Union shall only act within the limits of the competences conferred on it by the Member States by the **Treaties** to attain the objectives set out therein' (Article 5(2) TEU), and '**proportionality**', whereby 'the content and form of Union action shall not exceed what is necessary to achieve' those objectives (Article 5(4) TEU). The Lisbon Treaty has strengthened these principles by adding a de facto states' rights clause: 'Competences not conferred upon the Union in the Treaties remain with the Member States.' This latter proposition finds a parallel in the tenth amendment to the United States constitution and in Article 30 of the German constitution, both of which reserve to the states or *Länder* powers not specifically allocated to the federal government.

The intellectual antecedents of subsidiarity are said to lie in Pope Pius XI's encyclical letter *Quadragesima Anno* of 1931 – which talks of the 'principle of subsidiary function' – and in the writings of post-war German academics and Catholic thinkers, such as Hans Stadler, Oswald von Nell-Breuning and Gustav Gundlach. Before the Second World War, the Vatican found the concept useful in positing a limited role for the centralized state institutions that were eroding the Church's authority throughout Europe, not least in Italy. After the war, the German Christian Democrats sought to invoke subsidiarity to justify internal devolution within the new Federal Republic, as imposed by the 1949 constitution.

Subsidiarity only appeared on the European Community scene a quarter of a century later. The earliest reference to the concept in an official Community document is to be found in the **European Commission**'s submission to the **Tindemans Report** on **European Union** in June 1975. Paragraph 12 states: 'No more than the existing Communities have done so, European Union is not to give birth to a centralizing superstate. Consequently, and in accordance with the *principe de subsidiarité,* the Union will be given responsibility only for those matters which the Member States are no longer capable of dealing with efficiently.' The Commission's motive for invoking subsidiarity was to reassure those who feared that conversion of the Community into a Union would substantially erode the powers of national governments and parliaments. Perhaps because the Tindemans Report went less far than the Commission would have liked in proposing immediate steps towards Union, it did not take up the subsidiarity suggestion in its recommendations. Little more was heard of the notion, outside academic circles, for several years.

The notion of subsidiarity was taken up indirectly in the 1986 **Single European Act** (SEA), which inserted a new article into the Treaty of Rome: 'The Community shall take action relating to the environment to the extent to which [objectives] can be attained better at the Community level than at the level of individual Member States' (Article 130(r)4 EEC, since repealed). Although not yet of general application, the principle was increasingly invoked from the mid-1980s onwards by national governments intent upon finding ways of keeping Community competence in check. In December 1989, for example, the British government cited subsidiarity as one of several reasons for declining to sign the new Community **Social Charter**.

Subsidiarity emerged as a mainstream concept in Community circles when the impact of **German reunification** helped to reassert the centrality of federalism and states' rights in that country's political culture. The loss by the governing CDU–FDP coalition of its control of the upper chamber, the Bundesrat, made the presentation of the Bonn government's European policy as explicitly federalist more necessary for domestic consumption.

Germany became a stronger advocate of 'European Political Union' (EPU) to match **Economic and Monetary Union** (EMU), and in the course of the two parallel **Intergovernmental Conferences** (IGCs) held to draft treaty changes on these subjects in 1991, sought the inclusion of clauses guaranteeing both federalism and subsidiarity.

Whereas the British government saw these two principles as opposites, the Germans believed them to be coterminous. This difference of emphasis reflects the tendency of those most in favour of European integration to be federalists or devolutionists in their own member states, whilst those most sceptical of the European integration – such as Gaullists or Thatcherites – are most often centralizers at home. As a result, the British and German governments argued for differing wording in any subsidiarity clause: the first stressed that the Union should only undertake action which could not be *sufficiently achieved* at national level and the latter argued for Union action when it could be *better achieved* at supranational level. The final wording of what is now Article 5(3) TEU contains both propositions in quick succession, reflecting a classic Community compromise which satisfied nobody completely, but which was just about acceptable to all.

The resulting Maastricht Treaty, agreed in December 1991 and signed two months later, complemented the subsidiarity clause by describing the new European Union as one 'in which decisions are taken . . . as closely as possible to the citizen' (Article 1 TEU). The 1997 **Amsterdam Treaty** introduced a **protocol** on the application of the principles of subsidiarity and proportionality (Protocol 2 to the Treaties). This established a legal obligation on the Commission, when proposing legislation, to explain why 'a Union objective can be better achieved at Union level' and how the proposal complies with the two principles in question.

From the start, however, it was clear that applying the principle of subsidiarity would be far from easy. First, as the wording of the new article made clear, subsidiarity was to apply only to areas outside the 'exclusive competence' of the Community. Until such time as there was a reasonably clear-cut catalogue of which policy fields were matters of exclusive Union competence, and which were matters of shared competence between the Union and member states, there was bound to be ambiguity about the scope of the subsidiarity principle. Such a listing was only provided by the Lisbon Treaty over 15 years later.

Second, the wording of Article 5(3) TEU gives no guidance with regard to how an assessment can or should be made about whether an objective might be 'better achieved at Union level'. The lack of any objective standard, or even general criteria, by which to assess this question – with reliance instead on essentially subjective political judgements – made it difficult to apply the subsidiarity clause consistently within the EU institutions when drafting or enacting law, even assuming that there was sufficient political will to do so.

Third, the Maastricht Treaty did nothing to oblige the EU institutions to take subsidiarity into account in decision-making in any operational way. No arrangements were provided for the incorporation of a subsidiarity test in the law-making process. Instead, the burden of enforcing subsidiarity was to rest ex post facto with the **European Court of Justice** (ECJ). The seemingly sensible suggestion that an intermediate, external body – either a 'committee of wise men' (comprised of senior ex-politicians and lawyers) or a more formal tribunal – should subject each major draft proposal to a pre-legislative subsidiarity test, was rejected in the Political Union IGC.

Finally, it was unclear whether subsidiarity was sufficiently precise in point of substance or intent to be 'justiciable' at all. Some critics expressed the view that the subsidiarity clause was too general to use in specific rulings, whilst others feared that the Court would, in the absence of other guidance, tend simply to accept the expressed intention of law-makers in adopting any measure, so defeating the purpose of the initiative. The history of ECJ rulings on the catch-all **Article 352** TFEU, which allows the Union to legislate by unanimity in areas not otherwise provided for in the Treaties, suggested a distinct reluctance to invalidate legislation which the Commission, Council and Parliament had all endorsed.

In practice, as many predicted, the Court proved highly cautious in invoking subsidiarity in its rulings. Few cases were brought by plaintiffs on the subject, and in these, the Court declined to develop a distinctive case law in the field, concentrating mainly on procedural questions. The ECJ has yet to find that any action taken, or legislation adopted, by an EU institution has breached the subsidiarity principle. As a result, attention began to turn instead to whether **national parliaments** might play a bigger part in policing subsidiarity – an idea which usefully responded to growing political pressure for their closer involvement in EU decision-making more generally. In drafting the aborted **European Constitution**, the **Convention on the Future of Europe** (2003–4) included an amendment to Protocol 2 to give each national parliament an eight-week period during which it could send the Commission, Council or Parliament 'a reasoned opinion stating why it considers that the draft in question does not comply with the principle of subsidiarity'. Often called the 'yellow card' subsidiarity check, this was carried forward into the **Lisbon Treaty**. As a result, if one third of national parliaments provide reasoned opinions to this effect against a legislative proposal, 'the draft must be reviewed' by the Commission. For this purpose, each parliament is assigned two votes – with the two chambers of a bicameral parliament having one vote each – with a review currently requiring 18 votes out of 54. For measures in the field of police and judicial cooperation in criminal matters, only a quarter of national parliaments need to object for a review to be held (14 votes out of 54). After the review, the Commission 'may decide to maintain, amend or withdraw' its proposal.

The rejection of the Constitution in the **French and Dutch referenda** of May–June 2005 resulted in a strong push by some states, especially the Netherlands, for the 'yellow card' procedure to be strengthened before it even entered into effect. In consequence, the Lisbon Treaty further amended Protocol 2 to provide for a second, parallel 'orange card' process. If a simple majority, rather than just a third, of national parliaments (28 votes out of 54) objects on subsidiarity grounds to a proposal made under the **co-decision procedure** and the Commission chooses to maintain it, then the Council or Parliament must vote specifically on 'whether the legislative proposal is compatible with the principle of subsidiarity', before proceeding to a first-reading vote. If either 55 per cent of the member states in the Council or a simple majority in the Parliament consider that the proposal contravenes that principle, it 'shall not be given further consideration'. By early 2012, there had been no example yet of any Commission proposal provoking a reasoned opinion from a third, let alone a half, of national parliaments – although responses to a draft directive on the entry and residence of seasonal workers from third countries had come close to reaching the threshold.

The Lisbon Treaty also explicitly recognizes the (existing) right of any member state to bring a case in the ECJ to annul an EU legislative act on the grounds that it infringes the subsidiarity principle. Crucially, for the first time, it also allows each national parliament access to the Court: any member-state government may now introduce an action 'on behalf of [its] national Parliament or a chamber thereof' if the latter considers subsidiarity to have been infringed. The **Committee of the Regions** has been given a similar right to bring actions before the ECJ on these grounds (Article 8, Protocol 2).

Suez crisis

From the early 1950s, Europe's former colonial powers found themselves firmly in retreat in the Middle East and North Africa. In October 1951, the Egyptian government abrogated the Anglo-Egyptian Treaty of 1936, which gave the United Kingdom a 20-year lease on the Suez Canal zone. Egypt had been a British colony from 1882 to 1922, and after that the zone had become neutral territory under British protection. When General Gamal Abdel Nasser and fellow officers seized power in a military coup in July 1952, he made it clear that British troops would have to leave in 1956 and began to pursue an aggressive foreign policy which fomented discontent in other, pro-Western Arab countries and saw Egypt develop close links with the Soviet Union.

France, in turn, became increasingly anxious about the spillover of Egyptian policy in radicalizing opinion in its North African colonies and the Lebanon. The new Egyptian government gave public support and encouragement to the insurgency in Algeria, where France already had 400,000 troops.

When the United States, followed soon after by Britain, announced that it was withdrawing financial support for the Aswan Dam project – partly in response to Egypt's decision to recognize the People's Republic of China – Nasser retaliated on 26 July by forcibly nationalizing the Suez Canal Company, which was based in Paris and many of whose shareholders were French. Although Nasser had promised in 1954 that the status of the canal would remain unaltered, as the quid pro quo for British withdrawal, he now claimed that its revenues were needed to make up for the lost Anglo-American loans. A major international crisis followed. With over two-thirds of Europe's oil passing through this one conduit, both Britain and France were determined that the canal should remain under de facto Western control. Their interests converged with those of Israel, which wanted to restore access for its shipping to the canal, as well as to forestall any future Egyptian expansionism. Israel also saw an opportunity to align its interests with those of Europe's two largest powers and so wean Britain in particular away from its traditional Arabism.

The fundamental difficulty that Britain, France and Israel all faced was not military – the combined forces which they were soon to deploy, even in the very brief Suez adventure, amounted to a quarter of a million men – but geopolitical. Whilst the British prime minister, Anthony Eden, had convinced himself (and others) that Nasser would, unless contained and ideally toppled, emerge as a regional dictator, dominating the Middle East and directly threatening Western interests, that was not the prevailing view in Washington. The US Secretary of State, John Forster Dulles, was cautious about provoking any military confrontation, even if the nationalization of the canal gave Nasser an unwelcome advantage. He also feared that British diplomacy was accentuating divisions in the Middle East, allowing Egypt the opportunity to forge closer links with Libya, Syria and Saudi Arabia in the name of pan-Arab unity against a hostile West. Whatever the merits of the US position – and some pointed ironically to the CIA-led coup that had removed the Iranian leader, Mohammad Mossadeq, in 1953, after he had nationalized foreign oil interests in that country – the critical mistake made by Eden was to ignore the advice he had received from **Winston Churchill** when he succeeded him as prime minister in April 1955: 'never be separated from the Americans'. The British government wrongly assumed that US policymakers would turn a blind eye and accept any unilateral military action against Egypt as a useful fait accompli that contained a country that was not only destabilizing the region – by attempting to build what Nasser himself called 'a limitless strength extending from the Atlantic Ocean to the Arab Gulf' – but developing dangerous links with Communist states. The French and Israelis were inclined to accept Britain's reading of the likely US response.

Washington played for time, seeking to enmesh the British and French in a series of international discussions in the **United Nations** and the Suez Canal Users' Association. After two months of drift, London and Paris opened secret negotiations with the Israeli government – of which the Americans were not informed – about the possibility of launching a joint military action against Nasser. On 14 October, the French put a plan to Eden that they should prompt an Israeli invasion of Egypt and use this as a pretext to take control of the canal, with a subsequent international settlement preventing Egypt from exercising sovereignty over the zone. The details were thrashed out at a meeting between the British Foreign Secretary, Selwyn Lloyd, the French foreign minister, Christian Pineau, and the Israeli prime minister, David Ben-Gurion, held at a safe house outside Paris on 22 October.

The resulting agreement, signed by the three governments and known as the 'Sèvres protocol', provided that Israel would invade Egypt on 29 October and move to take key points along the Suez Canal. Britain and France would then invite both Israel and Egypt to pull their troops back from the canal and accept a temporary Anglo-French occupation of the zone 'to guarantee freedom of passage by vessels of all nations until a final settlement' could be negotiated. On the assumption that Egypt would refuse this request, Britain and France would 'launch military operations against the Egyptian forces in the early hours of the morning of 31 October', in order to protect the canal. The Americans first learned of the planned invasion two days after Sèvres through a seemingly unauthorized leak by the British Defence Secretary, Walter Monckton – who had serious reservations about the nature of the expedition – in a conversation with the US ambassador in London.

Despite a degree of mutual mistrust between the 'tripartite invaders', as they became known – hence the desire for a written document signed by each party – the Sèvres plan was put into effect almost exactly as agreed. However, once the Israeli invasion began on 29 October, rumours of a conspiracy started to circulate and the public reaction of the United States and elsewhere was much more negative than expected. One predictable factor was that General Eisenhower, facing re-election on 6 November and running as a 'peace President', was highly reluctant to get drawn into a new regional conflict. Less predictable was the almost simultaneous Soviet suppression of the anti-Communist uprising in Hungary. Eisenhower felt he could not credibly condemn a brutal suppression in Budapest whilst condoning what many saw as illegitimate aggression by his allies in the Middle East. The awkwardness of this situation was exposed in the UN Security Council on 31 October – the day the Anglo-French intervention was launched – when both countries were driven to veto US and Soviet resolutions calling for an immediate ceasefire and Israeli withdrawal.

Whilst London and Paris were being outmanoeuvred on the diplomatic front, Washington began to put significant economic pressure on Britain in particular. The US Treasury signalled that, without a ceasefire, it could not support the UK's request for a $ 1.0 billion loan from the International Monetary Fund (IMF), as it fought to defend the value of sterling by dissipating its gold and foreign currency reserves. Indeed, the US even threatened to start selling its substantial holdings of UK government debt, dating from the Second World War, making devaluation almost inevitable. (Half the Conservative parliamentary party outside government signed a motion describing American behaviour as 'gravely endangering' the Atlantic Alliance.) In parallel, Saudi Arabia announced an oil embargo on Britain and France, with the US indicating it would not make up any of the shortfall. As Anglo-French troops were progressing down the canal, establishing control, the British Chancellor of the Exchequer, Harold Macmillan, who had been one of the most hawkish advocates of invasion, informed Eden that the British economy could not sustain a continuation of the Suez adventure in the face of near unanimous international criticism, led by the United States, and the kind of economic reprisals now envisaged.

Just as the Americans had not been officially informed of the invasion in the first place, so now Eden decided to accept the call for a ceasefire, without any serious consultation of either the French or Israeli governments. The British prime minister's announcement, made on 7 November, effectively left his allies abandoned in midstream. With their troops under British command, the French had no choice but to accept London's decision, although Israel refused to do so (at least for some weeks). The same day, the General Assembly decided to create the UN's first-ever international peacekeeping force to take the place of the British and French troops.

Eden's hold on office quickly became untenable, as Britain was engulfed in its biggest and most divisive political crisis since the Second World War. The prime minister suffered a nervous breakdown and resigned in January 1957, to be replaced ironically by Macmillan, who had been 'first in, first out', as the media put it. Although Eden had enjoyed huge international esteem – founded on his resignation as Foreign Secretary over appeasement in 1938 and his long service in the same role to Churchill during and after the war – a series of grave errors of judgement over Suez now overshadowed his reputation. Not only had the expedition been a political disaster, even if militarily it was an almost faultless success, but the prime minister and his colleagues had lied to the House of Commons about the prior agreement between Britain, France and Israel to invade Egypt. The fact that documentary evidence of the Sèvres pact existed was, in the words of the British National Archives, 'a catastrophe – a smoking gun that exposed the full extent of collusion' between the three countries. The sheer personal animus of Eden towards Nasser looked demeaning once it was the latter, not the former, who survived in power. At one point, the prime minister shouted over the phone to Anthony Nutting, a junior Foreign Office minister who resigned over the crisis, on an open line at the Savoy Hotel, 'I want [Nasser] destroyed, don't you understand? I want him murdered' (Nutting, *No End of a Lesson: The Story of Suez*, 1966).

For both Britain and France, the Suez debacle marked the decisive moment when the limitations of their post-imperial power were thrown into stark relief. In the French case, it was one of a series of embarrassing reverses – from Diên Biên Phu in Indo-China in 1954 through to its enforced exit from Algeria in 1962 – which undermined the country's sense of its place in the world. Perhaps for this reason, Suez alone has a less vivid place in France's collective memory than it does in Britain's: the government of Socialist prime minister Guy Mollet survived, although, like Eden's, it faced intense criticism from many on the left. However, beyond that, the British and French political élites drew largely divergent conclusions from what had happened.

The reaction to Suez in London was generally one of alarm at the consequences of pursuing any major foreign-policy initiative without explicit US approval and support. The advice which Churchill had given Eden in 1954 was now to be taken more seriously. The country's shrinking possibilities on the international stage would require it to be less unilateral in its thinking and to keep close to Washington before launching any actions in the defence and security fields. Britain's willingness to accept that its 'independent' nuclear deterrent should become in effect an extension of the US programme was a powerful illustration of this tendency.

In Paris, by contrast, there were several distinct reactions, none of which pointed towards prioritizing the transatlantic link. Among the centrist figures who still dominated the declining Fourth Republic, the feeling was that closer cooperation with other continental countries – of the sort which was already embodied in the **European Coal and Steel Community** (ECSC) and would have characterized the aborted **European Defence Community** (EDC) – was now more necessary than ever, given the eroding power of individual European nation states. Although most politicians remained strongly committed to the Atlantic Alliance, they feared that the irrelevance of the **North Atlantic Treaty Organization** (NATO) during the Suez crisis suggested that Europe would need to act as a more cohesive force in the future if its interests were to count in a more complex world. Suez thus helped give greater impetus to the discussions already taking place about the creation of a **customs union** and **common market** among **the Six**, which led to the signing of the **Treaty of Rome** the following March. The German Chancellor, **Konrad Adenauer**, who was visiting Paris on 6 November, is said to have told Mollet and Pineau that, for France, Britain and indeed Germany, there remained 'only one way of playing a decisive role in the world. That is to unite Europe . . . We have no time to waste. Europe will be your revenge' (Pineau, *1956: Suez*, 1976).

For Gaullists, by contrast – and especially the future French President, **Charles de Gaulle**, himself – Suez confirmed the basic unreliability of Anglo-Saxons and the undesirability of any future reliance on the British or Americans as allies. It also pointed to the need to give greater attention to the interests of the leading nations in the Middle East. Whilst he agreed with the centrists on the desirability of a more cohesive Europe playing a bigger role in foreign policy, he objected strongly to their preference for this process to develop either within supranational institutions and/or the Atlantic Alliance. Once he returned to power in June 1958, the General sought to use Europe as a forum for maintaining the illusion of French leadership and as a means of reconciling domestic public opinion to the country's recent reverses abroad. To achieve this, he insisted that any European foreign policy should be structured entirely on intergovernmental terms and reflect French, rather than NATO, priorities. When this approach was rejected by others, he largely lost interest in the potential of the European Community as a vehicle for magnifying French power. At the same time, he loosened links with the United States, developing the French nuclear deterrent without their assistance and taking the country out of NATO's integrated military command structure a decade after Suez.

There is one parallelism, however, in the British and French reactions to Suez. For London, aligning with Washington was more complicated than it might first appear and did not necessarily point in an anti-European direction. Throughout the **Cold War**, the US administration had been actively encouraging the development of pan-European structures, initially of an intergovernmental kind, with which Britain felt broadly comfortable. However, from May 1950 on, the US accepted the logic of the **supranationalism** being pioneered by the Six and seriously regretted Britain's reluctance to become involved in either the ECSC or EDC. The welcome which Washington gave to the renewed, post-Suez impulse towards closer European integration – and specifically to the new **European Economic Community** (EEC), launched by the 1957 Treaty of Rome – was thus unambiguously positive. Conversely, US policy-makers were more sceptical about the UK's proposed alternative to the EEC, namely 'Plan G' for a **free trade area** encompassing all the countries of the **Organization for European Economic Cooperation** (OEEC). Macmillan's decision to apply three years later to join the new Community was driven in part by an awareness that 'never

[to] be separated from the Americans' now meant not being separated from continental Europeans either. The irony was that, by the time this realization dawned, it was already too late, as de Gaulle had returned to power in France and was to prove determined to keep Britain out of the Community.

Further reading: Keith Kyle, *Suez: Britain's End of Empire in the Middle East*, 1991; Hugh Thomas, *The Suez Affair*, 1967.

Summits

Meetings of heads of government are often referred to as summits. Until 1950, when **Winston Churchill** first used the word in this context, such meetings were usually termed 'conferences'. Advocating a meeting with Stalin, he said: 'It is not easy to see how matters could be worsened by a parley at the summit.' Significant summits had already been held in the form of the **Yalta and Potsdam Conferences** in February and July 1945, which Churchill himself had attended.

David Reynolds (see below) has argued that the golden age of summitry, largely between adversaries, lasted from the meeting between Neville Chamberlain and Aldolf Hitler in Munich in 1938 to those between Ronald Reagan and Mikhail Gorbachev in the 1980s. The development of the summit 'was made possible by air travel, made necessary by weapons of mass destruction, and made into household news by the mass media'. The end of the **Cold War**, the growth of terrorist networks and the development of new means of instant communication have conspired to render summitry more multilateral than bilateral, and more institutionalized than personal. This process is witnessed in the growing association of summits with the regular meetings of heads of government within various international organizations, notably the **Group of Eight** (G8) and **Group of Twenty** (G20), and Asia–Pacific Economic Cooperation (APEC). Such meetings are intensively prepared by civil servants, sometimes known as 'sherpas'. The former pattern of rivals meeting on an ad hoc basis with uncertain consequences has been superseded by large, orchestrated gatherings which often endorse routine conclusions agreed in advance.

The first summit meeting involving the heads of government of **the Six** member states of the European Community was held in Paris in February 1961. It was hosted by French President **Charles de Gaulle** to promote his **Fouchet Plan** for an intergovernmental political union in Europe. After a faltering start, summits were formalized in 1975 as meetings of the **European Council** and are now held at least four times a year. The **Lisbon Treaty** made the European Council a separate **institution** of the Union and established the formal post of **President of the European Council**, which is held by one individual for a term of 30 months, rather than for six months by the head of state or government from the member state occupying the rotating **presidency** of the **Council of Ministers**. The successive meetings of the European Council have, over time, become a powerful motor of European integration. They are sometimes marked by high political drama and offer perhaps the most visible public face of EU activity. Several such summits have been crucial in resolving major disputes between member states, not least on institutional or budgetary issues, and in defining the future path of EU policy.

In recent years, following Gaullist tradition, French President Nicolas Sarkozy proved active in trying to invent new forms of European summitry, outside a formal EU framework. In July 2008, he organized the founding summit of the Union for the Mediterranean (UfM). In October 2008, he brought together the heads of government of the four EU members of the **Group of Eight** (G8). In March 2011, he hosted a summit of the leaders of the EU member states supporting military action in Libya, together with the US Secretary of State and the Secretary General of the **United Nations**. With the onset of the economic and financial crisis in autumn 2008, Sarkozy insisted on hosting the first-ever summit of the leaders of **eurozone** countries – an initiative resisted then and for some time by Germany and the **European Commission**. After a series of ad hoc meetings in response to the developing **eurozone debt crisis**, in August 2011, Sarkozy persuaded the German Chancellor, Angela Merkel, of the necessity of holding eurozone summits on a regular basis. This approach was formalized by the European Council in October 2011, with a 'President of the Euro Summit' to be designated at the same time as the President of the European Council is chosen (with the implication that the two posts will be held by the same person). Such Euro Summits will henceforth usually be held immediately after European Council meetings, at least twice a year.

Further reading: David Dunn, *Diplomacy at the Highest Level: The Evolution of International Summitry*, 1996; David Reynolds, *Summits: Six Meetings that shaped the Twentieth Century*, 2007.

Supranationalism and intergovernmentalism

Supranationalism and intergovernmentalism are both theories of integration and terms used to describe specific institutional arrangements and decision-making procedures used at European level. Supranationalism envisages the existence of free-standing institutions, operating at a level above the nation state, which generate legally-binding acts from which no country can unilaterally resile. By contrast, intergovernmentalism foresees national governments choosing to cooperate in particular policy fields, whilst retaining a maximum degree of freedom from mutual obligation or constraint. Unlike supranationalism, intergovernmentalism avoids the use of international law and confines decision-making to the representatives of governments. Characteristically (although not necessarily) supranationalism foresees decisions being taken by some form of majority voting, whereas, by definition, intergovernmentalism requires **unanimity**, with each state retaining a formal right of veto. There is a close correlation between the supranational/intergovernmental divide and the distinction between **federalism and confederalism.**

The struggle between supranationalism and intergovernmentalism has been one of the major recurring themes in the history of post-war European integration. The question of how far international organizations should be tied to the nation states that create them – and whether they should enjoy the power to act independently of those states in certain spheres – is inherent in the decision to develop and pursue policies in common. The countries of western Europe were faced with this issue as soon as they began to work together after the Second World War and chose to draft treaties that would establish new institutions operating at a level above that of the nation state.

In the event, most of the organizations which evolved at European level in the early post-war years displayed strongly intergovernmental characteristics, reflecting a conscious desire by the United Kingdom and some other countries (as well as, to a lesser degree, the United States) to limit any explicit sharing of national **sovereignty**. For example, the **Organization for European Economic Cooperation** (OEEC), which became the OECD, the **Brussels Treaty** Organization, which became the **Western European Union** (WEU), and the **Council of Europe** were all founded on essentially intergovernmental principles, as was the (later) **European Free Trade Association** (EFTA). Although such organizations were equipped with central institutions and a permanent secretariat, the real power rested with the governments of the countries that chose to take part, a power symbolized by ministerial committees taking the final decisions. When it was necessary to adopt legally-binding acts, these would be undertaken on an ad hoc and voluntary basis through traditional international treaties, multilateral conventions or bilateral agreements. The Council of Europe was unusual in choosing to establish an internal court to adjudicate on cases relating to one such convention, the **European Convention on Human Rights** (ECHR).

The development of the **European Communities**, now European Union, represented a radical departure in that the initiative was based, explicitly, from the start, on a supranational, rather than intergovernmental, conception of how power should be exercised at international level. The '**Community method**' pioneered by **Jean Monnet** and others envisaged that **competence** in certain policy areas would be transferred from national to supranational level, where it would be exercised by free-standing institutions able, in these fields, to adopt and enforce their own European law. Such law would be proposed by an independent executive authority, be enacted in a ministerial forum where veto rights were to be limited, and be upheld by a dedicated court. Unlike traditional international law, Community legislation could extend rights to individuals directly, as well as impose obligations on states, thus in effect by-passing the latter.

For many years, the development of supranationalism at Community level was constrained by several factors. There were relatively few policy areas where the founding **Treaties** gave the EC exclusive or indeed shared **competence**, and they were also relatively peripheral to the central functions of the state. In most of these fields, French President **Charles de Gaulle** managed to limit or prevent the use of **qualified majority voting** (QMV) among governments in the **Council of Ministers**, through the **Luxembourg Compromise**, an arrangement which subsisted until the mid-1980s. The Community's executive body – first the **High Authority**, then the **European Commission** – frequently found itself on the defensive in the face of governments and chose increasingly to exercise its legislative powers with caution. The 'spillover' effect, whereby the success of one common policy was expected to generate momentum for new, linked, policies, was much less pronounced than many had hoped.

However, starting with the 1986 **Single European Act** (SEA), a series of treaty changes gradually widened Community competence, extended the scope of QMV (which soon operated both in theory and practice), and forced the Council increasingly to share its legislative power with the directly-elected **European Parliament**. Under President **Jacques Delors,** the Commission alighted on a project, the completion of the **single market** by 1992, which renewed confidence in the Community and asserted the logic for deeper sovereignty-sharing in other policy areas, notably the creation of a single currency. The British government, under prime ministers **Margaret Thatcher** and John Major, launched a staunch rearguard action against too rapid a move in a supranational direction, but with only limited success.

The 1992 **Maastricht Treaty** represented a hard-fought compromise between the advocates of supranationalism and intergovernmentalism in the future institutional design of Europe. The Treaty established the so-called '**pillared' structure** to the new European Union, with different pillars involving different levels of integration. The first – or European Community – pillar corresponded to existing Community activity, but with a strengthened supranational character. Conversely, the new second and third pillars – for respectively **Justice and Home Affairs** (JHA) and **Common Foreign and Security Policy** (CFSP) – were designed to deepen cooperation among the member states, but along essentially intergovernmental lines. They were an attempt to allow the development of common policies in certain sensitive fields, whilst keeping such action firmly within the ambit of the Council and out of the hands of the other institutions. As a general rule, in both JHA and CFSP, traditional forms of Community law would not apply, the Commission would not enjoy an exclusive **right of initiative**, unanimity would be required within the Council, there was to be no **co-decision** between the Council and Parliament, and the **European Court of Justice** (ECJ) would be denied the ability to arbitrate on disputes.

The Maastricht compromise never really satisfied either the supporters or opponents of closer institutional deepening. Most integationists remained suspicious of any divergence from the 'Community method', whilst many Eurosceptics feared that adherence to intergovernmentalism in the second and third pillars might be difficult to maintain in practice, once the principle had been conceded of there being EU policies in these fields. Soon after, the 1997 **Amsterdam Treaty** began the process of 'depillarizing' JHA: visas, asylum, immigration and judicial cooperation in civil matters were transferred to the first pillar, with the United Kingdom, Ireland and Denmark being given '**opt-outs**' from Community action in these fields. The nature of the CFSP pillar was also changed by both the Amsterdam Treaty, which created the position of **High Representative**, and the 2001 **Nice Treaty**, which instituted a **Common Security and Defence Policy** (CSDP). The **Lisbon Treaty** carries these processes still further, by abolishing both the second and third pillars, with an extended opt-out for the UK and Ireland in JHA and a replication of most of the intergovernmental features of CFSP in the new, single pillar, now called the European Union.

The Maastricht debate echoed two previous institutional struggles within the Community: integrationists had successfully resisted de Gaulle's **Fouchet Plan** (of 1960–62), designed to build an intergovernmental political union in parallel to the existing EC, and they had initially responded very coolly to the proposal made by a subsequent French President, **Valéry Giscard d'Estaing** (in 1974–5), to institute a system of regular **summit** meetings of EC heads of government. It required the intervention of Jean Monnet in support of Giscard's proposal, together with a commitment in return to institute direct elections to the European Parliament, for the idea of the new **European Council** to win acceptance. However, rather than intergovernmentalize the Community, regular summits had the opposite effect, as Monnet predicted – providing a forum for renewed leadership and dispute-resolution that neither the Commission nor the Council could provide on their own. See also **functionalism and neo-functionalism**, **positive and negative integration**.

Further reading: Andrew Moravcsik, *The Choice for Europe: Social Purpose and State Power from Messina to Maastricht*, 1998.

Supreme Headquarters Allied Powers Europe (SHAPE)

In December 1950, a Supreme Allied Commander Europe (SACEUR) was appointed within the framework of the **North Atlantic Treaty Organization** (NATO). SACEUR's headquarters, known as Supreme Headquarters Allied Powers Europe (SHAPE), were set up the following year in Rocquencourt, near Paris, to house the first international military force in the democratic world. When France withdrew from NATO's integrated military command structure in 1966, SHAPE was moved to its present site at Casteau, north of Mons in Belgium, the following year.

In 2002 and 2008, NATO reorganized its command structure on the basis of function, rather than geography. The two previous commands – called Allied Command Europe (ACE) and Allied Command Atlantic (ACA) to reflect their geographic spheres of activity – were replaced by Allied Command Operations (ACO) and Allied Command Transformation (ACT). The two commands are still based in Mons and Norfolk, Virginia, respectively. SHAPE, although retaining the reference to Europe in its title for historic reasons, is now the headquarters of ACO, which is tasked with coordinating all NATO military operations. SACEUR, as head of ACO, is, in NATO's words 'in overall command of NATO military operations and conducts the necessary military planning for operations, including the identification of forces required for the mission and requesting these forces from NATO countries', as authorized by NATO's North Atlantic Council and directed by its Military Committee.

ACE had two 'regional commands': Allied Forces North Europe, based in Brunssum, Netherlands, and headed by a British or German general; and Allied Forces South Europe, based in Naples, Italy, and headed by a US general. Each of these two regional commands had separate air and naval forces, as well as a series of sub-regional commands, located in various centres. Under the new system, the Brunssum and Naples facilities have become 'joint force commands' (JFCs) within ACO, with the first coordinating NATO operations in Afghanistan and the second, NATO operations in the Balkans. Each JFC now has access to the old sub-regional commands, although for practical purposes the latter remain assigned to one or other of the two JFCs.

By convention, the post of SACEUR is usually assigned to a US four-star general: notable holders of the post have included Dwight Eisenhower, Alexander Haig, Wesley Clark and James Jones. The current holder of the post, James Stavridis, is the first former admiral to be appointed. The positions of Deputy SACEUR and Chief of Staff normally go to a UK and German general respectively. Over 1,000 officers and 2,000 other service personnel (plus 1,500 civilians) make up the SHAPE staff, including the national military representatives accredited to SACEUR.

Suspension

The 1997 **Amsterdam Treaty** introduced a new provision under which a member state found guilty of a 'serious and persistent breach' of the 'principles of liberty, democracy, respect for human rights and fundamental freedoms, and the rule of law' (listed in Article 6 TEU) may be liable to forfeit 'certain of the rights' of EU membership, including explicitly its ability to vote in the **Council of Ministers** (Article 7 TEU). Responsibility for determining the existence of such a breach rests with the **European Council** of heads of government acting by **unanimity**, on a proposal from either the **European Commission** or at least one-third of the member states, and after securing the **consent** of the **European Parliament**. The decision with respect to which rights the offending state shall forfeit may be taken by **qualified majority voting** (QMV), as may any subsequent decisions to vary or revoke the penalty. The member state accused of a breach has the right to be heard, but at no stage in the proceedings is its vote taken into account. Article 7 makes it clear that the offending member state's 'obligations . . . under this Treaty continue to be binding on that state'.

Partly as a consequence of the 'Haider affair', during which 14 governments imposed diplomatic sanctions on Austria in 2000, the arrangements outlined above were supplemented by an additional 'early warning' provision in the 2001 **Nice Treaty**. The Council, acting by a four-fifths majority, may now 'determine that there is a clear risk of a serious breach' by a member state, in advance of such a breach actually existing. In this case, the Council may commission an independent report on the situation and address 'appropriate recommendations' to the state in question.

The introduction of a suspension clause must be seen as part of the European Union's attempt in recent years to strengthen its commitment to human rights, evidenced most notably in the adoption of the **Charter of Fundamental Rights**. It is also meant as a safeguard against the possibility that a member state might cease to conform to an acceptable pattern of democratic behaviour at some point in the future. The progressive **enlargement** of the Union makes the latter prospect more credible than in the past. Some might have preferred the simpler option of a country's possible exclusion from the Union, rather than the suspension of some of its rights. However, the intricate pattern of legal, financial and contractual obligations that has grown up between the Union and public and private bodies (and individuals), as a result of membership, means that there are real technical difficulties in the way of expelling a member state – setting aside the unpredictable political implications of doing so.

The suspension clause is a compromise between various schools of thought, and one which so far has never been formally invoked. However, the shadow of possible suspension hung over the disputes between France and the European Commission over the expulsion of Roma in autumn 2010 and between Hungary and the Commission over press freedom in spring 2011. In both cases, the Commission, with broad support in the European Parliament, was able to insist on respect for existing EU legal obligations, leading to adjustments in policy in both Paris and Budapest.

Switzerland

Swiss schizophrenia about its relationship with international organizations has a long and complicated history. Switzerland was the first country to assert its formal **neutrality**, a status enshrined in its constitution since 1815. During the inter-war years, the country was a founder member of the League of Nations, which it hosted in Geneva, but after the Second World War, it eschewed this approach, only joining the International Monetary Fund (IMF) and the World Bank in 1992, and remaining an observer member of the **United Nations** until 2002. When **the Six** agreed to establish a **customs union** and **common market** in Europe on an explicitly supranational basis in 1957, Switzerland chose to keep its distance from the new **Treaty of Rome**. However, the process of European integration posed a very serious challenge to Switzerland's post-war preference for non-involvement, especially given its high economic interdependence with the other countries of western Europe. On this basis, it decided to enter the intergovernmental alternative to the European Community, the **European Free Trade Association** (EFTA), in 1960, and to join the **Council of Europe** in 1963, some 15 years after most other European democracies. In 1972, with British, Danish and Irish **accession** to the Community imminent, Switzerland signed a **free trade agreement** with the Six, which has formed the basis of its economic relationship with the Community, now Union, ever since.

The advent of the ambitious programme to complete the European **single market** by 1992, underpinned by the 1986 **Single European Act** (SEA), renewed discussion in Switzerland about its relationship with the Union. Not only is the EU Switzerland's largest trading partner – representing almost half of the country's gross domestic product (GDP) – but Switzerland in turn is the fourth largest trading partner of the Union. This reflection on interdependence was given added force by the end of the **Cold War**, which cast in doubt traditional notions of neutrality. The result was a significant shift of thinking at élite level in the country, which was to prove unmatched among broader public opinion. In 1990–92, the Swiss government joined negotiations on the creation of a **European Economic Area** (EEA), which was designed to extend the opportunities and obligations of the single market to the remaining countries of EFTA. In the new mood of enthusiasm for closer links with the Union – and in fear that EFTA might soon be left as an empty shell – Switzerland then followed Austria, Finland and Sweden in submitting a formal application for EU membership in June 1992. When Swiss voters unexpectedly rejected – by a margin of 50.3 to 49.7 per cent – the ratification of the EEA Agreement in a national referendum on 6 December 1992, forcing the government in turn to suspend (but not withdraw) its application for EU membership, the country was left without any coherent approach to its relations with the Union. It would henceforth be outside both the Union and the EEA, and the only EFTA country not to be inside the EEA. From January 1995, Switzerland would be bordered on all sides by member states of the Union (other than by Liechtenstein). Unable to act independently of the EU, but still reluctant to become either part of it or to appear too dependent on it, Switzerland was left experiencing perhaps the most unusual relationship that currently exists between the Union and a non-member state.

Following the setbacks of 1992–5, the Swiss government sought to develop a new approach to its dealings with the Union. It aimed to secure as many of the benefits of membership as possible, but on a bilateral basis, outside the EEA framework, ostensibly between 'equal' negotiating partners. This approach had the simultaneous advantages of saving face for the Swiss government and being broadly acceptable to both the EU institutions and the Swiss public (who have usually chosen to back it, when necessary, in subsequent referenda). Starting in 1999, Switzerland proceeded to negotiate ten treaties with the Union (in two packages), dealing with issues such as the **free movement of persons**, **non-tariff barriers** to trade, air and road traffic, research and development, agriculture and **public procurement**. The practical effect of this complex process has been that, piece by piece, Switzerland has accepted several key elements of the ***acquis communautaire***, admittedly on a voluntary and selective basis, with even less influence on the content of **EU law** than that enjoyed by the three EEA countries (**Iceland**, Liechtenstein and **Norway**). Like EEA members, Switzerland has automatically to accept new EU legislation in these policy areas and it makes proportionate financial contribution towards the operational and administrative costs of the policy programmes or agencies in which it participates. However, a 'guillotine clause' gives the country the right to cancel the entire body of such bilateral treaties if any individual new obligation proves unacceptable. In addition, as a goodwill gesture towards the Union, in 2006, Switzerland established a special 'enlargement contribution' fund (of 1.26 billion Swiss francs) to assist the economic development of the new EU member states.

There are now over 120 specific agreements between Switzerland and the EU in different policy fields, managed through a series of 'joint committees', including several transit agreements to facilitate intra-EU trade. However, the attitude of the Swiss public towards free movement across and within their country, reflected in successive referenda, has proved somewhat erratic.

In February 1994, they voted to ban nearly all commercial road traffic through Switzerland with effect from 2004. This decision has led to the construction of a number of new railway tunnels under the Alps (notably the new Saint Gotthard base-route, due for completion in 2017), as well as the intensified development of combined road–rail transport. Conversely, in June 2005, the electorate endorsed the proposal that Switzerland join the **Schengen** zone from 2008 (with a 'yes' vote of 55.0 per cent). This latter move is already simplifying the lives of the nearly one million EU citizens who live or work in Switzerland, as well as the many more who drive through the country each year. In February 2009, the Swiss people, after a divisive referendum campaign, voted to open the country's labour market to citizens from Romania and Bulgaria. In addition to membership of Schengen, the Swiss have recently chosen to become involved in seven EU **Common Security and Defence Policy** (CSDP) missions in third countries (mainly in the western Balkans) and to join the EU in imposing sanctions on five countries.

One might imagine that the gradual convergence between Switzerland and the EU since the 1992 EEA referendum would mean that the question of membership of either the EEA or the Union itself might have come back onto the domestic political agenda. Formally speaking, Switzerland's application to join the EU is still pending, but ironically membership had been downgraded by the government in recent years from a 'strategic goal' to merely an 'option'. When a grass-roots, pro-European campaign, the 'Yes to Europe' initiative, sought to revive the application, forcing a premature referendum on 4 March 2001, the governing coalition was put in the embarrassing position of having to advocate a 'no' vote. The Swiss people voted by 76.8 per cent to 23.2 per cent against EU membership, making it very unlikely that the issue will be revisited for some time. In September 2010, the Swiss government signalled that it would prefer to continue with the sectoral approach to relations, building on existing bilateral agreements, for the foreseeable future. However, three months later, EU foreign ministers described the status quo as an unnecessarily 'complex system, which is creating legal uncertainty, has become unwieldy to manage and has clearly reached its limits'. The Luxembourg prime minister, Jean-Claude Junker, added for good measure that Swiss non-membership was a 'geo-strategic absurdity'.

Switzerland is a federation (although formally it still styles itself a confederation), with four official languages (German, French, Italian and Romance), in which a very strong sense of local identity coexists with an equally strong sense of national identity. Its mainstream political parties, from all language groups, cooperate in a permanent left–right coalition government at national level – a form of 'consociationalism', as the phenomenon is known in political science – in which the post of prime minister rotates between the parties annually. For these and other reasons, Switzerland has sometimes been held up as a model of how a united Europe could work, but it is a nation that has built up gradually over some 700 years on the basis of a very particular combination of geographic, political, religious and historical circumstances. It is governed at the federal, cantonal and communal levels, at each of which recourse may be had to a referendum under constitutional provisions introduced in 1874 as a means of limiting the power of central government. In recent years, tensions between French- and German-speaking parts of the country, together with the growth of far-right forces outside the consociational system, have put new strain on the Swiss 'model'.

Among the most prosperous countries in the world – with an annual GDP per head of over € 50,000 – Switzerland could easily meet the economic obligations of membership of the EU. What is less certain is whether the Swiss, with their lively attachment to direct democracy, neutrality and separate identity, will ever be prepared to adapt to a system in which supranational institutions play a pre-eminent role and which would require them to recognize the reality of the national **sovereignty** that they have already lost in practice, instead of maintaining the fiction of its survival in theory.

Further reading: Clive Church, *Switzerland and the European Union*, 2006.

Symbols of the Union

The various symbols of the European Union – notably a **European flag**, **European anthem** and Europe day – have developed piecemeal over several decades and are mainly borrowed from the intergovernmental **Council of Europe**. Recent efforts to give treaty status to these symbols failed when they were dropped from the **Lisbon Treaty**, the successor to the aborted **European Constitution**.

In 1955, the Council of Europe adopted a European flag – a circle of twelve five-pointed stars on a dark blue background – as a symbol of European unity. In 1972, it chose an orchestral arrangement of the 'Ode to Joy' in the last movement of Beethoven's Ninth Symphony as a European anthem. After the Council of Europe experienced difficulty in promoting their use, the European Community, now Union, in effect appropriated both the flag and anthem as its own symbols. This decision, taken by EC heads of government at the Milan **European Council** meeting in June 1985, on the recommendation of the **Adonnino Committee** for a People's Europe, led to a spectacular increase in the use of the flag, in all sorts of contexts, and to growing recognition of the anthem.

The Council of Europe's own Europe Day suffered a less happy fate. Since 1964, the Strasbourg-based intergovernmental body had marked 5 May – the anniversary of the signing of the Treaty of London, by which it was founded in 1949 – as Europe Day. However, at the Milan European Council in 1985, the European Council designated another date, which fell four days later, as a rival Europe day – the anniversary of the **Schuman Plan** for the **European Coal and Steel Community** (ECSC) on 9 May 1950. The second date has largely displaced the first, reflecting the increasing pre-eminence of the Union.

The draft European Constitution (Article I-8) listed a series of 'symbols of the Union', including not only the flag, anthem and Europe Day, but also a motto and the single currency, the **euro**, as well. It stated:

> *The flag of the Union shall be a circle of twelve golden stars on a blue background. The anthem of the Union shall be based on the 'Ode to Joy' from the Ninth Symphony by Ludwig van Beethoven. The motto of the Union shall be 'United in diversity'. The currency of the Union shall be the euro. Europe day shall be celebrated on 9 May throughout the Union.*

The motto 'united in diversity' won an unofficial competition for schoolchildren, held during the French **presidency** of the **Council of Ministers** in 2000, and it slowly entered into circulation thereafter. Some 80,000 pupils put forward over 2,000 slogans, with the final choice being made by a panel of 15 leading personalities (one from each member state), including **Jacques Delors**. The six other mottos on the shortlist were 'united in freedom', 'united for peace and democracy', 'peace, liberty, solidarity', 'our differences are our strengths', 'all different, all Europeans' and 'old continent, new hope'.

Following the rejection of the European Constitution in the **French and Dutch referenda** of May–June 2005, the reference to the symbols of the Union was removed by the **Intergovernmental Conference** (IGC) which drafted the Lisbon Treaty. The Dutch and several other governments argued that endowing such symbols with legal (especially treaty) status could raise the spectre of 'statehood' and give a hostage to fortune to critics of closer integration. The reference to the euro as the 'currency of the Union' was replaced by a more neutral formulation, describing it as the currency of the **Economic and Monetary Union** (EMU) (Article 3(4) TEU). This change tacitly acknowledged that, in any case, the currency was not really a 'symbol' at all. Formally speaking, only a physical representation of the currency, printed or stamped on the face of a note or coin, would have symbolic value.

In a declaration attached to the Lisbon Treaty, 16 member states (including Germany, Italy and Spain) indicated that 'for them' the symbols of the Union, as originally defined in the Constitution, would continue 'to express the sense of community of the people in the European Union and their allegiance to it'.

T

Tax harmonization

The process of tax harmonization within the EU has always been subsidiary to other treaty objectives and is almost wholly limited to indirect taxation. It involves the attempted alignment of the type, scope and rates of various taxes to prevent national differences in this field from acting as **non-tariff barriers** to trade. This process has long been advocated by the **European Commission** but equally strongly resisted by certain member-state governments. An indication of the sensitivity of the subject is the fact that, as an exception to what is now the general rule where **single market** measures are concerned, **unanimity** is still required in the **Council of Ministers** for the adoption of taxation measures, with the **European Parliament** limited to giving only an opinion under the **consultation procedure**.

Articles 110 to 112 TFEU require member states not to apply discriminatory taxes in order to favour domestically produced goods. Article 113 TFEU empowers the Council to 'adopt provisions for the harmonization of legislation concerning turnover taxes, excise duties and other forms of indirect taxation to the extent that such harmonization is necessary to ensure the establishment and the functioning of the internal market and to avoid distortion of competition'.

The first, and so far only, significant success for the tax harmonization agenda was the adoption in the 1960s and 1970s of **value-added tax** (VAT) as the standard form of sales tax throughout the European Community and its use as a component of the '**own resources**' for the financing of the Community **Budget**. The Commission proposed and the Council eventually adopted a series of **directives** that defined VAT and established the 'base' to be taxed, subject to a long list of possible exemptions. At this early stage, it proved impossible, however, to agree to any harmonization of the rate or rates at which VAT should be applied. Equally, no progress was registered in the Commission's parallel objective of harmonizing excise duties.

After a period of stasis, the effort to promote tax harmonization was renewed with the 1985 **Cockfield White Paper**, which inter alia identified the remaining fiscal barriers to trade within the single market. The Commission proposed that divergences in rates of VAT and excise duties should at least be limited, even if they could not be eliminated. After considerable wrangling, the **Ecofin Council** (of finance ministers) agreed in 1992 that henceforth every member state should be allowed to impose one standard rate, and up to two reduced rates, of VAT (including 'zero rating' in the United Kingdom and Ireland), and that the minima for these standard and reduced rates should be set at 15 and five per cent respectively. An informal maximum for the standard rate was set at 25 per cent.

In parallel, minimum rates of excise duty for alcohol, tobacco, cigarettes and mineral oil were established, although their impact was modest. (All these products are also subject to VAT.) The minimum rates for wine, beer and spirits were set at very low levels (at just above zero, in the case of wine). Although the total tax imposed on cigarettes must represent at least 57 per cent of the retail price of the product, the amount actually levied still permits a very wide divergence – by a factor of 15 – between the highest and lowest taxing countries, creating huge incentives for smuggling.

The only area of direct taxation where the Commission has so far attempted to introduce a measure of harmonization is the treatment of company profits. Limited proposals in this area were first put forward in 1960, but their legitimacy was contested. Piecemeal legislation has since been adopted on largely technical issues related to double taxation or cross-border activity (such as interest and royalty payments between associated companies in different member states). In December 1997, the Council reached agreement on a voluntary code of conduct to end 'harmful fiscal competition' between member states with respect to corporate taxation more generally. The code was meant to prefigure the establishment of a common corporate tax base and the setting of agreed minimum rates by January 2003, but this never happened. Several very different systems of corporation tax still operate within the Union – with divergences in the way profit is defined and in how depreciation or allowances are treated – and tax rates vary from 10 per cent in Bulgaria and Cyprus to 37.25 per cent in Italy. In August 2011, the French President, Nicolas Sarkozy, and German Chancellor, Angela Merkel, announced that they intended to adopt a common Franco-German régime for corporation tax by 2013.

The underlying problem in tax harmonization is that the varying rates of particular taxes in the member states – whether of VAT, excise duties or corporation tax, let alone of personal income tax or social contributions – are a product of very different traditions of how government is financed, reflecting in turn national political choices made over many decades. For example, whereas VAT accounts for over 27 per cent of government revenue in Cyprus, it comprises only 14 per cent in Italy. Equally, corporate taxes represent 15 per cent of revenue in Luxembourg, but less than 3 per cent in Germany. When combined with the continued need for unanimity in the Council, this problem appears to make significant further tax harmonization at EU level unlikely. When, in May 2010, the European Commission retabled a proposal which it had first put forward in the early 1990s for a Europe-wide carbon tax, it quickly disappeared without trace in the face of objections from several governments. Instead, recent discussion has tended to focus rather on whether a subgroup of member states with broadly common interests might, using arrangements for **enhanced cooperation**, attempt to establish a 'tax union', starting with corporate taxation. Under the **Lisbon Treaty**, a minimum of nine countries would be required, and even this threshold might prove very difficult to attain.

Thatcher, Margaret (born 1925)

Educated at her local grammar school in the East Midlands, before studying chemistry at Oxford University and training to be a barrister, Margaret Thatcher became a Conservative Member of Parliament in 1959, rising slowly up the ministerial hierarchy as a leadership loyalist. Having served as Education Secretary in the government of **Edward Heath** – with whom she shared a very similar, highly aspirational, lower middle-class background – she suddenly emerged as a right-wing critic of Heathite pragmatism when the Conservative party was unexpectedly defeated in the February 1974 general election (an outcome repeated in a second election eight months later). In the absence of more senior challengers, Thatcher stood against Heath in the party leadership election that followed in February 1975, drawing on a broad, but often unspoken, unease with his performance both in and out of power. In a spectacular upset, she polled more votes than the incumbent on the first ballot, forcing him out of the race, and then saw off a wider field of contestants on the second ballot, emerging as the winner by a decisive margin.

Even if some of her moderate supporters did not intend it, the advent of Margaret Thatcher as Conservative leader marked a significant shift in the centre of gravity of the party, heralding a new emphasis on free-market economics, fiscal discipline and a limited state, mixed with a more populist appeal on law and order, immigration and defence. Although Thatcher lacked the deep personal commitment to Europe of her predecessor, she was supportive of continued British membership of the European Community – unlike some on the right who had promoted her candidacy – and was critical of the Labour government's largely cosmetic **renegotiation** of the 'Tory terms' of entry in 1974–5. She campaigned conscientiously in favour of a 'yes' vote in the **British referendum on EC membership** of June 1975, speaking in the House of Commons of an 'organic, living Community . . . constantly developing the whole time, constantly responding to the interests of its members'. Already 'strong and already a major influence', she said, the Community 'opens windows on the world for us which since the war have been closing'.

Four years later, in May 1979, after a major economic crisis and the failure of Labour to contain the continued growth of trade union power, the Conservatives were returned to office under Thatcher's leadership. The following month, in the first direct elections to the **European Parliament**, the party won 60 of the country's 81 seats. The Conservative manifestos for both elections again struck a positive note on Europe, chastising the outgoing Labour government for its 'frequently obstructive and malevolent attitude' towards the Community and for refusing to take Britain into the **Exchange-Rate Mechanism** (ERM) of the new **European Monetary System** (EMS). 'We shall look for ways in which Britain can take her rightful place' within the ERM, the Euro-manifesto declared. Thatcher herself told the Commons that Britain's sole non-participation in the system was 'a sad day for Europe', reflecting the country's status as 'among the poorest and least influential members' of the Community. However, in the event, such language was to prove short-lived: the new prime minister's general approach to Europe during her 11 years in power was at best cautious and unsentimental, and often highly critical and confrontational. As a general rule, her increasingly adversarial style of politics proved ill-adapted to the conventions and procedures of a consensus-oriented decision-making system such as that of the Community.

Unlike James Callaghan, her immediate predecessor as prime minister, Thatcher made little effort to establish close personal relations with other European leaders. She was to suffer in turn from their indifference in her first quarrel with the Community, starting in November 1979, over the high level of the British net contribution to the annual **Budget**. The tone she struck in pursuing the **British Budget dispute** ignored conventional *communautaire* sensitivities, asserting the principle of and 'asking to have our own money back', as she put it. In turn, the dilatory manner in which her fellow leaders addressed the problem did little to inspire in her any respect or affection for the institutions and politics of the Community. The budget issue remained a growing source of tension until it was finally resolved through the **Fontainebleau Agreement** of June 1984, which instituted a permanent **abatement** that significantly reduced the UK's net contribution. Thatcher was initially frustrated in her parallel efforts to promote reform of the **Common Agricultural Policy** (CAP), although in 1983–5 the **European Commission** did propose the first of several rounds of changes designed to bring supply and demand for farm produce into better balance.

Lack of personal rapport with her continental opposite numbers, as well as an inability to 'think European', hampered Thatcher's ability to proactively shape the Community agenda, with sometimes comic results. Her then Foreign Secretary, Geoffrey Howe, describes her arguing at a European Council meeting for the need to ensure that legislation did not burden small business. 'I should know,' she said, 'I once worked in a firm that employed only three people.' 'I wonder what happened to the other two,' commented the Italian prime minister, Giulio Andreotti, dryly in an aside that was picked up in interpretation, much to Thatcher's irritation. On another occasion, in response to an upbeat intervention by the British prime minister, the French President, **François Mitterrand**, intervened ironically: 'I begin to wonder whether Madame Thatcher isn't even more intriguing when she is saying yes than when she is saying no.' (Both incidents are quoted in Howe's memoirs, *Conflict of Loyalty*, 1994.)

The appointment of the French finance minister, **Jacques Delors**, as Commission President from January 1985 marked an important turning-point in her relations with the rest of the Community, initially for the better and then decisively for the worse. (Thatcher had agreed to Delors taking the post with some hesitation, having previously opposed, along with some other heads of government, Mitterrand's initial suggestion that it go to the French foreign minister, Claude Cheysson.) In Delors' **single market** programme – launched in June 1985 and spearheaded by a British Conservative Commissioner, (Lord) Arthur Cockfield – she found, six years into her premiership, a Community objective to which she could give reasonably unequivocal support. Except for its advocacy of greater **tax harmonization**, the **Cockfield White Paper** embodied the kind of liberal economic thinking which she believed could revitalize the European economy through supply-side reform. However, Delors and others quickly alighted on the need to underpin completion of the single market with a number of institutional changes – notably the greater use of **qualified majority voting** (QMV) for decision-making in the **Council of Ministers** and certain extensions of Community **competence** – which challenged her essentially intergovernmental view of how the Community should be organized. In June 1985, Britain voted against the convening of the **Intergovernmental Conference** (IGC) that led to the **Single European Act** (SEA). Although Thatcher publicly supported the Act once it had been negotiated – and indeed her government heralded the outcome as a great British success – she was wary of the thinking which underpinned it.

In the event, against expectations – including those of Delors himself – the introduction of the Single Act played an important part in restoring confidence in the Community and led to progress on many fronts. QMV was accepted as the normal decision-making method wherever it was provided for in the **Treaties**, quickly resulting in the demise of the **Luxembourg Compromise**. The renewed sense of momentum gave Delors the political space in which to propose a substantial increase in **own resources** – to finance a doubling of **structural funds** and greater **cohesion** between rich and poorer member states – and, more importantly, concrete moves towards **Economic and Monetary Union** (EMU) and the development of a 'Social Europe'. In preparing this agenda, the Commission President worked closely with Mitterrand and the German Chancellor, **Helmut Kohl**. Despite the maintenance of civil and workmanlike relations, the British prime minister was largely viewed by all three leaders as a hostile force to be circumvented, rather than as a potential ally. Thatcher was later to argue that she had not been made fully aware of the institutional and policy implications of the Single Act by the Foreign Office and others, but in reality nobody could have wholly predicted the dramatic and sudden acceleration in European integration which took place from 1987 on.

Thatcher's basic instinct towards Europe resembled closely that of **Charles de Gaulle** two decades earlier, with its strong hostility to **supranationalism** as a philosophy and a corresponding preference for the pre-eminence of the nation state. In her view, the Council of Ministers, rather than the European Commission or European Parliament, should be the central forum for decision-making, with as many issues settled by **unanimity** as possible. She subsequently described nation states in Gaullist tones, as 'intractable political realities which it would be folly to seek to override or suppress in favour of a wider but as yet theoretical European nationhood'. Unlike the General, she had, of course, no desire to see a distinctive European foreign policy develop independently of the United States. She agreed with him, however, that the Community policies should be limited fairly strictly to the ones set down in the original **Treaty of Rome**, but emphasized those of a liberalizing character, notably the **free movement** of goods, services and capital, rather than the more interventionist and costly CAP. Conversely, Thatcher refused to acknowledge that the process of economic liberalization in Europe might itself have political consequences of a federalizing kind: in a barrier-free economy, there would be strong pressures for further integration – in a process known as 'spillover' – and the nation state might itself come to be seen as perhaps the ultimate supply-side constraint.

Although Thatcher's liberalizing policies reaped a significant political and economic dividend at home, she found herself increasingly on the defensive in the arena of Community politics, as the European agenda moved beyond the completion of the single market to the ambitious new priorities being defined and promoted by Delors. She reluctantly agreed to his reappointment as Commission President, confirmed at the June 1988 European Council, mainly because the only viable alternative, the veteran German foreign minister, Hans-Dietrich Genscher, was viewed as equally integrationist. This may, however, have been a serious miscalculation on her part: there was a general lack of understanding in Whitehall, as elsewhere, of quite how historically unique were Delors' political skills in being able to build a strong coalition of heads of government behind ambitious projects fashioned by the Commission in Brussels. Instead of attempting to force Delors out, Thatcher curiously insisted on the retirement of her own, highly successful, British Commissioner, Lord Cockfield.

At the same time, Thatcher began publicly to voice her doubts about closer European integration in general, and the Delors agenda in particular, with increasing force. Having managed, against huge vested interests, in liberalizing the British economy and limiting trade union power, she was fearful that her government's achievements might now be put at risk by what she saw as Delors' increasingly centralist and corporatist approach, especially in defining a new 'social dimension' for Europe. Starting in the summer of 1988, Thatcher made a series of controversial pronouncements designed to reshape public opinion and pull the mainstream of the Conservative party, seen historically as the 'party of Europe', behind her. The fullest expression of her views was given on 20 September, in the **Bruges speech**, which was consciously presented as a break with conventional British policy on Europe. Appealing directly to those who feared that European integration might promote Socialism on a continental scale, the prime minister asserted memorably: 'We have not successfully rolled back the frontiers of the state in Britain, only to see them reimposed at a European level, with a European super-state exercising a new dominance from Brussels.' The principal impact of such statements, however, was not to strengthen Thatcher's hand in the Community, but to help radicalize the debate on Europe in British politics, positively promoting the development of **Euroscepticism** in the Conservative party and beyond.

Against an increasingly difficult backdrop – where an ambitious new policy agenda in Brussels was matched by a more and more pugilistic prime minister at home, leading to a growing risk of British isolation in Europe – a significant difference of opinion began to open up within the government in London about the direction of the country's European policy in general, and the handling of moves towards EMU in particular. Both the Chancellor of the Exchequer, Nigel Lawson, and the Foreign Secretary, Geoffrey Howe, advocated early entry into the ERM – membership of which was now designated as part of 'stage one' of EMU – both on its own merits, and as an attempt to halt an early rush towards a single currency by others, without British involvement. Whilst her most senior ministers hoped to decouple the ERM from EMU, Thatcher, by contrast, was violently opposed to both, and simply rejected the Lawson–Howe strategy. Equally, Lawson's secret 'competing currencies' proposal – which would allow both a common currency and existing national currencies to circulate freely in competition with each other – was dismissed by Thatcher out of hand. Likewise, Howe's determination to keep open the option of Britain entering a single currency, whether or not it joined at the start, met with equally firm resistance from the prime minister, even if, like the commitment to Britain joining the ERM 'when the time is right', it in fact remained official government policy.

Tensions were apparent during the June 1989 European election campaign, when populist Conservative party posters sanctioned by the prime minister's office condemned Delors' Europe as a 'Diet of Brussels', whilst the more measured party election manifesto, authored by Geoffrey Howe and Chris Patten, spoke of Britain 'leading Europe into the 1990s'. At the launch of that manifesto, Howe served notice to Thatcher that her public position on the ERM 'could not, by definition, be maintained indefinitely'. She was indeed persuaded to agree, at the Madrid meeting of the **European Council** later that month, to British participation in the first stage of EMU and with it, make a commitment to join the ERM in the near term. She also had to accept that a majority of member states wished to convene an IGC on EMU by the end of 1990, although the future contours of any closer monetary integration were left open.

It was subsequently revealed that Howe and Lawson had jointly threatened to resign if Thatcher continued to rule out British membership of the ERM at Madrid. In July, she extracted her retribution by removing Howe from the Foreign Office in a botched reshuffle that led him, now as deputy prime minister, to emerge as de facto leader of the party's internal opposition to her policy on Europe (and on some other issues as well). She then unwisely invited a strong monetarist critic of the ERM, Alan Walters, to become her personal economic adviser at Number 10, as a counter-force to the Chancellor. In October 1989, Lawson suddenly resigned, worn down by her continued stalling on the ERM and opposition to his oblique policy of 'shadowing the Deutschmark', so delivering a substantial blow to her authority. Lawson used an unhelpful article by Walters as the immediate pretext for his departure, but noted ominously that 'it represented the tip of a singularly ill-concealed iceberg, with all the destructive potential that icebergs possess.' He warned Thatcher to 'seek the earliest practicable time to join [the ERM], rather than the latest for which a colourable case can be made'.

Thatcher's declining authority corresponded to a rising curve of public unpopularity, after a decade in power. Having won re-election with substantial parliamentary majorities in June 1983 and June 1987 – aided first by a divided opposition and then by evidence of growing economic success – the Conservative party's opinion poll lead began to falter in spring 1989. By early 1990, the Conservatives were some 20 per cent behind the opposition Labour party. Contributing decisively to this change of national mood was the introduction of a new 'poll tax' to finance local government, which doubled the number of direct taxpayers overnight and led to civil disobedience and violent unrest. The prime minister's determination to impose the 'Community Charge' in the face of serious misgivings within her own party was seen as evidence of her faltering political judgement, which the almost casual alienation of Howe and Lawson – who as her successive Chancellors had played such a central role in the successes of the Thatcher revolution – appeared to confirm.

Even the fall of the Berlin Wall in November 1989, which vindicated the resolute stand which Thatcher had taken against Communism during the latter part of the **Cold War**, ended up compounding the political malaise enveloping her premiership. She gave free rein to her deep and instinctive hostility to **German reunification**, sharing her misgivings with President Mitterrand, who, after initially concurring with her analysis in private, quickly chose to express a much more positive and pragmatic position in public. Britain's relationship with Germany became increasingly strained. In March 1990, the official record of a private seminar on Germany, organized for the prime minister at Chequers, was leaked: even if the overall assessment was positive, embarrassingly, it listed as German attributes, 'in alphabetical order, *Angst*, aggressiveness, assertiveness, bullying, egotism, inferiority complex, sentimentality'. In similar vein, the trade secretary, Nicholas Ridley – an early Thatcherite and emblematic Eurosceptic – was forced to resign in July 1990, when he spoke unguardedly of EMU as 'a German racket designed to take over the whole of Europe' and suggested that transferring power to the EU institutions was equivalent to giving it to Adolf Hitler.

In December 1989, Thatcher faced her first-ever challenge in the annual contest for the Conservative party leadership: 60 of the party's 374 MPs chose to vote for the maverick backbencher, Anthony Meyer, or to abstain, sending a warning signal to the prime minister that was largely ignored. In the same month, she found that her strident tone first on European integration, and now on German reunification, was visibly eroding her influence on Community decision-making. At the Strasbourg meeting of the European Council, her fellow leaders adopted the Community's new **Social Charter** without British support – the first time that a substantive policy position (as opposed to procedural decision) had been adopted by the European Council other than by unanimity. They also agreed, by simple majority, to convene the IGC on EMU by the end of 1990. In April 1990, the 'Dublin I' European Council welcomed a Mitterrand–Kohl proposal – from the preparation of which the UK was excluded – to move towards 'European Political Union' (EPU) in parallel to EMU. At the 'Dublin II' European Council two months later, heads of government decided to convene a political union IGC to run alongside the EMU one. Finally, at the 'Rome I' European Council in late October – only three weeks after she had finally acceded to Britain joining the ERM – Thatcher faced complete isolation when the 11 other member states decided on the principles that would guide the EMU IGC in designing a single currency and established a tentative timetable for its adoption. In response, she declared publicly for the first time that Britain would never join a single currency and famously shouted 'No, No, No', when she reported back to the House of Commons on her failure at the summit. On 1 November, Geoffrey Howe resigned as deputy prime minister, declaring that Thatcher's isolation in Europe and position on EMU had made it impossible for him to continue in her government. Twelve days later, he delivered a devastating resignation speech to his parliamentary colleagues, in which he spoke of the prime minister's attitude towards Europe 'running increasingly serious risks for the future of our nation'.

The interaction of Howe's departure and the imminence of the deadline for nominations in the annual Conservative leadership election was to prove fatal to Thatcher. Against the backdrop of deep and growing public hostility towards the poll tax, the opportunity existed for a serious challenge to her position. The former defence secretary, Michael Heseltine, who had resigned from the government during the 1986 Westland affair, stood as a candidate and won enough votes to deny the prime minister an outright victory on the first ballot. Thatcher hung on for two days – during which she signed the **Charter of Paris**, marking the formal end of the Cold War – before withdrawing from the contest, announcing her resignation on 22 November. The Chancellor, John Major, and Foreign Secretary, Douglas Hurd, ran against Heseltine in the second ballot. With Thatcher's informal backing, Major emerged with a plurality of the vote, but fell short of an absolute majority. Hurd was eliminated and Heseltine stood aside, averting the need for a third ballot, and Major was elected party leader and appointed prime minister. Soon after, on 14 December, the two IGCs on monetary and political union in Europe, which Thatcher had sought to avoid, began to meet, running for the following 12 months.

The sudden reversal of political fortune which overcame Thatcher and her supporters in November 1990 left them psychologically bruised, and, in some cases, eager for revenge. Although she promised to avoid 'backseat driving' and to allow her successor the opportunity to pursue his own policies – such as his proposal for a 'hard ECU' as an alternative to the single currency – Thatcher proved unable to resist the temptation, fuelled by the media, to allow her Euroscepticism full rein. So, whilst she initially professed herself 'thrilled for John' at his success, in December 1991, in negotiating a deal on the **Maastricht Treaty**, she soon played a key part in fomenting opposition to the new treaty in the House of Lords (to which she was elevated in June 1992), leading the campaign to subject its **ratification** to a referendum. Thatcher's willingness publicly to contradict her successor – just as Heath had criticized her in the past – did much to undermine Major's brittle authority, stoking the flames of the growing **Maastricht ratification crisis** which spiralled, after Britain's ejection from the ERM on **Black Wednesday** in September 1992, into a full-blown civil war within the Conservative party on Europe.

In retirement, Thatcher produced two volumes of memoirs, *The Downing Street Years* (1993) and *The Path to Power* (1995), as well as some reflections on foreign policy in *Statecraft: Strategies for a Changing World* (2002). In the latter book, she argued that British membership of the European Union had been 'a political error of historic magnitude', described the Union as 'fundamentally unreformable' and predicted that its 'inevitable destiny is failure'. She recommended that Britain should seek to negotiate additional **opt-outs** from certain key policies, notably the CAP and **Common Foreign and Security Policy** (CFSP), and that, if this could not be secured, the country should leave the Union on an amicable basis.

Further reading: Philip Stephens, *Politics and the Pound: The Tories, the Economy and Europe*, 1997; Stephen Wall, *A Stranger in Europe: Britain and the* EU *from Thatcher to Blair*, 2008; Hugo Young, *One of Us: Life of Margaret Thatcher*, 1993.

Tindemans Report

Commissioned by EC heads of government at the **European Council** meeting in Paris in December 1974 and presented 12 months later, the Tindemans Report was an ambitious and wide-ranging study of the possible shape of **European Union** and of the practical steps that could be taken to achieve a more integrated Europe closer to the citizen. Drawn up by Leo Tindemans, the Christian Democrat prime minister of Belgium, the 32-page report offered only a relatively vague definition of European Union – describing it as a 'qualitative change' in the relationship between member states, based on deeper external and internal policies, supported by stronger common institutions – the alternative to which was 'an unconvincing Europe without a future'. Such a Union could not be achieved, Tindemans argued, without a transfer of **competences** and resources and implied 'constraints, freely accepted certainly, but then enforced unreservedly'.

The report proposed to give **European Political Cooperation** (EPC) a formal legal basis and to develop it into a 'common foreign policy', underpinned by the de facto merger of EPC with existing Council discussion of external trade and **development policy**, and acceptance that ministers could discuss security and defence questions. It favoured resuming moves towards **Economic and Monetary Union** (EMU), initially by strengthening the 'Snake' (currency-management system), whilst accepting that not all member states would be able to participate in this field, at least initially. In a proposition which was radical at the time, Tindemans said that it was no longer possible to advance in this field if it was assumed that 'in every case, all stages should be reached by all the states at the same time', and argued that 'those states which are able to progress have a duty to forge ahead' until the others could catch up. Some accused the report of favouring a '**two-speed Europe**'. Less controversially, but equally ambitiously, the text also argued for greater action in the fields of energy, transport, research, social and regional policy, as well as the development of a 'Citizen's Europe', based on new policies for fundamental rights, consumer rights, higher education, and the 'gradual disappearance of frontier controls' to promote the **free movement of persons.**

Institutionally, the Tindemans Report argued that a directly-elected **European Parliament** should be given the right to approve the appointment of the President of the **European Commission** and allowed to share the **right of initiative** for legislative proposals with the Commission. The recently-created European Council should be harnessed to provide 'the impetus which is necessary for the construction of Europe'. Underpinning this, the **Council of Ministers** would be made more efficient: 'recourse to [**qualified**] **majority voting** . . . should become normal practice in the Community field', in effect overriding the **Luxembourg Compromise**; the rotating **presidency** of the Council would be extended from six months to one year; and **COREPER** would be allowed to adopt legislation on the Council's behalf, when ministerial discussion was unnecessary.

In preparing his report, Tindemans solicited contributions from the other EC institutions and a wide range of outside experts and organizations. The Commission's contribution was noteworthy in containing the first official reference to **subsidiarity** in a Community context. In his preface to the report, Tindemans commented on the 'distinct divergence' he had encountered between public opinion in most countries, which was 'extremely sceptical' towards the potential of European integration, and the views of political leaders, almost all of whom 'stated that they could not imagine a better future for their country than that offered by the building of Europe'.

In the event, few of Tindemans' recommendations were given immediate effect, although they did feed into a much bigger debate on institutional reform which gathered speed in the early 1980s. Many of the changes he proposed were eventually adopted in successive rounds of treaty reform, notably in the 1986 **Single European Act** (SEA) and 1992 **Maastricht Treaty**. (The direct election of the European Parliament had already been agreed in principle by heads of government in 1974.) The three main Tindemans proposals *not* to be adopted over time were the sharing of the Commission's right of initiative with the Parliament, the adoption of a one-year Council presidency and the right of COREPER to act on the Council's behalf.

Trade Policy Committee

The Trade Policy Committee, otherwise known as the Article 207 Committee, is the key decision-making body in the exercise of the European Union's exclusive **competence** in the field of **Common Commercial Policy** (CCP) or external trade. It is a committee of national officials from EU member-state governments, chaired by the rotating **presidency** of the **Council of Ministers**, which meets weekly to prepare the decisions of the Council in this policy field.

The fact that external trade ministers do not meet as a Council formation – with CCP issues left to foreign ministers, meeting in the **Foreign Affairs Council** (FAC) – gives the Trade Policy Committee a particularly strong influence over policy outcomes in this area. Article 207(3) TFEU obliges the Commission to secure a mandate from the Council before opening negotiations with third countries and international organizations, and to consult the Council continuously during the negotiating process. It also states that the 'Commission shall conduct these negotiations in consultation with a special committee appointed by the Council to assist the Commission in this task and within the framework of such directives as the Council may issue to it'. Until the introduction of the **Lisbon Treaty**, the committee was known successively as the Article 113 Committee (1961–97) and Article 133 Committee (1997–2009), reflecting the corresponding number of the treaty article relating to external trade policy at that time. When Lisbon entered into force, it was decided to use the name 'Trade Policy Committee', rather than Article 207 Committee, as its routine designation.

The committee meets at the level of national trade directors once a month, and at the level of their deputies during the other three weeks each month, usually on Fridays in Brussels. Its work covers, in the Commission's words, 'the full range of trade policy issues affecting the Community, from the strategic issues surrounding the launch of rounds of trade negotiations . . . to specific difficulties with the export of individual products, and considers the trade aspects of wider Community policies in order to ensure consistency of policy'. Agendas characteristically deal with the preparation of meetings within the **World Trade Organization** (WTO), as well as regional, bilateral and horizontal trade issues. Some tasks are delegated to expert working groups – covering such matters as services, textiles, steel and mutual recognition – or to negotiating groups that may convene at the WTO or in other international fora. There is a separate Council working group that looks at proposed external trade legislation before it is considered by the Trade Policy Committee and ministers. The committee produces an annual report for the Council on market access in third countries. See also **Common Customs Tariff**.

Transatlantic relations

The United States of America has always been broadly sympathetic to the idea of European unification. The country's status as the 'first new nation', in the striking phrase of Seymour Martin Lipset, together with its role in pioneering **federalism** on a continental scale, has given it an intuitive appreciation of the problems and possibilities of political integration. From the very beginning, many American officials and scholars, brought up on the history of their own political system, displayed an informed understanding of the European experiment in sharing **sovereignty**. It was no accident that two of the earliest and best studies of the nascent European Community – Ernst Haas's *The Uniting of Europe* (1958) and Leon Lindberg's *The Political Dynamics of European Economic Integration* (1963) – were written by Americans. Conversely, the idea of a **United States of Europe** was a source of inspiration to advocates of European unity from Victor Hugo to **Winston Churchill**, whilst the US Constitution served as an indirect model for several key concepts and phrases in the **Treaties**. For example, **Jean Monnet**, who worked in Washington during the Second World War, was much impressed by the role of independent regulatory agencies: the Interstate Commerce Commission and similar bodies served as a model for the **High Authority** of the **European Coal and Steel Community** (ECSC), the forerunner of the **European Commission.**

The United States itself played a central role in the efforts to bring together the shattered economies of the old continent after the Second World War. It was the **Marshall Plan** that led, at US insistence, to the founding of the first post-war, pan-European body, the **Organization for European Economic Cooperation** (OEEC). The earliest advocacy of a 'single large market' in western Europe came from US officials in 1949. Washington was also keen to engage western Europe in its own defence, promoting the signing of the **Brussels Treaty** in 1948: only the deepening of the **Cold War** and growing threat of **Communism** forced it, against its instincts, to provide a US-led protective shield through the creation of the **North Atlantic Treaty Organization** (NATO) in 1949. The Truman and Eisenhower Administrations strongly supported the establishment of the supranational ECSC in 1950–52 and regretted that Britain would not participate. They did nothing to resist the even more ambitious (but unsuccessful) plans for a **European Defence Community** (EDC) and **European Political Community** (EPC) in 1951–5, even if German membership of NATO was their first priority. In the debate soon thereafter about the creation of the **European Economic Community** (EEC), as opposed to the British plan for a wider **free trade area** in Europe, American support was decisively on the side of **the Six.**

Although the advent of NATO meant that the US and many European countries were firmly tied together in a security alliance, no comparable post-war structure developed for transatlantic relations in economics, trade and other 'domestic' policy areas. This problem was compounded by differences in the membership and philosophies of NATO and the new Community – the one firmly intergovernmental, the other supranational – and the absence (until the end of the Cold War) of any significant foreign or security policy role for the latter. The political and economic dimensions of the transatlantic relationship have therefore tended to proceed on distinct trajectories. Dense 'high politics' relations between member-state capitals and Washington have coexisted with a more amorphous, less visible, but increasingly important set of technical linkages on domestic issues between the EU institutions in Brussels and their US interlocutors.

There is no overall treaty or **association agreement** structuring relations between the European Union and United States, although **cooperation agreements** apply in several fields, such as customs, **competition policy**, public purchasing, air traffic, energy, science and technology, and higher education. EU–US relations were put on a more formal political basis by the 'Transatlantic Declaration' in November 1990, followed by agreement on a 'New Transatlantic Agenda' in December 1995. A framework was established for regular consultations between the **European Commission** and the US administration, on the one hand, and between EU foreign ministers and the US Secretary of State, on the other. An annual summit meeting was instituted between the US President and both the President of the European Commission and the prime minister of the member state holding the rotating **presidency** of the **Council of Ministers** (the latter place is now taken by the **President of the European Council**). A series of parallel 'dialogues' between policy stakeholders was also put in place: the Transatlantic Legislators' Dialogue (TLD) between the European Parliament and US House of Representatives; the Transatlantic Business Dialogue (TABD) between the chief executives of major corporations and senior officials; and the Transatlantic Consumer Dialogue (TCD) between consumer groups and officials.

Although Americans and Europeans have cooperated successfully, both bilaterally and in international institutions, on very many issues, there have been certain recurrent tensions in recent decades. In a NATO context, Washington has consistently pressurized its European partners since the 1980s to shoulder a bigger share of the burden of their own defence, accepting the possibility of a separate European defence capability through the EU if that can serve this purpose. In the economic sphere, regular disagreements have arisen with respect to trade policy (especially in agriculture), regulatory and competition policy issues (for example, in the Boeing/Airbus dispute), and periodic efforts by the US to assert the extraterritoriality of its domestic law. In these latter fields, the freedom of the US government has often been hindered by protectionist tendencies in Congress over which it has difficulty in exercising any control.

Commercial disagreements, although occasionally dramatic, conceal the sheer scale of mutual trade and investment between the EU and the US, and the high degree of economic interdependence that results. Together, the EU and US economies still account for over 50 per cent of the global economy and almost 40 per cent of world trade. In 2010, total EU–US trade in goods amounted to well over a billion euro per day, making it the most important bilateral trading relationship for both sides: the EU exported € 242 billion to the US and imported € 169 billion in return. The average level of tariffs was under three per cent. In services, the EU exported € 125 billion and imported € 131 billion. One third of EU–US trade was undertaken in 'intra-company' transfers, showing the strength of transatlantic multinational corporations in the two economies. The total stock of EU and US foreign direct investment (FDI) in each other's jurisdictions amounted to € 2.2 trillion, with US investment in the EU still running at three times the rate for Asia. The US invested more in Ireland than in all the BRICs during the decade 2000–9, and investment in Ireland was itself only seven per cent of total US investment in the Union. Some 13 million people are said to be employed in the 'transatlantic economy' in some way.

The EU and US have considered the possibility of creating a transatlantic **free trade area**. A proposal to this effect, known as the 'New Transatlantic Marketplace', was put forward in 1995 by Leon Brittan, the then European Commissioner for external trade, but was vetoed by France, mainly to protect agricultural interests. Advocates of closer economic links have since focused instead on creating a 'transatlantic single market', based on the removal of remaining **non-tariff barriers** (NTBs) to trade and investment, backed by greater regulatory convergence and closer alignment of competition policy. A recent survey suggested that removal of even half of such NTBs could increase joint EU–US GDP by over € 160 billion in a decade. To address these issues, the US and EU agreed on a new Transatlantic Economic Partnership (TEP) in 1998, and a Transatlantic Economic Council (TEC) was established by the European Commission and US administration in 2007. This meets six-monthly and its work feeds into the annual EU–US summit.

As EU **competence** has broadened over time, the range of policy areas covered by EU–US relations has expanded in parallel, creating new areas of both cooperation and tension across the Atlantic. A good example of this is the field of **Justice and Home Affairs** (JHA), where since 11 September 2001, the need and possibility for joint action has increased, whilst differing European and American attitudes about the balance to be struck between the competing needs of security and data protection have become apparent.

The 2009–10 'SWIFT affair' – in which the European Parliament vetoed an agreement on US monitoring of the bank transactions of European citizens – brought some of these problems into sharp relief.

The deepening of EU–US relations is still handicapped by strong competition between the larger EU member states for the exclusive attention of the US administration. The major national capitals have a strong vested interest in downplaying the significance of the Union in transatlantic relations, in favour of promoting privileged bilateral links of various kinds. This instinct is replayed in turn by Washington's persistent (and arguably outdated) emphasis on 'hard power' defence and security issues, rather than 'soft power' economic and domestic issues, in its thinking about the relevance of Europe. Even if Barack Obama has asserted that 'Europe is the cornerstone of our engagement in the world' and (at the time of writing) visited the continent nine times in his first 36 months as US President, none of his itineraries have yet included a stop in Brussels to visit the EU institutions.

Trans-European Networks (TENs)

From the early days of the Community, European-level funding for transnational infrastructure, including national infrastructure projects of European significance, was available to member states through the operations (successively) of the **European Investment Bank** (EIB), which started work in 1958, the **European Regional Development Fund** (ERDF), established in 1972–5, and the New Community Instrument (NCI) or 'Ortoli Facility', which provided loans for investment from 1977 to 1987. However, the 1992 **Maastricht Treaty** provided a specific legal basis for such support for the first time, by adding Articles 170–72 TFEU to the **Treaty of Rome**. Article 170 envisages 'the establishment and development of trans-European networks in the areas of transport, telecommunications and energy infrastructures'. The Union may take action aimed at 'promoting the interconnection and interoperability of national networks as well as access to such networks'. Particular account is to be taken of 'the need to link island, landlocked and peripheral regions with the central regions of the Union'.

Trans-European Networks are intended to complement the **single market** by allowing transport links, telecommunications networks and energy grids to be planned and developed on a Europe-wide basis. They also help underpin the Union's regional policy and promote territorial **cohesion**, by enabling outlying regions to be more efficiently linked with the centre. The Union may identify 'projects of common interest' and 'establish guidelines covering the objectives, priorities and broad lines' of action in the TENs field. It may support these projects through 'feasibility studies, loan guarantees or interest-rate subsidies' and by financing specific transport infrastructure projects under the Cohesion Fund. The **European Commission** may 'take any useful initiative' in this field, such as the identification of transport bottlenecks or the provision of technical assistance (Article 171 TFEU). Decision-making on Commission proposals for projects of common interest, guidelines and other measures is conducted under the **co-decision procedure** between the **Council of Ministers** and the **European Parliament**. No action that relates to the territory of a member state may be taken without the approval of the state in question (Article 172 TFEU).

An initial list of 14 transport and 10 energy TENs was established at the **European Council** meeting in Essen in December 1994, although this exercise was criticized for largely linking together existing national projects, rather than identifying from first principles strategic axes for future development. The list of priorities is updated periodically: the number of transport TENs has grown from 14 to 30 and of energy TENs from 10 to 15; those in the telecommunications field are chosen on a more ad hoc basis. Since the adoption of the 2007–13 Multiannual Financial Framework (MFF), greater funding has been available from the annual EU **Budget** for transport TENs, in particular, but the total is still only a fraction of what is required. Some € 51 billion is assigned for transport TENs over this seven-year period, matched by anticipated national funding of four times that amount (although the recent economic and financial crisis makes the latter figure increasingly unlikely). Only five of the 30 transport projects were complete by 2010, with 16 more expected to be finished over the next 15 years. Following the **enlargement** of the Union from 15 to 27 member states in 2004–7, greater priority has been attached to attempting to integrate the new member states into existing or planned infrastructure networks in western Europe.

Transport projects are collectively known as TEN-T, energy projects as TEN-E, and telecommunications projects as eTEN. The most prominent project in the transport field is the (almost complete) high-speed rail network (incorporating the Channel Tunnel) between London, Paris, Brussels, Cologne and Amsterdam. Other notable TEN-T projects include high-speed rail links in south-west France, Spain and Portugal; the new transalpine rail link from Lyon to Turin (and on to Venice, Trieste and Budapest); 'Nordic triangle' rail and road connections between Copenhagen, Oslo and Stockholm (including the multimodal Øresund bridge between Malmö and Copenhagen); improvements to the rail and ferry connections between Britain and Ireland; and the development of motorways from Gdansk to Athens, via Vienna and Budapest. The most important TEN projects in the energy field are a complex series of links between national electricity grids (for example, Ireland, the United Kingdom and France) and natural gas pipelines (for example, the UK, the Netherlands, Denmark and Germany), as well as the development of liquid natural gas terminals and storage capabilities across Europe. Some TEN-E projects link the Union with countries outside its borders: for example, the gas pipelines between Algeria and both Italy and Spain, and the Nabucco pipeline from Turkey to Austria. In the telecommunications field, the main emphasis has been on assisting the introduction of new digital exchanges, cross-border electronic clearing systems for banks and credit card operations, data transmission and mobile telephone networks.

Transitional period

The phrase 'transitional period' normally refers to the period of grace during which a new member state may be allowed progressively to introduce and apply European Union rules, the immediate adoption of which would cause difficulties. Agreement as to the length of any transitional periods and their field of application is reached in the course of the **enlargement** negotiations and laid down in the relevant **accession** treaty. In effect, the member state in question is given a temporary **derogation** from **EU law**. For example, when the United Kingdom entered the European Communities in 1973, it enjoyed a five-year transitional period during which agricultural exports from New Zealand were exempted from the **Common Customs Tariff** (CCT). More recently, there was a five-year transitional period (2004–9) during which Poland, Hungary and the Czech Republic were allowed to restrict the purchase of second homes by nationals of other EU member states (with a longer transition for agricultural land). The application of the rules for the **free movement of capital** in this field were thus deferred.

Since Spanish and Portuguese enlargement in 1986, some transitional periods have been applied to *existing* member states, offering them relief from rights which citizens of new entrants might otherwise exercise. There was a seven-year transitional period during which the pre-existing member states (EU15) could prevent the **free movement** of workers from the eight central and eastern European countries which joined the EU in 2004. (They could liberalize entry at the end of each of three phases, running from 2004–6, 2006–9 and 2009–11.) A similar arrangement applies to Bulgarian and Romanian workers from 2007 to 2014.

'Transitional period' also has a historic meaning in the context of the development of the European Community. Article 8 of the original **Treaty of Rome** required **the Six** to establish the **customs union** and **common market** 'during a transitional period of 12 years . . . divided into three stages of four years each'. Article 14 specified in detail the stages by which tariffs, customs duties and quantitative restrictions on trade between the founding member states were to be removed, starting on 1 January 1958. In the event, the process was completed ahead of schedule – after 10, rather than 12, years – on 1 July 1968. The treaty commitment to greater use of **qualified majority voting** (QMV) at the beginning of the third stage of the transitional period (on 1 January 1966) was a key cause of the 'empty chair crisis' in the second half of 1965, during which the French government boycotted meetings of the **Council of Ministers**. The crisis was resolved by the **Luxembourg Compromise** in January 1966.

Transport policy

The potential importance of transport as a means of facilitating cross-frontier exchange and improving the efficiency of the European economy was fully understood by the architects of the **Treaties**. The 1951 **Treaty of Paris**, which established the **European Coal and Steel Community** (ECSC), contained a brief reference to transport policy, and the ECSC **High Authority** sought to promote the strengthening of rail links. The creation of an intergovernmental European Conference of Ministers of Transport (ECMT) in 1953 reflected the perceived need for closer cooperation in this field. After the failure of the **European Defence Community** (EDC) in 1954, there was talk of creating a 'European Transport Community' as an alternative to a cross-sector **common market**. So, when the **Treaty of Rome** was drafted in 1956–7, it was natural that a title was included on the development of a 'common transport policy' (Articles 74–84 EEC, now Articles 90–100 TFEU).

In practice, however, progress towards the adoption of a transport policy at European level proved exceptionally slow during the early years of the Community. The **European Commission** was slow in proposing legislation in this field, partly because of the higher immediate priority it attached to pursuing other treaty objectives in the early 1960s, and partly because it appreciated that there were seriously divergent transport patterns and thus economic interests among **the Six**. France and Germany were heavily reliant on railways for the transport of their freight, for example, whilst the other states tended to use road transport. The political sensitivities and strong organized interests associated with the transport sector (often involving large state or private monopolies and powerful trade unions) induced a natural caution on the part of the Commission. Then transport policy became one of the principal casualties of the **Luxembourg Compromise**, agreed in January 1966, whereby decision-making could be postponed indefinitely on matters otherwise subject to **qualified majority voting** (QMV) in the **Council of Ministers**. QMV was supposed to apply from 1966 onwards in certain aspects of transport policy, but the 'veto culture' quickly became entrenched.

The success of the Community in promoting a very rapid growth of intra-Community trade in the 1960s and early 1970s meant that there was more and more pressure for transport issues to be addressed at supranational level. Equally, the **enlargement** of the Community in 1973 helpfully added three new member states – Denmark, Ireland and the United Kingdom – with a strong commitment to the development of a common transport policy along liberalizing lines. In 1982, in an attempt to break the impasse, the **European Parliament** took a path-breaking case to the **European Court of Justice** (ECJ) against the Council for its '**failure to act**' (under Article 175 EEC, now Article 265 TFEU). The resulting ECJ judgement in 1985 confirmed that the Council had failed to act in respect of certain specific rules foreseen in the Treaty of Rome, but ruled that the general obligation to establish a common transport policy was insufficiently precise to be enforceable. Although the Parliament did not win outright, momentum established by the case helped ensure that, as a part of the Commission's new programme to complete the **single market** by 1992, transport liberalization featured as a high priority. Crucially, the extension of QMV through the 1986 **Single European Act** (SEA) led quickly to the demise of the Luxembourg Compromise as an operating principle in Community law-making.

The original treaty provisions for a common transport policy could now more easily be put into effect. In the fields of rail, road and inland waterways, they allowed the Council to adopt, by QMV, 'common rules applicable to international transport' between or through member states and to 'the conditions under which non-resident carriers may operate' transport services within member states, as well as to adopt 'any other appropriate provisions'. The Council could also decide, by unanimity, to extend such common rules to air and sea transport. The 1992 **Maastricht Treaty** added the explicit right to enact 'measures to improve transport safety' to the list of common rules and allowed the Council to decide on air and sea transport by QMV. Since the 1997 **Amsterdam Treaty**, decision-making on transport legislation has been undertaken on the basis of **co-decision** between the Council and Parliament.

Even before the SEA came into force in 1987, some progress, admittedly limited, had been made in developing a common transport policy. In 1965, the Council took the first steps towards harmonizing competition rules for rail, road and inland waterway transport. Three years later, the normal treaty rules on **competition policy** were applied to this sector (even if many exemptions and **derogations** were still allowed). Article 93 TFEU has always permitted state aids to be maintained 'if they represent reimbursement for the discharge of certain obligations inherent in the concept of a public service'. This provision, of great importance to the railways, obviously required a common definition of a 'public service' and accounting systems that would allow revenues from state aids to be clearly identified. Both these aims were achieved in a series of regulations adopted from 1969 onwards.

Efforts were also made to promote 'common operating practices' in transport. Agreement was reached in 1969 on two regulations governing drivers' hours and the installation of recording equipment (the tachograph) in certain vehicles in commercial use. The technical specifications for road vehicles, most controversially heavy lorries, were increasingly defined. Maximum width, height, total weight and weight per axle were laid down in 1984, initially for international traffic between member states. Once QMV began to be used in practice, a step change occurred in this aspect of transport policy, as in others. A system of Community licences governing access to the market for commercial road transport was introduced in January 1993, replacing the restrictive and protectionist system of bilateral national quotas in force until that date. Progress was also made on the liberalization of *cabotage* regulations for goods and passenger transport: road freight carriers were allowed to take on business in countries they were passing through from 1998 onwards. Together these changes largely ended huge inefficiencies in road haulage, whereby lorries would often have to travel very long distances entirely empty.

In the rail sector, EU policy moved beyond the question of regulating subsidies and influencing pricing to a much broader strategy of trying to upgrade and encourage use of Europe's substantial rail network, both to take pressure off the roads and to reduce the need for short-haul air flights. Helped in part by their relatively modest impact on the environment and their economic use of energy, the railways have, for the first time in several decades, enjoyed a revival. The centrepiece of this policy has been Commission efforts to knit together the development of national high-speed rail services in Europe, by designating them as **Trans-European Networks** (TENs), even if the two main competing systems, the French TGV and the German ICE, still have compatibility problems. The length of the high-speed rail network in Europe more than doubled in the 2000s. The high-speed network already accounts for over a quarter of all rail passenger traffic, even if it represents only one twentieth of total track. A system of non-stop, long-distance international 'freightways', introduced in 1998, is intended to make the railways more attractive for the transport of goods and to improve peripheral regions' access to the principal markets. Eighteen of the 30 priority TENs transport projects involve the railways.

A series of three 'rail packages', adopted in 2001, 2004 and 2007, have gradually liberalized the provision of railway services within the Union, as well as improved safety and enhanced the interoperability of systems and equipment. (A European Railway Agency, based in Valenciennes, France, was created in 2004 for the latter purpose.) International rail freight within the EU has been totally liberalized since 2007, as has the operation of international passenger services since 2010, in both cases including *cabotage*. Operators may now pick up and set down passengers at any station on an international route, including at stations located in the same member state. The German railway company Deutsche Bahn will take advantage of this 'open access' right to compete with Eurostar to provide services on the London to Brussels high-speed route from 2013. Train drivers will also be able to operate anywhere in the EU, if they are in possession of a European driver's licence, based on certain minimum requirements. A set of EU-wide passenger rights has also been established. The Union's Marco Polo programme is channelling € 450 million between 2007 and 2013 towards projects which take freight off the roads and onto both rail and sea transport.

Despite this recent recovery in the EU's rail system, the volume of air traffic within the Union has continued to expand, not least because of the liberalization in air transport which the Union has promoted since the late 1980s. Even though air transport was not automatically included in the common transport policy, the **European Court of Justice** (ECJ) ruled in 1986, in the *Nouvelles Frontières case*, that competition rules applied to this sector (*Ministre Public* v *Asjes*, Cases 209–13/84). This opened up the possibility that the complex web of bilateral agreements between member states, which kept air fares unusually high, might be dismantled. The first of three packages of air transport liberalization measures was agreed in the Council in 1987, affecting flights by existing carriers on existing routes between member states. The Commission was also given supervisory and investigative powers similar to those it already possessed in other areas of competition policy. As a result, competition rules now broadly apply to the air transport sector, domestic and international, within the member states. Restrictions remained, however, on the access of new airlines to established routes, on the development of new routes and on *cabotage*. These problems were addressed in the second and third packages in 1989 and 1992. Initially, instead of both countries having to agree to the opening of a new route, this process could only be halted if both rejected any such proposal. Now any airline has the right to fly on any route for which they can obtain landing slots, at any fare it chooses to charge.

Now that liberalization has been largely achieved, the main thrust of EU air transport policy has shifted focus towards the rights and safety of passengers, and to limiting the environmental impact of air travel, especially by its inclusion in the European emissions trading scheme (ETS). The Union's 'Single European Sky' initiative has also attempted to develop a coherent air traffic management system in Europe: in 2002, it joined **Eurocontrol**, which it now uses as its service provider for the regulation of air space above the Union.

A common policy began to develop in the sea transport sector, which accounts for 40 per cent of intra-EU trade and 90 per cent of external trade in goods, in the mid-1980s. Four regulations were agreed in 1987, applying competition policy and extending freedom to supply services in this field. Starting in 1993, the Union began to become involved in maritime safety issues, including the setting of common rules for ship inspection, the construction of oil tankers, vessel and passenger registration, and the training and working hours of crews. A European Maritime Safety Agency (EMSA) was established in Lisbon in 2002. An important current EU objective in the sea transport sector is to create a 'maritime space without barriers', by simplifying administrative procedures and removing obstacles that still prevent maritime transport from being a viable alternative to road and air transport. One of the priorities under the transport dimension of TENs is the development of 'motorways of the sea'. Four maritime corridors have been designated – the Baltic, the Atlantic Arc, including the North and Irish Seas, and the West and East Mediterranean corridors – with a view to boosting infrastructure, so that high-capacity freight ferries, in particular, can relieve road traffic congestion and bypass bottlenecks on land, as well as improve transport links between islands.

Further reading: Hussein Kassim and Handley Stevens, *Air Transport and the European Union: Europeanization and its Limits*, 2009; Handley Stevens, *Transport Policy in the European Union*, 2003.

Treaties

The European Union is based upon and governed in accordance with a number of treaties concluded between the member states. These texts are the most fundamental part of the ***acquis commnunautaire*** and in every case have been the subject of (sometimes prolonged) negotiations leading to unanimous agreement among governments, and subsequently **ratification** by **national parliaments** and, in some cases, by **referendum** too. Often referred to as 'the Treaties', they serve as the Union's de facto constitution, defining its political institutions, assigning to it certain responsibilities or **competences**, and prescribing certain specific policy objectives, sometimes accompanied by a deadline or precise timetable for their achievement. This last feature (the definition of certain policies) is unusual among constitutions, although not entirely unknown, as is found in Switzerland and some US states.

The table below lists the main EU treaties adopted, in chronological order, since 1951, together with the date of entry into force of each and a brief summary of the institutional or other changes introduced. (Most of the treaties are the subject of separate entries in this *Companion*.) The first three treaties, establishing three legally distinct Communities, are often referred to as the 'founding treaties'. They have been amended and complemented by the successive treaties which have followed, each negotiated in an **Intergovernmental Conference** (IGC). Most of the treaties have **protocols** and declarations annexed to them: the former have the same legal status, whilst the latter do not.

Treaty	*Entry into force*	*Summary*
Treaty establishing the **European Coal and Steel Community** (ECSC). Known as the ECSC Treaty or the **Treaty of Paris**. Signed in Paris on 18 April 1951.	25 July 1952	Concluded for 50 years among **the Six** on the basis of the **Schuman Plan**; allowed to lapse on 23 July 2002.
Treaty establishing the **European Economic Community** (EEC). Originally known as the EEC Treaty or the **Treaty of Rome**, it was renamed the Treaty on the Functioning of the European Union (TFEU) by the Lisbon Treaty. Signed in Rome on 25 March 1957.	1 January 1958	Concluded on the model of the ECSC Treaty but for an unlimited duration and with a much broader range of objectives, instituting notably a **customs union** and **common market**. The most important of the Treaties, sometimes known simply as 'the Treaty'.
Treaty establishing the **European Atomic Energy Community** (EAEC). Known as the Euratom Treaty. Also signed in Rome on 25 March 1957, as a result of which the EEC and Euratom Treaties are together called the **Treaties of Rome**.	1 January 1958	A sector-specific treaty of limited application but unlimited duration.
Treaty establishing a single Council and a single Commission of the European Communities. Known as the **Merger Treaty**. Signed in Brussels on 8 April 1965.	1 July 1967	Amended the ECSC, EEC and Euratom Treaties to create a single **Council of Ministers** and a **European Commission** serving all three Communities. Superseded and repealed by the Amsterdam Treaty.
Treaty amending certain Budgetary Provisions of the Treaties establishing the European Communities. Known as the Treaty of Luxembourg or the 'First Budgetary Treaty'. Signed in Luxembourg on 22 April 1970.	1 January 1971	Laid down a new procedure for adopting the EC **Budget**, established distinction between **compulsory and non-compulsory expenditure**, and introduced the system of '**own resources**'.

Treaty amending certain Financial Provisions of the Treaties establishing the European Communities. Known as the 'Second Budgetary Treaty'. Signed in Brussels on 22 July 1975.	1 June 1977	Further refined the budgetary procedure to give the **European Parliament** the power to reject the EC Budget and set up the **Court of Auditors**.
Single European Act (SEA). Signed in Luxembourg on 17 February 1986.	1 July 1987	Amended and expanded the EEC Treaty, extended the scope of **qualified majority voting** (QMV) in the **Council of Ministers**, increased the legislative power of the European Parliament, laid down procedures for **European Political Cooperation** (EPC), widened **competence** to new policy fields, and provided a legal deadline (1992) for the completion of the **single market**.
Treaty on European Union (TEU). Known as the Treaty of Maastricht or **Maastricht Treaty**. Signed in Maastricht on 7 February 1992.	1 November 1993	Amended and expanded the EEC Treaty and renamed it EC Treaty, established a separate European Union, with intergovernmental '**pillars**' for **Common Foreign and Security Policy** (CFSP) and **Justice and Home Affairs** (JHA), provided for **Economic and Monetary Union** (EMU), extended QMV and increased the Parliament's legislative power by instituting the **co-decision procedure**, widened competence to new policy fields, and created **European citizenship**.

Treaty	*Entry into force*	*Summary*
Treaty of Amsterdam. Known as the **Amsterdam Treaty**. Signed in Amsterdam on 2 October 1997.	1 May 1999	Amended the Maastricht Treaty (TEU) and the EC Treaty, added new provisions on **enhanced cooperation** and **suspension** of member states, extended QMV and co-decision, 'communautarized' aspects of JHA, incorporated the **Schengen** *acquis* on frontier controls, created post of **High Representative** for CFSP, widened competence to new policy fields, and ended the UK opt-out from the **Social Chapter**.
Treaty of Nice. Known as the **Nice Treaty**. Signed in Nice on 26 February 2001.	1 February 2003	Amended the Maastricht Treaty (TEU) and the EC Treaty, reweighted QMV in the Council, reduced size of Commission, extended QMV and co-decision, and modified provisions on enhanced cooperation and suspension.
Treaty of Lisbon. Known as the **Lisbon Treaty**. Signed in Lisbon on 13 December 2007.	1 December 2009	Amended the Maastricht Treaty (TEU) and EC Treaty, renaming the latter the Treaty on the Functioning of the European Union (TFEU). Abolished the pillared structure of the Union and gave it **legal personality**, extended QMV and co-decision, created post of permanent **President of European Council**, enhanced post of High Representative, altered arrangements for chairing Councils, created **European External Action Service** (EEAS), incorporated **Charter of Fundamental Rights**, instituted a '**citizens' initiative**', introduced an **exit clause** and strengthened **national parliaments**.

In addition to the treaties listed here, a series of **accession** treaties – signed in 1972, 1979, 1985, 1994, 2003 and 2005 – have provided specific arrangements for each **enlargement**. There was also a 1984 Treaty on Greenland, as well as a series of free-standing protocols on the Netherlands Antilles (1962), the privileges and immunities of the Communities (1965) and on the Statute of the **European Investment Bank** (EIB) (1975). The 1976 **European Elections Act**, often cited as a treaty, is a **decision** of the **Council of Ministers** requiring ratification in the member states.

Not all treaties negotiated by the member states have entered into effect. The proposed Treaty establishing a **European Defence Community** (EDC) was abandoned after its rejection by the French National Assembly in August 1954. (The accompanying draft Treaty to create a **European Political Community** (EPC), never signed by the member states, fell by the wayside as a result.) Likewise, the ratification of the Treaty establishing a Constitution for Europe – otherwise known as the draft **European Constitution** – signed in Rome on 29 October 2004, had to be abandoned the following year, when it was rejected by the French and Dutch electorates in referenda in May–June 2005. Subsequently, many of the provisions of the proposed Constitution were incorporated in the Lisbon Treaty, which finally came into operation in December 2009. Only one treaty negotiation so far – that of the **Fouchet Plan** in 1960–62 – has failed to end in agreement among the member states, whether or not the subsequent treaty secured ratification.

The various EU Treaties apply throughout the territory of the 27 EU member states, with the exception of **Greenland and the Faeroes** and the British Sovereign Base Areas (of Akrotiri and Dhekelia) in Cyprus, and the partial exception of the Finnish Åland Islands, the Channel Islands and the Isle of Man (Article 355 TFEU). Special arrangements, differing from case to case, apply to all these territories and to Gibraltar. The Treaties also apply extraterritorially in the case of firms operating inside the member states but whose headquarters are outside – a principle established by the **European Court of Justice** (ECJ) in *ICI* v *Commission* (Case 48/69) and of great importance in **competition policy**.

As a result of the **eurozone debt crisis**, two treaties have been negotiated, and are currently being ratified, outside the EU framework. The first establishes a **European Stability Mechanism** (ESM) and the second, known as the **Fiscal Compact Treaty**, binds signatories in their approach to macroeconomic policy and decision-making within **Economic and Monetary Union** (EMU). The ESM treaty was concluded among the 17 member states within the **eurozone** on 2 February 2012. The Fiscal Compact Treaty includes eight of the ten other member states as well (the exceptions being the Czech Republic and the United Kingdom) and was signed on 2 March 2012.

Further reading: Clive Church and David Phinnemore, *The Penguin Guide to the European Treaties: From Rome to Maastricht, Amsterdam, Nice and Beyond*, 2002.

Treaty amendment, change or revision

See **Intergovernmental Conference** (IGC).

Treaty of Paris

Signed on 18 April 1951, the Treaty of Paris established the **European Coal and Steel Community** (ECSC) among **the Six**. The first of the founding **Treaties** and running to 100 articles, the Treaty of Paris was concluded for a period of 50 years, entered into force on 25 July 1952 and was allowed to lapse on 23 July 2002.

The ECSC, which owed its origins to the **Schuman Plan** of 9 May 1950, created a **common market** for coal and steel. Its path-breaking institutional design involved an independent, supranational executive authority, the **High Authority** (forerunner of the **European Commission**), a **Council of Ministers** capable of adopting binding supranational law by **qualified majority voting** (QMV), a Common Assembly (which became the **European Parliament**), and an embryo **European Court of Justice** (ECJ) to adjudicate on legal disputes. The ECSC provided the model for the two other **European Communities** – the **European Economic Community** (EEC) and the **European Atomic Energy Community** (EAEC or Euratom) – later established by the **Treaties of Rome** in 1957.

Treaty / Treaties of Rome

The Treaty of Rome – officially entitled the Treaty establishing the **European Economic Community** (EEC) – was signed by the Six on 25 March 1957 in the *Sala degli Orazi e Curiazi* in the *Palazzo dei Conservatori* in Rome and entered into force on 1 January 1958. A parallel treaty establishing the **European Atomic Energy Community** (EAEC or Euratom) was signed in the same place, at the same time, and took effect on the same date. The product of the **Messina Conference** and **Spaak Committee**, the two treaties together are sometimes referred to as the 'Treaties of Rome'. They were concluded for an unlimited period. The institutions and procedures laid down in the EEC and Euratom Treaties were modelled largely on the pre-existing **European Coal and Steel Community** (ECSC), established by the 1951 **Treaty of Paris**. The three treaties are often referred to collectively as the founding **Treaties**.

The EEC Treaty was renamed the Treaty establishing the European Community (EC) by the 1992 **Maastricht Treaty**, itself known as the Treaty on European Union (TEU). In turn, the EC Treaty was renamed the Treaty on the Functioning of the European Union (TFEU) by the 1997 Lisbon Treaty, which came into force in December 2009.

Troika

'Troika' is a Russian word meaning a sleigh drawn by three horses. It was first introduced into politics in the 1950s to signify the triumvirate that ruled the Soviet Union following Stalin's death, when the posts of head of state, prime minister and party leader were held by different individuals. In the early 1960s, the Soviet Union suggested that the position of Secretary General of the United Nations should be replaced by a troika composed of representatives of the Eastern bloc, the Western alliance and the non-aligned states.

In the European Union, the troika traditionally related to the six-month, rotating **presidency** of the **Council of Ministers**: it was a three-member group composed of the current president-in-office of the Council, together with his or her immediate predecessor and successor from other member states. Such groups first developed in the field of foreign affairs. The pattern was formally instituted under **European Political Cooperation** (EPC) in 1981, to promote a measure of continuity from one presidency to another, especially in ministerial-level discussions by the Community with third countries, notably at bilateral summits. During the 1990s, attempts to coordinate successive presidencies widened to other policy areas, with a troika approach becoming more common across the board. In December 1993, the **European Council** decided to introduce (from 1996) a system of rotation that would ensure that any three successive Council presidencies always contained at least one of the then five large member states. This system became unsustainable with the **enlargement** of the Union to 27 member states, only six of which were large.

In an effort to improve planning between presidencies, the **European Constitution** (negotiated by the **Convention on the Future of Europe** in 2002–3) envisaged a new troika principle, whereby in future the presidency of the Council of Ministers (other than of the **Foreign Affairs Council**) would 'be held by pre-established groups of three Member States for a period of 18 months'. Although each country would still take the chair for six months, the three successive presidencies would work together as a team. After ratification of the Constitution was abandoned, the Council decided to make unilateral arrangements for groups of three presidencies – which quickly become known as a 'Trio' – to adopt 18-month work programmes in turn. In September 2006, the Council amended its rules of procedure to provide that 'Every 18 months, the three Presidencies due to hold office shall prepare, in close cooperation with the Commission, and after appropriate consultations, a draft programme of Council activities for that period.' At the end of 2006, the upcoming German, Portuguese and Slovenian presidencies agreed a 69-page joint programme, which they formally submitted for Council endorsement, setting a pattern for the future. The demise of the classic rolling troika and its replacement by the new 18-month trio was further confirmed when, on the entry into force of the **Lisbon Treaty** in December 2009, the Council adopted a decision reproducing the wording on the trio system in the original Constitution.

Meanwhile, in the foreign affairs field, things were evolving in a rather different direction. The creation of the post of a **High Representative** for **Common Foreign and Security Policy** (CFSP) under the 1997 **Amsterdam Treaty** meant the troika model had, in any case, to be overhauled in external relations. The High Representative both needed to be included in the process and was able to embody the continuity previously offered by prior and succeeding presidencies of the Council. The **European Commission** also sought to take advantage of this change to secure recognition of its own standing in external relations, notably through the **Common Commercial Policy** (CCP) and **development policy**. The result was that a new notion of the troika evolved in the CFSP field, encompassing the current presidency of the Council, the High Representative and the relevant European Commissioner (with the successor presidency of the Council sometimes included, when necessary). A good example of this concept in action was the meeting of the 'EU–US Troika' – between the US Secretary of State, the High Representative, the Czech foreign minister and the Commissioner for external relations – held at the Council in Brussels in March 2009.

Although this form of troika was not the only framework in which the Council conducted its relations with third countries – the Council presidency or the High Representative could and did deal with them directly, just as the Commission does in its sphere of influence – it featured prominently from the late 1990s onwards. However, it was not entirely effective as a means of structuring dialogue. As one senior Council official put it: 'When you are having a meeting with the Americans or the Japanese, either the three people from Europe all say the same thing, which is boring, or they say different things, which is even worse.' Under the Lisbon Treaty, there is no need for the troika to continue, as the extended role of the High Representative now covers all previous Council and Commission responsibilities in the CFSP field at least.

The troika concept has, however, recently re-emerged in an entirely new context. With the onset of the **eurozone debt crisis**, any joint delegation of senior officials from the three international institutions – the European Commission, the **European Central Bank** (ECB) and the International Monetary Fund (IMF) – responsible for monitoring economic adjustment in EU member states receiving financial support under the various bail-out mechanisms is now known as a 'troika'. Visits by troika officials have become a regular feature of the Greek, Irish and Portuguese scenes, as a result.

Truman Doctrine

In an address to the United States Congress on 12 March 1947, President Harry Truman pledged his country 'to support free peoples who are resisting attempted subjugation by armed minorities or by outside pressures'. This commitment – which became known as the Truman Doctrine – represented a significant break with previous US policy in peacetime. As the central purpose of this activist foreign policy would be the containment of Communism, it marked what one commentator has described as an 'American declaration of the **Cold War**'. Truman immediately sought significant financial aid to bolster the Greek and Turkish governments in the face of attempted Communist subversion: Congress voted $400 and $100 million in civil and military assistance for the two countries respectively, although there was no deployment of US troops. Later in the year, the Truman administration proposed the **Marshall Plan**, which was to provide over $13 billion in financial aid for the reconstruction of western Europe, at a time when economic crisis was underpinning Communist electoral success in several countries. The Truman Doctrine developed into the prevailing philosophy in US foreign policy for the next quarter century, underpinning its prosecution of the Korean and Vietnam wars, as well as support for authoritarian régimes that were anti-Communist. Truman's decisions in 1947 and Congressional acceptance of them mark the formal assumption by the United States of its post-war role as a world power.

Turkey

Turkey first concluded an **association agreement** with the European Community in 1963, the second country to do so. This so-called 'Ankara Agreement', which had to be frozen during the period of military rule in Turkey (1980–83), foresaw a step-by-step move towards a **customs union** and the eventual possibility of membership. It was underpinned by three financial protocols – agreed in 1964, 1973 and 1977 – which provided assistance for the country's economic development.

By virtue of its membership of the **Council of Europe** (from 1949) and the **North Atlantic Treaty Organization** (NATO) (from 1952), Turkey has long been considered a European state, even though 96 per cent of its land mass is geographically in Asia. In April 1987, the Turkish government applied for membership of the Community. However, the opinion of the **European Commission**, delivered in December 1989, was unfavourable. Whilst acknowledging that Turkey was eligible to become a candidate, the Commission took the view that the size, relative poverty, high birth-rate and economic instability of the country made any successful **accession** impossible in the near term. The Commission also expressed doubts about whether the country's human rights record was consistent with Community standards, and whether membership might have 'negative effects' on the Greek–Turkish dispute over Cyprus. Instead, the Commission proposed to intensify relations within the existing association agreement. In March 1995, the EU–Turkey Association Council agreed to establish, from the following year, the customs union (other than for agricultural goods) envisaged in the association agreement. It was the first such arrangement between the European Union and a third country of any size.

By the mid-1990s, the applications for EU membership from the countries of central and eastern Europe led to renewed pressure on the Turkish government to pursue its own membership claim. To parry this approach, the Commission proposed a separate strategy for the 'further development' of relations with Turkey, to coincide with the publication, in July 1997, of its opinions on the applications from the former Communist states. Although the Commission said that the new customs union was 'working satisfactorily', it expressed serious concerns about human rights, relations between Greece and Turkey, and the need for a 'just and lasting settlement in Cyprus'. Instead of early accession, the Commission proposed to widen and deepen the customs union, supported by further structural reform of the Turkish economy. At the **European Council** meeting in Luxembourg in December 1997, it was agreed to invite Turkey to take part in a new 'European Conference' – a planned annual summit meeting of member states and applicant states, held for the first time in London in March 1998. However, the Turkish government declined this invitation, considering the gesture to be insulting.

The deterioration of EU-Turkish relations prompted a reappraisal on the European side, and the country was finally accepted as an applicant state at the Helsinki European Council in December 1999. A year later, Turkey was assured that if, by December 2004, it met the **Copenhagen criteria**, a firm date would be fixed for the start of accession negotiations. The path was smoothed by Turkey stating that it could accept the Annan Plan for Cypriot unity, so in effect ending its occupation of the northern part of the island. When Cyprus unexpectedly entered the Union in May 2004 whilst still divided, the situation became more complicated. However, both sides kept to the timeline envisaged, with the European Council agreeing in December 2004 to start negotiations the following year. In October 2005, eight 'chapters' of negotiation, out of a planned total of 35, were opened. However, Turkey's continued refusal to recognize the Republic of Cyprus as the legitimate government of the whole island, despite the country's accession to the Union – and specifically its unwillingness to open its ports and airports to Cypriot traffic – led to those chapters being frozen, at the instigation of the

Commission, in December 2006. Negotiations have progressed slowly in other areas since that date.

The question of Turkish membership is one of the most divisive issues in contemporary EU politics. It brings into relief a fundamental difference of opinion about whether the Union should be an 'open Europe' with relatively flexible borders, expressing certain universalist values and focused on adding value through its common policies, or rather a 'bounded Europe' that sees itself as a more protective force and draws on a strong and clear sense of its own identity. Most northern European states prefer the former concept, whereas many in France, Germany, Austria and Hungary, in particular, tend to the latter view. Leading advocates of Turkish enlargement – such as Swedish foreign minister Carl Bildt and former European Commissioner Chris Patten – argue that the EU has a strategic interest in the country's membership. Having proved a reliable partner in the West's defence over many decades, Turkey could now act as a bridge between Europe and the Muslim worlds, with the potential to be a powerful force in helping to stabilize the Middle East. In addition, its continuing economic development, sustained by a large and young population, could offer the ageing, low-growth Union a useful source of economic vitality for the future. Conversely, a rejected Turkey, disappointed in its European ambition, could equally drift off into a less benign orbit. Such considerations help explain the strong support given by successive US administrations to Turkey's prospective membership.

Echoing the European Commission's negative opinion in 1989, opponents of Turkish accession tend to highlight the country's size and relative poverty, rather than the fact that 99 per cent of its population is Muslim (70 per cent Sunni). Several much smaller, Balkan countries – notably Albania, Bosnia and Herzegovina, and Kosovo – also have substantial Muslim majority populations and this is not seen as an inherent barrier to their eventual membership. The key problem, they argue, is that, by 2020, Turkey's population will, on current trends, exceed that of Germany, whilst the country would still be one of the poorest in Europe. On entry, it would thus immediately become both the most powerful member state of the Union – notably in terms of voting power in the **Council of Ministers** – and the largest net recipient from the EU **Budget**. The political and financial strain this could put on existing members, notably France, Germany and the Benelux countries, could be considerable.

In March 2009, the French President, Nicholas Sarkozy, and German Chancellor, Angela Merkel, both publicly stated that Turkey should not be allowed to join the Union. Merkel declared at a joint press conference of the two leaders: 'Our common position is for a privileged partnership for Turkey, but not full membership.' Sarkozy added that instead of making 'empty promises' to Turkey, the Union should 'think about how we can create a large, common area and living space' that could include both Turkey and Russia. The French and Austrian governments have promised to hold domestic **referenda** before agreeing to Turkish enlargement, thus in effect installing a political safety catch designed to frustrate the enlargement process, if they wish to.

Two-speed Europe

The concept of a two-speed Europe – or *Europe à deux vitesses* – was first given credence by the **Tindemans Report** of 1975, drawn up by the then Belgian prime minister, Leo Tindemans. He sought to recognize that not all EC member states would be able or willing to proceed towards deeper integration at the same pace, and that some means should be found of allowing the more enthusiastic to make progress without being held back by the others. He wrote: 'It is impossible at the present time to submit a credible programme of action if it is deemed absolutely necessary that, in every case, all stages should be reached by all states at the same time.' Although the wording was ambiguous, the report appeared to limit the two-speed concept to the specific policy field of **Economic and Monetary Union** (EMU). Tindemans also insisted that those opting for the slower speed should do so on the basis of reasons recognized as valid by the **Council of Ministers**, on a proposal from the **European Commission**, and he enjoined those countries proceeding at the faster pace to lend as much assistance as possible to the rest.

Like much else in the Tindemans Report, the idea of a two-speed Europe found little immediate favour with either the Commission or the governments of the member states, especially those which feared that they might find themselves relegated to the second rank. If generalized, such an initiative would, it was argued, have damaging consequences for the uniform application of Community law, call into question the rights of member states to an equal share in decision-making, complicate the operation of the Community **Budget**, and undermine the perception of a common European interest, especially in external relations.

However, despite powerful objections of this kind, certain developments in the sphere of monetary cooperation in the 1970s pointed to the possibility of a two-speed Europe being more than simply a theoretical proposition among the advocates of full EMU. The 'Snake' currency management system, set up outside the **Treaties** in 1972, involved only some member states, whilst its ultimate successor, the **Exchange-Rate Mechanism** (ERM) of the **European Monetary System** (EMS), was established on the same basis in 1979. This tendency was repeated in another policy area, when the **Schengen** Agreement 'on the gradual abolition of controls at their common frontiers' was concluded, initially among five member states in 1985. Formal '**opt-outs**' were then extended to certain governments in the 1992 **Maastricht Treaty** and 1997 **Amsterdam Treaty** in relation not only to EMU, but to other sensitive policy fields, namely **Justice and Home Affairs** (JHA) and defence (and, for some years, to **social and employment policy**, too). Indeed the concept of membership of stage three of EMU itself being contingent on (those states that were not opted-out) meeting certain **convergence criteria** foreshadowed a long period in which the current and future members of the eurozone would be divided into two groups. Finally, the Amsterdam Treaty opened up the possibility of **enhanced cooperation** between groups of countries wishing to go further and faster than the rest in routine policy areas of the Union .

Strictly speaking, a two-speed Europe would be one in which two homogeneous sets of member states coexisted within the Union, with one group participating in all common policies and the other group taking part in only some. By contrast, a 'multi-speed Europe' would see member states free to 'mix and match' policies on more of a **variable geometry** or à la carte basis, provided that they accepted a minimum set of common obligations. The European Union today does not fall neatly into either category. However, the fact that the enhanced cooperation provisions introduced by the Amsterdam Treaty have scarcely been used, and equally that certain member states – notably the United Kingdom, Denmark and Ireland – have reiteratively received **opt-outs** of various kinds, suggests that the Union is currently closer to a two-speed than a multi-speed model. As Richard Corbett has pointed out, this ambiguous pattern is generated less by an *avant garde* pushing further and faster than others, than by a series of small, often overlapping, *arrières-gardes* (or rearguards), outside the **euro**, Schengen, JHA and defence cooperation.

In June 2010, former French President **Valéry Giscard d'Estaing** argued that a 'three-speed Europe' was emerging, with certain **eurozone** member states at the centre and the United Kingdom on the periphery. An intermediate group comprised those **eurozone** countries that did not wish to take a leadership role within the EU and others, notably the recent entrants from central and eastern Europe, which wished to adopt the single currency but were unable yet to do so. This analysis was reminiscent of the notion of a 'Europe of **concentric circles**' put forward in the 1990s and the idea of France, Germany and the **Benelux** countries constituting a 'hard core' of the European Union. Some criticized Giscard's analysis as conveniently avoiding the de facto emergence of a two- or three-speed eurozone, with member states in receipt of bail-outs struggling to stay within the system. However, the adoption at the March 2011 European Council of a 'Euro Plus Pact', by which all 17 eurozone countries, together with six other member states, committed to engage in deeper structural reform as part of the EMU process – leaving only the UK, the Czech Republic, Hungary and Sweden outside – suggests that Giscard's basic prophesy may yet prove to be valid.

One of the effects of the recent **eurozone debt crisis** has been to force the deepening of arrangements for **European economic governance** among the 17 states currently participating in stage three of EMU. The development since 1998 of the **Eurogroup** of finance ministers (caucusing before the full meetings of all 27 ministers in the **Ecofin Council**) has now been followed by the emergence since 2007 of regular eurozone summits, which were formalized in October 2011, on the basis that they should 'if possible' be held immediately following meetings of the **European Council** (of EU heads of government) at least twice a year. The new post of 'President of the Euro Summit' has been established, with the assumption that it will be held by the same individual serving as **President of the European Council**. The provisions of the **excessive deficit procedure** (EDP) – and the **Stability and Growth Pact** (SGP) more widely – have also been significantly strengthened. By these and other means, the institutional distinctiveness of the eurozone is being heightened, the policy obligations of **euro** membership have been made more demanding, and the centrality of EMU to the business of the Union is becoming more pronounced.

Traditionally, the United Kingdom has fought hard to avoid the perception that a two-speed Europe is developing, with Britain relegated to the outer tier. The eurozone debt crisis is making this perception, and indeed reality, increasingly difficult to avoid. Whereas Prime Minister Tony Blair made it clear that London would 'not accept a two-speed Europe' and his predecessor, John Major, had talked of a 'real danger in talk of . . . a two-tier Europe', the current British premier, David Cameron, has been less shy of the concept and more willing to allow it to evolve in practice. Soon after taking office in May 2010, his officials indicated that 'closer integration was for the eurozone only' – a notion not in fact shared by many other countries outside the single currency – whilst he chose not to attend eurozone summits or to contribute actively to 'bail outs' of countries in financial difficulty.

When, at the European Council on 9 December 2011, Cameron refused to accept a German request that the EU Treaties be amended so as to incorporate and make stringent the requirements of the SGP on eurozone states, his 'veto' did not stop the process, but simply resulted in the latter states deciding to negotiate a separate intergovernmental treaty open to as many non-eurozone countries as might wish to sign it. This spectacular negotiating reverse for Britain was 'self-inflicted' in two senses. First, in contrast to the instinctive reaction of previous premiers, Cameron chose to prioritize avoiding a domestic parliamentary vote over agreeing to a treaty that posed no obvious threat to domestic interests. Second, although the President of the European Council, Herman Van Rompuy, had specifically proposed a 'fast-track' route for limited treaty change that (by amending only **Protocol** 12 on eurozone arrangements) would not in fact require **ratification** in **national parliaments,** ironically this exemption could not be applied in Britain (alone) because of legislation that Cameron himself had introduced the previous year (the European Union Act 2010). The dramatic outcome of the December 2011 summit compounded the sense both of the eurozone as a separate political entity and of the United Kingdom as increasingly isolated within the EU political system. See also **Lamers–Schäuble paper**.

Further reading: Jean-Claude Piris, *The Future of Europe: Towards a Two-Speed EU?*, 2012.

U

Unanimity

The great majority of decisions taken in the EU **Council of Ministers** – and more recently a number of those formally assigned to the **European Council** – are now adopted by **qualified majority voting** (QMV). Indeed, since the **Lisbon Treaty** came into force, it is stated for the first time that the 'Council shall act by qualified majority except where the Treaties provide otherwise' (Article 16(3) TEU). However, when the **Treaty of Rome** was introduced in 1958, unanimity was the norm, so that in most policy fields, the individual member states retained a right of veto. The range of decisions subject to QMV was due to widen automatically in January 1966, but the then French President, **Charles de Gaulle**, forced the Community to agree to the **Luxembourg Compromise**, whereby wherever a member state considered that a 'particularly important national interest' was at stake, a decision could in practice be deferred indefinitely.

The 'veto culture' thus installed continued until the 1986 **Single European Act** (SEA), which widened the scope of QMV and in effect ended the writ of the Luxembourg Compromise. Successive treaty changes have since continued the shift towards QMV, to the point where unanimity is now confined mainly to questions of a politically sensitive nature, which raise issues of principle or where some (or all) of the member states fear that being outvoted could cause serious problems at home. When decisions are taken by unanimity, abstentions are not counted in the calculation (Article 238(4) TFEU).

There are currently about 75 specific references in the Treaties to decisions where unanimity in the Council of Ministers or the European Council is required. These include most aspects of **Common Foreign and Security Policy** (CFSP) and **Common Security and Defence Policy** (CSDP), some aspects of **Economic and Monetary Union** (EMU) and **Justice and Home Affairs** (JHA), and certain **international agreements**, as well as **tax harmonization**, social security, the use of **Article 352** TFEU (the competence-stretching 'flexibility clause'), the use of the ***passerelle* clauses** and decisions on the **language** régime in the EU institutions. Some particularly important unanimous decisions also require that, once taken, they be approved by the member states individually 'in accordance with their respective constitutional requirements', normally including at least endorsement by **national parliaments**. This latter category includes the **accession** of new member states, changes to the EU's system of **own resources**, the creation of new rights under **European citizenship**, and arrangements for a **uniform electoral system** for the **European Parliament**.

Under a specific arrangement for CFSP (including CDSP), set out in Article 23 TEU, any member state may engage in 'constructive abstention'. Instead of exercising a veto, it may decide to abstain and in return be absolved from applying the decision taken. If a third of member states, representing at least a third of the Union's population, engage in constructive abstention in any vote, 'the decision shall not be adopted'. Member states remain free to abstain in the normal way, without this being construed as 'constructive' within the meaning of Article 31 TEU.

In addition to the decisions taken in the Council of Ministers or European Council by unanimity, the Treaties also provide that certain decisions are adopted 'by common accord' of the representatives of member states' governments. Here, strictly speaking, the member states are *acting as governments* and not as members of an EU institution, even if that institution is being used as the vehicle for holding the vote. Unlike when a decision is taken by unanimity in the Council, if a government abstains in a vote requiring the common accord of governments, this action blocks the adoption of the measure. The most important decisions where common accord is required are the appointment of judges and advocates general of the **European Court of Justice** (ECJ) and the General Court, the location of the **seats of EU institutions**, and the conclusion of **Intergovernmental Conferences** (IGCs) under the 'ordinary revision procedure' to amend the Treaties. (By contrast, use of the 'simplified revision procedure' for treaty reform requires unanimity in the European Council.)

Uniform electoral procedure

The idea that the **European Parliament** should be elected on the basis of a standard or uniform electoral procedure (UEP) used throughout the member states is to be found in both the 1951 **Treaty of Paris** and the 1957 **Treaty of Rome**. The original wording of Article 138(3) EEC read: 'The European Parliament shall draw up proposals for elections by direct universal suffrage in accordance with a uniform procedure in all Member States.' However, in spite of several efforts to establish such a procedure, only a limited set of 'common principles' have so far been agreed. Apart from a general requirement to use proportional representation (PR), the quinquennial **European**

elections are still largely held on the basis of different national systems, with detailed arrangements remaining in the hands of national authorities.

The drawing up of proposals for a UEP is one of only three areas in which the European Parliament, not the **European Commission**, specifically enjoys the **right of initiative** in respect of legislation. (The other two are the 'statutes' for the European **Ombudsman** and for Members of the European Parliament (MEPs) themselves.) The Parliament submits its proposal to the **Council of Ministers**, which may agree the text or some variant of it, acting by **unanimity**. Since the 1997 **Amsterdam Treaty**, the Council's text must return to the Parliament for approval by an absolute majority of its membership, under the **consent procedure**. Once confirmed by the Parliament, the Council formally adopts the text, which must then be ratified in each member state (in effect by national parliamentary approval).

Under the Treaties of Paris and Rome, the European Parliament was originally composed of members (MEPs) nominated by and from the **national parliaments** of member states, pending the introduction of direct elections. With some difficulty, the nominated Parliament made several attempts to draw up proposals for a uniform electoral procedure, as a precursor to such elections, but on each occasion it met with no response from the Council. When eventually, in December 1974, the Paris **summit** of EC heads of government agreed that direct elections 'should take place in or after 1978', it was decided in effect to ignore the UEP requirement. The elections would be held every five years, but the choice of electoral system and many other details would be left to member states. The European Parliament urgently drafted new proposals for a UEP (in the Patijn Report of 1975); only some of these were included in the Council **decision** of September 1976, known as the European Elections Act, which provided the framework for the European elections held (in the event) in June 1979 and thereafter.

The European Elections Act set the number of MEPs, allocated by member state – a provision subsequently updated by successive treaties – and determined the frequency and timing of the elections, which would automatically be held in a predetermined four-day period every five years, unless the Council unanimously decided to vary the date. It also defined a list of offices incompatible with membership of the Parliament and provided for the verification of Members' credentials. Crucially, however, the Act left open the question of the method of election: in practice, all member states chose to use some variant of PR, except the United Kingdom, which adopted single-member constituencies in Great Britain and the single transferable vote (STV) system of PR in Northern Ireland. (An attempt by James Callaghan's minority Labour government to introduce PR for England, Scotland and Wales was defeated by a combination of Labour rebels and the Conservative opposition.)

The directly-elected European Parliament offered new proposals for a UEP in the Seitlinger and de Gucht reports of 1982 and 1992. However, the Parliament found it difficult to agree provisions that were sufficiently specific to meet a legal definition of uniformity: for example, it would not be enough for all member states to use some form of PR, as the Parliament was suggesting. Rather, they would all need to employ exactly the same form of PR for the system to be considered uniform. For example, whilst small countries had to use a single, national constituency, larger member states inevitably wished to be free to choose between national and regional constituencies, depending on their traditions and political cultures. Likewise, in some member states, there is a strong commitment to 'open' lists, where voters can alter the order of candidates offered by political parties; in others, 'closed' lists have long been the norm.

The reality is that electoral systems are founded upon historical and political assumptions that cannot easily be gainsaid, whilst every MEP, political party and national government approaches the issue with a view to their own political advantage. A notional treaty commitment to uniformity has not been strong enough to overcome these powerful forces. As a result, the only agreement that was possible within the Parliament avoided many difficult, detailed choices. The Council took the view that the Parliament's de Gucht report in 1992 embodied only 'general principles' and that 'much more specific provisions' would be required for it to represent a genuine proposal for a UEP.

There were legal difficulties too, springing from the meaning of the word 'procedure'. An electoral procedure is not just a voting system or a formula for translating votes into seats. Its scope goes much wider: it embraces, for example, the question of the voting age, the right to stand for election, the electoral threshold, disqualifications, the rules governing independent candidates, and so on. Many of these are sensitive issues in their own right. The **European Court of Justice** (ECJ) confirmed this view in its 1985 judgement in the case of *Les Verts* v *European Parliament* (Case 294/83). The Court ruled, in effect, that all provisions governed by law with a bearing on the equality of candidates' chances of being elected are covered by the notion of a 'procedure'.

Recognizing that these problems were potentially insuperable, the EU heads of government finally decided in effect to end the pretence of seeking a UEP by diluting the treaty requirement for uniformity. The Amsterdam Treaty allowed the Parliament to propose, as an alternative to a UEP, lighter arrangements drawn up 'in accordance with principles common to all Member States' (Article 223 TFEU). The Parliament quickly took advantage of this change, adopting a proposal based on common principles in July 1998. In June and September 2002, the Council agreed to modify the 1976 European

Elections Act to provide that MEPs would henceforth 'be elected on the basis of proportional representation, using the list system or the single transferable vote'. The United Kingdom had abandoned the single-member constituency system in June 1999 and did not object to this change being made permanent. Member states remained free to adopt national or regional, and open or closed lists, and were allowed to set a 'minimum threshold for the allocation of seats' of no more than five per cent of the national vote. The list of offices incompatible with membership of the European Parliament was widened to include national parliamentarians (from 2004), so ending the 'dual mandate'. (Exemptions were allowed in the 2004–9 Parliament for members of the British and Irish parliaments, where there are wholly or partially nominated upper chambers.)

United Nations (UN)

The successor body to the League of Nations, the United Nations was established in San Francisco in June 1945 by a treaty known as the UN Charter, which was ratified by 51 countries and entered force in October that year. The negotiations which resulted in the creation of the UN were, as Graham Evans and Richard Newnham have written, 'the first major international conference . . . not dominated by European states' and the resulting structure marked 'the formal end of the European states-system and its replacement by a genuinely global one' (*The Penguin Dictionary of International Relations*, 1998).

Now encompassing all 192 internationally-recognized states (except the Vatican City), the United Nations Organization (UNO), as it is officially known, has two main institutions, both based in New York. The UN General Assembly (UNGA) includes all member states and adopts non-binding resolutions by a two-thirds majority, on a 'one-state, one-vote' basis. Its approval is required for changes to the UN Charter and for new member states to join. The UN Security Council (UNSC) brings together five states enjoying permanent membership – the 'P5' of China, France, Russia, the United Kingdom and the United States – and ten other states rotating on a regional basis determined by the General Assembly. Any P5 state can exercise a veto over UNSC resolutions – otherwise adopted by nine positive votes (60 per cent) – which in specific circumstances are meant to be binding on all states or bodies to which they are addressed (including the European Union). As the League of Nations had been bedevilled by the requirement for strict unanimity among all its members, the selective veto system within the Security Council was designed to make it easier to reach decisions on difficult issues, whilst reflecting the realities of world power.

The UN's institutional structure also encompasses several other bodies, notably: i) the International Court of Justice, based in The Hague; ii) the Economic and Social Committee, with five regional commissions, including the **Economic Commission for Europe** (ECE), the latter based in Geneva; and iii) a 8,000-strong permanent UN secretariat, located in various centres and headed by the organization's Secretary General, who is appointed for a renewable five-year term. Five countries – the United States, Japan, Germany, United Kingdom and France (in that order) – contribute some 60 per cent of the UN's $ 5.0 billion annual administrative budget. Among the UN's principal operational programmes – which have separate, additional budgets – are the UN Conference on Trade and Development (UNCTAD), the UN Children's Fund (UNICEF), the UN Development Programme (UNDP), the Office of the UN High Commissioner for Refugees (UNHCR) and the World Food Programme (WFP). In addition, the UN undertakes peacekeeping operations in 14 countries worldwide (including Cyprus and Kosovo in Europe).

The United Nations also has an extensive network of autonomous specialized agencies and related bodies, some established by separate treaty but reporting to the central UN institutions. These include the International Atomic Energy Authority (IAEA, based in Vienna), World Health Organization (WHO, Geneva), International Labour Organization (ILO, Geneva), UN Educational, Scientific and Cultural Organization (UNESCO, Paris), Food and Agriculture Organization (FAO, Rome), World Trade Organization (WTO, Geneva), International Monetary Fund (IMF, Washington, DC) and World Bank (Washington, DC).

Since membership of the UN is only open to states (under Articles 2–3 of its Charter), the European Union can only enjoy observer status within the body's central institutions – as it has since the passage of UNGA resolution 3208 in 1974 – like any other international organization. (There are currently 67 'permanent observers' within UNGA, who are only permitted to speak after the 192 UN member states.) Starting in the 1960s, however, EC member states began to concert their positions and attempt to act as one within UN structures, in order to maximize European influence where possible. Regular coordination meetings were held in the various working places of the UN, and over time, the **European Commission** opened delegation offices for relations with UN bodies in New York, Geneva, Vienna, Rome, Paris and Nairobi. The **Council of Ministers** did the same in New York and Geneva. These offices have become single European Union delegation offices, as part of the new **European External Action Service** (EEAS), established under the **Lisbon Treaty**. Over a thousand coordination meetings, chaired by the EEAS, are now held each year, at ambassadorial level and below, in New York and Geneva. The Union regularly takes positions in the General Assembly, circulating texts and acting as a rallying-point, not only for the EU member states themselves, but for some other countries. As the EU member states collectively represent one eighth of the General Assembly (and contribute 40 per cent of its budget), their potential influence within the system can be substantial: for example, an EU-led campaign in 2010 forced Iran to withdraw its candidacy for the chairmanship of the UNSC.

The practice developed whereby the prime minister or foreign minister of the EU member state occupying the rotating **presidency** of the Council of Ministers would address the UN General Assembly, on behalf of the Union (but using the member state's own speaking time), during the opening of its annual plenary session each September. On occasion, the Commission President also did so, but only by taking up speaking time assigned to a member state. Since the introduction of the Lisbon Treaty in December 2009, either the **High Representative** or the **President of the European Council** speaks on behalf of the Union in this debate. Since the Union is in the unique position of being neither a state nor a conventional international organization, there has long been a strong case for upgrading its status within the General Assembly, something that the latter has within its power, by a two-thirds majority vote. In September 2010, the member states introduced a resolution to UNGA to this effect, but it was defeated on procedural grounds, mainly because certain third-world countries were fearful about the precedent that might be set for the treatment of other 'regional economic integration organizations' among the 67 observers. However, in May 2011, a revised version of this resolution was adopted by UNGA, allowing the EU representative to be called at an appropriate stage earlier in any UNGA debate, although not allowing the EU as such to co-sponsor resolutions or to vote in meetings. Similar arrangements will apply in international conferences convened under the auspices of UNGA.

Within the Security Council, any EU position on issues under discussion is, in the Commission's words, 'represented by EU member states, whether elected or permanent members'. Under Article 34(2) TEU, introduced by the 1992 **Maastricht Treaty**, those member states must 'concert', keep the other states 'fully informed', and more importantly 'defend the positions and the interests of the Union' in that body. Since the Lisbon Treaty came into effect, they 'shall request that the High Representative be invited to present the Union's position' in the Security Council, 'when the Union has defined a position on a subject which is on [its] agenda'.

The two EU member states that serve as permanent members of the Security Council – France and the United Kingdom – are extremely keen to retain a privileged status that reflects their global standing in 1945. It has been suggested that permanent membership should be extended to the Union as a whole, either in addition to the UK and France or in place of them. Germany has also requested that it be given permanent membership. As a single EU seat would ironically lead to the European presence in the Security Council being cut by half, it is more likely that a third seat may be adopted as part of a wider reform of the forum. Such a change might also see Brazil, Japan, India and/or South Africa gaining permanent member status.

Over time, the UN has accepted that in practice the European Community, now Union, acts on behalf of its member states in an increasing number of policy fields. It is a party to more than 50 multilateral agreements and conventions, as the only non-state participant, and has also been given special 'full participant' status in a number of major UN conferences, starting with the Rio 'Earth Summit' in 1992, and some standing bodies, such as the UN Commission on Sustainable Development. In 1991, the Community became a full member of the FAO, the only UN agency or body in which this status has so far been conceded.

Further reading: Michael Emerson et al., *Upgrading the EU's Role as Global Actor*, 2011; Katie Verlin Laatikainen and Karen Smith (editors), *The European Union at the United Nations: Intersecting Multilateralisms*, 2006.

'United States of Europe'

Although the best-known use of the phrase 'United States of Europe' is a passage in **Winston Churchill**'s 1946 **Zurich speech**, the origin of the idea is to be found much earlier. In 1849, Victor Hugo told a conference in Paris:

> *There will come a day when all of you – France, Russia, Italy, Britain, Germany – all you nations of this continent, without losing your distinctive qualities or your glorious individuality, will merge closely into a higher unity and will form the fraternity of Europe, just as Normandy, Brittany, Burgundy, Lorraine, Alsace, all our provinces, have merged to become France . . . Two huge groups will be seen, the United States of America and the United States of Europe, holding out their hands to one another across the ocean . . .* (quoted in Denis de Rougemont, *The Meaning of Europe*, 1965)

In fact, the period that followed this speech was marked by the apogée of nationalism and national rivalries in Europe, and by the channelling of Europe's energies into the acquisition of colonies overseas. The idea of a United States of Europe continued to be put forward as a way of resolving these rivalries; for example, the anthropologist J. G. Frazer, in an essay of 1906 entitled 'Pax Occidentis: A League of the West', called for

> *. . . a federation . . . among the European powers [which] beginning as a League of Peace and Defence between two or three states . . . might in time expand into a federation of the whole of Europe: the United States of Europe might stand beside the United States of America as friendly rivals in the promotion of civilization and peace.* (*The Gorgon's Head and other literary pieces*, 1927)

After the Second World War, the appeal of 'a kind of United States of Europe', as Churchill put it, lay in its easy invocation of what a successful united, democratic, continental political entity might resemble. As the **Cold War** deepened, there was also a strong desire among advocates of European integration to present any new European polity as a strong force to help 'stabilize the international system by balancing the existing superpowers', as Michael Hodges neatly summarized this view (*European Integration: Selected Readings*, 1972). The fact that **Jean Monnet** had spent much of the war working in Washington meant that prominent among the **founding fathers** was a figure with a deep understanding of the potential of the US federal system. Although the new **European Communities** took a rather more modest form, the hope that they might evolve into a more integrated '**European Union**' ensured that the US provided a continuing reference-point for Europe's possible institutional future.

In recent decades, the growing confidence of the European Communities, now Union, together with the end of the Cold War, has made transatlantic comparisons less necessary. The rapid development of the European Union as a distinctive political system means that there is less need to refer to the US as an inspiration or model. Equally, as academic study of EU institutions has deepened, there has been greater awareness of potentially misleading parallels between two rather different processes of integration: the one between relatively small, newly founded states enjoying a high degree of cultural and political homogeneity; the other between larger, more complex and long-established entities, each with its own distinctive history and traditions. A final factor has been the lively public debate about the nature of **federalism**, prompted notably by the **Maastricht ratification crisis** in the early 1990s.

The rise of **Euroscepticism** left defenders of the European Union keen to avoid any suggestion that it was or might become a 'federal state'. Comparisons with any explicitly federal system, notably the United States, thus became problematic. The German CDU removed a reference to creating a 'United States of Europe' from its statutes in 1995, and the centre-right European People's Party (EPP) followed suit in 2001. When **Valéry Giscard d'Estaing**, as chairman of the **Convention on the Future of Europe** (2002–3), suggested the 'United States of Europe' as one, among several, possible formulae to replace the title 'European Union', very few of his colleagues opted for it. However, debate in Belgium, itself reinvented as a federal state, seems to have been left untouched by this trend: in 2006, its prime minister, Guy Verhofstadt, published a personal manifesto on the future of Europe under the uncompromising title *The United States of Europe*. See also **Pan-Europa**.

Uri, Pierre (1911–92)

The French economist Pierre Uri was one of the key figures in the design of the founding **Treaties** of the **European Communities**. He worked as the close colleague and trusted confidant of **Jean Monnet**, both at the *Commissariat général au Plan* in Paris in the late 1940s and at the new **High Authority** of the **European Coal and Steel Community** (ECSC) during the 1950s. It was Monnet and Uri together who developed the concept of pooling French and German coal and steel production, which became the **Schuman Plan** of May 1950. Uri then helped Monnet to draft the text of the ECSC Treaty a year later. In 1955–6, he served as an influential member of the **Spaak Committee**, acting as its general **rapporteur** and evolving its detailed plans for relaunching European economic integration through a **common market** and **customs union**. He assisted in the drafting of the two **Treaties of Rome** establishing the **European Economic Community** (EEC) and the **European Atomic Energy Community** (EAEC or Euratom), which flowed from the Spaak Report. From the 1960s onwards, Uri wrote many books and articles on European issues and became a close associate of **François Mitterrand**, although he was too old by the time of the latter's accession to power in 1981 to be rewarded with governmental office.

Uri's obituary in *The Independent* in July 1992 described him as 'an admired if formidable academic and negotiating figure . . . without a trace of self-doubt'. In his *Memoirs* (1978), Monnet wrote of Uri's 'exceptional ability to think out new and rigorous solutions to the most complex problems. . . . [He] gets to the heart of them, where everything is simple; but this can only be done after going through the maze of details in which very intelligent people seem almost to enjoy losing their way.' Uri himself said: 'We cannot simplify the questions about Europe, but we must simplify the answers.' Uri was one of a group of self-confident French technocrats – including notably **Émile Noël**, Etienne Hirsch and Robert Marjolin – who played a decisive role, alongside the **founding fathers**, in shaping the early years of post-war European integration. Noël served as the first Secretary General of the **European Commission**, Hirsch was the first President of the Euratom Commission, and Marjolin successively the first Secretary General of the **Organization for European Economic Cooperation** (OEEC), the chief French negotiator on the EEC and Euratom Treaties, and one of the first EEC Commissioners.

V

Value-added tax (VAT)

Value-added tax was introduced in France in 1954: it is a consumption tax levied on the value added at each stage of production of any good or service. When the European Community was created, each of **the Six** founding member states was using a different form of sales or turnover tax. West Germany, Luxembourg and the Netherlands employed so-called 'cascade' taxes. The latter were, as the **European Commission** has described them, 'multi-stage taxes which were each levied on the actual value of output at each stage of the productive process, making it impossible to determine the real amount of tax actually included in the final price of a particular product'. As a result, there was a risk that member states would deliberately or inadvertently subsidize their exports by exaggerating the taxes due for refund on export. If there was to be a working **common market**, a 'transparent turnover tax system was required which ensured tax neutrality and allowed the exact amount of tax to be rebated at the point of export'.

Article 113 TFEU (previously Article 93 EC) allows the **Council of Ministers** to adopt measures for the harmonization of 'turnover taxes, excise duties and other forms of indirect taxation' where this is 'necessary to ensure the establishment and functioning of the internal market and to avoid distortion of competition'. In April 1967, the Community embarked on a process of indirect **tax harmonization**, with the Council agreeing two **directives** that required all member states to adopt a system of value-added tax. Since that date, the use of VAT has been a requirement of membership of the Community, now Union. Such is its appeal that VAT is now used by 57 countries in addition to the 27 member states of the Union, the only notable exception in the industrialized world being the United States (at federal level).

Since 1970, VAT-based revenue has also been an important, if diminishing, part of the '**own resources**' which are used to finance the Union (10.9 per cent in 2011, raising € 13.8 billion). Each member state pays a contribution to the EU **Budget** of 0.3 per cent, not of VAT actually collected, but of the VAT that would have been collected had it been applied at common rates to an agreed range of goods and services.

Initially, VAT rates differed very widely across the EU member states, as did the 'base' to which the tax was applied. Because these differences affected patterns of trade (and therefore competition) and encouraged member states to maintain fiscal controls at the Community's internal frontiers, the European Commission argued from the start for as much standardization of both the rates and coverage of VAT as practically possible. Some progress was made on the latter, when the Council adopted the sixth VAT directive in May 1977, which promoted the levying of the tax on the same transactions in different member states. However, certain goods and services were exempted from VAT altogether, notably medical care, education, postal services, public broadcasting, lending and insurance.

The major push for the approximation of VAT rates was made with the publication of the 1985 **Cockfield White Paper** on the completion of the **single market.** In 1987, abandoning hopes of securing a uniform rate of VAT or even the elimination of multiple rates, the Commission proposed that there should be 'standard' and 'reduced' rates for VAT, each permitted within a band of several percentage points (14–20 per cent and 5–9 per cent respectively). When certain member states strongly resisted this move, which could only be agreed by **unanimity** in the Council, a second proposal was made (in 1989) for a minimum 'standard' rate of 15 per cent. At a meeting of the **Ecofin Council** (of finance ministers) in October 1992, agreement was finally reached on this proposal, subject to its renewal every two years (now every five). At the same meeting, ministers agreed that each government would informally apply a maximum rate of 25 per cent. Member states were also allowed to apply one or two 'reduced' rates (of no lower than five per cent) to items from a specific list of goods and services (including foodstuffs, transport, broadcasting, hotel accommodation, social housing, funeral services and sporting events). Existing zero rates – a particular feature of the British and Irish systems – could be maintained but not extended. Zero rates are now treated as **derogations** that may continue so long as they meet three conditions: they were in force in December 1975, exist for clearly defined social reasons and benefit the final consumer.

At present, standard rates of VAT vary from the 15 per cent minimum in Cyprus and Luxembourg to the 25 per cent maximum in Denmark and Sweden. The average standard rate is just under 20 per cent. Only two countries, Denmark and Slovakia, have a single rate of VAT. Ten countries impose dual rates, whilst the others have three rates. There are periodic disputes about whether particular goods and services should be moved from the standard rate to a reduced rate, to boost their consumption. In 2006, for example, the Commission proposed and the Council agreed to allow member states to levy a lower rate, for a limited period, on two 'labour-intensive services' which must be 'mainly local' and provided direct to the consumer, drawn from a list of such services (including bicycle repairs, hairdressing, window and house cleaning, and domestic help). The French government fought an initially unsuccessful campaign to have restaurant and catering services included in this list, but in May 2009, it finally succeeded in getting these added, as well as house repairs. (The VAT rate on such services in France was subsequently reduced from 19.6 to 5.5 per cent.)

It is now clear in practice that, despite fears about potential distortions to competition, a single market can operate in the EU without the rates or scope of VAT being exactly the same in all countries. As a result, there is unlikely to be significant further pressure for VAT harmonization in the immediate future. However, one important outstanding issue is the question of whether to reform the way VAT is collected on products traded within the Union. In its 1985 White Paper, the Commission argued that, as part of the general removal of frontier controls, the point at which goods were taxed should be moved from the country of destination to the country of origin. This would mean that, whatever the differences in national tax systems and rates, adjustments to the amounts of tax paid would simply no longer have to be made between member states. In the event, the Council refused to embrace the 'origin' principle and opted instead for simply moving the payment of VAT from the exporter to the importer (at the local rate) and making this an ex post transaction coordinated by a VAT Information Exchange System. Although this 'transitional régime' did allow tax controls to be removed from internal EU frontiers, unfortunately, loopholes in the system, which depends ultimately on truthful registration of exports and imports by traders, have permitted the development of so-called 'carousel' fraud (or missing trader intra-Community VAT fraud), with lost tax revenue allegedly representing about one tenth of potential cross-border VAT receipts. VAT returns are themselves now the basis of statistics on trade within the Union, collected under a system known as Intrastat.

Certain parts of individual EU member states have been exempted from VAT, for political or practical reasons, notably the overseas departments of France, the Canary Islands, Cueta and Melilla (Spain), and Gibraltar and the Channel Islands (United Kingdom). Conversely Monaco (see **micro-states**), the Isle of Man and the British sovereign bases in Cyprus are treated as if they were within the EU for VAT purposes. **Greenland and the Faeroes** and the French overseas territories are outside the EU and do not use VAT, like Andorra, San Marino and Vatican City.

Van Duyn case

The van Duyn ruling by the **European Court of Justice** (ECJ) (*Yvonne van Duyn* v *Home Office*, Case 41/74) significantly defined and limited the ability of member states to constrain the right of **free movement of persons** within the European Union. It also provided a powerful illustration of the **direct effect** of **EU law**. The case concerned a Dutch citizen who in May 1973 was refused entry into the United Kingdom to take up employment at the Hubbard College of Scientology in East Grinstead. The British authorities justified their refusal on the grounds that it was 'undesirable' to admit persons intending to work for a cult which they considered to be a threat to public order. In this they relied upon the exceptions to the right of free movement of persons, on the grounds of 'public policy, public security or public health', set out in then Article 48 EEC, now Article 45 TFEU. Ms van Duyn argued that these exceptions, which had been defined more fully in a 1964 **directive**, could be applied only in relation to her personal conduct and did not have an institutional character. She also noted that there was no prohibition on British nationals working for the College of Scientology, and thus that the restriction on her was in effect discriminatory. In its ruling the following year, the Court held that Article 48 conferred a right of free movement directly on individuals without any need for implementing measures at the national level, a right that must be upheld by national courts.

Van Gend en Loos case
See **direct effect.**

Van Rompuy, Herman
See **President of the European Council.**

Variable geometry
The concept of 'variable geometry' or 'Europe *à la carte*' denotes a model of European integration in which member states of the European Union would decide freely whether or not to participate in a particular activity on a case-by-case basis, even if there would normally be a number of core activities in which all states take part. In the eyes of its advocates, such an approach would allow integration to reflect the political, economic or social diversity of the continent. If it were always the same states that chose not to take part in new activities, then this could lead to a '**two-speed Europe**'. If there were a variety of patterns, the result would be a 'multi-speed Europe'. (See also **Lamers–Schäuble paper** and **concentric circles.**) The expression 'Europe *à la carte*' was first used by the German sociologist and European Commissioner, Ralf Dahrendorf (1929–2009), writing under the pseudonym 'Wieland Europa' in *Die Zeit* in July 1971.

Vedel Report
In March 1972, at the invitation of the **European Commission**, a working-party of independent experts, chaired by the Professor Georges Vedel of the

Paris Faculty of Law, published a report on the possible future powers of the **European Parliament** in EC decision-making. The pretext for the report was the potential impact of the forthcoming **enlargement** (in 1973), the pending introduction of the new system of **own resources** (laid down in the 1970 Luxembourg Treaty) and the commitment of the finance ministers in March 1971 to move towards some form of **Economic and Monetary Union** (EMU) 'over the coming decade', following the **Werner Report**. The President of the Commission at the time, an Italian Christian Democrat, Franco Maria Malfatti, sensed that his institution had a strategic interest in strengthening the (then) largely advisory Parliament, which could become a long-term partner in promoting action at European level. This might help offset the legislative inertia of a **Council of Ministers** immobilized by the **Luxembourg Compromise**.

The Vedel working group comprised 14 academic lawyers and political scientists, including Mary Robinson, a future President of Ireland. It met 11 times between October 1971 and March 1972. The principal conclusion of its 87-page report – which despite its convoluted style still provides a valuable commentary on Community decision-making at the time, including the difficulty of securing outcomes from the Council – was that the legislative powers of the European Parliament should be substantially widened and deepened, in two phases, by treaty change. In the first phase, the Parliament would acquire a right of 'co-decision' with the Council – essentially meant as a post hoc right of veto (more akin to the **consent procedure** than to the **co-decision procedure**, in modern-day language). This new parliamentary power would apply to decisions to enlarge the Community, conclude **international agreements**, amend the **Treaties** and use the 'competence-stretching' Article 235 EEC (now **Article 352** TFEU). In more routine policy fields, the Parliament would be given a formal 'suspensory' power, to delay but not block Council decision-making. In the second phase, this delaying power would be replaced by a right of veto across the board.

The Vedel report also recommended that the Parliament should enjoy greater powers in respect of the Community **Budget** and be allowed formally to approve the member states' choice of President of the Commission, which could enhance the latter's authority in the process. It strongly endorsed an early move towards the direct election of the Parliament, as foreseen in the Treaties. It suggested the creation of a body, like COSAC (*Conférence des organes spécialisés dans les affaires communautaires*) today, which would bring together representatives of the European affairs committees of member-state parliaments, as part of a broader strengthening of links between the European Parliament and national parliaments once direct elections occurred (COSAC itself was formally established only in 1989).

In the event, apart from direct election of the Parliament, none of the main recommendations of the Vedel Report were followed up at the time. The EC heads of government, meeting at the Paris summit in October 1972, made no reference to the report in their conclusions, although they did express the desire to 'strengthen the supervisory powers' of the Parliament once it was elected. Many of the ideas in the report were, however, to suffuse the institutional debate in coming decades, finding favour in the successive treaty reforms that began with the **Single European Act** (SEA) in 1986.

Veto

See **unanimity, Luxembourg Compromise, consent procedure**.

Visegrád Group

The 'Visegrád states' are Poland, Hungary, the Czech Republic and Slovakia. In February 1991, the prime ministers of Hungary, Poland and what was then Czechoslovakia met in Visegrád, Hungary, to discuss their approach to European integration. They confirmed their wish for 'total integration into the European political, economic, security and legislative order' and agreed to cooperate in their progressive achievement of such integration. As a first step, each country concluded a Europe Agreement with the European Union (in 1991) and joined the **Council of Europe** (1990–93). The Visegrád states also concluded a **Central European Free Trade Agreement** (CEFTA) in Kraków, Poland, in December 1992, with the aim of creating a **free trade area** and a **single market** by 2001. After the Czech Republic and Slovakia became separate countries in January 1993, the resulting 'Visegrád Four' (V4), as they often call themselves, applied to join the European Union (in 1994–6). They had to leave CEFTA on their eventual **accession** to the Union in May 2004, by which time three other (Balkan) countries had joined the organization.

The Visegrád states formalized and reinforced their mutual cooperation by creating the Visegrád Group in May 1999. This arrangement promotes joint activity in a wide range of policy areas, including foreign affairs, justice and home affairs, education and culture, science and technology, and infrastructure and the environment. The Visegrád Group meets at the level of heads of government and foreign ministers twice a year, with the presidency rotating among the countries annually. Other ministers meet on an ad hoc basis. Cooperation is prepared at an official level by ambassadors meeting at least four times a year. The Visegrád Group has set up an International Visegrád Fund, to promote common cultural, scientific and educational projects, exchanges between young people, and the development of tourism. It has also established a 'regional partnership' with Austria and Slovenia and a 'V4 Plus' dialogue with its Eastern neighbours.

W

Warsaw Pact

In April 1955, the Western Allies recognized the independence of West Germany and admitted it to the **North Atlantic Treaty Organization** (NATO). In response, the following month, the Soviet Union formally annulled its wartime alliances with the United Kingdom (1942) and France (1944), and signed a mutual defence treaty with client states in central and eastern Europe, which became known as the Warsaw Pact. Concluded between the USSR, Albania, Bulgaria, Czechoslovakia, Hungary, Poland and Romania, the treaty required signatory states to assist each other in the case of 'armed aggression in Europe' and provided for 'a joint command of their armed forces'. Although the Soviet Union already had in fact mutual defence treaties with each of the signatories bilaterally, the new multilateral pact represented an important political assertion of 'bloc solidarity'. It marked the end of Soviet ambitions to 'neutralize' Germany, heralding a new hardening of attitudes in the **Cold War**.

The Warsaw Pact enabled the Soviet Union to station forces in the states of the 'Eastern Bloc' on a 'friendly' and ostensibly legitimate basis (as many as 20 Soviet divisions were based in East Germany). The USSR provided about three-quarters of the pact's forces, as well as successive commanders-in-chief. It was also a monopoly supplier of all military equipment used by member states, a feature which enhanced the interoperability and perceived readiness of their forces. When the Hungarian government attempted to leave the pact in November 1956 and become instead a neutral state, the successful Soviet crushing of the revolt clarified the implications of any attempted break with bloc solidarity. After the comparable ending of the 'Prague Spring' in Czechoslovakia 12 years later, the Soviet Union asserted the **Brezhnev Doctrine**, whereby intervention in bloc members was justified when the interests of the 'Socialist Commonwealth' were threatened by ideological disruption. The only country ever to leave the Warsaw Pact by mutual consent was Albania in 1968. East Germany became a member of the Warsaw Pact in 1956 and withdrew on being reunited with West Germany in 1990 (see

German reunification), by which time Communism had collapsed in most other member states. The pact was formally dissolved the following year.

Werner Report

The Werner Report of 1970 was an early blueprint for the achievement of **Economic and Monetary Union** (EMU) amongst **the Six**. It inspired a number of important initiatives, including the 1971 European currency management system known as the 'Snake' and a commitment by heads of government in 1972 to move to a single currency by 1980. The EMU process embarked upon was, however, unexpectedly disrupted by the successive effects of dollar instability in 1971 and the worldwide recession begun by the first oil crisis of 1973–4. By the mid-1970s there was little to show for this ambitious project, as it 'evaporated under adverse circumstances', in the words of economist Charles Goodhart.

Soon after the election in 1969 of Georges Pompidou as President of France and Willy Brandt as Chancellor of West Germany, political momentum began to emerge for renewed progress towards closer European integration. At more or less the same time, both the French and German currencies suffered substantial turbulence on the foreign-exchange markets, proving unable to remain within the 1.5 per cent fluctuation margins around the US dollar prescribed by agreements within the International Monetary Fund (IMF). In August 1969, the French franc was devalued by 11 per cent; in September, the Deutschmark was floated, and finally revalued by nine per cent the following month.

The **European Commission** saw in the economic and political changes of 1969 an opportunity to make EMU a major Community priority, something it did with surprising success. Raymond Barre, the Commissioner responsible for economic and financial affairs, brought forward specific plans to realize a policy objective that had neither featured in the **Treaty of Rome** nor been agreed by the member states at any point since 1958. In the so-called Barre Report of 1969, the Commission proposed that to counter currency instability, not only should macro-economic coordination be improved, but the fluctuation margins around the currencies of the Six should be eliminated as the first step towards fusing them into a single unit. This proposal was especially appealing to the new government in Paris, which was anxious to use the EMU goal as a means of bolstering the French franc on world markets and defending parities within the **Common Agricultural Policy** (CAP). It also appealed to all those who wanted to see Europe's economic dependence on the United States reduced at a time of growing financial strain across the Atlantic.

In December 1969, the heads of government, meeting in The Hague, decided that EMU should be a long-term Community objective. At the same **summit** – the only such meeting to be held between 1967 and 1972 – Pompidou announced the lifting of France's veto on British membership of the Community.

Work was put in hand within the **Ecofin Council** on devising transitional arrangements on the road to full EMU. The latter goal was agreed in February 1970 to be the adoption of a single currency. Early differences of opinion emerged, however, about the best way forward. France (backed by Barre in Brussels) favoured the rapid freezing of exchange rates as an interim measure, and argued that such a move would of itself promote the degree of convergence between member states' economies necessary before the adoption of a single currency. Germany argued the opposite case, proposing convergence as a precondition to a later locking of exchange rates, for fear that premature moves might generate disruptive side effects.

Germany also argued that, in order to provide a political foundation for EMU, **qualified majority voting** (QMV) should apply in the Ecofin Council on monetary matters, and that the **European Parliament** should be more closely associated with EMU decisions. Still managing the transition away from *gaullisme pur et dur*, the otherwise sympathetic French finance minister, **Valéry Giscard d'Estaing**, indicated that his government would have difficulty in accepting any institutional formula that made explicit the transfer of monetary **sovereignty** from national to European levels. Its preference was to leave institutional consolidation until later.

In March 1970, the Ecofin Council established a special study group under Pierre Werner, the prime minister and finance minister of Luxembourg, to review the EMU issue in greater detail and propose a concrete plan for moving ahead. Werner was a well-known advocate of closer monetary integration, and had floated some ideas of his own as early as September 1968, in what was known at the time as the Werner Plan. The study group, which included the chairman of the Committee of **Central Bank Governors** of the Six and the chairman of the **Monetary Committee**, completed its work very quickly. An interim report was presented to the Ecofin Council in June 1970, and the final report was delivered in October. The latter immediately became the baseline for all discussion of the issue.

The Werner Report trod a careful path between the competing French and German preferences on EMU. It proposed a three-stage move to full EMU, lasting from 1971 to 1980. The first stage would be directed at getting the economic underpinnings right and preparing the ground for any institutional development. The second stage would consolidate the economic and institutional progress of the first, leading in the third stage to the irrevocable fixing of exchange rates and finally the adoption of a single currency. The single currency end point was deemed to be desirable, but not strictly necessary for the project. During the first two stages, the domestic economic policies of member states would be increasingly closely coordinated at European level to promote convergence. In parallel, there would be a progressive narrowing of currency fluctuation bands, starting as soon as possible.

Institutional innovation would be kept to a minimum. There would be no need for a European central bank. Instead, a new **European Monetary Cooperation Fund** (EMCF) would be created in the second stage, to manage an increasing proportion of the reserves of member states and provide any short-term balance of payments support needed by weaker economies. The EMCF would be responsible to the existing Committee of Central Bank Governors – to be reconstituted as a 'Community system of central banks' – charged with coordinating monetary and exchange-rate policy. Macro-economic policy would need to be coordinated by an 'economic centre of decision' responsible to the European Parliament. There seemed no reason why this could not be accomplished by the existing Ecofin Council in revised form. The report stated delphically that 'a deeper study of institutions' was not within its remit, leaving open the precise content of any amendments to be made later to the Treaty of Rome.

Gaullist opposition to the Werner Report, spearheaded by former French prime minister Michel Debré, proved more intense than even Giscard had foreseen, and he was forced to indicate to the Ecofin Council in November 1970 that only a modest first stage would be acceptable to Paris. France could certainly agree to a managed currency arrangement, but institutional consolidation would have to be evolutionary and cautious. Although the other member states were sceptical of managing rates outside a binding framework, it seemed inconceivable that any progress could be made except on French terms. Anxious not to let the political initiative slip, Germany appeared willing to experiment in this way against its earlier better judgement.

In March 1971, the Ecofin Council duly agreed a lengthy resolution on attaining EMU 'during the coming decade' by stages, only the first of which (1971–4) was elaborated. The resolution identified a series of future Council decisions needed to bolster macro-economic coordination over the medium term. Mechanisms for closer cooperation between central banks were agreed. Most importantly, the member states committed themselves 'from the beginning of the first stage and on an experimental basis' to intervene to ensure that their currencies fluctuated against each other by less than the existing fluctuation margin allowed by the IMF against the US dollar: a 1.2 per cent band within a 1.5 per cent one. Germany insisted, successfully, that unless agreement was reached on the second and more substantive stage of EMU by January 1976, the monetary cooperation measures begun during the first stage would be discontinued.

The new exchange-rate arrangement – which was quickly dubbed the

'Snake' because the currencies of the Six were now tied to one another, rather than simply to the dollar, but on a flexible basis – had been agreed at what was to prove an extraordinarily unpropitious moment. In May 1971, the Deutschmark had to be revalued again, unilaterally, when strong upward pressure on the German currency followed a flight from the dollar, by now beset by serious balance-of-payments problems. The Snake's formal entry into effect in mid-June had to be postponed, as dollar instability returned on an even greater scale. In August, the dollar itself became a freely floating currency, and the whole Bretton Woods system of cross-rate parities against the dollar effectively collapsed. The anchor of the world monetary order was broken, and the whole EMU initiative looked stillborn.

In the course of 1972, efforts were made to salvage the project. The Snake was relaunched in April as the so-called 'Snake in the Tunnel' – perhaps a more accurate description of a narrow-band linkage operating within a wider one. (The phrase was attributed to Karl Schiller, the German finance minister at the time.) The new arrangement among central banks allowed each of the currencies of the nine current or future member states of the Community to move up or down within a 2.25 per cent band against the dollar, as opposed to the 4.5 per cent band laid down by the IMF. (The Smithsonian Agreement of December 1971 had devised the 4.5 per cent band as the basis for returning the dollar to 'fixed' exchange rates, although on a new, 'more realistic', set of parities.) Within a year, the currencies of four countries had withdrawn from the system: the United Kingdom and Ireland lasted only six weeks, with Denmark leaving soon after, followed by Italy in February 1973. Although Denmark managed to rejoin, France left in January 1974, only to re-enter the following year, and left once again in 1976. The Snake in the Tunnel continued until 1979, but the fact that its only participants were West Germany, the **Benelux** countries and Denmark made it in effect a wider Deutschmark zone. They chose to float collectively against the dollar, whilst retaining the reduced fluctuation margin among themselves.

For a while, the high politics of monetary union continued defiantly. The meeting of heads of government in Paris in October 1972 – in which the United Kingdom took part for the first time – strongly reaffirmed the Community's EMU objective, formally committing member states to its full realization by 1980. In the interim, 'fixed but adjustable parities' would be pursued. Already, however, the credibility of the whole exercise had been fatally prejudiced. When the European Commission duly proposed in April 1973 that the Community move to the second stage of EMU on schedule in 1974, there was no agreement in the Ecofin Council.

By the time the heads of government met again in Paris two years later, they could note only that 'internal and international difficulties have prevented in 1973 and 1974 the accomplishment of expected progress on the road to EMU.' Their assertion that 'their will has not weakened and that their objective has not changed since the [last] Paris conference' had a ritualistic air. The first, uncompleted stage of EMU was by now clearly in serious trouble. After the December 1974 declaration, nothing happened. Work on the Werner project was left in abeyance, and the 1980 EMU objective was quickly forgotten.

The only concrete achievements of the Werner Report and its follow-up by the Ecofin Council were, in addition to the March 1971 decision on strengthening cooperation among central banks, the creation of the EMCF in April 1973 along broadly the lines foreseen in the report (and in advance of the latter's timetable), and the adoption in February 1974 of a Council decision 'on the attainment of a high degree of convergence of the economic policies of the Member States'. The latter required the Council to examine the economic situation in the Community at least three times a year, to adopt an annual economic report drafted by the European Commission and to establish annual economic guidelines to be followed by the Community and member states. The Council could adopt such legislation as it deemed necessary to enforce these guidelines.

The Werner experience taught several important lessons about the economic and political difficulties of moving towards EMU. It suggested that a sustained record of both stable currency management and broad economic convergence was an indispensable precondition for any serious attempt to adopt a single currency. Equally, governments needed to enter into legally binding commitments, confirmed in treaty terms, if the objective were to stand much chance of being realized. Vague commitments in principle, without a firm timetable fixed in advance, were of little value. No lasting progress towards EMU could be achieved without appropriate institutional reforms guaranteeing a transfer of monetary sovereignty from national to European level. It is for these reasons that the **Delors Report** in 1989 recommended a much firmer, more legally-based move towards EMU, drawing on the success of the **European Monetary System** (EMS) at the time in establishing a quasi-fixed, exchange-rate régime within much of the European Community.

Further reading: Dennis Swann, *The Economics of the Common Market*, third edition, 1975.

Western European Union (WEU)

After the rejection by the French National Assembly of plans for a **European Defence Community** (EDC) in August 1954, Anthony Eden, then British Foreign Secretary, convened a meeting of the **Brussels Treaty** powers (the United Kingdom, France and the **Benelux** countries), together with West

Germany, Italy, Canada and the United States, to discuss ways of strengthening collective defence and extending cooperation into other areas. A ministerial conference was held in Paris in October 1954, and agreement was reached on modifications to the Brussels Treaty. In parallel, Italy and West Germany were to be invited to become signatories to the Treaty. West Germany was allowed to rearm and was admitted to the **North Atlantic Treaty Organization** (NATO), and the last vestiges of the Allied occupation were to be removed from the Federal Republic (although not from West Berlin, which had a separate status). A condition of German rearmament was a prohibition on the possession of atomic, biological and chemical weapons. The United Kingdom agreed to maintain a certain level of forces on mainland Europe. The signatories also agreed to establish an Assembly, comprised of their existing representatives (from national parliaments) to what is now called the Parliamentary Assembly of the **Council of Europe** (PACE), with a view to providing democratic oversight of activities in this field. With the ratification of these changes and the entry into force of the 'Modified Brussels Treaty' in May 1955, the Brussels Treaty Organization became the Western European Union, with its headquarters in London, and the new assembly became known as the WEU Assembly, based in Paris.

Just as the Brussels Treaty Organization had never developed any significant military or security role, having been quickly overshadowed by the **North Atlantic Treaty Organization** (NATO), so its successor fared little better. The WEU got off to an inauspicious start: its proposals to resolve the question of the **Saarland** were rejected by referendum in 1955. The new powers it had acquired under the modified Brussels Treaty for cooperation in the field of social and cultural affairs were scarcely activated and were then transferred to the Council of Europe in 1960. The WEU managed to carve out a limited role as the only European political forum in which France and the United Kingdom could meet regularly to discuss foreign policy and security issues. This was given greater importance after French President **Charles de Gaulle** removed his country from the integrated military command structure of NATO in 1966 and blocked the UK's application to join the European Community in 1963 and 1967.

During the 1980s, there was a growing debate about whether western European states were making an adequate contribution to their own defence. In October 1984, a WEU Council meeting in Rome decided to attempt to resuscitate the organization as a framework for the discussion of specifically European security questions. Three years later in The Hague, a 'Platform on European Security Interests' was adopted, which contained a commitment to develop a 'more cohesive European defence identity'. A discernible military role for the WEU began to emerge. The WEU coordinated a naval mission to escort shipping and clear the Strait of Hormuz of mines during the Iran–Iraq war. In 1990, the military response of west European countries to the Gulf crisis was coordinated through the WEU. In their 'Petersberg Declaration' of June 1992, the WEU foreign ministers widened the organization's remit to include humanitarian and rescue tasks, peacekeeping, and crisis management, including peacemaking. The operational capability of the WEU was drawn from a number of forces put at its disposal by member states. These were the **Eurocorps**, the European Operational Rapid Force (**EUROFOR**), the European Maritime Force (EUROMARFOR), the Belgian–German–Dutch–British Multinational Division, the German–Dutch corps, the British–Dutch amphibious force and the Italian amphibious force. In addition, the WEU could draw on NATO assets by joint agreement.

The seven original members of the WEU were joined by Portugal and Spain in 1990, and by Greece in 1995. Denmark and Ireland were observer members, together with (from 1995) Austria, Finland and Sweden. Associate status was extended to the other European members of NATO (at the time, **Iceland**, **Norway**, **Turkey**, the Czech Republic, Hungary and Poland) with seven other central and eastern European countries becoming 'associate partners'.

Ironically, the revival of the WEU led to its de facto and eventually its de jure takeover by another organization, the European Union. During the 1991 Intergovernmental Conference, the WEU emerged as a convenient vehicle for allowing non-NATO member states to accept the principle that defence cooperation should be added to the new **competences** of the Union. In the resulting 1992 **Maastricht Treaty**, the Union was allowed to request the WEU 'to elaborate and implement decisions and actions of the Union which have defence implications' (Article J.4 TEU, since repealed). In return, the WEU members, in a declaration annexed to the treaty, stated that the organization was 'prepared, at the request of the European Union' to perform such a role. The Maastricht Treaty also described the WEU as 'an integral part of the development of the Union' and, in their declaration, the WEU states said that the development of a 'genuine European security and defence identity' would 'be pursued through a gradual process' designed to 'build up [the] WEU in stages as the defence component of the European Union'.

As part of this process, the WEU's headquarters were transferred (between 1993 and 2001) from London to Brussels, so that the body could be 'co-located' with the Union and NATO. The WEU's Western European Armaments Group (WEAG) assumed responsibility for most of the work formerly done by the **Eurogroup** and the Independent European Programme Group (IEPG). With effect from 1998, the presidency of the WEU Council was aligned with the **presidency** of the EU **Council of Ministers** as far as possible (given that only ten of the then 15 EU member states were members of the WEU).

The 1997 **Amsterdam Treaty** took the process of WEU–EU convergence several steps further and clarified the relationship between the two. In a revised Article 17 TEU, the WEU was described as offering the Union 'access to an operational capability', notably in respect of the **Petersberg tasks**, which were for the first time spelt out in the treaty as an EU function, and as supporting the Union 'in framing the defence aspects' of its **Common Foreign and Security Policy** (CFSP). The Union would 'foster closer institutional relations with the WEU with a view to the possibility of the integration of the WEU into the Union, should the Council so decide'. When the Union 'avails itself of the WEU to elaborate and implement decisions of the Union', all member states, whether or not they belong to the WEU, were entitled 'to participate fully and on an equal footing in planning and decision-taking in the WEU'. A new WEU declaration annexed to the treaty specified that, when the WEU was taking action on the EU's behalf, it 'will act consistently with guidelines established by the European Council'.

Soon after the Anglo-French **Saint-Malo Declaration** of December 1988 – in which Europe's two largest military powers committed themselves to the development of an independent EU military capability, operating alongside, but outside, NATO structures – the EU heads of government decided to institute a **Common Security and Defence Policy** (CSDP), later formalized in the 2001 **Nice Treaty**. The conclusions of the Cologne European Council in June 1999 declared that the EU should, by the end of the following year, take over 'those functions of the WEU which will be necessary' for the former 'to fulfil its new responsibilities in the area of the Petersberg tasks'. It went on: 'In that event, the WEU as an organization would have completed its purpose. The different status of Member States with regard to collective defence guarantees will not be affected. The Alliance remains the foundation of the collective defence of its Member States.'

The Cologne meeting in effect killed the WEU as a meaningful body, but on a deferred basis. By the time that EU heads of government met six months later to define their defence plans in detail – setting the so-called **Helsinki Headline Goal** and creating new military structures for the Union – there was no longer any reference to the WEU in any of the documents. Javier Solana, the Union's new **High Representative** for CFSP, was appointed as Secretary General of the WEU, to help fold the one organization into the other. The WEU Council, meeting in Marseilles in November 2000, declared itself satisfied that the EU was able to assume the obligations set out in the Modified Brussels Treaty, especially the Article 5 commitment that, 'if any of the High Contracting Parties should be the object of an armed attack in Europe, the other High Contracting Parties will . . . afford the Party so attacked all the military and other aid and assistance in their power.'

Most of the remaining components of the WEU, other than the WEU

Assembly, were transferred to the European Union. As the WEU had no military forces permanently assigned to it, other than in a small central planning cell, this was a fairly simple operation. In January 2002, the EU Council of Ministers took over responsibility for the WEU Satellite Centre (SATCEN) in Torrejón de Ardoz, Spain, as well as the WEU Institute for Security Studies in Paris. The latter, renamed respectively the EU Satellite Centre (EUSC) and the EU Institute for Security Studies (EUISS), became 'second-pillar' **agencies** of the Union. The WEU planning cell was wound up. Formally, the WEU still existed as an international organization, with certain residual tasks administered by a small secretariat: these included organizing meetings of the WEU Assembly (see below), managing the Paris building which still housed both the Assembly and the EU Institute for Security Studies, and organizing certain legacy functions, such as archives and pensions. To oversee the phasing out of the WEU, the representatives of the relevant EU member states on the **Political and Security Committee** (PSC) were asked to assume a similar function towards the WEU Council, even if the latter never met.

The WEU Assembly managed to continue to operate for almost another decade, even though its sponsor had largely disappeared. The Assembly comprised 258 national parliamentarians drawn from all the 27 EU member states (even though the WEU only encompassed ten states), as well as the three European NATO members outside the EU (Iceland, Norway and Turkey) and nine other countries which were members of neither organization (Albania, Bosnia and Herzegovina, **Croatia**, FYR Macedonia, Moldova, Montenegro, the Russian Federation, Serbia and Ukraine). The 205 parliamentarians from EU member states were full members of the Assembly, the 20 from non-EU NATO countries 'associate members', and the 33 others 'partners'. Parliamentarians from three other countries (Armenia, Azerbaijan and Georgia) sat as observers. In all cases, the parliamentarians were also their countries' representatives in the Parliamentary Assembly of the Council of Europe.

The Assembly met in plenary session twice a year, with its six standing committees convening at other times. Although members sat alphabetically in meetings, most were members of one of three **political groups**: the Federated Group of Christian Democrats and European Democrats, the Socialist Group and the Liberal Group. The Assembly had a president and ten vice-presidents, who, together with political group leaders and heads of national delegation, met together in a Presidential Committee. The plenary adopted reports on defence and security issues which it communicated to ministers.

The merger of the WEU into the European Union left the WEU Assembly in search of a continuing role. At the time of the **Convention on the Future of Europe** (in 2002–3), some of the national parliamentarians sitting on the

Assembly attempted to gain recognition for it as a EU body, offering to provide parliamentary oversight in the emerging field of CSDP. When this proposal was declined – mainly as a result of resistance from Members of the European Parliament (MEPs) – the Assembly chose unilaterally to restyle itself as the 'European Security and Defence Assembly', even though this title had no official status and was not recognized by the EU institutions. Subsequently, the EU High Representative, as Secretary General of the WEU, declined to take part in its proceedings.

In March 2010, the governments of the ten high contracting parties to the WEU announced that they had 'collectively decided to terminate' the Modified Brussels Treaty, with a view to the organization ceasing to exist at the end of June 2011. The governments signalled that they regarded the new mutual assistance commitment between EU member states, introduced by the Lisbon Treaty (Article 42(7) TEU) as matching 'the principle of mutual defence' contained in Article 5 of the Modified Brussels Treaty. They encouraged national parliaments to develop new arrangements for inter-parliamentary dialogue in the fields of CFSP and CSDP, without indicating how this might be secured. The French National Assembly, supported by the two houses of the British Parliament, proposed that six members of each of the 27 national parliaments, together with six MEPs, should constitute a new forum, meeting once every six months. This formula proved unacceptable to the **European Parliament**, which felt it was being deliberately marginalized. A stand-off occurred at the EU Speakers' Conference in April 2011 and, so far, no arrangement has been agreed.

Further reading: Anne Deighton (editor), *Western European Union 1954–1997: Defence, Security, Integration*, 1997.

Y

Yalta and Potsdam Conferences

The Yalta and Potsdam Conferences, held in early and mid 1945 respectively, brought together the leaders of the three biggest Allied powers – the United States, Soviet Union and United Kingdom – to discuss the contours of a post-Second World War settlement. They agreed specific arrangements for the future of Germany, Poland and Austria; established general principles for the treatment of other countries that were under German occupation; and decided to create the **United Nations**, as a broader international framework for post-war cooperation. The two **summits** are highly controversial, because many of the agreements reached appear either to have reflected Soviet interests or entailed commitments from which Moscow was subsequently to resile. This reflected the reality of the USSR's growing influence, as its troops advanced across central and eastern Europe towards the end of the war, and its refusal to allow democratic government in those countries once liberated from Nazi rule.

The Yalta Conference took place on 4–11 February 1945 – at the Livadia Palace, just outside the Black Sea resort of Yalta in the Crimea – and was attended by US President Franklin D. Roosevelt, Soviet president and party leader Joseph Stalin, and British prime minister **Winston Churchill**. The 'big three' had previously met in Teheran in November 1943, when they had agreed in principle that the 'Curzon Line' would serve as the post-war border between the Soviet Union and Poland, thus accepting the Soviet annexation of Polish territory in 1939. At Yalta, this plan was confirmed, with the Oder–Neisse Line chosen as the new Polish–German border. The overall result would be to shift Poland over 150 kilometres to the west of its pre-war boundaries. In return, Moscow consented to enter the war against Japan in the Pacific three months after Germany had been defeated. The Allied leaders also agreed that France should join them as an equal partner in administering a defeated Germany, with the latter to be divided into occupation zones, and that democratic political systems would be established in all countries previously under German control. A successor organization to the League of Nations would be founded, in the form of the United Nations, with a special conference to be convened in April 1945 in San Francisco to draft its charter. To secure Soviet backing for the UN concept, it was secretly agreed that the four powers occupying Germany would also enjoy veto rights in the new UN Security Council.

The Potsdam Conference was held from 16 July to 2 August 1945 at the Cecilienhof on the southern outskirts of Berlin. In the five months since Yalta, much had happened: the Soviet Union had occupied an even larger part of central and eastern Europe, President Roosevelt had been replaced by Harry Truman, Germany had unconditionally surrendered on 8 May. During the Potsdam Conference itself, the United States successfully tested the first atomic bomb and Churchill's loss of the 1945 British general election was announced, with his untested successor, Clement Attlee, taking his place immediately.

Truman, Stalin and Attlee agreed at Potsdam that Germany should be democratized, 'de-Nazified', decentralized, demilitarized and in effect de-industrialized, with its capacity for heavy industrial production dismantled and traditional companies and cartels broken up. Reparations would be paid in kind, as part of the process of restructuring the German economy. Major war criminals were to be tried by military tribunal. All territories annexed by Germany before or during the war – notably Austria, the Sudetenland and Alsace-Lorraine – would be restored. Both Germany and Austria (and their capitals) were to be divided into four zones for Allied occupation: controversially, the boundaries agreed for the Soviet zone in Germany included areas that the Red Army had not occupied. Moreover, instead of all zones being under the single control of the new Inter-Allied Control Commission, each zone would be administered by its own occupying power separately. This meant, for example, that the recognition of political parties would depend on the decision of each occupying power.

In parallel, the Yalta understanding on the boundaries of Poland was confirmed – although the Soviets unilaterally annexed the northern part of East Prussia, an area they renamed Kaliningrad, which would otherwise have gone to Poland. With other changes, the effect of Poland's new boundaries was to reduce Germany's surface area by one quarter (compared with 1937) and gave the Soviet Union a direct border with Hungary and Czechoslovakia. Over nine million Germans living in the territories transferred to Poland (or the Soviet Union) were forcibly relocated to other parts of Germany. The new Soviet-controlled government in Warsaw, rather than the government-in-exile in London, was recognized as legitimate by the Allied powers. In return for the many concessions it received, the Soviet Union agreed to join the war against Japan, with the conference issuing an ultimatum that threatened the 'prompt and utter destruction' of that country unless it surrendered immediately. The United States dropped atomic bombs on Hiroshima and Nagasaki during the week following Potsdam.

The arrangements relating to Germany made at Potsdam were meant to be 'provisional', awaiting a final peace treaty with the Allies. However, no such treaty was ever signed. As the **Cold War** deepened, the trajectory of the Soviet zone diverged increasingly from that of the West. Two of the western zones merged to create the Anglo-American Bi-Zone ('Bizonia') in January 1947, whilst the **Marshall Plan** was extended to West Germany in June 1948 and a major currency reform was undertaken at the same time. The Soviets responded with the Berlin blockade of 1948–9, broken by the allied airlift. The Western powers created a Parliamentary Council to prepare the ground for the establishment of the Federal Republic in May 1949. In response, the Soviet zone was restyled the 'German Democratic Republic' five months later. The final boundaries of post-war Germany were only confirmed legally four decades later, as part of the process of **German reunification** in October 1990.

Further reading: Charles L. Mee, *Meeting at Potsdam*, 1975; S. M. Plokhy, *Yalta: The Price of Peace*, 2010.

'Year of Europe'

In a major speech at the Waldorf-Astoria Hotel in New York on 23 April 1972, the then US National Security Advisor, Henry Kissinger, designated 1973 as the 'Year of Europe'. US foreign policy would aim to strengthen **transatlantic relations**, with deeper cooperation on defence, security and economic issues, capped by the negotiation of a 'new Atlantic Charter setting the goals for the future'. Kissinger's initiative reflected a desire in Washington to engage European countries more actively in burden-sharing and in solving regional disputes, notably the Middle East, as well as to offset the corrosive impact of the Vietnam War on public attitudes towards the US across the continent. There were also fears about the possible effect of Britain's imminent **accession** to the European Community, under pro-European prime minister **Edward Heath**, in diluting the traditional UK–US 'special relationship'.

Dogging the Year of Europe from the start was the problem that the initiative was conceived unilaterally by the Americans, rather than negotiated in advance, and that it attached too much importance institutionally to the **North Atlantic Treaty Organization** (NATO), and too little to the emerging European Community. With France still outside NATO's integrated military command structure and the EC beginning to regain momentum as President Pompidou shifted from some traditional Gaullist positions, the potential existed to broaden the transatlantic relationship beyond the traditional sphere of military and foreign policy dialogue to a wider range of economic, trade, energy and development questions. Although the Americans professed a firm wish to move in this direction, the Year of Europe lacked any clear strategy for capitalizing on this opportunity.

In the event, on both sides of the Atlantic, 1973 turned out to be an unusually difficult year. The US President, Richard Nixon, became increasingly embroiled in the Watergate scandal, whilst the Paris peace accords, followed by the departure of American troops from Vietnam, served to underline the country's biggest post-war foreign policy failure. The Arab attack on Israel in the Yom Kippur war of October 1973 prompted a dramatic increase in the price of oil (on the import of which Europeans were much more dependent than the Americans). The war both polarized opinion on the Middle East and induced a rapid economic downturn. The West German government protested at the use of their ports to supply US armaments to Israel, and even Britain allegedly refused the Americans use of their sovereign air bases in Cyprus for reconnaissance flights on Israel's behalf. The maverick French foreign minister, Michel Jobert, seemed positively to relish the opportunity to point up differences with the US administration, whilst the domestic standing of most national governments in the EC was declining. Efforts by Kissinger, now Secretary of State, to negotiate the new Atlantic Charter and convene a major transatlantic summit were frustrated by the difficulties in eliciting any coherent European response.

By the end of 1973, there was a growing mood of mutual distrust and recrimination between American and European leaders. Some commentators called the impact of these events a kind of '**Suez crisis** in reverse', with Kissinger himself reported to have said that European governments had 'acted as though the [Atlantic] Alliance did not exist' and that 'I do not care what happens to NATO, I am so disgusted' (quoted in Z. 'The Year of Europe?', *Foreign Affairs*, January 1974). Reviewing events in 1973, a year-end editorial in *The New York Times* noted: 'What the United States had envisioned as the Year of Europe, a period of imaginative updating and refurbishing of the NATO alliance, capped with a new Atlantic Charter, has become instead the year in which Washington's relationship with its European partners has struck an all-time low.'

Further reading: Alistair Horne, *Kissinger's Year: 1973*, 2009.

Yugoslavia

The Kingdom of Serbs, Croats and Slovenes – as Yugoslavia was originally called – was created after the First World War out of the Kingdom of Serbia (with Montenegro) and territories formerly part of the Austro-Hungarian Empire, some of them Catholic (Slovenia, **Croatia**), others largely Orthodox or Muslim. Serbs made up almost half the population. The name Yugoslavia, adopted in order to play down ethnic divisions, dates from 1929. However, ethnic and other tensions characterized the political history of Yugoslavia throughout the 1920s and 1930s (the king was assassinated in 1934), many of them prompted by Croat and Macedonian separatist aspirations. The Second World War resulted in invasion, occupation by both Italy and Germany, and the creation in Croatia of a puppet state sympathetic to Germany. From 1945 until the break-up of the country, which began in early 1990, Yugoslavia was under Communist rule. As life president of the Socialist Federal Republic of Yugoslavia (SFRY), Marshal Tito succeeded in maintaining a substantial degree of independence from Moscow, whilst containing strong, historically-rooted, nationalist impulses in what was basically an artificial state. On his death in 1980, Tito was succeeded by a collective leadership which found this balancing act increasingly difficult to sustain.

The Serbs' long-standing desire for dominance of the region, mirrored by deep fears on the part of other ethnic groups at this prospect, re-emerged as soon as Communism collapsed in central and eastern Europe. The Yugoslav Communist party was dissolved in 1990, as tensions rose between the constituent states of the SFRY. Continued attempts by Serbia to retain overall control of the five other states of the federation, as well as of the autonomous provinces of Kosovo (where there was an Albanian majority) and Vojvodina, led to a strong showing of various nationalist forces in the first multi-party elections, followed by unilateral declarations of independence, first by Slovenia and Croatia in June 1991, and then by Bosnia and Herzegovina and Macedonia the following April. The refusal of the Belgrade régime, led by Slobodan Milosevic, to countenance the break-up of the Yugoslav state induced the European Union and the wider international community to recognize Slovenian and Croatian autonomy in January 1992. This move followed Germany's unilateral recognition the previous month, despite previous reluctance on the part of the United States, France and (to a lesser extent) Britain.

A complex web of armed conflicts ensued, both between the Serbs and the secessionist states, and within individual states, involving war crimes and 'ethnic cleansing' of minorities. A multi-dimensional civil war in Bosnia and Herzegovina (between Serbs, Croats, Bosnian Muslims and Bosnian Serbs) proved particularly vicious and intractable. The EU and **United Nations** imposed sanctions and diplomatic isolation on what was formally known from April 1992 as the Federal Republic of Yugoslavia (FRY), whose truncated territory incorporated Serbia, Montenegro, Kosovo and Vojvodina. However, there was a marked reluctance to countenance the use of force to defeat Serbia or even to separate the warring parties. A UN peacekeeping mission or protection force (UNPROFOR) was created in February 1992, with a contribution of manpower from the EU member states, but it had only a limited mandate, lacked both sufficient numbers on the ground and adequate air support, and sometimes found its members being taken hostage by combatants.

Successive EU and UN peace plans proved ineffective and tensions emerged between the Union and the United States about whether UNPROFOR should be supported by strategic air strikes against the Serbs, coordinated through the **North Atlantic Treaty Organization** (NATO). The latter's airpower was deployed in June 1993, but then only under 'dual key' control, in the sense that any strikes had to be authorized by both UN and NATO lines of command. The impasse on the ground reached an agonizing climax at Srebrenica – a Muslim enclave in a Serbian-dominated part of Bosnia and Herzegovina – on 13–15 July 1995, when over 7,000 Bosnian Muslims were massacred by Serbian forces under General Ratko Mladic. In response, reflecting a key change of US approach, NATO was mandated by the UN to intervene militarily to end the conflict. The rapid success of the resulting air campaign in August 1995, Operation Deliberate Force, coupled with pressure from Russia, paved the way for a peace agreement, signed in Dayton, Ohio, three months later. Under the Dayton accord, Bosnia and Herzegovina was divided internally into a Serb entity, the Republika Srpska (49 per cent of the territory), and the Federation of Bosnia and Herzegovina (BiH). NATO land forces, in the form of IFOR and SFOR, were deployed successively in Bosnia and Herzegovina until December 2004, when their mandate was assumed by the EU's Operation Althea.

In an innovative move, the town of Mostar in Bosnia and Herzegovina was placed under European Union administration in May 1994, as one of the first joint actions taken under the Union's new **Common Foreign and Security Policy** (CFSP). Supported by a police force provided by the **Western European Union** (WEU), the European Union Administration in Mostar (EUAM) was able to return the town to the control of an elected local authority three years later.

In April 1997, the EU Council of Ministers decided upon a 'regional approach' to the countries of south-eastern Europe, or the 'Western Balkans' as they became known. Encompassing the whole of the former Yugoslavia (other than FRY and Slovenia), together with Albania, the strategy held out the possibility of eventual membership of the Union in return for full implementation of the Dayton agreement, as well as the installation of democracy, respect for human and minority rights, economic stabilization, structural reform and cross-border cooperation. (Slovenia was not included in this process because it was already about to conclude a Europe Agreement with the Union as a prelude to starting **accession** negotiations in its own right.) Strengthening the Union's trade and aid relations and political contacts with the region was made conditional upon such progress, which was monitored by the Union's own monitoring mission (based in Sarajevo since July 1991) and the **European Commission**.

Despite progress in the region in general, the situation in FRY remained tense. The ethnic cleansing of Kosovar Albanians by the Yugoslav army, following an armed insurrection led by the Kosovan Liberation Army (KLA) in January 1999, led, in March–June 1999, after considerable agonizing in Western capitals, to a second NATO military operation against the Serbs. Although the NATO campaign itself did not have a UN Security Council mandate, the province of Kosovo was subsequently placed under UN administration, with a NATO force, KFOR, being stationed there since.

In June 2000, the European Council meeting in Feira sought to encourage pro-democracy forces in FRY, by affirming that 'a democratic, cooperative FRY, living in peace with its neighbours' would be 'a welcome member of the European family of democratic nations'. Sanctions were lifted four months later.

The Federal Republic of Yugoslavia was renamed Serbia and Montenegro in 2003, with Montenegro voting to become a separate state in June 2006, and (more controversially) Kosovo declaring independence in February 2008. As a result of the Balkans crisis in the 1990s and subsequent events, Yugoslavia has splintered into seven of the eight component units that Tito had defined at the end of the Second World War: Bosnia and Herzegovina, Croatia, Kosovo, FYR Macedonia, Montenegro, Serbia and Slovenia. Only Vojvodina remains with Serbia. Of the seven ex-Yugoslav republics, one (Slovenia) is already a member state of the European Union, a second (Croatia) is set to join in 2013, and three more are candidate countries (FYR Macedonia, Montenegro and Serbia).

Further reading: Mark Mazower, *The Balkans: From the End of Byzantium to the Present Day*, 2002.

Z

Zurich speech

In March 1946, **Winston Churchill** made his famous 'Iron Curtain' speech in Fulton, Missouri, in which he drew attention to the division of Europe – 'this is not the liberated Europe we fought to build up' – and the threat posed by the Soviet Union to world peace. Four months later, at a meeting of foreign ministers in Paris, relations between the United States and the USSR took a decisive turn for the worse, and it became clear that the idea of a lasting peace underwritten by the great powers was not likely to be realized – but a divided continent was. Churchill therefore returned to a theme which he had first explored before the Second World War and had touched on again in a speech to the Belgian parliament in November 1945, when he spoke of forging a '**United States of Europe**, which will unify this continent in a manner never known since the fall of the Roman Empire'.

Churchill's prime concern was to set out what Europe could do to contain the Soviet threat. In a speech given at Zurich University on 19 September 1946, he painted a characteristically broad and vivid picture of post-war devastation in Europe: 'Over wide areas a vast quivering mass of tormented, hungry, care-worn and bewildered human beings gape at the ruins of their cities and homes, and scan the dark horizons for the approach of some new peril, tyranny or terror.' But, he said, there was a 'sovereign remedy . . . to re-create the European family, or as much of it as we can, and provide it with a structure under which it can dwell in peace, in safety, and in freedom. We must build a kind of United States of Europe.' As he envisaged it, the 'United States of Europe' would be a regional organization within the **United Nations** that 'could give a sense of enlarged patriotism and common citizenship to the distracted peoples of this turbulent and mighty continent'.

Then followed the passage that, as Churchill was well aware, was the most striking of the whole speech:

> *I am now going to say something that will astonish you. The first step in the re-creation of the European family must be a partnership between France and Germany. In this*

way only can France recover the moral leadership of Europe. There can be no revival of Europe without a spiritually great France and a spiritually great Germany. The structure of the United States of Europe, if well and truly built, will be such as to make the material strength of a single state less important. Small nations will count as much as large ones and gain their honour by their contribution to the common cause.

The speech concluded with a practical suggestion: 'The first step is to form a **Council of Europe**. If at first all the states of Europe are not willing or able to join the Union, we must nevertheless proceed to assemble and combine those who will and those who can.'

Implicit in the Zurich speech was the possibility that the United Kingdom might not be part of any United States of Europe, but rather only one of the 'friends and sponsors of the new Europe', alongside the other victorious powers, including if possible 'Soviet Russia'. The wording about British involvement was ambiguous. In subsequent speeches before returning to power in 1951, Churchill expressed a greater willingness to see Britain actively participate in the process of European integration – for example, in the possible development, which he suggested, of a **European army**. Once back in government, however, his enthusiasm for such schemes waned.

The impact of the Zurich speech was enormous. As the historian David Cannadine has written: 'At a time when the full extent of Nazi atrocities was only just being revealed at the Nuremberg Trials', the idea that France and Germany 'must take the lead together' in defining a common European future 'was indeed an audacious idea' (*The Speeches of Winston Churchill*, 1990). Churchill called for 'an act of faith in the European family and an act of oblivion against all the crimes and follies of the past'. The fact that a statesman of Churchill's standing could look to a future of reconciliation, with no hint of recrimination, gave inspiration to many. His advocacy of the European cause gave it fresh impetus and made him the obvious choice as the man to preside over the **Congress of Europe**, held in The Hague, two years later. At the same time, the speech gave a potentially misleading impression of the extent to which the United Kingdom would in the longer term be prepared to become a partner in building institutions of a potentially supranational character in Europe.

Churchill sent a copy of his Zurich speech to **Charles de Gaulle**, with Duncan Sandys carrying it personally to Colombey. The General was less impressed than others with the text. He told Sandys that the speech had been ill received in France, that talk of a United States of Europe raised the spectre of 're-creating [a] kind of unified, centralized Reich', and that 'unless steps were taken to prevent the resuscitation of German power, there was a danger that a United Europe would become nothing else than an enlarged Germany' (quoted in Max Beloff, 'Churchill and Europe', in Robert Blake and William

Roger Louis, *Churchill*, 1993). Moves towards European integration should, de Gaulle argued, depend critically on both France and Britain being founder members of any new common entity. Ironically, 17 years later, de Gaulle vetoed Britain joining the European Community and signed the Franco-German **Elysée Treaty** in quick succession.

On 19 September 1996, Zurich University commemorated the 50th anniversary of Churchill's speech by playing an original recording to an invited audience in the exact setting in which it had been delivered. The impact on those present was said to be powerful. On the same day, a number of leading pro-European British Conservatives – including **Edward Heath**, Geoffrey Howe, Douglas Hurd and William Whitelaw – wrote a letter to *The Independent* newspaper in which they lamented the 'tragedy of Churchill's Zurich speech' in that its 'positive, internationalist vision of Europe's future' had not informed Britain's own post-war foreign policy. They noted that in subsequent years:

> *We sought to distance ourselves from Europe, rather than decisively to shape it, as we could and should have done. Our caution cost us dearly in the design of the new Europe. We eventually joined the European Community fifteen years too late. We have been working to catch up ever since. That is a mistake we must not make again . . . To commit ourselves, by contrast, to a positive role in the leadership of Europe is the most fitting tribute we can pay to Churchill's Zurich vision.*

Bibliography

Although the interested reader will find specific suggestions for further reading listed at the end of some of the individual entries in this *Companion*, the longer bibliography below offers a broad selection of English-language books on the European Union and the wider process of European integration. Reference is made to the most recent edition of any book, wherever possible.

Readers seeking a synoptic overview of recent developments in EU institutions and policies should refer to *The JCMS Annual Review of the European Union*, published each spring by the *Journal of Common Market Studies*.

Reference books, dictionaries and collections of documents or readings

Blair, Alasdair, *Companion to the European Union*, 2006.

de Giustino, David (editor), *A Reader in European Integration*, 1996.

Dinan, Desmond, *Encyclopedia of the European Union*, 2000.

Eilstrup-Sangiovanni, Mette, *Debates on European Integration: A Reader*, 2006.

Harryvan, Anjo, and Jan van der Harst (editors), *Documents on European Union*, 1997.

Hodges, Michael (editor), *European Integration*, 1972.

Jones, Alistair, *A Glossary of the European Union*, 2008.

Jørgensen, Knud, Mark Pollack and Ben Rosamond, *Handbook of European Union Politics*, 2007.

Leonard, Dick, with Leo Cendrowicz, *The Economist Guide to the European Union*, 2010.

Lipgens, Walter, *Documents on the History of European Integration:* Volume 1, *Continental Plans for European Union, 1939–1945*, 1985; Volume 2, *Plans for European Union in Great Britain and in Exile, 1939–1945*, 1986; Volume 3, *The Struggle for European Union by Political Parties and Pressure Groups in Western European Countries, 1945–1950*, 1988.

Nelsen, Brent, and Alexander Stubb, *The European Union: Readings on the Theory and Practice of European Integration*, 2003.

O'Neill, Michael, *The Politics of European Integration: A Reader*, 1996.
Phinnemore, David, and Lee McGowan, *A Dictionary of the European Union*, 2002.
Rossi, Ernest, and Barbara McCrea, *The European Political Dictionary*, 1985.
Stevenson, John (editor), *The Columbia Dictionary of European Political History since 1914*, 1992.
Unwin, Derek, *Dictionary of European History and Politics since 1945*, 1996.
Vanthoor, Wim, *A Chronological History of the European Union 1946–1998*, 1999.
Vaughan, Richard, *Post-War Integration in Europe: Documents of Modern History*, 1976.
Weigall, David, and Peter Stirk (editors), *The Origins and Development of European Integration*, 1999.
Young, John, *The Longman Companion to Cold War and Detente 1941–91*, 1993.

Introductory works and textbooks

Archer, Clive, *The European Union*, 2008.
Bache, Ian, and Stephen George, *Politics in the European Union*, 2006.
Bomberg, Elizabeth, John Peterson and Richard Corbett (editors), *The European Union: How does it work?*, 2011.
Bromley, Simon (editor), *Governing the European Union*, 2001.
Cini, Michelle, and Nieves Pérez-Solórzano Borragán (editors), *European Union Politics*, 2010.
Dinan, Desmond, *Ever Closer Union: An Introduction to European Integration*, 2010.
El-Agraa, Ali, *The European Union: Economics and Policies*, 2011.
George, Stephen, *Politics and Policy in the European Union*, 1996.
Hix, Simon, and Bjørn Høyland, *The Political System of the European Union*, 2011.
Lelieveldt, Herman, and Sebastiaan Princen, *The Politics of the European Union*, 2011.
Maclay, Michael, *The European Union*, 1998.
McCormick, John, *Understanding the European Union*, 2011.
Nugent, Neill, *The Government and Politics of the European Union*, 2010.
Peterson, John, and Michael Shackleton (editors), *The Institutions of the European Union*, 2012.
Pinder, John, and Simon Usherwood, *The European Union: A Very Short Introduction*, 2007.
Richardson, Jeremy, *European Union: Power and Policy-Making*, 2005.
Salmon, Trevor, and William Nicoll, *Building European Union: A Documentary History and Analysis*, 1997.
Wallace, Helen, Mark Pollack and Alasdair Young (editors), *Policy-Making in the European Union*, 2010.
Watts, Duncan, *The European Union*, 2008.

Nature and processes of European integration

Beetham, David, and Christopher Lord, *Political Legitimation and the European Union*, 1998.
Best, Edward, Thomas Christiansen and Pierpaolo Settembri (editors), *The Institutions of the Enlarged European Union: Continuity and Change*, 2008.
Chryssochoou, Dimitris, *Theorizing European Integration*, 2009.
Featherstone, Kevin, and Claudio Radaelli (editors), *The Politics of Europeanization: Theory and Analysis*, 2003.
Haller, Max, *European Integration as an Elite Process: The Failure of a Dream?*, 2008.
Harrison, David, *The Organisation of Europe: Developing a Continental Market Order*, 1995.
Hayward, Jack, and Anand Menon, *Governing Europe*, 2003.
Héritier, Adrienne, *Explaining Institutional Change in Europe*, 2007.
Hix, Simon, *What's Wrong with the European Union and How to Fix It*, 2008.
Holland, Martin, *European Integration*, 1994.
Jordan, Andrew, and Adriaan Schout, *The Coordination of the European Union: Exploring the Capacities of Networked Governance*, 2006.
Lord, Christopher, *Democracy in the European Union*, 1998.
Magnette, Paul, *What is the European Union?*, 2005.
Majone, Giandomenico, *Dilemmas of European Integration: The Ambiguities and Pitfalls of Integration by Stealth*, 2009.
— *Regulating Europe*, 1996.
Middlemas, Keith et al., *Orchestrating Europe: The Informal Politics of the European Union 1973–95*, 1995.
Moravcsik, Andrew, *The Choice for Europe: Social Purpose and State Power from Messina to Maastricht*, 1998.
Piris, Jean-Claude, *The Future of Europe: Towards a Two-Speed Europe?*, 2012.
Rosamond, Ben, *Theories of European Integration*, 2000.
Sandholtz, Wayne, and Alec Stone Sweet, *European Integration and Supranational Governance*, 1998.
Schmidt, Vivien, *Democracy in Europe: The EU and National Polities*, 2006.
Siedentop, Larry, *Democracy in Europe*, 2000.
Taylor, Paul, *The End of European Integration: Anti-Europeanism Examined*, 2008.
— *The European Union in the 1990s*, 1996.
— *The Limits of European Integration*, 1983.
Thomas, Hugh, *Ever Closer Union*, 1991.
Tsoukalis, Loukas, *What Kind of Europe?*, 2005.
Tugendhat, Christopher, *Making Sense of Europe*, 1986.
Versluis, Esther, et al., *Analysing the European Union Policy Process*, 2011

Wallace, William, *The Dynamics of European Integration*, 1990.
Weiner, Antje, and Thomas Diez (editors), *European Integration Theory*, 2004.

History of European integration

Albrecht-Carrié, R, *The Unity of Europe: An Historical Survey*, 1969.
Bond, Martyn, Julie Smith and William Wallace, *Eminent Europeans*, 1996.
Burgess, Michael, *Federalism and European Union: The Building of Europe 1950–2000*, 2000.
Davies, Norman, *Europe: A History*, 1996.
Dedman, Martin, *The Origins and Development of the European Union 1945–95*, 1996.
Deighton, Anne (editor), *Building Postwar Europe: National Decision-Makers and European Institutions, 1948–63*, 1995.
Dinan, Desmond, *Europe Recast: A History of European Union*, 2004
Dinan, Desmond (editor), *Origins and Evolution of the European Union*, 2006.
Dyson, Kenneth, and Kevin Featherstone, *The Road to Maastricht: Negotiating Economic and Monetary Union in Europe*, 1999.
Gillingham, John, *Coal, Steel, and the Rebirth of Europe, 1945–1955: The Germans and French from Ruhr Conflict to Economic Community*, 1991.
— *European Integration 1950–2003: Superstate or New Market Economy?*, 2003.
Hay, Denys, *Europe: the Emergence of an Idea*, 1968.
Hitchcock, William, *France Restored: Cold War Diplomacy and the Quest for Leadership in Europe, 1944–1954*, 1998.
Judt, Tony, *Postwar: A History of Europe since 1945*, 2006.
Kaiser, Wolfram, Brigitte Leucht and Morten Rasmussen, *The History of the European Union: Origins of a Trans- and Supranational Polity 1950–72*, 2008.
Kaiser, Wolfram, and Antonio Varsori (editors), *European Union History: Themes and Debates*, 2010.
King, Preston, and Andrea Bosco, *A Constitution for Europe: Comparative Study of Federal Constitutions and Plans for the United States of Europe*, 1991.
Lindsay, Kenneth, *European Assemblies: The Experimental Period 1949–1959*, 1960.
Mayne, Richard, *The Community of Europe*, 1962.
McAllister, Richard, *From EC to EU: An Historical and Political Survey*, 1997.
Milward Alan, *The European Rescue of the Nation State*, 1992.
— *The Reconstruction of Western Europe 1945–51*, 1984.
Milward, Alan et al., *The Frontier of National Sovereignty: History and Theory 1945–1992*, 1993.
Newhouse, John, *Collision in Brussels: The Common Market Crisis of 30 June 1965*, 1967.
Rosato, Sebastian, *Europe United: Power Politics and the Making of the European Community*, 2011.
Sampson, Anthony, *The New Europeans*, 1968.

Siebelink, Hanneke, *The 50 Days that Changed Europe*, 2011.
Stirk, P. M. R., *European Unity in Context: The Interwar Period*, 1989.
— *A History of European Integration since 1914*, 1996.
Sutton, Michael, *France and the Construction of Europe, 1944–2007*, 2007.
Urwin, Derek, *The Community of Europe: A History of European Integration since 1945*, 1992.
Willis, F. Roy, *France, Germany and the New Europe, 1945–1967*, 1968.
— *Italy Chooses Europe*, 1971.

United Kingdom and European Union

Bache, Ian, and Andrew Jordan, *The Europeanization of British Politics*, 2008.
Baker, David, and David Seawright (editors), *Britain for and against Europe: British Politics and the Question of European Integration*, 1998.
Black, Jeremy, *Convergence or Divergence? Britain and the Continent*, 1994.
Bullen, Roger, and M. E. Pelly, *Documents on British Policy Overseas*, Series 11, Volume 1, 1986 (Britain and the Schuman Plan).
Bulmer, Simon, and Martin Burch, *The Europeanisation of Whitehall: UK Central Government and the European Union*, 2009.
Butler, Michael, *Europe: More than a Continent*, 1986.
Camps, Miriam, *Britain and the European Community, 1955–1963*, 1964.
Charlton, Michael, *The Price of Victory*, 1983.
Daddow, Oliver, *Britain and Europe since 1945*, 2004.
Denman, Roy, *Missed Chances*, 1995.
Forster, Anthony, *Euroscepticism in Contemporary British Politics*, 2002.
Geddes, Andrew, *Britain in the European Community*, 1993.
George, Stephen, *An Awkward Partner: Britain in the EC*, 1998.
— *Britain and European Integration since 1945*, 1994.
Gowland, David, and Arthur Turner (editors), *Britain and European Integration, 1945–1998: A Documentary History*, 2000.
Gowland, David, Arthur Turner and Alex Wright, *Britain and European Integration since 1945: On the Sidelines*, 2010.
Kaiser, Wolfram, *Using Europe, Abusing the Europeans: Britain and European Integration, 1945–63*, 1996.
Kitzinger, Uwe, *Diplomacy and Persuasion: How Britain Joined the Common Market*, 1973.
— *The Second Try*, 1968.
Lord, Christopher, *Absent at the Creation: Britain and the Formation of the European Community, 1950–52*, 1996.
Ludlow, Piers, *Dealing with Britain: The Six and the First UK Application to the EEC*, 1997.
Menon, Anand (editor), *Britain and European Integration: Views from Within*, 2004.

Noakes, Jeremy, Peter Wende and Jonathan Wright (editors), *Britain and Germany in Europe 1949–1990*, 2002.

Nutting, Anthony, *Europe Will Not Wait: A Warning and a Way Out*, 1960.

O'Neill, Con, *Britain's Entry into the European Community: Report on the Negotiations of 1970–1972*, 2000.

Radice, Giles, *Offshore: Britain and the European Idea*, 1992.

Smith, Julie, and Mariana Tsatsas, *The New Bilateralism: The UK's Relations within the EU*, 2002.

Stephens, Philip, *Politics and the Pound: The Tories, the Economy and Europe*, 1997.

Wall, Stephen, *A Stranger in Europe: Britain and the EU from Thatcher to Blair*, 2008.

Wilkes, George (editor), *Britain's Failure to Enter the European Community, 1961–63*, 1997.

Young, Hugo, *This Blessed Plot: Britain and Europe from Churchill to Blair*, 1999.

Young, John W, *Britain and European Unity, 1945–1999*, 2000.

— *Britain, France and the Unity of Europe 1945–51*, 1984.

Economics, EMU and the single market

Armstrong, Kenneth, and Simon Bulmer, *The Governance of the Single European Market*, 1998.

Artis, Michael, and Frederick Nixson (editors), *Economics of the European Union: Policy and Analysis*, 2007.

Baldwin, Richard, and Charles Wyplosz, *The Economics of European Integration*, 2009.

Chang, Michele, *Monetary Integration in the European Union*, 2009.

Colchester, Nicholas, and David Buchan, *Europe Relaunched: Truths and Illusions on the Way to 1992*, 1990.

de Grauwe, Paul, *Economics of Monetary Union*, 2009.

Dyson, Kenneth, and Kevin Featherstone, *The Road to Maastricht: Negotiating Economic and Monetary Union in Europe*, 1999.

Dyson, Kenneth, and Martin Marcussen, *Central Banks in the Age of the Euro: Europeanization, Convergence, and Power*, 2009.

Eichengreen, Barry, *European Monetary Unification: Theory, Practice, and Analysis*, 1997.

Issing, Otmar, *The Birth of the Euro*, 2008.

Neal, Larry, *The Economics of Europe and of the European Union*, 2007.

Padoa-Schioppa, Tommaso, *Efficiency, Stability and Equity: A Strategy for the Evolution of the Economic System of the European Community*, 1987.

— *The Road to Monetary Union in Europe: The Emperor, the Kings and the Genies*, 1994.

Swann, Dennis, *The Economics of Europe: From Common Market to European Union*, 2000.
Tsoukalis, Loukas, *Governance and Legitimacy in EMU*, 2005.
— *The New European Economy: The Politics and Economics of Integration*, 1993.

Foreign Policy and external relations

Bickerton, Christopher J., *European Union Foreign Policy: From Effectiveness to Functionality*, 2011.
Bindi, Federiga (editor), *The Foreign Policy of the European Union*, 2010.
Bretherton, Charlotte, and John Vogler, *The European Union as a Global Actor*, 2006.
Cameron, Fraser, *An Introduction to European Foreign Policy*, 2007.
Carlsnaes, Walter, Helene Sjursen and Brian White, *Contemporary European Foreign Policy*, 2004.
Croci, Osvaldo, and Amy Verdun, *The Transatlantic Divide: Foreign and Security Policies in the Atlantic Alliance from Kosovo to Iraq*, 2006.
Cunningham, Dick, Peter Lichtenbaum and Julie Wolf, *The EU and World Trade*, 2001.
Emerson, Michael, et al., *Upgrading the EU's Role as Global Actor: Institutions, Law and the Restructuring of European Diplomacy*, 2011.
Gamble, Andrew, and David Lane, *The European Union and World Politics: Consensus and Division*, 2009.
Hill, Christopher, and Michael Smith (editors), *International Relations and the European Union*, 2005.
Holland, Martin, *The European Union and the Third World*, 2002.
Howorth, Jolyon, *Security and Defence Policy in the European Union*, 2007.
Keukeleire, Stephan, and Jennifer MacNaughtan, *The Foreign Policy of the European Union*, 2008.
Manners, Ian, and Richard Whitman (editors), *The Foreign Policies of European Union Member States*, 2000.
McGuire, Steven, and Michael Smith, *The European Union and the United States*, 2008.
Meunier, Sophie, *Trading Voices: The European Union in International Commercial Negotiations*, 2005.
Nuttall, Simon, *European Political Cooperation*, 1992.
Smith, Karen, *European Union Foreign Policy in a Changing World*, 2008.
Smith, Michael, *Europe's Foreign and Security Policy: The Institutionalization of Cooperation*, 2003.
Tonra, Ben, and Thomas Christiansen, *Rethinking European Union Foreign Policy*, 2004.
Whitman, Richard, *Pax Bruxellana? Multilateralism and EU Global Power and Influence*, 2009.

European Union law

Alter, Karen J., *Establishing the Supremacy of European Law: The Making of an International Rule of Law in Europe*, 2001.

— *The European Court's Political Power*, 2009.

Barnard, Catherine, *The Substantive Law of the EU: The Four Freedoms*, 2010.

Cappelletti, Mauro, Monica Seccombe and Joseph H. H. Weiler, *Integration through Law: Europe and the American Federal Experience*, 1988.

Chalmers, Damian, Gareth Davies and Giorgio Monti, *European Union Law: Text and Materials*, 2010.

Chalmers, Damian, and Adam Tomkins, *European Union Public Law: Text and Materials*, 2007.

Church, Clive, and David Phinnemore, *The Penguin Guide to the European Treaties: From Rome to Maastricht, Amsterdam, Nice and beyond*, 2002.

Craig, Paul, and Gráinne de Búrca, *EU Law: Text, Cases, and Materials*, 2011.

Craig, Paul, and Gráinne de Búrca (editors), *The Evolution of EU Law*, 2011.

Curtin, Deirdre, *Executive Power of the European Union: Law, Practices and the Living Constitution*, 2009.

De Lasser, Mitchel, *Judicial Transformation: The Rights Revolution in the Courts of Europe*, 2009.

Hartley, Trevor C., *Constitutional Problems of the European Union*, 1999.

— *European Union Law in a Global Context: Text, Cases and Materials*, 2004.

— *The Foundations of European Union Law*, 2010.

Horspool, Margot, and Matthew Humphreys, *European Union Law*, 2010.

Kaczorowska, Alina, *European Union Law*, 2011.

Lenaerts, Koen, and Piet Van Nuffel, *European Union Law*, 2011.

Rudden, Bernard, and Diarmuid Rossa Phelan, *Basic Community Cases*, 1997.

Schütze, Robert, *From Dual to Cooperative Federalism: The Changing Structure of European Law*, 2009.

Steiner, Josephine, and Lorna Woods, *EU Law*, 2009.

Stone Sweet, Alec, *The Judicial Construction of Europe*, 2004.

Toth, A. G., *The Oxford Encyclopaedia of European Community Law*, Volumes I and II, 1990 and 2005.

Tridimas, Takis, *The General Principles of EC Law*, 2006.

Ward, Ian, *A Critical Introduction to European Law*, 2009.

Weatherill, Stephen, *Cases and Materials on EU Law*, 2007.

Weatherill, Stephen, and Paul Beaumont, *EU Law*, 1999.

Weiler, Joseph H. H., *The Constitution of Europe: 'Do the New Clothes Have an Emperor?' and other essays on European Integration*, 1999.

Weiler, Joseph. H. H., and Marlene Wind, *European Constitutionalism Beyond the State*, 2003.

Synoptic Index

The following broad subject-headings are intended to help the reader find the main entries relevant to particular aspects of European Union. The lists are not exhaustive.

Institutions and organizations

Agencies
Committee of the Regions
COREPER
Council of Europe
Council of Ministers
Court of Auditors
European Atomic Energy Community
European Bank for Reconstruction and Development
European Central Bank
European Coal and Steel Community
European Commission
European Council
European Court of Justice
European Economic and Social Committee
European Economic Community
European External Action Service
European Investment Bank
European Parliament
European political parties
High Representative
National parliaments
North Atlantic Treaty Organization
Ombudsman
Organization for Economic Cooperation and Development
Permanent representation
Political groups
Presidency
President of the European Council

Political and institutional questions

European Constitution
European army
'European Union'
'Ever closer union'
Exit clause
Euroscepticism
Federalism and confederalism
Finalités politiques
Functionalism and neo-functionalism

Ioannina Compromise
Opt-out
Pillars and 'pillared structure'
Positive and negative integration
Seats of EU institutions
Sovereignty
Subsidiariy
Supranationalism and intergovernmentalism
Symbols of the Union
Transparency
Two-speed Europe
United States of Europe
Variable geometry

EMU and single market

Cassis de Dijon case
Cockfield White Paper
Competition policy
Customs union
Ecofin Council
Delors Report
Economic and Financial Committee
Economic and Monetary Union
Euro
Eurobonds
Eurogroup and Euro Summit
European Central Bank
European economic governance
European Financial Stabilisation Mechanism
European Financial Stability Facility and European Stability Mechanism
European Monetary Institute
European Monetary System
European Systemic Risk Board
Eurozone
Eurozone debt crisis
Excessive deficit procedure
Exchange-Rate Mechanism
Four freedoms
Fiscal Compact Treaty
Free movement
Free movement of capital, goods, persons, services
Freedom of establishment
Harmonization
Single market
Stability and Growth Pact
Tax harmonisation
Werner Report

Domestic policies

Budget
'Cohesion' and Cohesion Fund
Common Agricultural Policy
Common Fisheries Policy
Competition policy
Cultural policy
Economic and Monetary Union
Education policy
Energy policy
Environment policy
Equal treatment
European Regional Development Fund
European Social Fund
Justice and Home Affairs
Non-discrimination
Research and development policy
Schengen
Single market
Social and employment policy
Structural funds
Tax harmonisation
Trans-European Networks
Transport policy

Foreign policy and external relations

Association agreement
Common Commercial Policy
Common Foreign and Security Policy
Common Security and Defence Policy
Cooperation agreement
Development policy
European Neighbourhood Policy
European External Action Service
European Political Cooperation
EU Military Committee
Foreign Affairs Council
High Representative
International agreements
North Atlantic Treaty Organisation
Organisation for Security and Cooperation in Europe
Permanent Structured Cooperation in Defence
Petersberg tasks
Transatlantic relations
Western European Union

History

Black Wednesday
British Budget dispute
British referendum on EC membership
Cold War
Congress of Europe
Convention on Future of Europe
European army
European Defence Community
European Political Community
Franco-British union
French and Dutch referenda on European Constitution
French referendum on Maastricht Treaty
Fouchet Plan
Genscher-Colombo Plan
German reunification
Luxembourg Compromise
Maastricht ratification crisis
Marshall Plan
Messina Conference
Resignation of Santer Commission
Saarland
Schuman Plan
Spaak Committee
Stuttgart Declaration
Suez crisis
Yalta and Potsdam Conferences
Zurich speech

People

Adenauer, Konrad
Blair, Tony
Churchill, Winston
de Gasperi, Alcide
de Gaulle, Charles
Founding fathers
Giscard d'Estaing, Valéry
Hallstein, Walter
Heath, Edward
Jenkins, Roy
Kohl, Helmut
Monnet, Jean
Mitterrand, François
Schuman, Robert
Spaak, Paul-Henri
Spinelli, Altiero
Thatcher, Margaret

Procedures

Accession
Article 352
Budgetary process
Co-decision procedure
Consent procedure
Consultation procedure
Cooperation procedure
Enhanced cooperation
Enlargement
European elections
Intergovernmental Conference
Opt-out
Qualified majority voting
Rapporteur
Ratification
Referendum
Right of initiative
Unanimity
Uniform electoral procedure

Law

Acquis communautaire
Decision
Derogation
Direct effect
Directive
EU law
European Convention on Human Rights
'Failure to act'
Karlsruhe judgements
Legal act
Legal base
Legal certainty
Legal personality
Primacy
Proportionality
Regulation

Treaties and agreements

Amsterdam Treaty
Brussels Treaty
Charter of Fundamental Rights
Draft Treaty establishing the European Union
Dunkirk Treaty
Elysée Treaty
European Constitution
European Convention on Human Rights
European Economic Area
European Free Trade Association
Fiscal Compact Treaty
Inter-Institutional Agreement
Lisbon Treaty
Maastricht Treaty
Merger Treaty
Nice Treaty
Protocol
Ratification
Single European Act
Treaty of Paris
Treaty/Treaties of Rome